THE
RAMAYAN OF VALMIKI

THE
RAMAYAN OF VALMIKI

TRANSLATED INTO ENGLISH VERSE

BY

RALPH T. H. GRIFFITH, M. A., C. I. E.

GYAN

Published by

Gyan Publishing House
5, Ansari Road
Daryaganj, New Delhi-110002
Phone: 011-47034999, 9811692060
E-mail: books@gyanbooks.com

Distribution Network
gyanbooks.com
India, USA, Canada, UK, Australia

ISBN: 978-93-6208-065-3 (PB)
First Published, 1870

2nd Impression 2024

Printed at: Gyan Press, Delhi.

THE RAMAYAN OF VALMIKI
Author: VALMIKI, TRANSLATOR: RALPH T. H. GRIFFITH

THE
RÁMÁYAN OF VÁLMÍKI

TRANSLATED INTO ENGLISH VERSE

BY

RALPH T. H. GRIFFITH, M.A., C.I.E.

FORMER PRINCIPAL OF THE BENARES COLLEGE, AND LATE DIRECTOR PUBLIC INSTRUCTION N.-W. P. AND OUDH.

COMPLETE IN ONE VOLUME.

BENARES:

PRINTED AND PUBLISHED BY E. J. LAZARUS AND CO.

SOLD ALSO BY

LUZAC AND CO., LONDON.

1895.

TO

THE HONOURABLE

SIR WILLIAM MUIR, K. C. S. I., LL. D.

LIEUTENANT-GOVERNOR OF THE NORTH-WESTERN

PROVINCES OF INDIA

THIS TRANSLATION

OF

THE GREAT EPIC POEM OF THE HINDUS

IS RESPECTFULLY INSCRIBED.

CONTENTS.

NOTE.

a	is pronounced like	u	in	fun.
á	like	a	in	father.
e	like	a	in	fate.
i	like	i	in	fill.
í	like	ee	in	feel.
u	like	u	in	full.
ú	like	u	in	flute.
ai	like	i	in	fire.
au	like	ou	in	foul.

y is a consonant only.

ś is pronounced nearly as sh.

INTRODUCTION.

The subject of the Rámáyan, the great national epic of the Hindus, their one common and everlasting possesssion, is, as the name implies,[1] the life and adventures of Ráma. These adventures are briefly summarized in the introductory cantos of the poem and do not require to be dwelt upon here. The great exploit and main subject of the epic is the war which Ráma waged with the giant Rávaṇ, the fierce and mighty King of Lanká or Ceylon and the dread oppressor of Gods and nymphs and saints and men. 'The army,' to borrow the words of Gorresio, 'which Ráma led on this expedition was, as appears from the poem, gathered in great part from the region of the Vindhyan hills, but the races which he assembled are represented in the poem as monkeys, either out of contempt for their barbarism or because at that time they were little known to the Sanskrit-speaking Hindus. The people against whom Ráma waged war are, as the poem indicates in many places, different in origin, in civilization, and in worship, from the Sanskrit Indians; but the poet of the Rámáyan, in this respect like Homer who assigns to Troy customs, creeds, and worship similar to those of Greece, places in Ceylon, the seat of this alien and hostile people, names, habits, and worship similar to those of Sanskrit India. The poet calls the people whom Ráma attacked Rákshasas. Rákshasas, according to the popular Indian belief, are malignant beings, demons of many shapes, terrible and cruel, who disturb the sacrifices and the religious rites of the Bráhmans. It appears indubitable that the poet of the Rámáyan applied the hated name of Rákshasas to an abhorred and hostile people, and that this denomination is here rather an expression of hatred and horror than a real historical name.

Such, reduced to its bare simplicity, is the fundamental idea of the Rámáyan, a war of two hostile races differing in origin, civilization, and worship. But, as is the case in all primitive epopeas, around this idea as a nucleus have gathered elements of every kind drawn from the very vitals of Indian tradition, and worked up by the ancient poet to embody his lofty epic conception. The epopea received and incorporated the traditions, the ideas, the beliefs, the myths, the symbols of that civilization in the midst of which it arose, and by the weaving in and arranging of all these vast elements it became the complete and faithful expression of a whole ancient period; and in fact the epopea is nothing but a system which represents poetically those ideas of a people which the philosophical systems expound theoretically.'[2]

Other scholars will not concede even this historical basis to the exploits celebrated in the poem. 'Professor Weber is of opinion (Hist. of Ind. Lit. p. 181.) that the principal characters who figure in the Rámáyan are not historical personages at all,

---

[1] From *Ráma* and *ayana*, Ráma's Adventures. Schlegel Latinizes the Sanskrit title into Rámeis. In conformity with Indian custom I write Rámáyan with the dental or undotted 'n' and without the final 'a,' as we speak of the Iliad and Æneid and not of the Ilias and Æneis.

[2] GORRESIO, *Rámáyan, Vol. VI. Preface.*

but mere personifications of certain events and circumstances. Sítá (the furrow) he remarks, occurs both in the Rig-veda [R. V. IV. 57. 6] and in the Gṛihya ritual as an object of worship, and represents the A'ryan agriculture, while he regards Ráma as the ploughman personified. The Rámáyaṇa has only, he thinks, a historical character in so far as it refers to an actual occurrence, the diffusion of A'ryan civilization towards the south of the peninsula.'[1] To attempt to ascertain the date of the events, real or imaginary related in the Rámáyan would be a mere waste of time. I will only mention that Sir William Jones places Ráma in the year 2029 B. C., Tod in 1100, and Bentley in 950. Gorresio would place him about the thirteenth century before the Christian era.[2]

The introductory Cantos of the Rámáyan and general tradition ascribe the authorship of the poem to the inspired Saint Válmíki, one of the holy company of those whose eye could pierce 'The present, and the past, and the to-come,' who attained the science of secret things by

'Dreadful abstinence
And conquering penance of the mutinous flesh,
Deep contemplation, and unwearied study,
In years outstretched beyond the date of man.'[3]

The same authority makes Válmíki contemporary with Ráma, and assigns the composition of the poem to the age which saw the accomplishment of the great enterprise which forms its subject. 'Critical inquiry,' says Lassen, 'will not allow the actual authorship of Válmíki and the handing down of the poem unchanged from the beginning to pass current;'[4] while Gorresio maintains that 'the popular tradition which makes Válmíki contemporary with Ráma and relates all the particulars of the first propagation of the Rámáyan appears as probable and as worthy of credit as any other ancient fact historically related.' The internal evidence offered by the poem is sufficiently strong confirmation of its remote antiquity, although it is impossible to fix even approximately the date of its composition.[5] Portions of this and

---

[1] Muir's Sanskrit Texts, Vol. II. p. 438.

[2] 'From Ráma to Sumitra the contemporary, as it appears, of Vikramáditya (B. C. 57) fifty-six Kings ruled in succession. By allowing on a reasonable computation an average of a little more than twenty years to each reign we arrive at the thirteenth century before the Christian era. But to this opinion I do not intend to attribute more weight than that of a probable conjecture.'

GORRESIO, *Rámáyan*, *Vol.* 1. *Introduction.*

[3] Shelley's *Hellas.*

[4] *Indische Alterthumskunde*, 1. 484.

[5] 'The Greeks did not acquire any intimate knowledge of India. They applied themselves chiefly to describe the regions, situations, the climate, the natural productions of the Indian soil, the dress, the arms, and the customs of the inhabitants. No aid, then, can be hoped for from the Greeks to discover the age of the Rámáyan, as nothing can be concluded against its antiquity from our finding no mention of it in the works of those writers. Nor can precise data be obtained even from Indian writers, data impressed with a certain stamp of historical truth, sufficient by themselves to establish the indubitable age of the poem. Indian minds were always more inclined to meditate than to narrate, to launch themselves boldly into the regions of the ideal and the infinite rather than to consign to memory in their reality events

other evidence I will not lay before the reader, gathered chiefly from Gorresio's Introduction to his magnificent edition of the Rámáyan.

'What I have said,' observes Gorresio, 'with regard to the antiquity of Ráma may be applied to Válmíki the author of the Rámáyan, whose synchronism with Ráma is indicated, as I have pointed out, in the introduction to the poem, and confirmed by two passages of the poem itself. In such a case the question would be ended and the antiquity of the poem proved, although without determining its age with absolute precision, a difficult question not in the case of the Rámáyan only but in the poems of Homer themselves. But because there will be found some people to whom the testimony of the introduction to the poem will appear suspicious, and the authority of the two passages (not found in the Bengal recension) doubtful, I will here condense the indications and arguments which appear to me to confirm the antiquity of the Rámáyan. Passing over the Puráṇa period I come to the era of Vikramáditya (57 B. C.) Here I find a poem which celebrates in a compendious form the exploits sung in the Rámáyan, I mean the Raghuvanśa of Kálidása.[1] The poet himself in his introduction gives direct testimony that preceding poets have opened the way for him in this same subject. It is hardly necessary to say that amongst these poets Válmíki is certainly comprised, the copious and original source of all the poems which celebrate the deeds of Ráma. As I proceed beyond the age of Kálidása there appears before me a great epic monument to which Indian tradition ascribes a most remote antiquity so far as to make Vyaśa the compiler of the Vedas its author. This monument is the Mahábhárata. I bow before this colossal epic: but without wishing to detract from its antiquity, I do not hesitate to declare it less ancient than the Rámáyan. And here I first observe that when we speak of the antiquity of a literary monument, especially an epic one, we must distinguish the elements of which it is composed from the arranging hand which collected and put them together. These elements may be most ancient; and so are in fact the elements of the Mahábhárata: the work of arranging and uniting them may be more or less ancient. And it is precisely this work of union and arrangement in the Mahábhárata which I affirm to be later than that in the Rámáyan. If this posteriority were not declared in the Mahábhárata itself which says that the exploits of Ráma had already been sung by Válmíki inspired by Nárada, it would be sufficiently proved by the fact that there is embodied in the Mahábhárata a summary of the Rámáyan of Válmíki in the same order and very often in the same words. Besides the life and worship of Krishṇa celebrated in the Mahábhárata indicate an age later than the Rámáyan in which there is no mention of Krishṇa or Krishṇaism............ The invention of the *śloka* attributed to Válmíki in the introduction to the Rámáyan appears to confirm the antiquity of the poem..............It should be observed that the *śloka* is not only mentioned in the Rig-veda but the very metre is used. How can these apparent contradictions be reconciled? Tradition says that Válmíki was the inventor of the *śloka* and that he first made use of it in the Rámáyan: but in the Rámáyan the Vedas are very frequently spoken of in which the *śloka* is both mentioned and employed. It may be that the hymns referred to are later than the Rámáyan; but at present we must be content to leave the difficulty unsolved..........

The Rámáyan is mentioned in the Rájatarangíní (Rájatarangíní, Histoire des

---

circumscribed within narrow limits: in one word, history was checked by contemplation and poesy.' GORRESIO.

[1] A later date is by most scholars assigned to this poem.

Rois du Kachmir, par M. A. Troyer, Lib. I. Śl. 166.). Dámodara, second of that name among the kings of Kashmír, was cursed by certain Bráhmans. and the malediction was to cease on the day on which he should hear the entire Rámáyan recited. Now Dámodara the Second, in the series of the kings of Kashmír, precedes by five kings Gonarda the Third who according to the computation of M. Troyer, the sagacious and learned translator and commentator of the History of Kashmír, is to be placed in the year 1182 before Christ (Rájatarangini. Tom. II. p. 375), Reckoning backward from this point to Dámodara the Second through an interval of five reigns the average duration of each of which is about twenty-four years, we arrive at the beginning of the fourteenth century before the Christian era. I am far from wishing to attribute any great precision to these chronological computations, nor do I pretend to determine exactly the age of the Rámáyan, but I maintain that from the passage of the Rájataranginí cited the remote antiquity of the poem may with all confidence be inferred. This antiquity is confirmed by the various popular traditions diffused through the whole of India upon the epopea of Válmíki, upon the exploits which are celebrated in it, upon the principal actors in that great epic drama, since traditions and popular legends gather round ancient monuments as ivy and parasitical plants cling only to the trunks of aged oaks. The whole of India is full of such legends originated by the celebrity of the epic of Válmíki. The fame of Ráma and of Hanumán his mighty ally, accompanied with popular legends, has penetrated into the most remote parts of the southern regions of India and even into Tibet. A proof of the antiquity of the Rámáyan is the fact that many poets both dramatic and epic have had recourse to the great fountain of his poem as the Grecian poets have drawn their materials from the epics of Homer. The antiquity of the Rámáyan is proved by the numerous various readings which are found in it and which can have arisen only from its antiquity and its diffusion by many mouths through distant regions. And as an epic poem is the faithful image of the creeds, the cult, the customs of the age in which it arose, so finding no mention of a creed, a cult, a custom, or a region in an epic is a very probable indication that it did not exist when the poem was composed. It is worthy of being remarked that in the Rámáyan no traces are found of that mystic devotion which absorbs all the faculties of man, of that passionate, ardent worship called *bhakti* which is not of the greatest antiquity but still must have sprung up before our era, as it is mentioned in the Mahábhárata. There are indeed in the Rámáyan examples of prodigious austerities, but these have nothing to do with the religion called *bhakti*, and spring from another cause, a principle more profound. They appear to have been originated by an inner feeling, deeply rooted and of great antiquity in India, that is to say that expiation was to restore fallen human nature. Nor is there found in the Rámáyan any mention of Buddha or Buddhism, although other heterodox creeds are spoken of. Nor is the Island of Ceylon against which the expedition of Ráma was directed called Taprobane or Támraparṇí, or Palesimundu or Pálisímanta, names anterior by some centuries to the Christian era. Nor is it even called by the name of Sinhala (Seat of Lions) which name is connected with the occupation of the island by Vijaya several centuries before our era. The name which Ceylon bears in the Rámáyan is always the primitive, the most ancient, Lanká. I could adduce many other conjectural proofs of the antiquity of the Rámáyan, such for instance as the nature of the style, and its qualifying, as Homer does, with such epithets as venerable, benign, divine, the night, the day, the woods, the mountains, and the rivers.

Colonel Sykes, in his dissertation inserted in the Journal of the Royal Asiatic Society (Vol. VII. pp. 248 ff.), finding that the celebrated Chinese Buddhist Fa Hian who visited India at the end of the fourth and beginning of the fifth century after Christ makes no mention when in Ayodhyá, the capital of Ráma's kingdom, either of Ráma or the Rámáyan, thinks it may be doubted whether the poem existed at that time. If there is no more reason than this to doubt the antiquity of the Rámáyan we need not be alarmed. In fact what did the Chinese Buddhist see in his long journey through India, what has he observed or described, except Buddhist monasteries, Buddhist temples, Buddhist priests, Buddhist traditions, Buddhist doctrines, Buddhist heterodoxies? Everything that had no connection with Buddhism either of agreement or opposition was neglected by him as out of the line of his object.

One apparent difficulty seems to result from the mention of the Yavanas which is found in the first Book of the Rámáyan. The name of Yavanas, used in India to indicate the Greeks after the time of Alexander, may in this place appear subject to suspicion. With regard to this see the excellent remarks of von Schlegel (Rámáyan, Vol. I. Part II. p. 168). The name of Yavanas may have been anciently used by the Indians to denote the nations situated to the west of India; more recently, that is after the time of Alexander, it was applied principally to the Greeks.'[1]

It is not to be expected that every one will admit the cogency of all the arguments in favour of the great antiquity of the Rámáyan adduced by the ingenious and enthusiastic scholar from whom I have quoted; but few who have read the poem will refuse to concur at least in the sober judgment of the writer of an excellent article on the Rámáyan in Vol. L. of the Westminster Review: 'We are ignorant of the date of the poem, or rather of the era to which its older parts belong. Probably Válmíki and Homer were contemporaries; perhaps the Hindu was the earlier of the two, and sang his song while that Ilion was a reality, which to Homer rose in the back-ground of two or three generations. Our limits forbid us to enter into any detailed proof, nor indeed could any be quite satisfactory; the best arguments for its age are found in the poem itself, and the habits and manners which it describes. Thus the burning of widows on the funeral piles of their husbands, which the Greeks describe as an old custom when Alexander invaded India, B. C. 327, is utterly unknown in the Rámáyana, and one fact like this speaks volumes. In such poems as the Rámáyana and the Iliad we instinctively feel that they belong to the earlier world: we enter them as we enter a house in Pompeii—the colours may still seem fresh, and no mark of decay remind us of their age, but we feel that they belong not to us or ours, and a gulf of ages lies between us and our objects.'

The Rámáyan is divided into seven Books, but the action of the poem ends with the sixth, and there is every reason to believe that the seventh Book is a later addition. This last Book or Uttara Káṇḍa, 'contains various stories, legends, and traditions, which still have some connection of affinity with the principal poem. The mythical origin of the Rákshasas is there related............with the banishment of Sítá and her giving birth in the hermitage of Válmíki to twin sons, Kuśa and Lava, who were the first rhapsodists or 'aoidoi' of the Rámáyan, and other traditions and legends only distantly connected with the Rámáyan properly so called.'[2] The whole contains about 24,000 verses, chiefly ślokes or heroic distichs of thirty-two syllables each, with verses of a different metre occasionally introduced or interpolated, especially at the end of a canto.

---

[1] GORRESIO, *Rámáyan, Vol. I. Introduction.* [2] GORRESIO.

'The poem has evidently undergone considerable alteration since the time of its first composition, but still underneath all the subsequent additions the original elements are preserved, and careful criticism might perhaps separate the interpolations and present the more genuine parts as a whole by themselves. The task however, would be difficult, and perhaps as impracticable as it has proved in the Homeric poems. For many ages it is certain that the work existed only by oral tradition, and each rhapsodist added or altered at his pleasure, or to suit the taste or vanity of the princely families whom he served. The measure of the poem, moreover, is of a somewhat fatal facility, and many rhapsodists would naturally be ambitious of mingling their own songs with those of their bards, and the habit of repetition would at once supply them with a vocabulary of epic phrases to suit their purpose. Whole chapters thus betray their origin by their barrenness of thought and laborious mimicry of the epic spirit, which in the case of the old poets had spontaneously burst out of the heart's fulness like the free song of a child. But when the Indian Pisistratus arose who collected these separate songs and reduced them to their present shape, the genuine and spurious were alike included, and no Hindu critic ever appears to have attempted to discriminate between them. With regard to the Rámáyana it appears to have undergone two distinct revisions, one in Benares and the other in Bengal, and as the two were accomplished without any reference or relation to each other, they naturally present many varieties in their texts. The same thoughts and events are generally preserved in both, but the words and order of the verses continually differ, as would naturally be the case when the revisions were made from the oral traditions of two different schools of rhapsodists from each of which the poem had been undergoing a long series of alterations such as those we have suggested above.'[1]

Notwithstanding Gorresio's able and enthusiastic advocacy of what he considers the superior claims of the Bengal recension of the Rámáyan, it is generally allowed by European scholars that the Benares or North-West recension is the more genuine. Of the former there is a magnificent edition by Gorresio, published at the expense of Charles Albert, late King of Sardinia. The text is printed in a style that cannot be surpassed in an country, and an Italian prose translation of the whole accompanies it 'which may be equalled but not surpassed in any other of the languages of Europe. In his translation he has carefully preserved a Dantesque idiom and form of expression, free from all local patois; his rendering is most faithful, and his language elegent and spirited.'[2] The Benares recension has been less fortunate. In the years 1805—1810 Carey and Marshman, the venerable Missionaries of Serampore, published the text and English translation of two Books and a half or about one third of the entire poem,[3] but these volumes have long been out of print and unprocurable, and they 'are very inferior as productions of literary art, though no blame

[1] *Westminster Review*, *Vol.* L.

[2] *Calcutta Review*, *Vol. XXIII. The Rámáyana.*

[3] 'The gentlemen who compose the Committee (of the Asiatic Society of Bengal) have made choice of the Rámáyan of Válmíki to be the first in the series of translations from the Sanskrit. The reverence in which it is held, the extent of country through which it is circulated, and the interesting view which it exhibits of the religion, the doctrines, the mythology, the current ideas, and the manners and customs of the Hindus, combine to justify their election.' *Advertisement to Carey and Marshman's edition of the Rámáyan.*

attaches to the excellent men who publshed their work in the very dawn of oriental studies.'[1] In the year 1846 the great William von Schlegel published the text of the first two Books with a Latin translation of the first and part of the second. This edition is to some extent an eclectic one; it is founded on the North-West recension but sometimes admits passages from the Bengal recension when they are recommended by any special excellence. This work, as Gorresio justly says, 'bears the impress of that critical acumen, of that profound judgment, of that artistic sense, for which he is so renowned.' An admirable edition of the North-West recension with a commentary, has lately been lithographed at Bombay, and a rather inferior printed edition has been published in Calcutta. The late M. Hippolyte Fauche, the most intrepid and indefatigable of translators from the Sanskrit, has given to the world a French version of Gorresios' edition.[2] Thus the Bengal recension has been translated into Italian and French; but there is no English version of either recension, and only a small portion of the North-West recension has been translated into any European tongue. This fact alone will, I trust, be regarded as a sufficient reason or excuse for the present attempt to reproduce the Rámáyan in an English dress. The poem can hardly be denied a high place among the great epics of the world, and it is surely desirable that Englishmen—especially those who are more immediately connected with India—should at least be enabled, if they choose, to become acquainted with it.[3]

My first object has been to reproduce the original poem as faithfully as circumstances permit me to do. For this purpose I have preferred verse to prose. The translations of the Iliad by Chapman and Worsley--nay, even by translators of far inferior poetical powers—are, I think, much more Homeric than any literal prose

---

[1] Gorresio says: 'With regard to the merits of this work I will add nothing to the severe but just judgment passed upon it by the illustrious William von Schlegel who found it a work without skill or critical discernment, abounding in faults and worthless in every part.'

[2] One Canto, in the four versions, will be found in Appendix B.

[3] The Rámáyaṇa and Mahá-bhárata, unlike the Iliad and the Odysey, are closely connected with the present religious faith of millions; and these millions, be it remembered, acknowledge British sway, and have a right to expect the British public to take an interest in works which are the time-honoured repository of their legendary history and mythology, of their ancient customs and observances, as well as of their most cherished gems of poetry. It needs no argument to show that some knowledge of the two great Indian Epics ought to be required of all who hold office in India, whether in the Civil Service, or in any other capacity. Nor is it right, or even possible, for Englishmen generally to remain any longer wholly ignorant of the nature and contents of these poems. British India is now brought so close to us by steam and electricity, and the present condition of the Hindú community, social, political, and religious, forces itself so peremptorily on our attention, that the duty of studying the past history of our Eastern empire, so far as it can be collected from ancient Sanskrit literature, can no longer be evaded by educated men. Hitherto the Indian Epics, which, in the absence of all real history, are the only guides to the early condition of our Hindú fellow-subjects, have been sealed books to the majority of Englishmen.'

Indian Epic Poetry. By MONI ER WILLIAMS, M. A., *Preface, III, IV.*

rendering can possibly be. In the latter we may find the 'disjecti membra poetae,' but all the form and the life are gone, for 'the interpenetration of matter and manner constitute the very soul of poetry.' I have but seldom allowed myself to amplify or to condense, or omit apparently needless repetitions, but have attempted rather to give the poet as he is than to represent him as European taste might prefer him to be. Comparisons, therefore, which to English readers will appear vulgar or rediculous have been left unaltered, and long passages of unutterable tediousness re-appear in my version with, probably, their tediousness enhanced. I may observe, with all respect for Válmíki, that the Rámáyan, even in the sonorous and dignified Sanskrit, will hardly bear reading through, and I am sure that the translation will not. Válmíki's work is not much read even in India, although the Hindí refaccimento by the poet Tulsídás is more popular and more honoured by the people of the North-Western Provinces that the Bible is by the corresponding classes in England. The poem, it should be remembered, was in ancient times recited and not read; the audience that gathered round the rhapsodist might be continually changing, and each hearer would probably listen to a few consecutive cantos only. It is true that one unfortunate king mentioned in the Rájatarangini was condemned to remain under the malediction of the Bráhmans until he should have heard the whole Rámáyan recited at one sitting.[1] But it may be doubted which alternative he preferred; and this is quite an exceptional case.

The metre I have adopted has been chosen after long consideration and many experiments. It is not, I know, the exact equivalent of Válmíki's *śloka* or heroic distich, with which it cannot compare in gravity or grandeur. I would generally prefer other metres for free translations of short extracts or scenes from the poem, but for a translation of the entire work I am inclined to think that the octosyllabic metre fairly represents the original, and at the same time I find that it suits me best. The *śloka*, as I have already said, consists of two lines of sixteen syllables or, rather, four lines of eight syllables each, only four of which are fixed in quantity, the others being optionally long or short.[2] It corresponds then roughly to four lines of the

---

[1] This reminds one of Macaulay's story of the Italian criminal 'who was suffered to choose between Guicciardini and the galleys. He chose the History. But the war of Pisa was too much for him. He changed his mind, and went to the oar.'

[2] 'This verse is a stanza or Śloka, which, with some exceptions, consists of two lines or hemistichs: each of these is again subdivided into two parts: so that the entire stanza is for the most part a tetrastich, composed of four Pádas or Charaṇas, literally 'feet,' or, in our understanding of the term, lines or semi hemistichs; the intervals between the first and second, and third and fourth of which are not always so distinctly marked, as that between the second and third.........

This is by far the most frequent and useful form of Sanskrit verse. It is that in which the great body of metrical composition, whether narrative or didactic, exists. All works of considerable extent are written in it, relieved by the occasional introduction of other metres. It is the prevailing form of metre in the laws of Manu, the Mahábhárata, the Rámáyaṇa, and the Purános.........

Another rule given for the formation of the Anushṭup verse is, that the fifth syllable of each line shall be short, the sixth long and the seventh alternately long and short; whilst the first four syllables and the eighth are arbitrary. This will be

octosyllabic metre which will generally be found to reproduce it without, as a rule, either condensation or amplification. Blank verse, even if the translator could write it, would never represent the *śloka*, a verse generally commensurate with the sentence; and a Sanskrit distich must either be condensed into one heroic couplet or expanded to fill two.

For the first two Books I translate from Schlegel's edition, and from the Bombay edition for the remaining portion of the poem.

The notes, necessarily brief and simple, I owe chiefly to Schlegel and Gorresio: I have also borrowed freely from Wilson, Lassen, Muir, Max Müller, Goldstücker, and Professor Monier Williams. English readers will, I trust, remember that I write partly for Indians, and Indians that the notes which they may think superfluous are necessary to enable Europeans to understand the poem.

There are many archaisms in the original, and I have not entirely excluded them from my translation. My verses, I know, are frequently rough, prosaic, and dull, but I believe that any elaborate polish or the studied use of more modern poetical phraseology would only impair still further their likeness to the simple distichs of Válmíki.

Judged by a European standard there is but little true poetry in the first Book of the Rámáyan, and much of the aroma of that little has probably evaporated in the process of translation. Still, though fully aware of its many shortcomings, and only trusting that longer study, greater practice, and the lessons of intelligent criticism may make each succeeding volume less imperfect, I submit this first volume to the public with some confidence, as I am fully persuaded that the work when completed will supply a want which has long been felt in India if not in England.

I beg to offer my sincere thanks to the Governments of Bengal, the Punjab, Bombay, Mysore, the Central Provinces, and Oudh, for the liberal aid which, at the recommendation of the several Directors of Public Instruction, they have given to my undertaking; and more especially am I bound to render my best thanks to the very distinguished oriental scholar at the head of the Government of the North-Western Provinces—those Provinces in which Válmíki composed his immortal poem, and in which this first metrical translation of it has been begun and will, I hope, be completed.

---

found to be usually the form adopted, with occasional exceptions. The following, are examples:—

-⏑⏑|- ⏑ -| --||- - -|⏑⏑- |⏑-||
ásídidam tamobhútamaprájnátamalakshanam
- ⏑ - | ⏑⏑-|- -|| ⏑- ⏑|⏑⏑-|⏑-||
apratarkyamavijneyam prasuptamivasarvvatah

'This universe had become darkness, undiscerned, uncharacterised, indescribable, incomprehensible, as if everywhere in a deep sleep.' Manu.

- ⏑ -|- ⏑-| - ⏑||⏑⏑ -| - ⏑-|⏑-||
má nisháda pratishṭhám twamagamah śásvatí samáh,
- - ⏑|⏑ ⏑-|-⏑|| ⏑⏑ - |- ⏑-|⏑-||
yat kraunchamithunádekamabadhih kámamohitam

'Never, barbarian, mayest thou acquire fame for endless years, since thou hast slain one of these birds, heedless through passion.' Rámáyana. Tradition affirms of this that it is the first Śloka or anushṭup verse ever composed.'

WILSON'S Sanskrit Grammar, p. 436.

THE RÁMÁYAN.

INVOCATION.[1]

Praise to Válmíki,[2] bird of charming song,[3]
Who mounts on Poesy's sublimest spray,
And sweetly sings with accent clear and strong
Ráma, aye Ráma, in his deathless lay.

Where breathes the man can listen to the strain
That flows in music from Válmíki's tongue,
Nor feel his feet the path of bliss attain
When Ráma's glory by the saint is sung?

The stream Rámáyan leaves its sacred fount
The whole wide world from sin and stain to free.[1]
The Prince of Hermits is the parent mount,
The lordly Ráma is the darling sea.

Glory to him whose fame is ever bright!
Glory to him, Prachetas'[2] holy son!
Whose pure lips quaff with ever new delight
The nectar-sea of deeds by Ráma done.

Hail, arch-ascetic, pious, good, and kind!
Hail, Saint Válmíki, lord of every lore!
Hail, holy Hermit, calm and pure of mind!
Hail, First of Bards, Válmíki, hail once more!

[1] The MSS. vary very considerably in these stanzas of invocation: many lines are generally prefixed in which not only the poet, but those who play the chief parts in the poem are panegyrized. It is self-apparent that they are not by the author of the Rámáyan himself.

[2] 'Válmíki was the son of Varuṇa, the regent of the waters, one of whose names is Prachetas. According to the *Adhyátmá Rámáyaṇa*, the sage, although a Bráhman by birth, associated with foresters and robbers. Attacking on one occasion the seven Rishis, they expostulated with him successfully, and taught him the *mantra* of Ráma reversed, or *Mará, Mará*, in the inaudible repetition of which he remained immovable for thousands of years, so that when the sages returned to the same spot they found him still there, converted into a *valmík* or ant-hill, by the nests of the termites, whence his name of Válmíki.'

WILSON, *Specimens of the Hindu Theatre, Vol. I. p.* 313.

'Válmíki is said to have lived a solitary life in the woods: he is called both a *muni* and a *rishi*. The former word properly signifies an anchorite or hermit; the latter has reference chiefly to wisdom. The two words are frequently used promiscuously, and may both be rendered by the Latin *vates* in its earliest meaning of *seer*: Válmíki was both poet and seer, as he is said to have sung the exploits of Ráma by the aid of divining insight rather than of knowledge naturally acquired.' SCHLEGEL.

[3] Literally, *Kokila*, the Koïl, or Indian Cuckoo. Schlegel translates 'luscinium.'

[1] Comparison with the Ganges is implied, that river being called the purifier of the world.

[2] 'This name may have been given to the father of Válmíki allegorically. If we look at the derivation of the word (*pra*, before, and *chetas*, mind) it is as if the poet were called the son of Prometheus, the Forethinker.' SCHLEGEL.

BOOK I.[3]

CANTO I.

NÁRAD.[4]

OM.[5]

To sainted Nárad, prince of those
Whose lore in words of wisdom flows,
Whose constant care and chief delight
Were Scripture and ascetic rite,
The good Válmíki, first and best

[3] Called in Sanskrit also *Bála-Kánda*, and in Hindí *Bál-Kánd*, *i. e.* the Book describing Ráma's childhood, *bála* meaning a boy up to his sixteenth year.

[4] A divine saint, son of Brahmá. He is the eloquent messenger of the Gods, a musician of exquisite skill, and the inventor of the *viná* or Indian lute. He bears a strong resemblance to Hermes or Mercury.

[5] This mystic syllable, said to typify the supreme Deity, the Gods collectively, the Vedas, the three spheres of the world, the three holy fires, the three steps of Vishṇu etc., prefaces the prayers and most venerated writings of the Hindus.

Of hermit saints, these words addressed:[1]
'In all this world, I pray thee, who
Is virtuous, heroic, true?
Firm in his vows, of grateful mind,
To every creature good and kind?
Bounteous, and holy, just, and wise,
Alone most fair to all men's eyes?
Devoid of envy, firm, and sage,
Whose tranquil soul ne'er yields to rage?
Whom, when his warrior wrath is high,
Do Gods embattled fear and fly?
Whose noble might and gentle skill
The triple world can guard from ill?
Who is the best of princes, he
Who loves his people's good to see?
The store of bliss, the living mine
Where brightest joys and virtues shine?
Queen Fortune's[2] best and dearest friend,
Whose steps her choicest gifts attend?
Who may with Sun and Moon compare,
With Indra,[3] Vishṇu,[4] Fire, and Air?
Grant, Saint divine,[5] the boon I ask,
For thee, I ween, an easy task,
To whom the power is given to know
If such a man breathe here below.'

Then Nárad, clear before whose eye
The present, past, and future lie,[1]
Made ready answer: 'Hermit, where
Are graces found so high and rare?
Yet listen, and my tongue shall tell
In whom alone these virtues dwell.
From old Ikshváku's[2] line he came,
Known to the world by Ráma's name:
With soul subdued, a chief of might,
In Scripture versed, in glory bright.
His steps in virtue's paths are bent,
Obedient, pure, and eloquent.
In each emprise he wins success,
And dying foes his power confess.
Tall and broad-shouldered, strong of limb,
Fortune has set her mark on him.
Graced with a conch-shell's triple line,
His throat displays the auspicious sign.[3]

---

[1] This colloquy is supposed to have taken place about sixteen years after Ráma's return from his wanderings and occupation of his ancestral throne.

[2] Called also Śrí and Lakshmí, the consort of Vishṇu, the Queen of Beauty as well as the Dea Fortuna. Her birth 'from the full-flushed wave' is described in Canto XLV of this Book.

[3] One of the most prominent objects of worship in the Rig-veda, Indra was superseded in later times by the more popular deities Vishṇu and Śiva. He is the God of the firmament, and answers in many respects to the Jupiter Pluvius of the Romans. See *Additional Notes.*

[4] The second God of the Trimúrti or Indian Trinity. Derived from the root *viś* to penetrate, the meaning of the name appears to be *he who penetrates or pervades all things.* An embodiment of the preserving power of nature, he is worshipped as a Saviour who has nine times been incarnate for the good of the world and will descend on earth once more. See *Additional Notes* and Muir's Sanskrit Texts *passim.*

[5] In Sanskrit *devarshi. Rishi* is the general appellation of sages, and another word is frequently prefixed to distinguish the degrees. A *Brahmarshi* is a theologian or Bráhmanical sage; a Rájarshi is a royal sage or sainted king; a *Devarshi* is a divine or deified sage or saint.

[1] *Trikálajṅa.* Literally *knower of the three times.* Both Schlegel and Gorresio quote Homer's.

Ὃς ᾔδη τά τ' ἐόντα, τά τ' ἐσσόμενα, πρό τ' ἐόντα.

'That sacred seer, whose comprehensive view
The past, the present, and the future knew.'

The Bombay edition reads *trilokajṅa, who knows the three worlds* (earth, air and heaven.) 'It is by *tapas* (austere fervour) that rishis of subdued souls, subsisting on roots, fruits and air, obtain a vision of the three worlds with all things moving and stationary.' MANU, XI. 236.

[2] Son of Manu, the first king of Kośala and founder of the solar dynasty or family of the Children of the Sun, the God of that luminary being the father of Manu.

[3] The Indians paid great attention to the art of physiognomy and believed that character and fortune could be foretold not from the face only but from marks upon the neck and hands. Three lines under the chin like those at the mouth of a conch (*Śaṅkha*) were regarded as a peculiarly auspicious sign indicating, as did also the mark of Vishṇu's discus on the hand, one born to be a *chakravartin* or universal emperor. In the palmistry of Europe the line of fortune, as well as the line of life, is in the hand. Cardan says that marks on the nails and teeth also show what is to happen to us: 'Sunt etiam in nobis vestigia quædam futurorum eventuum in unguibus atque etiam in dentibus.' Though the palmy days of Indian chiromancy have passed away, the art is still to some extent studied and believed in.

High destiny is clear impressed
On massive jaw and ample chest,
His mighty shafts he truly aims,
And foemen in the battle tames.
Deep in the muscle, scarcely shown,
Embedded lies his collar-bone.
His lordly steps are firm and free,
His strong arms reach below his knee;[1]
All fairest graces join to deck
His head, his brow, his stately neck,
And limbs in fair proportion set:
The manliest form e'er fashioned yet.
Graced with each high imperial mark,
His skin is soft and lustrous dark.
Large are his eyes that sweetly shine
With majesty almost divine.
His plighted word he ne'er forgets;
On erring sense a watch he sets.
By nature wise, his teacher's skill
Has trained him to subdue his will.
Good, resolute and pure, and strong,
He guards mankind from scathe and wrong,
And lends his aid, and ne'er in vain,
The cause of justice to maintain.
Well has he studied o'er and o'er
The Vedas[2] and their kindred lore.
Well skilled is he the bow to draw,[1]
Well trained in arts and versed in law;
High-souled and meet for happy fate,
Most tender and compassionate;
The noblest of all lordly givers,
Whom good men follow, as the rivers
Follow the King of Floods, the sea:
So liberal, so just is he.
The joy of Queen Kauśalyá's[2] heart,
In every virtue he has part:
Firm as Himálaya's[3] snowy steep,
Unfathomed like the mighty deep;
The peer of Vishṇu's power and might,
And lovely as the Lord of Night;[4]
Patient as Earth, but, roused to ire,
Fierce as the world-destroying fire;
In bounty like the Lord of Gold,[5]
And Justice' self in human mould.

With him, his best and eldest son,
By all his princely virtues won
King Daśaratha[6] willed, to share
His kingdom as the Regent Heir.
But when Kaikeyí, youngest queen,
With eyes of envious hate had seen
The solemn pomp and regal state
Prepared the prince to consecrate,
She bade the hapless king bestow
Two gifts he promised long ago,
That Ráma to the woods should flee,
And that her child the heir should be.

By chains of duty firmly tied,
The wretched king perforce complied.

---

[1] Long arms were regarded as a sign of heroic strength.

[2] 'Veda means originally knowing or knowledge, and this name is given by the Bráhmans not to one work, but to the whole body of their most ancient sacred literature. Veda is the same word which appears in the Greek οἶδα, I know, and in the English wise, wisdom, to wit. The name of Veda is commonly given to four collections of hymns, which are respectively known by the names of Rig-veda, Yajur-veda, Sáma-veda, and Atharva-veda.'

'As the language of the Veda, the Sanskrit, is the most ancient type of the English of the present day, (Sanskrit and English are but varieties of one and the same language,) so its thoughts and feelings contain in reality the first roots and germs of that intellectual growth which by an unbroken chain connects our own generation with the ancestors of the Aryan race,—with those very people who at the rising and setting of the sun listened with trembling hearts to the songs of the Veda, that told them of bright powers above, and of a life to come after the sun of their own lives had set in the clouds of the evening. These men were the true ancestors of our race, and the Veda is the oldest book we have in which to study the first beginnings of our language, and of all that is embodied in language. We are by nature Aryan, Indo-European, not Semitic: our spiritual kith and kin are to be found in India, Persia, Greece, Italy, Germany; not in Mesopotamia, Egypt, or Palestine.'

Chips from a German Workshop, Vol. I. pp. 8, 4.

[1] As with the ancient Persians and Scythians, Indian princes were carefully instructed in archery which stands for military science in general, of which, among Hindu heroes, it was the most important branch.

[2] Chief of the three queens of Daśaratha and mother of Ráma.

[3] From *hima* snow, (Greek χειμ-ών Latin hiems) and *álaya* abode; the Mansion of Snow.

[4] The moon (*Soma, Indu, Chandra etc.*) is masculine with the Indians as with the Germans.

[5] Kuvera, the Indian Plutus, or God of Wealth.

[6] The events here briefly mentioned will be related fully in the course of the poem. The first four cantos are introductory, and are evidently the work of a later hand than Válmíki's.

Ráma, to please Kaikeyí went
Obedient forth to banishment.
Then Lakshman's truth was nobly shown,
Then were his love and courage known,
When for his brother's sake he dared
All perils, and his exile shared.
And Sítá, Ráma's darling wife,
Loved even as he loved his life,
Whom happy marks combined to bless,
A miracle of loveliness,
Of Janak's royal lineage sprung,
Most excellent of women, clung
To her dear lord, like Rohiṇí
Rejoicing with the Moon to be.[1]
The King and people, sad of mood,
The hero's car awhile pursued.
But when Prince Ráma lighted down
At Śringavera's pleasant town,
Where Gangá's holy waters flow,
He bade his driver turn and go.
Guha, Nishádas' king, he met,
And on the farther bank was set.
Then on from wood to wood they strayed,
O'er many a stream, through constant shade,
As Bharadvája bade them, till
They came to Chitrakúṭa's hill.
And Ráma there, with Lakshmaṇ's aid,
A pleasant little cottage made,
And spent his days with Sítá, dressed
In coat of bark and deerskin vest.[1]
And Chitrakúṭa grew to be
As bright with those illustrious three
As Meru's[2] sacred peaks that shine
With glory, when the Gods recline
Beneath them : Śiva's[3] self between
The Lord of Gold and Beauty's Queen.

The aged king for Ráma pined,
And for the skies the earth resigned.
Bharat, his son, refused to reign,
Though urged by all the twice-born[4] train.
Forth to the woods he fared to meet
His brother, fell before his feet,
And cried, 'Thy claim all men allow :
O come, our lord and king be thou.'
But Ráma nobly chose to be
Observant of his sire's decree.
He placed his sandals[5] in his hand
A pledge that he would rule the land :
And bade his brother turn again.
Then Bharat, finding prayer was vain,
The sandals took and went away ;
Nor in Ayodhyá would he stay.
But turned to Nandigráma, where
He ruled the realm with watchful care,
Still longing eagerly to learn
Tidings of Ráma's safe return.

Then lest the people should repeat
Their visit to his calm retreat,
Away from Chitrakúṭa's hill
Fared Ráma ever onward till

---

[1] 'Chandra, or the Moon, is fabled to have been married to the twenty-seven daughters of the patriarch Daksha, or Aśviní and the rest, who are in fact personifications of the Lunar Asterisms. His favourite amongst them was Rohiṇí to whom he so wholly devoted himself as to neglect the rest. They complained to their father, and Daksha repeatedly interposed, till, finding his remonstrances vain, he denounced a curse upon his son-in-law, in consequence of which he remained childless and became affected by consumption. The wives of Chandra having interceded in his behalf with their father, Daksha modified an imprecation which he could not recall, and pronounced that the decay should be periodical only, not permanent, and that it should alternate with periods of recovery. Hence the successive wane and increase of the Moon. *Padma Purána*, *Swarga-Khaṇḍa*, Sec. II. *Rohiṇí* in Astronomy is the fourth lunar mansion, containing five stars, the principal of which is Aldebaran.'

WILSON, *Specimens of the Hindu Theatre. Vol. I. p.* 234.

The Bengal recension has a different reading :

'Shone with her husband like the light
Attendant on the Lord of Night.'

[1] The garb prescribed for ascetics by Manu.

[2] 'Mount Meru, situated like Kailása in the lofty regions to the north of the Himálayas, is celebrated in the traditions and myths of India. Meru and Kailása are the two Indian Olympi. Perhaps they were held in such veneration because the Sanskrit-speaking Indians remembered the ancient home where they dwelt with the other primitive peoples of their family before they descended to occupy the vast plains which extend between the Indus and the Ganges.' GORRESIO.

[3] The third God of the Indian Triad, the God of destruction and reproduction. See *Additional Notes.*

[4] The epithet *dwija*, or *twice-born*, is usually appropriate to Bráhmans, but is applicable to the three higher castes. Investiture with the sacred thread and initiation of the neophyte into certain religious mysteries are regarded as his regeneration or second birth.

[5] His shoes to be a memorial of the absent heir and to maintain his right. Kálidása (Raghuvaṅśa, XII. 17.) says that they were to be *adhidevate* or guardian deities of the kingdom.

Beneath the shady trees he stood
Of Daṇḍaká's primeval wood.
Virádha, giant fiend, he slew,
And then Agastya's friendship knew.
Counselled by him he gained the sword
And bow of Indra, heavenly lord:
A pair of quivers too, that bore
Of arrows an exhaustless store.
While there he dwelt in greenwood shade
The trembling hermits sought his aid,
And bade him with his sword and bow
Destroy the fiends who worked them woe:
To come like Indra strong and brave,
A guardian God to help and save.
And Ráma's falchion left its trace
Deep cut on Śúrpaṇakhá's face:
A hideous giantess who came
Burning for him with lawless flame.
Their sister's cries the giants heard,
And vengeance in each bosom stirred:
The monster of the triple head,
And Dúshaṇ to the contest sped.
But they and myriad fiends beside
Beneath the might of Ráma died.

When Rávaṇ, dreaded warrior, knew
The slaughter of his giant crew:
Rávaṇ, the king, whose name of fear
Earth, hell, and heaven all shook to hear:
He bade the fiend Márícha aid
The vengeful plot his fury laid.
In vain the wise Márícha tried
To turn him from his course aside:
Not Rávaṇ's self, he said, might hope
With Ráma and his strength to cope.
Impelled by fate and blind with rage
He came to Ráma's hermitage.
There, by Márícha's magic art,
He wiled the princely youths apart,
The vulture[1] slew, and bore away
The wife of Ráma as his prey.
The son of Raghu[2] came and found
Jaṭáyu slain upon the ground.
He rushed within his leafy cot;
He sought his wife, but found her not.
Then, then the hero's senses failed;
In mad despair he wept and wailed.
Upon the pile that bird he laid,
And still in quest of Sítá strayed.
A hideous giant then he saw,
Kabandha named, a shape of awe.
The monstrous fiend he smote and slew,
And in the flame the body threw;
When straight from out the funeral flame
In lovely form Kabandha came,
And bade him seek in his distress
A wise and holy hermitess.
By counsel of this saintly dame
To Pampá's pleasant flood he came,
And there the steadfast friendship won
Of Hanumán the Wind-God's son.
Counselled by him he told his grief
To great Sugríva, Vánar chief,
Who, knowing all the tale, before
The sacred flame alliance swore.
Sugríva to his new-found friend
Told his own story to the end:
His hate of Báli for the wrong
And insult he had borne so long.
And Ráma lent a willing ear
And promised to allay his fear.
Sugríva warned him of the might
Of Báli, matchless in the fight,
And, credence for his tale to gain,
Showed the huge fiend[1] by Báli slain.
The prostrate corse of mountain size
Seemed nothing in the hero's eyes;
He lightly kicked it, as it lay,
And cast it twenty leagues[2] away.
To prove his might his arrows through
Seven palms in line, uninjured, flew.
He cleft a mighty hill apart,
And down to hell he hurled his dart.
Then high Sugríva's spirit rose,
Assured of conquest o'er his foes.
With his new champion by his side
To vast Kishkindhá's cave he hied.
Then, summoned by his awful shout,
King Báli came in fury out,
First comforted his trembling wife,
Then sought Sugríva in the strife.
One shaft from Ráma's deadly bow
The monarch in the dust laid low.
Then Ráma bade Sugríva reign
In place of royal Báli slain.
Then speedy envoys hurried forth
Eastward and westward, south and north,
Commanded by the grateful king
Tidings of Ráma's spouse to bring.

Then by Sampáti's counsel led,
Brave Hanumán, who mocked at dread,
Sprang at one wild tremendous leap
Two hundred leagues across the deep.
To Lanká's[3] town he urged his way,
Where Ravaṇ held his royal sway.

---

[1] Jaṭáyu, a semi-divine bird, the friend of Ráma, who fought in defence of Sítá.

[2] Raghu was one of the most celebrated ancestors of Ráma whose commonest appellation is, therefore, Rághava or descendant of Raghu. Kálidása in the *Raghuvaṅśa* makes him the son of Dilípa and great-grandfather of Ráma. See *Idylls from the Sanskrit*, 'Aja' and 'Dilípa.'

---

[1] Dundhubi.

[2] Literally *ten yojanas*. The *yojana* is a measure of uncertain length variously reckoned as equal to nine miles, five, and a little less.

[3] Ceylon.

There pensive 'neath Aśoka[1] boughs
He found poor Sítá, Ráma's spouse.
He gave the hapless girl a ring,
A token from her lord and king.
A pledge from her fair hand he bore;
Then battered down the garden door.
Five captains of the host he slew,
Seven sons of councillors o'erthrew;
Crushed youthful Aksha on the field,
Then to his captors chose to yield.
Soon from their bonds his limbs were free,
But honouring the high decree
Which Brahmá[2] had pronounced of yore,
He calmly all their insults bore.
The town he burnt with hostile flame,
And spoke again with Ráma's dame,
Then swiftly back to Ráma flew
With tidings of the interview.

Then with Sugríva for his guide,
Came Ráma to the ocean side.
He smote the sea with shafts as bright
As sunbeams in their summer height,
And quick appeared the Rivers' King[3]
Obedient to the summoning.
A bridge was thrown by Nala o'er
The narrow sea from shore to shore.[4]
They crossed to Lanká's golden town,
Where Ráma's hand smote Rávan down.
Vibhishan there was left to reign
Over his brother's wide domain.
To meet her husband Sítá came;
But Ráma, stung with ire and shame,
With bitter words his wife addressed
Before the crowd that round her pressed.
But Sítá, touched with noble ire,
Gave her fair body to the fire.
Then straight the God of Wind appeared,
And words from heaven her honour cleared.
And Ráma clasped his wife again,
Uninjured, pure from spot and stain,
Obedient to the Lord of Fire
And the high mandate of his sire.
Led by the Lord who rules the sky,
The Gods and heavenly saints drew nigh,
And honoured him with worthy meed,
Rejoicing in each glorious deed.
His task achieved, his foe removed,
He triumphed, by the Gods approved.
By grace of Heaven he raised to life
The chieftains slain in mortal strife;
Then in the magic chariot through
The clouds to Nandigráma flew.
Met by his faithful brothers there,
He loosed his votive coil of hair;
Thence fair Ayodhyá's town he gained,
And o'er his father's kingdom reigned.
Disease or famine ne'er oppressed
His happy people, richly blest
With all the joys of ample wealth,
Of sweet content and perfect health.
No widow mourned her well-loved mate,
No sire his son's untimely fate.
They feared not storm or robber's hand:
No fire or flood laid waste the land;
The Golden Age[1] had come again
To bless the days of Ráma's reign.

From him, the great and glorious king,
Shall many a princely scion spring.
And he shall rule, beloved by men,
Ten thousand years and hundreds ten,[2]
And when his life on earth is past
To Brahmá's world shall go at last.'

Whoe'er this noble poem reads
That tells the tale of Ráma's deeds,
Good as the Scriptures, he shall be
From every sin and blemish free.
Whoever reads the saving strain,
With all his kin the heavens shall gain.
Bráhmans who read shall gather hence
The highest praise for eloquence.
The warrior, o'er the land shall reign,
The merchant, luck in trade obtain;
And Śúdras listening[3] ne'er shall fail
To reap advantage from the tale.[4]

---

[1] The Jonesia Aśoka is a most beautiful tree bearing a profusion of red blossoms.

[2] *Brahmá*, the Creator, is usually regarded as the first God of the Indian Trinity, although, as Kálidása says:
'Of Brahmá, Vishnu, Śiva, each may be
First, second, third, amid the blessed Three.'

Brahmá had guaranteed Rávan's life against all enemies except man.

[3] Ocean personified.

[4] The rocks lying between Ceylon and the mainland are still called Ráma's Bridge by the Hindus.

[1] 'The Bráhmans, with a system rather cosmogonical than chronological, divide the present mundane period into four ages or *yugas* as they call them: the Krita, the Tretá, the Dwápara, and the Kali. The Krita, called also the Deva-yuga or that of the Gods, is the age of truth, the perfect age, the Tretá is the age of the three sacred fires, domestic and sacrificial; the Dwápara is the age of doubt; the Kali, the present age, is the age of evil.' GORRESIO.

[2] The ancient kings of India enjoyed lives of more than patriarchal length as will appear in the course of the poem.

[3] Śúdras, men of the fourth and lowest pure caste, were not allowed to read the poem, but might hear it recited.

[4] The three *ślokes* or distichs which these twelve lines represent are evidently a still later and very awkward addition to the introduction.

CANTO II.

BRAHMÁ'S VISIT.

Válmíki, graceful speaker, heard,
To highest admiration stirred.
To him whose fame the tale rehearsed
He paid his mental worship first;
Then with his pupil humbly bent
Before the saint most eloquent.
Thus honoured and dismissed the seer
Departed to his heavenly sphere.
Then from his cot Válmíki hied
To Tamasá's[1] sequestered side,
Not far remote from Gangá's tide.
He stood and saw the ripples roll
Pellucid o'er a pebbly shoal.
To Bharadvája[2] by his side
He turned in ecstasy, and cried:
'See, pupil dear, this lovely sight,
The smooth-floored shallow, pure and bright,
With not a speck or shade to mar,
And clear as good men's bosoms are.
Here on the brink thy pitcher lay,
And bring my zone of bark, I pray.
Here will I bathe: the rill has not,
To lave the limbs, a fairer spot.
Do quickly as I bid, nor waste
The precious time; away, and haste.'

Obedient to his master's hest
Quick from the cot he brought the vest;
The hermit took it from his hand,
And tightened round his waist the band;
Then duly dipped and bathed him there,
And muttered low his secret prayer.
To spirits and to Gods he made
Libation of the stream, and strayed
Viewing the forest deep and wide
That spread its shade on every side.
Close by the bank he saw a pair
Of curlews sporting fearless there.
But suddenly with evil mind
An outcast fowler stole behind,
And, with an aim too sure and true,
The male bird near the hermit slew.
The wretched hen in wild despair
With fluttering pinions beat the air,
And shrieked a long and bitter cry
When low on earth she saw him lie,
Her loved companion, quivering, dead,
His dear wings with his lifeblood red;
And for her golden-crested mate
She mourned, and was disconsolate.

The hermit saw the slaughtered bird,
And all his heart with ruth was stirred.
The fowler's impious deed distressed
His gentle sympathetic breast,
And while the curlew's sad cries rang
Within his ears, the hermit sang:
'No fame be thine for endless time,
Because, base outcast, of thy crime,
Whose cruel hand was fain to slay
One of this gentle pair at play!'
E'en as he spoke his bosom wrought
And laboured with the wondering thought
What was the speech his ready tongue
Had uttered when his heart was wrung.
He pondered long upon the speech,
Recalled the words and measured each,
And thus exclaimed the saintly guide
To Bharadvája by his side:
'With equal lines of even feet,
With rhythm and time and tone complete,
The measured form of words I spoke
In shock of grief be termed a śloke.'[1]
And Bharadvája, nothing slow
His faithful love and zeal to show,
Answered those words of wisdom, 'Be
The name, my lord, as pleases thee.'

As rules prescribe the hermit took
Some lustral water from the brook.
But still on this his constant thought
Kept brooding, as his home he sought;
While Bharadvája paced behind,
A pupil sage of lowly mind,
And in his hand a pitcher bore
With pure fresh water brimming o'er.
Soon as they reached their calm retreat
The holy hermit took his seat;
His mind from worldly cares recalled,
And mused in deepest thought enthralled.

Then glorious Brahmá,[2] Lord Most High,
Creator of the earth and sky,

---

[1] There are several rivers in India of this name, now corrupted into *Tonse*. The river here spoken of is that which falls into the Ganges a little below Allahabad.

[2] 'In Book II., Canto LIV., we meet with a saint of this name presiding over a convent of disciples in his hermitage at the confluence of the Ganges and the Jumna. Thence the later author of these introductory cantos has borrowed the name and person, inconsistently indeed, but with the intention of enhancing the dignity of the poet by ascribing to him so celebrated a disciple.' SCHLEGEL.

[1] The poet plays upon the similarity in sound of the two words: *śoka* means grief, *śloka*, the heroic measure in which the poem is composed. It need scarcely be said that the derivation is fanciful.

[2] Brahmá, the Creator, is usually regarded as the first person of the divine triad of India. The four heads with which he is represented are supposed to have allusion to the four corners of the earth which he is sometimes considered to personify. As an object of adoration Brahmá has been

The four-faced God, to meet the sage
Came to Válmíki's hermitage.
Soon as the mighty God he saw,
Up sprang the saint in wandering awe.
Mute, with clasped hands, his head he bent,
And stood before him reverent.
His honoured guest he greeted well,
Who bade him of his welfare tell;
Gave water for his blessed feet,
Brought offerings,[1] and prepared a seat.
In honoured place the God Most High
Sate down, and bade the saint sit nigh.
There sate before Válmíki's eyes
The Father of the earth and skies;
But still the hermit's thoughts were bent
On one thing only, all intent
On that poor curlew's mournful fate
Lamenting for her slaughtered mate;
And still his lips, in absent mood,
The verse that told his grief, renewed:
'Woe to the fowler's impious hand
That did the deed that folly planned;
That could to needless death devote
The curlew of the tuneful throat!'

The heavenly Father smiled in glee,
And said, 'O best of hermits, see,
A verse, unconscious, thou hast made;
No longer be the task delayed.
Seek not to trace, with labour vain,
The unpremeditated strain.
The tuneful lines thy lips rehearsed
Spontaneous from thy bosom burst.
Then come, O best of seers, relate
The life of Ráma good and great,
The tale that saintly Nárad told,
In all its glorious length unfold.
Of all the deeds his arm has done
Upon this earth, omit not one,
And thus the noble life record
Of that wise, brave, and virtuous lord.
His every act to day displayed,
His secret life to none betrayed:
How Lakshman, how the giants fought;
With high emprise and hidden thought:
And all that Janak's child[1] befell
Where all could see, where none could tell,
The whole of this shall truly be
Made known, O best of saints, to thee.
In all thy poem, through my grace,
No word of falsehood shall have place.
Begin the story, and rehearse
The tale divine in charming verse.
As long as in this firm-set land
The streams shall flow, the mountains stand,
So long throughout the world, be sure,
The great Rámáyan shall endure.[2]
While the Rámáyan's ancient strain
Shall glorious in the earth remain,
To higher spheres shalt thou arise
And dwell with me above the skies.'

He spoke, and vanished into air,
And left Válmíki wondering there.
The pupils of the holy man,
Moved by their love of him, began
To chant that verse, and ever more
They marvelled as they sang it o'er:
'Behold, the four-lined balanced rime,
Repeated over many a time,
In words that from the hermit broke
In shock of grief, becomes a śloke.'
This measure now Válmíki chose
Wherein his story to compose.
In hundreds of such verses, sweet
With equal lines and even feet,
The saintly poet, lofty-souled,
The glorious deeds of Ráma told.

CANTO III.

THE ARGUMENT.

The hermit thus with watchful heed
Received the poem's pregnant seed,
And looked with eager thought around
If fuller knowledge might be found.

---

entirely superseded by Śiva and Vishṇu. In the whole of India there is, I believe, but one temple dedicated to his worship. In this point the first of the Indian triad curiously resembles the last of the divine fraternity of Greece, Aïdes the brother of Zeus and Poseidon. 'In all Greece, says Pausanias, there is no single temple of Aïdes, except at a single spot in Elis.' See Gladstone's Juventus Mundi, p. 253.

[1] The *argha* or *arghya* was a libation or offering to a deity, a Bráhman, or other venerable personage. According to one authority it consisted of water, milk, the points of Kúsa-grass, curds, clarified butter, rice, barley, and white mustard; according to another, of saffron, bel, unbroken grain, flowers, curds, dúrbá-grass, kúsa-grass, and sesamum.

[1] Sítá, daughter of Janak king of Mithilá.

[2] 'I congratulate myself,' says Schlegel in the preface to his, alas, unfinished edition of the Rámáyan, 'that, by the favour of the Supreme Deity, I have been allowed to begin so great a work; I glory and make my boast that I too after so many ages have helped to confirm that ancient oracle declared to Válmíki by the Father of Gods and men:

Dum stabunt montes, campis dum flumina current,
Usque tuum toto carmen celebrabitur orbe.'

His lips with water first bedewed,[1]
He sate in reverent attitude
On holy grass,[2] the points all bent
Together toward the orient;[3]
And thus in meditation he
Entered the path of poesy.
Then clearly, through his virtue's might,
All lay discovered to his sight,
Whate'er befell, through all their life,
Ráma, his brother, and his wife:
And Daśaratha and each queen
At every time, in every scene:
His people too, of every sort;
The nobles of his princely court:
Whate'er was said, whate'er decreed,
Each time they sate, each plan and deed:
For holy thought and fervent rite
Had so refined his keener sight
That by his sanctity his view
The present, past, and future knew,
And he with mental eye could grasp,
Like fruit within his fingers' clasp,
The life of Ráma, great and good,
Roaming with Sítá in the wood.
He told, with secret-piercing eyes,
The tale of Ráma's high emprise,
Each listening ear that shall entice,
A sea of pearls of highest price.
Thus good Válmíki, sage divine,
Rehearsed the tale of Raghu's line,
As Nárad, heavenly saint, before
Had traced the story's outline o'er.
He sang of Ráma's princely birth,
His kindness and heroic worth;
His love for all, his patient youth,
His gentleness and constant truth,
And many a tale and legend old
By holy Viśvámitra told.
How Janak's child he wooed and won,
And broke the bow that bent to none.
How he with every virtue fraught
His namesake Ráma[4] met and fought.
The choice of Ráma for the throne;
The malice by Kaikeyí shown,
Whose evil counsel marred the plan
And drove him forth a banisht man.
How the king grieved and groaned, and cried,
And swooned away and pining died.
The subjects' woe when thus bereft;
And how the following crowds he left:
With Guha talked, and firmly stern
Ordered his driver to return.
How Gangá's farther shore he gained;
By Bharadvája entertained,
By whose advice he journeyed still
And came to Chitrakúṭa's hill.
How there he dwelt and built a cot;
How Bharat journeyed to the spot;
His earnest supplication made;
Drink-offerings to their father paid;
The sandals given by Ráma's hand,
As emblems of his right, to stand:
How from his presence Bharat went
And years in Nandigráma spent.
How Ráma entered Daṇḍak wood
And in Sutíkhṇa's presence stood.
The favour Anasúyá showed,
The wondrous balsam she bestowed.
How Śarabhanga's dwelling-place
They sought; saw Indra face to face;
The meeting with Agastya gained;
The heavenly bow from him obtained.
How Ráma with Virádha met;
Their home in Panchavaṭa set.
How Śúrpaṇakhá underwent
The mockery and disfigurement.
Of Triśirá's and Khara's fall,
Of Rávaṇ roused at vengeance' call.
Márícha doomed, without escape;
The fair Videhan[1] lady's rape.
How Ráma wept and raved in vain,
And how the Vulture-king was slain.
How Ráma fierce Kabandha slew;
Then to the side of Pampá drew,
Met Hanumán, and her whose vows
Were kept beneath the greenwood boughs.
How Raghu's son, the lofty-souled,
On Pampá's bank wept uncontrolled,
Then journeyed, Rishyamúk to reach,
And of Sugríva then had speech.
The friendship made, which both had sought;
How Báli and Sugríva fought.
How Báli in the strife was slain,
And how Sugríva came to reign.
The treaty, Tárá's wild lament;
The rainy nights in watching spent.
The wrath of Raghu's lion son;
The gathering of the hosts in one.
The sending of the spies about,
And all the regions pointed out.
The ring by Ráma's hand bestowed;
The cave wherein the bear abode.
The fast proposed, their lives to end;
Sampáti gained to be their friend.

---

[1] 'The sipping of water is a requisite introduction of all rites: without it, says the Sámba Puráṇa, all acts of religion are vain.' COLEBROOKE.

[2] The *darbha* or *kuśa* (Poa cynosuroides), a kind of grass used in sacrifice by the Hindus as *verbena* was by the Romans.

[3] The direction in which the grass should be placed upon the ground as a seat for the Gods, on occasion of offerings made to them.

[4] Paraśuráma or Ráma with the Axe. See Canto LXXIV.

[1] Sítá. Videha was the country of which Mithilá was the capital.

The scaling of the hill, the leap
Of Hanumán across the deep.
Ocean's command that bade them seek
Mainákka of the lofty peak.
The death of Sinhiká, the sight
Of Lanká with her palace bright.
How Hanumán stole in at eve;
His plan the giants to deceive.
How through the square he made his way
To chambers where the women lay,
Within the Aśoka garden came
And there found Ráma's captive dame.
His colloquy with her he sought,
And giving of the ring he brought.
How Sítá gave a gem o'erjoyed;
How Hanumán the grove destroyed.
How giantesses trembling fled,
And servant fiends were smitten dead.
How Hanumán was seized; their ire
When Lanká blazed with hostile fire.
His leap across the sea once more;
The eating of the honey store.
How Ráma he consoled, and how
He showed the gem from Sítá's brow.
With Ocean, Ráma's interview;
The bridge that Nala o'er it threw.
The crossing, and the sitting down
At night round Lanká's royal town.
The treaty with Vibhíshan made;
The plan for Rávan's slaughter laid.
How Kumbhakarna in his pride
And Meghanáda fought and died.
How Rávan in the fight was slain,
And captive Sítá brought again.
Vibhíshan set upon the throne;
The flying chariot Pushpak shown.
How Brahmá and the Gods appeared,
And Sítá's doubted honour cleared.
How in the flying car they rode
To Bharadvája's calm abode.
The Wind-God's son sent on afar;
How Bharat met the flying car.
How Ráma then was king ordained;
The legions their discharge obtained.
How Ráma cast his queen away;
How grew the people's love each day.
Thus did the saint Válmíki tell
Whate'er in Ráma's life befell,
And in the closing verses all
That yet to come will once befall.

CANTO IV.

THE RHAPSODISTS.

When to the end the tale was brought,
Rose in the sage's mind the thought;
'Now who throughout this earth will go,
And tell it forth that all may know?'
As thus he mused with anxious breast,
Behold, in hermit's raiment dressed,
Kuśá and Lava[1] came to greet
Their master and embrace his feet.
The twins he saw, that princely pair
Sweet-voiced, who dwelt beside him there.
None for the task could be more fit,
For skilled were they in Holy Writ;
And so the great Rámáyan, fraught
With lore divine, to these he taught:
The lay whose verses sweet and clear
Take with delight the listening ear,
That tell of Sítá's noble life
And Rávan's fall in battle strife.
Great joy to all who hear they bring,
Sweet to recite and sweet to sing.
For music's sevenfold notes are there,
And triple measure,[2] wrought with care,
With melody and tone and time,
And flavours[3] that enhance the rime:
Heroic might has ample place,
And loathing of the false and base,
With anger, mirth, and terror, blent
With tenderness, surprise, content.
When, half the hermit's grace to gain,
And half because they loved the strain,
The youths within their hearts had stored
The poem that his lips outpoured,
Válmíki kissed them on the head,
As at his feet they bowed, and said:
'Recite ye this heroic song
In tranquil shades where sages throng:
Recite it where the good resort,
In lowly home and royal court.'
The hermit ceased. The tuneful pair,
Like heavenly minstrels sweet and fair,
In music's art divinely skilled,
Their saintly master's word fulfilled.
Like Ráma's self, from whom they came,
They showed their sire in face and frame,

---

[1] The twin sons of Ráma and Sítá, born after Ráma had repudiated Sítá, and brought up in the hermitage of Válmíki. As they were the first rhapsodists the combined name Kuśílava signifies a reciter of poems, or an improvisatore, even to the present day.

[2] Perhaps the bass, tenor, and treble, or quick, slow and middle time. We know but little of the ancient music of the Hindus.

[3] 'Eight flavours or sentiments are usually enumerated, love, mirth, tenderness, anger, heroism, terror, disgust, and surprise: tranquillity or content, or paternal tenderness, is sometimes considered as the ninth.' WILSON. See the *Sáhitya Darpana* or *Mirror of Composition*, translated by Dr. Ballantyne and Bábú Pramadádása Mittra in the *Bibliotheca Indica*.

As though from some fair sculptured stone
Two selfsame images had grown.
Sometimes the pair rose up to sing,
Surrounded by a holy ring,
Where seated on the grass had met
Full many a musing anchoret.
Then tears bedimmed those gentle eyes,
As transport took them and surprise,
And as they listened every one
Cried in delight, Well done! Well done!
Those sages versed in holy lore
Praised the sweet minstrels more and more:
And wondered at the singers' skill,
And the bard's verses sweeter still,
Which laid so clear before the eye
The glorious deeds of days gone by.
Thus by the virtuous hermits praised,
Inspirited their voice they raised.
Pleased with the song this holy man
Would give the youths a water-can;
One gave a fair ascetic dress,
Or sweet fruit from the wilderness.
One saint a black-deer's hide would bring,
And one a sacrificial string:
One, a clay pitcher from his hoard,
And one, a twisted munja cord.[1]
One in his joy an axe would find,
One, braid, their plaited locks to bind.
One gave a sacrificial cup,
One rope to tie their fagots up;
While fuel at their feet was laid,
Or hermit's stool of fig-tree made.
All gave, or if they gave not, none
Forgot at least a benison.
Some saints, delighted with their lays,
Would promise health and length of days:
Others with surest words would add
Some boon to make their spirit glad.
In such degree of honour then
That song was held by holy men:
That living song which life can give,
By which shall many a minstrel live.
In seat of kings, in crowded hall,
They sang the poem, praised of all.
And Ráma chanced to hear their lay,
While he the votive steed[2] would slay,
And sent fit messengers to bring
The minstrel pair before the king.
They came, and found the monarch high
Enthroned in gold, his brothers nigh;
While many a minister below,
And noble, sate in lengthened row.

[1] Saccharum Munja is a plant from whose fibres is twisted the sacred string which a Bráhman wears over one shoulder after he has been initiated by a rite which in some respects answers to confirmation.

[2] A description of an Aśvamedha or Horse Sacrifice is given in Canto XIII. of this Book.

The youthful pair awhile he viewed
Graceful in modest attitude,
And then in words like these addressed
His brother Lakshman and the rest:
'Come, listen to the wondrous strain
Recited by these godlike twain,
Sweet singers of a story fraught
With melody and lofty thought.'
The pair, with voices sweet and strong,
Rolled the full tide of noble song,
With tone and accent deftly blent
To suit the changing argument.
Mid that assembly loud and clear
Rang forth that lay so sweet to hear,
That universal rapture stole
Through each man's frame and heart and soul.
'These minstrels, blest with every sign
That marks a high and princely line,
In holy shades who dwell,
Enshrined in Saint Válmíki's lay,
A monument to live for aye,
My deeds in song shall tell.'
Thus Ráma spoke: their breasts were fired,
And the great tale, as if inspired,
The youths began to sing,
While every heart with transport swelled,
And mute and rapt attention held
The concourse and the king.

CANTO V.

AYODHYÁ.

'Ikshváku's sons from days of old
Were ever brave and mighty-souled.
The land their arms had made their own
Was bounded by the sea alone.
Their holy works have won them praise,
Through countless years, from Manu's days.
Their ancient sire was Sagar, he
Whose high command dug out the sea:[1]
With sixty thousand sons to throng
Around him as he marched along.
From them this glorious tale proceeds:
The great Rámáyan tells their deeds.
This noble song whose lines contain
Lessons of duty, love, and gain,
We two will now at length recite,
While good men listen with delight.
On Sarjú's[2] bank, of ample size,
The happy realm of Kośal lies,

[1] This exploit is related in Canto XL.

[2] The Sarjú or Ghaghra, anciently called Sarayú, rises in the Himalayas, and after flowing through the province of Oudh, falls into the Ganges.

With fertile length of fair champaign
And flocks and herds and wealth of grain.
There, famous in her old renown,
Ayodhyá[1] stands, the royal town,
In bygone ages built and planned
By sainted Manu's[2] princely hand.
Imperial seat! her walls extend
Twelve measured leagues from end to end,
And three in width from side to side,
With square and palace beautified.
Her gates at even distance stand;
Her ample roads are wisely planned.
Right glorious is her royal street
Where streams allay the dust and heat.
On level ground in even row
Her houses rise in goodly show:
Terrace and palace, arch and gate
The queenly city decorate.
High are her ramparts, strong and vast,
By ways at even distance passed,
With circling moat, both deep and wide,
And store of weapons fortified.

King Daśaratha, lofty-souled,
That city guarded and controlled,
With towering Sál trees belted round,[3]
And many a grove and pleasure ground,
As royal Indra, throned on high,
Rules his fair city in the sky.[4]
She seems a painted city, fair
With chess-board line and even square.[5]
And cool boughs shade the lovely lake
Where weary men their thirst may slake.
There gilded chariots gleam and shine,
And stately piles the Gods enshrine.
There gay sleek people ever throng
To festival and dance and song.
A mine is she of gems and sheen,
The darling home of Fortune's Queen.
With noblest sort of drink and meat,
The fairest rice and golden wheat,
And fragrant with the chaplet's scent
With holy oil and incense blent.
With many an elephant and steed,
And wains for draught and cars for speed.
With envoys sent by distant kings,
And merchants with their precious things
With banners o'er her roofs that play,
And weapons that a hundred slay;[1]
All warlike engines framed by man,
And every class of artisan.
A city rich beyond compare
With bards and minstrels gathered there,
And men and damsels who entrance
The soul with play and song and dance.
In every street is heard the lute,
The drum, the tabret, and the flute,
The Veda chanted soft and low,
The ringing of the archer's bow;
With bands of godlike heroes skilled
In every warlike weapon, filled,
And kept by warriors from the foe,
As Nágas guard their home below.[2]
There wisest Bráhmans evermore
The flame of worship feed,
And versed in all the Vedas' lore,
Their lives of virtue lead.
Truthful and pure, they freely give;
They keep each sense controlled,
And in their holy fervour live
Like the great saints of old.

CANTO VI.

THE KING.

There reigned a king of name revered,
To country and to town endeared,
Great Daśaratha, good and sage.
Well read in Scripture's holy page:

---

[1] The ruins of the ancient capital of Ráma and the Children of the Sun may still be traced in the present Ajudhyá near Fyzabad. Ajudhyá is the Jerusalem or Mecca of the Hindus.

[2] A legislator and saint, the son of Brahmá or a personification of Brahmá himself, the creator of the world, and progenitor of mankind. Derived from the root *man* to think, the word means originally *man*, the thinker, and is found in this sense in the Rig-veda.

Manu as a legislator is identified with the Cretan Minos, as progenitor of mankind with the German Mannus: 'Celebrant carminibus antiquis, quod unum apud illos memoriæ et annalium genus est, Tuisconem deum terra editum, et filium Mannum, originem gentis conditoresque.' TACITUS, *Germania*, Cap. II.

[3] The Sál (Shorea Robusta) is a valuable timber tree of considerable height.

[4] The city of Indra is called Amarávatí or Home of the Immortals.

[5] Schlegel thinks that this refers to the marble of different colours with which the houses were adorned. It seems more natural to understand it as implying the regularity of the streets and houses.

[1] The *Śataghní i. e. centicide,* or slayer of a hundred, is generally supposed to be a sort of fire-arms, or the ancient Indian rocket; but it is also described as a stone set round with iron spikes.

[2] The Nágas (serpents) are demigods with a human face and serpent body. They inhabit Pátála or the regions under the earth. Bhogavatí is the name of their capital city. Serpents are still worshipped in India. See Fergusson's *Tree and Serpent Worship*.

Upon his kingdom's weal intent,
Mighty and brave and provident;
The pride of old Ikshváku's seed
For lofty thought and righteous deed.
Peer of the saints, for virtues famed,
For foes subdued and passions tamed;
A rival in his wealth untold
Of Indra and the Lord of Gold.
Like Manu first of kings, he reigned.
And worthily his state maintained.
For firm and just and ever true
Love, duty, gain he kept in view,
And ruled his city rich and free,
Like Indra's Amarávatí.
And worthy of so fair a place
There dwelt a just and happy race
With troops of children blest.
Each man contented sought no more,
Nor longed with envy for the store
By richer friends possessed.
For poverty was there unknown,
And each man counted as his own
Kine, steeds, and gold, and grain.
All dressed in raiment bright and clean,
And every townsman might be seen
With earrings, wreath, or chain.
None deigned to feed on broken fare,
And none was false or stingy there.
A piece of gold, the smallest pay,
Was earned by labour for a day.
On every arm were bracelets worn,
And none was faithless or forsworn,
A braggart or unkind.
None lived upon another's wealth,
None pined with dread or broken health,
Or dark disease of mind.
High-souled were all. The slanderous word,
The boastful lie, were never heard.
Each man was constant to his vows,
And lived devoted to his spouse.
No other love his fancy knew,
And she was tender, kind, and true.
Her dames were fair of form and face,
With charm of wit and gentle grace,
With modest raiment simply neat,
And winning manners soft and sweet.
The twice-born sages, whose delight
Was Scripture's page and holy rite,
Their calm and settled course pursued,
Nor sought the menial multitude.
In many a Scripture each was versed,
And each the flame of worship nursed,
And gave with lavish hand.
Each paid to Heaven the offerings due,
And none was godless or untrue
In all that holy band.
To Bráhmans, as the laws ordain,
The Warrior caste were ever fain
The reverence due to pay;
And these the Vaiśyas' peaceful crowd,
Who trade and toil for gain, were proud
To honour and obey;
And all were by the Śúdras[1] served,
Who never from their duty swerved,
Their proper worship all addressed
To Bráhman, spirits, God, and guest.
Pure and unmixt their rites remained,
Their race's honour ne'er was stained.[2]
Cheered by his grandsons, sons, and wife,
Each passed a long and happy life.
Thus was that famous city held
By one who all his race excelled,
Blest in his gentle reign,
As the whole land aforetime swayed
By Manu, prince of men, obeyed
Her king from main to main.
And heroes kept her, strong and brave,
As lions guard their mountain cave:
Fierce as devouring flame they burned,
And fought till death, but never turned.
Horses had she of noblest breed,
Like Indra's for their form and speed,
From Váhlí's[3] hills and Sindhu's[4] sand,
Vanáyu[5] and Kámboja's land.[6]

---

[1] The fourth and lowest pure caste, whose duty was to serve the three first classes.

[2] By forbidden marriages between persons of different castes.

[3] Váhlí or Váhlíka is Bactriana; its name is preserved in the modern Balkh.

[4] The Sanskrit word Sindhu is in the singular the name of the river Indus, in the plural of the people and territories on its banks. The name appears as *Hidhu* in the cuneiform inscription of Darius son of Hystaspes, in which the nations tributary to that king are enumerated.

The Hebrew form is *Hodda* (Esther, 1. I.) In Zend it appears as *Hendu* in a somewhat wider sense. With the Persians later the signification of *Hind* seems to have co-extended with their increasing acquaintance with the country. The weak Ionic dialect omitted the Persian *h*, and we find in Hecatæus and Herodotus Ἴνδος and ἡ Ἰνδική. In this form the Romans received the names and transmitted them to us. The Arabian geographers in their ignorance that Hind and Sind are two forms of the same word have made of them two brothers and traced their descent from Noah. See Lassen's Indische Alterthumskunde Vol. I. pp. 2, 3.

[5] The situation of Vanáyu is not exactly determined: it seems to have lain to the north-west of India.

[6] Kámboja was probably still further to the north-west. Lassen thinks that the

Her noble elephants had strayed
Through Vindhyan and Himálayan shade,
Gigantic in their bulk and height,
Yet gentle in their matchless might.
They rivalled well the world-spread fame
Of the great stock from which they came,
Of Váman, vast of size,
Of Mahápadma's glorious line,
Thine, Anjan, and, Airávat, thine,[1]
Upholders of the skies.
With those, enrolled in fourfold class,
Who all their mighty kin surpass,
Whom men Matangas name,
And Mrigas spotted black and white,
And Bhadras of unwearied might,
And Mandras hard to tame.[2]
Thus, worthy of the name she bore,[3]
Ayodhyá for a league or more
Cast a bright glory round,
Where Daśaratha wise and great
Governed his fair ancestral state,
With every virtue crowned.
Like Indra in the skies he reigned
In that good town whose wall contained
High domes and turrets proud,
With gates and arcs of triumph decked,
And sturdy barriers to protect
Her gay and countless crowd.

CANTO VII.

THE MINISTERS.

Two sages, holy saints, had he,
His ministers and priests to be:
Vaśishtha, faithful to advise,
And Vámadeva, Scripture-wise.
Eight other lords around him stood,
All skilled to counsel, wise and good:
Jayanta, Vijay, Dhrishṭi bold
In fight, affairs of war controlled:
Siddhárth and Arthasádhak true
Watched o'er expense and revenue,
And Dharmapál and wise Aśok
Of right and law and justice spoke.
With these the sage Sumantra, skilled
To urge the car, high station filled.
All these in knowledge duly trained
Each passion and each sense restrained:
With modest manners, nobly bred
Each plan and nod and look they read,
Upon their neighbours' good intent,
Most active and benevolent:
As sit the Vasus[1] round their king,
They sate around him counselling.
They ne'er in virtue's loftier pride
Another's lowly gifts decried.
In fair and seemly garb arrayed,
No weak uncertain plans they made.
Well skilled in business, fair and just,
They gained the people's love and trust,
And thus without oppression stored
The swelling treasury of their lord.
Bound in sweet friendship each to each,
They spoke kind thoughts in gentle speech.
They looked alike with equal eye
On every caste, on low and high.
Devoted to their king, they sought,
Ere his tongue spoke, to learn his thought,
And knew, as each occasion rose,
To hide their counsel or disclose.
In foreign lands or in their own
Whatever passed, to them was known.
By secret spies they timely knew
What men were doing or would do.
Skilled in the grounds of war and peace
They saw the monarch's state increase,
Watching his weal with conquering eye
That never let occasion by,
While nature lent her aid to bless
Their labours with unbought success.
Never for anger, lust, or gain,
Would they their lips with falsehood stain.
Inclined to mercy they could scan
The weakness and the strength of man.
They fairly judged both high and low,
And ne'er would wrong a guiltless foe;
Yet if a fault were proved, each one
Would punish e'en his own dear son.
But there and in the kingdom's bound
No thief or man impure was found:
None of loose life or evil fame,
No temper of another's dame.
Contented with their lot each caste

name is etymologically connected with *Cambyses* which in the cuneiform inscription of Behistun is written Ka(m)bujia.

[1] The elephants of Indra and other deities who preside over the four points of the compass.

[2] 'There are four kinds of elephants. 1 *Bhaddar*. It is well proportioned, has an erect head, a broad chest, large ears, a long tail, and is bold and can bear fatigue. 2 *Mand*. It is black, has yellow eyes, a uniformly sized body, and is wild and ungovernable. 3 *Mirg*. It has a whitish skin, with black spots. 4 *Mir*. It has a small head, and obeys readily. It gets frightened when it thunders.' *Aín-i-Akbarí*. Translated by H. Blochmann, Aín 41, *The Imperial Elephant Stables*.

[3] Ayodhyá means *not to be fought against*.

[1] Attendants of Indra, eight Gods whose names signify fire, light and its phenomena.

Calm days in blissful quiet passed;
And, all in fitting tasks employed,
Country and town deep rest enjoyed,
With these wise lords around his throne
The monarch justly reigned,
And making every heart his own
The love of all men gained.
With trusty agents, as beseems,
Each distant realm he scanned,
As the sun visits with his beams
Each corner of the land.
Ne'er would he on a mightier foe
With hostile troops advance,
Nor at an equal strike a blow
In war's delusive chance.
These lords in council bore their part
With ready brain and faithful heart,
With skill and knowledge, sense and tact,
Good to advise and bold to act.
And high and endless fame he won
With these to guide his schemes,
As, risen in his might, the sun
Wins glory with his beams.

CANTO VIII.

SUMANTRA'S SPEECH.

But splendid, just, and great of mind,
The childless king for offspring pined.
No son had he his name to grace,
Transmitter of his royal race.
Long had his anxious bosom wrought,
And as he pondered rose the thought:
'A votive steed 'twere good to slay,
So might a son the gift repay.'
Before his lords his plan he laid,
And bade them with their wisdom aid:
Then with these words Sumantra, best
Of royal counsellors, addressed:
'Hither, Vaśishṭha at their head,
Let all my priestly guides be led.'
To him Sumantra made reply:
'Hear, Sire, a tale of days gone by.
To many a sage in time of old,
Sanatkumár, the saint, foretold
How from thine ancient line, O King,
A son, when years came round, should spring.
'Here dwells,' 'twas thus the seer began,
'Of Kaśyap's[1] race, a holy man,
Vibháṇḍak named: to him shall spring
A son, the famous Rishyaśring.
Bred with the deer that round him roam,
The wood shall be that hermit's home.
To him no mortal shall be known
Except his holy sire alone.
Still by those laws shall he abide
Which lives of youthful Bráhmans guide,
Obedient to the strictest rule
That forms the young ascetic's school:
And all the wondering world shall hear
Of his stern life and penance drear;
His care to nurse the holy fire
And do the bidding of his sire.
Then, seated on the Angas'[1] throne,
Shall Lomapád to fame be known.
But folly wrought by that great king
A plague upon the land shall bring;
No rain for many a year shall fall
And grievous drought shall ruin all.
The troubled king with many a prayer
Shall bid the priests some cure declare:
'The lore of Heaven 'tis yours to know,
Nor are ye blind to things below:
Declare, O holy men, the way
This plague to expiate and stay.'
Those best of Bráhmans shall reply:
'By every art, O Monarch, try
Hither to bring Vibháṇḍak's child,
Persuaded, captured, or beguiled.
And when the boy is hither led
To him thy daughter duly wed.'
But how to bring that wondrous boy
His troubled thoughts will long employ,
And hopeless to achieve the task
He counsel of his lords will ask,
And bid his priests and servants bring
With honour saintly Rishyaśring.
But when they hear the monarch's speech,
All these their master will beseech,
With trembling hearts and looks of woe,
To spare them, for they fear to go.
And many a plan will they declare
And crafty plots will frame,
And promise fair to show him there,
Unforced, with none to blame.
On every word his lords shall say,
The king will meditate,
And on the third returning day
Recall them to debate.
Then this shall be the plan agreed,
That damsels shall be sent
Attired in holy hermits' weed,
And skilled in blandishment,
That they the hermit may beguile
With every art and amorous wile

[1] Kaśyap was a grandson of the God Brahmá. He is supposed to have given his name to Kashmír = Kaśyapa-míra, Kaśyap's Lake.

[1] The people of Anga. 'Anga is said in the lexicons to be Bengal; but here certainly another region is intended situated at the confluence of the Sarjú with the Ganges, and not far distant from Daśaratha's dominions.' GORRESIO. It comprised part of Behar and Bhagulpur.

Whose use they know so well,
And by their witcheries seduce
The unsuspecting young recluse
To live his father's cell.
Then when the boy with willing feet
Shall wander from his calm retreat
And in that city stand,
The troubles of the king shall end,
And streams of blessed rain descend
Upon the thirsty land.
Thus shall the holy Rishyaśring
To Lomapád, the mighty king,
By wedlock be allied;
For Śántá, fairest of the fair,
In mind and grace beyond compare,
Shall be his royal bride.
He, at the Offering of the Steed,
The flames with holy oil shall feed,
And for King Daśaratha gain
Sons whom his prayers have begged in vain.'
'I have repeated, Sire, thus far,
The words of old Sanatkumár,
In order as he spoke them then
Amid the crowd of holy men.'
Then Daśaratha cried with joy,
'Say how they brought the hermit boy.'

CANTO IX.

RISHYAŚRING.

The wise Sumantra, thus addressed,
Unfolded at the king's behest
The plan the lords in council laid
To draw the hermit from the shade:
'The priest, amid the lordly crowd,
To Lomapád thus spoke aloud:
'Hear, King, the plot our thoughts have framed,
A harmless trick by all unblamed.
Far from the world that hermit's child
Lives lonely in the distant wild:
A stranger to the joys of sense,
His bliss is pain and abstinence;
And all unknown are women yet
To him, a holy anchoret.
The gentle passions we will wake
That with resistless influence shake
The hearts of men; and he
Drawn by enchantment strong and sweet
Shall follow from his lone retreat,
And come and visit thee.
Let ships be formed with utmost care
That artificial trees may bear,
And sweet fruit deftly made;
Let goodly raiment, rich and rare,
And flowers, and many a bird be there
Beneath the leafy shade.
Upon the ships thus decked a band
Of young and lovely girls shall stand,
Rich in each charm that wakes desire,
And eyes that burn with amorous fire;
Well skilled to sing, and play, and dance,
And ply their trade with smile and glance.
Let these, attired in hermits' dress,
Betake them to the wilderness,
And bring the boy of life austere
A voluntary captive here.'
He ended; and the king agreed,
By the priest's counsel won.
And all the ministers took heed
To see his bidding done.
In ships with wondrous art prepared
Away the lovely women fared,
And soon beneath the shade they stood
Of the wild, lonely, dreary wood.
And there the leafy cot they found
Where dwelt the devotee,
And looked with eager eyes around
The hermit's son to see.
Still, of Vibhándak sore afraid,
They hid behind the creepers' shade.
But when by careful watch they knew
The elder saint was far from view,
With bolder steps they ventured nigh
To catch the youthful hermit's eye.
Then all the damsels, blithe and gay,
At various games began to play.
They tossed the flying ball about
With dance and song and merry shout,
And moved, their scented tresses bound
With wreaths, in mazy motion round.
Some girls as if by love possessed,
Sank to the earth in feigned unrest,
Up starting quickly to pursue
Their intermitted game anew.
It was a lovely sight to see
Those fair ones, as they played,
While fragrant robes were floating free,
And bracelets clashing in their glee
A pleasant tinkling made.
The anklet's chime, the Koïl's[1] cry
With music filled the place
As 'twere some city in the sky
Which heavenly minstrels grace.
With each voluptuous art they strove
To win the tenant of the grove,
And with their graceful forms inspire
His modest soul with soft desire.
With arch of brow, with beck and smile,
With every passion-waking wile

[1] The Koïl or *kokila* (Cuculus Indicus) as the harbinger of spring and love is a universal favourite with Indian poets. His voice when first heard in a glorious spring morning is not unpleasant, but becomes in the hot season intolerably wearisome to European ears.

Of glance and lotus hand,
With all enticements that excite
The longing for unknown delight
Which boys in vain withstand.
Forth came the hermit's son to view
The wondrous sight to him so new,
And gazed in rapt surprise,
For from his natal hour till then
On woman or the sons of men
He ne'er had cast his eyes.
He saw them with their waists so slim,
With fairest shape and faultless limb,
In variegated robes arrayed,
And sweetly singing as they played.
Near and more near the hermit drew,
And watched them at their game,
And stronger still the impulse grew
To question whence they came.
They marked the young ascetic gaze
With curious eye and wild amaze,
And sweet the long-eyed damsels sang,
And shrill their merry laughter rang.
Then came they nearer to his side,
And languishing with passion cried:
'Whose son, O youth, and who art thou,
Come suddenly to join us now?
And why dost thou all lonely dwell
In the wild wood? We pray thee, tell,
We wish to know thee, gentle youth;
Come, tell us, if thou wilt, the truth.'
He gazed upon that sight he ne'er
Had seen before, of girls so fair,
And out of love a longing rose
His sire and lineage to disclose:
'My father,' thus he made reply,
'Is Kaśyap's son, a saint most high,
Vibhándak styled; from him I came,
And Rishyaśring he calls my name.
Our hermit cot is near this place:
Come thither, O ye fair of face;
There be it mine, with honour due,
Ye gentle youths, to welcome you.'
They heard his speech, and gave consent,
And gladly to his cottage went.
Vibhándak's son received them well
Beneath the shelter of his cell
With guest-gift, water for their feet,
And woodland fruit and roots to eat,
They smiled, and spoke sweet words like these,
Delighted with his courtesies:
'We too have goodly fruit in store,
Grown on the trees that shade our door;
Come, if thou wilt, kind Hermit, haste
The produce of our grove to taste;
And let, O good Ascetic, first
This holy water quench thy thirst.'
They spoke, and gave him comfits sweet
Prepared ripe fruits to counterfeit;
And many a dainty cate beside
And luscious mead their stores supplied.
The seeming fruits, in taste and look,
The unsuspecting hermit took,
For, strange to him, their form beguiled
The dweller in the lonely wild.
Then round his neck fair arms were flung,
And there the laughing damsels clung,
And pressing nearer and more near
With sweet lips whispered at his ear;
While rounded limb and swelling breast
The youthful hermit softly pressed.
The pleasing charm of that strange bowl,
The touch of a tender limb,
Over his yielding spirit stole
And sweetly vanquished him.
But vows, they said, must now be paid;
They bade the boy farewell,
And, of the aged saint afraid,
Prepared to leave the dell.
With ready guile they told him where
Their hermit dwelling lay;
Then, lest the sire should find them there,
Sped by wild paths away.
They fled and left him there alone
By longing love possessed;
And with a heart no more his own
He roamed about distressed.
The aged saint came home, to find
The hermit boy distraught,
Revolving in his troubled mind
One solitary thought.
'Why dost thou not, my son,' he cried,
'Thy due obeisance pay?
Why do I see thee in the tide
Of whelming thought to-day?
A devotee should never wear
A mien so sad and strange.
Come, quickly, dearest child, declare
The reason of the change.'
And Rishyaśring, when questioned thus,
Made answer in this wise:
'O sire, there came to visit us
Some men with lovely eyes.
About my neck soft arms they wound
And kept me tightly held
To tender breasts so soft and round,
That strangely heaved and swelled.
They sing more sweetly as they dance
Than e'er I heard till now,
And play with many a sidelong glance
And arching of the brow.'
'My son,' said he, 'thus giants roam
Where holy hermits are,
And wander round their peaceful home
Their rites austere to mar.
I charge thee, thou must never lay
Thy trust in them, dear boy:
They seek thee only to betray,
And woo but to destroy.'
Thus having warned him of his foes
That night at home he spent,
And when the morrow's sun arose

Forth to the forest went.
But Rishyaśring with eager pace
Sped forth and hurried to the place
Where he those visitants had seen
Of daintly waist and charming mien.
When from afar they saw the son
Of Saint Vibhándak toward them run,
To meet the hermit boy they hied,
And hailed him with a smile, and cried:
'O come, we pray, dear lord, behold
Our lovely home of which we told:
Due honour there to thee we'll pay,
And speed thee on thy homeward way.'
Pleased with the gracious words they said
He followed where the damsels led.
As with his guides his steps he bent,
That Bráhman high of worth,
A flood of rain from heaven was sent
That gladdened all the earth.
Vibhándak took his homeward road,
And wearied by the heavy load
Of roots and woodland fruit he bore
Entered at last his cottage door.
Fain for his son he looked around,
But desolate the cell he found.
He stayed not then to bathe his feet,
Though fainting with the toil and heat,
But hurried forth and roamed about
Calling the boy with cry and shout.
He searched the wood, but all in vain;
Nor tidings of his son could gain.
One day beyond the forest's bound
The wandering saint a village found,
And asked the swains and neatherds there
Who owned the land so rich and fair,
With all the hamlets of the plain,
And herds of kine and fields of grain.
They listened to the hermit's words,
And all the guardians of the herds,
With suppliant hands together pressed,
This answer to the saint addressed:
The Angas' lord who bears the name
Of Lomapád, renowned by fame,
Bestowed these hamlets with their kine
And all their riches, as a sign
Of grace, on Rishyaśring: and he
Vibhándak's son is said to be.'
The hermit with exulting breast
The mighty will of fate confessed,
By meditation's eye discerned;
And cheerful to his home returned.
A stately ship, at early morn,
The hermit's son away had borne.
Loud roared the clouds, as on he sped,
The sky grew blacker overhead;
Till, as he reached the royal town,
A mighty flood of rain came down.
By the great rain the monarch's mind
The coming of his guest divined.
To meet the honoured youth he went,
And low to earth his head he bent.
With his own priest to lead the train,
He gave the gift high guests obtain.
And sought, with all who dwelt within
The city walls, his grace to win.
He fed him with the daintiest fare,
He served him with unceasing care,
And ministered with anxious eyes
Lest anger in his breast should rise;
And gave to be the Bráhman's bride
His own fair daughter, lotus-eyed.
Thus loved and honoured by the king,
The glorious Bráhman Rishyaśring
Passed in that royal town his life
With Śántá his beloved wife.'

CANTO X.

RISHYAŚRING INVITED.

'Again, O best of kings, give ear:
My saving words attentive hear,
And listen to the tale of old
By that illustrious Bráhman told.
'Of famed Ikshváku's line shall spring
('Twas thus he spoke) a pious king,
Named Daśaratha, good and great,
True to his word and fortunate.
He with the Angas' mighty lord
Shall ever live in sweet accord,
And his a daughter fair shall be,
Śántá of happy destiny.
But Lomapád, the Angas' chief,
Still pining in his childless grief,
To Daśaratha thus shall say:
'Give me thy daughter, friend, I pray,
Thy Śántá of the tranquil mind,
The noblest one of womankind.'
The father, swift to feel for woe,
Shall on his friend his child bestow;
And he shall take her and depart
To his own town with joyous heart.
The maiden home in triumph led,
To Rishyaśring the king shall wed.
And he with loving joy and pride
Shall take her for his honoured bride.
And Daśaratha to a rite
That best of Bráhmans shall invite
With supplicating prayer,
To celebrate the sacrifice
To win him sons and Paradise,[1]
That he will fain prepare.

[1] 'Sons and Paradise are intimately connected in Indian belief. A man desires above every thing to have a son to perpetuate his race, and to assist with sacrifices and funeral rites to make him worthy to obtain a lofty seat in heaven or to preserve that which he has already obtained.' GORRESIO.

From him the lord of men at length
The boon he seeks shall gain,
And see four sons of boundless strength
His royal line maintain.'
'Thus did the godlike saint of old
The will of fate declare,
And all that should befall unfold
Amid the sages there.
O Prince supreme of men, go thou,
Consult thy holy guide,
And win, to aid thee in thy vow,
This Bráhman to thy side.'
Sumantra's counsel, wise and good,
King Daśaratha heard,
Then by Vaśishṭha's side he stood
And thus with him conferred :
'Sumantra counsels thus : do thou
My priestly guide, the plan allow.'
Vaśishṭha gave his glad consent,
And forth the happy monarch went
With lords and servants on the road
That led to Rishyaśring's abode.
Forests and rivers duly past,
He reached the distant town at last
Of Lomapád the Angas' king,
And entered it with welcoming.
On through the crowded streets he came,
And, radiant as the kindled flame,
He saw within the monarch's house
The hermit's son most glorious.
There Lomapád, with joyful breast,
To him all honour paid,
For friendship for his royal guest
His faithful bosom swayed.
Thus entertained with utmost care
Seven days, or eight, he tarried there,
And then that best men thus broke
His purpose to the king, and spoke :
'O King of men, mine ancient friend,
(Thus Daśaratha prayed)
Thy Śántá with her husband send
My sacrifice to aid.'
Said he who ruled the Angas, Yea,
And his consent was won :
And then at once he turned away
To warn the hermit's son.
He told him of their ties beyond
Their old affection's faithful bond :
'This king,' he said, 'from days of old
A well beloved friend I hold.
To me this pearl of dames he gave
From childless woe mine age to save,
The daughter whom he loved so much,
Moved by compassion's gentle touch.
In him thy Śántá's father see :
As I am even so is he.
For sons the childless monarch yearns :
To thee alone for help he turns.
Go thou, the sacred rite ordain
To win the sons he prays to gain :
Go, with thy wife thy succour lend,
And give his vows a blissful end.'
The hermit's son with quick accord
Obeyed the Angas' mighty lord,
And with fair Śántá at his side
To Daśaratha's city hied.
Each king, with suppliant hands upheld,
Gazed on the other's face :
And then by mutual love impelled
Met in a close embrace.
Then Daśaratha's thoughtful care,
Before he parted thence,
Bade trusty servants homeward bear
The glad intelligence :
'Let all the town be bright and gay,
With burning incense sweet ;
Let banners wave, and water lay
The dust in every street.'
Glad were the citizens to learn
The tidings of their lord's return,
And through the city every man
Obedienly his task began.
And fair and bright Ayodhyá showed,
As following his guest he rode
Through the full streets where shell and
drum
Proclaimed aloud the king was come.
And all the people with delight
Kept gazing on their king,
Attended by that youth so bright,
The glorious Rishyaśring.
When to his home the king had brought
The hermit's saintly son,
He deemed that all his task was wrought,
And all he prayed for won.
And lords who saw that stranger dame
So beautiful to view,
Rejoiced within their hearts, and came
And paid her honour too.
There Rishyaśring passed blissful days,
Graced like the king with love and praise,
And shone in glorious light with her,
Sweet Śántá, for his minister,
As Brahmá's son Vaśishṭha, he
Who wedded Saint Arundhatí.[1]

CANTO XI.

THE SACRIFICE DECREED.

The Dewy Season[2] came and went ;
The spring returned again :
Then would the king, with mind intent,
His sacrifice ordain.

[1] One of the Pleiades and generally regarded as the model of wifely excellence.

[2] The Hindu year is divided into six seasons of two months each, spring, summer, rains, autumn, winter, and dews.

He came to Rishyaśring, and bowed
To him of look divine,
And bade him aid his offering vowed
For heirs, to save his line.
Nor would the youth his aid deny:
He spake the monarch fair,
And prayed him for that rite so high
All requisites prepare.
The king to wise Sumantra cried
Who stood aye ready near;
'Go summon quick each holy guide,
To counsel and to hear.'
Obedient to his lord's behest
Away Sumantra sped,
And brought Vaśishṭha and the rest,
In Scripture deeply read.
Suyajña, Vámadeva came,
Jáváli, Kaśyap's son,
And old Vaśishṭha, dear to fame,
Obedient every one.
King Daśaratha met them there
And duly honoured each,
And spoke in pleasant words his fair
And salutary speech:
'In childless longing doomed to pine,
No happiness, O lords, is mine.
So have I for this cause decreed
To slay the sacrificial steed.
Fain would I pay that offering high
Wherein the horse is doomed to die,
With Rishyaśring his aid to lend,
And with your glory to befriend.'
With loud applause each holy man
Received his speech, approved the plan,
And, by the wise Vaśishṭha led,
Gave praises to the king, and said:
'The sons thou cravest shalt thou see,
Of fairest glory, born to thee,
Whose holy feelings bid thee take
This righteous course for offspring's sake.'
Cheered by the ready praise of those
Whose aid he sought, his spirits rose,
And thus the king his speech renewed
With looks of joy and gratitude:
'Let what the coming rites require
Be ready as the priests desire,
And let the horse, ordained to bleed,
With fitting guard and priest, be freed.[1]
Yonder on Sarjú's northern side
The sacrificial ground provide;
And let the saving rites, that naught
Ill-omened may occur, be wrought.
The offering I announce to-day
Each lord of earth may claim to pay,
Provided that his care can guard
The holy rite by flaws unmarred.
For wandering fiends, whose watchful spite
Waits eagerly to spoil each rite,
Hunting with keenest eye detect
The slightest slip, the least neglect;
And when the sacred work is crossed
The workman is that moment lost.
Let preparation due be made:
Your powers the charge can meet:
That so the noble rite be paid
In every point complete.'
And all the Bráhmans answered, Yea,
His mandate honouring,
And gladly promised to obey
The order of the king.
They cried with voices raised aloud:
'Success attend thine aim!'
Then bade farewell, and lowly bowed,
And hastened whence they came.
King Daśaratha went within,
His well loved wives to see:
And said: 'Your lustral rites begin,
For these shall prosper me.
A glorious offering I prepare
That precious fruit of sons may bear.'
Their lily faces brightened fast
Those pleasant words to hear,
As lilies, when the winter's past,
In lovelier hues appear.

CANTO XII.

THE SACRIFICE BEGUN.

Again the spring with genial heat
Returning made the year complete.
To win him sons, without delay
His vow the king resolved to pay:
And to Vaśishṭha, saintly man,
In modest words this speech began:
'Prepare the rite with all things fit
As is ordained in Holy Writ,
And keep with utmost care afar
Whate'er its sacred forms might mar.
Thou art, my lord, my trustiest guide,
Kind-hearted, and my friend beside;
So is it meet thou undertake
This heavy task for duty's sake.'
Then he, of twice-born men the best,
His glad assent at once expressed:
'Fain will I do whate'er may be
Desired, O honoured King, by thee.'
To ancient priests he spoke, who, trained
In holy rites, deep skill had gained:
'Here guards be stationed, good and sage,
Religious men of trusted age.
And various workmen send and call,
Who frame the door and build the wall:
With men of every art and trade,
Who read the stars and ply the spade,

[1] It was essential that the horse should wander free for a year before immolation, as a sign that his master's paramount sovereignty was acknowledged by all neighbouring princes.

And mimes and minstrels hither bring,
And damsels trained to dance and sing.'
Then to the learned men he said,
In many a page of Scripture read:
'Be yours each rite performed to see
According to the king's decree.
And stranger Bráhmans quickly call
To this great rite that welcomes all.
Pavilions for the princes, decked
With art and ornament, erect,
And handsome booths by thousands made
The Bráhman visitors to shade,
Arranged in order side by side,
With meat and drink and all supplied.
And ample stables we shall need
For many an elephant and steed:
And chambers where the men may lie,
And vast apartments, broad and high,
Fit to receive the countless bands
Of warriors come from distant lands.
For our own people too provide
Sufficient tents, extended wide,
And stores of meat and drink prepare,
And all that can be needed there.
And food in plenty must be found
For guests from all the country round.
Of various viands presents make,
For honour, not for pity's sake,
That fit regard and worship be
Paid to each caste in due degree.
And let not wish or wrath excite
Your hearts the meanest guest to slight;
But still observe with special grace
Those who obtain the foremost place,
Whether for happier skill in art
Or bearing in the rite their part.
Do you, I pray, with friendly mind
Perform the task to you assigned,
And work the rite, as bids the law,
Without omission, slip, or flaw.'
They answered: 'As thou seest fit
So will we do and naught omit.'
The sage Vaśishtha then addressed
Sumantra called at his behest:
'The princes of the earth invite,
And famous lords who guard the rite,
Priest, Warrior, Merchant, lowly thrall,
In countless thousands summon all.
Where'er their home be, far or near,
Gather the good with honour here,
And Janak, whose imperial sway
The men of Míthilá[1] obey,
The firm of vow, the dread of foes,
Who all the lore of Scripture knows,
Invite him here with honour high,
King Daśaratha's old ally.
And Káśi's[1] lord of gentle speech,
Who finds a pleasant word for each,
In length of days our monarch's peer,
Illustrious king, invite him here.
The father of our ruler's bride,
Known for his virtues far and wide,
The king whom Kekaya's[2] realms obey,
Him with his son invite, I pray.
And Lomapád the Angas' king,
True to his vows and godlike, bring.
For be thine invitations sent
To west and south and orient.
Call those who rule Suráshṭra's[3] land,
Suvíra's[4] realm and Sindhu's strand,
And all the kings of earth beside
In friendship's bonds with us allied:
Invite them all to hasten in
With retinue and kith and kin.'
Vaśishṭha's speech without delay
Sumantra bent him to obey.
And sent his trusty envoys forth
Eastward and westward, south and north.
Obedient to the saint's request
Himself he hurried forth, and pressed
Each nobler chief and lord and king
To hasten to the gathering.
Before the saint Vaśishṭha stood
All those who wrought with stone and wood,
And showed the work which every one
In furtherance of the rite had done.
Rejoiced their ready zeal to see,
Thus to the craftsmen all said he:
'I charge ye, masters, see to this,
That there be nothing done amiss,
And this, I pray, in mind be borne,
That not one gift ye give in scorn:
Whenever scorn a gift attends
Great sin is his who thus offends.'
And now some days and nights had past,
And kings began to gather fast,
And precious gems in liberal store
As gifts to Daśaratha bore.
Then joy thrilled through Vaśishṭha's breast
As thus the monarch he addressed:
'Obedient to thy high decree
The kings, my lord, are come to thee.

---

[1] Called also Videha, later Tírabhukti, corrupted into the modern Tirhut, a province bounded on the west and east by the Gandakí and Kauśikí rivers, on the south by the Ganges, and on the north by the skirts of the Himálayas.

[1] The celebrated city of Benares. See Dr. Halls's learned and exhaustive Monograph in *the Sacred City of the Hindus*, by the Rev. M. A. Sherring.

[2] Kekaya is supposed to have been in the Panjáb. The name of the king was Aśvapati (Lord of Horses), father of Daśaratha's wife Kaikeyí.

[3] Surat.

[4] Apparently in the west of India not far from the Indus.

And it has been my care to greet
And honour all with reverence meet.
Thy servants' task is ended quite,
And all is ready for the rite.
Come forth then to the sacred ground
Where all in order will be found.'
Then Rishyaśring confirmed the tale:
Nor did their words to move him fail.
The stars propitious influence lent
When forth the world's great ruler went.
Then by the sage Vaśishṭha led
The priest began to speed
Those glorious rites wherein is shed
The lifeblood of the steed.

CANTO XIII.

THE SACRIFICE FINISHED.

The circling year had filled its course,
And back was brought the wandering horse:
Then upon Sarjú's northern strand
Began the rite the king had planned.
With Rishyaśring the forms to guide,
The Bráhmans to their task applied,
At that great offering of the steed
Their lofty-minded king decreed.
The priests, who all the Scripture knew,
Performed their part in order due,
And circled round in solemn train
As precepts of the law ordain.
Pravargya rites[1] were duly sped:
For Upasads[2] the flames were fed.
Then from the plant[3] the juice was squeezed,
And those high saints with minds well pleased
Performed the mystic rites begun
With bathing ere the rise of sun.
They gave the portion Indra's claim,
And hymned the King whom none can blame.
The mid-day bathing followed next,
Observed as bids the holy text.
Then the good priests with utmost care,
In form that Scripture's rules declare,
For the third time pure water shed
On high-souled Daśaratha's head.
Then Rishyaśring and all the rest
To Indra and the Gods addressed
Their sweet-toned hymn of praise and prayer,
And called them in the rite to share.
With sweetest song and hymn entoned
They gave the Gods in heaven enthroned,
As duty bids, the gifts they claim,
The holy oil that feeds the flame.
And many an offering there was paid,
And not one slip in all was made.
For with most careful heed they saw
That all was done by Veda law.
None, all those days, was seen oppressed
By hunger or by toil distressed.
Why speak of human kind? No beast
Was there that lacked an ample feast.
For there was store for all who came,
For orphan child and lonely dame:
The old and young were well supplied,
The poor and hungry satisfied.
Throughout the day ascetics fed,
And those who roam to beg their bread:
While all around the cry was still,
'Give forth, give forth,' and 'Eat you fill.'
'Give forth with liberal hand the meal,
And various robes in largess deal.'
Urged by these cries on every side
Unweariedly their task they plied:
And heaps of food like hills in size
In boundless plenty met the eyes:
And lakes of sauce, each day renewed,
Refreshed the weary multitude.
And strangers there from distant lands,
And women folk in crowded bands
The best of food and drink obtained
At the great rite the king ordained.
Apart from all, the Bráhmans there,
Thousands on thousands, took their share
Of various dainties sweet to taste,
On plates of gold and silver placed,
All ready set, as, when they willed,
The twice-born men their places filled.
And servants in fair garments dressed
Waited upon each Bráhman guest.
Of cheerful mind and mien were they,
With gold and jewelled earrings gay.
The best of Bráhmans praised the fare
Of countless sorts, of flavour rare:
And thus to Raghu's son they cried:
'We bless thee, and are satisfied.'
Between the rites some Bráhmans spent
The time in learned argument,

[1] 'The Pravargya ceremony lasts for three days, and is always performed twice a day, in the forenoon and afternoon. It precedes the animal and Soma sacrifices. For without having undergone it, no one is allowed to take part in the solemn Soma feast prepared for the gods.' HAUG'S *Aitareya Bráhmaṇam.* Vol. II. p. 41. note *q. v.*

[2] *Upasads.* 'The Gods said, Let us perform the burnt-offerings called Upasads (*i. e.* besieging). For by means of an *Upasad, i. e.* besieging, they conquer a large (fortified) town.'—*Ibid.* p. 52.

[3] The Soma plant, or Asclepias Acida. Its fermented juice was drunk in sacrifice by the priests and offered to the Gods who enjoyed the intoxicating draught.

With ready flow of speech, sedate,
And keen to vanquish in debate.[1]

There day by day the holy train
Performed all rites as rules ordain.
No priest in all that host was found
But kept the vows that held him bound :
None, but the holy Vedas knew,
And all their six-fold science[2] too.
No Bráhman there was found unfit
To speak with eloquence and wit.

And now the appointed time came near
The sacrificial posts to rear.
They brought them, and prepared to fix
Of Bel[3] and Khádir[4] six and six ;
Six, made of the Palása[5] tree,
Of Fig-wood one, apart to be :
Of Sleshmát[6] and of Devadár[7]
One column each, the mightiest far :
So thick the two, the arms of man
Their ample girth would fail to span.
All these with utmost care were wrought
By hand of priests in Scripture taught,
And all with gold were gilded bright
To add new splendour to the rite :
Twenty-and-one those stakes in all,
Each one-and-twenty cubits tall :
And one-and-twenty ribbons there
Hung on the pillars, bright and fair.
Firm in the earth they stood at last,
Where cunning craftsmen fixed them fast ;
And there unshaken each remained,
Octagonal and smoothly planed.
Then ribbons over all were hung,
And flowers and scent around them flung.
Thus decked they cast a glory forth
Like the great saints who star the north.[1]
The sacrificial altar then
Was raised by skilful twice-born men,
In shape and figure to behold
An eagle with his wings of gold,
With twice nine pits and formed three-fold.
Each for some special God, beside
The pillars were the victims tied ;
The birds that roam the wood, the air,
The water, and the land were there,
And snakes and things of reptile birth,
And healing herbs that spring from earth :
As texts prescribe, in Scripture found,
Three hundred victims there were bound.
The steed devoted to the host
Of Gods, the gem they honour most,
Was duly sprinkled. Then the Queen
Kauśalyá, with delighted mien,
With reverent steps around him paced,
And with sweet wreaths the victim graced;
Then with three swords in order due
She smote the steed with joy, and slew.
That night the queen, a son to gain,
With calm and steady heart was fain
By the dead charger's side to stay
From evening till the break of day.
Then came three priests, their care to lead
The other queens to touch the steed,
Upon Kauśalyá to attend,
Their company and aid to lend.
As by the horse she still reclined,
With happy mien and cheerful mind,
With Rishyaśring the twice-born came
And praised and blessed the royal dame.
The priest who well his duty knew,
And every sense could well subdue,
From out the bony chambers freed
And boiled the marrow of the steed.
Above the steam the monarch bent,
And, as he smelt the fragrant scent,
In time and order drove afar
All error that his hopes could mar.
Then sixteen priests together came
And cast into the sacred flame
The severed members of the horse,
Made ready all in ordered course.
On piles of holy Fig-tree raised

---

[1] 'Tum in cærimoniarum intervallis Brachmanæ facundi, sollertes, crebros sermones de rerum causis instituebant, alter alterum vincendi cupidi. This public disputation in the assembly of Bráhmans on the nature of things, and the almost fraternal connexion between theology and philosophy deserves some notice ; whereas the priests of some religions are generally but little inclined to show favour to philosophers, nay, sometimes persecute them with the most rancorous hatred, as we are taught both by history and experience... This *śloka* is found in the MSS. of different recensions of the Rámáyan, and we have, therefore, the most trustworthy testimony to the antiquity of philosophy among the Indians.' SCHLEGEL.

[2] The *Angas* or appendices of the Vedas, pronunciation, prosody, grammar, ritual, astronomy, and explanation of obscurities.

[3] In Sanskrit *vilva*, the *Ægle Marmelos*. 'He who desires food and wishes to grow fat, ought to make his Yúpa (sacrificial post) of Bilva wood.' HAUG'S *Aitareya Bráhmanam. Vol. II.* p. 73.

[4] The *Mimosa Catechu*. 'He who desires heaven ought to make his Yúpa of Khádira wood.'—*Ibid.*

[5] The *Butea Frondosa*. 'He who desires beauty and sacred knowledge ought to make his Yúpa of Palása wood.'—*Ibid.*

[6] The *Cardia Latifolia*.

[7] A kind of pine. The word means literally the tree of the Gods : Compare the Hebrew עצי יהוה 'trees of the Lord.'

[1] The Hindus call the constellation of Ursa Major the Seven Rishis or Saints.

The meaner victims' bodies blazed:
The steed, of all the creatures slain,
Alone required a pile of cane.
Three days, as is by law decreed,
Lasted that Offering of the Steed.
The Chatushṭom began the rite,
And when the sun renewed his light,
The Ukthya followed: after came
The Atirátra's holy flame.
These were the rites, and many more,
Arranged by light of holy lore,
The Aptoryám of mighty power,
And, each performed in proper hour,
The Abhijit and Viśvajit
With every form and service fit;
And with the sacrifice at night
The Jyotishṭom and Áyus rite.[1]

The task was done, as laws prescribe:
The monarch, glory of his tribe,
Bestowed the land in liberal grants
Upon the sacred ministrants.
He gave the region of the east,
His conquest, to the Hotri priest.
The west, the celebrant obtained:
The south, the priest presiding gained:
The northern region was the share
Of him who chanted forth the prayer.[1]
Thus did each priest obtain his meed
At the great Slaughter of the Steed,
Ordained, the best of all to be,
By self-existent deity.
Ikshváku's son with joyful mind
This noble fee to each assigned,
But all the priests with one accord
Addressed that unpolluted lord:
''Tis thine alone to keep the whole
Of this broad earth in firm control.

---

[1] A minute account of these ancient ceremonies would be out of place here. 'Agnishṭoma is the name of a sacrifice, or rather a series of offerings to fire for five days. It is the first and principal part of the Jyotishṭoma, one of the great sacrifices in which especially the juice of the Soma plant is offered for the purpose of obtaining Swarga or heaven.' GOLDSTÜCKER'S DICTIONARY. 'The *Agnishṭoma* is Agni. It is called so because they (the gods) praised him with this Stoma. They called it so to hide the proper meaning of the word; for the gods like to hide the proper meaning of words.'

'On account of four classes of gods having praised Agni with four Stomas, the whole was called *Chahtushṭoma* (containing four Stomas).'

'It (the Agnishṭoma) is called *Jyotishṭoma*, for they praised Agni when he had risen up (to the sky) in the shape of a light *(jyotis)*.'

'This (Agnishṭoma) is a sacrificial performance which has no beginning and no end.' HAUG'S *Aitareya Bráhmaṇam*.

The Atirátra, literally *lasting through the night*, is a division of the service of the Jyotishṭoma.

The Abhijit, *the everywhere victorious*, is the name of a sub-division of the great sacrifice of the Gavámanaya.

The Viśvajit, or *the all-conquering*, is a similar sub-division.

Áyus, is the name of a service forming a division of the Abhiplava sacrifice.

The *Aptoryám* is the seventh or last part of the Jyotishṭoma, for the performance of which it is not essentially necessary, but a voluntary sacrifice instituted for the attainment of a specific desire. The literal meaning of the word would be in conformity with the *Praudhamanoramá* 'a sacrifice which procures the attainment of the desired object. GOLDSTÜCKER'S DICTIONARY.

'The *Ukthya* is a slight modification of the Agnishṭoma sacrifice. The noun to be supplied to it is *kratu*. It is a Soma sacrifice also, and one of the seven Saṅsthas or component parts of the Jyotishṭoma. Its name indicates its nature. For *Ukthya* means "what refers to the Uktha," which is an older name for Shástra, *i. e.* recitation of one of the Hotṛi priests at the time of the Soma libations. Thus this sacrifice is only a kind of supplement to the Agnishṭoma.' HAUG. *Ai. B.*

[1] 'Four classes of priests were required in India at the most solemn sacrifices. 1. The officiating priests, manual labourers, and acolytes, who had chiefly to prepare the sacrificial ground, to dress the altar, slay the victims, and pour out the libations. 2. The choristers, who chant the sacred hymns. 3. The reciters or readers, who repeat certain hymns. 4. The overseers or bishops, who watch and superintend the proceedings of the other priests, and ought to be familiar with all the Vedas. The formulas and verses to be muttered by the first class are contained in the Yajur-veda-sanhitá. The hymns to be sung by the second class are in the Sama-veda-sanhitá. The Atharva-veda is said to be intended for the Brahman or overseer, who is to watch the proceedings of the sacrifice, and to remedy any mistake that may occur. The hymns to be recited by the third class are contained in the Rigveda.' *Chips from a German Workshop*.

No gift of lands from thee we seek :
To guard these realms our hands were weak.
On sacred lore our days are spent :
Let other gifts our wants content.'

The chief of old Ikshváku's line
Gave them ten hundred thousand kine,
A hundred millions of fine gold,
The same in silver four times told.
But every priest in presence there
With one accord resigned his share.
To Saint Vaśishṭha, high of soul,
And Rishyaśring they gave the whole.
That largess pleased those Bráhmans well,
Who bade the prince his wishes tell.
Then Daśaratha, mighty king,
Made answer thus to Rishyaśring :
'O holy Hermit, of thy grace,
Vouchsafe the increase of my race.'
He spoke ; nor was his prayer denied :
The best of Bráhmans thus replied :
'Four sons, O Monarch, shall be thine,
Upholders of thy royal line.'

CANTO XIV.

RÁVAṆ DOOMED.

The saint, well read in holy lore,
Pondered awhile his answer o'er,
And thus again addressed the king,
His wandering thoughts regathering :
'Another rite will I begin
Which shall the sons thou cravest win,
Where all things shall be duly sped
And first Atharva texts be read.'

Then by Vibháṇdak's gentle son
Was that high sacrifice begun,
The king's advantage seeking still
And zealous to perform his will.
Now all the Gods had gathered there,
Each one for his allotted share :
Brahmá, the ruler of the sky,
Stháṇu, Náráyaṇ, Lord most high,
And holy Indra men might view
With Maruts [1] for his retinue ;
The heavenly chorister, and saint,
And spirit pure from earthly taint,
With one accord had sought the place
The high-souled monarch's rite to grace.
Then to the Gods who came to take
Their proper share the hermit spake :
'For you has Daśaratha slain
The votive steed, a son to gain ;
Stern penance-rites the king has tried,
And in firm faith on you relied,
And now with undiminished care
A second rite would fain prepare.
But, O ye Gods, consent to grant
The longing of your supplicant.
For him beseeching hands I lift,
And pray you all to grant the gift,
That four fair sons of high renown
The offerings of the king may crown.'
They to the hermit's son replied :
'His longing shall be gratified.
For, Bráhman, in most high degree
We love the king and honour thee.'

These words the Gods in answer said,
And vanished thence by Indra led.
Thus to the Lord, the worlds who made,
The Immortals all assembled prayed :
'O Brahmá, mighty by thy grace,
Rávaṇ, who rules the giant race,
Torments us in his senseless pride,
And penance-loving saints beside.
For thou well pleased in days of old
Gavest the boon that makes him bold,
That God nor demon e'er should kill
His charmed life, for so thy will.
We, honouring that high behest,
Bear all his rage though sore distressed.
That lord of giants fierce and fell
Scourges the earth and heaven and hell.
Mad with thy boon, his impious rage
Smites saint and bard and God and sage.
The sun himself withholds his glow,
The wind in fear forbears to blow ;
The fire restrains his wonted heat
Where stand the dreaded Rávaṇ's feet,
And, necklaced with the wandering wave,
The sea before him fears to rave.
Kuvera's self in sad defeat
Is driven from his blissful seat.
We see, we feel the giant's might,
And woe comes o'er us and affright.
To thee, O Lord, thy suppliants pray
To find some cure this plague to stay.'

Thus by the gathered Gods addressed
He pondered in his secret breast,
And said : 'One only way I find
To slay this fiend of evil mind.
He prayed me once his life to guard
From demon, God, and heavenly bard,
And spirits of the earth and air,
And I consenting heard his prayer.
But the proud giant in his scorn
Recked not of man of woman born.
None else may take his life away,
But only man the fiend may slay.'
The Gods, with Indra at their head,
Rejoiced to hear the words he said.
Then, crowned with glory like a flame,
Lord Vishṇu to the council came ;
His hands shell, mace, and discus bore,
And saffron were the robes he wore.

[1] The Maruts are the winds, deified in the religion of the Veda like other mighty powers and phenomena of nature.

Riding his eagle through the crowd,
As the sun rides upon a cloud,
With bracelets of fine gold, he came
Loud welcomed by the Gods' acclaim.
His praise they sang with one consent,
And cried, in lowly reverence bent:
'O Lord whose hand fierce Madhu[1] slew,
Be thou our refuge, firm and true;
Friend of the suffering worlds art thou,
We pray thee help thy suppliants now.'
Then Vishṇu spake: 'Ye Gods, declare,
What may I do to grant your prayer?'

'King Daśaratha,' thus cried they,
'Fervent in penance many a day,
The sacrificial steed has slain,
Longing for sons, but all in vain.
Now, at the cry of us forlorn,
Incarnate as his seed be born.
Three queens has he: each lovely dame
Like Beauty, Modesty, or Fame.
Divide thyself in four, and be
His offspring by these noble three.
Man's nature take, and slay in fight
Rávaṇ who laughs at heavenly might:
This common scourge, this rankling thorn
Whom the three worlds too long have borne.
For Rávaṇ in the senseless pride
Of might unequalled has defied
The host of heaven, and plagues with woe
Angel and bard and saint below,
Crushing each spirit and each maid
Who plays in Nandan's[2] heavenly shade.
O conquering Lord, to thee we bow;
Our surest hope and trust art thou.
Regard the world of men below,
And slay the Gods' tremendous foe.'

When thus the suppliant Gods had prayed,
His wise reply Náráyaṇ[3] made:
'What task demands my presence there,
And whence this dread, ye Gods declare.'

The Gods replied: 'We fear, O Lord,
Fierce Rávaṇ, ravener abhorred.
Be thine the glorious task, we pray,
In human form this fiend to slay.
By thee of all the Blest alone
This sinner may be overthrown.
He gained by penance long and dire
The favour of the mighty Sire.
Then He who every gift bestows
Guarded the fiend from heavenly foes,
And gave a pledge his life that kept
From all things living, man except.
On him thus armed no other foe
Than man may deal the deadly blow.
Assume, O King, a mortal birth,
And strike the demon to the earth.'

Then Vishṇu, God of Gods, the Lord
Supreme by all the worlds adored,
To Brahmá and the suppliants spake:
'Dismiss your fear: for your dear sake
In battle will I smite him dead,
The cruel fiend, the Immortal's dread.
And lords and ministers and all
His kith and kin with him shall fall.
Then, in the world of mortal men,
Ten thousand years and hundreds ten
I as a human king will reign,
And guard the earth as my domain.'

God, saint, and nymph, and ministrel throng
With heavenly voices raised their song
In hymns of triumph to the God
Whose conquering feet on Madhu trod:

'Champion of Gods, as man appear,
This cruel Rávaṇ slay,
The thorn that saints and hermits fear,
The plague that none can stay.
In savage fury uncontrolled
His pride for ever grows:
He dares the Lord of Gods to hold
Among his deadly foes.'

CANTO XV.

THE NECTAR.

When wisest Vishṇu thus had given
His promise to the Gods of heaven,
He pondered in his secret mind
A suited place of birth to find.
Then he decreed, the lotus-eyed,
In four his being to divide,
And Daśaratha, gracious king,
He chose as sire from whom to spring.
That childless prince of high renown,
Who smote in war his foemen down,
At that same time with utmost care
Prepared the rite that wins an heir.[1]
Then Vishṇu, fain on earth to dwell,
Bade the Almighty Sire farewell,
And vanished while a reverent crowd
Of Gods and saints in worship bowed.

The monarch watched the sacred rite,
When a vast form of awful might,
Of matchless splendour, strength, and size
Was manifest before his eyes.

[1] A Titan or fiend whose destruction has given Vishṇu one of his well-known titles, Mádhava.

[2] The garden of Indra.

[3] One of the most ancient and popular of the numerous names of Vishṇu. The word has been derived in several ways, and may mean *he who moved on the (primordial) waters*, or *he who pervades or influences men or their thoughts*.

[1] The Horse-Sacrifice, just described.

From forth the sacrificial flame,
Dark, robed in red, the being came.
His voice was drumlike, loud and low,
His face suffused with rosy glow.
Like a huge lion's mane appeared
The long locks of his hair and beard.
He shone with many a lucky sign,
And many an ornament divine;
A towering mountain in his height,
A tiger in his gait and might.
No precious mine more rich could be,
No burning flame more bright than he.
His arms embraced in loving hold,
Like a dear wife, a vase of gold
Whose silver lining held a draught
Of nectar as in heaven is quaffed:
A vase so vast, so bright to view,
They scarce could count the vision true.
Upon the king his eyes he bent,
And said: 'The Lord of life has sent
His servant down, O Prince, to be
A messenger from heaven to thee.'
The king with all his nobles by
Raised reverent hands and made reply:
'Welcome, O glorious being! Say
How can my care thy grace repay.'
Envoy of Him whom all adore
Thus to the king he spake once more:
'The Gods accept thy worship: they
Give thee the blessed fruit to-day.
Approach and take, O glorious King,
This heavenly nectar which I bring,
For it shall give thee sons and wealth,
And bless thee with a store of health.
Give it to those fair queens of thine,
And bid them quaff the drink divine:
And they the princely sons shall bear
Long sought by sacrifice and prayer.'

'Yea, O my lord,' the monarch said,
And took the vase upon his head,
The gift of Gods, of fine gold wrought,
With store of heavenly liquor fraught.
He honoured, filled with transport new,
That wondrous being, fair to view,
As round the envoy of the God
With reverential steps he trod.[1]

His errand done, that form of light
Arose and vanished from the sight.
High rapture filled the monarch's soul,
Possessed of that celestial bowl,
As when a man by want distressed
With unexpected wealth is blest.
And rays of transport seemed to fall
Illuminating bower and hall,
As when the autumn moon rides high,
And floods with lovely light the sky.
Quick to the ladies' bower he sped,
And thus to Queen Kauśalyá said:
'This genial nectar take and quaff,'
He spoke, and gave the lady half.
Part of the nectar that remained
Sumitrá from his hand obtained.
He gave, to make her fruitful too,
Kaikeyí half the residue.
A portion yet remaining there,
He paused awhile to think.
Then gave Sumitrá, with her share,
The remnant of the drink.
Thus on each queen of those fair three
A part the king bestowed,
And with sweet hope a child to see
Their yearning bosoms glowed.
The heavenly bowl the king supplied
Their longing souls relieved,
And soon, with rapture and with pride,
Each royal dame conceived.
He gazed upon each lady's face,
And triumphed as he gazed,
As Indra in his royal place
By Gods and spirits praised.

CANTO XVI.

THE VÁNARS.

When Visnu thus had gone on earth,
From the great king to take his birth,
The self-existent Lord of all
Addressed the Gods who heard his call:
'For Vishnu's sake, the strong and true,
Who seeks the good of all of you,
Make helps, in war to lend him aid,
In forms that change at will, arrayed,
Of wizard skill and hero might,
Outstrippers of the wind in flight,
Skilled in the arts of counsel wise,
And Vishnu's peers in bold emprise;
With heavenly arts and prudence fraught,
By no devices to be caught;
Skilled in all weapon's lore and use
As they who drink the immortal juice.[1]

[1] To walk round an object keeping the right side towards it is a mark of great respect. The Sanskrit word for the observance is *pradakshiná*, from pra pro, and *daksha* right, Greek δεξίος, Latin dexter, Gaelic deas-il. A similar ceremony is observed by the Gaels.

'In the meantime she traced around him, with wavering steps, the propitiation, which some have thought has been derived from the Druidical mythology. It consists, as is well known, in the person who makes the *deasil* walking three times round the person who is the object of the ceremony, taking care to move according to the course of the sun.'

SCOTT. *The Two Drovers.*

[1] The *Amrit*, the nectar of the Indian Gods.

And let the nymphs supreme in grace,
And maidens of the minstrel race,
Monkeys and snakes, and those who rove
Free spirits of the hill and grove,
And wandering Daughters of the Air,
In monkey form brave children bear.
So erst the lord of bears I shaped,
Born from my mouth as wide I gaped.'

Thus by the mighty Sire addressed
They all obeyed his high behest,
And thus begot in countless swarms
Brave sons disguised in sylvan forms.
Each God, each sage became a sire,
Each minstrel of the heavenly quire,[1]
Each faun,[2] of children strong and good
Whose feet should roam the hill and wood.
Snakes, bards,[3] and spirits,[4] serpents bold
Had sons too numerous to be told.
Báli, the woodland hosts who led,
High as Mahendra's[5] lofty head,
Was Indra's child. That noblest fire,
The Sun, was great Sugríva's sire.
Tára, the mighty monkey, he
Was offspring of Vṛihaspati:[6]
Tára the matchless chieftain, boast
For wisdom of the Vánar host.
Of Gandhamádan brave and bold
The father was the Lord of Gold.
Nala the mighty, dear to fame,
Of skilful Viśvakarmá[7] came.
From Agni,[8] Níla bright as flame,
Who in his splendour, might, and worth,
Surpassed the sire who gave him birth.

The heavenly Aśvins,[1] swift and fair,
Were fathers of a noble pair,
Who, Dwivida and Mainda named,
For beauty like their sires were famed.
Varuṇ[2] was father of Sushen,
Of Sarabh, he who sends the rain.[3]
Hanúmán, best of monkey kind,
Was son of him who breathes the wind:
Like thunderbolt in frame was he,
And swift as Garuḍ's[4] self could flee.
These thousands did the Gods create
Endowed with might that none could mate,
In monkey forms that changed at will:
So strong their wish the fiend to kill.
In mountain size, like lions thewed,
Up sprang the wondrous multitude,
Auxiliar hosts in every shape,
Monkey and bear and highland ape.
In each the strength, the might, the mien
Of his own parent God were seen.
Some chiefs of Vánar mothers came,
Some of she-bear and minstrel dame,
Skilled in all arms in battle's shock;
The brandished tree, the loosened rock;
And prompt, should other weapons fail,
To fight and slay with tooth and nail.
Their strength could shake the hills amain,
And rend the rooted trees in twain,
Disturb with their impetuous sweep
The Rivers' Lord, the Ocean deep,
Rend with their feet the seated ground,
And pass wide floods with airy bound,
Or forcing through the sky their way
The very clouds by force could stay.
Mad elephants that wander through
The forest wilds, could they subdue,
And with their furious shout could scare
Dead upon earth the birds of air.
So were the sylvan chieftains formed;
Thousands on thousands still they swarmed.
These were the leaders honoured most,
The captains of the Vánar host,
And to each lord and chief and guide
Was monkey offspring born beside.
Then by the bears' great monarch stood
The other roamers of the wood,

---

[1] *Gandharvas* (Southey's Glendoveers) are celestial musicians inhabiting Indra's heaven and forming the orchestra at all the banquets of the principal deities.

[2] *Yakshas*, demigods attendant especially on Kuvera, and employed by him in the care of his garden and treasures.

[3] *Kimpurushas*, demigods attached also to the service of Kuvera, celestial musicians, represented like centaurs reversed with human figures and horses' heads.

[4] *Siddhas*, demigods or spirits of undefined attributes, occupying with the *Vidyádharas* the middle air or region between the earth and the sun.

Schlegel translates: 'Divi, Sapientes, Fidicines, Præpetes, illustres Genii, Præconesque procrearunt natos, masculos, silvicolas; angues porro, Hippocephali Beati, Aligeri, Serpentesque frequentes alacriter generavere prolem innumerabilem.'

[5] A mountain in the south of India.

[6] The preceptor of the Gods and regent of the planet Jupiter.

[7] The celestial architect, the Indian Hephæstus, Mulciber, or Vulcan.

[8] The God of Fire.

[1] Twin children of the Sun, the physicians of Swarga or Indra's heaven.

[2] The deity of the waters.

[3] Parjanya, sometimes confounded with Indra.

[4] The bird and vehicle of Vishṇu. He is generally represented as a being something between a man and a bird and considered as the sovereign of the feathered race. He may be compared with the Simurgh of the Persians, the 'Anká of the Arabs, the Griffin of chivalry, the Phœnix of Egypt, and the bird that sits upon the ash Yggdrasil of the Edda.

And turned, their pathless homes to seek,
To forest and to mountain peak.
The leaders of the monkey band
By the two brothers took their stand,
Sugríva, offspring of the Sun,
And Báli, Indra's mighty one.
They both endowed with Garuḍ's might,
And skilled in all the arts of fight,
Wandered in arms the forest through,
And lions, snakes, and tigers, slew.
But every monkey, ape, and bear
Ever was Báli's special care;
With his vast strength and mighty arm
He kept them from all scathe and harm.
And so the earth with hill, wood, seas,
Was filled with mighty ones like these,
Of various shape and race and kind,
With proper homes to each assigned,
With Ráma's champions fierce and strong
The earth was overspread,
High as the hills and clouds, a throng
With bodies vast and dread.[1]

CANTO XVII.

RISHYAŚRING'S RETURN.

Now when the high-souled monarch's rite,
The Aśvamedh, was finished quite,
Their sacrificial dues obtained,
The Gods their heavenly homes regained.
The lofty-minded saints withdrew,
Each to his place, with honour due,
And kings and chieftains, one and all,
Who came to grace the festival.
And Daśaratha, ere they went,
Addressed them thus benevolent:
'Now may you, each with joyful heart,
To your own realms, O Kings, depart.
Peace and good luck attend you there,
And blessing, is my friendly prayer;
Let cares of state each mind engage
To guard his royal heritage.
A monarch from his throne expelled
No better than the dead is held.
So he who cares for power and might
Must guard his realm and royal right.
Such care a meed in heaven will bring
Better than rites and offering.
Such care a king his country owes
As man upon himself bestows,
When for his body he provides
Raiment and every need besides.
For future days should kings foresee,
And keep the present error-free.'

Thus did the king the kings exhort:
They heard, and turned them from the court,
And, each to each in friendship bound,
Went forth to all the realms around.
The rites were o'er, the guests were sped:
The train the best of Bráhmans led,
In which the king with joyful soul,
With his dear wives, and with the whole
Of his imperial host and train
Of cars and servants turned again,
And, as a monarch dear to fame,
Within his royal city came.

Next, Rishyaśring, well-honoured sage,
And Śántá, sought their hermitage.
The king himself, of prudent mind,
Attended him, with troops behind.
And all her men the town outpoured
With Saint Vaśishṭha and their lord.
High mounted on a car of state,
O'ercanopied fair Śántá sate,
Drawn by white oxen, while a band
Of servants marched on either hand.
Great gifts of countless price she bore,
With sheep and goats and gems in store.
Like Beauty's self the lady shone
With all the jewels she had on,
As, happy in her sweet content,
Peerless amid the fair she went.
Not Queen Paulomí's[1] self could be
More loving to her lord than she.
She who had lived in happy ease,
Honoured with all her heart could please,
While dames and kinsfolk ever vied
To see her wishes gratified,
Soon as she knew her husband's will
Again to seek the forest, still
Was ready for the hermit's cot,
Nor murmured at her altered lot.
The king attended to the wild
That hermit and his own dear child,
And in the centre of a throng
Of noble courtiers rode along.
The sage's son had let prepare
A lodge within the wood, and there
While they lingered blithe and gay,
Then, duly honoured, went their way.
The glorious hermit Rishyaśring
Drew near and thus besought the king:

[1] This Canto will appear ridiculous to the European reader. But it should be remembered that the monkeys of an Indian forest, the 'bough-deer' as the poets call them, are very different animals from the 'turpissima bestia' that accompanies the itinerant organ-grinder or grins in the Zoological Gardens of London. Milton has made his hero, Satan, assume the forms of a cormorant, a toad, and a serpent, and I cannot see that this creation of semi-divine Vánars, or monkeys, is more ridiculous or undignified.

[1] The consort of Indra, called also Śachí and Indráṇí.

'Return, my honoured lord, I pray,
Return, upon thy homeward way.'
The monarch, with the waiting crowd,
Lifted his voice and wept aloud,
And with eyes dripping still to each
Of his good queens he spake this speech :

'Kauśalyá and Sumitrá dear,
And thou, my sweet Kaikeyí, hear.
All upon Śántá feast your gaze,
The last time for a length of days.'
To Śántá's arms the ladies leapt,
And hung about her neck and wept,
And cried, 'O, happy be the life
Of this great Bráhman and his wife.
The Wind, the Fire, the Moon on high,
The Earth, the Streams, the circling Sky,
Preserve thee in the wood, true spouse,
Devoted to thy husband's vows.
And O dear Śántá, ne'er neglect
To pay the dues of meek respect
To the great saint, thy husband's sire,
With all observance and with fire.
And, sweet one, pure of spot and blame,
Forget not thou thy husband's claim ;
In every change, in good and ill,
Let thy sweet words delight him still,
And let thy worship constant be :
Her lord is woman's deity.
To learn thy welfare, dearest friend,
The king will many a Bráhman send.
Let happy thoughts thy spirit cheer,
And be not troubled, daughter dear.'

These soothing words the ladies said,
And pressed their lips upon her head.
Each gave with sighs her last adieu,
Then at the king's command withdrew.
The king around the hermit went
With circling footsteps reverent,
And placed at Rishyaśring's command
Some soldiers of his royal band.
The Bráhman bowed in turn and cried,
'May fortune never leave thy side.
O mighty King, with justice reign,
And still thy people's love retain.'
He spoke, and turned away his face,
And, as the hermit went,
The monarch, rooted to the place,
Pursued with eyes intent.
But when the sage had past from view
King Daśaratha turned him too,
Still fixing on his friend each thought,
With such deep love his breast was fraught.
Amid his people's loud acclaim
Home to his royal seat he came,
And lived delighted there,
Expecting when each queenly dame,
Upholder of his ancient fame,
Her promised son should bear.
The glorious sage his way pursued
Till close before his eyes he viewed
Sweet Champá, Lomapád's fair town,
Wreathed with her Champacs'[1] leafy crown.
Soon as the saint's approach he knew,
The king, to yield him honour due,
Went forth to meet him with a band
Of priests and nobles of the land :
'Hail, Sage,' he cried, 'O joy to me!
What bliss it is, my lord, to see
Thee with thy wife and all thy train
Returning to my town again.
Thy father, honoured Sage, is well,
Who hither from his woodland cell
Has sent full many a messenger
For tidings both of thee and her.'
Then joyfully, for due respect,
The monarch bade the town be decked.
The king and Rishyaśring elate
Entered the royal city's gate :
In front the chaplain rode.
Then, loved and honoured with all care
By monarch and by courtier, there
The glorious saint abode.

CANTO XVIII.

RISHYAŚRING'S DEPARTURE.

The monarch called a Bráhman near
And said, 'Now speed away
To Kaśyap's son,[2] the mighty seer,
And with all reverence say
The holy child he holds so dear,
The hermit of the noble mind,
Whose equal it were hard to find,
Returned, is dwelling here.
Go, and instead of me do thou
Before that best of hermits bow,
That still he may, for his dear son,
Show me the favour I have won.'
Soon as the king these words had said,
To Kaśyap's son the Bráhman sped.
Before the hermit low he bent
And did obeisance, reverent ;
Then with meek words his grace to crave
The message of his lord he gave :
'The high-souled father of his bride
Had called thy son his rites to guide :
Those rites are o'er, the steed is slain ;
Thy noble child is come again.'
Soon as the saint that speech had heard
His spirit with desire was stirred
To seek the city of the king
And to his cot his son to bring.

[1] The *Michelia champaca*. It bears a scented yellow blossom :
'The maid of India blest again to hold
In her full lap the Champac's leaves of gold.'
Lallah Rookh.

[2] Vibháṇḍak, the father of Rishyaśring.

With young disciples at his side
Forth on his way the hermit hied,
While peasants from their hamlets ran
To reverence the holy man.
Each with his little gift of food,
Forth came the village multitude,
And, as they humbly bowed the head,
'What may we do for thee?' they said.
Then he, of Bráhmans first and best,
The gathered people thus addressed:
'Now tell me for I fain would know,
Why is it I am honoured so?'
They to the high-souled saint replied:
'Our ruler is with thee allied.
Our master's order we fulfil;
O Bráhman, let thy mind be still.'

With joy the saintly hermit heard
Each pleasant and delightful word,
And poured a benediction down
On king and ministers and town.
Glad at the words of that high saint
Some servants hastened to acquaint
Their king, rejoicing to impart
The tidings that would cheer his heart.
Soon as the joyful tale he knew
To meet the saint the monarch flew,
The guest-gift in his hand he brought,
And bowed before him and besought:
'This day by seeing thee I gain
Not to have lived my life in vain.
Now be not wroth with me, I pray,
Because I wiled thy son away.'[1]

The best of Bráhmans answer made:
'Be not, great lord of kings, afraid.
Thy virtues have not failed to win
My favour, O thou pure of sin.'
Then in the front the saint was placed,
The king came next in joyous haste,
And with him entered his abode,
Mid glad acclaim as on they rode.
To greet the sage the reverent crowd
Raised suppliant hands and humbly bowed.
Then from the palace many a dame
Following well-dressed Śántá came,
Stood by the mighty saint and cried:
'See, honour's source, thy son's dear bride.'
The saint, who every virtue knew,
His arms around his daughter threw,
And with a father's rapture pressed
The lady to his wondering breast.
Arising from the saint's embrace
She bowed her low before his face,
And then, with palm to palm applied,
Stood by her hermit father's side.
He for his son, as laws ordain,
Performed the rite that frees from stain,[2]
And, honoured by the wise and good,
With him departed to the wood.

CANTO XIX.

THE BIRTH OF THE PRINCES.

The seasons six in rapid flight
Had circled since that glorious rite.
Eleven months had passed away:
'Twas Chaitra's ninth returning day.[1]
The moon within that mansion shone
Which Aditi looks kindly on.
Raised to their apex in the sky
Five brilliant planets beamed on high.
Shone with the moon, in Cancer's sign,
Vrihaspati[2] with light divine.
Kauśalyá bore an infant blest
With heavenly marks of grace impressed;
Ráma, the universe's lord,
A prince by all the worlds adored.
New glory Queen Kauśalyá won
Reflected from her splendid son.
So Aditi shone more and more,
The Mother of the Gods, when she
The King of the Immortals[3] bore,
The thunder-wielding deity.

---

[1] A hemiśloka is wanting in Schlegel's text, which he thus fills up in his Latin translation.

[2] Rishyaśring, a Bráhman, had married Śántá who was of the Kshatriya or Warrior caste and an expiatory ceremony was necessary on account of this violation of the law.

[1] 'The poet no doubt intended to indicate the vernal equinox as the birthday of Ráma. For the month *Chaitra* is the first of the two months assigned to the spring; it corresponds with the latter half of March and the former half of April in our division of the year. *Aditi*, the mother of the Gods, is lady of the seventh lunar mansion which is called *Punarvasu*. The five planets and their positions in the Zodiac are thus enumerated by both commentators: the Sun in Aries, Mars in Capricorn, Saturn in Libra, Jupiter in Cancer, Venus in Pisces. ....I leave to astronomers to examine whether the parts of the description agree with one another, and, if this be the case, thence to deduce the date. The Indians place the nativity of Ráma in the confines of the second age (tretá) and the third (dwápara): but it seems that this should be taken in an allegorical sense.............. We may consider that the poet had an eye to the time in which, immediately before his own age, the aspects of the heavenly bodies were such as he has described.' SCHLEGEL.

[2] The regent of the planet Jupiter.

[3] Indra=Jupiter Tonans.

The lotus-eyed, the beauteous boy,
He came fierce Rávaṇ to destroy;
From half of Vishṇu's vigour born,
He came to help the worlds forlorn.
And Queen Kaikeyí bore a child
Of truest valour, Bharat styled,
With every princely virtue blest,
One fourth of Vishṇu manifest.
Sumitrá too a noble pair,
Called Lakshmaṇ and Śatrughna, bare,
Of high emprise, devoted, true,
Sharers in Vishṇu's essence too.
'Neath Pushya's[1] mansion, Mína's[2] sign,
Was Bharat born, of soul benign.
The sun had reached the Crab at morn
When Queen Sumitrá's babes were born,
What time the moon had gone to make
His nightly dwelling with the Snake.
The high-souled monarch's consorts bore
At different times those glorious four,
Like to himself and virtuous, bright
As Proshṭhapadá's[3] four-fold light.
Then danced the nymphs' celestial throng,
The minstrels raised their strain;
The drums of heaven pealed loud and long,
And flowers came down in rain.
Within Ayodhyá, blithe and gay,
All kept the joyous holiday.
The spacious square, the ample road
With mimes and dancers overflowed,
And with the voice of music rang
Where minstrels played and singers sang,
And shone, a wonder to behold,
With dazzling show of gems and gold.
Nor did the king his largess spare,
For minstrel, driver, bard, to share;
Much wealth the Bráhmans bore away,
And many thousand kine that day.

Soon as each babe was twelve days old
'Twas time the naming rite to hold.
When Saint Vaśishṭha, rapt with joy,
Assigned a name to every boy.
Ráma, to him the high-souled heir,
Bharat, to him Kaikeyí bare:
Of Queen Sumitrá one fair son
Was Lakshmaṇ, and Śatrughna[4] one.
Ráma, his sire's supreme delight,
Like some proud banner cheered his sight,
And to all creatures seemed to be
The self-existent deity.
All heroes, versed in holy lore,
To all mankind great love they bore.
Fair stores of wisdom all possessed,
With princely graces all were blest.
But mid those youths of high descent,
With lordly light preëminent,
Like the full moon unclouded, shone
Ráma, the world's dear paragon.
He best the elephant could guide,[1]
Urge the fleet car, the charger ride:
A master he of bowman's skill,
Joying to do his father's will.
The world's delight and darling, he
Loved Lakshmaṇ best from infancy;
And Lakshmaṇ, lord of lofty fate,
Upon his elder joyed to wait,
Striving his second self to please
With friendship's sweet observances.
His limbs the hero ne'er would rest
Unless the couch his brother pressed;
Except beloved Ráma shared
He could not taste the meal prepared.
When Ráma, pride of Reghu's race,
Sprang on his steed to urge the chase,
Behind him Lakshmaṇ loved to go
And guard him with his trusty bow.
As Ráma was to Lakshmaṇ dear
More than his life and ever near,
So fond Śatrughna prized above
His very life his Bharat's love.
Illustrious heroes, nobly kind
In mutual love they all combined,
And gave their royal sire delight
With modest grace and warrior might:
Supported by the glorious four
Shone Daśaratha more and more,
As though, with every guardian God
Who keeps the land and skies,
The Father of all creatures trod
The earth before men's eyes.

CANTO XX.

VIŚVÁMITRA'S VISIT.

Now Daśaratha's pious mind
Meet wedlock for his sons designed;

[1] 'Pushya is the name of a month; but here it means the eighth mansion. The ninth is called *Asleshá*, or the snake. It is evident from this that Bharat, though his birth is mentioned before that of the twins, was the youngest of the four brothers and Ráma's junior by eleven months.' SCHLEGEL.

[2] A fish, the Zodiacal sign *Pisces*.

[3] One of the constellations, containing stars in the wing of Pegasus.

[4] Ráma means the Delight (of the World); Bharat, the Supporter; Lakshmaṇ, the Auspicious; Śatrughna, the Slayer of Foes.

[1] Schlegel, in the *Indische Bibliothek*, remarks that the proficiency of the Indians in this art early attracted the attention of Alexander's successors, and natives of India were so long exclusively employed in this service that the name Indian was applied to any elephant-driver, to whatever country he might belong.

With priests and friends the king began
To counsel and prepare his plan.
Such thoughts engaged his bosom, when,
To see Ayodhyá's lord of men,
A mighty saint of glorious fame,
The hermit Viśvámitra[1] came.
For evil fiends that roam by night
Disturbed him in each holy rite,
And in their strength and frantic rage
Assailed with witcheries the sage.
He came to seek the monarch's aid
To guard the rites the demons stayed,
Unable to a close to bring
One unpolluted offering.
Seeking the king in this dire strait
He said to those who kept the gate:
'Haste, warders, to your master run,
And say that here stands Gádhi's son.'

Soon as they heard the holy man,
To the king's chamber swift they ran
With minds disordered all, and spurred
To wildest zeal by what they heard.
On to the royal hall they sped,
There stood and lowly bowed the head,
And made the lord of men aware
That the great saint was waiting there.

The king with priest and peer arose
And ran the sage to meet,
As Indra from his palace goes
Lord Brahmá's self to greet.
When glowing with celestial light
The pious hermit was in sight,
The king, whose mien his transport showed,
The honoured gift for guests bestowed.
Nor did the saint that gift despise,
Offered as holy texts advise;
He kindly asked the earth's great king
How all with him was prospering.
The son of Kuśik[2] bade him tell
If all in town and field were well,
All well with friends, and kith and kin,
And royal treasure stored within:
'Do all thy neighbours own thy sway?
Thy foes confess thee yet?
Dost thou continue still to pay
To Gods and men each debt?'
Then he, of hermits first and best,
Vaśishṭha with a smile[3] addressed,
And asked him of his welfare too,
Showing him honour as was due.
Then with the sainted hermit all
Went joyous to the monarch's hall,
And sate them down by due degree,
Each one, of rank and dignity.
Joy filled the noble prince's breast
Who thus bespoke the honoured guest:
'As amrit[1] by a mortal found,
As rain upon the thirsty ground,
As to an heirless man a son
Born to him of his precious one,
As gain of what we sorely miss,
As sudden dawn of mighty bliss,
So is thy coming here to me:
All welcome, mighty Saint, to thee.
What wish within thy heart hast thou?
If I can please thee, tell me how.
Hail, Saint, from whom all honours flow,
Worthy of all I can bestow.
Blest is my birth with fruit to-day,
Nor has my life been thrown away.
I see the best of Bráhman race
And night to glorious morn gives place.
Thou, holy Sage, in days of old
Among the royal saints enrolled,
Didst, penance-glorified, within
The Bráhman caste high station win.
'Tis meet and right in many a way
That I to thee should honour pay.
This seems a marvel to mine eyes:
All sin thy visit purifies;
And I by seeing thee, O Sage,
Have reaped the fruit of pilgrimage.
Then say what thou wouldst have me do,
That thou hast sought this interview.
Favoured by thee, my wish is still,
O Hermit, to perform thy will.
Nor needest thou at length explain
The object that thy heart would gain.
Without reserve I grant it now:
My deity, O Lord, art thou.'

The glorious hermit, far renowned,
With highest fame and virtue crowned,
Rejoiced these modest words to hear
Delightful to the mind and ear.

[1] The story of this famous saint is given at sufficient length in Cantos LI—LV. This saint has given his name to the district and city to the east of Benares. The original name, preserved in a land-grant on copper now in the Museum of the Benares College, has been Moslemized into Ghazeepore (the City of the Soldier-martyr).

[2] The son of Kuśik is Viśvámitra.

[3] At the recollection of their former enmity, to be described hereafter.

[1] The Indian nectar or drink of the Gods.

CANTO XXI.

VIŚVÁMITRA'S SPEECH.

The hermit heard with high content
That speech so wondrous eloquent,
And while each hair with joy arose,[2]

[2] Great joy, according to the Hindu belief, has this effect, not causing each particular hair to stand on end, but gently raising all the down upon the body.

He thus made answer at the close:
'Good is thy speech O noble King,
And like thyself in everything.
So should their lips be wisdom-fraught
Whom kings begot, Vaśishṭha taught.
The favour which I came to seek
Thou grantest ere my tongue can speak.
But let my tale attention claim,
And hear the need for which I came.
O King, as Scripture texts allow,
A holy rite employs me now.
Two fiends who change their forms at will
Impede that rite with cursed skill.[1]
Oft when the task is nigh complete,
These worst of fiends my toil defeat,
Throw bits of bleeding flesh. and o'er
The altar shed a stream of gore.
When thus the rite is mocked and stayed,
And all my pious hopes delayed,
Cast down in heart the spot I leave,
And spent with fruitless labour grieve.
Nor can I, checked by prudence, dare
Let loose my fury on them there:
The muttered curse, the threatening word,
In such a rite must ne'er be heard.
Thy grace the rite from check can free,
And yield the fruit I long to see.
Thy duty bids thee, King, defend
The suffering guest, the suppliant friend.
Give me thy son, thine eldest born,
Whom locks like raven's wings adorn.
That hero youth, the truly brave,
Of thee, O glorious King, I crave.
For he can lay those demons low
Who mar my rites and work me woe:
My power shall shield the youth from harm,
And heavenly might shall nerve his arm.
And on my champion will I shower
Unnumbered gifts of varied power,
Such gifts as shall ensure his fame
And spread through all the worlds his name.
Be sure those fiends can never stand
Before the might of Ráma's hand,
And mid the best and bravest none
Can slay that pair but Raghu's son.
Entangled in the toils of Fate
Those sinners, proud and obstinate,
Are, in their fury overbold,
No match for Ráma mighty-souled.
Nor let a father's breast give way
Too far to fond affection's sway.
Count thou the fiends already slain:
My word is pledged, nor pledged in vain.
I know the hero Ráma well
In whom high thoughts and valour dwell;
So does Vaśishṭha, so do these
Engaged in long austerities.
If thou would do the righteous deed,
And win high fame, thy virtue's meed,
Fame that on earth shall last and live,
To me, great King, thy Ráma give.
If to the words that I have said,
With Saint Vaśishṭha at their head
Thy holy men, O King, agree,
Then let thy Ráma go with me.
Ten nights my sacrifice will last,
And ere the stated time be past
Those wicked fiends, those impious twain,
Must fall by wondrous Ráma slain.
Let not the hours, I warn thee, fly,
Fixt for the rite, unheeded by;
Good luck have thou, O royal Chief,
Nor give thy heart to needless grief.'
Thus in fair words with virtue fraught
The pious glorious saint besought.
But the good speech with poignant sting
Pierced ear and bosom of the king,
Who, stabbed with pangs too sharp to bear,
Fell prostrate and lay fainting there.

CANTO XXII.

DAŚARATHA'S SPEECH.

His tortured senses all astray,
Awhle the hapless monarch lay,
Then slowly gathering thought and strengh
To Viśvámitra spoke at length:
'My son is but a child, I ween;
This year he will be just sixteen.
How is he fit for such emprise,
My darling with the lotus eyes?
A mghty army will I bring
That calls me master, lord, and king,
And with its countless squadrons fight
Against these rovers of the night.
My faithful heroes skilled to wield
The arms of war will take the field;
Their skill the demons' might may break:
Ráma, my child, thou must not take.
I, even I, my bow in hand,
Will in the van of battle stand,
And, while my soul is left alive,
With the night-roaming demons strive.
Thy guarded sacrifice shall be
Completed, from all hindrance free.
Thither will I my journey make:
Ráma, my child, thou must not take.
A boy unskilled, he knows not yet
The bounds to strength and weakness set.
No match is he for demon foes
Who magic arts to arms oppose.

[1] The Rákshasas, giants, or fiends who are represented as disturbing the sacrifice, signify here, as often elsewhere, merely the savage tribes which placed themselves in hostile opposition to Bráhmanical institutions.

O chief of saints, I have no power,
Of Ráma reft, to live one hour:
Mine aged heart at once would break:
Ráma, my child, thou must not take.
Nine thousand circling years have fled
With all their seasons o'er my head,
And as a hard-won boon, O Sage,
These sons have come to cheer mine age.
My dearest love amid the four
Is he whom first his mother bore,
Still dearer for his virtues' sake:
Ráma, my child, thou must not take.
But if, unmoved by all I say,
Thou needs must bear my son away,
Let me lead with him, I entreat,
A four-fold army[1] all complete.
What is the demons' might, O Sage?
Who are they? What their parentage?
What is their size? What beings lend
Their power to guard them and befriend?
How can my son their arts withstand?
Or I or all my armed band?
Tell me the whole that I may know
To meet in war each evil foe
Whom conscious might inspires with pride.'
And Viśvámitra thus replied:
'Sprung from Pulastya's race there came
A giant known by Rávaṇ's name.
Once favoured by the Eternal Sire
He plagues the worlds in ceaseless ire,
For peerless power and might renowned,
By giant bands encompassed round.
Viśravas for his sire they hold,
His brother is the Lord of Gold.
King of the giant hosts is he,
And worst of all in cruelty.
This Rávaṇ's dread commands impel
Two demons who in might excel,
Márícha and Suváhu hight,
To trouble and impede the rite.'
Then thus the king addressed the sage:
'No power have I, my lord, to wage
War with this evil-minded foe;
Now pity on my darling show,
And upon me of hapless fate,
For thee as God I venerate.
Gods, spirits, bards of heavenly birth,[2]
The birds of air, the snakes of earth
Before the might of Rávaṇ quail,
Much less can mortal man avail.
He draws, I hear, from out the breast
The valour of the mightiest.
No, ne'er can I with him contend,
Or with the forces he may send.
How can I then my darling lend,
Godlike, unskilled in battle? No,
I will not let my young child go.
Foes of thy rite, those mighty ones,
Sunda and Upasunda's sons,
Are fierce as Fate to overthrow:
I will not let my young child go.
Márícha and Suváhu fell
Are valiant and instructed well.
One of the twain I might attack
With all my friends their lord to back.'

CANTO XXIII.

VAŚISHṬHA'S SPEECH.

While thus the hapless monarch spoke,
Paternal love his utterance broke.
Then words like these the saint returned,
And fury in his bosom burned:
'Didst thou, O King, a promise make,
And wishest now thy word to break?
A son of Raghu's line should scorn
To fail in faith, a man forsworn.
But if thy soul can bear the shame
I will return e'en as I came.
Live with thy sons, and joy be thine,
False scion of Kakutstha's line.'
As Viśvámitra, mighty sage,
Was moved with this tempestuous rage,
Earth rocked and reeled throughout her frame,
And fear upon the Immortals came.
But Saint Vaśishṭha, wisest seer,
Observant of his vows austere,
Saw the whole world convulsed with dread,
And thus unto the monarch said:
'Thou, born of old Ikshváku's seed,
Art Justice' self in mortal weed.
Constant and pious, blest by fate,
The right thou must not violate.
Thou, Raghu's son, so famous through
The triple world as just and true,
Perform thy bounden duty still,
Nor stain thy race by deed of ill.
If thou have sworn and now refuse
Thou must thy store of merit lose.
Then, Monarch, let thy Ráma go,
Nor fear for him the demon foe.
The fiends shall have no power to hurt
Him trained to war or inexpert,
Nor vanquish him in battle field,
For Kuśik's son the youth will shield.
He is incarnate Justice, he
The best of men for bravery,
Embodied love of penance drear,
Among the wise without a peer.

---

[1] Consisting of horse, foot, chariots, and elephants.

[2] 'The Gandharvas, or heavenly bards, had originally a warlike character but were afterwards reduced to the office of celestial musicians cheering the banquets of the Gods. Dr. Kuhn has shown their identity with the Centaurs in name, origin, and attributes.' GORRESIO.

Full well he knows, great Kuśik's son,
The arms celestial, every one,
Arms from the Gods themselves concealed,
Far less to other men revealed.
These arms to him, when earth he swayed,
Mighty Kriśáśva, pleased, conveyed,
Kriśáśva's sons they are indeed,
Brought forth by Daksha's lovely seed,[1]
Heralds of conquest, strong and bold,
Brilliant, of semblance manifold.
Jayá and Vijayá, most fair,
And hundred splendid weapons bare.
Of Jayá. glorious as the morn,
First fifty noble sons were born,
Boundless in size yet viewless too,
They came the demons to subdue.
And fifty children also came
Of Vijayá the beauteous dame,
Sanháras named, of mighty force,
Hard to assail or check in course.
Of these the hermit knows the use,
And weapons new can he produce.
All these the mighty saint will yield
To Ráma's hand, to own and wield;
And armed with these, beyond a doubt
Shall Ráma put those fiends to rout.
For Ráma and the people's sake,
For thine own good my counsel take,
Nor seek, O King, with fond delay,
The parting of thy son to stay.'

CANTO XXIV.

THE SPELLS.

Vaśishṭha thus was speaking still:
The monarch, of his own free will,
Bade with quick zeal and joyful cheer
Ráma and Lakshmaṇ hasten near.
Mother and sire in loving care
Sped their dear son with rite and prayer:
Vaśishṭha blessed him ere he went;
O'er his loved head the father bent,
And then to Kuśik's son resigned
Ráma with Lakshmaṇ close behind.
Standing by Viśvámitra's side,
The youthful hero, lotus-eyed,
The Wind-God saw, and sent a breeze
Whose sweet pure touch just waved the trees.
There fell from heaven a flowery rain,
And with the song and dance the strain
Of shell and tambour sweetly blent
As forth the son of Raghu went.
The hermit led: behind him came
The bow-armed Ráma, dear to fame,
Whose locks were like the raven's wing:[1]
Then Lakshmaṇ, closely following.
The Gods and Indra, filled with joy,
Looked down upon the royal boy,
And much they longed the death to see
Of their ten-headed enemy.[2]
Ráma and Lakshmaṇ paced behind
That hermit of the lofty mind,
As the young Aśvins,[3] heavenly pair,
Follow Lord Indra through the air.
On arm and hand the guard they wore,
Quiver and bow and sword they bore;
Two fire-born Gods of War seemed they.[4]
He, Śiva's self who led the way.

Upon fair Sarjú's southern shore
They now had walked a league and more,
When thus the sage in accents mild
To Ráma said: 'Beloved child,
This lustral water duly touch:
My counsel will avail thee much.
Forget not all the words I say,
Nor let the occasion slip away.
Lo, with two spells I thee invest,
The mighty and the mightiest.
O'er thee fatigue shall ne'er prevail,
Nor age or change thy limbs assail.
Thee powers of darkness ne'er shall smite
In tranquil sleep or wild delight.
No one is there in all the land
Thine equal for the vigorous hand.

---

[1] These mysterious animated weapons are enumerated in Cantos XXIX and XXX. Daksha was the son of Brahmá and one of the Prajápatis, Demiurgi, or secondary authors of creation.

---

[1] Youths of the Kshatriya class used to leave unshorn the side locks of their hair. These were called *Káka-paksha*, or raven's wings.

[2] The Rákshas or giant Rávaṇ, king of Lanká.

[3] 'The meaning of Aśvins (from *aśva* a horse, Persian *asp*, Greek ἵππος, Latin *equus*, Welsh *ech*) is Horsemen. They were twin deities of whom frequent mention is made in the Vedas and the Indian myths. The Aśvins have much in common with the Dioscuri of Greece, and their mythical genealogy seems to indicate that their origin was astronomical. They were, perhaps, at first the morning star and evening star. They are said to be the children of the sun and the nymph Aśviní, who is one of the lunar asterisms personified. In the popular mythology they are regarded as the physicians of the Gods.' GORRESIO.

[4] The word *Kumára* (a young prince, a Childe) is also a proper name of Skanda or Kártikeya God of War, the son of Śiva and Umá. The babe was matured in the fire. See Appendix, *Kártikeii Generatio*

Thou, when thy lips pronounce the spell,
Shalt have no peer in heaven or hell.
None in the world with thee shall vie,
O sinless one, in apt reply,
In fortune, knowledge, wit, and tact,
Wisdom to plan and skill to act.
This double science take, and gain
Glory that shall for aye remain.
Wisdom and judgment spring from each
Of these fair spells whose use I teach.
Hunger and thirst unknown to thee,
High in the worlds thy rank shall be.
For these two spells with might endued,
Are the Great Father's heavenly brood,
And thee, O Chief, may fitly grace,
Thou glory of Kakutstha's race.
Virtues which none can match are thine,
Lord, from thy birth, of gifts divine,
And now these spells of might shall cast
Fresh radiance o'er the gifts thou hast.'
Then Ráma duly touched the wave,
Raised suppliant hands, bowed low his head,
And took the spells the hermit gave,
Whose soul on contemplation fed.
From him whose might these gifts enhanced,
A brighter beam of glory glanced:
So shines in all his autumn blaze
The Day-God of the thousand rays.
The hermit's wants those youths supplied,
As pupils use to holy guide.
And then the night in sweet content
On Sarjú's pleasant bank they spent.

CANTO XXV.

THE HERMITAGE OF LOVE.

Soon as appeared the morning light
Up rose the mighty anchorite,
And thus to youthful Ráma said,
Who lay upon his leafy bed:
'High fate is hers who calls thee son:
Arise, 'tis break of day;
Rise, Chief, and let those rites be done
Due at the morning's ray.'[1]
At that great sage's high behest
Up sprang the princely pair,
To bathing rites themselves addressed,
And breathed the holiest prayer.
Their morning task completed, they
To Viśvámitra came
That store of holy works, to pay
The worship saints may claim.
Then to the hallowed spot they went
Along fair Sarjú's side
Where mix her waters confluent
With three-pathed Gangá's tide.[1]
There was a sacred hermitage
Where saints devout of mind
Their lives through many a lengthened ago
To penance had resigned.
That pure abode the princes eyed
With unrestrained delight,
And thus unto the saint they cried,
Rejoicing at the sight:
'Whose is that hermitage we see?
Who makes his dwelling there?
Full of desire to hear are we:
O Saint, the truth declare.'
The hermit smiling made reply
To the two boys' request:
'Hear, Ráma, who in days gone by
This calm retreat possessed.
Kandarpa in apparent form,
Called Káma[2] by the wise,
Dared Umá's[3] new-wed lord to storm
And make the God his prize.
'Gainst Sthánu's[4] self, on rites austere
And vows intent,[5] they say,
His bold rash hand he dared to rear,
Though Sthánu cried, Away!
But the God's eye with scornful glare
Fell terrible on him,
Dissolved the shape that was so fair

---

[1] 'At the rising of the sun as well as at noon certain observances, invocations, and prayers were prescribed which might under no circumstances be omitted. One of these observances was the recitation of the Sávitrí, a Vedic hymn to the Sun of wonderful beauty.' GORRESIO.

[1] *Tripathaga*, *Three-path-go*, flowing in heaven, on earth, and under the earth. See Canto XLV.

[2] Tennyson's 'Indian Cama,' the God of Love, known also by many other names.

[3] *Umá, or Párvatí*, was daughter of Himálaya, Monarch of mountains, and wife of Śiva. See Kálidasa's *Kumára Sambhava*, or *Birth of the War-God*.

[4] *Sthánu*. The Unmoving one, a name of Śiva.

[5] 'The practice of austerities, voluntary tortures, and mortifications was anciently universal in India, and was held by the Indians to be of immense efficacy. Hence they mortified themselves to expiate sins, to acquire merits, and to obtain super-human gifts and powers; the Gods themselves sometimes exercised themselves in such austerities, either to raise themselves to greater power and grandeur, or to counteract the austerities of man which threatened to prevail over them and to deprive them of heaven............Such austerities were called in India *tapas* (burning ardour, fervent devotion) and he who practised them *tapasvin*.' GORRESIO.

And burnt up every limb.
Since the great God's terrific rage
Destroyed his form and frame,
Káma in each succeeding age
Has borne Ananga's[1] name.
So, where his lovely form decayed,
This land is Anga styled :
Sacred to him of old this shade,
And hermits undefiled.
Here Scripture-talking elders sway
Each sense with firm control,
And penance-rites have washed away
All sin from every soul.
One night, fair boy, we here will spend,
A pure stream on each hand,
And with to-morrow's light will bend
Our steps to yonder strand.
Here let us bathe, and free from stain
To that pure grove repair,
Sacred to Káma, and remain
One night in comfort there.'
With penance' far-discerning eye
The saintly men beheld
Their coming, and with transport high
Each holy bosom swelled.
To Kuśik's son the gift they gave
That honoured guest should greet,
Water they brought his feet to lave,
And showed him honour meet.
Ráma and Lakshmaṇ next obtained
In due degree their share.
Then with sweet talk the guests remained,
And charmed each listener there.
The evening prayers were duly said
With voices calm and low :
Then on the ground each laid his head
And slept till morning's glow.

CANTO XXVI.

THE FOREST OF TÁḌAKÁ.

When the fair light of morning rose
The princely tamers of their foes
Followed, his morning worship o'er,
The hermit to the river's shore.
The high-souled men with thoughtful care
A pretty barge had stationed there.
All cried, 'O lord, this barge ascend,
And with thy princely followers bend
To yonder side thy prosperous way
With naught to check thee or delay.'
Nor did the saint their rede reject :
He bade farewell with due respect,
And crossed, attended by the twain,
That river rushing to the main.
When now the bark was half way o'er,
Ráma and Lakshmaṇ heard the roar,
That louder grew and louder yet,
Of waves by dashing waters met.
Then Ráma asked the mighty seer :
'What is the tumult that I hear
Of waters cleft in mid career?'
Soon as the speech of Ráma, stirred
By deep desire to know, he heard,
The pious saint began to tell
What caused the waters' roar and swell :
'On high Kailása's distant hill
There lies a noble lake
Whose waters, born from Brahmá's will,
The name of Mánas[1] take.
Thence, hallowing where'er they flow,
The streams of Sarjú fall,
And wandering through the plains below
Embrace Ayodhyá's wall.
Still, still preserved in Sarjú's name
Sarovar's[2] fame we trace.
The flood of Brahmá whence she came
To run her holy race.
To meet great Gangá here she hies
With tributary wave :
Hence the loud roar ye hear arise,
Of floods that swell and rave.
Here, pride of Raghu's line, do thou
In humble adoration bow.'
He spoke. The princes both obeyed,
And reverence to each river paid.[3]
They reached the southern shore at last,
And gaily on their journey passed.
A little space beyond there stood
A gloomy awe-inspiring wood.
The monarch's noble son began
To question thus the holy man :
'Whose gloomy forest meets mine eye
Like some vast cloud that fills the sky?
Pathless and dark it seems to be,
Where birds in thousands wander free;
Where shrill cicalas' cries resound,

[1] *The Bodiless one.*

[1] 'A celebrated lake regarded in India as sacred. It lies in the lofty region between the northern highlands of the Himálayas and mount Kailása, the region of the sacred lakes. The poem, following the popular Indian belief, makes the river Sarayú (now Sarjú) flow from the Mánasa lake; the sources of the river are a little to the south about a day's journey from the lake. See Lassen, *Indische Alterthumskunde*, page 34.' GORRESIO. *Manas* means *mind; mánasa*, mental, mind-born.

[2] *Sarovar* means best of lakes. This is another of the poet's fanciful etymologies.

[3] The confluence of two or more rivers is often a venerated and holy place. The most famous is Prayág or Allahabad, where the Sarasvatí by an underground course is believed to join the Jumna and the Ganges.

And fowl of dismal note abound.
Lion, rhinoceros, and bear,
Boar, tiger, elephant, are there,
There shrubs and thorns run wild:
Dháo, Sál, Bignonia, Bel,[1] are found,
And every tree that grows on ground:
How is the forest styled?'
The glorious saint this answer made:
'Dear child of Raghu, hear
Who dwells within the horrid shade
That looks so dark and drear.
Where now is wood, long ere this day
Two broad and fertile lands,
Malaja and Karúsha lay,
Adorned by heavenly hands.
Here, mourning friendship's broken ties,
Lord Indra of the thousand eyes
Hungered and sorrowed many a day,
His brightness soiled with mud and clay,
When in a storm of passion he
Had slain his dear friend Namuchi.
Then came the Gods and saints who bore
Their golden pitchers brimming o'er
With holy streams that banish stain,
And bathed Lord Indra pure again.
When in this land the God was freed
From spot and stain of impious deed
For that his own dear friend he slew,
High transport thrilled his bosom through.
Then in his joy the lands he blessed,
And gave a boon they long possessed:
'Because these fertile lands retain
The washings of the blot and stain,'
'Twas thus Lord Indra sware,
'Malaja and Karúsha's name
Shall celebrate with deathless fame
My malady and care.'[2]
'So be it', all the Immortals cried,
When Indra's speech they heard,
And with acclaim they ratified
The names his lips conferred.
Long time, O victor of thy foes,
These happy lands had sweet repose,
And higher still in fortune rose.
At length a spirit, loving ill,
Tádaká, wearing shapes at will,
Whose mighty strength, exceeding vast,
A thousand elephants, surpassed,
Was to fierce Sunda, lord and head
Of all the demon armies, wed.
From her, Lord Indra's peer in might
Giant Máricha sprang to light:
And she, a constant plague and pest,
These two fair realms has long distressed.
Now dwelling in her dark abode
A league away she bars the road:
And we, O Ráma, hence must go
Where lies the forest of the foe.
Now on thine own right arm rely,
And my command obey:
Smite the foul monster that she die,
And take the plague away.
To reach this country none may dare,
Fallen from its old estate,
Which she, whose fury naught can bear,
Has left so desolate.
And now my truthful tale is told
How with accursed sway
The spirit plagued this wood of old,
And ceases not to-day.'

CANTO XXVII.

THE BIRTH OF TÁḌAKÁ.

When thus the sage without a peer
Had closed that story strange to hear,
Ráma again the saint addressed
To set one lingering doubt at rest:
'O holy man, 'tis said by all
That spirits' strength is weak and small;
How can she match, of power so slight,
A thousand elephants in might?'
And Viśvámitra thus replied
To Raghu's son the glorified:
'Listen, and I will tell thee how
She gained the strength that arms her now.
A mighty spirit lived of yore;
Suketu was the name he bore.
Childless was he, and free from crime
In rites austere he passed his time.
The mighty Sire was pleased to show
His favour, and a child bestow,
Tádaká named, most fair to see.
A pearl among the maids was she,
And matched, for such was Brahmá's dower,
A thousand elephants in power.
Nor would the Eternal Sire, although
The spirit longed, a son bestow
That maid in beauty's youthful pride
Was given to Sunda for a bride.
Her son, Máricha was his name,
A giant, through a curse, became.
She, widowed, dared with him molest

[1] The botanical names of the trees mentioned in the text are Grislea Tormentosa, Shorea Robusta, Echites Antidysenterica, Bignonia Suaveolens, Œgle Marmelos, and Diospyrus Glutinosa. I have omitted the *Kutaja* (Echites) and the *Tinduka* (Diospyrus).

[2] Here we meet with a fresh myth to account for the name of these regions. *Malaja* is probably a non-Aryan word signifying a hilly country: taken as a Sanskrit compound it means *sprung from defilement*. The word *Karúsha* appears to have a somewhat similar meaning.

Agastya,[1] of all saints the best.
Inflamed with hunger's wildest rage,
Roaring she rushed upon the sage.
When the great hermit saw her near,
On speeding in her fierce career,
He thus pronounced Máricha's doom:
'A giant's form and shape assume.'
And then, by mighty anger swayed,
On Táḍaká this curse he laid:
'Thy present form and semblance quit,
And wear a shape thy mood to fit;
Changed form and feature by my ban,
A fearful thing that feeds on man.'

She, by his awful curse possessed,
And mad with rage that fills her breast,
Has on this land her fury dealt
Where once the saint Agastya dwelt.
Go, Ráma, smite this monster dead,
The wicked plague, of power so dread,
And further by this deed of thine
The good of Bráhmans and of kine.
Thy hand alone can overthrow,
In all the worlds, this impious foe.
Nor let compassion lead thy mind
To shrink from blood of womankind;
A monarch's son must ever count
The people's welfare paramount.
And whether pain or joy he deal
Dare all things for his subjects' weal;
Yea, if the deed bring praise or guilt,
If life be saved or blood be spilt:
Such, through all time, should be the care
Of those a kingdom's weight who bear.
Slay, Ráma, slay this impious fiend,
For by no law her life is screened.
So Manthará, as bards have told,
Virochan's child, was slain of old
By Indra, when in furious hate
She longed the earth to devastate.
So Kávya's mother, Bhrigu's wife,
Who loved her husband as her life,
When Indra's throne she sought to gain,
By Vishnu's hand of yore was slain.
By these and high-souled kings beside,
Struck down, have lawless women died.'

[1] 'This is one of those indefinable mythic personages who are found in the ancient traditions of many nations, and in whom cosmogonical or astronomical notions are generally figured. Thus it is related of Agastya that the Vindhyan mountains prostrated themselves before him; and yet the same Agastya is believed to be regent of the star Canopus.' GORRESIO.

He will appear as the friend and helper of Ráma farther on in the poem.

CANTO XXVIII.

THE DEATH OF TÁḌAKÁ.

Thus spoke the saint. Each vigorous word
The noble monarch's offspring heard,
And, reverent hands together laid,
His answer to the hermit made:
'My sire and mother bade me aye
Thy word, O mighty Saint, obey.
So will I, O most glorious, kill
This Táḍaká who joys in ill,
For such my sire's, and such thy will.
To aid with mine avenging hand
The Bráhmans, kine, and all the land,
Obedient, heart and soul, I stand.'

Thus spoke the tamer of the foe,
And by the middle grasped his bow.
Strongly he drew the sounding string
That made the distant welkin ring.
Scared by the mighty clang the deer
That roamed the forest shook with fear.
And Táḍaká the echo heard,
And rose in haste from slumber stirred.
In wild amaze, her soul aflame
With fury toward the spot she came.
When that foul shape of evil mien
And stature vast as e'er was seen
The wrathful son of Raghu eyed,
He thus unto his brother cried:
'Her dreadful shape, O Lakshmaṇ, see,
A form to shudder at and flee.
The hideous monster's very view
Would cleave a timid heart in two.
Behold the demon hard to smite,
Defended by her magic might.
My hand shall stay her course to-day,
And shear her nose and ears away.
No heart have I her life to take:
I spare it for her sex's sake.
My will is but, with minished force,
To check her in her evil course.'
While thus he spoke, by rage impelled
  Roaring as she came nigh,
The fiend her course at Ráma held
  With huge arms tossed on high.
Her, rushing on, the seer assailed
  With a loud cry of hate;
And thus the sons of Raghu hailed:
  'Fight, and be fortunate.'
Then from the earth a horrid cloud
  Of dust the demon raised,
And for awhile in darkling shroud
  Wrapt Raghu's sons amazed.
Then calling on her magic power
  The fearful fight to wage,
She smote him with a stony shower,
  Till Ráma burned with rage.
Then pouring forth his arrowy rain
  That stony flood to stay,

With winged darts, as she charged amain,
He shore her hands away.
As Táḍaká still thundered near
Thus maimed by Ráma's blows,
Lakshmaṇ in fury severed sheer
The monster's ears and nose.
Assuming by her magic skill
A fresh and fresh disguise,
She tried a thousand shapes at will,
Then vanished from their eyes.
When Gádhi's son of high renown
Still saw the stony rain pour down
Upon each princely warrior's head,
With words of wisdom thus he said:
'Enough of mercy, Ráma, lest
This sinful evil-working pest,
Disturber of each holy rite,
Repair by magic arts her might.
Without delay the fiend should die,
For, see, the twilight hour is nigh.
And at the joints of night and day
Such giant foes are hard to slay.'
Then Ráma, skilful to direct
His arrow to the sound,
With shafts the mighty demon checked
Who rained her stones around.
She sore impeded and beset
By Ráma and his arrowy net,
Though skilled in guile and magic lore,
Rushed on the brothers with a roar.
Deformed, terrific, murderous, dread,
Swift as the levin on she sped,
Like cloudy pile in autumn's sky,
Lifting her two vast arms on high,
When Ráma smote her with a dart,
Shaped like a crescent, to the heart.
Sore wounded by the shaft that came
With lightning speed and surest aim,
Blood spouting from her mouth and side,
She fell upon the earth and died.
Soon as the Lord who rules the sky
Saw the dread monster lifeless lie,
He called aloud, Well done! well done!
And the Gods honoured Raghu's son.
Standing in heaven the Thousand-eyed,
With all the Immortals, joying cried:
'Lift up thine eyes, O Saint, and see
The Gods and Indra nigh to thee.
This deed of Ráma's boundless might
Has filled our bosoms with delight.
Now, for our will would have it so,
To Raghu's son some favour show.
Invest him with the power which naught
But penance gains and holy thought.
Those heavenly arms on him bestow
To thee entrusted long ago
By great Kriśáśva best of kings,
Son of the Lord of living things.
More fit recipient none can be
Than he who joys in following thee;
And for our sakes the monarch's seed
Has yet to do a mighty deed.'
He spoke; and all the heavenly train
Rejoicing sought their homes again,
While honour to the saint they paid.
Then came the evening's twilight shade,
The best of hermits overjoyed
To know the monstrous fiend destroyed,
His lips on Ráma's forehead pressed,
And thus the conquering chief addressed:
'O Ráma gracious to the sight,
Here will we pass the present night,
And with the morrow's earliest ray
Bend to my hermitage our way.'
The son of Daśaratha heard,
Delighted, Viśvámitra's word,
And as he bade, that night he spent
In Táḍaká's wild wood, content.
And the grove shone that happy day,
Freed from the curse that on it lay,
Like Chaitraratha[1] fair and gay.

CANTO XXIX.

THE CELESTIAL ARMS.

That night they slept and took their rest;
And then the mighty saint addressed,
With pleasant smile and accents mild
These words to Raghu's princely child:
'Well pleased am I. High fate be thine,
Thou scion of a royal line.
Now will I, for I love thee so,
All heavenly arms on thee bestow.
Victor with these, whoe'er oppose,
Thy hand shall conquer all thy foes,
Though Gods and spirits of the air,
Serpents and fiends, the conflict dare.
I'll give thee as a pledge of love
The mystic arms they use above,
For worthy thou to have revealed
The weapons I have learnt to wield.[2]

---

[1] The famous pleasure-garden of Kuvera the God of Wealth.

[2] 'The whole of this Canto together with the following one, regards the belief, formerly prevalent in India, that by virtue of certain spells, to be learnt and muttered, secret knowledge and superhuman powers might be acquired. To this the poet has already alluded in Canto xxiii. These incorporeal weapons are partly represented according to the fashion of those ascribed to the Gods and the different orders of demi-gods, partly are the mere creations of fancy; and it would not be easy to say what idea the poet had of them in his own mind, or what powers he meant to assign to each.' SCHLEGEL.

First, son of Raghu, shall be thine
The arm of Vengeance, strong, divine:
The arm of Fate, the arm of Right,
And Vishṇu's arm of awful might:
That, before which no foe can stand,
The thunderbolt of Indra's hand;
And Śiva's trident, sharp and dread,
And that dire weapon Brahmá's Head.
And two fair clubs, O royal child,
One Charmer and one Pointed styled
With flame of lambent fire aglow,
On thee, O Chieftain, I bestow.
And Fate's dread net and Justice' noose
That none may conquer, for thy use:
And the great cord, renowned of old,
Which Varuṇ ever loves to hold.
Take these two thunderbolts, which I
Have got for thee, the Moist and Dry.
Here Śiva's dart to thee I yield,
And that which Vishṇu wont to wield.
I give to thee the arm of Fire,
Desired by all and named the Spire.
To thee I grant the Wind-God's dart,
Named Crusher, O thou pure of heart,
This arm, the Horse's Head, accept,
And this, the Curlew's Bill yclept,
And these two spears, the best e'er flew,
Named the Invincible and True.
And arms of fiends I make thine own,
Skull-wreath and mace that smashes bone.
And Joyous, which the spirits bear,
Great weapon of the sons of air.
Brave offspring of the best of lords,
I give thee now the Gem of swords,
And offer next, thine hand to arm,
The heavenly bards' beloved charm.
Now with two arms I thee invest
Of never-ending Sleep and Rest,
With weapons of the Sun and Rain,
And those that dry and burn amain;
And strong Desire with conquering touch,
The dart that Káma prizes much.
I give the arm of shadowy powers
That bleeding flesh of men devours.
I give the arms the God of Gold
And giant fiends exult to hold.
This smites the foe in battle-strife,
And takes his fortune, strength, and life.
I give the arms called False and True,
And great Illusion give I too;
The hero's arm called Strong and Bright
That spoils the foeman's strength in fight.
I give thee as a priceless boon
The Dew, the weapon of the Moon,
And add the weapon, deftly planned,
That strengthens Viśvakarmá's hand.
The Mortal dart whose point is chill,
And Slaughter, ever sure to kill;
All these and other arms, for thou
Art very dear, I give thee now.
Receive these weapons from my hand,
Son of the noblest in the land.'

Facing the east, the glorious saint
Pure from all spot of earthly taint,
To Ráma, with delighted mind,
That noble host of spells consigned.
He taught the arms, whose lore is won
Hardly by Gods, to Raghu's son.
He muttered low the spell whose call
Summons those arms and rules them all,
And, each in visible form and frame,
Before the monarch's son they came.
They stood and spoke in reverent guise
To Ráma with exulting cries:
'O noblest child of Raghu, see,
Thy ministers and thralls are we.'

With joyful heart and eager hand
Ráma received the wondrous band,
And thus with words of welcome cried:
'Aye present to my will abide.'
Then hasted to the saint to pay
Due reverence, and pursued his way.

CANTO XXX.

THE MYSTERIOUS POWERS.[1]

Pure, with glad cheer and joyful breast,
Of those mysterious arms possessed,
Ráma, now passing on his way,
Thus to the saint began to say:
'Lord of these mighty weapons, I
Can scarce be harmed by Gods on high;
Now, best of saints, I long to gain
The powers that can these arms restrain.'
Thus spoke the prince. The sage austere,
True to his vows, from evil clear,
Called forth the names of those great charms
Whose powers restrain the deadly arms.
'Receive thou True and Truly-famed,
And Bold and Fleet: the weapons named

[1] 'In Sanskrit *Sanhára*, a word which has various significations but the primary meaning of which is *the act of seizing*. A magical power seems to be implied of employing the weapons when and where required. The remarks I have made on the preceding Canto apply with still greater force to this. The MSS. greatly vary in the enumeration of these *Sanháras*, and it is not surprising that copyists have incorrectly written the names which they did not well understand. The commentators throw no light upon the subject.' SCHLEGEL. I have taken the liberty of omitting four of these which Schlegel translates 'Scleromphalum, Euomphalum, Centiventrem, and Chrysomphalum.'

Warder and Progress, swift of pace,
Averted-head and Drooping-face;
The Seen, and that which Secret flies;
The weapon of the thousand eyes;
Ten-headed, and the Hundred-faced,
Star-gazer and the Layer-waste:
The Omen-bird, the Pure-from-spot,
The pair that wake and slumber not:
The Fiendish, that which shakes amain,
The Strong-of-Hand, the Rich-in-Gain:
The Guardian, and the Close-allied,
The Gaper, Love, and Golden-side:
O Raghu's son receive all these,
Bright ones that wear what forms they please;
Krisásva's mystic sons are they,
And worthy thou their might to sway.'
With joy the pride of Raghu's race
Received the hermit's proffered grace,
Mysterious arms, to check and stay,
Or smite the foeman in the fray.
Then, all with heavenly forms endued,
Nigh came the wondrous multitude.
Celestial in their bright attire
Some shone like coals of burning fire;
Some were like clouds of dusky smoke;
And suppliant thus they sweetly spoke:
'Thy thralls, O Ráma, here we stand:
Command, we pray, thy faithful band.'
'Depart,' he cried, 'where each may list,
But when I call you to assist,
Be present to my mind with speed,
And aid me in the hour of need.'
To Ráma then they lowly bent,
And round him in due reverence went,
To his command, they answered, Yea,
And as they came so went away.
When thus the arms had homeward flown,
With pleasant words and modest tone,
E'en as he walked, the prince began
To question thus the holy man:
'What cloudlike wood is that which near
The mountain's side I see appear?
O tell me, for I long to know;
Its pleasant aspect charms me so.
Its glades are full of deer at play,
And sweet birds sing on every spray.
Past is the hideous wild; I feel
So sweet a tremor o'er me steal,
And hail with transport fresh and new
A land that is so fair to view.
Then tell me all, thou holy Sage,
And whose this pleasant hermitage
In which those wicked ones delight
To mar and kill each holy rite.
And with foul heart and evil deed
Thy sacrifice, great Saint, impede.
To whom, O Sage, belongs this land
In which thine altars ready stand?
'Tis mine to guard them, and to slay
The giants who the rites would stay.
All this, O best of saints, I burn
From thine own lips, my lord, to learn.'

CANTO XXXI.

THE PERFECT HERMITAGE.

Thus spoke the prince of boundless might,
And thus replied the anchorite:
'Chief of the mighty arm, of yore
Lord Vishṇu whom the Gods adore,
For holy thought and rites austere
Of penance made his dwelling here.
This ancient wood was called of old
Grove of the Dwarf, the mighty-souled,
And when perfection he attained
The grove the name of Perfect gained.
Bali of yore, Virochan's son,
Dominion over Indra won,
And when with power his proud heart swelled,
O'er the three worlds his empire held.
When Bali then began a rite,
The Gods and Indra in affrght
Sought Vishṇu in this place of rest,
And thus with prayers the God addressed:
'Bali, Virochan's mighty son,
His sacrifice has now begun:
Of boundless wealth, that demon king
Is bounteous to each living thing.
Though suppliants flock from every side
The suit of none is e'er denied.
Whate'er, where'er howe'er the call,
He hears the suit and gives to all.
Now with thine own illusive art
Perform, O Lord, the helper's part:
Assume a dwarfish form, and thus
From fear and danger rescue us.'[1]

Thus in their dread the Immortals sued:
The God a dwarflike shape indued:[2]
Before Virochan's son he came,
Three steps of land his only claim.
The boon obtained, in wondrous wise
Lord Vishṇu's form increased in size;
Through all the worlds, tremendous, vast,
God of the Triple Step, he passed.[3]
The whole broad earth from side to side
He measured with one mighty stride,
Spanned with the next the firmament,
And with the third through heaven he went.

---

[1] I omit, after this line, eight *ślokes* which, as Schlegel allows, are quite out of place.

[2] This is the fifth of the *avatárs*, descents or incarnations of Vishṇu.

[3] This is a solar allegory. Vishṇu is the sun, the three steps being his rising, culmination, and setting.

Thus was the king of demons hurled
By Vishṇu to the nether world,
And thus the universe restored
To Indra's rule, its ancient lord.
And now because the immortal God
This spot in dwarflike semblance trod,
The grove has aye been loved by me
For reverence of the devotee.
But demons haunt it, prompt to stay
Each holy offering I would pay.
Be thine, O lion-lord, to kill
These giants that delight in ill.
This day, beloved child, our feet
Shall rest within the calm retreat:
And know, thou chief of Raghu's line,
My hermitage is also thine.'

He spoke; and soon the anchorite,
With joyous looks that beamed delight,
With Ráma and his brother stood
Within the consecrated wood.
Soon as they saw the holy man,
With one accord together ran
The dwellers in the sacred shade,
And to the saint their reverence paid,
And offered water for his feet,
The gift of honour and a seat;
And next with hospitable care
They entertained the princely pair.
The royal tamers of their foes
Rested awhile in sweet repose:
Then to the chief of hermits sued
Standing in suppliant attitude:
'Begin, O best of saints, we pray,
Initiatory rites to-day.
This Perfect Grove shall be anew
Made perfect, and thy words be true.'

Then, thus addressed, the holy man,
The very glorious sage, began
The high preliminary rite,
Restraining sense and appetite.
Calmly the youths that night reposed,
And rose when morn her light disclosed,
Their morning worship paid, and took
Of lustral water from the brook.
Thus purified they breathed the prayer,
Then greeted Viśvámitra where
As celebrant he sate beside
The flame with sacred oil supplied.

CANTO XXXII.

VIŚVÁMITRA'S SACRIFICE.

That conquering pair, of royal race,
Skilled to observe due time and place,
To Kúśik's hermit son addressed,
In timely words, their meet request:
'When must we, lord, we pray thee tell,
Those Rovers of the Night repel?
Speak, lest we let the moment fly,
And pass the due occasion by.'
Thus longing for the strife, they prayed,
And thus the hermits answer made:
Till the fifth day be come and past,
O Raghu's sons, your watch must last.
The saint his Dikshá[1] has begun,
And all that time will speak to none.'
Soon as the steadfast devotees
Had made reply in words like these,
The youths began, disdaining sleep,
Six days and nights their watch to keep.
The warrior pair who tamed the foe,
Unrivalled benders of the bow,
Kept watch and ward unwearied still
To guard the saint from scathe and ill.
'Twas now the sixth returning day,
The hour foretold had past away.
Then Ráma cried: 'O Lakshmaṇ, now
Firm, watchful, resolute be thou.
The fiends as yet have kept afar
From the pure grove in which we are;
Yet waits us, ere the day shall close,
Dire battle with the demon foes.'

While thus spoke Ráma borne away
By longing for the deadly fray,
See! bursting from the altar came
The sudden glory of the flame.
Round priest and deacon, and upon
Grass, ladles, flowers, the splendour shone,
And the high rite, in order due,
With sacred texts began anew.
But then a loud and fearful roar
Re-echoed through the sky;
And like vast clouds that shadow o'er
The heavens in dark July,
Involved in gloom of magic might
Two fiends rushed on amain,
Máricha, Rover of the Night,
Suváhu, and their train.
As on they came in wild career
Thick blood in rain they shed;
And Ráma saw those things of fear
Impending overhead.
Then soon as those accursed two
Who showered down blood he spied,
Thus to his brother brave and true
Spoke Ráma lotus-eyed:
'Now, Lakshmaṇ, thou these fiends shalt see,
Man-eaters, foul of mind,
Before my mortal weapon flee
Like clouds before the wind.'
He spoke. An arrow, swift as thought,
Upon his bow he pressed,
And smote, to utmost fury wrought,
Máricha on the breast.
Deep in his flesh the weapon lay
Winged by the mystic spell,

[1] Certain ceremonies preliminary to a sacrifice.

And, hurled a hundred leagues away,
In ocean's flood he fell.
Then Ráma, when he saw the foe
Convulsed and mad with pain
Neath the chill-pointed weapon's blow,
To Lakshman spoke again :
'See, Lakshman, see ! this mortal dart
That strikes a numbing chill,
Hath struck him senseless with the smart,
But left him breathing still.
But these who love the evil way,
And drink the blood they spill,
Rejoicing holy rites to stay,
Fierce plagues, my hand shall kill.'
He seized another shaft, the best,
Aglow with living flame;
It struck Suváhu on the chest,
And dead to earth he came.
Again a dart, the Wind-God's own,
Upon his string he laid,
And all the demons were o'erthrown,
The saints no more afraid.
When thus the fiends were slain in fight,
Disturbers of each holy rite,
Due honour by the saints was paid
To Ráma for his wondrous aid :
So Indra is adored when he
Has won some glorious victory.
Success at last the rite had crowned,
And Viśvámitra gazed around,
And seeing every side at rest,
The son of Raghu thus addressed :
'My joy, O Prince, is now complete :
Thou hast obeyed my will :
Perfect before, this calm retreat
In now more perfect still.'

CANTO XXXIII.

THE SONE.

Their task achieved, the princes spent
That night with joy and full content.
Ere yet the dawn was well displayed
Their morning rites they duly paid,
And sought, while yet the light was faint,
The hermits and the mighty saint.
They greeted first that holy sire
Resplendent like the burning fire,
And then with noble words began
Their sweet speech to the sainted man :
'Here stand, O Lord, thy servants true :
Command what thou wouldst have us do.'

The saints, by Viśvámitra led,
To Ráma thus in answer said :
'Janak the king who rules the land
Of fertile Mithilá has planned
A noble sacrifice, and we
Will thither go the rite to see.
Thou, Prince of men, with us shalt go,
And there behold the wondrous bow,
Terrific, vast, of matchless might,
Which, splendid at the famous rite,
The Gods assembled gave the king.
No giant, fiend, or God can string
That gem of bows, no heavenly bard ;
Then, sure, for man the task were hard.
When lords of earth have longed to know
The virtue of that wondrous bow,
The strongest sons of kings in vain
Have tried the mighty cord to strain.
This famous bow thou there shalt view,
And wondrous rites shalt witness too.
The high-souled king who lords it o'er
The realm of Mithilá of yore
Gained from the Gods this bow, the price
Of his imperial sacrifice.
Won by the rite the glorious prize
Still in the royal palace lies,
Laid up in oil of precious scent
With aloe-wood and incense blent.'

Then Ráma answering, Be it so,
Made ready with the rest to go.
The saint himself was now prepared,
But ere beyond the grove he fared,
He turned him and in words like these
Addressed the sylvan deities :
'Farewell ! each holy rite complete,
I leave the hermits' perfect seat :
To Gangá's northern shore I go
Beneath Himálaya's peaks of snow.'
With reverent steps he paced around
The limits of the holy ground,
And then the mighty saint set forth
And took his journey to the north.
His pupils, deep in Scripture's page,
Followed behind the holy sage,
And servants from the sacred grove
A hundred wains for convoy drove.
The very birds that winged that air,
The very deer that harboured there,
Forsook the glade and leafy brake
And followed for the hermit's sake.
They travelled far, till in the west
The sun was speeding to his rest,
And made, their portioned journey o'er,
Their halt on Śoṇa's[1] distant shore.
The hermits bathed when sank the sun,
And every rite was duly done,
Oblations paid to Fire, and then
Sate round their chief the holy men.
Ráma and Lakshmaṇ lowly bowed
In reverence to the hermit crowd,
And Ráma, having sate him down
Before the saint of pure renown,

[1] A river which rises in Bundelcund and falls into the Ganges near Patna. It is called also *Hiraṇyaváhu*, Golden-armed, and *Hiraṇyaváha*, Auriferous.

With humble palms together laid
His eager supplication made :
'What country, O my lord, is this,
Fair-smiling in her wealth and bliss?
Deign fully, O thou mighty Seer,
To tell me, for I long to hear.'
Moved by the prayer of Ráma, he
Told forth the country's history.

CANTO XXXIV.

BRAHMADATTA.

'A king of Brahmá's seed who bore
The name of Kuśa reigned of yore.
Just, faithful to his vows, and true,
He held the good in honour due.
His bride. a queen of noble name,
Of old Vidarbha's[1] monarchs came.
Like their own father, children four,
All valiant boys, the lady bore.
In glorious deeds each nerve they strained,
And well their Warrior part sustained.
To them most just, and true, and brave,
Their father thus his counsel gave :
'Beloved children, ne'er forget
Protection is a prince's debt :
The noble work at once begin,
High virtue and her fruits to win.'
The youths, to all the people dear,
Received his speech with willing ear ;
And each went forth his several way,
Foundations of a town to lay.
Kuśámba, prince of high renown,
Was builder of Kauśámbí's town,
And Kuśanábha, just and wise,
Bade high Mahodaya's towers arise.
Amúrtarajas chose to dwell
In Dharmáranya's citadel,
And Vasu bade his city fair
The name of Girivraja bear.[2]
This fertile spot whereon we stand
Was once the high-souled Vasu's land.
Behold! as round we turn our eyes,
Five lofty mountain peaks arise.
See! bursting from her parent hill,
Sumágadhí, a lovely rill,
Bright gleaming as she flows between
The mountains, like a wreath is seen,
And then through Magadh's plains and groves
With many a fair mæander roves.
And this was Vasu's old domain,
The fertile Magadh's broad champaign,
Which smiling fields of tilth adorn
And diadem with golden corn.
The queen Ghritáchí, nymph most fair,
Married to Kuśanábha, bare
A hundred daughters, lovely-faced,
With every charm and beauty graced.
It chanced the maidens, bright and gay
As lightning-flashes on a day
Of rain-time, to the garden went
With song and play and merriment,
And there in gay attire they strayed,
And danced, and laughed, and sang, and played.
The God of Wind who roves at will
All places, as he lists, to fill,
Saw the young maidens dancing there,
Of faultless shape and mien most fair.
'I love you all, sweet girls,' he cried,
And each shall be my darling bride.
Forsake, forsake your mortal lot,
And gain a life that withers not.
A fickle thing is youth's brief span,
And more than all in mortal man.
Receive unending youth, and be
Immortal, O my loves, with me.'
The hundred girls, to wonder stirred,
The wooing of the Wind-God heard,
Laughed, as a jest, his suit aside,
And with one voice they thus replied :
'O mighty Wind, free spirit who
All life pervadest, through and through,
Thy wondrous power we maidens know ;
Then wherefore wilt thou mock us so?
Our sire is Kuśanábha, King ;
And we, forsooth, have charms to bring
A God to woo us from the skies ;
But honour first we maidens prize.
Far may the hour, we pray, be hence,
When we, O thou of little sense,
Our truthful father's choice refuse,
And for ourselves our husbands choose.
Our honoured sire our lord we deem,
He is to us a God supreme,
And they to whom his high decree
May give us shall our husbands be.'
He heard the answer they returned,
And mighty rage within him burned.
On each fair maid a blast he sent :
Each stately form he bowed and bent.
Bent double by the Wind-God's ire
They sought the palace of their sire,

[1] The modern Berar.

[2] According to the Bengal recension the first (Kuśámba) is called Kuśáśva, and his city Kauśáśví. This name does not occur elsewhere. The reading of the northern recension is confirmed by Foĕ Kouĕ Ki; p. 385, where the city *Kiaoshangmi* is mentioned. It lay 500 *lis* to the south-west of *Prayága*, on the south bank of the Jumna. *Mahodaya* is another name of Kanyákubja; *Dharmáranya*, the wood to which the God of Justice is said to have fled through fear of Soma the Moon-God was in Magadh. Girivraja was in the same neighbourhood. See Lassen's I. A. Vol. I. p. 604.

There fell upon the ground with sighs,
While tears and shame were in their eyes.
The king himself, with troubled brow,
Saw his dear girls so fair but now,
A mournful sight all bent and bowed,
And grieving thus he cried aloud:
'What fate is this, and what the cause?
What wretch has scorned all heavenly laws?
Who thus your forms could curve and break?
You struggle, but no answer make.'

They heard the speech of that wise king
Of their misfortune questioning.
Again the hundred maidens sighed,
Touched with their heads his feet, and cried:
'The God of Wind, pervading space,
Would bring on us a foul disgrace,
And choosing folly's evil way
From virtue's path in scorn would stray.
But we in words like these reproved
The God of Wind whom passion moved:
'Farewell, O Lord! A sire have we,
No women uncontrolled and free.
Go, and our sire's consent obtain
If thou our maiden hands wouldst gain.
No self-dependent life we live:
If we offend, our fault forgive.'
'But led by folly as a slave,
He would not hear the rede we gave,
And even as we gently spoke
We felt the Wind-God's crushing stroke.'

The pious king, with grief distressed,
The noble hundred thus addressed:
'With patience, daughters, bear your fate,
Yours was a deed supremely great
When with one mind you kept from shame
The honour of your father's name.
Patience, when men their anger vent,
Is woman's praise and ornament;
Yet when the Gods inflict the blow
Hard is it to support the woe.
Patience, my girls, exceeds all price:
'Tis alms, and truth, and sacrifice.
Patience is virtue, patience fame:
Patience upholds this earthly frame.
And now, I think, is come the time
To wed you in your maiden prime.
Now, daughters, go where'er you will:
Thoughts for your good my mind shall fill.'

The maidens went, consoled, away:
The best of kings, that very day,
Summoned his ministers of state
About their marriage to debate.
Since then, because the Wind-God bent
The damsels' forms for punishment,
That royal town is known to fame
By Kanyákubja's[1] borrowed name.

[1] That is, the City of the Bent Virgins, the modern Kanauj or Canouge.

There lived a sage called Chúli then,
Devoutest of the sons of men;
His days in penance rites he spent,
A glorious saint, most continent.
To him absorbed in tasks austere
The child of Urmilá drew near,
Sweet Somadá, the heavenly maid
And lent the saint her pious aid.
Long time near him the maiden spent,
And served him meek and reverent,
Till the great hermit, pleased with her,
Thus spoke unto his minister:
'Grateful am I for all thy care:
Blest maiden, speak, thy wish declare.'
The sweet-voiced nymph rejoiced to see
The favour of the devotee,
And to that eloquent old man,
Most eloquent she thus began:
'Thou hast, by heavenly grace sustained,
Close union with the Godhead gained.
I long, O Saint, to see a son
By force of holy penance won.
Unwed, a maiden life I live:
A son to me, thy suppliant, give.'
The saint with favour heard her prayer,
And gave a son exceeding fair.
Him, Chúli's spiritual child,
His mother Brahmadatta[1] styled.
King Brahmadatta, rich and great,
In Kámpilí maintained his state,
Ruling, like Indra in his bliss,
His fortunate metropolis.
King Kuśanábha planned that he
His hundred daughters' lord should be.
To him, obedient to his call,
The happy monarch gave them all.
Like Indra then he took the hand
Of every maiden of the band.
Soon as the hand of each young maid
In Brahmadatta's palm was laid,
Deformity and cares away,
She shone in beauty bright and gay.
Their freedom from the Wind-God's might
Saw Kuśanábha with delight.
Each glance that on their forms he threw
Filled him with raptures ever new.
Then when the rites were all complete,
With highest marks of honour meet
The bridegroom with his brides he sent
To his great seat of government.

The nymph received with pleasant speech
Her daughters; and, embracing each,
Upon their forms she fondly gazed,
And royal Kuśanábha praised.

[1] Literally, Given by *Brahma* or devout contemplation.

CANTO XXXV.

VIŚVÁMITRA'S LINEAGE.

'The rites were o'er, the maids were wed,
The bridegroom to his home was sped.
The sonless monarch bade prepare
A sacrifice to gain an heir.
Then Kuśa, Brahmá's son, appeared,
And thus King Kuśanábha cheered:
'Thou shalt, my child, obtain a son
Like thine own self, O holy one.
Through him for ever, Gádhi named,
Shalt thou in all the worlds be famed.'
'He spoke, and vanished from the sight
To Brahmá's world of endless light.
Time fled, and, as the saint foretold,
Gádhi was born, the holy-souled.
My sire was he; through him I trace
My line from royal Kuśa's race.
My sister—elder-born was she—
The pure and good Satyavatí,[1]
Was to the great Richíka wed.
Still faithful to her husband dead,
She followed him, most noble dame,
And, raised to heaven in human frame,
A pure celestial stream became.
Down from Himálaya's snowy height,
In floods for ever fair and bright,
My sister's holy waves are hurled
To purify and glad the world.
Now on Himálaya's side I dwell
Because I love my sister well.
She, for her faith and truth renowned,
Most loving to her husband found,
High-fated, firm in each pure vow,
Is queen of all the rivers now.
Bound by a vow I left her side
And to the Perfect convent hied.
There, by the aid 'twas thine to lend,
Made perfect, all my labours end.
Thus, mighty Prince, I now have told
My race and lineage, high and old,
And local tales of long ago
Which thou, O Ráma, fain wouldst know
As I have sate rehearsing thus
The midnight hour is come on us.
Now, Ráma, sleep, that nothing may
Our journey of to-morrow stay.
No leaf on any tree is stirred:
Hushed in repose are beast and bird:
Where'er you turn, on every side,
Dense shades of night the landscape hide.
The light of eve is fled: the skies,
Thick-studded with their host of eyes,
Seem a star-forest overhead,
Where signs and constellations spread.
Now rises, with his pure cold ray,
The moon that drives the shades away,
And with his gentle influence brings
Joy to the hearts of living things.
Now, stealing from their lairs, appear
The beasts to whom the night is dear.
Now spirits walk, and every power
That revels in the midnight hour.'
  The mighty hermit's tale was o'er,
He closed his lips and spoke no more.
The holy men on every side,
'Well done! well done,' with reverence cried;
'The mighty men of Kuśa's seed
Were ever famed for righteous deed.
Like Brahmá's self in glory shine
The high-souled lords of Kuśa's line,
And thy great name is sounded most,
O Saint, amid the noble host.
And thy dear sister—fairest she
Of streams, the high-born Kauśikí—
Diffusing virtue where she flows,
New splendour on thy lineage throws.'
Thus by the chief of saints addressed
The son of Gádhi turned to rest;
So, when his daily course is done,
Sinks to his rest the beaming sun.
Ráma with Lakshmaṇ, somewhat stirred
To marvel by the tales they heard,
Turned also to his couch, to close
His eyelids in desired repose.

CANTO XXXVI.

THE BIRTH OF GANGÁ.

The hours of night now waning fast
On Śoṇa's pleasant shore they passed.
Then, when the dawn began to break,
To Ráma thus the hermit spake:
'The light of dawn is breaking clear,
The hour of morning rites is near.
Rise, Ráma, rise, dear son, I pray,
And make thee ready for the way.'
  Then Ráma rose, and finished all
His duties at the hermit's call,
Prepared with joy the road to take,
And thus again in question spake:
'Here fair and deep the Śoṇa flows,
And many an isle its bosom shows:
What way, O Saint, will lead us o'er
And land us on the farther shore?'
The saint replied: 'The way I choose
Is that which pious hermits use.'

---

[1] Now called Kośí (Cosy) corrupted from Kauśikí, daughter of Kuśa.

'This is one of those personifications of rivers so frequent in the Grecian mythology, but in the similar myths is seen the impress of the genius of each people, austere and profoundly religious in India, graceful and devoted to the worship of external beauty in Greece.' GORRESIO.

For many a league they journeyed on
Till, when the sun of mid-day shone,
The hermit-haunted flood was seen
Of Jáhnaví,[1] the Rivers' Queen.
Soon as the holy stream they viewed,
Thronged with a white-winged multitude
Of sárases[2] and swans,[3] delight
Possessed them at the lovely sight;
And then prepared the hermit band
To halt upon that holy strand.
They bathed as Scripture bids, and paid
Oblations due to God and shade.
To Fire they burnt the offerings meet,
And sipped the oil, like Amrit sweet.
Then pure and pleased they sate around
Saint Viśvámitra on the ground.
The holy men of lesser note,
In due degree, sate more remote,
While Raghu's sons took nearer place
By virtue of their rank and race.
Then Ráma said: 'O Saint, I yearn
The three-pathed Gangá's tale to learn.'

Thus urged, the sage recounted both
The birth of Gangá and her growth:
'The mighty hill with metals stored,
Himálaya, is the mountains' lord,
The father of a lovely pair
Of daughters fairest of the fair:
Their mother, offspring of the will
Of Meru, everlasting hill,
Mená, Himálaya's darling, graced
With beauty of her dainty waist.
Gangá was elder-born: then came
The fair one known by Umá's name.
Then all the Gods of heaven, in need
Of Gangá's help their vows to speed,
To great Himálaya came and prayed
The mountain King to yield the maid.
He, not regardless of the weal
Of the three worlds, with holy zeal
His daughter to the Immortals gave,
Gangá whose waters cleanse and save,
Who roams at pleasure, fair and free,
Purging all sinners, to the sea.
The three-pathed Gangá thus obtained,
The Gods their heavenly homes regained.
Long time the sister Umá passed
In vows austere and rigid fast,
And the king gave the devotee
Immortal Rudra's[4] bride to be,
Matching with that unequalled Lord
His Umá through the worlds adored.
So now a glorious station fills
Each daughter of the King of Hills:
One honoured as the noblest stream,
One mid the Goddesses supreme.
Thus Gangá, King Himálaya's child,
The heavenly river, undefiled,
Rose bearing with her to the sky
Her waves that bless and purify.'

[1] One of the names of the Ganges considered as the daughter of Jahnu. See Canto XLIV.
[2] The Indian Crane.
[3] Or, rather, geese.
[4] A name of the God Śiva.

CANTO XXXIX.

THE SONS OF SAGAR.

The saint in accents sweet and clear
Thus told his tale for Ráma's ear,
And thus anew the holy man
A legend to the prince began:
'There reigned a pious monarch o'er
Ayodhyá in the days of yore:
Sagar his name: no child had he,
And children much he longed to see.
His honoured consort, fair of face,
Sprang from Vidarbha's royal race,
Keśiní, famed from early youth
For piety and love of truth.
Arishṭanemi's daughter fair,
With whom no maiden might compare
In beauty, though the earth is wide,
Sumati, was his second bride.
With his two queens afar he went,
And weary days in penance spent,
Fervent, upon Himálaya's hill
Where springs the stream called Bhrigu's rill.
Nor did he fail that saint to please
With his devout austerities,
And, when a hundred years had fled,
Thus the most truthful Bhrigu said:
'From thee, O Sagar, blameless King,
A mighty host of sons shall spring,
And thou shalt win a glorious name
Which none, O Chief, but thou shall claim.
One of thy queens a son shall bear
Maintainer of thy race and heir;
And of the other there shall be
Sons sixty thousand born to thee.'
Thus as he spake, with one accord,
To win the grace of that high lord,
The queens, with palms together laid,
In humble supplication prayed:
'Which queen, O Bráhman, of the pair,
The many, or the one shall bear?
Most eager, Lord, are we to know,
And as thou sayest be it so.'

I am compelled to omit Cantos XXXVII and XXXVIII, THE GLORY OF UMÁ, and THE BIRTH OF KÁRTIKEYA, as both in subject and language offensive to modern taste. They will be found in Schlegel's Latin translation.

With his sweet speech the saint replied :
'Yourselves, O Queens, the choice decide.
Your own discretion freely use
Which shall the one or many choose :
One shall the race and name uphold,
The host be famous, strong, and bold.
Which will have which?' Then Keśiní
The mother of one heir would be.
Sumati, sister of the king[1]
Of all the birds that ply the wing,
To that illustrious Bráhman sued
That she might bear the multitude
Whose fame throughout the world should
sound
For mighty enterprise renowned.
Around the saint the monarch went,
Bowing his head, most reverent.
Then with his wives, with willing feet,
Resought his own imperial seat.
Time passed. The elder consort bare
A son called Asamanj, the heir.
Then Sumati, the younger, gave
Birth to a gourd,[2] O hero brave,
Whose rind, when burst and cleft in two,
Gave sixty thousand babes to view.
All these with care the nurses laid
In jars of oil ; and there they stayed,
Till, youthful age and strength complete,
Forth speeding from each dark retreat,
All peers in valour, years, and might,
The sixty thousand came to light.
Prince Asamanj, brought up with care,
Scourge of his foes, was made the heir.
But liegemen's boys he used to cast
To Sarjú's waves that hurried past,
Laughing the while in cruel glee
Their dying agonies to see.
This wicked prince who aye withstood
The counsel of the wise and good,
Who plagued the people in his hate,
His father banished from the state.
His son, kind-spoken, brave, and tall,
Was Anśumán, beloved of all.
Long years flew by. The king decreed
To slay a sacrificial steed.
Consulting with his priestly band
He vowed the rite his soul had planned,
And, Veda skilled, by their advice
Made ready for the sacrifice.

CANTO XL.

THE CLEAVING OF THE EARTH.

The hermit ceased : the tale was done :
Then in a transport Raghu's son
Again addressed the ancient sire
Resplendent as a burning fire :
'O holy man, I fain would hear
The tale repeated full and clear
How he from whom my sires descend
Brought the great rite to happy end.'
The hermit answered with a smile :
'Then listen, son of Raghu, while
My legendary tale proceeds
To tell of high-souled Sagar's deeds.
Within the spacious plain that lies
From where Himálaya's heights arise
To where proud Vindhya's rival chain
Looks down upon the subject plain—
A land the best for rites declared[1]—
His sacrifice the king prepared.
And Anśumán the prince—for so
Sagar advised—with ready bow
Was borne upon a mighty car
To watch the steed who roamed afar.
But Indra, monarch of the skies,
Veiling his form in demon guise,
Came down upon the appointed day
And drove the victim horse away.
Reft of the steek the priests, distressed,
The master of the rite addressed :
'Upon the sacred day by force
A robber takes the victim horse.
Haste, King ! now let the thief be slain ;
Bring thou the charger back again :
The sacred rite prevented thus
Brings scathe and woe to all of us.
Rise, monarch, and provide with speed
That naught its happy course impede.'
King Sagar in his crowded court
Gave ear unto the priests' report.
He summoned straightway to his side
His sixty thousand sons, and cried :
'Brave sons of mine, I knew not how
These demons are so mighty now :
The priests began the rite so well
All sanctified with prayer and spell.
If in the depths of earth he hide,
Or lurk beneath the ocean's tide,

---

1 Garuda.

2 Ikshváku, the name of a king of Ayodhyá who is regarded as the founder of the Solar race, means also *a gourd*. Hence, perhaps, the myth.

1 'The region here spoken of is called in the Laws of Manu *Madhyadeśa* or the middle region. 'The region situated between the Himálaya and the Vindhya Mountains.................is called *Madhyadeśa*, or the middle region ; the space comprised between these two mountains from the eastern to the western sea is called by sages Áryávartta, *the seat of honourable men.*' (MANU, II, 21, 22.) The Sanskrit Indians called themselves Áryans, which means *honourable, noble*. to distinguish themselves from the surrounding nations of different origin.' GORRESIO.

Pursue, dear sons, the robber's track ;
Slay him and bring the charger back.
The whole of this broad earth explore,
Sea-garlanded, from shore to shore :
Yea, dig her up with might and main
Until you see the horse again.
Deep let your searching labour reach,
A league in depth dug out by each.
The robber of our horse pursue,
And please your sire who orders you.
My grandson, I, this priestly train,
Till the steed comes, will here remain.'

Their eager hearts with transport burned
As to their task the heroes turned.
Obedient to their father, they
Through earth's recesses forced their way.
With iron arms' unflinching toil
Each dug a league beneath the soil.
Earth, cleft asunder, groaned in pain,
As emulous they plied amain
Sharp-pointed coulter, pick, and bar,
Hard as the bolts of Indra are.
Then loud the horrid clamour rose
Of monsters dying neath their blows,
Giant and demon, fiend and snake,
That in earth's core their dwelling make.
They dug, in ire that naught could stay,
Through sixty thousand leagues their way,
Cleaving the earth with matchless strength
Till hell itself they reached at length.
Thus digging searched they Jambudvíp[1]
With all its hills and mountains steep.
Then a great fear began to shake
The heart of God, bard, fiend, and snake,
And all distressed in spirit went
Before the Sire Omnipotent.
With signs of woe in every face
They sought the mighty Father's grace,
And trembling still and ill at ease
Addressed their Lord in words like these :
'The sons of Sagar, Sire benign,
Pierce the whole earth with mine on mine,
And as their ruthless work they ply
Innumerable creatures die.
'This is the thief,' the princes say,
'Who stole our victim steed away.
This marred the rite, and caused us ill,
And so their guiltless blood they spill.'

CANTO XLI.

KAPIL.

The father lent a gracious ear
And listened to their tale of fear,

[1] Said to be so called from the Jambu, or Rose Apple, abounding in it, and signifying according to the Puránas the central division of the world, the known world.

And kindly to the Gods replied
Whom woe and death had terrified :
'The wisest Vásudeva,[1] who
The Immortals' foe, fierce Madhu, slew,
Regards broad Earth with love and pride,
And guards, in Kapil's form, his bride.[2]
His kindled wrath will quickly fall
On the king's sons and burn them all.
This cleaving of the earth his eye
Foresaw in ages long gone by :
He knew with prescient soul the fate
That Sagar's children should await.'

The Three-and-thirty,[3] freed from fear,
Sought their bright homes with hopeful cheer.
Still rose the great tempestuous sound
As Sagar's children pierced the ground.
When thus the whole broad earth was cleft,
And not a spot unsearched was left,
Back to their home the princes sped,
And thus unto their father said :
'We searched the earth from side to side,
While countless hosts of creatures died.
Our conquering feet in triumph trod
On snake and demon, fiend and God ;
But yet we failed, with all our toil,
To find the robber and the spoil.
What can we more? If more we can,
Devise, O King, and tell thy plan.'

His children's speech King Sagar heard,
And answered thus, to anger stirred :
'Dig on, and ne'er your labour stay
Till through earth's depths you force your way.
Then smite the robber dead, and bring
The charger back with triumphing.'

[1] Here used as a name of Vishṇu

[2] Kings are called the husbands of their kingdoms or of the earth ; 'She and his kingdom were his only birdes.' *Raghuvaṅśa*.

'Doubly divorced! Bad men, you violate
A double marriage, 'twixt my crown and me,
And then between me and my married wife.'
King Richard II. Act V. Sc. I.

[3] The thirty-three Gods are said in the *Aitareya Bráhmaṇa*, Book I. ch. II. 10. to be the eight Vasus, the eleven Rudras, the twelve Ádityas, Prajápati, either Brahmá or Daksha, and Vashaṭkára or deified oblation. This must have been the actual number at the beginning of the Vedic religion gradually increased by successive mythical and religious creations till the Indian Pantheon was crowded with abstractions of every kind. Through the reverence with which the words of the Veda were regarded, the immense host of multiplied divinities, in later times, still bore the name of the Thirty-three Gods.

The sixty thousand chiefs obeyed :
Deep through the earth their way they made.
Deep as they dug and deeper yet
The immortal elephant they met,
Famed Virúpáksha[1] vast of size,
Upon whose head the broad earth lies :
The mighty beast who earth sustains
With shaggy hills and wooded plains.
When, with the changing moon, distressed,
And longing for a moment's rest,
His mighty head the monster shakes,
Earth to the bottom reels and quakes.
Around that warder strong and vast
With reverential steps they passed,
Nor, when the honour due was paid,
Their downward search through earth delayed.
But turning from the east aside
Southward again their task they plied.
There Mahápadma held his place,
The best of all his mighty race,
Like some huge hill, of monstrous girth,
Upholding on his head the earth.
When the vast beast the princes saw,
They marvelled and were filled with awe.
The sons of high-souled Sagar round
That elephant in reverence wound.
Then in the western region they
With might unwearied cleft their way.
There saw they with astonisht eyes
Saumanas, beast of mountain size.
Round him with circling steps they went
With greetings kind and reverent.
On, on—no thought of rest or stay—
They reached the seat of Soma's sway.
There saw they Bhadra, white as snow,
With lucky marks that fortune show,
Bearing the earth upon his head.
Round him they paced with solemn tread,
And honoured him with greetings kind ;
Then downward yet their way they mined.
They gained the tract 'twixt east and north
Whose fame is ever blazoned forth,[1]
And by a storm of rage impelled,
Digging through earth their course they held.
Then all the princes, lofty-souled,
Of wondrous vigour, strong and bold,
Saw Vásudeva[2] standing there
In Kapil's form he loved to wear,
And near the everlasting God
The victim charger cropped the sod.
They saw with joy and eager eyes
The fancied robber and the prize,
And on him rushed the furious band
Crying aloud, Stand, villain ! stand !
'Avaunt ! avaunt !' great Kapil cried,
His bosom flusht with passion's tide ;
Then by his might that proud array
All scorcht to heaps of ashes lay.[3]

CANTO XLII.

SAGAR'S SACRIFICE.

Then to the prince his grandson, bright
With his own fame's unborrowed light,
King Sagar thus began to say,
Marvelling at his sons' delay :
'Thou art a warrior skilled and bold,
Match for the mighty men of old.
Now follow on thine uncles' course
And track the robber of the horse.

---

[1] 'One of the elephants which, according to an ancient belief popular in India, supported the earth with their enormous backs ; when one of these elephants shook his wearied head the earth trembled with its woods and hills. An idea, or rather a mythical fancy, similar to this, but reduced to proportions less grand, is found in Virgil when he speaks of Enceladus buried under Ætna :

Fama est Enceladi semiustum fulmine corpus
Urgeri mole hac, ingentemque insuper Ætnam
Impositam, ruptis flammam expirare caminis ;
Et fessum quoties mutat latus, intremere omnem
Murmure Trinacriam, et cœlum subtexere fumo.' Æneid. Lib. III. GORRESIO.

[1] 'The Devas and Asuras (Gods and Titans) fought in the east, the south, the west, and the north, and the Devas were defeated by the Asuras in all these directions. They then fought in the north-eastern direction ; there the Devas did not sustain defeat. This direction is *aparájitá*, *i. e.* unconquerable. Thence one should do work in this direction, and have it done there ; for such a one (alone) is able to clear off his debts.' HAUG'S *Aitareya Bráhmaṇam*, Vol II., p. 33.

The debts here spoken of are a man's religious obligations to the Gods, the Pitaras or Manes, and men.

[2] Vishṇu.

[3] 'It appears to me that this mythical story has reference to the volcanic phenomena of nature. Kapil may very possibly be that hidden fiery force which suddenly unprisons itself and bursts forth in volcanic effects. Kapil is, moreover, one of the names of Agni the God of Fire.' GORRESIO.

To guard thee take thy sword and bow,
For huge and strong are beasts below.
There to the reverend reverence pay,
And kill the foes who check thy way;
Then turn successful home and see
My sacrifice complete through thee.'
Obedient to the high-souled lord
Grasped Ansumán his bow and sword,
And hurried forth the way to trace
With youth and valour's eager pace.
On sped he by the path he found
Dug by his uncles underground.
The warder elephant he saw
Whose size and strength pass Nature's law,
Who bears the world's tremendous weight,
Whom God, fiend, giant venerate,
Bird, serpent, and each flitting shade.
To him the honour meet he paid
With circling steps and greeting due,
And further prayed him, if he knew,
To tell him of his uncles' weal,
And who had dared the horse to steal.
To him in war and council tried
The warder elephant replied:
'Thou, son of Asamanj, shalt lead
In triumph back the rescued steed.'

As to each warder beast he came
And questioned all, his words the same,
The honoured youth with gentle speech
Drew eloquent reply from each,
That fortune should his steps attend,
And with the horse he home should wend.
Cheered with the grateful answer, he
Passed on with step more light and free,
And reached with careless heart the place
Where lay in ashes Sagar's race.
Then sank the spirit of the chief
Beneath that shock of sudden grief,
And with a bitter cry of woe
He mourned his kinsmen fallen so.
He saw, weighed down by woe and care,
The victim charger roaming there.
Yet would the pious chieftain fain
Oblations offer to the slain:
But, needing water for the rite,
He looked and there was none in sight.
His quick eye searching all around
The uncle of his kinsmen found,
King Garud, best beyond compare
Of birds who wing the fields of air.
Then thus unto the weeping man
The son of Vinatá[1] began:
'Grieve not, O hero, for their fall
Who died a death approved of all.
Of mighty strength, they met their fate
By Kapil's hand whom none can mate.
Pour forth for them no earthly wave,
A holier flood their spirits crave.
If, daughter of the Lord of Snow,
Gangá would turn her stream below,
Her waves that cleanse all mortal stain
Would wash their ashes pure again.
Yea, when her flood whom all revere
Rolls o'er the dust that moulders here,
The sixty thousand, freed from sin,
A home in Indra's heaven shall win.
Go, and with ceaseless labour try
To draw the Goddess from the sky.
Return, and with thee take the steed;
So shall thy grandsire's rite succeed.'

Prince Ansumán the strong and brave
Followed the rede Suparna[1] gave.
The glorious hero took the horse,
And homeward quickly bent his course.
Straight to the anxious king he hied,
Whom lustral rites had purified,
The mournful story to unfold
And all the king of birds had told.
The tale of woe the monarch heard,
Nor longer was the rite deferred:
With care and just observance he
Accomplished all, as texts decree.
The rites performed, with brighter fame,
Mighty in counsel, home he came.
He longed to bring the river down,
But found no plan his wish to crown.
He pondered long with anxious thought,
But saw no way to what he sought.
Thus thirty thousand years he spent,
And then to heaven the monarch went.

CANTO XLIII.

BHAGÍRATH.

When Sagar thus had bowed to fate,
The lords and commons of the state
Approved with ready heart and will
Prince Ansumán his throne to fill.
He ruled, a mighty king, unblamed,
Sire of Dilípa justly famed.
To him, his child and worthy heir,
The king resigned his kingdom's care,
And on Himálaya's pleasant side
His task austere of penance plied.
Bright as a God in clear renown
He planned to bring pure Gangá down.
There on his fruitless hope intent
Twice sixteen thousand years he spent,
And in the grove of hermits stayed
Till bliss in heaven his rites repaid.
Dilípa then, the good and great,
Soon as he learnt his kinsmen's fate,
Bowed down by woe, with troubled mind,

[1] Garuḍ was the son of Kaśyap and Vinatá.

[1] Garuḍ.

Pondering long no cure could find.
'How can I bring,' the mourner sighed,
'To cleanse their dust, the heavenly tide?
How can I give them rest, and save
Their spirits with the offered wave?'
Long with this thought his bosom skilled
In holy discipline was filled.
A son was born, Bhagírath named,
Above all men for virtue famed.
Dilípa many a rite ordained,
And thirty thousand seasons reigned.
But when no hope the king could see
His kinsmen from their woe to free,
The lord of men, by sickness tried,
Obeyed the law of fate, and died;
He left the kingdom to his son,
And gained the heaven his deeds had won
The good Bhagírath, royal sage,
Had no fair son to cheer his age.
He, great in glory, pure in will,
Longing for sons was childless still.
Then on one wish, one thought intent,
Planning the heavenly stream's descent,
Leaving his ministers the care
And burden of his state to bear,
Dwelling in far Gokarṇa[1] he
Engaged in long austerity.
With senses checked, with arms upraised,
Five fires[2] around and o'er him blazed.
Each weary month the hermit passed
Breaking but once his awful fast.
In winter's chill the brook his bed,
In rain, the clouds to screen his head.
Thousands of years he thus endured
Till Brahmá's favour was assured,
And the high Lord of living things
Looked kindly on his sufferings.
With trooping Gods the Sire came near
The king who plied his task austere:
'Blest Monarch, of a glorious race,
Thy fervent rites have won my grace.
Well hast thou wrought thine awful task:
Some boon in turn, O Hermit, ask.'

Bhagírath, rich in glory's light,
The hero with the arm of might,
Thus to the Lord of earth and sky
Raised suppliant hands and made reply:
'If the great God his favour deigns,
And my long toil its fruit obtains,
Let Sagar's sons receive from me
Libations that they long to see.
Let Gangá with her holy wave
The ashes of the heroes lave,
That so my kinsmen may ascend
To heavenly bliss that ne'er shall end.
And give, I pray, O God, a son,
Nor let my house be all undone.

[1] A famous and venerated region near the Malabar coast.

[2] That is four fires and the sun.

Sire of the worlds! be this the grace
Bestowed upon Ikshváku's race.'

The Sire, when thus the king had prayed,
In sweet kind words his answer made:
'High, high thy thought and wishes are,
Bhagírath of the mighty car!
Ikshváku's line is blest in thee,
And as thou prayest it shall be.
Gangá, whose waves in Swarga[1] flow,
Is daughter of the Lord of Snow.
Win Śiva that his aid be lent
To hold her in her mid descent,
For earth alone will never bear
Those torrents hurled from upper air;
And none may hold her weight but He,
The Trident-wielding deity.'
Thus having said, the Lord supreme
Addressed him to the heavenly stream;
And then with Gods and Maruts[2] went
To heaven above the firmament.

CANTO XLIV.

THE DESCENT OF GANGÁ.

The Lord of life the skies regained:
The fervent king a year remained
With arms upraised, refusing rest
While with one toe the earth he pressed,
Still as a post, with sleepless eye,
The air his food, his roof the sky.
The year had past. Then Umá's lord,[3]
King of creation, world-adored,
Thus spoke to great Bhagírath: 'I
Well pleased thy wish will gratify,
And on my head her waves shall fling
The daughter of the Mountains' King!'

He stood upon the lofty crest
That crowns the Lord of Snow,
And bade the river of the Blest
Descend on earth below.
Himálaya's child, adored of all,
The haughty mandate heard,
And her proud bosom, at the call,
With furious wrath was stirred.
Down from her channel in the skies
With awful might she sped
With a giant's rush, in a giant's size,
On Śiva's holy head.
'He calls me,' in her wrath she cried,
'And all my flood shall sweep
And whirl him in its whelming tide
To hell's profoundest deep.'
He held the river on his head,
And kept her wandering, where,
Dense as Himálaya's woods, were spread
The tangles of his hair.

[1] Heaven. [2] Wind-Gods. [3] Śiva.

No way to earth she found, ashamed,
Though long and sore she strove,
Condemned, until her pride were tamed,
Amid his locks to rove.
There, many lengthening seasons through,
The wildered river ran :
Bhagírath saw it, and anew
His penance dire began.
Then Śiva, for the hermit's sake,
Bade her long wanderings end,
And sinking into Vindu's lake
Her weary waves descend.
From Gangá, by the God set free,
Seven noble rivers came ;
Hládiní, Pávaní, and she
Called Naliní by name :
These rolled their lucid waves along
And sought the eastern side.
Suchakshu, Sítá fair and strong,
And Sindhu's mighty tide—[1]
These to the region of the west
With joyful waters sped :
The seventh, the brightest and the best,
Flowed where Bhagírath led.
On Śiva's head descending first
A rest the torrents found ;
Then down in all their might they burst
And roared along the ground.
On countless glittering scales the beam
Of rosy morning flashed,
Where fish and dolphins through the stream
Fallen and falling dashed.
Then bards who chant celestial lays
And nymphs of heavenly birth
Flocked round upon that flood to gaze
That streamed from sky to earth.
The Gods themselves from every sphere,
Incomparably bright,
Borne in their golden cars drew near
To see the wondrous sight.
The cloudless sky was all aflame
With the light of a hundred suns
Where'er the shining chariots came
That bore those holy ones.
So flashed the air with crested snakes
And fish of every hue
As when the lightning's glory breaks
Through fields of summer blue.
And white foam-clouds and silver spray
Were wildly tossed on high,
Like swans that urge their homeward way
Across the autumn sky.
Now ran the river calm and clear
With current strong and deep :
Now slowly broadened to a mere,
Or scarcely seemed to creep.
Now o'er a length of sandy plain
Her tranquil course she held ;
Now rose her waves and sank again,
By refluent waves repelled.
So falling first on Śiva's head,
Thence rushing to their earthly bed,
In ceaseless fall the waters streamed,
And pure with holy lustre gleamed.
Then every spirit, sage, and bard,
Condemned to earth by sentence hard,
Pressed eagerly around the tide
That Śiva's touch had sanctified.
Then they whom heavenly doom had hurled,
Accursed, to this lower world,
Touched the pure wave, and freed from sin
Resought the skies and entered in.
And all the world was glad, whereon
The glorious water flowed and shone,
For sin and stain were banished thence
By the sweet river's influence.
First, in a car of heavenly frame,
The royal saint of deathless name,
Bhagírath, very glorious rode,
And after him fair Gangá flowed.
God, sage , and bard, the chief in place
Of spirits and the Nága race,
Nymph, giant, fiend, in long array
Sped where Bhagírath led the way;
And all the hosts the flood that swim
Followed the stream that followed him.
Where'er the great Bhagírath led,
There ever glorious Gangá fled,
The best of floods, the rivers' queen,
Whose waters wash the wicked clean.
It chanced that Jahnu, great and good,
Engaged with holy offerings stood;
The river spread her waves around
Flooding his sacrificial ground.
The saint in anger marked her pride,
And at one draught her stream he dried.
Then God, and sage, and bard, afraid,
To noble high-souled Jahnu prayed,
And begged that he would kindly deem
His own dear child that holy stream.
Moved by their suit, he soothed their fears
And loosed her waters from his ears.
Hence Gangá through the world is styled
Both Jáhnaví and Jahnu's child.
Then onward still she followed fast,
And reached the great sea bank at last.
Thence deep below her way she made
To end those rites so long delayed.
The monarch reached the Ocean's side,
And still behind him Gangá hied.
He sought the depths which open lay
Where Sagar's sons had dug their way.
So leading through earth's nether caves
The river's purifying waves,

[1] The lake Vindu does not exist. Of the seven rivers here mentioned two only, the Ganges and the Sindhu or Indus, are known to geographers. Hládiní means the Gladdener, Pávaní the Purifier, Naliní the Lotus-clad, and Suchakshu the Fair-eyed.

Over his kinsmen's dust the lord
His funeral libation poured.
Soon as the flood their dust bedewed,
Their spirits gained beatitude,
And all in heavenly bodies dressed
Rose to the skies' eternal rest.

Then thus to King Bhagírath said
Brahmá, when, coming at the head
Of all his bright celestial train,
He saw those spirits freed from stain:
'Well done! great Prince of men, well done!
Thy kinsmen bliss and heaven have won.
The sons of Sagar mighty-souled,
Are with the Blest, as Gods, enrolled.
Long as the Ocean's flood shall stand
Upon the border of the land,
So long shall Sagar's sons remain,
And, godlike, rank in heaven retain.
Gangá thine eldest child shall be,
Called from thy name Bhágírathí;
Named also—for her waters fell
From heaven and flow through earth and hell—
Tripathagá, stream of the skies,
Because three paths she glorifies.
And, mighty King, 'tis given thee now
To free thee and perform thy vow.
No longer, happy Prince, delay
Drink-offerings to thy kin to pay.
For this the holiest Sagar sighed,
But mourned the boon he sought denied.
Then Ansumán, dear Prince! although
No brighter name the world could show,
Strove long the heavenly flood to gain
To visit earth, but strove in vain.
Nor was she by the sages' peer,
Blest with all virtues, most austere,
Thy sire Dilípa, hither brought,
Though with fierce prayers the boon he sought.
But thou, O King, earned success,
And won high fame which God will bless.
Through thee, O victor of thy foes,
On earth this heavenly Gangá flows,
And thou hast gained the meed divine
That waits on virtue such as thine.
Now in her ever holy wave
Thyself, O best of heroes, lave:
So shalt thou, pure from every sin,
The blessed fruit of merit win.
Now for thy kin who died of yore
The meet libations duly pour.
Above the heavens I now ascend:
Depart, and bliss thy steps attend.'

Thus to the mighty king who broke
His foemens' might, Lord Brahmá spoke,
And with his Gods around him rose
To his own heaven of blest repose.
The royal sage no more delayed,
But, the libation duly paid,
Home to his regal city hied
With water cleansed and purified.
There ruled he his ancestral state,
Best of all men, most fortunate.
And all the people joyed again
In good Bhagírath's gentle reign.
Rich, prosperous, and blest were they,
And grief and sickness fled away.
Thus, Ráma, I at length have told
How Gangá came from heaven of old.
Now, for the evening passes swift,
I wish thee each auspicious gift.
This story of the flood's descent
Will give—for 'tis most excellent—
Wealth, purity, fame, length of days,
And to the skies its hearers raise.'

CANTO XLV.

THE QUEST OF THE AMRIT.

High and more high their wonder rose
As the strange story reached its close,
And thus, with Lakshman, Ráma, best
Of Raghu's sons, the saint addressed:
'Most wondrous is the tale which thou
Hast told of heavenly Gangá, how
From realms above descending she
Flowed through the land and filled the sea.
In thinking o'er what thou hast said
The night has like a moment fled,
Whose hours in musing have been spent
Upon thy words most excellent:
So much, O holy Sage, thy lore
Has charmed us with this tale of yore.'

Day dawned. The morning rites were done
And the victorious Raghu's son
Addressed the sage in words like these,
Rich in his long austerities:
'The night is past: the morn is clear;
Told is the tale so good to hear;
Now o'er that river let us go,
Three-pathed, the best of all that flow.
This boat stands ready on the shore
To bear the holy hermits o'er,
Who of thy coming warned, in haste,
The barge upon the bank have placed.'

And Kuśik's son approved his speech,
And moving to the sandy beach,
Placed in the boat the hermit band,
And reached the river's farther strand.
On the north bank their feet they set,
And greeted all the saints they met.
On Gangá's shore they lighted down,
And saw Viśálá's lovely town.
Thither, the princes by his side,
The best of holy hermits hied.
It was a town exceeding fair

That might with heaven itself compare.
Then, suppliant palm to palm applied,
Famed Ráma asked his holy guide:
'O best of hermits, say what race
Of monarchs rules this lovely place.
Dear master, let my prayer prevail,
For much I long to hear the tale.'
Moved by his words, the saintly man
Viśálá's ancient tale began:
'List, Ráma, list, with closest heed
The tale of Indra's wondrous deed,
And mark me as I truly tell
What here in ancient days befell.
Ere Krita's famous Age[1] had fled,
Strong were the sons of Diti[2] bred;
And Aditi's brave children too
Were very mighty, good, and true.
The rival brothers fierce and bold
Were sons of Kaśyap lofty-souled.
Of sister mothers born, they vied,
Brood against brood, in jealous pride.
Once, as they say, band met with band,
And, joined in awful council, planned
To live, unharmed by age and time,
Immortal in their youthful prime.
Then this was, after due debate,
The counsel of the wise and great,
To churn with might the milky sea[3]
The life-bestowing drink to free.
This planned, they seized the Serpent King,
Vásuki, for their churning-string,
And Mandar's mountain for their pole,
And churned with all their heart and soul.
As thus, a thousand seasons through,
This way and that the snake they drew,
Biting the rocks, each tortured head
A very deadly venom shed.
Thence, bursting like a mighty flame,
A pestilential poison came,
Consuming, as it onward ran,
The home of God, and fiend, and man.
Then all the suppliant Gods in fear
To Śankar,[4] mighty lord, drew near.
To Rudra, King of Herds, dismayed,
'Save us, O save us, Lord!' they prayed.
Then Vishṇu, bearing shell, and mace,
And discus, showed his radiant face,
And thus addressed in smiling glee
The Trident-wielding deity:
What treasure first the Gods upturn
From troubled Ocean, as they churn,
Should—for thou art the eldest—be
Conferred, O best of Gods, on thee.

1 The first or Golden Age.

2 Diti and Aditi were wives of Kaśyap, and mothers respectively of Titans and Gods.

3 One of the seven seas surrounding as many worlds in concentric rings.

4 Śankar and Rudra are names of Śiva.

Then come, and for thy birthright's sake,
This venom as thy firstfruits take.'
He spoke, and vanished from their sight.
When Śiva saw their wild affright,
And heard his speech by whom is borne
The mighty bow of bending horn,[1]
The poisoned flood at once he quaffed
As 'twere the Amrit's heavenly draught.
Then from the Gods departing went
Śiva, the Lord pre-eminent.
The host of Gods and Asurs still
Kept churning with one heart and will.
But Mandar's mountain, whirling round,
Pierced to the depths below the ground.
Then Gods and bards in terror flew
To him who mighty Madhu slew.
'Help of all beings! more than all,
The Gods on thee for aid may call.
Ward off, O mighty-armed! our fate,
And bear up Mandar's threatening weight.'
Then Vishṇu, as their need was sore,
The semblance of a tortoise wore,
And in the bed of Ocean lay
The mountain on his back to stay.
Then he, the soul pervading all,
Whose locks in radiant tresses fall,
One mighty arm extended still,
And grasped the summit of the hill.
So ranged among the Immortals, he
Joined in the churning of the sea.
A thousand years had reached their close,
When calmly from the ocean rose
The gentle sage[2] with staff and can,
Lord of the art of healing man.
Then as the waters foamed and boiled,
As churning still the Immortals toiled,
Of winning face and lovely frame,
Forth sixty million fair ones came.
Born of the foam and water, these
Were aptly named Apsarases.[3]

1 'Śárṅgin, literally *carrying a bow of horn*, is a constantly recurring name of Vishṇu. The Indians also, therefore, knew the art of making bows out of the horns of antelopes or wild goats, which Homer ascribes to the Trojans of the heroic age.' SCHLEGEL.

2 Dhanvantari, the physician of the Gods.

3 The poet plays upon the word and fancifully derives it from *apsu*, the locative case plural of *ap*, water, and *rasa*, taste.........The word is probably derived from *ap*, water, and *sri*, to go, and seems to signify *inhabitants of the water*, nymphs of the stream; or, as Goldstücker thinks (Dict. s. v.) these divinities were originally personifications of the vapours which are attracted by the sun and form into mist or clouds.

Each had her maids. The tongue would fail—
So vast the throng—to count the tale.
But when no God or Titan wooed
A wife from all that multitude,
Refused by all, they gave their love
In common to the Gods above.
Then from the sea still vext and wild
Rose Surá,[1] Varuṇ's maiden child.
A fitting match she sought to find:
But Diti's sons her love declined,
Their kinsmen of the rival brood
To the pure maid in honour sued.
Hence those who loved that nymph so fair
The hallowed name of Suras bear.
And Asurs are the Titan crowd
Her gentle claims who disallowed.
Then from the foamy sea was freed
Uchchaiḥśravas,[2] the generous steed,
And Kaustubha, of gems the gem,[3]
And Soma, Moon God, after them.

At length when many a year had fled,
Up floated, on her lotus bed,
A maiden fair and tender-eyed,
In the young flush of beauty's pride.
She shone with pearl and golden sheen,
And seals of glory stamped her queen.
On each round arm glowed many a gem,
On her smooth brows, a diadem.
Rolling in waves beneath her crown
The glory of her hair flowed down.
Pearls on her neck of price untold,
The lady shone like burnisht gold.
Queen of the Gods, she leapt to land,
A lotus in her perfect hand,
And fondly, of the lotus-sprung,
To lotus-bearing Vishṇu clung.
Her Gods above and men below
As Beauty's Queen and Fortune know.[1]
Gods, Titans, and the minstrel train
Still churned and wrought the troubled main.
At length the prize so madly sought,
The Amrit, to their sight was brought.
For the rich spoil, 'twixt these and those
A fratricidal war arose,
And, host 'gainst host in battle, set,
Aditi's sons and Diti's met.
United, with the giants' aid,
Their fierce attack the Titans made,
And wildly raged for many a day
That universe-astounding fray.
When wearied arms were faint to strike,
And ruin threatened all alike,
Vishṇu, with art's illusive aid,
The Amrit from their sight conveyed.
That Best of Beings smote his foes
Who dared his deathless arm oppose:
Yea, Vishṇu, all-pervading God,
Beneath his feet the Titans trod
Aditi's race, the sons of light,
Slew Diti's brood in cruel fight.
Then town-destroying[2] Indra gained
His empire, and in glory reigned
O'er the three worlds, with bard and sage
Rejoicing in his heritage.

CANTO XLVI.

DITI'S HOPE.

But Diti, when her sons were slain,
Wild with a childless mother's pain,
To Kaśyap spake, Marícha's son,
Her husband: 'O thou glorious one!

[1] '*Surá*, in the feminine comprehends all sorts of intoxicating liquors, many kinds of which the Indians from the earliest times distilled and prepared from rice, sugar-cane, the palm tree, and various flowers and plants. Nothing is considered more disgraceful among orthodox Hindus than drunkenness, and the use of wine is forbidden not only to Bráhmans but the two other orders as well...So it clearly appears derogatory to the dignity of the Gods to have received a nymph so pernicious, who ought rather to have been made over to the Titans. However the etymological fancy has prevailed. The word *Sura*, a God, is derived from the indeclinable *Swar* heaven.' SCHLEGEL.

[2] Literally, high-eared, the horse of Indra. Compare the production of the horse from the sea by Neptune.

[3] 'And Kaustubha the best
Of gems that burns with living light
Upon Lord Vishṇu's breast.'
Churning of the Ocean.

[1] 'That this story of the birth of Lakshmí is of considerable antiquity is evident from one of her names *Kshírábdhi-tanayá*, daughter of the Milky Sea, which is found in *Amarasinha* the most ancient of Indian lexicographers. The similarity to the Greek myth of Venus being born from the foam of the sea is remarkable.'

'In this description of Lakshmí one thing only offends me, that she is said to have four arms. Each of Vishṇu's arms, single, as far as the elbow, there branches into two; but Lakshmí in all the brass seals that I possess or remember to have seen has two arms only. Nor does this deformity of redundant limbs suit the pattern of perfect beauty.' SCHLEGEL. I have omitted the offensive epithet.

[2] Purandhar, a common title of Indra.

Dead are the children, mine no more,
The mighty sons to thee I bore.
Long fervour's meed, I crave a boy
Whose arm may Indra's life destroy.
The toil and pain my care shall be:
To bless my hope depends on thee.
Give me a mighty son to slay
Fierce Indra, gracious lord! I pray.'
Then glorious Kaśyap thus replied
To Diti, as she wept and sighed:
'Thy prayer is heard, dear saint! Remain
Pure from all spot, and thou shalt gain
A son whose arm shall take the life
Of Indra in the battle strife.
For full a thousand years endure
Free from all stain, supremely pure;
Then shall thy son and mine appear,
Whom the three worlds shall serve with fear.'
These words the glorious Kaśyap said,
Then gently stroked his consort's head,
Blessed her, and bade a kind adieu,
And turned him to his rites anew.
Soon as her lord had left her side,
Her bosom swelled with joy and pride.
She sought the shade of holy boughs,
And there began her awful vows.
While yet she wrought her rites austere,
Indra, unbidden, hastened near,
With sweet observance tending her,
A reverential minister.
Wood, water, fire, and grass he brought,
Sweet roots and woodland fruit he sought,
And all her wants, the Thousand-eyed,
With never-failing care, supplied,
With tender love and soft caress
Removing pain and weariness.
When, of the thousand years ordained,
Ten only unfulfilled remained,
Thus to her son, the Thousand-eyed,
The Goddess in her triumph cried:
'Best of the mighty! there remain
But ten short years of toil and pain;
These years of penance soon will flee,
And a new brother thou shalt see.
Him for thy sake I'll nobly breed,
And lust of war his soul shall feed;
Then free from care and sorrow thou
Shalt see the worlds before him bow.'[1]

CANTO XLVII.

SUMATI.

Thus to Lord Indra, Thousand-eyed,
Softly beseeching Diti sighed.
When but a blighted bud was left,
Which Indra's hand in seven had cleft:[1]
'No fault, O Lord of Gods, is thine;
The blame herein is only mine.
But for one grace I fain would pray,
As thou hast reft this hope away.
This bud, O Indra, which a blight
Has withered ere it saw the light—
From this may seven fair spirits rise
To rule the regions of the skies.
Be theirs through heaven's unbounded space
On shoulders of the winds to race,
My children, drest in heavenly forms,
Far-famed as Maruts, Gods of storms.
One God to Brahmá's sphere assign,
Let one, O Indra, watch o'er thine;
And ranging through the lower air,
The third the name of Váyu[2] bear.
Gods let the four remaining be,
And roam through space, obeying thee.'
The Town-destroyer, Thousand-eyed,
Who smote fierce Bali till he died,
Joined suppliant hands, and thus replied:
'Thy children heavenly forms shall wear;
The names devised by thee shall bear,
And, Maruts called by my decree,
Shall Amrit drink and wait on me.
From fear and age and sickness freed,
Through the three worlds their wings shall speed.'
Thus in the hermits' holy shade
Mother and son their compact made,
And then, as fame relates, content,
Home to the happy skies they went.
This is the spot—so men have told—
Where Lord Mahendra[3] dwelt of old,
This is the blessed region where
His votaress mother claimed his care.
Here gentle Alambúshá bare
To old Ikshváku, king and sage,
Viśála, glory of his age,
By whom, a monarch void of guilt,
Was this fair town Viśálá built.

---

[1] A few verses are here left untranslated on account of the subject and language being offensive to modern taste.

[1] 'In this myth of Indra destrying the unborn fruit of Diti with his thunderbolt, from which afterwards came the Maruts or Gods of Wind and Storm, geological phenomena are, it seems, represented under mythical images. In the great Mother of the Gods is, perhaps, figured the dry earth: Indra the God of thunder rends it open, and there issue from its rent bosom the Maruts or exhalations of the earth. But such ancient myths are difficult to interpret with absolute certainty.' GORRESIO.

[2] Wind.

[3] Indra, with *mahá*, great, prefixed.

His son was Hemachandra, still
Renowned for might and warlike skill.
From him the great Suchandra came;
His son, Dhúmrásva, dear to fame.
Next followed royal Srinjay; then
Famed Sahadeva, lord of men.
Next came Kuśáśva, good and mild,
Whose son was Somadatta styled,
And Sumati, his heir, the peer
Of Gods above, now governs here.
And ever through Ikshváku's grace,
Viśálá's kings, his noble race,
Are lofty-souled, and blest with length
Of days, with virtue, and with strength.
This night, O prince, we here will sleep;
And when the day begins to peep,
Our onward way will take with thee,
The king of Mithilá to see.'

Then Sumati, the king, aware
Of Viśvámitra's advent there,
Came quickly forth with honour meet
The lofty-minded sage to greet.
Girt with his priest and lords the king
Did low obeisance, worshipping.
With suppliant hands, with head inclined,
Thus spoke he after question kind:
'Since thou hast deigned to bless my sight,
And grace awhile thy servant's seat,
High fate is mine, great Anchorite,
And none may with my bliss compete.'

CANTO XLVIII.

INDRA AND AHALYÁ.

When mutual courtesies had past,
Viśálá's ruler spoke at last:
'These princely youths, O Sage, who vie
In might with children of the sky,
Heroic, born for happy fate,
With elephants' or lions' gait,
Bold as the tiger or the bull,
With lotus eyes so large and full,
Armed with the quiver, sword, and bow,
Whose figures like the Aśvins[1] show,
Like children of the deathless Powers,
Come freely to these shades of ours,[2]—
How have they reached on foot this place?
What do they seek, and what their race?
As sun and moon adorn the sky,
This spot the heroes glorify.
Alike in stature, port, and mien,
The same fair form in each is seen.'

He spoke; and at the monarch's call
The best of hermits told him all,
How in the grove with him they dwelt,
And slaughter to the demons dealt.
Then wonder filled the monarch's breast,
Who tended well each royal guest.
Thus entertained, the princely pair
Remained that night and rested there,
And with the morn's returning ray
To Mithilá pursued their way.

When Janak's lovely city first
Upon their sight, yet distant, burst,
The hermits all with joyful cries
Hailed the fair town that met their eyes.
Then Ráma saw a holy wood,
Close, in the city's neighbourhood,
O'ergrown, deserted, marked by age,
And thus addressed the mighty sage:
'O reverend lord, I long to know
What hermit dwelt here long ago.'
Then to the prince his holy guide,
Most eloquent of men, replied:
'O Ráma, listen while I tell
Whose was this grove, and what befell
When in the fury of his rage
The high saint cursed the hermitage.
This was the grove—most lovely then—
Of Gautam, O thou best of men.
Like heaven itself, most honoured by
The Gods who dwell above the sky.
Here with Ahalyá at his side
His fervid task the ascetic plied.
Years fled in thousands. On a day
It chanced the saint had gone away,
When Town-destroying Indra came,
And saw the beauty of the dame.
The sage's form the God endued,
And thus the fair Ahalyá wooed:
'Love, sweet! should brook no dull delay
But snatch the moments when he may.'
She knew him in the saint's disguise,
Lord Indra of the Thousand eyes,
But touched by love's unholy fire,
She yielded to the God's desire.

'Now, Lord of Gods!' she whispered, 'flee,
From Gautam save thyself and me.'
Trembling with doubt and wild with dread
Lord Indra from the cottage fled;
But fleeing in the grove he met
The home-returning anchoret,
Whose wrath the Gods and fiends would shun,
Such power his fervent rites had won.
Fresh from the lustral flood he came,
In splendour like the burning flame,
With fuel for his sacred rites,
And grass, the best of eremites.
The Lord of Gods was sad of cheer
To see the mighty saint so near,
And when the holy hermit spied
In hermit's garb the Thousand-eyed,

[1] The Heavenly Twins.

[2] Not banished from heaven as the inferior Gods and demigods sometimes were.

He knew the whole, his fury broke
Forth on the sinner as he spoke:
'Because my form thou hast assumed,
And wrought this folly, thou art doomed.
For this my curse to thee shall cling,
Henceforth a sad and sexless thing.'
No empty threat that sentence came,
It chilled his soul and marred his frame,
His might and godlike vigour fled,
And every nerve was cold and dead.
Then on his wife his fury burst,
And thus the guilty dame he cursed:
'For countless years, disloyal spouse,
Devoted to severest vows,
Thy bed the ashes, air thy food,
Here shalt thou live in solitude.
This lonely grove thy home shall be,
And not an eye thy form shall see.
When Ráma, Daśaratha's child,
Shall seek these shades then drear and wild,
His coming shall remove thy stain,
And make the sinner pure again.
Due honour paid to him, thy guest,
Shall cleanse thy fond and erring breast,
Thee to my side in bliss restore,
And give thy proper shape once more.'[1]
Thus to his guilty wife he said,
Then far the holy Gautam fled,
And on Himálaya's lovely heights
Spent the long years in sternest rites.'

CANTO XLIX.

AHALYA' FREED.

Then Ráma, following still his guide,
Within the grove, with Lakshman, hied.
Her vows a wondrous light had lent
To that illustrious penitent.
He saw the glorious lady, screened
From eye of man, and God, and fiend,
Like some bright portent which the care
Of Brahmá launches through the air,
Designed by his illusive art
To flash a moment and depart:
Or like the flame that leaps on high
To sink involved in smoke and die:
Or like the full moon shining through
The wintry mist, then lost to view:
Or like the sun's reflection, cast
Upon the flood, too bright to last:
So was the glorious dame till then
Removed from Gods' and mortals' ken,
Till—such was Gautam's high decree—
Prince Ráma came to set her free.
Then, with great joy that dame to meet,
The sons of Raghu clasped her feet;
And she, remembering Gautam's oath,
With gentle grace received them both;
Then water for their feet she gave,
Guest-gift, and all that strangers crave.
The prince, of courteous rule aware,
Received, as meet, the lady's care.
Then flowers came down in copious rain,
And moving to the heavenly strain
Of music in the skies that rang,
The nymphs and minstrels danced and sang:
And all the Gods with one glad voice
Praised the great dame, and cried, 'Rejoice!
Through fervid rites no more defiled,
But with thy husband reconciled.'
Gautam, the holy hermit knew—
For naught escaped his godlike view—
That Ráma lodged beneath that shade,
And hasting there his homage paid.
He took Ahalyá to his side,
From sin and folly purified,
And let his new-found consort bear
In his austerities a share.
Then Ráma, pride of Raghu's race,
Welcomed by Gautam, face to face,
Who every highest honour showed,
To Mithilá pursued his road.

CANTO L.

JANAK.

The sons of Raghu journeyed forth,
Bending their steps 'twixt east and north.
Soon, guided by the sage, they found,
Enclosed, a sacrificial ground.
Then to the best of saints, his guide,
In admiration Ráma cried:
'The high-souled king no toil has spared,
But nobly for his rite prepared.
How many thousand Bráhmans here,
From every region, far and near,
Well read in holy lore, appear!
How many tents, that sages screen,
With wains in hundreds, here are seen!
Great Bráhman, let us find a place
Where we may stay and rest a space.'
The hermit did as Ráma prayed,
And in a spot his lodging made,

[1] 'Kumárila says: 'In the same manner, if it is said that Indra was the seducer of Ahalyá, this does not imply that the God Indra committed such a crime, but Indra means the sun, and Ahalyá (from ahan and li) the night; and as the night is seduced and ruined by the sun of the morning, therefore is Indra called the paramour of Ahalyá.' MAX MÜLLER, *History of Ancient Sanskrit Literature*, p. 530.

Far from the crowd, sequestered, clear,
With copious water flowing near.
Then Janak, best of kings, aware
Of Viśvámitra lodging there,
With Śatánanda for his guide—
The priest on whom he most relied,
His chaplain void of guile and stain—
And others of his priestly train,
Bearing the gift that greets the guest,
To meet him with all honour pressed.
The saint received with gladsome mind
Each honour and observance kind:
Then of his health he asked the king,
And how his rites were prospering.
Janak, with chaplain and with priest,
Addressed the hermits, chief and least,
Accosting all, in due degree,
With proper words of courtesy.
Then, with his palms together laid,
The king his supplication made:
'Deign, reverend lord, to sit thee down
With these good saints of high renown.'
Then sate the chief of hermits there,
Obedient to the monarch's prayer.
Chaplain and priest, and king and peer,
Sate in their order, far or near.
Then thus the king began to say:
'The Gods have blest my rite to-day,
And with the sight of thee repaid
The preparations I have made.
Grateful am I, so highly blest,
That thou, of saints the holiest,
Hast come, O Bráhman, here with all
These hermits to the festival.
Twelve days, O Bráhman Sage, remain—
For so the learned priests ordain—
And then, O heir of Kuśik's name,
The Gods will come their dues to claim.'

With looks that testified delight
Thus spake he to the anchorite,
Then with his suppliant hands upraised,
He asked, as earnestly he gazed:
'These princely youths, O Sage, who vie
In might with children of the sky,
Heroic, born for happy fate,
With elephants' or lions' gait,
Bold as the tiger and the bull,
With lotus eyes so large and full,
Armed with the quiver, sword and bow,
Whose figures like the Aśvins show,
Like children of the heavenly Powers,
Come freely to these shades of ours,—
How have they reached on foot this place?
What do they seek, and what their race?
As sun and moon adorn the sky,
This spot the heroes glorify:
Alike in stature, port, and mien,
The same fair form in each is seen.'[1]

Thus spoke the monarch, lofty-souled:
The saint, of heart unfathomed, told
How, sons of Daśaratha, they
Accompanied his homeward way,
How in the hermitage they dwelt,
And slaughter to the demons dealt:
Their journey till the spot they neared
Whence fair Viśálá's towers appeared:
Ahalyá seen and freed from taint;
Their meeting with her lord the saint;
And how they thither came, to know
The virtue of the famous bow.
Thus Viśvámitra spoke the whole
To royal Janak, great of soul.
And when this wondrous tale was o'er,
The glorious hermit said no more.

CANTO LI.

VIŚVÁMITRA.

Wise Viśvámitra's tale was done:
Then sainted Gautam's eldest son,
Great Śatánanda, far-renowned,
Whom long austerities had crowned
With glory,—as the news he heard
The down upon his body stirred,—
Filled full of wonder at the sight
Of Ráma, felt supreme delight.
When Śatánanda saw the pair
Of youthful princes seated there,
He turned him to the holy man
Who sate at ease, and thus began:
'And didst thou, mighty Sage, in truth
Show clearly to this royal youth
My mother, glorious far and wide,
Whom penance-rites have sanctified?
And did my glorious mother—she,
Heiress of noble destiny—
Serve her great guest with woodland store,
Whom all should honour evermore?
Didst thou the tale to Ráma tell
Of what in ancient days befell,
The sin, the misery, and the shame
Of guilty God and faithless dame?
And, O thou best of hermits, say,
Did Ráma's healing presence stay
Her trial? was the wife restored
Again to him, my sire and lord?
Say, Hermit, did that sire of mine
Receive her with a soul benign,
When long austerities in time
Had cleansed her from the taint of crime?

[1] 'The preceding sixteen lines have occurred before in Canto XLVIII. This Homeric custom of repeating a passage of several lines is strange to our poet. This is the only instance I remember. The repetition of single lines is common enough.' SCHLEGEL.

And, son of Kuśik, let me know,
Did my great-minded father show
Honour to Ráma, and regard,
Before he journeyed hitherward?'
The hermit with attentive ear
Marked all the questions of the seer:
To him for eloquence far-famed,
His eloquent reply he framed:
'Yea, 'twas my care no task to shun,
And all I had to do was done;
As Reṇuká and Bhrigu's child,
The saint and dame were reconciled.'
When the great sage had thus replied,
To Ráma Śatánanda cried:
'A welcome visit, Prince, is thine,
Thou scion of King Raghu's line,
With him to guide thy way aright,
This sage invincible in might,
This Bráhman sage, most glorious-bright,
By long austerities has wrought
A wondrous deed, exceeding thought:
Thou knowest well, O strong of arm,
This sure defence from scathe and harm.
None, Ráma, none is living now
In all the earth more blest than thou,
That thou hast won a saint so tried
In fervid rites thy life to guide.
Now listen, Prince, while I relate
His lofty deeds and wondrous fate.
He was a monarch pious-souled,
His foemen in the dust he rolled;
Most learned, prompt at duty's claim,
His people's good his joy and aim.
Of old the Lord of Life gave birth
To mighty Kuśa, king of earth.
His son was Kuśanábha, strong,
Friend of the right, the foe of wrong.
Gádhi, whose fame no time shall dim,
Heir of his throne was born to him,
And Viśvámitra, Gádhi's heir,
Governed the land with kingly care.
While years unnumbered rolled away
The monarch reigned with equal sway.
At length, assembling many a band,
He led his warriors round the land—
Complete in tale, a mighty force,
Cars, elephants, and foot, and horse.
Through cities, groves, and floods he passed,
O'er lofty hills, through regions vast.
He reached Vaśishṭha's pure abode,
Where trees, and flowers, and creepers glowed,
Where troops of sylvan creatures fed;
Which saints and angels visited.
Gods, fauns, and bards of heavenly race,
And spirits, glorified the place;
The deer their timid ways forgot,
And holy Bráhmans thronged the spot.
Bright in their souls, like fire, were these,
Made pure by long austerities,
Bound by the rule of vows severe,
And each in glory Brahmá's peer.
Some fed on water, some on air,
Some on the leaves that withered there.
Roots and wild fruit were others' food;
All rage was checked, each sense subdued,
There Bálakhilyas[1] went and came.
Now breathed the prayer, now fed the flame:
These, and ascetic bands beside,
The sweet retirement beautified.
Such was Vaśishṭha's blest retreat,
Like Brahmá's own celestial seat,
Which gladdened Viśvámitra's eyes,
Peerless for warlike enterprise.

CANTO LII.

VAŚISHṬHA'S FEAST.

Right glad was Viśvámitra when
He saw the prince of saintly men.
Low at his feet the hero bent,
And did obeisance, reverent.
The king was welcomed in, and shown
A seat beside the hermit's own,
Who offered him, when resting there,
Fruit in due course, and woodland fare.
And Viśvámitra, noblest king,
Received Vaśishṭha's welcoming,
Turned to his host, and prayed him tell
That he and all with him were well.
Vaśishṭha to the king replied
That all was well on every side,
That fire, and vows, and pupils throve,
And all the trees within the grove.
And then the son of Brahmá, best
Of all who pray with voice suppressed,
Questioned with pleasant words like these
The mighty king who sate at ease:
'And is it well with thee? I pray;
And dost thou win by virtuous sway
Thy people's love, discharging all
The duties on a king that fall?
Are all thy servants fostered well?
Do all obey, and none rebel?
Hast thou, destroyer of the foe,
No enemies to overthrow?
Does fortune, conqueror! still attend
Thy treasure, host, and every friend?
Is it all well? Does happy fate
On sons and children's children wait?'
He spoke. The modest king replied
That all was prosperous far and wide.

---

[1] Divine personages of minute size produced from the hair of Brahmá, and probably the origin of
'That small infantry
Warred on by cranes.'

Thus for awhile the two conversed,
As each to each his tale rehearsed,
And as the happy moments flew,
Their joy and friendship stronger grew.
When such discourse had reached an end,
Thus spoke the saint most reverened
To royal Viśvámitra, while
His features brightened with a smile:
'O mighty lord of men, I fain
Would banquet thee and all thy train
In mode that suits thy station high:
And do not thou my prayer deny.
Let my good lord with favour take
The offering that I fain would make,
And let me honour, ere we part,
My royal guest with loving heart.'

Him Viśvámitra thus addressed:
'Why make, O Saint, this new request?
Thy welcome and each gracious word
Sufficient honour have conferred.
Thou gavest roots and fruit to eat,
The treasures of this pure retreat,
And water for my mouth and feet;
And—boon I prize above the rest—
Thy presence has mine eyesight blest.
Honoured by thee in every way,
To whom all honour all should pay,
I now will go. My lord, Good-bye!
Regard me with a friendly eye.'

Him speaking thus Vaśishṭha stayed,
And still to share his banquet prayed.
The will of Gádhi's son he bent,
And won the monarch to consent,
Who spoke in answer, 'Let it be,
Great Hermit, as it pleases thee.'
When, best of those who breathe the prayer,
He heard the king his will declare,
He called the cow of spotted skin,
All spot without, all pure within.
'Come, Dapple-skin,' he cried, 'with speed;
Hear thou my words and help at need.
My heart is set to entertain
This monarch and his mighty train
With sumptuous meal and worthy fare;
Be thine the banquet to prepare.
Each dainty cate, each goodly dish,
Of six-fold taste[1] as each may wish—
All these, O cow of heavenly power,
Rain down for me in copious shower:
Viands and drink for tooth and lip,
To eat, to suck, to quaff, to sip—
Of these sufficient, and to spare,
O plenty-giving cow, prepare.'

[1] Sweet, salt, pungent, bitter, acid, and astringent.

CANTO LIII.

VIŚVÁMITRA'S REQUEST.

Thus charged, O slayer of thy foes,
The cow from whom all plenty flows,
Obedient to her saintly lord,
Viands to suit each taste, outpoured.
Honey she gave, and roasted grain,
Mead sweet with flowers, and sugar-cane.
Each beverage of flavour rare,
An food of every sort, were there:
Hills of hot rice, and sweetened cakes,
And curdled milk and soup in lakes.
Vast beakers foaming to the brim
With sugared drink prepared for him,
And dainty sweetmeats, deftly made,
Before the hermit's guests were laid.
So well regaled, so nobly fed,
The mighty army banqueted,
And all the train, from chief to least,
Delighted in Vaśishṭha's feast.
Then Viśvámitra, royal sage,
Surrounded by his vassalage,
Prince, peer, and counsellor, and all
From highest lord to lowest thrall,
Thus feasted, to Vaśishṭha cried
With joy, supremely gratified:
'Rich honour I, thus entertained,
Most honourable lord, have gained:
Now hear, before I journey hence,
My words, O skilled in eloquence.
Bought for a hundred thousand kine,
Let Dapple-skin, O Saint, be mine.
A wondrous jewel is thy cow,
And gems are for the monarch's brow.[1]
To me her rightful lord resign
This Dapple-skin thou callest thine.'

The great Vaśishṭha, thus addressed,
Arch-hermit of the holy breast,
To Viśvámitra answer made,
The king whom all the land obeyed:
Not for a hundred thousand,—nay,
Not if ten million thou wouldst pay,
With silver heaps the price to swell,—
Will I my cow, O Monarch, sell.
Unmeet for her is such a fate,
That I my friend should alienate.
As glory with the virtuous, she
For ever makes her home with me.
On her mine offerings which ascend
To Gods and spirits all depend:
My very life is due to her,
My guardian, friend, and minister.

[1] 'Of old hoards and minerals in the earth, the king is entitled to half by reason of his general protection, and because he is the lord paramount of the soil.'
MANU, Book VIII. 39.

The feeding of the sacred flame,[1]
The dole which living creatures claim.[2]
The mighty sacrifice by fire,
Each formula the rites require,[3]
And various saving lore beside,
Are by her aid, in sooth, supplied.
The banquet which thy host has shared,
Believe it, was by her prepared.
In her mine only treasures lie,
She cheers mine heart and charms mine eye.
And reasons more could I assign
Why Dapple-skin can ne'er be thine.'

The royal sage, his suit denied,
With eloquence more earnest cried:
'Tusked elephants, a goodly train,
Each with a golden girth and chain,
Whose goads with gold well fashioned shine—
Of these be twice seven thousand thine.
And four-horse cars with gold made bright,
With steeds most beautifully white,
Whose bells make music as they go,
Eight hundred, Saint, will I bestow.
Eleven thousand mettled steeds
From famous lands, of noble breeds—
These will I gladly give, O thou
Devoted to each holy vow.
Ten million heifers, fair to view,
Whose sides are marked with every hue—
These in exchange will I assign;
But let thy Dapple-skin be mine.
Ask what thou wilt, and piles untold
Of priceless gems and gleaming gold,
O best of Bráhmans, shall be thine;
But let thy Dapple-skin be mine.'

The great Vaśishṭha, thus addressed,
Made answer to the king's request:
'Ne'er will I give my cow away,
My gem, my wealth, my life and stay.
My worship at the moon's first show,
And at the full, to her I owe;
And sacrifices small and great,
Which largess due and gifts await.
From her alone, their root, O King,
My rites and holy service spring.
What boots it further words to say?
I will not give my cow away
Who yields me what I ask each day.'

CANTO LIV.

THE BATTLE.

As Saint Vaśishṭha answered so,
Nor let the cow of plenty go,
The monarch, as a last resource,
Began to drag her off by force.
While the king's servants tore away
Their moaning, miserable prey,
Sad, sick at heart, and sore distressed,
She pondered thus within her breast:
'Why am I thus forsaken? why
Betrayed by him of soul most high,
Vaśishṭha, ravished by the hands
Of soldiers of the monarch's bands?
Ah me! what evil have I done
Against the lofty-minded one,
That he, so pious, can expose
The innocent whose love he knows?'
In her sad breast as thus she thought,
And heaved deep sighs with anguish fraught,
With wondrous speed away she fled,
And back to Saint Vaśishṭha sped.
She hurled by hundreds to the ground
The menial crew that hemmed her round,
And flying swifter than the blast
Before the saint herself she cast.
There Dapple-skin before the saint
Stood moaning forth her sad complaint,
And wept and lowed: such tones as come
From wandering cloud or distant drum.
'O son of Brahmá,' thus cried she,
'Why hast thou thus forsaken me,
That the king's men, before thy face,
Bear off thy servant from her place?'

Then thus the Bráhman saint replied
To her whose heart with woe was tried,
And grieving for his favourite's sake.
As to a suffering sister spake:
'I leave thee not: dismiss the thought;
Nor, duteous, hast thou failed in aught
This king, o'erweening in the pride
Of power, has reft thee from my side.
Little, I ween, my strength could do
'Gainst him, a mighty warrior too.
Strong, as a soldier born and bred.—
Great, as a king whom regions dread.
See! what a host the conqueror leads,
With elephants, and cars, and steeds.
O'er countless bands his pennons fly;
So is he mightier far than I.'

---

[1] Ghí or clarified butter, 'holy oil,' being one of the essentials of sacrifice.

[2] 'A Bráhman had five principal duties to discharge every day: study and teaching the Veda, oblations to the manes or spirits of the departed, sacrifice to the Gods, hospitable offerings to men, and *a gift of food to all creatures.* The last consisted of rice or other grain which the Bráhman was to offer every day outside his house in the open air. MANU, Book III. 70.' GORRESIO.

[3] These were certain sacred words of invocation such a *sváhá vashat*, etc., pronounced at the time of sacrifice.

He spoke. Then she, in lowly mood,
To that high saint her speech renewed:
'So judge not they who wisest are:
The Bráhman's might is mightier far.
For Bráhmans strength from Heaven derive,
And warriors bow when Bráhmans strive.
A boundless power 'tis thine to wield:
To such a king thou shouldst not yield,
Who, very mighty though he be,—
So fierce thy strength,—must bow to thee.
Command me, Saint. Thy power divine
Has brought me here and made me thine;
And I, howe'er the tyrant boast,
Will tame his pride and slay his host.'
Then cried the glorious sage: 'Create
A mighty force the foe to mate.'

She lowed, and quickened into life,
Pahlavas,[1] burning for the strife,
King Viśvámitra's army slew
Before the very leader's view.
The monarch in excessive ire,
His eyes with fury darting fire,
Rained every missile on the foe
Till all the Pahlavas were low.
She, seeing all her champions slain,
Lying by thousands on the plain.
Created, by her mere desire,
Yavans and Śakas, fierce and dire.
And all the ground was overspread
With Yavans and with Śakas dread:
A host of warriors bright and strong,
And numberless in closest throng:
The threads within the lotus stem,
So densely packed, might equal them.
In gold-hued mail 'against war's attacks,
Each bore a sword and battle-axe.
The royal host, where'er these came,
Fell as if burnt with ravening flame.

The monarch, famous through the world
Again his fearful weapons hurled,
That made Kámbojas,[1] Barbars,[2] all,
With Yavans, troubled, flee and fall.

CANTO LV.

THE HERMITAGE BURNT.

So o'er the field that host lay strown,
By Viśvámitra's darts o'erthrown.
Then thus Vaśishtha charged the cow:
'Create with all thy vigour now.'

Forth sprang Kámbojas, as she lowed;
Bright as the sun their faces glowed.
Forth from her udder Barbars poured,—
Soldiers who brandished spear and sword,—
And Yavans with their shafts and darts,
And Śakas from her hinder parts.
And every pore upon her fell,
And every hair-producing cell,
With Mlechchhas[3] and Kirátas[4] teemed,
And forth with them Háritas streamed.
And Viśvámitra's mighty force,
Car, elephant, and foot, and horse,
Fell in a moment's time, subdued
By that tremendous multitude.
The monarch's hundred sons, whose eyes
Beheld the rout in wild surprise,
Armed with all weapons, mad with rage,
Rushed fiercely on the holy sage.
One cry he raised, one glance he shot,
And all fell scorched upon the spot:
Burnt by the sage to ashes, they
With horse, and foot, and chariot, lay.
The monarch mourned, with shame and pain,
His army lost, his children slain,
Like Ocean when his roar is hushed,
Or some great snake whose fangs are crushed:

---

[1] 'It is well known that the Persians were called Pahlavas by the Indians. The *Śakas* are nomad tribes inhabiting Central Asia, the Scythes of the Greeks, whom the Persians also, as Herodotus tells us, called Sakæ just as the Indians did. Lib. VII 64 οἱ γὰρ Πέρσαι πάντας τοὺς Σκύθας καλέουσι Σάκας. The name Yavans seems to be used rather indefinitely for nations situated beyond Persia to the west ....After the time of Alexander the Great the Indians as well as the Persians called the Greeks also Yavans.' SCHLEGEL.

Lassen thinks that the Pahlavas were the same people as the Πάκτυες of Herodotus, and that this non-Indian people dwelt on the north-west confines of India.

[1] See page 13, note 6.

[2] Barbarians, non-Sanskrit-speaking tribes.

[3] A comprehensive term for foreign or outcast races of different faith and language from the Hindus.

[4] The Kirátas and Háritas are savage aborigines of India who occupy hills and jungles and are altogether different in race and character from the Hindus. Dr. Muir remarks in his Sanskrit Texts, Vol. I. p. 488 (second edition) that it does not appear that it is the object of this legend to represent this miraculous creation as the origin of these tribes, and that nothing more may have been intended than that the cow called into existence large armies, of the same stock with particular tribes previously existing.

Or as in swift eclipse the Sun
Dark with the doom he cannot shun:
Or a poor bird with mangled wing—
So, reft of sons and host, the king.
No longer, by ambition fired,
The pride of war his breast inspired.
He gave his empire to his son—
Of all he had, the only one:
And bade him rule as kings are taught
Then straight a hermit-grove he sought.
Far to Himálaya's side he fled,
Which bards and Nágas visited,
And, Mahádeva's[1] grace to earn,
He gave his life to penance stern.
A lengthened season thus passed by,
When Śiva's self, the Lord most High,
Whose banner shows the pictured bull,[2]
Appeared, the God most bountiful:

'Why fervent thus in toil and pain?
What brings thee here? what boon to gain?
Thy heart's desire, O Monarch, speak:
I grant the boons which mortals seek.'
The king, his adoration paid,
To Mahádeva answer made:
'If thou hast deemed me fit to win
Thy favour, O thou void of sin,
On me, O mighty God, bestow
The wondrous science of the bow,
All mine, complete in every part,
With secret spell and mystic art.
To me be all the arms revealed
That Gods, and saints, and Titans wield,
And every dart that arms the hands
Of spirits, fiends and minstrel bands.
Be mine, O Lord supreme in place,
This token of thy boundless grace.'

The Lord of Gods then gave consent,
And to his heavenly mansion went.
Triumphant in the arms he held,
The monarch's breast with glory swelled.
So swells the ocean, when upon
His breast the full moon's beams have shone.
Already in his mind he viewed
Vaśishṭha at his feet subdued.
He sought that hermit's grove, and there
Launched his dire weapons through the air,
Till scorched by might that none could stay
The hermitage in ashes lay.
Where'er the inmates saw, aghast,
The dart that Viśvámitra cast,
To every side they turned and fled
In hundreds forth disquieted.
Vaśishṭha's pupils caught the fear,
And every bird and every deer,
And fled in wild confusion forth
Eastward and westward, south and north.
And so Vaśishṭha's holy shade
A solitary wild was made.
Silent awhile, for not a sound
Disturbed the hush that was around.

Vaśishṭha then, with eager cry,
Called, 'Fear not, friends, nor seek to fly.
This son of Gádhi dies to-day,
Like hoar-frost in the morning's ray.'
Thus having said, the glorious sage
Spoke to the king in words of rage:
'Because thou hast destroyed this grove
Which long in holy quiet throve,
By folly urged to senseless crime,
Now shalt thou die before thy time.'

[1] The Great God, Śiva.

[2] Nandi, the snow-white bull, the attendant and favourite vehicle of Śiva.

CANTO LVI.

VIŚVÁMITRA'S VOW.

But Viśvámitra, at the threat
Of that illustrious anchoret,
Cried, as he launched with ready hand
A fiery weapon, 'Stand, O Stand!'
Vaśishṭha, wild with rage and hate,
Raising, as 'twere the Rod of Fate,
His mighty Bráhman wand on high,
To Viśvámitra made reply:
'Nay, stand, O Warrior thou, and show
What soldier can, 'gainst Bráhman foe.
O Gádhi's son, thy days are told;
Thy pride is tamed, thy dart is cold.
How shall a warrior's puissance dare
With Bráhman's awful strength compare?
To-day, base Warrior, shalt thou feel
That God-sent might is more than steel.'
He raised his Bráhman staff, nor missed
The fiery dart that near him hissed:
And quenched the fearful weapon fell,
As flame beneath the billow's swell.

Then Gádhi's son in fury threw
Lord Varuṇ's arm and Rudra's too:
Indra's fierce bolt that all destroys;
That which the Lord of Herds employs:
The Human, that which minstrels keep,
The deadly Lure, the endless Sleep:
The Yawner, and the dart which charms;
Lament and Torture, fearful arms:
The Terrible, the dart which dries,
The Thunderbolt which quenchless flies,
And Fate's dread net, and Brahmá's noose,
And that which waits for Varuṇ's use:
The dart he loves who wields the bow
Pináka, and twin bolts that glow
With fury as they flash and fly,
The quenchless Liquid and the Dry:
The dart of Vengeance, swift to kill:
The Goblins' dart, the Curlew's Bill:

The discus both of Fate and Right,
And Vishnu's, of unerring flight:
The Wind-God's dart, the Troubler dread,
The weapon named the Horse's Head.
From his fierce hand two spears were
thrown,
And the great mace that smashes bone:
The dart of spirits of the air,
And that which Fate exults to bear:
The Trident dart which slaughters foes,
And that which hanging skulls compose:[1]
These fearful darts in fiery rain
He hurled upon the saint amain,
An awful miracle to view.
But as the ceaseless tempest flew,
The sage with wand of God-sent power
Still swallowed up that fiery shower.

Then Gádhi's son, when these had failed,
With Brahmá's dart his foe assailed.
The Gods, with Indra at their head,
And Nágas, quailed disquieted,
And saints and minstrels, when they saw
The king that awful weapon draw;
And the three worlds were filled with dread,
And trembled as the missile sped.

The saint, with Bráhman wand, em-
powered
By lore divine that dart devoured.
Nor could the triple world withdraw
Rapt gazes from that sight of awe:
For as he swallowed down the dart
Of Brahmá, sparks from every part,
From finest pore and hair-cell, broke
Enveloped in a veil of smoke.
The staff he waved was all aglow
Like Yama's ceptre, King below,
Or like the lurid fire of Fate
Whose rage the worlds will desolate.

The hermits, whom that sight had awed,
Extolled the saint with hymn and laud:
'Thy power, O Sage, is ne'er in vain:
Now with thy might thy might restrain.
Be gracious, Master, and allow
The worlds to rest from trouble now;
For Viśvámitra, strong and dread,
By thee has been discomfited.'

Then, thus addressed, the saint, well
pleased,
The fury of his wrath appeased.
The king, o'erpowered and ashamed,
With many a deep-drawn sigh exclaimed:
'Ah! Warriors' strength is poor and slight:
A Bráhman's power is truly might.
This Bráhman staff the hermit held
The fury of my darts has quelled.
This truth within my heart impressed,
With senses ruled and tranquil breast
My task austere will I begin,
And Bráhmanhood will strive to win.'

CANTO LVII.

TRIŚANKU.

Then with his heart consumed with woe,
Still brooding on his overthrow
By the great saint he had defied,
At every breath the monarch sighed
Forth from his home his queen he led,
And to a land far southward fled.
There, fruit and roots his only food,
He practised penance, sense-subdued,
And in that solitary spot
Four virtuous sons the king begot:
Havishyand, from the offering named,
And Madhushyand, for sweetness famed,
Mahárath, chariot-borne in fight,
And Dridhanetra strong of sight.

A thousand years had passed away,
When Brahmá, Sire whom all obey,
Addressed in pleasant words like these
Him rich in long austerities:
'Thou by the penance, Kuśik's son,
A place 'mid royal saints hast won.
Pleased with thy constant penance, we
This lofty rank assign to thee.'

Thus spoke the glorious Lord most High
Father of earth and air and sky,
And with the Gods around him spread
Home to his changeless sphere he sped.
But Viśvámitra scorned the grace,
And bent in shame his angry face.
Burning with rage, o'erwhelmed with grief,
Thus in his heart exclaimed the chief:
'No fruit, I ween, have I secured
By strictest penance long endured,
If Gods and all the saints decree
To make but royal saint of me.'
Thus pondering, he with sense subdued,
With sternest zeal his vows renewed.

---

[1] 'The names of many of these weapons which are mythical and partly allegorical have occurred in Canto XXIX. The general signification of the story is clear enough. It is a contest for supremacy between the regal or military order and Bráhmanical or priestly authority, like one of those struggles which our own Europe saw in the middle ages when without employing warlike weapons the priesthood frequently gained the victory.' SCHLEGEL.

For a full account of the early contests between the Bráhmans and the Kshattriyas, see Muir's Original Sanskrit Texts (second edition) Vol. I. Ch. IV.

Then reigned a monarch, true of soul,
Who kept each sense in firm control;
Of old Ikshváku's line he came,
That glories in Triśanku's[1] name.
Within his breast, O Raghu's child,
Arose a longing, strong and wild,
Great offerings to the Gods to pay,
And win, alive, to heaven his way.
His priest Vaśishṭha's aid he sought,
And told him of his secret thought.
But wise Vaśishṭha showed the hope
Was far beyond the monarch's scope.
Triśanku then, his suit denied,
Far to the southern region hied,
To beg Vaśishṭha's sons to aid
The mighty plan his soul had made.
There King Triśanku, far renowned,
Vaśishṭha's hundred children found,
Each on his fervent vows intent,
For mind and fame preëminent.
To these the famous king applied,
Wise children of his holy guide.
Saluting each in order due,
His eyes, for shame, he downward threw,
And reverent hands together pressed,
The glorious company addressed:
'I as a humble suppliant seek
Succour of you who aid the weak.
A mighty offering I would pay,
But sage Vaśishṭha answered, Nay.
Be yours permission to accord,
And to my rites your help afford.
Sons of my guide, to each of you
With lowly reverence here I sue;
To each, intent on penance-vow,
O Bráhmans, low my head I bow,
And pray you each with ready heart
In my great rite to bear a part,
That in the body I may rise
And dwell with Gods within the skies.
Sons of my guide, none else I see
Can give what he refuses me.
Ikshváku's children still depend
Upon their guide most reverend;
And you, as nearest in degree
To him, my deities shall be!'

[1] 'Triśanku, king of Ayodhyá, was seventh in descent from Ikshváku, and Daśaratha holds the thirty-fourth place in the same genealogy. See Canto LXX. We are thrown back, therefore, to very ancient times, and it occasions some surprise to find Vaśishṭha and Viśvámitra, actors in these occurrences, still alive in Ráma's time.'

CANTO LVIII.

TRIŚANKU CURSED.

Triśanku's speech the hundred heard,
And thus replied, to anger stirred:
'Why foolish King, by him denied,
Whose truthful lips have never lied,
Dost thou transgress his prudent rule,
And seek, for aid, another school?[1]
Ikshváku's sons have aye relied
Most surely on their holy guide:
Then how dost thou, fond Monarch, dare
Transgress the rule his lips declare?
'Thy wish is vain,' the saint replied,
And bade thee cast the plan aside.
Then how can we, his sons, pretend
In such a rite our aid to lend?
O Monarch, of the childish heart,
Home to thy royal town depart.
That mighty saint, thy priest and guide,
At noblest rites may well preside:
The worlds for sacrifice combined
A worthier priest could never find.'

Such speech of theirs the monarch heard,
Though rage distorted every word,
And to the hermits made reply:
'You, like your sire, my suit deny.
For other aid I turn from you:
So, rich in penance, Saints, adieu!'

Vaśishṭha's children heard, and guessed
His evil purpose scarce expressed,
And cried, while rage their bosoms burned,
'Be to a vile Chaṇḍála[2] turned!'

[1] "It does not appear how Triśanku, in asking the aid of Vaśishṭha's sons after applying in vain to their father, could be charged with resorting to another *śákhá* (School) in the ordinary sense of that word; as it is not conceivable that the sons should have been of another Śákhá from the father, whose cause they espouse with so much warmth. The commentator in the Bombay edition explains the word *Śákhántaram* as Yájanádiná rakshántaram, 'one who by sacrificing for thee, etc., will be another protector.' Gorresio's Gauḍa text, which may often be used as a commentary on the older one, has the following paraphrase of the words in question, ch. 60, 3. Múlam utsṛijya kasmát tvam sákhásv ichhasi lambitum. 'Why, forsaking the root, dost thou desire to hang upon the branches?'" MUIR, Sanskrit Texts Vol. I., p. 401.

[2] 'A Chaṇḍála was a man born of the illegal and impure union of a Śúdra with a woman of one of the three higher castes.

This said, with lofty thoughts inspired,
Each to his own retreat retired.

That night Triśanku underwent
Sad change in shape and lineament.
Next morn, an outcast swart of hue,
His dusky cloth he round him drew.
His hair had fallen from his head,
And roughness o'er his skin was spread.
Such wreaths adorned him as are found
To flourish on the funeral ground.
Each armlet was an iron ring :
Such was the figure of the king,
That every counsellor and peer,
And following townsman, fled in fear.

Alone, unyielding to dismay,
Though burnt by anguish night and day,
Great Viśvámitra's side he sought,
Whose treasures were by penance bought.

The hermit with his tender eyes
Looked on Triśanku's altered guise,
And grieving at his ruined state
Addressed him thus, compassionate :
'Great King,' the pious hermit said,
'What cause thy steps has hither led,
Ayodhyá's mighty Sovereign, whom
A curse has plagued with outcast's doom?'
In vile Chandála's shape, the king
Heard Viśvámitra's questioning,
And. suppliant palm to palm applied,
With answering eloquence he cried :
'My priest and all his sons refused
To aid the plan on which I mused.
Failing to win the boon I sought,
To this condition I was brought.
I, in the body, Saint, would fain
A mansion in the skies obtain.
I planned a hundred rites for this,
But still was doomed the fruit to miss.
Pure are my lips from falsehood's stain,
And pure they ever shall remain,—
Yea, by a Warrior's faith I swear,—
Though I be tried with grief and care.
Unnumbered rites to Heaven I paid,
With righteous care the sceptre swayed ;
And holy priest and high-souled guide
My modest conduct gratified.
But, O thou best of hermits, they
Oppose my wish these rites to pay ;
They one and all refuse consent,
Nor aid me in my high intent.
Fate is, I ween, the power supreme,
Man's effort but an idle dream.
Fate whirls our plans, our all away ;
Fate is our only hope and stay ;
Now deign, O blessed Saint, to aid
Me, even me by Fate betrayed,
Who come, a suppliant, sore distressed,
One grace, O Hermit, to request.
No other hope or way I see ;
No other refuge waits for me.
Oh, aid me in my fallen state,
And human will shall conquer Fate.'

The Chandála was regarded as the vilest and most abject of the men sprung from wedlock forbidden by the law (Mánava-dharmaśástra, Lib. X. 12.) ; a kind of social malediction weighed upon his head and rejected him from human society.' GORRESIO.

CANTO LIX.

THE SONS OF VAŚISHṬHA.

Then Kuśik's son, by pity warmed,
Spoke sweetly to the king transformed :
'Hail! glory of Ikshváku's line :
I know how bright thy virtues shine.
Dismiss thy fear, O noblest Chief,
For I myself will bring relief.
The holiest saints will I invite
To celebrate thy purposed rite :
So shall thy vow, O King, succeed,
And from thy cares shalt thou be freed.
Thou in the form which now thou hast,
Transfigured by the curse they cast,—
Yea, in the body, King, shalt flee,
Transported, where thou fain wouldst be.
O Lord of men, I ween that thou
Hast heaven within thy hand e'en now,
For very wisely hast thou done,
And refuge sought with Kuśik's son.'

Thus having said, the sage addressed
His sons, of men the holiest,
And bade the prudent saints whate'er
Was needed for the rite prepare.
The pupils he was wont to teach
He summoned next, and spoke this speech:
'Go bid Vaśishṭha's sons appear,
And all the saints be gathered here.
And what they one and all reply
When summoned by this mandate high,
To me with faithful care report,
Omit no word and none distort.'

The pupils heard, and prompt obeyed,
To every side their way they made.
Then swift from every quarter sped
The sages in the Vedas read.
Back to that saint the envoys came,
Whose glory shone like burning flame,
And told him in their faithful speech
The answer that they bore from each :
'Submissive to thy word, O Seer,
The holy men are gathering here.
By all was meet obedience shown :
Mahodaya[1] refused alone.

[1] This appellation, occuring nowhere else in the poem except as the name of a city, appears twice in this Canto as a name of Vaśishṭha.

And now, O Chief of hermits, hear
What answer, chilling us with fear,
Vaśishṭha's hundred sons returned,
Thick-speaking as with rage they burned:
'How will the Gods and saints partake
The offerings that the prince would make,
And he a vile and outcast thing,
His ministrant one born a king?
Can we, great Bráhmans, eat his food,
And think to win beatitude,
By Viśvámitra purified?'
Thus sire and sons in scorn replied,
And as these bitter words they said,
Wild fury made their eyeballs red.'

Their answer when the arch-hermit heard,
His tranquil eyes with rage were blurred;
Great fury in his bosom woke,
And thus unto the youths he spoke:
'Me, blameless me they dare to blame,
And disallow the righteous claim
My fierce austerities have earned:
To ashes be the sinners turned.
Caught in the noose of Fate shall they
To Yama's kingdom sink to-day.
Seven hundred times shall they be born
To wear the clothes the dead have worn.
Dregs of the dregs, too vile to hate.
The flesh of dogs their maws shall sate.
In hideous form, in loathsome weed,
A sad existence each shall lead,
Mahodaya too, the fool who fain
My stainless life would try to stain,
Stained in the world with long disgrace
Shall sink into a fowler's place.
Rejoicing guiltless blood to spill,
No pity through his breast shall thrill.
Cursed by my wrath for many a day,
His wretched life for sin shall pay.'

Thus, girt with hermit, saint, and priest,
Great Viśvámitra spoke—and ceased.

CANTO LX.

TRIŚANKU'S ASCENSION.

So with ascetic might, in ire,
He smote the children and the sire.
Then Viśvámitra, far-renowned,
Addressed the saints who gathered round:
'See by my side Triśanku stand,
Ikshváku's son, of liberal hand.
Most virtuous and gentle, he
Seeks refuge in his woe with me.
Now, holy men, with me unite,
And order so his purposed rite
That in the body he may rise
And win a mansion in the skies.'

They heard his speech with ready ear
And, every bosom filled with fear
Of Viśvámitra, wise and great,
Spoke each to each in brief debate:
'The breast of Kuśik's son, we know,
With furious wrath is quick to glow.
Whate'er the words he wills to say,
We must, be very sure, obey.
Fierce is our lord as fire, and straight
May curse us all infuriate.
So let us in these rites engage,
As ordered by the holy sage,
And with our best endeavour strive
That King Ikshváku's son, alive,
In body to the skies may go
By his great might who wills it so.'

Then was the rite begun with care:
All requisites and means were there:
And glorious Viśvámitra lent
His willing aid as president.
And all the sacred rites were done
By rule and use, omitting none.
By chaplain-priest, the hymns who knew
In decent form and order due.
Some time in sacrifice had past,
And Viśvámitra made, at last,
The solemn offering with the prayer
That all the Gods might come and share.
But the Immortals, one and all,
Refused to hear the hermit's call.

Then red with rage his eyeballs blazed:
The sacred ladle high he raised,
And cried to King Ikshváku's son:
'Behold my power, by penance won:
Now by the might my merits lend,
Ikshváku's child, to heaven ascend.
In living frame the skies attain,
Which mortals thus can scarcely gain.
My vows austere, so long endured,
Have, as I ween, some fruit assured.
Upon its virtue, King, rely,
And in thy body reach the sky.'

His speech had scarcely reached its close,
When, as he stood, the sovereign rose,
And mounted swiftly to the skies
Before the wondering hermits' eyes.

But Indra, when he saw the king
His blissful regions entering,
With all the army of the Blest
Thus cried unto the unbidden guest:
'With thy best speed, Triśanku, flee:
Here is no home prepared for thee.
By thy great master's curse brought low,
Go, falling headlong, earthward go.'

Thus by the Lord of Gods addressed,
Triśanku fell from fancied rest,
And screaming in his swift descent,
'O, save me, Hermit!' down he went.
And Viśvámitra heard his cry,
And marked him falling from the sky,
And giving all his passion sway,
Cried out in fury, 'Stay, O stay!'

By penance-power and holy lore,
Like Him who framed the worlds of yore,
Seven other saints he fixed on high
To star with light the southern sky.
Girt with his sages forth he went,
And southward in the firmament
New wreathed stars prepared to set
In many a sparkling coronet.
He threatened, blind with rage and hate,
Another Indra to create,
Or, from his throne the ruler hurled,
All Indraless to leave the world.
Yea, borne away by passion's storm,
The sage began new Gods to form.
But then each Titan, God, and saint,
Confused with terror, sick and faint,
To high souled Viśvámitra hied,
And with soft words to soothe him tried:
'Lord of high destiny, this king,
To whom his master's curses cling,
No heavenly home deserves to gain,
Unpurified from curse and stain.'

The son of Kuśik, underterred,
The pleading of the Immortals heard,
And thus in haughty words expressed
The changeless purpose of his breast:
'Content ye, Gods: I soothly sware
Triśanku to the skies to bear
Clothed in his body, nor can I
My promise cancel or deny.
Embodied let the king ascend
To life in heaven that ne'er shall end.
And let these new-made stars of mine
Firm and secure for ever shine.
Let these, my work, remain secure
Long as the earth and heaven endure.
This, all ye Gods, I crave: do you
Allow the boon for which I sue.'
Then all the Gods their answer made:
'So be it, Saint, as thou hast prayed.
Beyond the sun's diurnal way
Thy countless stars in heaven shall stay:
And 'mid them hung, as one divine,
Head downward shall Triśanku shine:
And all thy stars shall ever fling
Their rays attendant on the king.'[1]

The mighty saint, with glory crowned,
With all the sages compassed round,
Praised by the Gods, gave full assent,
And Gods and sages homeward went.

CANTO LXI.

ŚUNAHŚEPHA.

Then Viśvámitra, when the Blest
Had sought their homes of heavenly rest,
Thus, mighty Prince, his counsel laid
Before the dwellers of the shade:
'The southern land where now we are
Offers this check our rites to bar:[1]
To other regions let us speed,
And ply our tasks from trouble freed.
Now turn we to the distant west.
To Pushkar's[2] wood where hermits rest,
And there to rites austere apply,
For not a grove with that can vie.'

The saint, in glory's light arrayed,
In Pushkar's wood his dwelling made,
And living there on roots and fruit
Did penance stern and resolute.

The king who filled Ayodhyá's throne,
By Ambarísha's name far known,
At that same time, it chanced, began
A sacrificial rite to plan.
But Indra took by force away
The charger that the king would slay.
The victim lost, the Bráhman sped
To Ambarísha's side, and said:
'Gone is the steed, O King, and this
Is due to thee, in care remiss.

[1] 'The seven ancient *rishis* or saints, as has been said before, were the seven stars of Ursa Major. The seven other new saints which are here said to have been created by Viśvámitra, should be seven new southern stars, a sort of new Ursa. Von Schlegel thinks that this mythical fiction of new stars created by Viśvámitra may signify that these southern stars, unknown to the Indians as long as they remained in the neighbourhood of the Ganges, became known to them at a later date when they colonized the southern regions of Indra.' GORRESIO.

[1] 'This cannot refer to the events just related: for Viśvámitra was successful in the sacrifice performed for Triśanku. And yet no other impediment is mentioned. Still his restless mind would not allow him to remain longer in the same spot. So the character of Viśvámitra is ingeniously and skilfully shadowed forth; as he had been formerly a most warlike king, loving battle and glory, bold, active, sometimes unjust, and more frequently magnanimous, such also he always shows himself in his character of anchorite and ascetic.' SCHLEGEL.

[2] Near the modern city of Ajmere. The place is sacred still, and the name is preserved in the Hindí. Lassen, however, says that this Pushkala or Pushkara, called by the Grecian writers Πευκελαἵτις, the earliest place of pilgrimage mentioned by name, is not to be confounded with the modern Pushkara in Ajmere.

Such heedless faults will kings destroy
Who fail to guard what they enjoy.
The flaw is desperate: we need
The charger, or a man to bleed.
Quick! bring a man if not the horse,
That so the rite may have its course.'

The glory of Ikshváku's line
Made offer of a thousand kine,
And sought to buy at lordly price
A victim for the sacrifice.
To many a distant land he drove,
To many a people, town, and grove,
And holy shades where hermits rest,
Pursuing still his eager quest.
At length on Bhrigu's sacred height
The saint Richíka met his sight
Sitting beneath the holy boughs.
His children near him, and his spouse.

The mighty lord drew near, assayed
To win his grace, and reverence paid;
And then the sainted king addressed
The Bráhman saint with this request:
'Bought with a hundred thousand kine,
Give me, O Sage, a son of thine
To be a victim in the rite,
And thanks the favour shall requite.
For I have roamed all countries round,
Nor sacrificial victim found.
Then, gentle Hermit, deign to spare
One child amid the number there.'

Then to the monarch's speech replied
The hermit, penance-glorified:
'For countless kine, for hills of gold,
Mine eldest son shall ne'er be sold.'
But, when she heard the saint's reply,
The children's mother, standing nigh,
Words such as these in answer said
To Ambarísha, monarch dread:
'My lord, the saint, has spoken well:
His eldest child he will not sell.
And know, great Monarch, that above
The rest my youngest born I love.
'Tis ever thus: the father's joy
Is centred in his eldest boy.
The mother loves her darling best
Whom last she rocked upon her breast:
My youngest I will ne'er forsake.'

As thus the sire and mother spake,
Young Śunahśepha, of the three
The midmost, cried unurged and free:
'My sire withholds his eldest son,
My mother keeps her youngest one:
Then take me with thee, King: I ween
The son is sold who comes between.'
The king with joy his home resought,
And took the prize his kine had bought.
He bade the youth his car ascend,
And hastened back the rites to end.[1]

[1] 'Ambarísha is the twenty-ninth in descent from Ikshváku, and is therefore separated by an immense space of time from Triśanku in whose story Viśvámitra had played so important a part. Yet Richíka, who is represented as having young sons while Ambarísha was yet reigning being himself the son of Bhrigu and to be numbered with the most ancient sages, is said to have married the younger sister of Viśvámitra. But I need not again remark that there is a perpetual anachronism in Indian mythology.' SCHLEGEL.

'In the mythical story related in this and the following Canto we may discover, I think, some indication of the epoch at which the immolation of lower animals was substituted for human sacrifice.......... So when Iphigenia was about to be sacrificed at Aulis, one legend tells us that a hind was substituted for the virgin.' GORRESIO.

So the ram caught in the thicket took the place of Isaac, or, as the Musalmáns say, of Ishmael.

CANTO LXII.

AMBARÍSHA'S SACRIFICE.

As thus the king that youth conveyed,
His weary steeds at length he stayed
At height of noon their rest to take
Upon the bank of Pushkar's lake.
There while the king enjoyed repose
The captive Śunahśepha rose,
And hasting to the water's side
His uncle Viśvámitra spied,
With many a hermit 'neath the trees
Engaged in stern austerities.

Distracted with the toil and thirst,
With woeful mien, away he burst,
Swift to the hermit's breast he flew,
And weeping thus began to sue:
'No sire have I, no mother dear,
No kith or kin my heart to cheer:
As justice bids, O Hermit, deign
To save me from the threatened pain.
O thou to whom the wretched flee,
And find a saviour, Saint, in thee,
Now let the king obtain his will,
And me my length of days fulfil,
That rites austere I too may share,
May rise to heaven and rest me there.
With tender soul and gentle brow
Be guardian of the orphan thou,
And as a father pities, so
Preserve me from my fear and woe.'

When Viśvámitra, glorious saint,
Had heard the boy's heart-rending plaint,
He soothed his grief, his tears he dried,

Then called his sons to him, and cried:
'The time is come for you to show
The duty and the aid bestow
For which, regarding future life,
A man gives children to his wife.
This hermit's son, whom here you see
A suppliant, refuge seeks with me.
O sons, the friendless youth befriend,
And, pleasing me, his life defend.
For holy works you all have wrought,
True to the virtuous life I taught.
Go, and as victims doomed to bleed,
Die, and Lord Agni's hunger feed.
So shall the rite completed end,
This orphan gain a saving friend,
Due offerings to the Gods be paid,
And your own father's voice obeyed.'

Then Madhushyand and all the rest
Answered their sire with scorn and jest:
'What! aid to others' sons afford,
And leave thine own to die, my lord!
To us it seems a horrid deed,
As 'twere on one's own flesh to feed.'

The hermit heard his sons' reply,
And burning rage inflamed his eye.
Then forth his words of fury burst:
'Audacious speech, by virtue cursed!
It lifts on end each shuddering hair—
My charge to scorn! my wrath to dare!
You, like Vaśishṭha's evil brood,
Shall make the flesh of dogs your food
A thousand years in many a birth,
And punished thus shall dwell on earth.'

Thus on his sons his curse he laid,
Then calmed again that youth dismayed,
And blessed him with his saving aid:
'When in the sacred fetters bound,
And with a purple garland crowned,
At Vishṇu's post thou standest tied,
With lauds be Agni glorified.
And these two hymns of holy praise
Forget not, Hermit's son, to raise
In the king's rite, and thou shalt be
Lord of thy wish, preserved, and free.'

He learnt the hymns with mind intent,
And from the hermit's presence went.
To Ambarísha thus he spake:
'Let us our onward journey take.
Haste to thy home, O King, nor stay
The lustral rites with slow delay.'

The boy's address the monarch cheered,
And soon the sacred ground he neared.
The convocation's high decree
Declared the youth from blemish free;
Clothed in red raiment he was tied
A victim at the pillar's side.
There bound, the Fire-God's hymn he raised,
And Indra and Upendra praised.
Thousand-eyed Vishṇu, pleased to hear
The mystic laud, inclined his ear,
And won by worship, swift to save,
Long life to Śunahśepha gave.
The king in bounteous measure gained
The fruit of sacrifice ordained,
By grace of Him who rules the skies,
Lord Indra of the thousand eyes.

And Viśvámitra evermore.
Pursued his task on Pushkar's shore
Until a thousand years had past
In fierce austerity and fast.

CANTO LXIII.

MENAKÁ.

A thousand years had thus flown by
When all the Gods within the sky,
Eager that he the fruit might gain
Of fervent rite and holy pain,
Approached the great ascetic, now
Bathed after toil and ended vow.
Then Brahmá speaking for the rest
With sweetest words the sage addressed:
'Hail, Saint! This high and holy name
Thy rites have won, thy merits claim.'

Thus spoke the Lord whom Gods revere,
And sought again his heavenly sphere.
But Viśvámitra, more intent,
His mind to sterner penance bent.

So many a season rolled away,
When Menaká, fair nymph, one day
Came down from Paradise to lave
Her perfect limbs in Pushkar's wave.
The glorious son of Kuśik saw
That peerless shape without a flaw
Flash through the flood's translucent shroud
Like lightning gleaming through a cloud.
He saw her in that lone retreat,
Most beautiful from head to feet,
And by Kandarpa's[1] might subdued
He thus addressed her as he viewed:
'Welcome, sweet nymph! O deign, I pray,
In these calm shades awhile to stay.
To me some gracious favour show,
For love has set my breast aglow.'

He spoke. The fairest of the fair
Made for awhile her dwelling there,
While day by day the wild delight
Stayed vow austere and fervent rite
There as the winsome charmer wove
Her spells around him in the grove,
And bound him in a golden chain,
Five sweet years fled, and five again.
Then Viśvámitra woke to shame,
And, fraught with anguish, memory came
For quick he knew, with anger fired,
That all the Immortals had conspired

---

[1] The Indian Cupid.

To lap his careless soul in ease,
And mar his long austerities.
'Ten years have past, each day and night
Unheeded in delusive flight.
So long my fervent rites were stayed,
While thus I lay by love betrayed.'
As thus long sighs the hermit heaved,
And, touched with deep repentance, grieved,
He saw the fair one standing nigh
With suppliant hands and trembling eye.
With gentle words he bade her go,
Then sought the northern hills of snow.
With firm resolve he vowed to beat
The might of love beneath his feet.
Still northward to the distant side
Of Kauśikí,[1] the hermit hide,
And gave his life to penance there
With rites austere most hard to bear.
A thousand years went by, and still
He laboured on the northern hill
With pains so terrible and drear
That all the Gods were chilled with fear,
And Gods and saints, for swift advice,
Met in the halls of Paradise.
'Let Kuśik's son,' they counselled, 'be
A Mighty saint by just decree.'
His ear to hear their counsel lent
The Sire of worlds, omnipotent.
To him enriched by rites severe
He spoke in accents sweet to hear:
'Hail, Mighty Saint! dear son, all hail!
Thy fervour wins, thy toils prevail.
Won by thy vows and zeal intense
I give this high preëminence.'
He to the General Sire replied,
Not sad, nor wholly satisfied:
'When thou, O Brahmá, shalt declare
The title, great beyond compare,
Of Bráhman saint my worthy meed,
Hard earned by many a holy deed,
Then may I deem in sooth I hold
Each sense of body well controlled.'
Then Brahmá cried, 'Not yet, not yet:
Toil on awhile O Anchoret!'

Thus having said to heaven he went,
The saint, upon his task intent,
Began his labours to renew,
Which sterner yet and fiercer grew.
His arms upraised, without a rest,
With but one foot the earth he pressed;
The air his food, the hermit stood
Still as a pillar hewn from wood.
Around him in the summer days
Five mighty fires combined to blaze.
In floods of rain no veil was spread
Save clouds, to canopy his head.
In the dank dews both night and day
Couched in the stream the hermit lay.
Thus, till a thousand years had fled,
He plied his task of penance dread.
Then Vishṇu and the Gods with awe
The labours of the hermit saw,
And Śakra, in his troubled breast,
Lord of the skies, his fear confessed,
And brooded on a plan to spoil
The merits of the hermit's toil.
Encompassed by his Gods of Storm
He summoned Rambhá, fair of form,
And spoke a speech for woe and weal,
The saint to mar, the God to heal.

CANTO LXIV.

RAMBHÁ.

'A great emprise, O lovely maid,
To save the Gods, awaits thine aid:
To bind the son of Kuśik sure,
And take his soul with love's sweet lure.'
Thus orderd by the Thousand-eyed
The suppliant nymph in fear replied:
'O Lord of Gods, this mighty sage
Is very fierce and swift to rage.
I doubt not, he so dread and stern
On me his scorching wrath will turn.
Of this, my lord, am I afraid:
Have mercy on a timid maid.'
Her suppliant hands began to shake,
When thus again Lord Indra spake:
'O Rambhá, drive thy fears away,
And as I bid do thou obey.
In Koïl's form, who takes the heart
When trees in spring to blossom start,
I, with Kandarpa for my friend,
Close to thy side mine aid will lend.

[1] 'The same as she whose praises Viśvámitra has already sung in Canto XXXV, and whom the poet brings yet alive upon the scene in Canto LXI. Her proper name was *Satyavatí* (Truthful); the patronymic, Kauśikí was preserved by the river into which she is said to have been changed, and is still recognized in the corrupted forms Kuśa and Kuśí. The river flows from the heights of the Himálaya towards the Ganges, bounding on the east the country of Videha (Behar). The name is no doubt half hidden in the *Cosoagus* of Pliny and the *Kossoanos* of Arrian. But each author has fallen into the same error in his enumeration of these rivers (Condochatem, Erannoboam, Cosoagum, Sonum). The Erannoboas, (Hiraṇyaváha) and the Sone are not different streams, but well-known names of the same river. Moreover the order is disturbed, in which on the right and left they fall into the Ganges. To be consistent with geography it should be written: Erannoboam sive Sonum, Condochatem (Gandakí), Cosoagum.' SCHLEGEL.

Do thou thy beauteous splendour arm
With every grace and winsome charm,
And from his awful rites seduce
This Kuśik's son, the stern recluse.'

Lord Indra ceased. The nymph obeyed:
In all her loveliest charms arrayed,
With winning ways and witching smile
She sought the hermit to beguile.
The sweet note of that tuneful bird
The saint with ravished bosom heard,
And on his heart a rapture passed
As on the nymph a look he cast.
But when he heard the bird prolong
His sweet incomparable song,
And saw the nymph with winning smile,
The hermit's heart perceivd the wile.
And straight he knew the Thousand-eyed
A plot against his peace had tried.
Then Kuśik's son indignant laid
His curse upon the heavenly maid:
'Because thou wouldst my soul engage
Who fight to conquer love and rage,
Stand, till ten thousand years have flown,
Ill-fated maid, transformed to stone.
A Bráhman then, in glory strong,
Mighty through penance stern and long,
Shall free thee from thine altered shape:
Thou from my curse shalt then escape.'
But when the saint had cursed her so,
His breast was burnt with fires of woe,
Grieved that l ng effort to restrain
His mighty wrath was all in vain.
Cursed by the angry sage's power,
She stood in stone that selfsame hour.
Kandarpa heard the words he said,
And quickly from his presence fled.
His fall beneath his passion's sway
Had reft the hermit's meed away.
Unconquered yet his secret foes,
The humbled saint refused repose:
'No more shall rage my bosom fill,
Sealed be my lips, my tongue be still.
My very breath henceforth I hold
Until a thousand years are told:
Victorious o'er each erring sense,
I'll dry my frame with abstinence,
Until by penance duly done
A Bráhman's rank be bought and won.
For countless years, as still as death,
I taste no food, I draw no breath,
And as I toil my frame shall stand
Unharmed by time's destroying hand.'

CANTO LXV.

VIŚVÁMITRA'S TRIUMPH.

Then from Himálaya's heights of snow,
The glorious saint prepared to go,
And dwelling in the distant east
His penance and his toil increased.
A thousand years his lips he held
Closed by a vow unparalleled,
And other marvels passing thought,
Unrivalled in the world, he wrought.
In all the thousand years his frame
Dry as a log of wood became.
By many a cross and check beset,
Rage had not stormed his bosom yet.
With iron will that naught could bend
He plied his labour till the end.
So when the weary years were o'er,
Freed from his vow so stern and sore,
The hermit, all his penance sped,
Sate down to eat his meal of bread.
Then Indra, clad in Bráhman guise,
Asked him for food with hungry eyes.
The mighty saint, with steadfast soul,
To the false Bráhman gave the whole,
And when no scrap for him remained,
Fasting and faint, from speech refrained.
His silent vow he would not break:
No breath he heaved, no word he spake.
Then as he checked his breath, behold!
Around his brow thick smoke-clouds rolled
And the three worlds, as if o'erspread
With ravening flames, were filled with dread.
Then God and saint and bard, convened,
And Nága lord, and snake, and fiend,
Thus to the General Father cried,
Distracted, sad, and terrified:
'Against the hermit, sore assailed,
Lure, scathe, and scorn have naught availed,
Proof against rage and treacherous art
He keeps his vow with constant heart.
Now if his toils assist him naught
To gain the boon his soul has sought,
He through the worlds will ruin send
That fixt and moving things shall end.
The regions now are dark with doom,
No friendly ray relieves the gloom.
Each ocean foams with maddened tide,
The shrinking hills in fear subside.
Trembles the earth with feverous throes,
The wind in fitful tempest blows.
No cure we see with troubled eyes:
And atheist brood on earth may rise.
The triple world is wild with care,
Or spiritless in dull despair.
Before that saint the sun is dim,
His blessed light eclipsed by him.
Now ere the saint resolve to bring
Destruction on each living thing,
Let us appease, while yet we may,
Him bright as fire, like fire to slay.
Yea, as the fiery flood of Fate
Lays all creation desolate,
He o'er the conquered Gods may reign:
O, grant him what he longs to gain.'

Then all the Blest, by Brahmá led,
Approached the saint and sweetly said:
'Hail, Bráhman Saint! for such thy place:
Thy vows austere have won our grace.
A Bráhman's rank thy penance stern
And ceaseless labour richly earn.
I with the Gods of Storm decree
Long life, O Bráhman Saint, to thee.
May peace and joy thy soul possess:
Go where thou wilt in happiness.'

Thus by the General Sire addressed,
Joy and high triumph filled his breast.
His head in adoration bowed,
Thus spoke he to the Immortal crowd:
'If I, ye Gods, have gained at last
Both length of days and Bráhman caste,
Grant that the high mysterious name,
And holy Vedas, own my claim,
And that the formula to bless
The sacrifice, its lord confess.
And let Vaśishṭha, who excels
In Warriors' art and mystic spells,
In love of God without a peer.
Confirm the boon you promise here.'

With Brahmá's son Vaśishṭha, best
Of those who pray with voice repressed,
The Gods by earnest prayer prevailed,
And thus his new-made friend he hailed:
'Thy title now is sure and good
To rights of saintly Bráhmanhood.'
Thus spake the sage. The Gods, content,
Back to their heavenly mansions went.
And Viśvámitra, pious-souled,
Among the Bráhman saints enrolled,
On reverend Vaśishṭha pressed
The honours due to holy guest.
Successful in his high pursuit,
The sage, in penance resolute,
Walked in his pilgrim wanderings o'er
The whole broad land from shore to shore.
'Twas thus the saint, O Raghu's son,
His rank among the Bráhmans won.
Best of all hermits, Prince, is he;
In him incarnate Penance see.
Friend of the right, who shrinks from ill,
Heroic powers attend him still.'

The Bráhman, versed in ancient lore,
Thus closed his tale, and said no more.
To Śatánanda Kuśik's son
Cried in delight, Well done! well done!
Then Janak, at the tale amazed,
Spoke thus with suppliant hands upraised:
'High fate is mine, O Sage, I deem,
And thanks I owe for bliss supreme,
That thou and Raghu's children too
Have come my sacrifice to view.
To look on thee with blessed eyes
Exalts my soul and purifies.
Yea, thus to see thee face to face
Enriches me with store of grace.
Thy holy labours wrought of old,
And mighty penance, fully told,
Ráma and I with great delight
Have heard, O glorious Anchorite.
Unrivalled thine ascetic deeds:
Thy might, O Saint, all might exceeds.
No thought may scan, no limit bound
The virtues that in thee are found.
The story of thy wondrous fate
My thirsty ears can never sate.
The hour of evening rites is near:
The sun declines in swift career.
At early dawn, O Hermit, deign
To let me see thy face again.
Best of ascetics, part in bliss:
Do thou thy servant now dismiss.'

The saint approved, and glad and kind
Dismissed the king with joyful mind.
Around the sage King Janak went
With priests and kinsmen reverent.
Then Viśvámitra, honoured so,
By those high-minded, rose to go,
And with the princes took his way
To seek the lodging where they lay.

CANTO LXVI.

JANAK'S SPEECH.

With cloudless lustre rose the sun;
The king, his morning worship done,
Ordered his heralds to invite
The princes and the anchorite.
With honour, as the laws decree,
The monarch entertained the three.
Then to the youths and saintly man
Videha's lord this speech began:
'O blameless Saint, most welcome thou!
If I may please thee tell me how.
Speak, mighty lord, whom all revere,
'Tis thine to order, mine to hear.'

Thus he on mighty thoughts intent;
Then thus the sage most eloquent:
'King Daśaratha's sons, this pair
Of warriors famous everywhere,
Are come that best of bows to see
That lies a treasure stored by thee.
This, mighty Janak, deign to show,
That they may look upon the bow.
And then, contented, homeward go.'
Then royal Janak spoke in turn:
'O best of Saints, the story learn
Why this famed bow, a noble prize,
A treasure in my palace lies.
A monarch, Devarát by name,
Who sixth from ancient Nimi came,
Held it as ruler of the land,
A pledge in his successive hand.
This bow the mighty Rudra bore

At Daksha's[1] sacrifice of yore,
When carnage of the Immortals stained
The rite that Daksha had ordained,
Then as the Gods sore wounded fled,
Victorious Rudra, mocking, said :
'Because, O Gods, ye gave me naught
When I my rightful portion sought,
Your dearest parts I will not spare,
But with my bow your frames will tear.'

The Sons of Heaven, in wild alarm,
Soft flatteries tried his rage to charm.
Then Bhava, Lord whom Gods adore,
Grew kind and friendly as before,
And every torn and mangled limb
Was safe and sound restored by him.
Thenceforth this bow, the gem of bows,
That freed the God of Gods from foes,
Stored by our great forefathers lay
A treasure and a pride for aye.
Once, as it chanced, I ploughed the ground,
When sudden, 'neath the share was found
An infant springing from the earth,
Named Sítá from her secret birth.[2]
In strength and grace the maiden grew,
My cherished daughter, fair to view.
I vowed her, of no mortal birth,
Meet prize for noblest hero's worth.
In strength and grace the maiden grew,
And many a monarch came to woo.
To all the princely suitors I
Gave, mighty Saint, the same reply :
'I give not thus my daughter, she
Prize of heroic worth shall be.[3]
To Mithilá the suitors pressed
Their power and might to manifest.
To all who came with hearts aglow
I offered Siva's wondrous bow.
Not one of all the royal band
Could raise or take the bow in hand.
The suitors' puny might I spurned,
And back the feeble princes turned.
Enraged thereat, the warriors met,
With force combined my town beset.
Stung to the heart with scorn and shame,
With war and threats they madly came,
Besieged my peaceful walls, and long
To Mithilá did grievous wrong.
There, wasting all, a year they lay,
And brought my treasures to decay,
Filling my soul, O Hermit chief,
With bitter woe and hopeless grief.
At last by long-wrought penance I
Won favour with the Gods on high,
Who with my labours well content
A four-fold host to aid me sent.
Then swift the baffled heroes fled
To all the winds discomfited—
Wrong-doers, with their lords and host,
And all their valour's idle boast.
This heavenly bow, exceeding bright,
These youths shall see, O Anchorite.
Then if young Ráma's hand can string
The bow that baffled lord and king,
To him I give, as I have sworn,
My Sítá, not of woman born.'

CANTO LXVII.

THE BREAKING OF THE BOW.

Then spoke again the great recluse :
'This mighty bow, O King, produce.'
King Janak, at the saint's request,
This order to his train addressed :
'Let the great bow be hither borne,
Which flowery wreaths and scents adorn.'
Soon as the monarch's words were said,
His servants to the city sped :
Five thousand youths in number, all
Of manly strength and stature tall,
The ponderous eight-wheeled chest that held
The heavenly bow, with toil propelled.
At length they brought that iron chest,
And thus the godlike king addressed :
'This best of bows, O lord, we bring,
Respected by each chief and king,
And place it for these youths to see,
If, Sovereign, such thy pleasure be.'

With suppliant palm to palm applied
King Janak to the strangers cried :
'This gem of bows, O Bráhman Sage,
Our race has prized from age to age,
Too strong for those who yet have reigned,
Though great in might each nerve they strained.

[1] 'Daksha was one of the ancient Progenitors or Prajápatis created by Brahmá. The sacrifice which is here spoken of and in which Śankar or Śiva (called also here Rudra and Bhava) smote the Gods because he had not been invited to share the sacred oblations with them, seems to refer to the origin of the worship of Śiva, to its increase and to the struggle it maintained with other older forms of worship.' GORRESIO.

[2] Sítá means a furrow.

'Great Erectheus swayed,
That owed his nurture to the blue-eyed maid,
But from the teeming furrow took his birth,
The mighty offspring of the foodful earth.'
Iliad, Book II.

[3] 'The whole story of Sítá, as will be seen in the course of the poem has a great analogy with the ancient myth of Proserpine.' GORRESIO.

Titan and fiend its strength defies,
God, spirit, minstrel of the skies.
And bard above and snake below
Are baffled by this glorious bow.
Then how may human prowess hope
With such a bow as this to cope?
What man with valour's choicest gift
This bow can draw, or string, or lift?
Yet let the princes, holy Seer,
Behold it: it is present here.'

Then spoke the hermit pious-souled:
'Ráma, dear son, the bow behold.'
Then Ráma at his word unclosed
The chest wherein its might reposed,
Thus crying, as he viewed it: 'Lo!
I lay mine hand upon the bow:
May happy luck my hope attend
Its heavenly strength to lift or bend.'
'Good luck be thine,' the hermit cried:
'Assay the task!' the king replied.
Then Raghu's son, as if in sport,
Before the thousands of the court,
The weapon by the middle raised
That all the crowd in wonder gazed.
With steady arm the string he drew
Till burst the mighty bow in two.
As snapped the bow, an awful clang,
Loud as the shriek of tempests, rang.
The earth, affrighted, shook amain
As when a hill is rent in twain.
Then, senseless at the fearful sound,
The people fell upon the ground:
None save the king, the princely pair,
And the great saint, the shock could bear.

When woke to sense the stricken train,
And Janak's soul was calm again,
With suppliant hands and reverent head,
These words, most eloquent, he said:
'O Saint, Prince Ráma stands alone:
His peerless might he well has shown.
A marvel has the hero wrought
Beyond belief, surpassing thought.
My child, to royal Ráma wed,
New glory on our line will shed:
And true my promise will remain
That hero's worth the bride should gain.
Dearer to me than light and life,
My Sítá shall be Ráma's wife.
If thou, O Bráhman, leave concede,
My counsellors, with eager speed,
Borne in their flying cars, to fair
Ayodhyá's town the news shall bear,
With courteous message to entreat
The king to grace my royal seat.
This to the monarch shall they tell,
The bride is his who won her well:
And his two sons are resting here
Protected by the holy seer.
So, at his pleasure, let them lead
The sovereign to my town with speed.'

The hermit to his prayer inclined
And Janak, lord of virtuous mind,
With charges, to Ayodhyá sent
His ministers: and forth they went.

CANTO LXVIII.

THE ENVOYS' SPEECH.

Three nights upon the road they passed
To rest the steeds that bore them fast,
And reached Ayodhyá's town at last.
Then straight at Daśaratha's call
They stood within the royal hall,
Where, like a God, inspiring awe,
The venerable king they saw.
With suppliant palm to palm applied,
And all their terror laid aside,
They spoke to him upon the throne
With modest words, in gentle tone:
'Janak, Videha's king, O Sire,
Has sent us hither to inquire
The health of thee his friend most dear,
Of all thy priests and every peer.
Next Kuśik's son consenting, thus
King Janak speaks, dread liege, by us:
'I made a promise and decree
That valour's prize my child should be.
Kings, worthless found in worth's assay,
With mien dejected turned away.
Thy sons, by Viśvámitra led,
Unurged, my city visited,
And peerless in their might have gained
My daughter, as my vow ordained.
Full in a vast assembly's view
Thy hero Ráma broke in two
The gem of bows, of monstrous size,
That came a treasure from the skies.
Ordained the prize of hero's might,
Sítá my child is his by right.
Fain would I keep my promise made,
If thou, O King, approve and aid.
Come to my town thy son to see:
Bring holy guide and priest with thee.
O lord of kings, my suit allow,
And let me keep my promised vow.
So joying for thy children's sake
Their triumph too shalt thou partake,
With Viśvámitra's high consent.'
'Such words with friendship eloquent
Spoke Janak, fair Videha's king,
By Śatánanda's counselling.'

The envoys thus the king addressed,
And mighty joy his heart possessed.
To Vámadeva quick he cried,
Vaśishṭha, and his lords beside:
'Lakshman, and he, my princely boy
Who fills Kauśalyá's soul with joy,
By Viśvámitra guarded well
Among the good Videhans dwell.

Their ruler Janak, prompt to own
The peerless might my child has shown,
To him would knit in holy ties
His daughter, valour's lovely prize.
If Janak's plan seem good to you,
Come, speed we to his city too,
Nor let occasion idly by.'

He ceased. There came a glad reply
From priest and mighty saint and all
The councillors who thronged the hall.
Then cried the king with joyous heart:
'To-morrow let us all depart.'

That night the envoys entertained
With honour and all care remained.

CANTO LXIX.

DAŚARATHA'S VISIT.

Soon as the shades of night had fled,
Thus to the wise Sumantra said
The happy king, while priest and peer,
Each in his place, were standing near:
'Let all my treasurers to-day,
Set foremost in the long array,
With gold and precious gems supplied
In bounteous store, together ride.
And send you out a mighty force,
Foot, chariot, elephant, and horse.
Besides, let many a car of state,
And noblest steeds, my will await.
Vaśishṭha, Vámadeva sage,
And Márkaṇḍeya's reverend age,
Jáváli, Kaśyap's godlike seed,
And wise Kátyáyana, shall lead.
Thy care, Sumantra, let it be
To yoke a chariot now for me,
That so we part without delay:
These envoys hasten me away.'

So fared he forth. That host, with speed,
Quadruple, as the king decreed,
With priests to head the bright array,
Followed the monarch on his way.
Four days they travelled on the road,
And eve Videha's kingdom showed.
Janak had left his royal seat
The venerable king to greet,
And, noblest, with these words addressed
That noblest lord, his happy guest:
'Hail, best of kings: a blessed fate
Has led thee, Monarch, to my state.
Thy sons, supreme in high emprise,
Will gladden now their father's eyes.
And high my fate, that hither leads
Vaśishṭha, bright with holy deeds,
Girt with these sages far-renowned,
Like Indra with the Gods around.
Joy! joy! for vanquished are my foes:
Joy! for my house in glory grows,
With Raghu's noblest sons allied,
Supreme in strength and valour's pride.
To-morrow with its early light
Will shine on my completed rite.
Then, sanctioned by the saints and thee,
The marriage of thy Ráma see.'

Then Daśaratha, best of those
Whose speech in graceful order flows,
With gathered saints on every side,
Thus to the lord of earth replied:
'A truth is this I long have known,
A favour is the giver's own.
What thou shalt bid, O good and true,
We, as our power permits, will do.'

That answer of the truthful lord,
With virtuous worth and honour stored,
Janak, Videha's noble king,
Heard gladly, greatly marvelling.
With bosoms filled with pleasure met
Long-parted saint and anchoret,
And linked, in friendship's tie they spent
The peaceful night in great content.

Ráma and Lakshmaṇ thither sped,
By sainted Viśvámitra led,
And bent in filial love to greet
Their father, and embraced his feet.
The aged king, rejoiced to hear
And see again his children dear,
Honoured by Janak's thoughtful care,
With great enjoyment rested there.
King Janak, with attentive heed,
Consulted first his daughters' need,
And ordered all to speed the rite;
Then rested also for the night.

CANTO LXX.

THE MAIDENS SOUGHT.

Then with the morn's returning sun,
King Janak, when his rites were done,
Skilled all the charms of speech to know,
Spoke to wise Śatánanda so:
'My brother, lord of glorious fame,
My younger, Kuśadhwaj by name,
Whose virtuous life has won renown,
Has settled in a lovely town,
Sánkáśyá, decked with grace divine,
Whose glories bright as Pushpak's shine,
While Ikshumatí rolls her wave
Her lofty rampart's foot to lave.
Him, holy priest, I long to see:
The guardian of my rite is he:
That my dear brother may not miss
A share of mine expected bliss.'

Thus in the presence of the priest
The royal Janak spoke, and ceased.
Then came his henchmen, prompt and brave,

To whom his charge the monarch gave.
Soon as they heard his will, in haste
With fleetest steeds away they raced,
To lead with them that lord of kings,
As Indra's call Lord Vishṇu brings.
Sánkáśyá's walls they duly gained,
And audience of the king obtained.
To him they told the news they brought
Of marvels past and Janak's thought.
Soon as the king the story knew
From those good envoys swift and true,
To Janak's wish he gave assent,
And swift to Mithilá he went.
He paid to Janak reverence due,
And holy Śatánanda too,
Then sate him on a glorious seat
For kings or Gods celestial meet.
Soon as the brothers, noble pair
Peerless in might, were seated there,
They gave the wise Sudáman, best
Of councillors, their high behest:
'Go, noble councillor,' they cried,
'And hither to our presence guide
Ikshváku's son, Ayodhyá's lord,
Invincible by foeman's sword,
With both his sons, each holy seer,
And every minister and peer.'
Sudáman to the palace flew,
And saw the mighty king who threw
Splendour on Raghu's splendid race,
Then bowed his head with seemly grace:
'O King, whose hand Ayodhyá sways,
My lord, whom Mithilá obeys,
Yearns with desire, if thou agree,
Thee with thy guide and priest to see.'
Soon as the councillor had ceased,
The king, with saint and peer and priest,
Sought, speeding through the palace gate,
The hall where Janak held his state.
There, with his nobles round him spread,
Thus to Videha's lord he said:
'Thou knowest, King, whose aid divine
Protects Ikshváku's royal line.
In every need, whate'er befall,
The saint Vaśishṭha speaks for all.
If Viśvámitra so allow,
And all the saints around me now,
The sage will speak, at my desire,
As order and the truth require.'
  Soon as the king his lips had stilled,
Up rose Vaśishṭha, speaker skilled,
And to Videha's lord began
In flowing words that holy man:
'From viewless Nature Brahmá rose,
No change, no end, no waste he knows.
A son had he Maríchi styled,
And Kaśyap was Maríchi's child.
From him Vivasvat sprang: from him
Manu whose fame shall ne'er be dim.
Manu, who life to mortals gave,
Begot Ikshváku good and brave.
First of Ayodhyá's kings was he,
Pride of her famous dynasty.
From him the glorious Kukshi sprang,
Whose fame through all the regions rang.
Rival of Kukshi's ancient fame,
His heir, the great Vikukshi, came,
His son was Váṇa, lord of might;
His Anaraṇya, strong to fight.
His son was Prithu, glorious name;
From him the good Triśanku came.
He left a son renowned afar,
Known by the name of Dhundhumár.
His son, who drove the mighty car,
Was Yuvanáśva, feared in war.
He passed away. Him followed then
His son Mándhátá, king of men.
His son was blest in high emprise,
Susandhi, fortunate and wise.
Two noble sons had he, to wit
Dhruvasandhi and Prasenajit.
Bharat was Dhruvasandhi's son,
And glorious fame that monarch won.
The warrior Asit he begot.
Asit had warfare, fierce and hot,
With rival kings in many a spot,
Haihayas, Tálajanghas styled,
And Śaśivindus, strong and wild.
Long time he strove, but forced to yield
Fled from his kingdom and the field.
With his two wives away he fled
Where high Himálaya lifts his head,
And, all his wealth and glory past,
He paid the dues of Fate at last.
The wives he left had both conceived—
So is the ancient tale believed—
One, of her rival's hopes afraid
Fell poison in her viands laid.
It chanced that Chyavan, Bhrigu's child,
Had wandered to that pathless wild,
And there Himálaya's lovely height
Detained him with a strange delight.
There came the other widowed queen,
With lotus eyes and beauteous mien,
Longing a noble son to bear,
And wooed the saint with earnest prayer.
When thus Kálindí,[1] fairest dame,
With reverent supplication came,
To her the holy sage replied:
'Born with the poison from thy side,
O happy Queen, shall spring ere long
An infant fortunate and strong.
Then weep no more, and check thy sighs,
Sweet lady of the lotus eyes.'
The queen, who loved her perished lord,
For meet reply, the saint adored,
And, of her husband long bereaved,
She bore a son by him conceived.
Because her rival mixed the bane

[1] A different lady from the Goddess of the Jumna who bears the same name.

To render her conception vain,
And fruit unripened to destroy,
Sagar[1] she called her darling boy
To Sagar Asamanj was heir :
Bright Anśumán his consort bare.
Anśumán's son, Dilípa famed,
Begot a son Bhagírath named.
From him the great Kakutstha rose :
From him came Raghu, feared by foes,
Of him sprang Purushádak bold,
Fierce hero of gigantic mould :
Kalmáshapáda's name he bore,
Because his feet were spotted o'er.[2]
From him came Śankan, and from him
Sudarśan, fair in face and limb.
From beautiful Sudarśan came
Prince Agnivarṇa, bright as flame.
His son was Śíghraga, for speed
Unmatched ; and Maru was his seed.
Praśuśruka was Maru's child :
His son was Ambarísha styled.
Nahush was Ambarísha's heir,
The mighty lord of regions fair :
Nahush begot Yayáti : he,
Nábhág of happy destiny.
Son of Nábhág was Aja : his,
The glorious Daśaratha is,
Whose noble children boast to be
Ráma and Lakshmaṇ, whom we see.
Thus do those kings of purest race
Their lineage from Ikshváku trace :
Their hero lives the right maintained,
Their lips with falsehood ne'er were stained.
In Ráma's and in Lakshmaṇ's name
Thy daughters as their wives I claim,
So shall in equal bands be tied
Each peerless youth with peerless bride.'

CANTO LXXI.

JANAK'S PEDIGREE.

Then to the saint supremely wise
King Janak spoke in suppliant guise :
'Deign, Hermit, with attentive ear,
My race's origin to hear.
When kings a daughter's hand bestow,
'Tis right their line and fame to show.
There was a king whose deeds and worth
Spread wide his name through heaven and earth,
Nimi, most virtuous e'en from youth,
The best of all who love the truth.
His son and heir was Mithi, and
His Janak, first who ruled this land.
He left a son Udávasu,
Blest with all virtues, good and true.
His son was Nandivardhan, dear
For pious heart and worth sincere.
His son Suketu, hero brave,
To Devarát, existence gave.
King Devarát, a royal sage,
For virtue, glory of the age,
Begot Vrihadratha ; and he
Begot, his worthy heir to be,
The splendid hero Mahábír
Who long in glory governed here.
His son was Sudhriti, a youth
Firm in his purpose, brave in sooth.
His son was Dhrisṭaketu, blest
With pious will and holy breast.
The fame of royal saint he won :
Haryaśva was his princely son.
Haryaśva's son was Maru, who
Begot Pratíndhak, wise and true.
Next Kírtiratha held the throne,
His son, for gentle virtues known.
Then followed Devamídha, then
Vibudh, Mahándhrak, kings of men.
Mahándhrak's son, of boundless might,
Was Kírtirát, who loved the right.
He passed away, a sainted king,
And Mahároma following
To Swarṇaromá left the state.
Then Hraśvaromá, good and great,
Succeeded, and to him a pair
Of sons his royal consort bare.
Elder of these I boast to be :
Brave Kuśadhwaj is next to me.[1]
Me then, the elder of the twain,
My sire anointed here to reign.
He bade me tend my brother well,
Then to the forest went to dwell.
He sought the heavens, and I sustained
The burden as by law ordained,
And noble Kuśadhwaj, the peer
Of Gods, I ever held most dear.
Then came Sánkáśyá's mighty lord,
Sudhanvá, threatening siege and sword.
And bade me swift on him bestow
Śiva's incomparable bow,

[1] This is another fanciful derivation, *Sa*—with, and *gara*—poison.

[2] *Purushádak* means a cannibal. First called *Kalmáshapáda* on account of his spotted feet he is said to have been turned into a cannibal for killing the son of Vaśishṭha.

[1] 'In the setting forth of these royal genealogies the Bengal recension varies but slightly from the Northern. The first six names of the genealogy of the Kings of Ayodhyá are partly theogonical and partly cosmogonical ; the other names are no doubt in accordance with tradition and deserve the same amount of credence as the ancient traditional genealogies of other nations.' GORRESIO.

And Sítá of the lotus eyes :
But I refused each peerless prize.
Then, host to host, we met the foes,
And fierce the din of battle rose.
Sudhanvá, foremost of his band,
Fell smitten by my single hand.
When thus Sánkásyá's lord was slain,
I sanctified, as laws ordain,
My brother in his stead to reign,
Thus are we brothers, Saint most high
The younger he, the elder I.
Now, mighty Sage, my spirit joys
To give these maidens to the boys.
Let Sítá be to Ráma tied,
And Urmilá be Lakshman's bride.
First give, O King, the gift of cows,
As dowry of each royal spouse,
Due offerings to the spirits pay,
And solemnize the wedding-day.
The moon to-night, O royal Sage,
In Maghá's[1] House takes harbourage ;
On the third night his rays benign
In second Phálguni[2] will shine :
Be that the day, with prosperous fate,
The nuptial rites to celebrate.'

CANTO LXXII.

THE GIFT OF KINE.

When royal Janak's words were done,
Joined with Vaśishṭha Kuśik's son,
The mighty sage began his speech :
'No mind may scan, no thought can reach
The glories of Ikshváku's line,
Or, great Videha's King, of thine :
None in the whole wide world may vie
With them in fame and honours high.
Well matched, I ween, in holy bands,
These peerless pairs will join their hands.
But hear me as I speak once more :
Thy brother, skilled in duty's lore,
Has at his home a royal pair
Of daughters most divinely fair.
I for the hands of these sweet two
For Bharat and Śatrughna sue,
Both princes of heroic mould,
Wise, fair of form, and lofty-souled.
All Daśaratha's sons, I ween,
Own each young grace of form and mien:
Brave as the Gods are they, nor yield
To the great Lords the worlds who shield.
By these, good Prince of merits high,
Ikshváku's house with thine ally.'

The suit the holy sage preferred,
With willing ear the monarch heard :
Vaśishṭha's lips the counsel praised :
Then spake the king with hands upraised :
'Now blest indeed my race I deem,
Which your high will, O Saints supreme,
With Daśaratha's house unites
In bonds of love and marriage rites.
So be it done. My nieces twain
Let Bharat and Śatrughna gain,
And the four youths the selfsame day
Four maiden hands in theirs shall lay.
No day so lucky may compare,
For marriage—so the wise declare—
With the last day of Phálguni
Ruled by the genial deity.'
Then with raised hands in reverence due
To those arch-saints he spoke anew :
'I am your pupil, ever true :
To me high favour have ye shown ;
Come, sit ye on my royal throne,
For Daśaratha rules these towers
E'en as Ayodhyá now is ours.
Do with your own whate'er ye choose :
Your lordship here will none refuse.'

He spoke, and to Videha's king
Thus Daśaratha, answering:
'Boundless your virtues, lords, whose sway
The realms of Mithilá obey.
With honouring care you entertain
Both holy sage and royal train.
Now to my house my steps I bend—
May blessings still on you at end—
Due offerings to the shades to pay.'
Thus spoke the king, and turned away :
To Janak first he bade adieu,
Then followed fast those holy two.
The monarch reached his palace where
The rites were paid with solemn care.
When the next sun began to shine
He rose and made his gift of kine.
A hundred thousand cows prepared
For each young prince the Bráhmans shared.
Each had her horns adorned with gold ;
And duly was the number told,
Four hundred thousand perfect tale:
Each brought a calf, each filled a pail.
And when that glorious task was o'er,
The monarch with his children four,
Showed like the Lord of Life divine
When the worlds' guardians round him shine.

[1] The tenth of the lunar asterisms, composed of five stars.

[2] There are two lunar asterisms of this name, one following the other immediately, forming the eleventh and twelfth of the lunar mansions.

CANTO LXXIII.

THE NUPTIALS.

On that same day that saw the king
His gift of kine distributing,
The lord of Kekaya's son, by name
Yudhájit, Bharat's uncle, came,
Asked of the monarch's health, and then
Addressed the reverend king of men:
'The lord of Kekaya's realm by me
Sends greeting, noble King, to thee:
Asks if the friends thy prayers would bless
Uninterrupted health possess.
Right anxious, mighty King, is he
My sister's princely boy to see.
For this I sought Ayodhyá fair
The message of my sire to bear.
There learning, O my liege, that thou
With sons and noble kinsmen now
Wast resting here, I sought the place
Longing to see my nephew's face.'
The king with kind observance cheered
His friend by tender ties endeared,
And every choicest honour pressed
Upon his honourable guest.

That night with all his children spent,
At morn King Daśaratha went,
Behind Vaśishṭha and the rest,
To the fair ground for rites addressed.
Then when the lucky hour was nigh
Called Victory, of omen high,
Came Ráma, after vow and prayer
For nuptial bliss and fortune fair,
With the three youths in bright attire,
And stood beside his royal sire.
To Janak then Vaśishṭha sped,
And to Videha's monarch said:
'O King, Ayodhyá's ruler now
Has breathed the prayer and vowed the vow.
And with his sons expecting stands
The giver of the maidens' hands.
The giver and the taker both
Must ratify a mutual oath.
Perform the part for which we wait,
And rites of marriage celebrate.'

Skilled in the laws which Scriptures teach,
He answered thus Vaśishṭha's speech:
'O Saint, what warder bars the gate?
Whose bidding can the king await?
In one's own house what doubt is shown?
This kingdom, Sage, is all thine own.
E'en now the maidens may be found
Within the sacrificial ground:
Each vow is vowed and prayed each prayer,
And they, like fire, are shining there.
Here by the shrine my place I took
Expecting thee with eager look.
No bar the nuptial rites should stay:
What cause have we for more delay?'
When Janak's speech the monarch heard,
To sons and saints he gave the word,
And set them in the holy ring,
Then to Vaśishṭha spoke the king
Of Mithilá: 'O mighty Sage,
Now let this task thy care engage,
And lend thine aid and counsel wise
The nuptial rites to solemnize.'

The saint Vaśishṭha gave assent,
And quickly to the task he went,
With Viśvámitra, nothing loth,
And Śatánanda aiding both.
Then, as the rules prescribe, they made
An altar in the midst, and laid
Fresh wreaths of fragrant flowers thereon.
The golden ladles round it shone;
And many a vase, which branches hid
Fixed in the perforated lid,
And sprays, and cups, and censers there
Stood filled with incense rich and rare;
Shell-bowls, and spoons, and salvers dressed
With gifts that greet the honoured guest;
Piles of parched rice some dishes bore,
Others with corn prepared ran o'er;
And holy grass was duly spread
In equal lengths, while prayers were said.
Next chief of saints, Vaśishṭha came
And laid the offering in the flame.
Then by the hand King Janak drew
His Sítá, beautiful to view,
And placed her, bright in rich attire,
Ráma to face, before the fire,
Thus speaking to the royal boy
Who filled Kauśalyá's heart with joy:
'Here Sítá stands, my daughter fair,
The duties of thy life to share.
Take from her father, take thy bride;
Join hand to hand, and bliss betide!
A fathful wife, most blest is she,
And as thy shade will follow thee.'

Thus as he spoke the monarch threw
O'er her young limbs the holy dew,
While Gods and saints were heard to swell
The joyous cry, 'Tis well! 'Tis well!
His daughter Sítá thus bestowed,
O'er whom the sacred drops had flowed,
King Janak's heart with rapture glowed.
Then to Prince Lakshmaṇ thus he cried:
'Take Urmilá thine offered bride,
And clasp her hand within thine own
Ere yet the lucky hour be flown.'
Then to Prince Bharat thus cried he:
'Come, take the hand of Máṇḍaví.'
Then to Śatrughna: 'In thy grasp
The hand of Srutakírti clasp.
Now, Raghu's sons, may all of you
Be gentle to your wives and true;

Keep well the vows you make to-day,
Nor let occasion slip away.'

King Janak's word the youths obeyed;
The maidens' hands in theirs they laid.
Then with their brides the princes went
With ordered steps and reverent
Round both the fire and Janak, round
The sages and the sacred ground.

A flowery flood of lucid dyes
In rain descended from the skies,
While with celestial voices blent
Sweet strains from many an instrument,
And the nymphs danced in joyous throng
Responsive to the minstrel's song.
Such signs of exultation they
Saw on the princes' wedding-day.
Still rang the heavenly music's sound
When Raghu's sons thrice circled round
The fire, each one with reverent head,
And homeward then their brides they led.
They to the sumptuous palace hied
That Janak's care had seen supplied.
The monarch girt with saint and peer
Still fondly gazing followed near.

CANTO LXXIV.

RÁMA WITH THE AXE.[1]

Soon as the night had reached its close
The hermit Visvámitra rose;
To both the kings he bade adieu
And to the northern hill withdrew.
Ayodhyá's lord of high renown
Received farewell, and sought his town.
Then as each daughter left her bower
King Janak gave a splendid dower,
Rugs, precious silks, a warrior force,
Cars, elephants, and foot, and horse,
Divine to see and well arrayed;
And many a skilful tiring-maid,
And many a young and trusty slave
The father of the ladies gave.
Silver and coral, gold and pearls
He gave to his beloved girls.
These precious gifts the king bestowed
And sped his guest upon his road.
The lord of Mithilá's sweet town
Rode to his court and lighted down.

[1] This is another Ráma, son of Jamadagni, called Paraśuráma, or Ráma with the axe, from the weapon which he carried. He was while he lived the terror of the Warrior caste, and his name recalls long and fierce struggles between the sacerdotal and military order in which the latter suffered severely at the hands of their implacable enemy.

Ayodhyá's monarch, glad and gay,
Led by the seers pursued his way
With his dear sons of lofty mind:
The royal army marched behind.
As on he fared the voice he heard
Around of many a dismal bird,
And every beast in wild affright
Began to hurry to the right.
The monarch to Vaśishṭha cried:
'What strange misfortune will betide?
Why do the beasts in terror fly,
And birds of evil omen cry?
What is it shakes my heart with dread?
Why is my soul disquieted?'

Soon as he heard, the mighty saint
Thus answered Daśaratha's plaint
In sweetest tone: 'Now, Monarch, mark,
And learn from me the meaning dark.
The voices of the birds of air
Great peril to the host declare:
The moving beasts the dread allay,
So drive thy whelming fear away.'

As he and Daśaratha spoke
A tempest from the welkin broke,
That shook the spacious earth amain
And hurled high trees upon the plain.
The sun grew dark with murky cloud,
And o'er the skies was cast a shroud,
While o'er the army, faint with dread,
A veil of dust and ashes spread.
King, princes, saints their sense retained,
Fear-stupefied the rest remained.
At length, their wits returning, all
Beneath the gloom and ashy pall
Saw Jamadagni's son with dread,
His long hair twisted round his head,
Who, sprung from Bhrigu, loved to beat
The proudest kings beneath his feet.
Firm as Kailása's hill he showed,
Fierce as the fire of doom he glowed.
His axe upon his shoulder lay,
His bow was ready for the fray,
With thirsty arrows wont to fly
Like Lightnings from the angry sky.
A long keen arrow forth he drew,
Invincible like those which flew
From Śiva's ever-conquering bow
And Tripura in death laid low.

When his wild form, that struck with awe,
Fearful as ravening flame, they saw,
Vaśishṭha and the saints whose care
Was sacrifice and muttered prayer,
Drew close together, each to each,
And questioned thus with bated speech:
'Indignant at his father's fate
Will he on warriors vent his hate,
The slayers of his father slay,
And sweep the loathed race away?
But when of old his fury raged
Seas of their blood his wrath assuaged:

So doubtless now he has not planned
To slay all warriors in the land.'

Then with a gift the saints drew near
To Bhrigu's son whose look was fear,
And Ráma! Ráma! soft they cried.
The gift he took, no word replied.
Then Brigu's son his silence broke
And thus to Ráma Ráma spoke:

CANTO LXXV.

THE PARLE.

'Heroic Ráma, men proclaim
The marvels of thy matchless fame,
And I from loud-voiced rumour know
The exploit of the broken bow,
Yea, bent and broken, mighty Chief,
A feat most wondrous, past belief.
Stirred by thy fame thy face I sought:
A peerless bow I too have brought.
This mighty weapon, strong and dire,
Great Jamadagni owned, my sire.
Draw with its shaft my father's bow,
And thus thy might, O Ráma, show.
This proof of prowess let me see—
The weapon bent and drawn by thee;
Then single fight our strength shall try,
And this shall raise thy glory high.'

King Dasaratha heard with dread
The boastful speech, and thus he said;
Raising his hands in suppliant guise,
With pallid cheek and timid eyes:
'Forgetful of the bloody feud
Ascetic toils hast thou pursued;
Then, Bráhman, let my children be
Untroubled and from danger free.
Sprung of the race of Bhrigu, who
Read holy lore, to vows most true,
Thou swarest to the Thousand-eyed
And thy fierce axe was cast aside.
Thou turnedst to thy rites away
Leaving the earth to Kaśyap's sway,
And wentest far a grove to seek
Beneath Mahendra's[1] mountain peak.
Now, mighty Hermit, art thou here
To slay us all with doom severe?
For if alone my Ráma fall,
We share his fate and perish all.'

As thus the aged sire complained
The mighty chief no answer deigned.
To Ráma only thus he cried:
'Two bows, the Heavenly Artist's pride,
Celestial, peerless, vast, and strong,
By all the worlds were honoured long.
One to the Three-eyed God[1] was given,
By glory to the conflict driven,
Thus armed fierce Tripura he slew:
And then by thee 'twas burst in two.
The second bow, which few may brave,
The highest Gods to Vishṇu gave.
This bow I hold: before it fall
The foeman's fenced tower and wall.
Then prayed the Gods the Sire Most High
By some unerring proof to try
Were praise for might Lord Vishṇu's due,
Or his whose Neck is stained with Blue.[2]
The mighty Sire their wishes knew,
And he whose lips are ever true
Caused the two Gods to meet as foes.
Then fierce the rage of battle rose:
Bristled in dread each starting hair
As Śiva strove with Vishṇu there.
But Vishṇu raised his voice amain,
And Śiva's bowstring twanged in vain;
Its master of the Three bright Eyes
Stood fixt in fury and surprise.
Then all the dwellers in the sky,
Minstrel, and saint, and God drew nigh,
And prayed them that the strife might cease,
And the great rivals met in peace.
'Twas seen how Śiva's bow has failed
Unnerved, when Vishṇu's might assailed,
And Gods and heavenly sages thence
To Vishṇu gave preëminence.
Then glorious Śiva in his rage
Gave it to Devarát the sage
Who ruled Videha's fertile land,
To pass it down from hand to hand.
But this my bow, whose shafts smite down
The foeman's fenced tower and town.
To great Richíka Vishṇu lent
To be a pledge and ornament.
Then Jamadagni, Bráhman dread,
My sire, the bow inherited.
But Arjun stooped to treachery vile
And slew my noble sire by guile,
Whose penance awful strength had gained,
Whose hand the God-given bow retained.

---

[1] 'The author of the *Raghuvanśa* places the mountain Mahendra in the territory of the king of the Kalingans, whose palace commanded a view of the ocean. It is well known that the country along the coast to the south of the mouths of the Ganges was the seat of this people. Hence it may be suspected that this Mahendra is what Pliny calls "promontorium Calingon." The modern name *Cape Palmyras*, from the palmyras (Borassus flabelliformis) which abound there agrees remarkably with the description of the poet who speaks of the groves of these trees. *Raghuvanśa*, VI. 51.' SCHLEGEL.

[1] Śiva

[2] Śiva, God of the Azure Neck.

I heard indignant how he fell
By mournful fate, too sad to tell.
My vengeful fury since that time
Scourges all Warriors for the crime.
As generations spring to life
I war them down in endless strife.
All earth I brought beneath my sway,
And gave it for his meed and pay
To holy Kaśyap, when of yore
The rites performed by him were o'er.
Then to Mahendra's hill I turned
Strong in the strength that penance earned,
And toiled upon his lofty head
By Gods immortal visited.
The breaking of the bow I knew
From startled Gods conversing, through
The airy regions, of thy deed,
And hither came with swiftest speed.
Now, for thy Warrior's honour sake,
This best of bows, O Ráma, take:
This, owned by Vishnu's self of old,
My sire and grandsire loved to hold.
Drawn to its head upon the string
One town-destroying arrow bring;
If this thou can, O hero, I
In single fight thy strength will try.'

CANTO LXXVI.

DEBARRED FROM HEAVEN.

The haughty challenge, undeterred
The son of Daśaratha heard,
And cried, while reverence for his sire
Checked the full torrent of his ire:
'Before this day have I been told
The deed that stained thy hands of old.
But pity bids my soul forget:
Thy father, murdered, claimed the debt.
My strength, O Chief, thou deemest slight,
Too feeble for a Warrior's might.
Now will I show thy wondering eyes
The prowess which they dare despise.'

He hastened then with graceful ease
That mighty bow and shaft to seize.
His hand the weapon strung and swayed:
The arrow on the string was laid.
Then Jamadagni's son he eyed,
And thus in words of fury cried:
'Thou art a Bráhman, still to be
Most highly honoured, Chief, by me.
For Viśvámitra's sake beside
Shall reverence due be ne'er denied.
Though mine the power, I would not send
A dart at thee thy life to end.
But thy great power to wander free,
Which penance-rites have won for thee,
Or glorious worlds from thee to wrest,
Is the firm purpose of my breast.
And Vishnu's dart which now I strain
Can ne'er be shot to fall in vain:
It strikes the mighty, and it stuns
The madness of the haughty ones.'

Then Gods, and saints and heavenly choir
Preceded by the General Sire,
Met in the air and gazed below
On Ráma with that wondrous bow.
Nymph, minstrel, angel, all were there,
Snake-God, and spirit of the air,
Giant, and bard, and gryphon, met,
Their eyes upon the marvel set.
In senseless hush the world was chained
While Ráma's hand the bow retained.
And Jamadagni's son amazed
And powerless on the hero gazed.
Then when his swelling heart had shrunk,
And his proud strength in torpor sunk,
Scarce his voice ventured, low and weak,
To Ráma lotus-eyed, to speak:
'When long ago I gave away
The whole broad land to Kaśyap's sway,
He charged me never to remain
Within the limits of his reign.
Obedient to my guide's behest
On earth by night I never rest.
My choice is made. I will not dim
Mine honour and be false to him.
So, son of Raghu, leave me still
The power to wander where I will,
And swifter than the thought my flight
Shall place me on Mahendra's height.
My mansions of eternal joy,
By penance won, thou mayst destroy.
My path to these thy shaft may stay.
Now to the work! No more delay!
I know thee Lord of Gods; I know
Thy changeless might laid Madhu low.
All other hands would surely fail
To bend this bow. All hail! all hail!
See! all the Gods have left the skies
To bend on thee their eager eyes,
With whose achievements none compete,
Whose arm in war no God can meet.
No shame is mine, I ween, for thou,
Lord of the Worlds, hast dimmed my brow.
Now, pious Ráma, 'tis thy part
To shoot afar that glorious dart:
I, when the fatal shaft is shot,
Will seek that hill and tarry not.'

He ceased. The wondrous arrow flew,
And Jamadagni's offspring knew
Those glorious worlds to him were barred,
Once gained by penance long and hard.
Then straight the airy quarters cleared,
And the mid regions bright appeared,
While Gods and saints unnumbered praised
Ráma, the mighty bow who raised.
And Jamadagni's son, o'erawed,
Extolled his name with highest laud,

With reverent steps around him strode,
Then hastened on his airy road.
Far from the sight of all he fled,
And rested on Mahendra's head.

CANTO LXXVII.

BHARAT'S DEPARTURE.

Then Ráma with a cheerful mind
The bow to Varun's hand resigned.
Due reverence to the saints he paid,
And thus addressed his sire dismayed:
'As Bhrigu's son is far from view,
Now let the host its march pursue,
And to Ayodhyá's town proceed
In four-fold bands, with thee to lead.'

King Daśaratha thus addressed
His lips to Ráma's forehead pressed,
And held him to his aged breast.
Rejoiced in sooth was he to know
That Bhrigu's son had parted so,
And hailed a second life begun
For him and his victorious son.
He urged the host to speed renewed,
And soon Ayodhyá's gates he viewed.
High o'er the roofs gay pennons played;
Tabour and drum loud music made;
Fresh water cooled the royal road,
And flowers in bright profusion glowed.
Glad crowds with garlands thronged the ways
Rejoicing on their king to gaze.
And all the town was bright and gay
Exulting in the festive day.
People and Bráhmans flocked to meet
Their monarch ere he gained the street.
The glorious king amid the throng
Rode with his glorious sons along,
And passed within his dear abode
That like Himálaya's mountain showed.
And there Kauśalyá, noble queen,
Sumitrá with her lovely mien,
Kaikeyí of the dainty waist,
And other dames his bowers who graced,
Stood in the palace side by side
And welcomed home each youthful bride:
Fair Sítá, lofty-fated dame,
Urmilá of the glorious fame,
And Kuśadhwaja's children fair,
With joyous greeting and with prayer,
As all in linen robes arrayed
With offerings at the altars prayed.
Due reverence paid to Gods above,
Each princess gave her soul to love,
And hidden in her inmost bower
Passed with her lord each blissful hour.
The royal youths, of spirit high,
With whom in valour none could vie,
Lived each within his palace bounds
Bright as Kuvera's pleasure-grounds,
With riches, troops of faithful friends,
And bliss that wedded life attends:
Brave princes, trained in warlike skill,
And duteous to their father's will.
At length the monarch called one morn
Prince Bharat, of Kaikeyí born,
And cried: 'My son, within our gates
Lord Yudhájit thine uncle waits.
The son of Kekaya's king is he,
And came, my child, to summon thee.'

Then Bharat for the road prepared,
And with Śatrughna forth he fared.
First to his sire he bade adieu,
Brave Ráma, and his mothers too.
Lord Yudhájit with joyful pride
Went forth, the brothers by his side,
And reached the city where he dwelt:
And mighty joy his father felt.

Ráma and Lakshman honoured still
Their godlike sire with duteous will.
Two constant guides for Ráma stood,
His father's wish, the people's good.
Attentive to the general weal
He thought and wrought to please and heal.
His mothers too he strove to please
With love and sonly courtesies.
At every time, in every spot,
His holy guides he ne'er forgot.
So for his virtues kind and true
Dearer and dearer Ráma grew.
To Daśaratha, Bráhmans, all
In town and country, great and small.
And Ráma by his darling's side
Saw many a blissful season glide,
Lodged in her soul, each thought on her,
Lover, and friend, and worshipper.
He loved her for his father's voice
Had given her and approved the choice:
He loved her for each charm she wore
And her sweet virtues more and more.
So he her lord and second life
Dwelt in the bosom of his wife,
In double form, that, e'en apart,
Each heart could commune free with heart.

Still grew that child of Janak's race,
More goddess-fair in form and face,
The loveliest wife that e'er was seen,
In mortal mould sweet Beauty's Queen.
Then shone the son Kauśalyá bore,
With this bright dame allied,
Like Vishṇu whom the Gods adore,
With Lakshmí by his side.

BOOK II.

CANTO I.

THE HEIR APPARENT.

So Bharat to his grandsire went
Obedient to the message sent,
And for his fond companion chose
Śatrughna slayer of his foes.[1]
There Bharat for a time remained
With love and honour entertained,
King Aśvapati's constant care,
Beloved as a son and heir.
Yet ever, as they lived at ease,
While all around combined to please,
The aged sire they left behind
Was present to each hero's mind.
Nor could the king's fond memory stray
From his brave children far away,
Dear Bharat and Śatrughna dear,
Each Varuṇ's match or Indra's peer.

To all the princes, young and brave,
His soul with fond affection clave;
Around his loving heart they clung
Like arms from his own body sprung.[2]
But best and noblest of the four,
Good as the God whom all adore,
Lord of all virtues, undefiled,
His darling was his eldest child.
For he was beautiful and strong,
From envy free, the foe of wrong,
With all his father's virtues blest,
And peerless in the world confessed.
With placid soul he softly spoke:
No harsh reply could taunts provoke.
He ever loved the good and sage
Revered for virtue and for age,
And when his martial tasks were o'er
Sate listening to their peaceful lore.
Wise, modest, pure, he honoured eld,
His lips from lying tales withheld;
Due reverence to the Bráhmans gave,
And ruled each passion like a slave.
Most tender, prompt at duty's call,
Loved by all men he loved them all.
Proud of the duties of his race,
With spirit meet for Warrior's place,
He strove to win by glorious deed,
Throned with the Gods, a priceless meed.
With him in speech and quick reply
Vrihaspati might hardly vie,
But never would his accents flow
For evil or for empty show.
In art and science duly trained,
His student vow he well maintained;
He learnt the lore for princes fit,
The Vedas and their Holy Writ,
And with his well-drawn bow at last
His mighty father's fame surpassed.
Of birth exalted, truthful, just,
With vigorous hand, with noble trust,
Well taught by aged twice-born men
Who gain and right could clearly ken,
Full well the claims and bounds he knew
Of duty, gain, and pleasure too:
Of memory keen, of ready tact,
In civil business prompt to act.
Reserved, his features ne'er disclosed
What counsel in his heart reposed.
All idle rage and mirth controlled,
He knew the times to give and hold,
Firm in his faith, of steadfast will,
He sought no wrong, he spoke no ill:
Not rashly swift, not idly slow,
His faults and others' keen to know.
Each merit, by his subtle sense;
He matched with proper recompense.
He knew the means that wealth provide,
And with keen eye expense could guide.
Wild elephants could he reclaim,
And mettled steeds could mount and tame.
No arm like his the bow could wield,
Or drive the chariot to the field.
Skilled to attack, to deal the blow,
Or lead a host against the foe:
Yea, e'en infuriate Gods would fear
To meet his arm in full career.
As the great sun in noontide blaze
Is glorious with his world of rays,
So Ráma with these virtues shone
Which all men loved to gaze upon.

The aged monarch fain would rest,
And said within his weary breast,
'Oh that I might, while living yet,
My Ráma o'er the kingdom set,
And see, before my course be run,
The hallowed drops anoint my son;
See all this spacious land obey,
From side to side, my first-born's sway,
And then, my life and joy complete,
Obtain in heaven a blissful seat!'
In him the monarch saw combined
The fairest form, the noblest mind,
And counselled how his son might share,
The throne with him as Regent Heir.
For fearful signs in earth and sky,
And weakness warned him death was nigh:
But Ráma to the world endeared
By every grace his bosom cheered,

[1] Śatrughna means slayer of foes, and the word is repeated as an intensive epithet.

[2] Alluding to the images of Vishṇu, which have four arms, the four princes being portions of the substance of that God.

The moon of every eye, whose ray
Drove all his grief and fear away.
So duty urged that hour to seize,
Himself, his realm, to bless and please.

From town and country, far and near,
He summoned people, prince, and peer.
To each he gave a meet abode,
And honoured all and gifts bestowed.
Then, splendid in his king's attire,
He viewed them, as the general Sire,
In glory of a God arrayed,
Looks on the creatures he has made.
But Kekaya's king he called not then
For haste, nor Janak, lord of men;
For after to each royal friend
The joyful tidings he would send.
Mid crowds from distant countries met
The king upon his throne was set;
Then honoured by the people, all
The rulers thronged into the hall.
On thrones assigned, each king in place
Looked silent on the monarch's face.
Then girt by lords of high renown
And throngs from hamlet and from town
He showed in regal pride,
As, honoured by the rediant band
Of blessed Gods that round him stand,
Lord Indra, Thousand-eyed.

CANTO II.

THE PEOPLE'S SPEECH.

Then to the full assembly bowed
The monarch, and addressed the crowd
With gracious speech, in accents loud
As heavenly drum or thunder-cloud:

'Needs not to you who know declare
How ever with paternal care
My fathers of Ikshváku's line
Have ruled the realm which now is mine.
I too have taught my feet to tread
The pathway of the mighty dead,
And with fond care that never slept
Have, as I could, my people kept.
So toiling still, and ne'er remiss
For all my people's weal and bliss,
Beneath the white umbrella's[1] shade,
Old age is come and strength decayed.
Thousands of years have o'er me flown,
And generations round me grown
And passed away. I crave at length
Repose and ease for broken strength.
Feeble and worn I scarce can bear
The ruler's toil, the judge's care,
With royal dignity, a weight
That tries the young and temperate.
I long to rest, my labour done,
And in my place to set my son,
If to the twice-born gathered here
My counsel wise and good appear.
For greater gifts than mine adorn
Ráma my son, my eldest-born.
Like Indra brave, before him fall
The foeman's cities, tower and wall.
Him prince of men for power and might,
The best maintainer of the right,
Fair as the moon when nothing bars
His glory close to Pushya's stars,
Him with to-morrow's light I fain
Would throne the consort of my reign.
A worthy lord for you, I ween,
Marked as her own by Fortune's Queen.
The triple world itself would be
Well ruled by such a king as he.
To such high bliss and happy fate
Will I the country dedicate,
And my sad heart will cease to grieve
If he the precious charge receive.
Thus is my careful plan matured,
Thus for myself is rest secured;
Lieges, approve the words I say,
Or point ye out some wiser way.
Devise your prudent plan. My mind
Is fondly to this thought inclined,
But men by keen debating move
Some middle course which all approve.'

The monarch ceased. In answer came
The joyous princes' glad acclaim.
So peacocks in the rain rejoice
And hail the cloud with lifted voice.
Murmurs of joy from thousands round
Shook the high palace with the sound.
Then when the gathered throng had learned
His will who right and gain discerned,
Peasant and townsman, priest and chief,
All met in consultation brief,
And soon agreed with one accord
Gave answer to their sovereign lord:
'King of the land, we know thee old:
Thousands of years have o'er thee rolled.
Ráma thy son, we pray, anoint,
And at thy side his place appoint.
Our gallant prince, so brave and strong,
Riding in royal state along,
Our eyes with joyful pride will see
Screened by the shade that shelters thee.'
Then spoke the king again, as though
Their hearts' true wish he sought to know:
'These prayers for Ráma's rule suggest
One question to my doubting breast.
This thing, I pray, with truth explain:
Why would ye, while I justly reign,
That he, mine eldest son, should bear
His part with me as ruling heir?'
Then all the people made reply,
Peasant and townsman, low and high:
'Each noblest gift of form and mind,

[1] Chief of the insignia of imperial dignity.

O Monarch, in thy son we find.
Do thou the godlike virtues hear
Which Ráma to our hearts endear.
So richly blest with graces, none
In all the earth excels thy son:
Nay, who to match with him may claim
In truth, in justice, and in fame?
True to his promise, gentle, kind,
Unenvious, of grateful mind,
Versed in the law and firm of soul,
He keeps each sense with strict control.
With duteous care he loves to sit
By Bráhmans skilled in Holy Writ.
Hence brightest glory, ne'er to end,
And matchless fame his youth attend.
Skilled in the use of spear and shield,
And arms which heavenly warriors wield,
Supreme in war, unconquered yet
By man, fiend, God in battle met,
Whene'er in pomp of war he goes
'Gainst town or city of the foes,
He ever comes with Lakshmaṇ back
Victorious from the fierce attack.
Returning homeward from afar
Borne on his elephant or car,
He ever to the townsmen bends
And greets them as beloved friends,
Asks how each son, each servant thrives,
How fare our pupils, offerings, wives;
And like a father bids us tell,
Each for himself, that all is well.
If pain or grief the city tries
His heart is swift to sympathize.
When festive scenes our thoughts employ
He like a father shares the joy.
High is the fate, O King, that gave
Thy Ráma born to bless and save,
With filial virtues fair and mild
Like Kaśyap old Maríchi's child.
Hence to the kingdom's distant ends
One general prayer for him ascends.
Each man in town and country prays
For Ráma's strength, health, length of days.
With hearts sincere, their wish the same,
The tender girl, the aged dame,
Subject and stranger, peasant, hind,
One thought impressed on every mind,
At evening and at dawning day
To all the Gods for Ráma pray.
Do thou, O King, of grace comply,
And hear the people's longing cry,
And let us on the throne by thee
The lotus-tinted Ráma see.
O thou who givest boons, attend;
A gracious ear, O Monarch, lend
And for our weal install,
Consenting to our earnest prayer,
Thy godlike Ráma Regent Heir,
Who seeks the good of all.'

CANTO III.

DAŚARATHA'S PRECEPTS.

The monarch with the prayer complied
Of suppliant hands, on every side
Uplifted like a lotus-bed:
And then these gracious words he said:
'Great joy and mighty fame are mine
Because your loving hearts incline,
In full assembly clearly shown,
To place my Ráma on the throne.'
Then to Vaśishṭha, standing near,
And Vámadeva loud and clear
The monarch spoke that all might hear:
''Tis pure and lovely Chaitra now
When flowers are sweet on every bough,
All needful things with haste prepare
That Ráma be appointed heir.'

Then burst the people's rapture out
In loud acclaim and joyful shout;
And when the tumult slowly ceased
The king addressed the holy priest:
'Give order, Saint, with watchful heed
For what the coming rite will need.
This day let all things ready wait
Mine eldest son to consecrate.'
Best of all men of second birth
Vaśishṭha heard the lord of earth,
And gave commandment to the bands
Of servitors with lifted hands
Who waited on their master's eye:
'Now by to-morrow's dawn supply
Rich gold and herbs and gems of price
And offerings for the sacrifice,
Wreaths of white flowers and roasted rice,
And oil and honey, separate;
New garments and a car of state,
An elephant with lucky signs,
A fourfold host in ordered lines,
The white umbrella, and a pair
Of chowries,[1] and a banner fair;
A hundred vases, row on row,
To shine like fire in splendid glow,
A tiger's mighty skin, a bull
With gilded horns most beautiful.
All these, at dawn of coming day,
Around the royal shrine array,
Where burns the fire's undying ray.
Each palace door, each city gate
With wreaths of sandal decorate,
And with the garlands' fragrant scent
Let clouds of incense-smoke be blent.
Let food of noble kind and taste
Be for a hundred thousand placed;
Fresh curds with streams of milk bedewed
To feed the Bráhman multitude.

[1] Whisks, usually made of the long tails of the Yak.

With care be all their wants supplied,
And mid the twice-born chiefs divide
Rich largess, with the early morn,
And oil and curds and roasted corn.
Soon as the sun has shown his light
Pronounce the prayer to bless the rite,
And then be all the Bráhmans called
And in their ordered seats installed.
Let all musicians skilled to play,
And dancing-girls in bright array
Stand ready in the second ring
Within the palace of the king.
Each honoured tree, each holy shrine
With leaves and flowery wreaths entwine,
And here and there beneath the shade
Be food prepared and presents laid.
Then brightly clad, in warlike guise,
With long swords girt upon their thighs,
Let soldiers of the nobler sort
March to the monarch's splendid court.'

Thus gave command the twice-born pair
To active servants stationed there,
Then hastened to the king and said
That all their task was duly sped.
The king to wise Sumantra spake:
'Now quick, my lord, thy chariot take,
And hither with thy swiftest speed
My son, my noble Ráma lead.'

Sumantra, ere the word was given,
His chariot from the court had driven,
And Ráma, best of all who ride
In cars, came sitting by his side.
The lords of men had hastened forth
From east and west and south and north,
Áryan and stranger, those who dwell
In the wild wood and on the fell,
And as the Gods to Indra, they
Showed honour to the king that day.

Like Vásav, when his glorious form
Is circled by the Gods of storm,
Girt in his hall by kings he saw
His car-borne Ráma near him draw,
Like him who rules the minstrel band
Of heaven;[1] whose valour filled the land,
Of mighty arm and stately pride
Like a wild elephant in stride,
As fair in face as that fair stone
Dear to the moon, of moonbeams grown,[2]
With noble gifts and grace that took
The hearts of all, and chained each look,
World-cheering as the Lord of Rain
When floods relieve the parching plain.
The father, as the son came nigh,
Gazed with an ever-thirstier eye.
Sumantra helped the prince alight
From the good chariot passing bright,
And as to meet his sire he went
Followed behind him reverent.
Then Ráma clomb, the king to seek,
That terrace like Kailása's peak,
And reached the presence of the king,
Sumantra closely following.
Before his father's face he came,
Raised suppliant hands and named his name,[1]
And bowing lowly as is meet
Paid reverence to the monarch's feet.
But soon as Dasaratha viewed
The prince in humble attitude,
He raised him by the hand in haste
And his beloved son embraced,
Then signed him to a glorious throne,
Gem-decked and golden, near his own.
Then Ráma, best of Raghu's line,
Made the fair seat with lustre shine,
As when the orient sun upsprings
And his pure beam on Meru flings.
The glory flashed on roof and wall,
And with strange sheen suffused the hall,
As when the moon's pure rays are sent
Through autumn's star-lit firmament.
Then swelled his breast with joy and pride
As his dear son the father eyed,
E'en as himself more fair arrayed
In some clear mirror's face displayed.
The aged monarch gazed awhile,
Then thus addressed him with a smile,
As Kaśyap, whom the worlds revere,
Speaks for the Lord of Gods to hear:
'O thou of all my sons most dear,
In virtue best, thy father's peer,
Child of my consort first in place,
Mine equal in her pride of race,
Because the people's hearts are bound
To thee by graces in thee found,
Be thou in Pushya's favouring hour
Made partner of my royal power.
I know that thou by nature's bent
Both modest art and excellent,
But though thy gifts no counsel need
My love suggests the friendly rede.
Mine own dear son, be modest still,
And rule each sense with earnest will.
Keep thou the evils far away
That spring from love and anger's sway.
Thy noble course alike pursue
In secret as in open view,
And every nerve, the love to gain
Of ministers and subjects, strain.
The happy prince who sees with pride
His thriving people satisfied;
Whose arsenals with arms are stored,
And treasury with golden hoard,—

[1] Chitraratha, King of the Gandharvas.

[2] The Chandrakánta or Moonstone, a sort of crystal supposed to be composed of congealed moonbeams.

[1] A customary mark of respect to a superior.

His friends rejoice as joyed the Blest
When Amrit crowned their eager quest.
So well, my child, thy course maintain,
And from all ill thy soul refrain.'

The friends of Ráma, gathered nigh,
Longing their lord to gratify.
Ran to Kausalyá's bower to tell
The tidings that would please her well.
She, best of dames, with many a gem,
And gold, and kine rewarded them.

Then Ráma paid the reverence due,
Mounted the chariot, and withdrew,
And to his splendid dwelling drove
While crowds to show him honour strove.
The people, when the monarch's speech
Their willing ears had heard,
Were wild with joy as though on each
Great gifts had been conferred.
With meek and low salute each man
Turned to his home away,
And there with happy heart began
To all the Gods to pray.

CANTO IV.

RÁMA SUMMONED.

The crowd dismissed, to high debate
The monarch called his peers of state,
And, counsel from their lips obtained,
Firm in his will his will explained:
'To-morrow with auspicious ray
The moon in Pushya's sign will stay;
Be that the time with happy fate
Mine eldest son to consecrate,
And let my Ráma, lotus-eyed,
As Regent o'er the state preside.'

He sought, within, his charioteer,
And cried 'Again bring Ráma here.'
To Ráma's home Sumantra hied
Again to be the prince's guide.
His coming, told to Ráma's ear,
Suggested anxious doubt and fear.
He bade the messenger be led
That instant in, and thus he said:
'Tell me the cause, omitting naught,
Why thou again my house hast sought.'

The envoy answered: 'Prince, thy sire
Has sent thy presence to require.
My sender known, 'tis thine to say
If thou wilt go or answer nay.'
Then Ráma, when he heard his speech,
Made haste the royal court to reach.
Soon as the monarch was aware
His dearest son was waiting there,
Eager the parley to begin
He bade them lead the prince within.
Soon as he passed the chamber door
The hero bent him to the floor,
And at a distance from his seat
Raised his joined hands his sire to greet.
The monarch raised him from the ground,
And loving arms about him wound,
Then pointed to a seat that shone
With gold for him to rest upon.
'Aged am I,' he said, 'and worn;
In life's best joys my share have borne;
Rites to the Gods, in hundreds, paid,
With gifts of corn and largess made.
I yearned for sons: my life is blest
With them and thee of sons the best.
No debt to saints or Bráhamans, no,
Nor spirits, Gods, or self I owe.
One duty now remains alone,
To set thee on thy father's throne.
Now therefore, Ráma, hear my rede,
And mark my words with duteous heed:
This day the peoples' general voice,
Elects thee king of love and choice,
And I, consenting to the prayer,
Will make thee, darling, Regent Heir.
Dread visions, each returning night,
With evil omens scare my sight.
Red meteors with a fearful sound
Shoot wildly downward to the ground,
While tempests lash the troubled air;
And they who read the stars declare
That, leagued against my natal sign,
Ráhu,[1] the Sun,[2] and Mars combine.
When portents dire as these appear,
A monarch's death or woe is near.
Then while my senses yet are spared,
And thought and will are unimpaired,
Be thou, my son, anointed king:
Men's fancy is a fickle thing.
To-day the moon, in order due,
Entered the sign Punarvasu,[3]
To-morrow, as the wise foretell,
In Pushya's favouring stars will dwell:
Then on the throne shalt thou be placed:
My soul, prophetic, counsels haste:
Thee, O my son, to-morrow I
As Regent Heir will sanctify.
So till the coming night be passed
Do thou and Sítá strictly fast:
From worldly thoughts thy soul refrain,
And couched on holy grass remain.

[1] Ráhu, the ascending node, is in mythology a demon with the tail of a dragon whose head was severed from his body by Vishṇu, but being immortal, the head and tail retained their separate existence and being transferred to the stellar sphere became the authors of eclipses; the first especially by endeavouring to swallow the sun and moon.

[2] In eclipse.

[3] The seventh of the lunar asterisms.

And let thy trusted lords attend
In careful watch upon their friend.
For, unexpected, check and bar
Our weightiest counsels often mar.
While Bharat too is far away
Making with royal kin his stay,
I deem the fittest time of all
Thee, chosen Regent, to install.
It may be Bharat still has stood
True to the counsels of the good,
Faithful to thee with tender trust,
With governed senses, pure and just.
But human minds, too well I know,
Will sudden changes undergo,
And by their constant deeds alone
The virtue of the good is shown.
Now, Ráma, go. My son, good night!
Fixt is to-morrow for the rite.'

Then Ráma paid the reverence due,
And quickly to his home withdrew.
He passed within, nor lingered there,
But sought his mother's mansion, where
The dame in linen robes arrayed
Devoutly in the chapel prayed
To Fortune's Queen, with utterance checked,
That she her Ráma would protect.
There was Sumitrá too, and there
Was Lakshmaṇ led by loving care:
And when the royal choice they knew
Sítá in haste was summoned too.
Absorbed, with half-shut eyes, the queen
Attended by the three was seen.
She knew that Pushya's lucky hour
Would raise her son to royal power,
So fixed with bated breath each thought
On God supreme, by all men sought.
To her, as thus she knelt and prayed,
Ráma drew near, due reverence paid,
And then to swell his mother's joy,
Thus spoke her own beloved boy:
'O mother dear, my sire's decree
Entrusts the people's weal to me.
To-morrow I, for so his will,
Anointed king, the throne shall fill.
The few last hours till night shall end
Sítá with me must fasting spend,
For so my father has decreed,
And holy priests with him agreed.
What vows soever thou mayst deem
My consecration's eve beseem,
Do thou, sweet mother, for my sake
And for beloved Sítá's make.'

When the glad news Kauśalyá heard,
So long desired, so long deferred,
While tears of joy her utterance broke,
In answer to her son she spoke:
'Long be thy life, my darling: now
Thy prostrate foes before thee bow.
Live long and with thy bright success
My friends and dear Sumitrá's bless.
Surely the stars were wondrous fair
When thee, sweet son, thy mother bare,
That thy good gifts such love inspire
And win the favour of thy sire.
With thee I travailed not in vain;
Those lotus eyes reward my pain,
And all the glory of the line
Of old Ikshváku will be thine.'

He smiled, and on his brother gazed
Who sate with reverent hands upraised,
And said: 'My brother, thou must be
Joint-ruler of this land with me.
My second self thou, Lakshmaṇ, art,
And in my fortune bearest part.
Be thine, Sumitrá's son, to know
The joys from regal power that flow.
My life itself, the monarch's seat,
For thy dear sake to me are sweet.'

Thus Ráma to his brother said,
To both his mothers[1] bowed his head,
And then with Sítá by his side
To his own house the hero hied.

CANTO V.

RÁMA'S FAST.

Then Saint Vaśishṭha to the king
Came ready at his summoning.
'Now go,' exclaimed the monarch, thou
Enriched by fervent rite and vow,
For Ráma and his wife ordain
The fast, that joy may bless his reign.'

The best of those who Scripture know
Said to the king, 'My lord, I go.'
To Ráma's house Vaśishṭha hied,
The hero's fast by rule to guide,
And skilled in sacred texts to tell
Each step to him instructed well.
Straight to Prince Ráma's high abode,
That like a cloud pale-tinted showed,
Borne in his priestly car he rode.
Two courts he passed, and in the third
He stayed his car. Then Ráma heard
The holy sage was come, and flew
To honour him with honour due.
He hastened to the car and lent
His hand to aid the priest's descent.
Then spoke Vaśishṭha words like these,
Pleased with his reverent courtesies,
With pleasant things his heart to cheer
Who best deserved glad news to hear:
'Prince, thou hast won thy father's grace,
And thine will be the Regent's place:
Now with thy Sítá, as is right,
In strictest fasting spend the night,

[1] Kauśalyá and Sumitrá.

For when the morrow's dawn is fair
The king will consecrate his heir:
So Nahush,[1] as the wise relate,
Yayáti joyed to consecrate.'

Thus having said, Vaśishṭha next
Ordained the fast by rule and text,
For Ráma faithful to his vows
And the Videhan dame his spouse.
Then from the prince's house he hied
With courteous honours gratified.
Round Ráma gathered every friend
In pleasant talk a while to spend.
He bade good night to all at last,
And to his inner chamber passed.
Then Ráma's house shone bright and gay
With men and maids in glad array,
As in the morning some fair lake
When all her lotuses awake,
And every bird that loves the flood
Flits joyous round each opening bud.

Forth from the house Vaśishṭha drove,
That with the king's in splendour strove,
And all the royal street he viewed
Filled with a mighty multitude
The eager concourse blocked each square,
Each road and lane and thoroughfare,
And joyous shouts on every side
Rose like the roar of Ocean's tide,
As streams of men together came
With loud huzza and glad acclaim.
The ways were watered, swept and clean,
And decked with flowers and garlands green
And all Ayodhyá shone arrayed
With banners on the roofs that played.
Men, women, boys with eager eyes,
Expecting when the sun should rise,
Stood longing for the herald ray
Of Ráma's consecration-day,
To see, a source of joy to all,
The people-honoured festival.

The priest advancing slowly through
The mighty crowd he cleft in two,
Near to the monarch's palace drew.
He sought the terrace, by the stair,
Like a white cloud-peak high in air,
The reverend king of men to meet
Who sate upon his splendid seat:
Thus will Vrihaspati arise
To meet the monarch of the skies.
But when the king his coming knew,
He left his throne and near him drew.
Questioned by him Vaśishṭha said
That all his task was duly sped.
Then all who sate there, honouring
Vaśishṭha, rose as rose the king.
Vaśishṭha bade his lord adieu,
And all the peers, dismissed, withdrew.

Then as a royal lion seeks
His cave beneath the rocky peaks,
So to the chambers where abode
His consorts Daśaratha strode.
Full-thronged were those delightful bowers
With women richly dressed,
And splendid as the radiant towers
Where Indra loves to rest.
Then brighter flashed a thousand eyes
With the light his presence lent,
As, when the moon begins to rise,
The star thronged firmament.

CANTO VI.

THE CITY DECORATED.

Then Ráma bathed in order due,
His mind from worldly thoughts withdrew,
And with his large-eyed wife besought
Náráyan, as a votary ought.
Upon his head the brimming cup
Of holy oil he lifted up,
Then placed within the kindled fire
The offering to that heavenly Sire,
And as he sipped the remnant prayed
To Him for blessing and for aid.
Then with still lips and tranquil mind
With his Videhan he reclined,
In Vishṇu's chapel, on a bed
Where holy grass was duly spread,
While still the prince's every thought
The God supreme, Náráyan, sought.
One watch remained the night to close
When Ráma from his couch arose,
And bade the men and maids adorn
His palace for the solemn morn.
He heard the bards and heralds raise
Auspicious strains of joy and praise;
And breathed devout, with voice restrained,
The hymn for morning rites ordained;
Then, with his head in reverence bowed,
Praised Madhu's conquering foe aloud,
And, in pure linen robes arrayed,
The priests to raise their voices prayed.
Obedient to the summons they
Proclaimed to all the festal day.
The Bráhmans' voices, deep and sweet,
Resounded through the crowded street,
And echoed through Ayodhyá went
By many a loud-toned instrument.
Then all the people joyed to hear
That Ráma with his consort dear
Had fasted till the morning light
In preparation for the rite.
Swiftly the joyful tidings through
Ayodhyá's crowded city flew,
And soon as dawn appeared, each man
To decorate the town began.

[1] A king of the Lunar race, and father of Yayáti.

In all the temples bright and fair
As white clouds towering in the air,
In streets, and where the cross-ways met,
Where holy fig-trees had been set,
In open square, in sacred shade,
Where merchants' shops their wealth displayed,
On all the mansions of the great,
And householders of wealth and state,
Where'er the people loved to meet,
Where'er a tree adorned the street,
Gay banners floated to the wind,
And ribands round the staves were twined.
Then clear the singers' voices rang,
As, charming mind and ear, they sang.
Here players shone in bright attire,
There dancing women swelled the quire.
Each with his friend had much to say
Of Ráma's consecration-day;
Yea, even children, as they played
At cottage doors beneath the shade.
The royal street with flowers was strown
Which loving hands in heaps had thrown,
And here and there rich incense lent
Its fragrance to the garland's scent;
And all was fresh and fair and bright
In honour of the coming rite.
With careful foresight to illume
With borrowed blaze the midnight gloom,
The crowds erected here and there
Trees in each street gay lamps to bear.
The city thus from side to side
In festal guise was beautified.
The people of the town who longed
To view the rite together thronged,
And filling every court and square
Praised the good king in converse there:
'Our high-souled king! He throws a grace
On old Ikshváku's royal race.
He feels his years' increasing weight,
And makes his son associate.
Great joy to us the choice will bring
Of Ráma for our lord and king.
The good and bad to him are known,
And long will he protect his own.
No pride his prudent breast may swell,
Most just, he loves his brothers well,
And to us all that love extends,
Cherished as brothers and as friends.
Long may our lord in life remain,
Good Daśaratha, free from stain,
By whose most gracious favour we
Ráma anointed king shall see.'
Such were the words the townsmen spoke
Heard by the gathering countryfolk,
Who from the south, north, east, and west,
Stirred by the joyful tidings, pressed.
For by their eager longing led
To Ráma's consecration sped
The villagers from every side,
And filled Ayodhyá's city wide.
This way and that way strayed the crowd,
While rose a murmur long and loud,
As when the full moon floods the skies
And Ocean's waves with thunder rise.
That town, like Indra's city fair,
While peasants thronged her ways,
Tumultuous roared like Ocean, where
Each flood-born monster plays.

CANTO VII.

MANTHARÁ'S LAMENT.

It chanced a slave-born handmaid, bred
With Queen Kaikeyí, fancy-led,
Mounted the stair and stood upon
The terrace like the moon that shone.
Thence Manthará at ease surveyed
Ayodhyá to her eyes displayed,
Where water cooled the royal street,
Where heaps of flowers were fresh and sweet,
And costly flags and pennons hung
On roof and tower their shadow flung;
With covered ways prepared in haste,
And many an awning newly placed;
With sandal-scented streams bedewed,
Thronged by a new bathed multitude:
Whose streets were full of Bráhman bands
With wreaths and sweetmeats in their hands.
Loud instruments their music raised,
And through the town, where'er she gazed,
The doors of temples glittered white,
And the maid marvelled at the sight.
Of Ráma's nurse who, standing by,
Gazed with a joy-expanded eye,
In robes of purest white attired,
The wondering damsel thus inquired:
'Does Ráma's mother give away
Rich largess to the crowds to-day,
On some dear object fondly bent,
Or blest with measureless content?
What mean these signs of rare delight
On every side that meet my sight?
Say, will the king with joy elate
Some happy triumph celebrate?'
The nurse, with transport uncontrolled,
Her glad tale to the hump-back told:
'Our lord the king to-morrow morn
Will consecrate his eldest-born,
And raise, in Pushya's favouring hour,
Prince Ráma to the royal power.'
As thus the nurse her tidings spoke,
Rage in the hump-back's breast awoke.
Down from the terrace, like the head
Of high Kailása's hill, she sped.
Sin in her thoughts, her soul aflame,
Where Queen Kaikeyí slept, she came:

'Why sleepest thou?' she cried, 'arise,
Peril is near, unclose thine eyes.
Ah, heedless Queen, too blind to know
What floods of sin above thee flow!
Thy boasts of love and grace are o'er:
Thine is the show and nothing more.
His favour is an empty cheat,
A torrent dried by summer's heat.'

Thus by the artful maid addressed
In cruel words from raging breast,
The queen, sore troubled, spoke in turn;
'What evil news have I to learn?
That mournful eye, that altered cheek
Of sudden woe or danger speak.'

Such were the words Kaikeyí said:
Then Manthará, her eyeballs red
With fury, skilled with treacherous art
To grieve yet more her lady's heart,
From Ráma, in her wicked hate,
Kaikeyí's love to alienate,
Upon her evil purpose bent
Began again most eloquent:
'Peril awaits thee swift and sure,
And utter woe defying cure;
King Daśaratha will create
Prince Ráma Heir Associate.
Plunged in the depths of wild despair,
My soul a prey to pain and care,
As though the flames consumed me, zeal
Has brought me for my lady's weal,
Thy grief, my Queen, is grief to me:
Thy gain my greatest gain would be.
Proud daughter of a princely line,
The rights of consort queen are thine.
How art thou, born of royal race,
Blind to the crimes that kings debase?
Thy lord is gracious, to deceive,
And flatters, but thy soul to grieve,
While thy pure heart that thinks no sin
Knows not the snares that hem thee in.
Thy husband's lips on thee bestow
Soft soothing word, an empty show:
The wealth, the substance, and the power
This day will be Kauśalyá's dower.
With crafty soul thy child he sends
To dwell among thy distant friends,
And, every rival far from sight,
To Ráma gives the power and might.
Ah me! for thou, unhappy dame,
Deluded by a husband's name,
With more than mother's love hast pressed
A serpent to thy heedless breast,
And cherished him who works thee woe,
No husband but a deadly foe.
For like a snake, unconscious Queen,
Or enemy who stabs unseen,
King Daśaratha all untrue
Has dealt with thee and Bharat too.
Ah, simple lady, long beguiled
By his soft words who falsely smiled!
Poor victim of the guileless breast,
A happier fate thou meritest.
For thee and thine destruction waits
When he Prince Ráma consecrates.
Up, lady, while there yet is time;
Preserve thyself, prevent the crime.
Up, from thy careless ease, and free
Thyself, O Queen, thy son, and me!'

Delighted at the words she said,
Kaikeyí lifted from the bed,
Like autumn's moon, her radiant head,
And joyous at the tidings gave
A jewel to the hump-back slave;
And as she gave the precious toy
She cried in her exceeding joy:
'Take this, dear maiden, for thy news
Most grateful to mine ear, and choose
What grace beside most fitly may
The welcome messenger repay.
I joy that Ráma gains the throne:
Kauśalyá's son is as mine own.'

CANTO VIII.

MANTHARÁ'S SPEECH.

The damsel's breast with fury burned:
She answered, as the gift she spurned:
'What time, O simple Queen, is this
For idle dreams of fancied bliss?
Hast thou not sense thy state to know,
Engulfed in seas of whelming woe;
Sick as I am with grief and pain
My lips can scarce a laugh restrain
To see thee hail with ill-timed joy
A peril mighty to destroy.
I mourn for one so fondly blind:
What woman of a prudent mind
Would welcome, e'en as thou hast done,
The lordship of a rival's son,
Rejoiced to find her secret foe
Empowered, like death, to launch the blow;
I see that Ráma still must fear
Thy Bharat, to his throne too near.
Hence is my heart disquieted,
For those who fear are those we dread.
Lakshman, the mighty bow who draws,
With all his soul serves Ráma's cause;
And chains as strong to Bharat bind
Śatrughna, with his heart and mind,
Now next to Ráma, lady fair,
Thy Bharat is the lawful heir:
And far remote, I ween, the chance
That might the younger two advance.
Yes, Queen, 'tis Ráma that I dread,
Wise, prompt, in warlike science bred;
And oh, I tremble when I think
Of thy dear child on ruin's brink.

Blest with a lofty fate is she,
Kauśalyá; for her son will be
Placed, when the moon and Pushya meet,
By Bráhmans on the royal seat.
Thou as a slave in suppliant guise
Must wait upon Kauśalyá's eyes,
With all her wealth and bliss secured
And glorious from her foes assured.
Her slave with us who serve thee, thou
Wilt see thy son to Ráma bow,
And Sítá's friends exult o'er all,
While Bharat's wife shares Bharat's fall.'
As thus the maid in wrath complained,
Kaikeyí saw her heart was pained,
And answered eager in defence
Of Ráma's worth and excellence:
'Nay, Ráma, born the monarch's heir,
By holy fathers trained with care,
Virtuous, grateful, pure, and true,
Claims royal sway as rightly due.
He, like a sire, will long defend
Each brother, minister, and friend.
Then why, O hump-back, art thou pained
To hear that he the throne has gained?
Be sure when Ráma's empire ends,
The kingdom to my son descends,
Who, when a hundred years are flown,
Shall sit upon his fathers' throne.
Why is thine heart thus sad to see
The joy that is and long shall be,
This fortune by possession sure
And hopes which we may count secure?
Dear as the darling son I bore
Is Ráma, yea, or even more.
Most duteous to Kauśalyá, he
Is yet more dutiful to me.
What though he rule, we need not fear:
His brethren to his soul are dear.
And if the throne Prince Ráma fill
Bharat will share the empire still.'
She ceased. The troubled damsel sighed
Sighs long and hot, and thus replied:
'What madness has possessed thy mind,
To warnings deaf, to dangers blind?
Canst thou not see the floods of woe
That threaten o'er thine head to flow:
First Ráma will the throne acquire,
Then Ráma's son succeed his sire,
While Bharat will neglected pine
Excluded from the royal line.
Not all his sons, O lady fair,
The kingdom of a monarch share:
All ruling when a sovereign dies
Wild tumult in the state would rise.
The eldest, be he good or ill,
Is ruler by the father's will.
Know, tender mother, that thy son
Without a friend and all undone,
Far from the joyous ease of home
An alien from his race will roam.
I sped to thee for whom I feel,
But thy fond heart mistakes my zeal,
Thy hand a present would bestow
Because thy rival triumphs so.
When Ráma once begins his sway
Without a foe his will to stay,
Thy darling Bharat he will drive
To distant lands if left alive.
By thee the child was sent away
Beneath his grandsire's roof to stay.
Even in stocks and stones perforce
Will friendship spring from intercourse.
The young Śatrughna too would go
With Bharat, for he loved him so.
As Lakshman still to Ráma cleaves,
He his dear Bharat never leaves.
There is an ancient tale they tell:
A tree the foresters would fell
Was saved by reeds that round it stood,
For love that sprang of neighbourhood.
So Lakshman Ráma will defend,
And each on each for aid depend.
Such fame on earth their friendship wins
As that which binds the Heavenly Twins.
And Ráma ne'er will purpose wrong
To Lakshman, for their love is strong.
But Bharat, Oh, of this be sure,
Must evil at his hands endure.
Come, Ráma from his home expel
An exile in the woods to dwell.
The plan, O Queen, which I advise
Secures thy weal if thou be wise.
So we and all thy kith and kin
Advantage from thy gain shall win.
Shall Bharat, meet for happier fate,
Born to endure his rival's hate,
With all his fortune ruined cower
And dread his brother's mightier power?
Up, Queen, to save thy son, arise;
Prostrate at Ráma's feet he lies.
So the proud elephant who leads
His trooping consorts through the reeds
Falls in the forest shade beneath
The lion's spring and murderous teeth.
Scorned by thee in thy bliss and pride
Kauśalyá was of old defied,
And will she now forbear to show
The vengeful rancour of a foe?
O Queen, thy darling is undone
When Ráma's hand has once begun
Ayodhyá's realm to sway.
Come, win the kingdom for thy child
And drive the alien to the wild
In banishment to-day.'

CANTO IX.

THE PLOT.

As fury lit Kaikeyí's eyes
She spoke with long and burning sighs:

'This day my son enthroned shall see,
And Ráma to the woods shall flee.
But tell me, damsel, if thou can,
A certain way, a skilful plan
That Bharat may the empire gain,
And Ráma's hopes be nursed in vain.'

The lady ceased. The wicked maid
The mandate of her queen obeyed,
And darkly plotting Ráma's fall
Responded to Kaikeyí's call.

'I will declare, do thou attend,
How Bharat may his throne ascend.
Dost thou forget what things befell?
Or dost thou feign, remembering well?
Or wouldst thou hear my tongue repeat
A story for thy need so meet?
Gay lady, if thy will be so,
Now hear the tale of long ago,
And when my tongue has done its part
Ponder the story in thine heart.
When Gods and demons fought of old,
Thy lord, with royal saints enrolled,
Sped to the war with thee to bring
His might to aid the Immortals' King.
Far to the southern land he sped
Where Daṇḍaks mighty wilds are spread,
To Vaijayanta's city swayed
By Śambara, whose flag displayd
The hugest monster of the sea.
Lord of a hundred wiles was he;
With might which Gods could never blame
Against the King of Heaven he came.
Then raged the battle wild and dread,
And mortal warriors fought and bled;
The fiends by night with strength renewed
Charged, slew the sleeping multitude.
Thy lord, King Daśaratha, long
Stood fighting with the demon throng,
But long of arm, unmatched in strength,
Fell wounded by their darts at length.
Thy husband, senseless, by thine aid
Was from the battle field conveyed,
And wounded nigh to death thy lord
Was by thy care to health restored.
Well pleased the grateful monarch sware
To grant thy first and second prayer.
Thou for no favour then wouldst sue,
The gifts reserved for season due;
And he, thy high-souled lord, agreed
To give the boons when thou shouldst need.
Myself I knew not what befell,
But oft the tale have heard thee tell,
And close to thee in friendship knit
Deep in my heart have treasured it.
Remind thy husband of his oath,
Recall the boons and claim them both,
That Bharat on the throne be placed
With rites of consecration graced,
And Ráma to the woods be sent
For twice seven years of banishment.
Go, Queen, the mourner's chamber[1] seek,
With angry eye and burning cheek;
And with disordered robes and hair
On the cold earth lie prostrate there.
When the king comes still mournful lie,
Speak not a word nor meet his eye,
But let thy tears in torrent flow,
And lie enamoured of thy woe.
Well do I know thou long hast been,
And ever art, his darling queen.
For thy dear sake, O well-loved dame,
The mighty king would brave the flame,
But ne'er would anger thee, or brook
To meet his favourite's wrathful look.
Thy loving lord would even die
Thy fancy, Queen, to gratify,
And never could he arm his breast
To answer nay to thy request.
Listen and learn, O dull of sense,
Thine all-resistless, influence.
Gems he will offer, pearls and gold:
Refuse his gifts, be stern and cold.
Those proffered boons at length recall,
And claim them till he grants thee all.
And O my lady, high in bliss,
With heedful thought forget not this.
When from the ground his queen he lifts
And grants again the promised gifts,
Bind him with oaths he cannot break
And thy demands unflinching, make,
That Ráma travel to the wild
Five years and nine from home exiled,
And Bharat, best of all who reign,
The empire of the land obtain.
For when this term of years has fled
Over the banished Ráma's head,
Thy royal son to vigour grown
And rooted firm will stand alone.
The king, I know, is well inclined,
And this the hour to move his mind.
Be bold: the threatened rite prevent,
And force the king from his intent.'

She ceased. So counselled to her bane
Disguised beneath a show of gain,
Kaikeyí in her joy and pride
To Mantharā again replied:
'Thy sense I envy, prudent maid;
With sagest lore thy lids persuade.
No hump-back maid in all the earth,
For wise resolve, can match thy worth.
Thou art alone with constant zeal
Devoted to thy lady's weal.
Dear girl, without thy faithful aid
I had not marked the plot he laid.

---

[1] Literally *the chamber of wrath, a 'growlery,'* a small, dark, unfurnished room to which it seems, the wives and ladies of the king betook themselves when offended and sulky.

Full of all guile and sin and spite
Misshapen hump-backs shock the sight:
But thou art fair and formed to please,
Bent like a lily by the breeze.
I look thee o'er with watchful eye,
And in thy frame no fault can spy;
The chest so deep, the waist so trim,
So round the lines of breast and limb.[1]
Thy cheeks with moonlike beauty shine,
And the warm wealth of youth is thine.
Thy legs, my girl, are long and neat,
And somewhat long thy dainty feet,
While stepping out before my face
Thou seemest like a crane to pace.
The thousand wiles are in thy breast
Which Śambara the fiend possessed,
And countless others all thine own,
O damsel sage, to thee are known.
Thy very hump becomes thee too,
O thou whose face is fair to view,
For there reside in endless store
Plots, wizard wiles, and warrior lore.
A golden chain I'll round it fling
When Ráma's flight makes Bharat king:
Yea, polished links of finest gold,
When once the wished for prize I hold
With naught to fear and none to hate,
Thy hump, dear maid, shall decorate.
A golden frontlet wrought with care,
And precious jewels shalt thou wear:
Two lovely robes around thee fold,
And walk a Goddess to behold,
Bidding the moon himself compare
His beauty with a face so fair.
With scent of precious sandal sweet
Down to the nails upon thy feet,
First of the household thou shalt go
And pay with scorn each baffled foe.'
 Kaikeyí's praise the damsel heard,
And thus again her lady stirred,
Who lay upon her beauteous bed
Like fire upon the altar fed:
'Dear Queen, they build the bridge in vain
When swollen streams are dry again.
Arise, thy glorious task complete,
And draw the king to thy retreat.'
 The large-eyed lady left her bower
Exulting in her pride of power,
And with the hump-back sought the gloom
And silence of the mourner's room.
The string of priceless pearls that hung
Around her neck to earth she flung,
With all the wealth and lustre lent
By precious gem and ornament,
Then, listening to her slave's advice,
Lay, like a nymph from Paradise.
As on the ground her limbs she laid
Once more she cried unto the maid:
'Soon must thou to the monarch say
Kaikeyí's soul has past away,
Or, Ráma banished as we planned,
My son made king shall rule the land.
No more for gold and gems I care,
For brave attire or dainty fare.
If Ráma should the throne ascend,
That very hour my life will end.'
 The royal lady wounded through
The bosom with the darts that flew
 Launched from the hump-back's tongue
Pressed both her hands upon her side,
And o'er and o'er again she cried
 With wildering fury stung:
'Yes, it shall be thy task to tell
That I have hurried hence to dwell
 In Yama's realms of woe,
Or happy Bharat shall be king,
And doomed to years of wandering
 Kauśalyá's son shall go.
I heed not dainty viands now
Fair wreaths of flowers to twine my brow,
 Soft balm or precious scent:
My very life I count as naught,
Nothing on earth can claim my thought
 But Ráma's banishment.'
 She spoke these words of cruel ire;
Then stripping off her gay attire,
 The cold bare floor she pressed.
So, falling from her home on high,
Some lovely daughter of the sky
 Upon the ground might rest.
With darkened brow and furious mien,
Stripped of her gems and wreath, the queen
 In spotless beauty lay,
Like heaven obscured with gathering cloud,
When shades of midnight darkness shroud
 Each star's expiring ray.

CANTO X.

DAŚARATHA'S SPEECH.

As Queen Kaikeyí thus obeyed
The sinful counsel of her maid
She sank upon the chamber floor,
As sinks in anguish, wounded sore,
An elephant beneath the smart
Of the wild hunter's venomed dart.
The lovely lady in her mind
Revolved the plot her maid designed,
And prompt the gain and risk to scan
She step by step approved the plan.
Misguided by the hump-back's guile
She pondered her resolve awhile,
As the fair path that bliss secured
The miserable lady lured.

[1] In these four lines I do not translate faithfully, and I do not venture to follow Kaikeyí farther in her eulogy of the hump-back's charms.

Devoted to her queen, and swayed
By hopes of gain and bliss, the maid
Rejoiced her lady's purpose known,
And deemed the prize she sought her own.
Then bent upon her purpose dire,
Kaikeyí with her soul on fire,
Upon the floor lay, languid, down,
Her brows contracted in a frown.
The bright-hued wreath that bound her hair,
Chains, necklets, jewels rich and rare,
Stripped off by her own fingers lay
Spread on the ground in disarray,
And to the floor a lustre lent
As stars light up the firmament.
Thus prostrate in the mourner's cell,
In gerb of woe the lady fell,
Her long hair in a single braid,
Like some fair nymph of heaven dismayed.[1]

The monarch, Ráma to install,
With thoughtful care had ordered all,
And now within his home withdrew,
Dismissing first his retinue.
Now all the town has heard, thought he,
What joyful rite the morn will see,
So turned he to her bower to cheer
With the glad news his darling's ear.
Majestic, as the Lord of Night,
When threatened by the Dragon's might,
Bursts radiant on the evening sky
Pale with the clouds that wander by,
So Daśaratha, great in fame,
To Queen Kaikeyí's palace came.
There parrots flew from tree to tree,
And gorgeous peacocks wandered free,
While ever and anon was heard
The note of some glad water-bird.
Here loitered dwarf and hump-backed maid,
There lute and lyre sweet music played.
Here, rich in blossom, creepers twined
O'er grots with wondrous art designed,
There Champac and Aśoka flowers
Hung glorious o'er the summer bowers,
And mid the waving verdure rose
Gold, silver, ivory porticoes.
Through all the months in ceaseless store
The trees both fruit and blossom bore.
With many a lake the grounds were graced;
Seats, gold and silver, here were placed;
Here every viand wooed the taste.
It was a garden meet to vie
E'en with the home of Gods on high.
Within the mansion rich and vast
The mighty Daśaratha passed:
Not there was his beloved queen
On her fair couch reclining seen.
With love his eager pulses beat
For the dear wife he came to meet,
And in his blissful hopes deceived,
He sought his absent love and grieved.
For never had she missed the hour
Of meeting in her sumptuous bower,
And never had the king of men
Entered the empty room till then.
Still urged by love and anxious thought
News of his favourite queen he sought,
For never had his loving eyes
Found her or selfish or unwise.
Then spoke at length the warder maid,
With hands upraised and sore afraid:
'My Lord and King, the queen has sought
The mourner's cell with rage distraught.'

The words the warder maiden said
He heard with soul disquieted,
And thus as fiercer grief assailed,
His troubled senses wellnigh failed.
Consumed by torturing fires of grief
The king, the world's imperial chief,
His lady lying on the ground
In most unqueenly posture, found.
The aged king, all pure within,
Saw the young queen resolved on sin,
Low on the ground, his own sweet wife,
To him far dearer than his life,
Like some fair creeping plant uptorn,
Or like a maid of heaven forlorn,
A nymph of air or Goddess sent
From Swarga down in banishment.

As some wild elephant who tries
To soothe his consort as she lies
Struck by the hunter's venomed dart,
So the great king, disturbed in heart,
Strove with soft hand and fond caress
To soothe his darling queen's distress,
And in his love addressed with sighs
The lady of the lotus eyes:
'I know not, Queen, why thou shouldst be
Thus angered to the heart with me.
Say, who has slighted thee, or whence
Has come the cause of such offence
That in the dust thou liest low,
And rendest my fond heart with woe,
As if some goblin of the night
Had struck thee with a deadly blight,
And cast foul influence on her
Whose spells my loving bosom stir?
I have Physicians famed for skill,
Each trained to cure some special ill:
My sweetest lady, tell thy pain,
And they shall make thee well again.
Whom, darling, wouldst thou punished see?
Or whom enriched with lordly fee?

[1] These verses are evidently an interpolation. They contain nothing that has not been already related: the words only are altered. As the whole poem could not be recited at once, the rhapsodists at the beginning of a fresh recitation would naturally remind their hearers of the events immediately preceding.

Weep not, my lovely Queen, and stay
This grief that wears thy frame away.
Speak, and the guilty shall be freed,
The guiltless be condemned to bleed,
The poor enriched, the rich abased,
The low set high, the proud disgraced.
My lords and I thy will obey,
All slaves who own thy sovereign sway;
And I can ne'er my heart incline
To check in aught one wish of thine.
Now by my life I pray thee tell
The thoughts that in thy bosom dwell.
The power and might thou knowest well
Should from thy breast all doubt expel.
I swear by all my merit won,
Speak, and thy pleasure shall be done.
Far as the world's wide bounds extend
My glorious empire knows no end.
Mine are the tribes in eastern lands,
And those who dwell on Sindhu's sands:
Mine is Suráshṭra, far away,
Suvíra's realm admits my sway.
My hest the southern nations fear,
The Angas and the Vangas hear.
And as lord paramount I reign
O'er Magadh and the Matsyas' plain,
Kośal, and Káśí's wide domain:[1]
All rich in treasures of the mine,
In golden corn, sheep, goats, and kine.
Choose what thou wilt, Kaikeyí, thence:
But tell me, O my darling, whence
Arose thy grief, and it shall fly
Like hoar-frost when the sun is high.'

She, by his loving words consoled,
Longed her dire purpose to unfold,
And sought with sharper pangs to wring
The bosom of her lord the king.

CANTO XI.

THE QUEEN'S DEMAND.

To him enthralled by love, and blind,
Pierced by his darts who shakes the mind,[2]
Kaikeyí with remorseless breast
Her cruel purpose thus expressed:
'O King, no insult or neglect
Have I endured, or disrespect.
One wish I have, and fain would see
That longing granted, lord, by thee.
Now pledge thy word if thou incline
To listen to this prayer of mine,
Then I with confidence will speak,
And thou shalt hear the boon I seek.'

Ere she had ceased, the monarch fell
A victim to the lady's spell,
And to the deadly snare she set
Sprang, like a roebuck to the net.
Her lover raised her drooping head,
Smiled, playing with her hair, and said:
'Hast thou not learnt, wild dame, till now
That there is none so dear as thou
To me thy loving husband, save
My Ráma bravest of the brave?
By him my race's high-souled heir,
By him whom none can match, I swear,
Now speak the wish that on thee weighs:
By him whose right is length of days,
Whom if my fond paternal eye
Saw not one hour I needs must die,—
I swear by Ráma, my dear son,
Speak, and thy bidding shall be done.
Speak, darling; if thou choose, request
To have the heart from out my breast;
Regard my words, sweet love, and name
The wish thy mind thinks fit to frame.
Nor let thy soul give way to doubt:
My power should drive suspicion out.
Yea, by my merits won I swear,
Speak, darling, I will grant thy prayer.'

The queen, ambitious, overjoyed
To see him by her plot decoyed,
More eager still her aims to reach,
Spoke her abominable speech:
'A boon thou grantest, nothing loth,
And swearest with repeated oath.
Now let the thirty Gods and three
My witnesses, with Indra, be.
Let sun and moon and planets hear,
Heaven, quarters, day and night, give ear.
The mighty world, the earth outspread,
With bards of heaven and demons dread;
The ghosts that walk in midnight shade,
And household Gods, our present aid,
And every being great and small
To hear and mark the oath I call.'

When thus the archer king was bound
With treacherous arts and oaths enwound,
She to her bounteous lord subdued
By blinding love, her speech renewed:
'Remember, King, that long-past day
Of Gods' and demons' battle fray,
And how thy foe in doubtful strife
Had nigh bereft thee of thy life.
Remember, it was only I
Preserved thee when about to die,
And thou for watchful love and care
Wouldst grant my first and second prayer.
Those offered boons, pledged with thee then,
I now demand, O King of men,

[1] The *Śloka* or distich which I have been forced to expand into these nine lines is evidently spurious, but is found in all the commented MSS. which Schlegel consulted.

[2] Manmatha, Mind-disturber, a name of Káma or Love.

Of thee, O Monarch, good and just,
Whose righteous soul observes each trust.
If thou refuse thy promise sworn,
I die, despised, before the morn.
These rites in Ráma's name begun—
Transfer them, and enthrone my son.
The time is come to claim at last
That double boon of days long-past,
When Gods and demons met in fight,
And thou wouldst fain my care requite.
Now forth to Daṇḍak's forest drive
Thy Ráma for nine years and five,
And let him dwell a hermit there
With deerskin coat and matted hair.
Without a rival let my boy
The empire of the land enjoy,
And let mine eyes ere morning see
Thy Ráma to the forest flee.'

CANTO XII.

DAŚARATHA'S LAMENT.

The monarch, as Kaikeyí pressed
With cruel words her dire request,
Stood for a time absorbed in thought
While anguish in his bosom wrought.
'Does some wild dream my heart assail?
Or do my troubled senses fail?
Does some dire portent scare my view?
Or frenzy's stroke my soul subdue?'
Thus as he thought, his troubled mind
In doubt and dread no rest could find,
Distressed and trembling like a deer
Who sees the dreaded tigress near.
On the bare ground his limbs he threw,
And many a long deep sigh he drew,
Like a wild snake, with fury blind,
By charms within a ring confined.
Once as the monarch's fury woke,
'Shame on thee!' from his bosom broke,
And then in sense-bewildering pain
He fainted on the ground again.
At length, when slowly strength returned,
He answered as his eyeballs burned
With the wild fury of his ire
Consuming her, as 'twere, with fire:
'Fell traitress, thou whose thoughts design
The utter ruin of my line,
What wrong have I or Ráma done?
Speak murderess, speak thou wicked one,
Seeks he not evermore to please
Thee with all sonlike courtesies?
By what persuasion art thou led
To bring this ruin on his head?
Ah me, that fondly unaware
I brought thee home my life to snare,
Called daughter of a king, in truth
A serpent with a venomed tooth!
What fault can I pretend to find
In Ráma praised by all mankind,
That I my darling should forsake?
No, take my life, my glory take:
Let either queen be from me torn,
But not my well-loved eldest-born.
Him but to see is highest bliss,
And death itself his face to miss.
The world may sunless stand, the grain
May thrive without the genial rain,
But if my Ráma be not nigh
My spirit from its frame will fly.
Enough, thine impious plan forgo,
O thou who plottest sin and woe.
My head before thy feet, I kneel,
And pray thee some compassion feel.
O wicked dame, what can have led
Thy heart to dare a plot so dread?
Perchance thy purpose is to sound
The grace thy son with me has found;
Perchance the words that, all these days,
Thou still hast said in Ráma's praise,
Were only feigned, designed to cheer
With flatteries a father's ear.
Soon as thy grief, my Queen, I knew,
My bosom felt the anguish too.
In empty halls art thou possessed,
And subject to another's hest?
Now on Ikshváku's ancient race
Falls foul disorder and disgrace,
If thou, O Queen, whose heart so long
Has loved the good should choose the wrong.
Not once, O large-eyed dame, hast thou
Been guilty of offence till now,
Nor said a word to make me grieve,
Nor will I now thy sin believe.
With thee my Ráma used to hold
Like place with Bharat lofty-souled.
As thou so often, when the pair
Were children yet, wouldst fain declare.
And can thy righteous soul endure
That Ráma glorious, pious, pure,
Should to the distant wilds be sent
For fourteen years of banishment?
Yea, Ráma Bharat's self exceeds
In love to thee and sonlike deeds,
And, for deserving love of thee,
As Bharat, even so is he.
Who better than that chieftain may
Obedience, love, and honour pay,
Thy dignity with care protect,
Thy slightest word and wish respect?
Of all his countless followers none
Can breathe a word against my son;
Of many thousands not a dame
Can hint reproach or whisper blame.
All creatures feel the sweet control
Of Ráma's pure and gentle soul.
The pride of Manu's race he binds
To him the people's grateful minds.
He wins the subjects with his truth,

The poor with gifts and gentle ruth,
His teachers with his docile will,
The foemen with his archer skill.
Truth, purity, religious zeal,
The hand to give, the heart to feel,
The love that ne'er betrays a friend,
The rectitude that naught can bend,
Knowledge, and meek obedience grace
My Ráma pride of Raghu's race.
Canst thou thine impious plot design
'Gainst him in whom these virtues shine,
Whose glory with the sages vies,
Peer of the Gods who rule the skies?
From him no harsh or bitter word
To pain one creature have I heard,
And how can I my son address,
For thee, with words of bitterness?
Have mercy, Queen: some pity show
To see my tears of anguish flow,
And listen to my mournful cry,
A poor old man who soon must die.
Whate'er this sea-girt land can boast
Of rich and rare from coast to coast,
To thee, my Queen, I give it all:
But O, thy deadly words recall:
O see, my suppliant hands entreat,
Again my lips are on thy feet:
Save Ráma, save my darling child,
Nor kill me with this sin defiled.'
He grovelled on the ground, and lay
To burning grief a senseless prey,
And ever and anon, assailed
By floods of woe he wept and wailed,
Striving with eager speed to gain
The margent of his sea of pain.

With fiercer words she fiercer yet
The hapless father's pleading met:
'O Monarch, if thy soul repent
The promise and thy free consent,
How wilt thou in the world maintain
Thy fame for truth unsmirched with stain?
When gathered kings with thee converse,
And bid thee all the tale rehearse,
What wilt thou say, O truthful King,
In answer to their questioning?
'She to whose love my life I owe,
Who saved me smitten by the foe,
Kaikeyí, for her tender care,
Was cheated of the oath I sware.'
Thus wilt thou answer, and forsworn
Wilt draw on thee the princes' scorn.
Learn from that tale, the Hawk and Dove,[1]
How strong for truth was Saivya's love.
Pledged by his word the monarch gave
His flesh the suppliant bird to save.
So King Alarka gave his eyes,
And gained a mansion in the skies.
The Sea himself his promise keeps,
And ne'er beyond his limit sweeps.
My deeds of old again recall,
Nor let thy bond dishonoured fall.
The rights of truth thou wouldst forget,
Thy Ráma on the throne to set,
And let thy days in pleasure glide,
Fond King, Kauśalyá by thy side.
Now call it by what name thou wilt,
Justice, injustice, virtue, guilt,
Thy word and oath remain the same,
And thou must yield what thus I claim.
If Ráma be anointed, I
This very day will surely die,
Before thy face will poison drink,
And lifeless at thy feet will sink.
Yea, better far to die than stay
Alive to see one single day
The crowds before Kauśalyá stand
And hail her queen with reverent hand.
Now by my son, myself, I swear,
No gift, no promise whatsoe'er
My steadfast soul shall now content,
But only Ráma's banishment.'

So far she spake by rage impelled,
And then the queen deep silence held.
He heard her speech full fraught with ill,
But spoke no word bewildered still,
Gazed on his love once held so dear
Who spoke unlovely rede to hear;
Then as he slowly pondered o'er
The queen's resolve and oath she swore,
Once sighing forth. Ah Ráma! he
Fell prone as falls a smitten tree.
His senses lost like one insane,
Faint as a sick man weak with pain,
Or like a wounded snake dismayed,
So lay the king whom earth obeyed.
Long burning sighs he slowly heaved,
As, conquered by his woe, he grieved,
And thus with tears and sobs between
His sad faint words addressed the queen:

'By whom, Kaikeyí, wast thou taught
This flattering hope with ruin fraught?
Have goblins seized thy soul, O dame,
Who thus canst speak and feel no shame?
Thy mind with sin is sicklied o'er,
From thy first youth ne'er seen before.
A good and loving wife wast thou,
But all, alas! is altered now.
What terror can have seized thy breast
To make thee frame this dire request,
That Bharat o'er the land may reign,
And Ráma in the woods remain?
Turn from thine evil ways, O turn,
And thy perfidious counsel spurn,
If thou would fain a favour do
To people, lord, and Bharat too.
O wicked traitress, fierce and vile,
Who lovest deeds of sin and guile,

[1] This story is told in the Mahábhárat. A free version of it may be found in *Scenes from the Rámáyan, etc.*

What crime or grievance dost thou see,
What fault in Ráma or in me?
Thy son will ne'er the throne accept
If Ráma from his rights be kept,
For Bharat's heart more firmly yet
Than Ráma's is on justice set.
How shall I say, Go forth, and brook
Upon my Ráma's face to look,
See his pale cheek and ashy lips
Dimmed like the moon in sad eclipse?
How see the plan so well prepared
When prudent friends my counsels shared,
All ruined, like a host laid low
Beneath some foeman's murderous blow
What will these gathered princes say,
From regions near and far away?
'O'erlong endures the monarch's reign,
For now he is a child again.'
When many a good and holy sage
In Scripture versed, revered for age,
Shall ask for Ráma, what shall I
Unhappy, what shall I reply?
'By Queen Kaikeyí long distressed
I drove him forth and dispossessed.'
Although herein the truth I speak,
They all will hold me false and weak.
What will Kauśalyá say when she
Demands her son exiled by me?
Alas! what answer shall I frame,
Or how console the injured dame?
She like a slave on me attends,
And with a sister's care she blends
A mother's love, a wife's, a friend's.
In spite of all her tender care,
Her noble son, her face most fair,
Another queen I could prefer
And for thy sake neglected her.
But now, O Queen, my heart is grieved
For love and care by thee received,
E'en as the sickening wretch repents
His dainty meal and condiments.
And how will Queen Sumitrá trust
The husband whom she finds unjust,
Seeing my Ráma driven hence
Dishonoured, and for no offence?
Ah! the Videhan bride will hear
A double woe, a double fear,
Two whelming sorrows at one breath,
Her lord's disgrace, his father's death.
Mine aged bosom she will wring
And kill me with her sorrowing,
Sad as a fair nymph left to weep
Deserted on Himálaya's steep.
For short will be my days, I ween,
When I with mournful eyes have seen
My Ráma wandering forth alone
And heard dear Sítá sob and moan.
Ah me! my fond belief I rue.
Vile traitress, loved as good and true,
As one who in his thirst has quaffed,
Deceived by looks, a deadly draught.
Ah! thou hast slain me, murderess, while
Soothing my soul with words of guile,
As the wild hunter kills the deer
Lured from the brake his song to hear.
Soon every honest tongue will fling
Reproach on the dishonest king;
The people's scorn in every street
The seller of his child will meet,
And such dishonour will be mine
As whelms a Bráhman drunk with wine.
Ah me, for my unhappy fate,
Compelled thy words to tolerate!
Such woe is sent to scourge a crime
Committed in some distant time.
For many a day with sinful care
I cherished thee, thou sin and snare,
Kept thee, unwitting, like a cord
Destined to bind its hapless lord.
Mine hours of ease I spent with thee,
Nor deemed my love my death would be.
While like a heedless child I played,
On a black snake my hand I laid.
A cry from every mouth will burst
And all the world will hold me curst,
Because I saw my high-souled son
Unkinged, unfathered, and undone:
'The king by power of love beguiled
Is weaker than a foolish child,
His own beloved son to make
An exile for a woman's sake.
By chaste and holy vows restrained,
By reverend teachers duly trained,
When he his virtue's fruit should taste
He falls by sin and woe disgraced.'
Two words will all his answer be
When I pronounce the stern decree,
'Hence, Ráma, to the woods away,'
All he will say is, I obey.
O, if he would my will withstand
When banished from his home and land,
This were a comfort in my woe;
But he will ne'er do this, I know.
My Ráma to the forest fled,
And curses thick upon my head,
Grim Death will bear me hence away,
His world-abominated prey.
When I am gone and Ráma too,
How wilt thou those I love pursue?
What vengeful sin will be designed
Against the queens I leave behind?
When thou hast slain her son and me
Kauśalyá soon will follow: she
Will sink beneath her sorrows' weight,
And die like me disconsolate.
Exult, Kaikeyí, in thy pride,
And let thy heart be gratified,
When thou my queens and me hast hurled,
And children, to the under world.
Soon wilt thou rule as empress o'er
My noble house unvext before,
But then to wild confusion left,

Of Ráma and of me bereft.
If Bharat to thy plan consent
And long for Ráma's banishment,
Ne'er let his hands presume to pay
The funeral honours to my clay.
Vile foe, thou cause of all mine ill,
Obtain at last thy cursed will.
A widow soon shalt thou enjoy
The sweets of empire with thy boy.
O Princess, sure some evil fate
First brought thee here to devastate,
In whom the night of ruin lies
Veiled in a consort's fair disguise.
The scorn of all and deepest shame
Will long pursue my hated name,
And dire disgrace on me will press,
Misled by thee to wickedness.
How shall my Ráma, whom, before,
His elephant or chariot bore,
Now with his feet, a wanderer, tread
The forest wilds around him spread?
How shall my son, to please whose taste,
The deftest cooks, with earrings graced,
With rivalry and jealous care
The dainty meal and cates prepare—
How shall he now his life sustain
With acid fruit and woodland grain?
He spends his time unvext by cares,
And robes of precious texture wears;
How shall he, with one garment round
His limbs recline upon the ground?
Whose was this plan, this cruel thought
Unheard till now, with ruin fraught,
To make thy son Ayodhyá's king,
And send my Ráma wandering?
Shame, shame on women! Vile, untrue,
Their selfish ends they still pursue.
Not all of womankind I mean,
But more than all this wicked queen.
O worthless, cruel, selfish dame,
I brought thee home, my plague and woe.
What fault in me hast thou to blame,
Or in my son who loves thee so?
Fond wives may from their husbands flee,
And fathers may their sons desert,
But all the world would rave to see
My Ráma touched with deadly hurt.
I joy his very step to hear,
As though his godlike form I viewed;
And when I see my Ráma near
I feel my youth again renewed.
There might be life without the sun,
Yea, e'en if Indra sent no rain,
But, were my Ráma banished, none
Would, so I think, alive remain.
A foe that longs my life to take,
I brought thee here my death to be,
Caressed thee long, a venomed snake,
And through my folly die, Ah me!
Ráma and me and Lakshman slay,
And then with Bharat rule the state;
So bring the kingdom to decay,
And fawn on those thy lord who hate.
Plotter of woe, for evil bred,
For such a speech why do not all
Thy teeth from out thy wicked head
Split in a thousand pieces fall?
My Ráma's words are ever kind,
He knows not how to speak in ire:
Then how canst thou presume to find
A fault in him whom all admire?
Yield to despair, go mad, or die,
Or sink within the rifted earth;
Thy fell request will I deny,
Thou shamer of thy royal birth.
Thy longer life I scarce can bear,
Thou ruin of my home and race,
Who wouldst my heart and heartstrings tear,
Keen as a razor, false and base.
My life is gone, why speak of joy?
For what, without my son, were sweet?
Spare, lady, him thou canst destroy;
I pray thee as I touch thy feet.'
He fell and wept with wild complaint,
Heart-struck by her presumptuous speeech,
But could not touch, so weak and faint,
The cruel feet he strove to reach.

CANTO XIII.

DAŚARATHA'S DISTRESS.

Unworthy of his mournful fate,
The mighty king, unfortunate,
Lay prostrate in unseemly guise,
As, banished from the blissful skies,
Yayáti, in his evil day,
His merit all exhausted, lay.[1]
The queen, triumphant in the power
Won by her beauty's fatal dower,
Still terrible and unsubdued,
Her dire demand again renewed:
'Great Monarch, 'twas thy boast till now
To love the truth and keep the vow;
Then wherefore would thy lips refuse
The promised boon 'tis mine to choose?'
King Daśaratha, thus addressed,
With anger raging in his breast,
Sank for a while beneath the pain,
Then to Kaikeyí spoke again:

[1] Only the highest merit obtains a home in heaven for ever. Minor degrees of merit procure only leases of heavenly mansions terminable after periods proportioned to the fund which buys them. King Yayáti went to heaven and when his term expired was unceremoniously ejected, and thrown down to earth.

'Childless so long, at length I won,
With mighty toil, from Heaven a son,
Ráma, the mighty-armed; and how
Shall I desert my darling now?
A scholar wise, a hero bold,
Of patient mood, with wrath controlled,
How can I bid my Ráma fly,
My darling of the lotus eye?
In heaven itself I scarce could bear,
When asking of my Ráma there,
To hear the Gods his griefs declare,
And O, that death would take me hence
Before I wrong his innocence!'

As thus the monarch wept and wailed,
And maddening grief his heart assailed,
The sun had sought his resting-place,
And night was closing round apace.
But yet the moon-crowned night could bring
No comfort to the wretched king.
As still he mourned with burning sighs
And fixed his gaze upon the skies:
'O Night whom starry fires adorn,
I long not for the coming morn.
Be kind and show some mercy: see,
My suppliant hands are raised to thee.
Nay, rather fly with swifter pace;
No longer would I see the face
Of Queen Kaikeyí, cruel, dread,
Who brings this woe upon mine head.'
Again with suppliant hands he tried
To move the queen, and wept and sighed:
'To me, unhappy me, inclined
To good, sweet dame, thou shouldst be kind;
Whose life is well-nigh fled, who cling
To thee for succour, me thy king.
This, only this, is all my claim:
Have mercy, O my lovely dame.
None else have I to take my part:
Have mercy: thou art good at heart.
Hear, lady of the soft black eye,
And win a name that ne'er shall die:
Let Ráma rule this glorious land,
The gift of thine imperial hand.
O lady of the dainty waist,
With eyes and lips of beauty graced,
Please Ráma, me, each saintly priest,
Bharat, and all from chief to least.'
She heard his wild and mournful cry,
She saw the tears his speech that broke,
Saw her good husband's reddened eye,
But, cruel still, no word she spoke.
His eyes upon her face he bent,
And sought for mercy, but in vain:
She claimed his darling's banishment,
He swooned upon the ground again.

CANTO XIV.

RÁMA SUMMONED.

The wicked queen her speech renewed,
When rolling on the earth she viewed
Ikshváku's son, Ayodhyá's king,
For his dear Ráma sorrowing:
'Why, by a simple promise bound,
Liest thou prostrate on the ground,
As though a grievous sin dismayed
Thy spirit? Why so sore afraid!
Keep still thy word. The righteous deem
That truth, mid duties, is supreme:
And now in truth and honour's name
I bid thee own the binding claim.
Śaivya, a king whom earth obeyed,
Once to a hawk a promise made,
Gave to the bird his flesh and bone,
And by his truth made heaven his own.[1]
Alarka, when a Bráhman famed
For Scripture lore his promise claimed,
Tore from his head his bleeding eyes
And unreluctant gave the prize.
His narrow bounds prescribed restrain
The Rivers' Lord, the mighty main,
Who, though his waters boil and rave,
Keeps faithful to the word he gave.
Truth all religion comprehends,
Through all the world its might extends:
In truth alone is justice placed,
On truth the words of God are based:
A life in truth unchanging past
Will bring the highest bliss at last.
If thou the right would still pursue,
Be constant to thy word and true:
Let me thy promise fruitful see,
For boons, O King, proceed from thee.
Now to preserve thy righteous fame,
And yielding to my earnest claim—
Thrice I repeat it—send thy child,
Thy Ráma, to the forest wild.
But if the boon thou still deny,
Before thy face, forlorn, I die.'

Thus was the helpless monarch stung
By Queen Kaikeyí's fearless tongue,
As Bali strove in vain to loose
His limbs from Indra's fatal noose.
Dismayed in soul and pale with fear,
The monarch, like a trembling steer
Between the chariot's wheel and yoke,
Again to Queen Kaikeyí spoke,
With sad eyes fixt in vacant stare,
Gathering courage from despair:
'That hand I took, thou sinful dame,
With texts, before the sacred flame,
Thee and thy son, I scorn and hate,
And all at once repudiate.

---

[1] See *Additional Notes*, THE SUPPLIANT DOVE.

The night is fled: the dawn is near:
Soon will the holy priests be here
To bid me for the rite prepare
That with my son the throne will share.
The preparation made to grace
My Ráma in his royal place—
With this, e'en this, my darling for
My death the funeral flood shall pour.
Thou and thy son at least forbear
In offerings to my shade to share,
For by the plot thy guile has laid
His consecration will be stayed.
This very day how shall I brook
To meet each subject's altered look?
To mark each gloomy joyless brow
That was so bright and glad but now?'

While thus the high-souled monarch spoke
To the stern queen, the morning broke,
And holy night had slowly fled,
With moon and stars engarlanded.
Yet once again the cruel queen
Spoke words in answer fierce and keen,
Still on her evil purpose bent,
Wild with her rage and eloquent:
'What speech is this? Such words as these
Seem sprung from poison-sown disease.
Quick to thy noble Ráma send
And bid him on his sire attend.
When to my son the rule is given;
When Ráma to the woods is driven;
When not a rival copes with me,
From chains of duty thou art free.'

Thus goaded, like a generous steed
Urged by sharp spurs to double speed,
'My senses are astray,' he cried,
'And duty's bonds my hands have tied.
I long to see mine eldest son,
My virtuous, my beloved one.'

And now the night had past away;
Out shone the Maker of the Day,
Bringing the planetary hour
And moment of auspicious power.
Vaśishṭha, virtuous, far renowned,
Whose young disciples girt him round,
With sacred things without delay
Through the fair city took his way.
He traversed, where the people thronged.
And all for Ráma's coming longed,
The town as fair in festive show
As his who lays proud cities low.[1]
He reached the palace where he heard
The mingled notes of many a bird,
Where crowded thick high-honoured bands
Of guards with truncheons in their hands.
Begirt by many a sage, elate,
Vaśishṭha reached the royal gate,
And standing by the door he found
Sumantra, for his form renowned,
The king's illustrious charioteer
And noble counsellor and peer.
To him well skilled in every part
Of his hereditary art
Vasishṭha said: 'O charioteer,
Inform the king that I am here.
Here ready by my side behold
These sacred vessels made of gold,
Which water for the rite contain
From Gangá and each distant main.
Here for installing I have brought
The seat prescribed of fig-wood wrought,
All kinds of seed and precious scent
And many a gem and ornament;
Grain, sacred grass, the garden's spoil,
Honey and curds and milk and oil;
Eight radiant maids, the best of all
War elephants that feed in stall;
A four-horse car, a bow and sword,
A litter, men to bear their lord;
A white umbrella bright and fair
That with the moon may well compare;
Two chouries of the whitest hair;
A golden beaker rich and rare;
A bull high-humped and fair to view,
Girt with gold bands and white of hue;
A four-toothed steed with flowing mane,
A throne which lions carved sustain;
A tiger's skin, the sacred fire,
Fresh kindled, which the rites require;
The best musicians skilled to play,
And dancing-girls in raiment gay;
Kine, Bráhmans, teachers fill the court,
And bird and beast of purest sort.
From town and village, far and near,
The noblest men are gathered here;
Here merchants with their followers crowd,
And men in joyful converse loud,
And kings from many a distant land
To view the consecration stand.
The dawn is come, the lucky day;
Go bid the monarch haste away,
That now Prince Ráma may obtain
The empire, and begin his reign.'

Soon as he heard the high behest
The driver of the chariot pressed
Within the chambers of the king,
His lord with praises honouring.
And none of all the warders checked
His entrance for their great respect
Of him well known, in place so high,
Still fain their king to gratify.
He stood beside the royal chief,
Unwitting of his deadly grief,
And with sweet words began to sing
The praises of his lord and king:
'As, when the sun begins to rise,
The sparkling sea delights our eyes,
Wake, calm with gentle soul, and thus

[1] Indra, called also Purandara, Town-destroyer.

Give rapture, mighty King, to us.
As Mátali[1] this selfsame hour
Sang lauds of old to Indra's power,
When he the Titan hosts o'erthrew,
So hymn I thee with praises due.
The Vedas, with their kindred lore,
Brahmá their soul-born Lord adore,
With all the doctrines of the wise,
And bid him, as I bid thee, rise.
As, with the moon, the Lord of Day
Wakes with the splendour of his ray
Prolific Earth, who neath him lies,
So, mighty King, I bid thee rise.
With blissful words, O Lord of men,
Rise, radiant in thy form, as when
The sun ascending darts his light
From Meru's everlasting height.
May Śiva, Agni, Sun, and Moon
Bestow on thee each choicest boon,
Kuvera, Varuṇ, Indra bless
Kakutstha's son with all success.
Awake, the holy night is fled,
The happy light abroad is spread;
Awake, O best of kings, and share
The glorious task that claims thy care.
The holy sage Vaśishṭha waits,
With all his Bráhmans, at the gates.
Give thy decree, without delay,
To consecrate thy son to-day.
As armies, by no captain led,
As flocks that feed unshepherded,
Such is the fortune of a state
Without a king and desolate.'

Such were the words the bard addressed,
With weight of sage advice impressed;
And, as he heard, the hapless king
Felt deeper yet his sorrow's sting.
At length, all joy and comfort fled,
He raised his eyes with weeping red,
And, mournful for his Ráma's sake,
The good and glorious monarch spake:
'Why seek with idle praise to greet
The wretch for whom no praise is meet?
Thy words mine aching bosom tear,
And plunge me deeper in despair.'

Sumantra heard the sad reply,
And saw his master's tearful eye.
With reverent palm to palm applied
He drew a little space aside.
Then, as the king, with misery weak,
With vain endeavour strove to speak,
Kaikeyí, skilled in plot and plan,
To sage Sumantra thus began:
'The king, absorbed in joyful thought
For his dear son, no rest has sought:
Sleepless to him the night has past,
And now o'erwatched he sinks at last.
Then go, Sumantra, and with speed
The glorious Ráma hither lead:
Go, as I pray, nor longer wait;
No time is this to hesitate.'
'How can I go, O Lady fair,
Unless my lord his will declare?'
'Fain would I see him,' cried the king,
'Quick, quick, my beauteous Ráma bring.'
Then rose the happy thought to cheer
The bosom of the charioteer,
'The king, I ween, of pious mind,
The consecration has designed.'
Sumantra for his wisdom famed,
Delighted with the thought he framed,
From the calm chamber, like a bay
Of crowded ocean, took his way.
He turned his face to neither side,
But forth he hurried straight;
Only a little while he eyed
The guards who kept the gate.
He saw in front a gathered crowd
Of men of every class,
Who, parting as he came, allowed
The charioteer to pass.

[1] Indra's charioteer.

CANTO XV.

THE PREPARATIONS.

There slept the Bráhmans, deeply read
In Scripture, till the night had fled;
Then, with the royal chaplains, they
Took each his place in long array.
There gathered fast the chiefs of trade,
Nor peer nor captain long delayed,
Assembling all in order due
The consecrating rite to view.

The morning dawned with cloudless ray
On Pushya's high auspicious day,
And Cancer with benignant power
Looked down on Ráma's natal hour.
The twice-born chiefs, with zealous heed,
Made ready what the rite would need.
The well-wrought throne of holy wood
And golden urns in order stood.
There was the royal car whereon
A tiger's skin resplendent shone;
There water, brought for sprinkling thence
Where, in their sacred confluence,
Blend Jumná's waves with Gangá's tide,
From many a holy flood beside,
From brook and fountain far and near,
From pool and river, sea and mere.
And there were honey, curd, and oil,
Parched rice and grass, the garden's spoil,
Fresh milk, eight girls in bright attire,
An elephant with eyes of fire;
And urns of gold and silver made,
With milky branches overlaid,
All brimming from each sacred flood,
And decked with many a lotus bud.

And dancing-women fair and free,
Gay with their gems, were there to see,
Who stood in bright apparel by
With lovely brow and witching eye.
White flashed the jewelled chouri there,
And shone like moonbeams through the air;
The white umbrella overhead
A pale and moonlike lustre shed,
Wont in pure splendour to precede,
And in such rites the pomp to lead.
There stood the charger by the side
Of the great bull of snow-white hide;
There was all music soft and loud,
And bards and minstrels swelled the crowd.
For now the monarch bade combine
Each custom of his ancient line
With every rite Ayodhyá's state
Observed, her kings to consecrate.

Then, summoned by the king's behest,
The multitudes together pressed,
And, missing still the royal sire,
Began, impatient, to inquire:
'Who to our lord will tidings bear
That all his people throng the square?
Where is the king? the sun is bright,
And all is ready for the rite.'

As thus they spoke, Sumantra, tried
In counsel, to the chiefs replied,
Gathered from lands on every side:
'To Ráma's house I swiftly drave,
For so the king his mandate gave.
Our aged lord and Ráma too
In honour high hold all of you:
I in your words (be long your days!)
Will ask him why he thus delays.'

Thus spoke the peer in Scripture read,
And to the ladies' bower he sped.
Quick through the gates Sumantra hied,
Which access ne'er to him denied.
Behind the curtained screen he drew,
Which veiled the chamber from the view.
In benediction loud he raised
His voice, and thus the monarch praised:
'Sun, Moon, Kuvera, Śiva bless
Kakutstha's son with high success!
The Lords of air, flood, fire decree
The victory, my King, to thee!
The holy night has past away,
Auspicious shines the morning's ray.
Rise, Lord of men, thy part to take
In the great rite, awake! awake!
Bráhmans and captains, chiefs of trade,
All wait in festive garb arrayed;
For thee they look with eager eyes:
O Raghu's son, awake! arise'

To him in holy Scripture read,
Who hailed him thus, the monarch said,
Upraising from his sleep his head:
'Go. Ráma hither lead as thou
Wast ordered by the queen but now.
Come, tell me why my mandate laid
Upon thee thus is disobeyed.
Away! and Ráma hither bring;
I sleep not: make no tarrying.'

Thus gave the king command anew:
Sumantra from his lord withdrew;
With head in lowly reverence bent,
And filled with thoughts of joy, he went.
The royal street he traversed, where
Waved flag and pennon to the air,
And, as with joy the car he drove,
He let his eyes delighted rove.
On every side, where'er he came,
He heard glad words, their theme the same,
As in their joy the gathered folk
Of Ráma and the throning spoke.
Then saw he Ráma's palace bright
And vast as Mount Kailása's height,
That glorious in its beauty showed
As Indra's own supreme abode:
With folding doors both high and wide;
With hundred porches beautified:
Where golden statues towering rose
O'er gemmed and coralled porticoes:
Bright like a cave in Meru's side,
Or clouds through Autumn's sky that ride:
Festooned with length of bloomy twine,
Flashing with pearls and jewels' shine,
While sandal-wood and aloe lent
The mingled riches of their scent;
With all the odorous sweets that fill
The breezy heights of Dardar's hill.
There by the gate the Sáras screamed,
And shrill-toned peacocks' plumage gleamed.
Its floors with deftest art inlaid,
Its sculptured wolves in gold arrayed,
With its bright sheen the palace took
The mind of man and chained the look,
For like the sun and moon it glowed,
And mocked Kuvera's loved abode.
Circling the walls a crowd he viewed
Who stood in reverent attitude,
With throngs of countrymen who sought
Acceptance of the gifts they brought.
The elephant was stationed there,
Appointed Ráma's self to bear;
Adorned with pearls, his brow and cheek
Were sandal-dyed in many a streak,
While he, in stature, bulk, and pride,
With Indra's own Airávat[1] vied.
Sumantra, borne by coursers fleet,
Flashing a radiance o'er the street,
To Ráma's palace flew,
And all who lined the royal road,
Or thronged the prince's rich abode,
Rejoiced as near he drew.
And with delight his bosom swelled
As onward still his course he held

[1] The elephant of Indra.

Through many a sumptuous court
Like Indra's palace nobly made,
Where peacocks revelled in the shade,
And beasts of silvan sort.
Through many a hall and chamber wide,
That with Kailása's splendour vied,
Or mansions of the Blest,
While Ráma's friends, beloved and tried,
Before his coming stepped aside,
Still on Sumantra pressed.
He reached the chamber door, where stood
Around his followers young and good,
Bard, minstrel, charioteer,
Well skilled the tuneful chords to sweep,
With soothing strain to lull to sleep,
Or laud their master dear.
Then, like a dolphin darting through
Unfathomed depths of ocean's blue
With store of jewels decked,
Through crowded halls that rock-like rose,
Or as proud hills where clouds repose,
Sumantra sped unchecked—
Halls like the glittering domes on high
Reared for the dwellers of the sky
By heavenly architect.

CANTO XVI.

RÁMA SUMMONED.

So through the crowded inner door
Sumantra, skilled in ancient lore,
On to the private chambers pressed
Which stood apart from all the rest.
There youthful warriors, true and bold,
Whose ears were ringed with polished gold,
All armed with trusty bows and darts,
Watched with devoted eyes and hearts.
And hoary men, a faithful train,
Whose aged hands held staves of cane,
The ladies' guard, apparelled fair
In red attire, were stationed there.
Soon as they saw Sumantra nigh,
Each longed his lord to gratify,
And from his seat beside the door
Up sprang each ancient servitor.
Then to the warders quickly cried
The skilled Sumantra, void of pride:
'Tell Ráma that the charioteer
Sumantra waits for audience here.'
The ancient men with one accord
Seeking the pleasure of their lord,
Passing with speed the chamber door
To Ráma's ear the message bore.
Forthwith the prince with duteous heed
Called in the messenger with speed,
For 'twas his sire's command, he knew,
That sent him for the interview.
Like Lord Kuvera, well arrayed,
He pressed a couch of gold,
Wherefrom a covering of brocade
Hung down in many a fold.
Oil and the sandal's fragrant dust
Had tinged his body o'er
Dark as the stream the spearman's thrust
Drains from the wounded boar.
Him Sítá watched with tender care,
A chouri in her hand,
As Chitrá,[1] ever fond in fair,
Beside the Moon will stand.
Him glorious with unborrowed light,
A liberal lord of sunlike might,
Sumantra hailed in words like these,
Well skilled in gentle courtesies,
As, with joined hands in reverence raised,
Upon the beauteous prince he gazed:
'Happy Kauśalyá! Blest is she,
The Mother of a son like thee.
Now rise, O Ráma, speed away,
Go to thy sire without delay;
For he and Queen Kaikeyí seek
And interview with thee to speak.'

The lion-lord of men, the best
Of splendid heroes, thus addressed,
To Sítá spake with joyful cheer:
'The king and queen, my lady dear,
Touching the throning, for my sake
Some salutary counsel take.
The lady of the full black eye
Would fain her husband gratify,
And, all his purpose understood,
Counsels the monarch to my good.
A happy fate is mine, I ween,
When he, consulting with his queen,
Sumantra on this charge, intent
Upon my gain and good, has sent.
An envoy of so noble sort
Well suits the splendour of the court.
The consecration rite this day
Will join me in imperial sway.
To meet the lord of earth, for so
His order bids me, I will go.
Thou, lady, here in comfort stay,
And with thy maidens rest or play.'

Thus Ráma spake. For meet reply
The lady of the large black eye
Attended to the door her lord,
And blessings on his head implored:
'The majesty and royal state
Which holy Bráhmans venerate,
The consecration and the rite
Which sanctifies the ruler's might,
And all imperial powers should be
Thine by thy father's high decree,
As He, the worlds who formed and planned,
The kingship gave to Indra's hand.

---

[1] A star in the spike of Virgo: hence the name of the month Chaitra or Chait

Then shall mine eyes my king adore
When lustral rites and fast are o'er,
And black deer's skin and roebuck's horn
Thy lordly limbs and hand adorn.
May He whose hands the thunder wield
Be in the east thy guard and shield;
May Yama's care the south befriend,
And Varuṇ's arm the west defend;
And let Kuvera, Lord of Gold,
The north with firm protection hold.'
Then Ráma spoke a kind farewell,
And hailed the blessings as they fell
From Sítá's gentle lips; and then,
As a young lion from his den
Descends the mountain's stony side,
So from the hall the hero hied.
First Lakshmaṇ at the door he viewed
Who stood in reverent attitude,
Then to the central court he pressed
Where watched the friends who loved him best.
To all his dear companions there
He gave kind looks and greeting fair.
On to the lofty car that glowed
Like fire the royal tiger strode.
Bright as himself its silver shone:
A tiger's skin was laid thereon.
With cloudlike thunder, as it rolled,
It flashed with gems and burnished gold,
And, like the sun's meridian blaze,
Blinded the eye that none could gaze.
Like youthful elephants, tall and strong,
Fleet coursers whirled the car along:
In such a car the Thousand-eyed
Borne by swift horses loves to ride.
So like Parjanya,[1] when he flies
Thundering through the autumn skies,
The hero from the palace sped,
As leaves the moon some cloud o'erhead.
Still close to Ráma Lakshmaṇ kept,
Behind him to the car he leapt,
And, watching with fraternal care,
Waved the long chouri's silver hair,
As from the palace gate he came
Up rose the tumult of acclaim,
While loud huzza and jubilant shout
Pealed from the gathered myriads out.
Then elephants, like mountains vast,
And steeds who all their kind surpassed,
Followed their lord by hundreds, nay
By thousands, led in long array.
First marched a band of warriors trained,
With sandal dust and aloe stained;
Well armed was each with sword and bow,
And every breast with hope aglow,
And ever, as they onward went,
Shouts from the warrior train,
And every sweet-toned instrument
Prolonged the minstrel strain.

[1] The Rain-God.

On passed the tamer of his foes,
While well clad dames, in crowded rows,
Each chamber lattice thronged to view,
And chaplets on the hero threw.
Then all, of peerless face and limb,
Sang Ráma's praise for love of him,
And blent their voices, soft and sweet,
From palace high and crowded street:
'Now, sure, Kauśalyá's heart must swell
To see the son she loves so well,
Thee, Ráma, thee, her joy and pride,
Triumphant o'er the realm preside.'
Then—for they knew his bride most fair
Of all who part the soft dark hair,
His love, his life, possessed the whole
Of her young hero's heart and soul:—
'Be sure the lady's fate repays
Some mighty vow of ancient days,[1]
For blest with Ráma's love is she
As, with the Moon's, sweet Rohiṇí.'[2]
Such were the witching words that came
From lips of many a peerless dame
Crowding the palace roofs to greet
The hero as he gained the street.

CANTO XVII.

RÁMA'S APPROACH.

As Ráma, rendering blithe and gay
His loving friends, pursued his way,
He saw on either hand a press
Of mingled people numberless.
The royal street he traversed, where
Incense of aloe filled the air,
Where rose high palaces, that vied
With paly clouds, on either side;
With flowers of myriad colours graced,
And food for every varied taste,
Bright as the glowing path o'erhead
Which feet of Gods celestial tread.
Loud benedictions, sweet to hear,
From countless voices soothed his ear.
While he to each gave due salute
His place and dignity to suit:
'Be thou,' the joyful people cried,
'Be thou our guardian, lord and guide.
Throned and anointed king to-day,
Thy feet set forth upon the way
Wherein, each honoured as a God,
Thy fathers and forefathers trod.
Thy sire and his have graced the throne,
And loving care to us have shown:
Thus blest shall we and ours remain,
Yea still more blest in Ráma's reign.

[1] In a former life.

[2] One of the lunar asterisms, represented as the favourite wife of the Moon. See p. 4, note.

No more of dainty fare we need,
And but one cherished object heed,
That we may see our prince to-day
Invested with imperial sway.'

Such were the words and pleasant speech
That Ráma heard, unmoved, from each
Of the dear friends around him spread,
As onward through the street he sped.
For none could turn his eye or thought
From the dear form his glances sought,
With fruitless ardour forward cast
Even when Raghu's son had past.
And he who saw not Ráma nigh,
Nor caught a look from Ráma's eye,
A mark for scorn and general blame,
Reproached himself in bitter shame.
For to each class his equal mind
With sympathy and love inclined
Most fully of the princely four,
So greatest love to him they bore.

His circling course the hero bent
Round shrine and altar, reverent,
Round homes of Gods, where cross-roads met,
Where many a sacred tree was set.
Near to his father's house he drew
Like Indra's beautiful to view,
And with the light his glory gave
Within the royal palace drave.
Through three broad courts, where bowmen kept
Their watch and ward, his coursers swept.
Then through the two remaining went
On foot that prince preëminent.
Through all the courts the hero passed,
And gained the ladies' bower at last;
Then through the door alone withdrew,
And left without his retinue.
When thus the monarch's noble boy
Had gone his sire to meet,
The multitude, elate with joy,
Stood watching in the street,
And his return with eager eyes
Expected at the gates,
As for his darling moon to rise
The King of Rivers[1] waits.

CANTO XVIII.

THE SENTENCE.

With hopeless eye and pallid mien
There sat the monarch with the queen.
His father's feet with reverence due
He clasped, and touched Kaikeyí's too.
The king, with eyes still brimming o'er,
Cried Ráma! and could do no more.
His voice was choked, his eye was dim,
He could not speak or look on him.
Then sudden fear made Ráma shake
As though his foot had roused a snake,
Soon as his eyes had seen the change
So mournful, terrible, and strange.
For there, his reason well-nigh fled,
Sighing, with soul disquieted,
To torturing pangs a prey,
Dismayed, despairing, and distraught,
In a fierce whirl of wildering thought
The hapless monarch lay,
Like Ocean wave-engarlanded
Storm-driven from his tranquil bed,
The Sun-God in eclipse,
Or like a holy seer, heart-stirred
With anguish, when a lying word
Has passed his heedless lips.
The sight of his dear father, pained
With woe and misery unexplained,
Filled Ráma with unrest,
As Ocean's pulses rise and swell
When the great moon he loves so well
Shines full upon his breast.
So grieving for his father's sake,
To his own heart the hero spake:
'Why will the king my sire to-day
No kindly word of greeting say?
At other times, though wroth he be,
His eyes grow calm that look on me.
Then why does anguish wring his brow
To see his well-beloved now?'
Sick and perplexed, distraught with woe,
To Queen Kaikeyí bowing low,
While pallor o'er his bright cheek spread,
With humble reverence he said:
'What have I done, unknown, amiss
To make my father wroth like this?
Declare it, O dear Queen, and win
His pardon for my heedless sin.
Why is the sire I ever find
Filled with all love to-day unkind?
With eyes cast down and pallid cheek
This day alone he will not speak.
Or lies he prostrate neath the blow
Of fierce disease or sudden woe?
For all our bliss is dashed with pain,
And joy unmixt is hard to gain.
Does stroke of evil fortune smite
Dear Bharat, charming to the sight,
Or on the brave Śatrughna fall,
Or consorts, for he loves them all?
Against his words when I rebel,
Or fail to please the monarch well,
When deeds of mine his soul offend,
That hour I pray my life may end.
How should a man to him who gave
His being and his life behave?
The sire to whom he owes his birth
Should be his deity on earth.
Hast thou, by pride and folly moved,

[1] The Sea.

With bitter taunt the king reproved?
Has scorn of thine or cruel jest
To passion stirred his gentle breast?
Speak truly, Queen, that I may know
What cause has changed the monarch so.'
Thus by the high-souled prince addressed,
Of Raghu's sons the chief and best,
She cast all ruth and shame aside,
And bold with greedy words replied:
'Not wrath, O Ráma, stirs the king,
Nor misery stabs with sudden sting;
One thought that fills his soul has he,
But dares not speak for fear of thee.
Thou art so dear, his lips refrain
From words that might his darling pain.
But thou, as duty bids, must still
The promise of thy sire fulfil.
He who to me in days gone by
Vouchsafed a boon with honours high,
Dares now, a king, his word regret,
And caitiff-like disowns the debt.
The lord of men his promise gave
To grant the boon that I might crave,
And now a bridge would idly throw
When the dried stream has ceased to flow.
His faith the monarch must not break
In wrath, or e'en for thy dear sake.
From faith, as well the righteous know,
Our virtue and our merits flow.
Now, be they good or be they ill,
Do thou thy father's words fulfil:
Swear that his promise shall not fail,
And I will tell thee all the tale.
Yes, Ráma, when I hear that thou
Hast bound thee by thy father's vow,
Then, not till then, my lips shall speak,
Nor will he tell what boon I seek.'
He heard, and with a troubled breast
This answer to the queen addressed:
'Ah me, dear lady, canst thou deem
That words like these thy lips beseem?
I, at the bidding of my sire,
Would cast my body to the fire,
A deadly draught of poison drink,
Or in the waves of ocean sink:
If he command, it shall be done,—
My father and my king in one.
Then speak and let me know the thing
So longed for by my lord the king.
It shall be done: let this suffice;
Ráma ne'er makes a promise twice.'
He ended. To the princely youth
Who loved the right and spoke the truth,
Cruel, abominable came
The answer of the ruthless dame:
'When Gods and Titans fought of yore,
Transfixed with darts and bathed in gore
Two boons to me thy father gave
For the dear life 'twas mine to save.
Of him I claim the ancient debt,
That Bharat on the throne be set,
And thou, O Ráma, go this day
To Dandak forest far away.
Now, Ráma, if thou wilt maintain
Thy father's faith without a stain,
And thine own truth and honour clear,
Then, best of men, my bidding hear.
Do thou thy father's word obey,
Nor from the pledge he gave me stray.
Thy life in Dandak forest spend
Till nine long years and five shall end.
Upon my Bharat's princely head
Let consecrating drops be shed,
With all the royal pomp for thee
Made ready by the king's decree.
Seek Dandak forest and resign
Rites that would make the empire thine.
For twice seven years of exile wear
The coat of bark and matted hair.
Then in thy stead let Bharat reign
Lord of his royal sire's domain,
Rich in the fairest gems that shine,
Cars, elephants, and steeds, and kine.
The monarch mourns thy altered fate
And vails his brow compassionate:
Bowed down by bitter grief he lies
And dares not lift to thine his eyes.
Obey his word: be firm and brave,
And with great truth the monarch save.'
While thus with cruel words she spoke,
No grief the noble youth betrayed;
But forth the father's anguish broke,
At his dear Ráma's lot dismayed.

CANTO XIX.

RÁMA'S PROMISE.

Calm and unmoved by threatened woe
The noble conqueror of the foe
Answered the cruel words she spoke,
Nor quailed beneath the murderous stroke:
'Yea, for my father's promise sake
I to the wood my way will take,
And dwell a lonely exile there
In hermit dress with matted hair.
One thing alone I fain would learn,
Why is the king this day so stern?
Why is the scourge of foes so cold,
Nor gives me greeting as of old?
Now let not anger flush thy cheek:
Before thy face the truth I speak.
In hermit's coat with matted hair
To the wild wood will I repair.
How can I fail his will to do,
Friend, master, grateful sovereign too?
One only pang consumes my breast,
That his own lips have not expressed
His will, nor made his longing known
That Bharat should ascend the throne.

To Bharat I would yield my wife,
My realm and wealth, mine own dear life.
Unasked I fain would yield them all:
More gladly at my father's call,
More gladly when the gift may free
His honour and bring joy to thee.
Thus, lady, his sad heart release
From the sore shame, and give him peace.
But tell me, O, I pray thee, why
The lord of men, with downcast eye,
Lies prostrate thus, and one by one
Down his pale cheek the tear-drops run.
Let couriers to thy father speed
On horses of the swiftest breed,
And, by the mandate of the king,
Thy Bharat to his presence bring.
My father's words I will not stay
To question, but this very day
To Dandak's pathless wild will fare,
For twice seven years an exile there.'

When Ráma thus had made reply
Kaikeyí's heart with joy beat high.
She, trusting to the pledge she held,
The youth's departure thus impelled:
''Tis well. Be messengers despatched
On coursers ne'er for fleetness matched
To seek my father's home and lead
My Bharat back with all their speed.
And, Ráma, as I ween that thou
Wilt scarce endure to linger now,
So surely it were wise and good
This hour to journey to the wood.
And if, with shame cast down and weak,
No word to thee the king can speak,
Forgive, and from thy mind dismiss
A trifle in an hour like this.
But till thy feet in rapid haste
Have left the city for the waste,
And to the distant forest fled,
He will not bathe nor call for bread.'

'Woe! woe!' from the sad monarch burst,
In surging floods of grief immersed;
Then swooning, with his wits astray,
Upon the gold-wrought couch he lay.
And Ráma raised the aged king:
But the stern queen, unpitying,
Checked not her needless words, nor spared
The hero for all speed prepared,
But urged him with her bitter tongue
Like a good horse with lashes stung.
She spoke her shameful speech. Serene
He heard the fury of the queen,
And to her words so vile and dread
Gently, unmoved in mind, he said:
'I would not in this world remain
A grovelling thrall to paltry gain,
But duty's path would fain pursue,
True as the saints themselves are true.
From death itself I would not fly
My father's wish to gratify.
What deed soe'er his loving son
May do to please him, think it done.
Amid all duties, Queen, I count
This duty first and paramount,
That sons, obedient, aye fulfil
Their honoured fathers' word and will.
Without his word, if thou decree,
Forth to the forest will I flee,
And there shall fourteen years be spent
Mid lonely wilds in banishment.
Methinks thou couldst not hope to find
One spark of virtue in my mind,
If thou, whose wish is still my lord,
Hast for this grace the king implored.
This day I go, but, ere we part,
Must cheer my Sítá's tender heart,
To my dear mother bid farewell;
Then to the woods, a while to dwell.
With thee, O Queen, the care must rest
That Bharat hear his sire's behest,
And guard the land with righteous sway,
For such the law that lives for aye.'

In speechless woe the father heard,
Wept with loud cries, but spoke no word.
Then Ráma touched his senseless feet,
And hers, for honour most unmeet;
Round both his circling steps he bent,
Then from the bower the hero went.
Soon as he reached the gate he found
His dear companions gathered round.
Behind him came Sumitrá's child
With weeping eyes so sad and wild.
Then saw he all that rich array
Of vases for the glorious day.
Round them with reverent steps he paced,
Nor vailed his eye, nor moved in haste.
The loss of empire could not dim
The glory that encompassed him.
So will the Lord of Cooling Rays[1]
On whom the world delights to gaze,
Through the great love of all retain
Sweet splendour in the time of wane.
Now to the exile's lot resigned
He left the rule of earth behind:
As though all worldly cares he spurned
No trouble was in him discerned.
The chouries that for kings are used,
And white umbrella, he refused,
Dismissed his chariot and his men,
And every friend and citizen.
He ruled his senses, nor betrayed
The grief that on his bosom weighed,
And thus his mother's mansion sought
To tell the mournful news he brought.
Nor could the gay-clad people there
Who flocked round Ráma true and fair,
One sign of altered fortune trace
Upon the splendid hero's face.
Nor had the chieftain, mighty-armed,
Lost the bright look all hearts that charmed,

[1] The Moon.

As e'en from autumn moons is thrown
A splendour which is all their own.
With his sweet voice the hero spoke
Saluting all the gathered folk,
Then righteous-souled and great in fame
Close to his mother's house he came.
Lakshman the brave, his brother's peer
In princely virtues, followed near,
Sore troubled, but resolved to show
No token of his secret woe.
Thus to the palace Ráma went
Where all were gay with hope and joy;
But well he knew the dire event
That hope would mar, that bliss destroy.
So to his grief he would not yield
Lest the sad change their hearts might rend,
And, the dread tiding unrevealed,
Spared from the blow each faithful friend.

CANTO XX.

KAUŚALYÁ'S LAMENT.

But in the monarch's palace, when
Sped from the bower that lord of men,
Up from the weeping women went
A mighty wail and wild lament:
'Ah, he who ever freely did
His duty ere his sire could bid,
Our refuge and our sure defence,
This day will go an exile hence.
He on Kauśalyá loves to wait
Most tender and affectionate,
And as he treats his mother, thus
From childhood has he treated us.
On themes that sting he will not speak,
And when reviled is calm and meek.
He soothes the angry, heals offence:
He goes to-day an exile hence.
Our lord the king is most unwise,
And looks on life with doting eyes,
Who in his folly casts away
The world's protection, hope, and stay.'
Thus in their woe, like kine bereaved
Of their young calves,[1] the ladies grieved,
And ever as they wept and wailed
With keen reproach the king assailed.
Their lamentation, mixed with tears,
Smote with new grief the monarch's ears,
Who, burnt with woe too great to bear,
Fell on his couch and fainted there.
Then Ráma, smitten with the pain
His heaving heart could scarce restrain,
Groaned like an elephant and strode
With Lakshman to the queen's abode.
A warder there, whose hoary eld
In honour high by all was held,
Guarding the mansion, sat before
The portal, girt with many more.
Swift to their feet the warders sprang,
And loud the acclamation rang,
Hail, Ráma! as to him they bent,
Of victor chiefs preëminent.
One court he passed, and in the next
Saw, masters of each Veda text,
A crowd of Bráhmans, good and sage,
Dear to the king for lore and age.
To these he bowed his reverent head,
Thence to the court beyond he sped.
Old dames and tender girls, their care
To keep the doors, were stationed there.
And all, when Ráma came in view,
Delighted to the chamber flew,
To bear to Queen Kauśalyá's ear
The tidings that she loved to hear.
The queen, on rites and prayer intent,
In careful watch the night had spent,
And at the dawn, her son to aid,
To Vishnu holy offerings made.
Firm in her vows, serenely glad,
In robes of spotless linen clad,
As texts prescribe, with grace implored,
Her offerings in the fire she poured.
Within her splendid bower he came,
And saw her feed the sacred flame
There oil, and grain, and vases stood,
With wreaths, and curds, and cates, and wood,
And milk, and sesamum, and rice,
The elements of sacrifice.
She, worn and pale with many a fast
And midnight hours in vigil past,
In robes of purest white arrayed,
To Lakshmí Queen drink-offerings paid.
So long away, she flew to meet
The darling of her soul:
So runs a mare with eager feet
To welcome back her foal.
He with his firm support upheld
The queen, as near she drew,
And, by maternal love impelled,
Her arms around him threw.
Her hero son, her matchless boy
She kissed upon the head:
She blessed him in her pride and joy
With tender words, and said:

[1] The comparison may to a European reader seem a homely one. But Spenser likens an infuriate woman to a cow 'That is berobbed of her youngling dere.' Shakspeare also makes King Henry VI. compare himself to the calf's mother that 'Runs lowing up and down, Looking the way her harmless young one went.' 'Cows,' says De Quincey, 'are amongst the gentlest of breathing creatures; none show more passionate tenderness to their young, when deprived of them, and, in short, I am not ashamed to profess a deep love for these gentle creatures.'

'Be like thy royal sires of old,
The nobly good, the lofty-souled!
Their lengthened days and fame be thine,
And virtue, as beseems thy line!
The pious king, thy father, see
True to his promise made to thee:
That truth thy sire this day will show,
And regent's power on thee bestow.'
She spoke. He took the proffered seat,
And as she pressed her son to eat,
Raised reverent hands, and, touched with shame,
Made answer to the royal dame:
'Dear lady, thou hast yet to know
That danger threats, and heavy woe:
A grief that will with sore distress
On Sítá, thee, and Lakshmaṇ press.
What need of seats have such as I?
This day to Daṇḍak wood I fly.
The hour is come, a time, unmeet
For silken couch and gilded seat.
I must to lonely wilds repair,
Abstain from flesh, and living there
On roots, fruit, honey, hermit's food,
Pass twice seven years in solitude.
To Bharat's hand the king will yield
The regent power I thought to wield,
And me, a hermit, will he send
My days in Daṇḍak wood to spend.'
As when the woodman's axe has lopped
A Śal branch in the grove, she dropped:
So from the skies a Goddess falls
Ejected from her radiant halls.
When Ráma saw her lying low,
Prostrate by too severe a blow,
Around her form his arms he wound
And raised her fainting from the ground.
His hand upheld her like a mare
Who feels her load too sore to bear,
And sinks upon the way o'ertoiled,
And all her limps with dust are soiled.
He soothed her in her wild distress
With loving touch and soft caress.
She, meet for highest fortune, eyed
The hero watching by her side,
And thus, while Lakshmaṇ bent to hear,
Addressed her son with many a tear:
'If, Ráma, thou had ne'er been born
My child to make thy mother mourn,
Though reft of joy, a childless queen,
Such woe as this I ne'er had seen.
Though to the childless wife there clings
One sorrow armed with keenest stings,
'No child have I: no child have I,'
No second misery prompts the sigh.
When long I sought, alas, in vain,
My husband's love and bliss to gain,
In Ráma all my hopes I set
And dreamed I might be happy yet.
I, of the consorts first and best,
Must bear my rivals' taunt and jest,
And brook, though better far than they,
The soul distressing words they say.
What woman can be doomed to pine
In misery more sore than mine,
Whose hopeless days must still be spent
In grief that ends not and lament?
They scorned me when my son was nigh;
When he is banished I must die.
Me, whom my husband never prized,
Kaikeyí's retinue despised
With boundless insolence, though she
Tops not in rank nor equals me.
And they who do me service yet,
Nor old allegiance quite forget,
Whene'er they see Kaikeyí's son,
With silent lips my glances shun.
How, O my darling, shall I brook
Each menace of Kaikeyí's look,
And listen, in my low estate,
To taunts of one so passionate?
For seventeen years since thou wast born
I sat and watched, ah me, forlorn!
Hoping some blessed day to see
Deliverance from my woes by thee.
Now comes this endless grief and wrong,
So dire I cannot bear it long,
Sinking, with age and sorrow worn,
Beneath my rivals' taunts and scorn.
How shall I pass in dark distress
My long lone days of wretchedness
Without my Ráma's face, as bright
As the full moon to cheer my sight?
Alas, my cares thy steps to train,
And fasts, and vows, and prayers are vain,
Hard, hard, I ween, must be this heart
To bear this blow nor burst apart,
As some great river bank, when first
The floods of Rain-time on it burst.
No, Fate that speeds not will not slay,
Nor Yama's halls vouchsafe me room,
Or, like a lion's weeping prey,
Death now had borne me to my doom.
Hard is my heart and wrought of steel
That breaks not with the crushing blow,
Or in the pangs this day I feel
My lifeless frame had sunk below.
Death waits his hour, nor takes me now:
But this sad thought augments my pain,
That prayer and largess, fast and vow,
And Heavenward service are in vain.
Ah me, ah me! with fruitless toil
Of rites austere a child I sought:
Thus seed cast forth on barren soil
Still lifeless lies and comes to naught.
If ever wretch by anguish grieved
Before his hour to death had fled,
I mourning, like a cow bereaved,
Had been this day among the dead.'

CANTO XXI.

KAUŚALYÁ CALMED.

While thus Kauśalyá wept and sighed,
With timely words sad Lakshman cried:
'O honoured Queen I like it ill
That, subject to a woman's will,
Ráma his royal state should quit
And to an exile's doom submit.
The aged king, fond, changed, and weak,
Will as the queen compels him speak.
But why should Ráma thus be sent
To the wild woods in banishment?
No least offence I find in him,
I see no fault his fame to dim.
Not one in all the world I know,
Not outcast wretch, not secret foe,
Whose whispering lips would dare assail
His spotless life with slanderous tale.
Godlike and bounteous, just, sincere,
E'en to his very foemen dear:
Who would without a cause neglect
The right, and such a son reject?
And if a king such order gave,
In second childhood, passion's slave,
What son within his heart would lay
The senseless order, and obey?
Come, Ráma, ere this plot be known
Stand by me and secure the throne.
Stand like the King who rules below,
Stand aided by thy brother's bow:
How can the might of meaner men
Resist thy royal purpose then?
My shafts, if rebels court their fate,
Shall lay Ayodhyá desolate.
Then shall her streets with blood be dyed
Of those who stand on Bharat's side:
None shall my slaughtering hand exempt,
For gentle patience earns contempt.
If, by Kaikeyí's counsel changed,
Our father's heart be thus estranged,
No mercy must our arm restrain,
But let the foe be slain, be slain.
For should the guide, respected long,
No more discerning right and wrong,
Turn in forbidden paths to stray,
'Tis meet that force his steps should stay.
What power sufficient can he see,
What motive for the wish has he,
That to Kaikeyí would resign
The empire which is justly thine?
Can he, O conqueror of thy foes,
Thy strength and mine in war oppose?
Can he entrust, in our despite,
To Bharat's hand thy royal right?
I love this brother with the whole
Affection of my faithful soul.
Yea Queen, by bow and truth I swear,
By sacrifice, and gift, and prayer,
If Ráma to the forest goes,
Or where the burning furnace glows,
First shall my feet the forest tread,
The flames shall first surround my head.
My might shall chase thy grief and tears,
As darkness flies when morn appears.
Do thou, dear Queen, and Ráma too
Behold what power like mine can do.
My aged father I will kill,
The vassal of Kaikeyí's will,
Old, yet a child, the woman's thrall,
Infirm, and base, the scorn of all.'
 Thus Lakshman cried, the mighty-souled:
Down her sad cheeks the torrents rolled,
As to her son Kauśalyá spake;
 'Now thou hast heard thy brother, take
His counsel if thou hold it wise,
And do the thing his words advise.
Do not, my son, with tears I pray,
My rival's wicked word obey,
Leave me not here consumed with woe,
Nor to the wood, an exile, go.
If thou, to virtue ever true,
Thy duty's path would still pursue,
The highest duty bids thee stay
And thus thy mother's voice obey.
Thus Kaśyap's great ascetic son
A seat among the Immortals won:
In his own home, subdued, he stayed,
And honour to his mother paid.
If reverence to thy sire be due,
Thy mother claims like honour too,
And thus I charge thee, O my child,
Thou must not seek the forest wild.
Ah, what to me were life and bliss,
Condemned my darling son to miss?
But with my Ráma near, to eat
The very grass itself were sweet.
But if thou still wilt go and leave
Thy hapless mother here to grieve,
I from that hour will food abjure,
Nor life without my son endure.
Then it will be thy fate to dwell
In depth of world-detested hell,
As Ocean in the olden time
Was guilty of an impious crime
That marked the lord of each fair flood
As one who spills a Bráhman's blood.'[1]
 Thus spake the queen, and wept, and sighed;
Then righteous Ráma thus replied:
'I have no power to slight or break
Commandments which my father spake.
I bend my head, dear lady, low,
Forgive me, for I needs must go.
Once Kandu, mighty saint, who made
His dwelling in the forest shade,

[1] The commentators say that, in a former creation, Ocean grieved his mother and suffered in consequence the pains of hell.

A cow—and duty's claims he knew—
Obedient to his father, slew.
And in the line from which we spring,
When ordered by their sire the king,
Through earth the sons of Sagar cleft,
And countless things of life bereft.[1]
So Jamadagni's son[2] obeyed
His sire, when in the wood he laid
His hand upon his axe, and smote
Through Reṇuká his mother's throat.
The deeds of these and more beside,
Peers of the Gods, my steps shall guide,
And resolute will I fulfil
My father's word, my father's will.
Nor I, O Queen, unsanctioned tread
This righteous path, by duty led:
The road my footsteps journey o'er
Was traversed by the great of yore.
This high command which all accept
Shall faithfully by me be kept,
For duty ne'er will him forsake
Who fears his sire's command to break.'

Thus to his mother wild with grief:
Then thus to Lakshmaṇ spake the chief
Of those by whom the bow is bent,
Mid all who speak, most eloquent:
'I know what love for me thou hast,
What firm devotion unsurpassed:
Thy valour and thy worth I know,
And glory that appals the foe.
Blest youth, my mother's woe is great,
It bends her neath its matchless weight:
No claims will she, with blinded eyes,
Of truth and patience recognize.
For duty is supreme in place,
And truth is duty's noblest base.
Obedient to my sire's behest
I serve the cause of duty best.
For man should truly do whate'er
To mother, Bráhman, sire, he sware:
He must in duty's path remain,
Nor let his word be pledged in vain.
And, O my brother, how can I
Obedience to this charge deny?
Kaikeyí's tongue my purpose spurred,
But 'twas my sire who gave the word.
Cast these unholy thoughts aside
Which smack of war and Warriors' pride;
To duty's call, not wrath attend,
And tread the path which I commend.'

Ráma by fond affection moved
His brother Lakshmaṇ thus reproved;
Then with joined hands and reverent head
Again to Queen Kauśalyá said:
'I needs must go—do thou consent—
To the wild wood in banishment.
O give me, by my life I pray,
Thy blessing ere I go away.
I, when the promised years are o'er,
Shall see Ayodhyá's town once more.
Then, mother dear, thy tears restrain,
Nor let thy heart be wrung by pain:
In time, my father's will obeyed,
Shall I return from greenwood shade.
My dear Videhan, thou, and I
Lakshmaṇ, Sumitrá, feel this tie,
And must my father's word obey,
As duty bids that rules for aye.
Thy preparations now forgo,
And lock within thy breast thy woe,
Nor be my pious wish withstood
To go an exile to the wood.'

Calm and unmoved the prince explained
His duty's claim and purpose high,
The mother life and sense regained,
Looked on her son and made reply:
'If reverence be thy father's due,
The same by right and love is mine:
Go not, my charge I thus renew,
Nor leave me here in woe to pine.
What were such lonely life to me,
Rites to the shades, or deathless lot?
More dear, my son, one hour with thee
Than all the world where thou art not.'
As bursts to view, when brands blaze high,
Some elephant concealed by night,
So, when he heard his mother's cry,
Burnt Ráma's grief with fiercer might.
Thus to the queen, half senseless still,
And Lakshmaṇ, burnt with heart-felt pain,
True to the right, with steadfast will,
His duteous speech he spoke again:
'Brother, I know thy loving mind,
Thy valour and thy truth I know,
But now to claims of duty blind
Thou and my mother swell my woe.
The fruits of deeds in human life
Make love, gain, duty, manifest,
Dear when they meet as some fond wife
With her sweet babes upon her breast.
But man to duty first should turn
Whene'er the three are not combined:
For those who heed but gain we spurn,
And those to pleasure all resigned.
Shall then the virtuous disobey
Hests of an aged king and sire,
Though feverous joy that father sway,
Or senseless love or causeless ire?
I have no power, commanded thus,
To slight his promise and decree:
The honoured sire of both of us,
My mother's lord and life is he.
Shall she, while yet the holy king
Is living, on the right intent,—
Shall she, like some poor widowed thing,
Go forth with me to banishment!
Now, mother, speed thy parting son,
And let thy blessing soothe my pain,

[1] As described in Book I Canto XL.
[2] Paraśuráma.

That I may turn, mine exile done,
Like King Yayáti, home again.
Fair glory and the fruit she gives,
For lust of sway I ne'er will slight:
What, for the span a mortal lives,
Were rule of earth without the right?'
He soothed her thus, firm to the last
His counsel to his brother told:
Then round the queen in reverence passed,
And held her in his loving hold.

CANTO XXII.

LAKSHMAN CALMED.

So Ráma kept unshaken still
His noble heart with iron will.
To his dear brother next he turned,
Whose glaring eyes with fury burned,
Indignant, panting like a snake,
And thus again his counsel spake:
'Thine anger and thy grief restrain,
And firm in duty's path remain.
Dear brother, lay thy scorn aside,
And be the right thy joy and pride.
Thy ready zeal and thoughtful care
To aid what rites should grace the heir,—
These 'tis another's now to ask;
Come, gird thee for thy noble task,
That Bharat's throning rites may be
Graced with the things prepared for me.
And with thy gentle care provide
That her fond heart, now sorely tried
With fear and longing for my sake,
With doubt and dread may never ache.
To know that thoughts of coming ill
One hour that tender bosom fill
With agony and dark despair
Is grief too great for me to bear.
I cannot, brother, call to mind
One wilful fault or undesigned,
When I have pained in anything
My mothers or my sire the king.
The right my father keeps in view,
In promise, word, and action true;
Let him then all his fear dismiss,
Nor dread the loss of future bliss.
He fears his truth herein will fail:
Hence bitter thoughts his heart assail.
He trembles lest the rites proceed,
And at his pangs my heart should bleed.
So now this earnest wish is mine,
The consecration to resign,
And from this city turn away
To the wild wood with no delay.
My banishment to-day will free
Kaikeyí from her cares, that she,
At last contented and elate,
May Bharat's throning celebrate.
Then will the lady's trouble cease,
Then will her heart have joy and peace,
When wandering in the wood I wear
Deerskin, and bark, and matted hair.
Nor shall by me his heart be grieved
Whose choice approved, whose mind conceived
This counsel which I follow. No,
Forth to the forest will I go.
'Tis Fate, Sumitrá's son, confess,
That sends me to the wilderness.
'Tis Fate alone that gives away
To other hands the royal sway.
How could Kaikeyí's purpose bring
On me this pain and suffering,
Were not her change of heart decreed
By Fate whose will commands the deed?
I know my filial love has been
The same throughout for every queen,
And with the same affection she
Has treated both her son and me.
Her shameful words of cruel spite
To stay the consecrating rite,
And drive me banished from the throne,—
These I ascribe to Fate alone.
How could she, born of royal race,
Whom nature decks with fairest grace,
Speak like a dame of low degree
Before the king to torture me?
But Fate, which none may comprehend,
To which all life must bow and bend,
In her and me its power has shown,
And all my hopes are overthrown.
What man, Sumitrá's darling, may
Contend with Fate's resistless sway,
Whose all-commanding power we find
Our former deeds alone can bind?
Our life and death, our joy and pain,
Anger and fear, and loss and gain,
Each thing that is, in every state,
All is the work of none but Fate.
E'en saints, inspired with rigid zeal,
When once the stroke of Fate they feel,
In sternest vows no more engage,
And fall enslaved by love and rage.
So now the sudden stroke whose weight
Descends unlooked for, comes of Fate,
And with unpitying might destroys
The promise of commencing joys.
Weigh this true counsel in thy soul:
With thy firm heart thy heart control;
Then, brother, thou wilt cease to grieve
For hindered rites which now I leave.
So cast thy needless grief away,
And strictly my commands obey.
These preparations check with speed,
Nor let my throning rites proceed.
These urns that stand prepared to shed
King-making drops upon my head,
Shall with their pure lustrations now
Inaugurate my hermit's vow.

Yet what have I to do with things
That touch the state and pomp of kings?
These hands of mine shall water take
To sanctify the vow I make.
Now Lakshman, let thy heart no more
My fortune changed and lost deplore.
A forest life more joys may bring
Than those that wait upon a king.
Now though her arts successful mar
 My consecrating rite,
Let not the youngest queen too far
 Thy jealous fear excite.
Nor let one thought suggesting ill
 Upon our father fall,
But let thy heart remember still
 That Fate is lord of all.'

CANTO XXIII.

LAKSHMAN'S ANGER.

Thus Ráma to his brother said;
And Lakshman bent his drooping head.
In turns by grief and pride impelled,
A middle course of thought he held.
Then in a frown of anger, bent
His brows that chief most excellent,
And like a serpent in his hole,
Breathed fierce and fast in wrath of soul.
His threatening brows so darkly frowned,
His eyes so fiercely glanced around,
They made his glare, which none might brook,
Like some infuriate lion's look.
Like some wild elephant, full oft
He raised and shook his hand[1] aloft.
Now turned his neck to left and right
Now bent, now raised its stately height.
Now in his rage that sword he felt
Which mangling wounds to foemen dealt,
With sidelong glance his brother eyed,
And thus in burning words replied:
'Thy rash resolve, thy eager haste,
Thy mighty fear, are all misplaced:
No room is here for duty's claim,
No cause to dread the people's blame.
Can one so brave as thou consent
To use a coward's argument?
The glory of the Warrior race
With craven speech his lips debase?
Can one like thee so falsely speak,
Exalting Fate, confessed so weak?
Canst thou, undoubting still restrain
Suspicions of those sinful twain?
Canst thou, most duteous, fail to know
Their hearts are set on duty's show?
They with deceit have set their trains,
And now the fruit rewards their pains.
Had they not long ago agreed,
O Ráma, on this treacherous deed,
That promised boon, so long retained,
He erst had given and she had gained,
I cannot, O my brother, bear
To see another throned as heir
With rites which all our people hate:
Then, O, this passion tolerate.
This vaunted duty which can guide
Thy steps from wisdom's path aside,
And change the counsel of thy breast,
O lofty-hearted, I detest.
Wilt thou, when power and might are thine,
Submit to this abhorred design?
Thy father's impious hest fulfil,
That vassal of Kaikeyí's will?
But if thou still wilt shut thine eyes,
Nor see the guile herein that lies;
My soul is sad, I deeply mourn,
And duty seems a thing to scorn.
Canst thou one moment think to please
This pair who live for love and ease,
And 'gainst thy peace, as foes, allied,
With tenderest names their hatred hide
Now if thy judgment still refers
To Fate this plot of his and hers,
My mind herein can ne'er agree:
And O, in this be ruled by me.
Weak, void of manly pride are they
Who bend to Fate's imputed sway:
The choicest souls, the nobly great
Disdain to bow their heads to Fate.
And he who dares his Fate control
With vigorous act and manly soul,
Though threatening Fate his hopes assail,
Unmoved through all need never quail.
This day mankind shall learn aright
The power of Fate and human might,
So shall the gulf that lies between
A man and Fate be clearly seen.
The might of Fate subdued by me
This hour the citizens shall see,
Who saw its intervention stay
Thy consecrating rites to-day
My power shall turn this Fate aside,
That threatens, as, with furious stride,
An elephant who scorns to feel,
In rage unchecked, the driver's steel.
Not the great Lords whose sleepless might
Protects the worlds, shall stay the rite
Though earth, hell, heaven combine their powers:
And shall we fear this sire of ours?
Then if their minds are idly bent
To doom thee, King, to banishment,
Through twice seven years of exile they

[1] The Sanskrit word *hasta* signifies both *hand*, and the trunk of 'The beast that bears between his eyes a serpent for a hand.'

Shall in the lonely forest stay.
I will consume the hopes that fire
The queen Kaikeyí and our sire,
That to her son this check will bring
Advantage, making Bharat king.
The power of Fate will ne'er withstand
The might that arms my vigorous hand;
If danger and distress assail,
My fearless strength will still prevail.
A thousand circling years shall flee:
The forest then thy home shall be,
And thy good sons, succeeding, hold
The empire which their sire controlled.
The royal saints, of old who reigned,
For aged kings this rest ordained:
These to their sons their realm commit
That they, like sires, may cherish it.
O pious soul, if thou decline
The empire which is justly thine,
Lest, while the king distracted lies,
Disorder in the state should rise,
I,—or no mansion may I find
In worlds to hero souls assigned,—
The guardian of thy realm will be,
As the sea-bank protects the sea.
Then cast thine idle fears aside:
With prosperous rites be sanctified.
The lords of earth may strive in vain:
My power shall all their force restrain.
My pair of arms, my warrio's bow
Are not for pride of empty show:
For no support these shafts were made;
And binding up ill suits my blade:
To pierce the foe with deadly breach—
This is the work of all and each.
But small, methinks, the love I show
For him I count my mortal foe.
Soon as my trenchant steel is bare,
Flashing its lightning through the air,
I heed no foe, nor stand aghast
Though Indra's self the levin cast.
Then shall the ways be hard to pass,
Where chariots lie in ruinous mass;
When elephant and man and steed
Crushed in the murderous onslaught bleed,
And legs and heads fall, heap on heap,
Beneath my sword's tremendous sweep.
Struck by my keen brand's trenchant blade,
Thine enemies shall fall dismayed,
Like towering mountains rent in twain,
Or lightning clouds that burst in rain.
When armed with brace and glove I stand,
And take my trusty bow in hand,
Who then shall vaunt his might? who dare
Count him a man to meet me there?
Then will I loose my shafts, and strike
Man, elephant, and steed alike:
At one shall many an arrow fly,
And many a foe with one shall die.
This day the world my power shall see,
That none in arms can rival me:
My strength the monarch shall abase,
And set thee, lord, in lordliest place.
These arms which breathe the sandal's scent,
Which golden bracelets ornament,
These hands which precious gifts bestow,
Which guard the friend and smite the foe,
A nobler service shall assay,
And fight in Ráma's cause to-day,
The robbers of thy rights to stay.
Speak, brother, tell thy foeman's name
Whom I, in conquering strife,
May strip of followers and fame,
Of fortune, or of life.
Say, how may all this sea-girt land
Be brought to own thy sway:
Thy faithful servant here I stand
To listen and obey.'
Then strove the bride of Raghu's race
Sad Lakshman's heart to cheer,
While slowly down the hero's face,
Unchecked, there rolled a tear.
'The orders of my sire,' he cried,
'My will shall ne'er oppose:
I follow still, whate'er betide,
The path which duty shows.'

CANTO XXIV.

KAUŚALYÁ CALMED.

But when Kauśalyá saw that he
Resolved to keep his sire's decree,
While tears and sobs her utterance broke,
Her very righteous speech she spoke:
'Can he, a stranger yet to pain,
Whose pleasant words all hearts enchain,
Son of the king and me the queen,
Live on the grain his hands may glean;
Can he, whose slaves and menials eat
The finest cakes of sifted wheat—
Can Ráma in the forest live
On roots and fruit which woodlands give;
Who will believe, who will not fear
When the sad story smites his ear,
That one so dear, so noble held,
Is by the king his sire expelled?
Now surely none may Fate resist,
Which orders all as it may list,
If, Ráma, in thy strength and grace,
The woods become thy dwelling-place.
A childless mother long I grieved,
And many a sigh for offspring heaved,
With wistful longing weak and worn
Till thou at last, my son, wast born.
Fanned by the storm of that desire
Deep in my soul I felt the fire,
Whose offerings flowed from weeping eyes,
With fuel fed of groans and sighs,

While round the flame the smoke grew hot
Of tears because thou camest not.
Now reft of thee, too fiery fierce
The flame of woe my heart will pierce,
As, when the days of spring return,
The sun's hot beams the forest burn.
The mother cow still follows near
The wanderings of her youngling dear.
So close to thine my feet shall be,
Where'er thou goest following thee.'
Ráma, the noblest lord of men,
Heard his fond mother's speech, and then
In soothing words like these replied
To the sad queen who wept and sighed :
'Nay, by Kaikeyí's art beguiled,
When I am banished to the wild,
If thou, my mother, also fly,
The aged king will surely die.
When wedded dames their lords forsake,
Long for the crime their souls shall ache.
Thou must not e'en in thought within
Thy bosom frame so dire a sin.
Long as Kakutstha's son, who reigns
Lord of the earth, in life remains,
Thou must with love his will obey :
This duty claims, supreme for aye.
Yes, mother, thou and I must be
Submissive to my sire's decree,
King, husband, sire is he confessed,
The lord of all, the worthiest.
I in the wilds my days will spend
Till twice seven years have reached an end,
Then with great joy will come again,
And faithful to thy hests remain.'
Kauśalyá, by her son addressed,
With love and passion sore distressed,
Afflicted, with her eyes bedewed,
To Ráma thus her speech renewed :
'Nay, Ráma, but my heart will break
If with these queens my home I make.
Lead me too with thee ; let me go
And wander like a woodland roe.'
Then, while no tear the hero shed,
Thus to the weeping queen he said :
'Mother, while lives the husband, he
Is woman's lord and deity.
O dearest lady, thou and I
Our lord and king must ne'er deny;
The lord of earth himself have we
Our guardian wise and friend to be.
And Bharat, true to duty's call,
Whose sweet words take the hearts of all,
Will serve thee well, and ne'er forget
The virtuous path before him set.
Be this, I pray, thine earnest care,
That the old king my father ne'er,
When I have parted hence, may know,
Grieved for his son, a pang of woe.
Let not this grief his soul distress,
To kill him with the bitterness.
Wth duteous care, in every thing,
Love, comfort, cheer the aged king.
Though, best of womankind, a spouse
Keeps firmly all her fasts and vows,
Nor yet her husband's will obeys,
She treads in sin's forbidden ways.
She to her husband's will who bends
Goes to high bliss that never ends,
Yea, though the Gods have found in her
No reverential worshipper.
Bent on his weal, a woman still
Must seek to do her husband's will :
For Scripture, custom, law uphold
This duty Heaven revealed of old.
Honour true Bráhmans for my sake,
And constant offerings duly make,
With fire-oblations and with flowers,
To all the host of heavenly powers.
Look to the coming time, and yearn
For the glad hour of my return,
And still thy duteous course pursue,
Abstemious, humble, kind, and true.
The highest bliss shalt thou obtain
When I from exile come again,
If, best of those who keep the right,
The king my sire still see the light.'
The queen, by Ráma thus addressed,
Still with a mother's grief oppressed,
While her long eyes with tears were dim,
Began once more and answered him :
'Not by my pleading may be stayed
The firm resolve thy soul has made.
My hero, thou wilt go ; and none
The stern commands of Fate may shun.
Go forth, dear child whom naught can be nd
And may all bliss thy steps attend.
Thou wilt return, and that dear day
Will chase mine every grief away.
Thou wilt return, thy duty done,
Thy vows discharged, high glory won ;
From filial debt wilt thou be free,
And sweetest joy will come on me.
My son, the will of mighty Fate
At every time must dominate,
If now it drives thee hence to stray
Heedless of me who bid thee stay.
Go, strong of arm, go forth, my boy,
Go forth, again to come with joy.
And thine expectant mother cheer
With those sweet tones she loves to hear.
O that the blessed hour were nigh
When thou shalt glad this anxious eye,
With matted hair and hermit dress
Returning from the wilderness.'
Kauśalyá's conscious soul approved,
As her proud glance she bent
On Ráma constant and unmoved,
Resolved on banishment.
Such words, with happy omens fraught
To her dear son she said,
Invoking with each eager thought
A blessing on his head.

CANTO XXV.

KAUŚALYÁ'S BLESSING.

Her grief and woe she cast aside,
Her lips with water purified,
And thus her benison began
That mother of the noblest man:
'If thou wilt hear no words of mine,
Go forth, thou pride of Raghu's line.
Go, darling, and return with speed,
Walking where noble spirits lead.
May virtue on thy steps attend.
And be her faithful lover's friend.
May Those to whom thy vows are paid
In temple and in holy shade,
With all the mighty saints combine
To keep that precious life of thine.
The arms wise Viśvámitra[1] gave
Thy virtuous soul from danger save.
Long be thy life: thy sure defence
Shall be thy truthful innocence,
And that obedience, naught can tire,
To me thy mother and thy sire.
May fanes where holy fires are fed,
Altars with grass and fuel spread,
Each sacrificial ground, each tree,
Rock, lake, and mountain, prosper thee.
Let old Viráj,[2] and Him who made
The universe, combine to aid;
Let Indra and each guardian Lord
Who keeps the worlds, their help afford,
And be thy constant friend the Sun,
Lord Púshá, Bhaga, Aryaman.[3]
Fortnights and seasons, nights and days,
Years, months, and hours, protect thy ways,
Vrihaspati shall still be nigh,
The War-God, and the Moon on high,
And Nárad[4] and the sainted seven[5]
Shall watch thee from their starry heaven.
The mountains, and the seas which ring
The world, and Varuṇa the King,
Sky, ether, and the wind, whate'er
Moves not or moves, for thee shall care.
Each lunar mansion be benign,
With happier light the planets shine;
All gods, each light in heaven that glows,
Potect my child where'er he goes.
The twilight hours, the day and night,
Keep in the wood thy steps aright.
Watch, minute, instant, as they flee,
Shall all bring happiness to thee.
Celestials and the Titan brood
Protect thee in thy solitude,
And haunt the mighty wood to bless
The wanderer in his hermit dress.
Fear not, by mightier guardians screened,
The giant or night-roving fiend;
Nor let the cruel race who tear
Man's flesh for food thy bosom scare.
Far be the ape, the scorpion's sting,
Fly, gnat, and worm, and creeping thing.
Thee shall the hungry lion spare,
The tiger, elephant, and bear:
Safe from their furious might repose,
Safe from the horned buffaloes.
Each savage thing the forests breed,
That love on human flesh to feed,
Shall for my child its rage abate,
When thus its wrath I deprecate.
Blest be thy ways: may sweet success
The valour of my darling bless.
To all that Fortune can bestow,
Go forth, my child, my Ráma, go.
Go forth, O happy in the love
Of all the Gods below, above;
And in those guardian powers confide
Thy paths who keep, thy steps who guide.
May Śukra,[1] Yama, Sun, and Moon,
And He who gives each golden boon,[2]
Won by mine earnest prayers, be good
To thee, my son, in Daṇḍak wood.
Fire, wind, and smoke, each text and spell
From mouths of holy seers that fell,
Guard Ráma when his limbs he dips,
Or with the stream makes pure his lips!
May the great saints and He, the Lord
Who made the worlds, by worlds adored,
And every God in heaven beside
My banished Ráma keep and guide.'
 Thus with due praise the long-eyed dame,
Ennobled by her spotless fame,
With wreaths of flowers and precious scent
Worshipped the Gods, most reverent.
A high-souled Bráhman lit the fire,
And offered, at the queen's desire,
The holy oil ordained to burn
For Ráma's weal and safe return.
Kauśalyá, best of dames, with care
Set oil, wreaths, fuel, mustard, there.
Then when the rites of fire had ceased,
For Ráma's bliss and health, the priest,
Standing without, gave what remained
In general offering,[3] as ordained.

---

[1] See p. 41.
[2] The first progeny of Brahmá, or Brahmá himself.
[3] These are three names of the Sun.
[4] See p. 1.
[5] The saints who form the constellation of Ursa Major.

[1] The regent of the planet Venus.
[2] Kuvera.
[3] *Bali*, or the presentation of food to all created beings, is one of the five great sacraments of the Hindu religion: it consists in throwing a small parcel of the offering, *Ghee*, or rice, or the like, into the open air at the back of the house.

Dealing among the twice-born train
Honey, and curds, and oil, and grain,
He bade each heart and voice unite
To bless the youthful anchorite.
Then Ráma's mother, glorious dame
Bestowed, to meet the Bráhman's claim,
A lordly fee for duty done;
And thus again addressed her son:
'Such blessings as the Gods o'erjoyed
Poured forth, when Vritra[1] was destroyed,
On Indra of the thousand eyes,
Attend, my child, thine enterprise!
Yea, such as Vinatá once gave
To King Suparna[2] swift and brave,
Who sought the drink that cheers the skies,
Attend, my child, thine enterprise!
Yea, such as, when the Amrit rose,[3]
And Indra slew his Daitya foes,
The royal Aditi bestowed
On Him whose hand with slaughter glowed
Of that dire brood of monstrous size,
Attend, my child, thine enterprise!
E'en such as peerless Vishnu graced,
When with his triple step he paced,
Outbursting from the dwarf's disguise,[4]
Attend, my child, thine enterprise!
Floods, isles, and seasons as they fly,
Worlds, Vedas, quarters of the sky,
Combine, O mighty-armed, to bless
Thee destined heir of happiness!'
The long-eyed lady ceased: she shed
Pure scent and grain upon his head,
And that prized herb whose sovereign power
Preserves from dark misfortune's hour,
Upon the hero's arm she set,
To be his faithful amulet,
While holy texts she murmured low,
And spoke glad words though crushed by woe,
Concealing with obedient tongue
The pangs with which her heart was wrung.
She bent, she kissed his brow, she pressed
Her darling to her troubled breast:
'Firm in thy purpose, go,' she cried,
'Go Ráma, and may bliss betide.
Again returning safe and well,
Triumphant in Ayodhyá dwell.
Then shall my happy eyes behold
The empire by thy will controlled.
Then grief and care shall leave no trace,
Joy shall light up thy mother's face,
And I shall see my darling reign,
In moonlike glory come again.
These eyes shall fondly gaze on thee
So faithful to thy sire's decree,
When thou the forest wild shalt quit
On thine ancestral throne to sit.
Yea, thou shalt turn from exile back,
Nor choicest blessings ever lack,
Then fill with rapture ever new
My bosom and thy consort's too.
To Śiva and the heavenly host
My worship has been paid,
To mighty saint, to godlike ghost,
To every wandering shade.
Forth to the forest thou wilt hie,
Therein to dwell so long:
Let all the quarters of the sky
Protect my child from wrong.'
Her blessings thus the queen bestowed;
Then round him fondly paced,
And often, while her eyes o'erflowed,
Her dearest son embraced.
Kauśalyá's honoured feet he pressed,
As round her steps she bent,
And radiant with her prayers that blessed,
To Sítá's home he went.

[1] In mythology, a demon slain by Indra.
[2] Called also Garud, the King of the birds, offspring of Vinatá. See p. 53.
[3] See p. 56.
[4] See p. 43.

CANTO XXVI.

ALONE WITH SÍTÁ.

So Ráma, to his purpose true,
To Queen Kauśalyá bade adieu,
Received the benison she gave,
And to the path of duty clave.
As through the crowded street he passed,
A radiance on the way he cast,
And each fair grace, by all approved,
The bosoms of the people moved.

Now of the woeful change no word
The fair Videhan bride had heard;
The thought of that imperial rite
Still filled her bosom with delight.
With grateful heart and joyful thought
The Gods in worship she had sought,
And, well in royal duties learned,
Sat longing till her lord returned.
Not all unmarked by grief and shame
Within his sumptuous home he came,
And hurried through the happy crowd
With eye dejected, gloomy-browed.
Up Sítá sprang, and every limb
Trembled with fear at sight of him.
She marked that cheek where anguish fed,
Those senses care-disquieted.
For, when he looked on her, no more
Could his heart hide the load it bore,
Nor could the pious chief control
The paleness o'er his cheek that stole.
His altered cheer, his brow bedewed
With clammy drops, his grief she viewed,
And cried, consumed with fires of woe,
'What, O my lord, has changed thee so?

Vrihaspati looks down benign,
And the moon rests in Pushya's sign,
As Bráhmans sage this day declare:
Then whence, my lord, this grief and care?
Why does no canopy, like foam
For its white beauty, shade thee home,
Its hundred ribs spread wide to throw
Splendour on thy fair head below?
Where are the royal fans, to grace
The lotus beauty of thy face,
Fair as the moon or wild-swan's wing,
And waving round the new-made king?
Why do no sweet-toned bards rejoice
To hail thee with triumphant voice?
No tuneful heralds love to raise
Loud music in their monarch's praise?
Why do no Bráhmans, Scripture-read,
Pour curds and honey on thy head,
Anointed, as the laws ordain,
With holy rites, supreme to reign?
Where are the chiefs of every guild?
Where are the myriads should have filled
The streets, and followed home their king
With merry noise and triumphing?
Why does no gold-wrought chariot lead
With four brave horses, best for speed?
No elephant precede the crowd
Like a huge hill or thunder cloud,
Marked from his birth for happy fate,
Whom signs auspicious decorate?
Why does no henchman, young and fair,
Precede thee, and delight to bear
Entrusted to his reverent hold
The burthen of thy throne of gold?
Why, if the consecrating rite
Be ready, why this mournful plight?
Why do I see this sudden change,
This altered mien so sad and strange?'
To her, as thus she weeping cried,
Raghu's illustrious son replied:
'Sítá, my honoured sire's decree
Commands me to the woods to flee.
O high-born lady, nobly bred
In the good paths thy footsteps tread,
Hear, Janak's daughter, while I tell
The story as it all befell.
Of old my father true and brave
Two boons to Queen Kaikeyí gave.
Through these the preparations made
For me to-day by her are stayed,
For he is bound to disallow
This promise by that earlier vow.
In Dandak forest wild and vast
Must fourteen years by me be passed.
My father's will makes Bharat heir,
The kingdom and the throne to share.
Now, ere the lonely wild I seek,
I come once more with thee to speak.
In Bharat's presence, O my dame,
Ne'er speak with pride of Ráma's name:
Another's eulogy to hear
Is hateful to a monarch's ear.
Thou must with love his rule obey
To whom my father yields the sway.
With love and sweet observance learn
His grace, and more the king's, to earn.
Now, that my father may not break
The words of promise that he spake,
To the drear wood my steps are bent:
Be firm, good Sítá, and content.
Through all that time, my blameless spouse,
Keep well thy fasts and holy vows.
Rise from thy bed at break of day,
And to the Gods due worship pay.
With meek and lowly love revere
The lord of men, my father dear,
And reverence to Kauśalyá show,
My mother, worn with eld and woe:
By duty's law, O best of dames,
High worship from thy love she claims.
Nor to the other queens refuse
Observance, rendering each her dues:
By love and fond attention shown
They are my mothers like mine own.
Let Bharat and Śatrughna bear
In thy sweet love a special share:
Dear as my life, O let them be
Like brother and like son to thee.
In every word and deed refrain
From aught that Bharat's soul may pain:
He is Ayodhyá's king and mine,
The head and lord of all our line.
For those who serve and love them much
With weariless endeavour, touch
And win the gracious hearts of kings.
While wrath from disobedience springs.
Great monarchs from their presence send
Their lawful sons who still offend,
And welcome to the vacant place
Good children of an alien race.
Then, best of women, rest thou here,
And Bharat's will with love revere.
Obedient to thy king remain,
And still thy vows of truth maintain.
To the wide wood my steps I bend:
Make thou thy dwelling here;
See that thy conduct ne'er offend,
And keep my words, my dear.'

CANTO XXVII.

SÍTÁ'S SPEECH.

His sweetly-speaking bride, who best
Deserved her lord, he thus addressed.
Then tender love bade passion wake,
And thus the fair Videhan spake:
'What words are these that thou hast said?
Contempt of me the thought has bred.
O best of heroes, I dismiss
With bitter scorn a speech like this:

Unworthy of a warrior's fame
It taints a monarch's son with shame,
Ne'er to be heard from those who know
The science of the sword and bow.
My lord, the mother, sire, and son
Receive their lots by merit won;
The brother and the daughter find
The portions to their deeds assigned.
The wife alone, whate'er await,
Must share on earth her husband's fate.
So now the king's command which sends
Thee to the wild, to me extends.
The wife can find no refuge, none,
In father, mother, self, or son:
Both here, and when they vanish hence,
Her husband is her sole defence.
If, Raghu's son, thy steps are led
Where Dandak's pathless wilds are spread,
My feet before thine own shall pass
Through tangled thorn and matted grass.
Dismiss thine anger and thy doubt:
Like refuse water cast them out,
And lead me, O my hero, hence—
I know not sin—with confidence.
Whate'er his lot, 'tis far more sweet
To follow still a husband's feet
Than in rich palaces to lie,
Or roam at pleasure through the sky.
My mother and my sire have taught
What duty bids, and trained each thought,
Nor have I now mine ear to turn
The duties of a wife to learn.
I'll seek with thee the woodland dell
And pathless wild where no men dwell,
Where tribes of silvan creatures roam,
And many a tiger makes his home.
My life shall pass as pleasant there
As in my father's palace fair.
The worlds shall wake no care in me;
My only care be truth to thee.
There while thy wish I still obey,
True to my vows with thee I'll stray,
And there shall blissful hours be spent
In woods with honey redolent.
In forest shades thy mighty arm
Would keep a stranger's life from harm,
And how shall Sítá think of fear
When thou, O glorious lord, art near?
Heir of high bliss, my choice is made,
Nor can I from my will be stayed.
Doubt not; the earth will yield me roots,
These will I eat, and woodland fruits;
And as with thee I wander there
I will not bring thee grief or care.
I long, when thou, wise lord, art nigh,
All fearless, with delighted eye
To gaze upon the rocky hill,
The lake, the fountain, and the rill;
To sport with thee, my limbs to cool,
In some pure lily-covered pool,
While the white swan's and mallard's wings
Are plashing in the water-springs.
So would a thousand seasons flee
Like one sweet day, if spent with thee.
Without my lord I would not prize
A home with Gods above the skies:
Without my lord, my life to bless,
Where could be heaven or happiness?
 Forbid me not: with thee I go
  The tangled wood to tread.
 There will I live with thee, as though
  This roof were o'er my head.
 My will for thine shall be resigned;
  Thy feet my steps shall guide.
 Thou, only thou, art in my mind:
  I heed not all beside.
 Thy heart shall ne'er by me be grieved;
  Do not my prayer deny:
 Take me, dear lord; of thee bereaved
  Thy Sítá swears to die.'
 These words the duteous lady spake,
  Nor would he yet consent
 His faithful wife with him to take
  To share his banishment.
 He soothed her with his gentle speech;
  To change her will he strove;
 And much he said the woes to teach
  Of those in wilds who rove.

CANTO XXVIII.

THE DANGERS OF THE WOOD.

Thus Sítá spake, and he who knew
His duty, to its orders true,
Was still reluctant as the woes
Of forest life before him rose.
He sought to soothe her grief, to dry
The torrent from each brimming eye,
And then, her firm resolve to shake,
These words to pious hero spake:
'O daughter of a noble line,
Whose steps from virtue ne'er decline,
Remain, thy duties here pursue,
As my fond heart would have thee do.
Now hear me, Sítá, fair and weak,
And do the words that I shall speak.
Attend and hear while I explain
Each danger in the wood, each pain.
Thy lips have spoken: I condemn
The foolish words that fell from them.
This senseless plan, this wish of thine
To live a forest life, resign.
The names of trouble and distress
Suit well the tangled wilderness.
In the wild wood no joy I know,
A forest life is naught but woe.
The lion in his moutain cave
Answers the torrents as they rave,
And forth his voice of terror throws:
The wood, my love, is full of woes.

There mighty monsters fearless play,
And in their maddened onset slay
The hapless wretch who near them goes:
The wood, my love, is full of woes.
'Tis hard to ford each treacherous flood,
So thick with crocodiles and mud,
Where the wild elephants repose:
The wood, my love, is full of woes.
Or far from streams the wanderer strays
Through thorns and creeper-tangled ways,
While round him many a wild-cock crows:
The wood, my love, is full of woes.
On the cold ground upon a heap
Of gathered leaves condemned to sleep,
Toil-wearied, will his eyelids close:
The wood, my love, is full of woes.
Long days and nights must he content
His soul with scanty aliment,
What fruit the wind from branches blows:
The wood, my love, is full of woes.
O Sítá, while his strength may last,
The ascetic in the wood must fast,
Coil on his head his matted hair,
And bark must be his only wear.
To Gods and spirits day by day
The ordered worship he must pay,
And honour with respectful care
Each wandering guest who meets him there.
The bathing rites he ne'er must shun
At dawn, at noon, at set of sun,
Obedient to the law he knows:
The wood, my love, is full of woes.
To grace the altar must be brought
The gift of flowers his hands have sought—
The debt each pious hermit owes:
The wood, my love, is full of woes.
The devotee must be content
To live, severely abstinent,
On what the chance of fortune shows:
The wood, my love, is full of woes.
Hunger afflicts him evermore:
The nights are black, the wild winds roar;
And there are dangers worse than those:
The wood, my love, is full of woes.
There creeping things in every form
Infest the earth, the serpents swarm,
And each proud eye with fury glows:
The wood, my love, is full of woes.
The snakes that by the rives hide
In sinuous course like rivers glide,
And line the path with deadly foes:
The wood, my love, is full of woes.
Scorpions, and grasshoppers, and flies
Disturb the wanderer as he lies,
And wake him from his troubled doze:
The wood, my love, is full of woes.
Trees, thorny bushes, intertwined,
Their branches' ends together bind,
And dense with grass the thicket grows:
The wood, my dear, is full of woes,
With many ills the flesh is tried,
When these and countless fears beside
Vex those who in the wood remain:
The wilds are naught but grief and pain.
Hope, anger must be cast aside,
To penance every thought applied:
No fear must be of things to fear:
Hence is the wood for ever drear.
Enough, my love: thy purpose quit:
For forest life thou art not fit.
As thus I think on all, I see
The wild wood is no place for thee.'

CANTO XXIX.

SITA'S APPEAL.

Thus Ráma spake. Her lord's address
The lady heard with deep distress,
And, as the tear bedimmed her eye,
In soft low accents made reply:
'The perils of the wood, and all
The woes thou countest to appal,
Led by my love I deem not pain;
Each woe a charm, each loss a gain.
Tiger, and elephant, and deer,
Bull, lion, buffalo, in fear,
Soon as thy matchless form they see,
With every silvan beast will flee.
With thee, O Ráma, I must go:
My sire's command ordains it so.
Bereft of thee, my lonely heart
Must break, and life and I must part.
While thou, O mighty lord, art nigh,
Not even He who rules the sky,
Though He is strongest of the strong,
With all his might can do me wrong.
Nor can a lonely woman left
By her dear husband live bereft.
In my great love, my lord, I ween,
The truth of this thou mayst have seen.
In my sire's palace long ago
I heard the chief of those who know,
The truth-declaring Bráhmans, tell
My fortune, in the wood to dwell.
I heard their promise who divine
The future by each mark and sign,
And from that hour have longed to lead
The forest life their lips decreed.
Now, mighty Ráma, I must share
Thy father's doom which sends thee there;
In this I will not be denied,
But follow, love, where thou shalt guide.
O husband, I will go with thee,
Obedient to that high decree.
Now let the Bráhmans' words be true,
For this the time they had in view.
I know full well the wood has woes;
But they disturb the lives of those
Who in the forest dwell, nor hold
Their rebel senses well controlled.

In my sire's halls, ere I was wed,
I heard a dame who begged her bread
Before my mother's face relate
What griefs a forest life await.
And many a time in sport I prayed
To seek with thee the greenwood shade,
For O, my heart on this is set,
To follow thee, dear anchoret.
May blessings on thy life attend:
I long with thee my steps to bend,
For with such hero as thou art
This pilgrimage enchants my heart
Still close, my lord, to thy dear side
My spirit will be purified:
Love from all sin my soul will free;
My husband is a God to me.
So, love, with thee shall I have bliss
And share the life that follows this.
I heard a Bráhman, dear to fame,
This ancient Scripture text proclaim:
'The woman whom on earth below
Her parents on a man bestow,
And lawfully their hands unite
With water and each holy rite,
She in this world shall be his wife,
His also in the after life.'
Then tell me, O beloved, why
Thou wilt this earnest prayer deny,
Nor take me with thee to the wood,
Thine own dear wife so true and good.
But if thou wilt not take me there
Thus grieving in my wild despair,
To fire or water I will fly,
Or to the poisoned draught, and die.'

So thus to share his exile, she
Besought him with each earnest plea,
Nor could she yet her lord persuade
To take her to the lonely shade.
The answer of the strong-armed chief
Smote the Videhan's soul with grief,
And from her eyes the torrents came
Bathing the bosom of the dame.

CANTO XXX.

THE TRIUMPH OF LOVE.

The daughter of Videha's king,
While Ráma strove to soothe the sting
Of her deep anguish, thus began
Once more in furtherance of her plan:
And with her spirit sorely tried
By fear and anger, love and pride,
With keenly taunting words addressed
Her hero of the stately breast:
'Why did the king my sire, who reigns
O'er fair Videha's wide domains,
Hail Ráma son with joy unwise,
A woman in a man's disguise?
Now falsely would the people say,
By idle fancies led astray,
That Ráma's own are power and might,
As glorious as the Lord of Light.
Why sinkest thou in such dismay?
What fears upon thy spirit weigh,
That thou, O Ráma, fain wouldst flee
From her who thinks of naught but thee?
To thy dear will am I resigned
In heart and body, soul and mind,
As Sávitrí gave all to one,
Satyaván, Dyumatsena's son.[1]
Not e'en in fancy can I brook
To any guard save thee to look:
Let meaner wives their houses shame,
To go with thee is all my claim.
Like some low actor, deemst thou fit
Thy wife to others to commit—
Thine own, espoused in maiden youth,
Thy wife so long, unblamed for truth?
Do thou, my lord, his will obey
For whom thou losest royal sway,
To whom thou wouldst thy wife confide—
Not me, but thee, his wish may guide.
Thou must not here thy wife forsake,
And to the wood thy journey make,
Whether stern penance, grief, and care,
Or rule or heaven await thee there.
Nor shall fatigue my limbs distress
When wandering in the wilderness:
Each path which near to thee I tread
Shall seem a soft luxurious bed.
The reeds, the bushes where I pass,
The thorny trees, the tangled grass
Shall feel, if only thou be near,
Soft to my touch as skins of deer.
When the rude wind in fury blows,
And scattered dust upon me throws,
That dust, beloved lord, to me
Shall as the precious sandal be.
And what shall be more blest than I,
When gazing on the wood I lie
In some green glade upon a bed
With sacred grass beneath us spread?
The root, the leaf, the fruit which thou
Shalt give me from the earth or bough,
Scanty or plentiful, to eat,
Shall taste to me as Amrit sweet.
As there I live on flowers and roots
And every season's kindly fruits,
I will not for my mother grieve,
My sire, my home, or all I leave.
My presence, love, shall never add
One pain to make thy heart more sad;

[1] The story of Sávitrí, told in the Mahábhárat, has been admirably translated by Rückert, and elegantly epitomized by Mrs. Manning in *India, Ancient and Mediæval*. There is a free rendering of the story in *Idylls from the Sanskrit*.

I will not cause thee grief or care,
Nor be a burden hard to bear.
With thee is heaven, where'er the spot;
Each place is hell where thou art not.
Then go with me, O Ráma; this
Is all my hope and all my bliss.
If thou wilt leave thy wife who still
Entreats thee with undaunted will,
This very day shall poison close
The life that spurns the rule of foes.
How, after, can my soul sustain
The bitter life of endless pain,
When thy dear face, my lord, I miss?
No, death is better far than this.
Not for an hour could I endure
The deadly grief that knows not cure,
Far less a woe I could not shun
For ten long years, and three, and one.'

While fires of woe consumed her, such
Her sad appeal, lamenting much;
Then with a wild cry, anguish-wrung,
About her husband's neck she clung.
Like some she-elephant who bleeds
Struck by the hunter's venomed reeds,
So in her quivering heart she felt
The many wounds his speeches dealt.
Then, as the spark from wood is gained,[1]
Down rolled the tear so long restrained:
The crystal moisture, sprung from woe,
From her sweet eyes began to flow,
As runs the water from a pair
Of lotuses divinely fair.
And Sítá's face with long dark eyes,
Pure as the moon of autumn skies,
Faded with weeping, as the buds
Of lotuses when sink the floods.
Around his wife his arms he strained,
Who senseless from her woe remained,
And with sweet words, that bade her wake
To life again, the hero spake:
'I would not with thy woe, my Queen,
Buy heaven and all its blissful sheen.
Void of all fear am I as He,
The self-existent God, can be.
I knew not all thy heart till now,
Dear lady of the lovely brow
So wished not thee in woods to dwell;
Yet there mine arm can guard thee well.
Now surely thou, dear love, wast made
To dwell with me in green wood shade.
And, as a high saint's tender mind
Clings to its love for all mankind,
So I to thee will ever cling,
Sweet daughter of Videha's king.
The good, of old, O soft of frame,
Honoured this duty's sovereign claim,
And I its guidance will not shun,
True as light's Queen is to the Sun.
I cannot, pride of Janak's line,
This journey to the wood decline:
My sire's behest, the oath he sware,
The claims of truth, all lead me there.
One duty, dear the same for aye,
Is sire and mother to obey:
Should I their orders once transgress
My very life were weariness.
If glad obedience be denied
To father, mother, holy guide,
What rites, what service can be done
That stern Fate's favour may be won?
These three the triple world comprise,
O darling of the lovely eyes.
Earth has no holy thing like these
Whom with all love men seek to please.
Not truth, or gift, or bended knee,
Not honour, worship, lordly fee,
Storms heaven and wins a blessing thence
Like sonly love and reverence.
Heaven, riches, grain, and varied lore,
With sons and many a blessing more,
All these are made their own with ease
By those their elders' souls who please.
The mighty-souled, who ne'er forget,
Devoted sons, their filial debt,
Win worlds where Gods and minstrels are,
And Brahmá's sphere more glorious far.
Now as the orders of my sire,
Who keeps the way of truth, require,
So will I do, for such the way
Of duty that endures for aye:
To take thee, love, to Daṇḍak's wild
My heart at length is reconciled,
For thee such earnest thoughts impel
To follow, and with me to dwell.
O faultless form from feet to brows,
Come with me, as my will allows,
And duty there with me pursue,
Trembler, whose bright eyes thrill me through.
In all thy days, come good come ill,
Preserve unchanged such noble will,
And thou, dear love, wilt ever be
The glory of thy house and me.
Now, beauteous-armed, begin the tasks
The woodland life of hermits asks.
For me the joys of heaven above
Have charms no more without thee, love.
And now, dear Sítá, be not slow:
Food on good mendicants bestow,
And for the holy Bráhmans bring
Thy treasures and each precious thing.
Thy best attire and gems collect,
The jewels which thy beauty decked,
And every ornament and toy
Prepared for hours of sport and joy:
The beds, the cars wherein I ride,
Among our followers, next, divide.'

She conscious that her lord approved
Her going, with great rapture moved,

[1] Fire for sacrificial purposes is produced by the attrition of two pieces of wood.

Hastened within, without delay,
Prepared to give their wealth away.

CANTO XXXI.

LAKSHMAṆ'S PRAYER.

When Lakshmaṇ, who had joined them there,
Had heard the converse of the pair,
His mien was changed, his eyes o'erflowed,
His breast no more could bear its load.
The son of Raghu, sore distressed,
His brother's feet with fervour pressed,
While thus to Sítá he complained,
And him by lofty vows enchained:
'If thou wilt make the woods thy home,
Where elephant and roebuck roam,
I too this day will take my bow
And in the path before thee go.
Our way will lie through forest ground
Where countless birds and beasts are found.
I heed not homes of Gods on high,
I heed not life that cannot die,
Nor would I wish, with thee away,
O'er the three worlds to stretch my sway.'

Thus Lakshmaṇ spake, with earnest prayer
His brother's woodland life to share.
As Ráma still his prayer denied
With soothing words, again he cried:
'When leave at first thou didst accord,
Why dost thou stay me now, my lord?
Thou art my refuge: O, be kind,
Leave me not, dear my lord, behind.
Thou canst not, brother, if thou choose
That I still live, my wish refuse.'

The glorious chief his speech renewed
To faithful Lakshmaṇ as he sued,
And on the eyes of Ráma gazed
Longing to lead, with hands upraised:
'Thou art a hero just and dear,
Whose steps to virtue's path adhere,
Loved as my life till life shall end,
My faithful brother and my friend.
If to the woods thou take thy way
With Sítá and with me to-day,
Who for Kauśalyá will provide,
And guard the good Sumitrá's side?
The lord of earth, of mighty power,
Who sends good things in plenteous shower,
As Indra pours the grateful rain,
A captive lies in passion's chain.
The power imperial for her son
Has Aśvapati's daughter[1] won,
And she, proud queen, will little heed
Her miserable rivals' need.
So Bharat, ruler of the land,
By Queen Kaikeyí's side will stand,
Nor of those two will ever think,
While grieving in despair they sink.
Now, Lakshmaṇ, as thy love decrees,
Or else the monarch's heart to please,
Follow this counsel and protect
My honoured mother from neglect.
So thou, while not to me alone
Thy great affection will be shown,
To highest duty wilt adhere
By serving those thou shouldst revere.
Now, son of Raghu, for my sake
Obey this one request I make,
Or, of her darling son bereft,
Kauśalyá has no comfort left.'

The faithful Lakshmaṇ, thus addressed
In gentle words which love expressed,
To him in lore of language learned,
His answer, eloquent, returned:
'Nay, through thy might each queen will share
Attentive Bharat's love and care.
Should Bharat, raised as king to sway
This noblest realm, his trust betray,
Nor for their safety well provide,
Seduced by ill-suggesting pride,
Doubt not my vengeful hand shall kill
The cruel wretch who counsels ill—
Kill him and all who lend him aid,
And the three worlds in league arrayed.
And good Kauśalyá well can fee
A thousand champions like to me.
A thousand hamlets rich in grain
The station of that queen maintain.
She may, and my dear mother too,
Live on this ample revenue.
Then let me follow thee: herein:
Is naught that may resemble sin.
So shall I in my wish succeed,
And aid, perhaps, my brother's need.
My bow and quiver well supplied
With arrows hanging at my side,
My hands shall spade and basket bear,
And for thy feet the way prepare.
I'll bring thee roots and berries sweet,
And woodland fare which hermits eat.
Thou shalt with thy Videhan spouse
Recline upon the mountain's brows;
Be mine the toil, be mine to keep
Watch o'er thee waking or asleep.'

Filled by his speech with joy and pride,
Ráma to Lakshmaṇ thus replied:
'Go then, my brother, bid adieu
To all thy friends and retinue.
And those two bows of fearful might,
Celestial, which, at that famed rite,
Lord Varuṇ gave to Janak, king
Of fair Videha, with thee bring,
With heavenly coats of sword-proof mail,
Quivers, whose arrows never fail,

[1] Kaikeyí.

And golden-hilted swords so keen,
The rivals of the sun in sheen.
Tended with care these arms are all
Preserved in my preceptor's hall.
With speed, O Lakshman, go, produce,
And bring them hither for our use.'
So on a woodland life intent,
To see his faithful friends he went,
And brought the heavenly arms which lay
By Ráma's teacher stored away.
And Raghu's son to Ráma showed
Those wondrous arms which gleamed and glowed,
Well kept, adorned with many a wreath
Of flowers on case, and hilt, and sheath.
The prudent Ráma at the sight
Addressed his brother with delight:
'Well art thou come, my brother dear.
For much I longed to see thee here.
For with thine aid, before I go,
I would my gold and wealth bestow
Upon the Bráhmans sage, who school
Their lives by stern devotion's rule.
And for all those who ever dwell
Within my house and serve me well,
Devoted servants, true and good,
Will I provide a livelihood.
Quick, go and summon to this place
The good Vaśishtha's son,
Suyajna, of the Bráhman race
The first and holiest one.
To all the Bráhmans wise and good
Will I due reverence pay,
Then to the solitary wood
With thee will take my way.'

CANTO XXXII.

THE GIFT OF THE TREASURES.

That speech so noble which conveyed
His friendly wish, the chief obeyed.
With steps made swift by anxious thought
The wise Suyajna's home he sought.
Him in the hall of Fire[1] he found,
And bent before him to the ground:
'O friend, to Ráma's house return,
Who now performs a task most stern.'
He, when his noonday rites were done,
Went forth with fair Sumitrá's son,
And came to Ráma's bright abode
Rich in the love which Lakshmí showed.
The son of Raghu, with his dame,
With joined hands met him as he came,
Showing to him who Scripture knew
The worship that is Agni's due.

[1] The chapel where the sacred fire used in worship is kept.

With armlets, bracelets, collars, rings,
With costly pearls on golden strings,
With many a gem for neck and limb
The son of Raghu honoured him.
Then Ráma, at his wife's request,
The wise Suyajna thus addressed:
'Accept a necklace too to deck
With golden strings thy spouse's neck.
And Sítá here, my friend, were glad
A girdle to her gift to add.
And many a bracelet wrought with care,
And many an armlet rich and rare,
My wife to thine is fain to give,
Departing in the wood to live.
A bed by skilful workmen made,
With gold and various gems inlaid—
This too, before she goes, would she
Present, O saintly friend, to thee.
Thine be my elephant, so famed,
My uncle's present, Victor named;
And let a thousand coins of gold,
Great Bráhman, with the gift be told.'
Thus Ráma spoke: nor he declined
The noble gifts for him designed.
On Ráma, Lakshman, Sítá he
Invoked all high felicity.

In pleasant words then Ráma gave
His hest to Lakshman prompt and brave,
As Brahmá speaks for Him to hear
Who rules the Gods' celestial sphere:
'To the two best of Bráhmans run;
Agastya bring, and Kuśik's son,
And precious gifts upon them rain,
Like fostering floods upon the grain.
O long-armed Prince of Raghu's line,
Delight them with a thousand kine,
And many a fair and costly gem,
With gold and silver, give to them.
To him, so deep in Scripture, who,
To Queen Kauśalyá ever true,
Serves her with blessing and respect,
Chief of the Taittiríya sect[1]—
To him, with women-slaves, present
A chariot rich with ornament,
And costly robes of silk beside,
Until the sage be satisfied.
On Chitraratha, true and dear,
My tuneful bard and charioteer,
Gems, robes, and plenteous wealth confer—
Mine ancient friend and minister.
And these who go with staff in hand,
Grammarians trained, a numerous band,
Who their deep study only prize,
Nor think of other exercise,
Who toil not, loving dainty fare,
Whose praises e'en the good declare—
On these be eighty cars bestowed,
And each with precious treasures load.

[1] The students and teachers of the Taittiríya portion of the Yajur Veda.

A thousand bulls for them suffice,
Two hundred elephants of price,
And let a thousand kine beside
The dainties of each meal provide.
The throng who sacred girdles wear,
And on Kauśalyá wait with care—
A thousand golden coins shall please,
Son of Sumitrá, each of these.
Let all, dear Lakshmaṇ, of the train
These special gifts of honour gain:
My mother will rejoice to know
Her Bráhmans have been cherished so.'
  Then Raghu's son addressed the crowd
Who round him stood and wept aloud,
When he to all who thronged the court
Had dealt his wealth for their support:
'In Lakshmaṇ's house and mine remain,
And guard them till I come again.'
To all his people sad with grief,
In loving words thus spoke their chief,
Then bade his treasure-keeper bring
Gold, silver, and each precious thing.
Then straight the servants went and bore
Back to their chief the wealth in store.
Before the people's eyes it shone,
A glorius pile to look upon.
The prince of men with Lakshmaṇ's aid
Parted the treasures there displayed,
Gave to the poor, the young, the old,
And twice-born men, the gems and gold.
  A Bráhman, long in evil case,
Named Trijaṭ, born of Garga's race,
Earned ever toiling in a wood
With spade and plough his livelihood.
The youthful wife, his babes who bore,
Their indigence felt more and more.
Thus to the aged man she spake:
'Hear this my word: my counsel take.
Come, throw thy spade and plough away;
To virtuous Ráma go to-day,
And somewhat of his kindness pray.'

  He heard the words she spoke: around
His limbs his ragged cloth he wound,
And took his journey by the road
That led to Ráma's fair abode.
To the fifth court he made his way;
Nor met the Bráhman check or stay.
Brighu, Angiras[1] could not be
Brighter with saintly light than he.
To Ráma's presence on he pressed,
And thus the noble chief addressed:
'O Ráma, poor and weak am I,
And many children round me cry.
Scant living in the woods I earn:
On me thine eye of pity turn.'
And Ráma, bent on sport and jest,
The suppliant Bráhman thus addressed:
'O aged man, one thousand kine,
Yet undistributed, are mine.
The cows on thee will I bestow
As far as thou thy staff canst throw.'
  The Bráhman heard. In eager haste
He bound his cloth around his waist.
Then round his head his staff he whirled,
And forth with mightiest effort hurled.
Cast from his hand it flew, and sank
To earth on Sarjú's farther bank,
Where herds of kine in thousands fed
Near to the well-stocked bullock shed.
And all the cows that wandered o'er
The meadow, far as Sarjú's shore,
At Rámas word the herdsmen drove
To Trijaṭ's cottage in the grove.
He drew the Bráhman to his breast,
And thus with calming words addressed:
'Now be not angry, Sire, I pray:
This jest of mine was meant in play.
These thousand kine, but not alone.
Their herdsmen too, are all thine own.
And wealth beside I give thee: speak,
Thine shall be all thy heart can seek.'
  Thus Ráma spake. And Trijaṭ prayed
For means his sacrifice to aid.
And Ráma gave much wealth, required
To speed his offering as desired.

[1] Two of the ten divine personages called *Prajápatis* and *Brahmádikas* who were first created by Brahmá.

CANTO XXXIII.

THE PEOPLE'S LAMENT.

Thus Sítá and the princes brave
Much wealth to all the Bráhmans gave
Then to the monarch's house the three
Went forth the aged king to see.
The princes from two servants took
Those heavenly arms of glorious look,
Adorned with garland and with band
By Sítá's beautifying hand.
On each high house a mournful throng
Had gathered ere they passed along,
Who gazed in pure unselfish woe
From turret, roof, and portico.
So dense the crowd that blocked the ways,
The rest, unable there to gaze,
Were fain each terrace to ascend,
And thence their eyes on Ráma bend.
Then as the gathered multitude
On foot their well-loved Ráma viewed,
No royal shade to screen his head,
Such words, disturbed by grief, they said:
'O look, our hero, wont to ride
Leading a host in perfect pride—
Now Lakshmaṇ, sole of all his friends,
With Sítá on his steps attends.
Though he has known the sweets of power,
And poured his gifts in liberal shower,
From duty's path he will not swerve,

But still his father's truth preserve.
And she whose form so soft and fair
Was veiled from spirits of the air,
Now walks unsheltered from the day,
Seen by the crowds who throng the way.
Ah, for that gently-nurtured form!
How will it fade with sun and storm!
How will the rain, the cold, the heat
Mar fragrant breast and tinted feet!
Surely some demon has possessed
His sire, and speaks within his breast,
Or how could one that is a king
Thus send his dear son wandering?
It were a deed unkindly done
To banish e'en a worthless son:
But what, when his pure life has gained
The hearts of all, by love enchained?
Six sovereign virtues join to grace
Ráma the foremost of his race:
Tender and kind and pure is he,
Docile, religious, passion-free.
Hence misery strikes not him alone:
In bitterest grief the people moan,
Like creatures of the stream, when dry
In the great heat the channels lie.
The world is mournful with the grief
That falls on its beloved chief,
As, when the root is hewn away,
Tree, fruit, and flower, and bud decay.
The soul of duty, bright to see,
He is the root of you and me;
And all of us, who share his grief,
His branches, blossom, fruit, and leaf.
Now like the faithful Lakshmaṇ, we
Will follow and be true as he;
Our wives and kinsmen call with speed,
And hasten where our lord shall lead.
Yes, we will leave each well-loved spot,
The field, the garden, and the cot,
And, sharers of his weal and woe,
Behind the pious Ráma go.
Our houses, empty of their stores,
With ruined courts and broken doors,
With all their treasures borne away,
And gear that made them bright and gay:
O'errun by rats, with dust o'erspread,
Shrines, whence the deities have fled,
Where not a hand the water pours,
Or sweeps the long-neglected floors,
No incense loads the evening air,
No Bráhmans chant the text and prayer,
No fire of sacrifice is bright,
No gift is known, no sacred rite;
With floors which broken vessels strew,
As if our woes had crushed them too—
Of these be stern Kaikeyí queen,
And rule o'er homes where we have been.
The wood where Ráma's feet may roam
Shall be our city and our home,
And this fair city we forsake,
Our flight a wilderness shall make.
Each serpent from his hole shall hie,
The birds and beasts from mountain fly,
Lions and elephants in fear
Shall quit the woods when we come near,
Yield the broad wilds for us to range,
And take our city in exchange.
With Ráma will we hence, content
If, where he is, our days be spent.'
  Such were the varied words the crowd
Of all conditions spoke aloud.
And Ráma heard their speeches, yet
Changed not his purpose firmly set.
His father's palace soon he neared,
That like Kailása's hill appeared.
Like a wild elephant he strode
Right onward to the bright abode.
Within the palace court he stepped,
Where ordered bands their station kept,
And saw Sumantra standing near
With down-cast eye and gloomy cheer.

CANTO XXXIV.

RÁMA IN THE PALACE.

The dark incomparable chief
Whose eye was like a lotus leaf,
Cried to the mournful charioteer,
'Go tell my sire that I am here.'

  Sumantra, sad and all dismayed,
The chieftain's order swift obeyed.
Within the palace doors he hied
And saw the king, who wept and sighed.
Like the great sun when wrapped in shade,
Like fire by ashes overlaid,
Or like a pool with waters dried,
So lay the world's great lord and pride.
Awhile the wise Sumantra gazed
On him whose senses woe has dazed,
Grieving for Ráma. Near he drew
With hands upraised in reverence due.
With blessing first his king he hailed;
Then with a voice that well-nigh failed,
In trembling accents soft and low
Addressed the monarch in his woe:
'The prince of men, thy Ráma, waits
To see thee at the palace gates.
His wealth to Bráhmans he has dealt,
And all who in his home have dwelt.
Admit thy son. His friends have heard
His kind farewell and parting word.
He longs to see thee first, and then
Will seek the wilds, O King of men.
He, with each princely virtue's blaze,
Shines as the sun engirt by rays.'

  The truthful king who loved to keep
The law, profound as Ocean's deep,
And stainless as the dark blue sky,
Thus to Sumantra made reply:

'Go then, Sumantra, go and call
My wives and ladies one and all,
Drawn round me shall they fill the place
When I behold my Ráma's face.'
Quick to the inner rooms he sped,
And thus to all the women said,
'Come, at the summons of the king:
Come all, and make no tarrying.'
Their husband's word, by him conveyed,
Soon as they heard, the dames obeyed,
And following his guidance all
Came thronging to the regal hall.
In number half seven hundred, they,
All lovely dames, in long array,
With their bright eyes for weeping red,
To stand round Queen Kauśalyá, sped.
They gathered, and the monarch viewed
One moment all the multitude,
Then to Sumantra spoke and said:
'Now let my son be hither led.'
Sumantra went. Then Ráma came,
And Lakshman, and the Maithil dame,
And, as he led them on, their guide
Straight to the monarch's presence hied.
When yet far off the father saw
His son with raised palms toward him draw,
Girt by his ladies, sick with woes,
Swift from his royal seat he rose.
With all his strength the aged man
To meet his darling Ráma ran,
But trembling, wild with dark despair,
Fell on the ground and fainted there.
And Lakshman, wont in cars to ride,
And Ráma, threw them by the side
Of the poor miserable king,
Half lifeless with his sorrow's sting.
Throughout the spacious hall up went
A thousand women's wild lament:
'Ah Ráma!' thus they wailed and wept,
And anklets tinkled as they stepped.
Around his body, weeping, threw
Their loving arms the brothers two,
And then, with Sítá's gentle aid,
The king upon a couch was laid.
At length to earth's imperial lord,
When life and knowledge were restored,
Though seas of woe went o'er his head,
With suppliant hands thus Ráma said:
'Lord of us all, great King, thou art:
Bid me farewell before we part.
To Dandak wood this day I go:
One blessing and one look bestow.
Let Lakshman my companion be,
And Sítá also follow me.
With truthful pleas I sought to bend
Their purpose; but no ear they lend.
Now cast this sorrow from thy heart,
And let us all, great King, depart.
As Brahmá sends his children, so
Let Lakshman, me, and Sítá go.'
He stood unmoved, and watched intent
Until the king should grant consent.
Upon his son his eyes he cast,
And thus the monarch spake at last:
'O Ráma, by her arts enslaved,
I gave the boons Kaikeyí craved,
Unfit to reign, by her misled:
Be ruler in thy father's stead.'
Thus by the lord of men addressed,
Ráma, of virtue's friends the best,
In lore of language duly learned,
His answer, reverent, thus returned:
'A thousand years, O King, remain
O'er this our city still to reign.
I in the woods my life will lead:
The lust of rule no more I heed.
Nine years and five I there will spend,
And when the portioned days shall end,
Will come, my vows and exile o'er,
And clasp thy feet, my King, once more.'
A captive in the snare of truth,
Weeping, distressed with woe and ruth,
Thus spake the monarch, while the queen
Kaikeyí urged him on unseen:
'Go then, O Ráma, and begin
Thy course unvext by fear and sin:
Go, my beloved son, and earn
Success, and joy, and safe return.
So fast the bonds of duty bind,
O Raghu's son, thy truthful mind,
That naught can turn thee back, or guide
Thy will so strongly fortified.
But O, a little longer stay,
Nor turn thy steps this night away,
That I one little day—alas!
One only—with my son may pass.
Me and thy mother do not slight,
But stay, my son, with me to-night;
With every dainty please thy taste,
And seek to-morrow morn the waste.
Hard is thy task, O Raghu's son,
Dire is the toil thou wilt not shun,
Far to the lonely wood to flee,
And leave thy friends for love of me.
I swear it by my truth, believe,
For thee, my son, I deeply grieve,
Misguided by the traitress dame
With hidden guile like smouldering flame.
Now, by her wicked counsel stirred,
Thou fain wouldst keep my plighted word.
No marvel that my eldest born
Would hold me true when I have sworn.'
Then Ráma having calmly heard
His wretched father speak each word,
With Lakshman standing by his side
Thus, humbly, to the king replied:
'If dainties now my taste regale,
To-morrow must those dainties fail.
This day departure I prefer
To all that wealth can minister.
O'er this fair land, no longer mine,
Which I, with all her realms, resign,

Her multitudes of men, her grain,
Her stores of wealth, let Bharat reign.
And let the promised boon which thou
Wast pleased to grant the queen ere now,
Be hers in full. Be true, O King,
Kind giver of each precious thing.
Thy spoken word I still will heed,
Obeying all thy lips decreed;
And fourteen years in woods will dwell
With those who live in glade and dell.
No hopes of power my heart can touch,
No selfish joys attract so much
As, son of Raghu, to fulfil
With heart and soul my father's will.
Dismiss, dismiss thy needless woe,
Nor let those drowning torrents flow:
The Lord of Rivers in his pride
Keeps to the banks that bar his tide.
Here in thy presence I declare;
By thy good deeds, thy truth, I swear;
Nor lordship, joy, nor lands I prize;
Life, heaven, all blessings I despise;
I wish to see thee still remain
Most true, O King, and free from stain.
It must not, Sire, it must not be:
I cannot rest one hour with thee.
Then bring this sorrow to an end,
For naught my settled will can bend.
I gave a pledge that binds me too,
And to that pledge I still am true.
Kaikeyí bade me speed away:
She prayed me, and I answered yea.
Pine not for me, and weep no more;
The wood for us has joy in store,
Filled with the wild deer's peaceful herds
And voices of a thousand birds.
A father is the God of each,
Yea, e'en of Gods, so Scriptures teach:
And I will keep my sire's decree,
For as a God I honour thee.
O best of men, the time is nigh,
The fourteen years will soon pass by
And to thine eyes thy son restore:
Be comforted, and weep no more.
Thou with thy firmness shouldst support
These weeping crowds who throng the court;
Then why, O chief of high renown,
So troubled, and thy soul cast down?'

CANTO XXXV.

KAIKEYÍ REPROACHED.

Wild with the rage he could not calm,
Sumantra, grinding palm on palm,
His head in quick impatience shook,
And sighed with woe he could not brook.
He gnashed his teeth, his eyes were red,
From his changed face the colour fled.
In rage and grief that knew no law,
The temper of the king he saw.
With his word-arrows swift and keen
He shook the bosom of the queen.
With scorn, as though its lightning stroke
Would blast her body, thus he spoke:
'Thou, who, of no dread sin afraid,
Hast Daśaratha's self betrayed,
Lord of the world, whose might sustain
Each thing that moves or fixed remains,
What direr crime is left thee now?
Death to thy lord and house art thou,
Whose cruel deeds the king distress,
Mahendra's peer in mightiness,
Firm as the mountain's rooted steep,
Enduring as the Ocean's deep.
Despise not Daśaratha, he
Is a kind lord and friend to thee.
A loving wife in worth outruns
The mother of ten million sons.
Kings, when their sires have passed away,
Succeed by birthright to the sway.
Ikshváku's son still rules the state,
Yet thou this rule wouldst violate.
Yea, let thy son, Kaikeyí, reign,
Let Bharat rule his sire's domain.
Thy will, O Queen, shall none oppose:
We all will go where Ráma goes.
No Bráhman, scorning thee, will rest
Within the realm thou governest,
But all will fly indignant hence:
So great thy trespass and offence.
I marvel, when thy crime I see,
Earth yawns not quick to swallow thee;
And that the Bráhman saints prepare
No burning scourge thy soul to scare,
With cries of shame to smite thee, bent
Upon our Ráma's banishment.
The Mango tree with axes fell,
And tend instead the Neem tree well,
Still watered with all care the tree
Will never sweet and pleasant be.
Thy mother's faults to thee descend,
And with thy borrowed nature blend.
True is the ancient saw: the Neem
Can ne'er distil a honeyed stream.
Taught by the tale of long ago
Thy mother's hateful sin we know.
A bounteous saint, as all have heard,
A boon upon thy sire conferred,
And all the eloquence revealed
That fills the wood, the flood, the field.
No creature walked, or swam, or flew,
But he its varied language knew.
One morn upon his couch he heard
The chattering of a gorgeous bird,
And as he marked its close intent
He laughed aloud in merriment.
Thy mother furious with her lord,
And fain to perish by the cord,
Said to her husband: 'I would know,
O Monarch, why thou laughest so.'

The king in answer spake again :
'If I this laughter should explain,
This very hour would be my last,
For death, be sure, would follow fast.'
Again thy mother, flushed with ire,
To Kekaya spake, thy royal sire:
'Tell me the cause : then live or die :
I will not brook thy laugh, not I.'
Thus by his darling wife addressed,
The king whose might all earth confessed,
To that kind saint his story told
Who gave the wondrous gift of old.
He listened to the king's complaint,
And thus in answer spoke the saint :
'King, let her quit thy home or die,
But never with her prayer comply,'
The saint's reply his trouble stilled,
And all his heart with pleasure filled.
Thy mother from his home he sent,
And days like Lord Kuvera's spent.
So thou wouldst force the king, misled
By thee, in evil paths to tread,
And bent on evil wouldst begin,
Through folly, this career of sin.
Most true, methinks, in thee is shown
The ancient saw so widely known :
The sons their fathers' worth declare
And girls their mothers' nature share.
So be not thou. For pity's sake
Accept the word the monarch spake.
Thy husband's will, O Queen, obey,
And be the people's hope and stay,
O, do not, urged by folly, draw
The king to tread on duty's law,
The lord who all the world sustains,
Bright as the God o'er Gods who reigns.
Our glorious king, by sin unstained,
Will never grant what fraud obtained ;
No shade of fault in him is seen :
Let Ráma be anointed, Queen.
Remember, Queen, undying shame
Will through the world pursue thy name,
If Ráma leave the king his sire,
And, banished, to the wood retire.
Come, from thy breast this fever fling:
Of his own realm be Ráma king.
None in this city e'er can dwell
To tend and love thee half so well.
When Ráma sits in royal place,
True to the custom of his race
Our monarch of the mighty bow
A hermit to the woods will go.'[1]

[1] It was the custom of the kings of the solar dynasty to resign in their extreme old age the kingdom to the heir, and spend the remainder of their days in holy meditation in the forest:

'For such through ages in their life's decline
Is the good custom of Ikshváku's line.'
Raghuvanśa.

Sumantra thus, palm joined to palm,
Poured forth his words of bane and balm,
With keen reproach, with pleading kind,
Striving to move Kaikeyí's mind.
In vain he prayed, in vain reproved,
She heard unsoftened and unmoved.
Nor could the eyes that watched her view
One yielding look, one change of hue.

CANTO XXXVI.

SIDDHÁRTH'S SPEECH.

Ikshváku's son with anguish torn
For the great oath his lips had sworn,
With tears and sighs of sharpest pain
Thus to Sumantra spake again :
'Prepare thou quick a perfect force,
Cars, elephants, and foot, and horse,
To follow Raghu's scion hence
Equipped with all magnificence.
Let traders with the wealth they sell,
And those who charming stories tell,
And dancing-women fair of face,
The prince's ample chariots grace.
On all the train who throng his courts,
And those who share his manly sports,
Great gifts of precious wealth bestow,
And bid them with their master go.
Let noble arms, and many a wain,
And townsmen swell the prince's train ;
And hunters best for woodland skill
Their places in the concourse fill.
While elephants and deer he slays,
Drinking wood honey as he strays,
And looks on streams each fairer yet,
His kingdom he may chance forget.
Let all my gold and wealth of corn
With Ráma to the wilds be born ;
For it will soothe the exile's lot
To sacrifice in each pure spot,
Deal ample largess forth, and meet
Each hermit in his calm retreat.
The wealth shall Ráma with him bear :
Ayodhyá shall be Bharat's share.'

As thus Kakutstha's offspring spoke,
Fear in Kaikeyí's breast awoke.
The freshness of her face was dried,
Her trembling tongue was terror-tied.
Alarmed and sad, with bloodless cheek,
She turned to him and scarce could speak :
'Nay, Sire, but Bharat shall not gain
An empty realm where none remain,
My Bharat shall not rule a waste
Reft of all sweets to charm the taste—
The wine-cup's dregs, all dull and dead,
Whence the light foam and life are fled.'

Thus in her rage the long-eyed dame
Spoke her dire speech untouched by shame.

Then, answering, Daśaratha spoke:
'Why, having bowed me to the yoke,
Dost thou, must cruel, spur and goad
Me who am struggling with the load?
Why didst thou not oppose at first
This hope, vile Queen, so fondly nursed?'
Scarce could the monarch's angry speech
The ears of the fair lady reach,
When thus, with double wrath inflamed,
Kaikeyí to the king exclaimed:
'Sagar, from whom thy line is traced,
Drove forth his eldest son disgraced,
Called Asamanj, whose fate we know:
Thus should thy son to exile go.'
'Fie on thee, dame!' the monarch said;
Each of her people bent his head,
And stood in shame and sorrow mute:
She marked not, bold and resolute.
Then great Siddhárth, inflamed with rage,
The good old councillor and sage
On whose wise rede the king relied,
To Queen Kaikeyí thus replied:
'But Asamanj the cruel laid
His hands on infants as they played,
Cast them to Sarjú's flood, and smiled
For pleasure when he drowned a child.'[1]
The people saw, and, furious, sped
Straight the the king his sire and said:
'Choose us, O glory of the throne,
Choose us, or Asamanj alone.'
'Whence comes this dread?' the monarch cried;
And all the people thus replied:
'In folly, King, he loves to lay
Fierce hands upon our babes at play,
Casts them to Sarjú's flood, and joys
To murder our bewildered boys.'
With heedful ear the king of men
Heard each complaining citizen.
To please their troubled minds he strove,
And from the state his son he drove.
With wife and gear upon a car
He placed him quick, and sent him far.
And thus he gave commandment, 'He
Shall all his days an exile be.'
With basket and with plough he strayed
O'er mountain heights, through pathless shade,
Roaming all lands a weary time,
An outcast wretch defiled with crime.
Sagar, the righteous path who held,
His wicked offspring thus expelled.
But what has Ráma done to blame?
Why should his sentence be the same?
No sin his stainless name can dim;
We see no fault at all in him.
Pure as the moon, no darkening blot
On his sweet life has left a spot.
If thou canst see one fault, e'en one,
To dim the fame of Raghu's son,
That fault this hour, O lady, show,
And Ráma to the wood shall go.
To drive the guiltless to the wild,
Truth's constant lover, undefiled,
Would, by defiance of the right,
The glory e'en of Indra blight.
Then cease, O lady, and dismiss
Thy hope to ruin Ráma's bliss,
Or all thy gain, O fair of face,
Will be men's hatred, and disgrace.'

CANTO XXXVII.

THE COATS OF BARK.

Thus spake the virtuous sage; and then
Ráma addressed the king of men.
In laws of meek behaviour bred,
Thus to his sire he meekly said:
'King, I renounce all earthly care,
And live in woods on woodland fare.
What, dead to joys, have I to do
With lordly train and retinue?
Who gives his elephant and yet
Upon the girths his heart will set?
How can a cord attract his eyes
Who gives away the nobler prize?
Best of the good, with me be led
No host, my King, with banners spread.
All wealth, all lordship I resign:
The hermit's dress alone be mine.
Before I go, have here conveyed
A little basket and a spade.
With these alone I go, content,
For fourteen years of banishment.'
With her own hands Kaikeyí took
The hermit coats of bark, and, 'Look,'
She cried with bold unblushing brow
Before the concourse, 'Dress thee now.'
That lion leader of the brave
Took from her hand the dress she gave,
Cast his fine raiment on the ground,

[1] See Book I., Canto XXXIX. An Indian prince in more modern times appears to have diverted himself in a similar way.

It is still reported in Belgaum that Appay Deasy was wont to amuse himself "by making several young and beautiful women stand side by side on a narrow balcony, without a parapet, overhanging the deep reservoir at the new palace in Nipani. He used then to pass along the line of trembling creatures, and suddenly thrusting one of them headlong into the water below, he used to watch her drowning, and derive pleasure from her dying agonies."—History of the Belgaum District. By H. J. Stokes, M. S. C.

And round his waist the vesture bound.
Then quick the hero Lakshman too
His garment from his shoulders threw,
And, in the presence of his sire,
Indued the ascetic's rough attire.
But Sítá, in her silks arrayed,
Threw glances, trembling and afraid,
On the bark coat she had to wear,
Like a shy doe that eyes the snare.
Ashamed and weeping for distress
From the queen's hand she took the dress.
The fair one, by her husband's side
Who matched heaven's minstrel monarch,[1] cried:
'How bind they on their woodland dress,
Those hermits of the wilderness?'

There stood the pride of Janak's race
Perplexed, with sad appealing face.
One coat the lady's fingers grasped,
One round her neck she feebly clasped,
But failed again, again, confused
By the wild garb she ne'er had used.
Then quickly hastening Ráma, pride
Of all who cherish virtue, tied
The rough bark mantle on her, o'er
The silken raiment that she wore.

Then the sad women when they saw
Ráma the choice bark round her draw,
Rained water from each tender eye,
And cried aloud with bitter cry:
'O, not on her, beloved, not
On Sítá falls thy mournful lot.
If, faithful to thy father's will,
Thou must go forth, leave Sítá still.
Let Sítá still remaining here
Our hearts with her loved presence cheer.
With Lakshman by thy side to aid
Seek thou, dear son, the lonely shade.
Unmeet, one good and fair as she
Should dwell in woods a devotee.
Let not our prayers be prayed in vain:
Let beauteous Sítá yet remain;
For by thy love of duty tied
Thou wilt not here thyself abide.'

Then the king's venerable guide
Vaśishṭha, when he saw each coat
Enclose the lady's waist and throat,
Her zeal with gentle words repressed,
And Queen Kaikeyí thus addressed:
'O evil-hearted sinner, shame
Of royal Kekaya's race and name;
Who matchless in thy sin couldst cheat
Thy lord the king with vile deceit;
Lost to all sense of duty, know
Sítá to exile shall not go.
Sítá shall guard, as 'twere her own,
The precious trust of Ráma's throne.
Those joined by wedlock's sweet control
Have but one self and common soul.
Thus Sítá shall our empress be,
For Ráma's self and soul is she.
Or if she still to Ráma cleave
And for the woods the kingdom leave:
If naught her loving heart deter,
We and this town will follow her.
The warders of the queen shall take
Their wives and go for Ráma's sake.
The nation with its stores of grain,
The city's wealth shall swell his train.
Bharat, Śatrughna both will wear
Bark mantles, and his lodging share,
Still with their elder brother dwell
In the wild wood, and serve him well.
Rest here alone, and rule thy state
Unpeopled, barren, desolate;
Be empress of the land and trees,
Thou sinner whom our sorrows please.
The land which Ráma reigns not o'er
Shall bear the kingdom's name no more:
The woods which Ráma wanders through
Shall be our home and kingdom too.
Bharat, be sure, will never deign
O'er realms his father yields, to reign.
Nay, if the king's true son he be,
He will not, sonlike, dwell with thee.
Nay, shouldst thou from the earth arise,
And send thy message from the skies,
To his forefathers' custom true
No erring course would he pursue.
So hast thou, by thy grievous fault,
Offended him thou wouldst exalt.
In all the world none draws his breath
Who loves not Ráma, true to death.
This day, O Queen, shalt thou behold
Birds, deer, and beasts from lea and fold
Turn to the woods in Ráma's train,
And naught save longing trees remain.'

CANTO XXXVIII.

CARE FOR KAUŚALYÁ.

Then when the people wroth and sad
Saw Sítá in bark vesture clad,
Though wedded, like some widowed thing,
They cried out, 'Shame upon thee, King!'
Grieved by their cry and angry look
The lord of earth at once forsook
All hope in life that still remained,
In duty, self, and fame unstained.
Ikshváku's son with burning sighs
On Queen Kaikeyí bent his eyes,
And said: 'But Sítá must not flee
In garments of a devotee.
My holy guide has spoken truth:
Unfit is she in tender youth,

[1] Chitraratha, King of the celestial choristers.

So gently nurtured, soft and fair,
The hardships of the wood to share.
How has she sinned, devout and true,
The noblest monarch's child,
That she should garb of bark indue
And journey to the wild?
That she should spend her youthful days
Amid a hermit band,
Like some poor mendicant who strays
Sore troubled, through the land?
Ah, let the child of Janak throw
Her dress of bark aside,
And let the royal lady go
With royal wealth supplied.
Not such the pledge I gave before,
Unfit to linger here:
The oath, which I the sinner swore
Is kept, and leaves her clear.
Won from her childlike love this too
My instant death would be,
As blossoms on the old bamboo
Destroy the parent tree.[1]
If aught amiss by Ráma done
Offend thee, O thou wicked one,
What least transgression canst thou find
In her, thou worst of womankind?
What shade of fault in her appears,
Whose full soft eye is like the deer's?
What canst thou blame in Janak's child,
So gentle, modest, true, and mild?
Is not one crime complete, that sent
My Ráma forth to banishment?
And wilt thou other sins commit,
Thou wicked one, to double it?
This is the pledge and oath I swore,
What thou besoughtest, and no more,
Of Ráma—for I heard thee, dame—
When he for consecration came.
Now with this limit not content,
In hell should be thy punishment,
Who fain the Maithil bride wouldst press
To clothe her limbs with hermit dress.'
Thus spake the father in his woe;
And Ráma, still prepared to go,
To him who sat with drooping head
Spake in return these words and said:
'Just King, here stands my mother dear,
Kauśalyá, one whom all revere.
Submissive, gentle, old is she,
And keeps her lips from blame of thee.
For her, kind lord, of me bereft
A sea of whelming woe is left.
O, show her in her new distress
Still fonder love and tenderness.
Well honoured by thine honoured hand
Her grief for me let her withstand,
Who wrapt in constant thought of me
In me would live a devotee.
Peer of Mahendra, O, to her be kind,
And treat I pray, my gentle mother so,
That, when I dwell afar, her life resigned,
She may not pass to Yama's realm for woe.'

CANTO XXXIX.

COUNSEL TO SÍTÁ.

Scarce had the sire, with each dear queen,
Heard Ráma's pleading voice, and seen
His darling in his hermit dress
Ere failed his senses for distress.
Convulsed with woe, his soul that shook,
On Raghu's son he could not look;
Or if he looked with failing eye
He could not to the chief reply.
By pangs of bitter grief assailed,
The long-armed monarch wept and wailed,
Half dead a while and sore distraught,
While Ráma filled his every thought.
'This hand of mine in days ere now
Has reft her young from many a cow,
Or living things has idly slain:
Hence comes, I ween, this hour of pain.
Not till the hour is come to die
Can from its shell the spirit fly.
Death comes not, and Kaikeyí still
Torments the wretch she cannot kill,
Who sees his son before him quit
The fine soft robes his rank that fit,
And, glorious as the burning fire,
In hermit garb his limbs attire.
Now all the people grieve and groan
Through Queen Kaikeyí's deed alone,
Who, having dared this deed of sin,
Strives for herself the gain to win.'
He spoke. With tears his eyes grew dim,
His senses all deserted him.
He cried, O Ráma, once, then weak
And fainting could no further speak.
Unconscious there he lay: at length
Regathering his sense and strength,
While his full eyes their torrents shed,
To wise Sumantra thus he said:
'Yoke the light car, and hither lead
Fleet coursers of the noblest breed,
And drive this heir of lofty fate
Beyond the limit of the state.
This seems the fruit that virtues bear,
The meed of worth which texts declare—
The sending of the brave and good
By sire and mother to the wood.'
He heard the monarch, and obeyed,
With ready feet that ne'er delayed,
And brought before the palace gate
The horses and the car of state.
Then to the monarch's son he sped,
And raising hands of reverence said

[1] It is said that the bamboo dies after flowering.

That the light car which gold made fair,
With best of steeds, was standing there.
King Daśaratha called in haste
The lord o'er all his treasures placed.
And spoke, well skilled in place and time,
His will to him devoid of crime:
'Count all the years she has to live
Afar in forest wilds, and give
To Sítá robes and gems of price
As for the time may well suffice.'
Quick to the treasure-room he went,
Charged by that king most excellent,
Brought the rich stores, and gave them all
To Sítá in the monarch's hall.
The Maithil dame of high descent
Received each robe and ornament,
And tricked those limbs, whose lines foretold
High destiny, with gems and gold.
So well adorned, so fair to view,
A glory through the hall she threw:
So, when the Lord of Light upsprings,
His radiance o'er the sky he flings.
Then Queen Kauśalyá spake at last,
With loving arms about her cast,
Pressed lingering kisses on her head,
And to the high-souled lady said:
'Ah, in this faithless world below
When dark misfortune comes and woe,
Wives, loved and cherished every day,
Neglect their lords and disobey.
Yes, woman's nature still is this:—
After long days of calm and bliss
When some light grief her spirit tries,
She changes all her love, or flies.
Young wives are thankless, false in soul,
With roving hearts that spurn control.
Brooding on sin and quickly changed,
In one short hour their love estranged.
Not glorious deed or lineage fair,
Not knowledge, gift, or tender care
In chains of lasting love can bind
A woman's light inconstant mind.
But those good dames who still maintain
What right, truth, Scripture, rule ordain—
No holy thing in their pure eyes
With one beloved husband vies.
Nor let thy lord my son, condemned
To exile, be by thee contemned,
For be he poor or wealthy, he
Is as a God, dear child, to thee.'
When Sítá heard Kauśalyá's speech
Her duty and her gain to teach,
She joined her palms with reverent grace
And gave her answer face to face:
'All will I do, forgetting naught,
Which thou, O honoured Queen, hast taught,
I know, have heard, and deep have stored
The rules of duty to my lord.
Not me, good Queen, shouldst thou include
Among the faithless multitude.
Its own sweet light the moon shall leave
Ere I to duty cease to cleave.
The stringless lute gives forth no strain,
The wheelless car is urged in vain;
No joy a lordless dame, although
Blest with a hundred sons, can know.
From father, brother, and from son
A measured share of joy is won:
Who would not honour, love, and bless
Her lord, whose gifts are measureless?
Thus trained to think, I hold in awe
Scripture's command and duty's law.
Him can I hold in slight esteem?
Her lord is woman's God, I deem.'
Kauśalyá heard the lady's speech,
Nor failed those words her heart to reach.
Then, pure in mind, she gave to flow
The tear that sprang of joy and woe.
Then duteous Ráma forward came
And stood before the honoured dame,
And joining reverent hands addressed
The queen in rank above the rest:
'O mother, from these tears refrain;
Look on my sire and still thy pain.
To thee my days afar shall fly
As if sweet slumber closed thine eye,
And fourteen years of exile seem
To thee, dear mother, like a dream.
On me returning safe and well,
Girt by my friends, thine eyes shall dwell.'
Thus for their deep affection's sake
The hero to his mother spake,
Then to the half seven hundred too,
Wives of his sire, paid reverence due.
Thus Daśaratha's son addressed
That crowd of matrons sore distressed:
'If from these lips, while here I dwelt,
One heedless taunt you e'er have felt,
Forgive me, pray. And now adieu,
I bid good-bye to all of you.'
Then straight, like curlews' cries, upwent
The voices of their wild lament,
While, as he bade farewell, the crowd
Of royal women wept aloud,
And through the ample hall's extent,
Where erst the sound of tabour, blent
With drum and shrill-toned instrument,
In joyous concert rose,
Now rang the sound of wailing high,
The lamentation and the cry,
The shriek, the choking sob, the sigh
That told the ladies' woes.

CANTO XL.

RÁMA'S DEPARTURE.

Then Ráma, Sítá, Lakshman bent
At the king's feet, and sadly went

Round him with slow steps reverent.
When Ráma of the duteous heart
Had gained his sire's consent to part,
With Sítá by his side he paid
Due reverence to the queen dismayed.
And Lakshman, with affection meet,
Bowed down and clasped his mother's feet.
Sumitrá viewed him as he pressed
Her feet, and thus her son addressed:
'Neglect not Ráma wandering there,
But tend him with thy faithful care.
In hours of wealth, in time of woe,
Him, sinless son, thy refuge know.
From this good law the just ne'er swerve,
That younger sons the eldest serve,
And to this righteous rule incline
All children of thine ancient line—
Freely to give, reward each rite,
Nor spare their bodies in the fight.
Let Ráma Daśaratha be,
Look upon Sítá as on me,
And let the cot wherein you dwell
Be thine Ayodhyá. Fare thee well.'
Her blessing thus Sumitrá gave
To him whose soul to Ráma clave,
Exclaiming, when her speech was done,
'Go forth, O Lakshman, go, my son.
Go forth, my son, to win success,
High victory and happiness.
Go forth thy foemen to destroy,
And turn again at last with joy.'
As Mátali his charioteer
Speaks for the Lord of Gods to hear,
Sumantra, palm to palm applied,
In reverence trained, to Ráma cried:
'O famous Prince, my car ascend,—
May blessings on thy course attend,—
And swiftly shall my horses flee
And place thee where thou biddest me.
The fourteen years thou hast to stay
Far in the wilds, begin to-day;
For Queen Kaikeyí cries, Away.'
Then Sítá, best of womankind,
Ascended, with a tranquil mind,
Soon as her toilet task was done,
That chariot brilliant as the sun.
Ráma and Lakshman true and bold
Sprang on the car adorned with gold.
The king those years had counted o'er,
And given Sítá robes and store
Of precious ornaments to wear
When following her husband there.
The brothers in the car found place
For nets and weapons of the chase,
There warlike arms and mail they laid,
A leathern basket and a spade.
Soon as Sumantra saw the three
Were seated in the chariot, he
Urged on each horse of noble breed,
Who matched the rushing wind in speed.
As thus the son of Raghu went
Forth for his dreary banishment,
Chill numbing grief the town assailed,
All strength grew weak, all spirit failed.
Ayodhyá through her wide extent
Was filled with tumult and lament:
Steeds neighed and shook the bells they bore,
Each elephant returned a roar.
Then all the city, young and old,
Wild with their sorrow uncontrolled,
Rushed to the car, as, from the sun
The panting herds to water run.
Before the car, behind, they clung,
And there as eagerly they hung,
With torrents streaming from their eyes,
Called loudly with repeated cries:
'Listen, Sumantra: draw thy rein;
Drive gently, and thy steeds restrain.
Once more on Ráma will we gaze,
Now to be lost for many days.
The queen his mother has, be sure,
A heart of iron, to endure
To see her godlike Ráma go,
Nor feel it shattered by the blow.
Sítá, well done! Videha's pride,
Still like his shadow by his side;
Rejoicing in thy duty still
As sunlight cleaves to Meru's hill.
Thou, Lakshman, too, hast well deserved,
Who from thy duty hast not swerved,
Tending the peer of Gods above,
Whose lips speak naught but words of love.
Thy firm resolve is nobly great,
And high success on thee shall wait.
Yea, thou shalt win a priceless meed—
Thy path with him to heaven shall lead.'
As thus they spake, they could not hold
The tears that down their faces rolled,
While still they followed for a space
Their darling of Ikshváku's race.
There stood surrounded by a ring
Of mournful wives the mournful king;
For,' I will see once more,' he cried,
'Mine own dear son,' and forth he hied.
As he came near, there rose the sound
Of weeping, as the dames stood round.
So the she-elephants complain
When their great lord and guide is slain.
Kakutstha's son, the king of men,
The glorious sire, looked troubled then,
As the full moon is when dismayed
By dark eclipse's threatening shade.
Then Daśaratha's son, designed
For highest fate of lofty mind,
Urged to more speed the charioteer,
'Away, away! why linger here?
Urge on thy horses,' Ráma cried,
And 'Stay, O stay,' the people sighed.
Sumantra, urged to speed away,
The townsmen's call must disobey,
Forth as the long-armed hero went,

The dust his chariot wheels up sent
Was laid by streams that ever flowed
From their sad eyes who filled the road.
Then, sprung of woe, from eyes of all
The women drops began to fall,
As from each lotus on the lake
The darting fish the water shake.
When he, the king of high renown,
Saw that one thought held all the town,
Like some tall tree he fell and lay,
Whose root the axe has hewn away.
Then straight a mighty cry from those
Who followed Ráma's car arose,
Who saw their monarch fainting there
Beneath that grief too great to bear.
Then 'Ráma, Ráma!' with the cry
Of 'Ah, his mother!' sounded high,
As all the people wept aloud
Around the ladies' sorrowing crowd.
When Ráma backward turned his eye,
And saw the king his father lie
With troubled sense and failing limb,
And the sad queen, who followed him,
Like some young creature in the net,
That will not, in its misery, let
Its wild eyes on its mother rest,
So, by the bonds of duty pressed,
His mother's look he could not meet.
He saw them with their weary feet,
Who, used to bliss, in cars should ride,
Who ne'er by sorrow should be tried,
And, as one mournful look he cast,
'Drive on,' he cried, 'Sumantra, fast.'
As when the driver's torturing hook
Goads on an elephant, the look
Of sire and mother in despair
Was more than Ráma's heart could bear.
As mother kine to stalls return
Which hold the calves for whom they yearn,
So to the car she tried to run
As a cow seeks her little one.
Once and again the hero's eyes
Looked on his mother, as with cries
Of woe she called and gestures wild,
'O Sítá, Lakshman, O my child!'
'Stay,' cried the king, 'thy chariot stay:'
'On on,' cried Ráma, 'speed away.'
As one between two hosts, inclined
To neither was Sumantra's mind.
But Ráma spake these words again:
'A lengthened woe is bitterest pain.
On, on; and if his wrath grow hot,
Thine answer be, 'I heard thee not.''
Sumantra, at the chief's behest,
Dismissed the crowd that toward him pressed,
And, as he bade, to swiftest speed
Urged on his way each willing steed.
The king's attendants parted thence,
And paid him heart-felt reverence:
In mind, and with the tears he wept,
Each still his place near Ráma kept.
As swift away the horses sped,
His lords to Daśaratha said:
'To follow him whom thou again
Wouldst see returning home is vain.'
With failing limb and drooping mien
He heard their counsel wise:
Still on their son the king and queen
Kept fast their lingering eyes.[1]

CANTO XLI.

THE CITIZENS' LAMENT.

The lion chief with hands upraised
Was born from eyes that fondly gazed.
But then the ladies' bower was rent
With cries of weeping and lament:
'Where goes he now, our lord, the sure
Protector of the friendless poor,
In whom the wretched and the weak
Defence and aid were wont to seek?
All words of wrath he turned aside,
And ne'er, when cursed, in ire replied.
He shared his people's woe, and stilled
The troubled breast which rage had filled.
Our chief, on lofty thoughts intent,
In glorious fame preëminent:
As on his own dear mother, thus
He ever looked on each of us.
Where goes he now; His sire's behest,
By Queen Kaikeyí's guile distressed,
Has banished to the forest hence
Him who was all the world's defence.
Ah, senseless King, to drive away
The hope of men, their guard and stay,
To banish to the distant wood
Ráma the duteous, true, and good!'
The royal dames, like cows bereaved
Of their young calves, thus sadly grieved.
The monarch heard them as they wailed,
And by the fire of grief assailed
For his dear son, he bowed his head,
And all his sense and memory fled.
Then were no fires of worship fed,
Thick darkness o'er the sun was spread.
The cows their thirsty calves denied,
And elephants flung their food aside.

---

[1] 'Thirty centuries have passed since he began this memorable journey. Every step of it is known and is annually traversed by thousands: hero worship is not extinct. What can Faith do! How strong are the ties of religion when entwined with the legends of a country! How many a cart creeps creaking and weary along the road from Ayodhyá to Chitrakút. It is this that gives the Rámáyan a strange interest, the story still lives.' *Calcutta Review: Vol. XXIII.*

Triśanku,[1] Jupiter looked dread,
And Mercury and Mars the red,
In direful opposition met,
The glory of the moon beset.
The lunar stars withheld their light,
The planets were no longer bright,
But meteors with their horrid glare,
And dire Viśákhás[2] lit the air.
As troubled Ocean heaves and raves
When Doom's wild tempest sweeps the waves,
Thus all Ayodhyá reeled and bent
When Ráma to the forest went.
And chilling grief and dark despair
Fell suddenly on all men there.
Their wonted pastime all forgot,
Nor thought of food, or touched it not.
Crowds in the royal street were seen
With weeping eye and troubled mien:
No more a pe ple gay and glad,
Each head and heart was sick and sad.
No more the cool wind softly blew,
The moon no more was fair to view,
No more the sun with genial glow
Cherished the world now plunged in woe.
Sons, brothers, husbands, wedded wives
Forgot the ties that joined their lives;
No thought for kith and kin was spared,
But all for only Ráma cared.
And Ráma's friends who loved him best,
Their minds disordered and distressed.
By the great burthen of their woes
Turned not to slumber or repose.
Like Earth with all her hills bereft
Of Indra's guiding care.
Ayodhyá in her sorrow left
By him, the high souled heir,
Was bowed by fear and sorrow's force,
And shook with many a throe,
While warrior, elephant, and horse
Sent up the cry of woe.

CANTO XLII.

DAŚARATHA'S LAMENT.

While yet the dust was seen afar
That marked the course of Ráma's car,
The glory of Ikshváku's race
Turned not away his eager face.
While yet his duteous son he saw
He could not once his gaze withdraw,
But rooted to the spot remained
With eyes that after Ráma strained.
But when that dust no more he viewed,
Fainting he fell by grief subdued.

[1] See p. 72.

[2] Four stars of the sixteenth lunar asterism.

To his right hand Kauśalyá went,
And ready aid the lady lent,
While Bharat's loving mother tried
To raise him on the other side.
The king, within whose ordered soul
Justice and virtue held control,
To Queen Kaikeyí turned and said,
With every sense disquieted:
'Touch me not, thou whose soul can plot
All sin, Kaikeyí, touch me not.
No loving wife, no friend to me,
I ne'er again would look on thee;
Ne'er from this day have aught to do
With thee and all thy retinue;
Thee whom no virtuous thoughts restrain,
Whose selfish heart seeks only gain.
The hand I laid in mine, O dame,
The steps we took around the flame,[1]
And all that links thy life to mine
Here and hereafter I resign.
If Bharat too, thy darling son,
Joy in the rule thy art has won,
Ne'er may the funeral offerings paid
By his false hand approach my shade.'

Then while the dust upon him hung,
The monarch to Kauśalyá clung,
And she with mournful steps and slow
Turned to the palace, worn with woe.
As one whose hand has touched the fire,
Or slain a Bráhman in his ire,
He felt his heart with sorrow torn
Still thinking of his son forlorn.
Each step was torture, as the road
The traces of the chariot showed,
And as the shadowed sun grows dim
So care and anguish darkened him.
He raised a cry, by woe distraught,
As of his son again he thought,
And judging that the car had sped
Beyond the city, thus he said:
'I still behold the foot-prints made
By the good horses that conveyed
My son afar: these marks I see,
But high-souled Ráma, where is he?
Ah me, my son! my first and best,
On pleasant couches wont to rest,
With limbs perfumed with sandal, fanned
By many a beauty's tender hand:
Where will he lie with log or stone
Beneath him for a pillow thrown,
To leave at morn his earthy bed,
Neglected, and with dust o'erspread,
As from the flood with sigh and pant
Comes forth the husband elephant?
The men who make the woods their home
Shall see the long-armed hero roam
Roused from his bed, though lord of all,
In semblance of a friendless thrall.
Janak's dear child who ne'er has met

[1] In the marriage service.

With aught save joy and comfort yet,
Will reach to-day the forest, worn
And wearied with the brakes of thorn.
Ah, gentle girl, of woods unskilled,
How will her heart with dread be filled
At the wild beasts' deep roaring there,
Whose voices lift the shuddering hair!
Kaikeyí, glory in thy gain,
And, widow queen, begin to reign:
No will, no power to live have I
When my brave son no more is nigh.'
Thus pouring forth laments, the king
Girt by the people's crowded ring,
Entered the noble bower like one
New-bathed when funeral rites are done.
Where'er he looked naught met his gaze
But empty houses, courts, and ways.
Closed were the temples: countless feet
No longer trod the royal street,
And thinking of his son he viewed
Men weak and worn and woe-subdued.
As sinks the sun into a cloud,
So passed he on, and wept aloud,
Within that house no more to be
The dwelling of the banished three,
Brave Ráma, his Vedehan bride,
And Lakshman by his brother's side:
Like broad still waters, when the king
Of all the birds that ply the wing
Has swooped from heaven and borne away
The glittering snakes that made them gay.
With choking sobs and voice half spent
The king renewed his sad lament:
With broken utterance faint and low
Scarce could he speak these words of woe:
'My steps to Ráma's mother guide,
And place me by Kauśalyá's side:
There, only there my heart may know
Some little respite from my woe.'
The warders of the palace led
The monarch, when his words were said,
To Queen Kauśalyá's bower, and there
Laid him with reverential care.
But while he rested on the bed
Still was his soul disquieted.
In grief he tossed his arms on high
Lamenting with a piteous cry:
'O Ráma, Ráma,' thus said he,
'My son, thou hast forsaken me.
High bliss awaits those favoured men
Left living in Ayodhyá then,
Whose eyes shall see my son once more
Returning when the time is o'er.'
Then came the night, whose hated gloom
Fell on him like the night of doom.
At midnight Daśaratha cried
To Queen Kauśalyá by his side:
'I see thee not, Kauśalyá; lay
Thy gentle hand in mine, I pray.
When Ráma left his home my sight
Went with him, nor returns to-night.'

CANTO XLIII.

KAUŚALYÁ'S LAMENT.

Kauśalyá saw the monarch lie
With drooping frame and failing eye,
And for her banished son distressed
With these sad words her lord addressed:
'Kaikeyí, cruel, false, and vile
Has cast the venom of her guile
On Ráma lord of men, and she
Will ravage like a snake set free;
And more and more my soul alarm,
Like a dire serpent bent on harm.
For triumph crowns each dark intent,
And Ráma to the wild is sent.
Ah, were he doomed but here to stray
Begging his food from day to day,
Or do, enslaved, Kaikeyí's will,
This were a boon, a comfort still.
But she, as chose her cruel hate,
Has hurled him from his high estate,
As Bráhmans when the moon is new
Cast to the ground the demons' due.[1]
The long-armed hero, like the lord
Of Nágas, with his bow and sword
Begins, I ween, his forest life
With Lakshman and his faithful wife.
Ah, how will fare the exiles now,
Whom, moved by Queen Kaikeyí, thou
Hast sent in forests to abide,
Bred in delights, by woe untried?
Far banished when their lives are young,
With the fair fruit before them hung,
Deprived of all their rank that suits,
How will they live on grain and roots?
O, that my years of woe were passed,
And the glad hour were come at last
When I shall see my children dear,
Ráma, his wife, and Lakshman here!
When shall Ayodhyá, wild with glee,
Again those mighty heroes see,
And decked with wreaths her banners wave
To welcome home the true and brave?
When will the beautiful city view
With happy eyes the lordly two
Returning, joyful as the main
When the dear moon is full again?
When, like some mighty bull who leads
The cow exulting through the meads,
Will Ráma through the city ride,
Strong-armed, with Sítá at his side?
When will ten thousand thousand meet
And crowd Ayodhyá's royal street,
And grain in joyous welcome throw
Upon my sons who tame the foe?
When with delight shall youthful bands
Of Bráhman maidens in their hands

[1] The husks and chaff of the rice offered to the Gods.

Bear fruit and flowers in goodly show,
And circling round Ayodhyá go?
With ripened judgment of a sage,
And godlike in his blooming age,
When shall my virtuous son appear,
Like kindly rain, our hearts to cheer?
Ah, in a former life, I ween,
This hand of mine, most base and mean,
Has dried the udders of the kine
And left the thirsty calves to pine,
Hence, as the lion robs the cow,
Kaikeyí makes me childless now,
Exulting from her feebler foe
To rend the son she cherished so.
I had but him, in Scripture skilled,
With every grace his soul was filled.
Now not a joy has life to give,
And robbed of him I would not live:
Yea, all my days are dark and drear
If he, my darling, be not near,
And Lakshman brave, my heart to cheer.
As for my son I mourn and yearn,
The quenchless flames of anguish burn
And kill me with the pain,
As in the summer's noontide blaze
The glorious Day-God with his rays
Consumes the parching plain.'

CANTO XLIV.

SUMITRA'S SPEECH.

Kauśalyá ceased her sad lament,
Of beauteous dames most excellent.
Sumitrá who to duty clave,
In righteous words this answer gave:
'Dear Queen, all noble virtues grace
Thy son, of men the first in place.
Why dost thou shed these tears of woe
With bitter grief lamenting so?
If Ráma, leaving royal sway
Has hastened to the woods away,
'Tis for his high-souled father's sake
That he his premise may not break.
He to the path of duty clings
Which lordly fruit hereafter brings—
The path to which the righteous cleave—
For him, dear Queen, thou shouldst not grieve.
And Lakshman too, the blameless-souled,
The same high course with him will hold,
And mighty bliss on him shall wait,
So tenderly compassionate.
And Sítá, bred with tender care,
Well knows what toils await her there,
But in her love she will not part
From Ráma of the virtuous heart.
Now has thy son through all the world
The banner of his fame unfurled:
True, modest, careful of his vow,
What has he left to aim at now?
The sun will mark his mighty soul,
His wisdom, sweetness, self-control,
Will spare from pain his face and limb,
And with soft radiance shine for him.
For him through forest glades shall spring
A soft auspicious breeze, and bring
Its tempered heat and cold to play
Around him ever night and day.
The pure cold moonbeams shall delight
The hero as he sleeps at night,
And soothe him with the soft caress
Of a fond parent's tenderness.
To him, the bravest of the brave,
His heavenly arms the Bráhman gave,
When fierce Suváhu dyed the plain
With his life-blood by Ráma slain.
Still trusting to his own right arm
Thy hero son will fear no harm:
As in his father's palace, he
In the wild woods will dauntless be.
Whene'er he lets his arrows fly
His stricken foemen fall and die:
And is that prince of peerless worth
Too weak to keep and sway the earth?
His sweet pure soul, his beauty's charm,
His hero heart, his warlike arm,
Will soon redeem his rightful reign
When from the woods he comes again.
The Bráhmans on the prince's head
King-making drops shall quickly shed,
And Sítá, Earth, and Fortune share
The glories which await the heir.
For him, when forth his chariot swept,
The crowd that thronged Ayodhyá wept,
With agonizing woe distressed.
With him in hermit's mantle dressed
In guise of Sítá Lakshmí went.
And none his glory may prevent.
Yea, naught to him is high or hard,
Before whose steps, to be his guard,
Lakshman, the best who draws the bow,
With spear, shaft, sword rejoiced to go.
His wanderings in the forest o'er,
Thine eyes shall see thy son once more,
Quit thy faint heart, thy grief dispel,
For this, O Queen, is truth I tell.
Thy son returning, moonlike, thence,
Shall at thy feet do reverence,
And, blest and blameless lady, thou
Shalt see his head to touch them bow,
Yea, thou shalt see thy son made king
When he returns with triumphing,
And how thy happy eyes will brim
With tears of joy to look on him!
Thou, blameless lady, shouldst the whole
Of the sad people here console:
Why in thy tender heart allow
This bitter grief to harbour now?
As the long banks of cloud distil
Their water when they see the hill,

So shall the drops of rapture run
From thy glad eyes to see thy son
Returning, as he lowly bends
To greet thee, girt by all his friends.'
Thus soothing, kindly eloquent,
With every hopeful argument
Kauśalyá's heart by sorrow rent,
Fair Queen Sumitrá ceased.
Kauśalyá heard each pleasant plea,
And grief began to leave her free,
As the light clouds of autumn flee,
Their watery stores decreased.

CANTO XLV.

THE TAMASÁ.

Their tender love the people drew
To follow Ráma brave and true,
The high-souled hero, as he went
Forth from his home to banishment.
The king himself his friends obeyed,
And turned him homeward as they prayed.
But yet the people turned not back,
Still close on Ráma's chariot track.
For they who in Ayodhyá dwelt
For him such fond affection felt,
Decked with all grace and glories high,
The dear full moon of every eye.
Though much his people prayed and wept,
Kakutstha's son his purpose kept,
And still his journey would pursue
To keep the king his father true.
Deep in the hero's bosom sank
Their love, whose signs his glad eye drank.
He spoke to cheer them, as his own
Dear children, in a loving tone:
'If ye would grant my fond desire,
Give Bharat now that love entire
And reverence shown to me by all
Who dwell within Ayodhyá's wall.
For he, Kaikeyí's darling son,
His virtuous career will run,
And ever bound by duty's chain
Consult your weal and bliss and gain.
In judgment old, in years a child,
With hero virtues meek and mild,
A fitting lord is he to cheer
His people and remove their fear.
In him all kingly gifts abound,
More noble than in me are found:
Imperial prince, well proved and tried—
Obey him as your lord and guide.
And grant, I pray, the boon I ask:
To please the king be still your task,
That his fond heart, while I remain
Far in the woods, may feel no pain.'
The more he showed his will to tread
The path where filial duty led,
The more the people, round him thronged,
For their dear Ráma's empire longed.
Still more attached his followers grew,
As Ráma, with his brother, drew
The people with his virtues' ties,
Lamenting all with tear-dimmed eyes.
The saintly twice-born, triply old
In glory, knowledge, seasons told,
With hoary heads that shook and bowed,
Their voices raïsed and spake aloud:
'O steeds, who best and noblest are,
Who whirl so swiftly Ráma's car,
Go not, return: we call on you:
Be to your master kind and true.
For speechless things are swift to hear,
And naught can match a horse's ear.
O generous steeds, return, when thus
You hear the cry of all of us.
Each vow he keeps most firm and sure,
And duty makes his spirit pure.
Back with our chief! not wood-ward hence;
Back to his royal residence!'
Soon as he saw the aged band,
Exclaiming in their misery, stand,
And their sad cries around him rang,
Swift from his chariot Ráma sprang.
Then, still upon his journey bent,
With Sítá and with Lakshman went
The hero by the old men's side
Suiting to theirs his shortened stride.
He could not pass the twice-born throng
As weariedly they walked along:
With pitying heart, with tender eye,
He could not in his chariot fly.
When the steps of Ráma viewed
That still his onward course pursued,
Woe shook the troubled heart of each,
And burnt with grief they spoke this speech:
'With thee, O Ráma, to the wood
All Bráhmans go and Bráhmanhood:
Borne on our aged shoulders, see,
Our fires of worship go with thee.
Bright canopies that lend their shade
In Vájapeya[1] rites displayed,
In plenteous store are borne behind
Like cloudlets in the autumn wind.
No shelter from the sun hast thou,
And, lest his fury burn thy brow,
These sacrificial shades we bear
Shall aid thee in the noontide glare.
Our hearts, who ever loved to pore
On sacred text and Vedic lore,
Now all to thee, beloved, turn,
And for a life in forests yearn.
Deep in our aged bosoms lies
The Vedas' lore, the wealth we prize,
There still, like wives at home, shall dwell,
Whose love and truth protect them well.

---

[1] An important sacrifice at which seventeen victims were immolated.

To follow thee our hearts are bent;
We need not plan or argument.
All else in duty's law we slight,
For following thee is following right.
O noble Prince, retrace thy way:
O, hear us, Ráma, as we lay,
With many tears and many prayers,
Our aged heads and swan-white hairs
Low in the dust before thy feet;
O, hear us, Ráma, we entreat.
Full many of these who with thee run,
Their sacred rites had just begun.
Unfinished yet those rites remain;
But finished if thou turn again.
All rooted life and things that move
To thee their deep affection prove.
To them, when warmed by love, they glow
And sue to thee, some favour show
Each lowly bush, each towering tree
Would follow too for love of thee.
Bound by its root it must remain;
But—all it can—its boughs complain,
As when the wild wind rushes by
It tells its woe in groan and sign.
No more through air the gay birds flit,
But, foodless, melancholy sit
Together on the branch and call
To thee whose kind heart feels for all.'
As wailed the aged Bráhmans, bent
To turn him back, with wild lament,
Seemed Tamasá herself to aid,
Checking his progress, as they prayed.
Sumantra from the chariot freed
With ready hand each weary steed;
He groomed them with the utmost heed,
Their limbs he bathed and dried,
Then led them forth to drink and feed
At pleasure in the grassy mead
That fringed the river side.

CANTO XLVI.

THE HALT.

When Ráma, chief of Raghu's race,
Arrived at that delightful place,
He looked on Sítá first, and then
To Lakshman spake the lord of men:
'Now first the shades of night descend
Since to the wilds our steps we bend.
Joy to thee, brother! do not grieve
For our dear home and all we leave.
The woods unpeopled seem to weep
Around us, as their tenants creep
Or fly to lair and den and nest,
Both bird and beast, to seek their rest.
Methinks Ayodhyá's royal town
Where dwells my sire of high renown,
With all her men and dames to-night
Will mourn us vanished from their sight.
For, by his virtues won, they cling
In fond affection to their king,
And thee and me, O brave and true,
And Bharat and Śatrughna too.
I for my sire and mother feel
Deep sorrow o'er my bosom steal,
Lest mourning us, oppressed with fears,
They blind their eyes with endless tears.
Yet Bharat's duteous love will show
Sweet comfort in their hours of woe,
And with kind words their hearts sustain,
Suggesting duty, bliss, and gain.
I mourn my parents now no more:
I count dear Bharat's virtues o'er,
And his kind love and care dispel
The doubts I had, and all is well.
And thou thy duty wouldst not shun,
And, following me, hast nobly done;
Else, bravest, I should need a band
Around my wife as guard to stand.
On this first night, my thirst to slake,
Some water only will I take:
Thus, brother, thus my will decides,
Though varied store the wood provides.'
Thus having said to Lakshman, he
Addressed in turn Sumantra: Be
Most diligent to-night, my friend,
And with due care thy horses tend.'
The sun had set: Sumantra tied
His noble horses side by side,
Gave store of grass with liberal hand,
And rested near them on the strand.
Each paid the holy evening rite,
And when around them fell the night,
The charioteer, with Lakshmaṇ's aid,
A lowly bed for Ráma laid.
To Lakshmaṇ Ráma bade adieu,
And then by Sítá's side he threw
His limbs upon the leafy bed
Their care upon the bank had spread.
When Lakshmaṇ saw the couple slept,
Still on the strand his watch he kept,
Still with Sumantra there conversed,
And Ráma's varied gifts rehearsed.
All night he watched, nor sought repose,
Till on the earth the sun arose:
With him Sumantra stayed awake,
And still of Ráma's virtues spake.
Thus, near the river's grassy shore
Which herds unnumbered wandered o'er,
Repose, untroubled, Ráma found,
And all the people lay around.
The glorious hero left his bed,
Looked on the sleeping crowd, and said
To Lakshmaṇ, whom each lucky line
Marked out for bliss with surest sign:
'O brother Lakshmaṇ, look on these
Reclining at the roots of trees;
All care of house and home resigned,
Caring for us with heart and mind,
These people of the city yearn

To see us to our home return:
To quit their lives will they consent,
But never leave their firm intent.
Come, while they all unconscious sleep,
Let us upon the chariot leap,
And swiftly on our journey speed
Where naught our progress may impede,
That these fond citizens who roam
Far from Ikshváku's ancient home,
No more may sleep 'neath bush and tree,
Following still for love of me.
A prince with tender care should heal
The self-brought woes his people feel,
And never let his subjects share
The burthen he is forced to bear.'

Then Lakshman to the chief replied,
Who stood like Justice by his side:
'Thy rede, O sage, I well commend:
Without delay the car ascend.'
Then Ráma to Sumantra spoke:
'Thy rapid steeds, I pray thee, yoke.
Hence to the forest will I go:
Away, my lord, and be not slow.'

Sumantra, urged to utmost speed,
Yoked to the car each generous steed,
And then, with hand to hand applied,
He came before the chief and cried:
'Hail, Prince, whom mighty arms adorn,
Hail, bravest of the chariot-borne!
With Sítá and thy brother thou
Mayst mount: the car is ready now.'

The hero clomb the car with haste:
His bow and gear within were placed,
And quick the eddying flood he passed
Of Tamasá whose waves run fast.
Soon as he touched the farther side,
That strong-armed hero, glorified,
He found a road both wide and clear,
Where e'en the timid naught could fear.
Then, that the crowd might be misled,
Thus Ráma to Sumantra said:
'Speed north a while, then hasten back,
Returning in thy former track,
That so the people may not learn
The course I follow: drive and turn.'

Sumantra, at the chief's behest,
Quick to the task himself addressed;
Then near to Ráma came, and showed
The chariot ready for the road.
With Sítá, then, the princely two,
Who o'er the line of Raghu threw
A glory ever bright and new,
Upon the chariot stood.
Sumantra fast and faster drove
His horses, who in fleetness strove
Still onward to the distant grove,
The hermit-haunted wood.

CANTO XLVII.

THE CITIZENS' RETURN.

The people, when the morn shone fair,
Arose to find no Ráma there.
Then fear and numbing grief subdued
The senses of the multitude.
The woe-born tears were running fast
As all around their eyes they cast,
And sadly looked, but found no trace
Of Ráma, searching every place.
Bereft of Ráma good and wise,
With drooping cheer and weeping eyes,
Each woe-distracted sage gave vent
To sorrow in his wild lament:
'Woe worth the sleep that stole our sense
With its beguiling influence,
That now we look in vain for him
Of the broad chest and stalwart limb!
How could the strong-armed hero, thus
Deceiving all, abandon us?
His people so devoted see,
Yet to the woods, a hermit, flee?
How can he, wont our hearts to cheer,
As a fond sire his children dear,—
How can the pride of Raghu's race
Fly from us to some desert place!
Here let us all for death prepare,
Or on the last great journey fare;[1]
Of Ráma our dear lord bereft,
What profit in our lives is left?
Huge trunks of trees around us lie,
With roots and branches sere and dry,
Come let us set these logs on fire
And throw our bodies on the pyre.
What shall we speak? How can we say
We followed Ráma on his way,
The mighty chief whose arm is strong,
Who sweetly speaks, who thinks no wrong?
Ayodhyá's town with sorrow dumb,
Without our lord will see us come,
And hopeless misery will strike
Elder, and child, and dame alike.
Forth with that peerless chief we came,
Whose mighty heart is aye the same:
How, reft of him we love, shall we
Returning dare that town to see?'

Complaining thus with varied cry
They tossed their aged arms on high,
And their sad hearts with grief were wrung,
Like cows who sorrow for their young.
A while they followed on the road
Which traces of his chariot showed,
But when at length those traces failed,
A deep despair their hearts assailed.

---

[1] The great pilgrimage to the Himálayas, in order to die there.

The chariot marks no more discerned,
The hopeless sages backward turned:
'Ah, what is this? What can we more?
Fate stops the way, and all is o'er.'
With wearied hearts, in grief and shame
They took the road by which they came,
And reached Ayodhyá's city, where
From side to side was naught but care.
With troubled spirits quite cast down
They looked upon the royal town,
And from their eyes, oppressed with woe,
Their tears again began to flow.
Of Ráma reft, the city wore
No look of beauty as before.
Like a dull river or a lake
By Garud robbed of every snake.
Dark, dismal as the moonless sky,
Or as a sea whose bed is dry,
So sad, to every pleasure dead,
They saw the town, disquieted.
On to their houses, high and vast,
Where stores of precious wealth were massed,
The melancholy Bráhmans passed,
Their hearts with anguish cleft:
Aloof from all, they came not near
To stranger or to kinsman dear,
Showing in faces blank and drear.
That not one joy was left.

CANTO XLVIII.

THE WOMEN'S LAMENT.

When those who forth with Ráma went
Back to the town their steps had bent,
It seemed that death had touched and chilled
Those hearts which piercing sorrow filled.
Each to his several mansion came,
And girt by children and his dame,
From his sad eyes the water shed
That o'er his cheek in torrents spread.
All joy was fled: oppressed with cares
No bustling trader showed his wares.
Each shop had lost its brilliant look,
Each householder forbore to cook.
No hand with joy its earnings told,
None cared to win a wealth of gold,
And scarce the youthful mother smiled
To see her first, her new-born child.
In every house a woman wailed,
And her returning lord assailed
With keen taunt piercing like the steel
That bids the tusked monster kneel:
'What now to them is wedded dame,
What house and home and dearest aim,
Or son, or bliss, or gathered store,
Whose eyes on Ráma look no more!
There is but one in all the earth,
One man alone of real worth,
Lakshman, who follows, true and good,
Ráma, with Sítá, through the wood.
Made holy for all time we deem
Each pool and fountain, lake and stream,
If great Kakutstha's son shall choose
Their water for his bath to use.
Each forest, dark with lovely trees,
Shall yearn Kakutstha's son to please;
Each mountain peak and woody hill,
Each mighty flood and mazy rill,
Each rocky height, each shady grove
Where the blest feet of Ráma rove,
Shall gladly welcome with the best
Of all they have their honoured guest.
The trees that clustering blossoms bear,
And bright-hued buds to gem their hair,
The heart of Ráma shall delight,
And cheer him on the breezy height.
For him the upland slopes will show
The fairest roots and fruit that grow,
And all their wealth before him fling
Ere the due hour of ripening.
For him each earth-upholding hill
Its crystal water shall distil,
And all its floods shall be displayed
In many a thousand-hued cascade.
Where Ráma stands is naught to fear,
No danger comes if he be near;
For all who live on him depend,
The world's support, and lord, and friend.
Ere in too distant wilds he stray,
Let us to Ráma speed away,
For rich reward on those will wait
Who serve a prince of soul so great.
We will attend on Sítá there;
Be Raghu's son your special care.'
The city dames, with grief distressed,
Thus once again their lords addressed:
'Ráma shall be your guard and guide,
And Sítá will for us provide.
For who would care to linger here,
Where all is sad and dark and drear?
Who, mid the mourners, hope for bliss
In a poor soulless town like this?
If Queen Kaikeyí's treacherous sin,
Our lord expelled, the kingdom win,
We heed not sons or golden store,
Our life itself we prize no more.
If she, seduced by lust of sway,
Her lord and son could cast away,
Whom would she leave unharmed, the base
Defiler of her royal race?
We swear it by our children dear,
We will not dwell as servants here;
If Queen Kaikeyí live to reign,
We will not in her realm remain.
Bowed down by her oppressive hand,
The helpless, lordless, godless land,
Cursed for Kaikeyí's guilt will fall,
And swift destruction seize it all.

For, Ráma forced from home to fly,
The king his sire will surely die,
And when the king has breathed his last
Ruin will doubtless follow fast.
Sad, robbed of merits, drug the cup
And drink the poisoned mixture up,
Or share the exiled Ráma's lot,
Or seek some land that knows her not.
No reason, but a false pretence
Drove Ráma, Sítá, Lakshman hence,
And we to Bharat have been given
Like cattle to the shambles driven.'

While in each house the women, pained
At loss of Ráma, still complained,
Sank to his rest the Lord of Day,
And night through all the sky held sway.
The fires of worship all were cold,
No text was hummed, no tale was told,
And shades of midnight gloom came down
Enveloping the mournful town.
Still, sick at heart, the women shed,
As for a son or husband fled,
For Ráma tears, disquieted:
No child was loved as he.
And all Ayodhyá, where the feast,
Music, and song, and dance had ceased,
And merriment and glee,
Where every merchant's store was closed
That erst its glittering wares exposed,
Was like a dried up sea.

CANTO XLIX.

THE CROSSING OF THE RIVERS.

Now Ráma, ere the night was fled,
O'er many a league of road had sped,
Till, as his course he onward held,
The morn the shades of night dispelled.
The rites of holy dawn he paid,
And all the country round surveyed.
He saw, as still he hurried through
With steeds which swift as arrows flew,
Hamlets and groves with blossoms fair,
And fields which showed the tillers' care,
While from the clustered dwellings near
The words of peasants reached his ear:
'Fie on our lord the king, whose soul
Is yielded up to love's control!
Fie on the vile Kaikeyí! Shame
On that malicious sinful dame,
Who, keenly bent on cruel deeds,
No bounds of right and virtue heeds,
But with her wicked art has sent
So good a prince to banishment,
Wise, tender-hearted, ruling well
His senses, in the woods to dwell.
Ah cruel king! his heart of steel
For his own son no love could feel,
Who with the sinless Ráma parts,
The darling of the people's hearts.'

These words he heard the peasants say,
Who dwelt in hamlets by the way,
And, lord of all the realm by right,
Through Kośala pursued his flight.
Through the auspicious flood, at last,
Of Vedaśruti's stream he passed,
And onward to the place he sped
By Saint Agastya tenanted.
Still on for many an hour he hied,
And crossed the stream whose cooling tide
Rolls onward till she meets the sea,
The herd-frequented Gomatí.[1]
Borne by his rapid horses o'er,
He reached that river's farther shore,
And Syandiká's, whose swan-loved stream
Resounded with the peacock's scream.
Then as he journeyed on his road
To his Videhan bride he showed
The populous land which Manu old
To King Ikshváku gave to hold.
The glorious prince, the lord of men
Looked on the charioteer, and then
Voiced like a wild swan, loud and clear,
He spake these words and bade him hear:
'When shall I, with returning feet
My father and my mother meet?
When shall I lead the hunt once more
In bloomy woods on Sarjú's shore?
Most eagerly I long to ride
Urging the chase on Sarjú's side.
For royal saints have seen no blame
In this, the monarch's matchless game.'

Thus speeding on,—no rest or stay,—
Ikshváku's son pursued his way.
Oft his sweet voice the silence broke,
And thus on varied themes he spoke.

CANTO L.

THE HALT UNDER THE INGUDI.[2]

So through the wide and fair extent
Of Kośala the hero went.
Then toward Ayodhyá back he gazed,
And cried, with suppliant hands upraised:
'Farewell, dear city, first in place,
Protected by Kakutstha's race!
And Gods, who in thy temples dwell,
And keep thine ancient citadel!
I from his debt my sire will free,
Thy well-loved towers again will see,
And, coming from my wild retreat,
My mother and my father meet.'

---

[1] Known to Europeans as the Goomtee.
[2] A tree, commonly called *Ingua.*

Then burning grief inflamed his eye,
As his right arm he raised on high,
And, while hot tears his cheek bedewed,
Addressed the mournful multitude:
'By love and tender pity moved,
Your love for me you well have proved;
Now turn again with joy, and win
Success in all your hands begin.'
Before the high-souled chief they bent,
With circling steps around him went,
And then with bitter wailing, they
Departed each his several way.
Like the great sun engulfed by night,
The hero sped beyond their sight,
While still the people mourned his fate
And wept aloud disconsolate.
The car-borne chieftain passed the bound
Of Kośala's delightful ground,
Where grain and riches bless the land,
And people give with liberal hand:
A lovely realm unvexed by fear,
Where countless shrines and stakes[1] appear:
Where mango-groves and gardens grow,
And streams of pleasant water flow:
Where dwells content a well-fed race,
And countless kine the meadows grace:
Filled with the voice of praise and prayer:
Each hamlet worth a monarch's care.
Before him three-pathed Gangá rolled
Her heavenly waters bright and cold;
O'er her pure breast no weeds were spread,
Her banks were hermit-visited.
The car-borne hero saw the tide
That ran with eddies multiplied,
And thus the charioteer addressed:
'Here on the bank to-day we rest.
Not distant from the river, see!
There grows a lofty Ingudí
With blossoms thick on every spray:
There rest we, charioteer, to-day.
I on the queen of floods will gaze,
Whose holy stream has highest praise,
Where deer, and bird, and glittering snake,
God, Daitya, bard their pastime take.'
Sumantra, Lakshman gave assent,
And with the steeds they thither went.
When Ráma reached the lovely tree,
With Sítá and with Lakshman, he
Alighted from the car: with speed
Sumantra loosed each weary steed,
And, hand to hand in reverence laid,
Stood near to Ráma in the shade.
Ráma's dear friend, renowned by fame,
Who of Nisháda lineage came,
Guha, the mighty chief, adored
Through all the land as sovereign lord,
Soon as he heard that prince renowned
Was resting on Nisháda ground,
Begirt by counsellor and peer
And many an honoured friend drew near.
Soon as the monarch came in view,
Ráma and Lakshman toward him flew.
Then Guha, at the sight distressed,
His arms around the hero pressed,
Laid both his hands upon his head
Bowed to those lotus feet, and said:
'O Ráma, make thy wishes known,
And be this kingdom as thine own.
Who, mighty-armed, will ever see
A guest so dear as thou to me?'
He placed before him dainty fare
Of every flavour, rich and rare,
Brought forth the gift for honoured guest,
And thus again the chief addressed:
'Welcome, dear Prince, whose arms are strong;
These lands and all to thee belong.
Thy servants we, our lord art thou;
Begin, good king, thine empire now.
See, various food before thee placed,
And cups to drink and sweets to taste.
For thee soft beds are hither borne,
And for thy horses grass and corn.'
To Guha as he pressed and prayed,
Thus Raghu's son his answer made:
''Twas aye thy care my heart to please
With honour, love, and courtesies,
And friendship brings thee now to greet
Thy guest thus humbly on thy feet.'
Again the hero spake, as round
The king his shapely arms he wound:
'Guha, I see that all is well
With thee and those who with thee dwell;
That health and bliss and wealth attend
Thy realm, thyself, and every friend.
But all these friendly gifts of thine,
Bound to refuse, I must decline.
Grass, bark, and hide my only wear,
And woodland roots and fruit my fare,
On duty all my heart is set;
I seek the woods, an anchoret.
A little grass and corn to feed
The horses—this is all I need.
So by this favour, King, alone
Shall honour due to me be shown.
For these good steeds who brought me here
Are to my sire supremely dear;
And kind attention paid to these
Will honour me and highly please.'
Then Guha quickly bade his train
Give water to the steeds, and grain.
And Ráma, ere the night grew dark,
Paid evening rites in dress of bark,
And tasted water, on the strand,
Drawn from the stream by Lakshman's hand.
And Lakshman with observance meet
Bathed his beloved brother's feet,

[1] Sacrificial posts to which the victims were tied.

Who rested with his Maithil spouse :
Then sat him down 'neath distant boughs.
And Guha with his bow sat near
To Lakshman and the charioteer,
And with the prince conversing kept
His faithful watch while Ráma slept.
As Daśaratha's glorious heir,
Of lofty soul and wisdom rare,
Reclining with his Sítá there
Beside the river lay—
He who no troubles e'er had seen,
Whose life a life of bliss had been—
That night beneath the branches green
Passed pleasantly away.

CANTO LI.

LAKSHMAN'S LAMENT.

As Lakshman still his vigil held
By unaffected love impelled,
Guha, whose heart the sight distressed,
With words like these the prince addressed:
'Beloved youth, this pleasant bed
Was brought for thee, for thee is spread;
On this, my Prince, thine eyelids close,
And heal fatigue with sweet repose.
My men are all to labour trained,
But hardship thou hast ne'er sustained.
All we this night our watch will keep
And guard Kakutstha's son asleep.
In all the world there breathes not one
More dear to me than Raghu's son.
The words I speak, heroic youth,
Are true : I swear it by my truth.
Through his dear grace supreme renown
Will, so I trust, my wishes crown.
So shall my life rich store obtain
Of merit, blest with joy and gain.
While Raghu's son and Sítá lie
Entranced in happy slumber, I
Will, with my trusty bow in hand,
Guard my dear friend with all my band.
To me, who oft these forests range,
Is naught therein or new or strange.
We could with equal might oppose
A four-fold army led by foes.'
Then royal Lakshman made reply:
'With thee to stand as guardian nigh,
Whose faithful soul regards the right,
Fearless we well might rest to-night.
But how, when Ráma lays his head
With Sítá on his lowly bed,—
How can I sleep? how can I care
For life, or aught that's bright and fair?
Behold the conquering chief, whose might
Is match for Gods and fiends in fight;
With Sítá now he rests his head
Asleep on grass beneath him spread.
Won by devotion, text, and prayer,
And many a rite performed with care,
Chief of our father's sons he shines
Well marked, like him, with favouring signs.
Brief, brief the monarch's life will be
Now his dear son is forced to flee;
And quickly will the widowed state
Mourn for her lord disconsolate.
Each mourner there has wept her fill;
The cries of anguish now are still :
In the king's hall each dame, o'ercome
With weariness of woe is dumb.
This first sad night of grief, I ween,
Will do to death each sorrowing queen:
Scarce is Kauśalyá left alive;
My mother, too, can scarce survive.
If when her heart is fain to break,
She lingers for Śatrughna's sake,
Kauśalyá, mother of the chief,
Must sink beneath the chilling grief.
That town which countless thousands fill,
Whose hearts with love of Ráma thrill,—
The world's delight, so rich and fair,—
Grieved for the king, his death will share.
The hopes he fondly cherished, crossed,
Ayodhyá's throne to Ráma lost,—
With mournful cries, Too late, too late!
The king my sire will meet his fate.
And when my sire has passed away,
Most happy in their lot are they,
Allowed, with every pious care,
Part in his funeral rites to bear.
And O, may we with joy at last,—
These years of forest exile past,—
Turn to Ayodhyá's town to dwell
With him who keeps his promise well!'
While thus the hero mighty-souled,
In wild lament his sorrow told,
Faint with the load that on him lay,
The hours of darkness passed away.
As thus the prince, impelled by zeal
For his loved brother, prompt to feel
Strong yearnings for the people's weal,
His words of truth outspake,
King Guha, grieved to see his woe,
Heart-stricken, gave his tears to flow,
Tormented by the common blow,
Sad, as a wounded snake.

CANTO LII.

THE CROSSING OF GANGÁ.

Soon as the shades of night had fled,
Uprising from his lowly bed,
Ráma the famous, broad of chest,
His brother Lakshman thus addressed:
'Now swift upsprings the Lord of Ligh,
And fled is venerable night,

That dark-winged bird the Koïl now
Is calling from the topmost bough,
And sounding from the thicket nigh
Is heard the peacock's early cry.
Come, cross the flood that seeks the sea,
The swiftly flowing Jáhnaví.'[1]

King Guha heard his speech, agreed,
And called his minister with speed:
'A boat,' he cried, 'swift, strong, and fair,
With rudder, oars, and men, prepare,
And place it ready by the shore
To bear the pilgrims quickly o'er.'
Thus Guha spake: his followers all
Bestirred them at their master's call;
Then told the king that ready manned
A gay boat waited near the strand.
Then Guha, hand to hand applied,
With reverence thus to Ráma cried:
'The boat is ready by the shore:
How, tell me, can I aid thee more?
O lord of men, it waits for thee
To cross the flood that seeks the sea.
O godlike keeper of thy vow,
Embark: the boat is ready now.'

Then Ráma, lord of glory high,
Thus to King Guha made reply:
'Thanks for thy gracious care, my lord:
Now let the gear be placed on board.'
Each bow-armed chief, in mail encased,
Bound sword and quiver to his waist,
And then with Sítá near them hied
Down the broad river's shelving side.
Then with raised palms the charioteer,
In lowly reverence drawing near,
Cried thus to Ráma good and true:
'Now what remains for me to do?'
With his right hand, while answering,
The hero touched his friend:
'Go back,' he said, 'and on the king
With watchful care attend.
Thus far, Sumantra, thou wast guide;
Now to Ayodhyá turn,' he cried:
'Hence seek we leaving steeds and car,
On foot the wood that stretches far.'
Sumantra, when, with grieving heart,
He heard the hero bid him part,
Thus to the bravest of the brave,
Ikshváku's son, his answer gave:
'In all the world men tell of naught,
To match thy deed, by heroes wrought—
Thus with thy brother and thy wife
Thrall-like to lead a forest life.
No meet reward of fruit repays
Thy holy lore, thy saintlike days,
Thy tender soul, thy love of truth,
If woe like this afflicts thy youth.
Thou, roaming under forest boughs
With thy dear brother and thy spouse,
Shalt richer meed of glory gain
Than if three worlds confessed thy reign.
Sad is our fate, O Ráma: we,
Abandoned and repelled by thee,
Must serve as thralls Kaikeyí's will,
Imperious, wicked, born to ill.'
Thus cried the faithful charioteer,
As Raghu's son, in rede his peer,
Was fast departing on his road,—
And long his tears of anguish flowed.
But Ráma, when those tears were dried,
His lips with water purified,
And in soft accents, sweet and clear,
Again addressed the charioteer:
'I find no heart, my friend, like thine,
So faithful to Ikshváku's line.
Still first in view this object keep,
That ne'er for me my sire may weep.
For he, the world's far-ruling king,
Is old, and wild with sorrow's sting;
With love's great burthen worn and weak:
Deem this the cause that thus I speak
Whate'er the high-souled king decrees
His loved Kaikeyí's heart to please,
Yea, be his order what it may,
Without demur thou must obey,
For this alone great monarchs reign,
That ne'er a wish be formed in vain.
Then, O Sumantra, well provide
That by no check the king be tried:
Nor let his heart in sorrow pine:
This care, my faithful friend, be thine.
The honoured king my father greet,
And thus for me my words repeat
To him whose senses are controlled,
Untired till now by grief, and old:
'I, Sítá, Lakshman sorrow not,
O Monarch, for our altered lot:
The same to us, if here we roam,
Or if Ayodhyá be our home.
The fourteen years will quickly fly,
The happy hour will soon be nigh
When thou, my lord, again shalt see
Lakshman, the Maithil dame, and me.'
Thus having soothed, O charioteer,
My father and my mother dear,
Let all the queens my message learn,
But to Kaikeyí chiefly turn.
With loving blessings from the three,
From Lakshman, Sítá, and from me,
My mother, Queen Kauśalyá, greet
With reverence to her sacred feet.
And add this prayer of mine: 'O King,
Send quickly forth and Bharat bring,
And set him on the royal throne
Which thy decree has made his own.
When he upon the throne is placed,
When thy fond arms are round him laced,
Thine aged heart will cease to ache
With bitter pangs for Ráma's sake.'

[1] Daughter of Jahnu, a name of the Ganges. See p. 55.

And say to Bharat: 'See thou treat
The queens with all observance meet:
What care the king receives, the same
Show thou alike to every dame.
Obedience to thy father's will
Who chooses thee the throne to fill,
Will earn for thee a store of bliss
Both in the world to come and this.'
Thus Ráma bade Sumantra go
With thoughtful care instructed so.
Sumantra all his message heard,
And spake again, by passion stirred:
'O, should deep feeling mar in aught
The speech by fond devotion taught,
Forgive whate'er I wildly speak:
My love is strong, my tongue is weak.
How shall I, if deprived of thee,
Return that mournful town to see:
Where sick at heart the people are
Because their Ráma roams afar.
Woe will be theirs too deep to brook
When on the empty car they look,
As when from hosts, whose chiefs are slain,
One charioteer comes home again.
This very day, I ween, is food
Forsworn by all the multitude,
Thinking that thou, with hosts to aid,
Art dwelling in the wild wood's shade.
The great despair, the shriek of woe
They uttered when they saw thee go,
Will, when I come with none beside,
A hundred-fold be multiplied.
How to Kauśalyá can I say:
'O Queen, I took thy son away,
And with thy brother left him well:
Weep not for him; thy woe dispel?'
So false a tale I cannot frame,
Yet how speak truth and grieve the dame?
How shall these horses, fleet and bold,
Whom not a hand but mine can hold,
Bear others, wont to whirl the car
Wherein Ikshváku's children are!
Without thee, Prince, I cannot, no,
I cannot to Ayodhyá go.
Then deign, O Ráma, to relent,
And let me share thy banishment.
But if no prayers can move thy heart,
If thou wilt quit me and depart,
The flames shall end my car and me,
Deserted thus and reft of thee.
In the wild wood when foes are near,
When dangers check thy vows austere,
Borne in my car will I attend,
All danger and all care to end.
For thy dear sake I love the skill
That guides the steed and curbs his will:
And soon a forest life will be
As pleasant, for my love of thee.
And if these horses near thee dwell,
And serve thee in the forest well,
They, for their service, will not miss
The due reward of highest bliss.
Thine orders, as with thee I stray,
Will I with heart and head obey,
Prepared, for thee, without a sigh,
To lose Ayodhyá or the sky.
As one defiled with hideous sin,
I never more can pass within
Ayodhyá, city of our king,
Unless beside me thee I bring.
One wish is mine, I ask no more,
That, when thy banishment is o'er
I in my car may bear my lord,
Triumphant, to his home restored.
The fourteen years, if spent with thee,
Will swift as light-winged moments flee;
But the same years, without thee told,
Were magnified a hundred-fold.
Do not, kind lord, thy servant leave,
Who to his master's son would cleave,
And the same path with him pursue,
Devoted, tender, just and true.'
Again, again Sumantra made
His varied plaint, and wept and prayed.
Him Raghu's son, whose tender breast
Felt for his servants, thus addressed:
'O faithful servant, well my heart
Knows how attached and true thou art.
Hear thou the words I speak, and know
Why to the town I bid thee go.
Soon as Kaikeyí, youngest queen,
Thy coming to the town has seen,
No doubt will then her mind oppress
That Ráma roams the wilderness.
And so the dame, her heart content
With proof of Ráma's banishment,
Will doubt the virtuous king no more
As faithless to the oath he swore.
Chief of my cares is this, that she,
Youngest amid the queens, may see
Bharat her son securely reign
O'er rich Ayodhyá's wide domain.
For mine and for the monarch's sake
Do thou thy journey homeward take,
And, as I bade, repeat each word
That from my lips thou here hast heard.'
Thus spake the prince, and strove to cheer
The sad heart of the charioteer,
And then to royal Guha said
These words most wise and spirited:
'Guha, dear friend, it is not meet
That people throng my calm retreat:
For I must live a strict recluse,
And mould my life by hermits' use.
I now the ancient rule accept
By good ascetics gladly kept.
I go: bring fig-tree juice that I
In matted coils my hair may tie.'
Quick Guha hastened to produce,
For the king's son, that sacred juice.
Then Ráma of his long locks made,
And Lakshman's too, the hermit braid.

And the two royal brothers there
With coats of bark and matted hair,
Transformed in lovely likeness stood
To hermit saints who love the wood.
So Ráma, with his brother bold,
A pious anchorite enrolled,
Obeyed the vow which hermits take,
And to his friend, King Guha, spake:
'May people, treasure, army share,
And fenced forts, thy constant care:
Attend to all: supremely hard
The sovereign's task, to watch and guard.'

Ikshváku's son, the good and brave,
This last farewell to Guha gave,
And then, with Lakshman and his bride,
Determined, on his way he hied.
Soon as he viewed, upon the shore,
The bark prepared to waft them o'er
Impetuous Gangá's rolling tide,
To Lakshman thus the chieftain cried:
'Brother, embark; thy hand extend,
Thy gentle aid to Sítá lend:
With care her trembling footsteps guide,
And place the lady by thy side.'
When Lakshman heard, prepared to aid.
His brother's words he swift obeyed.
Within the bark he placed the dame,
Then to her side the hero came.
Next Lakshman's elder brother, lord
Of brightest glory, when on board,
Breathing a prayer for blessings, meet
For priest or warrior to repeat.
Then he and car-borne Lakshman bent,
Well-pleased, their heads, most reverent,
Their hands, with Sítá, having dipped,
As Scripture bids, and water sipped,
Farewell to wise Sumantra said,
And Guha, with the train he led.
So Ráma took, on board, his stand.
And urged the vessel from the land.
Then swift by vigorous arms impelled
Her onward course the vessel held,
And guided by the helmsman through
The dashing waves of Gangá flew.
Half way across the flood they came,
When Sítá, free from spot and blame,
Her reverent hands together pressed,
The Goddess of the stream addressed:
'May the great chieftain here who springs
From Daśaratha, best of kings,
Protected by thy care, fulfil
His prudent father's royal will.
When in the forest he has spent
His fourteen years of banishment,
With his dear brother and with me
His home again my lord shall see.
Returning on that blissful day,
I will to thee mine offerings pay,
Dear Queen, whose waters gently flow,
Who canst all blessed gifts bestow.
For, three-pathed Queen, though wandering here,
Thy waves descend from Brahmá's sphere
Spouse of the God o'er floods supreme,
Though rolling here thy glorious stream.
To thee, fair Queen, my head shall bend,
To thee shall hymns of praise ascend,
When my brave lord shall turn again,
And, joyful, o'er his kingdom reign.
To win thy grace, O Queen divine,
A hundred thousand fairest kine,
And precious robes and finest meal
Among the Bráhmans will I deal.
A hundred jars of wine shall flow,
When to my home, O Queen, I go;
With these, and flesh, and corn, and rice,
Will I, delighted, sacrifice.
Each hallowed spot, each holy shrine
That stands on these fair shores of thine,
Each fane and altar on thy banks
Shall share my offerings and thanks.
With me and Lakshman, free from harm,
May he the blameless, strong of arm,
Reseek Ayodhyá from the wild,
O blameless Lady undefiled!'
As, praying for her husband's sake,
The faultless dame to Gangá spake,
To the right bank the vessel flew
With her whose heart was right and true.
Soon as the bark had crossed the wave,
The lion leader of the brave,
Leaving the vessel on the strand,
With wife and brother leapt to land.
Then Ráma thus the prince addressed
Who filled with joy Sumitrá's breast:
'Be thine alike to guard and aid
In peopled spot, in lonely shade.
Do thou, Sumitrá's son, precede:
Let Sítá walk where thou shalt lead.
Behind you both my place shall be,
To guard the Maithil dame and thee.
For she, to woe a stranger yet,
No toil or grief till now has met;
The fair Videhan will assay
The pains of forest life to-day.
To-day her tender feet must tread
Rough rocky wilds around her spread:
No tilth is there, no gardens grow,
No crowding people come and go.'
The hero ceased: and Lakshman led
Obedient to the words he said:
And Sítá followed him, and then
Came Raghu's pride, the lord of men.
With Sítá walking o'er the sand
They sought the forest, bow in hand,
But still their lingering glances threw
Where yet Sumantra stood in view.
Sumantra, when his watchful eye
The royal youths no more could spy,
Turned from the spot whereon he stood
Homeward with Guha from the wood.'

Still on the brothers forced their way
Where sweet birds sang on every spray,
Though scarce the eye a path could find
Mid flowering trees where creepers twined.
Far on the princely brothers pressed,
And stayed their feet at length to rest
Beneath a fig-tree's mighty shade
With countless pendent shoots displayed.
Reclining there a while at ease,
They saw, not far, beneath fair trees
A lake with many a lotus bright
That bore the name of Lovely Sight.
Ráma his wife's attention drew,
And Lakshmaṇ's, to the charming view:
'Look, brother, look how fair the flood
Glows with the lotus, flower and bud!'
They drank the water fresh and clear,
And with their shafts they slew a deer.
A fire of boughs they made in haste,
And in the flame the meat they placed.
So Raghu's sons with Sítá shared
The hunter's meal their hands prepared,
Then counselled that the spreading tree
Their shelter and their home should be.

CANTO LIII.

RÁMA'S LAMENT.

When evening rites were duly paid,
Reclined beneath the leafy shade,
To Lakshmaṇ thus spake Ráma, best
Of those who glad a people's breast:
'Now the first night has closed the day
That saw us from our country stray,
And parted from the charioteer;
Yet grieve not thou, my brother dear.
Henceforth by night, when others sleep,
Must we our careful vigil keep,
Watching for Sítá's welfare thus,
For her dear life depends on us.
Bring me the leaves that lie around,
And spread them here upon the ground,
That we on lowly beds may lie,
And let in talk the night go by.'
So on the ground with leaves o'erspread,
He who should press a royal bed,
Ráma with Lakshmaṇ thus conversed,
And many a pleasant tale rehearsed:
'This night the king,' he cried, 'alas!
In broken sleep will sadly pass.
Kaikeyí now content should be,
For mistress of her wish is she.
So fiercely she for empire yearns,
That when her Bharat home returns,
She in her greed, may even bring
Destruction on our lord the king.
What can he do, in feeble eld,
Reft of all aid and me expelled,
His soul enslaved by love, a thrall
Obedient to Kaikeyí's call?
As thus I muse upon his woe
And all his wisdom's overthrow,
Love is, methinks, of greater might
To stir the heart than gain and right.
For who, in wisdom's lore untaught.
Could by a beauty's prayer be bought
To quit his own obedient son,
Who loves him, as my sire has done?
Bharat, Kaikeyí's child, alone
Will, with his wife, enjoy the throne,
And blissfully his rule maintain
O'er happy Kośala's domain.
To Bharat's single lot will fall
The kingdom and the power and all,
When fails the king from length of days,
And Ráma in the forest strays.
Whoe'er, neglecting right and gain,
Lets conquering love his soul enchain,
To him, like Daśaratha's lot,
Comes woe with feet that tarry not.
Methinks at last the royal dame,
Dear Lakshmaṇ, has secured her aim,
To see at once her husband dead,
Her son enthroned, and Ráma fled.
Ah me! I fear, lest borne away
By frenzy of success, she slay
Kauśalyá, through her wicked hate
Of me, bereft, disconsolate;
Or her who aye for me has striven
Sumitrá, to devotion given.
Hence, Lakshmaṇ, to Ayodhyá speed,
Returning in the hour of need.
With Sítá I my steps will bend
Where Daṇḍak's mighty woods extend.
No guardian has Kauśalyá now:
O, be her friend and guardian thou.
Strong hate may vile Kaikeyí lead
To many a base unrighteous deed,
Treading my mother 'neath her feet
When Bharat holds the royal seat.
Sure in some antenatal time
Were children, by Kauśalyá's crime,
Torn from their mothers' arms away,
And hence she mourns this evil day.
She for her child no toil would spare
Tending me long with pain and care;
Now in the hour of fruitage she
Has lost that son, ah, woe is me.
O Lakshmaṇ, may no matron e'er
A son so doomed to sorrow bear
As I, my mother's heart who rend
With anguish that can never end.
The Sáriká,[1] methinks, possessed
More love than glows in Ráma's breast,
Who, as the tale is told to us,
Addressed the stricken parrot thus:

[1] The *Mainá* or Gracula religiosa, a favourite cage-bird, easily taught to talk

'Parrot, the capturer's talons tear,
While yet alone thou flutterest there,
Before his mouth has closed on me:'
So cried the bird, herself to free.
Reft of her son, in childless woe,
My mother's tears for ever flow:
Ill-fated, doomed with grief to strive,
What aid can she from me derive?
Pressed down by care, she cannot rise
From sorrow's flood wherein she lies.
In righteous wrath my single arm
Could, with my bow, protect from harm
Ayodhyá's town and all the earth:
But what is hero prowess worth?
Lest breaking duty's law I sin,
And lose the heaven I strive to win,
The forest life to-day I choose,
And kingly state and power refuse.'
  Thus mourning in that lonely spot
The troubled chief bewailed his lot,
And filled with tears, his eyes ran o'er;
Then silent sat, and spake no more.
To him, when ceased his loud lament,
Like fire whose brilliant might is spent,
Or the great sea when sleeps the wave,
Thus Lakshmaṇ consolation gave:
'Chief of the brave who bear the bow,
E'en now Ayodhyá, sunk in woe,
By thy departure reft of light
Is gloomy as the moonless night.
Unfit it seems that thou, O chief,
Shouldst so afflict thy soul with grief,
So with thou Sítá's heart consign
To deep despair as well as mine.
Not I, O Raghu's son, nor she
Could live one hour deprived of thee:
We were, without thine arm to save,
Like fish deserted by the wave.
Although my mother dear to meet,
Śatrughna. and the king, were sweet,
On them, or heaven, to feed mine eye
Were nothing, if thou wert not by.'
  Sitting at ease, their glances fell
Upon the beds, constructed well,
And there the sons of virtue laid
Their limps beneath the fig-tree's shade.

CANTO LIV.

BHARADVÁJA'S HERMITAGE.

So there that night the heroes spent
Under the boughs that o'er them bent,
And when the sun his glory spread,
Upstarting, from the place they sped.
On to that spot they made their way,
Through the dense wood that round them lay,
Where Yamuná's[1] swift waters glide
To blend with Gangá's holy tide.
Charmed with the prospect ever new
The glorious heroes wandered through
Full many a spot of pleasant ground,
Rejoicing as they gazed around.
With eager eye and heart at ease,
On countless sorts of flowery trees.
And now the day was half-way sped
When thus to Lakshmaṇ Ráma said:
'There, there, dear brother, turn thine eyes;
See near Prayág[1] that smoke arise:
The banner of our Lord of Flames
The dwelling of some saint proclaims.
Near to the place our steps we bend
Where Yamuná and Gangá blend.
I hear and mark the deafening roar
When chafing floods together pour.
See, near us on the ground are left
Dry logs, by labouring woodmen cleft,
And the tall trees, that blossom near
Saint Bharadvája's home, appear.'
  The bow-armed princes onward pass ed,
And as the sun was sinking fast
They reached the hermit's dwelling, set
Near where the rushing waters met.
The presence of the warrior scared
The deer and birds as on he fared,
And struck them with unwonted awe:
Then Bharadvája's cot they saw.
The high-souled hermit soon they found
Girt by his dear disciples round:
Calm saint, whose vows had well been wrought,
Whose fervent rites keen sight had bought.
Duly had flames of worship blazed
When Ráma on the hermit gazed:
His suppliant hands the hero raised,
Drew nearer to the holy man
With his companions, and began,
Declaring both his name and race
And why they sought that distant place;
'Saint, Daśaratha's children we,
Ráma and Lakshmaṇ, come to thee.
This my good wife from Janak springs,
The best of fair Videha's kings;
Through lonely wilds, a faultless dame,
To this pure grove with me she came.
My younger brother follows still
Me banished by my father's will:
Sumitrá's son, bound by a vow,—
He roams the wood beside me now.
Sent by my father forth to rove,
We seek, O Saint, some holy grove,
Where lives of hermits we may lead,
And upon fruits and berries feed.'
  When Bharadvája, prudent-souled,
Had heard the prince his tale unfold,
Water he bade them bring, a bull,
And honour-gifts in dishes full,

[1] The Jumna.

[1] The Hindu name of Allahabad.

And drink and food of varied taste,
Berries and roots, before him placed,
And then the great ascetic showed
A cottage for the guests' abode.
The saint these honours gladly paid
To Ráma who had thither strayed,
Then compassed sat by birds and deer
And many a hermit resting near.
The prince received the service kind,
And sat him down rejoiced in mind.
Then Bharadvája silence broke,
And thus the words of duty spoke:
'Kakutstha's royal son, that thou
Hadst sought this grove I knew ere now.
Mine ears have heard thy story, sent
Without a sin to banishment.
Behold, O Prince, this ample space
Near where the mingling floods embrace,
Holy, and beautiful, and clear:
Dwell with us, and be happy here.'
  By Bharadvája thus addressed,
Ráma whose kind and tender breast
All living things would bless and save,
In gracious words his answer gave:
  'My honoured lord, this tranquil spot,
Fair home of hermits, suits me not:
For all the neighbouring people here
Will seek us when they know me near:
With eager wish to look on me,
And the Videhan dame to see,
A crowd of rustics will intrude
Upon the holy solitude.
Provide, O gracious lord, I pray,
Some quiet home that lies away,
Where my Videhan spouse may dwell
Tasting the bliss deserved so well.'
  The hermit heard the prayer he made:
A while in earnest thought he stayed,
And then in words like these expressed
His answer to the chief's request:
'Ten leagues away there stands a hill
Where thou mayst live, if such thy will:
A holy mount, exceeding fair;
Great saints have made their dwelling there:
There great Langúrs[1] in thousands play,
And bears amid the thickets stray;
Wide-known by Chitrakúṭa's name,
It rivals Gandhamádan's[2] fame.
Long as the man that hill who seeks
Gazes upon its sacred peaks,
To holy things his soul he gives
And pure from thought of evil lives.
There, while a hundred autumns fled,
Has many a saint with hoary head
Spent his pure life, and won the prize,
By deep devotion, in the skies:
Best home, I ween, if such retreat,
Far from the ways of men, be sweet:
Or let thy years of exile flee
Here in this hermitage with me.'
  Thus Bharadvája spake, and trained
In lore of duty, entertained
The princes and the dame, and pressed
His friendly gifts on every guest.
  Thus to Prayág the hero went,
Thus saw the saint preëminent,
And varied speeches heard and said:
Then holy night o'er heaven was spread.
And Ráma took, by toil oppressed,
With Sítá and his brother, rest;
And so the night, with sweet content,
In Bharadvája's grove was spent.
But when the dawn dispelled the night,
Ráma approached the anchorite,
And thus addressed the holy sire
Whose glory shone like kindled fire:
'Well have we spent, O truthful Sage,
The night within thy hermitage:
Now let my lord his guests permit
For their new home his grove to quit.'
  Then, as he saw the morning break,
In answer Bharadvája spake:
'Go forth to Chitrakúṭa's hill,
Where berries grow, and sweets distil:
Full well, I deem, that home will suit
Thee, Ráma, strong and resolute.
Go forth, and Chitrakúṭa seek,
Famed mountain of the Varied Peak.
In the wild woods that gird him round
All creatures of the chase are found:
Thou in the glades shalt see appear
Vast herds of elephants and deer.
With Sítá there shalt thou delight
To gaze upon the woody height;
There with expanding heart to look
On river, table-land, and brook,
And see the foaming torrent rave
Impetuous from the mountain cave.
Auspicious hill! where all day long
The lapwing's cry, the Koïl's song
  Make all who listen gay:
Where all is fresh and fair to see,
Where elephants and deer roam free,
  There, as a hermit, stay.'

CANTO LV.

THE PASSAGE OF YAMUNÁ.

The princely tamers of their foes
Thus passed the night in calm repose,
Then to the hermit having bent
With reverence, on their way they went.
High favour Bharadvája showed,
And blessed them ready for the road,

[1] The Langúr is a large monkey.
[2] A mountain said to lie to the east of Meru.

With such fond looks as fathers throw
On their own sons before they go.
Then spake the saint with glory bright
To Ráma peerless in his might:
'First, lords of men, direct your feet
Where Yamuná and Gangá meet;
Then to the swift Kálindí[1] go,
Whose westward waves to Gangá flow.
When thou shalt see her lovely shore
Worn by their feet who hasten o'er,
Then, Raghu's son, a raft prepare.
And cross the Sun-born river there.
Upon her farther bank a tree,
Near to the landing wilt thou see.
The blessed source of varied gifts,
There her green boughs that Fig-tree lifts:
A tree where countless birds abide,
By Śyáma's name known far and wide.
Sítá, revere that holy shade:
There be thy prayers for blessing prayed.
Thence for a league your way pursue,
And a dark wood shall meet your view,
Where tall bamboos their foliage show,
The Gum-tree and the Jujube grow.
To Chitrakúṭa have I oft
Trodden that path so smooth and soft,
Where burning woods no traveller scare,
But all is pleasant, green, and fair.'
When thus the guests their road had learned,
Back to his cot the hermit turned,
And Ráma, Lakshmaṇ, Sítá paid
Their reverent thanks for courteous aid.
Thus Ráma spake to Lakshmaṇ, when
The saint had left the lords of men:
'Great store of bliss in sooth is ours
On whom his love the hermit showers.'
As each to other wisely talked,
The lion lords together walked
On to Kálindí's woody shore;
And gentle Sítá went before.
They reached that flood, whose waters flee
With rapid current to the sea;
Their minds a while to thought they gave
And counselled how to cross the wave.
At length, with logs together laid,
A mighty raft the brothers made.
Then dry bamboos across were tied,
And grass was spread from side to side.
And the great hero Lakshmaṇ brought
Cane and Rose-Apple boughs and wrought,
Trimming the branches smooth and neat,
For Sítá's use a pleasant seat.
And Ráma placed thereon his dame
Touched with a momentary shame,
Resembling in her glorious mien
All-thought-surpassing Fortune's Queen
Then Ráma hastened to dispose,
Each in its place, the skins and bows,
And by the fair Videhan laid
The coats, the ornaments, and spade.
When Sítá thus was set on board,
And all their gear was duly stored,
The heroes, each with vigorous hand,
Pushed off the raft and left the land.
When half its way the raft had made,
Thus Sítá to Kálindí prayed:
'Goddess, whose flood I traverse now,
Grant that my lord may keep his vow.
For thee shall bleed a thousand kine,
A hundred jars shall pour their wine,
When Ráma sees that town again
Where old Ikshváku's children reign.'
Thus to Kálindí's stream she sued
And prayed in suppliant attitude.
Then to the river's bank the dame,
Fervent in supplication, came.
They left the raft that brought them o'er,
And the thick wood that clothed the shore,
And to the Fig-tree Śyáma made
Their way, so cool with verdant shade.
Then Sítá viewed that best of trees,
And reverent spake in words like these:
'Hail, hail, O mighty tree! Allow
My husband to complete his vow;
Let us returning, I entreat,
Kauśalyá and Sumitrá meet.'
Then with her hands together placed
Around the tree she duly paced.
When Ráma saw his blameless spouse
A suppliant under holy boughs,
The gentle darling of his heart,
He thus to Lakshmaṇ spake apart:
'Brother, by thee our way be led;
Let Sítá close behind thee tread:
I, best of men, will grasp my bow,
And hindmost of the three will go.
What fruits soe'er her fancy take,
Or flowers half hidden in the brake,
For Janak's child forget not thou
To gather from the brake or bough.'
Thus on they fared. The tender dame
Asked Ráma, as they walked, the name
Of every shrub that blossoms bore,
Creeper, and tree unseen before:
And Lakshmaṇ fetched, at Sítá's prayer,
Boughs of each tree with clusters fair.
Then Janak's daughter joyed to see
The sand-discoloured river flee,
Where the glad cry of many a bird,
The sáras and the swan, was heard.
A league the brothers travelled through
The forest: noble game they slew:
Beneath the trees their meal they dressed
And sat them down to eat and rest.
A while in that delightful shade
Where elephants unnumbered strayed,
Where peacocks screamed and monkeys played,

[1] Another name of the Jumna, daughter of the Sun.

They wandered with delight.
Then by the river's side they found
A pleasant spot of level ground,
Where all was smooth and fair around,
Their lodging for the night.

CANTO LVI.

CHITRAKÚṬA.

Then Ráma, when the morning rose,
Called Lakshmaṇ gently from repose:
'Awake, the pleasant voices hear
Of forest birds that warble near.
Scourge of thy foes, no longer stay;
The hour is come to speed away.'
The slumbering prince unclosed his eyes
When thus his brother bade him rise,
Compelling, at the timely cry,
Fatigue, and sleep, and rest to fly.
The brothers rose and Sítá too;
Pure water from the stream they drew,
Paid morning rites, then followed still
The road to Chitrakúṭa's hill.
Then Ráma as he took the road
With Lakshmaṇ, while the morning glowed,
To the Videhan lady cried,
Sítá the fair, the lotus-eyed:
'Look round thee, dear; each flowery tree
Touched with the fire of morning see:
The Kinśuk, now the Frosts are fled,—
How glorious with his wreaths of red!
The Bel-trees see, so loved of men,
Hanging their boughs in every glen,
O'erburthened with their fruit and flowers:
A plenteous store of food is ours.
See, Lakshmaṇ, in the leafy trees,
Where'er they make their home,
Down hangs, the work of labouring bees
The ponderous honeycomb.
In the fair wood before us spread
The startled wild-cock cries:
Hark, where the flowers are soft to tread,
The peacock's voice replies.
Where elephants are roaming free,
And sweet birds' songs are loud,
The glorious Chitrakúṭa see:
His peaks are in the cloud.
On fair smooth ground he stands displayed,
Begirt by many a tree:
O brother, in that holy shade
How happy shall we be!'[1]

Then Ráma, Lakshmaṇ, Sítá, each
Spoke raising suppliant hands this speech
To him, in woodland dwelling met,
Válmíki, ancient anchoret:
'O Saint, this mountain takes the mind,
With creepers, trees of every kind,
With fruit and roots abounding thus,
A pleasant life it offers us:
Here for a while we fain would stay,
And pass a season blithe and gay.'
Then the great saint, in duty trained,
With honour gladly entertained:
He gave his guests a welcome fair,
And bade them sit and rest them there.
Ráma of mighty arm and chest
His faithful Lakshmaṇ then addressed:
'Brother, bring hither from the wood
Selected timber strong and good,
And build therewith a little cot;
My heart rejoices in the spot
That lies beneath the mountain's side,
Remote, with water well supplied.'
Sumitrá's son his words obeyed,
Brought many a tree, and deftly made,
With branches in the forest cut,
As Ráma bade, a leafy hut.
Then Ráma, when the cottage stood
Fair, firmly built, and walled with wood,
To Lakshmaṇ spake, whose eager mind
To do his brother's will inclined:
'Now, Lakshmaṇ as our cot is made,
Must sacrifice be duly paid
By us, for lengthened life who hope,
With venison of the antelope.
Away, O bright-eyed Lakshmaṇ, speed:
Struck by thy bow a deer must bleed:
As Scripture bids, we must not slight
The duty that commands the rite.'
Lakshmaṇ, the chief whose arrows laid
His foemen low, his word obeyed;
And Ráma thus again addressed
The swift performer of his hest:
'Prepare the venison thou hast shot,
To sacrifice for this our cot.
Haste, brother dear, for this the hour,
And this the day of certain power.'
Then glorious Lakshmaṇ took the buck
His arrow in the wood had struck;
Bearing his mighty load he came,
And laid it in the kindled flame.

[1] 'We have often looked on that green hill: it is the holiest spot of that sect of the Hindu faith who devote themselves to this incarnation of Vishṇu. The whole neighbourhood is Ráma's country. Every headland has some legend, every cavern is connected with his name; some of the wild fruits are still called *Sítáphal*, being the reputed food of the exile. Thousands and thousands annually visit the spot, and round the hill is a raised foot-path, on which the devotee, with naked feet, treads full of pious awe.' *Calcutta Review*. Vol. XXIII.

Soon as he saw the meat was done,
And that the juices ceased to run
From the broiled carcass, Lakshmaṇ then
Spoke thus to Ráma best of men:
'The carcass of the buck, entire,
Is ready dressed upon the fire.
Now be the sacred rites begun
To please the God, thou godlike one.'
Ráma the good, in ritual trained,
Pure from the bath, with thoughts restrained,
Hasted those verses to repeat
Which make the sacrifice complete,
The hosts celestial came in view,
And Ráma to the cot withdrew,
While a sweet sense of rapture stole
Through the unequalled hero's soul.
He paid the Viśvedevas'[1] due,
And Rudra's right, and Vishṇu's too,
Nor wonted blessings, to protect
Their new-built home, did he neglect.
With voice repressed he breathed the prayer,
Bathed duly in the river fair,
And gave good offerings that remove
The stain of sin, as texts approve.
And many an altar there he made,
And shrines, to suit the holy shade,
All decked with woodland chaplets sweet,
And fruit and roots and roasted meat,
With muttered prayer, as texts require,
Water, and grass and wood and fire.
So Ráma, Lakshmaṇ, Sítá paid
Their offerings to each God and shade,
And entered then their pleasant cot
That bore fair signs of happy lot.
They entered, the illustrious three,
The well-set cottage, fair to see,
Roofed with the leaves of many a tree,
And fenced from wind and rain:
So, at their Father Brahmá's call,
The Gods of heaven, assembling all,
To their own glorious council hall
Advance in shining train.
So, resting on that lovely hill,
Near the fair lily-covered rill,
The happy prince forgot,
Surrounded by the birds and deer,
The woe, the longing, and the fear
That gloom the exile's lot.

CANTO LVII.

SUMANTRA'S RETURN.

When Ráma reached the southern bank,
King Guha's heart with sorrow sank:
He with Sumantra talked, and spent
With his deep sorrow, homeward went.
Sumantra, as the king decreed,
Yoked to the car each noble steed,
And to Ayodhyá's city sped
With his sad heart disquieted.
On lake and brook and scented grove
His glances fell, as on he drove:
City and village came in view
As o'er the road his coursers flew.
On the third day the charioteer,
When now the hour of night was near,
Came to Ayodhyá's gate, and found
The city all in sorrow drowned.
To him, in spirit quite cast down,
Forsaken seemed the silent town,
And by the rush of grief oppressed
He pondered in his mournful breast:
'Is all Ayodhyá burnt with grief,
Steed, elephant, and man, and chief?
Does her loved Ráma's exile so
Afflict her with the fires of woe?'
Thus as he mused, his steeds flew fast,
And swiftly through the gate he passed.
On drove the charioteer, and then
In hundreds, yea in thousands, men
Ran to the car from every side,
And, 'Ráma, where is Ráma?' cried.
Sumantra said: 'My chariot bore
The duteous prince to Gangá's shore;
I left him there at his behest,
And homeward to Ayodhyá pressed.'
Soon as the anxious people knew
That he was o'er the flood, they drew
Deep sighs, and crying, Ráma! all
Wailed, and big tears began to fall.
He heard the mournful words prolonged,
As here and there the people thronged:
'Woe, woe for us, forlorn, undone,
No more to look on Raghu's son!
His like again we ne'er shall see,
Of heart so true, of hand so free,
In gifts, in gatherings for debate,
When marriage pomps we celebrate.
What should we do? What earthly thing
Can rest, or hope, or pleasure bring?'
Thus the sad town, which Ráma kept
As a kind father, wailed and wept.
Each mansion, as the car went by,
Sent forth a loud and bitter cry,
As to the window every dame,
Mourning for banished Ráma, came.
As his sad eyes with tears o'erflowed,
He sped along the royal road
To Daśaratha's high abode.
There leaping down his car he stayed;
Within the gates his way he made;
Through seven broad courts he onward hied
Where people thronged on every side.
From each high terrace, wild with woe,
The royal ladies flocked below:

[1] Deities of a particular class in which five or ten are enumerated. They are worshipped particularly at the funeral obsequies in honour of deceased progenitors.

He heard them talk in gentle tone,
As each for Ráma made her moan:
'What will the charioteer reply
To Queen Kauśalyá's eager cry?
With Ráma from the gates he went;
Homeward alone, his steps are bent.
Hard is a life with woe distressed,
But difficult to win is rest,
If, when her son is banished, still
She lives beneath her load of ill.'
Such was the speech Sumantra heard
From them whom grief unfeigned had stirred.
As fires of anguish burnt him through,
Swift to the monarch's hall he drew,
Past the eighth court: there met his sight,
The sovereign in his palace bright,
Still weeping for his son, forlorn,
Pale, faint, and all with sorrow worn.
As there he sat, Sumantra bent
And did obeisance reverent,
And to the king repeated o'er
The message he from Ráma bore.
The monarch heard, and well-nigh brake
His heart, but yet no word he spake:
Fainting to earth he fell, and dumb,
By grief for Ráma overcome.
Rang through the hall a startling cry,
And women's arms were tossed on high,
When, with his senses all astray,
Upon the ground the monarch lay.
Kauśalyá, with Sumitrá's aid,
Raised from the ground her lord dismayed:
'Sire, of high fate,' she cried, O, why
Dost thou no single word reply
To Ráma's messenger who brings
News of his painful wanderings?
The great injustice done, art thou
Shame-stricken for thy conduct now?
Rise up, and do thy part: bestow
Comfort and help in this our woe.
Speak freely, King; dismiss thy fear,
For Queen Kaikeyí stands not near,
Afraid of whom thou wouldst not seek
Tidings of Ráma: freely speak.'
When the sad queen had ended so,
She sank, insatiate in her woe,
And prostrate lay upon the ground,
While her faint voice by sobs was drowned.
When all the ladies in despair
Saw Queen Kauśalyá wailing there,
And the poor king oppressed with pain,
They flocked around and wept again.

CANTO LVIII.

RÁMA'S MESSAGE.

The king a while had senseless lain,
When care brought memory back again.
Then straight he called, the news to hear
Of Ráma, for the charioteer.
With reverent hand to hand applied
He waited by the old man's side,
Whose mind with anguish was distraught
Like a great elephant newly caught.
The king with bitter pain distressed
The faithful charioteer addressed,
Who, sad of mien, with flooded eye,
And dust upon his limbs, stood by:
'Where will be Ráma's dwelling now
At some tree's foot, beneath the bough;
Ah, what will be the exile's food,
Bred up with kind solicitude?
Can he, long lapped in pleasant rest,
Unmeet for pain, by pain oppressed,
Son of earth's king, his sad night spend
Earth-couched, as one that has no friend?
Behind him, when abroad he sped,
Cars, elephant, and foot were led:
Then how shall Ráma dwell afar
In the wild woods where no men are?
How, tell me, did the princes there,
With Sítá good and soft and fair,
Alighting from the chariot, tread
The forest wilds around them spread?
A happy lot is thine, I ween,
Whose eyes my two dear sons have seen
Seeking on foot the forest shade,
Like the bright Twins to view displayed,
The heavenly Aśvins, when they seek
The woods that hang 'neath Mandar's peak.
What words, Sumantra, quickly tell,
From Ráma, Lakshman, Sítá, fell?
How in the wood did Ráma eat?
What was his bed, and what his seat?
Full answer to my questions give,
For I on thy replies shall live,
As with the saints Yayáti held
Sweet converse, from the skies expelled.'
Urged by the lord of men to speak,
Whose sobbing voice came faint and weak,
Thus he, while tears his utterance broke,
In answer to the monarch spoke:
'Hear then the words that Ráma said,
Resolved in duty's path to tread.
Joining his hands, his head he bent,
And gave this message, reverent:
'Sumantra, to my father go,
Whose lofty mind all people know:
Bow down before him, as is meet,
And in my stead salute his feet.
Then to the queen my mother bend,
And give the greeting that I send:
Ne'er may her steps from duty err,
And may it still be well with her.
And add this word: 'O Queen, pursue
Thy vows with faithful heart and true;
And ever at due season turn
Where holy fires of worship burn.
And, lady, on our lord bestow

Such honour as to Gods we owe.
Be kind to every queen: let pride
And thought of self be cast aside.
In the king's fond opinion raise
Kaikeyí, by respect and praise.
Let the young Bharat ever be
Loved, honoured as the king by thee:
Thy king-ward duty ne'er forget:
High over all are monarchs set.'
And Bharat, too, for me address:
Pray that all health his life may bless.
Let every royal lady share,
As justice bids, his love and care.
Say to the strong-armed chief who brings
Joy to Iksváku's line of kings:
'As ruling prince thy care be shown
Of him, our sire, who holds the throne.
Stricken in years he feels their weight;
But leave him in his royal state.
As regent heir content thee still,
Submissive to thy father's will.'
Ráma again his charge renewed,
As the hot flood his cheek bedewed:
'Hold as thine own my mother dear
Who drops for me the longing tear.'
Then Lakshman, with his soul on fire,
Spake breathing fast these words of ire:
'Say, for what sin, for what offence
Was royal Ráma banished thence?
He is the cause, the king; poor slave
To the light charge Kaikeyí gave.
Let right or wrong the motive be,
The author of our woe is he.
Whether the exile were decreed
Through foolish faith or guilty greed,
For promises or empire, still
The king has wrought a grievous ill.
Grant that the Lord of all saw fit
To prompt the deed and sanction it,
In Ráma's life no cause I see
For which the king should bid him flee.
His blinded eyes refused to scan
The guilt and folly of the plan,
And from the weakness of the king
Here and hereafter woe shall spring.
No more my sire: the ties that used
To bind me to the king are loosed.
My brother Ráma, Raghu's son,
To me is lord, friend, sire in one.
The love of men how can he win,
Deserting, by the cruel sin,
Their joy, whose heart is swift to feel
A pleasure in the people's weal?
Shall he whose mandate could expel
The virtuous Ráma, loved, so well,
To whom his subjects' fond hearts cling—
Shall he in spite of them be king?'
But Janak's child, my lord, stood by,
And oft the votaress heaved a sigh.
She seemed with dull and wandering sense,
Beneath a spirit's influence.
The noble princess, pained with woe
Which till that hour she ne'er could know,
Tears in her heavy trouble shed,
But not a word to me she said.
She raised her face which grief had dried,
And tenderly her husband eyed,
Gazed on him as he turned to go
While tear chased tear in rapid flow.'

CANTO LIX.

DAŚARATHA'S LAMENT.

As thus Sumantra, best of peers,
Told his sad tale with many tears,
The monarch cried, 'I pray thee, tell
At length again what there befell.'
Sumantra, at the king's behest,
Striving with sobs he scarce repressed,
His trembling voice at last controlled,
And thus his further tidings told:
'Their locks in votive coils they wound,
Their coats of bark upon them bound,
To Gangá's farther shore they went,
Thence to Prayág their steps were bent.
I saw that Lakshman walked ahead
To guard the path the two should tread.
So far I saw, no more could learn,
Forced by the hero to return.
Retracing slow my homeward course,
Scarce could I move each stubborn horse:
Shedding hot tears of grief he stood
When Ráma turned him to the wood.[1]
As the two princes parted thence
I raised my hands in reverence,
Mounted my ready car, and bore
The grief that stung me to the core.
With Guha all that day I stayed,
Still by the earnest hope delayed
That Ráma, ere the time should end,
Some message from the wood might send.
Thy realms, great Monarch, mourn the blow,
And sympathize with Ráma's woe.

---

[1] 'So in Homer the horses of Achilles lamented with many bitter tears the death of Patroclus slain by Hector:

Ἵπποι δ' Αἰακίδαο, μάχης ἀπάνευθεν ἐόντες,
Κλᾶιον, ἐπειδὴ πρῶτα πυθέσθην ἡνιόχοιο
'Εν κονίῃσι πεσόντος ὑφ' Ἕκτορος ἀνδροφόνοιο.

ILIAD. XVII. 426.

Ancient poesy frequently associated nature with the joys and sorrows of man.'

GORRESIO.

Each withering tree hangs low his head,
And shoot, and bud, and flower are dead.
Dried are the floods that wont to fill
The lake, the river, and the rill.
Drear is each grove and garden now,
Dry every blossom on the bough.
Each beast is still, no serpents crawl:
A lethargy of woe on all.
The very wood is silent: crushed
With grief for Ráma, all is hushed.
Fair blossoms from the water born,
Gay garlands that the earth adorn,
And every fruit that gleams like gold,
Have lost the scent that charmed of old.
Empty is every grove I see,
Or birds sit pensive on the tree.
Where'er I look, its beauty o'er,
The pleasance charms not as before.
I drove through fair Ayodhyá's street:
None flew with joy the car to meet.
They saw that Ráma was not there,
And turned them sighing in despair.
The people in the royal way
Wept tears of bitter grief, when they
Beheld me coming, from afar,
No Ráma with me in the car.
From palace roof and turret high
Each woman bent her eager eye;
She looked for Ráma, but in vain;
Gazed on the car and shrieked for pain.
Their long clear eyes with sorrow drowned
They, when this common grief was found,
Looked each on other, friend and foe,
In sympathy of levelling woe:
No shade of difference between
Foe, friend, or neutral, there was seen.
Without a joy, her bosom rent
With grief for Ráma's banishment,
Ayodhyá like the queen appears
Who mourns her son with many tears.'
He ended: and the king, distressed,
With sobbing voice that lord addressed:
'Ah me, by false Kaikeyí led,
Of evil race, to evil bred,
I took no counsel of the sage,
Nor sought advice from skill and age.
I asked no lord his aid to lend,
I called no citizen or friend.
Rash was my deed, bereft of sense,
Slave to a woman's influence.
Surely, my lord, a woe so great
Falls on us by the will of Fate;
It lays the house of Raghu low,
For Destiny will have it so.
I pray thee, if I e'er have done
An act to please thee, yea, but one,
Fly, fly, and Ráma homeward lead:
My life, departing, counsels speed.
Fly, ere the power to bid I lack,
Fly to the wood: bring Ráma back.
I cannot live for even one
Short hour bereaved of my son.
But ah, the prince, whose arms are strong,
Has journeyed far: the way is long:
Me, me upon the chariot place,
And let me look on Ráma's face.
Ah me, my son, mine eldest-born,
Where roams he in the wood forlorn,
The wielder of the mighty bow,
Whose shoulders like the lion's show?
O, ere the light of life be dim,
Take me to Sítá and to him.
O Ráma, Lakshman, and O thou
Dear Sítá, constant to thy vow,
Beloved ones, you cannot know
That I am dying of my woe.'
The king to bitter grief a prey,
That drove each wandering sense away,
Sunk in affliction's sea, too wide
To traverse, in his anguish cried:
'Hard, hard to pass, my Queen, this sea
Of sorrow raging over me:
No Ráma near to soothe mine eye,
Plunged in its lowest deeps I lie.
Sorrow for Ráma swells the tide,
And Sítá's absence makes it wide:
My tears its foamy flood distain,
Made billowy by my sighs of pain:
My cries its roar, the arms I throw
About me are the fish below.
Kaikeyí is the fire that feeds
Beneath: my hair the tangled weeds:
Its source the tears for Ráma shed:
The hump-back's words its monsters dread:
The boon I gave the wretch its shore,
Till Ráma's banishment be o'er.[1]
Ah me, that I should long to set
My eager eyes to-day
On Raghu's son, and he be yet
With Lakshman far away!'
Thus he of lofty glory wailed,
And sank upon the bed.
Beneath the woe his spirit failed,
And all his senses fled.

CANTO LX.

KAUŚALYÁ CONSOLED.

As Queen Kauśalyá, trembling much,
As blighted by a goblin's touch,
Still lying prostrate, half awoke
To consciousness, 'twas thus she spoke:
'Bear me away, Sumantra, far,
Where Ráma, Sítá, Lakshman are.
Bereft of them I have no power
To linger on a single hour.

[1] The lines containing this heap of forced metaphors are marked as spurious by Schlegel.

Again, I pray, thy steps retrace,
And me in Dandak forest place,
For after them I needs must go,
Or sink to Yama's realms below.'
His utterance choked by tears that rolled
Down from their fountains uncontrolled,
With suppliant hands the charioteer
Thus spake, the lady's heart to cheer:
'Dismiss thy grief, despair, and dread
That fills thy soul, of sorrow bred,
For pain and anguish thrown aside,
Will Ráma in the wood abide.
And Lakshman, with unfailing care
Will guard the feet of Ráma there,
Earning, with governed sense, the prize
That waits on duty in the skies.
And Sítá in the wild as well
As in her own dear home will dwell;
To Ráma all her heart she gives,
And free from doubt and terror lives.
No faintest sign of care or woe
The features of the lady show:
Methinks Videha's pride was made
For exile in the forest shade.
E'en as of old she used to rove
Delighted in the city's grove,
Thus, even thus she joys to tread
The woodlands uninhabited.
Like a young child, her face as fair
As the young moon, she wanders there.
What though in lonely woods she stray
Still Ráma is her joy and stay:
All his the heart no sorrow bends,
Her very life on him depends.
For, if her lord she might not see,
Ayodhyá like the wood would be.
She bids him, as she roams, declare
The names of towns and hamlets there,
Marks various trees that meet her eye,
And many a brook that hurries by,
And Janak's daughter seems to roam
One little league away from home
When Ráma or his brother speaks
And gives the answer that she seeks.
This, Lady, I remember well;
Nor angry words have I to tell:
Reproaches at Kaikeyí shot,
Such, Queen, my mind remembers not.'
The speech when Sítá's wrath was high,
Sumantra passed in silence by,
That so his pleasant words might cheer
With sweet report Kauśalyá's ear.
'Her moonlike beauty suffers not
Though winds be rude and suns be hot;
The way, the danger, and the toil
Her gentle lustre may not soil.
Like the red lily's leafy crown
Or as the fair full moon looks down,
So the Videhan lady's face
Still shines with undiminished grace.
What if the borrowed colours throw
O'er her fine feet no rosy glow,
Still with their natural tints they spread
A lotus glory where they tread.
In sportive grace she walks the ground
And sweet her chiming anklets sound.
No jewels clasp the faultless limb:
She leaves them all for love of him.
If in the woods her gentle eye
A lion sees, or tiger nigh,
Or elephant, she fears no ill
For Ráma's arm supports her still.
No longer be their fate deplored,
Nor thine, nor that of Kośal's lord,
For conduct such as theirs shall buy
Wide glory that can never die.
For casting grief and care away,
Delighting in the forest, they
With joyful spirits, blithe and gay,
Set forward on the ancient way
Where mighty saints have led:
Their highest aim, their dearest care
To keep their father's honour fair,
Observing still the oath he sware,
They roam, on wild fruit fed.'
Thus with persuasive art he tried
To turn her from her grief aside,
By soothing fancies won.
But still she gave her sorrow vent:
'Ah Ráma!,' was her shrill lament,
'My love, my son, my son!'

CANTO LXI.

KAUŚALYÁ'S LAMENT.

When, best of all who give delight,
Her Ráma wandered far from sight,
Kauśalyá weeping, sore distressed,
The king her husband thus addressed:
'Thy name, O Monarch, far and wide
Through the three worlds is glorified:
Yet Ráma's is the pitying mind,
His speech is true, his heart is kind.
How will thy sons, good lord, sustain
With Sítá all their care and pain?
How in the wild endure distress,
Nursed in the lap of tenderness?
How will the dear Videhan bear
The heat and cold when wandering there,
Bred in the bliss of princely state,
So young and fair and delicate?
The large-eyed lady, wont to eat
The best of finely seasoned meat—
How will she now her life sustain
With woodland fare of self-sewn grain?
Will she, with joys encompassed long,
Who loved the music and the song,
In the wild wood endure to hear
The ravening lion's voice of fear?
Where sleeps my strong-armed hero, where,

Like Lord Mahendra's standard, fair?
Where is, by Lakshmaṇ's side, his bed,
His club-like arm beneath his head?
When shall I see his flower-like eyes,
And face that with the lotus vies,
Feel his sweet lily breath, and view
His glorious hair and lotus hue?
The heart within my breast, I feel,
Is adamant or hardest steel,
Or, in a thousand fragments split,
The loss of him had shattered it,
When those I love, who should be blest,
Are wandering in the wood distressed,
Condemned their wretched lives to lead
In exile, by thy ruthless deed.
If, when the fourteen years are past,
Ráma reseeks his home at last,
I think not Bharat will consent
To yield the wealth and government.
At funeral feasts some mourners deal
To kith and kin the solemn meal,
And having duly fed them all
Some Bráhmans to the banquet call.
The best of Bráhmans, good and wise,
The tardy summoning despise,
And, equal to the Gods, disdain
Cups, e'en of Amrit, thus to drain.
Nay e'en when Bráhmans first have fed,
They loathe the meal for others spread,
And from the leavings turn with scorn,
As bulls avoid a fractured horn.
So Ráma, sovereign lord of men,
Will spurn the sullied kingship then:
He, born the eldest and the best,
His younger's leavings will detest,
Turning from tasted food away,
As tigers scorn another's prey.
The sacred post is used not twice,
Nor elements, in sacrifice.
But once the sacred grass is spread,
But once with oil the flame is fed:
So Ráma's pride will ne'er receive
The royal power which others leave,
Like wine when tasteless dregs are left,
Or rites of Soma juice bereft.
Be sure the pride of Raghu's race
Will never stoop to such disgrace:
The lordly lion will not bear
That man should beard him in his lair.
Were all the worlds against him ranged
His dauntless soul were still unchanged:
He, dutiful, in duty strong,
Would purge the impious world from wrong.
Could not the hero, brave and bold,
The archer, with his shafts of gold,
Burn up the very seas, as doom
Will in the end all life consume?
Of lion's might, eyed like a bull,
A prince so brave and beautiful,
Thou hast with wicked hate pursued,
Like sea-born tribes who eat their brood.
If thou, O Monarch, hadst but known
The duty all the Twice-born own,
If the good laws had touched thy mind,
Which sages in the Scriptures find,
Thou ne'er hadst driven forth to pine
This brave, this duteous son of thine.
First on her lord the wife depends,
Next on her son and last on friends:
These three supports in life has she,
And not a fourth for her may be.
Thy heart, O King, I have not won;
In wild woods roams my banished son;
Far are my friends: ah, hapless me,
Quite ruined and destroyed by thee.'

CANTO LXII.

DAŚARATHA CONSOLED.

The queen's stern speech the monarch heard,
As rage and grief her bosom stirred,
And by his anguish sore oppressed
Reflected in his secret breast.
Fainting and sad, with woe distraught,
He wandered in a maze of thought;
At length the queller of the foe
Grew conscious, rallying from his woe.
When consciousness returned anew
Long burning sighs the monarch drew.
Again immersed in thought he eyed
Kauśalyá standing by his side.
Back to his pondering soul was brought
The direful deed his hand had wrought,
When, guiltless of the wrong intent,
His arrow at a sound was sent.
Distracted by his memory's sting,
And mourning for his son, the king
To two consuming griefs a prey,
A miserable victim lay.
The double woe devoured him fast,
As on the ground his eyes he cast,
Joined suppliant hands, her heart to touch,
And spake in the answer, trembling much:
'Kauśalyá, for thy grace I sue,
Joining these hands as suppliants do.
Thou e'en to foes hast ever been
A gentle, good, and loving queen.
Her lord, with noble virtues graced,
Her lord, by lack of all debased,
Is still a God in woman's eyes,
If duty's law she hold and prize.
Thou, who the right hast aye pursued,
Life's changes and its chances viewed,
Shouldst never launch, though sorrow-stirred,
At me distressed, one bitter word.'
She listened, as with sorrow faint
He murmured forth his sad complaint:
Her brimming eyes with tears ran o'er,
As spouts the new-fallen water pour;

His suppliant hands, with fear dismayed
She gently clasped in hers, and laid,
Like a fair lotus, on her head,
And faltering in her trouble said:
'Forgive me; at thy feet I lie,
With low bent head to thee I cry.
By thee besought, thy guilty dame
Pardon from thee can scarcely claim.
She merits not the name of wife
Who cherishes perpetual strife
With her own husband good and wise,
Her lord both here and in the skies.
I know the claims of duty well,
I know thy lips the truth must tell.
All the wild words I rashly spoke,
Forth from my heart, through anguish, broke;
For sorrow bends the stoutest soul,
And cancels Scripture's high control.
Yea, sorrow's might all else o'erthrows
The strongest and the worst of foes.
'Tis thus with all: we keenly feel,
Yet bear the blows our foemen deal,
But when a slender woe assails
The manliest spirit bends and quails.
The fifth long night has now begun
Since the wild woods have lodged my son:
To me whose joy is drowned in tears,
Each day a dreary year appears.
While all my thoughts on him are set
Grief at my heart swells wilder yet:
With doubled might thus Ocean raves
When rushing floods increase his waves.'
  As from Kauśalyá reasoning well
The gentle words of wisdom fell,
The sun went down with dying flame,
And darkness o'er the landscape came.
His lady's soothing words in part
Relieved the monarch's aching heart,
Who, wearied out by all his woes,
Yielded to sleep and took repose.

CANTO LXIII.

THE HERMIT'S SON.

But soon by rankling grief oppressed
The king awoke from troubled rest,
And his sad heart was tried again
With anxious thought where all was pain.
Ráma and Lakshman's mournful fate
On Daśaratha, good and great
As Indra, pressed with crushing weight,
As when the demon's might assails
The Sun-God, and his glory pales.
Ere yet the sixth long night was spent,
Since Ráma to the woods was sent,
The king at midnight sadly thought
Of the old crime his hand had wrought,
And thus to Queen Kauśalyá cried
Who still for Ráma moaned and sighed:
'If thou art waking, give, I pray,
Attention to the words I say.
Whate'er the conduct men pursue,
Be good or ill the acts they do,
Be sure, dear Queen, they find the meed
Of wicked or of virtuous deed.
A heedless child we call the man
Whose feeble judgment fails to scan
The weight of what his hands may do,
Its lightness, fault, and merit too.
One lays the Mango garden low,
And bids the gay Paláśas grow:
Longing for fruit their bloom he sees,
But grieves when fruit should bend the trees.
Cut by my hand, my fruit-trees fell,
Paláśa trees I watered well.
My hopes this foolish heart deceive,
And for my banished son I grieve.
Kauśalyá, in my youthful prime
Armed with my bow I wrought the crime,
Proud of my skill, my name renowned,
An archer prince who shoots by sound.
The deed this hand unwitting wrought
This misery on my soul has brought,
As children seize the deadly cup
And blindly drink the poison up.
As the unreasoning man may be
Charmed with the gay Paláśa tree,
I unaware have reaped the fruit
Of joying at a sound to shoot.
As regent prince I shared the throne,
Thou wast a maid to me unknown.
The early Rain-time duly came,
And strengthened love's delicious flame.
The sun had drained the earth that lay
All glowing neath the summer day,
And to the gloomy clime had fled
Where dwell the spirits of the dead.[1]
The fervent heat that moment ceased,
The darkening clouds each hour increased
And frogs and deer and peacocks all
Rejoiced to see the torrents fall.
Their bright wings heavy from the shower,
The birds, new-bathed, had scarce the power
To reach the branches of the trees
Whose high tops swayed beneath the breeze.
The fallen rain, and falling still,
Hung like a sheet on every hill,
Till, with glad deer, each flooded steep
Showed glorious as the mighty deep.
The torrents down its wooded side
Poured, some unstained, while others dyed

[1] The southern region is the abode of Yama the Indian Pluto, and of departed spirits.

Gold, ashy, silver, ochre, bore
The tints of every mountain ore.
In that sweet time, when all are pleased,
My arrows and my bow I seized;
Keen for the chase, in field or grove,
Down Sarjú's bank my car I drove.
I longed with all my lawless will
Some elephant by night to kill,
Some buffalo that came to drink,
Or tiger, at the river's brink.
When all around was dark and still,
I heard a pitcher slowly fill,
And thought, obscured in deepest shade,
An elephant the sound had made.
I drew a shaft that glittered bright,
Fell as a serpent's venomed bite;
I longed to lay the monster dead,
And to the mark my arrow sped.
Then in the calm of morning, clear
A hermit's wailing smote my ear:
'Ah me, ah me,' he cried, and sank,
Pierced by my arrow, on the bank.
E'en as the weapon smote his side,
I heard a human voice that cried:
'Why lights this shaft on one like me,
A poor and harmless devotee?
I came by night to fill my jar
From this lone stream where no men are.
Ah, who this deadly shaft has shot?
Whom have I wronged, and knew it not?
Why should a boy so harmless feel
The vengeance of the winged steel?
Or who should slay the guiltless son
Of hermit sire who injures none,
Who dwells retired in woods, and there
Supports his life on woodland fare?
Ah me, ah me, why am I slain,
What booty will the murderer gain?
In hermit coils I bind my hair,
Coats made of skin and bark I wear.
Ah, who the cruel deed can praise
Whose idle toil no fruit repays,
As impious as the wretch's crime
Who dares his master's bed to climb?
Nor does my parting spirit grieve
But for the life which thus I leave:
Alas, my mother and my sire,—
I mourn for them when I expire.
Ah me, that aged, helpless pair,
Long cherished by my watchful care,
How will it be with them this day
When to the Five[1] I pass away?
Pierced by the self-same dart we die,
Mine aged mother, sire, and I.
Whose mighty hand, whose lawless mind
Has all the three to death consigned?'
When I, by love of duty stirred,
That touching lamentation heard,
Pierced to the heart by sudden woe,
I threw to earth my shafts and bow.
My heart was full of grief and dread
As swiftly to the place I sped,
Where, by my arrow wounded sore,
A hermit lay on Sarjú's shore.
His matted hair was all unbound,
His pitcher empty on the ground,
And by the fatal arrow pained,
He lay with dust and gore distained.
I stood confounded and amazed:
His dying eyes to mine he raised,
And spoke this speech in accents stern,
As though his light my soul would burn:
'How have I wronged thee, King, that I
Struck by thy mortal arrow die?
The wood my home, this jar I brought,
And water for my parents sought
This one keen shaft that strikes me through
Slays sire and aged mother too.
Feeble and blind, in helpless pain,
They wait for me and thirst in vain.
They with parched lips their pangs must bear,
And hope will end in blank despair.
Ah me, there seems no fruit in store
For holy zeal or Scripture lore,
Or else ere now my sire would know
That his dear son is lying low.
Yet, if my mournful fate he knew,
What could his arm so feeble do?
The tree, firm-rooted, ne'er may be
The guardian of a stricken tree.
Haste to my father, and relate
While time allows, my sudden fate,
Lest he consume thee, as the fire
Burns up the forest, in his ire.
This little path, O King, pursue:
My father's cot thou soon wilt view.
There sue for pardon to the sage.
Lest he should curse thee in his rage.
First from the wound extract the dart
That kills me with its deadly smart,
E'en as the flushed impetuous tide
Eats through the river's yielding side.'
I feared to draw the arrow out,
And pondered thus in painful doubt:
'Now tortured by the shaft he lies,
But if I draw it forth he dies.'
Helpless I stood, faint, sorely grieved:
The hermit's son my thought perceived;
As one o'ercome by direst pain
He scarce had strength to speak again,
With writhing limb and struggling breath,
Nearer and ever nearer death:
'My senses undisturbed remain,
And fortitude has conquered pain:
Now from one fear thy soul be freed,
Thy hand has made no Bráhman bleed.
Let not this pang thy bosom wring:
No twice-born youth am I, O King,

[1] The five elements of which the body consists, and to which it returns.

For of a Vaiśya sire I came,
Who wedded with a Śúdrá dame.'
These words the boy could scarcely say,
As tortured by the shaft he lay.
Twisting his helpless body round,
Then trembling senseless on the ground.
Then from his bleeding side I drew
The rankling shaft that pierced him through.
With death's last fear my face he eyed,
And, rich in store of penance, died.'

CANTO LXIV.

DAŚARATHA'S DEATH.

The son of Raghu to his queen
Thus far described the unequalled scene,
And, as the hermit's death he rued,
The mournful story thus renewed:
'The deed my heedless hand had wrought
Perplexed me with remorseful thought,
And all alone I pondered still
How kindly deed might salve the ill.
The pitcher from the ground I took,
And filled it from that fairest brook,
Then, by the path the hermit showed,
I reached his sainted sire's abode.
I came, I saw: the aged pair,
Feeble and blind, were sitting there,
Like birds with clipped wings, side by side,
With none their helpless steps to guide.
Their idle hours the twain beguiled
With talk of their returning child,
And still the cheering hope enjoyed,
The hope, alas, by me destroyed.
Then spoke the sage, as drawing near
The sound of footsteps reached his ear:
'Dear son, the water quickly bring;
Why hast thou made this tarrying?
Thy mother thirsts, and thou hast played,
And bathing in the brook delayed.
She weeps because thou camest not;
Haste, O my son, within the cot.
If she or I have ever done
A thing to pain thee, dearest son,
Dismiss the memory from thy mind:
A hermit thou, be good and kind.
On thee our lives, our all, depend:
Thou art thy friendless parents' friend.
The eyeless couple's eye art thou:
Then why so cold and silent now?'
With sobbing voice and bosom wrung
I scarce could move my faltering tongue,
And with my spirit filled with dread
I looked upon the sage, and said,
While mind, and sense, and nerve I strung
To fortify my trembling tongue,
And let the aged hermit know
His son's sad fate, my fear and woe:
'High-minded Saint, not I thy child,
A warrior, Daśaratha styled.
I bear a grievous sorrow's weight
Born of a deed which good men hate.
My lord, I came to Sarjú's shore,
And in my hand my bow I bore
For elephant or beast of chase
That seeks by night his drinking place.
There from the stream a sound I heard
As if a jar the water stirred.
An elephant, I thought, was nigh:
I aimed, and let an arrow fly.
Swift to the place I made my way,
And there a wounded hermit lay
Gasping for breath: the deadly dart
Stood quivering in his youthful heart.
I hastened near with pain oppressed;
He faltered out his last behest,
And quickly, as he bade me do,
From his pierced side the shaft I drew.
I drew the arrow from the rent,
And up to heaven the hermit went,
Lamenting, as from earth he passed,
His aged parents to the last.
Thus, unaware, the deed was done:
My hand, unwitting, killed thy son.
For what remains, O, let me win
Thy pardon for my heedless sin.'
As the sad tale of sin I told,
The hermit's grief was uncontrolled;
With flooded eyes, and sorrow-faint,
Thus spake the venerable saint:
I stood with hand to hand applied,
And listened as he spoke and sighed:
'If thou, O King, hadst left unsaid
By thine own tongue this tale of dread,
Thy head for hideous guilt accursed
Had in a thousand pieces burst.
A hermit's blood by warrior spilt,
In such a case, with purposed guilt,
Down from his high estate would bring
Even the thunder's mighty King.
And he a dart who concious sends
Against the devotee who spends
His pure life by the law of Heaven—
That sinner's head will split in seven.
Thou livest, for thy heedless hand
Has wrought a deed thou hast not planned,
Else thou and and all of Raghu's line
Had perished by this act of thine.
Now guide us,' thus the hermit said,
'Forth to the spot where he lies dead.
Guide us, this day, O Monarch, we
For the last time our son would see:
The hermit dress of skin he wore
Rent from his limbs distained with gore;
His senseless body lying slain,
His soul in Yama's dark domain.'
Alone the mourning pair I led,
Their souls with woe disquieted.
And let the dame and hermit lay

Their hands upon the breathless clay.
The father touched his son, and pressed
The body to his aged breast;
Then falling by the dead boy's side,
He lifted up his voice, and cried:
'Hast thou no word, my child, to say?
No greeting for thy sire to-day?
Why art thou angry, darling? why
Wilt thou upon the cold earth lie?
If thou, my son, art wroth with me,
Here, duteous child, thy mother see.
What! no embrace for me, my son?
No word of tender love—not one?
Whose gentle voice, so soft and clear,
Soothing my spirit, shall I hear
When evening comes, with accents sweet
Scripture or ancient lore repeat?
Who, having fed the sacred fire,
And duly bathed, as texts require,
Will cheer, when evening rites are done,
The father mourning for his son?
Who will the daily meal provide
For the poor wretch who lacks a guide,
Feeding the helpless with the best
Berries and roots, like some dear guest?
How can these hands subsistence find
For thy poor mother, old and blind?
The wretched votaress how sustain,
Who mourns her child in ceaseless pain?
Stay yet a while, my darling, stay,
Nor fly to Yama's realm to-day.
To-morrow I thy sire and she
Who bare thee, child, will go with thee.[1]
Then when I look on Yama, I
To great Vivasvat's son will cry:
'Hear, King of justice, and restore
Our child to feed us, I implore.
Lord of the world, of mighty fame,
Faithful and just, admit my claim,
And grant this single boon to free
My soul from fear, to one like me.'
Because, my son, untouched by stain,
By sinful hands thou fallest slain,
Win, through thy truth, the sphere where those
Who die by hostile darts repose.
Seek the blest home prepared for all
The valiant who in battle fall,
Who face the foe and scorn to yield,
In glory dying on the field.
Rise to the heaven where Dhundhumár
And Nahush, mighty heroes, are,
Where Janamejay and the blest
Dilípa, Sagar, Śaivya, rest:
Home of all virtuous spirits, earned
By fervent rites and Scripture learned:
By those whose sacred fires have glowed,
Whose liberal hands have fields bestowed:
By givers of a thousand cows,
By lovers of one faithful spouse:
By those who serve their masters well,
And cast away this earthly shell.
None of my race can ever know
The bitter pain of lasting woe.
But doomed to that dire fate is he
Whose guilty hand has slaughtered thee.'
Thus with wild tears the aged saint
Made many a time his piteous plaint,
Then with his wife began to shed
The funeral water for the dead.
But in a shape celestial clad,
Won by the merits of the lad,
The spirit from the body brake
And to the mourning parents spake:
'A glorious home in realms above
Rewards my care and filial love.
You, honoured parents, soon shall be
Partakers of that home with me.'
He spake, and swiftly mounting high,
With Indra near him, to the sky
On a bright car, with flame that glowed,
Sublime the duteous hermit rode.
The father, with his consort's aid,
The funeral rites with water paid,
And thus his speech to me renewed
Who stood in suppliant attitude:
'Slay me this day, O, slay me, King,
For death no longer has a sting.
Childless am I: thy dart has done
To death my dear, my only son.
Because the boy I loved so well
Slain by thy heedless arrow fell,
My curse upon thy soul shall press
With bitter woe and heaviness.
I mourn a slaughtered child, and thou
Shalt feel the pangs that kill me now.
Bereft and suffering e'en as I,
So shalt thou mourn thy son, and die.
Thy hand unwitting dealt the blow
That laid a holy hermit low,
And distant, therefore, is the time
When thou shalt suffer for the crime.
The hour shall come when, crushed by woes
Like these I feel, thy life shall close:
A debt to pay in after days
Like his the priestly fee who pays.'
This curse on me the hermit laid,
Nor yet his tears and groans were stayed.
Then on the pire their bodies cast
The pair; and straight to heaven they passed.
As in sad thought I pondered long
Back to my memory came the wrong
Done in wild youth, O lady dear,
When 'twas my boast to shoot by ear.

[1] So dying York cries over the body of Suffolk:
'Tarry, dear cousin Suffolk!
My soul shall thine keep company to heaven
Tarry, sweet soul, for mine, then fly abreast.'
King Henry V. Act IV. 6.

The deed has borne the fruit, which now
Hangs ripe upon the bending bough:
Thus dainty meats the palate please,
And lure the weak to swift disease.
Now on my soul return with dread
The words that noble hermit said,
That I for a dear son should grieve,
And of the woe my life should leave.'
Thus spake the king with many a tear;
Then to his wife he cried in fear:
'I cannot see thee, love; but lay
Thy gentle hand in mine, I pray.
Ah me, if Ráma touched me thus,
If once, returning home to us,
He bade me wealth and lordship give,
Then, so I think, my soul would live.
Unlike myself, unjust and mean
Have been my ways with him, my Queen,
But like himself is all that he,
My noble son, has done to me.
His son, though far from right he stray,
What prudent sire would cast away?
What banished son would check his ire,
Nor speak reproaches of his sire?
I see thee not: these eyes grow blind,
And memory quits my troubled mind.
Angels of Death are round me: they
Summon my soul with speed away.
What woe more grievous can there be,
That, when from light and life I flee,
I may not, ere I part, behold
My virtuous Ráma, true and bold?
Grief for my son, the brave and true,
Whose joy it was my will to do,
Dries up my breath, as summer dries
The last drop in the pool that lies.
Not men, but blessed Gods, are they
Whose eyes shall see his face that day;
See him, when fourteen years are past,
With earrings decked return at last.
My fainting mind forgets to think:
Low and more low my spirits sink.
Each from its seat, my senses steal:
I cannot hear, or taste, or feel.
This lethargy of soul o'ercomes
Each organ, and its function numbs:
So when the oil begins to fail,
The torch's rays grow faint and pale.
This flood of woe caused by this hand
Destroys me helpless and unmanned,
Resistless as the floods that bore
A passage through the river shore.
Ah Raghu's son, ah mighty-armed,
By whom my cares were soothed and charmed,
My son in whom I took delight,
Now vanished from thy father's sight!
Kauśalyá ah, I cannot see;
Sumitrá, gentle devotee!
Alas, Kaikeyí, cruel dame,
My bitter foe, thy father's shame!'
Kauśalyá and Sumitrá kept
Their watch beside him as he wept.
And Daśaratha moaned and sighed,
And grieving for his darling died.

CANTO LXV.

THE WOMEN'S LAMENT.

And now the night had past away,
And brightly dawned another day;
The minstrels, trained to play and sing,
Flocked to the chamber of the king:
Bards, who their gayest raiment wore,
And heralds famed for ancient lore:
And singers, with their songs of praise,
Made music in their several ways.
There as they poured their blessings choice,
And hailed their king with hand and voice,
Their praises with a swelling roar
Echoed through court and corridor.
Then as the bards his glory sang,
From beaten palms loud answer rang,
As glad applauders clapped their hands,
And told his deeds in distant lands.
The swelling concert woke a throng
Of sleeping birds to life and song:
Some in the branches of the trees,
Some caged in halls and galleries.
Nor was the soft string music mute;
The gentle whisper of the lute,
And blessings sung by singers skilled
The palace of the monarch filled.
Eunuchs and dames of life unstained,
Each in the arts of waiting trained,
Drew near attentive as before,
And crowded to the chamber door:
These skilful when and how to shed
The lustral stream o'er limb and head,
Others with golden ewers stood
Of water stained with sandal wood.
And many a maid, pure, young, and fair,
Her load of early offerings bare,
Cups of the flood which all revere,
And sacred things, and toilet gear.
Each several thing was duly brought
As rule of old observance taught,
And lucky signs on each impressed
Stamped it the fairest and the best.
There anxious, in their long array,
All waited till the shine of day:
But when the king nor rose nor spoke,
Doubt and alarm within them woke.
Forthwith the dames, by duty led,
Attendants on the monarch's bed,
Within the royal chamber pressed
To wake their master from his rest.
Skilled in the lore of dreaming, they
First touched the bed on which he lay.
But none replied: no sound was heard,

Nor hand, nor head, nor body stirred.
They trembled, and their dread increased,
Fearing his breath of life had ceased,
And bending low their heads, they shook
Like the tall reeds that fringe the brook.
In doubt and terror down they knelt,
Looked on his face, his cold hand felt,
And then the gloomy truth appeared
Of all their hearts had darkly feared.
Kauśalyá and Sumitrá, worn
With weeping for their sons, forlorn,
Woke not, but lay in slumber deep
And still as death's unending sleep.
Bowed down by grief, her colour fled,
Her wonted lustre dull and dead,
Kauśalyá shone not, like a star
Obscured behind a cloudy bar.
Beside the king's her couch was spread,
And next was Queen Sumitrá's bed.
Who shone no more with beauty's glow,
Her face bedewed with tears of woe.
There lapped in sleep each wearied queen,
There as in sleep, the king was seen;
And swift the troubling thought came o'er
Their spirits that he breathed no more.
At once with wailing loud and high
The matrons shrieked a bitter cry,
As widowed elephants bewail
Their dead lord in the woody vale.
At the loud shriek that round them rang,
Kauśalyá and Sumitrá sprang
Awakened from their beds, with eyes
Wide open in their first surprise.
Quick to the monarch's side they came,
And saw and touched his lifeless frame;
One cry, O husband! forth they sent,
And prostrate to the ground they went.
The king of Kośal's daughter[1] there
Writhed, with the dust on limb and hair,
Lustreless, as a star might lie
Hurled downward from the glorious sky.
When the king's voice in death was stilled,
The women who the chamber filled,
Saw, like a widow elephant slain,
Kauśalyá prostrate in her pain.
Then all the monarch's ladies led
By Queen Kaikeyí at their head,
Poured forth their tears, and weeping so,
Sank on the ground, consumed by woe.
The cry of grief so long and loud
Went up from all the royal crowd,
That, doubled by the matron train,
It made the palace ring again.
Filled with dark fear and eager eyes,
Anxiety and wild surmise;
Echoing with the cries of grief
Of sorrowing friends who mourned their
chief,
Dejected, pale with deep distress,
Hurled from their height of happiness:
Such was the look the palace wore
Where lay the king who breathed no more.

[1] Kauśalyá, daughter of the king of another Kośal.

CANTO LXVI.

THE EMBALMING.

Kauśalyá's eyes with tears o'erflowed,
Weighed down by varied sorrows' load;
On her dead lord her gaze she bent,
Who lay like fire whose might is spent,
Like the great deep with waters dry,
Or like the clouded sun on high.
Then on her lap she laid his head,
And on Kaikeyí looked and said:
'Triumphant now enjoy thy reign
Without a thorn thy side to pain.
Thou hast pursued thy single aim,
And killed the king, O wicked dame.
Far from my sight my Ráma flies,
My perished lord has sought the skies.
No friend, no hope my life to cheer,
I cannot tread the dark path here.
Who would forsake her husband, who
That God to whom her love is due,
And wish to live one hour, but she
Whose heart no duty owns, like thee?
The ravenous sees no fault: his greed
Will e'en on poison blindly feed.
Kaikeyí, through a hump-back maid,
This royal house in death has laid.
King Janak, with his queen, will hear
Heart-rent like me the tidings drear
Of Ráma banished by the king,
Urged by her impious counselling.
No son has he, his age is great,
And sinking with the double weight,
He for his darling child will pine,
And pierced with woe his life resign.
Sprung from Videha's monarch, she
A sad and lovely devotee,
Roaming the wood, unmeet for woe,
Will toil and trouble undergo.
She in the gloomy night with fear
The cries of beast and bird will hear,
And trembling in her wild alarm
Will cling to Ráma's sheltering arm.
Ah, little knows my duteous son
That I am widowed and undone—
My Ráma of the lotus eye,
Gone hence, gone hence, alas, to die.
Now, as a living wife and true,
I, e'en this day, will perish too:
Around his form these arms will throw,
And to the fire with him will go.'
Clasping her husband's lifeless clay
A while the weeping votaress lay,
Till chamberlains removed her thence

O'ercome by sorrow's violence.
Then in a cask of oil they laid
Him who in life the world had swayed,
And finished, as the lords desired,
All rites for parted souls required.
The lords, all-wise, refused to burn
The monarch ere his son's return;
So for a while the cropse they set
Embalmed in oil, and waited yet.
The women heard: no doubt remained,
And wildly for the king they plained.
With gushing tears that drowned each eye
Wildly they waved their arms on high,
And each her mangling nails impressed
Deep in her head and knee and breast:
'Of Ráma reft,—who ever spake
The sweetest words the heart to take,
Who firmly to the truth would cling,—
Why dost thou leave us, mighty King?
How can the consorts thou hast left
Widowed, of Raghu's son bereft,
Live with our foe Kaikeyí near,
The wicked queen we hate and fear?
She threw away the king, her spite
Drove Ráma forth and Lakshman's might,
And gentle Sítá: how will she
Spare any, whosoe'er it be?'
Oppressed with sorrow, tear-distained,
The royal women thus complained.
Like night when not a star appears,
Like a sad widow drowned in tears,
Ayodhyá's city, dark and dim,
Reft of her lord was sad for him.
When thus for woe the king to heaven had fled,
And still on earth his lovely wives remained.
With dying light the sun to rest had sped,
And night triumphant o'er the landscape reigned.

CANTO LXVII.

THE PRAISE OF KINGS.

That night of sorrow passed away,
And rose again the God of Day.
Then all the twice-born peers of state
Together met for high debate.
Jáváli, lord of mighty fame,
And Gautam, and Kátyáyan came,
And Márkandeya's reverend age,
And Vámadeva, glorious sage:
Sprung from Mudgalya's seed the one,
The other ancient Kaśyap's son.
With lesser lords these Bráhmans each
Spoke in his turn his several speech,
And turning to Vaśishtha, best
Of household priests, him thus addressed:
The night of bitter woe has past,
Which seemed a hundred years to last,
Our king, in sorrow for his son,
Reunion with the Five has won.
His soul is where the Blessed are,
While Ráma roams in woods afar,
And Lakshman, bright in glorious deeds,
Goes where his well-loved brother leads.
And Bharat and Śatrughna, they
Who smite their foes in battle fray,
Far in the realm of Kekaya stay,
Where their maternal grandsire's care
Keeps Rájagriha's city fair.
Let one of old Ikshváku's race
Obtain this day the sovereign's place,
Or havoc and destruction straight
Our kingless land will devastate.
In kingless lands no thunder's voice,
No lightning wreaths the heart rejoice,
Nor does Parjanya's heavenly rain
Descend upon the burning plain.
Where none is king, the sower's hand
Casts not the seed upon the land;
The son against the father strives,
And husbands fail to rule their wives.
In kingless realms no princes call
Their friends to meet in crowded hall;
No joyful citizens resort
To garden trim or sacred court.
In kingless realms no Twice-born care
To sacrifice with text and prayer,
Nor Bráhmans, who their vows maintain,
The great solemnities ordain.
The joys of happier days have ceased:
No gathering, festival, or feast
Together calls the merry throng
Delighted with the play and song.
In kingless lands it ne'er is well
With sons of trade who buy and sell:
No men who pleasant tales repeat
Delight the crowd with stories sweet.
In kingless realms we ne'er behold
Young maidens decked with gems and gold,
Flock to the gardens blithe and gay
To spend their evening hours in play.
No lover in the flying car
Rides with his love to woods afar.
In kingless lands no wealthy swain
Who keeps the herd and reaps the grain,
Lies sleeping, blest with ample store,
Securely near his open door.
Upon the royal roads we see
No tusked elephant roaming free,
Of three-score years, whose head and neck
Sweet tinkling bells of silver deck.
We hear no more the glad applause
When his strong bow each rival draws,
No clap of hands, no eager cries
That cheer each martial exercise.
In kingless realms no merchant bands
Who travel forth to distant lands,
With precious wares their wagons load,

And fear no danger on the road.
No sage secure in self-control,
Brooding on God with mind and soul,
In lonely wanderings finds his home
Where'er at eve his feet may roam.
In kingless realms no man is sure
He holds his life and wealth secure.
In kingless lands no warriors smite
The foeman's host in glorious fight.
In kingless lands the wise no more,
Well trained in Scripture's holy lore,
In shady groves and gardens meet
To argue in their calm retreat.
No longer, in religious fear,
Do they who pious vows revere,
Bring dainty cates and wreaths of flowers
As offerings to the heavenly powers.
No longer, bright as trees in spring,
Shine forth the children of the king
Resplendent in the people's eyes
With aloe wood and sandal dyes.
A brook where water once has been,
A grove where grass no more is green,
Kine with no herdsman's guiding hand—
So wretched is a kingless land.
The car its waving banner rears,
Banner of fire the smoke appears:
Our king, the banner of our pride,
A God with Gods is glorified.
In kingless lands no law is known,
And none may call his wealth his own,
Each preys on each from hour to hour,
As fish the weaker fish devour.
Then, fearless, atheists overleap
The bounds of right the godly keep,
And when no royal powers restrain,
Preëminence and lordship gain.
As in the frame of man the eye
Keeps watch and ward, a careful spy,
The monarch in his wide domains
Protects the truth, the right maintains.
He is the right, the truth is he,
Their hopes in him the well-born see.
On him his people's lives depend,
Mother is he, and sire, and friend.
The world were veiled in blinding night,
And none could see or know aright,
Ruled there no king in any state
The good and ill to separate.
We will obey thy word and will
As if our king were living still:
As keeps his bounds the faithful sea,
So we observe thy high decree.
O best of Bráhmans, first in place,
Our kingless land lies desolate:
Some scion of Ikshváku's race
Do thou as monarch consecrate.'

CANTO LXVIII.

THE ENVOYS.

Vaśishṭha heard their speech and prayer,
And thus addressed the concourse there,
Friends, Bráhmans, counsellors, and all
Assembled in the palace hall:
'Ye know that Bharat, free from care,
Still lives in Rájagriha[1] where
The father of his mother reigns:
Śatrughna by his side remains.
Let active envoys, good at need,
Thither on fleetest horses speed,
To bring the hero youths away:
Why waste the time in dull delay?'
Quick came from all the glad reply:
'Vaśishṭha, let the envoys fly.'
He heard their speech, and thus renewed
His charge before the multitude:
'Nandan, Aśok, Siddhárth, attend,
Your ears, Jayanta, Vijay, lend:
Be yours, what need requires, to do:
I speak these words to all of you.
With coursers of the fleetest breed
To Rájagriha's city speed.
Then rid your bosoms of distress,
And Bharat thus from me address:
'The household priest and peers by us
Send health to thee and greet thee thus:
Come to thy father's home with haste:
Thine absent time nô longer waste.'
But speak no word of Ráma fled,
Tell not the prince his sire is dead,
Nor to the royal youth the fate
That ruins Raghu's race relate.
Go quickly hence, and with you bear
Fine silken vestures rich and rare,
And gems and many a precious thing
As gifts to Bharat and the king.'
With ample stores of food supplied,
Each to his home the envoys hied,
Prepared, with steeds of swiftest race,
To Kekaya's land[2] their way to trace.
They made all due provision there,
And every need arranged with care,
Then ordered by Vaśishṭha, they
Went forth with speed upon their way.
Then northward of Pralamba, west
Of Apartála, on they pressed,
Crossing the Máliní that flowed
With gentle stream athwart the road.
They traversed Gangá's holy waves

---

[1] Rájagriha, or Girivraja was the capital of Aśvapati, Bharat's maternal grandfather.

[2] The Kekayas or Kaikayas in the Punjab appear amongst the chief nations in the war of the Mahábhárata; their king being a kinsman of Krishṇa.

Where she Hástinapura[1] laves,
Thence to Panchála[2] westward fast
Through Kurujángal's land[3] they passed.
On, on their course the envoys held
By urgency of task impelled,
Quick glancing at each lucid flood
And sweet lake gay with flower and bud.
Beyond, they passed unwearied o'er,
Where glad birds fill the flood and shore
Of Śaradaṇḍá racing fleet
With heavenly water clear and sweet,
Thereby a tree celestial grows
Which every boon on prayer bestows:
To its blest shade they humbly bent,
Then to Kulingá's town they went.
Then, having passed the Warrior's Wood,
In Abhikála next they stood,
O'er sacred Ikshumatí[4] came,
Their ancient kings' ancestral claim,
They saw the learned Bráhmans stand,
Each drinking from his hollowed hand,
And through Báhíka[5] journeying still
They reached at length Sudáman's hill:
There Vishṇu's footstep turned to see,
Vipáśá[6] viewed, and Śálmalí,
And many a lake and river met,
Tank, pool, and pond, and rivulet,
And lions saw, and tigers near,
And elephants and herds of deer,
And still, by prompt obedience led,
Along the ample road they sped.
Then when their course so swift and long,
Had worn their steeds though fleet and strong,
To Girivraja's splendid town
They came by night, and lighted down.

[1] Hástinapura was the capital of the kingdom of Kuru, near the modern Delhi.

[2] The Panchálas occupied the upper part of the Doab.

[3] 'Kurujángala and its inhabitants are frequently mentioned in the *Mahábhárata*, as in the *Ádi-parv.* 3789, 4337, *et al.*' WILSON'S *Vishṇu Puráṇa*, *Vol.* II. p. 176. DR. HALL'S Note.

[4] 'The 'Οξύματις of Arrian. See *As. Res.* Vol XV. p. 420, 421, also *Indische Alterthumskunde*, Vol. I. p. 602, first footnote.' WILSON'S *Vishṇu Puráṇa*, Vol. I. p. 421. DR. HALL'S Edition. The Íkshumatí was a river in Kurukshetra.

[5] 'The Báhíkas are described in the Mahábhárata, Karṇa Parvan, with some detail, and comprehend the different nations of the Punjab from the Sutlej to the Indus.' WILSON'S *Vishṇu Puráṇa*, Vol. I. p. 167.

[6] The Beas, Hyphasis, or Bibasis.

To please their master, and to guard
The royal race, the lineal right,
The envoys, spent with riding hard,
To that fair city came by night.[1]

CANTO LXIX.

BHARAT'S DREAM.

The night those messengers of state
Had past within the city's gate,
In dreams the slumbering Bharat saw
A sight that chilled his soul with awe.
The dream that dire events foretold
Left Bharat's heart with horror cold,

[1] It would be lost labour to attempt to verify all the towns and streams mentioned in Cantos LXVIII and LXXII. Professor Wilson observes (*Vishṇu Puráṇa*, p. 139. Dr. Hall's Edition) 'States, and tribes, and cities have disappeared, even from recollection; and some of the natural features of the country, especially the rivers, have undergone a total alteration .... Notwithstanding these impediments, however, we should be able to identify at least mountains and rivers, to a much greater extent than is now practicable, if our maps were not so miserably defective in their nomenclature. None of our surveyors or geographers have been oriental scholars. It may be doubted if any of them have been conversant with the spoken language of the country. They have, consequently, put down names at random, according to their own inaccurate appreciation of sounds carelessly, vulgarly, and corruptly uttered; and their maps of India are crowded with appellations which bear no similitude whatever either to past or present denominations. We need not wonder that we cannot discover Sanskrit names in English maps, when, in the immediate vicinity of Calcutta, Barnagore represents Baráhanagar, Dakshineśwar is metamorphosed into Duckinsore, and Ulubaría into Willoughbury...,.............There is scarcely a name in our Indian maps that does not afford proof of extreme indifference to accuracy in nomenclature, and of an incorrectness in estimating sounds, which is, in some degree, perhaps, a national defect.'

For further information regarding the road from Ayodhyá to Rájagriha, see *Additional Notes*.

And with consuming woes distraught,
Upon his aged sire he thought.
His dear companions, swift to trace
The signs of anguish on his face,
Drew near, his sorrow to expel,
And pleasant tales began to tell.
Some woke sweet music's cheering sound,
And others danced in lively round.
With joke and jest they strove to raise
His spirits, quoting ancient plays;
But Bharat still, the lofty-souled,
Deaf to sweet tales his fellows told,
Unmoved by music, dance, and jest,
Sat silent, by his woe oppressed.
To him, begirt by comrades near,
Thus spoke the friend he held most dear:
'Why ringed around by friends, art thou
So silent and so mournful now?'
'Hear thou,' thus Bharat made reply,
'What chills my heart and dims mine eye.
I dreamt I saw the king my sire
Sink headlong in a lake of mire
Down from a mountain high in air,
His body soiled, and loose his hair.
Upon the miry lake he seemed
To lie and welter, as I dreamed;
With hollowed hands full many a draught
Of oil he took, and loudly laughed.
With head cast down I saw him make
A meal on sesamum and cake;
The oil from every member dripped,
And in its clammy flood he dipped.
The ocean's bed was bare and dry,
The moon had fallen from the sky,
And all the world lay still and dead,
With whelming darkness overspread.
The earth was rent and opened wide,
The leafy trees were scorched, and died;
I saw the seated mountains split,
And wreaths of rising smoke emit.
The stately beast the monarch rode
His long tusks rent and splintered showed;
And flames that quenched and cold had lain
Blazed forth with kindled light again.
I looked, and many a handsome dame,
Arrayed in brown and sable came
And bore about the monarch, dressed,
On iron stool, in sable vest.
And then the king, of virtuous mind,
A blood-red wreath around him twined,
Forth on an ass-drawn chariot sped,
As southward still he bent his head.
Then, crimson-clad, a dame appeared
Who at the monarch laughed and jeered;
And a she-monster, dire to view,
Her hand upon his body threw.
Such is the dream I dreamt by night,
Which chills me yet with wild affright:
Either the king or Ráma, I
Or Lakshman now must surely die.
For when an ass-drawn chariot seems
To bear away a man in dreams,
Be sure above his funeral pyre
The smoke soon rears its cloudy spire.
This makes my spirit low and weak,
My tongue is slow and loth to speak:
My lips and throat are dry for dread,
And all my soul disquieted.
My lips, relaxed, can hardly speak,
And chilling dread has changed my cheek
I blame myself in aimless fears,
And still no cause of blame appears.
I dwell upon this dream of ill
Whose changing scenes I viewed,
And on the startling horror still
My troubled thoughts will brood.
Still to my soul these terrors cling,
Reluctant to depart,
And the strange vision of the king
Still weighs upon my heart.'

CANTO LXX.

BHARAT'S DEPARTURE.

While thus he spoke, the envoys borne
On horses faint and travel-worn
Had gained the city fenced around
With a deep moat's protecting bound.
An audience of the king they gained,
And honours from the prince obtained;
The monarch's feet they humbly pressed,
To Bharat next these words addressed:
'The household priest and peers by us
Send health to thee and greet thee thus:
'Come to thy father's house with haste:
Thine absent time no longer waste.
Receive these vestures rich and rare,
These costly gems and jewels fair,
And to thy uncle here present
Each precious robe and ornament.
These for the king and him suffice—
Two hundred millions is their price—
These, worth a hundred millions, be
Reserved, O large-eyed Prince, for thee.'
Loving his friends with heart and soul,
The joyful prince received the whole,
Due honour to the envoys paid,
And thus in turn his answer made:
'Of Daśaratha tidings tell:
Is the old king my father well?
Is Ráma, and is Lakshman, he
Of the high-soul, from sickness free?
And she who walks where duty leads,
Kauśalyá, known for gracious deeds,
Mother of Ráma, loving spouse,
Bound to her lord by well kept vows?
And Lakshman's mother too, the dame
Sumitrá skilled in duty's claim,
Who brave Śatrughna also bare,
Second in age,—her health declare.

And she, in self-conceit most sage,
With selfish heart most prone to rage,
My mother, fares she well? has she
Sent message or command to me?'
Thus Bharat spake, the mighty-souled,
And they in brief their tidings told:
'All they of whom thou askest dwell,
O lion lord, secure and well:
Thine all the smiles of fortune are:
Make ready; let them yoke the car.'
Thus by the royal envoys pressed,
Bharat again the band addressed:
'I go with you: no long delay,
A single hour I bid you stay.'
Thus Bharat, son of him who swayed
Ayodhyá's realm, his answer made,
And then bespoke, his heart to please,
His mother's sire in words like these:
'I go to see my father, King,
Urged by the envoys' summoning;
And when thy soul desires to see
Thy grandson, will return to thee.'
The king his grandsire kissed his head,
And in reply to Bharat said:
'Go forth, dear child; how blest is she,
The mother of a son like thee!
Greet well thy sire, thy mother greet,
O thou whose arms the foe defeat;
The household priest, and all the rest
Amid the Twice-born chief and best;
And Ráma and brave Lakshmaṇ, who
Shoot the long shaft with aim so true.'
To him the king high honour showed,
And store of wealth and gifts bestowed,
The choicest elephants to ride,
And skins and blankets deftly dyed,
A thousand strings of golden beads,
And sixteen hundred mettled steeds;
And boundless wealth before him piled
Gave Kekaya to Kaikeyí's child.
And men of counsel, good and tried,
On whose firm truth he aye relied,
King Aśvapati gave with speed
Prince Bharat on his way to lead.
And noble elephants, strong and young,
From sires of Indraśira sprung,
And others tall and fair to view
Of great Airávat's lineage true:
And well yoked asses fleet of limb
The prince his uncle gave to him.
And dogs within the palace bred,
Of body vast and massive head,
With mighty fangs for battle, brave,
The tiger's match in strength, he gave.
Yet Bharat's bosom hardly glowed
To see the wealth the king bestowed;
For he would speed that hour away,
Such care upon his bosom lay:
Those eager envoys urged him thence,
And that sad vision's influence.
He left his court-yard, crowded then
With elephants and steeds and men,
And, peerless in immortal fame,
To the great royal street he came.
He saw, as farther still he went,
The inner rooms most excellent,
And passed the doors, to him unclosed,
Where check nor bar his way oppossd.
There Bharat stayed to bid adieu
To grandsire and to uncle too,
Then, with Śatrughna by his side,
Mounting his car, away he hied.
The strong-wheeled cars were yoked, and they
More than a hundred, rolled away:
Servants, with horses, asses, kine,
Followed their lord in endless line.
So, guarded by his own right hand,
Forth high-souled Bharat hied,
Surrounded by a lordly band
On whom the king relied.
Beside him sat Śatrughna dear,
The scourge of trembling foes:
Thus from the light of Indra's sphere
A saint made perfect goes.

CANTO LXXI.

BHARAT'S RETURN.

Then Bharat's face was eastward bent
As from the royal town he went.
He reached Sudámá's farther side,
And glorious, gazed upon the tide;
Passed Hládiní, and saw her toss
Her westering billows hard to cross.
Then old Ikshváku's famous son
O'er Śatadrú[1] his passage won,
Near Ailadhána on the strand,
And came to Aparparyaṭ's land.
O'er Śilá's flood he hurried fast,
Akurvatí's fair stream he passed,
Crossed o'er Ágneya's rapid rill,
And Śalyakartan onward still.
Śiláva há's swift stream he eyed,
True to his vows and purified,
Then crossed the lofty hills, and stood
In Chaitraratha's mighty wood.
He reached the confluence where meet
Sarasvatí[2] and Gangá fleet,
And through Bhárunda forest, spread
Northward of Víramatsya, sped.
He sought Kalinda's child, who fills

[1] 'The Śatadrú, 'the hundred-channelled'—the Zaradrus of Ptolemy, Hesydrus of Pliny—is the Sutlej.' WILSON'S *Vishṇu Puráṇa*, Vol. II. p. 130.

[2] The Sarasvatí or Sursooty is a tributary of the Caggar or Guggur in Sirhind.

The soul with joy, begirt by hills,
Reached Yamuná, and passing o'er,
Rested his army on the shore:
He gave his horses food and rest,
Bathed reeking limb and drooping crest.
They drank their fill and bathed them there,
And water for their journey bare.
Thence through a mighty wood he sped
All wild and uninhabited,
As in fair chariot through the skies,
Most fair in shape a Storm-God flies.
At Anśudhána Gangá, hard
To cross, his onward journey barred,
So turning quickly thence he came
To Prágvaṭ's city dear to fame.
There having gained the farther side
To Kuṭikoshṭiká he hied:
The stream he crossed, and onward then
To Dharmavardhan brought his men.
Thence, leaving Toraṇ on the north,
To Jambuprastha journeyed forth.
Then onward to a pleasant grove
By fair Varútha's town he drove,
And when a while he there had stayed,
Went eastward from the friendly shade.
Eastward of Ujjiháná where
The Priyak trees are tall and fair,
He passed, and rested there each steed
Exhausted with the journey's speed.
There orders to his men addressed,
With quickened pace he onward pressed,
A while at Sarvatírtha spent,
Then o'er Uttániká he went.
O'er many a stream beside he sped
With coursers on the mountains bred,
And passing Hastiprishṭhak, took
The road o'er Kuṭiká's fair brook.
Then, at Lohitya's village, he
Crossed o'er the swift Kapívatí,
Then passed, where Ekaśála stands,
The Sthánumatí's flood and sands,
And Gomatí of fair renown
By Vinata's delightful town.
When to Kalinga near he drew,
A wood of Sál trees charmed the view;
That passed, the sun began to rise,
And Bharat saw with happy eyes,
Ayodhyá's city, built and planned
By ancient Manu's royal hand.
Seven nights upon the road had passed,
And when he saw the town at last
Before him in her beauty spread,
Thus Bharat to the driver said:
'This glorious city from afar,
Wherein pure groves and gardens are,
Seems to my eager eyes to-day
A lifeless pile of yellow clay.
Through all her streets where erst a throng
Of men and women streamed along,
Uprose the multitudinous roar:
To-day I hear that sonnd no more.
No longer do mine eyes behold
The leading people, as of old,
On elephants, cars, horses, go
Abroad and homeward, to and fro.
The brilliant gardens, where we heard
The wild note of each rapturous bird,
Where men and women loved to meet,
In pleasant shades, for pastime sweet,—
These to my eyes this day appear
Joyless, and desolate, and drear:
Each tree that graced the garden grieves,
And every path is spread with leaves.
The merry cry of bird and beast,
That spake aloud their joy, has ceased:
Still is the long melodious note
That charmed us from each warbling throat.
Why blows the blessed air no more,
The incense-breathing air that bore
Its sweet incomparable scent
Of sandal and of aloe blent?
Why are the drum and tabour mute?
Why is the music of the lute
That woke responsive to the quill,
Loved by the happy, hushed and still?
My boding spirit gathers hence
Dire sins of awful consequence,
And omens, crowding on my sight,
Weigh down my soul with wild affright.
Scarce shall I find my friends who dwell
Here in Ayodhyá safe and well:
For surely not without a cause
This crushing dread my soul o'erawes.'
  Heart-sick, dejected, every sense
Confused by terror's influence,
On to the town he quickly swept
Which King Ikshváku's children kept.
He passed through Vaijayanta's gate,
With weary steeds, disconsolate,
And all who near their station held,
His escort, crying Victory, swelled,
With heart distracted still he bowed
Farewell to all the following crowd,
Turned to the driver and began
To question thus the weary man:
'Why was I brought, O free from blame,
So fast, unknown for what I came?
Yet fear of ill my heart appals,
And all my wonted courage falls.
For I have heard in days gone by
The changes seen when monarchs die;
And all those signs, O charioteer,
I see to-day surround me here:
Each kinsman's house looks dark and grim,
No hand delights to keep it trim:
The beauty vanished, and the pride,
The doors, unkept, stand open wide.
No morning rites are offered there,
No grateful incense loads the air,
And all therein, with brows o'ercast,
Sit joyless on the ground and fast.
Their lovely chaplets dry and dead,

Their courts unswept, with dust o'erspread,
The temples of the Gods to-day
No more look beautiful and gay.
Neglected stands each holy shrne,
Each image of a Lord divine.
No shop where flowery wreaths are sold
Is bright and busy as of old.
The women and the men I mark
Absorbed in fancies dull and dark,
Their gloomy eyes with tears bedewed,
A poor afflicted multitude.'
His mind oppressed with woe and dread,
Thus Bharat to his driver said,
Viewed the dire signs Ayodhyá showed,
And onward to the palace rode.

CANTO LXXII.

BHARAT'S INQUIRY.

He entered in, he looked around,
Nor in the house his father found;
Then to his mother's dwelling, bent
To see her face, he quickly went.
She saw her son, so long away,
Returning after many a day,
And from her golden seat in joy
Sprang forward to her darling boy.
Within the bower, no longer bright,
Came Bharat lover of the right,
And bending with observance sweet
Clasped his dear mother's lovely feet.
Long kisses on his brow she pressed,
And held her hero to her breast,
Then fondly drew him to her knees,
And questioned him in words like these:
'How many nights have fled, since thou
Leftest thy grandsire's home, till now?
By flying steeds so swiftly borne,
Art thou not weak and travel-worn?
How fares the king my father, tell;
Is Yudhájit thine uncle well?
And now, my son, at length declare
The pleasures of the visit there.'
Thus to the offspring of the king
She spake with tender questioning,
And to his mother made reply
Young Bharat of the lotus eye:
'The seventh night has come and fled
Since from my grandsire's home I sped:
My mother's sire is well, and he,
Yudhájit, from all trouble free.
The gold and every precious thing
Presented by the conqueror king,
The slower guards behind convey:
I left them weary on the way.
Urged by the men my father sent,
My hasty course I hither bent:
Now, I implore, an answer deign,
And all I wish to know, explain.
Unoccupied I now behold
This couch of thine adorned with gold,
And each of King Ikshváku's race
Appears with dark and gloomy face.
The king is aye, my mother dear,
Most constant in his visits here.
To meet my sire I sought this spot:
How is it that I find him not?
I long to clasp my father's feet:
Say where he lingers, I entreat.
Perchance the monarch may be seen
Where dwells Kauśalyá, eldest queen.'
His father's fate, from him concealed,
Kaikeyí to her son revealed:
Told as glad news the story sad,
For lust of sway had made her mad:
'Thy father, O my darling, know,
Has gone the way all life must go:
Devout and famed, of lofty thought,
In whom the good their refuge sought.'
When Bharat pious, pure, and true,
Heard the sad words which pierced him through,
Grieved for the sire he loved so well
Prostrate upon the ground he fell:
Down fell the strong-armed hero, high
Tossing his arms, and a sad cry,
'Ah, woe is me, unhappy, slain!'
Burst from his lips again, again,
Afflicted for his father's fate
By grief's intolerable weight,
With every sense amazed and cowed
The splendid hero wailed aloud:
'Ah me, my royal father's bed
Of old a gentle radiance shed,
Like the pure sky when clouds are past,
And the moon's light is o'er it cast:
Ah, of its wisest lord bereft,
It shows to-day faint radiance left,
As when the moon has left the sky,
Or mighty Ocean's depths are dry.'
With choking sobs, with many a tear,
Pierced to the heart with grief sincere,
The best of conquerors poured his sighs,
And with his robe veiled face and eyes.
Kaikeyí saw him fallen there,
Godlike, afflicted, in despair,
Used every art to move him thence,
And tried him thus with eloquence:
'Arise, arise, my dearest; why
Wilt thou, famed Prince, so lowly lie?
Not by such grief as this are moved
Good men like thee, by all approved.
The earth thy father nobly swayed,
And rites to Heaven he duly paid.
At length his race of life was run:
Thou shouldst not mourn for him, my son.'
Long on the ground he wept, and rolled
From side to side, still unconsoled,
And then, with bitter grief oppressed,
His mother with these words addressed:

'This joyful hope my bosom fed
When from my grandsire's halls I sped—
'The king will throne his eldest son,
And sacrifice, as should be done.'
But all is changed, my hope was vain,
And this sad heart is rent in twain,
For my dear father's face I miss,
Who ever sought his loved ones' bliss.
But in my absence, mother, say,
What sickness took my sire away?
Ah, happy Ráma, happy they
Allowed his funeral rites to pay!
The glorious monarch has not learned
That I his darling have returned,
Or quickly had he hither sped,
And pressed his kisses on my head.
Where is that hand whose gentle touch,
Most soft and kind I loved so much,
The hand that loved to brush away
The dust that on his darling lay?
Quick, bear the news to Ráma's ear;
Tell the great chief that I am here:
Brother, and sire, and friend, and all
Is he, and I his trusty thrall.
For noble hearts, to virtue true,
Their sires in elder brothers view.
To clasp his feet I fain would bow:
He is my hope and refuge now.
What said my glorious sire, who knew
Virtue and vice, so brave and true?
Firm in his vows, dear lady, say,
What said he ere he passed away?
What was his rede to me? I crave
To hear the last advice he gave.'
Thus closely questioned by the youth,
Kaikeyí spoke the mournful truth:
'The high-souled monarch wept and sighed,
For Ráma, Sítá, Lakshman, cried,
Then, best of all who go to bliss,
Passed to the world which follows this.
'Ah, blessed are the people who
'Shall Ráma and his Sítá view,
And Lakshman of the mighty arm,
Returning free from scathe and harm.'
Such were the words, the last of all,
Thy father, ere he died, let fall,
By Fate and Death's dread coils enwound,
As some great elephant is bound.'
He heard, yet deeper in despair,
Her lips this double woe declare,
And with sad brow that showed his pain
Questioned his mother thus again:
'But where is he, of virtue tried,
Who fills Kauśalyá's heart with pride,
Where is the noble Ráma? where
Is Lakshman brave, and Sítá fair?'
Thus pressed, the queen began to tell
The story as each thing befell,
And gave her son in words like these,
The mournful news she meant to please:
'The prince is gone in hermit dress
To Daṇḍak's mighty wilderness,
And Lakshman brave and Sítá share
The wanderings of the exile there.'
Then Bharat's soul with fear was stirred
Lest Ráma from the right had erred,
And jealous for ancestral fame,
He put this quetion to the dame:
'Has Ráma grasped with lawless hold
A Bráhman's house, or land, or gold?
Has Ráma harmed with ill intent
Some poor or wealthy innocent?
Was Ráma, faithless to his vows,
Enamoured of anothers spouse?
Why was he sent to Daṇḍak's wild,
Like one who kills an unborn child?'
He questioned thus: and she began
To tell her deeds and crafty plan.
Deceitful-hearted, fond, and blind
As is the way of womankind:
'No Bráhman's wealth has Ráma seized,
No dame his wandering fancy pleased:
His very eyes he ne'er allows
To gaze upon a neighbour's spouse.
But when I heard the monarch planned
To give the realm to Ráma's hand,
I prayed that Ráma hence might flee,
And claimed the throne, my son, for thee.
The king maintained the name he bare,
And did according to my prayer,
And Ráma, with his brother, sent,
And Sítá, forth to banishment.
When his dear son was seen no more,
The lord of earth was troubled sore:
Too feeble with his grief to strive,
He joined the elemental Five.
Up then, most dutiful! maintain
The royal state, arise, and reign.
For thee, my darling son, for thee
All this was planned and wrought by me.
Come, cast thy grief and pain aside,
With manly courage fortified.
This town and realm are all thine own,
And fear and grief are here unknown.
Come, with Vaśishṭha's guiding aid,
And priests in ritual skilled
Let the king's funeral dues be paid,
And every claim fulfilled.
Perform his obsequies with all
That suits his rank and worth,
Then give the mandate to install
Thyself as lord of earth.'

CANTO LXXIII.

KAIKEYI REPROACHED.

But when he heard the queen relate
His brothers' doom, his father's fate,
Thus Bharat to his mother said
With burning grief disquieted:

'Alas, what boots it now to reign,
Struck down by grief and well-nigh slain?
Ah, both are gone, my sire, and he
Who was a second sire to me.
Grief upon grief thy hand has made,
And salt upon my gashes laid:
For my dear sire has died through thee,
And Ráma roams a devotee.
Thou camest like the night of Fate
This royal house to devastate.
Unwitting ill, my hapless sire
Placed in his bosom coals of fire,
And through thy crimes his death he met,
O thou whose heart on sin is set.
Shame of thy house! thy senseless deed
Has reft all joy from Raghu's seed.
The truthful monarch, dear to fame,
Received thee as his wedded dame,
And by thy act to misery doomed
Has died by flames of grief consumed.
Kauśalyá and Sumitrá too
The coming of my mother rue,
And if they live oppressed by woe,
For their dear sons their sad tears flow.
Was he not ever good and kind,—
That hero of the duteous mind?
Skilled in all filial duties, he
As a dear mother treated thee.
Kauśalyá too, the eldest queen,
Who far foresees with insight keen,
Did she not ever show thee all
A sister's love at duty's call?
And hast thou from the kingdom chased
Her son, with bark around his waist,
To the wild wood, to dwell therein,
And dost not sorrow for thy sin?
The love I bare to Raghu's son
Thou knewest not, ambitious one,
If thou hast wrought this impious deed
For royal sway, in lawless greed.
With him and Lakshman far away,
What power have I the realm to sway?
What hope will fire my bosom, when
I see no more those lords of men?
The holy king who loved the right
Relied on Rama's power and might,
His guardian and his glory: so
Joys Meru in his woods below.
How can I bear, a steer untrained,
The load his mightier strength sustained?
What power have I to brook alone
This weight on feeble shoulders thrown?
But if the needful power were bought
By strength of mind and brooding thought,
No triumph shall attend the dame
Who dooms her son to lasting shame.
Now should no doubt that son prevent
From quitting thee on evil bent,
But Ráma's love o'erpowers my will,
Who holds thee as his mother still.
Whence did the thought, O thou whose eyes
Are turned to sinful deeds, arise—
A plan our ancient sires would hate,
O fallen from thy virtuous state?
For in the line from which we spring
The eldest is anointed king:
No monarchs from the rule decline,
And, least of all, Ikshváku's line.
Our holy sires, to virtue true,
Upon our race a lustre threw,
But with subversive frenzy thou
Hast marred our lineal honour now.
Of lofty birth, a noble line
Of previous kings is also thine:
Then whence this hated folly? whence
This sudden change that steals thy sense?
Thou shalt not gain thine impious will,
O thou whose thoughts are bent on ill,
Thou from whose guilty hand descend
These sinful blows my life to end.
Now to the forest will I go,
Thy cherished plans to overthrow,
And bring my brother, free from stain,
His people's darling, home again.
And Ráma, when again he turns,
Whose glory like a beacon burns,
In me a faithful slave shall find
To serve him with contented mind.'

CANTO LXXIV.

BHARAT'S LAMENT.

When Bharat's anger-sharpened tongue
Reproaches on the queen had flung,
Again, with mighty rage possessed,
The guilty dame he thus addressed:
'Flee, cruel, wicked sinner, flee,
Let not this kingdom herbour thee.
Thou who hast thrown all right aside,
Weep thou for me when I have died.
Canst thou one charge against the king,
Or the most duteous Ráma, bring?
The one thy sin to death has sent,
The other chased to banishment.
Our line's destroyer, sin-defiled
Like one who kills an unborn child,
Ne'er with thy lord in heaven to dwell,
Thy portion shall be down in hell.
Because thy hand, that stayed for naught,
This awful wickedness has wrought,
And ruined him whom all held dear,
My bosom too is stirred with fear.
My father by thy sin is dead,
And Ráma to the wood is fled;
And of thy deed I bear the stain,
And fameless in the world remain.
Ambitious, evil-souled, in show
My mother, yet my direst foe,
My throning ne'er thine eyes shall bless,
Thy husband's wicked murderess.

Thou art not Aśvapati's child,
That righteous king, most sage and mild,
But thou wast born a fiend, a foe
My father's house to overthrow.
Thou who hast made Kauśalyá, pure,
Gentle, affectionate, endure
The loss of him who was her bliss,—
What worlds await thee, Queen, for this?
Was it not patent to thy sense
That Ráma was his friends' defence,
Kauśalyá's own true child most dear,
The eldest and his father's peer?
Men in the son not only trace
The father's figure, form, and face,
But in his heart they also find
The offspring of the father's mind;
And hence, though dear their kinsmen are,
To mothers sons are dearer far.
There goes an ancient legend how
Good Surabhi, the God-loved cow,
Saw two of her dear children strain,
Drawing a plough and faint with pain.
She saw them on the earth outworn,
Toiling till noon from early morn,
And as she viewed her children's woe,
A flood of tears began to flow.
As through the air beneath her swept
The Lord of Gods, the drops she wept,
Fine, laden with delicious smell,
Upon his heavenly body fell.
And Indra lifted up his eyes
And saw her standing in the skies,
Afflicted with her sorrow's weight,
Sad, weeping, all disconsolate.
The Lord of Gods in anxious mood
Thus spoke in suppliant attitude:
'No fear disturbs our rest, and how
Come this great dread upon thee now?
Whence can this woe upon thee fall,
Say, gentle one who lovest all?'
Thus spake the God who rules the skies,
Indra, the Lord supremely wise;
And gentle Surabhi, well learned
In eloquence, this speech returned:
'Not thine the fault, great God, not thine
And guiltless are the Lords divine:
I mourn two children faint with toil,
Labouring hard in stubborn soil.
Wasted and sad I see them now,
While the sun beats on neck and brow,
Still goaded by the cruel hind,—
No pity in his savage mind.
O Indra, from this body sprang
These children, worn with many a pang.
For this sad sight I mourn, for none
Is to the mother like her son.'
He saw her weep whose offspring feed
In thousands over hill and mead,
And knew that in a mother's eye
Naught with a son, for love, can vie.
He deemed her, when the tears that came
From her sad eyes bedewed his frame,
Laden with their celestial scent,
Of living things most excellent.
If she these tears of sorrow shed
Who many a thousand children bred,
Think what a life of woe is left
Kauśalyá, of her Ráma reft.
An only son was hers, and she
Is rendered childless now by thee.
Here and hereafter, for thy crime,
Woe is thy lot through endless time.
And now, O Queen, without delay,
With all due honour will I pay
Both to my brother and my sire
The rites their several fates require.
Back to Ayodhyá will I bring
The long-armed chief, her lord and king,
And to the wood myself betake
Where hermit saints their dwelling make.
For, sinner both in deed and thought!
This hideous crime which thou hast wrought
I cannot bear, or live to see
The people's sad eyes bent on me.
Begone, to Dandak wood retire,
Or cast thy body to the fire,
Or bind around thy neck the rope:
No other refuge mayst thou hope.
When Ráma, lord of valour true,
Has gained the earth, his right and due,
Then, free from duty's binding debt,
My vanished sin shall I forget.'

Thus like an elephant forced to brook
The goading of the driver's hook,
Quick panting like a serpent maimed,
He fell to earth with rage inflamed.

CANTO LXXV.

THE ABJURATION.

A while he lay: he rose at length,
And slowly gathering sense and strength,
With angry eyes which tears bedewed,
The miserable queen he viewed,
And spake with keen reproach to her
Before each lord and minister:
'No lust have I for kingly sway,
My mother I no more obey:
Naught of this consecration knew
Which Daśaratha kept in view.
I with Śatrughna all the time
Was dwelling in a distant clime:
I knew of Ráma's exile naught,
That hero of the noble thought:
I knew not how fair Sítá went,
And Lakshman, forth to banishment.'

Thus high-souled Bharat, mid the crowd,
Lifted his voice and cried aloud.

Kauśalyá heard, she raised her head,
And quickly to Sumitrá said:
'Bharat, Kaikeyí's son is here,—
Hers whose fell deeds I loathe and fear:
That youth of foresight keen I fain
Would meet and see his face again.'
Thus to Sumitrá spake the dame,
And straight to Bharat's presence came
With altered mien, neglected dress.
Trembling and faint with sore distress.
Bharat, Śatrughna by his side,
To meet her, toward her palace hied.
And when the royal dame they viewed
Distressed with dire solicitude,
Sad, fallen senseless on the ground,
About her neck their arms they wound.
The noble matron prostrate there,
Embraced, with tears, the weeping pair,
And with her load of grief oppressed,
To Bharat then these words addressed:
'Now all is thine, without a foe,
This realm for which thou longest so,
Ah, soon Kaikeyí's ruthless hand
Has won the empire of the land,
And made my guiltless Ráma flee
Dressed like some lonely devotee.
Herein what profit has the queen,
Whose eye delights in havoc, seen?
Me also, me 'twere surely good
To banish to the distant wood,
To dwell amid the shades that hold
My famous son with limbs like gold.
Nay, with the sacred fire to guide,
Will I, Sumitrá by my side,
Myself to the drear wood repair
And seek the son of Raghu there.
This land which rice and golden corn
And wealth of every kind adorn,
Car, elephant, and steed, and gem,—
She makes thee lord of it and them.'
With taunts like these her bitter tongue
The heart of blameless Bharat wrung
And direr pangs his bosom tore
Than when the lancet probes a sore.
With troubled senses all astray
Prone at her feet he fell and lay.
With loud lament a while he plained,
And slowly strength and sense regained.
With suppliant hand to hand applied
He turned to her who wept and sighed,
And thus bespake the queen, whose breast
With sundry woes was sore distressed:
'Why these reproaches, noble dame?
I, knowing naught, am free from blame.
Thou knowest well what love was mine
For Ráma, chief of Raghu's line.
O, never be his darkened mind
To Scripture's guiding lore inclined,
By whose consent the prince who led
The good, the truthful hero, fled.
May he obey the vilest lord,
Offend the sun with act abhorred.[1]
And strike a sleeping cow, who lent
His voice to Ráma's banishment.
May the good king who all befriends,
And, like his sons, the people tends,
Be wronged by him who gave consent
To noble Ráma's banishment.
On him that king's injustice fall,
Who takes, as lord, a sixth of all,
Nor guards, neglectful of his trust,
His people, as a ruler must.
The crime of those who swear to fee,
At holy rites, some devotee,
And then the promised gift deny,
Be his who willed the prince should fly.
When weapons clash and heroes bleed,
With elephant and harnessed steed,
Ne'er, like the good, be his to fight
Whose heart allowed the prince's flight.
Though taught with care by one expert
May he the Veda's text pervert,
With impious mind on evil bent,
Whose voice approved the banishment.
May he with traitor lips reveal
Whate'er he promised to conceal,
And bruit abroad his friend's offence,
Betrayed by generous confidence.
No wife of equal lineage born
The wretch's joyless home adorn:
Ne'er may he do one virtuous deed,
And dying see no child succeed.
When in the battle's awful day
Fierce warriors stand in dread array,
Let the base coward turn and fly,
And smitten by the foeman, die.
Long may he wander, rags his wear,
Doomed in his hand a skull to bear,
And like an idiot beg his bread,
Who gave consent when Ráma fled.
His sin who holy rites forgets,
Asleep when shows the sun and sets,
A load upon his soul shall lie
Whose will allowed the prince to fly.
His sin who loves his Master's dame,
His, kindler of destructive flame,
His who betrays his trusting friend
Shall, mingled all, on him descend.
By him no reverence due be paid
To blessed God or parted shade:
May sire and mother's sacred name
In vain from him obedience claim.
Ne'er may he go where dwell the good,
Nor win their fame and neighbourhood,
But lose all hopes of bliss to-day,
Who willed the prince should flee away.
May he deceive the poor and weak
Who look to him and comfort seek,

[1] *Súryamcha pratimehatu*, adversus solem mingat. An offence expressly forbidden by the Laws of Manu.

Betray the suppliants who complain,
And make the hopeful hope in vain.
Long may his wife his kiss expect,
And pine away in cold neglect.
May he his lawful love despise,
And turn on other dames his eyes,
Fool, on forbidden joys intent,
Whose will allowed the banishment.
His sin who deadly poison throws
To spoil the water as it flows,
Lay on the wretch its burden dread
Who gave consent when Ráma fled.'[1]

Thus with his words he undeceived
Kauśalyá's troubled heart, who grieved
For son and husband reft away;
Then prostrate on the ground he lay.
Him as he lay half-senseless there,
Freed by the mighty oaths he sware,
Kauśalyá, by her woe distressed,
With melancholy words addressed:
'Anew, my son, this sorrow springs
To rend my heart with keener stings:
These awful oaths which thou hast sworn
My breast with double grief have torn.
Thy soul, and faithful Lakshman's too,
Are still, thank Heaven! to virtue true.
True to thy promise, thou shalt gain
The mansions which the good obtain.'

Then to her breast that youth she drew,
Whose sweet fraternal love she knew,
And there in strict embraces held
The hero, as her tears outwelled.
And Bharat's heart grew sick and faint
With grief and oft-renewed complaint,
And all his senses were distraught
By the great woe that in him wrought.
Thus as he lay and still bewailed
With sighs and loud lament
Till all his strength and reason failed,
The hours of night were spent.

CANTO LXXVI.

THE FUNERAL.

The saint Vaśishṭha, best of all
Whose words with moving wisdom fall,
Bharat, Kaikeyí's son, addressed,
Whom burning fires of grief distressed:
'O Prince, whose fame is widely spread,
Enough of grief: be comforted.
The time is come: arise, and lay
Upon the pyre the monarch's clay.'

He heard the words Vaśishṭha spoke,
And slumbering resolution woke.
Then skilled in all the laws declare,
He bade his friends the rites prepare.
They raised the body from the oil,
And placed it, dripping, on the soil;
Then laid it on a bed, whereon
Wrought gold and precious jewels shone.
There, pallor o'er his features spread,
The monarch, as in sleep, lay dead.
Then Bharat sought his father's side,
And lifted up his voice and cried:
'O King, and has thy heart designed
To part and leave thy son behind?
Make Ráma flee, who loves the right,
And Lakshmaṇ of the arm of might?
Whither, great Monarch, wilt thou go
And leave this people in their woe.
Mourning their hero, wild with grief,
Of Ráma reft, their lion chief?
Ah, who will guard the people well
Who in Ayodhyá's city dwell,
When thou, my sire, hast sought the sky,
And Ráma has been forced to fly?
In widowed woe, bereft of thee,
The land no more is fair to see:
The city, to my aching sight,
Is gloomy as a moonless night.'

Thus, with o'erwhelming sorrow pained,
Sad Bharat by the bed complained:
And thus Vaśishṭha, holy sage,
Spoke his deep anguish to assuage:
'O Lord of men, no longer stay;
The last remaining duties pay:
Haste, mighty-armed, as I advise,
The funeral rites to solemnize.'

And Bharat heard Vaśishṭha's rede
With due attention and agreed.
He summoned straight from every side
Chaplain, and priest, and holy guide.
The sacred fires he bade them bring
Forth from the chapel of the king,
Wherein the priests in order due,
And ministers, the offerings threw.
Distraught in mind, with sob and tear,
They laid the body on a bier,
And servants, while their eyes brimmed o'er
The monarch from the palace bore.
Another band of mourners led
The long procession of the dead:
Rich garments in the way they cast,
And gold and silver, as they passed.
Then other hands the corse bedewed
With fragrant juices that exude
From sandal, cedar, aloe, pine,
And every perfume rare and fine.
Then priestly hands the mighty dead
Upon the pyre deposited,
The sacred fires they tended next,
And muttered low each funeral text;
And priestly singers who rehearse

[1] Bharat does not intend these curses for any particular person: he merely wishes to prove his own innocence by invoking them on his own head if he had any share in banishing Ráma.

The Sáman[1] sang their holy verse.
Forth from the town in litters came,
Or chariots, many a royal dame,
And honoured so the funeral ground,
With aged followers ringed around.
With steps in inverse order bent,[2]
The priests in sad procession went
Around the monarch's burning pyre
Who well had nursed each sacred fire:
With Queen Kauśalyá and the rest,
Their tender hearts with woe distressed.
The voice of women, shrill and clear
As screaming curlews, smote the ear,
As from a thousand voices rose
The shriek that tells of woman's woes.
Then weeping, faint, with loud lament,
Down Sarjú's shelving bank they went.
There standing on the river side
With Bharat, priest, and peer,
Their lips the women purified
With water fresh and clear.
Returning to the royal town,
Their eyes with tear-drops filled,
Ten days on earth they laid them down,
And wept till grief was stilled.

CANTO LXXVII.

THE GATHERING OF THE ASHES.

The tenth day passed: the prince again
Was free from every legal stain.
He bade them on the twelfth the great
Remaining honour celebrate.
Much gold he gave, and gems, and food,
To all the Bráhman multitude,
And goats whose hair was white and fine,
And many a thousand head of kine:
Slaves, men and damsels, he bestowed,
And many a car and fair abode:
Such gifts he gave the Bráhman race
His father's obsequies to grace.
Then when the morning's earliest ray
Appeared upon the thirteenth day,
Again the hero wept and sighed
Distraught and sorrow-stupefied;
Drew, sobbing in his anguish, near,
The last remaining debt to clear,
And at the bottom of the pyre,
He thus bespake his royal sire:
'O father, hast thou left me so,
Deserted in my friendless woe,
When he to whom the charge was given
To keep me, to the wood is driven?
Her only son is forced away
Who was his helpless mother's stay:
Ah, whither, father, art thou fled,
Leaving the queen uncomforted?'
He looked upon the pile where lay
The bones half-burnt and ashes grey,
And uttering a piteous moan,
Gave way, by anguish overthrown.
Then as his tears began to well,
Prostrate to earth the hero fell;
So from its seat the staff they drag,
And cast to earth some glorious flag.
The ministers approached again
The prince whom rites had freed from stain:
So when Yayáti fell, each seer,
In pity for his fate, drew near.
Śatrughna saw him lying low
O'erwhelmed beneath the rush of woe,
And as upon the king he thought,
He fell upon the earth distraught.
When to his loving memory came
Those noble gifts, that kingly frame,
He sorrowed, by his woe distressed,
As one by frenzied rage possessed:
'Ah me, this surging sea of woe
Has drowned us with its overflow:
The source is Manthará, dire and dark,
Kaikeyí is the ravening shark:
And the great boons the monarch gave
Lend conquering might to every wave.
Ah, whither wilt thou go, and leave
Thy Bharat in his woe to grieve,
Whom ever 'twas thy greatest joy
To fondle as a tender boy?
Didst thou not give with thoughtful care
Our food, our drink, our robes to wear?
Whose love will now for us provide,
When thou, our king and sire, hast died?
At such a time bereft, forlorn,
Why is not earth in sunder torn,
Missing her monarch's firm control,
His love of right, his lofty soul?
Ah me, for Ráma roams afar,
My sire is where the Blessed are:
How can I live deserted? I
Will pass into the fire and die.
Abandoned thus, I will not brook
Upon Ayodhyá's town to look,
Once guarded by Ikshváku's race:
The wood shall be my dwelling-place.'
Then when the princes' mournful train
Heard the sad brothers thus complain,
And saw their misery, at the view
Their grief burst wilder out anew.
Faint with lamenting, sad and worn,
Each like a bull with broken horn,
The brothers in their wild despair
Lay rolling, mad with misery, there.
Then old Vaśishtha good and true,
Their father's priest, all lore who knew,
Raised weeping Bharat on his feet,
And thus bespake with counsel meet:
'Twelve days, my lord, have past away

[1] The Sáma-veda, the hymns of which are chanted aloud.
[2] Walking from right to left.

Since flames consumed thy father's clay :
Delay no more : as rules ordain,
Gather what bones may yet remain.
Three constant pairs are ever found
To hem all mortal creatures round :[1]
Then mourn not thus, O Prince, for none
Their close companionship may shun.'
  Sumantra bade Śatrughna rise,
And soothed his soul with counsel wise,
And skilled in truth, his hearer taught
How all things are and come to naught.
When rose each hero from the ground,
A lion lord of men, renowned,
He showed like Indra's flag,[2] whereon
Fierce rains have dashed and suns have shone.
They wiped their red and weeping eyes,
And gently made their sad replies ;
Then, urged to haste, the royal pair
Performed the rites that claimed their care.

CANTO LXXVIII.

MANTHARÁ PUNISHED.

Śatrughna thus to Bharat spake
Who longed the forest road to take :
'He who in woe was wont to give
Strength to himself and all that live—
Dear Ráma, true and pure in heart,
Is banished by a woman's art.
Yet here was Lakshman, brave and strong,
Could not his might prevent the wrong?
Could not his arm the king restrain,
Or make the banished free again?
One loving right and fearing crime
Had checked the monarch's sin in time,
When, vassal of a woman's will,
His feet approached the path of ill.'
  While Lakshman's younger brother, dread
Śatrughna, thus to Bharat said,
Came to the fronting door, arrayed
In glittering robes, the hump-back maid.
There she, with sandal-oil besmeared,
In garments meet for queens appeared :
And lustre to her form was lent
By many a gem and ornament.
She girdled with her broidered zone,
And many a chain about her thrown,
Showed like a female monkey round
Whose body many a string is bound.
When on that cause of evil fell
The quick eye of the sentinel,
He grasped her in his ruthless hold,
And hastening in, Śatrughna told :
'Here is the wicked pest,' he cried,
'Through whom the king thy father died,
And Ráma wanders in the wood :
Do with her as thou deemest good.'
The warder spoke : and every word
Śatrughna's breast to fury stirred :
He called the servants, all and each,
And spake in wrath his hasty speech :
'This is the wretch my sire who slew,
And misery on my brothers drew :
Let her this day obtain the meed,
Vile sinner, of her cruel deed.'
He spake ; and moved by fury laid
His mighty hand upon the maid,
Who as her fellows ringed her round,
Made with her cries the hall resound.
Soon as the gathered women viewed
Śatrughna in his angry mood,
Their hearts disturbed by sudden dread,
They turned and from his presence fled.
'His rage,' they cried, 'on us will fall,
And ruthless, he will slay us all.
Come, to Kauśalyá let us flee :
Our hope, our sure defence is she,
Approved by all, of virtuous mind,
Compassionate, and good, and kind.'
  His eyes with burning wrath aglow,
Śatrughna, shatterer of the foe,
Dragged on the ground the hump-back maid
Who shrieked aloud and screamed for aid.
This way and that with no remorse
He dragged her with resistless force,
And chains and glittering trinkets burst
Lay here and there with gems dispersed,
Till like the sky of Autumn shone
The palace floor they sparkled on.
The lord of men, supremely strong,
Haled in his rage the wretch along :
Where Queen Kaikeyí dwelt he came,
And sternly then addressed the dame.
Deep in her heart Kaikeyí felt
The stabs his keen reproaches dealt,
And of Śatrughna's ire afraid,
To Bharat flew and cried for aid.
He looked and saw the prince inflamed
With burning rage, and thus exclaimed :
'Forgive! thine angry arm restrain :
A woman never may be slain.
My hand Kaikeyí's blood would spill,
The sinner ever bent on ill,
But Ráma, long in duty tried,
Would hate the impious matricide :
And if he knew thy vengeful blade
Had slaughtered e'en this hump-back maid,
Never again, be sure, would he
Speak friendly word to thee or me.'
  When Bharat's speech Śatrughna heard
He calmed the rage his breast that stirred,

[1] Birth and death, pleasure and pain, loss and gain.

[2] Erected upon a tree or high staff in honour of Indra.

Releasing from her dire constraint
The trembling wretch with terror faint.
Then to Kaikeyí's feet she crept,
And prostrate in her misery wept.
Kaikeyí on the hump-back gazed,
  And saw her weep and gasp,
Still quivering, with her senses dazed,
  From fierce Śatrughna's grasp.
With gentle words of pity she
  Assuaged her wild despair,
E'en as a tender hand might free
  A curlew from the snare.

CANTO LXXIX.

BHARAT'S COMMANDS.

Now when the sun's returning ray
Had ushered in the fourteenth day,
The gathered peers of state addressed
To Bharat's ear their new request:
'Our lord to heaven has parted hence,
Long served with deepest reverence;
Ráma, the eldest, far from home,
And Lakshman, in the forest roam.
O Prince, of mighty fame, be thou
Our guardian and our monarch now,
Lest secret plot or foeman's hate
Assail our unprotected state.
With longing eyes, O Lord of men,
To thee look friend and citizen,
And ready is each sacred thing
To consecrate our chosen king.
Come, Bharat, and accept thine own
Ancient hereditary throne.
Thee let the priests this day install
As monarch to preserve us all.'
  Around the sacred gear he bent
His circling footsteps reverent,
And, firm to vows he would not break,
Thus to the gathered people spake:
'The eldest son is ever king:
So rules the house from which we spring:
Nor should ye, Lords, like men unwise,
With words like these to wrong advise.
Ráma is eldest born, and he
The ruler of the land shall be.
Now to the woods will I repair,
Five years and nine to lodge me there.
Assemble straight a mighty force,
Cars, elephants, and foot and horse,
For I will follow on his track
And bring my eldest brother back.
Whate'er the rites of throning need
Placed on a car the way shall lead:
The sacred vessels I will take
To the wild wood for Ráma's sake.
I o'er the lion prince's head
The sanctifying balm will shed,
And bring him, as the fire they bring
Forth from the shrine, with triumphing.
Nor will I let my mother's greed
In this her cherished aim succeed:
In pathless wilds will I remain,
And Ráma here as king shall reign.
To make the rough ways smooth and clear
Send workman out and pioneer:
Let skilful men attend beside
Our way through pathless spots to guide.'
As thus the royal Bharat spake,
Ordaining all for Ráma's sake,
The audience gave with one accord
Auspicious answer to their lord:
'Be royal Fortune aye benign
To thee for this good speech of thine,
Who wishest still thine elder's hand
To rule with kingly sway the land.'
  Their glorious speech, their favouring
    cries
    Made his proud bosom swell:
  And from the prince's noble eyes
    The tears of rapture fell.[1]

CANTO LXXX.

THE WAY PREPARED.

All they who knew the joiner's art,
Or distant ground in every part;
Each busied in his several trade,
To work machines or ply the spade;
Deft workmen skilled to frame the wheel,
Or with the ponderous engine deal;
Guides of the way, and craftsmen skilled,
To sink the well, make bricks, and build;
And those whose hands the tree could hew,
And work with slips of cut bamboo,
Went forward, and to guide them, they
Whose eyes before had seen the way.
Then onward in triumphant mood
Went all the mighty multitude,
Like the great sea whose waves leap high
When the full moon is in the sky.
Then, in his proper duty skilled,
Each joined him to his several guild,
And onward in advance they went
With every tool and implement.
Where bush and tangled creeper lay
With trenchant steel they made the way;
They felled each stump, removed each
    stone,
And many a tree was overthrown.
In other spots, on desert lands,
Tall trees were reared by busy hands.
Where'er the line of road they took,
They plied the hatchet, axe, and hook.

[1] I follow in this stanza the Bombay edition in preference to Schlegel's which gives the tears of joy to the courtiers.

Others, with all their strength applied,
Cast vigorous plants and shrubs aside,
In shelving valleys rooted deep,
And levelled every dale and steep.
Each pit and hole that stopped the way
They filled with stones, and mud, and clay,
And all the ground that rose and fell
With busy care was levelled well.
They bridged ravines with ceaseless toil,
And pounded fine the flinty soil.
Now here, now there, to right and left,
A passage through the ground they cleft,
And soon the rushing flood was led
Abundant through the new-cut bed,
Which by the running stream supplied
With ocean's boundless waters vied.
In dry and thirsty spots they sank
Full many a well and ample tank,
And altars round about them placed
To deck the station in the waste.
With well-wrought plaster smoothly spread,
With bloomy trees that rose o'erhead,
With banners waving in the air,
And wild birds singing here and there,
With fragrant sandal-water wet,
With many a flower beside it set,
Like the Gods' heavenly pathway showed
That mighty host's imperial road.
Deft workmen, chosen for their skill
To do the high-souled Bharat's will,
In every pleasant spot where grew
Trees of sweet fruit and fair to view,
As he commanded, toiled to grace
With all delights his camping-place.
And they who read the stars, and well
Each lucky sign and hour could tell,
Raised carefully the tented shade
Wherein high-minded Bharat stayed.
With ample space of level ground,
With broad deep moat encompassed round;
Like Mandar in his towering pride,
With streets that ran from side to side;
Enwreathed with many a palace tall
Surrounded by its noble wall;
With roads by skilful workmen made,
Where many a glorious banner played;
With stately mansions, where the dove
Sat nestling in her cote above,
Rising aloft supremely fair
Like heavenly cars that float in air,
Each camp in beauty and in bliss
Matched Indra's own metropolis.
As shines the heaven on some fair night,
With moon and constellations filled,
The prince's royal road was bright,
Adorned by art of workmen skilled.

CANTO LXXXI.

THE ASSEMBLY.

Ere yet the dawn had ushered in
The day should see the march begin,
Herald and bard who rightly knew
Each nice degree of honour due,
Their loud auspicious voices raised,
And royal Bharat blessed and praised.
With sticks of gold the drum they smote,
Which thundered out its deafening note,
Blew loud the sounding shell, and blent
Each high and low-toned instrument.
The mingled sound of drum and horn
Through all the air was quickly borne,
And as in Bharat's ear it rang,
Gave the sad prince another pang.
Then Bharat, starting from repose,
Stilled the glad sounds that round him rose,
'I am not king: no more mistake:'
Then to Śatrughna thus he spake:
'O see what general wrongs succeed
Sprung from Kaikeyí's evil deed!
The king my sire has died and thrown
Fresh miseries on me alone.
The royal bliss, on duty based,
Which our just high-souled father graced,
Wanders in doubt and sore distress
Like a tossed vessel rudderless.
And he who was our lordly stay
Roams in the forest far away,
Expelled by this my mother, who
To duty's law is most untrue.'
As royal Bharat thus gave vent
To bitter grief in wild lament,
Gazing upon his face the crowd
Of pitying women wept aloud.
His lamentation scarce was o'er,
When Saint Vaśishṭha, skilled in lore
Of royal duty, dear to fame,
To join the great assembly came.
Girt by disciples ever true
Still nearer to that hall he drew,
Resplendent, heavenly to behold,
Adorned with wealth of gems and gold:
E'en so a man in duty tried
Draws near to meet his virtuous bride.
He reached his golden seat o'erlaid
With coverlet of rich brocade,
There sat, in all the Vedas read,
And called the messengers, and said:
'Go forth, let Bráhman, Warrior, peer,
And every captain gather here:
Let all attentive hither throng:
Go, hasten: we delay too long.
Śatrughna, glorious Bharat bring,
The noble children of the king,[1]

[1] The commentator says 'Śatrughna accompanied by the other sons of the king.

Yudhájit[1] and Sumantra, all
The truthful and the virtuous call.'
He ended: soon a mighty sound
Of thickening tumult rose around,
As to the hall they bent their course
With car, and elephant, and horse,
The people all with glad acclaim
Welcomed Prince Bharat as he came:
E'en as they loved their king to greet,
Or as the Gods Lord Indra[2] meet.
The vast assembly shone as fair
With Bharat's kingly face
As Daśaratha's self were there
To glorify the place.
It gleamed like some unruffled lake
Where monsters huge of mould
With many a snake their pastime take
O'er shells, sand, gems, and gold.

CANTO LXXXII.

THE DEPARTURE.

The prudent prince the assembly viewed
Thronged with its noble multitude,
Resplendent as a cloudless night
When the full moon is in his height;
While robes of every varied hue
A glory o'er the synod threw.
The priest in lore of duty skilled
Looked on the crowd the hall that filled,
And then in accents soft and grave
To Bharat thus his counsel gave:
'The king, dear son, so good and wise,
Has gone from earth and gained the skies,
Leaving to thee, her rightful lord,
This rich wide land with foison stored.
And still has faithful Ráma stood
Firm to the duty of the good,
And kept his father's hest aright,
As the moon keeps its own dear light.
Thus sire and brother yield to thee
This realm from all annoyance free:
Rejoice thy lords: enjoy thine own:
Anointed king, ascend the throne.
Let vassal Princes hasten forth
From distant lands, west, south, and north,
From Kerala,[3] from every sea,
And bring ten million gems to thee.'
As thus the sage Vaśishṭha spoke,
A storm of grief o'er Bharat broke.
And longing to be just and true,
His thoughts to duteous Ráma flew.
With sobs and sighs and broken tones,
E'en as a wounded mallard moans,
He mourned with deepest sorrow moved,
And thus the holy priest reproved:
'O, how can such as Bharat dare
The power and sway from him to tear,
Wise, and devout, and true, and chaste,
With Scripture lore and virtue graced?
Can one of Daśaratha's seed
Be guilty of so vile a deed?
The realm and I are Ráma's: thou
Shouldst speak the words of justice now.
For he, to claims of virtue true,
Is eldest born and noblest too:
Nahush, Dilípa could not be
More famous in their lives than he.
As Daśaratha ruled of right,
So Ráma's is the power and right.
If I should do this sinful deed
And forfeit hope of heavenly meed,
My guilty act would dim the shine
Of old Ikshváku's glorious line.
Nay, as the sin my mother wrought
Is grievous to my inmost thought,
I here, my hands together laid,
Will greet him in the pathless shade.
To Ráma shall my steps be bent,
My King, of men most excellent,
Raghu's illustrious son, whose sway
Might hell, and earth, and heaven obey.'
That righteous speech, whose every word
Bore virtue's stamp, the audience heard;
On Ráma every thought was set,
And with glad tears each eye was wet.
'Then, if the power I still should lack
To bring my noble brother back,
I in the wood will dwell, and share
His banishment with Lakshmaṇ there.
By every art persuasive I
To bring him from the wood will try,
And show him to your loving eyes,
O Brahmans noble, good, and wise.
E'en now, the road to make and clear,
Each labourer pressed, and pioneer
Have I sent forward to precede
The army I resolve to lead.'
Thus, by fraternal love possessed,
His firm resolve the prince expressed.
Then to Sumantra, deeply read
In holy texts, he turned and said:
'Sumantra, rise without delay,
And as I bid my words obey.
Give orders for the march with speed,
And all the army hither lead.'
The wise Sumantra, thus addressed,
Obeyed the high-souled chief's behest.
He hurried forth with joy inspired
And gave the orders he desired.
Delight each soldier's bosom filled,
And through each chief and captain thrilled,

[1] Not Bharat's uncle, but some councillor.

[2] *Śatakratu*, Lord of a hundred sacrifices, the performance of a hundred *Aśvamedhas* or sacrifices of a horse entitling the sacrificer to this exalted dignity.

[3] The modern Malabar.

To hear that march proclaimed, to bring
Dear Ráma back from wandering.
From house to house the tidings flew:
Each soldier's wife the order knew,
And as she listened blithe and gay
Her husband urged to speed away.
Captain and soldier soon declared
The host equipped and all prepared
With chariots matching thought for speed,
And wagons drawn by ox and steed.
When Bharat by Vaśishṭha's side,
His ready host of warriors eyed,
Thus in Sumantra's ear he spoke:
'My car and horses quickly yoke.'
Sumantra hastened to fulfil
With ready joy his master's will,
And quickly with the chariot sped
Drawn by fleet horses nobly bred.
Then glorious Bharat, true, devout,
Whose genuine valour none could doubt,
Gave in fit words his order out;
For he would seek the shade
Of the great distant wood, and there
Win his dear brother with his prayer:
'Sumantra, haste! my will declare
The host be all arrayed.
I to the wood my way will take,
To Ráma supplication make,
And for the world's advantage sake,
Will lead him home again.'
Then, ordered thus, the charioteer
Who listened with delighted ear,
Went forth and gave his orders clear
To captains of the train.
He gave the popular chiefs the word,
And with the news his friends he stirred,
And not a single man deferred
Preparing for the road.
Then Bráhman, Warrior, Merchant, thrall,
Obedient to Sumantra's call,
Each in his house arose, and all
Yoked elephant or camel tall,
Or ass or noble steed in stall,
And full appointed showed.

CANTO LXXXIII.

THE JOURNEY BEGUN.

Then Bharat rose at early morn,
And in his noble chariot borne
Drove forward at a rapid pace
Eager to look on Ráma's face.
The priests and lords, a fair array,
In sun-bright chariots led the way.
Behind, a well appointed throng,
Nine thousand elephants streamed along.
Then sixty thousand cars, and then,
With various arms, came fighting men.
A hundred thousand archers showed
In lengthened line the steeds they rode—
A mighty host, the march to grace
Of Bharat, pride of Raghu's race.
Kaikeyí and Śumitrá came,
And good Kauśalyá, dear to fame:
By hopes of Ráma's coming cheered
They in a radiant car appeared.
On fared the noble host to see
Ráma and Lakshmaṇ, wild with glee,
And still each other's ear to please,
Of Ráma spoke in words like these:
'When shall our happy eyes behold
Our hero true, and pure, and bold,
So lustrous dark, so strong of arm,
Who keeps the world from woe and harm?
The tears that now our eyeballs dim
Will vanish at the sight of him,
As the whole world's black shadows fly
When the bright sun ascends the sky.'
Conversing thus their way pursued
The city's joyous multitude,
And each in mutual rapture pressed
A friend or neighbour to his breast.
Thus every man of high renown,
And every merchant of the town,
And leading subjects, joyous went
Toward Ráma in his banishment.
And those who worked the potter's wheel,
And artists skilled in gems to deal;
And masters of the weaver's art,
And those who shaped the sword and dart;
And they who golden trinkets made,
And those who plied the fuller's trade;
And servants trained the bath to heat,
And they who dealt in incense sweet;
Physicians in their business skilled,
And those who wine and mead distilled;
And workmen deft in glass who wrought,
And those whose snares the peacock caught;
With them who bored the ear for rings,
Or sawed, or fashioned ivory things:
And those who knew to mix cement,
Or lived by sale of precious scent;
And men who washed, and men who sewed,
And thralls who mid the herds abode;
And fishers of the flood, and they
Who played and sang, and women gay;
And virtuous Bráhmans, Scripture-wise,
Of life approved in all men's eyes;
These swelled the prince's lengthened train,
Borne each in car or bullock wain.
Fair were the robes they wore upon
Their limbs where red-hued unguents shone.
These all in various modes conveyed
Their journey after Bharat made;
The soldiers' hearts with rapture glowed,
Following Bharat on his road
Their chief whose tender love would fain
Bring his dear brother home again.
With elephant, and horse, and car,
The vast procession travelled far,

And came where Gangá's waves below
The town of Śringavera[1] flow.
There, with his friends and kinsmen nigh,
Dwelt Guha, Ráma's dear ally,
Heroic guardian of the land
With dauntless heart and ready hand.
There for a while the mighty force
That followed Bharat stayed its course,
Gazing on Gangá's bosom stirred
By many a graceful water-bird.
When Bharat viewed his followers there,
And Gangá's water, blest and fair,
The prince, who lore of words possessed,
His councillors and lords addressed:
'The captains of the army call:
Proclaim this day a halt for all,
That so to-morrow, rested, we
May cross this flood that seeks the sea.
Meanwhile, descending to the shore,
The funeral stream I fain would pour
From Gangá's fair auspicious tide
To him, my father glorified.'
Thus Bharat spoke: each peer and lord
Approved his words with one accord,
And bade the weary troops repose
In separate spots where'er they chose.
There by the mighty stream that day,
Most glorious in its vast array
The prince's wearied army lay
In various groups reclined.
There Bharat's hours of night were spent,
While every eager thought he bent
On bringing home from banishment
His brother, great of mind.

CANTO LXXXIV.

GUHA'S ANGER.

King Guha saw the host spread o'er
The wide expanse of Gangá's shore,
With waving flag and pennon graced,
And to his followers spoke in haste:
'A mighty army meets my eyes,
That rivals Ocean's self in size:
Where'er I look my very mind
No limit to the host can find.
Sure Bharat with some evil thought
His army to our land has brought.
See, huge of form, his flag he rears,
That like an Ebony-tree appears.
He comes with bonds to take and chain,
Or triumph o'er our people slain:
And after, Ráma will he slay,—
Him whom his father drove away:
The power complete he longs to gain,
And—task too hard—usurp the reign.
So Bharat comes with wicked will
His brother Ráma's blood to spill.
But Ráma's slave and friend am I;
He is my lord and dear ally.
Keep here your watch in arms arrayed
Near Gangá's flood to lend him aid.
And let my gathered servants stand
And line with troops the river strand.
Here let the river keepers meet,
Who flesh and roots and berries eat;
A hundred fishers man each boat
Of the five hundred here afloat,
And let the youthful and the strong
Assemble in defensive throng.
But yet, if, free from guilty thought
'Gainst Ráma, he this land have sought,
The prince's happy host to day
Across the flood shall make its way.'
He spoke: then bearing in a dish
A gift of honey, meat, and fish,
The king of the Nishádas drew
Toward Bharat for an interview.
When Bharat's noble charioteer
Observed the monarch hastening near,
He duly, skilled in courteous lore,
The tidings to his master bore:
'This aged prince who hither bends
His footsteps with a thousand friends,
Knows, firm ally of Ráma, all
That may in Dandak wood befall:
Therefore, Kakutstha's son, admit
The monarch, as is right and fit:
For doubtless he can clearly tell
Where Ráma now and Lakshman dwell.'
When Bharat heard Sumantra's rede,
To his fair words the prince agreed:
'Go quickly forth,' he cried, 'and bring
Before my face the aged king.'
King Guha, with his kinsmen near,
Rejoiced the summoning to hear:
He nearer drew, bowed low his head,
And thus to royal Bharat said:
'No mansions can our country boast,
And unexpected comes thy host:
But what we have I give thee all:
Rest in the lodging of thy thrall.
See, the Nishádas here have brought
The fruit and roots their hands have sought:
And we have woodland fare beside,
And store of meat both fresh and dried.
To rest their weary limbs, I pray
This night at least thy host may stay:
Then cheered with all we can bestow
To-morrow thou with it mayst go.'

CANTO LXXXV.

GUHA AND BHARAT.

Thus the Nishádas' king besought:
The prince with spirit wisdom-fraught

[1] Now Sungroor, in the Allahabad district.

Replied in seemly words that blent
Deep matter with the argument:
'Thou, friend of him whom I revere,
With honours high hast met me here,
For thou alone wouldst entertain
And feed to-day so vast a train.'
In such fair words the prince replied,
Then, pointing to the path he cried:
'Which way aright will lead my feet
To Bharadvája's calm retreat;
For all this land near Gangá's streams
Pathless and hard to traverse seems?'
Thus spoke the prince: King Guha heard
Delighted every prudent word,
And gazing on that forest wide,
Raised suppliant hands, and thus replied:
'My servants, all the ground who know,
O glorious Prince, with thee shall go
With constant care thy way to guide,
And I will journey by thy side.
But this thy host so wide dispread
Wakes in my heart one doubt and dread,
Lest, threatening Ráma good and great,
Ill thoughts thy journey stimulate.'
But when King Guha, ill at ease,
Declared his fear in words like these,
As pure as is the cloudless sky
With soft voice Bharat made reply:
'Suspect me not: ne'er come the time
For me to plot so foul a crime!
He is my eldest brother, he
Is like a father dear to me.
I go to lead my brother thence
Who makes the wood his residence.
No thought but this thy heart should frame:
This simple truth my lips proclaim.'
Then with glad cheer King Guha cried,
With Bharat's answer gratified:
'Blessed art thou: on earth I see
None who may vie, O Prince, with thee,
Who canst of thy free will resign
The kingdom which unsought is thine.
For this, a name that ne'er shall die,
Thy glory through the worlds shall fly,
Who fain wouldst balm thy brother's pain
And lead the exile home again.'
As Guha thus, and Bharat, each
To other spoke in friendly speech,
The Day-God sank with glory dead,
And night o'er all the sky was spread.
Soon as King Guha's thoughtful care
Had quartered all the army there,
Well honoured, Bharat laid his head
Beside Śatrughna on a bed.
But grief for Ráma yet oppressed
High-minded Bharat's faithful breast—
Such torment little was deserved
By him who ne'er from duty swerved.
The fever raged through every vein
And burnt him with its inward pain:
So when in woods the flames leap free
The fire within consumes the tree.
From heat of burning anguish sprung
The sweat upon his body hung,
As when the sun with fervid glow
On high Himálaya melts the snow.
As, banished from the herd, a bull
Wanders alone and sorrowful,
Thus sighing and distressed,
In misery and bitter grief,
With fevered heart that mocked relief,
Distracted in his mind, the chief
Still mourned and found no rest.

CANTO LXXXVI.

GUHA'S SPEECH.

Guha the king, acquainted well
With all that in the wood befell,
To Bharat the unequalled told
The tale of Lakshman mighty-souled:
'With many an earnest word I spake
To Lakshman as he stayed awake,
And with his bow and shaft in hand
To guard his brother kept his stand:
'Now sleep a little, Lakshman, see
This pleasant bed is strewn for thee:
Hereon thy weary body lay,
And strengthen thee with rest, I pray,
Inured to toil are men like these,
But thou hast aye been nursed in ease.
Rest, duteous-minded! I will keep
My watch while Ráma lies asleep:
For in the whole wide world is none
Dearer to me than Raghu's son.
Harbour no doubt or jealous fear:
I speak the truth with heart sincere:
For from the grace which he has shown
Will glory on my name be thrown:
Great store of merit shall I gain,
And duteous, form no wish in vain.
Let me enforced by many a row
Of followers, armed with shaft and bow
For well-loved Ráma's weal provide
Who lies asleep by Sítá's side.
For through this wood I often go,
And all its shades conceal I know:
And we with conquering arms can meet
A four-fold host arrayed complete.'
'With words like these I spoke, designed
To move the high-souled Bharat's mind,
But he upon his duty bent,
Plied his persuasive argument:
'O, how can slumber close mine eyes
When lowly couched with Sítá lies
The royal Ráma? can I give
My heart to joy, or even live?
He whom no mighty demon, no,
Nor heavenly God can overthrow,
See, Guha, how he lies, alas,

With Sítá couched on gathered grass.
By varied labours, long, severe,
By many a prayer and rite austere,
He, Daśaratha's cherished son,
By Fortune stamped, from Heaven was won.
Now as his son is forced to fly,
The king ere long will surely die:
Reft of his guardian hand, forlorn
In widowed grief this land will mourn.
E'en now perhaps, with toil o'erspent,
The women cease their loud lament,
And cries of woe no longer ring
Throughout the palace of the king.
But ah for sad Kauśalyá! how
Fare she and mine own mother now?
How fares the king? this night, I think,
Some of the three in death will sink.
With hopes upon Śatrughna set
My mother may survive as yet,
But the sad queen will die who bore
The hero, for her grief is sore.
His cherished wish that would have made
Dear Ráma king, so long delayed,
'Too late! too late!' the king will cry,
And conquered by his misery die.
When Fate has brought the mournful day
Which sees my father pass away,
How happy in their lives are they
Allowed his funeral rites to pay.
Our excile o'er, with him who ne'er
Turns from the oath his lips may swear,
May we returning safe and well
Again in fair Ayodhyá dwell.'
Thus Bharat stood with many a sigh
Lamenting, and the night went by.
Soon as the morning light shone fair
In votive coils both bound their hair.
And then I sent them safely o'er
And left them on the farther shore.
With Sítá then they onward passed,
Their coats of bark about them cast,
Their locks like hermits' bound,
The mighty tamers of the foe,
Each with his arrows and his bow,
Went over the rugged ground,
Proud in their strength and undeterred
Like elephants that lead the herd,
And gazing oft around.

CANTO LXXXVII.

GUHA'S STORY.

That speech of Guha Bharat heard
With grief and tender pity stirred,
And as his ears the story drank,
Deep in his thoughtful heart it sank.
His large full eyes in anguish rolled,
His trembling limbs grew stiff and cold;
Then fell he, like a tree uptorn,
In woe too grievous to be borne.
When Guha saw the long-armed chief
Whose eye was like a lotus leaf,
With lion shoulders strong and fair,
High-mettled, prostrate in despair,—
Pale, bitterly afflicted, he
Reeled as in earthquake reels a tree.
But when Śatrughna standing nigh
Saw his dear brother helpless lie,
Distraught with woe his head he bowed,
Embraced him oft and wept aloud.
Then Bharat's mothers came, forlorn
Of their dear king, with fasting worn,
And stood with weeping eyes around
The hero prostrate on the ground.
Kauśalyá, by her woe oppressed,
The senseless Bharat's limbs caressed,
As a fond cow in love and fear
Caresses oft her youngling dear:
Then yielding to her woe she said,
Weeping and sore disquieted:
'What torments, O my son, are these
Of sudden pain or swift disease?
The lives of us and all the line
Depend, dear child, on only thine.
Ráma and Lakshman forced to flee,
I live by naught but seeing thee:
For as the king has past away
Thou art my only help to-day.
Hast thou, perchance, heard evil news
Of Lakshman, which thy soul subdues,
Or Ráma dwelling with his spouse—
My all is he—neath forest boughs?'
Then slowly gathering sense and strength
The weeping hero rose at length,
And words like these to Guha spake,
That bade Kauśalyá comfort take:
'Where lodged the prince that night? and where
Lakshman the brave, and Sítá fair?
Show me the couch whereon he lay,
Tell me the food he ate, I pray.'
Then Guha the Nishádas' king
Replied to Bharat's questioning:
'Of all I had I brought the best
To serve my good and honoured guest
Food of each varied kind I chose,
And every fairest fruit that grows.
Ráma the hero truly brave
Declined the gift I humbly gave:
His Warrior part he ne'er forgot,
And what I brought accepted not:
'No gifts, my friend, may we accept:
Our law is, Give, and must be kept.'
'The high-souled chief, O Monarch, thus
With gracious words persuaded us.
Then calm and still, absorbed in thought,
He drank the water Lakshman brought,
And then, obedient to his vows,
He fasted with his gentle spouse.
So Lakshman too from food abstained,

And sipped the water that remained :
Then with ruled lips, devoutly staid,
The three[1] their evening worship paid.
Then Lakshman with unwearied care
Brought heaps of sacred grass, and there
With his own hands he quickly spread,
For Ráma's rest, a pleasant bed,
And faithful Sítá's too, where they
Reclining each by other lay.
Then Lakshman bathed their feet, and drew
A little distance from the two.
Here stands the tree which lent them shade,
Here is the grass beneath it laid,
Where Ráma and his consort spent
The night together ere they went.
Lakshman, whose arms the foeman quell,
Watched all the night as sentinel,
And kept his great bow strung :
His hand was gloved, his arm was braced,
Two well-filled quivers at his waist,
With deadly arrows, hung.
I took my shafts and trusty bow,
And with that tamer of the foe
Stood ever wakeful near,
And with my followers, bow in hand,
Behind me ranged, a ready band,
Kept watch o'er Indra's peer.'

CANTO LXXXVIII.

THE INGUDI TREE.

When Bharat with each friend and peer
Had heard that tale so full and clear,
They went together to the tree
The bed which Ráma pressed to see.
Then Bharat to his mothers said :
'Behold the high-souled hero's bed :
These tumbled heaps of grass betray
Where he that night with Sítá lay :
Unmeet, the heir of fortune high
Thus on the cold bare earth should lie,
The monarch's son, in counsel sage,
Of old imperial lineage.
That lion-lord whose noble bed
With finest skins of deer was spread,—
How can he now endure to press
The bare earth, cold and comfortless !
This sudden fall from bliss to grief
Appears untrue, beyond belief :
My senses are distraught : I seem
To view the fancies of a dream.
There is no deity so great,
No power in heaven can master Fate,
If Ráma, Daśaratha's heir,
Lay on the ground and slumbered there ;
And lovely Sítá, she who springs
From fair Videha's ancient kings,
Ráma's dear wife, by all adored,
Lay on the earth beside her lord.
Here was his couch, upon this heap
He tossed and turned in restless sleep :
On the hard soil each manly limb
Has stamped the grass with signs of him.
That night, it seems, fair Sítá spent
Arrayed in every ornament,
For here and there my eyes behold
Small particles of glistering gold.
She laid her outer garment here,
For still some silken threads appear.
How dear in her devoted eyes
Must be the bed where Ráma lies,
Where she so tender could repose
And by his side forget her woes.
Alas, unhappy, guilty me !
For whom the prince was forced to flee,
And chief of Raghu's sons and best,
A bed like this with Sítá pressed.
Son of a royal sire whose hand
Ruled paramount o'er every land,
Could he who every joy bestows,
Whose body like the lotus shows,
The friend of all, who charms the sight,
Whose flashing eyes are darkly bright,
Leave the dear kingdom, his by right,
Unmeet for woe, the heir of bliss,
And lie upon a bed like this ?
Great joy and happy fate are thine,
O Lakshman, marked with each fair sign,
Whose faithful footsteps follow still
Thy brother in his hour of ill.
And blest is Sítá, nobly good,
Who dwells with Ráma in the wood.
Ours is, alas, a doubtful fate
Of Ráma reft and desolate.
My royal sire has gained the skies,
In woods the high-souled hero lies ;
The state is wrecked and tempest-tossed,
A vessel with her rudder lost.
Yet none in secret thought has planned
With hostile might to seize the land :
Though forced in distant wilds to dwell,
The hero's arm protects it well.
Unguarded, with deserted wall,
No elephant or steed in stall,
My father's royal city shows
Her portals open to her foes,
Of bold protectors reft and bare,
Defenceless in her dark despair :
But still her foes the wish restrain,
As men from poisoned cates refrain.
I from this hour my nights will pass
Couched on the earth or gathered grass,
Eat only fruit and roots, and wear
A coat of bark, and matted hair.
I in the woods will pass, content,
For him the term of banishment ;
So shall I still unbroken save
The promise which the hero gave.

[1] Ráma, Lakshman, and Sumantra.

While I remain for Ráma there,
Śatrughna will my exile share,
And Ráma in his home again,
With Lakshman, o'er Ayodhyá reign,
For him, to rule and guard the state,
The twice-born men shall consecrate.
O, may the Gods I serve incline
To grant this earnest wish of mine!
If when I bow before his feet
And with all moving arts entreat,
He still deny my prayer,
Then with my brother will I live:
He must, he must permission give,
Roaming in forests there.'

CANTO LXXXIX.

THE PASSAGE OF GANGÁ.

That night the son of Raghu lay
On Gangá's bank till break of day:
Then with the earliest light he woke
And thus to brave Śatrughna spoke:
'Rise up, Śatrughna, from thy bed:
Why sleepest thou? the night is fled.
See how the sun who chases night
Wakes every lotus with his light.
Arise, arise, and first of all
The lord of Śringavera call,
For he his friendly aid will lend
Our army o'er the flood to send.'
Thus urged, Śatrughna answered: 'I,
Remembering Ráma, sleepless lie.'
As thus the brothers, each to each,
The lion-mettled, ended speech,
Came Guha, the Nishádas' king,
And spoke with kindly questioning:
'Hast thou in comfort passed,' he cried,
'The night upon the river side?
With thee how fares it? and are these,
Thy soldiers, healthy and at ease?'
Thus the Nishádas' lord inquired
In gentle words which love inspired,
And Bharat, Ráma's faithful slave,
Thus to the king his answer gave:
'The night has sweetly passed, and we
Are highly honoured, King, by thee.
Now let thy servants boats prepare,
Our army o'er the stream to bear.'
The speech of Bharat Guha heard,
And swift to do his bidding stirred.
Within the town the monarch sped
And to his ready kinsmen said:
'Awake, each kinsman, rise, each friend!
May every joy your lives attend.
Gather each boat upon the shore
And ferry all the army o'er.'
Thus Guha spoke: nor they delayed,
But, rising quick, their lord obeyed,
And soon, from every side secured,
Five hundred boats were ready moored.
Some reared aloft the mystic sign,[1]
And mighty bells were hung in line:
Of firmest build, gay flags they bore,
And sailors for the helm and oar.
One such King Guha chose, whereon,
Of fair white cloth, an awning shone,
And sweet musicians charmed the ear,—
And bade his servants urge it near.
Then Bharat swiftly sprang on board,
And then Śatrughna, famous lord,
To whom, with many a royal dame,
Kauśalyá and Sumitrá came.
The household priest went first in place,
The elders, and the Bráhman race,
And after them the monarch's train
Of women borne in many a wain.
Then high to heaven the shouts of those
Who fired the army's huts,[2] arose,
With theirs who bathed along the shore,
Or to the boats the baggage bore.
Full freighted with that mighty force
The boats sped swiftly on their course,
By royal Guha's servants manned,
And gentle gales the banners fanned.
Some boats a crowd of dames conveyed,
In others noble coursers neighed;
Some chariots and their cattle bore,
Some precious wealth and golden store.
Across the stream each boat was rowed,
There duly disembarked its load,
And then returning on its way,
Sped here and there in merry play.
Then swimming elephants appeared
With flying pennons high upreared,
And as the drivers urged them o'er,
The look of winged mountains wore.
Some men in barges reached the strand,
Others on rafts came safe to land:
Some buoyed with pitchers crossed the tide,
And others on their arms relied.
Thus with the help the monarch gave
The army crossed pure Gangá's wave:
Then in auspicious hour it stood
Within Prayága's famous wood.
The prince with cheering words addressed
His weary men, and bade them rest
Where'er they chose: and he,
With priest and deacon by his side,
To Bharadvája's dwelling hied
That best of saints to see.

---

[1] The *svastika*, a little cross with a transverse line at each extremity.

[2] When an army marched it was customary to burn the huts in which it had spent the night.

CANTO XC.

THE HERMITAGE.

The prince of men a league away
Saw where the hermit's dwelling lay.
Then with his lords his path pursued,
And left his warrior multitude.
On foot, as duty taught his mind,
He left his warlike gear behind :
Two robes of linen cloth he wore,
And bade Vaśishṭha walk before.
Then Bharat from his lords withdrew
When Bharadvája came in view,
And toward the holy hermit went
Behind Vaśishṭha, reverent.
When Bharadvája, saint austere,
Saw good Vaśishṭha drawing near,
He cried, upspringing from his seat,
'The grace-gift bring, my friend to greet.'
When Saint Vaśishṭha near him drew,
And Bharat paid the reverence due,
The glorious hermit was aware
That Daśaratha's son was there.
The grace-gift, water for their feet
He gave, and offered fruit to eat ;
Then, duty-skilled, with friendly speech
In seemly order questioned each :
'How fares it in Ayodhyá now
With treasury and army ? how
With kith and kin and friends most dear,
With councillor, and prince, and peer ?
But, for he knew the king was dead,
Of Daśaratha naught he said.
Vaśishṭha and the prince in turn
Would of the hermit's welfare learn :
Of holy fires they fain would hear,
Of pupils, trees, and birds, and deer.
The glorious saint his answer made
That all was well in holy shade :
Then love of Ráma moved his breast,
And thus he questioned of his guest :
Why art thou here, O Prince, whose hand
With kingly sway protects the land ?
Declare the cause, explain the whole,
For yet some doubt disturbs my soul.
He whom Kauśalyá bare, whose might
The foemen slays, his line's delight,
He who with wife and brother sent
Afar now roams in banishment,
Famed prince, to whom his father spake
This order for a woman's sake :
'Away ! and in the forest spend
Thy life till fourteen years shall end'—
Hast thou the wish to harm him, bent
On sin against the innocent ?
Wouldst thou thine elder's realm enjoy
Without a thorn that can annoy ?'
'With sobbing voice and tearful eye
Thus Bharat sadly made reply :
'Ah lost am I, if thou, O Saint,
Canst thus in thought my heart attaint :
No warning charge from thee I need ;
Ne'er could such crime from me proceed.
The words my guilty mother spake
When fondly jealous for my sake—
Think not that I, to triumph moved,
Those words approve or e'er approved.
O Hermit, I have sought this place
To win the lordly hero's grace,
To throw me at my brother's feet
And lead him to his royal seat.
To this, my journey's aim and end,
Thou shouldst, O Saint, thy favour lend :
Where is the lord of earth ? do thou,
Most holy, say, where roams he now ?
Then, by the saint Vaśishṭha pressed,
And all the gathered priests beside,
To Bharat's dutiful request
The hermit graciously replied :
'Worthy of thee, O Prince, this deed,
True son of Raghu's ancient seed.
I know thee reverent, well-controlled,
The glory of the good of old.
I grant thy prayer : in this pursuit
I know thy heart is resolute.
'Tis for thy sake those words I said
That wider still thy fame may spread.
I know where Ráma, duty-tried,
His brother, and his wife abide.
Where Chitrakúṭa's heights arise
Thy brother Ráma's dwelling lies.
Go thither with the morning's light,
And stay with all thy lords to-night :
For I would show thee honour high,
And do not thou my wish deny.'

CANTO XCI.

BHARADVÁJA'S FEAST.

Soon as he saw the prince's mind
To rest that day was well inclined,
He sought Kaikeyí's son to please
With hospitable courtesies.
Then Bharat to the saint replied :
'Our wants are more than satisfied.
The gifts which honoured strangers greet,
And water for our weary feet
Hast thou bestowed with friendly care,
And every choice of woodland fare.'
Then Bharadvája spoke, a smile
Playing upon his lips the while :
'I know, dear Prince, thy friendly mind
Will any fare sufficient find,
But gladly would I entertain
And banquet all thine armed train :
Such is my earnest wish : do thou
This longing of my heart allow.
Why hast thou hither bent thy way,
And made thy troops behind thee stay ?

Why unattended? couldst thou not
With friends and army seek this spot?'
Bharat, with reverent hands raised high,
To that great hermit made reply:
'My troops, for awe of thee, O Sage,
I brought not to thy hermitage:
Troops of a king or monarch's son
A hermit's home should ever shun.
Behind me comes a mighty train
Wide spreading o'er the ample plain,
Where every chief and captain leads
Men, elephants, and mettled steeds
I feared, O reverend Sage, lest these
Might harm the holy ground and trees,
Springs might be marred and cots o'erthrown,
So with the priests I came alone.'
'Bring all thy host,' the hermit cried,
And Bharat, to his joy, complied.
Then to the chapel went the sire,
Where ever burnt the sacred fire,
And first, in order due, with sips
Of water purified his lips:
To Viśvakarmá then he prayed,
His hospitable feast to aid:
'Let Viśvakarmá hear my call,
The God who forms and fashions all:
A mighty banquet I provide,
Be all my wants this day supplied.
Lord Indra at their head, the three[1]
Who guard the worlds I call to me:
A mighty host this day I feed,
Be now supplied my every need.
Let all the streams that eastward go,
And those whose waters westering flow,
Both on the earth and in the sky,
Flow hither and my wants supply.
Be some with ardent liquor filled,
And some with wine from flowers distilled,
While some their fresh cool streams retain
Sweet as the juice of sugar-cane.
I call the Gods, I call the band
Of minstrels that around them stand:
I call the Háhá and Huhú,
I call the sweet Viśváyasu.
I call the heavenly wives of these
With all the bright Apsarases,
Alambushá of beauty rare,
The charmer of the tangled hair,
Ghritáchí and Viśváchí fair,
Hemá and Bhímá sweet to view,
And lovely Nágadantá too,
And all the sweetest nymphs who stand
By Indra or by Brahmá's hand—
I summon these with all their train
And Tumburu to lead the strain.
Here let Kuvera's garden rise
Which far in Northern Kuru[2] lies:
For leaves let cloth and gems entwine,
And let its fruit be nymphs divine.
Let Soma[1] give the noblest food
To feed the mighty multitude,
Of every kind, for tooth and lip,
To chew, to lick, to suck, and sip.
Let wreaths, where fairest flowers abound,
Spring from the trees that bloom around.
Each sort of wine to woo the taste,
And meats of every kind be placed.'
Thus spake the hermit self-restrained,
With proper tone by rules ordained,
On deepest meditation bent,
In holy might preëminent.
Then as with hands in reverence raised
Absorbed in thought he eastward gazed,
The deities he thus addressed
Came each in semblance manifest.
Delicious gales that cooled the frame
From Malaya and Dardar came,
That kissed those scented hills and threw
Auspicious fragrance where they blew.
Then falling fast in sweetest showers
Came from the sky immortal flowers,
And all the airy region round
With heavenly drums was made to sound.
Then breathed a soft celestial breeze,
Then danced the bright Apsarases,
The minstrels and the Gods advanced,
And warbling lutes the soul entranced.
The earth and sky that music filled,
And through each ear it softly thrilled,
As from the heavenly quills it fell
With time and tune attempered well.
Soon as the minstrels ceased to play
And airs celestial died away,
The troops of Bharat saw amazed
What Viśvakarmá's art had raised.
On every side, five leagues around,
All smooth and level lay the ground,
With fresh green grass that charmed the sight
Like sapphires blent with lazulite.
There the Wood-apple hung its load,
The Mango and the Citron glowed
The Bel and scented Jak were there,
And Aonlá with fruitage fair.
There, brought from Northern Kuru, stood
Rich in delights, the glorious wood,
And many a stream was seen to glide

[1] Yama, Varuṇa and Kuvera.

[2] A happy land in the remote north where 'the inhabitants enjoy a natural perfection attended with complete happiness obtained without exertion. There is there no vicissitude, nor decrepitude, nor death, nor fear: no distinction of virtue and vice, none of the inequalities denoted by the words best, worst, and intermediate, nor any change resulting from the succession of the four Yugas.' See MUIR'S *Sanskrit Texts*, Vol I. p. 492.

[1] The Moon.

With flowering trees along its side.
There mansions rose with four wide halls,
And elephants and chargers' stalls,
And many a house of royal state,
Triumphal arc and bannered gate.
With noble doorways, sought the sky,
Like a pale cloud, a palace high,
Which far and wide rare fragrance shed,
With wreaths of white engarlanded.
Square was its shape, its halls were wide,
With many a seat and couch supplied,
Drink of all kinds, and every meat
Such as celestial Gods might eat.
Then at the bidding of the seer
Kaikeyí's strong-armed son drew near,
And passed within that fair abode
Which with the noblest jewels glowed.
Then, as Vaśishṭha led the way,
The councillors, in due array,
Followed delighted and amazed
And on the glorious structure gazed.
Then Bharat, Raghu's son, drew near
The kingly throne, with prince and peer,
Whereby the chouri in the shade
Of ths white canopy was laid.
Before the throne he humbly bent
And honoured Ráma, reverent,
Then in his hand the chouri bore,
And sat where sits a councillor.
His ministers and household priest
Sat by degrees from chief to least,
Then sat the captain of the host
And all the men he honoured most.
Then when the saint his order gave,
Each river with enchanted wave
Rolled milk and curds divinely sweet
Before the princely Bharat's feet;
And dwellings fair on either side,
With gay white plaster beautified,
Their heavenly roofs were seen to lift,
The Bráhman Bharadvája's gift,
Then straight by Lord Kuvera sent,
Gay with celestial ornament
Of bright attire and jewels' shine,
Came twenty thousand nymphs divine:
The man on whom those beauties glanced
That moment felt his soul entranced.
With them from Nandan's blissful shades
Came twenty thousand heavenly maids.
Tumburu, Nárad, Gopa came,
And Sutanu, like radiant flame,
The kings of the Gandharva throng,
And ravished Bharat with their song.
Then spoke the saint, and swift obeyed
Alambushá, the fairest maid,
And Miśrakeśí bright to view,
Ramaṇá, Puṇḍaríká too,
And danced to him with graceful ease
The dances of Apsarases.
All chaplets that by Gods are worn,
Or Chaitraratha's groves adorn,
Bloomed by the saint's command arrayed
On branches in Prayága's shade.
When at the saint's command the breeze
Made music with the Vilva trees,
To wave in rhythmic beat began
The boughs of each Myrobolan,
And holy fig-trees wore the look
Of dancers, as their leaflets shook.
The fair Tamála, palm, and pine,
With trees that tower and plants that twine,
The sweetly varying forms displayed
Of stately dame or bending maid.
Here men the foaming winecup quaffed,
Here drank of milk full many a draught,
And tasted meats of every kind,
Well dressed, whatever pleased their mind.
Then beauteous women, seven or eight,
Stood ready by each man to wait:
Beside the stream his limbs they stripped
And in the cooling water dipped.
And then the fair ones, sparkling eyed,
With soft hands rubbed his limbs and dried,
And sitting on the lovely bank
Held up the winecup as he drank.
Nor did the grooms forget to feed
Camel and mule and ox and steed,
For there were stores of roasted grain,
Of honey and of sugar-cane.
So fast the wild excitement spread
Among the warriors Bharat led,
That all the mighty army through
The groom no more his charger knew,
And he who drove might seek in vain
To tell his elephant again.
With every joy and rapture fired,
Entranced with all the heart desired,
The myriads of the host that night
Revelled delirious with delight.
Urged by the damsels at their side
In wild delight the warriors cried:
'Ne'er will we seek Ayodhyá, no,
Nor yet to Daṇḍak forest go:
Here will we stay: may happy fate
On Bharat and on Ráma wait.'
Thus cried the army gay and free
Exulting in their lawless glee,
Both infantry and those who rode
On elephants, or steeds bestrode,
Ten thousand voices shouting, 'This
Is heaven indeed for perfect bliss.'
With garlands decked they idly strayed,
And danced and laughed and sang and played.
At length as every soldier eyed,
With food like Amrit satisfied,
Each dainty cate and tempting meat,
No longer had he care to eat.
Thus soldier, servant, dame, and slave
Received whate'er the wish might crave,
As each in new-wrought clothes arrayed
Enjoyed the feast before him laid.

Each man was seen in white attire
Unstained by spot or speck of mire:
None was athirst or hungry there,
And none had dust upon his hair.
On every side in woody dells
Was milky food in bubbling wells,
And there were all-supplying cows
And honey dropping from the boughs.
Nor wanted lakes of flower-made drink
With piles of meat upon the brink,
Boiled, stewed, and roasted, varied cheer,
Peachick and jungle-fowl and deer,
There was the flesh of kid and boar,
And dainty sauce in endless store,
With juice of flowers concocted well,
And soup that charmed the taste and smell,
And pounded fruits of bitter taste,
And many a bath was ready placed.
Down by each river's shelving side
There stood great basins well supplied,
And laid therein, of dazzling sheen,
White brushes for the teeth were seen,
And many a covered box wherein
Was sandal powdered for the skin.
And mirrors bright with constant care,
And piles of new attire were there,
And store of sandals and of shoes,
Thousands of pairs, for all to choose:
Eye-unguents, combs for hair and beard,
Umbrellas fair and bows appeared.
Lakes gleamed, that lent digestive aid,[1]
And some for pleasant bathing made,
With waters fair, and smooth incline
For camels, horses, mules, and kine.
There saw they barley heaped on high
The countless cattle to supply:
The golden grain shone fair and bright
As sapphires or the lazulite.
To all the gathered host it seemed
As if that magic scene they dreamed,
And wonder, as they gazed, increased
At Bharadvája's glorious feast.
  Thus in the hermit's grove they spent
That night in joy and merriment,
Blest as the Gods who take their ease
Under the shade of Nandan's trees.
Each minstrel bade the saint adieu,
And to his blissful mansion flew,
And every stream and heavenly dame
Returned as swiftly as she came.

CANTO XCII.

BHARAT'S FAREWELL.

So Bharat with his army spent
The watches of the night content,
And gladly, with the morning's light
Drew near his host the anchorite.
When Bharadvája saw him stand
With hand in reverence joined to hand,
When fires of worship had been fed,
He looked upon the prince and said:
'O blameless son, I pray thee tell,
Did the past night content thee well?
Say if the feast my care supplied
Thy host of followers gratified.'
  His hands he joined, his head he bent
And spoke in answer reverent
To the most high and radiant sage
Who issued from his hermitage:
'Well have I passed the night: thy feast
Gave joy to every man and beast;
And I, great lord, and every peer
Were satisfied with sumptuous cheer,
Thy banquet has delighted all
From highest chief to meanest thrall,
And rich attire and drink and meat
Banished the thought of toil and heat.
And now, O Hermit good and great,
A boon of thee I supplicate.
To Ráma's side my steps I bend:
Do thou with friendly eye commend.
O tell me how to guide my feet
To virtuous Ráma's lone retreat:
Great Hermit, I entreat thee, say
How far from here and which the way.'
  Thus by fraternal love inspired
The chieftain of the saint inquired:
Then thus replied the glorious seer
Of matchless might, of vows austere:
'Ere the fourth league from here be passed,
Amid a forest wild and vast,
Stands Chitrakúṭa's mountain tall,
Lovely with wood and waterfall.
North of the mountain thou wilt see
The beauteous stream Mandákiní,
Where swarm the waterfowl below,
And gay trees on the margin grow.
Then will a leafy cot between
The river and the hill be seen:
'Tis Ráma's, and the princely pair
Of brothers live for certain there.
Hence to the south thine army lead,
And then more southward still proceed,
So shalt thou find his lone retreat,
And there the son of Raghu meet.'
  Soon as the ordered march they knew,
The widows of the monarch flew,
Leaving their cars, most meet to ride,
And flocked to Bharadvája's side.
There with the good Sumitrá Queen
Kauśalyá, sad and worn, was seen,
Caressing, still with sorrow faint,
The feet of that illustrious saint,
Kaikeyí too, her longings crossed,
Reproached of all, her object lost,
Before the famous hermit came,

[1] The poet does not tell us what these lakes contained.

And clasped his feet, o'erwhelmed with shame.
With circling steps she humbly went
Around the saint preëminent,
And stood not far from Bharat's side
With heart oppressed, and heavy-eyed.
Then the great seer, who never broke
One holy vow, to Bharat spoke:
'Speak, Raghu's son: I fain would learn
The story of each queen in turn.'
Obedient to the high request
By Bharadvája thus addressed,
His reverent hands together laid,
He, skilled in speech, his answer made:
'She whom, O Saint, thou seest here
A Goddess in her form appear,
Was the chief consort of the king,
Now worn with fast and sorrowing.
As Aditi in days of yore
The all-preserving Vishṇu bore,
Kauśalyá bore with happy fate
Lord Ráma of the lion's gait.
She who, transfixed with torturing pangs,
On her left arm so fondly hangs,
As when her withering leaves decay
Droops by the wood the Cassia spray,
Sumitrá, pained with woe, is she,
The consort second of the three:
Two princely sons the lady bare,
Fair as the Gods in heaven are fair.
And she, the wicked dame through whom
My brothers' lives are wrapped in gloom,
And mourning for his offspring dear,
The king has sought his heavenly sphere,—
Proud, foolish-hearted, swift to ire,
Self-fancied darling of my sire,
Kaikeyí, most ambitious queen,
Unlovely with her lovely mien,
My mother she, whose impious will
Is ever bent on deeds of ill,
In whom the root and spring I see
Of all this woe which crushes me.'
Quick breathing like a furious snake,
With tears and sobs the hero spake,
With reddened eyes aglow with rage.
And Bharadvája, mighty sage,
Supreme in wisdom, calm and grave,
In words like these good counsel gave:
'O Bharat, hear the words I say;
On her the fault thou must not lay:
For many a blessing yet will spring
From banished Ráma's wandering.'
And Bharat, with that promise cheered,
Went circling round that saint revered,
He humbly bade farewell, and then
Gave orders to collect his men.
Prompt at the summons thousands flew
To cars which noble coursers drew,
Bright-gleaming, glorious to behold,
Adorned with wealth of burnished gold.
Then female elephants and male,
Gold-girthed, with flags that wooed the gale,
Marched with their bright bells' tinkling chime
Like clouds when ends the summer time:
Some cars were huge and some were light,
For heavy draught or rapid flight,
Of costly price, of every kind,
With clouds of infantry behind.
The dames, Kauśalyá at their head,
Were in the noblest chariots led,
And every gentle bosom beat
With hope the banished prince to meet.
The royal Bharat, glory-crowned,
With all his retinue around,
Borne in a beauteous litter rode,
Like the young moon and sun that glowed.
The army as it streamed along,
Cars, elephants, in endless throng,
Showed, marching on its southward way,
Like autumn clouds in long array.

CANTO XCIII.

CHITRAKUṬA IN SIGHT.

As through the woods its way pursued
That mighty bannered multitude,
Wild elephants in terror fled
With all the startled herds they led,
And bears and deer were seen on hill,
In forest glade, by every rill.
Wide as the sea from coast to coast,
The high-souled Bharat's mighty host
Covered the earth as cloudy trains
Obscure the sky when fall the rains.
The stately elephants he led,
And countless steeds the land o'erspread,
So closely crowded that between
Their serried ranks no ground was seen.
Then when the host had travelled far,
And steeds were worn who drew the car,
The glorious Bharat thus addressed
Vaśishtha, of his lords the best:
'The spot, methinks, we now behold
Of which the holy hermit told,
For, as his words described, I trace
Each several feature of the place:
Before us Chitrakuṭa shows,
Mandákiní beside us flows:
Afar umbrageous woods arise
Like darksome clouds that veil the skies.
Now tread these mountain-beasts of mine
On Chitrakúṭa's fair incline.
The trees their rain of blossoms shed
On table-lands beneath them spread,
As from black clouds the floods descend
When the hot days of summer end.
Śatrughna, look, the mountain see
Where heavenly minstrels wander free,

And horses browse beneath the steep,
Countless as monsters in the deep.
Scared by my host the mountain deer
Starting with tempest speed appear
Like the long lines of cloud that fly
In autumn through the windy sky.
See, every warrior shows his head
With fragrant blooms engarlanded;
All look like southern soldiers who
Lift up their shields of azure hue.
This lonely wood beneath the hill,
That was so dark and drear and still,
Covered with men in endless streams
Now like Ayodhyá's city seems.
The dust which countless hoofs excite
Obscures the sky and veils the light;
But see, swift winds those clouds dispel
As if they strove to please me well.
See, guided in their swift career
By many a skilful charioteer,
Those cars by fleetest coursers drawn
Race onward over glade and lawn.
Look, startled as the host comes near
The lovely peacocks fly in fear,
Gorgeous as if the fairest blooms
Of earth had glorified their plumes.
Look where the sheltering covert shows
The trooping deer, both bucks and does,
That occupy in countless herds
This mountain populous with birds.
Most lovely to my mind appears
This place which every charm endears:
Fair as the road where tread the Blest:
Here holy hermits take their rest.
Then let the army onward press
And duly search each green recess
For the two lion-lords, till we
Ráma once more and Lakshman see.'
Thus Bharat spoke: and hero bands
Of men with weapons in their hands
Entered the tangled forest: then
A spire of smoke appeared in ken.
Soon as they saw the rising smoke
To Bharat they returned and spoke:
'No fire where men are not: 'tis clear
That Raghu's sons are dwelling here.
Or if not here those heroes dwell
Whose mighty arms their foeman quell,
Still other hermits here must be
Like Ráma, true and good as he.'
His ears attentive Bharat lent
To their resistless argument,
Then to his troops the chief who broke
His foe's embattled armies spoke:
'Here let the troops in silence stay;
One step beyond they must not stray.
Come Dhrishṭi and Sumantra, you
With me alone the path pursue.'
Their leader's speech the warriors heard,
And from his place no soldier stirred.
And Bharat bent his eager eyes
Where curling smoke was seen to rise.
The host his order well obeyed,
And halting there in silence stayed
Watching where from the thicket's shade
They saw the smoke appear.
And joy through all the army ran,
'Soon shall we meet,' thought every man,
'The prince we hold so dear.'

CANTO XCIV.

CHITRAKÚṬA.

There long the son of Raghu dwelt
And love for hill and wood he felt.
Then his Videhan spouse to please
And his own heart of woe to ease,
Like some Immortal—Indra so
Might Swarga's charms to Śachí show—
Drew her sweet eyes to each delight
Of Chitrakúṭa's lovely height:
'Though reft of power and kingly sway,
Though friends and home are far away,
I cannot mourn my altered lot,
Enamoured of this charming spot.
Look, darling, on this noble hill
Which sweet birds with their music fill.
Bright with a thousand metal dyes
His lofty summits cleave the skies.
See, there a silvery sheen is spread,
And there like blood the rocks are red.
There shows a streak of emerald green,
And pink and yellow glow between.
There where the higher peaks ascend,
Crystal and flowers and topaz blend,
And others flash their light afar
Like mercury or some fair star:
With such a store of metals dyed
The king of hills is glorified.
There through the wild birds' populous
home
The harmless bear and tiger roam:
Hyænas range the woody slopes
With herds of deer and antelopes.
See, love, the trees that clothe his side
All lovely in their summer pride,
In richest wealth of leaves arrayed,
With flower and fruit and light and shade.
Look where the young Rose-apple glows;
What loaded boughs the Mango shows;
See, waving in the western wind
The light leaves of the Tamarind,
And mark that giant Peepul through
The feathery clump of tall bamboo.[1]

[1] These ten lines are a substitution for, and not a translation of the text which Carey and Marshman thus render: 'This mountain adorned with mango,[1] *jumboo*,[2] *usuna*,[3] lodhra,[4] *piala*,[5] *punusa*,[6] *dhava*,[7]

Look, on the level lands above,
Delighting in successful love
In sweet enjoyment many a pair
Of heavenly minstrels revels there,
While overhanging boughs support
Their swords and mantles as they sport:
Then see that pleasant shelter where
Play the bright Daughters of the Air.[1]
The mountain seems with bright cascade
And sweet rill bursting from the shade,
Like some majestic elephant o'er
Whose burning head the torrents pour.
Where breathes the man who would not feel
Delicious languor o'er him steal,
As the young morning breeze that springs
From the cool cave with balmy wings,
Breathes round him laden with the scent
Of bud and blossom dew-besprent?
If many autumns here I spent
With thee, my darling innocent,
And Lakshmaṇ, I should never know
The torture of the fires of woe,
This varied scene so charms my sight,
This mount so fills me with delight,
Where flowers in wild profusion spring,
And ripe fruits glow and sweet birds sing.
My beauteous one, a double good
Springs from my dwelling in the wood:
Loosed is the bond my sire that tied,
And Bharat too is gratified.
My darling, dost thou feel with me
Delight from every charm we see,
Of which the mind and every sense
Feel the enchanting influence?
My fathers who have passed away,
The royal saints, were wont to say
That life in woodland shades like this
Secures a king immortal bliss.
See, round the hill at random thrown,
Huge masses lie of rugged stone
Of every shape and many a hue,
Yellow and white and red and blue.
But all is fairer still by night:
Each rock reflects a softer light,
When the whole mount from foot to crest
In robes of lambent flame is dressed;
When from a million herbs a blaze
Of their own luminous glory plays,
And clothed in fire each deep ravine,
Each pinnacle and crag is seen.
Some parts the look of mansions wear,
And others are as gardens fair,
While others seem a massive block
Of solid undivided rock.
Behold those pleasant beds o'erlaid
With lotus leaves, for lovers made,
Where mountain birch and costus throw
Cool shadows on the pair below.
See where the lovers in their play
Have cast their flowery wreaths away,
And fruit and lotus buds that crowned
Their brows lie trodden on the ground.
North Kuru's realm is fair to see,
Vasvaukasárá,[1] Naliní,[2]
But rich in fruit and blossom still
More fair is Chitrakúṭa's hill.
Here shall the years appointed glide
With thee, my beauty, by my side,
  And Lakshmaṇ ever near;
Here shall I live in all delight,
Make my ancestral fame more bright,
Tread in their path who walk aright,
  And to my oath adhere.'

unkotha,[8] *bhuvya*,[9] *tinisha*,[10] *vilwa*,[11] *tindooka*,[12] bamboo,[13] *kashmaree*,[14] *urista*,[15] *vuruna*,[16] *madhooka*,[17] *tilaka*,[18] *vuduree*,[19] *amluka*,[20] *nipa*,[21] *vetra*,[22] *dhunwuna*,[23] *veejaka*,[24] and other trees affording flowers, and fruits, and the most delightful shade, how charming does it appear!'

[1] Mangifera Indica. [2] Eugenia Jambolifera. [3] Terminaliaalata tomentosa. [4] This tree is not ascertained. [5] Chironjia Sapida. [6] Artocarpus integrifolia. [7] Grislea tomentosa. [8] Allangium hexapetalum. [9] Averrhoa carimbola. [10] Dalbergia Oujeinensis. [11] Œgle marmelos. [12] Diospyrus melanoxylon. [13] Well known. [14] Gmelina Arborea. [15] Sapindus Saponaria. [16] Cratoeva tapia. [17] Bassia la tifolia. [18] Not yet ascertained. [19] Zizyphus jujuba. [20] Phyllanthus emblica. [21] Nauclea Orientalis. [22] Calamus-rotang. [23] Echites antidysenterica. [24] The citron tree.'

[1] *Vidyadharis*, Spirits of Air, sylphs.

CANTO XCV.

MANDÁKINÍ.

Then Ráma, like the lotus eyed,
Descended from the mountain side,
And to the Maithil lady showed
The lovely stream that softly flowed.
And thus Ayodhyá's lord addressed
His bride, of dames the loveliest,
Child of Videha's king, her face
Bright with the fair moon's tender grace;
'How sweetly glides, O darling, look,
Mandákiní's delightful brook,
Adorned with islets, blossoms gay,
And sárases and swans at play!

[1] A lake attached either to Amarávatí the residence of Indra, or Alaká that of Kuvera.

[2] The Ganges of heaven.

The trees with which her banks are lined
Show flowers and fruit of every kind:
The match in radiant sheen is she
Of King Kuvera's Naliní.[1]
My heart exults with pleasure new
The shelving band and ford to view,
Where gathering herds of thirsty deer
Disturb the wave that ran so clear.
Now look, those holy hermits mark
In skins of deer and coats of bark;
With twisted coils of matted hair,
The reverend men are bathing there,
And as they lift their arms on high
The Lord of Day they glorify:
These best of saints, my large-eyed spouse,
Are constant to their sacred vows.
The mountain dances while the trees
Bend their proud summits to the breeze,
And scatter many a flower and bud
From branches that o'erhang the flood.
There flows the stream like lucid pearl,
Round islets here the currents whirl,
And perfect saints from middle air
Are flocking to the waters there.
See, there lie flowers in many a heap
From boughs the whistling breezes sweep,
And others wafted by the gale
Down the swift current dance and sail.
Now see that pair of wild-fowl rise,
Exulting with their joyful cries:
Hark, darling, wafted from afar
How soft their pleasant voices are.
To gaze on Chitrakúṭa's hill,
To look upon this lovely rill,
To bend mine eyes on thee, dear wife,
Is sweeter than my city life.
Come, bathe we in the pleasant rill
Whose dancing waves are never still,
Stirred by those beings pure from sin,
The sanctities who bathe therein:
Come, dearest, to the stream descend,
Approach her as a darling friend,
And dip thee in the silver flood
Which lotuses and lilies stud.
Let this fair hill Ayodhyá seem,
Its silvan things her people deem,
And let these waters as they flow
Our own beloved Sarjú show.
How blest, mine own dear love, am I;
Thou, fond and true, art ever nigh,
And duteous, faithful Lakshmaṇ stays
Beside me, and my word obeys.
Here every day I bathe me thrice,
Fruit, honey, roots for food suffice,
And ne'er my thoughts with longing stray
To distant home or royal sway.
For who this charming brook can see
Where herds of roedeer wander free,
And on the flowery-wooded brink
Apes, elephants, and lions drink,
Nor feel all sorrow fly?'
Thus eloquently spoke the pride
Of Raghu's children to his bride,
And wandered happy by her side
Where Chitrakúṭa azure-dyed
Uprears his peaks on high.

CANTO XCVI.[1]

THE MAGIC SHAFT.

Thus Ráma showed to Janak's child
The varied beauties of the wild,
The hill, the brook and each fair spot,
Then turned to seek their leafy cot.
North of the mountain Ráma found
A cavern in the sloping ground,
Charming to view, its floor was strown
With many a mass of ore and stone,
In secret shadow far retired
Where gay birds sang with joy inspired,
And trees their graceful branches swayed
With loads of blossom downward weighed.
Soon as he saw the cave which took
Each living heart and chained the look,
Thus Ráma spoke to Síta who
Gazed wondering on the silvan view:
'Does this fair cave beneath the height,
Videhan lady, charm thy sight?
Then let us resting here a while
The languor of the way beguile.
That block of stone so smooth and square
Was set for thee to rest on there,
And like a thriving Keśar tree
This flowery shrub o'ershadows thee.'
Thus Ráma spoke, and Janak's child,
By nature ever soft and mild,
In tender words which love betrayed
Her answer to the hero made:
'O pride of Raghu's children, still
My pleasure is to do thy will.
Enough for me thy wish to know:
Far hast thou wandered to and fro.'
Thus Sítá spake in gentle tone,
And went obedient to the stone,
Of perfect face and faultless limb
Prepared to rest a while with him.
And Ráma, as she thus replied,
Turned to his spouse again and cried:
'Thou seest, love, this flowery shade
For silvan creatures' pleasure made.
How the gum streams from trees and plants
Torn by the tusks of elephants!

[1] Naliní, as here, may be the name of any lake covered with lotuses.

[1] This canto is allowed, by Indian commentators, to be an interpolation. It cannot be the work of Válmíki.

Through all the forest clear and high
Resounds the shrill cicala's cry.
Hark how the kite above us moans,
And calls her young in piteous tones;
So may my hapless mother be
Still mourning in her home for me.
There mounted on that lofty Sál
The loud Bhringráj[1] repeats his call:
How sweetly now he tunes his throat
Responsive to the Koïl's note.
Or else the bird that now has sung
May be himself the Koïl's young,
Linked with such winning sweetness are
The notes he pours irregular.
See, round the blooming Mango clings
That creeper with her tender rings,
So in thy love, when none is near,
Thine arms are thrown round me, my dear.'

Thus in his joy he cried; and she,
Sweet speaker, on her lover's knee,
Of faultless limb and perfect face,
Grew closer to her lord's embrace.
Reclining in her husband's arms,
A goddess in her wealth of charms,
She filled his loving breast anew
With mighty joy that thrilled him through.
His finger on the rock he laid,
Which veins of sanguine ore displayed,
And painted o'er his darling's eyes
The holy sign in mineral dyes.
Bright on her brow the metal lay
Like the young sun's first gleaming ray,
And showed her in her beauty fair
As the soft light of morning's air.
Then from the Kesar's laden tree
He picked fair blossoms in his glee,
And as he decked each lovely tress,
His heart o'erflowed with happiness.
So resting on that rocky seat
A while they spent in pastime sweet,
Then onward neath the shady boughs
Went Ráma with his Maithil spouse.
She roaming in the forest shade
Where every kind of creature strayed
Observed a monkey wandering near,
And clung to Ráma's arm in fear.
The hero Ráma fondly laced
His mighty arms around her waist,
Consoled his beauty in her dread,
And scared the Monkey till he fled.
That holy mark of sanguine ore
That gleamed on Sítá's brow before,
Shone by that close embrace impressed
Upon the hero's ample chest.
Then Sítá, when the beast who led
The monkey troop, afar had fled,
Laughed loudly in light-hearted glee
That mark on Ráma's chest to see.

[1] A fine bird with a strong, sweet note, and great imitative powers.

A clump of bright Aśokas fired
The forest in their bloom attired:
The restless blossoms as they gleamed
A host of threatening monkeys seemed.
Then Sítá thus to Ráma cried,
As longingly the flowers she eyed:
'Pride of thy race, now let us go
Where those Aśoka blossoms grow.'
He on his darling's pleasure bent
With his fair goddess thither went
And roamed delighted through the wood
Where blossoming Aśokas stood,
As Śiva with Queen Umá roves
Through Himaván's majestic groves.
Bright with purpureal glow the pair
Of happy lovers sported there,
And each upon the other set
A flower-inwoven coronet.
There many a crown and chain they wove
Of blooms from that Aśoka grove,
And in their graceful sport the two
Fresh beauty o'er the mountain threw.
The lover let his love survey
Each pleasant spot that round them lay,
Then turned they to their green retreat
Where all was garnished, gay, and neat.
By brotherly affection led,
Sumitrá's son to meet them sped,
And showed the labours of the day
Done while his brother was away.
There lay ten black-deer duly slain
With arrows pure of poison stain,
Piled in a mighty heap to dry,
With many another carcass nigh.
And Lakshman's brother saw, o'erjoyed,
The work that had his hands employed,
Then to his consort thus he cried:
'Now be the general gifts supplied.'
Then Sítá, fairest beauty, placed
The food for living things to taste,
And set before the brothers meat
And honey that the pair might eat.
They ate the meal her hands supplied,
Their lips with water purified:
Then Janak's daughter sat at last
And duly made her own repast.
The other venison, to be dried,
Piled up in heaps was set aside,
And Ráma told his wife to stay
And drive the flocking crows away.
Her husband saw her much distressed
By one more bold than all the rest,
Whose wings where'er he chose could fly,
Now pierce the earth, now roam the sky.
Then Ráma laughed to see her stirred
To anger by the plaguing bird:
Proud of his love the beauteous dame
With burning rage was all aflame.
Now here, now there, again, again
She chased the crow, but all in vain,
Enraging her, so quick to strike

With beak and wing and claw alike:
Then how the proud lip quivered, how
The dark frown marked her angry brow!
When Ráma saw her cheek aglow
With passion, he rebuked the crow.
But bold in impudence the bird,
With no respect for Ráma's word,
Fearless again at Sítá flew:
Then Ráma's wrath to fury grew.
The hero of the mighty arm
Spoke o'er a shaft the mystic charm,
Laid the dire weapon on his bow
And launched it at the shameless crow.
The bird, empowered by Gods to spring
Through earth itself on rapid wing,
Through the three worlds in terror fled
Still followed by that arrow dread.
Where'er he flew, now here now there,
A cloud of weapons filled the air.
Back to the high-souled prince he fled
And bent at Ráma's feet his head,
And then, as Sítá looked, began
His speech in accents of a man:
O pardon, and for pity's sake
Spare, Ráma, spare my life to take!
Where'er I turn, where'er I flee,
No shelter from this shaft I see.'
The chieftain heard the crow entreat
Helpless and prostrate at his feet,
And while soft pity moved his breast,
With wisest speech the bird addressed:
'I took the troubled Sítá's part,
And furious anger filled my heart.
Then on the string my arrow lay
Charmed with a spell thy life to slay.
Thou seekest now my feet, to crave
Forgiveness and thy life to save.
So shall thy prayer have due respect:
The suppliant I must still protect.
But ne'er in vain this dart may flee:
Yield for thy life a part of thee,
What portion of thy body, say,
Shall this mine arrow rend away?
Thus far, O bird, thus far alone
On thee my pity may be shown.
Forfeit a part thy life to buy:
'Tis better so to live than die.'
Thus Ráma spoke: the bird of air
Pondered his speech with anxious care,
And wisely deemed it good to give
One of his eyes that he might live.
To Raghu's son he made reply:
'O Ráma, I will yield an eye.
So let me in thy grace confide
And live hereafter single-eyed.'
Then Ráma charged the shaft, and lo,
Full in the eye it smote the crow.
And the Videhan lady gazed
Upon the ruined eye amazed.
The crow to Ráma humbly bent,
Then where his fancy led he went.
Ráma with Lakshman by his side
With needful work was occupied.

CANTO XCVII.

LAKSHMAN'S ANGER.

Thus Ráma showed his love the rill
Whose waters ran beneath the hill,
Then resting on his mountain seat
Refreshed her with the choicest meat.
So there reposed the happy two:
Then Bharat's army nearer drew:
Rose to the skies a dusty cloud,
The sound of trampling feet was loud.
The swelling roar of marching men
Drove the roused tiger from his den,
And scared amain the serpent race
Flying to hole and hiding-place.
The herds of deer in terror fled,
The air was filled with birds o'erhead,
The bear began to leave his tree,
The monkey to the cave to flee.
Wild elephants were all amazed
As though the wood around them blazed.
The lion oped his ponderous jaw,
The buffalo looked round in awe.
The prince, who heard the deafening sound,
And saw the silvan creatures round
Fly wildly startled from their rest,
The glorious Lakshman thus addressed:
'Sumitrá's noble son most dear,
Hark, Lakshman, what a roar I hear,
The tumult of a coming crowd,
Appalling, deafening, deep, and loud!
The din that yet more fearful grows
Scares elephants and buffaloes,
Or frightened by the lions, deer
Are flying through the wood in fear.
I fain would know who seeks this place:
Comes prince or monarch for the chase?
Or does some mighty beast of prey
Frighten the silvan herds away?
'Tis hard to reach this mountain height,
Yea, e'en for birds in airy flight.
Then fain, O Lakshman, would I know
What cause disturbs the forest so.'
Lakshman in haste, the wood to view,
Climbed a high Sál that near him grew,
The forest all around he eyed,
First gazing on the eastern side.
Then northward when his eyes he bent
He saw a mighty armament
Of elephants, and cars, and horse,
And men on foot, a mingled force,
And banners waving in the breeze,
And spoke to Ráma words like these:
'Quick, quick, my lord, put out the fire,
Let Sítá to the cave retire.

Thy coat of mail around thee throw,
Prep are thine arrows and thy bow.'
In eager haste thus Lakshmaṇ cried,
And Ráma, lion lord, replied:
'Still closer be the army scanned,
And say who leads the warlike band.'
Lakshmaṇ his answer thus returned,
As furious rage within him burned,
Exciting him like kindled fire
To scorch the army in his ire:
''Tis Bharat: he has made the throne
By consecrating rites his own:
To gain the whole dominion thus
He comes in arms to slaughter us.
I mark tree-high upon his car
His flagstaff of the Kovidár,[1]
I see his glittering banner glance,
I see his chivalry advance:
I see his eager warriors shine
On elephants in lengthened line.
Now grasp we each the shafts and bow,
And higher up the mountain go.
Or in this place, O hero, stand
With weapons in each ready hand.
Perhaps beneath our might may fall
This leader of the standard tall,
And Bharat I this day may see
Who brought this mighty woe on thee,
Sítá, and me, who drove away
My brother from the royal sway.
Bharat our foe at length is nigh,
And by this hand shall surely die:
Brother, I see no sin at all
If Bharat by my weapon fall.
No fault is his who slays the foe
Whose hand was first to strike he blow:
With Bharat now the crime begins
Who against thee and duty sins.
The queen athirst for royal sway
Will see her darling son to-day
Fall by this hand, like some fair tree
Struck by an elephant, slain by me.
Kaikeyí's self shall perish too
With kith and kin and retinue,
And earth by my avenging deed
Shall from this mass of sin be freed.
This day my wrath, too long restrained,
Shall fall upon the foe, unchained,
Mad as the kindled flame that speeds
Destroying through the grass and reeds.
This day mine arrows keen and fierce
The bodies of the foe shall pierce:
The woods on Chitrakúṭa's side
Shall run with torrents crimson-dyed.
The wandering beasts of pray shall feed
On heart-cleft elephant and steed,
And drag to mountain caves away
The bodies that my arrows slay.
Doubt not that Bharat and his train
Shall in this mighty wood be slain:
So shall I pay the debt my bow
And these my deadly arrows owe.

CANTO XCVIII.

LAKSHMAṆ CALMED.

Then Ráma nobly calm allayed
The wrath that Lakshmaṇ's bosom swayed:
'What need have we the sword to wield,
To bend the bow or lift the shield,
If Bharat brave, and wise, and good,
Himself has sought this sheltering wood?
I sware my father's will to do,
And if I now my brother slew
What gain in kingship should I find,
Despised and scorned by all mankind?
Believe me, e'en as I would shrink
From poisoned meat or deadly drink,
No power or treasure would I win
By fall of friend or kith or kin.
Brother, believe the words I speak:
For your dear sakes alone I seek
Duty and pleasure, wealth and gain,
A holy life, a happy reign.
If royal sway my heart desires,
My brothers' weal the wish inspires:
Their bliss and safety is my care,
By this uplifted bow I swear.
'Twere not so hard for me to gain
This broad land girdled by the main,
But even Indra's royal might
Should ne'er be mine in duty's spite.
If any bliss my soul can see
Deprived of dear Śatrughna, thee,
And Bharat, may the flame destroy
With ashy gloom the selfish joy.
Far dearer than this life of mine,
Knowing the custom of our line,
His heart with fond affection fraught,
Bharat Ayodhyá's town resougt,
And hearing when he came that I,
With thee and Sítá, forced to fly
With matted hair and hermit dress
Am wandering in the wilderness,
While grief his troubled senses storms,
And tender love his bosom warms,
From every thought of evil clear,
Is come to meet his brother here.
Some grievous words perchance he spoke
Kaikeyí's anger to provoke,
Then won the king, and comes to lay
Before my feet the royal sway.
Hither, methinks, in season due
Comes Bharat for an interview,
Nor in his secret heart has he
One evil thought 'gainst thee or me.
What has he done ere now, reflect!
How failed in love or due respect

[1] Bauhinea variegata, a species of ebony.

To make thee doubt his faith and lay
This evil to his charge to-day?
Thou shouldst not join with Bharat's name
So harsh a speech and idle blame.
The blows thy tongue at Bharat deals,
My sympathizing bosom feels.
How, urged by stress of any ill.
Should sons their father's life-blood spill,
Or brother slay in impious strife
A brother dearer than his life?
If thou these cruel words hast said
By strong desire of empire led,
My brother Bharat will I pray
To give to thee the kingly sway.
'Give him the realm', my speech shall be,
And Bharat will, methinks, agree.'
Thus spoke the prince whose chief delight
Was duty, and to aid the right:
And Lakshman keenly felt the blame,
And shrank within himself for shame:
And then his answer thus returned,
With downcast eye and cheek that burned:
'Brother, I ween, to see thy face
Our sire himself has sought this place.'
Thus Lakshman spoke and stood ashamed,
And Ráma saw and thus exclaimed:
'It is the strong-armed monarch: he
Is come, methinks, his sons to see,
To bid us both the forest quit
For joys for which he deems us fit:
He thinks on all our care and pain,
And now would lead us home again.
My glorious father hence will bear
Sítá who claims all tender care.
I see two coursers fleet as storms,
Of noble breed and lovely forms.
I see the beast of mountain size
Who bears the king our father wise,
The aged Victor, march this way
In front of all the armed array.
But doubt and fear within me rise,
For when I look with eager eyes
I see no white umbrella spread,
World-famous, o'er the royal head.
Now, Lakshman, from the tree descend,
And to my words attention lend.'
Thus spoke the pious prince: and he
Descended from the lofty tree,
And reverent hand to hand applied,
Stood humbly by his brother's side.
The host, compelled by Bharat's care,
The wood from trampling feet to spare,
Dense crowding half a league each way
Encamped around the mountain lay.
Below the tall hill's shelving side
Gleamed the bright army far and wide
Spread o'er the ample space,
By Bharat led who firmly true
In duty from his bosom threw
All pride, and near his brother drew
To win the hero's grace,

CANTO XCIX.

BHARAT'S APPROACH.

Soon as the warriors took their rest
Obeying Bharat's high behest,
Thus Bharat to Śatrughna spake:
'A band of soldiers with thee take,
And with these hunters o'er and o'er
The thickets of the wood explore.
With bow, sword, arrows in their hands
Let Guha with his kindred bands
Within this grove remaining trace
The children of Kakutstha's race.
And I meanwhile on foot will through
This neighbouring wood my way pursue,
With elders and the twice-born men,
And every lord and citizen.
There is, I feel, no rest for me
Till Ráma's face again I see,
Lakshman, in arms and glory great,
And Sítá born to happy fate:
No rest, until his cheek as bright
As the fair moon rejoice my sight,
No rest until I see the eye
With which the lotus petals vie;
Till on my head those dear feet rest
With signs of royal rank impressed;
None, till my kingly brother gain
His old hereditary reign,
Till o'er his limbs and noble head
The consecrating drops be shed.
How blest is Janak's daughter, true
To every wifely duty, who
Cleaves faithful to her husband's side
Whose realm is girt by Ocean's tide!
This mountain too above the rest
E'en as the King of Hills is blest,—
Whose shades Kakutstha's scion hold
As Nandan charms the Lord of Gold.
Yea, happy is this tangled grove
Where savage beasts unnumbered rove,
Where, glory of the Warrior race,
King Ráma finds a dwelling-place.'
Thus Bharat, strong-armed hero, spake,
And walked within the pathless brake.
O'er plains where gay trees bloomed he went,
Through boughs in tangled net-work bent,
And then from Ráma's cot appeared
The banner which the flame upreared.
And Bharat joyed with every friend
To mark those smoky wreaths ascend:
'Here Ráma dwells,' he thought; 'at last
The ocean of our toil is passed.'
Then sure that Ráma's hermit cot
Was on the mountain's side
He stayed his army on the spot,
And on with Guha hied,

CANTO C.

THE MEETING.

Then Bharat to Śatrughna showed
The spot, and eager onward strode,
First bidding Saint Vaśishtha bring
The widowed consorts of the king.
As by fraternal love impelled
His onward course the hero held,
Sumantra followed close behind
Śatrughna with an anxious mind:
Not Bharat's self more fain could be
To look on Ráma's face than he.
As, speeding on, the spot he neared,
Amid the hermits' homes appeared
His brother's cot with leaves o'erspread,
And by its side a lowly shed.
Before the shed great heaps were left
Of gathered flowers and billets cleft,
And on the trees hung grass and bark
Ráma and Lakshmaṇ's path to mark:
And heaps of fuel to provide
Against the cold stood ready dried.
The long-armed chief, as on he went
In glory's light preëminent,
With joyous words like these addressed
The brave Śatrughna and the rest:
'This is the place, I little doubt,
Which Bharadvája pointed out,
Not far from where we stand must be
The woodland stream, Mandákiní.
Here on the mountain's woody side
Roam elephants in tusked pride,
And ever with a roar and cry
Each other, as they meet, defy.
And see those smoke-wreaths thick and dark:
The presence of the flame they mark,
Which hermits in the forest strive
By every art to keep alive.
O happy me! my task is done,
And I shall look on Raghu's son,
Like some great saint, who loves to treat
His elders with all reverence meet.'
Thus Bharat reached that forest rill,
Thus roamed on Chitrakúṭa's hill;
Then pity in his breast awoke,
And to his friends the hero spoke:
'Woe, woe upon my life and birth!
The prince of men, the lord of earth
Has sought the lonely wood to dwell
Sequestered in a hermit's cell.
Through me, through me these sorrows fall
On him the splendid lord of all:
Through me resigning earthly bliss
He hides him in a home like this.
Now will I, by the world abhorred,
Fall at the dear feet of my lord,
And at fair Sítá's too, to win
His pardon for my heinous sin.'
As thus he sadly mourned and sighed,
The son of Daśaratha spied
A bower of leafy branches made,
Sacred and lovely in the shade,
Of fair proportions large and tall,
Well roofed with boughs of palm and Sál,
Arranged in order due o'erhead
Like grass upon an altar spread.
Two glorious bows were gleaming there,
Like Indra's[1] in the rainy air,
Terror of foemen, backed with gold,
Meet for the mightiest hand to hold:
And quivered arrows cast a blaze
Bright gleaming like the Day-God's rays:
Thus serpents with their eyes aglow
Adorn their capital below.[2]
Great swords adorned the cottage, laid
Each in a case of gold brocade;
There hung the trusty shields, whereon
With purest gold the bosses shone.
The brace to bind the bowman's arm,
The glove to shield his hand from harm,
A lustre to the cottage lent
From many a golden ornament:
Safe was the cot from fear of men
As from wild beasts the lion's den.
The fire upon the altar burned,
That to the north and east was turned.
Bharat his eager glances bent
And gazed within the cot intent;
In deerskin dress, with matted hair,
Ráma his chief was sitting there:
With lion-shoulders broad and strong,
With lotus eyes, arms thick and long,
The righteous sovereign, who should be
Lord paramount from sea to sea,
High-minded, born to lofty fate,
Like Brahmá's self supremely great;
With Lakshmaṇ by his side, and her,
Fair Sítá, for his minister.
And Bharat gazing, overcome
By sorrow for a while was dumb,
Then, yielding to his woe, he ran
To Ráma and with sobs began:
'He who a royal seat should fill
With subjects round to do his will,
My elder brother,—see him here,
With silvan creatures waiting near.
The high-souled hero, wont to wear
The costliest robes exceeding fair,
Now banished, in a deerskin dress,
Here keeps the path of righteousness.
How brooks the son of Raghu now
The matted locks which load his brow,
Around whose princely head were twined
Sweet blossoms of the rarest kind?
The prince whose merits grew, acquired

[1] The rainbow is called the bow of Indra.

[2] Bhogavatí, the abode of the Nágas or Serpent race.

By rites performed as he desired,
Would now a store of merit gain
Bought by his body's toil and pain.
Those limbs to which pure sandal lent
The freshness of its fragrant scent,
Exposed to sun, and dust, and rain,
Are now defiled with many a stain.
And I the wretched cause why this
Falls on the prince whose right is bliss?
Ah me, that ever I was born
To be the people's hate and scorn!'
  Thus Bharat cried: of anguish sprung,
Great drops upon his forehead hung.
He fell o'erpowered—his grief was such—
Ere he is brother's feet could touch.
As on the glorious prince he gazed
In vain his broken voice he raised:
'Dear lord'—through tears and sobbing came,
The only words his lips could frame.
And brave Śatrughna wept aloud,
As low at Ráma's feet he bowed.
Then Ráma, while his tears ran fast,
His arms around his brothers cast.
Guha, Sumantra came to meet
The princes in their wild retreat.
  Vrihaspati and Śukra bright
    Their greeting thus rejoice to pay
  To the dear Lord who brings the night,
    And the great God who rules the day.
  Then wept the dwellers of the shade,
    Whose eyes the princes, meet to ride
  On mighty elephants, surveyed;
    And cast all thought of joy aside.

CANTO CI.

BHARAT QUESTIONED.

Then Ráma gazed, and scarcely knew
Bharat so worn and changed in hue.
He raised him, kissed him on the head,
Embraced him, and thus kindly said:
'Where was thy father, brother dear,
That thou art come to seek me here?
Unmeet, if he be living yet,
Thy feet within the wood to set.
I pray thee now the cause declare
Why thou hast left the kingdom there.
With matted locks and deerskin dress
To roam the distant wilderness.'
  Thus questioned by the prince, at length
Kaikeyí's son regained his strength,
And hand to hand in reverence laid,
To Ráma thus his answer made:
'The great-armed monarch, O my lord,
Has dared to do a thing abhorred,
Left us, and grieving for his son,
A home among the Gods has won.
My mother Queen Kaikeyí gave
The order to the king her slave,
And at the bidding of the dame
He wrought the sin which mars his fame
Athirst for sway, her hopes are crossed,
She mourns her son, her husband lost,
And through her impious crime will go
For punishment to hell below.
Now O my lord, forgive me all;
Be gracious to thy lowly thrall:
Anointed king, accept to-day
Like Indra's self, the royal sway.
Be gracious, Prince, to lord and peer,
And widowed queens who seek thee here.
Accept the kingdom thine by right,
And so thy faithful friends delight.
Let the broad land no longer be
All widowed and forlorn of thee:
Let the full moon of autumn reign
Triumphant o'er the night again.
These lords and I before thee bend:
O Ráma, to our prayer attend.
O do not thou this grace deny:
Thy brother, pupil, slave am I.
Look on this venerable ring,
Advisers of our sire the king,
From age to age so honoured: thou
Shouldst grant their supplication now.'
  As weeping thus the hero prayed,
His head at Ráma's feet he laid.
Like a mad elephant he sighed:
And Ráma gazed and thus replied:
'How, brother, can a man of worth,
True to his vows, of noble birth—
A man like me, commit a sin
The lordship of the land to win?
No slightest shade of fault I see,
O tamer of thy foes, in thee.
But ne'er shouldst thou in childish thought
The queen thy mother blame in aught.
O brother wise and sinless, know
The sacred laws would have it so,
That from good wife and son require
Obedience to their lord and sire.
And we are all the king's, for thus
The virtuous ever reckon us:
Yea brother, be it known to thee,
His wives, and sons, and pupils we.
His is the right, if he deem fit,
To bid me, throned as monarch, sit,
Or in a coat of bark expel,
And deerskin, in the wood to dwell.
And O remember, best of all
Who act as claims of duty call,
As to a virtuous sire is due,
Such honour claims a mother too.
So they whose lives have ever been
By duty led, the king and queen,
Said, 'Ráma, seek the forest shade:'
And I (what could I else?) obeyed.
Thou must the royal power retain,

And o'er the famed Ayodhyá reign :
I dressed in bark my days will spent
Where Dandak's forest wilds extend.
So Daśaratha spoke, our king,
His share to each apportioning
Before his honoured servants, eyes :
Then, heir of bliss, he sought the skies.
The righteous monarch's honoured will,
Whom all revered, must guide thee still,
And thou must still enjoy the share
Assigned thee by our father's care.
So I till twice seven years are spent
Will roam this wood in banishment,
Contented with the lot which he,
My high-souled sire, has given me.
The charge the monarch gave, endeared
To all mankind, by all revered,
Peer of the Lord Supreme,
Far better, richer far in gain
Of every blessing than to reign
O'er all the worlds I deem.'

CANTO CII.

BHARAT'S TIDINGS.

He spoke : and Bharat thus replied :
'If, false to every claim beside,
I ne'er in kingly duties fail,
What will my royal life avail ?
Still should the custom be observed,
From which our line has never swerved,
Which to the younger son ne'er gives
The kingdom while the elder lives.
Now to Ayodhyá rich and fair
With me, O Raghu's son, repair,
And to protect and gladden all
Our house, thyself as king install.
A king the world's opinion deems
A man : to me a God he seems,
Whose life in virtuous thoughts and deeds
The lives of other men exceeds.
When I in distant Kekaya stayed,
And thou hadst sought the forest shade,
Our father died, the saints' delight,
So constant in each holy rite.
Scarce with thy wife and Lakshman thou
Hadst journeyed forth to keep the vow,
When mourning for his son, forspent,
To heavenly rest the monarch went.
Then up, O lord of men, away !
His funeral rites of water pay :
I and Śatrughna, ere we came,
Neglected not the sacred claim.
But in the spirit-world, they say,
That gift alone is fresh for aye
Which best beloved hands have poured ;
And thou his dearest art, my lord.
For thee he longed, for thee he grieved,
His every thought on thee was bent,
And crushed by woe, of thee bereaved,
He thought of thee as hence he went.'

CANTO CIII.

THE FUNERAL LIBATION.

When Ráma heard from Bharat each
Dark sorrow of his mournful speech,
And tidings of his father dead,
His spirits fell, his senses fled.
For the sad words his brother spoke
Struck on him like a thunder stroke,
Fierce as the bolt which Indra throws,
The victor of his Daitya foes.
Raising his arms in anguish, he,
As when the woodman hews a tree
With its fair flowery branches crowned,
Fainted and fell upon the ground.
Lord of the earth to earth he sank,
Helpless, as when a towering bank
With sudden ruin buries deep
An elephant who lay asleep.
Then swift his wife and brothers flew,
And water, weeping, o'er him threw.
As slowly sense and strength he gained,
Fast from his eyes the tears he rained,
And then in accents sad and weak
Kakutstha's son began to speak,
And mourning for the monarch dead,
With righteous words to Bharat said :
'What calls me home, when he, alas,
Has gone the way which all must pass ?
Of him, the best of kings bereft
What guardian has Ayodhyá left ?
How may I please his spirit ? how
Delight the high-souled monarch now,
Who wept for me and went above
By me ungraced with mourning love ?
Ah, happy brothers ! you have paid
Due offerings to his parting shade.
E'en when my banishment is o'er,
Back to my home I go no more,
To look upon the widowed state
Reft of her king, disconsolate.
E'en then, O tamer of the foe,
If to Ayodhyá's town I go,
Who will direct me as of old,
Now other worlds our father hold ?
From whom, my brother, shall I hear
Those words which ever charmed mine ear
And filled my bosom with delight
Whene'er he saw me act aright ?'
Thus Ráma spoke : then nearer came
And looking on his moonbright dame,
'Sítá, the king is gone,' he said :
'And Lakshman, know thy sire is dead,

And with the Gods on high enrolled:
This mournful news has Bharat told.'
He spoke: the noble youths with sighs
Rained down the torrents from their eyes.
And then the brothers of the chief
With words of comfort soothed his grief:
'Now to the king our sire who swayed
The earth be due libations paid.'
Soon as the monarch's fate she knew,
Sharp pangs of grief smote Sítá through:
Nor could she look upon her lord
With eyes from which the torrents poured.
And Ráma strove with tender care
To soothe the weeping dame's despair,
And then, with piercing woe distressed,
The mournful Lakshman thus addressed:
'Brother, I pray thee bring for me
The pressed fruit of the Ingudí,
And a bark mantle fresh and new,
That I may pay this offering due.
First of the three shall Sítá go,
Next thou, and I the last: for so
Moves the funereal pomp of woe.'[1]

Sumantra of the noble mind,
Gentle and modest, meek and kind,
Who, follower of each princely youth,
To Ráma clung with constant truth,
Now with the royal brothers' aid
The grief of Ráma soothed and stayed,
And lent his arm his lord to guide
Down to the river's holy side.
That lovely stream the heroes found,
With woods that ever blossomed crowned,
And there in bitter sorrow bent
Their footsteps down the fair descent.
Then where the stream that swiftly flowed
A pure pellucid shallow showed,
The funeral drops they duly shed,
And 'Father, this be thine,' they said.
But he, the lord who ruled the land,
Filled from the stream his hollowed hand,
And turning to the southern side
Stretched out his arm and weeping cried:
'This sacred water clear and pure,
An offering which shall aye endure,
To thee, O lord of kings, I give:
Accept it where the spirits live!'

Then, when the solemn rite was o'er,
Came Ráma to the river shore,
And offered, with his brothers' aid,
Fresh tribute to his father's shade.
With jujube fruit he mixed the seed
Of Ingudís from moisture freed,
And placed it on a spot o'erspread
With sacred grass, and weeping said:
'Enjoy, great King, the cake which we
Thy children eat and offer thee!
For ne'er do blessed Gods refuse
To share the food which mortals use.'

Then Ráma turned him to retrace
The path that brought him to the place,
And up the mountain's pleasant side
Where lovely lawns lay fair, he hied.
Soon as his cottage door he gained,
His brothers to his breast he strained,
From them and Sítá in their woes
So loud the cry of weeping rose,
That like the roar of lions round
The mountain rolled the echoing sound.
And Bharat's army shook with fear
The weeping of the chiefs to hear.
'Bharat,' the soldiers cried, ''tis plain,
His brother Ráma meets again,
And with these cries that round us ring
They sorrow for their sire the king.'
Then leaving car and wain behind,
One eager thought in every mind,
Swift toward the weeping, every man,
As each could find a passage, ran.
Some thither bent their eager course
With car, and elephant, and horse,
And youthful captains on their feet
With longing sped their lord to meet,
As though the new-come prince had been
An exile for long years unseen.
Earth beaten in their frantic zeal
By clattering hoof and rumbling wheel,
Sent forth a deafening noise as loud
As heaven when black with many a cloud
Then, with their consorts gathered near,
Wild elephants in sudden fear
Rushed to a distant wood, and shed
An odour round them as they fled.
And every silvan thing that dwelt
Within those shades the terror felt,
Deer, lion, tiger, boar and roe,
Bison, wild-cow, and buffalo.
And when the tumult wild they heard,
With trembling pinions flew each bird,
From tree, from thicket, and from lake,
Swan, koïl, curlew, crane, and drake.
With men the ground was overspread,
With startled birds the sky o'erhead.
Then on his sacrificial ground
The sinless, glorious chief was found.
Loading with curses deep and loud
The hump-back and the queen, the crowd
Whose cheeks were wet, whose eyes were dim,
In fond affection ran to him.
While the big tears their eyes bedewed,
He looked upon the multitud e,

---

[1] 'The order of the procession on these occasions is that the children precede according to age, then the women and after that the men according to age, the youngest first and the eldest last: when they descend into the water this is reversed and resumed when they come out of it.'

CAREY AND MARSHMAN.

And then as sire and mother do,
His arms about his loved ones threw.
Some to his feet with reverence pressed,
Some in his arms he strained:
Each friend, with kindly words addressed,
Due share of honour gained.
Then, by their mighty woe o'ercome,
The weeping heroes' cry
Filled, like the roar of many a drum,
Hill, cavern, earth, and sky.

CANTO CIV.

THE MEETING WITH THE QUEENS.

Vaśishṭha with his soul athirst
To look again on Ráma, first
In line the royal widows placed,
And then the way behind them traced.
The ladies moving, faint and slow,
Saw the fair stream before them flow,
And by the bank their steps were led
Which the two brothers visited.
Kauśalyá with her faded cheek
And weeping eyes began to speak,
And thus in mournful tones addressed
The queen Sumitrá and the rest:
'See in the wood the bank's descent,
Which the two orphan youths frequent,
Whose noble spirits never fail,
Though woes surround them, reft of all.
Thy son with love that never tires
Draws water hence which mine requires.
This day, for lowly toil unfit,
His pious task thy son should quit.'
As on the long-eyed lady strayed,
On holy grass, whose points were laid
Directed to the southern sky,
The funeral offering met her eye.
When Ráma's humble gift she spied
Thus to the queens Kauśalyá cried:
'The gift of Ráma's hand behold,
His tribute to the king high-souled,
Offered to him, as texts require,
Lord of Ikshváku's line, his sire!
Not such I deem the funeral food
Of kings with godlike might endued.
Can he who knew all pleasures, he
Who ruled the earth from sea to sea,
The mighty lord of monarchs, feed
On Ingudí's extracted seed?
In all the world there cannot be
A woe, I ween, more sad to see,
Than that my glorious son should make
His funeral gift of such a cake.
The ancient text I oft have heard
This day is true in every word:
'Ne'er do the blessed Gods refuse
To eat the food their children use.'
The ladies soothed the weeping dame:
To Ráma's hermitage they came,
And there the hero met their eyes
Like a God fallen from the skies.
Him joyless, reft of all, they viewed,
And tears their mournful eyes bedewed.
The truthful hero left his seat,
And clasped the ladies' lotus feet,
And they with soft hands brushed away
The dust that on his shoulders lay.
Then Lakshmaṇ, when he saw each queen
With weeping eyes and troubled mien,
Near to the royal ladies drew
And paid them gentle reverence too.
He, Daśaratha's offspring, signed
The heir of bliss by Fortune kind,
Received from every dame no less
Each mark of love and tenderness.
And Sítá came and bent before
The widows, while her eyes ran o'er,
And pressed their feet with many a tear.
They when they saw the lady dear
Pale, worn with dwelling in the wild,
Embraced her as a darling child:
'Daughter of royal Janak, bride
Of Daśaratha's son,' they cried,
'How couldst thou, offspring of a king,
Endure this woe and suffering
In the wild forest? When I trace
Each sign of trouble on thy face—
That lotus which the sun has dried,
That lily by the tempest tried,
That gold whereon the dust is spread,
That moon whence all the light is fled—
Sorrow assails my heart, alas!
As fire consumes the wood and grass.'
Then Ráma, as she spoke distressed,
The feet of Saint Vaśishṭha pressed,
Touched them with reverential love,
Then near him took his seat:
Thus Indra clasps in realms above
The Heavenly Teacher's[1] feet.
Then with each counsellor and peer,
Bharat of duteous mind,
With citizens and captains near,
Sat humbly down behind.
When with his hands to him upraised,
In devotee's attire,
Bharat upon his brother gazed
Whose glory shone like fire,
As when the pure Mahendra bends
To the great Lord of Life,
Among his noble crowd of friends
This anxious thought was rife:
'What words to Raghu's son to-day
Will royal Bharat speak,
Whose heart has been so prompt to pay
Obeisance fond and meek?'
Then steadfast Ráma, Lakshmaṇ wise,
Bharat for truth renowned,

[1] Vrihaspati, the preceptor of the Gods.

Shone like three fires that heavenward rise
  With holy priests around.

CANTO CV.

RÁMA'S SPEECH.

A while they sat, each lip compressed,
Then Bharat thus his chief addressed:
'My mother here was made content;
To me was given the government.
This now, my lord, I yield to thee:
Enjoy it, from all trouble free.
Like a great bridge the floods have rent,
Impetuous in their wild descent,
All other hands but thine in vain
Would strive the burthen to maintain.
In vain the ass with steeds would vie,
With Tárkshya,[1] birds that wing the sky;
So, lord of men, my power is slight
To rival thine imperial might.
Great joys his happy days attend
On whom the hopes of men depend,
But wretched is the life he leads
Who still the aid of others needs.
And if the seed a man has sown,
With care and kindly nurture grown,
Rear its huge trunk and spring in time
Too bulky for a dwarf to climb,
Yet, with perpetual blossom gay,
No fruit upon its boughs display,
Ne'er can that tree, thus nursed in vain,
Approval of the virtuous gain.
The simile is meant to be
Applied, O mighty-armed, to thee,
Because, our lord and leader, thou
Protectest not thy people now.
O, be the longing wish fulfilled
Of every chief of house and guild,
To see again their sun-bright lord
Victorious to his realm restored!
As thou returnest through the crowd
Let roars of elephants be loud,
And each fair woman lift her voice
And in her new-found king rejoice.'
  The people all with longing moved,
The words that Bharat spoke approved,
And crowding near to Ráma pressed
The hero with the same request.
The steadfast Ráma, when he viewed
His glorious brother's mournful mood,
With each ambitious thought controlled,
Thus the lamenting prince consoled:
'I cannot do the things I will,
For Ráma is but mortal still.
Fate with supreme, resistless law
This way and that its slave will draw.
All gathered heaps must waste away,
All lofty lore and powers decay.
Death is the end of life, and all,
Now firmly joined, apart must fall.
One fear the ripened fruit must know,
To fall upon the earth below;
So every man who draws his breath
Must fear inevitable death.
The pillared mansion, high, compact,
Must fall by Time's strong hand attacked;
So mortal men, the gradual prey
Of eld and ruthless death, decay.
The night that flies no more returns:
Yamuná for the Ocean yearns:
Swift her impetuous waters flee,
But roll not backward from the sea.
The days and nights pass swiftly by
And steal our moments as they fly,
E'en as the sun's unpitying rays
Drink up the floods in summer blaze.
Then for thyself lament and leave
For death of other men to grieve,
For if thou go or if thou stay,
Thy life is shorter day by day.
Death travels with us: death attends
Our steps until our journey ends,
Death, when the traveller wins the goal,
Returns with the returning soul.
The flowing hair grows white and thin,
And wrinkles mark the altered skin.
The ills of age man's strength assail:
Ah, what can mortal power avail?
Men joy to see the sun arise,
They watch him set with joyful eyes:
But ne'er reflect, too blind to see,
How fast their own brief moments flee.
With lovely change for ever new
The seasons' sweet return they view,
Nor think with heedless hearts the while
That lives decay as seasons smile.
As haply on the boundless main
Meet drifting logs and part again,
So wives and children, friends and gold,
Ours for a little time we hold:
Soon by resistless laws of fate
To meet no more we separate.
In all this changing world not one
The common lot of all can shun:
Then why with useless tears deplore
The dead whom tears can bring no more?
As one might stand upon the way
And to a troop of travellers say:
'If ye allow it, sirs, I too
Will travel on the road with you:'
So why should mortal man lament
When on that path his feet are bent
Which all men living needs must tread,
Where sire and ancestors have led?
Life flies as torrents downward fall
Speeding away without recall,
So virtue should our thoughts engage,
For bliss[1] is mortals' heritage.

---

[1] Garud, the king of birds.

[1] To be won by virtue.

By ceaseless care and earnest zeal
For servants and for people's weal,
By gifts, by duty nobly done,
Our glorious sire the skies has won.
Our lord the king, o'er earth who reigned,
A blissful home in heaven has gained
By wealth in ample largess spent,
And many a rite magnificent;
With constant joy from first to last
A long and noble life he passed,
Praised by the good, no tears should dim
Our eyes, O brother dear, for him.
His human body, worn and tried
By length of days, he cast aside,
And gained the godlike bliss to stray
In Brahma's heavenly home for aye.
For such the wise as we are, deep
In Veda lore, should never weep.
Those who are firm and ever wise
Spurn vain lament and idle sighs.
Be self-possessed: thy grief restrain:
Go, in that city dwell again.
Return, O best of men, and be
Obedient to our sire's decree,
While I with every care fulfil
Our holy father's righteous will,
Observing in the lonely wood
His charge approved by all the good.'
Thus Ráma of the lofty mind
To Bharat spoke his righteous speech,
By every argument designed
Obedience to his sire to teach,

CANTO CVI.

BHARAT'S SPEECH.

Good Bharat, by the river side,
To virtuous Ráma's speech replied,
And thus with varied lore addressed
The prince, while nobles round him pressed:
'In all this world whom e'er can we
Find equal, scourge of foes, to thee?
No ill upon thy bosom weighs,
No thoughts of joy thy spirit raise.
Approved art thou of sages old,
To whom thy doubts are ever told.
Alike in death and life, to thee
The same to be and not to be.
The man who such a soul can gain
Can ne'er be crushed by woe or pain.
Pure as the Gods, high-minded, wise,
Concealed from thee no secret lies.
Such glorious gifts are all thine own,
And birth and death to thee are known,
That ill can ne'er thy soul depress
With all-subduing bitterness.
O let my prayer, dear brother, win
Thy pardon for my mother's sin,
Wrought for my sake who willed it not
When absent in a distant spot.

Duty alone with binding chains
The vengeance due to crime restrains,
Or on the sinner I should lift
My hand in retribution swift.
Can I who know the right, and spring
From Daśaratha, purest king—
Can I commit a heinous crime,
Abhorred by all through endless time?
The aged king I dare not blame,
Who died so rich in holy fame,
My honoured sire, my parted lord,
E'en as a present God adored.
Yet who in lore of duty skilled
So foul a crime has ever willed,
And dared defy both gain and right
To gratify a woman's spite?
When death draws near, so people say,
The sense of creatures dies away;
And he has proved the ancient saw
By acting thus in spite of law.
But O my honoured lord, be kind,
Dismiss the trespass from thy mind,
The sin the king committed, led
By haste, his consort's wrath, and dread.
For he who veils his sire's offence
With tender care and reverence—
His sons approved by all shall live:
Not so their fate who ne'er forgive.
Be thou, my lord, the noble son,
And the vile deed my sire has done,
Abhorred by all the virtuous, ne'er
Resent, lest thou the guilt too share.
Preserve us, for on thee we call,
Our sire, Kaikeyí, me and all
Thy citizens, thy kith and kin;
Preserve us and reverse the sin.
To live in woods a devotee
Can scarce with royal tasks agree,
Nor can the hermit's matted hair
Suit fitly with a ruler's care.
Do not, my brother, do not still
Pursue this life that suits thee ill.
Mid duties of a king we count
His consecration paramount,
That he with ready heart and hand
May keep his people and his land.
What Warrior born to royal sway
From certain good would turn away,
A doubtful duty to pursue,
That mocks him with the distant view?
Thou wouldst to duty cleave, and gain
The meed that follows toil and pain.
In thy great task no labour spare:
Rule the four castes with justest care.
Mid all the four, the wise prefer
The order of the householder:[1]

[1] The four religious orders, referable to different times of life are, that of the student, that of the householder, that of the anchorite, and that of the mendicant.

Canst thou, whose thoughts to duty cleave,
The best of all the orders leave?
My better thou in lore divine,
My birth, my sense must yield to thine:
While thou, my lord, art here to reign,
How shall my hands the rule maintain?
O faithful lover of the right,
Take with thy friends the royal might,
Let thy sires' realm, from trouble free,
Obey her rightful king in thee.
Here let the priests and lords of state
Our monarch duly consecrate,
With prayer and holy verses blessed
By saint Vaśishṭha and the rest.
Anointed king by us, again
Seek fair Ayodhyá, there to reign,
And like imperial Indra girt
By Gods of Storm, thy might assert.
From the three debts[1] acquittance earn,
And with thy wrath the wicked burn,
O'er all of us thy rule extend,
And cheer with boons each faithful friend.
Let thine enthronement, lord, this day
Make all thy lovers glad and gay,
And let all those who hate thee flee
To the ten winds for fear of thee.
Dear lord, my mother's words of hate
With thy sweet virtues expiate,
And from the stain of folly clear
The father whom we both revere.
Brother, to me compassion show,
I pray thee with my head bent low,
And to these friends who on thee call,—
As the Great Father pities all.
But if my tears and prayers be vain,
And thou in woods wilt still remain,
I will with thee my path pursue
And make my home in forests too.'

Thus Bharat strove to bend his will
With suppliant head, but he,
Earth's lord, inexorable still
Would keep his sire's decree.
The firmness of the noble chief
The wondering people moved,
And rapture mingling with their grief,
All wept and all approved.
'How firm his steadfast will,' they cried,
'Who keeps his promise thus!
Ah, to Ayodhyá's town,' they sighed,
'He comes not back with us.'
The holy priests, the swains who tilled
The earth, the sons of trade,
And e'en the mournful queens were filled
With joy as Bharat prayed,
And bent their heads, their weeping stilled
A while, his prayers to aid.

[1] To Gods, men, and Manes.

CANTO CVII.

RÁMA'S SPEECH.

Thus, by his friends encompassed round,
He spoke, and Ráma, far renowned,
To his dear brother thus replied,
Whom holy rites had purified:
'O thou whom Queen Kaikeyí bare
The best of kings, thy words are fair.
Our royal father, when of yore
He wed her, to her father swore
The best of kingdoms to confer,
A noble dowry meet for her;
Then, grateful, on the deadly day
Of heavenly Gods' and demons' fray,
A future boon on her bestowed
To whose sweet care his life he owed.
She to his mind that promise brought,
And then the best of kings besought
To bid me to the forest flee,
And give the rule, O Prince, to thee.
Thus bound by oath, the king our lord
Gave her those boons of free accord,
And bade me, O thou chief of men,
Live in the woods four years and ten.
I to this lonely wood have hied
With faithful Lakshmaṇ by my side,
And Sítá by no fears deterred,
Resolved to keep my father's word.
And thou, my noble brother, too
Shouldst keep our father's promise true:
Anointed ruler of the state
Maintain his word inviolate.
From his great debt, dear brother, free
Our lord the king for love of me,
Thy mother's breast with joy inspire,
And from all woe preserve thy sire.
'Tis said, near Gayá's holy town[1]
Gaya, great saint of high renown,
This text recited when he paid
Due rites to each ancestral shade:
'A son is born his sire to free
From Put's infernal pains:
Hence, saviour of his father, he
The name of Puttra gains.'[2]
Thus numerous sons are sought by prayer,
In Scripture trained with graces fair,

[1] Gayá is a very holy city in Behar. Every good Hindu ought once in his life to make funeral offerings in Gayá in honour of his ancestors.

[2] *Put* is the name of that region of hell to which men are doomed who leave no son to perform the funeral rites which are necessary to assure the happiness of the departed. *Putra*, the common word for a son, is said by the highest authority to be derived from *Put* and *tra* deliverer.

That of the number one some day
May funeral rites at Gayá pay.
The mighty saints who lived of old
This holy doctrine ever hold.
Then, best of men, our sire release
From pains of hell, and give him peace.
Now Bharat, to Ayodhyá speed,
The brave Śatrughna with thee lead,
Take with thee all the twice-born men,
And please each lord and citizen.
I now, O King, without delay
To Daṇḍak wood will bend my way,
And Lakshmaṇ and the Maithil dame
Will follow still, our path the same.

Now, Bharat, lord of men be thou,
And o'er Ayodhyá reign :
The silvan world to me shall bow,
King of the wild domain.
Yea, let thy joyful steps be bent
To that fair town to-day,
And I as happy and content,
To Daṇḍak wood will stray.
The white umbrella o'er thy brow
Its cooling shade shall throw :
I to the shadow of the bough
And leafy trees will go.
Śatrughna, for wise plans renowned,
Shall still on thee attend ;
And Lakshmaṇ, ever faithful found,
Be my familiar friend.
Let us his sons, O brother dear,
The path of right pursue,
And keep the king we all revere
Still to his promise true.'

CANTO CVIII.

JÁVÁLI'S SPEECH.

Thus Ráma soothed his brother's grief :
Then virtuous Jáváli, chief
Of twice-born sages, thus replied
In words that virtue's law defied :
'Hail, Raghu's princely son, dismiss
A thought so weak and vain as this.
Canst thou, with lofty heart endowed,
Think with the dull ignoble crowd ?
For what are ties of kindred ? can
One profit by a brother man ?
Alone the babe first opes his eyes,
And all alone at last he dies.
The man, I ween, has little sense
Who looks with foolish reverence
On father's or on mother's name :
In others, none a right may claim.
E'en as a man may leave his home
And to a distant village roam,
Then from his lodging turn away
And journey on the following day,
Such brief possession mortals hold
In sire and mother, house and gold,
And never will the good and wise
The brief uncertain lodging prize.
Nor, best of men, shouldst thou disown
Thy sire's hereditary throne,
And tread the rough and stony ground
Where hardship, danger, woes abound.
Come, let Ayodhyá rich and bright
See thee enthroned with every rite :
Her tresses bound in single braid [1]
She waits thy coming long delayed.
O come, thou royal Prince, and share
The kingly joys that wait thee there,
And live in bliss transcending price
As Indra lives in Paradise.
The parted king is naught to thee,
Nor right in living man has he :
The king is one, thou, Prince of men,
Another art : be counselled then.
Thy royal sire, O chief, has sped
On the long path we all must tread.
The common lot of all is this,
And thou in vain art robbed of bliss.
For those—and only those—I weep
Who to the path of duty keep ;
For here they suffer ceaseless woe,
And dying to destruction go.
With pious care, each solemn day,
Will men their funeral offerings pay :
See, how the useful food they waste :
He who is dead no more can taste.
If one is fed, his strength renewed
Whene'er his brother takes his food,
Then offerings to the parted pay :
Scarce will they serve him on his way.
By crafty knaves these rules were framed,
And to enforce men's gifts proclaimed :
'Give, worship, lead a life austere,
Keep lustral rites, quit pleasures here.'
There is no future life : be wise,
And do, O Prince, as I advise.
Enjoy, my lord, the present bliss,
And things unseen from thought dismiss.
Let this advice thy bosom move,
The counsel sage which all approve ;
To Bharat's earnest prayer incline,
And take the rule so justly thine.'

CANTO CIX.

THE PRAISES OF TRUTH.

By sage Jáváli thus addressed,
Ráma of truthful hearts the best,

---

[1] It was the custom of Indian women when mourning for their absent husbands to bind their hair in a long single braid.

Carey and Marshman translate, 'the one-tailed city.'

With perfect skill and wisdom high
Thus to his speech made fit reply:
'Thy words that tempt to bliss are fair,
But virtue's garb they falsely wear.
For he from duty's path who strays
To wander in forbidden ways,
Allured by doctrine false and vain,
Praise from the good can never gain.
Their lives the true and boaster show,
Pure and impure, and high and low.
Else were no mark to judge between
Stainless and stained and high and mean;
They to whose lot fair signs may fall
Were but as they who lack them all,
And those to virtuous thoughts inclined
Were but as men of evil mind.
If in the sacred name of right
I do this wrong in duty's spite;
The path of virtue meanly quit,
And this polluting sin commit,
What man who marks the bounds between
Virtue and vice with insight keen,
Would rank me high in after time,
Stained with this soul-destroying crime?
Whither could I, the sinner, turn,
How hope a seat in heaven to earn,
If I my plighted promise break,
And thus the righteous path forsake?
This world of ours is ever led
To walk the ways which others tread,
And as their princes they behold,
The subjects too their lives will mould.
That truth and mercy still must be
Beloved of kings, is Heaven's decree.
Upheld by truth the monarch reigns,
And truth the very world sustains.
Truth evermore has been the love
Of holy saints and Gods above,
And he whose lips are truthful here
Wins after death the highest sphere.
As from a serpent's deadly tooth,
We shrink from him who scorns the truth.
For holy truth is root and spring
Of justice and each holy thing,
A might that every power transcends,
Linked to high bliss that never ends.
Truth is all virtue's surest base,
Supreme in worth and first in place.
Oblations, gifts men offer here,
Vows, sacrifice, and rites austere,
And Holy Writ, on truth depend:
So men must still that truth defend.
Truth, only truth protects the land,
By truth unharmed our houses stand;
Neglect of truth makes men distressed,
And truth in highest heaven is blessed.
Then how can I, rebellious, break
Commandments which my father spake—
I ever true and faithful found,
And by my word of honour bound?
My father's bridge of truth shall stand
Unharmed by my destructive hand:
Not folly, ignorance, or greed
My darkened soul shall thus mislead.
Have we not heard that God and shade
Turn from the hated offerings paid
By him whose false and fickle mind
No pledge can hold, no promise bind?
Truth is all duty: as the soul,
It quickens and supports the whole.
The good respect this duty: hence
Its sacred claims I reverence.
The Warrior's duty I despise
That seeks the wrong in virtue's guise:
Those claims I shrink from, which the base,
Cruel, and covetous embrace.
The heart conceives the guilty thought,
Then by the hand the sin is wrought,
And with the pair is leagued a third,
The tongue that speaks the lying word.
Fortune and land and name and fame
To man's best care have right and claim;
The good will aye to truth adhere,
And its high laws must men revere.
Base were the deed thy lips would teach,
Approved as best by subtle speech.
Shall I my plighted promise break,
That I these woods my home would make?
Shall I, as Bharat's words advise,
My father's solemn charge despise?
Firm stands the oath which then before
My father's face I soothly swore,
Which Queen Kaikeyí's anxious ear
Rejoiced with highest joy to hear.
Still in the wood will I remain,
With food prescribed my life sustain,
And please with fruit and roots and flowers
Ancestral shades and heavenly powers.
Here every sense contented, still
Heeding the bounds of good and ill,
My settled course will I pursue,
Firm in my faith and ever true.
Here in this wild and far retreat
Will I my noble task complete;
And Fire and Wind and Moon shall be
Partakers of its fruit with me.
A hundred offerings duly wrought
His rank o'er Gods for Indra bought,
And mighty saints their heaven secured
By torturing years on earth endured.'

That scoffing plea the hero spurned,
  And thus he spake once more,
Chiding, the while his bosom burned,
  Jáváli's impious lore:
'Justice, and courage ne'er dismayed,
  Pity for all distressed,
Truth, loving honour duly paid
  To Bráhman, God, and guest—
In these, the true and virtuous say,
  Should lives of men be passed:
They form the right and happy way
  That leads to heaven at last.

My father's thoughtless act I chide
  That gave thee honoured place,
Whose soul, from virtue turned aside,
  Is faithless, dark, and base.
We rank the Buddhist with the thief,[1]
  And all the impious crew
Who share his sinful disbelief,
  And hate the right and true.
Hence never should wise kings who seek
  To rule their people well,
Admit, before their face to speak,
  The cursed infidel.
But twice-born men in days gone by,
  Of other sort than thou,
Have wrought good deeds, whose glories high
  Are fresh among us now:
This world they conquered, nor in vain
  They strove to win the skies:
The twice-born hence pure lives maintain,
  And fires of worship rise.
Those who in virtue's path delight,
  And with the virtuous live,—
Whose flames of holy zeal are bright,
  Whose hands are swift to give,
Who injure none, and good and mild
  In every grace excel,
Whose lives by sin are undefiled,
  We love and honour well.'
Thus Ráma spoke in righteous rage
  Jáváli's speech to chide,
When thus again the virtuous sage
  In truthful words replied:
'The atheist's lore I use no more,
  Not mine his impious creed:
His words and doctrine I abhor,
  Assumed at time of need.
E'en as I rose to speak with thee,
  The fit occasion came
That bade me use the atheist's plea
  To turn thee from thine aim.
The atheist creed I disavow,
  Unsay the words of sin,
And use the faithful's language now
  Thy favour, Prince, to win.

CANTO CX.

THE SONS OF IKSHVÁKU.[2]

Then spake Vaśishṭha who perceived
That Ráma's soul was wroth and grieved:
'Well knows the sage Jáváli all
The changes that the world befall;
And but to lead thee to revoke
Thy purpose were the words he spoke.
Lord of the world, now hear from me
How first this world began to be.
First water was, and naught beside;
There earth was formed that stretches wide.
Then with the Gods from out the same
The Self-existent Brahmá came.
Then Brahmá[1] in a boar's disguise
Bade from the deep this earth arise;
Then, with his sons of tranquil soul,
He made the world and framed the whole.
From subtlest ether Brahmá rose:
No end, no loss, no change he knows.
A son had he, Maríchi styled,
And Kaśyap was Maríchi's child.
From him Vivasvat sprang: from him
Manu, whose fame shall ne'er be dim.
Manu, who life to mortals gave,
Begot Ikshváku good and brave:
First of Ayodhyá's kings was he,
Pride of her famous dynasty.
From him the glorious Kukshi sprang,
Whose fame through all the regions rang.
Rival of Kukshi's ancient fame,
His heir the great Vikukshi came.
His son was Váṇa, lord of might,
His Anaraṇya, strong in fight.
No famine marred his blissful reign,
No drought destroyed the kindly grain;
Amid the sons of virtue chief,
His happy realm ne'er held a thief,
His son was Prithu, glorious name,
From him the wise Triśanku came;
Embodied to the skies he went
For love of truh preëminent.
He left a son renowned afar,
Known by the name of Dhundhumár,
His son succeeding bore the name
Of Yuvanáśva dear to fame.
He passed away. Him followed then
His son Mándhátá, king of men.
His son was blest in high emprise,
Susandhi, fortunate and wise.
Two noble sons had he, to wit
Dhruvasandhi and Prasenajit.
Bharat was Dhruvasandhi's son:
His glorious arm the conquest won.
Against his son King Asit, rose
In fierce array his royal foes,
Haihayas, Tálajanghas styled,
And Śaśivindhus fierce and wild.

[1] The verses in a different metre with which some cantos end are all to be regarded with suspicion. Schlegel regrets that he did not exclude them all from his edition. These lines are manifestly spurious. See *Additional Notes.*

[2] This genealogy is a repetition with slight variation of that given in Book I. Canto LXX.

[1] In Gorresio's recension identified with Vishṇu. See Muir's *Sanskrit Texts, Vol. IV. pp* 29, 30.

Long time he strove, but forced to yield
Fled from his kingdom and the field.
The wives he left had both conceived—
So is the ancient tale believed :—
One, of her rival's hopes afraid,
Fell poison in the viands laid.
It chanced that Chyavan, Bhrigu's child,
Had wandered to the pathless wild
Where proud Himálaya's lovely height
Detained him with a strange delight.
Then came the other widowed queen
With lotus eyes and beauteous mien,
Longing a noble son to bear,
And wooed the saint with earnest prayer.
When thus Kálindí, fairest dame
With reverent supplication came,
To her the holy sage replied :
'O royal lady, from thy side
A glorious son shall spring ere long,
Righteous and true and brave and strong ;
He, scourge of foes and lofty-souled,
His ancient race shall still uphold.'
Then round the sage the lady went,
And bade farewell, most reverent.
Back to her home she turned once more,
And there her promised son she bore.
Because her rival mixed the bane
To render her conception vain,
And her unripened fruit destroy,
Sagar she called her rescued boy.[1]
He, when he paid that solemn rite,[2]
Filled living creatures with affright :
Obedient to his high decree
His countless sons dug out the sea.
Prince Asamanj was Sagar's child :
But him with cruel sin defiled
And loaded with the people's hate
His father banished from the state.
To Asamanj his consort bare
Bright Anśumán his valiant heir.
Anśumán's son, Dilípa famed,
Begot a son Bhagírath named.
From him renowned Kakutstha came :
Thou bearest still the lineal name.
Kakutstha's son was Raghu : thou
Art styled the son of Raghu now.
From him came Purushádak bold,
Fierce hero of gigantic mould :
Kalmáshapáda's name he bore,
Because his feet were spotted o'er.
Śankhan his son, to manhood grown,
Died sadly with his host o'erthrown,
But ere he perished sprang from him
Sudarśan fair in face and limb.
From beautiful Sudarśan came
Prince Agnivarna, bright as flame.
His son was Śíghraga, for speed
Unmatched ; and Maru was his seed.
Praśuśruka was Maru's child :
His son was Ambarísha styled.
Nahush was Ambarísha's heir
With hand to strike and heart to dare.
His son was good Nábhág, from youth
Renowned for piety and truth.
From great Nábhág sprang children two,
Aja and Suvrat pure and true.
From Aja Daśaratha came,
Whose virtuous life was free from blame.
His eldest son art thou : his throne,
O famous Ráma, is thine own.
Accept the sway so justly thine,
And view the world with eyes benign.
For ever in Ikshváku's race
The eldest takes his father's place,
And while he lives no son beside
As lord and king is sanctified.
The rule by Raghu's children kept
Thou must not spurn to-day.
This realm of peerless wealth accept,
And like thy father sway.'

CANTO CXI.

COUNSEL TO BHARAT.

Thus said Vaśishṭha, and again
To Ráma spake in duteous strain :
'All men the light of life who see
With high respect should look on three :
High honour ne'er must be denied
To father, mother, holy guide.
First to their sires their birth they owe,
Nursed with maternal love they grow :
Their holy guides fair knowledge teach :
So men should love and honour each.
Thy sire and thou have learned of me,
The sacred guide of him and thee,
And if my word thou wilt obey
Thou still wilt keep the virtuous way.
See, with the chiefs of every guild
And all thy friends, this place is filled :
All these, as duty bids, protect;
So still the righteous path respect.
O, for thine aged mother feel,
Nor spurn the virtuous dame's appeal :
Obey, O Prince, thy mother dear,
And still to virtue's path adhere.
Yield thou to Bharat's fond request,
With earnest supplication pressed,
So wilt thou to thyself be true,
And faith and duty still pursue.'
Thus by his saintly guide addressed
With pleas in sweetest tones expressed,
The lord of men in turn replied
To wise Vaśishṭha by his side :
'The fondest son's observance ne'er
Repays the sire and mother's care :

[1] From *sa* with, and *gara* poison.
[2] See Book I. Canto XL.

The constant love that food provides,
And dress, and every need besides:
Their pleasant words still soft and mild,
Their nurture of the helpless child:
The word which Daśaratha spake,
My king and sire, I ne'er will break.'

Then Bharat of the ample chest
The wise Sumantra thus addressed:
'Bring sacred grass, O charioteer,
And strew it on the level here.
For I will sit and watch his face
Until I win my brother's grace.
Like a robbed Bráhman will I lie,[1]
Nor taste of food nor turn my eye,
In front of Ráma's leafy cot,
And till he yield will leave him not.'
When Bharat saw Sumantra's eye
Looked up to Ráma for reply,
The Prince himself in eager haste
The sacred grass in order placed.
Him great and mighty Ráma, best
Of royal saints, in turn addressed:
'What, Bharat, have I done, that thou
Besiegest me,[2] a suppliant now?
Thus streched, to force redress for wrongs
To men of Bráhman birth belongs,
Not those upon whose kingly head
The consecrating drops are shed.
Up, lord of men! arise, and quit
This fearful vow for thee unfit.
Go, brother, seek Ayodhyá's town,
Fair city of supreme renown.'
But Bharat, as his seat he took,
Cast all around an eager look:
'O people, join your prayers with mine,
And so his stubborn heart incline.'
And all the people answered thus:
'Full well is Ráma known to us.
Right is the word he speaks, and he
Is faithful to his sire's decree;
Nor can we rashly venture now
To turn him from his purposed vow.'
Then Ráma spoke: 'O Bharat, heed
Thy virtuous friends, and mark their rede.
Mark well what I and these advise,
And duty view with clearer eyes.
Thy hand on mine, O hero, place,
Touch water, and thy sin efface.'
Then Bharat rose: his hand he dipped,
And purifying water sipped:
'Each citizen,' he cried, 'give ear,
Attend, each counsellor and peer.
My mother planned, by me untaught,
To win the sway I never sought:
Ne'er Raghu's son could I despise,
In duty's lore supremely wise.
Now if obedience to our sire
This dwelling in the woods require,
I, till the destined years be spent,
Will dwell alone in banishment.'
The virtuous Ráma, wonder-stirred,
The faithful speech of Bharat heard,
And thus the hero's feelings found
Due utterance, as he gazed around:
'Still to my father's word I hold,
Whate'er he bought, or pledged, or sold:
Ne'er shall his living promise be
Annulled by Bharat or by me.
Not thus my task will I evade,
My exile on another laid:
Most wise was Queen Kaikeyí's rede,
And just and good my father's deed.
Dear Bharat's patient soul I know,
How reverence due he loves to show;
In him, high-souled and faithful found,
Must each auspicious grace abound.
When from the woods I turn again
I with his aid shall nobly reign,
With one so good, of peerless worth,
A glorious lord of happy earth.
Her boon Kaikeyí sought and won:
I, as my father swore, have done:
And O, do thou, my brother dear,
The monarch's name from falsehood clear.

[1] A practice which has frequently been described, under the name of *dherna*, by European travellers in India.

[2] Compare Milton's '*beseeching or besieging.*'

CANTO CXII.

THE SANDALS.

High wonder mingled with delight
Took the great sages at the sight,
Thrilling their breasts who came to view
The meeting of the peerless two.
The saints and sages' holy train
Departed to their home again,
And high each holy voice was raised,
And thus the glorious brothers praised.
'High fate is his, the sire of two
Most virtuous sons, so brave and true:
With wonder and with joy intense
Our ears have heard their conference.
Then the great sages, longing all
To see the ten-necked tyrant[1] fall,
To Bharat, bravest of the brave,
Their salutary counsel gave:
'O thou of lofty lineage born,
Whom wisdom, conduct, fame adorn,
Thou for thy honoured father's sake
Shouldst Ráma's righteous counsel take.

[1] Ten-headed, ten-necked, ten faced, are common epithets of Rávaṇ the giant king of Lanká.

All debts to Queen Kaikeyí paid,
Thy sire his home in heaven has made,
So virtuous Ráma we would see
From filial obligation free.'
Thus gave each royal sage advice,
High saint, and bard of Paradise;
Then quickly vanishing from view
Each to his proper home withdrew.
Then Ráma's face his rapture showed,
And his full heart with joy o'erflowed.
While, as the sages parted thence,
He paid his humble reverence.
  Then Bharat shook in every limb
As suppliant thus he spake to him:
'The duty of a king respect,
Held by our race in high respect:
And O, thy gracious ear incline
To heed my mother's prayer and mine.
The mighty realm to rule and guard
For me alone is task too hard.
No power have I the love to gain
Of noble, citizen, and swain.
All those who know thee, warrior, friend,
On thee their eager glances bend,
As labouring hinds who till the plain
Look fondly for the Lord of Rain.
O wisest Prince, thy realm secure,
And make its firm foundations sure.
Kakutstha's son, thy mighty arm
Can keep the nation free from harm.'
He spoke, and fell in sorrow drowned
At Ráma's feet upon the ground,
And there the hero sued and sighed,
And 'Hear me, Raghu's son,' he cried.
  Then Ráma raised him up, and pressed
His brother to his loving breast,
And sweetly as a wild swan cried
To Bharat dark and lotus-eyed:
  So just and true thy generous soul,
Thy hand may well this earth control:
But many a sage his aid will lend.
With counsellor, and peer, and friend:
With these advise: their counsel ask,
And so perform thy arduous task.
The moon his beauty may forgo,
The cold forsake the Hills of Snow,
And Ocean o'er his banks may sweep,
But I my father's word will keep.
Now whether love of thee or greed
Thy mother led to plan the deed,
Forth from thy breast the memory throw,
And filial love and reverence show.'
  Thus spake Kauśalyá's son: again
Bharat replied in humble strain
To him who matched the sun in might
And lovely as the young moon's light:
'Put, noble brother, I entreat,
These sandals on thy blessed feet:
These, lord of men, with gold-bedecked,
The realm and people will protect.'
  Then Ráma, as his brother prayed
Beneath his feet the sandals laid,
And these with fond affection gave
To Bharat's hand, the good and brave.
Then Bharat bowed his reverent head
And thus again to Ráma said:
'Through fourteen seasons will I wear
The hermit's dress and matted hair:
With fruit and roots my life sustain,
And still beyond the realm remain,
Longing for thee to come again.
The rule and all affairs of state
I to these shoes will delegate.
And if, O tamer of thy foes,
When fourteen years have reached their close,
I see thee not that day return,
The kindled fire my frame shall burn.'
  Then Ráma to his bosom drew
Dear Bharat and Satrughna too:
'Be, never wroth,' he cried, 'with her,
Kaikeyí's guardian minister:
This, glory of Ikshváku's line,
Is Sítá's earnest prayer and mine.'
He spoke, and as the big tears fell,
To his dear brother bade farewell.
Round Ráma, Bharat strong and bold
    In humble reverence paced,
  When the bright sandals wrought with gold
    Above his brows were placed.
  The royal elephant who led
    The glorious pomp he found,
  And on the monster's mighty head
    Those sandals duly bound.
  Then noble Ráma, born to swell
    The glories of his race,
  To all in order bade farewell
    With love and tender grace—
  To brothers, counsellers, and peers,—
    Still firm, in duty proved,
  Firm, as the Lord of Snow uprears
    His mountains unremoved.
  No queen, for choking sobs and sighs,
    Could say her last adieu:
  Then Ráma bowed, with flooded eyes,
    And to his cot withdrew.

CANTO CXIII.

BHARAT'S RETURN.

Bearing the sandals on his head
Away triumphant Bharat sped,
And clomb, Śatrughna by his side,
The car wherein he wont to ride.
Before the mighty army went
The lords for counsel eminent,
Vaśishtha, Vámadeva next,
Jáváli, pure with prayer and text.

Then from that lovely river they
Turned eastward on their homeward way:
With reverent steps from left to right
They circled Chitrakúṭa's height,
And viewed his peaks on every side
With stains of thousand metals dyed.
Then Bharat saw, not far away.
Where Bhardvája's dwelling lay,
And when the chieftain bold and sage
Had reached that holy hermitage,
Down from the car he sprang to greet
The saint, and bowed before his feet.
High rapture filled the hermit's breast,
Who thus the royal prince addressed:
'Say, Bharat, is thy duty done?
Hast thou with Ráma met, my son?'
  The chief whose soul to virtue clave
This answer to the hermit gave:
'I prayed him with our holy guide:
But Raghu's son our prayer denied,
And long besought by both of us
He answered Saint Vaśishṭha thus:
'True to my vow, I still will be
Observant of my sire's decree:
Till fourteen years complete their course
That promise shall remain in force.'
The saint in highest wisdom taught,
These solemn words with wisdom fraught,
To him in lore of language learned
Most eloquent himself returned:
'Obey my rede: let Bharat hold
This pair of sandals decked with gold:
They in Ayodhyá shall ensure
Our welfare, and our bliss secure.'
When Ráma heard the royal priest
He rose, and looking to the east
Consigned the sandals to my hand
That they for him might guard the land.
Then from the high-souled chief's abode
I turned upon my homeward road,
Dismissed by him, and now this pair
Of sandals to Ayodhyá bear.'
  To him the hermit thus replied,
By Bharat's tidings gratified:
'No marvel thoughts so just and true,
Thou best of all who right pursue,
Should dwell in thee, O Prince of men,
As waters gather in the glen.
He is not dead: we mourn in vain:
Thy blessed father lives again,
Whose noble son we thus behold
Like Virtue's self in human mould.'
  He ceased: before him Bharat fell
To clasp his feet, and said farewell:
His reverent steps around him bent,
And onward to Ayodhyá went.
His host of followers stretching far
With many an elephant and car,
Waggon and steed, and mighty train,
Traversed their homeward way again.
O'er holy Yamuná they sped,
Fair stream, with waves engarlanded,
And then once more the rivers' queen,
The blessed Gangá's self was seen.
Then making o'er that flood his way,
Where crocodiles and monsters lay,
The king to Śringavera drew
His host and royal retinue.
His onward way he thence pursued,
And soon renowned Ayodhyá viewed.
Then burnt by woe and sad of cheer
Bharat addressed the charioteer:
'Ah, see, Ayodhyá dark and sad,
Her glory gone, once bright and glad:
Of joy and beauty reft, forlorn,
In silent grief she seems to mourn.'

CANTO CXIV.

BHARAT'S DEPARTURE.

Deep, pleasant was the chariot's sound
As royal Bharat, far renowned,
Whirled by his mettled coursers fast
Within Ayodhyá's city passed.
There dark and drear was every home
Where cats and owls had space to roam,
As when the shades of midnight fall
With blackest gloom, and cover all:
As Rohiṇí, dear spouse of him
Whom Ráhu hates,[1] grows faint and dim,
When, as she shines on high alone
The demon's shade is o'er her thrown;
As burnt by summer's heat a rill
Scarce trickling from her parent hill,
With dying fish in pools half dried,
And fainting birds upon her side:
As sacrificial flames arise
When holy oil their food supplies,
But when no more the fire is fed
Sink lustreless and cold and dead:
Like some brave host that filled the plain,
With harness rent and captains slain,
When warrior, elephant, and steed
Mingled in wild confusion bleed:
As when, all spent her store of worth,
Rocks from her base the loosened earth:
Like a sad fallen star no more
Wearing the lovely light it wore:
So mournful in her lost estate
Was that sad town disconsolate.
Then car-borne Bharat, good and brave,
Thus spake to him the steeds who drave:
'Why are Ayodhyá's streets so mute?
Where is the voice of lyre and lute?
Why sounds not, as of old, to-day
The music of the minstrel's lay?

[1] The spouse of Rohiṇí is the Moon: Ráhu is the demon who causes eclipses.

Where are the wreaths they used to twine?
Where are the blossoms and the wine?
Where is the cool refreshing scent
Of sandal dust with aloe blent?
The elephant's impatient roar,
The din of cars, I hear no more:
No more the horse's pleasant neigh
Rings out to meet me on my way.
Ayodhyá's youths, since Ráma's flight,
Have lost their relish for delight:
Her men roam forth no more, nor care
Bright garlands round their necks to wear.
All grieve for banished Ráma: feast,
And revelry and song have ceased:
Like a black night when floods pour down,
So dark and gloomy is the town.
When will he come to make them gay
Like some auspicious holiday?
When will my brother, like a cloud
At summer's close, make glad the crowd?'
  Then through the streets the hero rode,
And passed within his sire's abode,
Like some deserted lion's den,
Forsaken by the lord of men.
Then to the inner bowers he came,
Once happy home of many a dame,
  Now gloomy, sad, and drear,
Dark as of old that sunless day
When wept the Gods in wild dismay; [1]
  There poured he many a tear.

CANTO CXV.

NANDIGRÁM.[2]

Then when the pious chief had seen
Lodged in her home each widowed queen,
Still with his burning grief oppressed
His holy guides he thus addressed:
'I go to Nundigrám: adieu,
This day, my lords to all of you:
I go, my load of grief to bear,
Reft of the son of Raghu, there.
The king my sire, alas, is dead,
And Ráma to the forest fled;
There will I wait till he, restored,
Shall rule the realm, its rightful lord.'
  They heard the high-souled prince's speech,
And thus with ready answer each
Of those great lords their cheif addressed,
With saint Vaśishṭha and the rest:
'Good are the words which thou hast said,
By brotherly affection led,
Like thine own self, a faithful friend,
True to thy brother to the end:
A heart like thine must all approve,
Which naught from virtue's path can move.'
  Soon as the words he loved to hear
Fell upon Bharat's joyful ear,
Thus to the charioteer he spoke:
'My car with speed, Sumantra, yoke.'
Then Bharat with delighted mien
Obeisance paid to every queen,
And with Satrughna by his side
Mounting the car away he hied.
With lords, and priests in long array
The brothers hastened on their way.
And the great pomp the Bráhmans led
With Saint Vaśishṭha at their head.
Then every face was eastward bent
As on to Nundigrám they went.
Behind the army followed, all
Unsummoned by their leader's call,
And steeds and elephants and men
Streamed forth with every citizen.
As Bharat in his chariot rode
His heart with love fraternal glowed,
And with the sandals on his head
To Nundigrám he quickly sped.
Within the town he swiftly pressed,
Alighted, and his guides addressed:
'To me in trust my brother's hand
Consigned the lordship of the land,
When he these gold-wrought sandals gave
As emblems to protect and save.'
Then Bharat bowed, and from his head
The sacred pledge deposited,
And thus to all the people cried
Who ringed him round on every side:
'Haste, for these sandals quickly bring
The canopy that shades the king.
Pay ye to them all reverence meet
As to my elder brother's feet,
For they will right and law maintain
Until King Ráma come again.
My brother with a loving mind
These sandals to my charge consigned:
I till he come will guard with care
The sacred trust for Raghu's heir.
My watchful task will soon be done,
The pledge restored to Raghu's son;
Then shall I see, his wanderings o'er,
These sandals on his feet once more.
My brother I shall meet at last,
The burthen from my shoulders cast,
To Ráma's hand the realm restore
And serve my elder as before.
When Ráma takes again this pair
Of sandals kept with pious care,
And here his glorious reign begins,
I shall be cleansed from all my sins,

---

[1] 'Once,' says the Commentator Tírtha, 'in the battle between the Gods and demons the Gods were vanquished, and the sun was overthrown by Ráhu. At the request of the Gods Atri undertook the management of the sun for a week.'

[2] Now Nundgaon, in Oudh.

When the glad people's voices ring
With welcome to the new-made king,
Joy will be mine four-fold as great
As if supreme I ruled the state.'
Thus humbly spoke in sad lament
The chief in fame preëminent:
Thus, by his reverent lords obeyed,
At Nandigrám the kingdom swayed.
With hermit's dress and matted hair
He dwelt with all his army there.
The sandals of his brother's feet
Installed upon the royal seat,
He, all his powers to them referred,
Affairs of state administered.
In every care, in every task,
When golden store was brought,
He first, as though their rede to ask,
Those royal sandals sought.

CANTO CXVI.

THE HERMIT'S SPEECH.

When Bharat took his homeward road
Still Ráma in the wood abode:
But soon he marked the fear and care
That darkened all the hermits there.
For all who dwelt before the hill
Were sad with dread of coming ill:
Each holy brow was lined by thought,
And Ráma's side they often sought.
With gathering frowns the prince they eyed,
And then withdrew and talked aside.
Then Raghu's son with anxious breast
The leader of the saints addressed:
'Can aught that I have done displease,
O reverend Sage, the devotees?
Why are their loving looks, O say,
Thus sadly changed or turned away?
Has Lakshman through his want of heed
Offended with unseemly deed?
Or is the gentle Sítá, she
Who loved to honour you and me—
Is she the cause of this offence,
Failing in lowly reverence?'
One sage, o'er whom, exceeding old,
Had many a year of penance rolled,
Trembling in every aged limb
Thus for the rest replied to him:
'How could we, O beloved, blame
Thy lofty-souled Videhan dame,
Who in the good of all delights,
And more than all of anchorites?
But yet through thee a numbing dread
Of fiends among our band has spread;
Obstructed by the demons' art
The trembling hermits talk apart.
For Rávan's brother, overbold,
Named Khara, of gigantic mould,
Vexes with fury fierce and fell
All those in Janasthán[1] who dwell.
Resistless in his cruel deeds,
On flesh of men the monster feeds:
Sinful and arrogant is he,
And looks with special hate on thee.
Since thou, beloved son, hast made
Thy home within this holy shade,
The fiends have vexed with wilder rage
The dwellers of the hermitage.
In many a wild and dreadful form
Around the trembling saints they swarm,
With hideous shape and foul disguise
Their terrify our holy eyes.
They make our loathing souls endure
Insult and scorn and sights impure,
And flocking round the altars stay
The holy rites we love to pay.
In every spot throughout the grove
With evil thoughts the monsters rove,
Assailing with their secret might
Each unsuspecting anchorite.
Ladle and dish away they fling,
Our fires with floods extinguishing,
And when the sacred flame should burn
They trample on each water-urn.
Now when they see their sacred wood
Plagued by this impious brotherhood,
The troubled saints away would roam
And seek in other shades a home:
Hence will we fly, O Ráma, ere
The cruel fiends our bodies tear.
Not far away a forest lies
Rich in the roots and fruit we prize,
To this will I and all repair
And join the holy hermits there:
Be wise, and with us thither flee
Before this Khara injure thee.
Mighty art thou, O Ráma, yet
Each day with peril is beset,
If with thy consort by thy side
Thou in this wood wilt still abide.'
He ceased: the words the hero spake
The hermit's purpose failed to break:
To Raghu's son farewell he said,
And blessed the chief and comforted;
Then with the rest the holy sage
Departed from the hermitage.
So from the wood the saints withdrew,
And Ráma bidding all adieu
In lowly reverence bent:
Instructed by their friendly speech,
Blest with the gracious love of each,
To his pure home he went.
Nor would the son of Raghu stray
A moment from that grove away
From which the saints had fled.
And many a hermit thither came
Attracted by his saintly fame
And the pure life he led.

[1] A part of the great Daṇḍak forest.

CANTO CXVII.

ANASU'YA'.

But dwelling in that lonely spot
Left by the hermits pleased him not.
'I met the faithful Bharat here,
The townsmen, and my mother dear:
The painful memory lingers yet,
And stings me with a vain regret.
And here the host of Bharat camped,
And many a courser here has stamped,
And elephants with ponderous feet
Have trampled through the calm retreat.'
So forth to seek a home he hied,
His spouse and Lakshmaṇ by his side.
He came to Atri's pure retreat,
Paid reverence to his holy feet,
And from the saint such welcome won
As a fond father gives his son.
The noble prince with joy unfeigned
As a dear guest he entertained,
And cheered the glorious Lakshmaṇ too
And Sítá with observance due.
Then Anasúyá at the call
Of him who sought the good of all,
His blameless venerable spouse,
Delighting in her holy vows,
Came from her chamber to his side:
To her the virtuous hermit cried:
'Receive, I pray, with friendly grace
This dame of Maithil monarchs' race:
To Ráma next made known his wife,
The devotee of saintliest life:
'Ten thousand years this votaress bent
On sternest rites of penance spent;
She when the clouds withheld their rain,
And drought ten years consumed the plain,
Caused grateful roots and fruit to grow
And ordered Gangá here to flow:
So from their cares the saints she freed,
Nor let these checks their rites impede.
She wrought in Heaven's behalf, and made
Ten nights of one, the Gods to aid:[1]
Let holy Anasúyá be
An honoured mother, Prince, to thee.
Let thy Videhan spouse draw near
To her whom all that live revere,
Stricken in years, whose loving mind
Is slow to wrath and ever kind.'
He ceased: and Ráma gave assent,
And said, with eyes on Sítá bent:
'O Princess, thou hast heard with me
This counsel of the devotee:
Now that her touch thy soul may bless,
Approach the saintly votaress:
Come to the venerable dame,
Far known by Anasúyá's name:
The mighty things that she has done
High glory in the world have won.'
Thus spoke the son of Raghu: she
Approached the saintly devotee,
Who with her white locks, old and frail,
Shook like a plantain in the gale.
To that true spouse she bowed her head,
And 'Lady, I am Sítá,' said:
Raised suppliant hands and prayed her tell
That all was prosperous and well.
The aged matron, when she saw
Fair Sítá true to duty's law,
Addressed her thus: 'High fate is thine
Whose thoughts to virtue still incline.
Thou, lady of the noble mind,
Hast kin and state and wealth resigned
To follow Ráma forced to tread
Where solitary woods are spread.
Those women gain high spheres above
Who still unchanged their husbands love,
Whether they dwell in town or wood,
Whether their hearts be ill or good.
Though wicked, poor, or led away
In love's forbidden paths to stray,
The noble matron still will deem
Her lord a deity supreme.
Regarding kin and friendship, I
Can see no better, holier tie,
And every penance-rite is dim
Beside the joy of serving him.
But dark is this to her whose mind
Promptings of idle fancy blind,
Who led by evil thoughts away
Makes him who should command obey.
Such women, O dear Maithil dame,
Their virtue lose and honest fame,
Enslaved by sin and folly, led
In these unholy paths to tread.
But they who good and true like thee
The present and the future see,
Like men by holy deeds will rise
To mansions in the blissful skies.
So keep thee pure from taint of sin,
Still to thy lord be true,
And fame and merit shalt thou win,
To thy devotion due.'

CANTO CXVIII.

ANASU'YA'S GIFTS.

Thus by the holy dame addressed
Who banished envy from her breast,
Her lowly reverence Sítá paid,
And softly thus her answer made:
'No marvel, best of dames, thy speech
The duties of a wife should teach;

[1] When the saint Máṇḍavya had doomed some saint's wife, who was Anasúyá's friend, to become a widow on the morrow.

Yet I, O lady, also know
Due reverence to my lord to show.
Were he the meanest of the base,
Unhonoured with a single grace,
My husband still I ne'er would leave,
But firm through all to him would cleave:
Still rather to a lord like mine
Whose virtues high-exalted shine,
Compassionate, of lofty soul,
With every sense in due control,
True in his love, of righteous mind,
Like a dear sire and mother kind.
E'en as he ever loves to treat
Kauśalyá with observance meet,
Has his behaviour ever been
To every other honoured queen.
Nay, more, a sonlike reverence shows
The noble Ráma e'en to those
On whom the king his father set
His eyes one moment, to forget.
Deep in my heart the words are stored,
Said by the mother of my lord,
When from my home I turned away
In the lone fearful woods to stray.
The counsel of my mother deep
Impressed upon my soul I keep,
When by the fire I took my stand,
And Ráma clasped in his my hand.
And in my bosom cherished yet,
My friends' advice I ne'er forget:
Woman her holiest offering pays
When she her husband's will obeys.
Good Sávitrí her lord obeyed,
And a high saint in heaven was made,
And for the self-same virtue thou
Hast heaven in thy possession now.
And she with whom no dame could vie,
Now a bright Goddess in the sky,
Sweet Rohiṇí the Moon's dear Queen,
Without her lord is never seen:
And many a faithful wife beside
For her pure love is glorified.'
  Thus Sítá spake: soft rapture stole
Through Anasúyá's saintly soul:
Kisses on Sítá's head she pressed,
And thus the Maithil dame addressed:
'I by long rites and toils endured
Rich store of merit have secured:
From this my wealth will I bestow
A blessing ere I let thee go.
So right and wise and true each word
That from thy lips mine ears have heard,
I love thee: be my pleasing task
To grant the boon that thou shalt ask.'
  Then Sítá marvelled much, and while
Played o'er her lips a gentle smile,
'All has been done, O Saint,' she cried,
And naught remains to wish beside.
  She spake; the lady's meek reply
Swelled Anasúyá's rapture high;
'Sítá,' she said, 'my gift to-day
Thy sweet contentment shall repay.
Accept this precious robe to wear,
Of heavenly fabric, rich and rare,
These gems thy limbs to ornament,
This precious balsam sweet of scent.
O Maithil dame, this gift of mine
Shall make thy limbs with beauty shine,
And breathing o'er thy frame dispense
Its pure and lasting influence.
This balsam on thy fair limbs spread
New radiance on thy lord shall shed,
As Lakshmí's beauty lends a grace
To Vishṇu's own celestial face.'
  Then Sítá took the gift the dame
Bestowed on her in friendship's name,
The balsam, gems, and robe divine,
And garlands wreathed of bloomy twine;
Then sat her down, with reverence meet,
At saintly Anasúyá's feet.
The matron rich in rites and vows
Turned her to Ráma's Maithil spouse,
And questioned thus in turn to hear
A pleasant tale to charm her ear:
'Sítá, 'tis said that Raghu's son
Thy hand, mid gathered suitors, won.
I fain would hear thee, lady, tell
The story as it all befell:
Do thou repeat each thing that passed,
Reviewing all from first to last.'
  Thus spake the dame to Sítá: she
Replying to the devotee,
'Then, lady, thy attention lend,'
Rehearsed the story to the end:
'King Janak, just and brave and strong,
Who loves the right and hates the wrong,
Well skilled in what the law ordains
For Warriors, o'er Videha reigns.
Guiding one morn the plough, his hand
Marked out for rites the sacred land,
When, as the ploughshare cleft the earth,
Child of the king I leapt to birth.
Then as the ground he smoothed and cleared,
He saw me all with dust besmeared,
And on the new-found babe, amazed
The ruler of Videha gazed.
In childless love the monarch pressed
The welcome infant to his breast:
'My daughter,' thus he cried, 'is she:'
And as his child he cared for me.
Forth from the sky was heard o'erhead
As 'twere a human voice that said:
'Yea, even so: great King, this child
Henceforth thine own be justly styled.'
Videha's monarch, virtuous-souled,
Rejoiced o'er me with joy untold,
Delighting in his new-won prize,
The darling of his heart and eyes.
To his chief queen of saintly mind
The precious treasure he consigned,
And by her side she saw me grow,
Nursed with the love which mothers know.'

Then as he saw the seasons fly,
And knew my marriage-time was nigh,
My sire was vexed with care, as sad
As one who mourns the wealth he had :
'Scorn on the maiden's sire must wait
From men of high and low estate :
The virgin's father all despise,
Though Indra's peer, who rules the skies.'
More near he saw, and still more near,
The scorn that filled his soul with fear,
On trouble's billowy ocean tossed,
Like one whose shattered bark is lost.
My father knowing how I came,
No daughter of a mortal dame,
In all the regions failed to see
A bridegroom meet to match with me.
Each way with anxious thought he scanned,
And thus at length the monarch planned :
'The Bride's Election will I hold,
With every rite prescribed of old.'
It pleased King Varuṇ to bestow
Quiver and shafts and heavenly bow
Upon my father's sire who reigned,
When Daksha his great rite ordained.
Where was the man might bend or lift
With utmost toil that wondrous gift?
Not e'en in dreams could mortal king
Strain the great bow or draw the string.
Of this tremendous bow possessed,
My truthful father thus addressed
The lords of many a region, all
Assembled at the monarch's call :
'Whoe'er this bow can manage, he
The husband of my child shall be.'
The suitors viewed with hopeless eyes
That wondrous bow of mountain size,
Then to my sire they bade adieu,
And all with humbled hearts withdrew.
At length with Viśvámitra came
This son of Raghu, dear to fame,
The royal sacrifice to view
Near to my father's home he drew,
His brother Lakshmaṇ by his side,
Ráma, in deeds heroic tried.
My sire with honour entertained
The saint in lore of duty trained,
Who thus in turn addressed the king :
'Ráma and Lakshmaṇ here who spring
From royal Daśaratha, long
To see thy bow so passing strong.'
  Before the prince's eyes was laid
That marvel, as the Bráhman prayed.
One moment on the bow he gazed,
Quick to the notch the string he raised,
Then, in the wandering people's view,
The cord with mighty force he drew.
Then with an awful crash as loud
As thunderbolts that cleave the cloud,
The bow beneath the matchless strain
Of arms heroic snapped in twain.
Thus, giving purest water, he,
My sire, to Ráma offered me.
The prince the offered gift declined
Till he should learn his father's mind;
So horsemen swift Ayodhyá sought
And back her aged monarch brought.
Me then my sire to Ráma gave,
Self-ruled, the bravest of the brave.
And Urmilá, the next to me,
Graced with all gifts, most fair to see,
My sire with Raghu's house allied,
And gave her to be Lakshmaṇ's bride.
Thus from the princes of the land
Lord Ráma won my maiden hand,
And him exalted high above
Heroic chiefs I truly love.'

CANTO CXIX.

THE FOREST.

When Anasúyá, virtuous-souled,
Had heard the tale by Sítá told,
She kissed the lady's brow and laced
Her loving arms around her waist.
'With sweet-toned words distinct and clear
Thy pleasant tale has charmed mine ear,
How the great king thy father held
That Maiden's Choice unparalleled.
But now the sun has sunk from sight,
And left the world to holy Night.
Hark! how the leafy thickets sound
With gathering birds that twitter round :
They sought their food by day, and all
Flock homeward when the shadows fall.
See, hither comes the hermit band,
Each with his pitcher in his hand :
Fresh from the bath, their locks are wet,
Their coats of bark are dripping yet.
Here saints their fires of worship tend,
And curling wreaths of smoke ascend :
Borne on the flames they mount above,
Dark as the brown wings of the dove.
The distant trees, though well-nigh bare,
Gloom thickenend by the evening air,
And in the faint uncertain light
Shut the horizon from our sight.
The beasts that prowl in darkness rove
On every side about the grove,
And the tame deer, at ease reclined
Their shelter near the altars find.
The night o'er all the sky is spread,
With lunar stars engarlanded,
And risen in his robes of light
The moon is beautifully bright.
Now to thy lord I bid thee go :
Thy pleasant tale has charmed me so :
One thing alone I needs must pray,
Before me first thyself array :
Here in thy heavenly raiment shine,
And glad, dear love, these eyes of mine.'

Then like a heavenly Goddess shone
Fair Sítá with that raiment on.
She bowed her to the matron's feet,
Then turned away her lord to meet.
The hero prince with joy surveyed
His Sítá in her robes arrayed,
As glorious to his arms she came
With love-gifts of the saintly dame.
She told him how the saint to show
Her fond affection would bestow
That garland of celestial twine,
Those ornaments and robes divine.
Then Ráma's heart, nor Lakshmaṇ's less,
Was filled with pride and happiness,
For honours high had Sítá gained,
Which mortal dames have scarce obtained.
There honoured by each pious sage
Who dwelt within the hermitage,
Beside his darling well content
That sacred night the hero spent.
The princes, when the night had fled,
Farewell to all the hermits said,
Who gazed upon the distant shade,
Their lustral rites and offerings paid.
The saints who made their dwelling there
In words like these addressed the pair:
'O Princes, monsters fierce and fell
Around that distant forest dwell:
On blood from human veins they feed,
And various forms assume at need,
With savage beasts of fearful power
That human flesh and blood devour.
Our holy saints they rend and tear
When met alone or unaware,
And eat them in their cruel joy:
These chase, O Ráma, or destroy.
By this one path our hermits go
To fetch the fruits that yonder grow:
By this, O Prince, thy feet should stray
Through pathless forests far away.'
Thus by the reverent saints addressed,
And by their prayers auspicious blessed,
He left the holy crowd:
His wife and brother by his side,
Within the mighty wood he hied.
So sinks the Day-God in his pride
Beneath a bank of cloud.

BOOK III.

CANTO I.

THE HERMITAGE.

When Ráma, valiant hero, stood
In the vast shade of Daṇḍak wood,
His eyes on every side he bent
And saw a hermit settlement,
Where coats of bark were hung around,
And holy grass bestrewed the ground.
Bright with Bráhmanic lustre glowed
That circle where the saints abode:
Like the hot sun in heaven it shone,
Too dazzling to be looked upon.
Wild creatures found a refuge where
The court, well-swept, was bright and fair,
And countless birds and roedeer made
Their dwelling in the friendly shade.
Beneath the boughs of well-loved trees
Oft danced the gay Apsarases.[1]
Around was many an ample shed
Wherein the holy fire was fed;
With sacred grass and skins of deer,
Ladles and sacrificial gear,
And roots and fruit, and wood to burn,
And many a brimming water-urn.
Tall trees their hallowed branches spread,
Laden with pleasant fruit, o'erhead;
And gifts which holy laws require,[2]
And solemn offerings burnt with fire,[3]
And Veda chants on every side
That home of hermits sanctified.
There many a flower its odour shed,
And lotus blooms the lake o'erspred.
There, clad in coats of bark and hide,—
Their food by roots and fruit supplied,—
Dwelt many an old and reverend sire
Bright as the sun or Lord of Fire,
All with each worldly sense subdued,
A pure and saintly multitude.
The Veda chants, the saints who trod
The sacred ground and mused on God,
Made that delightful grove appear
Like Brahmá's own most glorious sphere.
As Raghu's splendid son surveyed
That hermit home and tranquil shade,
He loosed his mighty bow-string, then
Drew nearer to the holy men.

---

1 Heavenly nymphs.

2 The *bali*, or present of food to all created beings.

3 The clarified butter &c. cast into the sacred fire.

With keen celestial sight endued
Those mighty saints the chieftain viewed,
With joy to meet the prince they came,
And gentle Sítá dear to fame.
They looked on virtuous Ráma, fair
As Soma[1] in the evening air,
And Lakshmaṇ by his brother's side,
And Sítá long in duty tried,
And with glad blessings every sage
Received them in the hermitage.
Then Ráma's form and stature tall
Entranced the wondering eyes of all,—
His youthful grace, his strength of limb,
And garb that nobly sat on him.
To Lakshmaṇ too their looks they raised,
And upon Sítá's beauty gazed
With eyes that closed not lest their sight
Should miss the vision of delight.
Then the pure hermits of the wood,
Rejoicing in all creatures' good,
Their guest, the glorious Ráma, led
Within a cot with leaves o'erhead.
With highest honour all the best
Of radiant saints received their guest,
With kind observance, as is meet,
And gave him water for his feet.
To highest pitch of rapture wrought
Their stores of roots and fruit they brought.
They poured their blessings on his head,
And 'All we have is thine,' they said.
Then, reverent hand to hand applied,[2]
Each duty-loving hermit cried:
'The king is our protector, bright
In fame, maintainer of the right.
He bears the awful sword, and hence
Deserves an elder's reverence.
One fourth of Indra's essence, he
Preserves his realm from danger free.
Hence honoured by the world, of right
The king enjoys each choice delight.
Thou shouldst to us protection give,
For in thy realm, dear lord, we live:
Whether in town or wood thou be,
Thou art our king, thy people we.
Our wordly arms are laid aside,
Our hearts are tamed and purified.
To thee our guardian, we who earn
Our only wealth by penance turn.'
Then the pure dwellers in the shade
To Raghu's son due honour paid,
And Lakshman, bringing store of roots,
And many a flower, and woodland fruits.
And others strove the prince to please
With all attentive courtesies.

[1] The Moon-God: 'he is,' says the commentator, 'the special deity of Bráhmans.'

[2] 'Because he was an incarnation of the deity,' says the commentator, 'otherwise such honour paid by men of the sacerdotal caste to one of the military would be improper.'

CANTO II.

VIRÁDHA.

Thus entertained he passed the night,
Then, with the morning's early light,
To all the hermits bade adieu
And sought his onward way anew.
He pierced the mighty forest where
Roamed many a deer and pard and bear:
Its ruined pools he scarce could see.
For creeper rent and prostrate tree,
Where shrill cicala's cries were heard,
And plaintive notes of many a bird.
Deep in the thickets of the wood
With Lakshmaṇ and his spouse he stood.
There in the horrid shade he saw
A giant passing nature's law:
Vast as some mountain-peak in size,
With mighty voice and sunken eyes,
Huge, hideous, tall, with monstrous face,
Most ghastly of his giant race.
A tiger's hide the Rákshas wore
Still reeking with the fat and gore:
Huge-faced, like Him who rules the dead,
All living things he struck with dread.
Three lions, tigers four, ten deer
He carried on his iron spear,
Two wolves, an elephant's head beside
With mighty tusks which blood-drops dyed.
When on the three his fierce eye fell,
He charged them with a roar and yell
As furious as the grisly King
When stricken worlds are perishing
Then with a mighty roar that shook
The earth beneath their feet, he took
The trembling Sítá to his side.
Withdrew a little space, and cried:
'Ha, short-lived wretches! ye who dare,
In hermit dress with matted hair,
Armed each with arrows, sword, and bow,
Through Daṇḍak's pathless wood to go:
How with one dame, I bid you tell,
Can you among ascetics dwell?
Who are ye, sinners, who despise
The right, in holy men's disguise?
The great Virádha, day by day
Through this deep-tangled wood I stray,
And ever, armed with trusty steel,
I seize a saint to make my meal.
This woman young and fair of frame
Shall be the conquering giant's dame:
Your blood, ye things of evil life,
My lips shall quaff in battle strife.'
He spoke: and Janak's hapless child,
Scared by his speech so fierce and wild,

Trembled for terror, as a frail
Young plantain shivers in the gale.
When Ráma saw Virádha clasp
Fair Sítá in his mighty grasp,
Thus with pale lips that terror dried
The hero to his brother cried :
'O see Virádha's arm enfold
My darling in its cursed hold,—
The child of Janak best of kings,
My spouse whose soul to virtue clings,
Sweet princess, with pure glory bright,
Nursed in the lap of soft delight.
Now falls the blow Kaikeyí meant,
Successful in her dark intent:
This day her cruel soul will be
Triumphant over thee and me.
Though Bharat on the throne is set,
Her greedy eyes look farther yet :
Me from my home she dared expel,
Me whom all creatures loved so well.
This fatal day at length, I ween,
Brings triumph to the younger queen.
I see with bitterest grief and shame
Another touch the Maithil dame.
Not loss of sire and royal power
So grieves me as this mournful hour.'
Thus in his anguish cried the chief :
Then drowned in tears, o'erwhelmed by grief,
Thus Lakshman in his anger spake,
Quick panting like a spell-bound snake :
'Canst thou, my brother, Indra's peer,
When I thy minister am near,
Thus grieve like some forsaken thing,
Thou, every creature's lord and king?
My vengeful shaft the fiend shall slay,
And earth shall drink his blood to-day.
The fury which my soul at first
Upon usurping Bharat nursed,
On this Virádha will I wreak
As Indra splits the mountain peak.
Winged by this arm's impetuous might
My shaft with deadly force
The monster in the chest shall smite,
And fell his shattered corse.'

CANTO III.

VIRÁDHA ATTACKED.

Virádha with a fearful shout
That echoed through the wood, cried out :
'What men are ye, I bid you say,
And whither would ye bend your way?'
To him whose mouth shot fiery flame
The hero told his race and name :
'Two Warriors, nobly bred, are we,
And through this wood we wander free.
But who art thou, how born and styled,
Who roamest here in Daṇḍak's wild?'

To Ráma, bravest of the brave,
His answer thus Virádha gave :
'Hear, Raghu's son, and mark me well,
And I my name and race will tell.
Of Śatahradá born, I spring
From Java as my sire, O King :
Me, of this lofty lineage, all
Giants on earth Virádha call.
The rites austere I long maintained
From Brahmá's grace the boon have gained
To bear a charmed frame which ne'er
Weapon or shaft may pierce or tear.
Go as ye came, untouched by fear,
And leave with me this woman here :
Go, swiftly from my presence fly,
Or by this hand ye both shall die.'
Then Ráma with his fierce eyes red
With fury to the giant said:
'Woe to thee, sinner, fond and weak,
Who madly thus thy death wilt seek!
Stand, for it waits thee in the fray :
With life thou ne'er shalt flee away.'
He spoke, and raised the cord whereon
A pointed arrow flashed and shone,
Then, wild with anger, from his bow
He launched the weapon on the foe.
Seven times the fatal cord he drew,
And forth seven rapid arrows flew,
Shafts winged with gold that left the wind
And e'en Suparṇa's[1] self behind.
Full on the giant's breast they smote,
And purpled like the peacock's throat,
Passed through his mighty bulk and came
To earth again like flakes of flame.
The fiend the Maithil dame unclasped ;
In his fierce hand his spear he grasped,
And wild with rage, pierced through and through,
At Ráma and his brother flew.
So loud the roar which chilled with fear,
So massy was the monster's spear,
He seemed, Like Indra's flagstaff, dread
As the dark God who rules the dead.
On huge Virádha fierce as He[2]
Who smites, and worlds have ceased to be,
The princely brothers poured amain
Their fiery flood of arrowy rain.
Unmoved he stood, and opening wide
His dire mouth laughed unterrified,
And ever as the monster gaped
Those arrows from his jaws escaped.
Preserving still his life unharmed,
By Brahmá's saving promise charmed,
His mighty spear aloft in air
He raised, and rushed upon the pair.
From Ráma's bow two arrows flew
And cleft that massive spear in two,

---

[1] The King of birds.

[2] *Kálántakayamopamam,* resembling Yama the destroyer.

Dire as the flaming levin sent
From out the cloudy firmament.
Cut by the shafts he guided well
To earth the giant's weapon fell:
As when from Meru's summit, riven
By fiery bolts, a rock is driven.
Then swift his sword each warrior drew,
Like a dread serpent black of hue,
And gathering fury for the blow
Rushed fiercely on the giant foe.
Around each prince an arm he cast,
And held the dauntless heroes fast;
Then, though his gashes gaped and bled,
Bearing the twain he turned and fled.
Then Ráma saw the giant's plan,
And to his brother thus began:
'O Lakshman, let Virádha still
Hurry us onward as he will,
For look, Sumitrá's son, he goes
Along the path we freely chose.'
He spoke: the rover of the night
Upraised them with terrific might,
Till, to his lofty shoulders swung,
Like children to his neck they clung.
Then sending far his fearful roar,
The princes through the wood he bore,—
A wood like some vast cloud to view,
Where birds of every plumage flew,
And mighty trees o'erarching threw
Dark shadows on the ground;
Where snakes and silvan creatures made
Their dwelling, and the jackal strayed
Through tangled brakes around.

CANTO IV.

VIRÁDHA'S DEATH.

But Sítá viewed with wild affright
The heroes hurried from her sight.
She tossed her shapely arms on high,
And shrieked aloud her bitter cry:
'Ah, the dread giant bears away
The princely Ráma as his prey,
Truthful and pure, and good and great,
And Lakshman shares his brother's fate.
The brindled tiger and the bear
My mangled limbs for food will tear.
Take me, O best of giants, me,
And leave the sons of Raghu free.'
Then, by avenging fury spurred,
Her mournful cry the heroes heard,
And hastened, for the lady's sake,
The wicked monster's life to take.
Then Lakshman with resistless stroke
The foe's left arm that held him broke,
And Ráma too, as swift to smite,
Smashed with his heavy hand the right.
With broken arms and tortured frame
To earth the fainting giant came,
Like a huge cloud, or mighty rock
Rent, sundered by the levin's shock.
Then rushed they on, and crushed and beat
Their foe with arms and fists and feet,
And nerved each mighty limb to pound
And bray him on the level ground.
Keen arrows and each biting blade
Wide rents in breast and side had made;
But crushed and torn and mangled, still
The monster lived they could not kill.
When Ráma saw no arms might slay
The fiend who like a mountain lay,
The glorious hero, swift to save
In danger, thus his counsel gave:
'O Prince of men, his charmed life
No arms may take in battle strife:
Now dig we in this grove a pit
His elephantine bulk to fit,
And let the hollowed earth enfold
The monster of gigantic mould.'
This said, the son of Raghu pressed
His foot upon the giant's breast.
With joy the prostrate monster heard
Victorious Ráma's welcome word,
And straight Kakutstha's son, the best
Of men, in words like these addressed:
'I yield, O chieftain, overthrown
By might that vies with Indra's own.
Till now my folly-blinded eyes
Thee, hero, failed to recognize.
Happy Kauśalyá! blest to be
The mother of a son like thee!
I know thee well, O chieftain, now:
Ráma, the prince of men, art thou.
There stands the high-born Maithil dame,
There Lakshman, lord of mighty fame.
My name was Tumburu,[1] for song
Renowned among the minstrel throng:
Cursed by Kuvera's stern decree
I wear the hideous shape you see.
But when I sued, his grace to crave,
The glorious God this answer gave:
'When Ráma, Daśaratha's son,
Destroys thee and the fight is won,
Thy proper shape once more assume,
And heaven again shall give thee room.'
When thus the angry God replied,
No prayers could turn his wrath aside,
And thus on me his fury fell
For loving Rambhá's[2] charms too well.
Now through thy favour am I freed
From the stern fate the God decreed,
And saved, O tamer of the foe,

[1] Somewhat inconsistently with this part of the story Tumburu is mentioned in Book II. Canto XII as one of the Gandharvas or heavenly minstrels summoned to perform at Bharadvája's feast.

[2] Rambhá appears in Book I. Canto LXIV as the temptress of Viśvámitra.

By thee, to heaven again shall go.
A league, O Prince, beyond this spot
Stands holy Śarabhanga's cot:
The very sun is not more bright
Than that most glorious anchorite:
To him, O Ráma, quickly turn,
And blessings from the hermit earn.
First under earth my body throw,
Then on thy way rejoicing go.
Such is the law ordained of old
For giants when their days are told:
Their bodies laid in earth, they rise
To homes eternal in the skies.'
Thus, by the rankling dart oppressed,
Kakutstha's offspring he addressed:
In earth his mighty body lay,
His spirit fled to heaven away.
Thus spake Virádha ere he died;
And Ráma to his brother cried:
'Now dig we in this grove a pit
His elephantine bulk to fit.
And let the hollowed earth enfold
This mighty giant fierce and bold.'
This said, the valiant hero put
Upon the giant's neck his foot.
His spade obedient Lakshman plied,
And dug a pit both deep and wide
By lofty-souled Virádha's side.
Then Raghu's son his foot withdrew,
And down the mighty form they threw;
One awful shout of joy he gave
And sank into the open grave.
The horoes, to their purpose true,
In fight the cruel demon slew,
And radiant with delight
Deep in the hollowed earth they cast
The monster roaring to the last,
In their resistless might.
Thus when they saw the warrior's steel
No life-destroying blow might deal,
The pair, for lore renowned,
Deep in the pit their hands had made
The unresisting giant laid,
And killed him neath the ground.
Upon himself the monster brought
From Ráma's hand the death he sought
With strong desire to gain:
And thus the rover of the night
Told Ráma, as they strove in fight,
That swords might rend and arrows smite
Upon his breast in vain.
Thus Ráma, when his speech he heard,
The giant's mighty form interred,
Which mortal arms defied.
With thundering crash the giant fell,
And rock and cave and forest dell
With echoing roar replied.
The princes, when their task was done
And freedom from the peril won,
Rejoiced to see him die.
Then in the boundless wood they strayed,
Like the great sun and moon displayed
Triumphant in the sky.[1]

CANTO V.

ŚARABHANGA.

Then Ráma, having slain in fight
Virádha of terrific might,
With gentle words his spouse consoled,
And clasped her in his loving hold.
Then to his brother nobly brave
The valiant prince his counsel gave:
'Wild are these woods around us spread;
And hard and rough the ground to tread:
We, O my brother, ne'er have viewed
So dark and drear a solitude:
To Śarabhanga let us haste,
Whom wealth of holy works has graced.'

Thus Ráma spoke, and took the road
To Śarabhanga's pure abode.
But near that saint whose lustre vied
With Gods, by penance purified,
With startled eyes the prince beheld
A wondrous sight unparalleled.
In splendour like the fire and sun
He saw a great and glorious one.
Upon a noble car he rode,
And many a God behind him glowed:
And earth beneath his feet unpressed[1]
The monarch of the skies confessed.
Ablaze with gems, no dust might dim
The bright attire that covered him.
Arrayed like him, on every side
High saints their master glorified.
Near, borne in air, appeared in view
His car which tawny coursers drew,
Like silver cloud, the moon, or sun
Ere yet the day is well begun.
Wreathed with gay garlands, o'er his head
A pure white canopy was spread,
And lovely nymphs stood nigh to hold
Fair chouris with their sticks of gold,
Which, waving in each gentle hand,
The forehead of their monarch fanned.
God, saint, and bard, a radiant ring,
Sang glory to their heavenly King:
Forth into joyful lauds they burst
As Indra with the sage conversed.
Then Ráma, when his wondering eyes
Beheld the monarch of the skies,

---

[1] The conclusion of this Canto is all a vain repetition: it is manifestly spurious and a very feeble imitation of Válmíki's style. See *Additional Notes*.

[1] 'Even when he had alighted,' says the commentator. The feet of Gods do not touch the ground.

To Lakshman quickly called, and showed
The car wherein Lord Indra rode:
'See, brother, see that air-borne car,
Whose wondrous glory shines afar:
Wherefrom so bright a lustre streams
That like a falling sun it seems.
These are the steeds whose fame we know,
Of heavenly race through heaven they go:
These are the steeds who bear the yoke
Of Śakra,[1] Him whom all invoke.
Behold these youths, a glorious band,
Toward every wind a hundred stand:
A sword in each right hand is borne,
And rings of gold their arms adorn.
What might in every broad deep chest
And club-like arm is manifest!
Clothed in attire of crimson hue
They show like tigers fierce to view.
Great chains of gold each warder deck,
Gleaming like fire beneath his neck.
The age of each fair youth appears
Some score and five of human years:
The ever-blooming prime which they
Who live in heaven retain for aye:
Such mien these lordly beings wear,
Heroic youths, most bright and fair.
Now, brother, in this spot, I pray,
With the Videhan lady stay,
Till I have certain knowledge who
This being is, so bright to view.'

He spoke, and turning from the spot
Sought Śarabhanga's hermit cot.
But when the lord of Śachí[2] saw
The son of Raghu near him draw,
He hastened of the sage to take
His leave, and to his followers spake:
'See, Ráma bends his steps this way,
But ere he yet a word can say,
Come, fly to our celestial sphere;
It is not meet he see me here.
Soon victor and triumphant he
In fitter time shall look on me.
Before him still a great emprise,
A task too hard for others, lies.'

Then with all marks of honour high
The Thunderer bade the saint good-bye,
And in his car which coursers drew
Away to heaven the conqueror flew.
Then Ráma, Lakshman, and the dame,
To Śarabhanga nearer came,
Who sat beside the holy flame.
Before the ancient sage they bent,
And clasped his feet most reverent:
Then at his invitation found
A seat beside him on the ground.
Then Ráma prayed the sage would deign
Lord Indra's visit to explain;
And thus at length the holy man
In answer to his prayer began:
'This Lord of boons has sought me here
To waft me hence to Brahmá's sphere,
Won by my penance long and stern,—
A home the lawless ne'er can earn.
But when I knew that thou wast nigh,
To Brahmá's world I could not fly
Until these longing eyes were blest
With seeing thee, mine honoured guest.
Since thou, O Prince, hast cheered my sight,
Great-hearted lover of the right,
To heavenly spheres will I repair
And bliss supreme that waits me there.
For I have won, dear Prince, my way
To those fair worlds which ne'er decay,
Celestial seat of Brahmá's reign:
Be thine, with me, those worlds to gain.'

Then master, of all sacred lore,
Spake Ráma to the saint once more:
'I, even I, illustrious sage,
Will make those worlds mine heritage:
But now, I pray, some home assign
Within this holy grove of thine.'

Thus Ráma, Indra's peer in might,
Addressed the aged anchorite;
And he, with wisdom well endued,
To Raghu's son his speech renewed:
'Sutíkshṇa's woodland home is near,
A glorious saint of life austere,
True to the path of duty: he
With highest bliss will prosper thee.
Against the stream thy course must be
Of this fair brook Mandákiní,
Whereon light rafts like blossoms glide;
Then to his cottage turn aside.
There lies thy path: but ere thou go,
Look on me, dear one, till I throw
Aside this mould that girds me in,
As casts the snake his withered skin.'

He spoke, the fire in order laid,
With holy oil due offerings made,
And Śarabhanga, glorious sire,
Laid down his body in the fire.
Then rose the flame above his head,
On skin, blood, flesh, and bones it fed,
Till forth, transformed, with radiant hue
Of tender youth, he rose anew.
Far-shining in his bright attire
Came Śarabhanga from the pyre:
Above the home of saints, and those
Who feed the quenchless flame,[1] he rose:
Beyond the seat of Gods he passed,
And Brahmá's sphere was gained at last.

---

[1] A name of Indra.

[2] Śachí is the consort of Indra.

[1] The spheres or mansions gained by those who have duly performed the sacrifices required of them. Different situations are assigned to these spheres, some placing them near the sun, others near the moon.

The noblest of the twice-born race,
For holy works supreme in place,
The Mighty Father there beheld
Girt round by hosts unparalleled;
And Brahmá joying at the sight
Welcomed the glorious anchorite.

CANTO VI.

RÁMA'S PROMISE.

When he his heavenly home had found,
The holy men who dwelt around
To Ráma flocked, whose martial fame
Shone glorious as the kindled flame:
Vaikhánasas [1] who love the wild,
Pure hermits Bálakhilyas [2] styled,
Good Samprakshálas, [3] saints who live
On rays which moon and daystar give:
Those who with leaves their lives sustain
And those who pound with stones their grain:
And they who lie in pools, and those
Whose corn, save teeth, no winnow knows:
Those who for beds the cold earth use,
And those who every couch refuse:
And those condemned to ceaseless pains,
Whose single foot their weight sustains:
And those who sleep neath open skies,
Whose food the wave or air supplies,
And hermits pure who spend their nights
On ground prepared for sacred rites;
Those who on hills their vigil hold,
Or dripping clothes around them fold:
The devotees who live for prayer,
Or the five fires [4] unflinching bear,
On contemplation all intent,
With light that heavenly knowledge lent,
They came to Ráma, saint and sage,
In Śarabhaga's hermitage.
The hermit crowd around him pressed,
And thus the virtuous chief addressed:
'The lordship of the earth is thine,
O Prince of old Ikshváku's line.
Lord of the Gods is Indra, so
Thou art our lord and guide below.
Thy name, the glory of thy might,
Throughout the triple world are bright:
Thy filial love so nobly shown,
Thy truth and virtue well are known.
To thee, O lord, for help we fly,
And on thy love of right rely:
With kindly patience hear us speak,
And grant the boon we humbly seek.
That lord of earth were most unjust,
Foul traitor to his solemn trust,
Who should a sixth of all [1] require,
Nor guard his people like a sire.
But he who ever watchful strives
To guard his subjects' wealth and lives,
Dear as himself or, dearer still,
His sons, with earnest heart and will,—
That king, O Raghu's son, secures
High fame that endless years endures,
And he to Brahmá's world shall rise,
Made glorious in the eternal skies.
Whate'er, by duty won, the meed
Of saints whom roots and berries feed,
One fourth thereof, for tender care
Of subjects, is the monarch's share.
These, mostly of the Bráhman race,
Who make the wood their dwelling-place.
Although a friend in thee they view,
Fall friendless neath the giant crew.
Come, Ráma, come, and see hard by
The holy hermits' corpses lie,
Where many a tangled pathway shows
The murderous work of cruel foes.
These wicked fiends the hermits kill
Who live on Chitrakúṭa's hill,
And blood of slaughtered saints has dyed
Mandákiní and Pampá's side.
No longer can we bear to see
The death of saint and devotee
Whom through the forest day by day
These Rákshases unpitying slay.
To thee, O Prince, we flee, and crave
Thy guardian help our lives to save.
From these fierce rovers of the night
Defend each stricken anchorite.
Throughout the world 'twere vain to seek
An arm like thine to aid the weak.
O Prince, we pray thee hear our call,
And from these fiends preserve us all.'
The son of Raghu heard the plaint
Of penance-loving sage and saint,
And the good prince his speech renewed
To all the hermit multitude:
'To me, O saints, ye need not sue:
I wait the hests of all of you.
I by mine own occasion led
This mighty forest needs must tread,

[1] Hermits who live upon roots which they dig out of the earth: literally *diggers*, derived from the prefix *vi* and *khan* to dig.

[2] Generally, divine personages of the height of a man's thumb, produced from Brahmá's hair: here, according to the commentator followed by Gorresio, hermits who when they have obtained fresh food throw away what they had laid up before.

[3] Sprung from the washings of Vishṇu's feet.

[4] Four fires burning round them, and the sun above.

[1] The tax allowed to the king by the Laws of Manu.

And while I keep my sire's decree
Your lives from threatening foes will free.
I hither came of free accord
To lend the aid by you implored,
And richest meed my toil shall pay,
While here in forest shades I stay.
I long in battle strife to close,
And slay these fiends, the hermits' foes,
That saint and sage may learn aright
My prowess and my brother's might.'
Thus to the saints his promise gave
That prince who still to virtue clave
With never-wandering thought:
And then with Lakshmaṇ by his side,
With penance-wealthy men to guide,
Sutíkshṇa's home he sought.

CANTO VII.

SUTÍKSHṆA.

So Raghu's son, his foemen's dread,
With Sítá and his brother sped,
Girt round by many a twice-born sage,
To good Sutíkshṇa's hermitage.[1]
Through woods for many a league he passed,
O'er rushing rivers full and fast,
Until a mountain fair and bright
As lofty Meru rose in sight.
Within its belt of varied wood
Ikshváku's sons and Sítá stood,
Where trees of every foliage bore
Blossom and fruit in endless store.
There coats of bark, like garlands strung,
Before a lonely cottage hung,
And there a hermit, dust-besmeared,
A lotus on his breast, appeared.
Then Ráma with obeisance due
Addressed the sage, as near he drew:
'My name is Ráma, lord; I seek
Thy presence, saint, with thee to speak.
O sage, whose merits ne'er decay,
Some word unto thy servant say.'
The sage his eyes on Ráma bent,
Of virtue's friends preëminent;
Then words like these he spoke, and pressed
The son of Raghu to his breast:
'Welcome to thee, illustrious youth,
Best champion of the rights of truth!
By thine approach this holy ground
A worthy lord this day has found.
I could not quit this mortal frame
Till thou shouldst come, O dear to fame:
To heavenly spheres I would not rise,
Expecting thee with eager eyes.
I knew that thou, unkinged, hadst made
Thy home in Chitrakúṭa's shade.
E'en now, O Ráma, Indra, lord
Supreme by all the Gods adored,
King of the Hundred Offerings,[1] said,
When he my dwelling visited,
That the good works that I have done
My choice of all the worlds have won.
Accept this meed of holy vows,
And with thy brother and thy spouse,
Roam, through my favour, in the sky
Which saints celestial glorify.'
To that bright sage, of penance stern,
The high-souled Ráma spake in turn,
As Vásava[2] who rules the skies
To Brahmá's gracious speech replies:
'I of myself those worlds will win,
O mighty hermit pure from sin:
But now, O saint, I pray thee tell
Where I within this wood may dwell:
For I by Śarabhanga old,
The son of Gautama, was told
That thou in every lore art wise,
And seest all with loving eyes.'
Thus to the saint, whose glories high
Filled all the world, he made reply:
And thus again the holy man
His pleasant speech with joy began:
'This calm retreat, O Prince, is blest
With many a charm: here take thy rest.
Here roots and kindly fruits abound,
And hermits love the holy ground.
Fair silvan beasts and gentle deer
In herds unnumbered wander here:
And as they roam, secure from harm,
Our eyes with grace and beauty charm:
Except the beasts in thickets bred,
This grove of ours has naught to dread.'
The hermit's speech when Ráma heard,—
The hero ne'er by terror stirred,—
On his great bow his hand he laid,
And thus in turn his answer made:
'O saint, my darts of keenest steel,
Armed with their murderous barbs, would deal
Destruction mid the silvan race
That flocks around thy dwelling-place.
Most wretched then my fate would be
For such dishonour shown to thee:
And only for the briefest stay
Would I within this grove delay.'
He spoke and ceased. With pious care
He turned him to his evening prayer,
Performed each customary rite,
And sought his lodging for the night,
With Sítá and his brother laid

[1] Near the celebrated Rámagiri or Ráma's Hill, now Rám-ṭek, near Nagpore —the scene of the Yaksha's exile in the *Messenger Cloud*.

[1] A hundred *Aśvamedhas* or sacrifices of a horse raise the sacrificer to the dignity of Indra.

[2] Indra.

Beneath the grove's delightful shade,
First good Sutíkshṇa, when he saw
The shades of night around them draw,
With hospitable care
The princely chieftains entertained
With store of choicest food ordained
For holy hermit's fare.

CANTO VIII.

THE HERMITAGE.

So Ráma and Sumitrá's son,
When every honour due was done,
Slept through the night. When morning broke,
The heroes from their rest awoke.
Betimes the son of Raghu rose,
With gentle Sítá, from repose,
And sipped the cool delicious wave
Sweet with the scent the lotus gave,
Then to the Gods and sacred flame
The heroes and the lady came,
And bent their heads in honour meet
Within the hermit's pure retreat.
When every stain was purged away,
They saw the rising Lord of Day:
Then to Sutíkhṇa's side they went,
And softly spoke, most reverent:
'Well have we slept, O holy lord,
Honoured of thee by all adored:
Now leave to journey forth we pray:
These hermits urge us on our way.
We haste to visit, wandering by,
The ascetics' homes that round you lie,
And roaming Daṇdak's mighty wood
To view each saintly brotherhood.
For thy permission now we sue,
With these high saints to duty true,
By penance taught each sense to tame,—
In lustre like the smokeless flame.
Ere on our brows the sun can beat
With fierce intolerable heat,
Like some unworthy lord who wins
His power by tyranny and sins,
O saint, we fain would part.' The three
Bent humbly to the dovotee.
He raised the princes as they pressed
His feet, and strained them to his breast;
And then the chief of devotees
Bespake them both in words like these:
'Go with thy brother, Ráma, go,
Pursue thy path untouched by woe:
Go with thy faithful Sítá, she
Still like a shadow follows thee.
Roam Daṇdak wood observing well
The pleasant homes where hermits dwell,—
Pure saints whose ordered souls adhere
To penance rites and vows austere.
There plenteous roots and berries grow,
And noble trees their blossoms show,
And gentle deer and birds of air
In peaceful troops are gathered there.
There see the full-blown lotus stud
The bosom of the lucid flood,
And watch the joyous mallard shake
The reeds that fringe the pool and lake.
See with delighted eye the rill
Leap sparkling from her parent hill,
And hear the woods that round thee lie
Reëcho to the peacock's cry.
And as I bid thy brother, so,
Sumitrá's child, I bid thee go.
Go forth, these varied beauties see,
And then once more return to me.'
Thus spake the sage Sutíkshṇa: both
The chiefs assented, nothing loth.
Round him with circling steps they paced,
Then for the road prepared with haste.
There Sítá stood, the dame long-eyed,
Fair quivers round their waists she tied,
And gave each prince his trusty bow,
And sword which ne'er a spot might know.
Each took his quiver from her hand,
And clanging bow and gleaming brand:
Then from the hermits' home the two
Went forth each woodland scene to view.
Each beauteous in the bloom of age,
Dismissed by that illustrious sage,
With bow and sword accoutred, hied
Away, and Sítá by their side.

CANTO IX.

SÍTÁ'S SPEECH.

Blest by the sage, when Raghu's son
His onward journey had begun,
Thus in her soft tone Sítá, meek
With modest fear, began to speak:
'One little slip the great may lead
To shame that follows lawless deed:
Such shame, my lord, as still must cling
To faults from low desire that spring.
Three several sins defile the soul,
Born of desire that spurns control:
First, utterance of a lying word,
Then, viler both, the next, and third:
The lawless love of other's wife,
The thirst of blood uncaused by strife.
The first, O Raghu's son, in thee
None yet has found, none e'er shall see.
Love of another's dame destroys
All merit, lost for guilty joys:
Ráma, such crime in thee, I ween,
Has ne'er been found, shall ne'er be seen:
The very thought, my princely lord,
Is in thy secret soul abhorred.

For thou hast ever been the same
Fond lover of thine own dear dame,
Content with faithful heart to do
Thy father's will, most just and true:
Justice, and faith, and many a grace
In thee have found a resting-place.
Such virtues, Prince, the good may gain
Who empire o'er each sense retain;
And well canst thou, with loving view
Regarding all, each sense subdue.
But for the third, the lust that strives,
Insatiate still, for others' lives,—
Fond thirst of blood where hate is none,—
This, O my lord, thou wilt not shun.
Thou hast but now a promise made,
The saints of Danndak wood to aid;
And to protect their lives from ill
The giants' blood in fight wilt spill:
And from thy promise lasting fame
Will glorify the forest's name.
Armed with thy bow and arrows thou
Forth with thy brother journeyest now,
While as I think how true thou art
Fears for thy bliss assail my heart,
And all my spirit at the sight
Is troubled with a strange affright.
I like it not—it seems not good—
Thy going thus to Dandak wood:
And I, if thou wilt mark me well,
The reason of my fear will tell.
Thou with thy brother, bow in hand,
Beneath those ancient trees wilt stand,
And thy keen arrows will not spare
Wood-rovers who will meet thee there.
For as the fuel food supplies
That bids the dormant flame arise,
Thus when the warrior grasps his bow
He feels his breast with ardour glow.
Deep in a holy grove, of yore,
Where bird and beast from strife forbore,
Śuchi beneath the sheltering boughs,
A truthful hermit, kept his vows.
Then Indra, Śachí's heavenly lord,
Armed like a warrior with a sword,
Came to his tranquil home to spoil
The hermit of his holy toil,
And left the glorious weapon there
Entrusted to the hermit's care,
A pledge for him to keep, whose mind
To fervent zeal was all resigned.
He took the brand: with utmost heed
He kept it for the warrior's need:
To keep his trust he fondly strove
When roaming in the neighbouring grove:
Whene'er for roots and fruit he strayed
Still by his side he bore the blade:
Still on his sacred charge intent,
He took his treasure when he went.
As day by day that brand he wore,
The hermit, rich in merit's store,
From penance rites each thought withdrew,
And fierce and wild his spirit grew.
With heedless soul he spurned the right,
And found in cruel deeds delight.
So, living with the sword, he fell,
A ruined hermit, down to hell.
This tale applies to those who deal
Too closely with the warrior's steel:
The steel to warriors is the same
As fuel to the smouldering flame.
Sincere affection prompts my speech:
I honour where I fain would teach.
Mayst thou, thus armed with shaft and bow,
So dire a longing never know
As, when no hatred prompts the fray,
These giants of the wood to slay:
For he who kills without offence
Shall win but little glory thence.
The bow the warrior joys to bend
Is lent him for a nobler end,
That he may save and succour those
Who watch in woods when pressed by foes.
What, matched with woods, is bow or steel?
What, warrior's arm with hermit's zeal?
We with such might have naught to do:
The forest rule should guide us too.
But when Ayodhyá hails thee lord,
Be then thy warrior life restored:
So shall thy sire [1] and mother joy
In bliss that naught may e'er destroy.
And if, resigning empire, thou
Submit thee to the hermit's vow,
The noblest gain from virtue springs,
And virtue joy unending brings.
All earthly blessings virtue sends:
On virtue all the world depends.
Those who with vow and fasting tame
To due restraint the mind and frame,
Win by their labour, nobly wise,
The highest virtue for their prize.
Pure in the hermit's grove remain,
True to thy duty, free from stain.
But the three worlds are open thrown
To thee, by whom all things are known.
Who gave me power that I should dare
His duty to my lord declare?
'Tis woman's fancy, light as air,
  That moves my foolish breast.
Now with thy brother counsel take,
Reflect, thy choice with judgment make,
  And do what seems the best.'

[1] Gorresio observes that Daśaratha was dead and that Sítá had been informed of his death. In his translation he substitutes for the words of the text 'thy relations and mine.' This is quite superfluous. Daśaratha though in heaven still took a loving interest in the fortunes of his son.

CANTO X.

RÁMA'S REPLY.

The words that Sítá uttered, spurred
By truest love, the hero heard :
Then he who ne'er from virtue strayed
To Janak's child his answer made:
' In thy wise speech, sweet love, I find
True impress of thy gentle mind,
Well skilled the warrior's path to trace,
Thou pride of Janak's ancient race.
What fitting answer shall I frame
To thy good words, my honoured dame ?
Thou sayst the warrior bears the bow
That misery's tears may cease to flow ;
And those pure saints who love the shade
Of Dandak wood are sore dismayed.
They sought me of their own accord,
With suppliant prayers my aid implored :
They, fed on roots and fruit, who spend
Their lives where bosky wilds extend,
My timid love, enjoy no rest
By these malignant fiends distressed.
These make the flesh of man their meat:
The helpless saints they kill and eat.
The hermits sought my side, the chief
Of Bráhman race declared their grief.
I heard, and from my lips there fell
The words which thou rememberest well :
I listened as the hermits cried,
And to their prayers I thus replied :
' Your favour, gracious lords, I claim,
O'erwhelmed with this enormous shame
That Bráhmans, great and pure as you,
Who should be sought, to me should sue.'
And then before the saintly crowd,
' What can I do?' I cried aloud.
Then from the trembling hermits broke
One long sad cry, and thus they spoke:
' Fiends of the wood, who wear at will
Each varied shape, afflict us still.
To thee in our distress we fly :
O help us, Ráma, or we die.
When sacred rites of fire are due,
When changing moons are full or new,
These fiends who bleeding flesh devour
Assail us with resistless power.
They with their cruel might torment
The hermits on their vows intent:
We look around for help and see
Our surest refuge, Prince, in thee.
We, armed with powers of penance, might
Destroy the rovers of the night:
But loth were we to bring to naught
The merit years of toil have bought.
Our penance rites are grown too hard,
By many a check and trouble barred,
But though our saints for food are slain
The withering curse we yet restrain.
Thus many a weary day distressed
By giants who this wood infest,
We see at length deliverance, thou
With Lakshman art our guardian now.'
As thus the troubled hermits prayed,
I promised, dame, my ready aid,
And now—for truth I hold most dear—
Still to my word must I adhere.
My love, I might endure to be
Deprived of Lakshman, life, and thee,
But ne'er deny my promise, ne'er
To Bráhmans break the oath I sware.
I must, enforced by high constraint,
Protect them all. Each suffering saint
In me, unasked, his help had found ;
Still more in one by promise bound.
I know thy words, mine own dear dame,
From thy sweet heart's affection came :
I thank thee for thy gentle speech,
For those we love are those we teach.
'Tis like thyself, O fair of face,
'Tis worthy of thy noble race :
Dearer than life, thy feet are set
In righteous paths they ne'er forget.'
Thus to the Maithil monarch's child,
His own dear wife, in accents mild
The high-souled hero said :
Then to the holy groves which lay
Beyond them fair to see, their way
The bow-armed chieftain led.

CANTO XI.

AGASTYA.

Ráma went foremost of the three,
Next Sítá, followed, fair to see,
And Lakshman with his bow in hand
Walked hindmost of the little band.
As onward through the wood they went,
With great delight their eyes were bent
On rocky heights beside the way
And lofty trees with blossoms gay;
And streamlets running fair and fast
The royal youths with Sítá passed.
They watched the sáras and the drake
On islets of the stream and lake,
And gazed delighted on the floods
Bright with gay birds and lotus buds.
They saw in startled herds the roes,
The passion-frenzied buffaloes,
Wild elephants who fiercely tore
The tender trees, and many a boar.
A length of woodland way they passed,
And when the sun was low at last
A lovely stream-fed lake they spied,
Two leagues across from side to side.
Tall elephants fresh beauty gave
To grassy bank and lilied wave,

By many a swan and sáras stirred,
Mallard, and gay-winged water-bird.
From those sweet waters, loud and long,
Though none was seen to wake the song,
Swelled high the singer's music blent
With each melodious instrument.
Ráma and car-borne Lakshman heard
The charming strain, with wonder stirred,
Turned on the margent of the lake
To Dharmabhrit[1] the sage, and spake:
'Our longing souls, O hermit, burn
This music of the lake to learn:
We pray thee, noblest sage, explain
The cause of the mysterious strain.'
He, as the son of Raghu prayed,
With swift accord his answer made,
And thus the hermit, virtuous-souled,
The story of the fair lake told:

'Through every age 'tis known to fame,
Panchápsaras[2] its glorious name,
By holy Mándakarṇi wrought
With power his rites austere had bought.
For he, great votarist, intent
On strictest rule his stern life spent.
Ten thosand years the stream his bed,
Ten thousand years on air he fed.
Then on the blessed Gods who dwell
In heavenly homes great terror fell:
They gathered all, by Agni led,
And counselled thus disquieted:
'The hermit by ascetic pain
The seat of one of us would gain.'
Thus with their hearts by fear oppressed
In full assembly spoke the Blest,
And bade five loveliest nymphs, as fair
As lightning in the evening air,
Armed with their winning wiles, seduce
From his stern vows the great recluse.
Though lore of earth and heaven he knew,
The hermit from his task they drew,
And made the great ascetic slave
To conquering love, the Gods to save.
Each of the heavenly five became,
Bound to the sage, his wedded dame;
And he, for his beloved's sake,
Formed a fair palace neath the lake.
Under the flood the ladies live,
To joy and ease their days they give,
And lap in bliss the hermit wooed
From penance rites to youth renewed.
So when the sportive nymphs within
Those secret bowers their play begin,
You hear the singers' dulcet tones
Blend sweetly with their tinkling zones.'

'How wondrous are these words of thine!'
Cried the famed chiefs of Raghu's line,
As thus they heard the sage unfold
The marvels of the tale he told.
As Ráma spake, his eyes were bent
Upon a hermit settlement
With light of heavenly lore endued,
With sacred grass and vesture strewed.
His wife and brother by his side,
Within the holy bounds he hied,
And there, with honour entertained
By all the saints, a while remained.
In time, by due succession led,
Each votary's cot he visited,
And then the lord of martial lore,
Returned where he had lodged before.
Here for the months, content, he stayed,
There for a year his visit paid:
Here for four months his home would fix,
There, as it chanced, for five or six.
Here for eight months and there for three
The son of Raghu's stay would be:
Here weeks, there fortnights, more or less,
He spent in tranquil happiness.
As there the hero dwelt at ease
Among those holy devotees,
In days untroubled o'er his head
Ten circling years of pleasure fled.
So Raghu's son in duty trained
A while in every cot remained,
Then with his dame retraced the road
To good Sutíkshṇa's calm abode.
Hailed by the saints with honours due
Near to the hermit's home he drew,
And there the tamer of his foes
Dwelt for a time in sweet repose.
One day within that holy wood
By saint Sutíkshṇa Ráma stood,
And thus the prince with reverence meek
To that high sage began to speak:
'In the wide woodlands that extend
Around us, lord most reverend,
As frequent voice of rumour tells,
Agastya, saintliest hermit, dwells.
So vast the wood, I cannot trace
The path to reach his dwelling place,
Nor, searching unassisted, find
That hermit of the thoughtful mind.
I with my wife and brother fain
Would go, his favour to obtain,
Would seek him in his lone retreat
And the great saint with reverence greet.
This one desire, O Master, long
Cherished within my heart, is strong,
That I may pay of free accord
My duty to that hermit lord.'
As thus the prince whose heart was bent
On virtue told his firm intent,
The good Sutíkshṇa's joy rose high,
And thus in turn he made reply:
The very thing, O Prince, which thou
Hast sought, I wished to urge but now,
Bid thee with wife and brother see

[1] One of the hermits who had followed Ráma.

[2] The lake of the five nymphs.

Agastya, glorious devotee.
I count this thing an omen fair
That thou shouldst thus thy wish declare,
And I, my Prince, will gladly teach
The way Agastya's home to reach.
Southward, dear son, direct thy feet
Eight leagues beyond this still retreat:
Agastya's hermit brother there
Dwells in a home most bright and fair.
'Tis on a knoll of woody ground,
With many a branching Pippal[1] crowned:
There sweet birds' voices ne'er are mute,
And trees are gay with flower and fruit.
There many a lake gleams bright and cool,
And lilies deck each pleasant pool.
While swan, and crane, and mallard's wings
Are lovely in the water-springs.
There for one night, O Ráma, stay,
And with the dawn pursue thy way.
Still farther, bending southward, by
The thicket's edge thy course must lie,
And thou wilt see, two leagues from thence
Agastya's lovely residence,
Set in the woodland's fairest spot,
All varied foliage decks the cot:
There Sítá, Lakshmaṇ thou, at ease
May spend sweet hours neath shady trees,
For all of noblest growth are found
Luxuriant on that bosky ground.
If it be still thy firm intent
To see that saint preëminent,
O mighty counsellor, this day
Depart upon thine onward way.'
The hermit spake, and Ráma bent
His head, with Lakshmaṇ, reverent,
And then with him and Janak's child
Set out to trace the forest wild.
He saw dark woods that fringed the road,
And distant hills like clouds that showed,
And, as the way he followed, met
With many a lake and rivulet.
So passing on with ease where led
The path Sutíkshṇa bade him tread,
The hero with exulting breast
His brother in these words addressed:
'Here, surely, is the home, in sight,
Of that illustrious anchorite:
Here great Agastya's brother leads
A life intent on holy deeds.
Warned of each guiding mark and sign,
I see them all herein combine:
I see the branches bending low
Beneath the flowers and fruit they show.
A soft air from the forest springs,
Fresh from the odorous grass, and brings
A spicy fragrance as it flees
O'er the ripe fruit of Pippal trees.
See, here and there around us high
Piled up in heaps cleft billets lie,
And holy grass is gathered, bright
As strips of shining lazulite.
Full in the centre of the shade
The hermits' holy fire is laid:
I see its smoke the pure heaven streak
Dense as a big cloud's dusky peak.
The twice-born men their steps retrace
From each sequestered bathing-place,
And each his sacred gift has brought
Of blossoms which his hands have sought.
Of all these signs, dear brother, each
Agrees with good Sutíkshṇa's speech,
And doubtless in this holy bound
Agastya's brother will be found.
Agastya once, the worlds who viewed
With love, a Deathlike fiend subdued,
And armed with mighty power, obtained
By holy works, this grove ordained
To be a refuge and defence
From all oppressors' violence.
In days of yore within this place
Two brothers fierce of demon race,
Vátápi dire and Ilval, dwelt,
And slaughter mid the Bráhmans dealt.
A Bráhman's form, the fiend to cloak,
Fierce Ilval wore, and Sanskrit spoke,
And twice-born sages would invite
To solemnize some funeral rite.
His brother's flesh, concealed within
A ram's false shape and borrowed skin,—
As men are wont at funeral feasts,—
He dressed, and fed those gathered priests.
The holy men, unweeting ill,
Took of the food and ate their fill.
Then Ilval with a mighty shout
Exclaimed 'Vátápi, issue out.'
Soon as his brother's voice he heard,
The fiend with ram-like bleating stirred:
Rending in pieces every frame,
Forth from the dying priests he came.
So they who changed their forms at will
Thousands of Bráhmans dared to kill,—
Fierce fiends who loved each cruel deed,
And joyed on bleeding flesh to feed.
Agastya, mighty hermit, pressed
To funeral banquet like the rest,
Obedient to the Gods' appeal
Ate up the monster at a meal.
''Tis done, 'tis done,' fierce Ilval cried,
And water for his hands supplied:
Then lifting up his voice he spake:
'Forth, brother, from thy prison break.'
Then him who called the fiend, who long
Had wrought the suffering Bráhmans wrong,
Thus thoughtful-souled Agastya, best
Of hermits, with a smile addressed:
'How, Rákshas, is the fiend empowered
To issue forth whom I devoured?
Thy brother in a ram's disguise
Is gone where Yama's kingdom lies.'

[1] The holy fig-tree.

When from the words Agastya said
He knew his brother fiend was dead,
His soul on fire with vengeful rage,
Rushed the night-rover at the sage.
One lightning glance of fury, hot
As fire, the glorious hermit shot,
As the fiend neared him in his stride,
And straight, consumed to dust, he died.
In pity for the Bráhmans' plight
Agastya wrought this deed of might:
This grove which lakes and fair trees grace
In his great brother's dwelling place.
As Ráma thus the tale rehearsed,
And with Sumitrá's son conversed,
The setting sun his last rays shed,
And evening o'er the land was spread.
A while the princely brothers stayed
And even rites in order paid,
Then to the holy grove they drew
And hailed the saint with honour due.
With courtesy was Ráma met
By that illustrious anchoret,
And for one night he rested there
Regaled with fruit and hermit fare.
But when the night had reached its close,
And the sun's glorious circle rose,
The son of Raghu left his bed
And tothe hermit's brother said:
'Well rested in thy hermit cell,
I stand, O saint, to bid farewell;
For with thy leave I journey hence
Thy broher saint to reverence.'
'Go, Ráma go,' the sage replied:
Then from the cot the chieftain hied,
And while the pleasant grove he viewed,
The path the hermit showed, pursued.
Of every leaf, of changing hue,
Plants, trees by hundreds round him grew,
With joyous eyes he looked on all,
Then Jak,[1] the wild rice, and Sál;[2]
He saw the red Hibiscus glow,
He saw the flower-tipped creeper throw
The glory of her clusters o'er
Tall trees that loads of blossom bore.
Some, elephants had prostrate laid,
In some the monkeys leapt and played,
And through the whole wide forest rang
The charm of gay birds as they sang.
Then Ráma of the lotus eye
To Lakshman turned who followed nigh,
And thus the hero youth impressed
With Fortune's favouring signs, addressed:
'How soft the leaves of every tree,
How tame each bird and beast we see!
Soon the fair home shall we behold
Of that great hermit tranquil-souled.
The deed the good Agastya wrought
High fame throughout the world has bought:
I see, I see his calm retreat
That balms the pain of weary feet.
Where white clouds rise from flames beneath,
Where bark-coats lie with many a wreath,
Where silvan things, made gentle, throng,
And every bird is loud in song.
With ruth for suffering creatures filled,
A deathlike fiend with might he killed,
And gave this southern realm to be
A refuge, from oppression free.
There stands his home, whose dreaded might
Has put the giant crew to flight,
Who view with envious eyes afar
The peaceful shades they cannot mar.
Since that most holy saint has made
His dwelling in this lovely shade.
Checked by his might the giant brood
Have dwelt in peace with souls subdued.
And all this southern realm, within
Whose bounds no fiend may entrance win,
Now bears a name which naught may dim,
Made glorious through the worlds by him.
When Vindhya, best of hills, would stay
The journey of the Lord of Day,
Obedient to the saint's behest
He bowed for aye his humbled crest.
That hoary hermit, world-renowned
For holy deeds, within this ground
Has set his pure and blessed home,
Where gentle silvan creatures roam.
Agastya, whom the worlds revere,
Pure saint to whom the good are dear,
To us his guests all grace will show,
Enriched with blessings ere we go.
I to this aim each thought will turn,
The favour of the saint to earn,
That here in comfort may be spent
The last years of our banishment.
Here sanctities and high saints stand,
Gods, minstrels of the heavenly band;
Upon Agastya's will they wait,
And serve him, pure and temperate.
The liar's tongue, the tyrant's mind
Within these bounds no home may find:
No cheat, no sinner here can be:
So holy and so good is he.
Here birds and lords of serpent race,
Spirits and Gods who haunt the place,
Content with scanty fare remain,
As merit's meed they strive to gain.
Made perfect here, the saints supreme,
On cars that mock the Day-God's gleam,—
Their mortal bodies cast aside,—
Sought heaven transformed and glorified.
Here Gods to living things, who win
Their favour, pure from cruel sin,
Give royal rule and many a good,

[1] The bread-fruit tree, Artocarpus integrifolia.

[2] A fine timber tree, Shorea robusta.

Immortal life and spirithood.
Now, Lakshman, we are near the place :
Do thou precede a little space,
And tell the mighty saint that I
With Sítá at my side am nigh.'

CANTO XII.

THE HEAVENLY BOW.

He spoke : the younger prince obeyed :
Within the bounds his way he made,
And thus addressed, whom first he met,
A pupil of the anchoret :
'Brave Ráma, eldest born, who springs
From Daśaratha, hither brings
His wife the lady Sítá : he
Would fain the holy hermit see.
Lakshman am I—if happy fame
E'er to thine ears has brought the name—
His younger brother, prompt to do
His will, devoted, fond, and true.
We, through our royal sire's decree,
To the dread woods were forced to flee.
Tell the great Master, I entreat,
Our earnest wish our lord to greet.'
He spoke : the hermit rich in store
Of fervid zeal and sacred lore,
Sought the pure shrine which held the fire,
To bear his message to the sire.
Soon as he reached the saint most bright
In sanctity's surpassing might,
He cried, uplifting reverent hands :
'Lord Ráma near thy cottage stands.'
Then spoke Agastya's pupil dear
The message for his lord to hear :
'Ráma and Lakshman, chiefs who spring
From Daśaratha, glorious king,
Thy hermitage e'en now have sought,
And lady Sítá with them brought.
The tamers of the foe are here
To see thee, Master, and revere.
'Tis thine thy further will to say :
Deign to command, and we obey.'
When from his pupil's lips he knew
The presence of the princely two,
And Sítá born to fortune high,
The glorious hermit made reply :
'Great joy at last is mine this day
That Ráma hither finds his way,
For long my soul has yearned to see
The prince who comes to visit me.
Go forth, go forth, and hither bring
The royal three with welcoming :
Lead Ráma in and place him near :
Why stands he not already here ?'
Thus ordered by the hermit, who,
Lord of his thoughts, all duty knew,
His reverent hands together laid,
The pupil answered and obeyed.
Forth from the place with speed he ran,
To Lakshman came and thus began :
'Where is he? let not Ráma wait,
But speed, the sage to venerate.'
Then with the pupil Lakshman went
Across the hermit settlement,
And showed him Ráma where he stood
With Janak's daughter in the wood.
The pupil then his message spake
Which the kind hermit bade him take ;
Then led the honoured Ráma thence
And brought him in with reverence.
As nigh the royal Ráma came
With Lakshman and the Maithil dame,
He viewed the herds of gentle deer
Roaming the garden free from fear.
As through the sacred grove he trod
He viewed the seat of many a God,
Brahmá and Agni,[1] Sun and Moon,
And His who sends each golden boon ;[2]
Here Vishṇu's stood, there Bhaga's[3] shrine,
And there Mahendra's, Lord divine ;
Here His who formed this earthly frame,[4]
His there from whom all beings came.[5]
Váyu's,[6] and His who loves to hold
The great noose, Varuṇ[7] mighty-souled :
Here was the Vasus'[8] shrine to see,
Here that of sacred Gáyatri,[9]
The king of serpents[10] here had place,
And he who rules the feathered race.[11]
Here Kártikeya,[12] warrior lord,
And there was Justice' King adored.
Then with disciples girt about
The mighty saint himself came out :
Through fierce devotion bright as flame
Before the rest the Master came :
And then to Lakshman, fortune blest,
Ráma these hasty words addressed :
'Behold, Agastya's self draws near,
The mighty saint whom all revere :
With spirit raised I meet my lord
With richest wealth of penance stored.'
The strong-armed hero spake, and ran
Forward to meet the sunbright man.
Before him, as he came, he bent
And clasped his feet most reverent,
Then rearing up his stately height
Stood suppliant by the anchorite,
While Lakshman's strength and Sítás grace
Stood by the pride of Raghu's race.

---

[1] The God of fire.

[2] Kuvera, the God of riches.

[3] The Sun. [4] Brahmá, the creator.

[5] Śiva. [6] The Wind-God.

[7] The God of the sea.

[8] A class of demi-gods, eight in number.

[9] The holiest text of the Vedas, deified.

[10] Vásuki. [11] Garuḍ.

[12] The War-God.

The sage his arms round Ráma threw
And welcomed him with honours due,
Asked, was all well, with question sweet,
And bade the hero to a seat.
With holy oil he fed the flame,
He brought the gifts which strangers claim,
And kindly waiting on the three
With honours due to high degree,
He gave with hospitable care
A simple hermit's woodland fare.
Then sat the reverend father, first
Of hermits, deep in duty versed,
And thus to suppliant Ráma, bred
In all the lore of virtue, said:
'Did the false hermit, Prince, neglect
To hail his guest with due respect,
He must,—the doom the perjured meet,—
His proper flesh hereafter eat.
A car-borne king, a lord who sways
The earth, and virtue's law obeys,
Worthy of highest honour, thou
Hast sought, dear guest, my cottage now.'
He spoke: with fruit and hermit fare,
With every bloom the branches bare,
Agastya graced his honoured guest,
And thus with gentle words addressed:
'Accept this mighty bow, divine,
Whereon red gold and diamonds shine;
'Twas by the Heavenly Artist planned
For Vishṇu's own almighty hand;
This God-sent shaft of sunbright hue,
Whose deadly flight is ever true,
By Lord Mahendra given of yore:
This quiver with its endless store,
Keen arrows hurtling to their aim
Like kindled fires that flash and flame:
Accept, in golden sheath encased,
This sword with hilt of rich gold graced.
Armed, whilom, with this best of bows
Lord Vishṇu slew his demon foes,
And mid the dwellers in the skies
Won brilliant glory for his prize.
The bow, the quivers, shaft, and sword
Received from me, O glorious lord:
These conquest to thine arm shall bring,
As thunder to the thunder's King.'
The splendid hermit bade him take
The noble weapons as he spake,
And as the prince accepted each
In words like these renewed his speech:

CANTO XIII.

AGASTYA'S COUNSEL.

'O Ráma, great delight I feel,
Pleased, Lakshmaṇ, with thy faithful zeal,
That you within these shades I see
With Sítá come to honour me.
But wandering through the rough rude wild
Has wearied Janak's gentle child:
With labours of the way oppressed
The Maithil lady longs for rest.
Young, delicate, and soft, and fair,
Such toils as these untrained to bear,
Her wifely love the dame has led
The forest's troubled ways to tread.
Here, Ráma, see that naught annoy
Her easy hours of tranquil joy:
A glorious task has she assayed,
To follow thee through woodland shade.
Since first from Nature's hand she came,
A woman's mood is still the same,
When Fortune smiles, her love to show,
And leave her lord in want and woe.
No pity then her heart can feel,
She arms her soul with warrior's steel,
Swift as the storm or Feathered King,
Uncertain as the lightning's wing.
Not so thy spouse: her purer mind
Shrinks from the faults of womankind;
Like chaste Arundhatí[1] above,
A paragon of faithful love.
Let these blest shades, dear Ráma, be
A home for Lakshmaṇ, her, and thee.'
With raised hands reverently meek
He heard the holy hermit speak,
And humbly thus addressed the sire
Whose glory shone like kindled fire:
'How blest am I, what thanks I owe
That our great Master deigns to show
His favour, that his heart can be
Content with Lakshmaṇ, Sítá, me.
Show me, I pray, some spot of ground
Where thick trees wave and springs abound,
That I may raise my hermit cell
And there in tranquil pleasure dwell.'
Then thus replied Agastya, best
Of hermits, to the chief's request:
When for a little he had bent
His thoughts, upon that prayer intent:
'Beloved son, four leagues away
Is Panchavaṭí bright and gay:
Thronged with its deer, most fair it looks
With berries, fruit, and water-brooks.
There build thee with thy brother's aid
A cottage in the quiet shade,
And faithful to thy sire's behest,
Obedient to the sentence, rest.
For well, O sinless chieftain, well
I know thy tale, how all befell:
Stern penance and the love I bore
Thy royal sire supply the lore.
To me long rites and fervid zeal
The wish that stirs thy heart reveal,
And hence my guest I bade thee be,
That this pure grove might shelter thee.

[1] One of the Pleiades generally regarded as the model of wifely excellence.

So now, thereafter, thus I speak:
The shades of Panchavaṭí seek;
That tranquil spot is bright and fair,
And Sítá will be happy there.
Not far romote from here it lies,
A grove to charm thy loving eyes.
Godávarí's pure stream is nigh:
There Sítá's days will sweetly fly.
Pure, lovely, rich in many a charm,
O hero of the mighty arm,
'Tis gay with every plant and fruit,
And throngs of gay birds never mute.
Thou, true to virtue's path, hast might
To screen each trusting anchorite,
And wilt from thy new home defend
The hermits who on thee depend.
Now yonder, Prince, direct thine eyes
Where dense Madhúka[1] woods arise:
Pierce their dark shade, and issuing forth
Turn to a fig-tree on the north:
Then onward up a sloping mead
Flanked by a hill the way will lead:
There Panchavaṭí, ever gay
With ceaseless bloom, thy steps will stay.'
The hermit ceased: the princely two
With seemly honours bade adieu:
With reverential awe each youth
Bowed to the saint whose word was truth,
And then, dismissed with Sítá, they
To Panchavaṭí took their way.
Thus when each royal prince had grasped
His warrior's mighty bow, and clasped
His quiver to his side,
With watchful eyes along the road
The glorious saint Agastya showed,
Dauntless in fight the brothers strode,
And Sítá with them hied.

CANTO XIV.

JAṬÁYUS.

Then as the son of Raghu made
His way to Panchavaṭí's shade,
A mighty vulture he beheld
Of size and strength unparalleled.
The princes, when the bird they saw,
Approached with reverence and awe,
And as his giant form they eyed,
'Tell who thou art,' in wonder cried.
The bird, as though their hearts to gain,
Addressed them thus in gentlest strain:
'In me, dear sons, the friend behold
Your royal father loved of old.'
He spoke: nor long did Ráma wait
His sire's dear friend to venerate:

[1] The Madhúka, or, as it is now called, Mahuwá, is the Bassia latifolia, a tree from whose blossoms a spirit is extracted.

He bade the bird declare his name
And the high race of which he came.
When Raghu's son had spoken, he
Declared his name and pedigree,
His words prolonging to disclose
How all the things that be arose:
'List while I tell, O Raghu's son,
The first-born Fathers, one by one,
Great Lords of Life, whence all in earth
And all in heaven derive their birth.
First Kardam heads the glorious race
Where Vikrit holds the second place,
With Śesha, Sanśray next in line,
And Bahuputra's might divine.
Then Stháṇu and Maríchi came,
Atri, and Kratu's forceful frame.
Pulastya followed, next to him
Angiras' name shall ne'er be dim.
Prachetas, Pulah next, and then
Daksha, Vivasvat praised of men:
Arishṭanemi next, and last
Kaśyap in glory unsurpassed.
From Daksha,—fame the tale has told—:
Three-score bright daughters sprang of old
Of these fair-waisted nymphs the great
Lord Kaśyap sought and wedded eight,
Aditi, Diti, Kálaká,
Támrá, Danú, and Analá,
And Krodhavaśá swift to ire,
And Manu[1] glorious as her sire.
Then when the mighty Kaśyap cried
Delighted to each tender bride:
'Sons shalt thou bear, to rule the three
Great worlds, in might resembling me,'

[1] 'I should have doubted whether Manu could have been the right reading here, but that it occurs again in verse 29, where it is in like manner followed in verse 31 by Analá, so that it would certainly seem that the name Manu is intended to stand for a female, the daughter of Daksha. The Gauḍa recension, followed by Signor Gorresio (III 20, 12), adopts an entirely different reading at the end of the line, viz. *Balám Atibalám api,* "Balá and Atibilá," instead of Manu and Analá. I see that Professor Roth s. v. adduces the authority of the Amara Kosha and of the Commentator on Páṇini for stating that the word sometimes means "the wife of Manu." In the following text of the Mahábhárata I. 2553, also, Manu appears to be the name of a female: *Anavadyám, Manum, Vanśám, Asurám, Márgaṇapriyám, Anúpám, Subhagám, Bhásím iti Prádhá vyajáyata* ‖ "Prádhá (daughter of Daksha) bore Anavadyá, Manu, Vanśá, Márgaṇapriyá, Anúpá, Subhagá, and Bhási."' *Muir's Sanskrit Text,* Vol. I. p. 116.

Aditi, Diti, and Danú
Obeyed his will as consorts true,
And Kálaká ; but all the rest
Refused to hear their lord's behest.
First Aditi conceived, and she,
Mother of thirty Gods and three,
The Vasus and Ádityas bare,
Rudras, and Aśvins, heavenly pair.
Of Diti sprang the Daityas : fame
Delights to laud their ancient name.
In days of yore their empire dread
O'er earth and woods and ocean spread.
Danú was mother of a child,
O hero, Aśvagríva styled,
And Narak next and Kálak came
Of Kálaká, celestial dame.
Of Támrá, too, five daughters bright
In deathless glory sprang to light.
Ennobling fame still keeps alive
The titles of the lovely five :
Immortal honour still she claims
For Kraunchí, Bhásí, Śyení's names,
And wills not that the world forget
Śukí or Dhritaráshṭrí yet.
Then Kraunchí bare the crane and owl,
And Bhásí tribes of water fowl :
Vultures and hawks that race through air
With storm-fleet pinions Śyení bare.
All swans and geese on mere and brook
Their birth from Dhritaráshṭrí took,
And all the river-haunting brood
Of ducks, a countless multitude.
From Śukí Nalá sprang, who bare
Dame Vinatá surpassing fair.
From fiery Krodhavaśá ten
Bright daughters sprang, O King of men:
Mrigí and Mrigamandá named,
Harí and Bhadramadá famed,
Śárdúlí, Śvetá fair to see,
Mátangí bright, and Surabhí,
Surasá marked with each fair sign,
And Kadrumá, all maids divine.
Mrigí, O Prince without a peer,
Was mother of the herds of deer.
The bear, the Yak, the mountain roe
Their birth to Mrigamandá owe ;
And Bhadramadá joyed to be
Mother of fair Irávatí,
Who bare Airávat,[1] huge of mould,
Mid warders of the earth enrolled.
From Harí lordly lions trace,
With monkeys of the wild, their race.
From the great dame Śárdúlí styled
Sprang pards, Lángúrs,[2] and tigers wild.
Mátangí, Prince, gave birth to all
Mátangas, elephants strong and tall,

[1] The elephant of Indra.

[2] *Golángúlas*, described as a kind of monkey, of a black colour, and having a tail like a cow.

And Śvetá bore the beasts who stand
One at each wind, earth's warder band.[1]
Next Surabhí the Goddess bore
Two heavenly maids, O Prince, of yore,
Gandharví—dear to fame is she—
And her sweet sister Rohiṇí.
With kine this daughter filled each mead,
And bright Gandharví bore the steed.[2]
Surasá bore the serpents :[3] all
The snakes Kadrú their mother call.
Then Manu, high-souled Kaśyap's[4] wife,
To all the race of men gave life,
The Bráhmans first, the Kshatriya caste,
Then Vaiśyas, and the Śúdras last.
Sprang from her mouth the Brahman race ;
Her chest the Kshatriyas' natal place :
The Vaiśyas from her thighs, 'tis said,
The Śúdras from her feet were bred.
From Analá all trees that hang
Their fair fruit-laden branches sprang.
The child of beauteous Śukí bore
Vinatá, as I taught before :
And Surasá and Kadrú were
Born of one dame, a noble pair.
Kadrú gave birth to countless snakes
That roam the earth in woods and brakes.
Aruṇ and Garuḍ swift of flight
By Vinatá were given to light,
And sons of Aruṇ red as morn
Sampáti first, then I was born.
Me then, O tamer of the foe,
Jaṭáyus, son of Śyení, know.
Thy ready helper will I be,
And guard thy house, if thou agree :
When thou and Lakshmaṇ urge the chase
By Sítá's side shall be my place.'

With courteous thanks for promised aid,
  The prince, to rapture stirred,
Bent low, and due obeisance paid,
  Embraced the royal bird.

[1] Eight elephants attached to the four quarters and intermediate points of the compass, to support and guard the earth.

[2] Some scholars identify the centaurs with the Gandharvas.

[3] The hooded serpents, says the commentator Tírtha, were the offspring of Surasá : all others of Kadrú.

[4] 'The text reads Káśyapa, "a descendant of Kaśyapa," who according to Rám. II. 10, 6, ought to be Vivasvat. But as it is stated in the preceding part of this passage III. 14, 11 f. that Manu was one of Kaśyapa's eight wives, we must here read Kaśyapa. The Gauḍa recension reads (III. 20, 30) *Manur manushyáms cha tathá janayámása Rághava*, instead of the corresponding line in the Bombay edition.' *Muir's Sanskrit Text, Vol. I. p.* 117.

He often in the days gone by
Had heard his father tell
How, linked with him in friendship's tie,
He loved Jaṭáyus well.
He hastened to his trusted friend
His darling to confide,
And through the wood his steps to bend
By strong Jaṭáyus' side.
On to the grove, with Lakshmaṇ near,
The prince his way pursued,
To free those pleasant shades from fear
And slay the giant brood.

CANTO XV.

PANCHAVAṬI.

Arrived at Panchavaṭí's shade
Where silvan life and serpents strayed,
Ráma in words like these addressed
Lakshmaṇ of vigour unrepressed:
'Brother, our home is here: behold
The grove of which the hermit told:
The bowers of Panchavaṭí see
Made fair by every blooming tree.
Now, brother, bend thine eyes around;
With skilful glance survey the ground:
Here be some spot selected, best
Approved for gentle hermits' rest,
Where thou, the Maithil dame, and I
May dwell while seasons sweetly fly.
Some pleasant spot be chosen where
Pure waters gleam and trees are fair,
Some nook where flowers and wood are found
And sacred grass and springs abound.'
Then Lakshmaṇ, Sítá standing by,
Raised reverent hands, and made reply:
'A hundred years shall flee, and still
Will I obey my brother's will:
Select thyself a pleasant spot;
Be mine the care to rear the cot.'
The glorious chieftain, pleased to hear
That loving speech that soothed his ear,
Selected with observant care
A spot with every charm most fair.
He stood within that calm retreat,
A shade for hermits' home most meet,
And thus Sumitrá's son addressed,
While his dear hand in his he pressed:
'See, see this smooth and lovely glade
Which flowery trees encircling shade:
Do thou, beloved Lakshmaṇ rear
A pleasant cot to lodge us here.
I see byond that feathery brake
The gleaming of a lilied lake,
Where flowers in sunlike glory throw
Fresh odours from the wave below.
Agastya's words now find we true,
He told the charms which here we view:
Here are the trees that blossom o'er
Godávarí's most lovely shore,
Whose pleasant flood from side to side
With swans and geese is beautified,
And fair banks crowded with the deer
That steal from every covert near.
The peacock's cry is loud and shrill
From many a tall and lovely hill,
Green-belted by the trees that wave
Full blossoms o'er the rock and cave.
Like elephants whose huge fronts glow
With painted streaks, the mountains show
Long lines of gold and silver sheen
With copper's darker hues between.
With every tree each hill is graced,
Where creepers blossom interlaced.
Look where the Sál's long branches sway,
And palms their fanlike leaves display;
The date-tree and the Jak are near,
And their long stems Tamálas rear.
See the tall Mango lift his head,
Aśokas all their glory spread,
The Ketak her sweet buds unfold,
And Champacs hang their cups of gold.[1]
The spot is pure and pleasant: here
Are multitudes of birds and deer.
O Lakshmaṇ, with our father's friend
What happy hours we here shall spend!'
He spoke: the conquering Lakshmaṇ heard,
Obedient to his brother's word.
Raised by his toil a cottage stood
To shelter Ráma in the wood.
Of ample size, with leaves o'erlaid,
Of hardened earth the walls were made.
The strong bamboos his hands had felled
For pillars fair the roof upheld,
And rafter, beam, and lath supplied
Well interwrought from side to side.
Then Śamí[2] boughs he deftly spread
Enlaced with knotted cord o'erhead,
Well thatched above from ridge to eaves
With holy grass, and reed, and leaves.
The mighty chief with careful toil
Had cleared the ground and smoothed the soil

---

[1] The original verses merely name the trees. I have been obliged to amplify slightly and to omit some quas versu dicere non est; *e. g.* the *tiniśa* (Dalbergia ougeiniensis), *punnága* (Rottleria tinctoria) *tilaka* (not named), *syandana* (Dalbergia ougeiniensis again) *vandana* (unknown) *nípa* (Nauclea Kadamba) *lakucha* (Artœarpus lacucha), *dhava* (Grislea tomentosa) Aśvakarṇa (another name for the Sál), *Śamí* (Acacia Suma) *khadira* (Mimosa catechu) *kinśuka* (Butea frondosa) *páṭala* (Bignonia suaveolens).

[2] Acacia Suma.

Where now, his loving labour done,
Rose a fair home for Raghu's son.
Then when his work was duly wrought,
Godávarís sweet stream he sought,
Bathed, plucked the lilies, and a store
Of fruit and berries homeward bore.
Then sacrifice he duly paid,
And wooed the Gods their hopes to aid,
And then to Ráma proudly showed
The cot prepared for his abode.
Then Raghu's son with Sítá gazed
Upon the home his hands had raised,
And transport thrilled his bosom through
His leafy hermitage to view.
The glorious son of Raghu round
His brother's neck his arms enwound,
And thus began his sweet address
Of deep-felt joy and gentleness:
'Well pleased am I, dear lord, to see
This noble work performed by thee.
For this,—sole grace I can bestow,—
About thy neck mine arms I throw.
So wise art thou, thy breast is filled
With grateful thoughts, in duty skilled,
Our mighty father, free from stain,
In thee, his offspring, lives again.'

Thus spoke the prince, who lent a grace
To fortune, pride of Raghu's race;
Then in that spot whose pleasant shade
Gave store of fruit, content he stayed.
With Lakshmaṇ and his Maithil spouse
He spent his days neath sheltering boughs,
As happy as a God on high
Lives in his mansion in the sky.

CANTO XVI.

WINTER.

While there the high-souled hero spent
His tranquil hours in sweet content,
The glowing autumn passed, and then
Came winter so beloved of men.

One morn, to bathe, at break of day
To the fair stream he took his way.
Behind him, with the Maithil dame
Bearing a pitcher Lakshmaṇ came,
And as he went the mighty man
Thus to his brother chief began:

'The time is come, to thee more dear
Than all the months that mark the year:
The gracious seasons' joy and pride,
By which the rest are glorified.
A robe of hoary rime is spread
O'er earth, with corn engarlanded.
The streams we loved no longer please,
But near the fire we take our ease.
Now pious men to God and shade
Offer young corn's fresh sprouted blade,
And purge away their sins with rice
Bestowed in humble sacrifice.
Rich stores of milk delight the swain,
And hearts are cheered that longed for gain.
Proud kings whose breasts for conquests glow
Lead bannered troops to smite the foe.
Dark is the north: the Lord of Day
To Yama's south[1] has turned away:
And she—sad widow—shines no more,
Reft of the bridal mark[2] she wore.
Himálaya's hill, ordained of old
The treasure-house of frost and cold,
Scarce conscious of the feebler glow,
Is truly now the Lord of Snow.
Warmed by the noontide's genial rays
Delightful are the glorious days:
But how we shudder at the chill
Of evening shadows and the rill!
How weak the sun, how cold the breeze!
How white the rime on grass and trees!
The leaves are sere, the woods have lost
Their blossoms killed by nipping frost.
Neath open skies we sleep no more:
December's nights with rime are hoar:
Their triple watch[3] in length extends
With hours the shortened daylight lends.
No more the moon's sun-borrowed rays
Are bright, involved in misty haze,
As when upon the mirror's sheen
The breath's obscuring cloud is seen.
E'en at the full the faint beams fail
To struggle through the darksome veil:
Changed like her hue, they want the grace
That parts not yet from Sítá's face.
Cold is the western wind, but how
Its piercing chill is heightened now,
Blowing at early morning twice
As furious with its breath of ice!
See how the dewy tears they weep
The barley, wheat, and woodland steep,
Where, as the sun goes up the sky,
The curlew and the sáras cry.
See where the rice plants scarce uphold
Their full ears tinged with paly gold,
Bending their ripe heads slowly down
Fair as the date tree's flowery crown.
Though now the sun has mounted high
Seeking the forehead of the sky,
Such mist obscures his struggling beams,
No bigger than the moon he seems.
Though weak at first, his rays at length
Grow pleasant in their noonday strength,
And where a while they chance to fall
Fling a faint splendour over all.

[1] The south is supposed to be the residence of the departed.

[2] The sun.

[3] The night is divided into three watches of four hours each.

See, o'er the woods where grass is wet
With hoary drops that cling there yet,
With soft light clothing earth and bough
There steals a tender glory now.
Yon elephant who longs to drink,
Still standing on the river's brink,
Plucks back his trunk in shivering haste
From the cold wave he fain would taste.
The very fowl that haunt the mere
Stand doubtful on the bank, and fear
To dip them in the wintry wave
As cowards dread to meet the brave.
The frost of night, the rime of dawn
Bind flowerless trees and glades of lawn:
Benumbed in apathetic chill
Of icy chains they slumber still.
You hear the hidden sáras cry
From floods that wrapped in vapour lie,
And frosty-shining sands reveal
Where the unnoticed rivers steal.
The hoary rime of dewy night,
And suns that glow with tempered light
Lend fresh cool flavours to the rill
That sparkles from the tompost hill.
The cold has killed the lily's pride:
Leaf, filament, and flower have died:
With chilling breath rude winds have blown,
The withered stalk is left alone.
At this gay time, O noblest chief,
The faithful Bharat, worn by grief,
Lives in the royal town where he
Spends weary hours for love of thee.
From titles, honour, kingly sway,
From every joy he turns away:
Couched on cold earth, his days are passed
With scanty fare and hermit's fast.
This moment from his humble bed
He lifts, perhaps, his weary head,
And girt by many a follower goes
To bathe where silver Sarjú flows.
How, when the frosty morn is dim,
Shall Sarjú be a bath for him
Nursed with all love and tender care,
So delicate and young and fair?
How bright his hue! his brilliant eye
With the broad lotus leaf may vie.
By fortune stamped for happy fate,
His graceful form is tall and straight.
In duty skilled, his words are truth:
He proudly rules each lust of youth.
Though his strong arm smites down the foe,
In gentle speech his accents flow.
Yet every joy has he resigned
And cleaves to thee with heart and mind.
Thus by the deeds that he has done
A home in heaven has Bharat won,
For in his life he follows yet
Thy steps, O banished anchoret.
Thus faithful Bharat, nobly wise,
The proverb of the world belies:
'No men, by mothers' guidance led,
The footsteps of their fathers tread.'
How could Kaikeyí, blest to be
Spouse of the king our sire, and see
A son like virtuous Bharat, blot
Her glory with so foul a plot!'
Thus in fraternal love he spoke,
And from his lips reproaches broke:
But Ráma grieved to hear him chide
The absent mother, and replied:
'Cease, O beloved, cease to blame
Our royal father's second dame.
Still speak of Bharat first in place
Of old Ikshváku's princely race.
My heart, so firmly bent but now
To dwell in woods and keep my vow,
Half melting as I hear thee speak
Of Bharat's love, grows soft and weak.
With tender joy I bring to mind
His speeches ever sweet and kind,
That dear as Amrit took the sense
With most enchanting influence.
Ah, when shall I, no more to part,
Meet Bharat of the mighty heart?
When, O my brother, when shall we
The good and brave Śatrughna see!'
Thus as he poured his fond lament
The son of Raghu onward went:
They reached the river, and the three
Bathed them in fair Godávarí.
Libations of the stream they paid
To every deity and shade,
With hymns of praise, the Sun on high
And sinless Gods to glorify.
Fresh from the purifying tide
Resplendent Ráma came,
With Lakshman ever by his side,
And the sweet Maithil dame.
So Rudra shines by worlds adored,
In glory undefiled,
When Nandi[1] stands beside his lord,
And King Himálaya's child.[2]

CANTO XVII.

ŚÚRPAṆAKHÁ.

The bathing and the prayer were o'er:
He turned him from the grassy shore,
And with his brother and his spouse
Sought his fair home beneath the boughs.
Sítá and Lakshman by his side,
On to his cot the hero hied,
And after rites at morning due
Within the leafy shade withdrew.

[1] The chief chamberlain and attendant of Śiva or Rudra.

[2] Umá or Párvatí, the consort of Śiva.

Then, honoured by the devotees,
As royal Ráma sat at ease,
With Sítá near him, o'er his head
A canopy of green boughs spread,
He shone as shines the Lord of Night
By Chitrá's[1] side, his dear delight.
With Lakshmaṇ there he sat and told
Sweet stories of the days of old,
And as the pleasant time he spent
With heart upon each tale intent,
A giantess, by fancy led,
Came wandering to his leafy shed.
Fierce Śúrpaṇakhá,—her of yore
The Ten-necked tyrant's mother bore,—
Saw Ráma with his noble mien
Bright as the Gods in heaven are seen;
Him from whose brow a glory gleamed,
Like lotus leaves his full eyes beamed:
Long-armed, of elephantine gait,
With hair close coiled in hermit plait:
In youthful vigour, nobly framed,
By glorious marks a king proclaimed:
Like some bright lotus lustrous-hued,
With young Kandarpa's[2] grace endued:
As there like Indra's self he shone,
She loved the youth she gazed upon.
She grim of eye and foul of face
Loved his sweet glance and forehead's grace:
She of unlovely figure, him
Of stately form and shapely limb:
She whose dim locks disordered hung,
Him whose bright hair on high brows clung:
She whose fierce accents counselled fear,
Him whose soft tones were sweet to hear:
She whose dire form with age was dried,
Him radiant in his youthful pride:
She whose false lips maintained the wrong,
Him in the words of virtue strong:
She cruel-hearted, stained with sin,
Him just in deed and pure within:
She, hideous fiend, a thing to hate,
Him formed each eye to captivate:
Fierce passion in her bosom woke,
And thus to Raghu's son she spoke:

'With matted hair above thy brows,
With bow and shaft and this thy spouse,
How hast thou sought in hermit dress
The giant-haunted wilderness?
What dost thou here? The cause explain:
Why art thou come, and what to gain?'
As Śúrpaṇakhá questioned so,
Ráma, the terror of the foe,
In answer to the monster's call,
With fearless candour told her all.
'King Daśaratha reigned of old,
Like Gods celestial brave and bold.
I am his eldest son and heir,
And Ráma is the name I bear.
This brother, Lakshmaṇ, younger born,
Most faithful love to me has sworn.
My wife, this princess, dear to fame,
Is Sítá the Videhan dame.
Obedient to my sire's behest
And by the queen my mother pressed,
To keep the law and merit win,
I sought this wood to harbour in.
But speak, for I of thee in turn
Thy name, and race, and sire would learn.
Thou art of giant race, I ween,
Changing at will thy form and mien.
Speak truly, and the cause declare
That bids thee to these shades repair.'
Thus Ráma spoke: the demon heard,
And thus replied by passion spurred:
'Of giant race, what form soe'er
My fancy wills, 'tis mine to wear.
Named Śúrpaṇakhá here I stray,
And where I walk spread wild dismay.
King Rávaṇ is my brother: fame
Has taught perchance his dreaded name.
Strong Kumbhakarṇa slumbering deep
In chains of never-ending sleep:
Vibhíshaṇ of the duteous mind,
In needs unlike his giant kind:
Dúshaṇ and Khara, brave and bold
Whose fame by every tongue is told:
Their might by mine is far surpassed:
But when, O best of men, I cast
These fond eyes on thy form, I see
My chosen love and lord in thee.
Endowed with wondrous might am I:
Where'er my fancy leads I fly.
The poor misshapen Sítá leave,
And me, thy worthier bride receive.
Look on my beauty, and prefer
A spouse more meet than one like her:
I'll eat that ill-formed woman there:
Thy brother too her fate shall share.
But come, beloved; thou shalt roam
With me through all our woodland home:
Each varied grove with me shalt seek,
And gaze upon each mountain peak.'
As thus she spoke, the monster gazed
With sparkling eyes where passion blazed:
Then he, in lore of language learned,
This answer eloquent returned:

CANTO XVIII.

THE MUTILATION.

On her ensnared in Káma's net
His eyes the royal Ráma set,

[1] A star, one of the favourites of the Moon.

[2] The God of love.

And thus, her passion to beguile,
Addressed her with a gentle smile:
'I have a wife: behold her here,
My Sítá ever true and dear:
And one like thee will never brook
Upon a rival spouse to look.
But there my brother Lakshmaṇ stands:
Unchained is he by nuptial bands:
A youth heroic, loved of all,
Gracious and gallant, fair and tall.
With winning looks, most nobly bred,
Unmatched till now, he longs to wed.
Meet to enjoy thy youthful charms,
O take him to thy loving arms,
Enamoured on his bosom lie,
Fair damsel of the radiant eye,
As the warm sunlight loves to rest
Upon her darling Meru's breast.'
The hero spoke, the monster heard,
While passion still her bosom stirred.
Away from Ráma's side she broke,
And thus in turn to Lakshmaṇ spoke:
Come, for thy bride take me who shine
In fairest grace that suits with thine.
Thou by my side from grove to grove
Of Daṇḍak's wild in bliss shalt rove.'
Then Lakshmaṇ, skilled in soft address,
Wooed by the amorous giantess,
With art to turn her love aside,
To Súrpaṇakhí thus replied:
'And can so high a dame agree
The slave-wife of a slave to be?
I, lotus-hued! in good and ill
Am bondsman to my brother's will.
Be thou, fair creature radiant-eyed,
My honoured brother's younger bride:
With faultless tint and dainty limb,
A happy wife, bring joy to him.
He from his spouse grown old and grey,
Deformed, untrue, will turn away,
Her withered charms will gladly leave,
And to his fair young darling cleave.
For who could be so fond and blind,
O loveliest of all female kind,
To love another dame and slight
Thy beauties rich in all delight?'
Thus Lakshmaṇ praised in scornful jest
The long-toothed fiend with loathly breast,
Who fondly heard his speech, nor knew
His mocking words were aught but true.
Again inflamed with love she fled
To Ráma, in his leafy shed
Where Sítá rested by his side,
And to the mighty victor cried:
'What, Ráma, canst thou blindly cling
To this old false misshapen thing?
Wilt thou refuse the charms of youth
For withered breast and grinning tooth!
Canst thou this wretched creature prize
And look on me with scornful eyes?
This aged crone this very hour
Before thy face will I devour:
Then joyous, from all rivals free,
Through Daṇḍak will I stray with thee.'
She spoke, and with a glance of flame
Rushed on the fawn-eyed Maithil dame:
So would a horrid meteor mar
Fair Rohiṇí's soft beaming star.
But as the furious fiend drew near,
Like Death's dire noose which chills with fear,
The mighty chief her purpose stayed,
And spoke, his brother to upbraid:
'Ne'er should we jest with creatures rude,
Of savage race and wrathful mood.
Think, Lakshmaṇ, think how nearly slain
My dear Videhan breathes again.
Let not the hideous wretch escape
Without a mark to mar her shape.
Strike, lord of men, the monstrous fiend,
Deformed, and foul, and evil-miened.'
He spoke: then Lakshmaṇ's wrath rose high,
And there before his brother's eye,
He drew that sword which none could stay,
And cleft her nose and ears away.
Noseless and earless, torn and maimed,
With fearful shrieks the fiend exclaimed,
And frantic in her wild distress
Resought the distant wilderness.
Deformed, terrific, huge, and dread,
As on she moved, her gashes bled,
And groan succeeded groan as loud
As roars, ere rain, the thunder cloud.
Still on the fearful monster passed,
While streams of blood kept falling fast,
And with a roar, and arms outspread
Within the boundless wood she fled.
To Janasthán the monster flew;
Fierce Khara there she found,
With chieftains of the giant crew
In thousands ranged around.
Before his awful feet she bent
And fell with piercing cries,
As when a bolt in swift descent
Comes flashing from the skies.
There for a while with senses dazed
Silent she lay and scared:
At length her drooping head she raised,
And all the tale declared,
How Ráma, Lakshmaṇ, and the dame
Had reached that lonely place:
Then told her injuries and shame,
And showed her bleeding face.

CANTO XIX.

THE ROUSING OF KHARA.

When Khara saw his sister lie
With blood-stained limbs and troubled eye,

Wild fury in his bosom woke,
And thus the monstrous giant spoke;
'Arise, my sister; cast away
This numbing terror and dismay,
And straight the impious hand declare
That marred those features once so fair.
For who his finger tip will lay
On the black snake in childish play,
And unattacked, with idle stroke
His poison-laden fang provoke?
Ill-fated fool, he little knows
Death's noose around his neck he throws,
Who rashly met thee, and a draught
Of life-destroying poison quaffed.
Strong, fierce as death, 'twas thine to choose
Thy way at will, each shape to use;
In power and might like one of us:
What hand has maimed and marred thee thus?
What God or fiend this deed has wrought,
What bard or sage of lofty thought
Was armed with power supremely great
Thy form to mar and mutilate?
In all the worlds not one I see
Would dare a deed to anger me:
Not Indra's self, the Thousand-eyed,
Beneath whose hand fierce Páka[1] died.
My life-destroying darts this day
His guilty breath shall rend away,
E'en as the thirsty wild swan drains
Each milk-drop that the wave retains.
Whose blood in foaming streams shall burst
O'er the dry ground which lies athirst,
When by my shafts transfixed and slain
He falls upon the battle plain?
From whose dead corpse shall birds of air
The mangled flesh and sinews tear,
And in their gory feast delight,
When I have slain him in the fight?
Not God or bard or wandering ghost,
No giant of our mighty host
Shall step between us, or avail
To save the wretch when I assail.
Collect each scattered sense, recall
Thy troubled thoughts, and tell me all.
What wretch attacked thee in the way,
And quelled thee in victorious fray?'
His breast with burning fury fired,
Thus Khara of the fiend inquired:
And then with many a tear and sigh
Thus Śúrpaṇakhá made reply:
''Tis Daśaratha's sons, a pair
Strong, resolute, and young, and fair:
In coats of dark and blackdeer's hide,
And like the radiant lotus eyed:
On berries roots and fruit they feed,
And lives of saintly virtue lead:
With ordered senses undefiled,
Ráma and Lakshmaṇ are they styled.
Fair as the Minstrels' King[1] are they,
And stamped with signs of regal sway.
I know not if the heroes trace
Their line from Gods or Dánav[2] race.
There by these wondering eyes between
The noble youths a dame was seen,
Fair, blooming, young, with dainty waist,
And all her bright apparel graced.
For her with ready heart and mind
The royal pair their strength combined,
And brought me to this last distress,
Like some lost woman, comfortless.
Perfidious wretch! my soul is fain
Her foaming blood and theirs to drain.
O let me head the vengeful fight,
And with this hand my murderers smite.
Come, brother, hasten to fulfil
This longing of my eager will.
On to the battle! Let me drink
Their lifeblood as to earth they sink.'
Then Khara, by his sister pressed,
Inflamed with fury, gave his hest
To twice seven giants of his crew,
Fierce as the God of death to view:
'Two men equipped with arms, who wear
Deerskin and bark and matted hair,
Leading a beauteous dame, have strayed
To the wild gloom of Daṇḍak's shade.
These men, this cursed woman slay,
And hasten back without delay,
That this my sister's lips may be
Red with the lifeblood of the three.
Giants, my wounded sister longs
To take this vengeance for her wrongs.
With speed her dearest wish fulfil,
And with your might these creatures kill.
Soon as your matchless strength shall lay
These brothers dead in battle fray,
She in triumphant joy will laugh,
And their hearts' blood delighted quaff.'
The giants heard the words he said,
And forth with Śúrpaṇakhá sped,
As mighty clouds in autumn fly
Urged by the wind along the sky.

CANTO XX.

THE GIANTS' DEATH.

Fierce Śúrpaṇakhá with her train
To Ráma's dwelling came again,
And to the eager giants showed
Where Sítá and the youths abode.
Within the leafy cot they spied
The hero by his consort's side,
And faithful Lakshmaṇ ready still
To wait upon his brother's will.

[1] A demon slain by Indra.

[1] Chitraratha, King of the Gandharvas.

[2] Titanic.

Then noble Ráma raised his eye
And saw the giants standing nigh,
And then, as nearer still they pressed.
His glorious brother thus addressed,
'Be thine a while, my brother dear,
To watch o'er Śítá's safety here,
And I will slay these creatures who
The footsteps of my spouse pursue.'
He spoke, and reverent Lakshmaṇ heard
Submissive to his brother's word.
The son of Raghu, virtuous-souled,
Strung his great bow adorned with gold,
And, with the weapon in his hand,
Addressed him to the giant band:
'Ráma and Lakshmaṇ we, who spring
From Daśaratha, mighty king;
We dwell a while with Śítá here
In Daṇḍak forest wild and drear.
On woodland roots and fruit we feed,
And lives of strictest rule we lead.
Say why would ye our lives oppress
Who sojourn in the wilderness.
Sent hither by the hermits' prayer
With bow and darts unused to spare,
For vengeance am I come to slay
Your sinful band in battle fray.
Rest as ye are: remain content,
Nor try the battle's dire event.
Unless your offered lives ye spurn,
O rovers of the night, return.'
They listened while the hero spoke,
And fury in each breast awoke.
The Bráhman-slayers raised on high
Their mighty spears and made reply:
They spoke with eyes aglow with ire,
While Ráma's burnt with vengeful fire,
And answered thus, in fury wild,
That peerless chief whose tones were mild:
'Nay thou hast angered, overbold,
Khara our lord, the mighty-souled,
And for thy sin, in battle strife
Shalt yield to us thy forfeit life.
No power hast thou alone to stand
Against the numbers of our band.
'Twere vain to match thy single might
Against us in the front of fight.
When we equipped for fight advance
With brandished pike and mace and lance,
Thou, vanquished in the desperate field,
Thy bow, thy strength, thy life shalt yield.'
With bitter words and threatening mien
Thus furious spoke the fierce fourteen,
And raising scymitar and spear
On Ráma rushed in wild career.
Their levelled spears the giant crew
Against the matchless hero threw.
His bow the son of Raghu bent,
And twice seven shafts to meet them sent,
And every javelin sundered fell
By the bright darts he aimed so well.
The hero saw: his anger grew
To fury: from his side he drew
Fresh sunbright arrows pointed keen,
In number, like his foes, fourteen.
His bow he grasped, the string he drew,
And gazing on the giant crew,
As Indra casts the levin, so
Shot forth his arrows at the foe.
The hurtling arrows, stained with gore,
Through the fiends' breasts a passage tore,
And in the earth lay buried deep
As serpents through an ant-hill creep.
Like trees uptorn by stormy blast
The shattered fiends to earth were cast,
And there with mangled bodies they,
Bathed in their blood and breathless, lay.
With fainting heart and furious eye
The demon saw her champions die.
With drying wounds that scarcely bled
Back to her brother's home she fled.
Oppressed with pain, with loud lament
At Khara's feet the monster bent.
There like a plant whence slowly come
The trickling drops of oozy gum,
With her grim features pale with pain
She poured her tears in ceaseless rain.
There routed Śúrpaṇakhá lay,
And told her brother all,
The issue of the bloody fray,
Her giant champions' fall.

CANTO XXI.

THE ROUSING OF KHARA.

Low in the dust he saw her lie,
And Khara's wrath grew fierce and high.
Aloud he cried to her who came
Disgracefully with baffled aim:
'I sent with thee at thy request
The bravest of my giants, best
Of all who feed upon the slain:
Why art thou weeping here again?
Still to their master's interest true,
My faithful, noble, loyal crew,
Though slaughtered in the bloody fray,
Would yet their monarch's word obey.
Now I, my sister, fain would know
The cause of this thy fear and woe,
Why like a snake thou writhest there,
Calling for aid in wild despair.
Nay, lie not thus in lowly guise:
Cast off thy weakness and arise!'
With soothing words the giant chief
Assuaged the fury of her grief.
Her weeping eyes she slowly dried
And to her brother thus replied:
'I sought thee in my shame and fear
With severed nose and mangled ear:
My gashes like a river bled,
I sought thee and was comforted.

Those twice seven giants, brave and strong,
Thou sentest to avenge the wrong,
To lay the savage Ráma low,
And Lakshman who misused me so.
But ah, the shafts of Ráma through
The bodies of my champions flew:
Though madly fierce their spears they plied,
Beneath his conquering might they died.
I saw them, famed for strength and speed,
I saw my heroes fall and bleed:
Great trembling seized my every limb
At the great deed achieved by him.
In trouble, horror, doubt, and dread,
Again to thee for help I fled.
While terror haunts my troubled sight,
I seek thee, rover of the night.
And canst thou not thy sister free
From this wide waste of troublous sea
Whose sharks are doubt and terror, where
Each wreathing wave is dark despair?
Low lie on earth thy giant train
By ruthless Ráma's arrows slain,
And all the mighty demons, fed
On blood, who followed me are dead.
Now if within thy breast may be
Pity for them and love for me,
If thou, O rover of the night,
Have valour and with him can fight,
Subdue the giants' cruel foe
Who dwells where Daṇḍak's thickets grow.
But if thine arm in vain assay
This queller of his foes to slay,
Now surely here before thine eyes,
Wronged and ashamed thy sister dies.
Too well, alas, too well I see
That, strong in war as thou mayst be,
Thou canst not in the battle stand
When Ráma meets thee hand to hand.
Go forth, thou hero but in name,
Assuming might thou canst not claim;
Call friend and kin, no longer stay:
Away from Janasthán, away!
Shame of thy race! the weak alone
Beneath thine arm may sink o'erthrown;
Fly Ráma and his brother: they
Are men too strong for thee to slay.
How canst thou hope, O weak and base,
To make this grove thy dwelling-place?
With Ráma's might unmeet to vie,
O'ermastered thou wilt quickly die.
A hero strong in valorous deed
Is Ráma, Daśaratha's seed;
And scarce of weaker might than he
His brother chief who mangled me.'
Thus wept and wailed in deep distress
The grim misshapen giantess:
Before her brother's feet she lay
O'erwhelmed with grief, and swooned away.

CANTO XXII

KHARA'S WRATH.

Roused by the taunting words she spoke,
The mighty Khara's wrath awoke,
And there, while giants girt him round,
In these fierce words an utterance found:
'I cannot, peerless one, contain
Mine anger at this high disdain,
Galling as salt when sprinkled o'er
The rawness of a bleeding sore.
Ráma in little count I hold,
Weak man whose days are quickly told.
The caitiff with his life to-day
For all his evil deeds shall pay.
Dry, sister, dry each needless tear,
Stint thy lament and banish fear,
For Ráma and his brother go
This day to Yama's realm below.
My warrior's axe shall stretch him slain,
Ere set of sun, upon the plain,
Then shall thy sated lips be red
With his warm blood in torrents shed.'
As Khara's speech the demon heard,
With sudden joy her heart was stirred:
She fondly praised him as the boast
And glory of the giant host.
First moved to ire by taunts and stings,
Now soothed by gentle flatterings,
To Dúshan, who his armies led,
The demon Khara spoke, and said:
'Friend, from the host of giants call
Full fourteen thousand, best of all,
Slaves of my will, of fearful might,
Who never turn their backs in fight:
Fiends who rejoice to slay and mar,
Dark as the clouds of autumn are:
Make ready quickly, O my friend,
My chariot and the bows I bend,
My swords, my shafts of brilliant sheen,
My divers lances long and keen.
On to the battle will I lead
These heroes of Pulastya's seed,
And thus, O famed for warlike skill,
Ráma my wicked foeman kill.'
He spoke, and ere his speech was done,
His chariot glittering like the sun,
Yoked and announced, by Dúshaṇ's care,
With dappled steeds was ready there.
High as a peak from Meru rent
It burned with golden ornament:
The pole of lazulite, of gold
Were the bright wheels whereon it rolled.
With gold and moonstone blazoned o'er,
Fish, flowers, trees, rocks, the panels bore:
Auspicious birds embossed thereon,
And stars in costly emblem shone.
O'er flashing swords his banner hung,
And sweet bells, ever tinkling, swung.

That mighty host with sword and shield
And car was ready for the field :
And Khara saw, and Dúshan cried,
'Forth to the fight, ye giants, ride.'
Then banners waved, and shield and sword
Flashed as the host obeyed its lord.
From Janasthán they sallied out
With eager speed, and din, and shout,
Armed with the mace for close attacks,
The bill, the spear, the battle-axe,
Steel quoit and club that flashed afar,
Huge bow and sword and scymitar,
The dart to pierce, the bolt to strike,
The murderous bludgeon, lance, and pike.
So forth from Janasthán, intent
On Khara's will, the monsters went.
He saw their awful march : not far
Behind the host he drove his car.
Ware of his master's will, to speed
The driver urged each gold-decked steed.
Then forth the warrior's coursers sprang,
And with tumultuous murmur rang
Each distant quarter of the sky
And realms that intermediate lie.
High and more high within his breast
  His pride triumphant rose,
While terrible as Death he pressed
  Onward to slay his foes.
'More swiftly yet,' as on they fled,
  He cried in thundering tones
Loud as a cloud that overhead
  Hails down a flood of stones.

CANTO XXIII.

THE OMENS.

As forth upon its errand went
That huge ferocious armament,
An awful cloud, in dust and gloom,
With threatening thunders from its womb
Poured in sad augury a flood
Of rushing water mixt with blood.
The monarch's steeds, though strong and
  fleet,
Stumbled and fell : and yet their feet
Passed o'er the bed of flowers that lay
Fresh gathered on the royal way.
No gleam of sunlight struggled through
The sombre pall of midnight hue,
Edged with a line of bloody red,
Like whirling torches overhead.
A vulture, fierce, of mighty size,
Terrific with his cruel eyes,
Perched on the staff enriched with gold,
Whence hung the flag in many a fold.
Each ravening bird, each beast of prey
Where Janasthán's wild thickets lay,
Rose with a long discordant cry
And gathered as the host went by,
And from the south long, wild, and shrill,
Came spirit voices boding ill.
Like elephants in frantic mood,
Vast clouds terrific, sable-hued,
Hid all the sky where'er they bore
Their load of water mixt with gore.
Above, below, around were spread
Thick shades of darkness strange and dread,
Nor could the wildered glance descry
A point or quarter of the sky.
Then came o'er heaven a sanguine hue,
Though evening's flush not yet was due,
While each ill-omened bird that flies
Assailed the king with harshest cries.
There screamed the vulture and the crane,
And the loud jackal shrieked again.
Each hideous thing that bodes aright
Disaster in the coming fight,
With gaping mouth that hissed and flamed,
The ruin of the host proclaimed.
Eclipse untimely reft away
The brightness of the Lord of Day,
And near his side was seen to glow
A mace-like comet boding woe.
Then while the sun was lost to view
A mighty wind arose and blew,
And stars like fireflies shed their light,
Nor waited for the distant night.
The lilies drooped, the brooks were dried,
The fish and birds that swam them died,
And every tree that was so fair
With flower and fruit was stripped and bare.
The wild wind ceased, yet, raised on high,
Dark clouds of dust involved the sky.
In doleful twitter long sustained
The restless Sárikás[1] complained,
And from the heavens with flash and flame
Terrific meteors roaring came.
Earth to her deep foundation shook
With rock and tree and plain and brook,
As Khara with triumphant shout,
Borne in his chariot, sallied out.
His left arm throbbed : he knew full well
That omen, and his visage fell.
Each awful sign the giant viewed,
And sudden tears his eye bedewed.
Care on his brow sat chill and black,
Yet mad with wrath he turned not back.
Upon each fearful sight that raised
The shuddering hair the chieftain gazed,
And laughing in his senseless pride
Thus to his giant legions cried :
'By sense of mightiest strength upborne,
These feeble signs I laugh to scorn.
I could bring down the stars that shine
In heaven with these keen shafts of mine.
Impelled by warlike fury I
Could cause e'en Death himself to die.

[1] The Sáriká is the Maina, a bird like a starling.

I will not seek my home again
Until my pointed shafts have slain
This Raghu's son so fierce in pride,
And Lakshman by his brother's side.
And she, my sister, she for whom
These sons of Raghu meet their doom,
She with delighted lips shall drain
The lifeblood of her foemen slain.
Fear not for me: I ne'er have known
Defeat, in battle overthrown.
Fear not for me, O giants; true
Are the proud words I speak to you.
The king of Gods who rules on high,
If wild Airávat bore him nigh,
Should fall before me bolt in hand:
And shall these two my wrath withstand!'
He ended and the giant host
Who heard their chief's triumphant boast,
Rejoiced with equal pride elate,
Entangled in the noose of Fate.
Then met on high in bright array,
With eyes that longed to see the fray,
God and Gandharva, sage and saint,
With beings pure from earthly taint.
Blest for good works aforetime wrought,
Thus each to other spake his thought:
'Now joy to Bráhmans, joy to kine,
And all whom world count half divine!
May Raghu's offspring slay in fight
Pulastya's sons who roam by night!'
In words like these and more, the best
Of high-souled saints their hopes expressed,
Bending their eager eyes from where
Car-borne with Gods they rode in air.
Beneath them stretching far, they viewed
The giants' death-doomed multitude.
They saw where, urged with fury, far
Before the host rolled Khara's car,
And close beside their leader came
Twelve giant peers of might and fame.[1]
Four other chiefs[2] before the rest
Behind their leader Dúshan pressed.
Impetuous, cruel, dark, and dread,
All thirsting for the fray,
The hosts of giant warriors sped
Onward upon their way.
With eager speed they reached the spot
Where dwelt the princely two,—
Like planets in a league to blot
The sun and moon from view.

[1] Their names which are rather unmanageable and of no importance are Syenagámí, Prithuśyáma, Yajnaśatru, Vihangama, Durjaya, Paravíráksha, Purusha, Kálakámuka, Meghamáli, Mahámáli, Varásya, Rudhiráśana.

[2] Mahákapála, Sthúláksha, Pramátha, Triśiras.

CANTO XXIV.

THE HOST IN SIGHT.

While Khara, urged by valiant rage,
Drew near that little hermitage,
Those wondrous signs in earth and sky
Smote on each prince's watchful eye.
When Ráma saw those signs of woe
Fraught with destruction to the foe,
With bold impatience scarce repressed
His brother chief he thus addressed:
'These fearful signs, my brother bold,
Which threaten all our foes, behold:
All laden, as they strike the view,
With ruin to the fiendish crew.
The angry clouds are gathering fast,
Their skirts with dusty gloom o'ercast,
And harsh with loud-voiced thunder, rain
Thick drops of blood upon the plain.
See, burning for the coming fight,
My shafts with wreaths of smoke are white,
And my great bow embossed with gold
Throbs eager for the master's hold.
Each bird that through the forest flies
Sends out its melancholy cries.
All signs foretell the dangerous strife,
The jeopardy of limb and life.
Each sight, each sound gives warning clear
That foemen meet and death is near.
But courage, valiant brother! well
The throbbings of mine arm foretell
That ruin waits the hostile powers,
And triumph in the fight is ours.
I hail the welcome omen: thou
Art bright of face and clear of brow.
For Lakshman, when the eye can trace
A cloud upon the warrior's face
Stealing the cheerful light away,
His life is doomed in battle fray.
List, brother, to that awful cry:
With shout and roar the fiends draw nigh.
With thundering beat of many a drum
The savage-hearted giants come.
The wise who value safety know
To meet, prepared, the coming blow:
In paths of prudence trained aright
They watch the stroke before it smite.
Take thou thine arrows and thy bow,
And with the Maithil lady go
For shelter to the mountain cave
Where thickest trees their branches wave.
I will not have thee, Lakshman, say
One word in answer, but obey.
By all thy honour for these feet
Of mine, dear brother, I entreat.
Thy warlike arm, I know could, smite
To death these rovers of the night;
But I this day would fight alone
Till all the fiends be overthrown.'

He spake: and Lakshmaṇ answered naught:
His arrows and his bow he brought,
And then with Sítá following hied
For shelter to the mountain side.
As Lakshmaṇ and the lady through
The forest to the cave withdrew,
'Tis well,' cried Ráma. Then he braced
His coat of mail around his waist.
When, bright as blazing fire, upon
His mighty limbs that armour shone,
The hero stood like some great light
Uprising in the dark of night.
His dreadful shafts were by his side;
His trusty bow he bent and plied.
Prepared he stood: the bowstring rang,
Filling the welkin with the clang.

The high-souled Gods together drew
The wonder of the fight to view,
The saints made free from spot and stain,
And bright Gandharvas' heavenly train.
Each glorious sage the assembly sought,
Each saint divine of loftiest thought,
And filled with zeal for Ráma's sake,
Thus they whose deeds were holy spake:
'Now be it well with Bráhmans, now
Well with the worlds and every cow!
Let Ráma in the deadly fray
The fiends who walk in darkness slay,
As He who bears the discus[1] slew
The chieftains of the Asur crew.'

Then each with anxious glances viewed
His fellow and his speech renewed:
'There twice seven thousand giants stand
With impious heart and cruel hand:
Here Ráma stands, by virtue known:
How can the hero fight alone?'

Thus royal sage and Bráhman saint,
Spirit, and Virtue free from taint,
And all the Gods of heaven who rode
On golden cars, their longing showed.
Their hearts with doubt and terror rent,
They saw the giants' armament,
And Ráma clothed in warrior might,
Forth standing in the front of fight.
Lord of the arm no toil might tire,
He stood majestic in his ire,
Matchless in form as Rudra[2] when
His wrath is fierce on Gods or men.

While Gods and saints in close array
Held converse of the coming fray,
The army of the fiends drew near
With sight and sound that counselled fear.
Long, loud and deep their war-cry pealed,
As on they rushed with flag and shield,
Each, of his proper valour proud,
Urging to fight the demon crowd.
His ponderous bow each warrior tried,
And swelled his bulk with martial pride.
'Mid shout and roar and trampling feet,
And thunder of the drums they beat,
Loud and more loud the tumult went
Throughout the forest's vast extent,
And all the life that moved within
The woodland trembled at the din.
In eager haste all fled to find
Some tranquil spot, nor looked behind.

With every arm of war supplied,
On-rushing wildly like the tide
Of some deep sea, the giant host
Approached where Ráma kept his post.
Then he, in battle skilled and tried,
Bent his keen eye on every side,
And viewed the host of Khara face
To face before his dwelling-place.
He drew his arrows forth, and reared
And strained that bow which foemen feared,
And yielded to the vengeful sway
Of fierce desire that host to slay.
Terrific as the ruinous fire
That ends the worlds, he glowed in ire,
And his tremendous form dismayed
The Gods who roam the forest shade.
For in the furious wrath that glowed
Within his soul the hero showed
Like Śiva when his angry might
Stayed Daksha's sacrificial rite.[1]
Like some great cloud at dawn of day
When first the sun upsprings,
And o'er the gloomy mass each ray
A golden radiance flings:
Thus showed the children of the night,
Whose mail and chariots threw,
With gleam of bows and armlets bright,
Flashes of flamy hue.

CANTO XXV.

THE BATTLE.

When Khara with the hosts he led
Drew near to Ráma's leafy shed,
He saw that queller of the foe
Stand ready with his ordered bow.
He saw, and burning at the view
His clanging bow he raised and drew,
And bade his driver urge apace
His car to meet him face to face.
Obedient to his master's hest
His eager steeds the driver pressed
On to the spot where, none to aid,
The strong-armed chief his weapon swayed.
Soon as the children of the night
Saw Khara rushing to the fight,

[1] Vishṇu, who bears a *chakra* or discus.

[2] Śiva.

[1] See *Additional Notes*—DAKSHA SACRIFICE.

His lords with loud unearthly cry
Followed their chief and gathered nigh.
As in his car the leader rode
With all his lords around, he showed
Like the red planet fiery Mars
Surrounded by the lesser stars.
Then with a horrid yell that rent
The air, the giant chieftain sent
A thousand darts in rapid shower
On Ráma matchless in his power.
The rovers of the night, impelled
By fiery rage which naught withheld,
Upon the unconquered prince, who strained
His fearful bow, their arrows rained.
With sword and club, with mace and pike,
With spear and axe to pierce and strike,
Those furious fiends on every side
The unconquerable hero plied.
The giant legions huge and strong,
Like clouds the tempest drives along,
Rushed upon Ráma with the speed
Of whirling car, and mounted steed,
And hill-like elephant, to slay
The matchless prince in battle fray.
Then upon Ráma thick and fast
The rain of mortal steel they cast,
As labouring clouds their torrents shed
Upon the mountain-monarch's[1] head.
As near and nearer round him drew
The warriors of the giant crew,
He showed like Śiva girt by all
His spirits when night's shadows fall.
As the great deep receives each rill
And river rushing from the hill,
He bore that flood of darts, and broke
With well-aimed shaft each murderous stroke.
By stress of arrowy storm assailed,
And wounded sore, he never failed,
Like some high mountain which defies
The red bolts flashing from the skies.
With ruddy streams each limb was dyed
From gaping wounds in breast and side,
Showing the hero like the sun
'Mid crimson clouds ere day is done.
Then, at that sight of terror, faint
Grew God, Gandharva, sage, and saint,
Trembling to see the prince oppose
His single might to myriad foes.
But waxing wroth, with force unspent,
He strained his bow to utmost bent,
And forth his arrows keen and true
In hundreds, yea in thousands flew,—
Shafts none could ward, and none endure:
Death's fatal noose was scarce so sure.
As 'twere in playful ease he shot
His gilded shafts, and rested not.
With swiftest flight and truest aim
Upon the giant hosts they came.
Each smote, each stayed a foeman's breath,
As fatal as the coil of Death.
Each arrow through a giant tore
A passage, and besmeared with gore,
Pursued its onward way and through
The air with flamy brilliance flew.
Unnumbered were the arrows sent
From the great bow which Ráma bent,
And every shaft with iron head
The lifeblood of a giant shed.
Their pennoned bows were cleft, nor mail
Nor shield of hide could aught avail.
For Ráma's myriad arrows tore
Through arms, and bracelets which they wore,
And severed mighty warriors' thighs
Like trunks of elephants in size,
And cut resistless passage sheer
Through gold-decked horse and charioteer,
Slew elephant and rider, slew
The horseman and the charger too,
And infantry unnumbered sent
To dwell 'neath Yama's government.
Then rose on high a fearful yell
Of rovers of the night, who fell
Beneath that iron torrent, sore
Wounded by shafts that rent and tore.
So mangled by the ceaseless storm
Of shafts of every kind and form,
Such joy they found, as forests feel
When scorched by flame, from Ráma's steel.
The mightiest still the fight maintained,
And furious upon Ráma rained
Dart, arrow, spear, with wild attacks
Of mace, and club, and battle-axe.
But the great chief, unconquered yet,
Their weapons with his arrows met,
Which severed many a giant's head,
And all the plain with corpses spread.
With sundered bow and shattered shield
Headless they sank upon the field,
As the tall trees, that felt the blast
Of Garuḍ's wing, to earth were cast.
The giants left unslaughtered there
Where filled with terror and despair,
And to their leader Khara fled
Faint, wounded, and discomfited.
These fiery Dúshaṇ strove to cheer,
And poised his bow to calm their fear;
Then fierce as He who rules the dead,
When wroth, on angered Ráma sped.
By Dúshaṇ cheered, the demons cast
Their dread aside and rallied fast.
With Sáls, rocks, palm-trees in their hands,
With nooses, maces, pikes, and brands,
Again upon the godlike man
The mighty fiends infuriate ran,
These casting rocks like hail, and these
A whelming shower of leafy trees.
Wild, wondrous fight, the eye to scare,
And raise on end each shuddering hair,

[1] Himálaya.

As with the fiends who loved to rove
By night heroic Ráma strove!
The giants in their fury plied
Ráma with darts on every side.
Then, by the gathering demons pressed
From north and south and east and west,
By showers of deadly darts assailed
From every quarter fiercely hailed,
Girt by the foes who swarmed around,
He raised a mighty shout whose sound
Struck terror. On the giant crew
His great Gándharva[1] arrow flew.
A thousand mortal shafts were rained
From the orbed bow the hero strained,
Till east and west and south and north
Were filled with arrows volleyed forth.
They heard the fearful shout: they saw
His mighty hand the bowstring draw,
Yet could no wounded giant's eye
See the swift storm of arrows fly.
Still firm the warrior stood and cast
His deadly missiles thick and fast.
Dark grew the air with arrowy hail
Which hid the sun as with a veil.
Fiends wounded, falling, fallen, slain,
All in a moment, spread the plain,
And thousands scarce alive were left
Mangled, and gashed, and torn, and cleft.
Dire was the sight, the plain o'erspread
With trophies of the mangled dead.
There lay, by Ráma's missiles rent,
Full many a priceless ornament,
With severed limb and broken gem,
Hauberk and helm and diadem.
There lay the shattered car, the steed,
The elephant of noblest breed,
The splintered spear, the shivered mace,
Chouris and screens to shade the face.
The giants saw with bitterest pain
Their warriors weltering on the plain,
Nor dared again his might oppose
Who scourged the cities of his foes.

CANTO XXVI.

DU'SHAṆ'S DEATH.

When Dúshaṇ saw his giant band
Slaughtered by Ráma's conquering hand,
He called five thousand fiends, and gave
His orders. Bravest of the brave,
Invincible, of furious might,
Ne'er had they turned their backs in flight.
They, as their leader bade them seize
Spears, swords, and clubs, and rocks, and
  trees,
Poured on the dauntless prince again
A ceaseless shower of deadly rain.
The virtuous Ráma, undismayed,
Their missiles with his arrows stayed,
And weakened, ere it fell, the shock
Of that dire hail of tree and rock,
And like a bull with eyelids closed,
The pelting of the storm opposed.

Then blazed his ire: he longed to smite
To earth the rovers of the night.
The wrath that o'er his spirit came
Clothed him with splendour as of flame,
While showers of mortal darts he poured
Fierce on the giants and their lord.
Dúshaṇ, the foeman's dusky dread,
By frenzied rage inspirited,
On Raghu's son his missiles cast
Like Indra's bolts which rend and blast.
But Ráma with a trenchant dart
Cleft Dúshaṇ's ponderous bow apart.
And then the gold-decked steeds who drew
The chariot, with four shafts he slew.
One crescent dart he aimed which shred
Clean from his neck the driver's head;
Three more with deadly skill addressed
Stood quivering in the giant's breast.
Hurled from his car, steeds, driver slain,
The bow he trusted cleft in twain,
He seized his mace, strong, heavy, dread,
High as a mountain's towering head.
With plates of gold adorned and bound,
Embattled Gods it crushed and ground.
Its iron spikes yet bore the stains
Of mangled foemen's blood and brains.
Its heavy mass of jagged steel
Was like a thunderbolt to feel.
It shattered, as on foes it fell,
The city where the senses dwell.[1]
Fierce Dúshaṇ seized that ponderous mace
Like monstrous form of serpent race,
And all his savage soul aglow
With fury, rushed upon the foe.
But Raghu's son took steady aim,
And as the rushing giant came,
Shore with two shafts the arms whereon
The demon's glittering bracelets shone.
His arm at each huge shoulder lopped,
The mighty body reeled and dropped,
And the great mace to earth was thrown
Like Indra's staff when storms have blown.
As some vast elephant who lies
Shorn of his tusks, and bleeding dies,
So, when his arms were rent away,
Low on the ground the giant lay.
The spirits saw the monster die,
And loudly rang their joyful cry,
'Honour to Ráma! nobly done!
Well hast thou fought, Kakutstha's son!

---

[1] One of the mysterious weapons given to Ráma.

[1] A periphrasis for the body.

But the great three, the host who led,
Enraged to see their chieftain dead,
As though Death's toils were round them cast,
Rushed upon Ráma fierce and fast.
Mahákapála seized, to strike
His foeman down, a ponderous pike:
Sthúláksha charged with spear to fling,
Pramáthi with his axe to swing.
When Ráma saw, with keen darts he
Received the onset of the three,
As calm as though he hailed a guest
In each, who came for shade and rest.
Mahákapála's monstrous head
Fell with the trenchant dart he sped.
His good right hand in battle skilled
Sthúláksha's eyes with arrows filled,
And trusting still his ready bow
He laid the fierce Pramáthi low,
Who sank as some tall tree falls down
With bough and branch and leafy crown.
Then with five thousand shafts he slew
The rest of Dúshaṇ's giant crew:
Five thousand demons, torn and rent,
To Yama's gloomy realm he sent.
When Khara knew the fate of all
The giant band and Dúshaṇ's fall,
He called the mighty chiefs who led
His army, and in fury said:
'Now Dúshaṇ and his armèd train
Lie prostrate on the battle plain.
Lead forth an army mightier still,
Ráma, this wretched man, to kill.
Fight ye with darts of every shape,
Nor let him from your wrath escape.'
Thus spoke the fiend, by rage impelled,
And straight his course toward Ráma held.
With Śyenagámí and the rest
Of his twelve chiefs he onward pressed,
And every giant as he went
A storm of well-wrought arrows sent.
Then with his pointed shafts that came
With gold and diamond bright as flame,
Dead to the earth the hero threw
The remnant of the demon crew.
Those shafts with feathers bright as gold,
Like flames which wreaths of smoke enfold,
Smote down the fiends like tall trees rent
By red bolts from the firmament.
A hundred shafts he pointed well:
By their keen barbs a hundred fell:
A thousand,—and a thousand more
In battle's front lay drenched in gore.
Of all defence and guard bereft,
With sundered bows and harness cleft,
Their bodies red with bloody stain
Fell the night-rovers on the plain,
Which, covered with the loosened hair
Of bleeding giants prostrate there,
Like some great altar showed, arrayed
For holy rites with grass o'erlaid.
The darksome wood, each glade and dell
Where the wild demons fought and fell,
Was like an awful hell whose floor
Is thick with mire and flesh and gore.
Thus twice seven thousand fiends, a band
With impious heart and bloody hand,
By Raghu's son were overthrown,
A man, on foot, and all alone.
Of all who met on that fierce day,
Khara, great chief, survived the fray,
The monster of the triple head,[1]
And Raghu's son, the foeman's dread.
The other demon warriors, all
Skilful and brave and strong and tall,
In front of battle, side by side,
Struck down by Lakshmaṇ's brother died.
When Khara saw the host he led
Triumphant forth to fight
Stretched on the earth, all smitten dead,
By Ráma's nobler might,
Upon his foe he fiercely glared,
And drove against him fast,
Like Indra when his arm is bared
His thundering bolt to cast.

CANTO XXVII.

THE DEATH OF TRIŚIRAS.

But Triśiras,[2] a chieftain dread,
Marked Khara as he onward sped,
And met his car and cried, to stay
The giant from the purposed fray:
'Mine be the charge: let me attack,
And turn thee from the contest back.
Let me go forth, and thou shalt see
The strong-armed Ráma slain by me.
True are the words I speak, my lord:
I swear it as I touch my sword:
That I this Ráma's blood will spill,
Whom every giant's hand should kill.
This Ráma will I slay, or he
In battle fray shall conquer me.
Restrain thy spirit: check thy car,
And view the combat from afar.
Thou, joying o'er the prostrate foe,
To Janasthán again shalt go,
Or, if I fall in battle's chance,
Against my conqueror advance.'
Thus Triśiras for death who yearned:
And Khara from the conflict turned.
'Go forth to battle,' Khara cried;
And toward his foe the giant hied.
Borne on a car of glittering hue
Which harnessed coursers fleetly drew,
Like some huge hill with triple peak
He onward rushed the prince to seek,

[1] Triśiras. [2] The Three-headed.

Still, like a big cloud, sending out
His arrowy rain with many a shout
Like the deep sullen roars that come
Discordant from a moistened drum.
But Raghu's son, whose watchful eye
Beheld the demon rushing nigh,
From the great bow he raised and bent
A shower of shafts to meet him sent.
Wild grew the fight and wilder yet
As fiend and man in combat met,
As when in some dark wood's retreat
An elephant and a lion meet.

The giant bent his bow, and true
To Ráma's brow three arrows flew.
Then, raging as he felt the stroke,
These words in anger Ráma spoke:
'Heroic chief! is such the power
Of fiends who rove at midnight hour?
Soft as the touch of flowers I feel
The gentle blows thine arrows deal.
Receive in turn my shafts, and know
What arrows fly from Ráma's bow.'
Thus as he spoke his wrath grew hot,
And twice seven deadly shafts he shot,
Which, dire as serpent's deadly fang,
Straight to the giant's bosom sprang.
Four arrows more,—each shaped to deal
A mortal wound with barbèd steel,—
The glorious hero shot, and slew
The four good steeds the car that drew.
Eight other shafts flew straight and fleet,
And hurled the driver from his seat,
And in the dust the banner laid
That proudly o'er the chariot played.
Then as the fiend prepared to bound
Forth from his useless car to ground,
The hero smote him to the heart,
And numbed his arm with deadly smart.
Again the chieftain, peerless-souled,
Sent forth three rapid darts, and rolled
With each keen arrow, deftly sped,
Low in the dust a monstrous head.
Then yielding to each deadly stroke,
Forth spouting streams of blood and smoke,
The headless trunk bedrenched with gore
Fell to the ground and moved no more.
The fiends who yet were left with life,
Routed and crushed in battle strife,
To Khara's side, like trembling deer
Scared by the hunter, fled in fear.
King Khara saw with furious eye
His scattered giants turn and fly;
Then rallying his broken train
At Raghu's son he drove amain,
Like Ráhu[1] when his deadly might
Comes rushing on the Lord of Night.

[1] The demon who causes eclipses.

CANTO XXVIII.

KHARA DISMOUNTED.

But when he turned his eye where bled
Both Triśiras and Dúshaṇ dead,
Fear o'er the giant's spirit came
Of Ráma's might which naught could tame.
He saw his savage legions, those
Whose force no creature dared oppose,—
He saw the leader of his train
By Ráma's single prowess slain.
With burning grief he marked the few
Still left him of his giant crew.
As Namuchi[1] on Indra, so
Rushed the dread demon on his foe.
His mighty bow the monster strained,
And angrily on Ráma rained
His mortal arrows in a flood,
Like serpent fangs athirst for blood.
Skilled in the bowman's warlike art,
He plied the string and poised the dart.
Here, on his car, and there, he rode,
And passages of battle showed,
While all the skyey regions grew
Dark with his arrows as they flew.
Then Ráma seized his ponderous bow,
And straight the heaven was all aglow
With shafts whose stroke no life might bear,
That filled with flash and flame the air,
Thick as the blinding torrents sent
Down from Parjanya's[2] firmament.
In space itself no space remained,
But all was filled with arrows rained
Incessantly from each great bow
Wielded by Ráma and his foe.
As thus in furious combat, wrought
To mortal hate, the warriors fought,
The sun himself grew faint and pale,
Obscured behind that arrowy veil.

As when beneath the driver's steel
An elephant is forced to kneel,
So from the bard and pointed head
Of many an arrow Ráma bled.
High on his car the giant rose
Prepared in deadly strife to close,

[1] 'This Asura was a friend of Indra; and taking advantage of his friend's confidence, he drank up Indra's strength along with a draught of wine and Soma. Indra then told the Aśvins and Sarasvatí that Namuchi had drunk up his strength. The Aśvins in consequence gave Indra a thunderbolt in the form of a foam, with which he smote off the head of Namuchi.' GARRETT'S *Classical Dictionary of India.* See also Book I. p. 39.

[2] Indra.

And all the spirits saw him stand
Like Yama with his noose in hand.
For Khara deemed in senseless pride
That he, beneath whose hand had died
The gaint legions, failed at length
Slow sinking with exhausted strength.
But Ráma, like a lion, when
A trembling deer comes nigh his den,
Feared not the demon mad with hate,—
Of lion might and lion gait.
Then in his lofty car that glowed
With sunlike brilliance Khara rode
At Ráma : madly on he came
Like a poor moth that seeks the flame.
His archer skill the fiend displayed,
And at the place where Ráma laid
His hand, an arrow cleft in two
The mighty bow the hero drew.
Seven arrows by the giant sent,
Bright as the bolts of Indra, rent
Their way through mail and harness joints,
And pierced him with their iron points.
On Ráma, hero unsurpassed,
A thousand shafts smote thick and fast,
While as each missile struck, rang out
The giant's awful battle-shout.
His knotted arrows pierced and tore
The sunbright mail the hero wore,
Till, band and buckle rent away,
Glittering on the ground it lay.
Then pierced in shoulder, breast, and side,
Till every limb with blood was dyed,
The chieftain in majestic ire
Shone glorious as the smokeless fire.
Then loud and long the war-cry rose
Of Ráma, terror of his foes,
As, on the giant's death intent,
A ponderous bow he strung and bent,—
Lord Vishṇu's own, of wondrous size,—
Agastya gave the heavenly prize.
Then, rushing on the demon foe,
He raised on high that mighty bow,
And with his well-wrought shafts, whereon
Bright gold between the feathers shone,
He struck the pennon fluttering o'er
The chariot, and it waved no more.
That glorious flag whose every fold
Was rich with blazonry and gold,
Fell as the sun himself by all
The Gods' decree might earthward fall.
From wrathful Khara's hand, whose art
Well knew each vulnerable part,
Four keenly-piercing arrows flew,
And blood in Ráma's bosom drew,
With every limb distained with gore
From deadly shafts which rent and tore,
From Khara's clanging bowstring shots,
The prince's wrath waxed wondrous hot.
His hand upon his bow that best
Of mighty archers firmly pressed,
And from the well-drawn bowstring, true
Each to its mark, six arrows flew.
One quivered in the giant's head,
With two his brawny shoulders bled ;
Three, with the crescent heads they bore,
Deep in his breast a passage tore.
Thirteen, to which the stone had lent
The keenest point, were swiftly sent
On the fierce giant, every one
Destructive, gleaming like the sun.
With four the dappled steeds he slew ;
One cleft the chariot yoke in two,
One, in the heat of battle sped,
Smote from the neck the driver's head.
The poles were rent apart by three ;
Two broke the splintered axle-tree.
Then from the hand of Ráma, while
Across his lips there came a smile,
The twelfth, like thunderbolt impelled,
Cut the great hand and bow it held.
Then, scarce by Indra's self surpassed,
He pierced the giant with the last.
The bow he trusted cleft in twain,
His driver and his horses slain,
Down sprang the giant, mace in hand,
On foot against the foe to stand.
  The Gods and saints in bright array
    Close gathered in the skies,
  The prince's might in battle-fray
    Beheld with joyful eyes.
  Uprising from their golden seats,
    Their hands in honour raised,
  They looked on Ráma's noble feats,
    And blessed him as they praised.

CANTO XXIX.

KHARA'S DEFEAT.

When Ráma saw the giant nigh,
On foot, alone, with mace reared high,
In mild reproof at first he spoke,
Then forth his threatening anger broke :
'Thou with the host 'twas thine to lead,
With elephant and car and steed,
Hast wrought an act of sin and shame,
An act which all who live must blame.
Know that the wretch whose evil mind
Joys in the grief of human kind,
Though the three worlds confess him lord,
Must perish dreaded and abhorred.
Night-rover, when a villain's deeds
Distress the world he little heeds,
Each hand is armed his life to take,
And crush him like a deadly snake.
The end is near when men begin
Through greed or lust a life of sin,
E'en as a Bráhman's dame, unwise,
Eats of the fallen hail[1] and dies.

[1] Popularly supposed to cause death.

Thy hand has slain the pure and good,
The hermit saints of Daṇḍak wood,
Of holy life, the heirs of bliss ;
And thou shalt reap the fruit of this.
Not long shall they whose cruel breasts
Joy in the sin the world detests
Retain their guilty power and pride,
But fade like trees whose roots are dried.
Yes, as the seasons come and go,
Each tree its kindly fruit must show,
And sinners reap in fitting time
The harvest of each earlier crime.
As those must surely die who eat
Unwittingly of poisoned meat,
They too whose lives in sin are spent
Receive ere long the punishment.
And know, thou rover of the night,
That I, a king, am sent to smite
The wicked down, who court the hate
Of men whose laws they violate.
This day my vengeful hand shall send
Shafts bright with gold to tear and rend,
And pass with fury through thy breast
As serpents pierce an emmet's nest.
Thou with thy host this day shalt be
Among the dead below, and see
The saints beneath thy hand who bled,
Whose flesh thy cruel maw has fed.
They, glorious on their seats of gold,
Their slayer shall in hell behold.
Fight with all strength thou callest thine,
Mean scion of ignoble line,
Still, like the palm-tree's fruit, this day
My shafts thy head in dust shall lay.'
  Such were the words that Ráma said :
Then Khara's eyes with wrath glowed red,
Who, maddened by the rage that burned
Within him, with a smile returned :
  'Thou Daśaratha's son, hast slain
The meaner giants of my train:
And canst thou idly vaunt thy might
And claim the praise not thine by right?
Not thus in self-laudation rave
The truly great, the nobly brave :
No empty boasts like thine disgrace
The foremost of the human race.
The mean of soul, unknown to fame,
Who taint their warrior race with shame,
Thus speak in senseless pride as thou,
O Raghu's son, hast boasted now,
What hero, when the war-cry rings,
Vaunts the high race from which he springs,
Or seeks, when warriors meet and die,
His own descent to glorify?
Weakness and folly show confessed
In every vaunt thou utterest,
As when the flames fed high with grass
Detect the simulating brass,
Dost thou not see me standing here
Armed with the mighty mace I rear,
Firm as an earth-upholding hill
Whose summit veins of metal fill?
Lo, here I stand before thy face
To slay thee with my murderous mace,
As Death, the universal lord,
Stands threatening with his fatal cord.
Enough of this. Much more remains
That should be said: but time constrains.
Ere to his rest the sun descend,
And shades of night the combat end,
The twice seven thousand of my band
Who fell beneath thy bloody hand
Shall have their tears all wiped away
And triumph in thy fall to-day.'
  He spoke, and loosing from his hold
His mighty mace ringed round with gold,
Like some red bolt alive with fire,
Hurled it at Ráma, mad with ire.
The ponderous mace which Khara threw
Sent fiery flashes as it flew.
Trees, shrubs were scorched beneath the blast,
As onward to its aim it passed.
But Ráma, watching as it sped
Dire as His noose who rules the dead,
Cleft it with arrows as it came
On rushing with a hiss and flame.
Its fury spent and burnt away,
Harmless upon the ground it lay
Like a great snake in furious mood
By herbs of numbing power subdued.

CANTO XXX.

KHARA'S DEATH.

When Ráma, pride of Raghu's race,
Virtue's dear son, had cleft the mace,
Thus with superior smile the best
Of chiefs the furious fiend addressed :

'Thou, worst of giant blood, at length
Hast shown the utmost of thy strength,
And forced by greater might to bow,
Thy vaunting threats are idle now.
My shafts have cut thy club in twain :
Useless it lies upon the plain,
And all thy pride and haughty trust
Lie with it levelled in the dust.
The words that thou hast said to-day,
That thou wouldst wipe the tears away
Of all the giants I have slain,
My deeds shall render void and vain.
Thou meanest of the giants' breed,
Evil in thought and word and deed,
My hand shall take that life of thine
As Garuḍ[1] seized the juice divine.

[1] Garuḍ, the King of Birds, carried off the Amrit or drink of Paradise from Indra's custody.

Thou, rent by shafts, this day shalt die :
Low on the ground thy corse shall lie,
And bubbles from the cloven neck
With froth and blood thy skin shall deck.
With dust and mire all rudely dyed,
Thy torn arms lying by thy side,
While streams of blood each limb shall steep,
Thou on earth's breast shalt take thy sleep
Like a fond lover when he strains
The beauty whom at length he gains.
Now when thy heavy eyelids close
For ever in thy deep repose,
Again shall Daṇḍak forest be
Safe refuge for the devotee.
Thou slain, and all thy race who held
The realm of Janasthán expelled,
Again shall happy hermits rove,
Fearing no danger, through the grove.
Within those bounds, their brethren slain,
No giant shall this day remain,
But all shall fly with many a tear
And fearing, rid the saints of fear.
This bitter day shall misery bring
On all the race that calls thee king.
Fierce as their lord, thy dames shall know,
Bereft of joys, the taste of woe.
Base, cruel wretch, of evil mind,
Plaguer of Bráhmans and mankind,
With trembling hands each devotee
Feeds holy fires in dread of thee.'
Thus with wild fury unrepressed
Raghu's brave son the fiend addressed ;
And Khara, as his wrath grew high,
Thus thundered forth his fierce reply :
'By senseless pride to madness wrought,
By danger girt thou fearest naught,
Nor heedest, numbered with the dead,
What thou shouldst say and leave unsaid.
When Fate's tremendous coils enfold
The captive in resistless hold,
He knows not right from wrong, each sense
Numbed by that deadly influence.'
He spoke, and when his speech was done
Bent his fierce brows on Raghu's son.
With eager eyes he looked around
If lethal arms might yet be found.
Not far away and full in view
A Sál-tree towering upward grew.
His lips in mighty strain compressed,
He tore it up with root and crest,
With huge arms waved it o'er his head
And hurled it shouting, Thou art dead.
But Rama, unsurpassed in might,
Stayed with his shafts its onward flight,
And furious longing seized his soul
The giant in the dust to roll.
Great drops of sweat each limb bedewed,
His red eyes showed his wrathful mood.
A thousand arrows, swiftly sent,
The giant's bosom tore and rent.
From every gash his body showed
The blood in foamy torrents flowed.
As springing from their caverns leap
Swift rivers down the mountain steep.
When Khara felt each deadened power
Yielding beneath that murderous shower,
He charged, infuriate with the scent
Of blood, in dire bewilderment.
But Ráma watched. with ready bow,
The onset of his bleeding foe,
And ere the monster reached him, drew
Backward in haste a yard or two.
Then from his side a shaft he took
Whose mortal stroke no life might brook :
Of peerless might, it bore the name
Of Brahmá's staff, and glowed with flame :
Lord Indra, ruler of the skies,
Himself had given the glorious prize.
His bow the virtuous hero drew,
And at the fiend the arrow flew.
Hissing and roaring like the blast
Of tempest through the air it passed,
And fixed, by Ráma's vigour sped,
In the foe's breast its pointed head.
Then fell the fiend : the quenchless flame
Burnt furious in his wounded frame.
So burnt by Rudra Andhak[1] fell
In Śvetáraṇya's silvery dell :
So Namuchi and Vritra[2] died
By steaming bolts that tamed their pride :
So Bala[3] fell by lightning sent
By Him who rules the firmament.
Then all the Gods in close array
With the bright hosts who sing and play,
Filled full of rapture and amaze,
Sang hymns of joy in Ráma's praise,
Beat their celestial drums and shed
Rain of sweet flowers upon his head.
For three short hours had scarcely flown,
And by his pointed shafts o'erthrown
The twice seven thousand fiends, whose will
Could change their shapes, in death were still,
With Triśiras and Dúshaṇ slain,
And Khara. leader of the train.
'O wondrous deed,' the bards began,
'The noblest deed of virtuous man!
Heroic strength that stood alone,
And firmness e'en as Vishṇu's own!'
Thus having sung, the shining train
Turned to their heavenly homes again.

---

[1] A demon, son of Kaśyap and Diti, slain by Rudra or Śiva when he attempted to carry off the tree of Paradise.

[2] Namuchi and Vritra were two demons slain by Indra. Vritra personifies drought, the enemy of Indra, who imprisons the rain in the cloud.

[3] Another demon slain by Indra.

Then the high saints of royal race
And loftiest station sought the place,
And by the great Agastya led,
With reverence to Ráma said:
'For this, Lord Indra, glorious sire,
Majestic as the burning fire,
Who crushes cities in his rage,
Sought Śarabhanga's hermitage.
Thou wast, this great design to aid,
Led by the saints to seek this shade,
And with thy mighty arm to kill
The giants who delight in ill.
Thou, Daśaratha's noble son,
The battle for our sake hast won,
And saints in Daṇḍak's wild who live
Their days to holy tasks can give.'
Forth from the mountain cavern came
The hero Lakshmaṇ with the dame.
And rapture beaming from his face,
Resought the hermit dwelling-place.
Then when the mighty saints had paid
Due honour for the victor's aid,
The glorious Ráma honoured too
By Lakshmaṇ to his cot withdrew.
When Sítá looked upon her lord,
His foemen slain, the saints restored,
In pride and rapture uncontrolled
She clasped him in her loving hold.
On the dead fiends her glances fell:
She saw her lord alive and well,
Victorious after toil and pain,
And Janak's child was blest again.
Once more, once more with new delight
Her tender arms she threw
Round Ráma whose victorious might
Had crushed the demon crew.
Then as his grateful reverence paid
Each saint of lofty soul,
O'er her sweet face, all fears allayed,
The flush of transport stole.

CANTO XXXI.

RÁVAṆ.

But of the host of giants one,
Akampan, from the field had run
And sped to Lanká[1] to relate
In Rávaṇ's ear the demons' fate:
'King, many a giant from the shade
Of Janasthán in death is laid:
Khara the chief is slain, and I
Could scarcely from the battle fly.'
Fierce anger, as the monarch heard,
Inflamed his look, his bosom stirred,
And while with scorching glance he eyed
The messenger, he thus replied:
'What fool has dared, already dead,
Strike Janasthán, the general dread?
Who is the wretch shall vainly try
In earth, heaven, hell, from me to fly?
Vaiśravaṇ,[1] Indra, Vishṇu, He
Who rules the dead, must reverence me;
For not the mightiest lord of these
Can brave my will and live at ease.
Fate finds in me a mightier fate
To burn the fires that devastate.
With unresisted influence I
Can force e'en Death himself to die,
With all-surpassing might restrain
The fury of the hurricane,
And burn in my tremendous ire
The glory of the sun and fire.'
As thus the fiend's hot fury blazed,
His trembling hands Akampan raised,
And with a voice which fear made weak,
Permission craved his tale to speak.
King Rávaṇ gave the leave he sought,
And bade him tell the news he brought.
His courage rose, his voice grew bold,
And thus his mournful tale he told:
'A prince with mighty shoulders, sprung
From Daśaratha, brave and young,
With arms well moulded, bears the name
Of Ráma with a lion's frame.
Renowned, successful, dark of limb,
Earth has no warrior equals him.
He fought in Janasthán and slew
Dúshaṇ the fierce and Khara too.'
Rávaṇ the giants' royal chief,
Received Akampan's tale of grief.
Then, panting like an angry snake,
These words in turn the monarch spake:
'Say quick, did Ráma seek the shade
Of Janasthán with Indra's aid,
And all the dwellers in the skies
To back his hardy enterprise?'
Akampan heard, and straight obeyed
His master, and his answer made.
Then thus the power and might he told
Of Raghu's son the lofty-souled:
'Best is that chief of all who know
With deftest art to draw the bow.
His are strange arms of heavenly might,
And none can match him in the fight.
His brother Lakshmaṇ brave as he,
Fair as the rounded moon to see,
With eyes like night and voice that comes
Deep as the roll of beaten drums,
By Ráma's side stands ever near,
Like wind that aids the flame's career.
That glorious chief, that prince of kings,
On Janasthán this ruin brings.
No Gods were there,—dismiss the thought
No heavenly legions came and fought.
His swift-winged arrows Ráma sent,
Each bright with gold and ornament.
To serpents many-faced they turned:

[1] The capital of the giant king Rávaṇ.

[1] Kuvera, the God of gold.

The giant hosts they ate and burned.
Where'er these fled in wild dismay
Ráma was there to strike and slay.
By him O King of high estate,
Is Janasthán left desolate.'
Akampan ceased: in angry pride
The giant monarch thus replied:
'To Janasthán myself will go
And lay these daring brothers low.'
Thus spoke the king in furious mood:
Akampan then his speech renewed:
'O listen while I tell at length
The terror of the hero's strength.
No power can check, no might can tame
Ráma, a chief of noblest fame.
He with resistless shafts can stay
The torrent foaming on its way.
Sky, stars, and constellations, all
To his fierce might would yield and fall.
His power could earth itself uphold
Down sinking as it sank of old.[1]
Or all its plains and cities drown,
Breaking the wild sea's barrier down;
Crush the great deep's impetuous will,
Or bid the furious wind be still.
He glorious in his high estate
The triple world could devastate,
And there, supreme of men, could place
His creatures of a new-born race.
Never can mighty Ráma be
O'ercome in fight, my King, by thee.
Thy giant host the day might win
From him, if heaven were gained by sin.
If Gods were joined with demons, they
Could ne'er, I ween, that hero slay,
But guile may kill the wondrous man:
Attend while I disclose the plan.
His wife, above all women graced,
Is Sítá of the dainty waist,
With limbs to fair proportion true,
And a soft skin of lustrous hue.
Round neck and arm rich gems are twined:
She is the gem of womankind.
With her no bright Gandharví vies,
No nymph or Goddess in the skies;
And none to rival her would dare
'Mid dames who part the long black hair.
That hero in the wood beguile,
And steal his lovely spouse the while.
'Reft of his darling wife, be sure,
Brief days the mourner will endure.'
With flattering hope of triumph moved
The giant king that plan approved,
Pondered the counsel in his breast,
And then Akampan thus addressed:
'Forth in my car I go at morn,
None but the driver with me borne,
And this fair Sítá will I bring
Back to my city triumphing.'
Forth in his car by asses drawn
The giant monarch sped at dawn,
Bright as the sun, the chariot cast
Light through the sky as on it passed.
Then high in air that best of cars
Traversed the path of lunar stars,
Sending a fitful radiance pale
As moonbeams shot through cloudy veil.
Far on his airy way he flew:
Near Táḍakeya's[1] grove he drew.
Máricha welcomed him, and placed
Before him food which giants taste,
With honour led him to a seat,
And brought him water for his feet;
And then with timely words addressed
Such questiion to his royal guest:
'Speak, is it well with thee whose sway
The giant multitudes obey?
I know not all, and ask in fear
The cause, O King, why thou art here.'
Rávaṇ, the giants' mighty king,
Heard wise Máricha's questioning,
And told with ready answer, taught
In eloquence, the cause he sought:
'My guards, the bravest of my band,
Are slain by Ráma's vigorous hand,
And Janasthán, that feared no hate
Of foes, is rendered desolate.
Come, aid me in the plan I lay
To steal the conqueror's wife away.'
Máricha heard the king's request,
And thus the giant chief addressed:
'What foe in friendly guise is he
Who spoke of Sítá's name to thee?
Who is the wretch whose thought would bring
Destruction on the giants' king?
Whose is the evil counsel, say,
That bids thee bear his wife away,
And careless of thy life provoke
Earth's loftiest with threatening stroke?
A foe is he who dared suggest
This hopeless folly to thy breast,
Whose ill advice would bid thee draw
The venomed fang from serpent's jaw.
By whose unwise suggestion led
Wilt thou the path of ruin tread?
Whence falls the blow that would destroy
Thy gentle sleep of ease and joy?
Like some wild elephant is he
That rears his trunk on high,
Lord of an ancient pedigree,
Huge tusks, and furious eye.
Rávaṇ, no rover of the night
With bravest heart can brook,
Met in the front of deadly fight,
On Raghu's son to look.

---

[1] In the great deluge.

[1] The giant Máricha, son of Táḍaká. Táḍaká was slain by Ráma. See p. 39.

The giant hosts were brave and strong,
Good at the bow and spear :
But Ráma slew the routed throng,
A lion 'mid the deer.
No lion's tooth can match his sword,
Or arrows fiercely shot:
He sleeps, he sleeps—the lion lord ;
Be wise and rouse him not.
O Monarch of the giants, well
Upon my counsel think,
Lest thou for ever in the hell
Of Ráma's vengeance sink :
A hell, where deadly shafts are sent
From his tremendous bow,
While his great arms all flight prevent,
Like deepest mire below:
Where the wild floods of battle rave
Above the foeman's head,
And each with many a feathery wave
Of shafts is garlanded.
O, quench the flames that in thy breast
With raging fury burn :
And pacified and self-possessed
To Lanká's town return.
Rest thou in her imperial bowers
With thine own wives content,
And in the wood let Ráma's hours
With Sítá still be spent.'
The lord of Lanká's isle obeyed
The counsel, and his purpose stayed.
Borne on his car he parted thence
And gained his royal residence.

CANTO XXXII.

RÁVAṆ ROUSED.

But Súrpaṇakhá saw the plain
Spread with the fourteen thousand slain,
Doers of cruel deeds o'erthrown
By Ráma's mighty arm alone,
And Triśiras and Dúshaṇ dead,
And Khara, with the hosts they led.
Their death she saw, and mad with pain,
Roared like a cloud that brings the rain,
And fled in anger and dismay
To Lanká, seat of Rávaṇ's sway.
There on a throne of royal state
Exalted sat the potentate,
Begirt with counsellor and peer,
Like Indra with the Storm-Gods near.
Bright as the sun's full splendour shone
The glorious throne he sat upon,
As when the blazing fire is red
Upon a golden altar fed.
Wide gaped his mouth at every breath,
Tremendous as the jaws of Death.
With him high saints of lofty thought,
Gandharvas, Gods, had vainly fought.
The wounds were on his body yet
From wars where Gods and demons met,
And scars still marked his ample chest
By fierce Airávat's[1] tusk impressed.
A score of arms, ten necks, had he,
His royal gear was brave to see.
His massive form displayed each sign
That marks the heir of kingly line.
In stature like a mountain height,
His arms were strong, his teeth were white,
And all his frame of massive mould
Seemed lazulite adorned with gold.
A hundred seams impressed each limb
Where Vishṇu's arm had wounded him,
And chest and shoulder bore the print
Of sword and spear and arrow dint,
Where every God had struck a blow
In battle with the giant foe.
His might to wildest rage could wake
The sea whose faith naught else can shake,
Hurl towering mountains to the earth,
And crush e'en foes of heavenly birth.
The bonds of law and right he spurned :
To others' wives his fancy turned.
Celestial arms he used in fight,
And loved to mar each holy rite.
He went to Bhogavatí's town,[2]
Where Vásuki was beaten down,
And stole, victorious in the strife,
Lord Takshaka's beloved wife.
Kailása's lofty crest he sought,
And when in vain Kuvera fought,
Stole Pushpak thence, the car that through
The air, as willed the master, flew.
Impelled by furious anger, he
Spoiled Nandan's[3] shade and Naliní,
And Chaitraratha's heavenly grove,
The haunts where Gods delight to rove.
Tall as a hill that cleaves the sky,
He raised his mighty arms on high
To check the blessed moon, and stay
The rising of the Lord of Day.
Ten thousand years the giant spent
On dire austerities intent,
And of his heads an offering, laid
Before the Self-existent, made.
No God or fiend his life could take,
Gandharva, goblin, bird or snake :
Safe from all fears of death, except
From human arm, that life was kept.
Oft when the priests began to raise
Their consecrating hymns of praise,
He spoiled the Soma's sacred juice
Poured forth by them in solemn use.

[1] Indra's elephant.

[2] Bhogavatí, in Pátála in the regions under the earth, is the capital of the serpent race whose king is Vásuki.

[3] The grove of Indra.

The sacrifice his hands o'erthrew,
And cruelly the Bráhmans slew.
His was a heart that naught could melt,
Joying in woes which others felt.
She saw the ruthless monster there,
Dread of the worlds, unused to spare.
In robes of heavenly texture dressed,
Celestial wreaths adorned his breast.
He sat a shape of terror, like
Destruction ere the worlds it strike.
She saw him in his pride of place,
The joy of old Pulastya's[1] race,
Begirt by counsellor and peer,
Rávaṇ, the foeman's mortal fear,
And terror in her features shown,
The giantess approached the throne.
Then Súrpaṇakhá bearing yet
Each deeply printed trace
Where the great-hearted chief had set
A mark upon her face,
Impelled by terror and desire,
Still fierce, no longer bold,
To Rávaṇ of the eyes of fire
Her tale, infuriate, told.

CANTO XXXIII.

SU'RPAṆAKHA'S SPEECH.

Burning with anger, in the ring
Of counsellors who girt their king,
To Rávaṇ, ravener of man,
With bitter words she thus began:
'Wilt thou absorbed in pleasure, still
Pursue unchecked thy selfish will:
Nor turn thy heedless eyes to see
The coming fate which threatens thee?
The king who days and hours employs
In base pursuit of vulgar joys
Must in his people's sight be vile
As fire that smokes on funeral pile.
He who when duty calls him spares
No time for thought of royal cares,
Must with his realm and people all
Involved in fatal ruin fall.
As elephants in terror shrink
From the false river's miry brink,
Thus subjects from a monarch flee
Whose face their eyes may seldom see,
Who spends the hours for toil ordained
In evil courses unrestrained.
He who neglects to guard and hold
His kingdom by himself controlled,
Sinks nameless like a hill whose head
Is buried in the ocean's bed.
Thy foes are calm and strong and wise,
Fiends, Gods, and warriors of the skies,—
How, heedless, wicked, weak, and vain,
Wilt thou thy kingly state maintain?
Thou, lord of giants, void of sense,
Slave of each changing influence,
Heedless of all that makes a king,
Destruction on thy head wilt bring.
O conquering chief, the prince, who boasts,
Of treasury and rule and hosts,
By others led, though lord of all,
Is meaner than the lowest thrall.
For this are monarchs said to be
Long-sighted, having power to see
Things far away by faithful eyes
Of messengers and loyal spies.
But aid from such thou wilt not seek:
Thy counsellors are blind and weak,
Or thou from these hadst surely known
Thy legions and thy realm o'erthrown.
Know, twice seven thousand, fierce in might,
Are slain by Ráma in the fight,
And they, the giant host who led,
Khara and Dúshaṇ, both are dead.
Know, Ráma with his conquering arm
Has freed the saints from dread of harm,
Has smitten Janasthán and made
Asylum safe in Daṇḍak's shade.
Enslaved and dull, of blinded sight,
Intoxicate with vain delight,
Thou closest still thy heedless eyes
To dangers in thy realm that rise.
A king besotted, mean, unkind,
Of niggard hand and slavish mind,
Will find no faithful followers heed
Their master in his hour of need.
The friend on whom he most relies,
In danger, from a monarch flies,
Imperious in his high estate,
Conceited, proud, and passionate;
Who ne'er to state affairs attends
With wholesome fear when woe impends,
Most weak and worthless as the grass,
Soon from his sway the realm will pass.
For rotting wood a use is found,
For clods and dust that strew the ground,
But when a king has lost his sway,
Useless he falls, and sinks for aye.
As raiment by another worn,
As faded garland crushed and torn,
So is, unthroned, the proudest king,
Though mighty once, a useless thing.
But he who every sense subdues
And each event observant views,
Rewards the good and keeps from wrong,
Shall reign secure and flourish long.
Though lulled in sleep his senses lie
He watches with a ruler's eye,
Untouched by favour, ire, and hate,
And him the people celebrate.
O weak of mind, without a trace

[1] Pulastya is considered as the ancestor of the Rakshases or giants, as he is the father of Viśravas, the father of Rávaṇ and his brethren.

Of virtues that a king should grace,
Who hast not learnt from watchful spy
That low in death the giants lie.
Scorner of others, but enchained
By every base desire,
By thee each duty is disdained
Which time and place require.
Soon wilt thou, if thou canst not learn,
Ere yet it be too late,
The good from evil to discern,
Fall from thy high estate.'
As thus she ceased not to upbraid
The king with cutting speech,
And every fault to view displayed,
Naming and marking each,
The monarch of the sons of night,
Of wealth and power possessed,
And proud of his imperial might,
Long pondered in his breast.

CANTO XXXIV.

SU'RPAṆAKHA'S SPEECH.

Then forth the giant's fury broke
As Súrpaṇakhá harshly spoke.
Girt by his lords the demon king
Looked on her, fiercely questioning:
'Who is this Ráma, whence, and where?
His form, his might, his deeds declare.
His wandering steps what purpose led
To Daṇḍak forest, hard to tread?
What arms are his that he could smite
In fray the rovers of the night,
And Trisiras and Dúshaṇ lay
Low on the earth, and Khara slay?
Tell all, my sister, and declare
Who maimed thee thus, of form most fair.'
Thus by the giant king addressed,
While burnt her fury unrepressed,
The giantess declared at length
The hero's form and deeds and strength:
'Long are his arms and large his eyes:
A black deer's skin his dress supplies.
King Daśaratha's son is he,
Fair as Kandarpa's self to see.
Adorned with many a golden band,
A bow, like Indra's, arms his hand,
And shoots a flood of arrows fierce
As venomed snakes to burn and pierce.
I looked, I looked, but never saw
His mighty hand the bowstring draw
That sent the deadly arrows out,
While rang through air his battle-shout.
I looked, I looked, and saw too well
How with that hail the giants fell,
As falls to earth the golden grain,
Struck by the blows of Indra's rain.
He fought, and twice seven thousand, all
Terrific giants, strong and tall,
Fell by the pointed shafts o'erthrown
Which Ráma shot on foot, alone.
Three little hours had scarcely fled,—
Khara and Dúshaṇ both were dead,
And he had freed the saints and made
Asylum sure in Daṇḍak's shade.
Me of his grace the victor spared,
Or I the giants' fate had shared.
The high-souled Ráma would not deign
His hand with woman's blood to stain.
The glorious Lakshmaṇ, justly dear,
In gifts and warrior might his peer,
Serves his great brother with the whole
Devotion of his faithful soul:
Impetuous victor, bold and wise,
First in each hardy enterprise,
Still ready by his side to stand,
A second self or better hand.
And Ráma has a large-eyed spouse,
Pure as the moon her cheek and brows,
Dearer than life in Ráma's sight,
Whose happiness is her delight.
With beauteous hair and nose the dame
From head to foot has naught to blame.
She shines the wood's bright Goddess, Queen
Of beauty with her noble mien.
First in the ranks of women placed
Is Sítá of the dainty waist.
In all the earth mine eyes have ne'er
Seen female form so sweetly fair.
Goddess nor nymph can vie with her,
Nor bride of heavenly chorister.
He who might call this dame his own,
Her eager arms about him thrown,
Would live more blest in Sítá's love
Than Indra in the world above.
She, peerless in her form and face
And rich in every gentle grace,
Is worthy bride, O King, for thee,
As thou art meet her lord to be.
I even I, will bring the bride
In triumph to her lover's side—
This beauty fairer than the rest,
With rounded limb and heaving breast.
Each wound upon my face I owe
To cruel Lakshmaṇ's savage blow.
But thou, O brother, shalt survey
Her moonlike loveliness to-day,
And Káma's piercing shafts shall smite
Thine amorous bosom at the sight.
If in thy breast the longing rise
To make thine own the beauteous prize,
Up, let thy better foot begin
The journey and the treasure win.
If, giant Lord, thy favouring eyes
Regard the plan which I advise,
Up, cast all fear and doubt away
And execute the words I say.
Come, giant King, this treasure seek,
For thou art strong and they are weak.

Let Sítá of the faultless frame
Be borne away and be thy dame.
Thy host in Janasthán who dwelt
Forth to the battle hied,
And by the shafts which Ráma dealt
They perished in their pride.
Dúshaṇ and Khara breathe no more,
Laid low upon the plain.
Arise, and ere the day be o'er
Take vengeance for the slain.'

CANTO XXXV.

RÁVAṆ'S JOURNEY.

When Rávaṇ, by her fury spurred,
That terrible advice had heard,
He bade his nobles quit his side,
And to the work his thought applied.
He turned his anxious mind to scan
On every side the hardy plan:
The gain against the risk he laid,
Each hope and fear with care surveyed,
And in his heart at length decreed
To try performance of the deed.
Then steady in his dire intent
The giant to the courtyard went.
There to his charioteer he cried,
'Bring forth the car whereon I ride.'
Aye ready at his master's word
The charioteer the order heard,
And yoked with active zeal the best
Of chariots at his lord's behest.
Asses with heads of goblins drew
That wondrous car where'er it flew.
Obedient to the will it rolled
Adorned with gems and glistering gold.
Then mounting, with a roar as loud
As thunder from a labouring cloud,
The mighty monarch to the tide
Of Ocean, lord of rivers, hied.
White was the shade above him spread,
White chouris waved around his head,
And he with gold and jewels bright
Shone like the glossy lazulite.
Ten necks and twenty arms had he:
His royal gear was good to see.
The heavenly Gods' insatiate foe,
Who made the blood of hermits flow,
He like the Lord of Hills appeared
With ten huge heads to heaven upreared.
In the great car whereon he rode,
Like some dark cloud the giant showed,
When round it in their close array
The cranes 'mid wreaths of lightning play.
He looked, and saw, from realms of air,
The rocky shore of ocean, where
Unnumbered trees delightful grew
With flower and fruit of every hue.
He looked on many a lilied pool
With silvery waters fresh and cool,
And shores like spacious altars meet
For holy hermits' lone retreat.
The graceful palm adorned the scene,
The plantain waved her glossy green.
There grew the sál and betel, there
On bending boughs the flowers were fair.
There hermits dwelt who tamed each sense
By strictest rule of abstinence:
Gandharvas, Kinnars,[1] thronged the place,
Nágas and birds of heavenly race.
Bright minstrels of the ethereal quire,
And saints exempt from low desire,
With Ájas, sons of Brahmá's line,
Maríchipas of seed divine,
Vaikhánasas and Máshas strayed,
And Bálakhilyas[2] in the shade.
The lovely nymphs of heaven were there,
Celestial wreaths confined their hair,
And to each form new grace was lent
By wealth of heavenly ornament.
Well skilled was each in play and dance
And gentle arts of dalliance.
The glorious wife of many a God
Those beautiful recesses trod,
There Gods and Dánavs, all who eat
The food of heaven, rejoiced to meet.
The swan and Sáras thronged each bay
With curlews, ducks, and divers gay,
Where the sea spray rose soft and white
O'er rocks of glossy lazulite.
As his swift way the fiend pursued
Pale chariots of the Gods he viewed,
Bearing each lord whose rites austere
Had raised him to the heavenly sphere.
Thereon celestial garlands hung,
There music played and songs were sung.
Then bright Gandharvas met his view,
And heavenly nymphs, as on he flew.
He saw the sandal woods below,
And precious trees of odorous flow,
That to the air around them lent
Their riches of delightful scent;
Nor failed his roving eye to mark
Tall aloe trees in grove and park.
He looked on wood with cassias filled,
And plants which balmy sweets distilled,
Where her fair flowers the betel showed
And the bright pods of pepper glowed.
The pearls in many a silvery heap
Lay on the margin of the deep,
And grey rocks rose amid the red
Of coral washed from ocean's bed.

---

[1] Beings with the body of a man and the head of a horse.

[2] Ájas, Maríchipas, Vaikhánasas, Máshas, and Bálakhilyas are classes of supernatural beings who lead the lives of hermits.

High soared the mountain peaks that bore
Treasures of gold and silver ore,
And leaping down the rocky walls
Came wild and glorious waterfalls.
Fair towns which grain and treasure held,
And dames who every gem excelled,
He saw outspread beneath him far,
With steed, and elephant, and car.
That ocean shore he viewed that showed
Fair as the blessed Gods' abode
Where cool delightful breezes played
O'er levels in the freshest shade.
He saw a fig-tree like a cloud
With mighty branches earthward bowed.
It stretched a hundred leagues and made
For hermit bands a welcome shade.
Thither the feathered king of yore
An elephant and tortoise bore,
And lighted on a bough to eat
The captives of his taloned feet.
The bough unable to sustain
The crushing weight and sudden strain,
Loaded with sprays and leaves of spring
Gave way beneath the feathered king.
Under the shadow of the tree
Dwelt many a saint and devotee,
Ajas, the sons of Brahmá's line,
Máshas Maríchipas divine,
Vaikhánasas, and all the race
Of Bálakhilyas, loved the place.
But pitying their sad estate
The feathered monarch raised the weight
Of the huge bough, and bore away
The loosened load and captured prey.
A hundred leagues away he sped,
Then on his monstrous booty fed,
And with the bough he smote the lands
Where dwell the wild Nisháda bands.
High joy was his because his deed
From jeopardy the hermits freed.
That pride for great deliverance wrought
A double share of valour brought.
His soul conceived the high emprise
To snatch the Amrit from the skies.
He rent the nets of iron first,
Then through the jewel chamber burst,
And bore the drink of heaven away
That watched in Indra's palace lay.
Such was the hermit-sheltering tree
Which Rávan turned his eye to see.
Still marked where Garuḍ sought to rest,
The fig-tree bore the name of Blest.
When Rávan stayed his chariot o'er
The ocean's heart-enchanting shore,
He saw a hermitage that stood
Sequestered in the holy wood.
He saw the fiend Márícha there
With deerskin garb, and matted hair
Coiled up in hermit guise, who spent
His days by rule most abstinent.
As guest and host are wont to meet,
They met within that lone retreat.
Before the king Márícha placed
Food never known to human taste.
He entertained his guest with meat
And gave him water for his feet.
And then addressed the giant king
With timely words of questioning:
'Lord, is it well with thee, and well
With those in Lanká's town who dwell?
What sudden thought, what urgent need
Has brought thee with impetuous speed?'
The fiend Márícha thus addressed
Rávan the king, his mighty guest,
And he, well skilled in arts that guide
The eloquent, in turn replied:

CANTO XXXVI.

RÁVAṆ'S SPEECH.

'Hear me, Márícha, while I speak,
And tell thee why thy home I seek.
Sick and distressed am I, and see
My surest hope and help in thee.
Of Janasthán I need not tell,
Where Súrpaṇakhá, Khara, dwell,
And Dúshaṇ with the arm of might,
And Triśiras, the fierce in fight,
Who feeds on human flesh and gore,
And many noble giants more,
Who roam in dark of midnight through
The forest, brave and strong and true.
By my command they live at ease
And slaughter saints and devotees.
Those twice seven thousand giants, all
Obedient to their captain's call,
Joying in war and ruthless deeds
Follow where mighty Khara leads.
Those fearless warrior bands who roam
Through Janasthán their forest home,
In all their terrible array
Met Ráma in the battle fray.
Girt with all weapons forth they sped
With Khara at the army's head.
The front of battle Ráma held:
With furious wrath his bosom swelled.
Without a word his hate to show
He launched the arrows from his bow.
On the fierce hosts the missiles came,
Each burning with destructive flame.
The twice seven thousand fell o'erthrown
By him, a man, on foot, alone.
Khara the army's chief and pride,
And Dúshaṇ, fearless warrior, died,
And Triśiras the fierce was slain,
And Daṇḍak wood was free again.
He, banished by his angry sire,
Roams with his wife in mean attire.
This wretch, his Warrior tribe's disgrace,
Has slain the best of giant race.

Harsh, wicked, fierce, and greedy-souled,
A fool, with senses uncontrolled,
No thought of duty stirs his breast:
He joys to see the world distressed.
He sought the wood with fair pretence
Of truthful life and innocence,
But his false hand my sister left
Mangled, of nose and ears bereft.
This Ráma's wife who bears the name
Of Sítá, in her face and frame
Fair as a daughter of the skies,—
Her will I seize and bring the prize
Triumphant from the forest shade:
For this I seek thy willing aid.
If thou, O mighty one, wilt lend
Thy help and stand beside thy friend,
I with my brothers may defy
All Gods embattled in the sky.
Come, aid me now, for thine the power
To succour in the doubtful hour.
Thou art in war and time of fear,
For heart and hand, without a peer.
For thou art skilled in art and wile,
A warrior brave and trained in guile.
With this one hope, this only aim,
O Rover of the Night, I came.
Now let me tell what aid I ask
To back me in my purposed task.
In semblance of a golden deer
Adorned with silver spots appear.
Go, seek his dwelling: in the way
Of Ráma and his consort stray.
Doubt not the lady, when she sees
The wondrous deer amid the trees,
Will bid her lord and Lakshman take
The creature for its beauty's sake.
Then when the chiefs have parted thence,
And left her lone, without defence,
As Ráhu storms the moonlight, I
Will seize the lovely dame and fly.
Her lord will waste away and weep
For her his valour could not keep.
Then boldly will I strike the blow
And wreak my vengeance on the foe.'
When wise Márícha heard the tale
His heart grew faint, his cheek was pale,
He stared with open orbs, and tried
To moisten lips which terror dried,
And grief, like death, his bosom rent
As on the king his look he bent.
The monarch's will he strove to stay,
Distracted with alarm,
For well he knew the might that lay
In Ráma's matchless arm.
With suppliant hands Márícha stood
And thus began to tell
His counsel for the tyrant's good,
And for his own as well:

CANTO XXXVII.

MÁRÍCHA'S SPEECH.

Márícha gave attentive ear
The ruler of the fiends to hear:
Then, trained in all the rules that teach
The eloquent, began his speech:
''Tis easy task, O King, to find
Smooth speakers who delight the mind.
But they who urge and they who do
Distasteful things and wise, are few.
Thou hast not learnt, by proof untaught,
And borne away by eager thought,
That Ráma, formed for high emprise,
With Varuṇ or with Indra vies.
Still let thy people live in peace,
Nor let their name and lineage cease,
For Ráma with his vengeful hand
Can sweep the giants from the land.
O, let not Janak's daughter bring
Destruction on the giant king.
Let not the lady Sítá wake
A tempest, on thy head to break.
Still let the dame, by care untried,
Be happy by her husband's side,
Lest swift avenging ruin fall
On glorious Lanká, thee, and all.
Men such as thou with wills unchained,
Advised by sin and unrestrained,
Destroy themselves, the king, the state,
And leave the people desolate.
Ráma, in bonds of duty held,
Was never by his sire expelled.
He is no wretch of greedy mind,
Dishonour of his Warrior kind.
Free from all touch of rancorous spite,
All creatures' good is his delight.
He saw his sire of truthful heart
Deceived by Queen Kaikeyí's art,
And said, a true and duteous son,
'What thou hast promised shall be done.'
To gratify the lady's will,
His father's promise to fulfil,
He left his realm and all delight
For Daṇḍak wood, an anchorite.
No cruel wretch, no senseless fool
Is Ráma, unrestrained by rule.
This groundless charge has ne'er been heard,
Nor shouldst thou speak the slanderous word.
Ráma in truth and goodness bold
Is Virtue's self in human mould,
The sovereign of the world confessed
As Indra rules among the Blest.
And dost thou plot from him to rend
The darling whom his arms defend?
Less vain the hope to steal away
The glory of the Lord of Day.

O Rávaṇ, guard thee from the fire
Of vengeful Ráma's kindled ire,—
Each spark a shaft with deadly aim,
While bow and falchion feed the flame.
Cast not away in hopeless strife
Thy realm, thy bliss, thine own dear life.
O Rávaṇ of his might beware,
A God of Death who will not spare.
That bow he knows so well to draw
Is the destroyer's flaming jaw,
And with his shafts which flash and glow
He slays the armies of the foe.
Thou ne'er canst win—the thought forego—
From the safe guard of shaft and bow
King Janak's child, the dear delight
Of Ráma unapproached in might.
The spouse of Raghu's son, confessed
Lion of men with lion chest,—
Dearer than life, through good and ill
Devoted to her husband's will,
The slender-waisted, still must be
From thy polluting touches free.
Far better grasp with venturous hand
The flame to wildest fury fanned.
What, King of giants, canst thou gain
From this attempt so wild and vain?
If in the fight his eye he bend
Upon thee, Lord, thy days must end,
So life and bliss and royal sway,
Lost beyond hope, will pass away.
Summon each lord of high estate,
And chief, Vibhíshaṇ[1] to debate.
With peers in lore of counsel tried
Consider, reason, and decide.
Scan strength and weakness, count the cost,
What may be gained and what be lost.
Examine and compare aright
Thy proper power and Ráma's might,
Then if thy weal be still thy care.
Thou wilt be prudent and forbear.
O giant King, the contest shun,
  Thy force is all too weak
The lord of Kosál's mighty son
  In deadly fray to seek.
King of the hosts that rove at night,
  O hear what I advise:
My prudent counsel do not slight;
  Be patient and be wise.'

[1] 'The younger brother of the giant Rávaṇ; when he and his brother had practised austerities for a long series of years, Brahmá appeared to offer them boons: Vibhíshaṇa asked that he might never meditate any unrighteousness......... On the death of Rávaṇ Vibhíshaṇa was installed as Rája of Lanká.' GARRETT'S *Classical Dictionary of India*.

CANTO XXXVIII.

MÁRÍCHA'S SPEECH.

'Once in my strength and vigour's pride
I roamed this earth from side to side,
And towering like a mountain's crest,
A thousand Nágas'[1] might possessed.
Like some vast sable cloud I showed:
My golden armlets flashed and glowed.
A crown I wore, an axe I swayed,
And all I met were sore afraid.
I roved where Daṇḍak wood is spread;
On flesh of slaughtered saints I fed.
Then Viśvámitra, sage revered,
Holy of heart, my fury feared.
To Daśaratha's court he sped
And went before the king and said:[2]
'With me, my lord, thy Ráma send
On holy days his aid to lend.
Máricha fills my soul with dread
And keeps me sore disquieted.'
The monarch heard the saint's request
And thus the glorious sage addressed:
'My boy as yet in arms untrained
The age of twelve has scarce attained.
But I myself a host will lead
To guard thee in the hour of need.
My host with fourfold troops complete,
The rover of the night shall meet,
And I, O best of saints, will kill
Thy foeman and thy prayer fulfil.'
The king vouchsafed his willing aid:
The saint again this answer made:
'By Ráma's might, and his alone,
Can this great fiend be overthrown.
I know in days of yore the Blest
Thy saving help in fight confessed.
Still of thy famous deeds they tell
In heaven above, in earth, and hell.
A mighty host obeys thy hest:
Here let it still, I pray thee, rest.
Thy glorious son, though yet a boy,
Will in the fight that fiend destroy.
Ráma alone with me shall go:
Be happy, victor of the foe.'
He spoke: the monarch gave assent,
And Ráma to the hermit lent.
So to his woodland home in joy
Went Viśvámitra with the boy.
With ready bow the champion stood
To guard the rites in Daṇḍak wood.
With glorious eyes, most bright to view,
Beardless as yet and dark of hue;
A single robe his only wear,
His temples veiled with waving hair,

[1] Serpent-gods.

[2] See p. 33.

Around his neck a chain of gold,
He grasped the bow he loved to hold;
And the young hero's presence made
A glory in the forest shade.
Thus Ráma with his beauteous mien,
Like the young rising moon was seen.
I, like a cloud which tempest brings,
My arms adorned with golden rings,
Proud of the boon which lent me might,
Approached where dwelt the anchorite.
But Ráma saw me venturing nigh,
Raising my murderous axe on high;
He saw, and fearless of the foe,
Strung with calm hand his trusty bow.
By pride of conscious strength beguiled,
I scorned him as a feeble child,
And rushed with an impetuous bound
On Viśvámitra's holy ground.
A keen swift shaft he pointed well,
The foeman's rage to check and quell,
And hurled a hundred leagues away
Deep in the ocean waves I lay.
He would not kill, but, nobly brave,
My forfeit life he chose to save.
So there I lay with wandering sense
Dazed by that arrow's violence.
Long in the sea I lay: at length
Slowly returned my sense and strength,
And rising from my watery bed
To Lanká's town again I sped.
Thus was I spared, but all my band
Fell slain by Ráma's conquering hand,—
A boy, untrained in warrior skill,
Of iron arm and dauntless will.
If thou with Ráma still, in spite
Of warning and of prayer, wilt fight,
I see terrific woes impend,
And dire defeat thy days will end.
Thy giants all will feel the blow
And share the fatal overthrow,
Who love the taste of joy and play,
The banquet and the festal day.
Thine eyes will see destruction take
Thy Lanká, lost for Sítá's sake,
And stately pile and palace fall
With terrace, dome, and jewelled wall.
The good will die: the crime of kings
Destruction on the people brings:
The sinless die, as in the lake
The fish must perish with the snake.
The prostrate giants thou wilt see
Slain for this folly wrought by thee,
Their bodies bright with precious scent
And sheen of heavenly ornament;
Or see the remnant of thy train
Seek refuge far, when help is vain,
And with their wives, or widowed, fly
To every quarter of the sky;
Thy mournful eyes, where'er they turn,
Will see thy stately city burn,
When royal homes with fire are red,
And arrowy nets around are spread.
A sin that tops all sins in shame
Is outrage to another's dame.
A thousand wives thy palace fill,
And countless beauties wait thy will.
O rest contented with thine own,
Nor let thy race be overthrown.
If thou, O King, hast still delight
In rank and wealth and power and might,
In noble wives, in troops of friends,
In all that royal state attends,
I warn thee, cast not all away,
Nor challenge Ráma to the fray.
If deaf to every friendly prayer,
 Thou still wilt seek the strife,
And from the side of Ráma tear
 His lovely Maithil wife,
Soon will thy life and empire end
 Destroyed by Ráma's bow,
And thou, with kith and kin and friend,
 To Yama's realm must go.'

CANTO XXXIX.

MÁRÍCHA'S SPEECH.

'I told thee of that dreadful day
When Ráma smote and spared to slay.
Now hear me, Rávan, while I tell
What in the after time befell.
At length, restored to strength and pride,
I and two mighty fiends beside
Assumed the forms of deer and strayed
Through Dandak wood in lawn and glade.
I reared terrific horns: beneath
Were flaming tongue and pointed teeth.
I roamed where'er my fancy led,
And on the flesh of hermits fed,
In sacred haunt, by hallowed tree,
Where'er the ritual fires might be.
A fearful shape, I wandered through
The wood, and many a hermit slew.
With ruthless rage the saints I killed
Who in the grove their tasks fulfilled.
When smitten to the earth they sank,
Their flesh I ate, their blood I drank,
And with my cruel deeds dismayed
All dwellers in the forest shade,
Spoiling their rites in bitter hate,
With human blood inebriate.
Once in the wood I chanced to see
Ráma again, a devotee,
A hermit, fed on scanty fare,
Who made the good of all his care.
His noble wife was by his side,
And Lakshman in the battle tried.
In senseless pride I scorned the might
Of that illustrious anchorite,
And heedless of a hermit foe,
Recalled my earlier overthow.

I charged him in my rage and scorn
To slay him with my pointed horn,
In heedless haste, to fury wrought
As on my former wounds I thought.
Then from the mighty bow he drew
Three foe-destroying arrows flew,
Keen-pointed, leaping from the string
Swift as the wind or feathered king.
Dire shafts, on flesh of foemen fed,
Like rushing thunderbolts they sped.
With knots well smoothed and barbs well bent,
Shot e'en as one, the arrows went.
But I who Ráma's might had felt,
And knew the blows the hero dealt,
Escaped by rapid flight. The two
Who lingered on the spot, he slew.
I fled from mortal danger, freed
From the dire shaft by timely speed.
Now to deep thought my days I give,
And as a humble hermit live.
In every shrub, in every tree
I view that noblest devotee.
In every knotted trunk I mark
His deerskin and his coat of bark,
And see the bow-armed Ráma stand
Like Yama with his noose in hand.
I tell thee Rávaṇ, in my fright
A thousand Rámas mock my sight.
This wood with every bush and bough
Seems all one fearful Ráma now.
Throughout the grove there is no spot
So lonely where I see him not.
He haunts me in my dreams by night,
And wakes me with the wild affright.
The letter that begins his name
Sends terror through my startled frame.
The rapid cars whereon we ride,
The rich rare jewels, once my pride,
Have names[1] that strike upon mine ear
With hated sound that counsels fear.
His mighty strength too well I know,
Nor art thou match for such a foe.
Too strong were Raghus's son in fight
For Namuchi or Bali's might.
Then Ráma to the battle dare,
Or else be patient and forbear;
But, wouldst thou see me live in peace,
Let mention of the hero cease.
The good whose holy lives were spent
In deepest thought, most innocent,
With all their people many a time
Have perished through another's crime.
So in the common ruin, I
Must for another's folly die,
Do all thy strength and courage can,
But ne'er will I approve the plan.
For he, in might supremely great,
The giant world could extirpate,
Since, when impetuous Khara sought
The grove of Janasthán and fought
For Súrpaṇakhá's sake, he died
By Ráma's hand in battle tried.
How has he wronged thee? Soothly swear,
And Ráma's fault and sin declare.
I warn thee, and my words are wise,
I seek thy people's weal:
But if this rede thou wilt despise,
Nor hear my last appeal,
Thou with thy kin and all thy friends
In fight this day wilt die,
When his great bow the hero bends,
And shafts unerring fly.'

CANTO XL.

RÁVAṆ'S SPEECH.

But Rávaṇ scorned the rede he gave
In timely words to warn and save,
E'en as the wretch who hates to live
Rejects the herb the leeches give.
By fate to sin and ruin spurred,
That sage advice the giant heard,
Then in reproaches hard and stern
Thus to Márícha spoke in turn:
'Is this thy counsel, weak and base,
Unworthy of thy giant race?
Thy speech is fruitless, vain, thy toil
Like casting seed on barren soil.
No words of thine shall drive me back
From Ráma and the swift attack.
A fool is he, inured to sin,
And more, of human origin.
The craven, at a woman's call
To leave his sire, his mother, all
The friends he loved, the power and sway,
And hasten to the woods away!
But now his anger will I rouse,
Stealing away his darling spouse.
I in thy sight will ravish her
From Khara's cruel murderer.
Upon this plan my soul is bent,
And naught shall move my firm intent,
Not if the way through demons led
And Gods with Indra at their head.
'Tis thine, when questioned, to explain
The hope and fear, the loss and gain,
And, when thy king thy thoughts would know,
The triumph or the danger show.
A prudent counsellor should wait,
And speak when ordered in debate,
With hands uplifted, calm and meek,
If honour and reward he seek.
Or, when some prudent course he sees
Which, spoken, may his king displease,

[1] The Sanskrit words for car and jewels begin with *ra*.

He should by hints of dexterous art
His counsel to his lord impart.
But prudent words are said in vain
When the blunt speech brings grief and pain.
A high-souled king will scarcely thank
The man who shames his royal rank.
Five are the shapes that kings assume,
Of majesty, of grace, and gloom:
Like Indra now, or Agni, now
Like the dear Moon, with placid brow:
Like mighty Varuṇ now they show,
Now fierce as He who rules below.
O giant, monarchs lofty-souled
Are kind and gentle, stern and bold,
With gracious love their gifts dispense
And swiftly punish each offence.
Thus subjects should their rulers view
With all respect and honour due.
But folly leads thy heart to slight
Thy monarch and neglect his right.
Thou hast in lawless pride addressed
With bitter words thy royal guest.
I asked thee not my strength to scan,
Or loss and profit in the plan.
I only spoke to tell the deed
O mighty one, by me decreed,
And bid thee in the peril lend
Thy succour to support thy friend.
Hear me again, and I will tell
How thou canst aid my venture well.
In semblance of a golden deer
Adorned with silver drops, appear:
And near the cottage in the way
Of Ráma and his consort stray.
Draw nigh, and wandering through the brake
With thy strange form her fancy take.
The Maithil dame with wondering eyes
Will look upon thy fair disguise,
And quickly bid her husband go
And bring the deer that charms her so.
When Raghu's son has left the place,
Still pressing onward in the chase,
Cry out, 'O Lakshmaṇ! Ah, mine own!'
With voice resembling Ráma's tone.
When Lakshmaṇ hears his brother's cry,
Impelled by Sítá he will fly,
Restless with eager love, to aid
The hunter in the distant shade.
When both her guards have left her side,
Even as Indra, thousand-eyed,
Clasps Śachí, will I bear away
The Maithil dame an easy prey.
When thou, my friend, this aid hast lent,
Go where thou wilt and live content.
True servant, faithful to thy vow,
With half my realm I thee endow.
Go forth, may luck thy way attend
That leads thee to the happy end.
I in my car will quickly be
In Dandak wood, and follow thee.
So will I cheat this Ráma's eyes
And win without a blow the prize;
And safe return to Lanká's town
With thee, my friend, this day shall crown.
But if thou wilt not aid my will,
My hand this day thy blood shall spill.
Yea, thou must share the destined task,
For force will take the help I ask.
No bliss that rebel's life attends
Whose stubborn will his lord offends.
Thy life, if thou the task assay,
In jeopardy may stand;
Oppose me, and this very day
Thou diest by this hand.
Now ponder all that thou hast heard
Within thy prudent breast:
Reflect with care on every word,
And do what seems the best.'

CANTO XLI.

MÁRÍCHA'S REPLY.

Against his judgment sorely pressed
By his imperious lord's behest,
Márícha threats of death defied
And thus with bitter words replied:
'Ah, who, my King, with sinful thought
This wild and wicked counsel taught,
By which destruction soon will fall
On thee, thy sons, thy realm and all?
Who is the guilty wretch who sees
With envious eye thy blissful ease,
And by this plan, so falsely shown,
Death's gate for thee has open thrown?
With souls impelled by mean desire
Thy foes against thy life conspire.
They urge thee to destruction's brink,
And gladly would they see thee sink.
Who with base thought to work thee woe
This fatal road has dared to show,
And, triumph in his wicked eye,
Would see thee enter in and die?
To all thy counsellors, untrue,
The punishment of death is due,
Who see thee tempt the dangerous way,
Nor strain each nerve thy foot to stay.
Wise lords, whose king, by passion led,
The path of sin begins to tread,
Restrain him while there yet is time:
But thine,—they see nor heed the crime.
These by their master's will obtain
Merit and fame and joy and gain.
''Tis only by their master's grace
That servants hold their lofty place.
But when the monarch stoops to sin
They lose each joy they strove to win,
And all the people high and low
Fall in the common overthrow.

Merit and fame and honour spring,
Best of the mighty, from the king.
So all should strive with heart and will
To keep the king from every ill.
Pride, violence, and sullen hate
Will ne'er maintain a monarch's state,
And those who cruel deeds advise
Must perish when their master dies,
Like drivers with their cars o'erthrown
In places rough with root and stone.
The good whose holy lives were spent
On duty's highest laws intent,
With wives and children many a time
Have perished for another's crime.
Hapless are they whose sovereign lord,
Opposed to all, by all abhorred,
Is cruel-hearted, harsh, severe:
Thus might a jackal tend the deer.
Now all the giant race await,
Destroyed by thee, a speedy fate,
Ruled by a king so cruel-souled,
Foolish in heart and uncontrolled.
Think not I fear the sudden blow
That threatens now to lay me low:
I mourn the ruin that I see
Impending o'er thy host and thee.
Me first perchance will Ráma kill,
But soon his hand thy blood will spill.
I die, and if by Ráma slain
And not by thee, I count it gain.
Soon as the hero's face I see
His angry eyes will murder me,
And if on her thy hands thou lay
Thy friends and thou are dead this day.
If with my help thou still must dare
The lady from her lord to tear,
Farewell to all! our days are o'er,
Lanká and giants are no more.
In vain, in vain, an earnest friend,
I warn thee, King, and pray.
Thou wilt not to my prayers attend,
Or heed the words I say.
So men, when life is fleeting fast
And death's sad hour is nigh,
Heedless and blinded to the last
Reject advice and die.'

CANTO XLII.

MÁRÍCHA TRANSFORMED.

Márícha thus in wild unrest
With bitter words the king addressed,
Then to his giant lord in dread,
'Arise, and let us go,' he said.
'Ah, I have met that mighty lord
Armed with his shafts and bow and sword,
And if again that bow he bend
Our lives that very hour will end.
For none that warrior can provoke
And think to fly his deadly stroke.
Like Yama with his staff is he,
And his dread hand will slaughter thee.
What can I more? My words can find
No passage to thy stubborn mind.
I go, great King, thy task to share,
And my success attend thee there.'
With that reply and bold consent
The giant king was well content.
He strained Márícha to his breast
And thus with joyful words addressed:
'There spoke a hero dauntless still,
Obedient to his master's will,
Márícha's proper self once more:
Some other took thy shape before.
Come, mount my jewelled car that flies,
Well-governed, through the yielding skies.
These asses, goblin-faced, shall bear
Us quickly through the fields of air.
Attract the lady with thy shape,
Then through the wood, at will, escape.
And I, when she has no defence,
Will seize the dame and bear her thence.
Again Márícha made reply,
Consent and will to signify.
With rapid speed the giants two
From the calm hermit dwelling flew,
Borne in that wondrous chariot, meet
For some great God's celestial seat.
They from their airy path looked down
On many a wood and many a town,
On lake and river, brook and rill,
City and realm and towering hill.
Soon he whom giant hosts obeyed,
Márícha by his side, surveyed
The dark expanse of Daṇḍak wood
Where Ráma's hermit cottage stood.
They left the flying car, whereon
The wealth of gold and jewels shone,
And thus the giant king addressed
Márícha as his hand he pressed:
'Márícha, look! before our eyes
Round Ráma's home the plantains rise.
His hermitage is now in view:
Quick to the work we came to do!'
Thus Rávaṇ spoke, Márícha heard
Obedient to his master's word,
Threw off his giant shape and near
The cottage strayed a beauteous deer.
With magic power, by rapid change,
His borrowed form was fair and strange.
A sapphire tipped each horn with light;
His face was black relieved with white.
The turkis and the ruby shed
A glory from his ears and head.
His arching neck was proudly raised,
And lazulites beneath it blazed.
With roseate bloom his flanks were dyed,
And lotus tints adorned his hide.
His shape was fair, compact, and slight;

His hoofs were carven lazulite.
His tail with every changing glow
Displayed the hues of Indra's bow.
With glossy skin so strangely flecked,
With tints of every gem bedecked.
A light o'er Ráma's home he sent,
And through the wood, where'er he went.
The giant clad in that strange dress
That took the soul with loveliness,
To charm the fair Videhan's eyes
With mingled wealth of mineral dyes,
Moved onward, cropping in his way,
The grass and grain and tender spray.
His coat with drops of silver bright,
A form to gaze on with delight,
He raised his fair neck as he went
To browse on bud and filament.
Now in the Cassia grove he strayed,
Now by the cot in plantains' shade.
Slowly and slowly on he came
To catch the glances of the dame,
And the tall deer of splendid hue
Shone full at length in Sítá's view.
He roamed where'er his fancy chose
Where Ráma's leafy cottage rose.
Now near, now far, in careless ease,
He came and went among the trees.
Now with light feet he turned to fly,
Now, reassured, again drew nigh:
Now gambolled close with leap and bound,
Now lay upon the grassy ground:
Now sought the door, devoid of fear,
And mingled with the troop of deer;
Led them a little way, and thence
Again returned with confidence.
Now flying far, now turning back
Emboldened on his former track,
Seeking to win the lady's glance
He wandered through the green expanse.
Then thronging round, the woodland deer
Gazed on his form with wondering fear;
A while they followed where he led,
Then snuffed the tainted gale and fled.
The giant, though he longed to slay
The startled quarry, spared the prey,
And mindful of the shape he wore
To veil his nature, still forbore.
Then Sítá of the glorious eye,
Returning from her task drew nigh:
For she had sought the wood to bring
Each loveliest flower of early spring.
Now would the bright-eyed lady choose
Some gorgeous bud with blending hues,
Now plucked the mango's spray, and now
The bloom from an Asoka bough.
She with her beauteous form, unmeet
For woodland life and lone retreat,
That wondrous dappled deer beheld
Gemmed with rich pearls, unparalleled.
His silver hair the lady saw,
His radiant teeth and lips and jaw,
And gazed with rapture as her eyes
Expanded in their glad surprise.
And when the false deer's glances fell
On her whom Ráma loved so well,
He wandered here and there, and cast
A luminous beauty as he passed;
And Janak's child with strange delight
Kept gazing on the unwonted sight.

CANTO XLIII.

THE WONDROUS DEER.

She stooped, her hands with flowers to fill,
But gazed upon the marvel still:
Gazed on its back and sparkling side
Where silver hues with golden vied.
Joyous was she of faultless mould,
With glossy skin like polished gold,
And loudly to her husband cried
And bow-armed Lakshmaṇ by his side:
Again, again she called in glee:
'O come this glorious creature see;
Quick, quick, my lord, this deer to view,
And bring thy brother Lakshmaṇ too.'
As through the wood her clear tones rang,
Swift to her side the brothers sprang.
With eager eyes the grove they scanned,
And saw the deer before them stand.
But doubt was strong in Lakshmaṇ's breast,
Who thus his thought and fear expressed:
'Stay, for the wondrous deer we see
The fiend Márícha's self may be.
Ere now have kings who sought this place
To take their pastime in the chase,
Met from his wicked art defeat,
And fallen slain by like deceit.
He wears, well trained in magic guile,
The figure of a deer a while,
Bright as the very sun, or place
Where dwell the gay Gandharva race.
No deer, O Ráma, e'er was seen
Thus decked with gold and jewels' sheen.
'Tis magic, for the world has ne'er,
Lord of the world, shown aught so fair.'
But Sítá of the lovely smile,
A captive to the giant's wile,
Turned Lakshmaṇ's prudent speech aside
And thus with eager words replied:
My honoured lord, this deer I see
With beauty rare enraptures me.
Go, chief of mighty arm, and bring
For my delight this precious thing.
Fair creatures of the woodland roam
Untroubled near our hermit home.
The forest cow and stag are there,
The fawn, the monkey, and the bear,
Where spotted deer delight to play,

And strong and beauteous Kinnars[1] stray.
But never, as they wandered by,
Has such a beauty charmed mine eye
As this with limbs so fair and slight,
So gentle, beautiful and bright.
O see, how fair it is to view
With jewels of each varied hue:
Bright as the rising moon it glows,
Lighting the wood where'er it goes.
Ah me, what form and grace are there!
Its limbs how fine, its hues how fair!
Transcending all that words express,
It takes my soul with loveliness.
O, if thou would, to please me, strive
To take the beauteous thing alive,
How thou wouldst gaze with wondering eyes
Delighted on the lovely prize!
And when our woodland life is o'er,
And we enjoy our realm once more,
The wondrous animal will grace
The chambers of my dwelling-place,
And a dear treasure will it be
To Bharat and the queens and me,
And all with rapture and amaze
Upon its heavenly form will gaze.
But if the beauteous deer, pursued,
Thine arts to take it still elude,
Strike it, O chieftain, and the skin
Will be a treasure, laid within.
O, how I long my time to pass
Sitting upon the tender grass,
With that soft fell beneath me spread
Bright with its hair of golden thread!
This strong desire, this eager will,
Befits a gentle lady ill:
But when I first beheld, its look
My breast with fascination took.
See, golden hair its flank adorns,
And sapphires tip its branching horns.
Resplendent as the lunar way,
Or the first blush of opening day,
With graceful form and radiant hue
It charmed thy heart, O chieftain, too.'
He heard her speech with willing ear,
He looked again upon the deer.
Its lovely shape his breast beguiled
Moved by the prayer of Janak's child,
And yielding for her pleasure's sake,
To Lakshmaṇ Ráma turned and spake:
'Mark, Lakshmaṇ, mark how Sítá's breast
With eager longing is possessed.
To-day this deer of wondrous breed
Must for his passing beauty bleed,
Brighter than e'er in Nandan strayed,
Or Chaitraratha's heavenly shade.
How should the groves of earth possess
Such all-surpassing loveliness!
The hair lies smooth and bright and fine,
Or waves upon each curving line,
And drops of living gold bedeck
The beauty of his side and neck.
O look, his crimson tongue between
His teeth like flaming fire is seen,
Flashing, whene'er his lips he parts,
As from a cloud the lightning darts.
O see his sunlike forehead shine
With emerald tints and almandine,
While pearly light and roseate glow
Of shells adorn his neck below.
No eye on such a deer can rest
But soft enchantment takes the breast:
No man so fair a thing behold
Ablaze with light of radiant gold,
Celestial, bright with jewels' sheen,
Nor marvel when his eyes have seen.
A king equipped with bow and shaft
Delights in gentle forest craft,
And as in boundless woods he strays
The quarry for the venison slays.
There as he wanders with his train
A store of wealth he oft may gain.
He claims by right the precious ore,
He claims the jewels' sparkling store.
Such gains are dearer in his eyes
Than wealth that in his chamber lies,
The dearest things his spirit knows,
Dear as the bliss which Sukra chose.
But oft the rich expected gain
Which heedless men pursue in vain,
The sage, who prudent counsels know,
Explain and in a moment show.
This best of deer, this gem of all,
To yield his precious spoils must fall,
And tender Sítá by my side
Shall sit upon the golden hide.
Ne'er could I find so rich a coat
On spotted deer or sheep or goat.
No buck or antelope has such,
So bright to view, so soft to touch.
This radiant deer and one on high
That moves in glory through the sky,
Alike in heavenly beauty are,
One on the earth and one a star.
But, brother, if thy fears be true,
And this bright creature that we view
Be fierce Márícha in disguise,
Then by this hand he surely dies.
For that dire fiend who spurns control
With bloody hand and cruel soul,
Has roamed this forest and dismayed
The holiest saints who haunt the shade.
Great archers, sprung of royal race,
Pursuing in the wood the chase,
Have fallen by his wicked art,
And now my shaft shall strike his heart.
Vátápi, by his magic power

[1] A race of beings of human shape but with the heads of horses, like centaurs reversed.

Made heedless saints his flesh devour,
Then, from within, their frames he rent
Forth bursting from imprisonment.
But once his art in senseless pride
Upon the mightiest saint he tried,
Agastya's self, and caused him taste
The baited meal before him placed.
Vátápi, when the rite was o'er,
Would take the giant form he wore,
But Saint Agastya knew his wile,
And checked the giant with a smile:
'Vátápi, thou with cruel spite
Hast conquered many an anchorite,
The noblest of the Bráhman caste,—
And now thy ruin comes at last.'
Now if my power he thus defies,
This giant, like Vátápi, dies,
Daring to scorn a man like me,
A self-subduing devotee.
Yea, as Agastya slew the foe,
My hand shall lay Márícha low.
Clad in thine arms, thy bow in hand,
To guard the Maithil lady stand,
With watchful eye and thoughtful breast
Keeping each word of my behest.
I go, and hunting through the brake
This wondrous deer will bring or take.
Yea, surely I will bring the spoil
Returning from my hunter's toil.
See, Lakshmaṇ, how my consort's eyes
Are longing for the lovely prize.
This day it falls, that I may win
The treasure of so fair a skin.
Do thou and Sítá watch with care
Lest danger seize you unaware.
Swift from my bow one shaft will fly;
The stricken deer will fall and die.
Then quickly will I strip the game
And bring the trophy to my dame.
Jaṭáyus, guardian good and wise,
Our old and faithful friend,
The best and strongest bird that flies,
His willing aid will lend.
The Maithil lady well protect,
For every chance provide,
And in thy tender care suspect
A foe on every side.'

CANTO XLIV.

MÁRÍCHA'S DEATH.

Thus having warned his brother bold
He grasped his sword with haft of gold,
And bow with triple flexure bent,
His own delight and ornament;
Then bound two quivers to his side,
And hurried forth with eager stride.
Soon as the antlered monarch saw
The lord of monarchs near him draw,
A while with trembling heart he fled,
Then turned and showed his stately head.
With sword and bow the chief pursued
Where'er the flying deer he viewed
Sending from dell and lone recess
The splendour of his loveliness.
Now full in view the creature stood,
Now vanished in the depth of wood;
Now luring with a languid flight,
Now like a meteor lost to sight.
With trembling limbs away he sped;
Then like the moon with clouds o'erspread
Gleamed for a moment bright between
The trees, and was again unseen.
Thus in the magic deer's disguise
Márícha lured him to the prize,
And seen a while, then lost to view,
Far from his cot the hero drew.
Still by the flying game deceived
The hunter's heart was wroth and grieved,
And wearied with the fruitless chase
He stayed him in a shady place.
Again the rover of the night
Enraged the chieftain, full in sight,
Slow moving in the coppice near,
Surrounded by the woodland deer.
Again the hunter sought the game
That seemed a while to court his aim:
But seized again with sudden dread,
Beyond his sight the creature fled.
Again the hero left the shade,
Again the deer before him strayed.
With surer hope and stronger will
The hunter longed his prey to kill.
Then, as his soul impatient grew,
An arrow from his side he drew,
Resplendent at the sunbeam's glow,
The crusher of the smitten foe.
With skilful heed the mighty lord
Fixed well the shaft and strained the cord.
Upon the deer his eyes he bent,
And like a fiery serpent went
The arrow Brahmá's self had framed,
Alive with sparks that hissed and flamed,
Like Indra's flashing levin, true
To the false deer the missile flew.
Cleaving his flesh, that wondrous dart
Stood quivering in Márícha's heart.
Scarce from the ground one foot he sprang,
Then stricken fell with deadly pang.
Half lifeless, as he pressed the ground,
He gave a roar of awful sound.
And ere the wounded giant died
He threw his borrowed form aside.
Remembering still his lord's behest
He pondered in his heart how best
Sítá might send her guard away,
And Rávaṇ seize the helpless prey.
The monster knew the time was nigh,
And called aloud with eager cry,
'Ho, Sítá, Lakshmaṇ!' and the tone

He borrowed was like Ráma's own.
So by that matchless arrow cleft,
The deer's bright form Máricha left,
Resumed his giant shape and size
And closed in death his languid eyes.
When Ráma saw his awful foe
Gasp, smeared with blood, in deadly throe,
His anxious thoughts to Sitá sped,
And the wise words that Lakshman said,
That this was false Máricha's art,
Returned again upon his heart,
He knew the foe he triumphed o'er
The name of great Máricha bore.
'The fiend,' he pondered, 'ere he died,
'Ho, Lakshman! ho, my Sítá!' cried.
Ah, if that cry has reached her ear,
How dire must be my darling's fear!
And Lakshman of the mighty arm,
What thinks he in his wild alarm?
As thus he thought in sad surmise,
Each startled hair began to rise;
And when he saw the giant slain
And thought upon that cry again,
His spirit sank and terror pressed
Full sorely on the hero's breast.
Another deer he chased and struck:
He bore away the fallen buck,
To Janasthán then turned his face
And hastened to his dwelling-place.

CANTO XLV.

LAKSHMAN'S DEPARTURE.

But Sitá hearing, as she thought,
Her husband's cry with anguish fraught,
Called to her guardian, 'Lakshman, run
And in the wood seek Raghu's son.
Scarce can my heart retain its throne,
Scarce can my life be called mine own,
As all my powers and senses fail
At that long, loud and bitter wail.
Haste to the wood with all thy speed
And save thy brother in his need.
Go, save him in the distant shade
Where loud he calls for timely aid.
He falls beneath some giant foe—
A bull whom lions overthrow.'
Deaf to her prayer, no step he stirred
Obedient to his brother's word.
Then Janak's child, with ire inflamed,
In words of bitter scorn exclaimed:
'Sumitrá's son, a friend in show,
Thou art in truth thy brother's foe,
Who canst at such an hour deny
Thy succour and neglect his cry.
Yes, Lakshman, smit with love of me
Thy brother's death thou fain wouldst see.
This guilty love thy heart has swayed
And makes thy feet so loth to aid.
Thou hast no love for Ráma, no:
Thy joy is vice, thy thoughts are low.
Hence thus unmoved thou yet canst stay
While my dear lord is far away.
If aught of ill my lord betide
Who led thee here, thy chief and guide,
Ah, what will be my hapless fate
Left in the wild wood desolate!'
Thus spoke the lady sad with fear,
With many a sigh and many a tear,
Still trembling like a captured doe:
And Lakshman spoke to calm her woe:
'Videhan Queen, be sure of this,—
And at the thought thy fear dismiss,—
Thy husband's mightier power defies
All Gods and angels of the skies,
Gandharvas, and the sons of light,
Serpents, and rovers of the night.
I tell thee, of the sons of earth,
Of Gods who boast celestial birth,
Of beasts and birds and giant hosts,
Of demigods, Gandharvas, ghosts,
Of awful fiends, O thou most fair,
There lives not one whose heart would dare
To meet thy Ráma in the fight,
Like Indra's self unmatched in might.
Such idle words thou must not say:
Thy Ráma lives whom none may slay.
I will not, cannot leave thee here
In the wild wood till he be near.
The mightiest strength can ne'er withstand
His eager force, his vigorous hand:
No, not the triple world allied
With all the immortal Gods beside.
Dismiss thy fear, again take heart,
Let all thy doubt and woe depart.
Thy lord, be sure, will soon be here
And bring thee back that best of deer.
Not his, not his that mournful cry,
Nor haply came it from the sky:
Some giant's art was busy there
And framed a castle based on air.
A precious pledge art thou, consigned
To me by him of noblest mind;
Nor can I, fairest dame, forsake
The pledge which Ráma bade me take.
Upon our heads, O Queen, we drew
The giants' hate when Ráma slew
Their chieftain Khara, and the shade
Of Janasthán in ruin laid.
Through all this mighty wood they rove
With varied cries from grove to grove.
On rapine bent they wander here:
But O, dismiss thy causeless fear.'
Bright flashed her eye as Lakshman spoke,
And forth her words of fury broke
Upon her truthful guardian, flung
With bitter taunts that pierced and stung:
'Shame on such false compassion, base
Defiler of thy glorious race!
'Twere joyous sight, I ween, to thee

My lord in direst strait to see.
Thou knowest Ráma sore bested,
Or word like this thou ne'er hadst said.
No marvel if we find such sin
In rivals false to kith and kin.
Wretches like thee of evil kind,
Concealing crime with crafty mind.
Thou, wretch, thine aid wilt still deny,
And leave my lord alone to die.
Has love of me unnerved thy hand,
Or Bharat's art this ruin planned?
But be the treachery his or thine,
In vain, in vain the base design.
For how shall I, the chosen bride
Of dark-hued Ráma, lotus-eyed,
The queen who once called Ráma mine,
To love of other men decline?
Believe me, Lakshmaṇ, Ráma's wife
Before thine eyes will quit this life,
And not a moment will she stay
If her dear lord have passed away.'
  The lady's bitter speech, that stirred
Each hair upon his frame, he heard.
With lifted hands together laid,
His calm reply he gently made:
  'No words have I to answer now:
My deity, O Queen, art thou.
But 'tis no marvel, dame, to find
Such lack of sense in womankind.
Throughout this world, O Maithil dame,
Weak women's hearts are still the same.
Inconstant, urged by envious spite,
They sever friends and hate the right.
I cannot brook, Videhan Queen,
Thy words intolerably keen.
Mine ears thy fierce reproaches pain
As boiling water seethes the brain.
And now to bear me witness all
The dwellers in the wood I call,
That, when with words of truth I plead,
This harsh reply is all my meed.
Ah, woe is thee! Ah, grief, that still
Eager to do my brother's will,
Mourning thy woman's nature, I
Must see thee doubt my truth and die.
I fly to Ráma's side, and Oh,
May bliss attend thee while I go!
May all attendant wood-gods screen
Thy head from harm, O large-eyed Queen!
And though dire omens meet my sight
And fill my soul with wild affright,
May I return in peace and see
The son of Raghu safe with thee!'
  The child of Janak heard him speak,
And the hot tear-drops down her cheek,
Increasing to a torrent, ran,
As thus once more the dame began:
'O Lakshmaṇ, if I widowed be
Godávarí's flood shall cover me,
Or I will die by cord, or leap,
Life-weary, from yon rocky steep;
Or deadly poison will I drink,
Or 'neath the kindled flames will sink,
But never, reft of Ráma, can
Consent to touch a meaner man.'
  The Maithil dame with many sighs,
And torrents pouring from her eyes,
The faithful Lakshmaṇ thus adressed,
And smote her hands upon her breast.
Sumitrá's son, o'erwhelmed by fears,
    Looked on the large-eyed queen:
  He saw that flood of burning tears,
    He saw that piteous mien.
  He yearned sweet comfort to afford,
    He strove to soothe her pain:
  But to the brother of her lord
    She spoke no word again.
  His reverent hands once more he raised
    His head he slightly bent,
  Upon her face he sadly gazed,
    And then toward Ráma went.

CANTO XLVI.

THE GUEST.

The angry Lakshmaṇ scarce could brook
Her bitter words, her furious look.
With dark forebodings in his breast
To Ráma's side he quickly pressed.
  Then ten-necked Rávaṇ saw the time
Propitious for his purposed crime.
A mendicant in guise he came
And stood before the Maithil dame.
His garb was red, with tufted hair
And sandalled feet a shade he bare,
And from the fiend's left shoulder slung
A staff and water-vessel hung.
Near to the lovely dame he drew,
While both the chiefs were far from view
As darkness takes the evening air
When neither sun nor moon is there.
He bent his eye upon the dame,
A princess fair, of spotless fame:
So might some baleful planet be
Near Moon-forsaken Rohiṇí.[1]
As the fierce tyrant nearer drew,
The trees in Janasthán that grew
Waved not a leaf for fear and woe,
And the hushed wind forbore to blow.
Godávarí's waters as they fled,
Saw his fierce eye-balls flashing red,
And from each swiftly-gliding wave
A melancholy murmur gave.
Then Rávaṇ, when his eager eye
Beheld the longed-for moment nigh,
In mendicant's apparel dressed
Near to the Maithil lady pressed.

---

[1] The favourite wife of the Moon.

In holy guise, a fiend abhorred,
He found her mourning for her lord.
Thus threatening draws Śaniśchar[1] nigh
To Chitrá[2] in the evening sky;
Thus the deep well by grass concealed
Yawns treacherous in the verdant field.
He stood and looked upon the dame
Of Ráma, queen of spotless fame.
With her bright teeth and each fair limb
Like the full moon she seemed to him,
Sitting within her leafy cot,
Weeping for woe that left her not.
Thus, while with joy his pulses beat,
He saw her in her lone retreat,
Eyed like the lotus, fair to view
In silken robes of amber hue.
Pierced to the core by Káma's dart
He murmured texts with lying art,
And questioned with a soft address
The lady in her loneliness.
The fiend essayed with gentle speech
The heart of that fair dame to reach,
Pride of the worlds, like Beauty's Queen
Without her darling lotus seen:
'O thou whose silken robes enfold
A form more fare than finest gold,
With lotus garland on thy head,
Like a sweet spring with bloom o'erspread,
Who art thou, fair one, what thy name,
Beauty, or Honour, Fortune, Fame,
Spirit, or nymph, or Queen of love
Descended from thy home above?
Bright as the dazzling jasmine shine
Thy small square teeth in level line.
Like two black stars aglow with light
Thine eyes are large and pure and bright.
Thy charms of smile and teeth and hair
And winning eyes, O thou most fair,
Steal all my spirit, as the flow
Of rivers mines the bank below.
How bright, how fine each flowing trees!
How firm those orbs beneath thy dress!
That dainty waist with ease were spanned,
Sweet lady, by a lover's hand.
Mine eyes, O beauty, ne'er have seen
Goddess or nymph so fair of mien,
Or bright Gandharva's heavenly dame,
Or woman of so perfect frame.
In youth's soft prime thy years are few,
And earth has naught so fair to view.
I marvel one like thee in face
Should make the woods her dwelling-place.
Leave, lady, leave this lone retreat
In forest wilds for thee unmeet,
Where giants fierce and strong assume
All shapes and wander in the gloom.
These dainty feet were formed to tread
Some palace floor with carpets spread,
Or wander in trim gardens where
Each opening bud perfumes the air
The richest robe thy form should deck,
The rarest gems adorn thy neck.
The sweetest wreath should bind thy hair,
The noblest lord thy bed should share.
Art thou akin, O fair of form,
To Rudras,[1] or the Gods of storm,[2]
Or to the glorious Vasus[3]? How
Can less than these be bright as thou?
But never nymph or heavenly maid
Or Goddess haunts this gloomy shade.
Here giants roam, a savage race;
What led thee to so dire a place?
Here monkeys leap from tree to tree,
And bears and tigers wander free;
Here ravening lions prowl, and fell
Hyenas in the thickets yell,
And elephants infuriate roam,
Mighty and fierce, their woodland home.
Dost thou not dread, so soft and fair,
Tiger and lion, wolf and bear?
Hast thou, O beauteous dame, no fear
In the wild wood so lone and drear?
Whose and who art thou? whence and why,
Sweet lady, with no guardian nigh,
Dost thou this awful forest tread
By giant bands inhabited?'
The praise the high-souled Rávaṇ spoke
No doubt within her bosom woke.
His saintly look and Bráhman guise
Deceived the lady's trusting eyes.
With due attention on the guest
Her hospitable rites she pressed.
She bade the stranger to a seat,
And gave him water for his feet.
The bowl and water-pot he bare,
And garb which wandering Bráhmans wear
Forbade a doubt to rise.
Won by his holy look she deemed
The stranger even as he seemed
To her deluded eyes.
Intent on hospitable care,
She brought her best of woodland fare.
And showed her guest a seat.
She bade the saintly stranger lave
His feet in water which she gave,
And sit and rest and eat.
He kept his eager glances bent
On her so kindly eloquent,
Wife of the noblest king;
And longed in heart to steal her thence,
Preparing by the dire offence,
Death on his head to bring.

---

[1] The planet Saturn.

[2] Another favourite of the Moon; one of the lunar mansions.

[1] The Rudras, agents in creation, are eight in number; they sprang from the forehead of Brahmá.

[2] Maruts, the attendants of Indra.

[3] Radiant demi-gods.

The lady watched with anxious face
For Ráma coming from the chase
  With Lakshman by his side :
But nothing met her wandering glance
Save the wild forest's green expanse
  Extending far and wide.

CANTO XLVII.

RÁVAN'S WOOING.

As, clad in mendicant's disguise,
He questioned thus his destined prize,
She to the seeming saintly man
The story of her life began.
'My guest is he,' she thought, 'and I,
To 'scape his curse, must needs reply :'
'Child of a noble sire I spring
From Janak, fair Videha's king.
May every good be thine! my name
Is Sítá, Ráma's cherished dame.
Twelve winters with my lord I spent
Most happily with sweet content
In the rich home of Raghu's line,
And every earthly joy was mine.
Twelve pleasant years flew by, and then
His peers advised the king of men,
Ráma, my lord, to consecrate
Joint ruler of his ancient state.
But when the rites were scarce begun,
To consecrate Ikshváku's son,
The queen Kaikeyí, honoured dame,
Sought of her lord an ancient claim.
Her plea of former service pressed,
And made him grant her new request,
To banish Ráma to the wild
And consecrate instead her child.
This double prayer on him, the best
And truest king, she strongly pressed :
'Mine eyes in sleep I will not close,
Nor eat, nor drink, nor take repose.
This very day my death shall bring
If Ráma be anointed king.'
As thus she spake in envious ire,
The aged king, my husband's sire,
Besought with fitting words; but she
Was cold and deaf to every plea.
As yet my days are few; eighteen
The years of life that I have seen;
And Ráma, best of all alive,
Has passed of years a score and five—
Ráma the great and gentle, through
All region famed as pure and true,
Large-eyed and mighty-armed and tall.
With tender heart that cares for all.
But Daśaratha, led astray
By woman's wile and passion's sway,
By his strong love of her impelled,
The consecrating rites withheld.
When, hopeful of the promised grace,
My Ráma sought his father's face,
The queen Kaikeyí, ill at ease,
Spoke to my lord brief words like these :
'Hear, son of Raghu, hear from me
The words thy father says to thee:
'I yield this day to Bharat's hand,
Free from all foes, this ancient land.
Fly from this home no longer thine,
And dwell in woods five years and nine.
Live in the forest and maintain
Mine honour pure from falsehood's stain.'
Then Ráma spoke, untouched by dread :
'Yea, it shall be as thou hast said.'
And answered, faithful to his vows,
Obeying Daśaratha's spouse :
'The offered realm I would not take,
But still keep true the words he spake.'
Thus, gentle Bráhman, Ráma still
Clung to his vow with firmest will.
And valiant Lakshman, dear to fame,
His brother by a younger dame,
Bold victor in the deadly fray,
Would follow Ráma on his way.
On sternest vows his heart was set,
And he, a youthful anchoret,
Bound up in twisted coil his hair
And took the garb which hermits wear;
Then with his bow to guard us, he
Went forth with Ráma and with me.
By Queen Kaikeyí's art bereft
The kingdom and our home we left,
And bound by stern religious vows
We sought this shade of forest boughs.
Now, best of Bráhmans, here we tread
These pathless regions dark and dread.
But come, refresh thy soul, and rest
Here for a while an honoured guest.
For he, my lord, will soon be here
With fresh supply of woodland cheer,
Large store of venison of the buck,
Or some great boar his hand has struck.
Meanwhile, O stranger, grant my prayer :
Thy name, thy race, thy birth declare,
And why with no companion thou
Roamest in Dandak forest now.'
  Thus questioned Sítá, Ráma's dame.
Then fierce the stranger's answer came:
'Lord of the giant legions, he
From whom celestial armies flee,—
The dread of hell and earth and sky,
Rávan the Rákshas king am I.
Now when thy gold-like form I view
Arrayed in silks of amber hue,
My love, O thou of perfect mould,
For all my dames is dead and cold.
A thousand fairest women, torn
From many a land my home adorn.
But come, loveliest lady, be
The queen of every dame and me.
My city Lanká, glorious town,
Looks from a mountain's forehead down

Where ocean with his flash and foam
Beats madly on mine island home.
With me, O Sítá, shalt thou rove
Delighted through each shady grove,
Nor shall thy happy breast retain
Fond memory of this life of pain.
In gay attire, a glittering band,
Five thousand maids shall round thee stand,
And serve thee at thy beck and sign,
If thou, fair Sítá, wilt be mine.'
Then forth her noble passion broke
As thus in turn the lady spoke:
'Me, me the wife of Ráma, him
The lion lord with lion's limb,
Strong as the sea, firm as the rock,
Like Indra in the battle shock;
The lord of each auspicious sign,
The glory of his princely line,
Like some fair Lodh tree strong and tall,
The noblest and the best of all,
Ráma, the heir of happy fate
Who keeps his word inviolate,
Lord of the lion gait, possessed
Of mighty arm and ample chest,
Ráma the lion-warrior, him
Whose moon bright face no fear can dim,
Ráma, his bridled passions' lord,
The darling whom his sire adored,—
Me, me the true and loving dame
Of Ráma, prince of deathless fame,—
Me wouldst thou vainly woo and press?
A jackal woo a lioness!
Steal from the sun his glory! such
Thy hope Lord Ráma's wife to touch.
Ha! thou hast seen the trees of gold,
The sign which dying eyes behold,
Thus seeking, weary of thy life,
To win the love of Ráma's wife.
Fool! wilt thou dare to rend away
The famished lion's bleeding prey,
Or from the threatening jaws to take
The fang of some envenomed snake?
What, wouldst thou shake with puny hand
Mount Mandar,[1] towering o'er the land,
Put poison to thy lips and think
The deadly cup a harmless drink?
With pointed needle touch thine eye,
A razor to thy tongue apply,
Who wouldst pollute with impious touch
The wife whom Ráma loves so much?
Be round thy neck a millstone tied,
And swim the sea from side to side;
Or raising both thy hands on high
Pluck sun and moon from yonder sky;
Or let the kindled flame be pressed,
Wrapt in thy garment, to thy breast;
More wild the thought that seeks to win
Ráma's dear wife who knows not sin.
The fool who thinks with idle aim
To gain the love of Ráma's dame,
With dark and desperate footing makes
His way o'er points of iron stakes.
As Ocean to a bubbling spring,
The lion to a fox, the king
Of all the birds that ply the wing
To an ignoble crow.
As gold to lead of little price,
As to the drainings of the rice
The drink they quaff in Paradise,
The Amrit's heavenly flow,
As sandal dust with perfume sweet
Is to the mire that soils our feet,
A tiger to a cat,
As the white swan is to the owl,
The peacock to the waterfowl,
An eagle to a bat,
Such is my lord compared with thee;
And when with bow and arrows he,
Mighty as Indra's self shall see
His foeman, armed to slay,
Thou, death-doomed like the fly that sips
The oil that on the altar drips,
Shalt cast the morsel from thy lips
And lose thy half-won prey.'
Thus in high scorn the lady flung
The biting arrows of her tongue
In bitter words that pierced and stung
The rover of the night.
She ceased. Her gentle cheek grew pale,
Her loosened limbs began to fail,
And like a plantain in the gale
She trembled with affright.
He terrible as Death stood nigh,
And watched with fierce exulting eye
The fear that shook her frame.
To terrify the lady more,
He counted all his triumphs o'er,
Proclaimed the titles that he bore,
His pedigree and name.

CANTO XLVIII.

RÁVAṆ'S SPEECH.

With knitted brow and furious eye
The stranger made his fierce reply:
'In me O fairest dame, behold
The brother of the King of Gold.
The Lord of Ten Necks my title, named
Rávaṇ, for might and valour famed.
Gods and Gandharva hosts I scare;
Snakes, spirits, birds that roam the air
Fly from my coming, wild with fear,
Trembling like men when Death is near.
Vaiśravaṇ once, my brother, wrought
To ire, encountered me and fought,

[1] The mountain which was used by the Gods as a churning stick at the Churning of the Ocean.

But yielding to superior might
Fled from his home in sore affright.
Lord of the man-drawn chariot, still
He dwells on famed Kailása's hill.
I made the vanquished king resign
The glorious car which now is mine,—
Pushpak, the far-renowned, that flies
Will-guided through the buxom skies.
Celestial hosts by Indra led
Flee from my face disquieted,
And where my dreaded feet appear
The wind is hushed or breathless is fear.
Where'er I stand, where'er I go
The troubled waters cease to flow,
Each spell-bound wave is mute and still
And the fierce sun himself is chill.
Beyond the sea my Lanká stands
Filled with fierce forms and giant bands,
A glorious city fair to see
As Indra's Amarávatí.
A towering height of solid wall,
Flashing afar, surrounds it all,
Its golden courts enchant the sight,
And gates aglow with lazulite.
Steeds, elephants, and cars are there,
And drums' loud music fills the air,
Fair trees in lovely gardens grow
Whose boughs with varied fruitage glow.
Thou, beauteous Queen, with me shalt dwell
In halls that suit a princess well,
Thy former fellows shalt forget
Nor think of women with regret,
No earthly joy thy soul shall miss,
And take its fill of heavenly bliss.
Of mortal Ráma think no more,
Whose terms of days will soon be o'er.
King Daśaratha looked in scorn
On Ráma though the eldest born,
Sent to the woods the weakling fool,
And set his darling son to rule.
What, O thou large-eyed dame, hast thou
To do with fallen Ráma now,
From home and kingdom forced to fly,
A wretched hermit soon to die?
Accept thy lover, nor refuse
The giant king who fondly woos.
O listen, nor reject in scorn
A heart by Káma's arrows torn.
If thou refuse to hear my prayer,
Of grief and coming woe beware;
For the sad fate will fall on thee
Which came on hapless Urvaśí,
When with her foot she chanced to touch
Purúravas, and sorrowed much.[1]
My little finger raised in fight
Were more than match for Ráma's might.
O fairest, blithe and happy be
With him whom fortune sends to thee.'
Such were the words the giant said,
And Sítá's angry eyes were red.
She answered in that lonely place
The monarch of the giant race:
'Art thou the brother of the Lord
Of Gold by all the world adored,
And sprung of that illustrious seed
Wouldst now attempt this evil deed?
I tell thee, impious Monarch, all
The giants by thy sin will fall,
Whose reckless lord and king thou art,
With foolish mind and lawless heart.
Yea, one may hope to steal the wife
Of Indra and escape with life.
But he who Ráma's dame would tear
From his loved side must needs despair.
Yea, one may steal fair Śachí, dame
Of Him who shoots the thunder flame,
May live successful in his aim
And length of day may see;
But hope, O giant King, in vain,
Though cups of Amrit thou may drain,
To shun the penalty and pain
Of wronging one like me.'

CANTO XLIX.

THE RAPE OF SÍTÁ.

The Rákshas monarch, thus addressed,
His hands a while together pressed,
And straight before her startled eyes
Stood monstrous in his giant size.
Then to the lady, with the lore
Of eloquence, he spoke once more:
'Thou scarce,' he cried, 'hast heard aright
The glories of my power and might.
I borne sublime in air can stand
And with these arms upheave the land,
Drink the deep flood of Ocean dry
And Death with conquering force defy,
Pierce the great sun with furious dart
And to her depths cleave earth apart.
See, thou whom love and beauty blind,
I wear each form as wills my mind.'
As thus he spake in burning ire
His glowing eyes were red with fire.
His gentle garb aside was thrown
And all his native shape was shown.
Terrific, monstrous, wild, and dread
As the dark God who rules the dead,
His fiery eyes in fury rolled,
His limbs were decked with glittering gold.
Like some dark cloud the monster showed,
And his fierce breast with fury glowed.
The ten-faced rover of the night,
With twenty arms exposed to sight,
His saintly guise aside had laid
And all his giant height displayed.

[1] The story will be found in GARRETT'S *Classical Dictionary*. See ADDITIONAL NOTES

Attired in robes of crimson dye
He stood and watched with angry eye
The lady in her bright array
Resplendent as the dawn of day
When from the east the sunbeams break,
And to the dark-haired lady spake:
'If thou would call that lord thine own
Whose fame in every world is known,
Look kindly on my love, and be
Bride of a consort meet for thee.
With me let blissful years be spent,
For ne'er thy choice shalt thou repent.
No deed of mine shall e'er displease
My darling as she lives at ease.
Thy love for mortal man resign,
And to a worthier lord incline.
Ah foolish lady, seeming wise
In thine own weak and partial eyes,
By what fair graces art thou held
To Ráma from his realm expelled?
Misfortunes all his life attend,
And his brief days are near their end.
Unworthy prince, infirm of mind!
A woman spoke, and he resigned
His home and kingdom and withdrew
From troops of friends and retinue,
And sought this forest dark and dread
By savage beasts inhabited.'

Thus Rávaṇ urged the lady meet
For love, whose words were soft and sweet.
Near and more near the giant pressed
As love's hot fire inflamed his breast.
The leader of the giant crew
His arm around the lady threw:
Thus Budha[1] with ill-omened might
Steals Rohiṇí's delicious light.
One hand her glorious tresses grasped,
One with its ruthless pressure clasped
The body of his lovely prize,
The Maithil dame with lotus eyes.
The silvan Gods in wild alarm
Marked his huge teeth and ponderous arm,
And from that Death-like presence fled,
Of mountain size and towering head.
Then seen was Rávaṇ's magic car
Aglow with gold which blazed afar,—
The mighty car which asses drew
Thundering as it onward flew.
He spared not harsh rebuke to chide
The lady as she moaned and cried,
Then with his arm about her waist
His captive in the car he placed.
In vain he threatened: long and shrill
Rang out her lamentation still,
O Ráma! which no fear could stay:
But her dear lord was far away.
Then rose the fiend, and toward the skies
Bore his poor helpless struggling prize:
Hurrying through the air above
The dame who loathed his proffered love
So might a soaring eagle bear
A serpent's consort through the air.
As on he bore her through the sky
She shrieked aloud her bitter cry.
As when some wretch's lips complain
In agony of maddening pain;
'O Lakshmaṇ, thou whose joy is still
To do thine elder brother's will,
This fiend, who all disguises wears,
From Ráma's side his darling tears.
Thou who couldst leave bliss, fortune, all,
Yea life itself at duty's call,
Dost thou not see this outrage done
To hapless me, O Raghu's son?
'Tis thine, O victor of the foe,
To bring the haughtiest spirit low,
How canst thou such an outrage see
And let the guilty fiend go free?
Ah, seldom in a moment's time
Comes bitter fruit of sin and crime,
But in the day of harvest pain
Comes like the ripening of the grain.
So thou whom fate and folly lead
To ruin for this guilty deed,
Shalt die by Ráma's arm ere long
A dreadful death for hideous wrong.
Ah, too successful in their ends
Are Queen Kaikeyí and her friends,
When virtuous Ráma, dear to fame,
Is mourning for his ravished dame.
Ah me, ah me! a long farewell
To lawn and glade and forest dell
In Janasthán's wild region, where
The Cassia trees are bright and fair!
With all your tongues to Ráma say
That Rávaṇ bears his wife away.
Farewell, a long farewell to thee,
O pleasant stream Godávarí,
Whose rippling waves are ever stirred
By many a glad wild water-bird!
All ye to Ráma's ear relate
The giant's deed and Sítá's fate.
O all ye Gods who love this ground
Where trees of every leaf abound,
Tell Ráma I am stolen hence,
I pray you all with reverence.
On all the living things beside
That these dark boughs and coverts hide,
Ye flocks of birds, ye troops of deer,
I call on you my prayer to hear.
All ye to Ráma's ear proclaim
That Rávaṇ tears away his dame
With forceful arms,—his darling wife,
Dearer to Ráma than his life.
O, if he knew I dwelt in hell,
My mighty lord, I know full well,
Would bring me, conqueror, back to-day,
Though Yama's self reclaimed his prey.'

Thus from the air the lady sent

[1] Mercury: to be carefully distinguished from Buddha.

With piteous voice her last lament,
And as she wept she chanced to see
The vulture on a lofty tree.
As Rávan bore her swiftly by,
On the dear bird she bent her eye,
And with a voice which woe made faint
Renewed to him her wild complaint:
'O see, the king who rules the race
Of giants, cruel, fierce and base,
Rávan the spoiler bears me hence
The helpless prey of violence.
This fiend who roves in midnight shade
By thee, dear bird, can ne'er be stayed,
For he is armed and fierce and strong
Triumphant in the power to wrong.
For thee remains one only task,
To do, kind friend, the thing I ask.
To Ráma's ear by thee be borne
How Sítá from her home is torn,
And to the valiant Lakshman tell
The giant's deed and what befell.'

CANTO L.

JAṬÁYUS.

The vulture from his slumber woke
And heard the words which Sítá spoke.
He raised his eye and looked on her,
Looked on her giant ravisher.
That noblest bird with pointed beak,
Majestic as a mountain peak,
High on the tree addressed the king
Of giants, wisely counselling:
'O Ten-necked lord, I firmly hold
To faith and laws ordained of old,
And thou, my brother, shouldst refrain
From guilty deeds that shame and stain.
The vulture king supreme in air,
Jaṭáyus is the name I bear.
Thy captive, known by Sítá's name,
Is the dear consort and the dame
Of Ráma Daśaratha's heir
Who makes the good of all his care.
Lord of the world, in might he vies
With the great Gods of seas and skies.
The law he boasts to keep allows
No king to touch another's spouse,
And, more than all, a prince's dame
High honour and respect may claim.
Back to the earth thy way incline,
Nor think of one who is not thine.
Heroic souls should hold it shame
To stoop to deeds which others blame,
And all respect by them is shown
To dames of others as their own.
Not every case of bliss and gain
The Scripture's holy texts explain,
And subjects, when that light is dim,
Look to their prince and follow him.
The king is bliss and profit, he
Is store of treasures fair to see,
And all the people's fortunes spring,
Their joy and misery, from the king.
If, lord of giant race, thy mind
Be fickle, false, to sin inclined,
How wilt thou kingly place retain?
High thrones in heaven no sinners gain.
The soul which gentle passions sway
Ne'er throws its nobler part away,
Nor will the mansion of the base
Long be the good man's dwelling-place.
Prince Ráma, chief of high renown,
Has wronged thee not in field or town.
Ne'er has he sinned against thee: how
Canst thou resolve to harm him now?
If moved by Súrpaṇkhá's prayer
The giant Khara sought him there,
And fighting fell with baffled aim,
His and not Ráma's is the blame.
Say, mighty lord of giants, say
What fault on Ráma canst thou lay?
What has the world's great master done
That thou should steal his precious one?
Quick, quick the Maithil dame release;
Let Ráma's consort go in peace,
Lest scorched by his terrific eye
Beneath his wrath thou fall and die
Like Vritra when Lord Indra threw
The lightning flame that smote and slew.
Ah fool, with blinded eyes to take
Home to thy heart a venomed snake!
Ah foolish eyes, too blind to see
That Death's dire coils entangle thee!
The prudent man his strength will spare,
Nor lift a load too great to bear.
Content is he with wholsome food
Which gives him life and strength renewed
But who would dare the guilty deed
That brings no fame or glorious meed,
Where merit there is none to win
And vengeance soon o'ertakes the sin?
My course of life, Pulastya's son,
For sixty thousand years has run.
Lord of my kind I still maintain
Mine old hereditary reign.
I, worn by years, am older far
Than thou, young lord of bow and car,
In coat of glittering mail encased
And armed with arrows at thy waist,
But not unchallenged shalt thou go,
Or steal the dame without a blow.
Thou canst not, King, before mine eyes
Bear off unchecked thy lovely prize,
Safe as the truth of Scripture bent
By no close logic's argument.
Stay if thy courage let thee, stay
And meet me in the battle fray,
And thou shalt stain the earth with gore
Falling as Khara fell before.
Soon Ráma, clothed in bark, shall smite.

Thee, his proud foe, in deadly fight,—
Ráma, from whom have oft times fled
The Daitya hosts discomfited.
No power have I to kill or slay:
The princely youths are far away,
But soon shalt thou with fearful eye
Struck down beneath their arrows lie.
But while I yet have life and sense,
Thou shalt not, tyrant, carry hence
Fair Sítá, Ráma's honoured queen,
With lotus eyes and lovely mien.
Whate'er the pain, whate'er the cost,
Though in the struggle life be lost,
The will of Raghu's noblest son
And Daśaratha must be done.
Stay for a while, O Rávan, stay,
One hour thy flying car delay,
And from that glorious chariot thou
Shalt fall like fruit from shaken bough,
For I to thee, while yet I live,
The welcome of a foe will give.'

CANTO LI.

THE COMBAT.

Rávan's red eyes in fury rolled:
Bright with his armlets' flashing gold,
In high disdain, by passion stirred
He rushed against the sovereign bird.
With clash and din and furious blows
Of murderous battle met the foes:
Thus urged by winds two clouds on high
Meet warring in the stormy sky.
Then fierce the dreadful combat raged
As fiend and bird in war engaged,
As if two winged mountains sped
To dire encounter overhead.
Keen pointed arrows thick and fast,
In never ceasing fury cast,
Rained hurtling on the vulture king
And smote him on the breast and wing.
But still that noblest bird sustained
The cloud of shafts which Rávan rained,
And with strong beak and talons bent
The body of his foeman rent.
Then wild with rage the ten-necked king
Laid ten swift arrows on his string,—
Dread as the staff of Death were they,
So terrible and keen to slay.
Straight to his ear the string he drew,
Straight to the mark the arrows flew,
And pierced by every iron head
The vulture's mangled body bled.
One glance upon the car he bent
Where Sítá wept with shrill lament,
Then heedless of his wounds and pain
Rushed at the giant king again.
Then the brave vulture with the stroke
Of his resistless talons broke
The giant's shafts and bow whereon
The fairest pearls and jewels shone.
The monster paused, by rage unmanned:
A second bow soon armed his hand,
Whence pointed arrows swift and true
In hundreds, yea in thousands, flew.
The monarch of the vultures, plied
With ceaseless darts on every side.
Showed like a bird that turns to rest
Close covered by the branch-built nest.
He shook his pinions to repel
The storm of arrows as it fell;
Then with his talons snapped in two
The mighty bow which Rávan drew.
Next with terrific wing he smote
So fiercely on the giant's coat,
The harness, glittering with the glow
Of fire, gave way beneath the blow.
With storm of murderous strokes he beat
The harnessed asses strong and fleet,—
Each with a goblin's monstrous face
And plates of gold his neck to grace.
Then on the car he turned his ire,—
The will-moved car that shone like fire,
And broke the glorious chariot, broke
The golden steps and pole and yoke.
The chouris and the silken shade
Like the full moon to view displayed,
Together with the guards who held
Those emblems, to the ground he felled.
The royal vulture hovered o'er
The driver's head, and pierced and tore
With his strong beak and dreaded claws
His mangled brow and cheek and jaws.
With broken car and sundered bow,
His charioteer and team laid low,
One arm about the lady wound,
Sprang the fierce giant to the ground.
Spectators of the combat, all
The spirits viewed the monster's fall:
Lauding the vulture every one
Cried with glad voice, Well done! well done!
But weak with length of days, at last
The vulture's strength was failing fast.
The fiend again assayed to bear
The lady through the fields of air.
But when the vulture saw him rise
Triumphant with his trembling prize,
Bearing the sword that still was left
When other arms were lost or cleft,
Once more, impatient of repose,
Swift from the earth her champion rose,
Hung in the way the fiend would take,
And thus addressing Rávan spake:
'Thou, King of giants, rash and blind,
Wilt be the ruin of thy kind,
Stealing the wife of Ráma, him
With lightning scars on chest and limb.
A mighty host obeys his will
And troops of slaves his palace fill;

His lords of state are wise and true,
Kinsmen has he and retinue.
As thirsty travellers drain the cup,
Thou drinkest deadly poison up.
The rash and careless fool who heeds
No coming fruit of guilty deeds,
A few short years of life shall see,
And perish doomed to death like thee.
Say whither wilt thou fly to loose
Thy neck from Death's entangling noose,
Caught like the fish that finds too late
The hook beneath the treacherous bait?
Never, O King—of this be sure—
Will Raghu's fiery sons endure,
Terrific in their vengeful rage,
This insult to their hermitage.
Thy guilty hands this day have done
A deed which all reprove and shun,
Unworthly of a noble chief,
The pillage loved by coward thief.
Stay, if thy heart allow thee, stay
And meet me in the deadly fray.
Soon shalt thou stain the earth with gore,
And fall as Khara fell before:
The fruits of former deeds o'erpower
The sinner in his dying hour:
And such a fate on thee, O King,
Thy tyranny and madness bring.
Not e'en the Self-existent Lord,
Who reigns by all the worlds adored,
Would dare attempt a guilty deed
Which the dire fruits of crime succeed.'
 Thus brave Jaṭáyus, best of birds,
Addressed the fiend with moving words,
Then ready for the swift attack
Swooped down upon the giant's back.
Down to the bone the talons went:
With many a wound the flesh was rent:
Such blows infuriate drivers deal
Their elephants with pointed steel.
Fixed in his back the strong beak lay,
The talons stripped the flesh away.
He fought with claws and beak and wing,
And tore the long hair of the king.
Still as the royal vulture beat
The giant with his wings and feet,
Swelled the fiend's lips, his body shook
With furious rage too great to brook.
About the Maithil dame he cast
One huge left arm and held her fast.
In furious rage to frenzy fanned
He struck the vulture with his hand.
Jaṭáyus mocked the vain assay,
And rent his ten left arms away.
Down dropped the severed limbs: anew
Ten others from his body grew:
Thus bright with pearly radiance glide
Dread serpents from the hillock side,
Again in wrath the giant pressed
The lady closer to his breast,
And foot and fist sent blow on blow
In ceaseless fury at the foe.
So fierce and dire the battle, waged
Between those mighty champions, raged:
Here was the lord of giants, there
The noblest of the birds of air.
Thus, as his love of Ráma taught,
The faithful vulture strove and fought.
But Rávaṇ seized his sword and smote
His wings and side and feet and throat.
At mangled side and wing he bled;
He fell, and life was almost fled.
The lady saw her champion lie,
His plumes distained with gory dye,
And hastened to the vulture's side
Grieving as though a kinsman died.
The lord of Lanká's island viewed
 The vulture as he lay:
Whose back like some dark cloud was hued,
 His breast a paly grey,
Like ashes, when by none renewed,
 The flame has died away.
The lady saw with mournful eye.
 Her champion press the plain,—
The royal bird, her true ally
 Whom Rávaṇ's might had slain.
Her soft arms locked in strict embrace
 Around his neck she kept,
And lovely with her moon-bright face
 Bent o'er her friend and wept.

CANTO LII.

RÁVAṆ'S FLIGHT.

Fair as the lord of silvery rays
Whom every star in heaven obeys,
The Maithil dame her plaint renewed
O'er him by Rávaṇ's might subdued:
'Dreams, omens, auguries foreshow
Our coming lot of weal and woe:
But thou, my Ráma, couldst not see
The grievous blow which falls on thee.
The birds and deer desert the brakes
And show the path my captor takes,
And thus e'en now this royal bird
Flew to mine aid by pity stirred.
Slain for my sake in death he lies,
The broad-winged rover of the skies.
O Ráma, haste, thine aid I crave:
O Lakshmaṇ, why delay to save?
Brave sons of old Ikshváku, hear
And rescue in this hour of fear.'
 Her flowery wreath was torn and rent,
Crushed was each sparkling ornament.
She with weak arms and trembling knees
Clung like a creeper to the trees,
And like some poor deserted thing
With wild shrieks made the forest ring.
But swift the giant reached her side,

As loud on Ráma's name she cried.
Fierce as grim Death one hand he laid
Upon her tresses' lovely braid.
That touch, thou impious King, shall be
The ruin of thy race and thee.
The universal world in awe
That outrage on the lady saw.
All nature shook convulsed with dread,
And darkness o'er the land was spread.
The Lord of Day grew dark and chill,
And every breath of air was still.
The Eternal Father of the sky
Beheld the crime with heavenly eye,
And spake with solemn voice, 'The deed,
The deed is done, of old decreed.'
Sad were the saints within the grove,
But triumph with their sorrow strove.
They wept to see the Maithil dame
Endure the outrage, scorn, and shame:
They joyed because his life should pay
The penalty incurred that day.
Then Rávaṇ raised her up, and bare
His captive through the fields of air,
Calling with accents loud and shrill
On Ráma and on Lakshmaṇ still.
With sparkling gems on arm and breast,
In silk of paly amber dressed,
High in the air the Maithil dame
Gleamed like the lightning's flashing flame.
The giant, as the breezes blew
Upon her robes of amber hue,
And round him twined that gay attire,
Showed like a mountain girt with fire.
The lady, fairest of the fair,
Had wreathed a garland round her hair;
Its lotus petals bright and sweet
Rained down about the giant's feet.
Her vesture, bright as burning gold,
Gave to the wind each glittering fold,
Fair as a gilded cloud that gleams
Touched by the Day-God's tempered beams.
Yet struggling in the fiend's embrace,
The lady with her sweet pure face,
Far from her lord, no longer wore
The light of joy that shone before.
Like some sad lily by the side
Of waters which the sun has dried:
Like the pale moon uprising through
An autumn cloud of darkest hue,
So was her perfect face between
The arms of giant Rávaṇ seen:
Fair with the charm of braided tress
And forehead's finished loveliness;
Fair with the ivory teeth that shed
White lustre through the lips' fine red,
Fair as the lotus when the bud
Is rising from the parent flood.
With faultless lip and nose and eye,
Dear as the moon that floods the sky
With gentle light, of perfect mould,
She seemed a thing of burnished gold,
Though on her cheek the traces lay
Of tears her hand had brushed away.
But as the moon-beams swiftly fade
Ere the great Day-God shines displayed,
So in that form of perfect grace
Still trembling in the fiend's embrace,
From her beloved Ráma reft,
No light of pride or joy was left.
The lady with her golden hue
O'er the swart fiend a lustre threw,
As when embroidered girths enfold
An elephant with gleams of gold.
Fair as the lily's bending stem,—
Her arms adorned with many a gem,
A lustre to the fiend she lent
Gleaming from every ornament,
As when the cloud-shot flashes light
The shadows of a mountain height.
Whene'er the breezes earthward bore
The tinkling of the zone she wore,
He seemed a cloud of darkness hue
Sending forth murmurs as it flew.
As on her way the dame was sped
From her sweet neck fair flowers were shed,
The swift wind caught the flowery rain
And poured it o'er the fiend again.
The wind-stirred blossoms, sweet to smell,
On the dark brows of Rávaṇ fell,
Like lunar constellations set
On Meru for a coronet.
From her small foot an anklet fair
With jewels slipped, and through the air,
Like a bright circlet of the flame
Of thunder, to the valley came.
The Maithil lady, fair to see
As the young leaflet of a tree
Clad in the tender hues of spring,
Flashed glory on the giant king,
As when a gold-embroidered zone
Around an elephant is thrown.
While, bearing far the lady, through
The realms of sky the giant flew,
She like a gleaming meteor cast
A glory round her as she passed.
Then from each limb in swift descent
Dropped many a sparkling ornament;
On earth they rested dim and pale
Like fallen stars when virtues fail.[1]
Around her neck a garland lay
Bright as the Star-God's silvery ray:
It fell and flashed like Gangá sent
From heaven above the firmament.[2]
The birds of every wing had flocked
To stately trees by breezes rocked:

[1] The spirits of the good dwell in heaven until their store of accumulated merit is exhausted. Then they redescend to earth in the form of falling stars.

[2] See The Descent of Gangá, Book I. Canto XLIV.

These bowed their wind-swept heads and
said:
'My lady sweet, be comforted.'
With faded blooms each brook within
Whose waters moved no gleamy fin,
Stole sadly through the forest dell
Mourning the dame it loved so well.
From every woodland region near
Came lions, tigers, birds, and deer,
And followed, each with furious look,
The way her flying shadow took.
For Sítá's loss each lofty hill
Whose tears were waterfall, and rill,
Lifting on high each arm-like steep,
Seemed in the general woe to weep.
When the great sun, the lord of day,
Saw Rávan tear the dame away,
His glorious light began to fail
And all his disk grew cold and pale.
'If Rávan from the forest flies
With Ráma's Sítá as his prize,
Justice and truth have vanished hence,
Honour and right and innocence:'
Thus rose the cry of wild despair
From spirits as they gathered there.
In trembling troops in open lawns
Wept, wild with woe, the startled fawns,
And a strange terror changed the eyes
They lifted to the distant skies.
On silvan Gods who love the dell
A sudden fear and trembling fell,
As in the deepest woe they viewed
The lady by the fiend subdued.
Still in loud shrieks was heard afar
That voice whose sweetness naught could
mar,
While eager looks of fear and woe
She bent upon the earth below.
The lady of each winning wile
With pearly teeth and lovely smile,
Seized by the lord of Lanká's isle,
Looked down for friends in vain.
She saw no friend to aid her, none,
Not Ráma nor the younger son
Of Daśaratha, and undone
She swooned with fear and pain.

CANTO LIII.

SITA'S THREATS.

Soon as the Maithil lady knew
That high through air the giant flew,
Distressed with grief and sore afraid
Her troubled spirit sank dismayed.
Then, as anew the waters welled
From those red eyes which sorrow swelled,
Forth in keen words her passion broke,
And to the fierce-eyed fiend she spoke:
'Canst thou attempt a deed so base,
Untroubled by the deep disgrace.—
To steal me from my home and fly,
When friend or guardian none was nigh?
Thy craven soul that longed to steal,
Fearing the blows that warriors deal,
Upon a magic deer relied
To lure my husband from my side,
Friend of his sire, the vulture king
Lies low on earth with mangled wing,
Who gave his aged life for me
And died for her he sought to free.
Ah, glorious strength indeed is thine,
Thou meanest of thy giant line,
Whose courage dared to tell thy name
And conquer in the fight a dame.
Does the vile deed that thou hast done
Cause thee no shame, thou wicked one—
A woman from her home to rend
When none was near his aid to lend?
Through all the worlds, O giant King,
The tidings of this deed will ring,
This deed in law and honour's spite
By one who claims a hero's might.
Shame on thy boasted valour, shame!
Thy prowess is an empty name.
Shame, giant, on this cursed deed
For which thy race is doomed to bleed!
Thou fliest swifter than the gale,
For what can strength like thine avail?
Stay for one hour, O Rávan, stay;
Thou shalt not flee with life away.
Soon as the royal chieftains' sight
Falls on the thief who roams by night,
Thou wilt not, tyrant, live one hour
Though backed by all thy legions' power.
Ne'er can thy puny strength sustain
The tempest of their arrowy rain:
Have e'er the trembling birds withstood
The wild flames raging in the wood?
Hear me, O Rávan, let me go,
And save thy soul from coming woe.
Or if thou wilt not set me free,
Wroth for this insult done to me.
With his brave brother's aid my lord
Against thy life will raise his sword.
A guilty hope inflames thy breast
His wife from Ráma's home to wrest.
Ah fool, the hope thou hast is vain;
Thy dreams of bliss shall end in pain.
If torn from all I love by thee
My godlike lord no more I see,
Soon will I die and end my woes,
Nor live the captive of my foes.
Ah fool, with blinded eyes to choose
The evil and the good refuse!
So the sick wretch with stubborn will
Turns fondly to the cates that kill,
And madly draws his lips away
From medicine that would check decay.
About thy neck securely wound

The deadly coil of Fate is bound,
And thou, O Rávan, dost not fear
Although the hour of death is near.
With death-doomed sight thine eyes behold
The gleaming of the trees of gold,—
See dread Vaitaraṇi, the flood
That rolls a stream of foamy blood,—
See the dark wood by all abhorred—
Its every leaf a threatening sword.
The tangled thickets thou shalt tread
Where thorns with iron points are spread.
For never can thy days be long,
Base plotter of this shame and wrong
To Ráma of the lofty soul:
He dies who drinks the poisoned bowl.
The coils of death around thee lie:
They hold thee and thou canst not fly.
Ah whither, tyrant, wouldst thou run
The vengeance of my lord to shun?
By his unaided arm alone
Were twice seven thousand fiends o'erthrown:
Yes, in the twinkling of an eye
He forced thy mightiest fiends to die.
And shall that lord of lion heart,
Skilled in the bow and spear and dart,
Spare thee, O fiend, in battle strife,
The robber of his darling wife?'
These were her words, and more beside,
By wrath and bitter hate supplied.
Then by her woe and fear o'erthrown
She wept again and made her moan.
As long she wept in grief and dread,
Scarce conscious of the words she said,
The wicked giant onward fled
And bore her through the air.
As firm he held the Maithil dame,
Still wildly struggling, o'er her frame
With grief and bitter misery came
The trembling of despair.

CANTO LIV.

LANKÁ.

He bore her on in rapid flight,
And not a friend appeared in sight.
But on a hill that o'er the wood
Raised its high top five monkeys stood.
From her fair neck her scarf she drew,
And down the glittering vesture flew.
With earring, necklet, chain, and gem,
Descending in the midst of them:
'For these,' she thought, 'my path may show,
And tell my lord the way I go.'
Nor did the fiend, in wild alarm,
Mark when she drew from neck and arm
And foot the gems and gold, and sent
To earth each gleaming ornament.
The monkeys raised their tawny eyes
That closed not in their first surprise,
And saw the dark-eyed lady, where
She shrieked above them in the air.
High o'er their heads the giant passed
Holding the weeping lady fast.
O'er Pampá's flashing flood he sped
And on to Lanká's city fled.
He bore away in senseless joy
The prize that should his life destroy,
Like the rash fool who hugs beneath
His robe a snake with venomed teeth.
Swift as an arrow from a bow,
Speeding o'er lands that lay below,
Sublime in air his course he took
O'er wood and rock and lake and brook.
He passed at length the sounding sea
Where monstrous creatures wander free,—
Seat of Lord Varuṇ's ancient reign,
Controller of the eternal main.
The angry waves were raised and tossed
As Rávaṇ with the lady crossed,
And fish and snake in wild unrest
Showed flashing fin and gleaming crest.
Then from the blessed troops who dwell
In air celestial voices fell;
'O ten-necked King,' they cried, 'attend:
This guilty deed will bring thine end.'
Then Rávaṇ speeding like the storm,
Bearing his death in human form,
The struggling Sítá, lighted down
In royal Lanká's glorious town;
A city bright and rich, that showed
Well-ordered street and noble road;
Arranged with just division, fair
With multitudes in court and square.
Thus, all his journey done, he passed
Within his royal home at last.
There in a queenly bower he placed
The black-eyed dame with dainty waist:
Thus in her chamber Maya laid
The lovely Máyá, demon maid.
Then Rávaṇ gave command to all
The dread she-fiends who filled the hall:
'This captive lady watch and guard
From sight of man and woman barred.
But all the fair one asks beside
Be with unsparing hand supplied:
As though 'twere I that asked, withhold
No pearls or dress or gems or gold.
And she among you that shall dare
Of purpose or through want of care
One word to vex her soul to say,
'Throws her unvalued life away.'
Thus spake the monarch of their race
To those she-fiends who thronged the place,
And pondering on the course to take
Went from the chamber as he spake.
He saw eight giants, strong and dread,
On flesh of bleeding victims fed,
Proud in the boon which Brahmá gave,

And trusting in its power to save.
He thus the mighty chiefs addressed
Of glorious power and strength possessed:
'Arm, warriors, with the spear and bow;
With all your speed from Lanká go,
For Janasthán, our own no more,
Is now defiled with giants' gore;
The seat of Khara's royal state
Is left unto us desolate.
In your brave hearts and might confide,
And cast ignoble fear aside.
Go, in that desert region dwell
Where the fierce giants fought and fell.
A glorious host that region held,
For power and might unparalleled,
By Dúshan and brave Khara led,—
All, slain by Ráma's arrows, bled.
Hence boundless wrath that spurns control
Reigns paramount within my soul,
And naught but Ráma's death can sate
The fury of my vengeful hate.
I will not close my slumbering eyes
Till by this hand my foeman dies.
And when mine arm has slain the foe
Who laid those giant princes low,
Long will I triumph in the deed,
Like one enriched in utmost need.
Now go; that I this end may gain,
In Janasthán, O chiefs, remain.
Watch Ráma there with keenest eye,
And all his deeds and movements spy.
Go forth, no helping art neglect,
Be brave and prompt and circumspect,
And be your one endeavour still
To aid mine arm this foe to kill.
Oft have I seen your warrior might
Proved in the forehead of the fight,
And sure of strength I know so well
Send you in Janasthán to dwell.'
  The giants heard with prompt assent
    The pleasant words he said,
  And each before his master bent
    For meet salute, his head.
  Then as he bade, without delay,
    From Lanká's gate they passed,
  And hurried forward on their way
    Invisible and fast.

CANTO LV.

SÍTÁ IN PRISON.

Thus Rávan his commandment gave
To those eight giants strong and brave,
So thinking in his foolish pride
Against all dangers to provide.
Then with his wounded heart aflame
With love he thought upon the dame,
And took with hasty steps the way
To the fair chamber where she lay.
He saw the gentle lady there
Weighed down by woe too great to bear,
Amid the throng of fiends who kept
Their watch around her as she wept:
A pinnace sinking neath the wave
When mighty winds around her rave:
A lonely herd-forsaken deer,
When hungry dogs are pressing near,
Within the bower the giant passed:
Her mournful looks were downward cast
As there she lay with streaming eyes
The giant bade the lady rise,
And to the shrinking captive showed
The glories of his rich abode,
Where thousand women spent their days
In palaces with gold ablaze;
Where wandered birds of every sort,
And jewels flashed in hall and court,
Where noble pillars charmed the sight
With diamond and lazulite,
And others glorious to behold
With ivory, crystal, silver, gold.
There swelled on high the tambour's sound
And burnished ore was bright around.
He led the mournful lady where
Resplendent gold adorned the stair,
And showed each lattice fair to see
With silver work and ivory:
Showed his bright chambers, line on line
Adorned with nets of golden twine.
Beyond he showed the Maithil dame
His gardens bright as lightning's flame,
And many a pool and lake he showed
Where blooms of gayest colour glowed.
Through all his home from view to view
The lady sunk in grief he drew.
Then trusting in her heart to wake
Desire of all she saw, he spake:
'Three hundred million giants, all
Obedient to their master's call,
Not counting young and weak and old,
Serve me with spirits fierce and bold.
A thousand culled from all of these
Wait on the lord they long to please.
This glorious power, this pomp and sway
Dear lady, at thy feet I lay:
Yea, with my life I give the whole,
O dearer than my life and soul.
A thousand beauties fill my hall:
Be thou my wife and rule them all.
O hear my supplication! why
This reasonable prayer deny?
Some pity to thy suitor show,
For love's hot flames within me glow.
This isle a hundred leagues in length,
Encompassed by the ocean's strength,
Would all the Gods and fiends defy
Though led by Him who rules the sky.
No God in heaven, no sage on earth,
No minstrel of celestial birth,

No spirit in the worlds I see
A match in power and might for me.
What wilt thou do with Ráma, him
Whose days are short, whose light is dim,
Expelled from home and royal sway,
Who treads on foot his weary way?
Leave the poor mortal to his fate,
And wed thee with a worthier mate.
My timid love, enjoy with me
The prime of youth before it flee.
Do not one hour the hope retain
To look on Ráma's face again.
For whom would wildest thought beguile
To seek thee in the giants' isle?
Say who is he has power to bind
In toils of net the rushing wind.
Whose is the mighty hand will tame
And hold the glory of the flame?
In all the worlds above, below,
Not one, O fair of form, I know
Who from this isle in fight could rend
The lady whom these arms defend.
Fair Queen, o'er Lanká's island reign,
Sole mistress of the wide domain.
Gods, rovers of the night like me,
And all the world thy slaves will be.
O'er thy fair brows and queenly head
Let consecrating balm be shed,
And sorrow banished from thy breast,
Enjoy my love and take thy rest.
Here never more thy soul shall know
The memory of thy former woe,
And here shalt thou enjoy the meed
Deserved by every virtuous deed.
Here garlands glow of flowery twine,
With gorgeous hues and scent divine.
Take gold and gems and rich attire:
Enjoy with me thy heart's desire.
There stand, of chariots far the best,
The car my brother once possessed.
Which, victor in the stricken field,
I forced the Lord of Gold to yield.
'Tis wide and high and nobly wrought,
Bright as the sun and swift as thought.
Therein, O Sítá, shalt thou ride
Delighted by thy lover's side.
But sorrow mars with lingering trace
The splendour of thy lotus face.
A cloud of woe is o'er it spread,
And all the light of joy is fled.'
  The lady, by her woe distressed,
One corner of her raiment pressed
To her sad cheek like moonlight clear,
And wiped away a falling tear.
The rover of the night renewed
His eager pleading as he viewed
The lady stand like one distraught,
Striving to fix her wandering thought:
  'Think not, sweet lady, of the shame
Of broken vows, nor fear the blame.
The saints approve with favouring eyes
This union knit with marriage ties.
O beauty, at thy radiant feet
I lay my heads, and thus entreat.
One word of grace, one look I crave:
Have pity on thy prostrate slave.
These idle words I speak are vain,
Wrung forth by love's consuming pain,
And ne'er of Rávaṇ be it said
He wooed a dame with prostrate head.'
Thus to the Maithil lady sued
The monarch of the giant brood,
And 'She is now mine own,' he thought,
In Death's dire coils already caught.

CANTO LVI.

SÍTÁ'S DISDAIN.

His words the Maithil lady heard
Oppressed by woe but undeterred.
Fear of the fiend she cast aside,
And thus in noble scorn replied:
'His word of honour never stained
King Daśaratha nobly reigned,
The bridge of right, the friend of truth.
His eldest son, a noble youth,
Is Ráma, virtue's faithful friend,
Whose glories through the worlds extend.
Long arms and large full eyes has he,
My husband, yea a God to me.
With shoulders like the forest king's,
From old Ikshváku's line he springs.
He with his brother Lakshmaṇ's aid
Will smite thee with the vengeful blade.
Hadst thou but dared before his eyes
To lay thine hand upon the prize,
Thou stretched before his feet hadst lain
In Janasthán like Khara slain.
Thy boasted rovers of the night
With hideous shapes and giant might,—
Like serpents when the feathered king
Swoops down with his tremendous wing,—
Will find their useless venom fail
When Ráma's mighty arms assail.
The rapid arrows bright with gold,
Shot from the bow he loves to hold,
Will rend thy frame from flank to flank
As Gangá's waves erode the bank.
Though neither God nor fiend have power
To slay thee in the battle hour,
Yet from his hand shall come thy fate,
Struck down before his vengeful hate.
That mighty lord will strike and end
The days of life thou hast to spend.
Thy days are doomed, thy life is sped
Like victim's to the pillar led.
Yea, if the glance of Ráma bright
With fury on thy form should light,
Thou scorched this day wouldst fall and die

Like Káma slain by Rudra's eye.[1]
He who from heaven the moon could throw,
Or bid its bright rays cease to glow,—
He who could drain the mighty sea
Will set his darling Sítá free
Fled is thy life, thy glory, fled
Thy strength and power: each sense is dead.
Soon Lanká widowed by thy guilt
Will see the blood of giants spilt.
This wicked deed, O cruel King,
No triumph, no delight will bring.
Thou with outrageous might and scorn
A woman from her lord hast torn.
My glorious husband far away,
Making heroic strength his stay,
Dwells with his brother, void of fear,
In Dandak forest lone and drear.
No more in force of arms confide:
That haughty strength, that power and pride
My hero with his arrowy rain
From all thy bleeding limbs will drain.
When urged by Fate's dire mandate, nigh
Comes the fixt hour for men to die.
Caught in Death's toils their eyes are blind,
And folly takes each wandering mind.
So for the outrage thou hast done
The fate is near thou canst not shun,—
The fate that on thyself and all
Thy giants and thy town shall fall.
I spurn thee: can the altar dight
With vessels for the sacred rite,
O'er which the priest his prayer has said,
Be sullied by an outcaste's tread?
So me, the consort dear and true
Of him who clings to virtue too,
Thy hated touch shall ne'er defile,
Base tyrant lord of Lanká's isle.
Can the white swan who floats in pride
Through lilies by her consort's side,
Look for one moment, as they pass,
On the poor diver in the grass?
This senseless body waits thy will,
To torture, chain, to wound or kill.
I will not, King of giants, strive
To keep this fleeting soul alive.
But never shall they join the name
Of Sítá with reproach and shame.'

Thus as her breast with fury burned
Her bitter speech the dame returned.
Such words of rage and scorn, the last
She uttered, at the fiend she cast.
Her taunting speech the giant heard,
And every hair with anger stirred;
Then thus with fury in his eye
He made in threats his fierce reply:
'Hear Maithil lady, hear my speech;
List to my words and ponder each.
If o'er thy head twelve months shall fly
And thou thy love wilt still deny.
My cooks shall mince thy flesh with steel
And serve it for my morning meal.'

Thus with terrific threats to her
Spake Rávan, cruel ravener.
Mad with the rage her answer woke
He called the fiendish train and spoke:
'Take her, ye Rákshas dames, who fright
With hideous form and mien the sight,
Who make the flesh of men your food,—
And let her pride be soon subdued.'
He spoke, and at his word the band
Of fiendish monsters raised each hand
In reverence to the giant king,
And pressed round Sítá in a ring.
Rávan once more with stern behest
To those she-fiends his speech addressed
Shaking the earth beneath his tread,
He stamped his furious foot and said:
'To the Asoka garden bear
The dame, and guard her safely there
Until her stubborn pride be bent
By mingled threat and blandishment.
See that ye watch her well, and tame,
Like some she-elephant, the dame.'

They led her to that garden where
The sweetest flowers perfumed the air,
Where bright trees bore each rarest fruit,
And birds, enamoured, ne'er were mute.
Bowed down with terror and distress,
Watched by each cruel giantess,—
Like a poor solitary deer
When ravening tigresses are near,—
The hapless lady lay distraught
Like some wild thing but newly caught,
And found no solace, no relief
From agonizing fear and grief;
Not for one moment could forget
Each terrifying word and threat,
Or the fierce eyes upon her set
By those who watched around.
She thought of Ráma far away,
She mourned for Lakshman as she lay
In grief and terror and dismay
Half fainting on the ground.

CANTO LVII.

SITA' COMFORTED.

Soon as the fiend had set her down
Within his home in Lanká's town
Triumph and joy filled Indra's breast,
Whom thus the Eternal Sire addressed:
'This deed will free the worlds from wo
And cause the giants' overthrow,
The fiend has borne to Lanká's isle
The lady of the lovely smile,
True consort, born to happy fate,
Well nurtured, fair and delicate.

[1] See Book I, Canto XXV.

She looks and longs for Ráma's face,
But sees a crowd of demon race,
And guarded by the giant's train
Pines for her lord and weeps in vain.
But Lanká founded on a steep
Is girdled by the mighty deep.
And how will Ráma know his fair
And blameless wife is prisoned there?
She on her woe will sadly brood
And pine away in solitude,
And heedless of herself will cease
To live, despairing of release.
Yes, pondering on her fate, I see
Her gentle life in jeopardy.
Go, Indra, swiftly seek the place,
And look upon her lovely face.
Within the city make thy way:
Let heavenly food her spirit stay.'
Thus Brahmá spake: and He who slew
The cruel demon Páka, flew
Where Lanká's royal city lay,
And Sleep went with him on his way.
'Sleep,' cried the heavenly Monarch, 'close
Each giant's eye in deep repose.'
Thus Indra spoke, and Sleep fulfilled
With joy his mandate, as he willed.
To aid the plan the Gods proposed,
The demons' eyes in sleep she closed.
Then Sachí's lord, the Thousand-eyed,
To the Asoka garden hied.
He came and stood where Sítá lay,
And gently thus began to say:
'Lord of the Gods who hold the sky,
Dame of the lovely smile, am I.
Weep no more, lady, weep no more;
Thy days of woe will soon be o'er.
I come, O Janak's child, to be
The helper of thy lord and thee.
He through my grace, with hosts to aid,
This sea-girt land will soon invade.
'Tis by my art that slumbers close
The eyelids of thy giant foes.
Now I, with Sleep, this place have sought,
Videhan lady, and have brought
A gift of heaven's ambrosial food
To stay thee in thy solitude.
Receive it from my hand, and taste,
O lady of the dainty waist:
For countless ages thou shalt be
From pangs of thirst and hunger free.'
But doubt within her bosom woke
As to the Lord of Gods she spoke:
'How may I know for truth that thou
Whose form I see before me now
Art verily the King adored
By heavenly Gods, and Śachí's lord?
With Raghu's sons I learnt to know
The certain signs which Godhead show.
These marks before mine eyes display
If o'er the Gods thou bear the sway.'
The heavenly lord of Śachí heard,
And did according to her word.
Above the ground his feet were raised;
With eyelids motionless he gazed.
No dust upon his raiment lay,
And his bright wreath was fresh and gay.
Nor was the lady's glad heart slow
The Monarch of the Gods to know,
And while the tears unceasing ran
From her sweet eyes she thus began:
'My lord has gained a friend in thee,
And I this day thy presence see
Shown clearly to mine eyes, as when
Ráma and Lakshman, lords of men,
Beheld it, and their sire the king,
And Janak too from whom I spring.
Now I, O Monarch of the Blest,
Will eat this food at thy behest,
Which thou hast brought me, of thy grace,
To aid and strengthen Raghu's race.'
She spoke, and by his words relieved,
The food from Indra's hand received.
Yet ere she ate the balm he brought,
On Lakshman and her lord she thought.
'If my brave lord be still alive,
If valiant Lakshman yet survive,
May this my taste of heavenly food
Bring health to them and bliss renewed!'
She ate, and that celestial food
Stayed hunger, thirst, and lassitude,
And all her strength restored.
Great joy her hopeful spirit stirred
At the glad tidings newly heard
Of Lakshman and her lord.
And Indra's heart was joyful too:
He bade the Maithil dame adieu,
His saving errand done.
With Sleep beside him parting thence
He sought his heavenly residence
To prosper Raghu's son.

CANTO LVIII.

THE BROTHERS' MEETING.

When Ráma's deadly shaft had struck
The giant in the seeming buck.
The chieftain turned him from the place
His homeward way again to trace.
Then as he hastened onward, fain
To look upon his spouse again,
Behind him from a thicket nigh
Rang out a jackal's piercing cry.
Alarmed he heard the startling shriek
That raised his hair and dimmed his cheek,
And all his heart was filled with doubt
As the shrill jackal's cry rang out:
'Alas, some dire disaster seems
Portended by the jackal's screams.
O may the Maithil dame be screened
From outrage of each hungry fiend!

Alas, if Lakshmaṇ chanced to hear
That bitter cry of woe and fear
What time Márícha, as he died,
With voice that mocked my accents cried,
Swift to my side the prince would flee
And quit the dame to succour me.
Too well I see the demon band
The slaughter of my love have planned.
Me far from home and Sítá's view
The seeming deer Márícha drew.
He led me far through brake and dell
Till wounded by my shaft he fell,
And as he sank rang out his cry,
'O save me, Lakshmaṇ, or I die.'
May it be well with both who stayed
In the great wood with none to aid,
For every fiend is now my foe
For Janasthán's great overthrow,
And many an omen seen to-day
Has filled my heart with sore dismay.'
Such were the thoughts and sad surmise
Of Ráma at the jackal's cries,
And all his heart within him burned
As to his cot his steps he turned.
He pondered on the deer that led
His feet to follow where it fled,
And sad with many a bitter thought
His home in Janasthán he sought.
His soul was dark with woe and fear
When flocks of birds and troops of deer
Move round him from the left, and raised
Discordant voices as they gazed.
The omens which the chieftain viewed
The terror of his soul renewed,
When lo, to meet him Lakshmaṇ sped
With brows whence all the light had fled.
Near and more near the princes came,
Each brother's heart and look the same;
Alike on each sad visage lay
The signs of misery and dismay,
Then Ráma by his terror moved
His brother for his fault reproved
In leaving Sítá far from aid
In the wild wood where giants strayed.
Lakshmaṇ's left hand he took, and then
In gentle tones the prince of men,
Though sharp and fierce their tenour ran,
Thus to his brother chief began:
'O Lakshmaṇ, thou art much to blame
Leaving alone the Maithil dame,
And flying hither to my side:
O, may no ill my spouse betide!
But ah, I know my wife is dead,
And giants on her limbs have fed,
So strange, so terrible are all
The omens which my heart appal.
O Lakshmaṇ, may we yet return
The safety of my love to learn,
To find the child of Janak still
Alive and free from scathe and ill!
Each bird with notes of warning screams,
Though the hot sun still darts his beams,
The moan of deer, the jackal's yell
Of some o'erwhelming misery tell.
O mighty brother, still may she,
My princess, live from danger free!
That semblance of a golden deer
Allured me far away,
I followed nearer and more near,
And longed to take the prey.
I followed where the quarry fled:
My deadly arrow flew,
And as the dying creature bled,
The giant met my view.
Great fear and pain oppress my heart
That dreads the coming blow,
And through my left eye keenly dart
The throbs that herald woe.
Ah Lakshmaṇ, all these signs dismay.
My soul that sinks with dread.
I know my love is torn away,
Or, haply, she is dead.'

CANTO LIX.

RÁMA'S RETURN.

When Ráma saw his brother stand
With none beside him, all unmanned,
Eager he questioned why he came
So far without the Maithil dame:
'Where is my wife, my darling, she
Who to the wild wood followed me?
Where hast thou left my lady, where
The dame who chose my lot to share?
Where is my love who balms my woe
As through the forest wilds I go,
Unkinged and banished and disgraced,—
My darling of the dainty waist?
She nerves my spirit for the strife,
She, only she gives zest to life,
Dear as my breath is she who vies
In charms with daughters of the skies.
If Janak's child be mine no more,
In splendour fair as virgin ore,
The lordship of the skies and earth
To me were prize of little worth.
Ah, lives she yet, the Maithil dame,
Dear as the soul within this frame?
O, let not all my toil be vain,
The banishment, the woe and pain!
O, let not dark Kaikeyí win
The guerdon of her treacherous sin,
If, Sítá lost, my days I end,
And thou without me homeward wend!
O, let not good Kauśalyá shed
Her bitter tears to mourn me dead,
Nor her proud rival's hest obey,
Strong in her son and queenly sway!
Back to my cot will I repair
If Sítá live to greet me there,

But if my wife have perished, I
Reft of my love will surely die,
O Lakshmaṇ, if I seek my cot,
Look for my love and find her not
Sweet welcome with her smile to give,
I tell thee, I will cease to live.
O answer,—let thy words be plain,—
Lives Sitá yet, or is she slain?
Didst thou thy sacred trust betray
Till ravening giants seized the prey?
Ah me, so young, so soft and fair,
Lapped in all bliss, untried by care,
Rent from her own dear husband, how
Will she support her misery now?
That voice, O Lakshmaṇ smote thine ear,
And filled, I ween, thy heart with fear,
When on thy name for succour cried
The treacherous giant ere he died.
That voice too like mine own, I ween,
Was heard by the Videhan queen.
She bade thee seek my side to aid,
And quickly was the hest obeyed,
But ah, thy fault I needs must blame,
To leave alone the helpless dame,
And let the cruel giants sate
The fury of their murderous hate.
Those blood-devouring demons all
Grieve in their souls for Khara's fall,
And Sítá, none to guard her side,
Torn by their cruel hands has died.
I sink, O tamer of thy foes,
Deep in the sea of whelming woes.
What can I now? I must endure
The mighty grief that mocks at cure.'
Thus, all his thoughts on Sítá bent,
To Janasthán the chieftain went,
Hastening on with eager stride,
And Lakshmaṇ hurried by his side.
With toil and thirst and hunger worn,
His breast with doubt and anguish torn,
He sought the well-known spot.
Again, again he turned to chide
With quivering lips which terror dried:
He looked, and found her not.
Within his leafy home he sped,
Each pleasant spot he visited
Where oft his darling strayed.
'Tis as I feared', he cried, and there,
Yielding to pangs too great to bear,
He sank by grief dismayed.

CANTO LX.

LAKSHMAṆ REPROVED.

But Ráma ceased not to upbraid
His brother for untimely aid,
And thus, while anguish wrung his breast,
The chief with eager question pressed:
'Why, Lakshmaṇ, didst thou hurry hence
And leave my wife without defence?
I left her in the wood with thee,
And deemed her safe from jeopardy.
When first thy form appeared in view,
I marked that Sítá come not too.
With woe my troubled soul was rent,
Prophetic of the dire event.
Thy coming steps afar I spied,
I saw no Sítá by thy side.
And felt a sudden throbbing dart
Through my left eye, and arm, and heart.'
Lakshmaṇ, with Fortune's marks impressed,
His brother mournfully addressed:
'Not by my heart's free impulse led,
Leaving thy wife to thee I sped;
But by her keen reproaches sent,
O Ráma, to thine aid I went.
She heard afar a mournful cry,
'O save me, Lakshmaṇ, or I die.'
The voice that spoke in moving tone
Smote on her ear and seemed thine own.
Soon as those accents reached her ear
She yielded to her woe and fear,
She wept o'ercome by grief, and cried,
'Fly, Lakshmaṇ, fly to Ráma's side.'
Though many a time she bade me speed,
Her urgent prayer I would not heed.
I bade her in thy strength confide,
And thus with tender words replied:
'No giant roams the forest shade
From whom thy lord need shrink dismayed.
No human voice, believe me, spoke
Those words thy causeless fear that woke.
Can he whose might can save in woe
The heavenly Gods e'er stoop so low,
And with those piteous accents call
For succour like a caitiff thrall?
And why should wandering giants choose
The accents of thy lord to use,
In alien tones my help to crave,
And cry aloud, O Lakshmaṇ, save?
Now let my words thy spirit cheer,
Compose thy thoughts and banish fear.
In hell, in earth, or in the skies
There is not, and there cannot rise
A champion whose strong arm can slay
Thy Ráma in the battle fray.
To heavenly hosts he ne'er would yield
Though Indra led them to the field.'
To soothe her thus I vainly sought:
Her heart with woe was still distraught.
While from her eyes the waters ran
Her bitter speech she thus began:
'Too well I see thy dark intent;
Thy lawless thoughts on me are bent.
Thou hopest, but thy hope is vain,
To win my love, thy brother slain.
Not love, but Bharat's dark decree
To share his exile counselled thee,

Or hearing now his bitter cry
Thou surely to his aid wouldst fly.
For love of me, a stealthy foe
Thou choosest by his side to go,
And now thou longest that my lord
Should die, and wilt no help afford.'
Such were the words the lady said:
With angry fire my eyes were red.
With pale lips quivering in my rage
I hastened from the hermitage.'
He ceased; and frenzied by his pain
The son of Raghu spoke again:
'O brother, for thy fault I grieve,
The Maithil dame alone to leave.
Thou knowest that my arm is strong
To save me from the giant throng,
And yet couldst leave the cottage, spurred
To folly by her angry word.
For this thy deed I praise thee not,—
To leave her helpless in the cot,
And thus thy sacred charge forsake
For the wild words a woman spake.
Yea thou art all to blame herein,
And very grievous is thy sin.
That anger swayed thy faithless breast
And made thee false to my behest.
An arrow speeding from my bow
Has laid the treacherous giant low,
Who lured me eager for the chase
Far from my hermit dwelling-place.
The string with easy hand I drew,
The arrow as in pastime flew,
The wounded quarry bled.
The borrowed form was cast away,
Before mine eyes a giant lay
With bright gold braceleted.
My arrow smote him in the chest:
The giant by the pain distressed
Raised his loud voice on high.
Far rang the mournful sound: mine own,
It seemed, were accent, voice, and tone,
They made thee leave my spouse alone
And to my rescue fly.'

CANTO LXI.

RAMA'S LAMENT.

As Ráma sought his leafy cot
Through his left eye keen throbbings shot,
His wonted strength his frame forsook,
And all his body reeled and shook.
Still on those dreadful signs he thought,—
Sad omens with disaster fraught,
And from his troubled heart he cried,
'O, may no ill my spouse betide!'
Longing to gaze on Sítá's face
He hastened to his dwelling-place,
Then sinking neath his misery's weight,
He looked and found it desolate.
Tossing his mighty arms on high
He sought her with an eager cry.
From spot to spot he wildly ran
Each corner of his home to scan.
He looked, but Sítá was not there;
His cot was disolate and bare,
Like streamlet in the winter frost,
The glory of her lilies lost.
With leafy tears the sad trees wept
As a wild wind their branches swept.
Mourned bird and deer, and every flower
Drooped fainting round the lonely bower.
The silvan deities had fled
The spot where all the light was dead,
Where hermit coats of skin displayed,
And piles of sacred grass were laid,
He saw, and maddened by his pain
Cried in lament again, again:
'Where is she, dead or torn away,
Lost, or some hungry giant's prey?
Or did my darling chance to rove
For fruit and blossoms though the grove?
Or has she sought the pool or rill,
Her pitcher from the wave to fill?'
His eager eyes on fire with pain
He roamed about with maddened brain.
Each grove and glade he searched with care,
He sought, but found no Sítá there.
He wildly rushed from hill to hill;
From tree to tree, from rill to rill.
As bitter woe his bosom rent
Still Ráma roamed with fond lament:
'O sweet Kadamba, say has she
Who loved thy bloom been seen by thee?
If thou have seen her face most fair,
Say, gentle tree, I pray thee, where.
O Bel tree with thy golden fruit
Round as her breast, no more be mute.
Where is my radiant darling, gay
In silk that mocks thy glossy spray?
O Arjun, say, where is she now
Who loved to touch thy scented bough?
Do not thy graceful friend forget,
But tell me, is she living yet?
Speak, Basil, thou must surely know,
For like her limbs thy branches show,—
Most lovely in thy fair array
Of twining plant and tender spray.
Sweet Tila, fairest of the trees,
Melodious with the hum of bees,
Where is my darling Sítá, tell,—
The dame who loved thy flowers so well?
Aśoka, act thy gentle part,—
Named Heartsease,[1] give me what thou art,
To these sad eyes my darling show
And free me from this load of woe.
O Palm, in rich ripe fruitage dressed
Round as the beauties of her breast,

[1] *Aśoka* is compounded of *a* not and *śoka* grief.

If thou have heart to know and feel,
My peerless consort's fate reveal.
Hast thou, Rose-apple, chanced to view
My darling bright with golden hue?
If thou have seen her quickly speak,
Where is the dame I wildly seek?
O glorious Cassia, thou art gay
With all thy loveliest bloom to-day,
Where is my dear who loved to hold
In her full lap thy flowery gold?'
To many a tree and plant beside,
To Jasmin, Mango, Sál, he cried.
'Say, hast thou seen, O gentle deer,
The fawn-eyed Sítá wandering here?
It may be that my love has strayed
To sport with fawns beneath the shade.
If thou, great elephant, have seen
My darling of the lovely mien,
Whose rounded limbs are soft and fine
As is that lissome trunk of thine,
O noblest of wild creatures, show
Where is the dame thou needs must know.
O tiger, hast thou chanced to see
My darling? very fair is she.
Cast all thy fear away, declare,
Where is my moon-faced darling, where?
There, darling of the lotus eye,
I see thee, and 'tis vain to fly.
Wilt thou not speak, dear love? I see
Thy form half hidden by the tree.
Stay if thou love me, Sítá, stay
In pity cease thy heartless play.
Why mock me now? thy gentle breast
Was never prone to cruel jest.
'Tis vain behind yon bush to steal;
Thy shimmering silks thy path reveal.
Fly not. mine eyes pursue thy way;
For pity's sake, dear Sítá, stay.
Ah me, ah me, my words are vain;
My gentle love is lost or slain.
How could her tender bosom spurn
Her husband on his home-return?
Ah no, my love is surely dead,
Fierce giants on her flesh have fed,
Rending the soft limbs of their prey
When I her lord was far away.
That moon-bright face, that polished brow,
Red lips, bright teeth—what are they now?
Alas. my darling's shapely neck
She loved with chains of gold to deck,—
That neck that mocked the sandal scent,
The ruthless fiends have grasped and rent
Alas, 'twas vain those arms to raise
Soft as the young tree's tender sprays
Ah. dainty meal for giants' lips
Were arms and quivering finger tips.
Ah, she who counted many a friend
Was left for fiends to seize and rend,
Was left by me without defence
From ravening giants' violence.
O Lakshman of the arm of might,
Say. is my darling love in sight?
O dearest Sítá. where art thou?
Where is my darling consort now?'
Thus as he cried in wild lament
From grove to grove the mourner went.
Here for a moment sank to rest.
Then started up and onward pressed.
Thus roaming on like one distraught
Still for his vanished love he sought.
He searched in wood and hill and glade,
By rock and brook and wild cascade.
Through groves with restless step he sped
And left no spot unvisited.
Through lawns and woods of vast extent
Still searching for his love he went
With eager steps and fast.
For many a weary hour he toiled,
Still in his fond endeavour foiled,
Yet hoping to the last.

CANTO LXII.

RÁMA'S LAMENT.

When all the toil and search was vain
He sought his leafy home again.
'Twas empty still: all scattered lay
The seats of grass in disarray.
He raised his shapely arms on high
And spoke aloud with bitter cry:
'Where is the Maithil dame?' he said,
'O, whither has my darling fled?
Who can have borne away my dame,
Or feasted on her tender frame?
If, Sítá, hidden by some tree,
Thou joyest still to mock at me,
Cease, cease thy cruel sport, and take
Compassion, or my heart will break.
Bethink thee, love, the gentle fawns
With whom thou playest on the lawns,
Impatient for thy coming wait
With streaming eyes disconsolate.
Reft of my love, I needs must go
Hence to the shades weighed down by woe.
The king our sire will see me there,
And cry, 'O perjured Ráma, where,
Where is thy faith, that thou canst speed
From exile ere the time decreed?
Ah Sítá, whither hast thou fled
And left me here disquieted,
A hapless mourner, reft of hope,
Too feeble with my woe to cope?
E'en thus indignant Glory flies
The wretch who stains his soul with lies.
If thou, my love, art lost to view,
I in my woe must perish too.'
Thus Ráma by his grief distraught
Wept for the wife he vainly sought.
And Lakshman whose fraternal breast
Longed for his weal, the chief addressed,

Whose soul gave way beneath the pain
When all his eager search was vain.
Like some great elephant who stands
Sinking upon the treacherous sands:
'Not yet, O wisest chief, despair;
Renew thy toil with utmost care.
This noble hill where trees are green
Has many a cave and dark ravine.
The Maithil lady day by day
Delighted in the woods to stray.
Deep in the grove she wanders still,
Or walks by blossom-covered rill,
Or fish-loved river stealing through
Tall clusters of the dark bamboo.
Or else the dame with arch design
To prove thy mood, O Prince, and mine,
Far in some sheltering thicket lies
To frighten ere she meet our eyes.
Then come, renew thy labour, trace
The lady to her lurking-place,
And search the wood from side to side
To know where Sítá loves to hide.
Collect thy thoughts, O royal chief,
Nor yield to unavailing grief.'
Thus Lakshman, by affection stirred,
To fresh attempts his brother spurred,
And Ráma, as he ceased, began
With Lakshman's aid each spot to scan.
In eager search their way they took
Through wood, o'er hill, by pool and brook.
They roamed each mount, nor spared to seek
On ridge and crag and towering peak.
They sought the dame in every spot;
But all in vain; they found her not.
Above, below, on every side
They ranged the hill, and Ráma cried,
'O Lakshman, O my brother still
No trace of Sítá on the hill!'
Then Lakshman as he roamed the wood
Beside his glorious brother stood,
And while fierce grief his bosom burned
This answer to the chief returned:
'Thou, Ráma, after toil and pain
Wilt meet the Maithil dame again,
As Vishnu, Bali's might subdued,
His empire of the earth renewed.'[1]
Then Ráma cried in mournful tone,
His spirit by his woe o'erthrown:
'The wood is searched from side to side,
No distant spot remains untried,
No lilied pool, no streamlet where
The lotus buds are fresh and fair.
Our eyes have searched the hill with all
His caves and every waterfall,—
But ah, not yet I find my wife,
More precious than the breath of life.'
As thus he mourned his vanished dame
A mighty trembling seized his frame,
And by o'erpowering grief assailed,
His troubled senses reeled and failed.
Too great to bear his misery grew,
And many a long hot sigh he drew,
Then as he wept and sobbed and sighed,
'O Sítá, O my love!' he cried.
Then Lakshman, joining palm to palm,
Tried every art his woe to calm.
But Ráma in his anguish heard
Or heeded not one soothing word,
Still for his spouse he mourned, and shrill
Rang out his lamentation still.

CANTO LXIII.

RÁMA'S LAMENT.

Thus for his wife in vain he sought:
Then, his sad soul with pain distraught,
The hero of the lotus eyes
Filled all the air with frantic cries.
O'erpowered by love's strong influence, he
His absent wife still seemed to see,
And thus with accents weak and faint
Renewed with tears his wild complaint:
'Thou, fairer than their bloom, my spouse,
Art hidden by Aśoka boughs.
Those blooms have power to banish care,
But now they drive me to despair.
Thine arms are like the plantain's stem:
Why let the plantain cover them?
Thou art not hidden, love; thy feet
Betray thee in thy dark retreat.
Thou runnest in thy girlish sport
To flowery trees, thy dear resort.
But cease, O cease, my love, I pray,
To vex me with thy cruel play.
Such mockery in a holy spot
Where hermits dwell beseems thee not.
Ah, now I see thy fickle mind
To scornful mood too much inclined.
Come, large-eyed beauty, I implore;
Lone is the cot so dear before.
No, she is slain by giants; they
Have stolen or devoured their prey,
Or surely at my mournful cry
My darling to her lord would fly.
O Lakshman, see those troops of deer:
In each sad eye there gleams a tear.
Those looks of woe too clearly say
My consort is the giants' prey.
O noblest, fairest of the fair,
Where art thou, best of women, where?
This day will dark Kaikeyí find
Fresh triumph for her evil mind,
When I who with my Sítá came
Return alone, without my dame.
But ne'er can I return to see
Those chambers where my queen should be
And hear the scornful people speak

[1] See Book I. Canto XXXI.

Of Ráma as a coward weak.
For mine will be the coward's shame
Who let the foeman steal his dame.
How can I seek my home, or brook
Upon Videha's king to look?
How listen, when he bids me tell,
My wanderings o'er, that all is well?
He, when I meet his eager view,
Will mark that Sítá comes not too,
And when he hears the mournful tale
His wildered sense will reel and fail.
'O Daśaratha,' will he cry,
'Blest in thy mansion in the sky!'
Ne'er to that town my steps shall bend,
That town which Bharat's arms defend,
For e'en the blessed homes above
Would seem a waste without my love.
Leave me, my brother, here, I pray;
To fair Ayodhyá bend thy way.
Without my love I cannot bear
To live one hour in blank despair.
Round Bharat's neck thy fond arms twine,
And greet him with these words of mine:
'Dear brother, still the power retain,
And o'er the land as monarch reign.'
With salutation next incline
Before thy mother, his, and mine.
Still, brother, to my words attend,
And with all care each dame befriend.
To my dear mother's ear relate
My mournful tale and Sítá's fate.'
Thus Ráma gave his sorrow vent,
And from a heart which anguish rent,
Mourned for his wife in loud lament,—
Her of the glorious hair,
From Lakshman's cheek the colour fled,
And o'er his heart came sudden dread,
Sick, faint, and sore disquieted
By woe too great to bear.

CANTO LXIV.

RÁMA'S LAMENT.

Reft of his love, the royal chief,
Weighed down beneath his whelming grief,
Desponding made his brother share
His grievous burden of despair.
Over his sinking bosom rolled
The flood of sorrow uncontrolled,
And as he wept and sighed,
In mournful accents faint and slow
With words congenial to his woe,
To Lakshman thus he cried:
'Brother, I ween, beneath the sun,
Of all mankind there lives not one
So full of sin, whose hand has done
Such cursed deeds as mine.
For my sad heart with misery bleeds,
As, guerdon of those evil deeds,
Still greater woe to woe succeeds
In never-ending line.
A life of sin I freely chose,
And from my past transgression flows
A ceaseless flood of bitter woes
My folly to repay.
The fruit of sin has ripened fast,
Through many a sorrow have I passed,
And now the crowning grief at last
Falls on my head to-day.
From all my faithful friends I fled,
My sire is numbered with the dead,
My royal rank is forfeited,
My mother far away.
These woes on which I sadly think
Fill, till it raves above the brink,
The stream of grief in which I sink,—
The flood which naught can stay.
Ne'er, brother, ne'er have I complained;
Though long by toil and trouble pained,
Without a murmur I sustained
The woes of woodland life.
But fiercer than the flames that rise
When crackling wood the food supplies,—
Flashing a glow through evening skies,—
This sorrow for my wife.
Some crued fiend has seized the prey
And torn my trembling love away,
While, as he bore her through the skies,
She shrieked aloud with frantic cries,
It tones of fear which, wild and shrill,
Retained their native sweetness still.
Ah me, that breast so soft and sweet,
For sandal's precious perfume meet,
Now all distained with dust and gore,
Shall meet my fond caress no more.
That face, whose lips with tones so clear
Made pleasant music, sweet to hear,—
With soft locks plaited o'er the brow,—
Some giant's hand is on it now.
It smiles not, as the dear light fails
When Ráhu's jaw the moon assails.
Ah, my true love! that shapely neck
She loved with fairest chains to deck,
The cruel demons rend, and drain
The lifeblood from each mangled vein.
Ah, when the savage monsters came
And dragged away the helpless dame,
The lady of the long soft eye
Called like a lamb with piteous cry.
Beneath this rock, O Lakshman, see,
My peerless consort sat with me,
And gently talked to thee the while,
Her sweet lips opening with a smile.
Here is that fairest stream which she
Loved ever, bright Godávarí.
Ne'er can the dame have passed this way:
So far alone she would not stray,
Nor has my darling, lotus-eyed,
Sought lilies by the river's side,
For without me she ne'er would go

To streamlets where the wild flowers grow,
Tell me not, brother, she has strayed
To the dark forest's distant shade
Where blooming boughs are gay and sweet,
And bright birds love the cool retreat.
Alone my love would never dare,—
My timid love,—to wander there.
O Lord of Day whose eye sees all
We act and plan, on thee I call:
For naught is hidden from thy sight,—
Great witness thou of wrong and right.
Where is she, lost or torn away?
Dispel my torturing doubt and say.
And O thou Wind who blowest free,
The worlds have naught concealed from
thee.
List to my prayer, reveal one trace
Of her, the glory of her race.
Say, is she stolen hence, or dead,
Or do her feet the forest tread?'
Thus with disordered senses, faint
With woe he poured his sad complaint,
And then, a better way to teach,
Wise Lakshmaṇ spoke in seemly speech:
'Up, brother dear, thy grief subdue,
With heart and soul thy search renew.
When woes oppress and dangers threat
Brave effort ne'er was fruitless yet.'
He spoke, but Ráma gave no heed
To valiant Lakshmaṇ's prudent rede.
With double force the flood of pain
Rushed o'er his yielding soul again.

CANTO LXV.

RÁMA'S WRATH.

With piteous voice, by woe subdued,
Thus Raghu's son his speech renewed:
'Thy steps, my brother, quickly turn
To bright Godávarí and learn
If Sítá to the stream have hied
To cull the lilies on its side.'
Obedient to the words he said,
His brother to the river sped.
The shelving banks he searched in vain,
And then to Ráma turned again.
'I searched, but found her not,' he cried;
'I called aloud, but none replied.
Where can the Maithil lady stray,
Whose sight would chase our cares away?
I know not where, her steps untraced,
Roams Sítá of the dainty waist.'
When Ráma heard the words he spoke
Again he sank beneath the stroke,
And with a bosom anguish-fraught
Himself the lovely river sought.
There standing on the shelving side,
'O Sítá, where art thou?' he cried.
No spirit voice an answer gave,
No murmur from the trembling wave
Of sweet Godávarí declared
The outrage which the fiend had dared.
'O speak!' the pitying spirits cried,
But yet the stream their prayer denied,
Nor dared she, coldly mute, relate
To the sad chief his darling's fate.
Of Rávaṇ's awful form she thought,
And the dire deed his arm had wrought,
And still withheld by fear dismayed,
The tale for which the mourner prayed.
When hope was none, his heart to cheer,
That the bright stream his cry would hear,
While sorrow for his darling tore
His longing soul he spake once more:
'Though I have sought with tears and sighs
Godávarí no word replies,
O say, what answer can I frame
To Janak father of my dame?
Or how before her mother stand
Leading no Sítá by the hand?
Where is my loyal love who went
Forth with her lord to banishment?
Her faith to me she nobly held
Though from my realm and home expel-
led,—
A hermit, nursed on woodland fare,—
She followed still and soothed my care.
Of all my friends am I bereft,
Nor is my faithful consort left.
How slowly will the long nights creep
While comfortless I wake and weep!
O, if my wife may yet be found,
With humble love I'll wander round
This Janasthán, Praśravaṇ's hill,
Mandákiní's delightful rill.
See how the deer with gentle eyes
Look on my face and sympathize.
I mark their soft expression: each
Would soothe me, if it could, with speech.'
A while the anxious throng he eyed,
And 'Where is Sítá, where?' he cried.
Thus while hot tears his utterance broke
The mourning son of Raghu spoke.
The deer in pity for his woes
Obeyed the summons and arose.
Upon his right thy stood, and raised
Their sad eyes up to heaven and gazed.
Each to that quarter bent her look
Which Rávaṇ with his captive took.
Then Raghu's son again they viewed,
And toward that point their way pursued.
Then Lakshmaṇ watched their looks intent
As moaning on their way they went,
And marked each sign which struck his
sense
With mute expressive influence,
Then as again his sorrow woke
Thus to his brother chief he spoke:
'Those deer thy eager question heard

And rose at once by pity stirred:
See, in thy search their aid they lend,
See, to the south their looks they bend.
Arise, dear brother, let us go
The way their eager glances show,
If haply sign or trace descried
Our footsteps in the search may guide.'
The son of Raghu gave assent,
And quickly to the south they went;
With eager eyes the earth he scanned,
And Lakshman followed close at hand.
As each to other spake his thought,
And round with anxious glances sought,
Scattered before them in the way,
Blooms of a fallen garland lay.
When Ráma saw that flowery rain
He spoke once more with bitterest pain:
'O Lakshman every flower that lies
Here on the ground I recognize.
I culled them in the grove, and there
My darling twined them in her hair.
The sun, the earth, the genial breeze
Have spared these flowers my soul to please.'
Then to that woody hill he prayed,
Whence flashed afar each wild cascade:
'O best of mountains, hast thou seen
A dome of perfect form and mien
In some sweet spot with trees o'ergrown,—
My darling whom I left alone?'
Then as a lion threats a deer
He thundered with a voice of fear:
'Reveal her, mountain, to my view
With golden limbs and golden hue.
Where is my darling Sítá? speak
Before I rend thee peak from peak.'
The mountain seemed her track to show,
But told not all he sought to know.
Then Daśaratha's son renewed
His summons as the mount he viewed:
'Soon as my flaming arrows fly,
Consumed to ashes shalt thou lie
Without a herb or bud or tree,
And birds no more shall dwell in thee.
And if this stream my prayer deny,
My wrath this day her flood shall dry,
Because she lends no aid to trace
My darling of the lotus face.'
Thus Ráma spake as though his ire
Would scorch them with his glance of fire;
Then searching farther on the ground
The footprint of a fiend he found,
And small light traces here and there,
Where Sítá in her great despair,
Shrieking for Ráma's help, had fled
Before the giant's mighty tread.
His careful eye each trace surveyed
Which Sítá and the fiend had made,—
The quivers and the broken bow
And ruined chariot of the foe,—
And told, distraught by fear and grief,
His tidings to his brother chief;
'O Lakshman, here,' he cried 'behold
My Sítá's earrings dropped with gold.
Here lie her garlands torn and rent,
Here lies each glittering ornament.
O look, the ground on every side
With blood-like drops of gold is dyed.
The fiends who wear each strange disguise
Have seized, I ween, the helpless prize.
My lady, by their hands o'erpowered,
Is slaughtered, mangled, and devoured.
Methinks two fearful giants came
And waged fierce battle for the dame.
Whose, Lakshman, was this mighty bow
With pearls and gems in glittering row?
Cast to the ground the fragments lie,
And still their glory charms the eye.
A bow so mighty sure was planned
For heavenly God or giant's hand.
Whose was this coat of golden mail
Which, though its lustre now is pale.
Shone like the sun of morning, bright
With studs of glittering lazulite?
Whose, Lakshman, was this bloom-wreathed shade
With all its hundred ribs displayed?
This screen, most meet for royal brow,
With broken staff lies useless now.
And these tall asses, goblin-faced,
With plates of golden harness graced,
Whose hideous forms are stained with gore
Who is the lord whose yoke they bore?
Whose was this pierced and broken car
That shoots a flame-like blaze afar?
Whose these spent shafts at random spread,
Each fearful with its iron head,—
With golden mountings fair to see,
Long as a chariot's axle-tree?
These quivers see, which, rent in twain,
Their sheaves of arrows still contain.
Whose was this driver? Dead and cold,
His hands the whip and reins still hold.
See, Lakshman, here the foot I trace
Of man, nay, one of giant race.
The hatred that I nursed of old
Grows mightier now a hundred fold
Against these giants, fierce of heart,
Who change their forms by magic art.
Slain, eaten by the giant press,
Or stolen is the votaress,
Nor could her virtue bring defence
To Sítá seized and hurried hence.
O, if my love be slain or lost
All hope of bliss for me is crossed.
The power of all the worlds were vain
To bring one joy to soothe my pain.
The spirits with their blinded eyes
Would look in wonder, and despise
The Lord who made the worlds, the great
Creator when compassionate.
And so, I ween, the Immortals turn
Cold eyes upon me now, and spurn

The weakling prompt at pity's call,
Devoted to the good of all.
But from this day behold me changed,
From every gentle grace estranged.
Now be it mine all life to slay,
And sweep these cursed fiends away.
As the great sun leaps up the sky,
And the cold moonbeams fade and die,
So vengeance rises in my breast.
One passion conquering all the rest.
Gandharvas in their radiant place,
The Yakshas, and the giant race,
Kinnars and men shall look in vain
For joy they ne'er shall see again.
The anguish of my great despair,
O Lakshman, fills the heaven and air;
And I in wrath all life will slay
Within the triple world to-day.
Unless the Gods in heaven who dwell
Restore my Sítá safe and well,
I armed with all the fires of Fate.
The triple world will devastate.
The troubled stars from heaven shall fall,
The moon be wrapped in gloomy pall,
The fire be quenched, the wind be stilled,
The radiant sun grow dark and chilled:
Crushed every mountain's towering pride,
And everg lake and river dried,
Dead every creeper, plant, and tree,
And lost for aye the mighty sea.
Thou shalt the word this day behold
In wild disorder uncontrolled,
With dying life which naught defends
From the fierce storm my bowstring sends.
My shafts this day, for Sítá's sake,
The life of every fiend shall take.
The Gods this day shall see the force
That wings my arrows on their course,
And mark how far that course is held,
By my unsparing wrath impelled.
No God, not one of Daitya strain,
Goblin or Rákshas shall remain.
My wrath shall end the worlds, and all
Demons and Gods therewith shall fall.
Each world which Gods, the Dánav race,
And giants make their dwelling place,
Shall fall beneath my arrows sent
In fury when my bow is bent.
The arrows loosened from my string
Confusion on the worlds shall bring.
For she is lost or breathes no more,
Nor will the Gods my love restore.
Hence all on earth with life and breath
This day I dedicate to death.
All, till my darling they reveal,
The fury of my shafts shall feel.'
Thus as he spake by rage impelled,
Red grew his eyes, his fierce lips swelled.
His bark coat round his form he drew
And coiled his hermit braids anew.
Like Rudra when he yearned to slay
The demon Tripur[1] in the fray.
So looked the hero brave and wise,
The fury flashing from his eyes.
Then Ráma, conqueror of the foe,
From Lakshmaṇ's hand received his bow,
Strained the great string, and laid thereon
A deadly dart that flashed and shone,
And spake these words as fierce in ire
As He who ends the worlds with fire:
'As age and time and death and fate
All life with checkless power await,
So Lakshmaṇ in my wrath to-day
My vengeful might shall brook no stay,
Unless this day I see my dame
In whose sweet form is naught to blame,—
Yea, as before, my love behold
Fair with bright teeth and perfect mould,
This world shall feel a deadly blow
Destroyed with ruthless overthrow,
And serpent lords and Gods of air,
Gandharvas, men, the doom shall share.'

CANTO LXVI.

LAKSHMAṆ'S SPEECH.

He stood incensed with eyes of flame,
Still mourning for his ravished dame,
Determined, like the fire of Fate,
To leave the wide world desolate.
His ready bow the hero eyed,
And as again, again he sighed,
The triple world would fain consume
Like Hara[2] in the day of doom.
Then Lakshmaṇ moved with sorrow viewed
His brother in unwonted mood,
And reverent palm to palm applied,
Thus spoke with lips which terror dried
'Thy heart was ever soft and kind,
To every creature's good inclined.
Cast not thy tender mood away,
Nor yield to anger's mastering sway.
The moon for gentle grace is known,
The sun has splendour all his own,
The restless wind is free and fast,
And earth in patience unsurpassed.
So glory with her noble fruit
Is thine eternal attribute.
O, let not, for the sin of one,
The triple world be all undone.
I know not whose this car that lies
In fragments here before our eyes,
Nor who the chiefs who met and fought,
Nor what the prize the foemen sought;
Who marked the ground with hoof and wheel,

[1] An Asur or demon, king of Tripura, the modern Tipperah.

[2] Śiva.

Or whose the hand that plied the steel
Which left this spot, the battle o'er,
Thus sadly dyed with drops of gore.
Searching with utmost care I view
The signs of one and not of two.
Where'er I turn mine eyes I trace
No mighty host about the place.
Then mete not out for one offence
This all-involving recompense.
For kings should use the sword they bear,
But mild in time should learn to spare,
Thou, ever moved by misery's call,
Wast the great hope and stay of all.
Throughout this world who would not blame
This outrage on thy ravished dame?
Gandharvas, Dánavs, Gods, the trees,
The rocks, the rivers, and the seas,
Can ne'er in aught thy soul offend,
As one whom holiest rites befriend.
But him who dared to steal the dame
Pursue, O King, with ceaseless aim,
With me, the hermits' holy band,
And thy great bow to arm thy hand
By every mighty flood we'll seek,
Each wood, each hill from base to peak.
To the fair homes of Gods we'll fly,
And bright Gandharvas in the sky,
Until we reach, where'er he be,
The wretch who stole thy spouse from thee.
Then if the Gods will not restore
Thy Sítá when the search is o'er,
Then, royal lord of Kośal's land,
No longer hold thy vengeful hand.
If meekness, prayer, and right be weak
To bring thee back the dame we seek,
Up, brother, with a deadly shower
Of gold-bright shafts thy foes o'erpower,
Fierce as the flashing levin sent
From King Mahendra's firmament.

CANTO LXVII.

RÁMA APPEASED.

As Ráma, pierced by sorrow's sting,
Lamented like a helpless thing,
And by his mighty woe distraught
Was last in maze of troubled thought,
Sumitrá's son with loving care
Consoled him in his wild despair,
And while his feet he gently pressed
With words like these the chief addressed:
'For sternest vow and noblest deed
Was Daśaratha blessed with seed.
Thee for his son the king obtained,
Like Amrit by the Gods regained.
Thy gentle graces won his heart,
And all too weak to live apart
The monarch died, as Bharat told,
And lives on high mid Gods enrolled.
If thou, O Ráma, wilt not bear
This grief which fills thee with despair,
How shall a weaker man e'er hope,
Infirm and mean, with woe to cope?
Take heart, I pray thee, noblest chief;
What man who breathes is free from grief?
Misfortunes come and burn like flame,
Then fly as quickly as they came.
Yayáti son of Nahush reigned
With Indra on the throne he gained,
But falling for a light offence
He mourned a while the consequence.
Vaśishṭha, reverend saint and sage,
Priest of our sire from youth to age,
Begot a hundred sons, but they
Were smitten in a single day.[1]
And she, the queen whom all revere,
The mother whom we hold so dear,
The earth herself not seldom feels
Fierce fever when she shakes and reels.
And those twin lights, the world's great eyes,
On which the universe relies,—
Does not eclipse at times assail
Their brilliance till their fires grow pale?
The mighty Powers, the Immortal Blest
Bend to a law which none contest.
No God, no bodied life is free
From conquering Fate's supreme decree.
E'en Śakra's self must reap the meed
Of virtue and of sinful deed.
And O great lord of men, wilt thou
Helpless beneath thy misery bow?
No, if thy dame be lost or dead,
O hero, still be comforted,
Nor yield for ever to thy woe
O'ermastered like the mean and low.
Thy peers, with keen far-reaching eyes,
Spend not their hours in ceaseless sighs;
In dire distress, in whelming ill
Their manly looks are hopeful still.
To this, great chief, thy reason bend,
And earnestly the truth perpend.
By reason's aid the wisest learn
The good and evil to discern.
With sin and goodness scarcely known
Faint light by chequered lives is shown;
Without some clear undoubted deed
We mark not how the fruits succeed.
In time of old, O thou most brave,
To me thy lips such counsel gave.
Vrihaspati[2] can scarcely find
New wisdom to instruct thy mind.
For thine is wit and genious high
Meet for the children of the sky.
I rouse that heart benumbed by pain
And call to vigorous life again.
Be manly godlike vigour shown;
Put forth that noblest strength, thine own.

---

[1] See Book I. Canto LIX.

[2] The preceptor of the Gods.

Strive, best of old Ikshváku's strain,
Strive till the conquered foe be slain.
Where is the profit or the joy
If thy fierce rage the worlds destroy?
Search till thou find the guilty foe,
Then let thy hand no mercy show.'

CANTO LXVIII.

JAṬÁYUS.

Thus faithful Lakshmaṇ strove to cheer
The prince with counsel wise and clear,
Who, prompt to seize the pith of all,
Let not that wisdom idly fall.
With vigorous effort he restrained
The passion in his breast that reigned,
And leaning on his bow for rest
His brother Lakshmaṇ thus addressed:
'How shall we labour now, reflect;
Whither again our search direct?
Brother, what plan canst thou devise
To bring her to these longing eyes?'
To him by toil and sorrow tried
The prudent Lakshmaṇ thus replied:
'Come, though our labour yet be vain,
And search through Janasthán again,—
A realm where giant foes abound.
And trees and creepers hide the ground.
For there are caverns deep and dread,
By deer and wild birds tenanted,
And hills with many a dark abyss,
Grotto and rock and precipice.
There bright Gandharvas love to dwell,
And Kinnars in each bosky dell.
With me thy eager search to aid
Be every hill and cave surveyed.
Great chiefs like thee, the best of men,
Endowed with sense and piercing ken,
Though tried by trouble never fail,
Like rooted hills that mock the gale.'
Then Ráma, pierced by anger's sting,
Laid a keen arrow on his string,
And by the faithful Lakshmaṇ's side
Roamed through the forest far and wide.
Jaṭáyus there with blood-drops dyed,
Lying upon the ground he spied,
Huge as a mountain's shattered crest,
Mid all the birds of air the best.
In wrath the mighty bird he eyed,
And thus the chief to Lakshmaṇ cried:
'Ah me, these signs the truth betray;
My darling was the vulture's prey.
Some demon in the bird's disguise
Roams through the wood that round us lies,
On large-eyed Sítá he has fed,
And rests him now with wings outspread.
But my keen shafts, whose flight is true,
Shall pierce the ravenous monster through.'
An arrow on the string he laid,
And rushing near the bird surveyed,
While earth to ocean's distant side
Trembled beneath his furious stride.
With blood and froth on neck and beak
The dying bird essayed to speak,
And with a piteous voice, distressed,
Thus Daśaratha's son addressed:
'She whom like some sweet herb of grace
Thou seekest in this lonely place,
Fair lady, is fierce Rávaṇ's prey,
Who took, beside, my life away.
Lakshmaṇ and thou had parted hence
And left the dame without defence,
I saw her swiftly borne away
By Rávaṇ's might which none could stay.
I hurried to the lady's aid,
I crushed his car and royal shade,
And putting forth my warlike might
Hurled Rávaṇ to the earth in fight.
Here, Ráma, lies his broken bow,
Here lie the arrows of the foe.
There on the ground before thee are
The fragments of his battle car.
There bleeds the driver whom my wings
Beat down with ceaseless buffetings.
When toil my aged strength subdued,
His sword my weary pinions hewed.
Then lifting up the dame he bare
His captive through the fields of air.
Thy vengeful blows from me restrain,
Already by the giant slain.'
When Ráma heard the vulture tell
The tale that proved his love so well,
His bow upon the ground he placed,
And tenderly the bird embraced:
Then to the earth he fell o'erpowered,
And burning tears both brothers showered,
For double pain and anguish pressed
Upon the patient hero's breast.
The solitary bird he eyed
Who in the lone wood gasped and sighed,
And as again his anguish woke
Thus Ráma to his brother spoke:
'Expelled from power the woods I tread
My spouse is lost, the bird is dead.
A fate so sad. I ween, would tame
The vigour of the glorious flame.
If I to cool my fever tried
To cross the deep from side to side,
The sea,—so hard my fate,—would dry
His waters as my feet came nigh.
In all this world there lives not one
So cursed as I beneath the sun;
So strong a net of misery cast
Around me holds the captive fast,
Best of all birds that play the wing,
Loved, honoured by our sire the king,
The vulture, in my fate enwound,
Lies bleeding, dying on the ground.'
Then Ráma and his brother stirred

By pity mourned the royal bird,
And, as their hands his limbs caressed,
Affection for a sire expressed.
And Ráma to his bosom strained
The bird with mangled wings distained,
With crimson blood-drops dyed.
He fell, and shedding many a tear,
'Where is my spouse than life more dear?
Where is my love?' he cried.

CANTO LXIX.

THE DEATH OF JAṬÁYUS.

As Ráma viewed with heart-felt yain
The vulture whom the fiend had slain,
In words with tender love impressed
His brother chief he thus addressed:
'This royal bird with faithful thought
For my advantage strove and fought.
Slain by the fiend in mortal strife
For me he yields his noble life.
See, Lakshmaṇ, how his wounds have bled;
His struggling breath will soon have fled.
Faint is his voice, and near to die,
He scarce can lift his trembling eye.
Jaṭáyus, if thou still can speak,
Give, give the answer that I seek.
The fate of ravished Sítá tell,
And how thy mournful chance befell.
Say why the giant stole my dame:
What have I done that he could blame?
What fault in me has Rávaṇ seen
That he should rob me of my queen?
How looked the lady's moon-bright cheek?
What were the words she found to speak?
His strength, his might, his deeds declare:
And tell the form he loves to wear.
To all my questions make reply:
Where does the giant's dwelling lie?'
The noble bird his glances bent
On Ráma as he made lament,
And in low accents faint and weak
With anguish thus began to speak:
'Fierce Rávaṇ, king of giant race,
Stole Sítá from thy dwelling-place.
He calls his magic art to aid
With wind and cloud and gloomy shade.
When in the fight my power was spent
My wearied wings he cleft and rent.
Then round the dame his arms he threw,
And to the southern region flew.
O Raghu's son, I gasp for breath,
My swimming sight is dim in death.
E'en now before my vision pass
Bright trees of gold with hair of grass.
The hour the impious robber chose
Brings on the thief a flood of woes.
The giant in his haste forgot
'Twas Vinda's hour,[1] or heeded not.
Those robbed at such a time obtain
Their plundered store and wealth again.
He, like a fish that takes the bait,
In briefest time shall meet his fate.
Now be thy troubled heart controlled
And for thy lady's loss consoled,
For thou wilt slay the fiend in fight
And with thy dame have new delight.'
With senses clear, though sorely tried,
The royal vulture thus replied,
While as he sank beneath his pain
Forth rushed the tide of blood again.
'Him,[2] brother of the Lord of Gold,
Viśravas' self begot of old.'
Thus spoke the bird, and stained with gore
Resigned the breath that came no more.
'Speak, speak again!' thus Ráma cried,
With reverent palm to palm applied,
But from the frame the spirit fled
And to the skiey regions sped.
The breath of life had passed away,
Stretched on the ground the body lay.

When Ráma saw the vulture lie,
Huge as a hill, with darksome eye,
With many a poignant woe distressed
His brother chief he thus addressed:
'Amid these haunted shades content
Full many a year this bird has spent.
His life in home of giants passed,
In Daṇḍak wood he dies at last.
The years in lengthened course have fled
Untroubled o'er the vulture's head,
And now he lies in death, for none
The stern decrees of Fate may shun.
See, Lakshmaṇ, how the vulture fell
While for my sake he battled well,
And strove to free with onset bold
My Sítá from the giant's hold.
Supreme amid the vulture kind
His ancient rule the bird resigned,
And conquered in the fruitless strife
Gave for my sake his noble life.
O Lakshmaṇ, many a time we see
Great souls who keep the law's decree,
With whom the weak sure refuge find,
In creatures of inferior kind.
The loss of her, my darling queen,
Strikes with a pang less fiercely keen
Than now this slaughtered bird to see
Who nobly fought and died for me.
As Daśaratha, good and great,
Was glorious in his high estate,
Honoured by all, to all endeared,
So was this royal bird revered.
Bring fuel for the funeral rite;
These hands the solemn fire shall light

[1] From the root *vid*, to find.
[2] Rávaṇ.

And on the burning pyre shall lay
The bird who died for me to-day.
Now on the gathered wood shall lie
The lord of all the birds that fly,
And I will burn with honours due
My champion whom the giant slew.
O royal bird of noblest heart,
Graced with all funeral rites depart
To bright celestial seats above,
Rewarded for thy faithful love.
Dwell in thy happy home with those
Whose constant fires of worship rose.
Live blest amid the unyielding brave,
And those who land in largess gave.'
  Sore grief upon his bosom weighed
As on the pyre the bird he laid,
And bade the kindled flame ascend
To burn the body of his friend.
Then with his brother by his side
The hero to the forest hied.
There many a stately deer he slew,
The flesh around the bird to strew.
The venison into balls he made,
And on fair grass before him laid.
Then that the parted soul might rise
And find free passage to the skies,
Each solemn word and text he said
Which Bráhmans utter o'er the dead.
Then hastening went the princely pair
To bright Godávarí, and there
Libations of the stream they poured
In honour of the vulture lord,
With solemn ritual to the slain,
As scripture's holy texts ordain.
Thus offerings to the bird they gave
And bathed their bodies in the wave.
  The vulture monarch having wrought
  A hard and glorious feat,
Honoured by Ráma sage in thought,
  Soared to his blissful seat.
The brothers, when each rite was paid
  To him of birds supreme,
Their hearts with new-found comfort stayed,
  And turned them from the stream.
Like sovereigns of celestial race
  Within the wood they came,
Each pondering the means to trace,
  The captor of the dame.

CANTO LXX.

KABANDHA.

When every rite was duly paid
The princely brothers onward strayed,
An eager in the lady's quest
They turned their footsteps to the west.
Through lonely woods that round them lay
Ikshváku's children made their way,
And armed with bow and shaft and brand
Pressed onward to the southern land.
Thick trees and shrubs and creepers grew
In the wild grove they hurried through.
'Twas dark and drear and hard to pass
For tangled thorns and matted grass.
Still onward with a southern course
They made their way with vigorous force,
And passing through the mazes stood
Beyond that vast and fearful wood.
With toil and hardship yet unspent
Three leagues from Janasthán they went,
And speeding on their way at last
Within the wood of Krauncha[1] passed:
A fearful forest wild and black
As some huge pile of cloudy rack,
Filled with all birds and beasts, where grew
Bright blooms of every varied hue.
On Sítá bending every thought
Through all the mighty wood they sought,
And at the lady's loss dismayed
Here for a while and there they stayed.
Then turning farther eastward they
Pursued three leagues their weary way,
Passed Krauncha's wood and reached the grove
Where elephants rejoiced to rove.
The chiefs that awful wood surveyed
Where deer and wild birds filled each glade,
Where scarce a step the foot could take
For tangled shrub and tree and brake.
There in a mountain's woody side
A cave the royal brothers spied,
With dread abysses deep as hell,
Where darkness never ceased to dwell.
When, pressing on, the lords of men
Stood near the entrance of the den,
They saw within the dark recess
A huge misshapen giantess;
A thing the timid heart that shook
With fearful shape and savage look.
Terrific fiend, her voice was fierce,
Long were her teeth to rend and pierce.
The monster gorged her horrid feast
Of flesh of many a savage beast,
While her long locks, at random flung,
Dishevelled o'er her shoulders hung.
Their eyes the royal brothers raised,
And on the fearful monster gazed.
Forth from her den she came and glanced
At Lakshmaṇ as he first advanced,
Her eager arms to hold him spread,
And 'Come and be my love' she said,
Then as she held him to her breast,
The prince in words like these addressed:
'Behold thy treasure fond and fair:
Ayomukhí[2] the name I bear.

[1] Or Curlews' Wood.

[2] Iron-faced.

In thickets of each lofty hill,
On islets of each brook and rill,
With me delighted shalt thou play,
And live for many a lengthened day.'
Enraged he heard the monster woo;
His ready sword he swiftly drew,
And the sharp steel that quelled his foes
Cut through her breast and ear and nose.
Thus mangled by his vengeful sword
In rage and pain the demon roared,
And hideous with her awful face
Sped to her secret dwelling place.
Soon as the fiend had fled from sight,
The brothers, dauntless in their might,
Reached a wild forest dark and dread
Whose tangled ways were hard to tread.
Then bravest Lakshman, virtuous youth,
The friend of purity and truth,
With reverent palm to palm applied
Thus to his glorious brother cried:
'My arm presaging throbs amain,
My troubled heart is sick with pain,
And cheerless omens ill portend
Where'er my anxious eyes I bend.
Dear brother, hear my words: advance
Resolved and armed for every chance,
For every sign I mark to-day
Foretells a peril in the way.
This bird of most ill-omened note,
Loud screaming with discordant throat,
Announces with a warning cry
That strife and victory are nigh.'
Then as the chiefs their search pursued
Throughout the dreary solitude,
They heard amazed a mighty sound
That broke the very trees around.
As though a furious tempest passed
Crushing the wood beneath its blast.
Then Ráma raised his trusty sword,
And both the hidden cause explored.
There stood before their wondering eyes
A fiend broad-chested, huge of size.
A vast misshapen trunk they saw
In height surpassing nature's law.
It stood before them dire and dread
Without a neck, without a head.
Tall as some hill aloft in air,
Its limbs were clothed with bristling hair,
And deep below the monster's waist
His vast misshapen mouth was placed.
His form was huge, his voice was loud
As some dark-tinted thunder cloud.
Forth from his ample chest there came
A brilliance as of gushing flame.
Beneath long lashes, dark and keen
The monster's single eye was seen.
Deep in his chest, long, fiercely bright,
It glittered with terrific light.
He swallowed down his savage fare
Of lion, bird, and slaughtered bear,
And with huge teeth exposed to view
O'er his great lips his tongue he drew.
His arms unshapely, vast and dread,
A league in length, he raised and spread.
He seized with monstrous hands a herd
Of deer and many a bear and bird.
Among them all he picked and chose,
Drew forward these, rejected those.
Before the princely pair he stood
Barring their passage through the wood.
A league of shade the chiefs had passed
When on the fiend their eyes they cast.
A monstrous shape without a head
With mighty arms before him spread,
They saw that hideous trunk appear
That struck the trembling eye with fear.
Then, stretching to their full extent
His awful arms with fingers bent,
Round Raghu's princely sons he cast
Each grasping limb and held them fast.
Though strong of arm and fierce in fight,
Each armed with bow and sword to smite,
The royal brothers, brave and bold,
Were helpless in the giant's hold.
Then Raghu's son, heroic still,
Felt not a pang his bosom thrill;
But young, with no protection near,
His brother's heart was sad with fear,
And thus with trembling tongue he said
To Ráma, sore disquieted:
'Ah me, ah me, my days are told:
O see me in the giant's hold.
Fly, son of Raghu, swiftly flee,
And thy dear self from danger free.
Me to the fiend an offering give;
Fly at thine ease thyself and live.
Thou, great Kakutstha's son, I ween,
Wilt find ere long thy Maithil queen,
And when thou holdest, throned again,
Thine old hereditary reign.
With servants prompt to do thy will,
O think upon thy brother still.'
As thus the trembling Lakshman cried,
The dauntless Ráma thus replied;
'Brother, from causeless dread forbear.
A chief like thee should scorn despair.'
He spoke to soothe his wild alarm;
Then fierce Kabandha[1] long of arm,
Among the Dánavs[2] first and best,
The sons of Raghu thus addressed:
'What men are you, whose shoulders show
Broad as a bull's, with sword and bow,
Who roam this dark and horrid place,
Brought by your fate before my face?
Declare by what occasion led
These solitary wilds you tread,
With swords and bows and shafts to pierce,

[1] Kabandha means a trunk.

[2] A class of mythological giants. In the Epic period they were probably personifications of the aborigines of India.

Like bulls whose horns are strong and fierce.
Why have you sought this forest land
Where wild with hunger's pangs I stand?
Now as your steps my path have crossed
Esteem your lives already lost.'
The royal brothers heard with dread
The words which fierce Kabandha said.
And Ráma to his brother cried,
Whose cheek by blanching fear was dried.
'Alas, we fall, O valiant chief,
From sorrow into direr grief.
Still mourning her I hold so dear
We see our own destruction near.
Mark, brother, mark what power has time
O'er all that live, in every clime.
Now, lord of men, thyself and me
Involved in fatal danger see.
'Tis not, be sure, the might of Fate
That crushes all with deadly weight.
Ne'er can the brave and strong, who know
The use of spear and sword and bow,
The force of conquering time withstand,
But fall like barriers built of sand.'
Thus in calm strength which naught could shake
The son of Daśaratha spake,
With glory yet unstained
Upon Sumitrá's son he bent
His eyes, and firm in his intent
His dauntless heart maintained.

CANTO LXXI.

KABANDHA'S SPEECH.

Kabandha saw each chieftain stand
Imprisoned by his mighty hand,
Which like a snare around him pressed
And thus the royal pair addressed:
'Why, warriors, are your glances bent
On me whom hungry pangs torment?
Why stand with wildered senses? Fate
Has brought you now my maw to sate.'
When Lakshmaṇ heard, a while appalled,
His ancient courage he recalled,
And to his brother by his side
With seasonable counsel cried:
'This vilest of the giant race
Will draw us to his side apace.
Come, rouse thee; let the vengeful sword
Smite off his arms, my honoured lord.
This awful giant, vast of size,
On his huge strength of arm relies,
And o'er the world victorious, thus
With mighty force would slaughter us.
But in cold blood to slay, O King,
Discredit on the brave would bring,
As when some victim in the rite
Shuns not the hand upraised to smite.'
The monstrous fiend, to anger stirred,
The converse of the brothers heard.
His horrid mouth he opened wide
And drew the princes to his side.
They, skilled due time and place to note,
Unsheathed their glittering swords and smote,
Till from the giant's shoulders they
Had hewn the mighty arms away.
His trenchant falchion Ráma plied
And smote him on the better side,
While valiant Lakshmaṇ on the left
The arm that held him prisoned cleft.
Then to the earth dismembered fell
The monster with a hideous yell,
And like a cloud's his deep roar went
Through earth and air and firmament.
Then as the giant's blood flowed fast,
On his cleft limbs his eye he cast,
And called upon the princely pair
Their names and lineage to declare.
Him then the noble Lakshmaṇ, blest
With fortune's favouring marks, addressed,
And told the fiend his brother's name
And the high blood of which he came:
'Ikshváku's heir here Ráma stands,
Illustrious through a hundred lands.
I, younger brother of the heir,
O fiend, the name of Lakshmaṇ bear.
His mother stole his realm away
And drove him forth in woods to stray.
Thus through the mighty forest he
Roamed with his royal wife and me.
While glorious as a God he made
His dwelling in the greenwood shade,
Some giant stole away his dame,
And seeking her we hither came.
But tell me who thou art, and why
With headless trunk that towered so high.
With flaming face beneath thy chest,
Thou liest crushed, in wild unrest.'
He heard the words that Lakshmaṇ spoke,
And memory in his breast awoke,
Recalling Indra's words to mind
He spoke in gentle tones and kind:
'O welcome, best of men, are ye
Whom, blest by fate, this day I see.
A blessing on each trenchant blade
That low on earth these arms has laid!
Thou, lord of men, incline thine ear
The story of my woe to hear,
While I the rebel pride declare
Which doomed me to the form I wear.'

CANTO LXXII.

KABANDHA'S TALE.

'Lord of the mighty arm, of yore
A shape transcending thought I wore,
And through the triple world's extent
My fame for might and valour went.

Scarce might the sun and moon on high,
Scarce Śakra, with my beauty vie.
Then for a time this form I took,
And the great world with trembling shook.
The saints in forest shades who dwelt
The terror of my presence felt.
But once I stirred to furious rage
Great Sthúlaśiras, glorious sage.
Culling in woods his hermit food
My hideous shape with fear he viewed.
Then forth his words of anger burst
That bade me live a thing accursed:
'Thou, whose delight is others' pain,
This grisly form shalt still retain.'
Then when I prayed him to relent
And fix some term of punishment,—
Prayed that the curse at length might cease,
He bade me thus expect release:
'Let Ráma cleave thine arms away
And on the pyre thy body lay,
And then shalt thou, set free from doom,
Thine own fair shape once more assume.'
O Lakshman, hear my words: in me
The world-illustrious Danu see.
By Indra's curse, subdued in fight,
I wear this form which scares the sight.
By sternest penance long maintained
The mighty Father's grace I gained.
When length of days the God bestowed,
With foolish pride my bosom glowed.
My life, of lengthened years assured,
I deemed from Śakra's might secured.
Let by my senseless pride astray
I challenged Indra to the fray.
A flaming bolt with many a knot
With his terrific arm he shot,
And straight my head and thighs compressed
Were buried in my bulky chest.
Deaf to each prayer and piteous call
He sent me not to Yama's hall.
'Thy prayers and cries,' he said, 'are vain;
The Father's word must true remain.'
'But how may lengthened life be spent
By one thy bolt has torn and rent?
How can I live,' I cried, 'unfed,
With shattered face and thighs and head?'
As thus I spoke his grace to crave,
Arms each a league in length he gave,
And opened in my chest beneath
This mouth supplied with fearful teeth.
So my huge arms I used to cast
Round woodland creatures as they passed,
And fed within the forest here
On lion, tiger, pard, and deer.
Then Indra spake to soothe my grief:
'When Ráma and his brother chief
From thy huge bulk those arms shall cleave,
Then shall the skies thy soul receive.'
Disguised in this terrific shape
I let no woodland thing escape,
And still my longing soul was pleased
Whene'er my arms a victim seized,
For in these arms I fondly thought
Would Ráma's self at last be caught.
Thus hoping, toiling many a day
I yearned to cast my life away,
And here, my lord, thou standest now:
Blessings be thine! for none but thou
Could cleave my arms with trenchant stroke:
True are the words the hermit spoke.
Now let me, best of warriors, lend
My counsel, and thy plans befriend,
And aid thee with advice in turn
If thou with fire my corse wilt burn.'
As thus the mighty Danu prayed
With offer of his friendly aid,
While Lakshman gazed with anxious eye,
The virtuous Ráma made reply:
'Lakshmaṇ and I through forest shade
From Janasthán a while had strayed.
When none was near her, Rávaṇ came
And bore away my glorious dame.
The giant's form and size unknown,
I learn as yet his name alone.
Not yet the power and might we know
Or dwelling of the monstrous foe.
With none our helpless feet to guide
We wander here by sorrow tried.
Let pity move thee to requite
Our service in the funeral rite.
Our hands shall bring the boughs that, dry
Where elephants have rent them, lie,
Then dig a pit, and light the fire
To burn thee as the laws require.
Do thou as meed of this declare
Who stole my spouse, his dwelling where.
O, if thou can, I pray thee say,
And let this grace our deeds repay.'
Danu had lent attentive ear
The words which Ráma spoke to hear,
And thus, a speaker skilled and tried,
To that great orator replied:
'No heavenly lore my soul endows,
Naught know I of thy Maithil spouse.
Yet will I, when my shape I wear,
Him who will tell thee all declare.
Then, Ráma, will my lips disclose
His name who well that giant knows.
But till the flames my corse devour
This hidden knowledge mocks my power.'
For through that curse's withering taint
My knowledge now is small and faint.
Unknown the giant's very name
Who bore away the Maithil dame.
Cursed for my evil deeds I wore
A shape which all the worlds abhor.
Now ere with wearied steeds the sun
Through western skies his course have run,
Deep in a pit my body lay

And burn it in the wonted way.
When in the grave my corse is placed,
With fire and funeral honours graced,
Then I, great chief, his name will tell
Who knows the giant robber well.
With him, who guides his life aright,
In league of trusting love unite,
And he, O valiant prince, will be
A faithful friend and aid to thee.
For, Ráma, to his searching eyes
The triple world uncovered lies.
For some dark cause of old, I ween,
Through all the spheres his ways have been.'

CANTO LXXIII.

KABANDHA'S COUNSEL.

The monster ceased: the princely pair
Heard great Kabandha's eager prayer.
Within a mountain cave they sped,
Where kindled fire with care they fed.
Then Lakshman in his mighty hands
Brought ample store of lighted brands,
And to a pile of logs applied
The flame that ran from side to side.
The spreading glow with gentle force
Consumed Kabandha's mighty corse,
Till the unresting flames had drunk
The marrow of the monstrous trunk,
As balls of butter melt away
Amid the fires that o'er them play.
Then from the pyre, like flame that glows
Undimmed by cloudy smoke, he rose,
In garments pure of spot or speck,
A heavenly wreath about his neck.
Resplendent in his bright attire
He sprang exultant from the pyre.
While from neck, arm, and foot was sent
The flash of gold and ornament.
High on a chariot, bright of hue,
Which swans of fairest pinion drew,
He filled each region of the air
With splendid glow reflected there.
Then in the sky he stayed his car
And called to Ráma from afar:
'Hear, chieftain, while my lips explain
The means to win thy spouse again.
Six plans, O prince, the wise pursue
To reach the aims we hold in view.[1]
When evils ripening sorely press
They load the wretch with new distress.
So thou and Lakshman, tried by woe,
Have felt at last a fiercer blow,
And plunged in bitterest grief to-day
Lament thy consort torn away.
There is no course but this: attend;
Make, best of friends, that chief thy friend.
Unless his prospering help thou gain
Thy plans and hopes must all be vain.
O Ráma, hear my words, and seek,
Sugríva, for of him I speak.
His brother Báli, Indra's son,
Expelled him when the fight was won.
With four great chieftains, faithful still,
He dwells on Rishyamúka's hill,—
Fair mountain, lovely with the flow
Of Pampá's waves that glide below,—
Lord of the Vánars[1] just and true,
Strong, very glorious, bright to view,
Unmatched in counsel, firm and meek,
Bound by each word his lips may speak,
Good, splendid, mighty, bold and brave,
Wise in each plan to guide and save.
His brother, fired by lust of sway,
Drove forth the prince in woods to stray.
In all thy search for Sítá he
Thy ready friend and help will be.
With him to aid thee in thy quest
Dismiss all sorrow from thy breast.
Time is a mighty power, and none
His fixed decree can change or shun.
So rich reward thy toil shall bless,
And naught can stay thy sure success.
Speed hence, O chief, without delay,
To strong Sugríva take thy way.
This hour thy footsteps onward bend,
And make that mighty prince thy friend.
With him before the attesting flame
In solemn truth alliance frame.
Nor wilt thou, if thy heart be wise,
Sugríva, Vánar king, despise.
Of boundless strength, all shapes he wears,
He hearkens to a suppliant's prayers,
And, grateful for each kindly deed,
Will help and save in hour of need.
And you, I ween, the power possess
To aid his hopes and give redress.
He, let his cause succeed or fail,
Will help you, and you must prevail.
A banished prince, in fear and woe
He roams where Pampá's waters flow,
True offspring of the Lord of Light
Expelled by Báli's conquering might.
Go, Raghu's son, that chieftain seek
Who dwells on Rishyamúka's peak.
Before the flame thy weapons cast
And bind the bonds of friendship fast.
For, prince of all the Vánar race,
He in his wisdom knows each place
Where dwell the fierce gigantic brood
Who make the flesh of man their food.
To him, O Raghu's son, to him
Naught in the world is dark or dim,
Where'er the mighty Day-God gleams
Resplendent with a thousand beams.

---

1 Peace, war, marching, halting, sowing dissensions, and seeking protection.

1 See Book I, Canto XVI.

He over rocky height and hill,
Through gloomy cave, by lake and rill,
Will with his Vánars seek the prize,
And tell thee where thy lady lies.
And he will send great chieftains forth
To east and west and south and north,
To seek the distant spot where she
All desolate laments for thee.
He even in Rávaṇ's halls would find
Thy Sítá, gem of womankind.
Yea, if the blameless lady lay
On Meru's loftiest steep,
Or, far removed from light of day,
Where hell is dark and deep,
That chief of all the Vánar race
His way would still explore,
Meet the cowed giants face to face
And thy dear spouse restore.'

CANTO LXXIV.

KABANDHA'S DEATH.

When wise Kabandha thus had taught
The means to find the dame they sought,
And urged them onward in the quest,
He thus again the prince addressed:
'This path, O Raghu's son, pursue
Where those fair trees which charm the view,
Extending westward far away,
The glory of their bloom display,
Where their bright leaves Rose-apples show,
And the tall Jak and Mango grow.
Whene'er you will, those trees ascend,
Or the long branches shake and bend.
Their savoury fruit like Amrit eat,
Then onward speed with willing feet.
Beyond this shady forest, decked
With flowering trees, your course direct.
Another grove you then will find
With every joy to take the mind,
Like Nandan with its charms displayed,
Or Northern Kuru's blissful shade;
Where trees distil their balmy juice,
And fruit through all the year produce;
Whose shades with seasons ever fair
With Chaitraratha may compare;
Where trees whose sprays with fruit are bowed
Rise like a mountain or a cloud.
There, when you list, from time to time,
The loaded trees may Lakshmaṇ climb,
Or from the shaken boughs supply
Sweet fruit that may with Amrit vie.
The onward path pursuing still
From wood to wood, from hill to hill,
Your happy eyes at length will rest
On Pampá's lotus-covered breast.
Her banks with gentle slope descend,
Nor stones nor weed the eyes offend,
And o'er smooth beds of silver sand
Lotus and lily blooms expand.
There swans and ducks and curlews play,
And keen-eyed ospreys watch their prey,
And from the limpid waves are heard
Glad notes of many a water-bird.
Untaught a deadly foe to fear
They fly not when a man is near,
And fat as balls of butter they
Will, when you list, your hunger stay.
Then Lakshmaṇ with his shafts will take
The fish that swim the brook and lake,
Remove each bone and scale and fin,
Or strip away the speckled skin,
And then on iron skewers broil
For thy repast the savoury spoil.
Thou on a heap of flowers shalt rest
And eat the meal his hands have dressed.
There shalt thou lie on Pampá's brink,
And Lakshmaṇ's hand shall give thee drink,
Filling a lotus leaf with cool
Pure water from the crystal pool,
To which the opening blooms have lent
The riches of divinest scent.
Beside thee at the close of day
Will Lakshmaṇ through the woodland stray,
And show thee where the monkeys sleep
In caves beneath the mountain steep.
Lurd-voiced as bulls they forth will burst
And seek the flood, oppressed by thirst;
Then rest a while, their wants supplied,
Their well-fed bands on Pampá's side.
Thou roving there at eve shalt see
Rich clusters hang on shrub and tree,
And Pampá flushed with roseate glow,
And at the view forget thy woe.
There shalt thou mark with strange delight
Each loveliest flower that blooms by night,
While lily buds that shrink from day
Their tender loveliness display.
In that far wild no hand but thine
Those peerless flowers in wreaths shall twine:
Immortal in their changeless pride,
Ne'er fade those blooms and ne'er are dried.
There erst on holy thoughts intent
Their days Matanga's pupils spent.
Once for their master food they sought,
And store of fruit and berries brought.
Then as they laboured through the dell
From limb and brow the heat-drops fell:
Thence sprang and bloomed those wondrous trees;
Such holy power have devotees.
Thus, from the hermits' heat-drops sprung,
Their growth is ever fresh and young.
There Śavarí is dwelling yet,
Who served each vanished anchoret.

Beneath the shade of holy boughs
That ancient votaress keeps her vows.
Her happy eyes on thee will fall,
O godlike prince, adored by all,
And she, whose life is pure from sin,
A blissful seat in heaven will win.
But cross, O son of Raghu, o'er,
And stand on Pampá's western shore.
A tranquil hermitage that lies
Deep in the woods will meet thine eyes,
No wandering elephants invade
The stillness of that holy shade,
But checked by saint Matanga's power
They spare each consecrated bower.
Through many an age those trees have stood
World-famous as Matanga's wood.
Still, Raghu's son, pursue thy way:
Through shades where birds are vocal stray,
Fair as the blessed wood where rove
Immortal Gods, or Nandan's grove.
Near Pampá eastward, full in sight,
Stands Rishyamúka's wood-crowned height.
'Tis hard to climb that towering steep
Where serpents unmolested sleep.
The free and bounteous, formed of old
By Brahmá of superior mould,
Who sink when day is done to rest
Reclining on that mountain crest,—
What wealth or joy in dreams they view,
Awaking find the vision true.
But if a villain stained with crime
That holy hill presume to climb,
The giants in their fury sweep
From the hill top the wretch asleep.
There loud and long is heard the roar
Of elephants on Pampá's shore,
Who near Matanga's dwelling stray
And in those waters bathe and play.
A while they revel by the flood,
Their temples stained with streams like blood,
Then wander far away dispersed,
Dark as huge clouds before they burst.
But ere they part they drink their fill
Of bright pure water from the rill,
Delightful to the touch, where meet
Scents of all flowers divinely sweet,
Then speeding from the river side
Deep in the sheltering thicket hide.
Then bears and tigers shalt thou view
Whose soft skins show the sapphire's hue,
And silvan deer that wander nigh
Shall harmless from thy presence fly.
High in that mountains wooded side
Is a fair cavern deep and wide,
Yet hard to enter: piles of rock
The portals of the cavern block.[1]
Fast by the eastern door a pool
Gleams with broad waters fresh and cool,
Where stores of roots and fruit abound,
And thick trees shade the grassy ground.
This mountain cave the virtuous-souled
Sugríva and his Vánars hold,
And oft the mighty chieftain seeks
The summits of those towering peaks.'
Thus spake Kabandha high in air
His counsel to the royal pair.
Still on his neck that wreath he bore,
And radiance like the sun's he wore.
Their eyes the princely brothers raised
And on that blissful being gazed:
'Behold, we go: no more delay;
Begin,' they cried, 'thy heavenward way.'
'Depart,' Kabandha's voice replied,
'Pursue your search, and bliss betide.'
Thus to the happy chiefs he said,
Then on his heavenward journey sped.
Thus once again Kabandha won
A shape that glittered like the sun
Without a spot or stain.
Thus bade he Ráma from the air
To great Sugríva's side repair
His friendly love to gain.

CANTO LXXV.

ŚAVARÍ.

Thus counselled by their friendly guide
On through the wood the princes hied,
Pursuing still the eastern road
To Pampá which Kabandha showed,
Where trees that on the mountains grew
With fruit like honey charmed the view.
They rested weary for the night
Upon a mountain's wooded height,
Then onward with the dawn they hied
And stood on Pampá's western side,
Where Śavarí's fair home they viewed
Deep in that shady solitude.
The princes reached the holy ground
Where noble trees stood thick around,
And joying in the lovely view
Near to the aged votaress drew.
To meet the sons of Raghu came,
With hands upraised, the pious dame,
And bending low with reverence meet
Welcomed them both and pressed their feet.
Then water, as beseems, she gave,
Their lips to cool, their feet to lave.
To that pure saint who never broke
One law of duty Ráma spoke:
'I trust no cares invade thy peace,
While holy works and zeal increase;
That thou content with scanty food
All touch of ire hast long subdued;
That all thy vows are well maintained

[1] Or as the commentator Tírtha says, Śilápidháná, rock-covered, may be the name of the cavern.

While peace of mind is surely gained:
That reverence of the saints who taught
Thy faithful heart due fruit has brought.'
The aged votaress pure of taint,
Revered by every perfect saint,
Rose to her feet by Ráma's side
And thus in gentle tones replied:
'My penance' meed this day I see
Complete, my lord, in meeting thee.
This day the fruit of birth I gain,
Nor have I served the saints in vain.
I reap rich fruits of toil and vow,
And heaven itself awaits me now,
When I, O chief of men, have done
Honour to thee the godlike one.
I feel, great lord, thy gentle eye
My earthly spirit purify,
And I, brave tamer of thy foes,
Shall through thy grace in bliss repose.
Thy feet by Chitrakúṭa strayed
When those great saints whom I obeyed,
In dazzling chariots bright of hue,
Hence to their heavenly mansions flew.
As the high saints were borne away
I heard their holy voices say:
'In this pure grove, O devotee,
Prince Ráma soon will visit thee.
When he and Lakshmaṇ seek this shade,
Be to thy guests all honour paid.
Him shalt thou see, and pass away
To those blest worlds which ne'er decay.'
To me, O mighty chief, the best
Of lofty saints these words addressed.
Laid up within my dwelling lie
Fruits of each sort which woods supply,—
Food culled for thee in endless store
From every tree on Pampá's shore.'
Thus to her virtuous guest she sued
And he, with heavenly lore endued,
Words such as these in turn addressed
To her with equal knowledge blest:
'Danu himself the power has told
Of thy great masters lofty-souled.
Now, if thou will, mine eyes would fain
Assurance of their glories gain.'
She heard the prince his wish declare:
Then rose she, and the royal pair
Of brothers through the wood she led
That round her holy dwelling spread.
'Behold Matanga's wood,' she cried,
'A grove made famous far and wide.
Dark as thick clouds and filled with herds
Of wandering deer, and joyous birds.
In this pure spot each reverend sire
With offerings fed the holy fire.
See, here the western altar stands
Where daily with their trembling hands
The aged saints, so long obeyed
By me, their gifts of blossoms laid.
The holy power, O Raghu's son,
By their ascetic virtue won,
Still keeps their well-loved altar bright,
Filling the air with beams of light.
And those seven neighbouring lakes behold
Which, when the saints infirm and old,
Worn out by fasts, no longer sought,
Moved hither drawn by power of thought.
Look, Ráma, where the devotees
Hung their bark mantles on the trees,
Fresh from the bath: those garments wet
Through many a day are dripping yet.
See, through those aged hermits' power
The tender spray, the bright-hued flower
With which the saints their worship paid,
Fresh to this hour nor change nor fade.
Here thou hast seen each lawn and dell,
And heard the tale I had to tell:
Permit thy servant, lord, I pray,
To cast this mortal shell away,
For I would dwell, this life resigned,
With those great saints of lofty mind,
Whom I within this holy shade
With reverential care obeyed.'
When Ráma and his brother heard
The pious prayer the dame preferred,
Filled full of transport and amazed
They marvelled as her words they praised.
Then Ráma to the votaress said
Whose holy vows were perfected:
'Go, lady, where thou fain wouldst be,
O thou who well hast honoured me.'
Her locks in hermit fashion tied,
Clad in bark coat and black deer's hide,
When Ráma gave consent, the dame
Resigned her body to the flame.
Then, like the fire that burns and glows,
To heaven the sainted lady rose,
In all her heavenly garments dressed,
Immortal wreaths on neck and breast,
Bright with celestial gems she shone
Most beautiful to look upon,
And like the flame of lightning sent
A glory through the firmament.
That holy sphere the dame attained,
By depth of contemplation gained,
Where roam high saints with spirits pure
In bliss that shall for aye endure.

CANTO LXXVI.

PAMPÁ.

When Śavarí had sought the skies
And gained her splendid virtue's prize,
Ráma with Lakshmaṇ stayed to brood
O'er the strange scenes their eyes had viewed.
His mind upon those saints was bent,
For power and might preëminent.
And he to musing Lakshmaṇ spoke
The thoughts that in his bosom woke:

'Mine eyes this wondrous home have viewed
Of those great saints with souls subdued,
Where peaceful tigers dwell and birds,
And deer abound in heedless herds.
Our feet upon the banks have stood
Of those seven lakes within the wood,
Where we have duly dipped, and paid
Libations to each royal shade.
Forgotten now are thoughts of ill
And joyful hopes my bosom fill.
Again my heart is light and gay
And grief and care have passed away.
Come, brother, let us hasten where
Bright Pampá's flood is fresh and fair,
And towering in their beauty near
Mount Rishyamúka's heights appear,
Which, offspring of the Lord of Light,
Still fearing Báli's conquering might,
With four brave chiefs of Vánar race
Sugríva makes his dwelling-place.
I long with eager heart to find
That leader of the Vánar kind,
For on that chief my hopes depend
That this our quest have prosperous end.'
Thus Ráma spoke, in battle tried,
And thus Sumitrá's son replied:
'Come, brother, come, and speed away:
My spirit brooks no more delay.'
Thus spake Sumitrá's son, and then
Forth from the grove the king of men
With his dear brother by his side
To Pampá's lucid waters hied.
He gazed upon the woods where grew
Trees rich in flowers of every hue.
From brake and dell on every side
The curlew and the peacock cried,
And flocks of screaming parrots made
Shrill music in the bloomy shade.
His eager eyes, as on he went,
On many a pool and tree were bent.
Inflamed with love he journeyed on
Till a fair flood before him shone.
He stood upon the water's side
Which streams from distant hills supplied:
Matanga's name that water bore:
There bathed he from the shelving shore.
Then, each on earnest thoughts intent,
Still farther on their way they went.
But Ráma's heart once more gave way
Beneath his grief and wild dismay.
Before him lay the noble flood
Adorned with many a lotus bud.
On its fair banks Ásokas glowed,
And all bright trees their blossoms showed.
Green banks that silver waves confined
With lovely groves were fringed and lined.
The crystal waters in their flow
Showed level sands that gleamed below.
There glittering fish and tortoise played,
And bending trees gave pleasant shade.
There creepers on the branches hung
With lover-like embraces clung.
There gay Gandharvas loved to meet
And Kinnar sought the calm retreat.
There wandering Yakshas found delight,
Snake-gods and rovers of the night.
Cool were the pleasant waters, gay
Each tree with creeper, flower, and spray.
There flushed the lotus darkly red,
Here their white glory lilies spread,
Here sweet buds showed their tints of blue:
So carpets gleam with many a hue.
A grove of Mangoes blossomed nigh,
Echoing with the peacock's cry.
When Ráma by his brother's side
The lovely flood of Pampá eyed,
Decked like a beauty, fair to see
With every charm of flower and tree,
His mighty heart with woe was rent
And thus he spoke in wild lament:
'Here, Lakshman, on this beauteous shore,
Stands, dyed with tints of many an ore,
The mountain Rishyamúka bright
With flowery trees that crown each height.
Sprung from the chief who, famed of yore,
The name of Riksharajas bore,
Sugríva, chieftain strong and dread,
Dwells on that mountain's towering head.
Go to him, best of men, and seek
That prince of Vánars on the peak,
I cannot longer brook my pain,
Or, Sítá lost, my life retain.'
Thus by the pangs of love distressed,
His thoughts on Sítá bent,
His faithful brother he addressed,
And cried in wild lament.
He reached the lovely ground that lay
On Pampá's wooded side,
And told in anguish and dismay,
The grief he could not hide.
With listless footsteps faint and slow
His way the chief pursued,
Till Pampá with her glorious show
Of flowering woods he viewed.
Through shades were every bird was found
The prince with Lakshman passed,
And Pampá with her groves around
Burst on his eyes at last.

BOOK IV.[1]

CANTO I.

RÁMA'S LAMENT.

The princes stood by Pampá's side[2]
Which blooming lilies glorified.
With troubled heart and sense o'erthrown
There Ráma made his piteous moan.
As the fair flood before him lay
The reason of the chief gave way;
And tender thoughts within him woke,
As to Sumitrá's son he spoke:
'How lovely Pampá's waters show,
Where streams of lucid crystal flow!
What glorious trees o'erhang the flood
Which blooms of opening lotus stud!
Look on the banks of Pampá where
Thick groves extend divinely fair;
And piles of trees, like hills in size,
Lift their proud summits to the skies.
But thought of Bharat's[3] pain and toil,
And my dear spouse the giant's spoil,
Afflict my tortured heart and press
My spirit down with heaviness.
Still fair to me though sunk in woe
Bright Pampá and her forest show,
Where cool fresh waters charm the sight,
And flowers of every hue are bright.
The lotuses in close array
Their passing loveliness display,
And pard and tiger, deer and snake
Haunt every glade and dell and brake.
Those grassy spots display the hue
Of topazes and sapphires' blue,
And, gay with flowers of every dye,
With richly broidered housings vie.
What loads of bloom the high trees crown,
Or weigh the bending branches down!
And creepers tipped with bud and flower
Each spray and loaded limb o'erpower.
Now cool delicious breezes blow,
And kindle love's voluptuous glow,
When balmy sweetness fills the air,
And fruit and flowers and trees are fair.
Those waving woods, that shine with bloom,
Each varied tint in turn assume.
Like labouring clouds they pour their showers
In rain of ever-changing flowers.
Behold, those forest trees, that stand
High upon rock and table-land,
As the cool gales their branches bend,
Their floating blossoms downward send.
See, Lakshman, how the breezes play
With every floweret on the spray,
And sport in merry guise with all
The fallen blooms and those that fall.
See, brother, where the merry breeze
Shakes the gay boughs of flowery trees,
Disturbed amid their toil a throng
Of bees pursue him, loud in song.
The Koïls,[1] mad with sweet delight,
The bending trees to dance invite;
And in its joy the wild wind sings
As from the mountain cave he springs.
On speed the gales in rapid course,
And bend the woods beneath their force,
Till every branch and spray they bind
In many a tangled knot entwined.
What balmy sweets those gales dispense
With cool and sacred influence!
Fatigue and trouble vanish: such
The magic of their gentle touch.
Hark, when the gale the boughs has bent
In woods of honey redolent,
Through all their quivering sprays the trees
Are vocal with the murmuring bees.
The hills with towering summits rise,
And with their beauty charm the eyes,
Gay with the giant trees which bright
With blossom spring from every height:
And as the soft wind gently sways
The clustering blooms that load the sprays,
The very trees break forth and sing
With startled wild bees' murmuring.
Thine eyes to yonder Cassias[2] turn
Whose glorious clusters glow and burn.

---

[1] Or Kishkindhá Káṇda. Kishkindhá, the city of Báli the elder brother and enemy of Sugríva, is supposed to have been situated north of Mysore.

[2] Pampá is said by the commentator to be the name both of a lake and a brook which flows into it. The brook is said to rise in the hill Rishyamúka.

[3] Who was acting as Regent for Ráma and leading an ascetic life while he mourned for his absent brother.

[1] The Indian Cuckoo.

[2] The Cassia Fistula or Amaltás is a splendid tree like a giant laburnum covered with a profusion of chains and tassels of gold. Dr. Roxburgh well describes it as "uncommonly beautiful when in flower, few trees surpassing it in the elegance of its numerous long pendulous racemes of large bright-yellow flowers intermixed with the young lively green foliage." It is remarkable also for its curious cylindrical black seed-pods about two feet long, which are called monkeys' walking-sticks.

Those trees in yellow robes behold,
Like giants decked with burnished gold.
Ah me, Sumitrá's son, the spring,
Dear to sweet birds who love and sing,
Wakes in my lonely breast the flame
Of sorrow as I mourn my dame.
Love strikes me through with darts of fire,
And wakes in vain the sweet desire.
Hark, the loud Koïl swells his throat,
And mocks me with his joyful note.
I hear the happy wild-cock call
Beside the shady waterfall.
His cry of joy afflicts my breast
By love's absorbing might possessed.
My darling from our cottage heard
One morn in spring this shrill-toned bird,
And called me in her joy to hear
The happy cry that charmed her ear.
See, birds of every varied voice
Around us in the woods rejoice,
On creeper, shrub, and plant alight,
Or wing from tree to tree their flight.
Each bird his kindly mate has found,
And loud their notes of triumph sound,
Blending in sweetest music like
The distant warblings of the shrike.
See how the river banks are lined
With birds of every hue and kind.
Here in his joy the Koïl sings,
There the glad wild-cock flaps his wings.
The blooms of bright Aśokas[1] where
The song of wild bees fills the air,
And the soft whisper of the boughs
Increase my longing for my spouse.
The vernal flush of flower and spray
Will burn my very soul away.
What use, what care have I for life
If I no more may see my wife,
Soft speaker with the glorious hair,
And eyes with silken lashes fair?
Now is the time when all day long
The Koïls fill the woods with song,
And gardens bloom at spring's sweet touch
Which my beloved loved so much.
Ah me, Sumitrá's son, the fire
Of sorrow, sprung from soft desire,
Fanned by the charms the spring-time shows,
Will burn my heart and end my woes,
Whose sad eyes look on each fair tree,
But my sweet love no more may see.
Ah me, Ah me, from hour to hour
Love in my soul will wax in power,
And spring, upon whose charms I gaze,
Whose breath the heat of toil allays,
With thoughts of her for whom I strain
My hopeless eyes, increase my pain.
As fire in summer rages through
The forests thick with dry bamboo,
So will my fawn-eyed love consume
My soul o'erwhelmed with thoughts of gloom.
Behold, beneath each spreading tree
The peacocks dance[1] in frantic glee,
And, stirred by all the gales that blow,
Their tails with jewelled windows glow,
Each bird, in happy love elate,
Rejoices with his darling mate.
But sights like these of joy and peace
My pangs of hopeless love increase.
See on the mountain slope above
The peahen languishing with love.
Behold her now in amorous dance
Close to her consort's side advance.
He with a laugh of joy and pride
Displays his glittering pinions wide;
And follows through the tangled dell
The partner whom he loves so well.
Ah happy bird! no giant's hate
Has robbed him of his tender mate;
And still beside his loved one he
Dances beneath the shade in glee.
Ah, in this month when flowers are fair
My widowed woe is hard to bear.
See, gentle love a home may find
In creatures of inferior kind.
See how the peahen turns to meet
Her consort now with love-drawn feet.

[1] "The Jonesia Asoca is a tree of considerable size, native of southern India. It blossoms in February and March with large erect compact clusters of flowers, varying in colour from pale-orange to scarlet, almost to be mistaken, on a hasty glance, for immense trusses of bloom of an Ixora. Mr. Fortune considered this tree, when in full bloom, superior in beauty even to the Amherstia.

The first time I saw the Asoc in flower was on the hill where the famous rock-cut temple of Kârlî is situated, and a large concourse of natives had assembled for the celebration of some Hindoo festival. Before proceeding to the temple the Mahratta women gathered from two trees, which were flowering somewhat below, each a fine truss of blossom, and inserted it in the hair at the back of her head. ....As they moved about in groups it is impossible to imagine a more delightful effect than the rich scarlet bunches of flowers presented on their fine glossy jet-black hair." FIRMINGER, *Gardening for India.*

[1] No other word can express the movements of peafowl under the influence of pleasing excitement, especially when after the long drought they hear the welcome roar of the thunder and feel that the rain is near.

So, Lakshman, if my large-eyed dear,
The child of Janak still were here,
She, by love's thrilling influence led,
Upon my breast would lay her head.
These blooms I gathered from the bough
Without my love are useless now.
A thousand blossoms fair to see
With passing glory clothe each tree
That hangs its cluster-burthened head
Now that the dewy months[1] are fled,
But, followed by the bees that ply
Their fragrant task, they fall and die.
A thousand birds in wild delight
Their rapture-breathing notes unite;
Bird calls to bird in joyous strain,
And turns my love to frenzied pain.
O, if beneath those alien skies
There be a spring where Sítá lies,
I know my prisoned love must be
Touched with like grief, and mourn with me.
But ah, methinks that dreary clime
Knows not the touch of spring's sweet time.
How could my black-eyed love sustain,
Without her lord, so dire a pain?
Or if the sweet spring come to her
In distant lands a prisoner,
How may his advent aid her, met
On every side with taunt and threat?
Ah, if the springtide's languor came
With soft enchantment o'er my dame,
My darling of the lotus eye,
My gently speaking love, would die;
For well my spirit knows that she
Can never live bereft of me.
With love that never wavered yet
My Sítá's heart on me is set,
Who, with a soul that ne'er can stray,
With equal love her love repay.
In vain, in vain the soft wind brings
Sweet blossoms on his balmy wings;
Delicious from his native snow,
To me like fire he seems to glow.
O, how I loved a breeze like this
When darling Sítá shared the bliss!
But now in vain for me it blows
To fan the fury of my woes.
That dark-winged bird that sought the skies
Foretelling grief with warning cries,
Sits on the tree where buds are gay,
And pours glad music from the spray.
That rover of the fields of air
Will aid my love with friendly care,
And me with gracious pity guide
To my large-eyed Videhan's side.[1]
Hark, Lakshman, how the woods around
With love-inspiring chants resound,
Where birds in every bloom-crowned tree
Pour forth their amorous minstrelsy.
As though an eager gallant wooed
A gentle maid by love subdued,
Enamoured of her flowers the bee
Darts at the wind-rocked Tila tree.[2]
Aśoka, brightest tree that grows,
That lends a pang to lovers' woes,
Hangs out his gorgeous bloom in scorn
And mocks me as I weep forlorn.
O Lakshman, turn thine eye and see
Each blossom-laden Mango tree,
Like a young lover gaily dressed
Whom fond desire forbids to rest.
Look, son of Queen Sumitrá, through
The forest glades of varied hue,
Where blooms are bright and grass is green
The Kinnars[3] with their loves are seen.
See, brother, see where sweet and bright
Those crimson lilies charm the sight,
And o'er the flood a radiance throw
Fair as the morning's roseate glow.
See, Pampá, most divinely sweet,
The swan's and mallard's loved retreat,
Shows her glad waters bright and clear,
Where lotuses their heads uprear
From the pure wave, and charm the view
With mingled tints of red and blue.
Each like the morning's early beams
Reflected in the crystal, gleams;
And bees on their sweet toil intent
Weigh down each tender filament.
There with gay lawns the wood recedes;
There wildfowl sport amid the reeds,
There roedeer stand upon the brink,
And elephants descend to drink.
The rippling waves which winds make fleet
Against the bending lilies beat,
And opening bud and flower and stem
Gleam with the drops that hang on them.
Life has no pleasure left for me
While my dear queen I may not see,

[1] The Dewy Season is one of the six ancient seasons of the Indian year, lasting from the middle of January to the middle of March.

[1] Ráma appears to mean that on a former occasion a crow flying high overhead was an omen that indicated his approaching separation from Sítá; and that now the same bird's perching on a tree near him may be regarded as a happy augury that she will soon be restored to her husband.

[2] A tree with beautiful and fragrant blossoms.

[3] A race of semi-divine musicians attached to the service of Kuvera, represented as centaurs reversed with human figures and horses' heads.

Who loved so well those blooms that vie
With the full splendour of her eye.
O tyrant Love, who will not let
My bosom for one hour forget
The lost one whom I yearn to meet,
Whose words were ever kind and sweet.
Ah, haply might my heart endure
This hopeless love that knows not cure,
If spring with all his trees in flower
Assailed me not with ruthless power.
Each lovely scene, each sound and sight
Wherein, with her, I found delight,
Has lost the charm so sweet of yore,
And glads my widowed heart no more.
On lotus buds I seem to gaze,
Or blooms that deck Palásá[1] sprays;
But to my tortured memory rise
The glories of my darling's eyes.
Cool breezes through the forest stray
Gathering odours on their way,
Enriched with all the rifled scent
Of lotus flower and filament.
Their touch upon my temples falls
And Sítá's fragrant breath recalls.
Now look, dear brother, on the right
Of Pampá towers a mountain height
Where fairest Cassia trees unfold
The treasures of their burnished gold.
Proud mountain king! his woody side
With myriad ores is decked and dyed,
And as the wind-swept blossoms fall
Their fragrant dust is stained with all.
To yon high lands thy glances turn:
With pendent fire they flash and burn,
Where in their vernal glory blaze
Palásá flowers on leafless sprays.
O Lakshmaṇ, look! on Pampá's side
What fair trees rise in blooming pride!
What climbing plants above them show
Or hang their flowery garlands low!
See how the amorous creeper rings
The wind-rocked trees to which she clings,
As though a dame by love impelled
With clasping arms her lover held.
Drunk with the varied scents that fill
The balmy air, from hill to hill,
From grove to grove, from tree to tree,
The joyous wind is wandering free.
These gay trees wave their branches bent
By blooms, of honey redolent.
There, slowly opening to the day,
Buds with dark lustre deck the spray.
The wild bee rests a moment where
Each tempting flower is sweet and fair,
Then, coloured by the pollen dyes,
Deep in some odorous blossom lies.
Soon from his couch away he springs:
To other trees his course he wings,
And tastes the honeyed blooms that grow
Where Pampá's lucid waters flow.
See, Lakshmaṇ, see, how thickly spread
With blossoms from the trees o'erhead,
That grass the weary traveller woos
With couches of a thousand hues,
And beds on every height arrayed
With red and yellow tints are laid,
No longer winter chills the earth:
A thousand flowerets spring to birth,
And trees in rivalry assume
Their vernal garb of bud and bloom.
How fair they look, how bright and gay
With tasselled flowers on every spray!
While each to each proud challenge flings
Borne in the song the wild bee sings.
That mallard by the river edge
Has bathed amid the reeds and sedge:
Now with his mate he fondly plays
And fires my bosom as I gaze.
Mandákiní[1] is far renowned:
No lovelier flood on earth is found;
But all her fairest charms combined
In this sweet stream enchant the mind,
O, if my love were here to look
With me upon this lovely brook,
Ne'er for Ayodhyá would I pine,
Or wish that Indra's lot were mine.
If by my darling's side I strayed
O'er the soft turf which decks the glade,
Each craving thought were sweetly stilled,
Each longing of my soul fulfilled.
But, now my love is far away,
Those trees which make the woods so gay,
In all their varied beauty dressed,
Wake thoughts of anguish in my breast.
That lotus-covered stream behold
Whose waters run so fresh and cold,

---

[1] Butea Frondosa. A tree that bears a profusion of brilliant red flowers which appear before the leaves.

I omit five *ślokas* which contain nothing but a list of trees for which, with one or two exceptions, there are no equivalent names in English. The following is Gorresio's translation of the corresponding passage in the Bengal recension:—

"Oh come risplendono in questa stagione di primavera i vitici, le galedupe, le bassie, le dalbergie, i diospyri...............le tile, le michelie, le rottlerie, le pentaptere ed i pterospermi, i bombaci, le grislee, gli abri, gli amaranti e le dalbergie; i sirii, le galedupe, le barringtonie ed i palmizi, i xanthocymi, il pepebetel, le verbosine e le ficaie, le nauclee le erythrine, gli asochi, e le tapie fanno d'ogni intorno pompa de' lor fiori."

[1] A sacred stream often mentioned in the course of the poem. See Book II. Canto XCV.

Sweet rill, the wildfowl's loved resort,
Where curlew, swan, and diver sport;
Where with his consort plays the drake,
And tall deer love their thirst to slake,
While from each woody bank is heard
The wild note of each happy bird.
The music of that joyous quire
Fills all my soul withsoft desire;
And, as I hear, my sad thoughts fly
To Sítá of the lotus eye,
Whom, lovely with her moonbright cheek,
In vain mine eager glances seek.
Now turn, those chequered lawns survey
Where hart and hind together stray.
Ah, as they wander at their will
My troubled breast with grief they fill,
While torn by hopeless love I sigh
For Sítá of the fawn-like eye.
If in those glades where, touched by spring,
Gay birds their amorous ditties sing,
Mine own beloved I might see,
Then, brother, it were well with me:
If by my side she wandered still,
And this cool breeze that stirs the rill
Touched with its gentle breath the brows
Of mine own dear Videhan spouse.
For, Lakshman, O how blest are those
On whom the breath of Pampá blows,
Dispelling all their care and gloom
With sweets from where the lilies bloom!
How can my gentle love remain
Alive amid the woe and pain,
Where prisoned far away she lies,—
My darling of the lotus eyes?
How shall I dare her sire to greet
Whose lips have never known deceit?
How stand before the childless king
And meet his eager questioning?
When banished by my sire's decree,
In low estate, she followed me.
So pure, so true to every vow,
Where is my gentle darling now?
How can I bear my widowed lot,
And linger on where she is not,
Who followed when from home I fled
Distracted, disinherited?
My spirit sinks in hopeless pain
When my fond glances yearn in vain
For that dear face with whose bright eye
The worshipped lotus scarce can vie.
Ah when, my brother, shall I hear
That voice that rang so soft and clear,
When, sweetly smiling as she spoke,
From her dear lips gay laughter broke?
When worn with toil and love I strayed
With Sítá through the forest shade,
No trace of grief was seen in her,
My kind and thoughtful comforter.
How shall my faltering tongue relate
To Queen Kauśalyá Sítá's fate?
How answer when in wild despair
She questions, Where is Sítá, where?
Haste, brother, haste: to Bharat hie,
On whose fond love I still rely.
My life can be no longer borne,
Since Sítá from my side is torn.'

Thus like a helpless mourner, bent
By sorrow, Ráma made lament;
And with wise counsel Lakshman tried
To soothe his care, and thus replied:
'O best of men, thy grief oppose,
Nor sink beneath thy weight of woes.
Not thus despond the great and pure
And brave like thee, but still endure.
Reflect what anguish wrings the heart
When loving souls are forced to part;
And, mindful of the coming pain,
Thy love within thy breast restrain.
For earth, though cooled by wandering streams,
Lies scorched beneath the midday beams.
Rávan his steps to hell may bend,
Or lower yet in flight descend;
But be thou sure, O Raghu's son,
Avenging death he shall not shun.
Rise, Ráma, rise: the search begin,
And track the giant foul with sin.
Then shall the fiend, though far he fly,
Resign his prey or surely die.
Yea, though the trembling monster hide
With Sítá close to Diti's[1] side,
E'en there, unless he yield the prize,
Slain by this wrathful hand he dies.
Thy heart with strength and courage stay,
And cast this weakling mood away.
Our fainting hopes in vain revive
Unless with firm resolve we strive.
The zeal that fires the toiler's breast
Mid earthly powers is first and best.
Zeal every check and bar defies,
And wins at length the loftiest prize.
In woe and danger, toil and care,
Zeal never yields to weak despair.
With zealous heart thy task begin,
And thou once more thy spouse shalt win.
Cast fruitless sorrow from thy soul,
Nor let this love thy heart control.
Forget not all thy sacred lore,
But be thy noble self once more.'

He heard, his bosom rent by grief,
The counsel of his brother chief;
Crushed in his heart the maddening pain,
And rose resolved and strong again.
Then forth upon his journey went
The hero on his task intent,
Nor thought of Pampá's lovely brook,

---

[1] A daughter of Daksha who became one of the wives of Kaśyapa and mother of the Daityas. She is termed the general mother of Titans and malignant beings. See Book I Cantos XLV, XLVI.

Or trees which murmuring breezes shook,
Though on dark woods his glances fell,
On waterfall and cave and dell ;
And still by many a care distressed
The son of Raghu onward pressed.
As some wild elephant elate
Moves through the woods in pride,
So Lakshman with majestic gait
Strode by his brother's side.
He, for his lofty spirit famed,
Admonished and consoled ;
Showed Raghu's son what duty claimed,
And bade his heart be bold.
Then as the brothers strode apace
To Rishyamúka's height,
The sovereign of the Vánar race[1]
Was troubled at the sight.
As on the lofty hill he strayed
He saw the chiefs draw near ;
A while their glorious forms surveyed,
And mused in restless fear.
His slow majestic step he stayed
And gazed upon the pair.
And all his spirit sank dismayed
By fear too great to bear.
When in their glorious might the best
Of royal chiefs came nigh,
The Vánars in their wild unrest
Prepared to turn and fly.
They sought the hermit's sacred home[2]
For peace and bliss ordained,
And there, where Vánars loved to roam,
A sure asylum gained.

CANTO II.

SUGRÍVA'S ALARM.

Sugríva moved by wondering awe
The high-souled sons of Raghu saw,
In all their glorious arms arrayed ;
And grief upon his spirit weighed.
To every quarter of the sky
He turned in fear his anxious eye,
And roving still from spot to spot
With troubled steps he rested not.
He durst not, as he viewed the pair,
Resolve to stand and meet them there ;
And drooping cheer and quailing breast
The terror of the chief confessed.
While the great fear his bosom shook,
Brief counsel with his lords he took ;
Each gain and danger closely scanned,
What hope in flight, what power to stand.
While doubt and fear his bosom rent,
On Raghu's sons his eyes he bent,
And with a spirit ill at ease
Addressed his lords in words like these :
'Those chiefs with wandering steps invade
The shelter of our pathless shade,
And hither come in fair disguise
Of hermit garb as Báli's spies.'
Each lord beheld with troubled heart
Those masters of the bowman's art,
And left the mountain side to seek
Sure refuge on a loftier peak.
The Vánar chief in rapid flight
Found shelter on a towering height,
And all the band with one accord
Were closely gathered round their lord.
Their course the same, with desperate leap
Each made his way from steep to steep,
And speeding on in wild career
Filled every height with sudden fear.
Each heart was struck with mortal dread,
As on their course the Vánars sped,
While trees that crowned the steep were bent
And crushed beneath them as they went.
As in their eager flight they pressed
For safety to each mountain crest,
The wild confusion struck with fear
Tiger and cat and wandering deer.
The lords who watched Sugríva's will
Were gathered on the royal hill,
And all with reverent hands upraised
Upon their king and leader gazed.
Sugríva feared some evil planned,
Some train prepared by Báli's hand.
But, skilled in words that charm and teach,
Thus Hanumán[1] began his speech :
'Dismiss, dismiss thine idle fear,
Nor dread the power of Báli here.
For this is Malaya's glorious hill[2]
Where Báli's might can work no ill.
I look around but nowhere see
The hated foe who made thee flee,
Fell Báli, fierce in form and face :
Then fear not, lord of Vánar race.
Alas, in thee I clearly find
The weakness of the Vánar kind,

---

[1] Sugríva, the ex-king of the Vánars, foresters, or monkeys, an exile from his home, wandering about the mountain Rishyamúka with his four faithful ex-ministers.

[2] The hermitage of the Saint Matanga which his curse prevented Báli, the present king of the Vánars, from entering. The story is told at length in Canto XI. of this Book.

[1] Hanumán, Sugríva's chief general, was the son of the God of Wind. See Book I. Canto XVI.

[2] A range of hills in Malabar ; the Western Gháts in the Deccan.

That loves from thought to thought to range,
Fix no belief, and welcome change.
Mark well each hint and sign, and scan,
Discreet and wise, thine every plan.
How may a king, with sense denied,
The subjects of his sceptre guide?'
Hanúmán,[1] wise in hour of need,
Urged on the chief his prudent rede.
His listening ear Sugríva bent,
And spake in words more excellent:
'Where is the dauntless heart that free
From terror's chilling touch can see
Two stranger warriors, strong as those,
Equipped with swords and shafts and bows,
With mighty arms and large full eyes,
Like glorious children of the skies?
Báli my foe, I ween, has sent
These chiefs to aid his dark intent.
Hence doubt and fear disturb me still,
For thousands serve a monarch's will.
In borrowed garb they come, and those
Who walk disguised are counted foes.
With secret thoughts they watch their time,
And wound fond hearts that fear no crime.
My foe in state affairs is wise,
And prudent kings have searching eyes.
By other hands they strike the foe:
By meaner tools the truth they know.
Now to those stranger warriors turn,
And, less than king, their purpose learn.
Mark well the trick and look of each;
Observe his form and note his speech.
With care their mood and temper sound,
And, if their minds be friendly found,
With courteous looks and words begin
Their confidence and love to win.
Then as my friend and envoy speak,
And question what the strangers seek.
Ask why equipped with shaft and bow
Through this wild maze of wood they go.
If they, O chief, at first appear
Pure of all guile, in heart sincere,
Detect in speech and look the sin
And treachery that lurk within.'
He spoke: the Wind-God's son obeyed.
With ready zeal he sought the shade,
And reached with hasty steps the wood
Where Raghu's son and Lakshman stood.[2]

[1] Válmíki makes the second vowel in this name long or short to suit the exigencies of the verse. Other Indian poets have followed his example, and the same licence will be used in this translation.

[2] I omit a recapitulatory and interpolated verse in a different metre, which is as follows:—Reverencing with the words, So be it, the speech of the greatly terrified and unequalled monkey king, the magnanimous Hanumán then went where (stood) the very mighty Ráma with Lakshman.

CANTO III.

HANUMAN'S SPEECH.

The envoy in his faithful breast
Pondered Sugríva's high behest.
From Rishyamúka's peak he hied
And placed him by the princes' side.
The Wind-God's son with cautious art
Had laid his Vánar form apart,
And wore, to cheat the strangers' eyes,
A wandering mendicant's disguise.[1]
Before the heroes' feet he bent
And did obeisance reverent,
And spoke, the glorious pair to praise,
His words of truth in courteous phrase,
High honour duly paid, the best
Of all the Vánar kind addressed,
With free accord and gentle grace,
Those glories of their warrior race:
'O hermits, blest in vows, who shine
Like royal saints or Gods divine,
O best of young ascetics, say
How to this spot you found your way,
Scaring the troops of wandering deer
And silvan things that harbour here
Searching amid the trees that grow
Where Pampá's gentle waters flow,
And lending from your brows a gleam
Of glory to the lovely stream.
Who are you, say, so brave and fair,
Clad in the bark which hermits wear?
I see you heave the frequent sigh,
I see the deer before you fly,
While you, for strength and valour dread,
The earth, like lordly lions, tread,
Each bearing in his hand a bow,
Like Indra's own, to slay the foe,
With the grand paces of a bull,
So bright and young and beautiful.
The mighty arms you raise appear
Like trunks which elephants uprear,
And as you move this mountain-king[2]
Is glorious with the light you bring.
How have you reached, like Gods in face
Best lords of earth, this lonely place,

[1] The semi-divine Hanumán possesses like the Gods and demons, the power of wearing all shapes at will. He is one of the *Kámarúpís*.

Like Milton's good and bad angels
"as they please
They limb themselves, and colour, shape
or size
Assume as likes them best, condense
or rare."

[2] Himálaya is of course *par excellence* the Monarch of mountains, but the complimentary title is frequently given to other hills as here to Malaya.

With tresses coiled in hermit guise,[1]
And splendours of those lotus eyes?
As God's who leave their heavenly sphere,
Alike your beauteous forms appear.
The Lords of Day and Night[2] might thus
Stray from the skies to visit us.
Heroic youth, so broad of chest,
Fair with the beauty of the Blest,
With lion shoulders, tall and strong,
Like bulls who lead the lowing throng,
Your arms, unmatched for grace and length,
With massive clubs may vie in strength.
Why do no gauds those limbs adorn
Where priceless gems were meetly worn?
Each noble youth is fit, I deem,
To guard this earth, as lord supreme,
With all her woods and seas, to reign
From Meru's peak to Vindhya's chain.
Your smooth bows decked with dyes and gold
Are glorious in their masters' hold,
And with the arms of Indra[3] vie
Which diamond splendours beautify.
Your quivers glow with golden sheen,
Well stored with arrows fleet and keen,
Each gleaming like a fiery snake
That joys the foeman's life to take.
As serpents cast their sloughs away
And all their new-born sheen display,
So flash your mighty swords inlaid
With burning gold on hilt and blade.
Why are you silent, heroes? Why
My questions hear nor deign reply?
Sugríva, lord of virtuous mind.
The foremost of the Vánar kind,
An exile from his royal state,
Roams through the land disconsolate.
I, Hanumán, of Vánar race.
Sent by the king have sought this place,
For he, the pious, just, and true,
In friendly league would join with you.
Know, godlike youths, that I am one
Of his chief lords, the Wind-God's son.
With course unchecked I roam at will,
And now from Rishyamúka's hill.
To please his heart, his hope to speed,
I came disguised in beggar's weed.'
Thus Hanúmán, well trained in lore
Of language, spoke, and said no more.
The son of Raghu joyed to hear
The envoy's speech, and bright of cheer
He turned to Lakshman by his side,
And thus in words of transport cried:
'The counsellor we now behold
Of King Sugríva righteous-souled.
His face I long have yearned to see,
And now his envoy comes to me.
With sweetest words in courteous phrase
Answer this mighty lord who slays
His foemen, by Sugríva sent,
This Vánar chief most eloquent.
For one whose words so sweetly flow
The whole Rig-veda[1] needs must know,
And in his well-trained memory store
The Yajush and the Sáman's lore.
He must have bent his faithful ear
All grammar's varied rules to hear.
For his long speech how well he spoke!
In all its length no rule he broke.
In eye, on brow, in all his face
The keenest look no guile could trace.
No change of hue, no pose of limb
Gave sign that aught was false in him.
Concise, unfaltering, sweet and clear,
Without a word to pain the ear.
From chest to throat, nor high nor low,
His accents came in measured flow.
How well he spoke with perfect art
That wondrous speech that charmed the heart,
With finest skill and order graced
In words that knew nor pause nor haste!
That speech, with consonants that spring
From the three seats of uttering,[2]
Would charm the spirit of a foe
Whose sword is raised for mortal blow.
How may a ruler's plan succeed
Who lacks such envoy good at need?
How fail, if one whose mind is stored
With gifts so rare assist his lord?
What plans can fail, with wisest speech
Of envoy's lips to further each?'
Thus Ráma spoke; and Lakshman, taught
In all the art that utters thought,
To King Sugríva's learned spy
Thus made his eloquent reply:
'Full well we know the gifts that grace
Sugríva, lord of Vánar race,
And hither turn our wandering feet
That we that high-souled king may meet.
So now our pleasant task shall be
To do the words he speaks by thee.'
His prudent speech the Vánar heard,
And all his heart with joy was stirred.
And hope that league with them would bring
Redress and triumph to his king.

---

[1] Twisted up in a matted coil as was the custom of ascetics.

[2] The sun and moon.

[3] The rainbow.

[1] The Vedas are four in number, the Rich or Rig-veda, the Yajush or Yajur-veda; the Sáman or Sáma-veda, and the Atharvan or Atharva-veda. See p. 3. Note.

[2] The chest, the throat, and the head.

CANTO IV.

LAKSHMAṆ'S REPLY.

Cheered by the words that Ráma spoke,
Joy in the Vánar's breast awoke,
And, as his friendly mood he knew,
His thoughts to King Sugríva flew:
'Again,' he mused, 'my high-souled lord
Shall rule, to kingly state restored;
Since one so mighty comes to save,
And freely gives the help we crave.'
Then joyous Hanumán, the best
Of all the Vánar kind, addressed
These words to Ráma, trained of yore
In all the arts of speakers' lore:[1]
'Why do your feet this forest tread
By silvan life inhabited,
This awful maze of tree and thorn
Which Pampá's flowering groves adorn?'
He spoke: obedient to the eye
Of Ráma Lakshmaṇ made reply,
The name and fortune to unfold
Of Raghu's son the lofty-souled:
'True to the law, of fame unstained,
The glorious Daśaratha reigned,
And, steadfast in his duty, long
Kept the four castes[2] from scathe and wrong.
Through his wide realm his will was done,
And, loved by all, he hated none.
Just to each creature great and small,
Like the Good Sire he cared for all.
The Agnishṭom,[3] as priests advised,
And various rites he solemnized,
Where ample largess ever paid
The Bráhmans for their holy aid.
Here Ráma stands, his heir by birth,
Whose name is glorious in the earth:
Sure refuge he of all oppressed,
Most faithful to his sire's behest.
He, Daśaratha's eldest born
Whom gifts above the rest adorn,
Lord of each high imperial sign,[1]
The glory of his kingly line,
Reft of his right, expelled from home,
Came forth with me the woods to roam.
And Sítá too, his faithful dame,
Forth with her virtuous husband came,
Like the sweet light when day is done
Still cleaving to her lord the sun.
And me his sweet perfections drew
To follow as his servant true,
Named Lakshmaṇ, brother of my lord
Of grateful heart with knowledge stored.
Most meet is he all bliss to share,
Who makes the good of all his care.
While, power and lordship cast away,
In the wild wood he chose to stay,
A giant came,—his name unknown,—
And stole the princess left alone.
Then Diti's son[2] who, cursed of yore,
The semblance of a Rakshas wore,
To King Sugríva bade us turn
The robber's name and home to learn,
For he, the Vánar chief, would know
The dwelling of our secret foe.
Such words of hope spake Diti's son,
And sought the heaven his deeds had won.
Thou hast my tale. From first to last
Thine ears have heard whate'er has past.
Ráma the mighty lord and I
For refuge to Sugríva fly.
The prince whose arm bright glory gained,
O'er the whole earth as monarch reigned,
And richest gifts to others gave,
Is come Sugríva's help to crave;
Son of a king the surest friend
Of virtue, him who loved to lend
His succour to the suffering weak,
Is come Sugríva's aid to seek.
Yes, Raghu's son whose matchless hand
Protected all this sea-girt land,
The virtuous prince, my holy guide,
For refuge seeks Sugríva's side.
His favour sent on great and small
Should ever save and prosper all.
He now to win Sugríva's grace
Has sought his woodland dwelling-place.

---

[1] "In our own metrical romances, or wherever a poem is meant not for readers but for chanters and oral reciters, these *formulæ*, to meet the same recurring case, exist by scores. Thus every woman in these metrical romances who happens to be young, is described as "so bright of ble," or complexion; always a man goes "the mountenance of a mile" before he overtakes or is overtaken. And so on through a vast bead-roll of cases. In the same spirit Homer has his eternal τον δ'αρ' ὑποδρα ιδων, or τον δ'απαμειβομενος προσεφη, &c.

To a reader of sensibility, such recurrences wear an air of child-like simplicity, beautifully recalling the features of Homer's primitive age. But they would have appeared faults to all commonplace critics in literary ages."

DE QUINCEY. *Homer and the Homeridæ.*

[2] Bráhmans the sacerdotal caste. Kshatriyas the royal and military, Vaiśyas the mercantile, and Śudras the servile.

[3] A protracted sacrifice extending over several days. See Book I. p. 24 Note.

[1] Possessed of all the auspicious personal marks that indicate capacity of universal sovereignty. See Book I. p. 2, and Note 3.

[2] Kabandha. See Book III. Canto LXXIII.

Son of a king of glorious fame;—
Who knows not Daśaratha's name!—
From whom all princes of the earth
Received each honour due to worth;—
Heir of that best of earthly kings,
Ráma the prince whose glory rings
Through realms below and earth and skies,
For refuge to Sugríva flies.
Nor should the Vánar king refuse
The boon for which the suppliant sues,
But with his forest legions speed
To save him in his utmost need.'
Sumitrá's son, his eyes bedewed
With piteous tears, thus sighed and sued.
Then, trained in all the arts that guide
The speaker, Hanumán replied:
'Yea, lords like you of wisest thought,
Whom happy fate has hither brought,
Who vanquish ire and rule each sense,
Must of our lord have audience.
Reft of his kingdom, sad, forlorn,
Once Báli's hate now Báli's scorn,
Defeated, severed from his spouse,
Wandering under forest boughs,
Child of the Sun, our lord and king
Sugríva will his succours bring,
And all our Vánar hosts combined
Will trace the dame you long to find.'
With gentle tone and winning grace
Thus spake the chief of Vánar race,
And then to Raghu's son he cried:
'Come, haste we to Sugrívá's side.'
He spoke, and for his words so sweet
Good Lakshman paid all honour meet;
Then turned and cried to Raghu's son:
'Now deem thy task already done,
Because this chief of Vánar kind,
Son of the God who rules the wind,
Declares Sugríva's self would be
Assisted in his need by thee.
Bright gleams of joy his cheek o'erspread
As each glad word of hope he said;
And ne'er will one so valiant deign
To cheer our hearts with hope in vain.'
He spoke, and Hanumán the wise
Cast off his mendicant disguise,
And took again his Vánar form,
Son of the God of wind and storm.
High on his ample back in haste
Raghu's heroic sons he placed;
And turned with rapid steps to find
The sovereign of the Vánar kind.

CANTO V.

THE LEAGUE.

From Rishyamúka's rugged side
To Malaya's hill the Vánar hied,
And to his royal chieftain there
Announced the coming of the pair:
'See, here with Lakshman Ráma stands
Illustrious in a hundred lands,
Whose valiant heart will never quail
Although a thousand foes assail;
King Daśaratha's son, the grace
And glory of Ikshváku's race.
Obedient to his father's will
He cleaves to sacred duty still.
With rites of royal pomp and pride
His sire the Fire-God gratified;
Ten hundred thousand kine he freed,
And priests enriched with ample meed;
And the broad land protected, famed
For truthful lips and passions tamed.
Through woman's guile his son has made
His dwelling in the forest shade,
Where, as he lived with every sense
Subdued in hermit abstinence,
Fierce Rávan stole his wife, and he
Is come a suppliant, lord, to thee.
Now let all honour due be paid
To these great chiefs who seek thine aid.'
Thus spake the Vánar prince, and, stirred
With friendly thoughts, Sugríva heard.
The light of joy his face o'erspread,
And thus to Raghu's son he said:
'O Prince, in rules of duty trained,
Caring for all with love unfeigned,
Hanúmán's tongue has truly shown
The virtues that are thine alone.
My chiefest glory, gain, and bliss,
O stranger Prince, I reckon this,
That Raghu's son will condescend
To seek the Vánar for his friend.
If thou my true ally wouldst be
Accept the pledge I offer thee.
This hand in sign of friendship take,
And bind the bond we ne'er will break.'
He spoke, and joy thrilled Ráma's breast;
Sugríva's hand he seized and pressed;
And, transport beaming from his eye,
Held to his heart his new ally.
In wanderer's weed disguised no more,
His proper form Hanúmán wore.
Then, wood with wood engendering,[1] came
Neath his deft hands the kindled flame.
Between the chiefs that fire he placed

[1] Fire for sacred purposes is produced by the attrition of two pieces of wood. In marriage and other solemn covenants fire is regarded as the holy witness in whose presence the agreement is made. Spenser in a description of a marriage, has borrowed from the Roman rite what he calls the housling, or sacramental fire:

With wreaths of flowers and worship graced,
And round its blazing glory went
The friends with slow steps reverent.
Thus each to other pledged and bound
In solemn league new transport found,
And bent upon his dear ally
The gaze he ne'er could satisfy.
'Friend of my soul art thou : we share
Each other's joy, each other's care ;'
Thus in the bliss that thrilled his breast
Sugríva Raghu's son addressed.
From a high Sál a branch he tore
Which many a leaf and blossom bore,
And the fine twigs beneath them laid
A seat for him and Ráma made.
Then Hanumán with joyous mind,
Son of the God who rules the wind,
To Lakshman gave, his seat to be,
The gay branch of a Sandal tree.
Then King Sugríva with his eyes
Still trembling with the sweet surprise
Of the great joy he could not hide,
To Raghu's noblest scion cried :
'O Ráma, racked with woe and fear,
Spurned by my foes, I wander here.
Reft of my spouse, forlorn I dwell
Here in my forest citadel.
Or wild with terror and distress
Roam through the distant wilderness.
Vext by my brother Báli long
My soul has borne the scathe and wrong.
Do thou, whose virtues all revere,
Release me from my woe and fear.
From dire distress thy friend to free
Is a high task and worthy thee.'

He spoke, and Raghu's son who knew
All sacred duties men should do.
The friend of justice, void of guile,
Thus answered with a gentle smile :
'Great Vánar, friends who seek my aid
Still find their trust with fruit repaid.
Báli, thy foe, who stole away
Thy wife, this vengeful hand shall slay.
These shafts which sunlike flash and burn,
Winged with the feathers of the hern,
Each swift of flight and sure and dread,
With even knot and pointed head,
Fierce as the crashing fire-bolt sent
By him who rules the firmament,[1]
Shall reach thy wicked foe and like
Infuriate serpents hiss and strike.
Thou, Vánar King, this day shalt see
The foe who long has injured thee
Lie, like a shattered mountain, low,
Slain by the tempest of my bow.'
Thus Ráma spake : Sugríva heard,
And mighty joy his bosom stirred :
As thus his champion he addressed :
'Now by thy favour, first and best
Of heroes, shall thy friend obtain
His realm and darling wife again
Recovered from the foe.
Check thou mine elder brother's might,
That ne'er again his deadly spite
May rob me of mine ancient right,
Or vex my soul with woe.'
The league was struck, a league to bring
To Sítá fiends, and Vánar king[1]
Apportioned bliss and bale.
Through her left eye quick throbbings shot,[2]
Glad signs the lady doubted not,
That told their hopeful tale.
The bright left eye of Báli felt
An inauspicious throb that dealt
A deadly blow that day.
The fiery left eyes of the crew
Of demons felt the throb, and knew
The herald of dismay.

"His owne two hands the holy knots did knit
That none but death for ever can divide.
His owne two hands, for such a turn most fit,
The housling fire did kindle and provide.'
Faery Queen, Book I. XII. 37.

[1] Indra.

CANTO VI.

THE TOKENS.

With joy that sprang from hope restored.
To Ráma spake the Vánar lord :
'I know, by wise Hanúmán taught,
Why thou the lonely wood hast sought.
Where with thy brother Lakshman thou
Hast sojourned, bound by hermit vow ;
Have heard how Sítá, Janak's child,
Was stolen in the pathless wild,
How by a roving Rákshas she
Weeping was reft from him and thee ;
How, bent on death, the gaint slew
The vulture king, her guardian true,
And gave thy widowed breast to know
A solitary mourner's woe.
But soon, dear Prince, thy heart shall be
From every trace of sorrow free ;

[1] Báli the king *de facto*.

[2] With the Indians, as with the ancient Greeks, the throbbing of the right eye in a man is an auspicious sign, the throbbing of the left eye is the opposite. In a woman the significations of signs are reversed.

On the alliance between Ráma and the monkeys, see ADDITIONAL NOTES.

For I thy darling will restore,
Lost like the prize of holy lore.[1]
Yea, though in heaven the lady dwell,
Or prisoned in the depths of hell,
My friendly care her way shall track
And bring thy ransomed darling back.
Let this my promise soothe thy care,
Nor doubt the words I truly swear.
Saints, fiends, and dwellers of the skies
Shall find thy wife a bitter prize,
Like the rash child who rues too late
Thy treacherous lure of poisoned cate.
No longer, Prince, thy loss deplore :
Thy darling wife will I restore.
'Twas she I saw : my heart infers
That shrinking form was doubtless hers,
Which giant Rávan, fierce and dread,
Bore swiftly through the clouds o'erhead
Still writhing in his strict embrace
Like helpless queen oft serpent race,[2]
And from her lips that sad voice came
Shrieking thine own and Lakshman's name.
High on a hill she saw me stand
With comrades twain on either hand.
Her outer robe to earth she threw,
And with it sent her anklets too.
We saw the glittering tokens fall,
We found them there and kept them all.
These will I bring : perchance thine eyes
The treasured spoils will recognze.'
He ceased ; then Raghu's son replied
To the glad tale, and eager cried :
'Bring them with all thy speed : delay
No more, dear friend, but haste away.'
Thus Ráma spoke. Sugríva hied
Within the mountain's caverned side,
Impelled by love that stirred each thought
The precious tokens quickly brought,
And said to Raghu's son, Behold
This garment and these rings of gold.
In Ráma's hand with friendly haste
The jewels and the robe he placed.
Then, like the moon by mist assailed,
The tear-dimmed eyes of Ráma failed ;
That burst of woe unmanned his frame,
Woe sprung from passion for his dame,
And with his manly strength o'erthrown,
He fell and cried, Ah me ! mine own !
Again, again close to his breast
The ornaments and robe he pressed,
While the quick pants that shook his frame
As from a furious serpent came.
On his dear brother standing nigh
He turned at length his piteous eye ;
And, while his tears increasing ran,
In bitter wail he thus began :
'Look, brother, and behold once more
The ornaments and robe she wore,
Dropped while the giant bore away
In cruel arms his struggling prey,
Dropped in some quiet spot, I ween,
Where the young grass was soft and green
For still untouched by spot or stain
Their former beauty all retain.'
He spoke with many a tear and sigh,
And thus his brother made reply :
'The bracelets thou hast fondly shown,
And earrings, are to me unknown,
But by long service taught I greet
The anklets of her honoured feet.'[1]
Then to Sugríva Ráma, best
Of Raghu's sons, these words addressed :
'Say to what quarter of the sky
The cruel fiend was seen to fly,
Bearing afar my captured wife,
My darling dearer than my life.
Speak, Vánar King, that I may know
Where dwells the cause of all my woe ;
The fiend for whose transgression all
The giants by this hand shall fall.
He who the Maithil lady stole
And kindled fury in my soul,
Has sought his fate in senseless pride
And opened Death's dark portal wide.
Then tell me, Vánar lord, I pray,
The dwelling of my foe,
And he, beneath this hand, to-day
To Yama's halls shall go.'

---

[1] The Vedas stolen by the demons Madhu and Kaitabha.

* The text has नष्टां वेदश्रुतिम् which signifies literally "the lost vedic tradition." It seems that allusion is here made to the Vedas submerged in the depth of the sea, but promptly recovered by Vishnu in one of his incarnation, as the brahmanic legend relates, with which the ordhodoxy of the Bráhmans intended perhaps to allude to the prompt restoration and uninterrupted continuity of the ancient vedic tradition." GORRESIO.

[2] Like the wife of a Nága or Serpent-God carried off by an eagle. The enmity between the King of birds and the serpent is of very frequent occurrence. It seems to be a modification of the strife between the Vedic Indra and the Ahi, the serpent or drought-fiend ; between Apollôn, and the Pythôn, Adam and the Serpent.

[1] He means that he has never venture to raise his eyes to her arms and face though he has ever been her devote servant.

CANTO VII.

RÁMA CONSOLED.

With longing love and woe oppressed
The Vánar chief he thus addressed;
And he, while sobs his utterance broke,
Raised up his reverent hands and spoke:
'O Raghu's son, I cannot tell
Where now that cruel fiend may dwell,
Declare his power and might, or trace
The author of his cursed race.
Still trust the promise that I make
And let thy breast no longer ache.
So will I toil, nor toil in vain,
That thou thy consort mayst regain.
So will I work with might and skill
That joy anew thy heart shall fill:
The valour of my soul display,
And Rávan and his legions slay.
Awake, awake! unmanned no more
Recall the strength was thine of yore.
Beseems not men like thee to wear
A weak heart yielding to despair.
Like troubles, too, mine eyes have seen,
Lamenting for a long-lost queen;
But, by despair unconquered yet,
My strength of mind I ne'er forget.
Far more shouldst thou of lofty soul
Thy passion and thy tears control,
When I, of Vánar's humbler strain,
Weep not for her in ceaseless pain.
Be firm, be patient, nor forget
The bounds the brave of heart have set
In loss, in woe, in strife, in fear,
When the dark hour of death is near.
Up? with thine own brave heart advise:
Not thus despond the firm and wise.
But he who gives his childish heart
To choose the coward's weakling part,
Sinks, like a foundered vessel, deep
In waves of woe that o'er him sweep.
See, suppliant hand to hand I lay,
And, moved by faithful love, I pray.
Give way no more to grief and gloom,
But all thy native strength resume.
No joy on earth, I ween, have they
Who yield their souls to sorrow's sway.
Their glory fades in slow decline:
'Tis not for thee to grieve and pine.
I do but hint with friendly speech
The wiser part I dare not teach.
This better path, dear friend, pursue,
And let not grief thy soul subdue.'
Sugríva thus with gentle art
And sweet words soothed the mourner's heart,
Who brushed off with his mantle's hem
Tears from the eyes bedewed with them.
Sugríva's words were not in vain,
And Ráma was himself again;
Around the king his arms he threw,
And thus began his speech anew:
'Whate'er a friend most wise and true,
Who counsels for the best, should do,
Whate'er his gentle part should be,
Has been performed, dear friend, by thee.
Taught by thy counsel, O my lord,
I feel my native strength restored.
A friend like thee is hard to gain,
Most rare in time of grief and pain.
Now strain thine utmost power to trace
The Maithil lady's dwelling place,
And aid me in my search to find
Fierce Rávan of the impious mind.
Trust thou, in turn, thy loyal friend,
And say what aid this arm can lend
To speed thy hopes, as fostering rain
Quickens in earth the scattered grain.
Deem not those words, that seemed to spring
From pride, are false, O Vánar King.
None from these lips has ever heard,
None e'er shall hear, one lying word.
Again I promise and declare,
Yea, by my truth, dear friend, I swear.'
Then glad was King Sugríva's breast,
And all his lords their joy confessed,
Stirred by sure hope of Ráma's aid,
And promise which the prince had made.

CANTO VIII.

RÁMA'S PROMISE.

Doubt from Sugríva's heart had fled,
And thus to Raghu's son he said:
'No bliss the Gods of heaven deny,
Each views me with a favouring eye,
When thou, whom all good gifts attend,
Hast sought me and become my friend.
Leagued, friend, with thee in bold emprise
My arm might win the conquered skies;
And shall our banded strength be weak
To gain the realm which now I seek?
A happy fate was mine above
My kith and kin and all I love,
When, near the witness fire, I won
Thy friendship, Raghu's glorious son.
Thou too in ripening time shalt see
Thy friend not all unworthy thee.
What gifts I have shall thus be shown:
Not mine the tongue to make them known.
Strong is the changeless bond that binds
The friendly faith of noble minds.
In woe, in danger, firm and sure
Their constancy and love endure.
Gold, silver, jewels rich and rare
They count as wealth for friends to share.

Yea, be they rich or poor and low,
Blest with all joys or sunk in woe,
Stained with each fault or pure of blame,
Their friends the nearest place may claim;
For whom they leave at friendship's call,
Their gold, their bliss, their homes and all.
He spoke by generous impulse moved,
And Raghu's son his speech approved,
Glancing at Lakshman by his side,
Like Indra in his beauty's pride.
The Vánar monarch saw the pair
Of mighty brothers standing there,
And turned his rapid eye to view
The forest trees that near him grew.
He saw, not far from where he stood,
A Sál tree towering o'er the wood.
Amid the thick leaves many a bee
Graced the scant blossoms of the tree,
From whose dark shade a bough, that bore
A load of leafy twigs, he tore,
Which on the grassy ground he laid
And seats for him and Ráma made.
Hanúmán saw them sit, he sought
A Sál tree's leafy bough and brought
The burthen, and with meek request
Entreated Lakshman, too, to rest.
There on the noble mountain's brow,
Strewn with the young leaves of the bough,
Sat Raghu's son in placid ease
Calm as the sea when sleeps the breeze.
Sugríva's heart with rapture swelled,
And thus, by eager love impelled,
He spoke in gracious tone, that, oft
Checked by his joy, was low and soft:
'I, by my brother's might oppressed,
By ceaseless woe and fear distressed,
Mourning my consort far away,
On Rishyamúka's mountain stray.
Expelled by Báli's cruel hate
I wander here disconsolate.
Do thou to whom all sufferers flee,
From his dread hand deliver me.'
He spoke, and Ráma, just and brave,
Whose pious soul to virtue clave,
Smiled as in conscious might he eyed
The king of Vánars, and replied:
'Best fruit of friendship is the deed
That helps the friend in hour of need;
And this mine arm in death shall lay
Thy robber ere the close of day.
For see, these feathered darts of mine
Whose points so fiercely flash and shine,
And shafts with golden emblem, came
From dark woods known by Skanda's name,[1]
Winged from the pinion of the hern
Like Indra's bolts they strike and burn.
With even knots and piercing head
Each like a furious snake is sped;
With these, to-day, before thine eye
Shall, like a shattered mountain, lie
Báli, thy dread and wicked foe,
O'erwhelmed in hideous overthrow.'
He spoke: Sugríva's bosom swelled
With hope and joy unparalleled.
Then his glad voice the Vánar raised,
And thus the son of Raghu praised:
'Long have I pined in depth of grief;
Thou art the hope of all, O chief.
Now, Raghu's son, I hail thee friend,
And bid thee to my woes attend;
For, by my truth I swear it, now
Not life itself is dear as thou,
Since by the witness fire we met
And friendly hand in hand was set.
Friend communes now with friend, and hence
I tell with surest confidence,
How woes that on my spirit weigh
Consume me through the night and day.'
For sobs and sighs he scarce could speak,
And his sad voice came low and weak,
As, while his eyes with tears o'erflowed,
The burden of his soul he showed.
Then by strong effort, bravely made,
The torrent of his tears he stayed,
Wiped his bright eyes, his grief subdued,
And thus, more calm, his speech renewed;
'By Báli's conquering might oppressed,
Of power and kingship dispossessed,
Loaded with taunts of scorn and hate
I left my realm and royal state.
He tore away my consort: she
Was dearer than my life to me,
And many a friend to me and mine
In hopeless chains was doomed to pine.
With wicked thoughts, unsated still,
Me whom he wrongs he yearns to kill;
And spies of Vánar race, who tried
To slay me, by this hand have died.
Moved by this constant doubt and fear
I saw thee, Prince, and came not near.
When woe and peril gather round
A foe in every form is found.
Save Hanumán, O Raghu's son,
And these, no friend is left me, none.
Through their kind aid, a faithful band
Who guard their lord from hostile hand,
Rest when their chieftain rests and bend
Their steps where'er he lists to wend,—
Through them alone, in toil and pain,
My wretched life I still sustain.

---

[1] The wood in which Skanda or Kártikeya was brought up:

'The Warrior-God
Whose infant steps amid the thickets strayed
Where the reeds wave over the holy sod.'
Meghadúta.

See also Book I. Canto XXIX.

Enough, for thou hast heard in brief
The story of my pain and grief.
His mighty strength all regions know,
My brother, but my deadly foe.
Ah, if the proud oppressor fell,
His death would all my woe dispel.
Yea, on my cruel conqueror's fall
My joy depends, my life, my all.
This were the end and sure relief,
O Ráma, of my tale of grief.
Fair be his lot or dark with woe,
No comfort like a friend I know.'
Then Ráma spoke ; 'O friend, relate
Whence sprang fraternal strife and hate,
That duly taught by thee, I may
Each foeman's strength and weakness weigh :
And skilled in every chance restore
The blissful state thou hadst before.
For, when I think of all the scorn
And bitter woe thou long hast borne,
My soul indignant swells with pain
Like waters flushed with furious rain.
Then, ere I string this bended bow,
Tell me the tale I long to know,
Ere from the cord my arrow fly,
And low in death thy foeman lie.'
He spoke : Sugríva joyed to hear,
Nor less his lords were glad of cheer :
And thus to Ráma mighty-souled
The cause that moved their strife he told :

CANTO IX.

SUGRÍVA'S STORY.[1]

'My brother, known by Báli's name,
Had won by might a conqueror's fame.
My father's eldest-born was he,
Well honoured by his sire and me.
My father died, and each sage lord
Named Báli king with one accord ;
And he, by right of birth ordained,
The sovereign of the Vánars reigned.
He in his royal place controlled
The kingdom of our sires of old,
And I all faithful service lent
To aid my brother's government.
The fiend Máyáví,—him of yore
To Dundubhi[2] his mother bore,—
For woman's love in strife engaged,
A deadly war with Báli waged.
When sleep had chained each weary frame
To vast Kishkindhá's[1] gates he came,
And, shouting through the shades of night,
Challenged his foeman to the fight.
My brother heard the furious shout,
And wild with rage rushed madly out,
Though fain would I and each sad wife
Detain him from the deadly strife.
He burned his demon foe to slay,
And rushed impetuous to the fray.
His weeping wives he thrust aside,
And forth, impelled by fury, hied ;
While, by my love and duty led,
I followed where my brother sped.
Máyáví looked, and at the sight
Fled from his foes in wild affright.
The flying fiend we quickly viewed,
And with swift feet his steps pursued.
Then rose the moon, whose friendly ray
Cast light upon our headlong way.
By the soft beams was dimly shown
A mighty cave with grass o'ergrown.
Within its depths he sprang, and we
The demon's form no more might see.
My brother's breast was all aglow
With fury when he missed the foe,
And, turning, thus to me he said
With senses all disquieted :
'Here by the cavern's mouth remain ;
Keep ear and eye upon the strain,
While I the dark recess explore
And dip my brand in foeman's gore.'
I heard his angry speech, and tried
To turn him from his plan aside.
He made me swear by both his feet,
And sped within the dark retreat.
While in the cave he stayed, and I
Watched at the mouth, a year went by.
For his return I looked in vain,
And, moved by love, believed him slain.
I mourned, by doubt and fear distressed,
And greater horror seized my breast
When from the cavern rolled a flood,
A carnage stream of froth and blood ;
And from the depths a sound of fear,
The roar of demons, smote mine ear ;
But never rang my brother's shout
Triumphant in the battle rout.
I closed the cavern with a block,
Huge as a hill, of shattered rock,
Gave offerings due to Báli's shade,
And sought Kishkindhá, sore dismayed.
Long time with anxious care I tried
From Báli's lords his fate to hide,
But they, when once the tale was known,
Placed me as king on Báli's throne.
There for a while I justly reigned

[1] "Sugríva's story paints in vivid colours the manners, customs and ideas of the wild mountain tribes which inhabited Kishkindhya or the southern hills of the Deccan, of the people whom the poem calls monkeys, tribes altogether different in origin and civilization from the Indo-Sanskrit race." GORRESIO.

[2] A fiend slain by Báli.

[1] Báli's mountain city.

And all with equal care ordained,
When joyous from the demon slain
My brother Báli came again.
He found me ruling in his stead,
And, fired with rage, his eyes grew red.
He slew the lords who made me king,
And spoke keen words to taunt and sting.
The kingly rank and power I held
My brother's rage with ease had quelled,
But still, restrained by old respect
For claims of birth, the thought I checked.
Thus having struck the demon down
Came Báli to his royal town.
With meek respect, with humble speech,
His haughty heart I strove to reach.
But all my arts were tried in vain,
No gentle word his lips would deign.
Though to the ground I bent and set
His feet upon my coronet;
Still Báli in his rage and pride
All signs of grace and love denied.'

CANTO X.

SUGRÍVA'S STORY.

'I strove to soothe and lull to rest
The fury of his troubled breast:
'Well art thou come, dear lord,' I cried,
'By whose strong arm thy foe has died.
Forlorn I languished here, but now
My saviour and defence art thou.
Once more receive this regal shade[1]
Like the full moon in heaven displayed;
And let the chouries,[2] thus restored,
Wave glorious o'er the rightful lord.
I kept my watch, thy word obeyed,
And by the cave a year I stayed.
But when I saw that stream of blood
Rush from the cavern in a flood,
My sad heart broken with dismay,
And every wandering sense astray,
I barred the entrance with a stone,—
A crag from some high mountain thrown—
Turned from the spot I watched in vain,
And to Kishkindhá came again.
My deep distress and downcast mien
By citizen and lord were seen.
They made me king against my will:
Forgive me if the deed was ill.
True as I ever was I see
My honoured king once more in thee;
I only ruled a while the state
When thou hadst left us desolate.
This town with people, lords, and lands,
Lay as a trust in guardian hands;
And now, my gracious lord, accept
The kingdom which thy servant kept.
Forgive me. victor of the foe,
Nor let thy wrath against me glow.
See joining suppliant hands I pray,
And at thy feet my head I lay.
Believe my words: against my will
The royal seat they made me fill.
Unkinged they saw the city, hence
They made me lord for her defence.'

But Báli, though I humbly sued,
Reviled me in his furious mood:
'Out on thee, wretch!' in wrath he cried,
With many a bitter taunt beside.
He summoned every lord, and all
His subjects gathered at his call.
Then forth his burning anger broke,
And thus amid his friends he spoke:
'I need not tell, for well ye know,
How fierce Máyávi, fiend and foe,
Came to Kishkindhá's gate by night,
And dared me in his wrath to fight.
I heard each word the demon said:
Forth from my royal hall I sped;
And, foe in brother's guise concealed,
Sugríva followed to the field.
The mighty demon through the shade
Beheld me come with one to aid;
Then shrinking from unequal fight.
He turned his back in swiftest flight.
From vengeful foes his life to save
He sought the refuge of a cave.
Then when I saw the fiend had fled
Within that cavern dark and dread,
Thus to my brother cruel-eyed,
Impatient in my wrath, I cried:
'I seek no more my royal town
Till I have struck the demon down.
Here by the cavern's mouth remain
Until my hand the foe have slain.'
Upon his faith my heart relied,
And swift within the depths I hied.
A year went by: in every spot
I sought the fiend, but found him not.
At length my foe I saw and slew.
Whom long I feared when lost to view;
And all his kinsmen by his side
Beneath my vengeful fury died.
The monster, as he reeled and fell,
Poured forth his blood with roar and yell;
And, filling all the cavern, dyed
The portal with the crimson tide.
Upon my foeman slain at last
One look, one pitying look, I cast.
I sought again the light of day:
The cave was closed and left no way.
To the barred mouth I sadly came,
And called aloud Sugríva's name.
But all was still: no voice replied,

[1] The canopy or royal umbrella, one of the usual Indian regalia.

[2] Whisks made of the hair of the Yak or Bos grunniers, also regal insignia.

And hope within my bosom died.
With furious efforts, vain at first,
Through bars of rock my way I burst.
Then, free once more, the path that brought
My feet in safety home I sought.
'Twas thus Sugríva dared despise
The claim of brothers' friendly ties.
With crags of rock he barred me in,
And for himself the realm would win.'
Thus Báli spoke in words severe;
And then, unmoved by ruth or fear,
Left me a single robe and sent
His brother forth in banishment.
He cast me out with scathe and scorn,
And from my side my wife was torn.
Now in great fear and ill at ease
I roam this land with woods and seas,
Or dwell on Rishyamúka's hill,
And sorrow for my consort still.
Thou hast the tale how first arose
This bitter hate of brother foes.
Such are the griefs neath which I pine,
And all without a fault of mine.
O swift to save in hour of fear,
My prayer who dread this Báli, hear.
With gracious love assistance deign,
And mine oppressor's arm restrain.'
Then Raghu's son, the good and brave,
With a gay laugh his answer gave:
'These shafts of mine which ne'er can fail,
Before whose sheen the sun grows pale,
Winged by my fury, fleet and fierce,
The wicked Báli's heart shall pierce.
Yea, mark the words I speak, so long
Shall live that wretch who joys in wrong,
Until these angered eyes have seen
The robber of thy darling queen.
I, taught by equal suffering, know
What waves of grief above thee flow.
This hand thy captive wife shall free,
And give thy kingdom back to thee.'
Sugríva joyed as Ráma spoke,
And valour in his breast awoke.
His eye grew bright, his heart grew bold,
And thus his wondrous tale he told:

CANTO XI.

DUNDUBHI.

'I doubt not, Prince, thy peerless might,
Armed with these shafts so keen and bright,
Like all-destroying fires of fate,
The worlds could burn and devastate.
But lend thou first thy mind and ear
Of Báli's power and might to hear.
How bold, how firm, in battle tried,
Is Báli's heart; and then decide.
From east to west, from south to north
On restless errand hurrying forth,
From farthest sea to sea he flies
Before the sun has lit the skies.
A mountain top he oft will seek,
Tear from its root a towering peak,
Hurl it aloft, as 'twere a ball,
And catch it ere to earth it fall;
And many a tree that long has stood
In health and vigour in the wood,
His single arm to earth will throw,
The marvels of his might to show.
Shaped like a bull, a monster bore
The name of Dundubhi of yore:
He matched in size a mountain height,
A thousand elephants in might.
By pride of wondrous gifts impelled,
And strength he deemed unparalleled,
To Ocean, lord of stream and brook,
Athirst for war, his way he took.
He reached the king of rolling waves
Whose gems are piled in sunless caves,
And threw his challenge to the sea:
'Come forth, O King, and fight with me.'
He spoke, and from his ocean bed
The righteous[1] monarch heaved his head,
And gave, sedate, his calm reply
To him whom fate impelled to die:
'Not mine, not mine the power,' he cried,
'To cope with thee in battle tried;
But listen to my voice, and seek
The worthier foe of whom I speak.
The Lord of Hills, where hermits live
And love the home his forests give,
Whose child is Śankar's darling queen,[2]
The King of Snows is he I mean.
Deep caves has he, and dark boughs shade
The torrent and the wild cascade.
From him expect the fierce delight
Which heroes feel in equal fight.'
He deemed that fear checked ocean's king,
And, like an arrow from the string,
To the wild woods that clothe the side
Of Lord Himálaya's hills he hied.
Then Dundubhi, with hideous roar,
Huge fragments from the summit tore
Vast as Airávat,[3] white with snow,
And hurled them to the plains below.
Then like a white cloud soft, serene,
The Lord of Mountains' form was seen.
It sat upon a lofty crest,
And thus the furious fiend addressed:
'Beseems thee not, O virtue's friend,
My mountain tops to rive and rend;

---

[1] Righteous because he never transgresses his bounds, and
"over his great tides
Fidelity presides."

[2] Himálaya, the Lord of Snow, is the father of Umá the wife of Śiva or Śankar.

[3] Indra's celestial elephant.

For I, the hermit's calm retreat,
For deeds of war am all unmeet.'
The demon's eye with rage grew red,
And thus in furious tone he said:
'If thou from fear or sloth decline
To match thy strength in war with mine,
Where shall I find a champion, say,
To meet me burning for the fray?'
He spoke: Himálaya, skilled in lore
Of eloquence, replied once more,
And, angered in his righteous mind,
Addressed the chief of demon kind:
'The Vánar Báli, brave and wise,
Son of the God who rules the skies,[1]
Sways, glorious in his high renown,
Kishkindhá his imperial town.
Well may that valiant lord who knows
Each art of war his might oppose
To thine, in equal battle set,
As Namuchi[2] and Indra met.
Go, if thy soul desire the fray;
To Báli's city speed away,
And that unconquered hero meet
Whose fame is high for warlike feat.'
He listened to the Lord of Snow,
And, his proud heart with rage aglow,
Sped swift away and lighted down
By vast Kishkindhá, Báli's town.
With pointed horns to strike and gore
The semblance of a bull he bore,
Huge as a cloud that downward bends
Ere the full flood of rain descends.
Impelled by pride and rage and hate,
He thundered at Kishkindhá's gate;
And with his bellowing, like the sound
Of pealing drums, he shook the ground.
He rent the earth and prostrate threw
The trees that near the portal grew.
King Báli from the bowers within
Indignant heard the roar and din.
Then, moonlike mid the stars, with all
His dames he hurried to the wall;
And to the fiend this speech, expressed
In clear and measured words, addressed:
'Know me for monarch, Báli styled,
Of Vánar tribes that roam the wild.
Say why dost thou this gate molest,
And bellowing thus disturb our rest?
I know thee, mighty fiend: beware
And guard thy life with wiser care.'
He spoke: and thus the fiend returned,
While red with rage his eyeballs burned:
'What! speak when all thy dames are nigh
And hero-like thy foe defy?
Come, meet me in the fight this day,
And learn my strength by bold assay.
Or shall I spare thee, and relent
Until the coming night be spent?
Take then the respite of a night
And yield thee to each soft delight.
Then, monarch of the Vánar race,
With loving arms thy friends embrace.
Gifts on thy faithful lords bestow,
Bid each and all farewell, and go.
Show in the streets once more thy face,
Instal thy son to fill thy place.
Dally a while with each dear dame;
And then my strength thy pride shall tame
For, should I smite thee drunk with wine
Enamoured of those dames of thine,
Beneath diseases bowed and bent,
Or weak, unarmed, or negligent,
My deed would merit hate and scorn
As his who slays the child unborn.'
Then Báli's soul with rage was fired,
Queen Tárá and the dames retired;
And slowly, with a laugh of pride,
The king of Vánars thus replied:
'Me, fiend, thou deemest drunk with wine:
Unless thy fear the fight decline,
Come, meet me in the fray, and test
The spirit of my valiant breast.'
He spoke in wrath and high disdain:
And, laying down his golden chain,
Gift of his sire Mahendra, dared
The demon, for the fray prepared;
Seized by the horns the monster, vast
As a huge hill, and held him fast,
Then fiercely dragged him round and round,
And, shouting, hurled him to the ground.
Blood streaming from his ears, he rose,
And wild with fury strove the foes.
Then Báli, match for Indra's might,
With every arm renewed the fight.
He fought with fists, and feet, and knees,
With fragments of the rock, and trees.
At last the monster's strength, assailed
By Śakra's[1] conquering offspring, failed.
Him Báli raised with mighty strain,
And dashed upon the ground again;
Where, bruised and shattered, in a tide
Of rushing blood, the demon died.
King Báli saw the lifeless corse,
And, bending, with tremendous force
Raised the huge bulk from where it lay,
And hurled it full a league away.
As through the air the body flew,
Some blood-drops, caught by gales that blew,
Welled from his shattered jaw and fell
By Saint Matanga's hermit cell:
Matanga saw, illustrious sage,
Those drops defile his hermitage,

[1] Báli was the son of Indra. See p. 28.

[2] An Asur slain by Indra. See p. 261 Note. He is, like Vritra, a form of the demon of drought destroyed by the beneficent God of the firmament.

[1] Another name of Indra or Mahendra.

And, as he marvelled whence they came,
Fierce anger filled his soul with flame :
'Who is the villain, evil-souled,
With childish thoughts unwise and bold,
Who is the impious wretch,' he cried,
'By whom my grove with blood is dyed?'
Thus spoke Matanga in his rage,
And hastened from the hermitage,
When lo, before his wondering eyes
Lay the dead bull of mountain size.
His hermit soul was nothing slow
The doer of the deed to know,
And thus the Vánar in a burst
Of wild tempestuous wrath he cursed :
'Ne'er let that Vánar wander here,
For, if he come, his death is near.
Whose impious hand with blood has dyed
The holy place where I abide,
Who threw this demon corse and made
A ruin of the pleasant shade.
If e'er he plant his wicked feet
Within one league of my retreat ;
Yea, if the villain come so nigh
That very hour he needs must die.
And let the Vánar lords who dwell
In the dark woods that skirt my cell
Obey my words, and speeding hence
Find them some meeter residence.
Here if they dare to stay, on all
The terrors of my curse shall fall.
They spoil the tender saplings, dear
As children which I cherish here,
Mar root and branch and leaf and spray,
And steal the ripening fruit away.
One day I grant, no further hour,
To-morrow shall my curse have power,
And then each Vánar I may see
A stone through countless years shall be.'
The Vánars heard the curse and hied
From sheltering wood and mountain side.
King Báli marked their haste and dread,
And to the flying leaders said :
'Speak, Vánar chiefs, and tell me why
From Saint Matanga's grove ye fly
To gather round me: is it well
With all who in those woodlands dwell?'
He spoke : the Vánar leaders told
King Báli with his chain of gold
What curse the saint had on them laid,
Which drove them from their ancient shade.
Then royal Báli sought the sage,
With reverent hands to soothe his rage.
The holy man his suppliant spurned,
And to his cell in anger turned.
That curse on Báli sorely pressed,
And long his conscious soul distressed.
Him still the curse and terror keep
Afar from Rishyamúka's steep.
He dares not to the grove draw nigh,
Nay scarce will hither turn his eye.
We know what terrors warm him hence,
And roam these woods in confidence.
Look, Prince, before thee white and dry
The demon's bones uncovered lie,
Who, like a hill in bulk and length,
Fell ruind for his pride of strength.
See those high Sál trees seven in row
That droop their mighty branches low,
These at one grasp would Báli seize,
And leafless shake the trembling trees.
These tales I tell, O Prince, to show
The matchless power that arms the foe.
How canst thou hope to slay him? how
Meet Báli in the battle now?'
Sugríva spoke and sadly sighed :
And Lakshman with a laugh replied :
'What show of power, what proof and test
May still the doubts that fill thy breast?'
He spoke. Sugríva thus replied :
'See yonder Sál trees side by side.
King Báli here would take his stand
Grasping his bow with vigorous hand,
And every arrow, keen and true,
Would strike its tree and pierce it through
If Ráma now his bow will bend,
And through one trunk an arrow send ;
Or if his arm can raise and throw
Two hundred measures of his bow,
Grasped by a foot and hurled through air,
The demon bull that moulders there,
My heart will own his might and fain
Believe my foe already slain.'
Sugríva spoke inflamed with ire,
Scanned Ráma with a glance of fire,
Pondered a while in silent mood.
And thus again his speech renewed :
'All lands with Báli's glories ring,
A valiant, strong, and mighty king ;
In conscious power unused to yield,
A hero first in every field.
His wondrous deeds his might declare,
Deeds Gods might scarcely do or dare ;
And on this power reflecting still
I roam on Rishyamúka's hill.
Awed by my brother's might I rove,
In doubt and fear, from grove to grove,
While Hanumán, my chosen friend,
And faithful lords my steps attend ;
And now, O true to friendship's tie,
I hail in thee my best ally.
My surest refuge from my foes,
And steadfast as the Lord of Snows.
Still, when I muse how strong and bold
Is cruel Báli, evil-souled,
But ne'er, O chief of Raghu's line,
Have seen what strength in war is thine,
Though in my heart I may not dare
Doubt thy great might, despise, compare,
Thoughts of his fearful deeds will rise
And fill my soul with sad surmise.
Speech, form, and trust which naught may
move

Thy secret strength and glory prove,
As smouldering ashes dimly show
The dormant fires that live below.'
He ceased: and Ráma answered, while
Played o'er his lips a gracious smile:
'Not yet convinced? This clear assay
Shall drive each lingering doubt away.'
Thus Ráma spoke his heart to cheer,
To Dundubhi's vast frame drew near;
He touched it with his foot in play
And sent it twenty leagues away.
Sugríva marked what easy force
Hurled through the air that demon's corse
Whose mighty bones were white and dried,
And to the son of Raghu cried:
'My brother Báli, when his might
Was drunk and weary from the fight,
Hurled forth the monster body, fresh
With skin and sinews, blood and flesh.
Now flesh and blood are dried away,
The crumbling bones are light as hay,
Which thou, O Raghu's son, hast sent
Flying through air in merriment.
This test alone is weak to show
If thou be stronger or the foe.
By thee a heap of mouldering bone,
By him the recent corse was thrown.
Thy strength, O Prince, is yet untried:
Come, pierce one tree: let this decide.
Prepare thy ponderous bow and bring
Close to thine ear the straining string.
On yonder Sál tree fix thine eye,
And let the mighty arrow fly,
I doubt not, chief, that I shall see
Thy pointed shaft transfix the tree.
Then come, assay the easy task,
And do for love the thing I ask.
Best of all lights, the Day-God fills
With glory earth and sky:
Himálaya is the lord of hills
That heave their heads on high.
The royal lion is the best
Of beasts that tread the earth;
And thou, O hero, art confessed
First in heroic worth.'

CANTO XII.

THE PALM TREES.

Then Ráma, that his friend might know
His strength unrivalled, grasped his bow,
That mighty bow the foe's dismay,—
And on the string an arrow lay.
Next on the tree his eye he bent,
And forth the hurtling weapon went.
Loosed from the matchless hero's hold,
That arrow, decked with burning gold,
Cleft the seven palms in line, and through
The hill that rose behind them flew:
Six subterranean realms it passed,
And reached the lowest depth at last,
Whence speeding back through earth and air
It sought the quiver, and rested there.[1]
Upon the cloven trees, amazed,
The sovereign of the Vánars gazed.
With all his chains and gold outspread
Prostrate on earth he laid his head.
Then, rising, palm to palm he laid
In reverent act, obeisance made,
And joyously to Ráma, best
Of war-trained chiefs, these words addressed:
'What champion, Raghu's son, may hope
With thee in deadly fight to cope,
Whose arrow, leaping from the bow,
Cleaves tree and hill and earth below?
Scarce might the Gods, arrayed for strife
By Indra's self, escape, with life
Assailed by thy victorious hand:
And how may Báli hope to stand?
All grief and care are past away,
And joyous thoughts my bosom sway,
Who have in thee a friend, renowned,
As Varun[2] or as Indra, found.
Then on! subdue,—'tis friendship's claim,—
My foe who bears a brother's name.
Strike Báli down beneath thy feet:
With suppliant hands I thus entreat.'
Sugríva ceased, and Ráma pressed
The grateful Vánar to his breast;
And thoughts of kindred feeling woke
In Lakshman's bosom, as he spoke:
'On to Kishkindhá, on with speed!
Thou, Vánar King, our way shalt lead,
Then challenge Báli forth to fight.
Thy foe who scorns a brother's right.'
They sought Kishkindhá's gate and stood
Concealed by trees in densest wood,
Sugríva, to the fight addressed,
More closely drew his cinctured vest,
And raised a wild sky-piercing shout

[1] The Bengal recension makes it return in the form of a swan.

[2] Varuna is one of the oldest of the Vedic Gods, corresponding in name and partly in character to the Οὐρανός of the Greeks and is often regarded as the supreme deity. He upholds heaven and earth, possesses extraordinary power and wisdom, sends his messengers through both worlds, numbers the very winkings of men's eyes, punishes transgressors whom he seizes with his deadly noose, and pardons the sins of those who are penitent. In later mythology he has become the God of the sea.

To call the foeman Báli out.
  Forth came impetuous Báli, stirred
To fury by the shout he heard.
So the great sun, ere night has ceased,
Springs up impatient to the east.
Then fierce and wild the conflict raged
As hand to hand the foes engaged,
As though in battle mid the stars
Fought Mercury and fiery Mars.[1]
To highest pitch of frenzy wrought
With fists like thunderbolts they fought,
While near them Ráma took his stand,
And viewed the battle, bow in hand.
Alike they stood in form and might,
Like heavenly Asvins[2] paired in fight,
Nor might the son of Raghu know
Where fought the friend and where the foe;
So, while his bow was ready bent,
No life-destroying shaft he sent.
Crushed down by Báli's mightier stroke
Sugríva's force now sank and broke,
Who, hoping naught from Ráma's aid,
To Rishyamúka fled dismayed,
Weary, and faint, and wounded sore,
His body bruised and dyed with gore,
From Báli's blows, in rage and dread,
Afar to sheltering woods he fled.
  Nor Báli farther dared pursue,
The curbing curse too well he knew.
'Fled from thy death!' the victor cried,
And home the mighty warrior hied.
Hanúmán, Lakshman, Raghu's son
Beheld the conquered Vánar run,
And followed to the sheltering shade
Where yet Sugríva stood dismayed.
Near and more near the chieftains came,
Then, for intolerable shame,
Not daring yet to lift his eyes,
Sugríva spoke with burning sighs:
'Thy matchless strength I first beheld,
And dared my foe, by thee impelled.
Why hast thou tried me with deceit
And urged me to a sure defeat?
Thou shouldst have said, 'I will not slay
Thy foeman in the coming fray.'
For had I then thy purpose known
I had not waged the fight alone.'
  The Vánar sovereign, lofty-souled,
In plaintive voice his sorrows told.
Then Ráma spake: 'Sugríva, list,
All anger from thy heart dismissed,
And I will tell the cause that stayed
Mine arrow, and withheld the aid.
In dress, adornment, port, and height,
In splendour, battle-shout, and might,
No shade of difference could I see
Between thy foe, O King, and thee.
So like was each, I stood at gaze,
My senses lost in wildering maze,
Nor loosened from my straining bow
A deadly arrow at the foe,
Lest in my doubt the shaft should send
To sudden death our surest friend.
O, if this hand in heedless guilt
And rash resolve thy blood had spilt,
Through every land, O Vánar King,
My wild and foolish act would ring.
Sore weight of sin on him must lie
By whom a friend is made to die;
And Lakshman, I, and Sítá, best
Of dames, on thy protection rest.
On, warrior! for the fight prepare;
Nor fear again thy foe to dare.
Within one hour thine eye shall view
My arrow strike thy foeman through;
Shall see the stricken Báli lie
Low on the earth, and gasp and die.
But come, a badge about thee bind,
O monarch of the Vánar kind,
That in the battle shock mine eyes
The friend and foe may recognize.
Come, Lakshman, let that creeper deck
With brightest bloom Sugríva's neck,
And be a happy token, twined
Around the chief of lofty mind.'
  Upon the mountain slope there grew
A spreading creeper fair to view,
And Lakshman plucked the bloom and round
Sugríva's neck a garland wound.
Graced with the flowery wreath he wore,
The Vánar chief the semblance bore
Of a dark cloud at close of day
Engarlanded with cranes at play,
In glorious light the Vánar glowed
As by his comrade's side he strode,
And, still on Ráma's words intent,
His steps to great Kishkindhá bent.

---

[1] Budha, not to be confounded with the great reformer Buddha, is the son of Soma or the Moon, and regent of the planet Mercury. Angára is the regent of Mars who is called the red or the fiery planet. The encounter between Michael and Satan is similarly said to have been as if

"Two planets rushing from aspect malign
Of fiercest opposition in midsky
Should combat, and their jarring spheres compound."

Paradise Lost, Book VI.

[2] The Asvins or Heavenly Twins, the Dioskuri or Castor and Pollux of the Hindus, have frequently been mentioned. See p. 36, Note.

CANTO XIII.

THE RETURN TO KISHKINDHA'.

Thus with Sugríva, from the side
Of Rishyamúka, Ráma hied,
And stood before Kishkindhá's gate
Where Báli kept his regal state.
The hero in his warrior hold
Raised his great bow adorned with gold,
And drew his pointed arrow bright
As sunbeams, finisher of fight.
Strong-necked Sugríva led the way
With Lakshman mighty in the fray.
Nala and Níla came behind
With Hanumán of lofty mind,
And valiant Tára, last in place,
A leader of the Vánar race.
They gazed on many a tree that showed
The glory of its pendent load,
And brook and limpid rill that made
Sweet murmurs as they seaward strayed.
They looked on caverns dark and deep,
On bower and glen and mountain steep,
And saw the opening lotus stud
With roseate cup the crystal flood,
While crane and swan and coot and drake
Made pleasant music on the lake,
And from the reedy bank was heard
The note of many a happy bird.
In open lawns, in tangled ways,
They saw the tall deer stand at gaze,
Or marked them free and fearless roam,
Fed with sweet grass, their woodland home.
At times two flashing tusks between
The wavings of the wood were seen,
And some mad elephant, alone,
Like a huge moving hill, was shown.
And scarcely less in size appeared
Great monkeys all with dust besmeared.
And various birds that roam the skies,
And silvan creatures, met their eyes,
As through the wood the chieftains sped,
And followed where Sugríva led.
Then Ráma, as their way they made,
Saw near at hand a lovely shade,
And, as he gazed upon the trees,
Spake to Sugríva words like these:
'Those stately trees in beauty rise
Fair as a cloud in autumn skies.
I fain, my friend, would learn from thee
What pleasant grove is that I see.'
Thus Ráma spake, the mighty souled;
And thus his tale Sugríva told:
'That, Ráma, is a wide retreat
That brings repose to weary feet.
Bright streams and fruit and roots are there,
And shady gardens passing fair.
There, neath the roof of hanging boughs,
The sacred Seven maintained their vows.
Their heads in dust were lowly laid,
In streams their nightly beds were made.
Each seventh night they broke their fast,
But air was still their sole repast,
And when seven hundred years were spent
To homes in heaven the hermits went.
Their glory keeps the garden yet,
With walls of stately trees beset.
Scarce would the Gods and demons dare,
By Indra led, to enter there.
No beast that roams the wood is found,
No bird of air, within the bound;
Or, thither if they idly stray,
They find no more their homeward way.
You hear at times mid dulcet tones
The chime of anklets, rings, and zones.
You hear the song and music sound.
And heavenly fragrance breathes around.
There duly burn the triple fires[1]
Where mounts the smoke in curling spires,
And, in a dun wreath, hangs above
The tall trees, like a brooding dove.
Round branch and crest the vapours close
Till every tree enveloped shows
A hill of lazulite when clouds
Hang round it with their misty shrouds.
With Lakshman, lord of Raghu's line,
In reverent guise thine head incline,
And with fixt heart and suppliant hand
Give honour to the sainted band.
They who with faithful hearts revere
The holy Seven who harboured here,
Shall never, son of Raghu, know
In all their lives an hour of woe.'
Then Ráma and his brother bent,
And did obeisance reverent
With suppliant hand and lowly head,
Then with Sugríva onward sped.
Beyond the sainted Seven's abode
Far on their way the chieftains strode,
And great Kishkindhá's portal gained,
The royal town where Báli reigned.
Then by the gate they took their stand
All ready armed a noble band,
And burning every one
To slay in battle, hand to hand,
Their foeman, Indra's son.

CANTO XIV.

THE CHALLENGE.

They stood where trees of densest green
Wove round their forms a veiling screen.
O'er all the garden's pleasant shade
The eyes of King Sugríva strayed,

[1] Called respectively Gárhapatya, A'havaníya, and Dakshina, household, sacrificial, and southern.

And, as on grass and tree he gazed,
The fires of wrath within him blazed.
Then like a mighty cloud on high,
When roars the tempest through the sky,
Girt by his friends he thundered out
His dread sky-rending battle-shout.
Like some proud lion in his gait,
Or as the sun begins his state,
Sugríva let his quick glance rest
On Ráma whom he thus addressed:
'There is the seat of Báli's sway,
Where flags on wall and turret play,
Which mighty bands of Vánars hold,
Rich in all arms and store of gold.
Thy promise to thy mind recall
That Báli by thy hand shall fall.
As kindly fruits adorn the bough,
So give my hopes their harvest now.'
In suppliant tone the Vánar prayed,
And Raghu's son his answer made:
'By Lakshman's hand this flowery twine
Was wound about thee for a sign.
The wreath of giant creeper throws
About thy form its brillant glows,
As though about the sun were set
The bright stars for a coronet.
One shaft of mine this day, dear friend,
Thy sorrow and thy fear shall end,
And, from the bowstring freed, shall be
Giver of freedom, King, to thee.
Then come, Sugríva, quickly show,
Where'er he lie, thy bitter foe;
And let my glance the wretch descry
Whose deeds a brother's name belie.
Yea, soon in dust and blood o'erthrown
Shall Báli fall and gasp and groan.
Once let this eye the foeman see,
Then, if he live to turn and flee,
Despise my puny strength, and shame
With foul opprobrium Ráma's name.
Hast thou not seen this hand, O King,
Through seven tall trees one arrow wing?
Still in that strength securely trust,
And deem thy foeman in the dust.
In all my days, though sorely tried
By grief and woe, I ne'er have lied;
And still by duty's law restrained
Will ne'er with falsehood's charge be stained.
Cast doubt away: the oath I sware
Its kindly fruit shall quickly bear,
As smiles the land with golden grain
By mercy of the Lord of rain.
On, warrior, to the gate! defy
Thy foe with shout and battle-cry,
Till Báli with his chain of gold
Come speeding from his royal hold.
Proud hearts, with warlike fire aglow,
Brook not the challenge of a foe:
Each on his power and might relies,
And most before his ladies' eyes,
King Báli loves the fray too well
To linger in his citadel,
And, when he hears thy battle-shout,
All wild for war will hasten out.'

He spoke. Sugríva raised a cry
That shook and rent the echoing sky,
A shout so fierce and loud and dread
That stately bulls in terror fled,
Like dames who fly from threatened stain
In some ignoble monarch's reign.
The deer in wild confusion ran
Like horses turned in battle's van.
Down fell the birds, like Gods who fall
When merits fail,[1] at that dread call.
So fiercely, boldened for the fray,
The offspring of the Lord of Day
Sent forth his furious shout as loud
As thunder from a labouring cloud,
Or, where the gale blows fresh and free,
The roaring of the troubled sea.

CANTO XV.

TÁRÁ.

That shout, which shook the land with fear,
In thunder smote on Báli's ear,
Where in the chamber barred and closed
The sovereign with his dame reposed.
Each amorous thought was rudely stilled,
And pride and rage his bosom filled.
His angry eyes flashed darkly red,
And all his native brightness fled,
As when, by swift eclipse assailed,
The glory of the sun has failed.
While in his fury uncontrolled
He ground his teeth, his eyeballs rolled,
He seemed a lake wherein no gem
Of blossom decks the lotus stem.
He heard, and with indignant pride
Forth from the bower the Vánar hied.
And the earth trembled at the beat
And fury of his hastening feet.
But Tárá to her consort flew,
Her loving arms around him threw,
And, trembling and bewildered, gave
Wise counsel that might heal and save:
O dear my lord, this rage control
That like a torrent floods thy soul,
And cast these idle thoughts away
Like faded wreaths of yesterday,
O tarry till the morning light,
Then, if thou wilt, go forth and fight.

---

[1] The store of merit accumulated by a holy or austere life secures only a temporary seat in the mansions of bliss. When by the lapse of time this store is exhausted, return to earth is unavoidable.

Think not I doubt thy valour, no ;
Or deem thee weaker than thy foe,
Yet for a while would have thee stay
Nor see thee tempt the fight to-day.
Now list, my loving lord, and learn
The reason why I bid thee turn.
Thy foeman came in wrath and pride,
And thee to deadly fight defied.
Thou wentest out : he fought, and fled
Sore wounded and discomfited.
But yet, untaught by late defeat,
He comes his conquering foe to meet,
And calls thee forth with cry and shout :
Hence spring, my lord, this fear and doubt.
A heart so bold that will not yield,
But yearns to tempt the desperate field,
Such loud defiance, fiercely pressed,
On no uncertain hope can rest.
So lately by thine arm o'erthrown,
He comes not back, I ween, alone.
Some mightier comrade guards his side,
And spurs him to this burst of pride.
For nature made the Vánar wise:
On arms of might his hope relies ;
And never will Sugríva seek
A friend whose power to save is weak.
Now listen while my lips unfold
The wondrous tale my Angad told.
Our child the distant forest sought,
And, learnt from spies, the tidings brought.
Two sons of Dasaratha, sprung
From old Ikshváku, brave and young,
Renowned in arms, in war untamed—
Ráma and Lakshman are they named—
Have with thy foe Sugríva made
A league of love and friendly aid.
Now Ráma, famed for exploit high,
Is bound thy brother's firm ally.
Like fires of doom[1] that ruin all
He makes each foe before him fall.
He is the suppliant's sure defence,
The tree that shelters innocence.
The poor and wretched seek his feet :
In him the noblest glories meet.
With skill and knowledge vast and deep
His sire's commands he loved to keep ;
With princely gifts and graces stored
As metals deck the Mountains' Lord.[2]
Thou canst not, O my hero, stand
Before the might of Ráma's hand ;
For none may match his power, or dare
With him in deeds of war compare.
Hear, I entreat, the words I say,
Nor lightly turn my rede away.
O let fraternal discord cease,
And link you in the bonds of peace.
Let consecrating rites ordain
Sugríva partner of thy reign.
Let war and thoughts of conflict end,
And be thou his and Ráma's friend.
Each soft approach of love begin,
And to thy soul thy brother win ;
For whether here or there he be,
Thy brother still, dear lord, is he.
Though far and wide these eyes I strain
A friend like him I seek in vain.
Let gentle words his heart incline,
And gifts and honours make him thine,
Till, foes no more, in love allied,
You stand as brothers side by side.
Thou in high rank wast wont to hold
Sugríva, formed in massive mould :
Then come, thy brother's love regain,
For other aids are weak and vain.
If thou would please my soul, and still
Preserve me from all fear and ill,
I pray thee by thy love be wise
And do the thing which I advise.
Assuage thy fruitless wrath, and shun
The mightier arms of Raghu's son ;
For Indra's peer in might is he,
A foe too strong, my lord, for thee.'

CANTO XVI.

THE FALL OF BÁLI.

Thus Tárá with the starry eyes[1]
Her counsel gave with burning sighs,
But Báli, by her prayers unmoved,
Spurned her advice, and thus reproved :
'How may this insult, scathe, and scorn
By me, dear love, be tamely born ?
My brother, yea my foe, comes nigh
And dares me forth with shout and cry.
Learn, trembler! that the valiant, they
Who yield no step in battle fray,
Will die a thousand deaths but ne'er
An unavenged dishonour bear.
Nor, O my love, be thou dismayed
Though Ráma lend Sugríva aid ;
For one so pure and duteous, one
Who loves the right, all sin will shun.
Release me from thy soft embrace,
And with thy dames thy steps retrace ;
Enough already, O mine own.
Of love and sweet devotion shown.
Drive all thy fear and doubt away ;
I seek Sugríva in the fray
His boisterous rage and pride to still,
And tame the foe I would not kill.
My fury, armed with brandished trees,
Shall strike Sugríva to his knees :

[1] The conflagration which destroys the world at the end of a Yuga or age.
[2] Himálaya.

[1] Tárá means 'star'. The poet plays upon the name by comparing her beauty to that of the Lord of Stars, the Moon.

Nor shall the humbled foe withstand
The blows of my avenging hand,
When, nerved by rage and pride, I beat
The traitor down beneath my feet.
Thou, love, hast lent thine own sweet aid,
And all thy tender care displayed;
Now by my life, by these who yearn
To serve thee well, I pray thee turn.
But for a while, dear dame, I go
To come triumphant o'er the foe.'

Thus Báli spake in gentlest tone:
Soft arms about his neck were thrown;
Then round her lord the lady went
With sad steps slow and reverent.
She stood in solemn guise to bless
With prayers for safety and success,
Then with her train her chamber sought
By grief and racking fear distraught.

With serpent's pantings fierce and fast
King Báli from the city passed.
His glance, as each quick breath he drew,
Around to find the foe he threw,
And saw where fierce Sugríva showed
His form with golden hues that glowed,
And, as a fire resplendent, stayed
To meet his foe in arms arrayed.
When Báli, long-armed chieftain, found
Sugríva stationed on the ground,
Impelled by warlike rage he braced
His warrior garb about his waist,
And with his mighty arm raised high
Rushed at Sugríva with a cry.
But when Sugríva, fierce and bold,
Saw Báli with his chain of gold,
His arm he heaved, his hand he closed,
And face to face his foe opposed.
To him whose eyes with fury shone,
In charge impetuous rushing on,
Skilled in each warlike art and plan,
Báli with hasty words began:
'My ponderous hand, to fight addressed,
With fingers clenched and firm compressed,
Shall on thy death-doomed brow descend
And, crashing down, thy life shall end.'
He spoke; and, wild with rage and pride,
The fierce Sugríva thus replied:
'Thus let my arm begin the strife
And from thy body crush the life.'

Then Báli, wounded and enraged,
With furious blows the battle waged.
Sugríva seemed, with blood-streams dyed,
A hill with fountains in his side.
But with his native force unspent
A Sál tree from the earth he rent,
And like the bolt of Indra smote
On Báli's head and chest and throat.
Bruised by the blows he could not shield,
Half vanquished Báli sank and reeled,
As sinks a vessel with her freight
Borne down by overwhelming weight.
Swift as Suparna's[1] swiftest flight
In awful strength they rushed to fight:
So might the sun and moon on high
Encountering battle in the sky.
Fierce and more fierce, as fought the foes,
The furious rage of combat rose.
They warred with feet and arms and knees,
With nails and stones and boughs and trees,
And blows descending fast as rain
Dyed each dark form with crimson stain,
While like two thunder-clouds they met
With battle-cry and shout and threat.
Then Ráma saw Sugríva quail,
Marked his worn strength grow weak and fail,
Saw how he turned his wistful eye
To every quarter of the sky.
His friend's defeat he could not brook,
Bent on his shaft an eager look,
Then burned to slay the conquering foe,
And laid his arrow on the bow.
As to an orb the bow he drew
Forth from the string the arrow flew
Like Fate's tremendous discus hurled
By Yama[2] forth to end the world.
So loud the din that every bird
The bow-string's clang with terror heard,
And wildly fled the affrighted deer
As though the day of doom were near.
So, deadly as the serpent's fang,
Forth from the string the arrow sprang.
Like the red lightning's flash and flame
It flew unerring to its aim,
And, hissing murder through the air,
Pierced Báli's breast, and quivered there.
Struck by the shaft that flew so well
The mighty Vánar reeled and fell,
As earthward Indra's flag they pull
When Asviní's fair moon is full.[3]

CANTO XVII.

BÁLI'S SPEECH.

Like some proud tree before the blast
Brave Báli to the ground was cast,
Where prostrate in the dust he rolled
Clad in the sheen of glistering gold,

[1] Suparna, the Well-winged, is another name of Garuḍa the King of Birds. See p. 28, Note.

[2] The God of Death.

[3] The flag-staff erected in honour of the God Indra is lowered when the festival is over. Asviní in astronomy is the head of Aries or the first of the twenty-eight lunar mansions or asterisms.

As when uptorn the standard lies
Of the great God who rules the skies.
When low upon the earth was laid
The lord whom Vánar tribes obeyed,
Dark as a moonless sky no more
His land her joyous aspect wore.
Though low in dust and mire was rolled
The form of Báli lofty-souled,
Still life and valour, might and grace
Clung to their well-loved dwelling-place.
That golden chain with rich gems set,
The choicest gift of Śakra,[1] yet
Preserved his life nor let decay
Steal strength and beauty's light away.
Still from that chain divinely wrought
His dusky form a glory caught,
As a dark cloud, when day is done,
Made splendid by the dying sun.
As fell the hero, crushed in fight,
There beamed afar a triple light
From limbs, from chain, from shaft that drank
His life-blood as the warrior sank.
The never-failing shaft, impelled
By the great bow which Ráma held,
Brought bliss supreme. and lit the way
To Brahmá's worlds which ne'er decay.[2]
Ráma and Lakshman nearer drew
The mighty fallen foe to view,
Mahendra's son, the brave and bold,
The monarch with his chain of gold,
With lustrous face and tawny eyes,
Broad chest, and arms of wondrous size,
Like Lord Mahendra fierce in fight,
Or Vishnu's never-conquered might,
Now fallen like Yayáti[3] sent
From heaven, his store of merit spent,
Like the bright flame that pales and dies,
Like the great sun who fires the skies,
Doomed in the general doom to fall
When time shall end and ruin all.
The wounded Báli, when he saw
Ráma and Lakshman nearer draw,
Keen words to Raghu's son, impressed
With justice' holy stamp, addressed:
'What fame, from one thou hast not slain
In front of battle, canst thou gain,
Whose secret hand has laid me low
When madly fighting with my foe?
From every tongue thy glory rings,
A scion of a line of kings,
True to thy vows, of noblest race,
With every gentle gift and grace:
Whose tender heart for woe can feel,
And joy in every creature's weal:
Whose breast with high ambition swells,
Knows duty's claim and ne'er rebels.
They praise thy valour, patience, ruth,
Thy firmness, self-restrain, and truth:
Thy hand prepared for sin's control,
All virtues of a princely soul.
I thought of all these gifts of thine,
And glories of an ancient line,
I set my Tárá's tears at naught,
I met Sugríva and we fought.
O Ráma, till this fatal morn
I held that thou wouldst surely scorn
To strike me as I fought my foe
And thought not of a stranger's blow.
But now thine evil heart is shown,
A yawning well with grass o'ergrown.
Thou wearest virtue's badge,[1] but guile
And meanest sin thy soul defile.
I took thee not for treacherous fire,
A sinner clad in saint's attire;
Nor deemed thou idly wouldst profess
The show and garb of righteousness.
In fenced town, in open land,
Ne'er hast thou suffered at this hand,
Nor canst of proud contempt complain:
Then wherefore is the guiltless slain?
My harmless life in woods I lead,
On forest fruits and roots I feed.
My foeman in the field I sought,
And ne'er with thee, O Ráma, fought.
Upon thy limbs, O King, I see
The raiment of a devotee;
And how can one like thee, who springs
From a proud line of ancient kings,
Beneath fair virtue's mask, disgrace
His lineage by a deed so base?
From Raghu is thy long descent,
For duteous deeds prëeminent:
Why, sinner clad in saintly dress,
Roamest thou through the wilderness?
Truth, valour, justice free from spot,
The hand that gives and grudges not,
The might that strikes the sinner down,
These bring a prince his best renown.
Here in the woods, O King, we live
On roots and fruit which branches give.[2]

---

[1] Indra the father of Báli.

[2] It is believed that every creature killed by Ráma obtained in consequence immediate beatitude.

'And blessed the hand that gave se dear a death.'

[3] "Yayáti was invited to heaven by Indra, and conveyed on the way thither by Mátali, Indra's charioteer. He afterwards returned to earth where, by his virtuous administration he rendered all his subjects exempt from passion and decay." GARRETT'S C. D. OF INDIA.

[1] The ascetic's dress which he wore during his exile.

[2] There is much inconsistency in the passages of the poem in which the Vánars are spoken of, which seems to point to two

Thus nature framed our harmless race :
Thou art a man supreme in place.
Silver and gold and land provoke
The fierce attack, the robber's stroke.
Canst thou desire this wild retreat,
The berries and the fruit we eat?
'Tis not for mighty kings to tread
The flowery path, by pleasure led.
Theirs be the arm that crushes sin,
Theirs the soft grace to woo and win:
The steadfast will that guides the state,
Wise favour to the good and great;
And for all time are kings renowned
Who blend these arts and ne'er confound.
But thou art weak and swift to ire,
Unstable, slave of each desire.
Thou tramplest duty in the dust,
And in thy bow is all thy trust.
Thou carest naught for noble gain,
And treatest virtue with disdain,
While every sense its captive draws
To follow pleasure's changing laws.
I wronged thee not in word or deed,
But by thy deadly dart I bleed.
What wilt thou, mid the virtuous, say
To purge thy lasting stain away?
All these, O King, must sink to hell,
The regicide, the infidel,
He who in blood and slaughter joys,
A Bráhman or a cow destroys,
Untimely weds in law's despite
Scorning an elder brother's right,[1]
Who dares his Teacher's bed ascend,
The miser, spy, and treacherous friend.
These impious wretches, one and all,
Must to the hell of sinners fall.
My skin the holy may not wear,
Useless to thee my bones and hair;
Nor may my slaughtered body be
The food of devotees like thee.
These five-toed things a man may slay
And feed upon the fallen prey;
The mailed rhinoceros may die,
And, with the hare his food supply.
Iguanas he may kill and eat,
With porcupine and tortoise meat.[1]
But all the wise account it sin
To touch my bones and hair and skin.
My flesh they may not eat; and I
A useless prey, O Ráma, die.
In vain my Tárá reasoned well,
On dull deaf ears her counsel fell.
I scorned her words though sooth and sweet,
And hither rushed my fate to meet.
Ah for the land thou rulest! she
Finds no protection, lord, from thee,
Neglected like some noble dame
By a vile husband dead to shame.
Mean-hearted coward, false and vile,
Whose cruel soul delights in guile,
Could Daśaratha, noblest king,
Beget so mean and base a thing?
Alas! an elephant, in form
Of Ráma, in a maddening storm
Of passion casting to the ground
The girth of law[2] that clipped him round,
Too wildly passionate to feel
The prick of duty's guiding steel,[3]
Has charged me unawares, and dead
I fall beneath his murderous tread.
How, stained with this my base defeat,
How wilt thou dare, where good men meet,
To speak, when every tongue will blame
With keen reproach this deed of shame?
Such hero strength and valour, shown
Upon the innocent alone,
Thou hast not proved in manly strife
On him who robbed thee of thy wife.
Hadst thou but fought in open field
And met me boldly unconcealed,
This day had been thy fate to fall,
Slain by this hand, to Yama's hall.
In vain I strove, and struck by thee
Fell by a hand I could not see.
Thus bites a snake, for sins of yore,
A sleeping man who wakes no more.
Sugríva's foeman thou hast killed,
And thus his heart's desire fulfilled:
But, Ráma, hadst thou sought me first,
And told the hope thy soul has nursed,
That very day had I restored
The Maithil lady to her lord;
And, binding Rávan with a chain,
Had laid him at thy feet unslain.

---

widely different legends. The Vánars are generally represented as semi-divine beings with preternatural powers, living in houses and eating and drinking like men, sometimes as here, as monkeys pure and simple, living in woods and eating fruit and roots.

[1] For a younger brother to marry before the elder is a gross violation of Indian law and duty. The same law applied to daughters with the Hebrews: "It must not be so done in our country to give the younger before the first-born." GENESIS, xxix. 26.

[1] "The hedgehog and porcupine, the lizard, the rhinoceros, the tortoise, and the rabbit or hare, wise legislators delare lawful food among five-toed animals."
MANU, v. 18.

[2] "He can not buckle his distempered cause
Within the belt of rule." MACBETH.

[3] The *Ankuś* or iron hook with which an elephant is driven and guided.

Yea, were she sunk in deepest hell,
Or whelmed beneath the ocean's swell,
I would have followed on her track
And brought the rescued lady back,
As Hayagríva[1] once set free
From hell the white Ásvatarí.[2]
That when my spirit wings its flight
Sugríva reign, is just and right.
But most unjust, O King, that I,
Slain by thy treacherous hand, should lie.
Be still, my heart: this earthly state
Is darkly ruled by sovereign Fate.
The realm is lost and won: defy
Thy questioners with apt reply.'[3]

CANTO XVIII.

RÁMA'S REPLY.

He ceased: and Ráma's heart was stirred
At every keen reproach he heard.
There Báli lay, a dim dark sun,
His course of light and glory run:
Or like the bed of Ocean dried
Of his broad floods from side to side,
Or helpless, as the dying fire,
Hushed his last words of righteous ire.
Then Ráma, with his spirit moved,
The Vánar king in turn reproved:
'Why dost thou Báli, thus revile,
And castest not a glance the while
On claims of duty, love, and gain,
And customs o'er the world that reign?
Why dost thou blame me, rash and blind,
Fickle as all thy Vánar kind,
Slighting each rule of ancient days
Which all the good and prudent praise?
This land, each hill and woody chase,
Belongs to old Ikshváku's race:
With bird and beast and man, the whole
Is ours to cherish and control.
Now Bharat, prompt at duty's call,
Wise, just, and true, is lord of all
Each claim of law, love, gain he knows,
And wrath and favour duly shows.
A king from truth who never bends,
And grace with vigour wisely blends;
With valour worthy of his race,
He knows the claims of time and place.
Now we and other kings of might,
By his ensample taught aright,
The lands of every region tread
That justice may increase and spread.
While royal Bharat, wise and just,
Rules the broad earth, his glorious trust,
Who shall attempt, while he is lord,
A deed by Justice held abhorred?
We now, as Bharat has decreed,
Let justice guide our every deed,
And toil each sinner to repress
Who scorns the way of righteousness.
Thou from that path hast turned aside,
And virtue's holy law defied,
Left the fair path which kings should tread,
And followed pleasure's voice instead.
The man who cleaves to duty's law
Regards these three with filial awe—
The sire, the elder brother, third
Him from whose lips his lore he heard.
Thus too, for duty's sake, the wise
Regard with fond paternal eyes
The well-loved younger brother, one
Their lore has ripened, and a son.
Fine are the laws which guide the good,
Abstruse, and hardly understood;
Only the soul, enthroned within
The breast of each, knows right from sin.
But thou art wild and weak of soul,
And spurnest, like thy race, control:
The true and right thou canst not find,
The blind consulting with the blind.
Incline thine ear and I will teach
The cause that prompts my present speech.
This tempest of thy soul assuage,
Nor blame me in thine idle rage.
On this great sin thy thoughts bestow,
The sin for which I lay thee low.
Thou, Báli, in thy brother's life
Hast robbed him of his wedded wife,
And keepest, scorning ancient right
His Rumá for thine own delight.
Thy son's own wife should scarcely be
More sacred in thine eyes than she.
All duty thou hast scorned, and hence
Comes punishment for dire offence.
For those who blindly do amiss
There is, I ween, no way but this:
To check the rash who dare to stray
From customs which the good obey,
I may not, sprung of Kshatriya line,

[1] Hayagríva, Horse-necked, is a form of Vishnu

[2] "Ásvatara is the name of a chief of the Nágas or serpents which inhabit the regions under the earth; it is also the name of a Gandharva. Ásvatarí ought to be the wife of one of the two, but I am not sure that this conjecture is right. The commentator does not say who this Asvatarí is, or what tradition or myth is alluded to. Vimalabódha reads Ásvatari in the nominative case, and explains, Ásvatarí is the sun, and as the sun with his rays brings back the moon which has been sunk in the ocean and the infernal regions, so will I bring back Sítá." GORRESIO.

[3] That is, 'Consider what answer you can give to your accusers when they charge you with injustice in killing me.'

Forgive this heinous sin of thine :
The laws for those who sin like thee
The penalty of death decree.
Now Bharat rules with sovereign sway,
And we his royal word obey.
There was no hope of pardon, none,
For the vile deed that thou hast done,
That wisest monarch dooms to die
The wretch whose crimes the law defy ;
And we, chastising those who err,
His righteous doom administer.
My soul accounts Sugríva dear
E'en as my brother Lakshman here.
He brings me blessing, and I swore
His wife and kingdom to restore :
A bond in solemn honour bound
When Vánar chieftains stood around.
And can a king like me forsake
His friend, and plighted promise break ?
Reflect, O Vánar, on the cause,
The sanction of eternal laws,
And, justly smitten down, confess
Thou diest for thy wickedness.
By honour was I bound to lend
Assistance to a faithful friend;
And thou hast met a righteous fate
Thy former sins to expiate.
And thus wilt thou some merit win
And make atonement for thy sin.
For hear me, Vánar King, rehearse
What Manu[1] spake in ancient verse,—
This holy law, which all accept
Who honour duty, have I kept :
'Pure grow the sinners kings chastise,
And, like the virtuous, gain the skies;
By pain or full atonement freed,
They reap the fruit of righteous deed,
While kings who punish not incur
The penalties of those who err.'
Mándhátá[2] once, a noble king,
Light of the line from which I spring,
Punished with death a devotee
When he had stooped to sin like thee ;
And many a king in ancient time
Has punished frantic sinners' crime,
And, when their impious blood was spilt,
Has washed away the stain of guilt.
Cease, Báli, cease : no more complain :
Reproaches and laments are vain,
For thou art justly punished : we
Obey our king and are not free.
Once more, O Báli, lend thine ear
Another weightiest plea to hear.
For this, when heard and pondered well,
Will all complaint and rage dispel.
My soul will ne'er this deed repent,
Nor was my shaft in anger sent.
We take the silvan tribes beset
With snare and trap and gin and net,
And many a heedless deer we smite
From thickest shade, concealed from sight.
Wild for the slaughter of the game,
At stately stags our shafts we aim.
We strike them bounding scared away,
We strike them as they stand at bay,
When careless in the shade they lie,
Or scan the plain with watchful eye.
They turn away their heads : we aim,
And none the eager hunter blame.
Each royal saint, well trained in law
Of duty, loves his bow to draw
And strike the quarry, e'en as thou
Hast fallen by mine arrow now,
Fighting with him or unaware,—
A Vánar thou.—I little care.[1]
But yet, O best of Vánars, know
That kings who rule the earth bestow
Fruit of pure life and virtuous deed,
And lofty duty's hard-won meed.
Harm not thy lord the king : abstain
From act and word that cause him pain ;
For kings are children of the skies
Who walk this earth in men's disguise.
But thou, in duty's claims untaught,
Thy breast with blinding passion fraught,
Assailest me who still have clung
To duty, with thy bitter tongue.'

He ceased : and Báli sore distressed
The sovereign claims of law confessed,
And freed, o'erwhelmed with woe and shame,
The lord of Raghu's race from blame.
Then, reverent palm to palm applied,
To Ráma thus the Vánar cried :
'True, best of men, is every word
That from thy lips these ears have heard.
It ill beseems a wretch like me
To bandy empty words with thee.
Forgive the angry taunts that broke
From my wild bosom as I spoke.
And lay not to my charge, O King,

---

[1] Manu, Book VIII. 318. "But men who have committed offences and have received from kings the punishment due to them, go pure to heaven and become as clear as those who have done well."

[2] Mándhátá was one of the earlier descendants of Ikshváku. His name is mentioned in Ráma's genealogy, p. 81.

[1] I cannot understand how Válmíki could put such an excuse as this into Ráma's mouth. Ráma with all solemn ceremony, has made a league of alliance with Báli's younger brother whom he regards as a dear friend and almost as an equal, and now he winds up his reasons for killing Báli by coolly saying : 'Besides you are only a monkey, you know, after all, and as such I have every right to kill you how, when, and where I like.'

My mad reproaches' idle sting.
Thou, in the truth by trial trained,
Best knowledge of the right hast gained:
And layest, just and pure within,
The meetest penalty on sin,
Through every bond of law I burst,
The boldest sinner and the worst.
O let thy right-instructing speech
Console my heart and wisely teach.'
Like some sad elephant who stands
Fast sinking in the treacherous sands,
Thus Báli raised despairing eyes;
Then spake again with sobs and sighs:
'Not for myself, O King, I grieve,
For Tárá or the friends I leave,
As for sweet Angad, my dear son,
My noble, only little one.
For, nursed in luxury and bliss,
His father he will mourn and miss,
And like a stream whose fount is dry
Will waste away and sink and die,—
My own dear child, my only boy,
His mother Tárás hope and joy.
Spare him, O son of Raghu, spare
The child entrusted to thy care.
My Angad and Sugríva treat
E'en as thy heart considers meet,
For thou, O chief of men, art strong
To guard the right and punish wrong.
O, if thou wilt thine ear incline
To hear these dying words of mine,
He and Sugríva will to thee
As Bharat and as Lakshman be.
Let not my Tárá, left forlorn,
Weep for Sugríva's wrathful scorn;
Nor let him, for her lord's offence,
Condemn her faithful innocence.
And well and wisely may he reign
If thy dear grace his power sustain:
If, following thee his friend and guide,
He turn not from thy hest aside:
Thus may he reign with glory, nay
Thus to the skies will win his way.
Though stayed by Tárá's fond recall,
By thy dear hand I longed to fall.
Against my brother rushed and fought,
And gained the death I long have sought.'
Then Ráma thus the prince consoled
From whose clear eyes the mists were rolled:
'Grieve not for those thou leavest thus,
Nor tremble for thyself or us,
For we will deal with thine and thee
As duty and the laws decree.
He who exacts and he who pays,
Is justly slain or justly slays,
Shall in the life to come have bliss;
For each has done his task in this.
Thou, wandering from the right, art made
Pure by the forfeit thou hast paid.
Thy weight of sins is cast aside,
And duty's claim is satisfied.
Then grieve no more, O Prince, but clear
Thy bosom from all doubt and fear,
For fate, inexorably stern,
Thou hast no power to move or turn.
Thy princely Angad still will share
My tender love, Sugríva's care;
And to thy offspring shall be shown
Affection that shall match thine own.'

CANTO XIX.

TÁRÁ'S GRIEF.

No answer gave the Vánar king
To Ráma's prudent counselling.
Battered and bruised by tree and stone,
By Ráma's arrow overthrown,
Fainting upon the ground he lay,
Gasping his troubled life away.
But Tárá in the Vánar's hall
Heard tidings of her husband's fall;
Heard that a shaft from Ráma's bow
Had laid the royal Báli low.
Her darling Angad by her side,
Distracted from her home she hied.
Then nigh the place of battle drew
The Vánars, Angad's retinue.
They saw the bow-armed Ráma: dread
Fell on them, and they turned and fled.
Like helpless deer, their leaders slain,
So wildly fled the startled train.
But Tárá saw, and nearer pressed.
And thus the flying band addressed:
'O Vánars, ye who ever stand
About our king, a trusty band,
Where is the lion master? why
Forsake ye thus your lord and fly?
Say, lies he dead upon the plain,
A brother by a brother slain,
Or pierced by shafts from Ráma's bow
That rain from far upon the foe?'
Thus Tárá questioned, and was still:
Then, wearers of each shape at will,
The Vánars thus with one accord
Answered the Lady of their lord:
'Turn, Tárá turn, and half undone
Save Angad thy beloved son.
There Ráma stands in death's disguise,
And conquered Báli faints and dies.
He by whose strong arm, thick and fast,
Uprooted trees and rocks were cast,
Lies smitten by a shaft that came
Resistless as the lightning flame.
When he, whose splendour once could vie
With Indra's, regent of the sky,
Fell by that deadly arrow, all
The Vánars fled who marked his fall.
Let all our chiefs their succours bring,
And Angad be anointed king;

For all who come of Vánar race
Will serve him set in Báli's place.
Or else our conquering foes to-day
Within our wall will force their way,
Polluting with their hostile feet
The chambers of thy loved retreat.
Great fear is on us, all and one.
Those who have wives and who have none,
They lust for power, are fierce and bold,
Or hate us for the strife of old.'
She heard their speech as, sore afraid,
Arrested in their flight, they stayed,
And gave her answer as became
The spirit of so true a dame:
'Nay, what have I to do with pelf,
With son, with kingdom, or with self,
When he, my noble lord, who leads
The Vánars like a loin, bleeds?
His high-souled victor will I meet,
And throw me prostrate at his feet.'
She hastened forth, her bosom rent
With anguish, weeping as she went,
And striking, mastered by her woes,
Her head and breast with frantic blows.
She hurried to the field and found
Her husband postrate on the ground,
Who quelled the hostile Vánars' might,
Whose back was never turned in flight:
Whose arm a massy rock could throw
As Indra hurls his bolts below:
Fierce as the rushing tempest, loud
As thunder from a labouring cloud:
Whene'er he roared his voice of fear
Struck terror on the boldest ear:
Now slain, as hungry for the prey,
A tiger might a lion slay:
Or when, his serpent foe to seek,
Suparṇa[1] with his furious beak
Tears up a sacred hillock, long
The reverence of a village throng,
Its altar with their offerings spread,
And the gay flag that waved o'erhead.
She looked and saw the victor stand
Resting upon his bow his hand:
And fierce Sugriva she descried,
And Lakshmaṇ by his brother's side.
She passed them by, nor stayed to view,
Swift to her husband's side she flew;
Then as she looked, her strength gave way,
And in the dust she fell and lay.
Then, as if startled ere the close
Of slumber, from the earth she rose.
Upon her dying husband, round
Whose soul the coils of Death were wound,
Her eyes in agony she bent
And called him with a shrill lament.
Sugríva, when he heard her cries,
And saw the queen with weeping eyes,
And youthful Angad standing there,
His load of grief could hardly bear.

CANTO XX.

TÁRA'S LAMENT.

Again she bent her to the ground,
Her arms about her husband wound,
Sobbed on his breast, and sick and faint
With anguish poured her wild complaint:
'Brave in the charge of battle, boast
And glory of the Vánar host,
Why on the cold earth wilt thou lie
And give no answer when I cry?
Up, warrior, from thy lowly bed!
A meeter couch for thee is spread.
It ill beseems a glorious king
On the bare ground his limbs to fling.
Ah, surely must thy love be strong
For her whom thou hast governed long,
If thou, my hero, canst recline
On her cold breast forsaking mine.
Or, famed for justice through the land,
Thou on the road to heaven hast planned
Some city fairer far than this
To be thy new metropolis.
Are all our pleasures ended now,
With those delicious hours which thou
And I, dear lord, together spent
In woods that breathed the honey's scent?
Whelmed in my sorrow's boundless sea,
There is no joy, no hope, for me,
When my beloved lord, who led
The Vánars to the fight, is dead.
My widowed heart is stern and cold,
Or, at the sight mine eyes behold,
O'ermastered would it end this ache
And in a thousand fragments break.
Ah noble Vánar, doomed to pay
The penalty of all to-day—
Sugríva from his home expelled,
And Rumá[1] from his arms withheld.
Our Vánar race and thee to save,
Wise counsel for thy weal I gave;
But thou, by wildest folly stirred,
Wouldst give no credence to my word,
And now wilt woo the nymphs above,
And shake their souls with pangs of love.
Ah, never could it be that thou
Beneath Sugríva's power shouldst bow,
Thy conqueror is none but Fate
Whose mandates all who breathe await.
And does no thrill of anguish run
Through the stern breast of Raghu's son,
Whose base hand dealt a coward's blow,
And smote thee fighting with thy foe?
Reft of my lord my days, alas!

[1] A name of Garuḍa the king of birds, the great enemy of the Serpents.

[1] Sugríva's wife.

In bitter bitter woe will pass:
And I, long blest with every good,
Must bear my dreary widowhood.
And when his uncle's brow is stern,
When his fierce eyes with fury burn,
Ah, what will be my Angad's fate,
So fair and young and delicate?
Come, darling, for the last sad sight.
Of thy dear sire who loved the right;
For soon thine eyes will long in vain
A look at that loved face to gain.
And, hero, as thy child draws near,
With tender words his spirit cheer;
Thy dying wishes gently speak,
And kiss him on the brows and cheek.
High fame, I ween, has Ráma won
By this great deed his hand has done,
His debt to brave Sugríva paid
And kept the promise that he made.
Be happy, King Sugríva, lord
Of Rumá to thine arms restored:
Enjoy uninterrupted reign,
For he, thy foe, at length is slain.
Dost thou not hear me speak, and why
Hast thou no word of soft reply?
Wilt thou not lift thine eyes and see
These dames who look to none but thee?'
From their sad eyes, as Tárá spoke,
The floods of bitter sorrow broke:
Then, pressing close to Angad's side,
Each lifted up her voice and cried:
'How couldst thou leave thine Angad thus,
And go, for ever go, from us—
Thy child so dear in brave attire,
Graced with the virtues of his sire?
If e'er in want of thought, O chief,
One deed of mine have caused thee grief,
Forgive my folly, I entreat,
And with my head I touch thy feet.'
Again the hapless Tárá wept
As to her husband's side she crept,
And wild with sorrow and dismay
Sat on the ground where Báli lay.

CANTO XXI.

HANUMA'N'S SPEECH.

There, like a fallen star, the dame
Fell by her lord's half lifeless frame;
And Hanumán drew softly near,
And strove her grieving heart to cheer:
'By changeless law our bliss and woe
From ancient worth and folly flow.
What fruits soe'er we cull, the seeds
Were scattered by our former deeds.[1]
Why mourn another's mournful fate,
And weep, thyself unfortunate?
Be calm, O thou whose heart is wise,
For none deserves another's sighs.
Look up, with idle sorrow strive:
Thy child, his heir, is yet alive.
Let needful rites be duly done,
Nor in thy woe forget thy son.
Regard the law which all obey:
They spring to life, they pass away.
Begin the task that bids thee rise,
And stay these tears, for thou art wise.
Our lord the king is doomed to die,
On whom ten million hearts rely.
Kind, liberal, patient, true, and just
Was he in whom they place their trust,
And now he seeks the land of those
Who for the right subdue their foes.
Each Vánar lord with all his train,
Each ranger of this wild domain,
And Angad here, thy darling, see
A governor and friend in thee.
These twain[1] whose hearts with sorrow ache
The funeral rites shall undertake,
And Angad by his mother's care
Be king, his father's rightful heir.
Now let him pay, as laws require,
His sacred duty to his sire,
Nor one solemnity omit
Of all that mighty kings befit.
And when thy fond eye sees thine own
Dear Angad on his father's throne,
Then, lightened of its load of pain,
Thy spirit will have rest again.'
She heard his speech, she heaved her head,
Looked upon Hanumán and said:
'Sweeter my slain lord's limbs to touch,
Than Angad or a hundred such.
No rule or right, a widowed dame,
O'er Angad or the realm I claim.
Sugríva is the uncle, he
In every act supreme must be.
I pray thee, chief, this plan resign,
Nor claim from me what ne'er is mine.
The father with his tender care
Guards the dear child the mother bare,
Where'er I be, no sweeter task,
No happier joy I hope or ask
Than thus to sit with loving eyes
And watch the bed where Báli lies.'

CANTO XXII.

BA'LI DEAD.

There breathing still with slow faint sighs
Lay Báli on the ground: his eyes,

[1] "Our deeds still follow with us from afar.
And what we have been makes us what we are."

[1] Sugríva and Angad.

Damp with the tears of death, he raised,
On conquering Sugríva gazed,
And then in clearest speech expressed
The tender feelings of his breast:
'Not to my charge, Sugríva, lay
Thine injuries avenged to-day;
But rather blame resistless Fate
That urged me on infuriate.
Fate ne'er agreed our lives to bless
With simultaneous happiness:
To dwell like brothers side by side
In tender love was still denied.
The Vánars' realm is thine to-day:
Begin, O King, thy rightful sway;[1]
For I must go at Yama's call
To sojourn in his gloomy hall;
Must part and leave this very hour
My life, my realm, my kingly power,
And go instead of these to gain
Bright glory free from spot and stain.
Now at thy hands one boon I seek
With the last words my lips shall speak,
And, though it be no easy thing,
Perform the task I give thee, King.
This son of mine, no foolish boy,
Worthy of bliss and nursed in joy,—
See, prostrate on the ground he lies,
The hot tears welling from his eyes—
The child I love so well, more sweet
Than life itself, for woe unmeet,—
To him be kindly favour shown:
O guard and keep him as thine own.
Retain him ever by thy side,
His father, helper, friend, and guide.
From fear and woe his young life save,
And give him all his father gave.
Then Tárá's son in time shall be
Brave, resolute, and famed like thee,
And march before thee to the fight
Where stricken fiends shall own his might.
While yet a tender stripling, fame
Shall bruit abroad his warrior name,
And brightly shall his glory shine
For exploits worthy of his line.
Child of Sushen,[2] my Tárá well
Obscurest lore can read and tell:
And, trained in wondrous art, divines
Each mystery of boding signs.
Her solemn warning ne'er despise,
Do boldly what her lips advise;
For things to come her eye can see,
And with her words events agree.
And for the son of Raghu's sake
The toil and danger undertake:
For breach of faith were grievous wrong,
Nor wouldst thou be unpunished long.
Now, brother, take this chain of gold,
Gift of celestial hands of old,
Or when I die its charm will flee,
And all its might be lost with me.'
  The loving speech Sugríva heard,
And all his heart with woe was stirred.
Remorse and gentle pity stole
Each thought of triumph from his soul:
Thus fades the light when Ráhu[1] mars
The glory of the Lord of Stars.[2]
All angry thoughts were staved and stilled
And kindly love his bosom filled.
His brother's word the chief obeyed
And took the chain as Báli prayed.
On little Angad standing nigh
The dying hero fixed his eye.
And, ready from this world to part,
Spoke the fond utterance of his heart:
  'Let time and place thy thoughts employ:
In woe be strong, be meek in joy.
Accept both pain and pleasure, still
Obedient to Sugríva's will.
Thou hast, my darling, from the first
With tender care been softly nursed;
But harder days, if thou wouldst win
Sugríva's love, must now begin.
To those who hate him ne'er incline,
Nor count his foe a friend of thine.
In all thy thoughts his welfare seek,
Obedient, lowly, faithful, meek.
Let no rash suit his bosom pain,
Nor yet from due requests abstain.[3]
Each is a grievous fault, between
The two is found the happy mean.'
  Then Báli ceased: his eyeballs rolled
In stress of anguish uncontrolled
His massive teeth were bared to view,
And from the frame the spirit flew.
Their lord and leader dead, the crowd
Of noblest Vánars shrieked aloud:
'Since thou, O King, hast sought the skies
All desolate Kishkindhá lies.
Her woods, where Vánars loved to rove,
Are empty now, and hill and grove.
From every eye the light is fled,
Since thou, our mighty lord, art dead.
Thine was the unwearied arm that bore
The brunt of deadly fight of yore
With Golabh the Gandharva, when,
Lasting through five long years and ten,

[1] Angad himself, being too young to govern, would be Yuvarája or heir-apparent.

[2] Sushena was the son of Varuna the God of the sea.

[1] A demon with the tail of a dragon, that causes eclipses by endeavouring to swallow the sun and moon.

[2] The Lord of Stars is the Moon.

[3] Or the passage may be interpreted: 'Be neither to obsequious or affectionate, nor wanting in due respect or love.'

The dreadful conflict knew no stay
In gloom of night, in glare of day;
And when the fifteenth year had past
Thy dire opponent fell at last.
If such a foeman fell beneath
Our hero's arm and awful teeth
Who freed us from our terror, how
Is conquering Báli fallen now?'
  Then when they saw their leader slain
Great anguish seized the Vánar train,
Weeping their mighty chief, as when
In pastures near a lion's den
The cows by sudden fear are stirred,
Slain the bold bull who led the herd.
And hapless Tárá sank below
The whelming waters of her woe,
Looked upon Báli's face and fell
Beside him whom she loved so well,
Like a young creeper clinging round
A tall tree prostrate on the ground.

CANTO XXIII.

TÁRÁ'S LAMENT.

She kissed her lifeless husband's face,
She clasped him in a close embrace,
Laid her soft lips upon his head;
Then words like these the mourner said:
  'No words of mine wouldst thou regard,
And now thy bed is cold and hard.
Upon the rude rough ground o'erthrown,
Beneath thee naught but sand and stone.
To thee the earth is dearer far
Than I and my caresses are,
If thou upon her breast wilt tie,
And to my words make no reply.
Ah my beloved, good and brave,
Bold to attack and strong to save,
Fate is Sugríva's thrall, and we
In him our lord and master see.
Lo, by thy bed, a mournful band,
Thy Vánar chiefs lamenting stand.
O hear thy nobles' groans and cries,
O mark thy Angad's weeping eyes,
O list to my entreaties, break
The chains of slumber and awake.
Ah me, my lord, this lowly bed
Where rest thy limbs and fallen head,
Is the cold couch where smitten lay
Thy foemen in the bloody fray.
O noble heart from blemish free,
Lover of war, beloved by me,
Why hast thou fled away and left
Thy Tárá of all hope bereft?
Unwise the father who allows
His child to be a warrior's spouse,
For, hero, see thy consort's fate,
A widow now most desolate,
For ever broken is my pride,
My hope of lasting bliss has died,
And sinking in the lowest deep
Of sorrow's sea I pine and weep.
Ah, surely not of earthly mould,
This stony heart is stern and cold,
Or, in a hundred pieces rent,
It had not lingered to lament.
Dead, dead! my husband, friend, and lord
In whom my loving hopes were stored,
First in the field, his foemen's dread,
My own victorious Báli, dead!
A woman when her lord has died.
Though children flourish by her side,
Though stores of gold her coffers fill,
Is called a lonely widow still.
Alas, thy bleeding gashes make
Around thy limbs a purple lake:
Thus slumbering was thy wont to lie
On cushions bright with crimson dye.
Dark streams of welling blood besmear
Thy limbs where dust and mire adhere,
Nor have I strength, weighed down by woe,
Mine arms about thy form to throw.
The issue of this day has brought
Sugríva all his wishes sought,
For Ráma shot one shaft and he
Is freed from fear and jeopardy.
Alas, alas, I may not rest
My head upon thy wounded breast,
Obstructed by the massive dart
Deep buried in thy bleeding heart.'
  Then Níla from his bosom drew
The fatal shaft that pierced him through,
Like some tremendous serpent deep
In caverns of a hill asleep.
As from the hero's wound it came,
Shot from the shaft a gleam of flame,
Like the last flashes of the sun
Descending when his course is run.
From the wide rent in crimson flood
Rushed the full stream of Báli's blood,
Like torrents down a mountain's side
With golden ore and copper dyed.
Then Tárá brushed with tender care
The dust of battle from his hair,
While her sad eyes poured down their rain
Upon her lord untimely slain.
Once more she looked upon the dead;
Then to her bright-eyed child she said:
'Turn hither, turn thy weeping eyes
Where low in death thy father lies.
By sinful deed and bitter hate
Our lord has met his mournful fate.
Bright as the sun at early morn
To Yama's halls is Báli borne.
Then go, my child, salute the king,
From whom our bliss and honour spring.'
  Obedient to his mother's hest
His father's feet he gently pressed

With twining arms and lingering hands :
'Father', he cried, 'here Angad stands.'
Then Tárá : 'Art thou stern and mute,
Regardless of thy child's salute?
Hast thou no blessing for thy son,
No word for little Angad, none?
O hero, at thy lifeless feet
Here with my boy I take my seat,
As some sad mother of the herd,
By the fierce lion undeterred,
Lies moaning by the grassy dell
Wherein her lord and leader fell.
How, having wrought that awful rite,
The sacrifice of deadly fight.
Wherein the shaft by Ráma sped
Supplied the place of water shed,
How hast thou bathed thee at the end
Without thy wife her aid to lend?[1]
Why do mine eyes no more behold
Thy bright beloved chain of gold,
Which, pleased with thee, the Immortals' King
About thy neck vouchsafed to fling?
Still lingering on thy lifeless face
I see the pride of royal race :
Thus when the sun has set, his glow
Still rests upon the Lord of Snow.
Alas my hero! undeterred
Thou wouldst not listen to my word.
With tears and prayers I sued in vain :
Thou wouldst not listen, and art slain.
Gone is my bliss, my glory : I
And Angad now with thee will die.'

[1] Sacrifices and all religious rites begin and end with ablution, and the wife of the officiating Brahman takes an important part in the performance of the holy ceremonies.

CANTO XXIV.

SUGRIVA'S LAMENT.

But when Sugriva saw her weep
O'erwhelmed in sorrow's rushing deep,
Swift through his bosom pierced the sting
Of anguish for the fallen king.
At the sad sight his eyes beheld
A flood of bitter tears outwelled,
And, with his bosom racked and rent,
To Ráma with his train he went.
He came with faltering steps and slow
Where Ráma held his mighty bow
And arrow like a venomed snake,
And to the son of Raghu spake :
'Well hast thou kept, O King, thy vow :
The promised fruit is gathered now.
But life is marred, my soul to-day
Turns sickening from all joy away.
For, while this queen laments and sighs
Amid a mourning people's cries,
And Angad weeps his father slain,
How can my heart delight to reign?
For outrage, fury, senseless pride,
My brother, doomed of yore, has died.
Yet, Raghu's son, in bitter woe
I mourn his fated overthrow.
Ah, better far in pain and ill
To dwell on Rishyamúka still
Than gain the heaven of Gods and all
Its pleasures by my brother's fall.
Did not he cry,—great-hearted foe,—
'Go, for I will not slay thee, Go'?
With his brave soul those words agree :
My speech, my deeds, are worthy me.
How can a brother counterweigh
His grievous loss with joys of sway,
And see with dull unpitying eye
So brave and good a brother die?
His lofty soul was nobly blind :
My death alas, he ne'er designed ;
But I, urged blindly on by hate,
Sought with his life my rage to sate.
He smote me with a splintered tree :
I groaned aloud and turned to flee,
From stern reproaches he forbore,
And gently bade me sin no more.
Serene and dutiful and good,
He kept the laws of brotherhood :
I, fierce and greedy, vengeful, base,
Showed all the vices of our race.
Ah me, dear friend, my brother's fate
Lays on my soul a crushing weight:
A sin no heart should e'er conceive,
But at the thought each soul should grieve:
Sin such as Indra's when his blow
Laid heavenly Viśvarúpa[1] low.
Yet earth, the waters of the seas,
The race of women and the trees
Were fain upon themselves to take
The weight of sin for Indra's sake.
But who a Vánar's soul will free,
Or ease the load that crushes me?
Wretch that I am, I may not claim
The reverence due to royal name.
How shall I reign supreme, or dare
Affect the power I should not share?
Ah me, I sorrow for my sin,
The ruin of my race and kin,
Polluted by a hideous crime
World-hated till the end of time.
Alas, the floods of sorrow roll
With whelming force upon my soul ;
So gathers the descending rain
In the deep hollow of the plain.

[1] Viśvarúpa, a son of Twashṭri or Viśvakarma the heavenly architect, was a three-headed monster slain by Indra.

CANTO XXV.

RÁMA'S SPEECH.

Then Raghu's son, whose feeling breast
Shared the great woe that moved the rest,
Strove with wise charm their grief to ease
And gently spoke in words like these:
'You ne'er can raise the dead to bliss
By agony of grief like this.
Cease your lament, nor leave undone
The funeral task you may not shun.
As nature orders o'er the dead
Your tributary tears are shed,
But Fate, directing each event,
Is still the lord preëminent.
Yes, all obey the changeless laws
Of Fate the universal cause.
By Fate, the lives of all proceed,
That governs every word and deed,
None acts, none sees his hest obeyed,
But each and all by Fate are swayed.
The world its ordered course maintains,
And o'er that course Fate ever reigns.
Fate ne'er exceeds the rule of Fate:
Is ne'er too swift, is ne'er too late,
And making nature its ally
Forgets no life, nor passes by.
No kith and kin, no power and force
Can check or stay its settled course,
No friend or client, grace or charm,
That victor of the world disarm.
So all who see with prudent eyes
The hand of Fate must recognize,
For virtue rules, or love, or gain,
As Fate's unchanged decrees ordain.
Báli has died and won the meed
That waits in heaven on noble deed,
Throned in the seats the brave may reach
By liberal hand and gentle speech,
True to a warrior's duty, bold
In fight, the hero lofty-souled
Deigned not to guard his life: he died,
And now in heaven is glorified.
Then cease these tears and wild despair:
Turn to the task that claims your care,
For Báli's is the glorious fate
Which warriors count most fortunate.'

When Rama's speech had found a close.
Brave Lakshman, terror of his foes.
With wise and soothing words addressed
Sugríva still with woe oppressed:
'Arise Sugríva,' thus he said,
'Perform the service of the dead.
Prepare with Tárá and her son
That Báli's rites be duly done.
A store of funeral wood provide
Which wind and sun and time have dried
And richest sandal fit to grace
The pyre of one of royal race.
With words of comfort soft and kind
Console poor Angad's troubled mind,
Nor let thy heart be thus cast down,
For thine is now the Vánars' town.
Let Angad's care a wreath supply,
And raiment rich with varied dye,
And oil and perfumes for the fire,
And all the solemn rites require.
Go, hasten to the town, O King,
And Tára's little quickly bring.
A virtue is despatch: and speed
Is best of all in hour of need.
Go, let a chosen band prepare
The litter of the dead to bear,
For stout and tall and strong of limb
Must be the cheifs who carry him.'

He spoke,—his friends' delight and pride,—
Then stood again by Ráma's side.
When Tára[1] heard the words he said
Within the town he quickly sped,
And brought, on stalwart shoulders laid,
The litter for the rites arrayed,
Framed like a car for Gods, complete
With painted sides and royal seat,
With latticed windows deftly made,
And golden birds and trees inlaid:
Well joined and wrought in every part,
A marvel of ingenious art,
Where pleasure mounds in carven wood
And many a groven figure stood.
The best of jewels o'er it hung,
And wreaths of flowers around it clung,
And over all was raised on high
A canopy of saffron dye,
While like the sun of morning shone
The billiant blooms that lay thereon.
That glorious litter Ráma eyed.
And spake to Lakshman by his side:
'Let Báli on the bier be placed
And with all funeral service graced.'
Sugríva then with many a tear
Drew Báli's body to the bier
Whereon, with weeping Angad's aid,
The relics of the chief were laid
Neath many a vesture's varied fold,
And wreaths and ornaments and gold.
Then King Sugríva bade them speed
The obsequies by law decreed:
'Let Vánars lead the way and throw
Rich gems around them as they go,
And be the chosen bearers near
Behind them laden with the bier.
No costly rite may you deny,
Used when the proudest monarchs die:
As for a king of widest sway,
Perform his obsequies to-day.'

---

[1] The Vánar chief, not to be confounded with Tárá.

Sugríva gave his high behest ;
Then Princely Tára and the rest,
With little Angad weeping, led
The long procession of the dead.
Behind the funeral litter came,
With Tárá first, each widowed dame,
In tears and shrieks her loss deplored,
And cried aloud, My lord! My lord!
While wood and hill and valley sent
In echoes back the shrill lament.
Then on a low and sandy isle
Was reared the hero's funeral pile
By crowds of toiling Vánars, where
The mountain stream ran fresh and fair,
The Vánar chiefs, a noble band,
Had laid the litter on the sand,
And stood a little space apart,
Each mourning in his inmost heart.
But Tárá, when her weeping eye
Saw Báli, on the litter lie,
Laid his dear head upon her lap,
And wailed aloud her dire mishap:
'O mighty Vánar, lord and king,
To whose fond breast I loved to cling,
Of goodly arms, wise, brave, and bold,
Rise, look upon me as of old,
Rise up, my sovereign, dost thou see
A crowd of subjects weep for thee?
Still o'er thy face, though breath has fled,
The joyous light of life is spread :
Thus around the sun, although he set,
A crimson glory lingers yet.
Death clad in Ráma's form to-day
Hast dragged thee from the world away.
One shaft from his tremendous bow
Dooms us to widowhood and woe.
Hast thou, O Vánar King, no eyes
Thy weeping wives to recognize,
Who for the length of way unmeet
Have followed thee with weary feet?
Yet every moon-faced beauty here
By thee, O King, was counted dear.
Lord of the Vánar race, hast thou
No eyes to see Sugríva now?
About thee stands in mournful mood
A sore-afflicted multitude,
And Tára and thy lords of state
Around their monarch weep and wait,
Arise my lord, with gentle speech,
As was thy wont, dismissing each,
Then in the forest will we play
And love shall make our spirits gay.'
The Vánar dames raised Tárá, drowned
In floods of sorrow, from the ground ;
And Angad with Sugríva's aid,
O'erwhelmed with anguish and dismayed,
Weeping for his departed sire,
Placed Báli's body on the pyre :
Then lit the flame, and round the dead
Passed slowly with a mourner's tread.
Thus with full rites the funeral train
Performed the service for the slain,
Then sought the flowing stream and made
Libations to the parted shade.
There, setting Angad first in place,
The chieftains of the Vánar race,
With Tárá and Sugríva, shed
The water that delights the dead.

CANTO XXVI.

THE CORONATION.

Each Vánar councillor and peer
In crowded numbers gathered near
Sugríva, mournful king, while yet
His vesture from the wave was wet,
Before the chief of Raghu's seed
Unwearied in each arduous deed,
They stood and raised the reverent hand
As saints bef re Lord Brahmá stand.
Then Hanumán of massive mould,
Like some tall hill of glistering gold,
Son of the God whose wild blasts shake
The forest, thus to Ráma spake :
'By thy kind favour, O my lord,
Sugríva, to his home restored
Triumphant, has regained to-day
His rank and power and royal sway.
He now will call each faithful friend,
Enter the city, and attend
With sage advice and prudent care
To every task that waits him there.
Then balm and unguent shall anoint
Our monarch, as the laws appoint,
And gems and precious wreaths shall be
His grateful offering, King, to thee.
Do thou, O Ráma, with thy friend
Thy steps within the city bend ;
Our ruler on his throne install,
And with thy presence cheer us all.'
Then, skilled in lore and arts that guide
The speaker, Raghu's son replied :
'For fourteen years I might not break
The mandate that my father spake ;
Nor can I, till that time be fled,
The street of town or village tread.
Let King Sugríva seek the town
Most worthy of her high renown,
There let him be without delay
Anointed, and begin his sway.
This answered, to Sugríva then
Thus spake anew the king of men :
'Do thou who knowest right ordain
Prince Angad consort of thy reign ;
For he is noble, true, and bold,
And trained a righteous course to hold.
Gifts like his sire's that youth adorn
Born eldest to the eldest born.

This is the month of Śrávaṇ,[1] first
Of those that see the rain-clouds burst.
Four months, thou knowest well, extends
The season when the rain descends.
No time for deeds of war is this:
Seek thou thy fair metropolis,
And I with Lakshmaṇ, O my friend,
The time upon this hill will spend.
An ample cavern opens there
Made lovely by the mountain air,
And lotuses and lilies fill
The pleasant lake and murmuring rill.
When Kártik's[2] month shall clear the skies,
Then tempt the mighty enterprise.
Now, chieftain to thy home repair,
And be anointed sovereign there.'
Sugríva heard: he bowed his head:
Within the lovely town he sped
Which Báli's royal will had swayed,
Where thousand Vánar chiefs arrayed
Gathered in order round their king,
And led him on with welcoming.
Low on the earth the lesser crowd
Fell in prostration as they bowed.
Sugríva looked with grateful eyes,
Spake to them all and bade them rise.
Then through the royal bowers he strode
Wherein the monarch's wives abode.
Soon from the inner chambers came
The Vánar of exalted fame;
And joyful friends drew near and shed
King-making balm upon his head,
Like Gods anointing in the skies
Their sovereign of the thousand eyes.[3]
Then brought they, o'er their king to hold
The white umbrella decked with gold,
And chouries with their waving hair
In golden handles wondrous fair;
And fragrant herbs and seed and spice,
And sparkling gems exceeding price,
And every bloom from woods and leas,
And gum distilled from milky trees;
And precious ointment white as milk,
And spotless robes of cloth and silk,
Wreaths of sweet flowers whose glories gleam
In grassy grove, on lake or stream,
And fragrant sandal and each scent
That makes the soft breeze redolent;
Grain, honey, odorous seed, and store
Of oil and curd and golden ore;
A noble tiger's skin, a pair
Of sandals wrought with costliest care.
Eight pairs of damsels drawing nigh
Brought unguents stained with varied dye.
Then gems and cates and robes displayed
Before the twice-born priests were laid,
That they would deign in order due
To consecrate the king anew.
The sacred grass was duly spread
And sacrificial flame was fed,
Which Scripture-learned priests supplied
With oil which texts had sanctified.
Then, with all rites ordained of old,
High on the terrace bright with gold,
Whereon a glorious carpet lay,
And fresh-culled garlands sweet and gay,
Placed on his throne, Sugríva bent
His looks toward the Orient.
In horns from forehead of the bull,
In pitchers bright and beautiful,
In urns of gold the Vánars took
Pure water brought from stream and brook,
From every consecrated strand
And every sea that beats the land.
Then, as prescribed by sacred lore
And many a mighty sage of yore,[1]
The leaders of the Vánars poured
The sacred water on their lord.[2]
From every Vánar at the close
Of that imperial rite arose
Shouts of glad triumph, loud and long
Repeated by the high-souled throng.
Sugríva, when the rite was done,
Obeyed the hest of Raghu's son,
Prince Angad to his breast he strained,
And partner of his sway ordained.
Once more from all the host rang out
The loud huzza and joyful shout.
'Well done! well done! each Vánar cried,
And good Sugríva glorified.

[1] Śrávaṇ: July-August. But the rains begin a month earlier, and what follows must not be taken literally. The text has: *púrvo' yam várshiko másah Śrávaṇah salilágamah.* The Bengal recension has the same, and Gorresio translates: 'E questo il mese Srâvana (luglio-agosto) primo della stagione piovosa, in cui dilagano le acque.'

[2] Kártik: October-November.

[3] "Indras, as the nocturnal sun, hides himself, transformed, in the starry heavens: the stars are his eyes. The hundred-eyed or all-seeing (panoptês) Argos placed as a spy over the actions of the cow beloved by Zeus, is the Hellenic equivalent of this form of Indras." DE GUBERNATIS, *Zoological Mythology*, Vol. I. p. 418.

[1] Baudháyana and others.

[2] Sugríva appears to have been consecrated with all the ceremonies that attended the *Abhisheka* or coronation of an Indian prince of the Aryan race. Compare the preparations made for Ráma's consecration, Book II. Canto III. Thus Homer frequently introduces into Troy the rites of Hellenic worship.

Then with glad voices loudly raised
Were Ráma and his brother praised;
And bright Kishkindhá shone that day
With happy throngs and banners gay.

CANTO XXVII.

RÁMA ON THE HILL.

But when the solemn rite was o'er,
And bold Sugríva reigned once more,
The sons of Raghu sought the hill,
Prasravaṇ of the rushing rill,
Where roamed the tiger and the deer,
And lions raised their voice of fear;
Thick set with trees of every kind,
With trailing shrubs and plants entwined;
Home of the ape and monkey, lair
Of mountain cat and pard and bear.
In cloudy gloom against the sky
The sanctifying hills rose high.
Pierced in their crest, a spacious cave
To Raghu's sons a shelter gave.
Then Ráma, pure from every crime,
In words well suited to the time
To Lakshmaṇ spake, whose faithful zeal
Watched humbly for his brother's weal:
'I love this spacious cavern where
There breathes a fresh and pleasant air.
Brave brother, let us here remain
Throughout the season of the rain.
For in mine eyes this mountain crest
Is above all, the loveliest.
Where copper-hued and black and white
Show the huge blocks that face the height;
Where gleams the shine of varied ore,
Where dark clouds hang and torrents roar;
Where waving woods are fair to see,
And creapers climb from tree to tree;
Where the gay peacock's voice is shrill,
And sweet birds carol on the hill;
Where odorous breath is wafted far
From Jessamine and Sinduvár;[1]
And opening flowers of every hue
Give wondrous beauty to the view.
See, too, this pleasant water near
Our cavern home is fresh and clear;
And lilies gay with flower and bud
Are glorious on the lovely flood.
This cave that faces north and east
Will shelter us till rain has ceased;
And towering hills that rise behind
Will screen us from the furious wind.
Close by the cavern's portal lies
And level stone of ample size
And sable hue, a mighty block
Long severed from the parent rock.
Now let thine eye bent northward rest
A while upon that mountain crest,
High as a cloud that brings the rain,
And dark as iron rent in twain.
Look southward, brother, now and view
A cloudy pile of paler hue
Like Mount Kailása's topmost height
Where ores of every tint are bright.
See, Lakshmaṇ, see before our cave
That clear brook eastward roll its wave
As though 'twere Gangá's infant rill
Down streaming from the three-peaked hill.
See, by the water's gentle flow
Aśoka, sál, and sandal grow.
And every lovely tree most fair
With leaf and bud and flower is there.
See where, beneath the bending trees
That fringe her bank, the river flees,
Clothed with their beauty like a maid
In all her robes and gems arrayed,
While from the sedgy banks are heard
The soft notes of each amorous bird.
O see what lovely islets stud
Like gems the bosom of the flood,
And sárases and wild swans crowd
About her till she laughs aloud.
See, lotus blooms the brook o'erspread,
Some tender blue, some dazzling red,
And opening lilies white as snow
Their buds in rich profusion show.
There rings the joyous peacock's scream,
There stands the curlew by the stream,
And holy hermits love to throng
Where the sweet waters speed along.
Ranged on the grassy margin shine
Gay sandal trees in glittering line,
And all the wondrous verdure seems
The offspring of creative dreams,
O conquering Prince, there cannot be
A lovelier place than this we see.
Here sheltered on the beauteous height
Our days will pass in calm delight.
Nor is Kishkindhá's city, gay
With grove and garden, far away.
Thence will the breeze of evening bring
Sweet music as the minstrels sing;
And, when the Vánars dance, will come
The sound of tabour and of drum.
Again to spouse and realm restored,
Girt by his friends, the Vánar lord
Great glory has acquired; and how
Can he be less than happy now?'

This said, the son of Raghu made
His dwelling in that pleasant shade
Upon the mountain's shelving side
That sweetly all his wants supplied.
But still the hero's troubled mind
No comfort in his woe could find,
Yet mourning for his stolen wife
Dearer to Ráma than his life,
Chief when he saw the Lord of Night
Rise slowly o'er the eastern height,

[1] Vitex Negundo.

He tossed upon his leafy bed
With eyes by sleep unvisited.
Outwelled the tears in ceaseless flow,
And every sense was numbed by woe.
Each pang that pierced the mourner through
Smote Lakshman's faithful bosom too,
Who, troubled for his brother's sake,
With wisest words the prince bespake:
'Arise, my brother, and be strong:
Thy hero heart has mourned too long.
Thou knowest well that tears and sighs
Will mar the mightiest enterprise.
Thine was the soul that loved to dare:
To serve the Gods was still thy care;
And ne'er may sorrow's sting subdue
A heart so resolute and true.
How canst thou hope to slay in fight
The giant cruel in his might?
Unwearied must the champion be
Who strives with such a foe as he.
Tear out this sorrow by the root:
Again be bold and resolute.
Arise, my brother, and subdue
The demon and his wicked crew.
Thou canst destroy the earth, her seas,
Her rooted hills and giant trees
Unseated by thy furious hand:
And shall one fiend thy power withstand?
Wait through this season of the rain
Till suns of autumn dry the plain,
Then shall thy giant foe, and all
His host and realm, before thee fall.
I wake thy valour that has slept
Amid the tears thine eyes have wept;
As drops of oil in worship raise
The dormant flame to sudden blaze.'

The son of Raghu heard: he knew
His brother's rede was wise and true;
And, honouring his friendly guide,
In gentle words he thus replied:
'Whate'er a hero firm and bold,
Devoted, true, and lofty-souled
Should speak by deep affection led,
Such are the words which thou hast said.
I cast away each pensive thought
That brings the noblest plans to naught,
And each uninjured power will strain
Until the purposed end we gain.
Thy prudent words will I obey,
And till the close of rain-time stay,
When King Sugríva will invite
To action, and the streams be bright.
The hero saved in hour of need
Repays the debt with friendly deed:
But hated by the good are they
Who take the boon and ne'er repay.'

CANTO XXVIII.

THE RAINS.

'See, brother, see' thus Ráma cried
On Málvavat's[1] dark-wooded side,
'A chain of clouds, like lofty hills,
The sky with gathering shadow fills.
Nine months those clouds have borne the load
Conceived from sunbeams as they glowed,
And, having drunk the seas, give birth,
And drop their offspring on the earth.
Easy it seems at such a time
That flight of cloudy stairs to climb,
And, from their summit, safely won,
Hang flowery wreaths about the sun.
See how the flash of evening's red
Fringes the fleecy clouds o'erhead
Till all the sky is streaked and lined
With bleeding wounds incarnadined.
Or the wide firmament above
Shows like a lover sick with love,
And, pale with cloudlets, heaves a sigh
In the soft breeze that wanders by.
See, by the fervent heat embrowned,
Now drenched with recent showers, the ground
Pours out in floods her gushing tears,
Like Sítá wild with torturing fears.
So softly blows this cloud-born breeze
Cool through the boughs of camphor trees
That one might hold it in the cup
Of hollowed hands and drink it up.
See, brother, where that rocky steep,
Where odorous shrubs in rain-drops weep,
Shows like Sugríva when they shed
The royal balm upon his head.
Like students at their task appear
Those hills whose misty peaks are near:
Black deerskin[2] garments wrought of cloud
Their forms with fitting mantles shroud;
Each torrent from the summit poured
Supplies the place of sacred cord;[3]
And winds that in their caverns moan

[1] Málvavat: "The name of this mountain appears to me to be erroneous, and I think that instead of Málvavat should be read Malayavat. Malaya is a group of mountains situated exactly in that southern part of India where Ráma now was while Málvavat is placed to the north east." GORRESIO.

[2] Mantles of the skin of the black antelope were the prescribed dress of ascetics and religious students.

[3] The sacred cord worn as the badge of religious initiation by men of the three twice-born castes.

Sound like the voice's undertone.[1]
From east to west red lightnings flash,
And, quivering neath the golden lash,
The great sky like a generous steed
Groans inly at each call to speed.
Yon lightning, as it flashes through
The giant cloud of sable hue,
Recalls my votaress Sítá pressed
Mid struggles to the demon's breast.
See, on those mountain ridges stand
Sweet shrubs that bud and bloom expand.
The soft rain ends their pangs of grief.
And drops its pearls on flower and leaf.
But all their raptures stab me through
And wake my pining love anew.[2]
Now through the air no wild bird flies,
Each lily shuts her weary eyes;
And blooms of opening jasmin show
The parting sun has ceased to glow.
No captain now for conquest burns,
But homeward with his host returns;
For roads and kings' ambitious dreams
Have vanished neath descending streams.
This is the watery month[3] wherein
The Sáman's[4] sacred chants begin.
Áshádha[5] past, now Kosal's lord[6]
The harvest of the spring has stored,[7]
And dwells within his palace freed
From every care of pressing need.
Full is the moon, and fierce and strong
Impetuous Sarjú[1] roars along
As though Ayodhyá's crowds ran out
To greet their king with echoing shout.
In this sweet time of ease and rest
No care disturbs Sugríva's breast,
The foe that marred his peace o'erthrown,
And queen and realm once more his own.
Alas, a harder fate is mine,
Reft both of realm and queen to pine,
And, like the bank which floods erode,
I sink beneath my sorrow's load.
Sore on my soul my miseries weigh,
And these long rains our action stay,
While Rávan seems a mightier foe
Than I dare hope to overthrow.
I saw the roads were barred by rain,
I knew the hopes of war were vain;
Nor could I bid Sugríva rise,
Though prompt to aid my enterprise.
E'en now I scarce can urge my friend
On whom his house and realm depend,
Who, after toil and peril past,
Is happy with his queen at last.
Sugríva after rest will know
The hour is come to strike the blow,
Nor will his grateful soul forget
My succour, or deny the debt.
I know his generous heart, and hence
Await the time with confidence
When he his friendly zeal will show,
And brooks again untroubled flow.'[2]

1 The hum with which students con their tasks.

2 I omit here a long general description of the rainy season which is not found in the Bengal recension and appears to have been interpolated by a far inferior and much later hand than Válmíki's. It is composed in a metre different from that of the rest of the Canto, and contains figures of poetical rhetoric and commonplaces which are the delight of more recent poets.

3 Praushṭhapada or Bhadra, the modern Bhádon, corresponds to half of August and half of September.

4 The Sáman or Sáma-veda, the third of the four Vedas, is really merely a reproduction of parts of the Rig-veda, transposed and scattered about piece-meal, only 78 verses in the whole being, it is said, untraceable to the present recension of the Rig-veda.

5 Áshádha is the month corresponding to parts of June and July.

6 Bharat, who was regent during Ráma's absence.

7 Or with Gorresio, following the gloss of another commentary, "Has completed every holy rite and accumulated stores of merit."

CANTO XXIX.

HANUMÁN'S COUNSEL.

No flash of lightning lit the sky,
No cloudlet marred the blue on high.
The Sáras[3] missed the welcome rain,
The moon's full beams were bright again.
Sugríva, lapped in bliss, forgot
The claims of faith, or heeded not;
And by alluring joys misled
The path of falsehood learned to tread.
In careless ease he passed each hour,
And dallied in his lady's bower:
Each longing of his heart was stilled,
And every lofty hope fulfilled.
With royal Rumá by his side,
Or Tárá yet a dearer bride,

1 The river on which Ayodhyá was built.

2 I omit a *śloka* or four lines on gratitude and ingratitude repeated word for word from the last Canto.

3 The Indian crane; a magnificent bird easily domesticated.

He spent each joyous day and night
In revelry and wild delight,
Like Indra whom the nymphs entice
To taste the joys of Paradise.
The power to courtiers' hands resigned,
To all their acts his eyes were blind.
All doubt, all fear he cast aside
And lived with pleasure for his guide.
But sage Hanúmán, firm and true,
Whose heart the lore of Scripture knew,
Well trained to meet occasion, trained
In all by duty's law ordained,
Strove with his prudent speech to find
Soft access to the monarch's mind.
He, skilled in every gentle art
Of eloquence that wins the heart,
Sugríva from his trance to wake,
His salutary counsel spake:
'The realm is won, thy name advanced,
The glory of thy house enhanced.
And now thy foremost care should be
To aid the friends who succoured thee.
He who is firm and faithful found
To friendly ties in honour bound,
Will see his name and fame increase
And his blest kingdom thrive in peace.
Wide sway is his who truly boasts
That friends and treasure, self and hosts,
All blent in one harmonious whole,
Are subject to his firm control.
Do thou, whose footsteps never stray
From the clear bounds of duty's way,
Assist, as honour bids thee, now
Thy friends, observant of thy vow.
For if all cares we lay not by,
And to our friend's assistance fly,
We, after, toil in idle haste,
And all the late endeavour waste.
Up! nor the promised help delay
Until the hour have slipped away.
Up! and with Raghu's son renew
The search for Sítá lost to view.
The hour is come: he hears the call,
But not on thee reproaches fall
From him who labours to repress
His eager spirit's restlessness.
Long joined to thee in friendly ties
He made thy fame and fortune rise,
In gentle gifts by none excelled,
In splendid might unparalleled.
Up, to his succour, King! repay
The favour of that prosperous day,
And to thy bravest captains send
Prompt mandates to assist thy friend.
The cry for help thou wilt not spurn
Although no grace demands return:
And wilt thou not thine aid afford
To him who realm and life restored?
Exert thy power, and thou hast won
The love of Daśaratha's son:
And wilt thou for his summons wait,
And, till he call thee, hesitate?
Think not the hero needs thy power
To save him in the desperate hour
He with his arrows could subdue
The Gods and all the demon crew,
And only waits that he may see
Redeemed the promise made by thee.
For thee he risked his life and fought,
For thee that great deliverance wrought.
Then let us trace through earth and skies
His lady wheresoe'er she lies.
Through realms above, beneath, we flee,
And plant our footsteps on the sea.
Then why, O Lord of Vánars, still
Delay us waiting for thy will?
Give thy commands, O King, and say
What task has each, and where the way.
Before thee myriad Vánars stand
To sweep through heaven, o'er seas and land.'
Sugríva heard the timely rede
That roused him in the day of need,
And thus to Níla prompt and brave
His best the imperial Vánar gave:
'Go, Níla, to the distant hosts
That keep in arms their several posts,
And all the armies that protect
The quarters,[1] with their chiefs, collect.
To all the limitaries placed
In intermediate regions haste,
And bid each captain rise and lead
His squadrons to their king with speed.
Do thou meanwhile with strictest care
All that the time requires prepare.
The loitering Vánar who delays
To gather here ere thrice five days,
Shall surely die for his offence,
Condemned for sinful negligence.'

CANTO XXX.

RÁMA'S LAMENT.

But Ráma in the autumn night
Stood musing on the mountain height,
While grief and love that scorned control
Shook with wild storms the hero's soul.
Clear was the sky, without a cloud
The glory of the moon to shroud.
And bright with purest silver shone
Each hill the soft beams looked upon.
He knew Sugríva's heart was bent
On pleasure, gay and negligent.
He thought on Janak's child forlorn
From his fond arms for ever torn.
He mourned occasion slipping by,
And faint with anguish heaved each sigh.

[1] The troops who guard the frontiers on the north, south, east, and west.

He sat where many a varied streak
Of rich ore marked the mountain peak,
He raised his eyes the sky to view,
And to his love his sad thoughts flew.
He heard the Sáras cry, and faint
With sorrow poured his love-born plaint:
'She, she who mocked the softest tone
Of wild birds' voices with her own,—
Where strays she now, my love who played
So happy in our hermit shade?
How can my absent love behold
The bright trees with their flowers of gold,
And all their gleaming glory see
With eyes that vainly look for me?
How is it with my darling when
From the deep tangles of the glen
Float carols of each bird elate
With rapture singing to his mate?
In vain my weary glances rove
From lake to hill, from stream to grove:
I find no rapture in the scene,
And languish for my fawn-eyed queen.
Ah, does strong love with wild unrest,
Born of the autumn, stir her breast?
And does the gentle lady pine
Till her bright eyes shall look in mine?'
Thus Raghu's son in piteous tone,
O'erwhelmed with sorrow, made his moan,
E'en as the bird that drinks the rains [1]
To Indra thousand-eyed complains.
Then Lakshman who had wandered through
The copses where the berries grew,
Returning to the cavern found
His brother chief in sorrow drowned,
And pitying the woes that broke
The spirit of the hero spoke:
'Why cast thy strength of soul away,
And weakly yield to passion's sway?
Arise, my brother, do and dare
Ere action perish in despair.
Recall the firmness of thy heart,
And nerve thee for a hero's part.
Whose is the hand unscathed to seize
The red flame quickened by the breeze?
Where is the foe will dare to wrong
Or keep the Maithil lady long?'
Then with pale lips that sorrow dried
The son of Raghu thus replied:
Lord Indra thousand-eyed has sent
The sweet rain from the firmament,
Sees the rich promise of the grain,
And turns him to his rest again.
The clouds with voices loud and deep,
Veiling each tree upon the steep,
Up on the thirsty earth have shed
Their precious burthen, and are fled.

[1] The Chátaka, Cuculus Melanoleucus, is supposed to drink nothing but the water of the clouds.

Now in kings' hearts ambition glows:
They rush to battle with their foes; [1]
But in Sugríva's sloth I see
No care for deeds of chivalry.
See, Lakshman, on each breezy height
A thousand autumn blooms are bright.
See how the wings of wild swans gleam
On every islet of the stream.
Four months of flood and rain are past:
A hundred years they seemed to last
To me whom toil and trouble tried,
My Sítá severed from my side.
She, gentlest woman, weak and young,
Still to her lord unwearied clung.
Still by the exile's side she stood
In the wild ways of Daṇḍak wood,
Like a fond bird disconsolate
If parted from her darling mate.
Sugríva, lapped in soft repose,
Untouched by pity for my woes,
Scorns the poor exile, dispossessed,
By Rávan's mightier arm oppressed,
The wretch who comes to sue and pray
From his lost kingdom far away.
Hence falls on me the Vánar's scorn,
A suitor friendless and forlorn.
The time is come: with heedless eye
He sees the hour of action fly,—
Unmindful, now his hopes succeed,
Of promise made in stress of need.
Go seek him sunk in bliss and sloth,
Forgetful of his royal oath,
And as mine envoy thus upbraid
The monarch for his help delayed:
'Vile is the wretch who will not pay
The favour of an earlier day,
Hope in the suppliant's breast awakes,
And then his plighted promise breaks.
Noblest, mid all of women born,
Who keeps the words his lips have sworn,
Yea, if those words be good or ill,
Maintains his faith unbroken still.
The thankless who forget to aid
The friend who helped them when they prayed,
Dishonoured in their death shall lie,
And dogs shall pass their corpses by.
Sure thou wouldst see my strained arm hold
My bow of battle backed with gold,
Wouldst gaze upon its awful form
Like lightning flashing through the storm,
And hear the clanging bowstring loud
As thunder from a labouring cloud.'
His valour and his strength I know,
But pleasure's sway now sinks them low.
With thee, my brother, for ally.
That strength and valour I defy.

[1] The time for warlike expeditions began when the rains had ceased.

He promised, when the rains should end,
The succour of his arm to lend.
Those months are past: he dares forget,
And, lapped in pleasure, slumbers yet.
No thought disturbs his careless breast
For us impatient and distressed,
And, while we sadly wait and pine,
Girt by his lords he quaffs the wine.
Go, brother, go, his palace seek,
And boldly to Sugríva speak.
Thus give the listless king to know
What waits him if my anger glow:
Still open, to the gloomy God,
Lies the sad path that Báli trod.
'Still to thy plighted word be true,
Lest thou, O King, that path pursue.
I launched the shaft I pointed well,
And Báli, only Báli, fell.
But, if from truth thou dare to stray,
Both thee and thine this hand shall slay.'
Thus be the Vánar king addressed,
Then add thyself what seems the best.

CANTO XXXI.

THE ENVOY.

Thus Ráma spoke, and Lakshman then
Made answer to the prince of men:
'Yea, if the Vánar, underterred
By fear of vengeance, break his word,
Loss of his royal power ere long
Shall pay the traitor for the wrong,
Nor deem I him so void of sense
To brave the bitter consequence.
But if enslaved to joy he lie,
And scorn thy grace with blinded eye,
Then let him join his brother slain:
Unmeet were such a wretch to reign.
Quick rises, kindling in my breast,
The wrath that will not be repressed,
And bids me in my fury slay
The breaker of his faith to-day.
Let Báli's son thy consort trace
With bravest chiefs of Vánar race.'
Thus spoke the hero, and aglow
With rage of battle seized his bow,
But Ráma thus in gentler mood
With fitting words his speech renewed;
'No hero with a soul like thine
To paths of sin will e'er incline.
He who his angry heart can tame
Is worthiest of a hero's name.
Not thine, my brother, be the part
So alien from the tender heart,
Nor let thy feet by wrath misled
Forsake the path they loved to tread.
From harsh and angry words abstain;
With gentle speech a hearing gain,
And tax Sugríva with the crime
Of failing faith and wasted time.'
Then Lakshman, bravest of the brave,
Obeyed the best that Ráma gave,
To whom devoting every thought
The Vánar's royal town he sought.
As Mandar's mountain heaves on high
His curved peak soaring to the sky,
So Lakshman showed, his dread bow ben[t]
Like Indra's[1] in the firmament.
His brother's wrath, his brother's woe
Inflamed his soul to fiercest glow.
The tallest trees to earth were cast
As furious on his way he passed,
And where he stepped, so fiercely fleet,
The stones were shivered by his feet.
He reached Kishkindhá's city deep
Embosomed where the hills were steep,
Where street and open square were lined
With legions of the Vánar kind.
Then, as his lips with fury swelled,
The lord of Raghu's line beheld
A stream of Vánar chiefs outpoured
To do obeisance to their lord.
But when the mighty prince in view
Of the thick coming Vánars drew,
They turned them in amaze to seize
Crags of the rock and giant trees.
He saw, and fiercer waxed his ire,
As oil lends fury to the fire.
Scarce had the Vánar chieftains seen
That wrathful eye, that troubled mien
Fierce as the God's who rules the dead,
When, turned in wild affright, they fled.
Speeding in breathless terror all
Sought King Sugríva's council hall,
And there made known their tale of fea[r]
That Lakshman, wild with rage, was nea[r].
The king, untroubled by alarms,
Held Tárá in his amorous arms,
And in the distant bower with her
Heard not each clamorous messenger.
Then, summoned at the lords' behest,
Forth from the city portals pressed,
Each like some elephant or cloud,
The Vánars in a trembling crowd:
Fierce warriors all, with massive jaws
And terrors of their tiger claws.
Some matched ten elephants, and some
A hundred's strength could overcome.
Some chieftains, mightier than the rest,
Ten times a hundred's force possessed.
With eyes of fury Lakshman viewed
The Vánars' tree-armed multitude.
Thus garrisoned from side to side
The city walls assault defied.
Beyond the moat that girt the wall
Advanced the Vánar chiefs; and all
Upon the plain in firm brigade,
Impetuous warriors, stood arrayed.

1 The rainbow.

Red at the sight flashed Lakshman's eyes,
His bosom heaved tumultuous sighs,
And forth the fire of fury broke
Like flame that flashes through the smoke.
Like some fierce snake the hero stood :
His bow recalled the expanded hood,
And in his shaft-head bright and keen
The flickering of its tongue was seen :
And in his own all-conquering might
The venom of its deadly bite.
Prince Angad marked his angry look,
And every hope his heart forsook.
Then, his large eyes with fury red,
To Angad Lakshman turned and said :
'Go tell the king that Lakshman waits
For audience at the city gates,
Whose heart, O tamer of thy foes,
Is heavy with his brother's woes.
Bid him to Ráma's word attend,
And ask if he will aid his friend.
Go, let the king my message learn :
Then hither with all speed return.'
Prince Angad heard and wild with grief
Cried as he looked upon the chief :
''Tis Lakshman's self : impelled by ire
He seeks the city of my sire.'
At the fierce words and furious look
Of Raghu's son he quailed and shook.
Back through the city gates he sped,
And, laden with the tale of dread,
Sought King Sugríva, filled his ears
And Rumá's with his doubts and fears.
To Rumá and the king he bent,
And clasped their feet most reverent,
Clasped the dear feet of Tárá, too,
And told the startling tale anew.
But King Sugríva's ear was dulled,
By love and wine and languor lulled,
Nor did the words that Angad spake
The slumberer from his trance awake.
But soon as Raghu's son came nigh
The startled Vánars raised a cry,
And strove to win his grace, while dread
Each anxious heart disquieted.
They saw, and, as they gathered round,
Rose from the mighty throng a sound
Like torrents when they downward dash,
Or thunder with the lightning's flash.
The shouting of the Vánars broke
Sugríva's slumber, and he woke :
Still with the wine his eyes were red,
His neck with flowers was garlanded.
Roused at the voice of Angad came
Two Vánar lords of rank and fame ;
One Yaksha, one Prabháva hight,—
Wise counsellors of gain and right.
They came and raised their voices high,
And told that Raghu's son was nigh :
'Two brothers steadfast in their truth,
Each glorious in the bloom of youth,
Worthy of rule, have left the skies,
And clothed their forms in men's disguise.
One at thy gates, in warlike hands
Holding his mighty weapon, stands.
His message is the charioteer
That brings the eager envoy near,
Urged onward by his bold intent,
And by the hest of Ráma sent.[1]
The gathered Vánars saw and fled,
And raised aloud their cry of dread.
Son of Queen Tárá, Angad ran
To parley with the godlike man.
Still fiery-eyed with rage and hate
Stands Lakshman at the city gate,
And trembling Vánars scarce can fly
Scathed by the lightning of his eye.
Go with thy son, thy kith and kin,
The favour of the prince to win,
And bow thy reverent head that so
His fiery wrath may cease to glow.
What righteous Ráma bids thee. do,
And to thy plighted word be true.'

CANTO XXXII.

HANUMAN'S COUNSEL.

Sugríva heard, and, trained and tried
In counsel, to his lords replied :
'No deed of mine, no hasty word
The anger of the prince has stirred.
But haply some who hate me still
And watch their time to work me ill,
Have slandered me to Raghu's son,
Accused of deeds I ne'er have done.
Now, O my lords—for you are wise—
Speak truly what your hearts advise,
And, pondering each event, inquire
The reason of the prince's ire.
No fear have I of Lakshman : none :
No dread of Raghu's mightier son.
But wrath, that fires a friendly breast
Without due cause, distrubs my rest.
With labour light is friendship gained,
But with severest toil maintained.
And doubt is strong, and faith is weak,

[1] In a note on the corresponding passage in the Bengal recension Gorresio says : 'The text here makes use of a strange and something more than bold metaphor which I have sought to modify. The text says : "Here is Lakshman the charioteer of words who by the orders of Ráma has come hither upon the car of resolution." In his Italian translation he renders the passage : "Here is Lakshman, the brother of Ráma who by his orders comes hither the determined bearer of words."

And friendship dies when traitors speak.
Hence is my troubled bosom cold
With fear of Ráma lofty-souled;
For heavy on my spirit weigh
His favours I can ne'er repay.'
He ceased: and Hanumán of all
The Vánars in the council hall
In wisdom first, and rank, expressed
The thoughts that filled his prudent breast:
'No marvel thou rememberest yet
The service thou shouldst ne'er forget,
How the brave prince of Raghu's seed
Thy days from fear and peril freed;
And Báli for thy sake o'erthrew,
Whom Indra's self might scarce subdue.
I doubt not Ráma's anger burns
For the scant love thy heart returns.
For this he sends his brother, him
Whose glory never waxes dim.
Sunk in repose thy careless eye
Marks not the seasons as they fly,
Nor sees that autumn has begun
With dark blooms opening to the sun.
Clear is the sky: no cloudlet mars
The splendour of the shining stars.
The balmy air is soft and still,
And clear and bright are lake and rill.
Thou heedest not with blinded eyes
The hour for warlike enterprise.
Hence Lakshman hither comes to break
Thy slothful trance and bid thee wake.
Then, Monarch, with a patient ear
The high-souled Ráma's message hear,
Which, reft of wife and realm and friends,
Thus by another's mouth he sends.
Thou, Vánar King, hast done amiss:
And now I see no way but this:
Before his envoy humbly stand
And sue for peace with suppliant hand.
High duty bids a courtier seek
His master's weal, and freely speak.
So by no thought of fear controlled
My speech, O King, is free and bold.
For Ráma, if his anger glow,
Can, with the terrors of his bow,
This earth with all the Gods subdue,
Gandharvas,[1] and the demon crew.
Unwise to stir his wrathful mood
Whose favour must again be wooed.
And, most of all, unwise for one
Grateful like thee for service done.
Go with thy son and kinsmen: bend
Thy humble head and greet thy friend.
And, like a fond obedient spouse,
Be faithful to thy plighted vows.'

[1] Indra's associates in arms, and musicians of his heaven.

CANTO XXXIII.

LAKSHMAN'S ENTRY.

Through the fair city Lakshman came,
Invited in Sugríva's name.
Within the gates the guardian bands,
Of Vánars raised their suppliant hands,
And in their ordered ranks, amazed,
Upon the princely hero gazed.
They marked each burning breath he drew,
The fury of his soul they knew.
Their hearts were chilled with sudden fear:
They gazed, but dared not venture near.
Before his eyes the city, gay
With gems and flowery gardens, lay,
Where fane and palace rose on high,
And things of beauty charmed the eye.
Where trees of every blossom grew
Yielding their fruit in season due
To Vánars of celestial seed
Who wore each varied form at need,
Fair-faced and glorious with the shine
Of heavenly robes and wreaths divine.
There sandal, aloe, lotus bloomed,
And there delicious breath perfumed
The city's broad street, redolent
Of sugary mead[1] and honey scent.
There many a lofty palace rose
Like Vindhya or the Lord of Snows,
And with sweet murmur sparkling rills
Leapt lightly down the sheltering hills.
On many a glorious palace, raised
For prince and noble,[2] Lakshman gazed:
Like clouds of paly hue they shone
With fragrant wreaths that hung thereon;
There wealth of jewels was enshrined,
And fairer gems of womankind.
There gleamed, of noble height and size,
Like Indra's mansion in the skies,
Protected by a crystal fence
Of rock, the royal residence,
With roof and turret high and bright
Like Mount Kailása's loftiest height.
There blooming trees, Mahendra's gift,
High o'er the walls were seen to lift
Their golden-fruited boughs, that made
With leaf and flower delicious shade.
He saw a band of Vánars wait,

[1] Maireya, a spirituous liquor from the blossoms of the Lythrum fruticosum, with sugar, &c.

[2] Their names are as follows:
Angad, Mainda, Dwida, Gavaya, Gaváksha, Gaja, Sarabha, Vidyunmáli, Sampáti, Súryáksa, Hanumán, Vírabáhu, Subáhu, Nala, Kúmuda, Sushena, Tára, Jámbuvatu, Dadhivakra, Níla, Supátala, and Sunetra.

Wielding their weapons, at the gate
Where golden portals flashed between
Celestial garlands red and green.
Within Sugríva's fair abode
Unchecked the mighty hero strode,
As when the sun of autumn shrouds
His glory in a pile of clouds.
Through seven wide courts he quickly passed,
And reached the royal bower at last,
Where seats were set with couch and bed
Of gold and silver richly spread.
While the young chieftain's feet drew near
The sound of music reached his ear,
As the soft breathings of the flute
Came blending with the voice and lute.
Then beauty showed her youth and grace
And varied charm of form and face:
Soft bright-eyed creatures, fair and young,—
Gay garlands round their necks were hung,
And greater charms to each were lent
By richest dress and ornament.
He saw the calm attendants wait
About their lord in careless state,
Heard women's girdles chime in sweet
Accordance with their tinkling feet.
He heard the anklet's silvery sound,
He saw the calm that reigned around,
And o'er him, as he listened, came
A rush of rage, a flood of shame.
He drew his bowstring: with the clang
From east to west the welkin rang:
Then in his modest mood withdrew
A little from the ladies' view.
And sternly silent stood apart,
While wrath for Ráma filled his heart.
Sugríva knew the sounding string,
And at the call the Vánar king
Sprang swiftly from his golden seat,
And feared the coming prince to meet.
Then with cold lips that terror dried
To beauteous Tárá thus he cried:
'What cause of anger, O my spouse
Fair with the charm of lovely brows,
Sets Lakshman's gentle breast on fire,
And brings him in unwonted ire?
Say, canst thou see, O faultless dame,
A cause to fill his soul with flame?
For there must be a reason when
Such fury stirs the king of men.
Reveal the sin, if sin of mine
Anger the lord of Raghu's line.
Or go thyself, his rage subdue,
And with soft words his favour woo.
Soon as on thee his eyes are set
His heart this anger will forget,
For men like him of lofty mind
Are never stern with womankind.
First let thy gentle speech disarm
His fury, and his spirit charm,
And I, from fear of peril free,
The conqueror of his foes will see.'
She heard: with faltering steps and slow,
With eyes that shone with trembling glow,
With gold-girt body gently bent
To meet the stranger prince she went.
When Lakshmaṇ saw the Vánar queen
With tranquil eyes and modest mien,
Before the dame he bent his head,
And anger, at her presence, fled.
Made bold by draughts of wine, and cheered
By Lakshmaṇ's look, no more she feared,
And in the trust his favour lent
She thus addressed him eloquent:
'Whence springs thy burning fury? say:
Who dares thy will to disobey?
Who checks the maddened flames that seize
On forests full of withered trees?
Then Lakshmaṇ spoke, her mind to ease,
His kind reply in words like these:
'Thy lord his days in pleasure spends,
Heedless of duty and of friends.
Nor dost thou mark, though fondly true,
The evil path his steps pursue.
He cares not for affairs of state,
Nor us forlorn and desolate,
But sits a mere spectator still,
A sensual slave to pleasure's will.
Four months were fixed, the time agreed
When he should help us in our need:
But, bound in toils of pleasure fast,
He sees not that the months are past.
Where beats the heart which draughts of wine
To virtue or to gain incline?
Hast thou not heard those draughts destroy
Virtue and gain and love and joy?
For those who, helped at need, refuse
Their aid in turn, their virtue lose:
And they who scorn a friend disdain
A treasure naught may buy again.
Thy lord has cast his friend away,
Nor feared from virtue's path to stray.
If this be true, declare, O dame
Who knowest duty's every claim,
What further work remains for us
Deceived and disappointed thus.'
She listened, for his words were kind,
Where virtue showed with gain combined,
And thus in turn the prince addressed,
As hope was rising in his breast:
'No time, no cause of wrath I see
With those who love and honour thee;
And thou shouldst bear without offence
Thy servant's fitful negligence.
I know the seasons glide away,
While Ráma maddens at delay.
I know what deed our thanks has earned,
I know that grace should be returned.
But still I know, whate'er befall,
That conquering love is lord of all;

Know where Sugríva's thoughts, possessed
By one absorbing passion, rest.
But he whom sensual joys debase
Heeds not the claim of time and place,
And sees not with his blinded sight
His duty or his gain aright.
O pardon him who loves me! spare
The Vánar caught in pleasure's snare,
And once again let Ráma grace
With favour him who rules our race.
E'en royal saints, whose chief delight
Was penance and austerest rite,
At love's commandment have unbent,
Beguiled by sweetest blandishment.
And know, Sugríva, roused at last,
The order to his lords has passed,
And, long by love and bliss delayed,
Wakes all on fire your hopes to aid.
A countless host his city fills,
New-gathered from a thousand hills:
Impetuous chiefs, who wear at need
Each varied form, his legions lead.
Come then, O hero, kept aloof
By modest awe, nor fear reproof:
A faithful friend untouched by blame
May look upon another's dame.'
He passed within, by Tárá pressed,
And by his own impatient breast.
Refulgent there in sunlike sheen
Sugríva on his throne was seen.
Gay garlands round his neck were twined,
And Rumá by her lord recline.

CANTO XXXIV.

LAKSHMAN'S SPEECH.

Sugríva started from his rest
With doubt and terror in his breast.
He heard the prince's furious tread
He saw his eyes glow fiercely red.
Swift sprang the monarch to his feet
Upstarting from his golden seat.
Rose Rumá and her fellows, too,
And closely round Sugríva drew,
As round the moon's full glory stand
Attendant stars in glittering band.
Sugríva glanced with reddened eyes,
Raised his joined hands in suppliant guise
Flew to the door, and rooted there
Stood like the tree that grants each prayer.[1]
And Lakshman saw, and, fiercely moved,
With angry speech the king reproved:

' Famed is the prince who loves the truth
Whose soul is touched with tender ruth,
Who, liberal, keeps each sense subdued,
And pays the debt of gratitude.
But all unmeet a king to be,
The meanest of the mean is he
Who basely breaks the promise made
To trusting friends who lent him aid.
He sins who for a steed has lied,
As if a hundred steeds had died:
Or if he lie, a cow to win,
Tenfold as heavy is the sin.
But if the lie a man betray,
Both he and his shall all decay.[1]
O Vánar King, the thankless man
Is worthy of the general ban.
Who takes assistance of his friends,
And in his turn no service lends.
This verse of old by Brahmá sung
Is echoed now by every tongue.
Hear what He cried in angry mood
Bewailing man's ingratitude:
'For draughts of wine, for slaughtered cows
For treacherous theft, for broken vows
A pardon is ordained: but none
For thankless scorn of service done.'
Ungrateful, Vánar King, art thou,
And faithless to thy plighted vow.
For Ráma brought thee help, and yet
Thou shunnest to repay the debt:
Or, grateful, thou hadst surely pressed
To aid the hero in his quest.
Thou art, in vulgar pleasures drowned,
False to thy bond in honour bound.
Nor yet has Ráma's guileless heart
Discerned thee for the thing thou art—
A snake who holds the frogs that cries
And lures fresh victims as it dies.
Brave Ráma, born for glorious fate,
Has set thee in thy high estate,
And to the Vánars' throne restored,
Great-souled himself, their mean-souled lord.
Now if thy pride disown what he,
High-thoughted prince, has done for thee,
Struck by his arrows shalt thou fall,
And Báli meet in Yama's hall.
Still open, to the gloomy God,
Lies the sad path thy brother trod.
Then to thy plighted word be true,
Nor let thy steps that path pursue.
Methinks the shafts of Ráma, shot
Like thunderbolts, thou heedest not,
Who canst, absorbed in sensual bliss,
Thy promise from thy mind dismiss.'

---

[1] The Kalpadruma or Wishing-tree is one of the trees of Svarga or Indra's Paradise: it has the power of granting all desires.

[1] The meaning is that if a man promises to give a horse and then breaks his word he commits a sin as great as if he had killed a hundred horses.

CANTO XXXV.

TÁRA'S SPEECH.

He ceased: and Tárá starry-eyed
Thus to the angry prince replied:
'Not to my lord shouldst thou address
A speech so fraught with bitterness:
Not thus reproached my lord should be,
And least of all, O Prince, by thee.
He is no thankless coward—no—
With spirit dead to valour's glow.
From paths of truth he never strays,
Nor wanders in forbidden ways.
Ne'er will Sugríva's heart forget,
By Ráma saved, the lasting debt.
Still in his grateful breast will live
The succour none but he could give.
Restored to fame by Ráma's grace,
To empire o'er the Vánar race,
From ceaseless dread and toil set free,
Restored to Rumá and to me:
By grief and care and exile tried,
New to the bliss so long denied,
Like Viśvámitra once, alas,
He marks not how the seasons pass.
That saint ten thousand years remained,
By sweet Ghritáchí's[1] love enchained,
And deemed those years, that flew away
So lightly, but a single day.
O, if those years unheeded flew
By him who times and seasons knew,
Unequalled for his lofty mind,
What marvel meaner eyes are blind?
Then be not angry, Raghu's son,
And let thy brother feel for one
Who many a weary year has spent
Stranger to love and blandishment.
Let not this wrath thy soul inflame,
Like some mean wretch unknown to fame:
For high and noble hearts like thine
Love mercy and to ruth incline,
Calm and deliberate, and slow
With anger's raging fire to glow.
At length, O righteous prince, relent,
Nor let my words in vain be spent.
This sudden blaze of fury slake,
I pray thee for Sugríva's sake.
He would renounce at Ráma's call
Rumá and Angad, me and all
Who call him lord: his gold and grain,
The favour of his friend to gain.
His arm shall slay the fiend more base
In soul than all his impious race,
And happy Ráma reunite
To Sítá, rival in delight
Of the triumphant Moon when he
Rejoins his darling Rohiṇí.[1]
Ten million million demons guard
The gates of Lanká firmly barred.
All hope until that host be slain,
To smite the robber king is vain.
Nor with Sugríva's aid alone
May king and host be overthrown.
Thus ere he died—for well he knew—
Spake Báli, and his words are true.
I know not what his proofs might be,
But speak the words he spake to me.
Hence far and wide our lords are sent
To raise the mightiest armament.
For their return Sugríva waits
Ere he can sally from his gates.
Still is the oath Sugríva swore
Kept firmly even as before:
And the great host this day will be
Assembled by the king's decree,
Ten thousand thousand troops, who wear
The form of monkey and of bear,
Prepared for thee the war to wage:
Then let thy wrath no longer rage.
The matrons of the Vánar race
See marks of fury in thy face;
They see thine eyes like blood are red,
And will not yet be comforted.'

CANTO XXXVI.

SUGRÍVA'S SPEECH.

She ceased: and Lakshman gave assent,
Won by her gentle argument.
So Tárá's pleading, just and mild,
His softening heart had reconciled.
His altered mood Sugríva saw,
And cast aside the fear and awe
Like raiment heavy with the rain
Which on his troubled soul had lain.
Then quickly to the ground he threw
His flowery garland, bright of hue,
Which round his royal neck he wore,
And, sobered, was himself once more.
Then turning to the princely man
In soothing words the king began:
'My glory, wealth, and royal sway
To other hands had passed away:
But Ráma to my rescue came,
And gave me back my power and fame.
O Lakshman, say, whose grateful heart

[1] The story is told in Book I. Canto LXIII., but the charmer there is called Menaká.

[1] Rohiṇí is the name of the ninth Nakshatra or lunar asterism personified as a daughter of Daksha, and the favourite wife of the Moon.

Aldebaran is the principal star in the constellation.

Could nurse the hope to pay in part,
By service of a life, the deed
Of Ráma sprung of heavenly seed?
His foeman Rávaṇ shall be slain,
And Sítá shall be his again.
The hero's side I will not leave,
But he the conquest shall achieve.
What need of help has he who drew
His bow, and one great arrow flew
Trough seven tall trees, a mountain rent,
And cleft the earth with force unspent?
What aid needs he who shook his bow,
And at the sound the earth below
With hill and wood and rooted rock
Quaked feverous with the thunder shock?
Yet all my legions will I bring,
And follow close the warrier king
Marching on his impetuous way
Fierce Rávan and his hosts to slay.
If I be guilty of offence,
Careless through love or neligence,
Let him his loyal slave forgive;
For error cleaves to all who live.'

Thus king Sugríva, good and brave,
In humble words his answer gave,
Softened was Lakshmaṇ's angry mood
Who thus his friendly speech renewed:
'My brother, Vánar King, will see
A champion and a friend in thee.
So strong art thou, so brave and bold,
So pure in thought, so humble-souled,
That thou deservest well to reign
And all a monarch's bliss to gain.
Lend thou my brother aid, and all
His foes beneath his arm will fall.
Full well the words thou speakest suit
A chieftain wise and resolute,
With grateful heart that loves the right,
And foot that never yields in fight.
O come, and my sad brother cheer
Who mourns the wife he holds so dear.
O pardon, friend, my harsh address,
And Ráma's frantic bitterness.'

CANTO XXXVII.

THE GATHERING.

He ceased: and King Sugríva cried
To sage Hanúmán[1] by his side:
'Summon the Vánar legions, those
Who dwell about the Lord of Snows:
Those who in Vindhyan groves delight,
Kailása's, or Mahendra's height,
Dwell on the Five bright Peaks, or where
Mandar's white summit cleaves the air:
Wherever they are wandring free
In highlands by the western sea,
On that east hill whence springs the sun,
Or where he sinks when day is done.
Call the great chiefs whose legions fill
The forests of the Lotus Hill,[1]
Where every one in strength and size
With the stupendous Anjan[2] vies.
Call those, with tints of burnished gold,
Whom Mahásaila's caverns hold:
Those who on Dhúmra roam, or hide
In the wild woods on Meru's side.
Call those who, brilliant as the sun,
On high Mahárun leap and run,
Quaffing sweet juices that distil
From odorous trees upon the hill.
Call those whom tranquil haunts delight,
Where dwell the sage and anchorite
In groves that through their wide extent
Exhale a thousand blossoms' scent.
Send out, send out: from coast to coast
Assemble all the Vánar host:
With force, with words, with gifts of price
Compel, admonish and entice.
Already envoys have been sent
To warn them of their lord's intent.
Let others urged by thee repeat
My mandate that their steps be fleet.
Those lords who yielding to the sway
Of love's delight would fain delay,
Urge hither with the utmost speed,
Or with thee to my presence lead:
And those who linger to the last
Until ten days be come and passed,
And dare their sovereign to defy,
For their offence shall surely die.
Thousands, yea millions, shall there be,
Obedient to their king's decree,
The lions of the Vánar race,
Assembled from each distant place.
Forth shall they haste like hills in size,
Or mighty clouds that veil the skies,
And swiftly speeding on their way
Bring all our legions in array.'

[1] Válmíki and succeeding poets make the second vowel in this name long or short at their pleasure.

[1] Some of the mountains here mentioned are fabulous and others it is impossible to identify. Sugríva means to include all the mountains of India from Kailás the residence of the God Kuvera, regarded as one of the loftiest peaks of the Himálayas, to Mahendra in the extreme south, from the mountain in the east where the sun is said to rise to Astáchal or the western mountain where he sets. The commentators give little assistance: that Mahásaila, &c. are certain mountains is about all the information they give.

[2] One of the celestial elephants of the Gods who protect the four quarters and intermediate points of the compass.

He ceased: the son of Váyu[1] heard,
Submissive to his sovereign's word;
And sent his rapid envoys forth
To east and west and south and north.
They bent their airy course afar
Along the paths of bird and star,
And sped through ether farther yet
Where Vishṇu's splendid sphere is set.[2]
By sea, on hill, by wood and lake
They called to arms for Ráma's sake,
As each with terror in his breast
Obeyed his awful king's behest.
Three million Vánars, fierce and strong
As Anjan's self, a wondrous throng,
Sped from the spot where Ráma still
Gazed restless from the woody hill.
Ten million others, brave and bold,
With coats that shone like burning gold,
Came flying from the mountain crest
Where sinks the weary sun to rest.
Impetuous from the northern skies,
Where Mount Kailása's summits rise,
Ten hundred millions hasted, hued
Like manes of lions, ne'er subdued:
The dwellers on Himálaya's side,
Whose food his roots and fruit supplied,
With rangers of the Vindhyan chain
And neighbours of the Milky Main.[3]
Some from the palm groves where they fed,
Some from the woods of betel sped:
In countless numbers, fierce and brave,
They came from mountain, lake, and cave.

As on their way the Vánars went
To rouse each distant armament,
They chanced that wondrous tree to view
That on Himálaya's summit grew.
Of old upon that sacred height
Was wrought Maheśvar's[4] glorious rite,
Which every God in heaven beheld,
And his glad heart with triumph swelled.
There from pure seed at random sown
Bright plants with luscious fruit had grown,
And, sweet as Amrit to the taste,
The summit of the mountain graced.
Who once should eat the virtuous fruit
That sprang from so divine a root,
One whole revolving moon should be
From every pang of hunger free.
The Vánars culled the fruit they found
Ripe on the sacrificial ground
With rare celestial odours sweet,
To lay them at Sugríva's feet.
Those noble envoys scoured the land
To summon every Vánar band
Then swiftly homeward at the head
Of countless armaments they sped.
They gathered by Kishkindhá's wall,
They thronged Sugríva's palace hall,
And, richly laden, bare within
That fruit of heavenly origin.
Their gifts before their king they spread,
And thus in tones of triumph said:
'Through every land our way we took
To visit hill and wood and brook,
And all thy hosts from east to west
Flock hither at their lord's behest.'
Sugríva with delighted look
The present of his envoys took,
Then bade them go, with gracious speech
Rewarding and dismissing each.

CANTO XXXVIII.

SUGRÍVA'S DEPARTURE.

Thus all the princely Vánars, true
To their appointed tasks, withdrew.
Sugríva deemed already done
The work he planned for Raghu's son.
Then Lakshmaṇ gently spoke and cheered
Sugríva for his valour feared:
'Now, chieftain, if thy will be so,
Forth from Kishkindhá let us go.'
Sugríva's heart swelled high with pride
As to the prince he thus replied:
'Come, speed we forth without delay:
'Tis mine thy mandate to obey.'
Sugríva bade the dames adieu,
And Tárá and the rest withdrew.
Then at their chieftain's summons came
The Vánars first in rank and fame,
A trusty brave and reverent band,
Meet e'en before a queen to stand.
They at his call made haste to bring
The litter of the glorious king.
'Mount, O my friend,' Sugríva cried,
And straight Sumitrá's son complied.
Then took by Lakshmaṇ's side his place
The sovereign of the woodland race,
Upraised by Vánars, fleet and strong,
Who bore the glittering load along.
On high above his royal head
A paly canopy was spread,
And chouries white in many a hand
The forehead of the monarch fanned,
And shell and drum and song and shout
Pealed round him as the king passed out.

[1] Váyu or the Wind was the father of Hanumán.

[2] The path or station of Vishṇu is the space between the seven Rishis or Ursa Major, and Dhruva or the polar star.

[3] One of the seven seas which surround the earth in concentric circles.

[4] The title of Maheśvar or Mighty Lord is sometimes given to Indra, but more generally to Śiva whom it here denotes.

About the monarch went a throng
Of Vánar warriors brave and strong,
As onward to the mountain shade
Where Ráma dwelt his way he made.
Soon as the lovely spot he viewed
Where Ráma lived in solitude,
The Vánar monarch, far-renowed,
With Lakshmaṇ, lightly stepped to ground,
And to the son of Raghu went
Joining his raised hands reverent.
As their great leader raised his hands,
So suppliant stood the Vánar bands.
Well pleased the son of Raghu saw
Those legions, hushed in reverent awe,
Stand silent like the tranquil floods
That raise their hands of lotus buds.
But Ráma, when the king, to greet
His friend, had bowed him at his feet,
Raised him who ruled the Vánar race,
And held him in a close embrace:
Then, when his arms he had unknit,
Besought him by his side to sit,
And thus with gentle words the best
Of men the Vánar king addressed:
'The prince who well his days divides,
And knows aright the times and tides
To follow duty, joy, or gain,
He, only he, deserves to reign.
But he who wealth and virtue leaves,
And every hour to pleasure cleaves,
False from his bliss like him who wakes
From slumber on a branch that breaks.
True king is he who smites his foes,
And favour to his servants shows,
And of that fruit makes timely use
Which virtue, wealth, and joy produce.
The hour is come that bids thee rise
To aid me in my enterprise.
Then call thy nobles to debate,
And with their help deliberate.'

'Lost was my power,' the king replied,
'All strength had fled, all hope had died:
The Vánars owned another lord,
But by thy grace was all restored.
All this, O conqueror of the foe,
To thee and Lakshmaṇ's aid I owe
And his should be the villain's shame
Who durst deny the sacred claim.
These Vánar chiefs of noblest birth
Have at my bidding roamed the earth,
And brought from distant regions all
Our legions at their monarch's call:
Fierce bears with monkey troops combined,
And apes of every varied kind,
Terrific in their forms, who dwell
In grove and wood and bosky dell:
The bright Gandharvas' brood, the seed
Of Gods,[1] they change their shapes at need.
Each with his legions in array,
Hither, O Prince, they make their way.
They come: and tens of millions swell
To numbers that no tongue may tell.[1]
For thee their armies will unite
With chiefs, Mahendra's peers in might.
From Meru and from Vindhya's chain
They come like clouds that bring the rain.
These round thee to the war will go,
To smite to earth thy demon foe;
Will slay the Rákshas and restore
Thy consort when the fight is o'er.'

[1] See Book I. Canto XVI.

CANTO XXXIX.

THE VÁNAR HOST.

Then Ráma, best of all who guide
Their steps by duty, thus replied:
'What marvel if Lord Indra send
The kindly rain, O faithful friend?
If, thousand-rayed, the God of Day
Drive every darksome cloud away?
Or, rising high, the Lord of Night
Flood the broad heaven with silver light?
What marvel, King, that one like thee
The glory of his friends should be?
No marvel, O my lord, that thou
Hast shown thy noble nature now.
Thy heart, Sugríva, well I know:
Naught from thy lips but truth may flow.
With thee for friend and champion all
My foes beneath my arm will fall.
The Rákshas, when my queen he stole,
Brought sure destruction on his soul,
Like Anuhláda[2] who beguiled
Queen Śachí called Puloma's child.
Yes, near, Sugríva, is the day
When I my demon foe shall slay,
As conquering Indra in his ire
Slew Queen Paulomí's haughty sire.'[3]

[1] The numbers are unmanageable in English verse. The poet speaks of hundreds of *arbudas;* and an *arbuda* is a hundred millions.

[2] Anuhláda or Anuhráda is one of the four sons of the mighty Hiraṇyakaśipu, an Asur or a Daitya son of Kaśyapa and Diti and killed by Vishṇu in his incarnation of the Man-Lion *Narasinha.* According to the Bhágavata Puráṇa the Daitya or Asur Hiraṇyakaśipu and Hiraṇyáksha his brother, both killed by Vishṇu, were born again as Rávaṇ and Kumbhakarṇa his brother."

[3] Puloma, a demon, was the father-in-law of Indra who destroyed him in order to avert an imprecation. Paulomií is a patronymic denoting Śachí the daughter of Puloma.

He ceased : thick clouds of dust rose high
To every quarter of the sky :
The very sun grew faint and pale
Behind the darkly-gathering veil.
The mighty clouds that hung o'erhead
From east to west thick darkness spread,
And earth to her foundations shook
With hill and forest, lake and brook.
Then hidden was the ground beneath
Fierce warriors armed with fearful teeth,
Hosts numberless, each lord in size
A match for him who rules the skies :
From many a sea and distant hill,
From rock and river, lake and rill.
Some like the morning sun were bright,
Some, like the moon, were silver white :
These green as lotus fibres, those
White-coated from their native snows.[1]
Then Śatabali came in view
Girt by a countless retinue.
Like some gold mountain high in air
Tárá's illustrious sire[2] was there.
There Rumá's father,[3] far-renowned,
With tens of thousands ranged around.
There, tinted like the tender green
Of lotus filaments, was seen,
Compassed by countless legions, one
Whose face was as the morning sun,
Hanúmán's father good and great,
Kesarí,[4] wisest in debate.
There the proud king Gavákshа, feared
For his strong warrior arm, appeared.
There Dhúmra, mighty lord, the dread
Of foes, his ursine legions led.
There Panas, first for warlike fame,
With twenty million warriors came.
There glorious Níla, dark of hue,
Arrayed his countless troops in view.
There moved lord Gavaya brave and bold,
Resplendent like a hill of gold,
And near him Darímukha stood
With millions from the hill and wood.
And Dwivid famed for strength and speed,
And Mainda, both of Aśvin seed.
There Gaja, strong and glorious, led
The countless troops around him spread,
And Jámbaván[5] the king whose sway
The bears delighted to obey,
With swarming myriads onward pressed
True to his lord Sugríva's hest ;
And princely Ruman, dear to fame,
Led millions whom no hosts could tame.
All these and many a chief beside[1]
Came onward fierce in warlike pride.
They covered all the plain, and still
Pressed forward over wood and hill.
In rows for many a league around
They rested on the grassy ground ;
Or to Sugríva made their way,
Like clouds about the Lord of Day,
And to the king their proud heads bent
In power and might preëminent.
Sugríva then to Ráma sped,
And raised his reverent hands, and said
That every chief from coast to coast
Was present with his warrior host.

CANTO XL.

THE ARMY OF THE EAST.

With practised eye the king reviewed
The Vánars' countless multitude,
And, joying that his hest was done,
Thus spake to Raghu's mighty son :
'See, all the Vánar hosts who fear
My sovereign might are gathered here.
Chiefs strong as Indra's self, who speed
Wher'er they list, these armies lead.
Fierce and terrific to the view
As Daityas or the Dánav[2] crew,

---

1 "Observe the variety of colours which the poem attributes to all these inhabitants of the different mountainous regions, some white, others yellow, &c. Such different colours were perhaps peculiar and distinctive characteristics of those various races." GORRESSIO.

2 Sushen. 3 Tára.

4 Kesarí was the husband of Hanumán's mother, and is here called his father.

5 "I here unite under one heading two animals of very diverse nature and race, but which from some gross resemblances, probably helped by an equivoque in the language, are closely affiliated in the Hindoo myth......a reddish colour of the skin, want of symmetry and ungainliness of form, strength in hugging with the fore paws or arms, the faculty of climbing, shortness of tail (?), sensuality, capacity of instruction in dancing and in music, are all characteristics which more or less distinguish and meet in bears as well as in monkeys. In the *Rámáyaṇam*, the wise Jámbavant, the Odysseus of the expedition of Lanká, is called now king of the bears (rikshapárthivah), now great monkey (*Mahákapih*). DE GUBERNATIS : *Zoological Mythology*, Vol. II. p. 97.

1 Gandhamádana, Angad, Tára, Indrajánu, Rambha, Durmukha, Hanumán, Nala, Darímukha, Śarabha, Kumuda, Vahni.

2 Daityas and Dánavas are fiends and enemies of the Gods, like the Titans of Greek mythology.

Famed in all lands for souls afire
With lofty thoughts, they never tire,
O'er hill and vale they wander free,
And islets of the distant sea.
And these gathered myriads, all
Will serve thee, Ráma, at thy call.
Whate'er thy heart advises, say:
Thy mandates will the host obey.'
Then answered Ráma, as he pressed
The Vánar monarch to his breast:
'O search for my lost Sítá, strive
To find her if she still survive:
And in thy wondrous wisdom trace
Fierce Rávaṇ to his dwelling-place.
And when by toil and search we know
Where Sítá lies and where the foe,
With thee, dear friend, will I devise
Fit means to end the enterprise.
Not mine, not Lakshmaṇ's is the power
To guide us in the doubtful hour.
Thou, sovereign of the Vánars, thou
Must be our hope and leader now.'
He ceased: at King Sugríva's call
Near came a Vánar strong and tall,
Huge as a towering mountain, loud
As some tremendous thunder cloud,
A prince who war like legions led:
To him his sovereign turned and said:
'Go, take ten thousand[1] of our race
Well trained in lore of time and place,
And search the eastern region; through
Groves, woods, ane hills thy way pursue.
There seek for Sítá, trace the spot
Where Rávaṇ hides, and weary not.
Search for the captive in the caves
Of mountains, and by woods and waves.
To Surjú,[2] Kauśikí,[3] repair,
Bhagírath's daughter[4] fresh and fair.
Search mighty Yámun's[5] peak, explore
Swift Yamuná's[6] delightful shore,
Sarasvatí[7] and Sindhu's[8] tide,
And rapid Śoṇa's[1] pebbly side.
Then roam afar by Mahí's[2] bed
Where Kálamahí's groves are spread.
Go where the silken tissue shines,
Go to the land of silver mines.[3]
Visit each isle and mountain steep
And city circled by the deep,
And distant villages that high
About the peaks of Mandar lie.
Speed over Yavadwípa's land,[4]
And see Mount Śiśir[5] proudly stand
Uplifting to the skies his head
By Gods and Dánavs visited.
Search each ravine and mountain pass,
Each tangled thicket deep in grass.
Search every cave with utmost care
If haply Ráma's queen be there.
Then pass beyond the sounding sea
Where heavenly beings wander free,
And Śoṇa's[6] waters swift and strong
With ruddy billows foam along.
Search where his shelving banks descend,
Search where the hanging woods extend:
Try if the pathless thickets screen
The robber and the captive queen.
Search where the torrent floods that rend
The mountain to the plains descend:
Search dark abysses where they rave,
Search mountain slope and wood and cave.
Then on with rapid feet, and gain
The islands of the fearful main
Where, tortured by the tempest's lash,
Against rude rocks the billows dash:
An ocean like a sable cloud,
Whose margent monstrous serpents crowd:

[1] I reduce the unwieldy numbers of the original to more modest figures.

[2] Sarayú now Sarjú is the river on which Ayodhyá was built.

[3] Kauśikí is a river which flows through Behar, commonly called Kosi.

[4] Bhagírath's daughter is Ganga or the Ganges. The legend is told at length in Book I. Canto XLIV. *The Descent of Gangá.*

[5] A mountain not identified.

[6] The Jumna. The river is personified as the twin sister of Yama, and hence regared as the daughter of the Sun.

[7] The Sarasvatí (corruptly called Sursooty, is supposed to join the Ganges and Jumna at Prayág or Allahabad. It rises in the mountains bounding the north-east part of the province of Dehli, and running in a south-westerly direction becomes lost in the sands of the great desert.

[8] The Sindhu is the Indus, the Sanskrit *s* becoming *h* in Persian and being in this instance dropped by the Greeks.

[1] The Sone which rises in the district of Nagpore and falls into the Ganges above Patna.

[2] Mahí is a river rising in Malwa and falling into the gulf of Cambay after a westerly course of 280 miles.

[3] There is nothing to show what parts of the country the poet intended to denote as silk-producing and silver-producing.

[4] Yavadwípa means the island of Yava, wherever that may be.

[5] Śiśir is said to be a mountain ridge projecting from the base of Meru on the south. WILSON'S *Vishṇu Puráṇa*, ed. Hall, Vol. II. p. 117.

[6] This appears to be some mythical stream and not the well-known Sone. The name means red-coloured.

An ocean rising with a roar
To beat upon an iron shore.
On, onward still! your feet shall tread
Shores of the sea whose waves are red,
Where spreading wide your eyes shall see
The guilt-tormenting cotton tree [1]
And the wild spot where Garud[2] dwells
Which gems adorn and ocean shells,
High as Kailása, nobly decked,
Wrought by the heavenly architect.[3]
Huge giants named Mandehas[4] there
In each foul shape they love to wear,
Numbing the soul with terror's chill,
Hang from the summit of the hill.
When darts the sun his earliest beam
They plunge them in the ocean stream,
New vigour from his rays obtain,
And hang upon the rocks again.
Speed onward still: your steps shall be
At length beside the Milky Sea
Whose every ripple as it curls
Gleams glorious with its wealth of pearls.
Amid that sea like pale clouds spread
The white Mount Rishabh[5] rears his head.
About the mountain's glorious waist
Woods redolent of bloom are braced.
A lake where lotuses unfold
Their silver buds with threads of gold,
Sudarśan ever bright and fair
Where white swans sport, lies gleaming there,
The wandering Kinnar's[6] dear resort,
Where heavenly nymphs and Yakshas[7] sport.

[1] A fabulous thorny rod of the cotton tree used for torturing the wicked in hell. The tree gives its name, Sálmalí, to one of the seven Dwípas or great divisions of the known continent: and also to a hell where the wicked are tormented with the pickles of the tree.

[2] The king of the feathered creation.

[3] Viśvakarmá, the Mulciber of the Indian heaven.

[4] "The terrific fiends named Mandehas attempt to devour the sun: for Brahmá denounced this curse upon them, that without the power to perish they should die every day (and revive by night) and therefore a fierce contest occurs (daily) between them and the sun."

WILSON'S *Vishṇu Puráṇa*, Vol. II. p. 250.

[5] Said in the *Vishṇu Puráṇa* to be a ridge projecting from the base of Meru to the north.

[6] Kinnars are centaurs reversed, beings with equine heads and human bodies.

[7] Yakshas are demi-gods attendant on Kuvera the God of wealth.

On! leave the Milky Sea behind:
Another flood your search shall find,
A waste of waters, wild and drear,
That chills each living heart with fear.
There see the horse's awful head,
Wrath-born, that flames in Ocean's bed.[1]
There rises up a fearful cry
From the sea things that move thereby,
When, helpless, powerless for flight,
They gaze upon the horrid sight.
Past to the northern shore, and then
Beyond the flood three leagues and ten
Your wondering glances will behold
Mount Játarúpa[2] bright with gold.
There like the young moon pale of hue
The monstrous serpent[3] will ye view,
The earth's supporter, whose bright eyes
Resemble lotus leaves in size.
He rests upon the mountain's brow,
And all the Gods before him bow.
Ananta with a thousand heads
His length in robes of azure spreads.
A triple-headed palm of gold—
Meet standard for the lofty-souled—
Springs towering from the mountain's crest
Beneath whose shade he loves to rest,
So that in eastern realms each God
May use it as a measuring-rod.
Beyond, with burning gold aglow,
The eastern steep his peaks will show,
Which in unrivalled glory rise
A hundred leagues to pierce the skies,
And all the neighbouring air is bright
With golden trees that clothe the height.
A lofty peak uprises there
Ten leagues in height and one league square
Saumanas, wrought of glistering gold,
Ne'er to be loosened from its hold.
There his first step Lord Vishṇu placed
When through the universe he paced,
And with his second lightly pressed
The loftiest peak of Meru's crest.
When north of Jambudwíp[4] the sun

[1] Aurva was one of the descendants of Bhrigu. From his wrath proceeded a flame that threatened to destroy the world, had not Aurva cast it into the ocean where it remained concealed, and having the face of a horse. The legend is told in the *Mahábhárat*, I. 6802.

[2] The word Játarúpa means gold.

[3] The celebrated mythological serpent king Sesha, called also Ananta or the infinite, represented as bearing the earth on one of his thousand heads.

[4] Jambudwípa is in the centre of the seven great *dwípas* or continents into which the world is divided, and in the centre of Jambudwípa is the golden

A portion of his course has run,
And hangs above this mountain height,
Then creatures see the genial light.
Vaikhánases,[1] saints far renowned,
And Bálakhilyas[2] love the ground
Where in their glory half divine,
Touched by the morning glow, they shine
The light that flashes from that steep
Illumines all Sudarśandwíp,[3]
And on each creature, as it glows,
The sight and strength of life bestows.
Search well that mountain's woody side
If Rávaṇ there his captive hide.
The rising sun, the golden hill
The air with growing splendours fill,
Till flashes from the east the red
Of morning with the light they shed.
This, where the sun begins his state,
Is earth and heaven's most eastern gate.
Through all the mountain forest seek
By waterfall and cave and peak.
Search every nook and bosky dell,
If Rávaṇ there with Sítá dwell.
There, Vánars, there your steps must stay:
No farther eastward can ye stray.
Beyond no sun, no moon gives light,
But all is sunk in endless night.
Thus far, O Vánar lords, may you
O'er sea and land your search pursue.
But wild and dark and known to none
Is the drear space beyond the sun.
That mountain whence the sun ascends
Your long and weary journey ends.[4]
Now go, and in a month return,
And let success my praises earn.
He who beyond the month shall stay
Will with his life the forfeit pay.'

mountain Meru 84,000 yojans high, and crowned by the great city of Brahmá. See WILSON'S *Vishṇu Puráṇa,* Vol. II. p. 110.

[1] Vaikhánases are a race of hermit saints said to have sprung from the nails of Prajápati.

[2] "The wife of Kratu, Samnati, brought forth the sixty thousand Válakhilyas, pigmy sages, no bigger than a joint of the thumb, chaste, pious, resplendent as the rays of the Sun." WILSON'S *Vishṇu Puráṇa.*

[3] The continent in which Sudarśan or Meru stands, *i. e.* Jambudwíp.

[4] The names of some historical peoples which occur in this Canto and in the Cantos describing the south and north will be found in the ADDITIONAL NOTES. They are bare lists, not susceptible of a metrical version.

CANTO XLI.

THE ARMY OF THE SOUTH.

He gathered next a chosen band
For service in the southern land.
He summoned Níla son of Fire,
And, offspring of the eternal Sire,
Jámbaván bold and strong and tall,
And Hanumán, the best of all,
And many a valiant lord beside,[1]
With Angad for their chief and guide.
'Go forth,' he cried, 'with all this host
Exploring to the southern coast:
The thousand peaks that Vindhya shows
Where every tree and creeper grows:
Where Narmadá's[2] sweet waters run,
And serpents bask them in the sun:
Where Krishṇaveṇí[3] currents flee,
And sparkles fair Godávarí.[4]
Through Mekhal[5] pass and Utkal's[6] land:
Go where Daśárna's[7] cities stand.
Avantí[8] seek, of high renown,
And Abravantí's[9] glorious town.
Search every hill and brook and cave
Where Dandak's woods their branches wave
Ayomukh's[10] woody hill explore
Whose sides are bright with richest ore,
Lifting his glorious head on high
From bloomy groves that round him lie.

[1] Suhotra, Śarári, Śaragulma, Gaja, Gaváksha, Gavaya, Sushena, Gandhamádana, Ulkámukha, and Ananga.

[2] The modern Nerbudda.

[3] Krishṇaveṇí is mentioned in the *Vishṇu Puraṇa* as "the deep Krishṇaveṇi" but there appears to be no clue to its identification.

[4] The modern Godavery,

[5] The Mekhalas or Mekalas according to the Puráṇas live in the Vindhya hills, but here they appear among the peoples of the south.

[6] Utkal is still the native name of Orissa.

[7] The land of the people of the 'ten forts.' Professor Hall in a note on WILSON'S *Vishṇu Puraṇa,* Vol. II. p. 160 says: "The oral traditions of the vicinity to this day assign the name of Daśárná to a region lying to the east of the District of Chundeyree."

[8] Avantí is one of the ancient names of the celebrated Ujjayin or Oujein in Central India.

[9] Not identified.

[10] Ayomukh means iron faced. The mountain is not identified,

Search well his forests where the breeze
Blows fragrant from the sandal trees.
Then will you see Káverí's[1] stream
Whose pleasant waters glance and gleam,
And to the lovely banks entice
The sportive maids of Paradise.
High on the top of Malaya's[2] hill,
In holy musing, calm and still,
Sits, radiant as the Lord of Light,
Agastya,[3] noblest anchorite.
Soon as that lofty-thoughted lord
His high permission shall accord,
Pass Támraparṇí's[4] flood whose isles
Are loved by basking crocodiles.
The sandal woods that fringe her side
Those islets and her waters hide;
While, like an amorous matron, she
Speeds to her own dear lord the sea.
Thence hasting on your way behold
The Pándyas'[5] gates of pearl and gold.
Then, with your task maturely planned,
On ocean's shore your feet will stand.
Where, by Agastya's high decree,
Mahendra,[6] planted in the sea,
With tinted peaks against the tide
Rises in solitary pride,
And glorious in his golden glow
Spurns back the waves that beat below.
Fair mountain, bright with creepers' bloom
And every tint that trees assume,
Where Yaksha, God, and heavenly maid
Meet wandering in the lovely shade,
At changing moon and solemn tide
By Indra's presence glorified.
One hundred leagues in fair extent
An island[7] fronts the continent:
No man may tread its glitering shore:
With utmost heed that isle explore,
For the fair country owns the sway
Of Rávaṇ whom we burn to slay.
A mighty monster stands to keep
The passage of the southern deep.
Lifting her awful arms on high
She grasps e'en shadows as they fly.
Speed through that isle, and onward still
Where in mid sea the Flowery Hill[1]
Raises on high his bloomy head
By saints and angels visited.
There, with a hundred gleaming peaks
Bright as the sun, the sky he seeks,
One glorious peak the Lord of Day
Gilds ever with his loving ray:
Thereon ne'er yet the glances fell
Of thankless wretch or infidel.
Bow to that hill in reverence due,
And then once more your search pursue.
Beyond that glorious mountain hie,
And Súryaván,[2] proud hill is nigh.
Your rapid course yet farther bend
Where Vaidyut's[3] airy peaks ascend.
There trees of noblest sort, profuse
Of wealth, their kindly gifts produce.
Their precious fruits, O Vánars, taste,
The honey sip, and onward haste.
Next will ye see Mount Kunjar rise,
Who cheers with beauty hearts and eyes.
There is Agastya's[4] mansion, decked
By heaven's all moulding architect.
Near Bhogavatí[5] stands, the place
Where dwell the hosts of serpent race:
A broad-wayed city, walled and barred,
Which watchful legions keep and guard,
The fiercest of the serpent youth,
Each awful for his venomed tooth:
And throned in his imperial hall
Is Vásuki[6] who rules them all.
Explore the serpent city well,
Search town and tower and citadel,
And scan each field and wood that lies
Around it, with your watchful eyes.
Beyond that spot your way pursue:
A noble mountain shall ye view,
Named Rishabh, like a mighty bull,
With gems made bright and beautiful.

---

[1] The Káverí or modern Cauvery is well known and has always borne the same appellation, being the Chaberis of Ptolemy.

[2] One of the seven principal mountain chains: the southern portion of the Western Gháts.

[3] Agastya is the great sage who has already frequently appeared as Ráma's friend and benefactor.

[4] Támraparṇi is a river rising in Malaya.

[5] The Pándyas are a people of the Deccan.

[6] Mahendra is the chain of hills that extends from Orissa and the northern Sircars to Gondwána, part of which near Ganjam is still called Mahendra Malay or hills of Mahendra.

[7] Lanká, Sinhaladvípa, Sarandib, or Ceylon.

[1] The Flowery Hill of course is mythical.

[2] The whole of the geography south of Lanká is of course mythical. Súryaván means Sunny.

[3] Vaidyut means connected with lightning.

[4] Agastya is here placed far to the south of Lanká. Earlier in this Canto he was said to dwell on Malaya.

[5] Bhogavatí has been frequently mentioned: it is the capital of the serpent Gods or demons, and usually represented as being in the regions under the earth.

[6] Vásuki is according to some accounts the king of the Nágas or serpent Gods.

All trees of sandal flourish there
Of heavenly fragrance, rich and rare.
But, though they tempt your longing eyes,
Avoid to touch them, and be wise.
For Rohitas, a guardian band
Of fierce Gandharvas, round them stand,
Who five bright sovereign lords[1] obey,
In glory like the God of Day.
Here by good deeds a home is won,
With shapes like fire, the moon, the sun.
Here they who merit heaven by worth
Dwell on the confines of the earth.
There stay: beyond it, dark and drear,
Lies the departed spirits' sphere,
And, girt with darkness, far from bliss,
Is Yama's sad metropolis.[2]
So far, my lords, o'er land and sea
Your destined course is plain and free.
Beyond your steps you may not set,
Where living thing ne'er journeyed yet.
With utmost care these realms survey,
And all you meet upon the way.
And, when the lady's course is traced,
Back to your king, O Vánars, haste.
And he who tells me he has seen,
After long search, the Maithil queen,
Shall gain a noble guerdon: he
In power and bliss shall equal me.
Dear as my very life, above
His fellows in his master's love;
I call him, yea though stained with crime,
My kinsman from that happy time.'

[1] Śailúsha, Gramíní, Siksha, Suka, Babhru.

[2] The distant south beyond the confines of the earth is the home of departed spirits and the city of Yama the God of Death.

CANTO XLII.

THE ARMY OF THE WEST.

Then to Sushen Sugríva bent,
And thus addressed him reverent:
'Two hundred thousand of our best
With thee, my lord, shall seek the west.
Explore Suráshṭra's[3] distant plain,
Explore Váhlíka's[4] wild domain,
And all the pleasant brooks that flee
Through mountains to the western sea.
Search clustering groves on mountain heights,
And woods the whom of anchorites.
Search where the breezy hills are high,
Search where the desert regions lie.
Search all the western land beset
With woody mountains like a net.
The country's farthest limit reach,
And stand upon the ocean beach.
There wander through the groves of palm
Where the soft air is full of balm.
Through grassy dell and dark ravine
Seek Rávaṇ and the Maithil queen.
Go visit Somagiri's[1] steep
Where Sindhu[2] mingles with the deep.
There lions, borne on swift wings, roam
The levels of their mountain home,
And elephants and monsters bear,
Caught from the ocean, to their lair.
You Vánars, changing forms at will,
With rapid search must scour the hill,
And his sky-kissing peak of gold
Where loveliest trees their blooms unfold.
There golden-peaked, ablaze with light,
Uprises Páriyátra's[3] height
Where wild Gandharvas, fierce and fell,
In bands of countless myriads dwell.
Pluck ye no fruit within the wood;
Beware the impious neighbourhood,
Where, very mighty, strong, and hard
To overcome, the fruit they guard.
Yet search for Janak's daughter still,
For Vánars there need fear no ill.
Near, bright as turkis, Vajra[4] named,
There stands a hill of diamond framed.
Soaring a hundred leagues in pride,
With trees and creepers glorified.
Search there each cave and dark abyss
By waterfall and precipice.
Far in that sea the wild waves beat
On Chakraván's[5] firm-rooted feet.
Where the great discus,[6] thousand rayed,
By Viśvakarmá's[7] art was made.
When Panchajan[8] the fiend was slain,
And Hayagríva,[9] fierce in vain,

[3] Suráshṭra, the 'good country,' is the modern Surat.

[4] A country north-west of Afghanistan, Balkh.

[1] The Moon-mountain here is mythical.

[2] Sindhu is the Indus.

[3] Páriyátra, or as more usually written Páripátra, is the central or western portion of the Vindhya chain which skirts the province of Malwa.

[4] Vajra means both diamond and thunderbolt, the two substances being supposed to be identical.

[5] Chakraván means the discus-bearer.

[6] The discus is the favourite weapon of Vishṇu.

[7] The Indian Hephaistos or Vulcan.

[8] Panchajan was a demon who lived in the sea in the form of a conch shell. WILSON'S *Vishṇu Puráṇa*, V. 21.

[9] Hayagríva, Horse-necked, is the name of a Daitya who at the dissolution of the universe caused by Brahmá's sleep, seized and carried off the Vedas. Vishṇu slew him and recovered the sacred treasures,

Thence taking shell and discus went
Lord Vishṇu, God preëminent.
On! sixty thousand hills of gold
With wondering eyes shall ye behold,
Where in his glory every one
Is brilliant as the morning sun.
Full in the midst King Meru.[1] best
Of mountains, lifts his lofty crest,
On whom of yore, as all have heard,
The sun well-pleased this boon conferred:
'On thee, O King, on thee and thine
Light, day and night, shall ever shine.
Gandharvas, Gods who love thee well
And on thy sacred summits dwell,
Undimmed in lustre, bright and fair,
The golden sheen shall ever share.'
The Viśvas,[2] Vasus,[3] they who ride
The tempest,[4] every God beside,
Draw nigh to Meru's lofty crest
When evening darkens in the west,
And to the parting Lord of Day
The homage of their worship pay,
Ere yet a while, unseen of all,
Behind Mount Asta's[5] peaks he fall.
Wrought by the heavenly artist's care
A glorious palace glitters there,
And round about it sweet birds sing
Where the gay trees are blossoming:
The home of Varuṇ[1] high souled-lord,
Wrist-girded with his deadly cord.[2]
With ten tall stems, a palm between
Meru and Asta's hill is seen:
Pure silver from the base it springs,
And far and wide its lustre flings.
Seek Rávaṇ and the dame by brook,
In pathless glen, in leafy nook.
On Meru's crest a hermit lives
Bright with the light that penance gives:
Sávarṇi[3] is he named, renowned
As Brahmá's peer, with glory crowned.
There bowing down in reverence speak
And ask him of the dame you seek.
Thus far the splendid Lord of Day
Pursues through heaven his ceaseless way,
Shedding on every spot his light;
Then sinks behind Mount Asta's height.
Thus far advance: the sunless sea
Beyond is all unknown to me.
Sushen of mighty arm, long tried
In peril, shall your legions guide.
Receive his words with high respect,
And ne'er his lightest wish neglect.
He is my consort's sire, and hence
Deserves the utmost reverence.'

CANTO XLIII.

THE ARMY OF THE NORTH.

Forth went the legions of the west:
And wise Sugríva then addressed
Śatabal, summoned from the crowd,
To whom the sovereign cried aloud:
'Go forth, O Vánar chief, go forth,
Explore the regions of the north.
Thy host a hundred thousand be,
And Yama's sons[4] attend on thee.
With dauntless courage, strength, and skill
Search every river, wood, and hill.
Through every land in order go
Right onward to the Hills of Snow.
Search mid the peaks that shine afar,
In woods of Lodh and Deodár.[5]
Search if with Janak's daughter, screened
By sheltering rocks, there lie the fiend.

[1] Meru stands in the centre of Jambudwípa and consequently of the earth. "The sun travels round the world, keeping Meru always on his right. To the spectator who fronts him, therefore, as he rises Meru must be always on the north; and as the sun's rays do not penetrate beyond the centre of the mountain, the regions beyond, or to the north of it must be in darkness, whilst those on the south of it must be in light: north and south being relative, not absolute, terms, depending on the position of the spectator with regard to the Sun and Meru." WILSON'S *Vishṇu Puráṇa*, Vol. II. p. 243. Note.

[2] The Viśvadevas are a class of deities to whom sacrifices should be daily offered, as part of the ordinary worship of the householder. According to the *Váyu Puráṇa*, this is a privilege conferred on them by Brahmá and the Pitris as a reward for religious austerities practised by them upon Himálaya.

[3] The eight Vasus were originally personifications like other Vedic deities, of natural phenomena, such as Fire, Wind, &c. Their appellations are variously given by different authorities.

[4] The Maruts or Storm-Gods, frequently addressed and worshipped as the attendants and allies of Indra.

[5] The mountain behind which the sun sets.

[1] One of the oldest and mightiest of the Vedic deities; in later mythology regarded as the God of the sea.

[2] The knotted noose with which he seizes and punishes transgressors.

[3] Sávarṇi is a Manu, offspring of the Sun by Chháyá.

[4] The poet has not said who the sons of Yama are.

[5] The Lodhra or Lodh (Symplocos Racemosa) and the Devadáru or Deodar are well known trees.

The holy grounds of Soma tread
By Gods and minstrels visited.
Reach Kála's mount, and flats that lie
Among the peaks that tower on high.
Then leave that hill that gleams with ore,
And fair Sudarśan's heights explore
Then on to Devasakhá[1] hie,
Loved by the children of the sky.
A dreary land you then will see
Without a hill or brook or tree,
A hundred leagues, bare, wild, and dread
In lifeless desolation, spread.
Pursue your onward way, and haste
Through the dire horrors of the waste
Until triumphant with delight
You reach Kailása's glittering height.
There stands a palace decked with gold,
For King Kuvera[2] wrought of old,
A home the heavenly artist planned
And fashioned with his cunning hand.
There lotuses adorn the flood
With full-blown flower and opening bud
Where swans and mallards float, and gay
Apsarases[3] come down to play.
There King Vaiśravan's[4] self, the lord
By all the universe adored,
Who golden gifts to mortals sends,
Lives with the Guhyakas[5] his friends.
Search every cavern in the steep,
And green glens where the moonbeams sleep,
If haply in that distant ground
The robber and the dame be found.
Then on to Krauncha's hill,[6] and through
His fearful pass your way pursue:
Though dark and terrible the vale
Your wonted courage must not fail.
There through abyss and cavern seek,
On lofty ridge, and mountain peak.
On, on! pursue your journey still
By valley, lake, and towering hill.
Reach the North Kurus' land, where rest
The holy spirits of the blest:
Where golden buds of lilies gleam
Resplendent on the silver stream,
And leaves of azure turkis throw
Soft splendour on the waves below.
Bright as the sun at early morn
Fair pools that happy clime adorn,
Where shine the loveliest flowers on stems
Of crystal and all valued gems.
Blue lotuses through all the land
The glories of their blooms expand,
And the resplendent earth is strown
With peerless pearl and precious stone.
There stately trees can scarce uphold
The burthen of their fruits of gold,
And ever flaunt their gay attire
Of flower and leaf like flames of fire.
All there sweet lives untroubled spend
In bliss and joy that know not end,
While pearl-decked maidens laugh, or sing
To music of the silvery string.[1]
Still on your forward journey keep,
And rest you by the northern deep,
Where springing from the billows high
Mount Somagiri[2] seeks the sky,
And lightens with perpetual glow
The sunless realm that lies below.
There, present through all life's extent,
Dwells Brahmá Lord preëminent,
And round the great God, manifest
In Rudra[3] forms high sages rest.
Then turn, O Vánars: search no more,
Nor tempt the sunless, boundless shore.'

CANTO XLIV.

THE RING.

But special counselling he gave
To Hanumán the wise and brave:

[1] The hills mentioned are not identifiable. Soma means the Moon, Kála, black; Sudaraśan, fair to see; and Devasakhá, friend of the Gods.

[2] The God of Wealth.

[3] The nymphs of Paradise.

[4] Kuvera the son of Viśravas.

[5] A class of demigods who, like the Yakshas, are the attendants of Kuvera, and the guardians of his treasures.

[6] Situated in the eastern part of the Himálaya chain, on the north of Assam. The mountain was torn asunder and the pass formed by the War-God Kártikeya and Paraśuráma.

[1] "The Uttara Kurus, it should be remarked, may have been a real people, as they are mentioned in the Aitareya Bráhmana, VIII. 14......"Wherefore the several nations who dwell in this northern quarter, beyond the Himavat, the Uttara Kurus and the Uttara Madras are consecrated to glorious dominion, and people term them the glorious. In another passage of the same work, however, the Uttara Kurus are treated as belonging to the domain of mythology." MUIR's *Sanskrit Texts*, Vol. I. p. 494. See ADDITIONAL NOTES.

[2] The Moon-mountain.

[3] The Rudras are the same as the storm winds, more usually called Maruts, and are often associated with Indra. In the later mythology the Rudras are regarded as inferior manifestations of Śiva, and most of their names are also names of Śiva.

To him on whom his soul relied,
With friendly words the monarch cried:
'O best of Vánars, naught can stay
By land or sea thy rapid way,
Who through the air thy flight canst bend,
And to the Immortals' home ascend.
All realms, I ween, are known to thee
With every mountain, lake and sea.
In strength and speed which naught can tire
Thou, worthy rival of thy sire
The mighty monarch of the wind,
Where'er thou wilt a way canst find.
Exert thy power, O swift and strong,
Bring back the lady lost so long.
For time and place, O thou most wise,
Lie open to thy searching eyes.'
When Ráma heard that special hest
To Hanumán above the rest,
He from the monarch's favour drew
Hope of success and trust anew
That he on whom his lord relied,
In toil and peril trained and tried,
Would to a happy issue bring
The task commanded by the king.
He gave the ring that bore his name,
A token for the captive dame,
That the sad lady in her woe
The missive of her lord might know.
'This ring,' he said, 'my wife will see,
Nor fear an envoy sent by me.
Thy valour and thy skill combined,
Thy resolute and vigorous mind,
And King Sugríva's high behest,
With joyful hopes inspire my breast.'

CANTO XLV.

THE DEPARTURE.

Away, away the Vánars sped
Like locusts o'er the land outspread.
To northern realms where rising high
The King of Mountains cleaves the sky,
Fierce Śatabal with vast array
Of Vánar warriors led the way.
Far southward, as his lord decreed,
Wise Hanumán, the Wind-God's seed,
With Angad his swift way pursued,
And Tára's warlike multitude,
Strong Vinata with all his band
Betook him to the eastern land,
And brave Sushen in eager quest
Sped swiftly to the gloomy west.
Each Vánar chieftain sought with speed
The quarter by his king decreed,
While from his legions rose on high
The shout and boast and battle cry:
'We will restore the dame and beat
The robber down beneath our feet,
My arm alone shall win the day
From Rávaṇ met in single fray,
Shall rob the robber of his life,
And rescue Ráma's captive wife
All trembling in her fear and woe.
Here, comrades, rest: no farther go:
For I will vanquish hell, and she
Shall by this arm again be free.
The rooted mountains will I rend,
The mightiest trees will break and bend,
Earth to her deep foundations cleave,
And make the calm sea throb and heave.
A hundred leagues from steep to steep
In desperate bound my feet shall leap.
My steps shall tread unchecked and free.
Through woods, o'er land and hill and sea,
Range as they list from flood to fell.
And wander through the depths of hell.'

CANTO XLVI.

SUGRÍVA'S TALE.

'How, King,' cried Ráma, 'didst thou gain
Thy lore of sea and hill and plain?'
'I told thee how,' Sugríva said,
'From Báli's arm Máyáví fled[1]
To Malaya's hill, and strove to save
His life by hiding in the cave.
I told how Báli sought, to kill
His foe, the hollow of the hill;
Nor need I, King, again unfold
The wondrous tale already told.
Then, wandering forth, my way I took
By many a town and wood and brook.
I roamed the earth from place to place,
Till, like a mirror's polished face,
The whole broad disk, that lies between
Its farthest bounds, mine eyes had seen.
I wandered first to eastern skies
Where fairest trees rejoiced mine eyes,
And many a cave and wooded hill
Where lilies robed the lake and rill.
There metal dyes that hill[2] adorn
Whence springs the sun to light the morn.
There, too, I viewed the Milky sea,
Where nyphs of heaven delight to be.
Then to the south I made my way
From regions of the rising day,
And roamed o'er Vindhya, where the breeze
Is odorous of sandal trees.
Still in my fear I found no rest:
I sought the regions of the west,
And gazed on Asta,[3] where the sun

---

[1] Canto IX.

[2] Udayagiri or the hill from which the sun rises.

[3] Asta is the mountain behind which the sun sets.

Sinks when his daily course is run.
Then from that noblest hill I fled
And to the nothern country sped,
Saw Himaván,[1] and Meru's steep,
And stood beside the northern deep.
But when, by Báli's might oppressed,
E'en in those wilds I could not rest,
Came Hanumán the wise and brave,
And thus his prudent counsel gave:
'I told thee how Matanga[2] cursed
Thy tyrant, that his head should burst
In pieces, should he dare invade
The precincts of that tranquil shade.
There may we dwell in peace and be
From thy oppressor's malice free.'
We went to Rishyamúka's hill,
And spent our days secure from ill
Where, with that curse upon his head,
The cruel Báli durst not tread.'

CANTO XLVII.

THE RETURN.

Thus forth in quest of Sítá went
The legions King Sugríva sent.
To many a distant town they hied
By many a lake and river's side.
As their great sovereign's order taught,
Through valleys, plains, and groves they sought.
They toiled unresting through the day:
At night upon the ground they lay
Where the tall trees, whose branches swayed
Beneath their fruit, gave pleasant shade.
Then, when a weary month was spent,
Back to Prasravaṇ's hill they went,
And stood with faces of despair
Before their king Sugríva there.
Thus, having wandered through the east,
Great Vinata his labours ceased,
And weary of the fruitless pain
Returned to meet the king again.
Brave Satabali to the north
Had led his Vánar legions forth.
Now to Sugríva back he sped
With all his host dispirited.
Sushen the western realms had sought,
And homeward now his legions brought.
All to Sugríva came, where still
He sat with Ráma on the hill,
Before their sovereign humbly bent
And thus addressed him reverent:
'On every hill our steps have been,
By wood and cave and deep ravine;
And all the wandering brooks we know
Throughout the land that seaward flow.
Our feet by thy command have traced
The tangled thicket and the waste,
And dens and dingles hard to pass
For creeping plants and matted grass.
Well have we searched with toil and pain,
And monstrous creatures have we slain.
But Hanumán of noblest mind
The Maithil lady yet will find;
For to his quarter of the sky[1]
The robber fiend was seen to fly.'

CANTO XLVIII.

THE ASUR'S DEATH.

But Hanumán still onward pressed
With Tára, Angad, and the rest,
Through Vindhya's pathless glens he sped
And left no spot unvisited.
He gazed from every mountain height,
He sought each cavern dark as night,
And wandered through the bloomy shade
By pool and river and cascade,
But, though they sought in every place,
Of Sítá yet they found no trace.
On fruit and woodland berries fed
Through many a lonely wild they sped,
And reached at last, untouched by fear,
A desert terrible and drear:
A fruitless waste, a land of gloom
Where trees were bare of leaf and bloom;
Where every scanty stream was dried,
And niggard earth her roots denied.
No elephants through all the ground,
No buffaloes or deer are found.
There roams no tiger, pard, or bear,
No creature of the wood is there.
No bird displays his glittering wings,
No tree, no shrub, no creeper springs.
There rise no lilies from the flood,
Resplendent with their flower and bud,
Where the delighted bees may throng
About the fragrance with their song.
There lived a hermit Kaṇḍu named,
For truth and wealth of penance famed,
Whom fervent zeal and holy rite
Had dowered with all-surpassing might.
His little son, a ten year child—
So chanced it—perished in the wild.
His death with fury stirred the sage,
Who cursed the forest in his rage,
Doomed from that hour to shelter none,
A waste for bird and beast to shun.

---

[1] Himálaya, the Hills of Snow.

[2] Canto XI.

[1] Hanumán was the leader of the army of the south which was under the nominal command of Angad the heir apparent

They searched by every forest edge,
They searched each cave and mountain ledge,
And thickets whence the water fell
Wandering through the tangled dell.
Striving to do Sugríva's will
They roamed along each leafy rill.
But vain were all endeavours, vain
The careful search, the toil and pain.
Through one dark grove they scarce could wind,
So thick were creepers intertwined.
There as they struggled through the wood
Before their eyes an Asur[1] stood.
High as a towering hill, his pride
The very Gods in heaven defied.
When on the fiend their glances fell
Each braced him for the combat well.
The demon raised his arm on high,
And rushed upon them with a cry.
Him Angad smote,—for, sure, he thought
This was the fiend they long had sought.
From his huge mouth by Angad felled,
The blood in rushing torrents welled,
As, like a mountain from his base
Uptorn, he dropped upon his face.
Thus fell the mighty fiend : and they
Through the thick wood pursued their way;
Then, weary with the toil, reclined
Where leafy boughs to shade them twined.

CANTO XLIX.

ANGAD'S SPEECH.

Then Angad spake : 'We Vánars well
Have searched each valley, cave, and dell,
And hill, and brook, and dark recess,
And tangled wood, and wilderness.
But all in vain : no eye has seen
The robber or the Maithil queen.
A dreary time has passed away,
And stern is he we all obey.
Come, cast your grief and sloth aside:
Again be every effort tried ;
So haply may our toil attain
The sweet success that follows pain.
Laborious effort, toil, and skill,
The firm resolve, the constant will
Secure at last the ends we seek :
Hence, O my friends, I boldly speak.
Once more then, noble hearts, once more
Let us to-day this wood explore,
And, languor and despair subdued,
Purchase success with toil renewed.
Sugríva is a king austere,
And Ráma's wrath we needs must fear.
Come, Vánars, if ye think it wise,
And do the thing that I advise.'
Then Gandhamádan thus replied
With lips that toil and thirst had dried :
'Obey his words, for wise and true
Is all that he has counselled you.
Come, let your hosts their toil renew
And search each grove and desert through,
Each towering hill and forest glade.
By lake and brook and white cascade,
Till every spot, as our great lord
Commanded, be again explored.'
Uprose the Vánars one and all,
Obedient to the chieftain's call,
And over the southern region sped
Where Vindhya's tangled forests spread.
They clomb that hill that towers on high
Like a huge cloud in autumn's sky,
Where many a cavern yawns, and streaks
Of radiant silver deck the peaks.
In eager search they wandered through
The forests where the Lodh trees grew.
Where the dark leaves were thick and green,
But found not Ráma's darling queen.
Then faint with toil, their hearts depressed,
Descending from the mountain's crest,
Their weary limbs a while to ease
They lay beneath the spreading trees.

CANTO L.

THE ENCHANTED CAVE.

Angad and Tára by his side,
Again rose Hanumán and tried
Each mountain cavern, dark and deep,
And stony pass and wooded steep.
The lion's and the tiger's home,
By rushing torrents white with foam.
Then with new ardour, south and west,
O'er Vindhya's height the search they pressed.
The day prescribed was near, and they
Still wandered on their weary way.
They reached the southern land beset
With woody mountains like a net.
At length a mighty cave they spied
That opened in a mountain's side.
Where many a verdant creeper grew
And o'er the mouth its tendrils threw.
Thence issued crane, and swan, and drake,
And trooping birds that love the lake.
The Vánars rushed within to cool
Their fevered lips in spring or pool.
Vast was the cavern dark and dread,
Where not a ray of light was shed :
Yet not the more their eyesight failed,

[1] The Bengal recension—Gorresio's edition—calls this Asur or demon the son of Máricha.

Their courage sank or valour quailed.
On through the gloom the Vánars pressed
With hunger, thirst, and toil distressed,
Poor helpless wanderers, sad, forlorn,
With wasted faces wan and worn.
At length, when life seemed lost for aye,
They saw a splendour as of day,
A wondrous forest, fair and bright,
Where golden trees shot flamy light.
And lotus-covered pools were there
With pleasant waters fresh and fair,
And streams their rippling currents rolled
By seats of silver and of gold.
Fair houses reared their stately height
Of burnished gold and lazulite,
And glorious was the lustre thrown
Through lattices of precious stone.
And there were flowers and fruit on stems
Of coral decked with rarest gems,
And emerald leaves on silver trees,
And honeycomb and golden bees.
Then as the Vánars nearer drew,
A holy woman met their view.
Around her form was duly tied
A garment of the blackdeer's hide.[1]
Pure votaress she shone with light
Of fervent zeal and holy rite.
Then Hanumán before the rest
With reverent words the dame addressed:
'Who art thou? say: and who is lord
Of this vast cave with treasures stored?'

CANTO LI.

SVAYAMPRABHÁ.

'Assailed by thirst and hunger, dame,
Within a gloomy vault we came.
We saw the cavern opening wide,
And straight within its depths we hied.
But utterly amazed are we
At all the marvels that we see.
Whose are the golden trees that gleam
With splendour like the morning's beam?
These cates of noblest sort? these roots?
This wondrous store of rarest fruits?
Whose are these calm and cool retreats,
These silver homes and golden seats,
And lattices of precious stones?
Who is the happy lord that owns
The golden trees, of rarest scent,
Neath loads of fruit and blossom bent?
Who, strong in holy zeal, had power
To deck the streams with richest dower,
And bade the lilies bright with gold
The glory of their blooms unfold,
Where fish in living gold below
The sheen of changing colours show?
Thine is the holy power, I ween,
That beautified the wondrous scene;
But if another's, lady, deign
To tell us, and the whole explain.'

To him the lady of the cave
In words like these her answer gave:
'Skilled Maya framed in days of old
This magic wood of growing gold.
The chief artificer in place
Was he of all the Dánav race.
He, for his wise enchantments famed,
This glorious dwelling planned and framed.
He for a thousand years endured
The sternest penance, and secured
From Brahmá of all boons the best,
The knowledge Uśanas[1] possessed.
Lord, by that boon, of all his will,
He fashioned all with perfect skill;
And, with his blissful state content,
In this vast grove a season spent.
By Indra's jealous bolt he fell
For loving Hemá's[2] charms too well.
And Brahmá on that nymph bestowed
The treasures of this fair abode,
Wherein her tranquil days to spend
In happiness that ne'er may end.
Sprung of a lineage old and high,
Merusávarṇi's[3] daughter, I
Guard ever for that heavenly dame
This home, Svayamprabhá[4] my name,—
For I have loved the lady long,
So skilled in arts of dance and song.
But say what cause your steps has led
The mazes of this grove to tread.

[1] The skin of the black antelope was the ascetic's proper garb.

[1] Uśanas is the name of a sage mentioned in the Vedas. In the epic poems he is identified with Śukra, the regent of the planet Venus, and described as the preceptor of the Asuras or Daityas, and possessor of vast knowledge.

[2] Hemá is one of the nymphs of Paradise.

[3] Merusávarṇi is a general name for the last four of the fourteen Manus.

[4] Svayamprabhá, the "self-luminous" is according to DE GUBERNATIS the moon: "In the *Svayamprabhâ* too, we meet with the moon as a good fairy who, from the golden palace which she reserves for her friend Hemâ (the golden one:) is during a month the guide, in the vast cavern of Hanumant and his companions, who have lost their way in the search of the dawn Sitá." This is not quite accurate: Hanumán and his companions wander for a month in the cavern without a guide and then Svayamprabhá leads them out.

How, strangers, did ye chance to spy
The wood concealed from wanderer's eye?
Tell clearly why ye come; but first
Eat of this fruit and quench your thirst.'

CANTO LII.

THE EXIT.

'Ráma,' he cried, 'a prince whose sway
All peoples of the earth obey,
To Daṇḍak's tangled forest came
With his brave brother and his dame.
From that dark shade of forest boughs
The giant Rávaṇ stole his spouse.
Our king Sugríva's orders send
These Vánars forth to aid his friend,
That so the lady be restored
Uninjured to her sorrowing lord.
With Angad and the rest this band
Has wandered through the southern land,
With careful search in every place
The lady and the fiend to trace.
We roamed the southern region o'er,
And stood upon the ocean's shore.
By hunger pressed our strength gave way;
Beneath the spreading trees we lay,
And cried, worn out with toil and woe,
'No farther, comrades, can we go.'
Then as our sad eyes looked around
We spied an opening in the ground,
Where all was gloomy dark behind
The creeping plants that o'er it twined.
Forth trooping from the dark recess
Came swans and mallards numberless,
With drops upon their shining wings
As newly bathed where water springs.
'On, comrades, to the cave,' I cried
And all within the portal hied.
Each clasping fast another's hand
Far onward pressed the Vánar band;
And still, as thirst and hunger drove,
We traced the mazes of the grove.
Here thou with hospitable care
Hast fed us with the noblest fare,
Preserving us, about to die,
With this thy plentiful supply.
But how, O pious lady, say,
May we thy gracious boon repay?'
He ceased: the ascetic dame replied:
'Well, Vánars, am I satisfied.
A life of holy works I lead,
And from your hands no service need.'
Then spake again the Vánar chief:
'We came to thee and found relief.
Now listen to a new distress,
And aid us, holy votaress.
Our wanderings in this vasty cave
Exhaust the time Sugríva gave.
Once more then, lady, grant release,
And let thy suppliants go in peace
Again upon their errand sped.
For King Sugríva's ire we dread.
And the great task our sovereign set,
Alas, is unaccomplished yet.'
Thus Hanumán their leader prayed,
And thus the dame her answer made:
Scarce may the living find their way
Returning hence to light of day;
But I will free you through the might
Of penance, fast, and holy rite.
Close for a while your eyes, or ne'er
May you return to upper air.'
She ceased: the Vánars all obeyed;
Their fingers on their eyes they laid,
And, ere a moment's time had fled,
Were through the mazy cavern led.
Again the gracious lady spoke,
And joy in every bosom woke:
'Lo, here again is Vindhya's hill,
Whose valleys trees and creepers fill;
And, by the margin of the sea,
Prasravaṇ where you fain would be.'
With blessings then she bade adieu,
And swift within the cave withdrew.

CANTO LIII.

ANGAD'S COUNSEL.

They looked upon the boundless main
The awful seat of Varuṇ's reign,
And heard his waters roar and rave
Terrific with each crested wave.
Then, in the depths of sorrow drowned,
They sat upon the bosky ground,
And sadly, as they pondered, grieved
For days gone by and naught achieved.
Pain pierced them through with sharper sting
When, gazing on the trees of spring,
They saw each waving bough that showed
The treasures of its glorious load,
And helpless, fainting with the weight
Of woe they sank disconsolate.
Then, lion-shouldered, stout and strong,
The noblest of the Vánar throng,
Angad the prince imperial rose,
And, deeply stricken by the woes
That his impetuous spirit broke,
Thus gently to the chieftains spoke:
'Mark ye not, Vánars, that the day
Our monarch fixed has passed away?
The month is lost in toil and pain,
And now, my friends, what hopes remain?
On you, in lore of counsel tried,
Our king Sugríva most relied.
Your hearts, with strong affection fraught,

His weal in every labour sought,
And the true valour of your band
Was blazoned wide in every land.
Forth on the toilsome search you sped,
By me—for so he willed it—led.
To us, of every hope bereft,
Death is the only refuge left.
For none a happy life may see
Who fails to do our king's decree.
Come, let us all from food abstain,
And perish thus, since hope is vain.
Stern is our king and swift to ire,
Imperious, proud, and fierce like fire,
And ne' er will pardon us the crime
Of fruitless search and wasted time.
Far better thus to end our lives,
And leave our wealth, our homes and wives,
Leave our dear little ones and all,
Than by his vengeful hand to fall.
Think not Sugríva's wrath will spare
Me Báli's son, imperial heir:
For Raghu's royal son, not he,
To this high place anointed me.
Sugríva, long my bitter foe,
With eager hand will strike the blow,
And, mindful of the old offence,
Will slay me now for negligence,
Nor will my pitying friends have power
To save me in the deadly hour.
No—here, O chieftains, will I lie
By ocean's marge, and fast and die.'
They heard the royal prince declare
The purpose of his fixt despair;
And all, by common terror moved,
His speech in these sad words approved:
'Sugriva's heart is hard and stern,
And Ráma's thoughts for Sítá yearn.
Our forfeit lives will surely pay
For idle search and long delay,
And our fierce king will bid us die
The favour of his friend to buy.'
Then Tára softly spake to cheer
The Vánars' hearts oppressed by fear:
'Despair no more, your doubts dispel:
Come in this ample cavern dwell.
There may we live in blissful ease
Mid springs and fruit and bloomy trees,
Secure from every foe's assault,
For magic framed the wondrous vault.
Protected there we need not fear
Though Ráma and our king come near;
Nor dread e'en him who batters down
The portals of the foeman's town.'[1]

[1] Purandara, the destroyer of cities; the cities being the clouds which the God of the firmament bursts open with his thunderbolts, to release the waters imprisoned in these fortesses of the demons of drought.

CANTO LIV.

HANUMÁN'S SPEECH.

But Hanumán, while Tára, best
Of splendid chiefs his thought expressed,
Perceived that Báli's princely son
A kingdom for himself had won.[1]
His keen eye marked in him combined
The warrior's arm, the ruler's mind,
And every noble gift should grace
The happy sovereign of his race:
Marked how he grew with ripening age
More glorious and bold and sage,—
Like the young moon that night by night
Shines on with ever waxing light,—
Brave as his royal father, wise
As he who counsels in the skies:[2]
Marked how, forwearied with the quest,
He heeded not his liege's hest,
But Tára's every word obeyed
Like Indra still by Sukra[3] swayed.
Then with his prudent speech he tried
To better thoughts the prince to guide,
And by division's skilful art
The Vánars and the youth to part:
'Illustrious Angad, thou in fight
Hast far surpassed thy father's might,
Most worthy, like thy sire of old,
The empire of our race to hold.
The Vánars' fickle people range
From wish to wish and welcome change.
Their wives and babes they will not leave
And to their new-made sovereign cleave.
No art, no gifts will draw away
The Vánars from Sugriva's sway,
Through hope of wealth, through fear of pain
Still faithful will they all remain.
Thou fondly hopest in this cave
The vengeance of the foe to brave.
But Lakshman's arm a shower will send
Of deadly shafts those walls to rend.
Like Indra's bolts his shafts have power
To cleave the mountain like a flower.
O Angad, mark my counsel well:
If in this cave thou choose to dwell,

[1] Perceived that Angad had secured through the love of the Vánars, the reversion of Sugríva's kingdom; or, as another commentator explains it, perceived that Angad had obtained a new kingdom in the enchanted cave which the Vánars, through love of him, would consent to occupy.

[2] Váchaspati, Lord of Speech, the Preceptor of the Gods.

[3] Sukra is the regent of the planet Venus, and the preceptor of the Daityas.

These Vánar hosts with one accord
Will quit thee for their lawful lord,
And turn again with thirsty eyes
To wife and babe and all they prize.
Thou in the lonely cavern left
Of followers and friends bereft,
Wilt be in all thy woe, alas,
Weak as a blade of trembling grass:
And Lakshmaṇ's arrows, keen and fierce
From his strong bow, thy heart will pierce.
But if in lowly reverence meek
Sugríva's court with us thou seek,
He, as thy birth demands, will share
The kingdom with the royal heir.
Thy loving kinsman, true and wise,
Looks on thee still with favouring eyes.
Firm in his promise, pure is he,
And ne'er will vex or injure thee.
He loves thy mother, lives for her
A faithful friend and worshipper.
That mother's love thou mayst not spurn:
Her only child, return, return.'

CANTO LV.

ANGAD'S REPLY.

'What truth or justice canst thou find,'
Cried Angad, 'in Sugríva's mind?
Where is his high and generous soul,
His purity and self-control?
How is he worthy of our trust,
Righteous, and true, and wise, and just,
Who, shrinking not from sin and shame,
Durst take his living brother's dame?
Who, when, in stress of mortal strife
His noble brother fought for life,
Against the valiant warrior barred
The portal which he stood to guard?
Can he be grateful—he who took
The hand of Ráma, and forsook
That friend who saved him in his woes,
To whom his life and fame he owes?
Ah no! his heart is cold and mean,
What bids him search for Ráma's queen?
Not honour's law, not friendship's debt,
But angry Lakshman's timely threat.
No prudent heart will ever place
Its trust in one so false and base,
Who heeds not friendship, kith or kin,
Who scorns the law and cleaves to sin.
But true or false, whate'er he be,
One consequence I clearly see:
Me, in my youth anointed heir
Against his wish, he will not spare.
But strike with eager hand the blow
That rids him of a household foe.
Shall I of power and friends despoiled,
In all my purpose crossed and foiled,—
Shall I Kishkindhá seek, and wait,
Like some poor helpless thing, my fate?
The cruel wretch through lust of sway
Will seize upon his hapless prey,
And to a prison's secret gloom
The remnant of my years will doom.
'Tis better far to fast and die
Than hopeless bound in chains to lie,
Your steps, O Vánars, homeward bend,
And leave me here my life to end.
Better to die of hunger here
Than meet at home the fate I fear.
Go, bow you at Sugríva's feet,
And in my name the monarch greet.
Before the sons of Raghu bend,
And give the greeting that I send.
Greet kindly Rumá too, for she
A son's affection claims from me,
And gently calm with friendly care
My mother Tárá's wild despair;
Or when she hears her darling's fate
The queen will die disconsolate.'
Thus Angad bade the chiefs adieu:
Then on the ground his limbs he threw
Where sacred Darbha[1] grass was spread,
And wept as every hope had fled.
The moving words of Angad drew
Down aged cheeks the piteous dew.
And, as the chieftains' eyes grew dim,
They swore to stay and die with him.
On holy grass whose every blade
Was duly, pointing southward, laid,
The Vánars sat them down and bent
Their faces to the orient,
While 'Here, O comrades, let us die
With Angad,' was the general cry.

CANTO LVI.

SAMPÁTI.

Then came the vultures' mighty king
Where sat the Vánars sorrowing,—
Sampáti,[2] best of birds that fly
On sounding pinions through the sky,
Jaṭáyus' brother, famed of old,
Most glorious and strong and bold.
Upon the slope of Vindhya's hill
He saw the Vánars calm and still.

---

[1] The name of various kinds of grass used at sacrificial ceremonies, especially, of the Kuśa grass, Poa cynosuroides, which was used to strew the ground in preparing for a sacrifice, the officiating Brahmans being purified by sitting on it.

[2] Sampáti is the eldest son of the celebrated Garuḍa the king of birds.

These words he uttered while the sight
Filled his fierce spirit with delight:
'Behold how Fate with changeless laws
Within his toils the sinner draws,
And brings me, after long delay,
A rich and noble feast to-day,
These Vánars who are doomed to die
My hungry maw to satisfy.'
He spoke no more: and Angad heard
The menace of the mighty bird;
And thus, while anguish filled his breast,
The noble Hanumán addressed:
'Vivasvat's[1] son has sought this place
For vengeance on the Vánar race.
See, Yama, wroth for Sítá's sake,
Is come our gulity lives to take.
Our king's decree is left undone,
And naught achieved for Raghu's son.
In duty have we failed, and hence
Comes punishment for dire offence.
Have we not heard the marvels wrought
By King Jaṭáyus,[2] how he fought
With Rávaṇ's might, and, nobly brave,
Perished, the Maithil queen to save?
There is no living creature, none,
But loves to die for Raghu's son,
And in long toils and dangers we
Have placed our lives in jeopardy.
Blest is Jaṭáyus, he who gave
His life the Maithil queen to save,
And proved his love for Ráma well
When by the giant's hand he fell.
Now raised to bliss and high renown
He fears not fierce Sugríva's frown.
Alas, alas! what miseries spring
From that rash promise of the king![3]
His own sad death, and Ráma sent
With Lakshmaṇ forth to banishment:
The Maithil lady borne away:
Jaṭáyus slain in mortal fray:
The fall of Báli when the dart
Of Ráma quivered in his heart:
And, after toil and pain and care,
Our misery and deep despair.'
He ceased: the feathered monarch heard,
His heart with ruth and wonder stirred:
'Whose is that voice,' the vulture cried,
'That tells me how Jaṭáyus died,
And shakes my inmost soul with woe
For a loved brother's overthrow?
After long days at length I hear
The glorious name of one so dear.
Once more, O Vánar chieftains, tell
How King Jaṭáyus fought and fell.
But first your aid, I pray you, lend,
And from this peak will I descend.
The sun has burnt my wings, and I
No longer have the power to fly.'

[1] Vivasvat or the Sun is the father of Yama the God of Death.

[2] Book III. Canto LI.

[3] Daśaratha's rash oath and fatal promise to his wife Kaikeyí.

CANTO LVII.

ANGAD'S SPEECH.

Though grief and woe his utterance broke,
They trusted not the words he spoke;
But, looking still for secret guile,
Reflected in their hearts a while:
'If on our mangled limbs he feed,
We gain the death ourselves decreed.'
Then rose the Vánar chiefs, and lent
Their arms to aid the bird's descent;
And Angad spake: There lived of yore
A noble Vánar king who bore
The name of Riksharajas, great
And brave and strong and fortunate.
His sons were like their father: fame
Knows Báli and Sugríva's name.
Praised in all lands, a glorious king
Was Báli, and from him I spring.
Brave Ráma. Daśaratha's heir,
A glorious prince beyond compare,
His sire and duty's law obeyed.
And sought the depths of Daṇḍaks' shade.
Sítá his well-beloved dame.
And Lakshmaṇ, with the wanderer came.
A giant watched his hour, and stole
The sweet delight of Ráma's soul.
Jaṭáyus, Daśaratha's friend,
Swift succour to the dame would lend.
Fierce Rávaṇ from his car he felled,
And for a time the prize withheld.
But bleeding, weak with years, and tired,
Beneath the demon's blows expired,
Due rites at Ráma's hands obtained,
And bliss that ne'er shall minish, gained.
Then Ráma with Sugríva made
A covenant for mutual aid,
And Báli, to the field defied,
By conquering Ráma's arrow died.
Sugríva then, by Ráma's grace,
Was monarch of the Vánar race.
By his command a mighty host
Seeks Ráma's queen from coast to coast.
Sent forth by him, in every spot
We looked for her, but find her not.
Vain is the toil, as though by night
We sought to find the Day-God's light.
In lands unknown at length we found
A spacious cavern under ground,
Whose vaults that stretch beneath the hill
Were formed by Maya's magic skill.
Through the dark maze our steps were bent,
And wandering there a month we spent,

And lost, in fruitless error, thus
The days our king allotted us.
Thus we though faithful have transgressed,
And failed to keep our lord's behest.
No chance of safety can we see,
No lingering hope of life have we.
Sugríva's wrath and Ráma's hate
Press on our souls with grievous weight:
And we, because 'tis vain to fly,
Resolve at length to fast and die.'

CANTO LVIII.

TIDINGS OF SÍTÁ.

The piteous tears his eye bedewed
As thus his speech the bird renewed:
'Alas my brother, slain in fight
By Rávan's unresisted might!
I, old and wingless, weak and worn,
O'er his sad fate can only mourn.
Fled is my youth: in life's decline
My former strength no more is mine.
Once on the day when Vritra[1] died,
We brothers, in ambitious pride,
Sought, mounting with adventurous flight,
The Day-God garlanded with light.
On, ever on we urged our way
Where fields of ether round us lay,
Till, by the fervent heat assailed,
My brother's pinions flagged and failed.
I marked his sinking strength, and spread
My stronger wings to screen his head,
Till, all my feathers burnt away,
On Vindhya's hill I fell and lay.
There in my lone and helpless state
I heard not of my brother's fate.'
Thus King Sampáti spoke and sighed:
And royal Angad thus replied:
'If, brother of Jatáyus, thou
Hast heard the tale I told but now,
Obedient to mine earnest prayer
The dwelling of that fiend declare.
O, say where cursed Rávan dwells,
Whom folly to his death impels.'

He ceased. Again Sampáti spoke,
And hope in every breast awoke:
'Though lost my wings, and strength decayed,
Yet shall my words lend Ráma aid.
I know the worlds where Vishnu trod,[1]
I know the realm of Ocean's God;
How Asurs fought with heavenly foes,
And Amrit from the churning rose.[2]
A mighty task before me lies,
To prosper Ráma's enterprise,
A task too hard for one whom length
Of days has rifled of his strength.
I saw the cruel Rávan bear
A gentle lady through the air.
Bright was her form, and fresh and young,
And sparkling gems about her hung.
'O Ráma, Ráma!' cried the dame,
And shrieked in terror Lakshman's name,
As, struggling in the giant's hold,
She dropped her gauds of gems and gold.
Like sun-light on a mountain shone
The silken garments she had on,
And glistened o'er his swarthy form
As lightning flashes through the storm.
That giant Rávan, famed of old,
Is brother of the Lord of Gold.[3]
The southern ocean roars and swells
Round Lanká, where the robber dwells
In his fair city nobly planned
And built by Visvakarmá's[4] hand.
Within his bower securely barred,
With monsters round her for a guard,
Still in her silken vesture clad
Lies Sítá, and her heart is sad.
A hundred leagues your course must be
Beyond this margin of the sea.
Still to the south your way pursue,
And there the giant Rávan view.
Then up, O Vánars, and away!
For by my heavenly lore I say,
There will you see the lady's face.
And hither soon your steps retrace.
In the first field of air are borne
The doves and birds that feed on corn.
The second field supports the crows
And birds whose food on branches grows.
Along the third in balanced flight
Sail the keen osprey and the kite.
Swift through the fourth the falcon springs
The fifth the slower vulture wings.
Up to the sixth the gay swans rise,

[1] Vritra, 'the coverer, hider, obstructer (of rain)' is the name of the Vedic personification of an imaginary malignant influence, or demon of darkness and drought supposed to take possession of the clouds, causing them to obstruct the clearness of the sky and keep back the waters. Indra is represented as battling with this evil influence, and the pent-up clouds being practically represented as mountains or castles are shattered by his thunderbolt and made to open their receptacles.

[1] Frequent mention has been made of the three steps of Vishnu typifying the rising culmination, and setting of the sun.

[2] For the *Churning of the Sea*, see Book I. Canto XLV.

[3] Kuvera, the God of Wealth.

[4] The Architect of the Gods.

Where royal Vainateya[1] flies.
We too, O chiefs, of vulture race,
Our line from Vinatá may trace,
Condemned, because we wrought a deed
Of shame, on flesh and blood to feed.
But all Suparna's[2] wondrous powers
And length of keenest sight are ours,
That we a hundred leagues away
Through fields of air descry our prey.
Now from this spot my gazing eye
Can Rávaṇ and the dame descry.
Devise some plan to overleap
This barrier of the briny deep,
Find the Videhan lady there,
And joyous to your home repair.
Me too, O Vánars, to the side
Of Varuṇ's[3] home the ocean, guide,
Where due libations shall be paid
To my great-hearted brother's shade.'

CANTO LIX.

SAMPATI'S STORY.

They heard his counsel to the close,
Then swiftly to their feet they rose;
And Jámbaván with joyous breast
The vulture king again addressed:
'Where, where is Sítá? who has seen,
Who borne away the Maithil queen?
Who would the lightning flight withstand
Of arrows shot by Lakshmaṇ's hand?'
Again Sampáti spoke to cheer
The Vánars as they bent to hear:
'Now listen, and my words shall show
What of the Maithil dame I know,
And in what distant prison lies
The lady of the long dark eyes.
Scorched by the fiery God of Day,
High on this mighty hill I lay.
A long and weary time had passed,
And strength and life were failing fast.
Yet, ere the breath had left my frame,
My son, my dear Supárśva, came.
Each morn and eve he brought me food,
And filial care my life renewed.
But serpents still are swift to ire,
Gandharvas slaves to soft desire,
And we, imperial vultures, need
A full supply our maws to feed.
Once he turned at close of day,
Stood by my side, but brought no prey.
He looked upon my ravenous eye,
Heard my complaint and made reply:
'Borne on swift wings ere day was light
I stood upon Mahendra's[1] height,
And, far below, the sea I viewed
And birds in countless multitude.
Before mine eyes a giant flew
Whose monstrous form was dark of hue
And struggling in his grasp was borne
A lady radiant as the morn.
Swift to the south his course he bent,
And cleft the yielding element.
The holy spirits of the air
Came round me as I marvelled there,
And cried as their bright legions met:
'O say, is Sítá living yet?'
Thus cried the saints and told the name
Of him who held the struggling dame.
Then while mine eye with eager look
Pursued the path the robber took,
I marked the lady's streaming hair,
And heard her cry of wild despair.
I saw her silken vesture rent
And stripped of every ornament,
Thus, O my father, fled the time:
Forgive, I pray, the heedless crime.'
In vain the mournful tale I heard
My pitying heart to fury stirred.
What could a helpless bird of air,
Reft of his boasted pinions, dare?
Yet can I aid with all that will
And words can do, and friendly skill.'

CANTO LX.

SAMPATI'S STORY.

Then from the flood Sampáti paid
Due offerings to his brother's shade.
He bathed him when the rites were done,
And spake again to Báli's son:
'Now listen, Prince, while I relate
How first I learned the lady's fate.
Burnt by the sun's resistless might
I fell and lay on Vindhya's height.
Seven nights in deadly swoon I passed,
But struggling life returned at last.
Around I bent my wondering view,
But every spot was strange and new.
I scanned the sea with eager ken,
And rock and brook and lake and glen,
I saw gay trees their branches wave,
And creepers mantling o'er the cave.
I heard the wild birds' joyous song,
And waters as they foamed along,
And knew the lovely hill must be
Mount Vindhya by the southern sea.

[1] Garuḍa, son of Vinatá, the sovereign of the birds.

[2] 'The well winged one,' Garuḍa.

[3] The God of the sea.

[1] Mahendra is chain of mountains generally identified with part of the Gháts of the Peninsula.

Revered by heavenly beings, stood
Near where I lay, a sacred wood,
Where great Niśákar dwelt of yore
And pains of awful penance bore.
Eight thousand seasons winged their flight
Over the toiling anchorite—
Upon that hill my days were spent,—
And then to heaven the hermit went.
At last, with long and hard assay,
Down from that height I made my way,
And wandered through the mountain pass
Rough with the spikes of Darbha grass.
I with my misery worn, and faint
Was eager to behold the saint:
For often with Jaṭáyus I
Had sought his home in days gone by.
As nearer to the grove I drew
The breeze with cooling fragrance blew,
And not a tree that was not fair,
With richest flower and fruit was there.
With anxious heart a while I stayed
Beneath the trees' delightful shade,
And soon the holy hermit, bright
With fervent penance, came in sight.
Behind him bears and lions, tame
As those who know their feeder, came,
And tigers, deer, and snakes pursued
His steps, a wondrous multitude,
And turned obeisant when the sage
Had reached his shady hermitage.
Then came Niśákar to my side
And looked with wondering eyes, and cried:
'I knew thee not, so dire a change
Has made thy form and feature strange.
Where are thy glossy feathers? where
The rapid wings that cleft the air?
Two vulture brothers once I knew:
Each form at will could they endue.
They of the vulture race were kings,
And flew with Mátariśva's[1] wings.
In human shape they loved to greet
Their hermit friend, and clasp his feet.
The younger was Jaṭáyus, thou
The elder whom, I gaze on now.
Say, has disease or foeman's hate
Reduced thee from thy high estate?

CANTO LXI.

SAMPATI'S STORY.

'Ah me! o'erwhelmed with shame and weak
With wounds,' I cried, 'I scarce can speak.
My hapless brother once and I
Our strength of flight resolved to try,

[1] Mátariśva is identified with Váyu, the wind.

And by our foolish pride impelled
Our way through realms of ether held.
We vowed before the saints who tread
The wilds about Kailása's head,
That we with follwing wings would chase
The swift sun to his resting place.
Up on our soaring pinions through
The fields of cloudless air we flew.
Beneath us far, and far away,
Like chariot wheels bright cities lay,
Whence in wild snatches rose the song
Of women mid the gay-clad throng,
With sounds of sweetest music blent
And many a tinkling ornament.
Then as our rapid wings we strained
The pathway of the sun we gained.
Beneath us all the earth was seen
Clad in her garb of tender green,
And every river in her bed
Meandered like a silver thread.
We looked on Meru far below,
And Vindhya and the Lord of Snow,
Like elephants that bend to cool
Their fever in a lilied pool.
But fervent heat and toil o'ercame
The vigour of each yielding frame,
Our weary hearts began to quail,
And wildered sense to reel and fail.
We knew not, fainting and distressed,
The north or south or east or west.
With a great strain mine eyes I turned
Where the fierce sun before me burned,
And seemed to my astonished eyes
The equal of the earth in size.[1]
At length, o'erpowered, Jaṭáyus fell
Without a word to say farewell,
And when to earth I saw him hie
I followed headlong from the sky.[2]
With sheltering wings I intervened
And from the sun his body screened,
But lost, for heedless folly doomed,
My pinions which the heat consumed.
In Janasthán, I hear them say,
My hapless brother fell and lay.
I, pinionless and faint and weak,
Dropped upon Vindhya's woody peak.
Now with my swift wings burnt away,
Reft of my brother and my sway,
From this tall mountain's summit I
Will cast me headlong down and die.

[1] Of course not equal to the whole earth, says the Commentator, but equal to Janasthán.

[2] This appears to be the Indian form of the stories of Phaethon and Dædalus and Icarus.

CANTO LXII.

SAMPATI'S STORY.

'As to the saint I thus complained
My bitter tears fell unrestrained.
He pondered for a while, then broke
The silence, and thus calmly spoke:
'Forth from thy sides again shall spring,
O royal bird, each withered wing,
And all thine ancient power and might
Return to thee with strength of sight.
A noble deed has been foretold
In prophecy pronounced of old:
Nor dark to me are future things,
Seen by the light which penance brings.
A glorious king shall rise and reign,
The pride of old Ikshváku's strain.
A good and valiant prince, his heir,
Shall the dear name of Ráma bear.
With his brave brother Lakshman he
An exile in the woods shall be,
Where Rávan, whom no God may slay,[1]
Shall steal his darling wife away,
In vain the captive will be wooed
With proffered love and dainty food,
She will not hear, she will not taste:
But, lest her beauty wane and waste,
Lord Indra's self will come to her
With heavenly food, and minister.
Then envoys of the Vánar race
By Ráma sent will seek this place.
To them, O roamer of the air,
The lady's fate shalt thou declare.
Thou must not move—so maimed thou art
Thou canst not from this spot depart.
Await the day and moment due,
And thy burnt wings will sprout anew.
I might this day the boon bestow
And bid again thy pinions grow,
But wait until thy saving deed
The nations from their fear have freed.
Then for this glorious aid of thine
The princes of Ikshváku's line,
And Gods above and saints below
Eternal gratitude shall owe.
Fain would mine aged eyes behold
That pair of whom my lips have told,
Yet wearied here I must not stay,
But leave my frame and pass away.'

CANTO LXIII.

SAMPATI'S STORY.

'With this and many a speech beside
My failing heart he fortified,
With glorious hope my breast inspired,
And to his holy home retired.
I scaled the mountain height, to view
The region round, and looked for you.
In ceaseless watchings night and day
A hundred seasons passed away,
And by the sage's words consoled
I wait the hour and chance foretold.
But since Nisákar sought the skies,
And cast away all earthly ties,
Full many a care and doubt has pressed
With grievous weight upon my breast.
But for the saint who turned aside
My purpose I had surely died.
Those hopeful words the hermit spake,
That bid me live for Ráma's sake,
Dispel my anguish as the light
Of lamp and torch disperse the night.'
He ceased: and in the Vánars' view
Forth from his side young pinions grew,
And boundless rapture filled his breast
As thus the chieftains he addressed:
'Joy, joy! the pinions, which the Lord
Of Day consumed, are now restored
Through the dear grace & boundless might
Of that illustrious anchorite.
The fire of youth within me burns,
And all my wonted strength returns.
Onward, ye Vánars, toil strive,
And you shall find the dame alive.
Look on these new-found wings, and hence
Be strong in surest confidence.'
Swift from the crag he sprang to try
His pinions in his native sky.
His words the chieftains' doubts had stilled?
And every heart with courage filled.[1]

CANTO LXIV.

THE SEA.

Shouts of triumphant joy outrang
As to their feet the Vánars sprang:
And, on the mighty task intent,
Swift to the sea their steps they bent.
They stood and gazed upon the deep,
Whose billows with a roar and leap
On the sea banks were wildly hurled,—
The mirror of the mighty world.
There on the strand the Vánars stayed
And with sad eyes the deep surveyed.
Here, as in play, his billows rose,
And there he slumbered in repose.
Here leapt the boisterous waters, high
As mountains, menacing the sky,
And wild infernal forms between
The ridges of the waves were seen.

---

[1] According to the promise given him by Brahmá. See Book I. Canto XIV.

[1] In the Bengal recension the fourth Book ends here, the remaining Cantos being placed in the fifth.

They saw the billows rave and swell,
And their sad spirits sank and fell;
For ocean in their deep despair
Seemed boundless as the fields of air.
Then noble Angad spake to cheer
The Vánars and dispel their fear:
'Faint not: despair should never find
Admittance to a noble mind.
Despair, a serpent's mortal bite,
Benumbs the hero's power and might.'
Then passed the weary night, and all
Assembled at their prince's call,
And every lord of high estate
Was gathered round him for debate.
Bright was the chieftains' glorious band
Round Angad on the ocean strand,
As when the mighty Storm-Gods meet
Round Indra on his golden seat.
Then princely Angad looked on each,
And thus began his prudent speech:
'What chief of all our host will leap
A hundred leagues across the deep?
Who, O illustrious Vánars, who
Will make Sugríva's promise true,
And from our weight of fear set free
The leaders of our band and me?
To whom, O warriors, shall we owe
A sweet release from pain and woe,
And proud success, and happy lives
With our dear children and our wives,
Again permitted by his grace
To look with joy on Ráma's face,
And noble Lakshman, and our lord
The king, to our sweet homes restored?'
Thus to the gathered lords he spoke;
But no reply the silence broke.
Then with a sterner voice he cried:
'O chiefs, the nation's boast and pride,
Whom valour strength and power adorn,
Of most illustrious lineage born,
Where'er you will you force a way,
And none your rapid course can stay.
Now come, your several powers declare,
And who this desperate leap will dare?

CANTO LXV.

THE COUNCIL.

But none of all the host was found
To clear the sea with desperate bound,
Though each, as Angad bade, declared
His proper power and what he dared.[1]
Then spake good Jámbaván the sage,
Chief of them all for reverend age;
'I, Vánar chieftains, long ago
Limbs light to leap could likewise show,
But now on frame and spirit weighs
The burthen of my length of days.
Still task like this I may not slight,
When Ráma and our king unite.
So listen while I tell, O friends,
What lingering strength mine age attends.
If my poor leap may aught avail,
Of ninety leagues, I will not fail.
Far other strength in youth's fresh prime
I boasted, in the olden time,
When, at Prahláda's[1] solemn rite,
I circled in my rapid flight
Lord Vishṇu, everlasting God,
When through the universe he trod.
But now my limbs are weak and old,
My youth is fled, its fire is cold,
And these exhausted nerves to strain
In such a task were idle pain.'

Then Angad due obeisance paid,
And to the chief his answer made:
'Then I, ye noble Vánars, I
Myself the mighty leap will try;
Although perchance the power I lack
To leap from Lanká's island back.'

Thus the impetuous chieftain cried,
And Jámbaván the sage replied;
'Whate'er thy power and might may be,
This task, O Prince, is not for thee.
Kings go not forth themselves, but send
The servants who their hest attend.
Thou art the darling and the boast,
The honoured lord of all the host.
In thee the root, O Angad, lies
Of our appointed enterprise;
And thee, on whom our hopes depend,
Our care must cherish and defend.'

Then Báli's noble son replied;
'Needs must I go, whate'er betide,
For, if no chief this exploit dare,
What waits us all save blank despair,—
Upon the ground again to lie
In hopeless misery, fast, and die?
For not a hope of life I see
If we neglect our king's decree.'
Then spoke the aged chief again:
'Nay, our attempt shall not be vain,
For to the task will I incite
A chieftain of sufficient might.'

---

[1] Each chief comes forward and says how far he can leap. Gaja says he can leap ten yojans, Gaváksha can leap twenty, Gavaya thirty, and so on up to ninety.

[1] Prahláda, the son of Hiraṇyakaśipu, was a pious Datya remarkable for his devotion to Vishṇu, and was on this account persecuted by his father.

CANTO LXVI.

HANUMAN.

The chieftain turned his glances where
The legions sat in mute despair;
And then to Hanumán, the best
Of Vánar lords, these words addressed:
'Why still, and silent, and apart,
O hero of the dauntless heart?
Thou keepest treasured in thy mind
The laws that rule the Vánar kind,
Strong as our king Sugríva, brave
As Ráma's self to slay or save.
Through every land thy praise is heard,
Famous as that illustrious bird,
Arishṭanemi's son,[1] the king
Of every fowl that plies the wing.
Oft have I seen the monarch sweep
With sounding pinions o'er the deep,
And in his mighty talons bear
Huge serpents struggling through the air.
Thy arms, O hero, match in might
The ample wings he spreads for flight;
And thou with him mayst well compare
In power to do, in heart to dare.
Why, rich in wisdom, power, and skill,
O hero, art thou lingering still?
An Apsaras,[2] the fairest found
Of nymphs for heavenly charms renowned,
Sweet Punjikasthalá, became
A noble Vánar's wedded dame.
Her heavenly title heard no more,
Anjaná was the name she bore,
When, cursed by Gods, from heaven she fell
In Vánar form on earth to dwell,
New-born in mortal shape the child
Of Kunjar monarch of the wild.
In youthful beauty wondrous fair,
A crown of flowers about her hair,
In silken robes of richest dye
She roamed the hills that kiss the sky.
Once in her tinted garments dressed
She stood upon the mountain crest,
The God of Wind beside her came,
And breathed upon the lovely dame.
And as he fanned her robe aside
The wondrous beauty that he eyed
In rounded lines of breast and limb
And neck and shoulder ravished him;
And captured by her peerless charms
He strained her in his amorous arms.
Then to the eager God she cried
In trembling accents, terrified:
'Whose impious love has wronged a spouse
So constant to her nuptial vows?'
He heard, and thus his answer made:
'O, be not troubled, nor afraid.
But trust, and thou shalt know ere long
My love has done thee, sweet, no wrong
So strong and brave and wise shall be
The glorious child I give to thee.
Might shall be his that naught can tire,
And limbs to spring as springs his sire.'
Thus spoke the God: the conquered dame
Rejoiced in heart nor feared the shame.
Down in a cave beneath the earth
The happy mother gave thee birth.
Once o'er the summit of the wood
Before thine eyes the new sun stood.
Thou sprangest up in haste to seize
What seemed the fruitage of the trees.
Up leapt the child, a wondrous bound,
Three hundred leagues above the ground,
And, though the angered Day-God shot
His fierce beams on him, feared him not.
Then from the hand of Indra came
A red bolt winged with wrath and flame.
The child fell smitten on a rock.
His cheek was shattered by the shock,
Named Hanumán[1] thenceforth by all
In memory of the fearful fall.
The wandering Wind-God saw thee lie
With bleeding cheek and drooping eye,
And stirred to anger by thy woe
Forbade each scented breeze to blow.
The breath of all the worlds was stilled,
And the sad Gods with terror filled
Prayed to the Wind, to calm the ire
And soothe the sorrow of the sire.
His fiery wrath no longer glowed,
And Brahmá's self the boon bestowed
That in the brunt of battle none
Should slay with steel the Wind-God's son.
Lord Indra, sovereign of the skies,
Bent on thee all his thousand eyes,
And swore that ne'er the bolt which he
Hurls from the heaven should injure thee.
'Tis thine, O mighty chief, to share
The Wind-God's power, his son and heir.
Sprung from that glorious father thou,
And thou alone, canst aid us now.
This earth of yore, through all her climes,
I circled one-and-twenty times,
And gathered, as the Gods decreed,
Great store of herbs from hill and mead,
Which, scattered o'er the troubled wave,
The Amrit to the toilers gave.

[1] The Bengal recension calls him Arishṭanemi's brother. "The commentator says "Arishṭanemi is Aruṇa." Aruṇa the charioteer of the sun is the son of Kaśyapa and Vinatá and by consequence brother of Garuḍa called Vainateya from Vinatá his mother." GORRESIO.

[2] A nymph of Paradise.

[1] Hanu or Hanú means jaw. Hanumán or Hanúmán means properly one with a large jaw.

But now my days are wellnigh told,
My strength is gone, my limbs are old,
And thou, the bravest and the best,
Art the sure hope of all the rest.
Now, mighty chief, the task assay:
Thy matchless power and strength display.
Rise up, O prince, our second king,
And o'er the flood of ocean spring.
So shall the glorious exploit vie
With his who stepped through earth and sky.'[1]
He spoke: the younger chieftain heard,
His soul to vigorous effort stirred,
And stood before their joyous eyes
Dilated in gigantic size.

CANTO LXVII.

HANUMÁN'S SPEECH.

Soon as his stature they beheld,
Their fear and sorrow were dispelled;
And joyous praises loud and long
Rang out from all the Vánar throng.
On the great chief their eyes they bent
In rapture and astonishment,
As, when his conquering foot he raised,
The Gods upon Náráyan[2] gazed.
He stood amid the joyous crowd,
Bent to the chiefs, and cried aloud:
'The Wind-God, Fire's eternal friend,
Whose blasts the mountain summits rend,
With boundless force that none may stay,
Takes where he lists his viewless way.
Sprung from that glorious father, I
In power and speed with him may vie,
A thousand times with airy leap
Can circle loftiest Meru's steep:
With my fierce arms can stir the sea
Till from their bed the waters flee
And rush at my command to drown
This land with grove and tower and town.
I through the fields of air can spring
Far swifter than the feathered King,
And leap before him as he flies
On sounding pinions through the skies.
I can pursue the Lord of Light
Uprising from the eastern height,
And reach him ere his course be sped
With burning beams engarlanded.
I will dry up the mighty main,
Shatter the rocks and rend the plain.
O'er earth and ocean will I bound,
And every flower that grows on ground,

[1] Vishṇu, the God of the Three Steps.

[2] Náráyaṇ, 'He who moved upon the waters,' is Vishṇu. The allusion is to the famous three steps of that God.

And bloom of climbing plants shall show
Strewn on the ground, the way I go,
Bright as the lustrous path that lies
Athwart the region of the skies.[1]
The Maithil lady will I find,—
Thus speaks mine own prophetic mind,—
And cast in hideous ruin down
The shattered walls of Lanká's town.'
Still on the chief in rapt surprise
The Vánar legions bent their eyes,
And thus again sage Jámbaván
Addressed the glorious Hanumán:
'Son of the Wind, thy promise cheers
The Vánars' hearts, and calms their fears,
Who, rescued from their dire distress,
With prospering vows thy way will bless.
The holy saints their favour lend,
And all our chiefs the deed commend
Urging thee forward on thy way:
Arise then, and the task assay.
Thou art our only refuge; we.
Our lives and all, depend on thee.'
Then sprang the Wind-God's son the best
Of Vánars, on Mahendra's crest,
And the great mountain rocked and swayed
By that unusual weight dismayed,
As reels an elephant beneath
The lion's spring and rending teeth.
The shady wood that crowned him shook,
The trembling birds the boughs forsook,
And ape and pard and lion fled
From brake and lair disquieted.

[1] The Milky Way.

BOOK V.[1]

CANTO I.

HANUMAN'S LEAP.

Thus Rávan's foe resolved to trace
The captive to her hiding-place
Through airy pathways overhead
Which heavenly minstrels visited.
With straining nerve and eager brows,
Like some strong husband of the cows,
In ready might he stood prepared
For the bold task his soul has dared.
O'er gem-like grass that flashed and glowed
The Vánar like a lion strode.
Roused by the thunder of his tread,
The beasts to shady coverts fled.
Tall trees he crushed or hurled aside,
And every bird was terrified.
Around him loveliest lilies grew,
Pale pink, and red, and white, and blue,
And tints of many a metal lent
The light of varied ornament.
Gandharvas, changing forms at will,
And Yakshas roamed the lovely hill,
And countless Serpent-Gods were seen
Where flowers and grass were fresh and green.
As some resplendent serpent takes
His pastime in the best of lakes,
So on the mountain's woody height
The Vánar wandered with delight.
Then, standing on the flowery sod,
He paid his vows to saint and God.
Swayambhu[2] and the Sun he prayed,
And the swift Wind to lend him aid,
And Indra, sovereign of the skies,
To bless his hardy enterprise.
Then once again the chief addressed
The Vánars from the mountain crest:
'Swift as a shaft from Ráma's bow
To Rávan's city will I go,
And if she be not there will fly
And seek the lady in the sky;
Or, if in heaven she be not found,
Will hither bring the giant bound.'
He ceased; and mustering his might
Sprang downward from the mountain height,
While, shattered by each mighty limb,
The trees unrooted followed him.
The shadow on the ocean cast
By his vast form, as on he passed,
Flew like a ship before the gale
When the strong breeze has filled the sail,
And where his course the Vánar held
The sea beneath him raged and swelled.
Then Gods and all the heavenly train
Poured flowerets down in gentle rain;
Their voices glad Gandharvas raised,
And saints in heaven the Vánar praised.
Fain would the Sea his succour lend
And Raghu's noble son befriend.
He, moved by zeal for Ráma's sake,
The hill Maináka[1] thus bespake:
'O strong Maináka, heaven's decree
In days of old appointed thee
To be the Asurs' bar, and keep
The rebels in the lowest deep.
Thou guardest those whom heaven has cursed
Lest from their prison-house they burst,
And standest by the gates of hell
Their limitary sentinel.
To thee is given the power to spread
Or spring above thy watery bed.
Now, best of noble mountains, rise
And do the thing that I advise.
E'en now above thy buried crest
Flies mighty Hanumán, the best
Of Vánars, moved for Ráma's sake
A wondrous deed to undertake.
Lift up thy head that he may stay
And rest him on his weary way.'
He heard, and from his watery shroud,
As bursts the sun from autumn cloud,
Rose swiftly, crowned with plant and tree,
And stood above the foamy sea.[2]
There with his lofty peaks upraised
Bright as a hundred suns he blazed,
And crest and crag of burnished gold
Flashed on the flood that round him rolled.

[1] This Book is called Sundar or the Beatiful. To a European taste it is the most intolerably tedious of the whole poem, abounding in repetition, overloaded description, and long and useless speeches which impede the action of the poem. Manifest interpolations of whole Cantos also occur. I have omitted none of the action of the Book, but have occasionally omitted long passages of common-place description, lamentation, and long stories which have been again and again repeated.

[2] Brahmá the Self-Existent.

[1] Maináka was the son of Himálaya and Mená or Menaká.

[2] Thus Milton makes the hills of heaven self-moving at command:

'At his commad the uprooted hills retired
Each to his place, they heard his voice and went
Obsequious.'

The Vánar thought the mountain rose
A hostile bar to interpose,
And, like a wind-swept cloud, o'erthrew
The glittering mountain as he flew.
Then from the falling hill rang out
A warning voice and joyful shout.
Again he raised him high in air
To meet the flying Vánar there,
And standing on his topmost peak
In human form began to speak :[1]
'Best of the Vánars' noblest line,
A mighty task, O chief, is thine.
Here for a while, I pray thee, light
And rest upon the breezy height.
A prince of Raghu's line was he
Who gave his glory to the Sea,[2]
Who now to Ráma's envoy shows
High honour for the debt he owes.
He bade me lift my buried head
Uprising from my watery bed,
And woo the Vánar chief to rest
A moment on my glittering crest.
Refresh thy weary limbs, and eat
My mountain fruits for they are sweet.
I too, O chieftain, know thee well ;
Three worlds thy famous virtues tell ;
And none, I ween, with thee may vie
Who spring impetuous through the sky.
To every guest, though mean and low,
The wise respect and honour show ;
And how shall I neglect thee, how
Slight the great guest so near me now ?
Son of the Wind, 'tis thine to share
The might of him who shakes the air ;
And,—for he loves his offspring,—he
Is honoured when I honour thee.
Of yore, when Krita's age[3] was new,
The little hills and mountains flew
Where'er they listed, borne on wings
More rapid the feathered king's.[4]
But mighty terror came on all
The Gods and saints who feared their fall,
And Indra in his anger rent
Their pinions with the bolts he sent.
When in his ruthless fury he
Levelled his flashing bolt at me,
The great-souled Wind inclined to save,
And laid me neath the ocean's wave.
Thus by the favour of the sire
I kept my cherished wings entire ;
And for this deed of kindness done
I honour thee his noble son.
O come, thy weary limbs relieve,
And honour due from me receive.'
'I may not rest,' the Vánar cried ;'
'I must not stay or turn aside.
Yet pleased am I, thou noblest hill,
And as the deed accept thy will.'
Thus as he spoke he lightly pressed
With his broad hand the mountain's crest,
Then bounded upward to the height
Of heaven, rejoicing in his might,
And through the fields of boundless blue,
The pathway of his father, flew.
Gods, saints, and heavenly bards beheld
That flight that none had paralleled,
Then to the Nágas' mother[1] came
And thus addressed the sun-bright dame :
'See, Hanumán with venturous leap
Would spring across the mighty deep,—
A Vánar prince, the Wind-God's seed :
Come, Surasá, his course impede.
In Rákshas form thy shape disguise,
Terrific, like a hill in size :
Let thy red eyes with fury glow,
And high as heaven thy body grow.
With fearful tusks the chief defy,
That we his power and strength may try.
He will with guile thy hold elude,
Or own thy might, by thee subdued.'
Pleased with the grateful honours paid,
The godlike dame their words obeyed.
Clad in a shape of terror she
Sprang from the middle of the sea,
And, with fierce accents that appalled
All creatures, to the Vánar called :
'Come, prince of Vánars, doomed to be
My food this day by heaven's decree.
Such boon from ages long ago
To Brahmá's favouring will I owe.'
She ceased, and Hanumán replied,
By shape and threat unterrified :
'Brave Ráma with his Maithil spouse
Lodged in the shade of Dandak's boughs.
Thence Rávan king of giants stole
Sítá the joy of Ráma's soul.

---

[1] The spirit of the mountain is separable from the mountain. Himálaya has also been represented as standing in human on one of his own peaks.

[2] Ságar or the Sea is said to have derived its name from Sagar. The story is fully told in Book I. Cantos XLII., XLIII., and XLIV.

[3] Kritu is the first of the four ages of the world, the golden age, also called Satya.

[4] *Parvata* means a mountain and in the Vedas a cloud. Hence in later mythology the mountain have taken the place of the clouds as the objects of the attacks of ndra the Sun-God. The feathered king Garuḍa.

[1] "The children of Surasá were a thousand mighty many-headed serpents, traversing the sky."

WILSON'S *Vishnu Puráṇa*, Vol. II. p. 73.

By Ráma's high behest to her
I go a willing messenger;
And never shouldst thou hinder one
Who toils for Daśaratha's son.
First captive Sítá will I see,
And him who sent and waits for me,
Then come and to thy will submit,
Yea, by my truth I promise it.'
'Nay, hope not thus thy life to save;
Not such the boon that Brahmá gave.
Enter my mouth,' was her reply,
'Then forward on thy journey hie!'[1]

'Stretch, wider stretch thy jaws,' exclaimed
The Vánar chief, to ire inflamed;
And, as the Rákshas near him drew,
Ten leagues in height his stature grew.
Then straight, her threatening jaws between,
A gulf of twenty leagues was seen.
To fifty leagues he waxed, and still
Her mouth grew wider at her will.
Then smaller than a thumb became,
Shrunk by his power, the Vánar's frame.[2]
He leaped within, and turning round
Sprang through the portal at a bound.
Then hung in air a moment, while
He thus addressed her with a smile:
'O Daksha's child,[3] farewell at last!
For I within thy mouth have passed.
Thou hast the gift of Brahmá's grace:
I go, the Maithil queen to trace.'
Then, to her former shape restored,
She thus addressed the Vánar lord:
'Then forward to the task, and may
Success and joy attend thy way!
Go, and the rescued lady bring
In triumph to her lord and king.'

Then hosts of spirits as they gazed
The daring of the Vánar praised.
Through the broad fields of ether, fast
Garuḍ's royal self, he passed,
The region of the cloud and rain,
Loved by the gay Gandharva train,
Where mid the birds that came and went
Shone Indra's glorious bow unbent,
And like a host of wandering stars
Flashed the high Gods' celestial cars.
Fierce Sinhiká[1] who joyed in ill
And changed her form to work her will,
Descried him on his airy way
And marked the Vánar for her prey.
'This day at length,' the demon cried,
'My hunger shall be satisfied,'
And at his passing shadow caught
Delighted with the cheering thought.
The Vánar felt the power that stayed
And held him as she grasped his shade,
Like some tall ship upon the main
That struggles with the wind in vain.
Below, above, his eye he bent
And scanned the sea and firmament.
High from the briny deep upreared
The monster's hideous form appeared.
'Sugríva's tale,' he cried, 'is true:
This is the demon dire to view
Of whom the Vánar monarch told,
Whose grasp a passing shade can hold.'
Then, as a cloud in rain-time grows,
His form, dilating, swelled and rose.
Wide as the space from heaven to hell
Her jaws she opened with a yell,
And rushed upon her fancied prey
With cloud-like roar to seize and slay.
The Vánar swift as thought compressed
His borrowed bulk of limb and chest,
And stood with one quick bound inside
The monstrous mouth she opened wide.
Hid like the moon when Ráhu[2] draws
The orb within his ravening jaws.
Within that ample cavern pent
The demon's form he tore and rent,
And, from the mangled carcass freed,
Came forth again with thought-like speed.[3]

---

[1] She means, says the Commentator, pursue thy journey if thou can.

[2] If Milton's spirits are allowed the power of infinite self-extension and compression the same must be conceded to Válmíki's supernatural beings. Given the power as in Milton the result in Válmíki is perfectly consistent.

[3] "Daksha is the son of Brahmá and one of the Prajápatis or divine progenitors. He had sixty daughters, twenty-seven of whom married to Kaśyapa produced, according to one of the Indian cosmogonies, all mundane beings. Does the epithet, Descendent of Daksha, given to Surasá, mean that she is one of those daughters? I think not. This epithet is perhaps an appellation common to all created beings as having sprung from Daksha." GORRESIO.

[1] Sinhiká is the mother of Ráhu the dragon's head or ascending node, the chief agent in eclipses.

[2] Ráhu is the demon who causes eclipses by attempting to swallow the sun and moon.

[3] According to De Gubernatis, the author of the very learned, ingenious, and interesting though too fanciful *Zoological Mythology*, Hanumán here represents the sun entering into and escaping from a cloud. The biblical Jonah, according to him, typifies the same phenomenon. Śá'df,

Thus with his skill the fiend he slew,
Then to his wonted stature grew.
The spirits saw the demon die,
And hailed the Vánar from the sky:
'Well hast thou fought a wondrous fight
Nor spared the fiend's terrific might.
On, on! perform the blameless deed,
And in thine every wish succeed.
Ne'er can they fail in whom combine
Such valour, thought, and skill as thine.'
Pleased with their praises as they sang,
Again through fields of air he sprang,
And now, his travail wellnigh done,
The distant shore was almost won.
Before him on the margent stood
In long dark line a waving wood,
And the fair island, bright and green
With flowers and trees, was clearly seen,
And every babbling brook that gave
Her lord the sea a tribute wave.
He lighted down on Lamba's peak
Which tinted metals stain and streak,
And looked where Lanká's splendid town
Shone on the mountain like a crown.

CANTO II.

LANKÁ.

The glorious sight a while he viewed,
Then to the town his way pursued.
Around the Vanar as he went
Breathed from the wood delicious scent,
And the soft grass beneath his feet
With gem-like flowers was bright and sweet.
Still as the Vánar nearer drew
More clearly rose the town to view.
The palm her fan-like leaves displayed,
Priyálas[1] lent their pleasant shade,
And mid the lower greenery far
Conspicuous rose the Kovidár.[2]
A thousand trees mid flowers that glowed
Hung down their fruit's delicious load,[3]
And in their crests that rocked and swayed
Sweet birds delightful music made.
And there were pleasant pools whereon
The glories of the lotus shone;
And gleams of sparkling fountains, stirred
By many a joyous water-bird.
Around, in lovely gardens grew
Blooms sweet of scent and bright of hue,
And Lanká, seat of Rávan's sway,
Before the wondering Vánar lay:
With stately domes and turrets tall,
Encircled by a golden wall,
And moats whose waters were aglow
With lily blossoms bright below:
For Sítá's sake defended well
With bolt and bar and sentinel,
And Rákshases who roamed in bands
With ready bows in eager hands.
He saw the stately mansions rise
Like pale-hued clouds in autumn skies:
Where noble streets were broad and bright,
And banners waved on every height.
Her gates were glorious to behold,
Rich with the shine of burnished gold:
A lovely city planned and decked
By heaven's creative arhitect,[1]
Fairest of earthly cities meet
To be the Gods' celestial seat.
The Vánar by the northern gate
Thus in his heart began debate:
'Our mightiest host would strive in vain
To take this city on the main:
A city that may well defy
The chosen warriors of the sky;
A city never to be won
E'en by the arm of Raghu's son.
Here is no hope by guile to win
The hostile hearts of those within.
'Twere vain to war, or bribe, or sow
Dissension mid the Vánar foe.
But now my search must I pursue
Until the Maithil queen I view;
And, when I find the captive dame,
Make victory mine only aim.
But, if I wear my present shape,
How shall I enter and escape
The Rákshas troops, their guards and spies,
And sleepless watch of cruel eyes?
The fiends of giant race who hold
This mighty town are strong and bold;
And I must labour to elude
The fiercely watchful multitude.
I in a shape to mock their sight
Must steal within the town by night,
Blind with my art the demons' eyes,
And thus achieve my enterprise.
How may I see, myself unseen
Of the fierce king, the captive queen,
And meet her in some lonely place,
With none beside her, face to face?'
When the bright sun had left the skies
The Vánar dwarfed his mighty size,

---

speaking of sunset, says *Yùnas andar-i-dihán-i máhí shud:* Jonas was within the fish's mouth. See ADDITIONAL NOTES.

[1] The Buchanania Latifolia.

[2] The Bauhinia Variegata.

[3] Through the power that Rávan's stern mortifications had won for him his trees bore flowers and fruit simultaneously.

[1] Viśvakarmá is the architect of the Gods.

And, in the straitest bounds restrained,
The bigness of a cat retained.[1]
Then, when the moon's soft light was spread,
Within the city's walls he sped.

CANTO III.

THE GUARDIAN GODDESS.

There from the circling rampart's height
He gazed upon the wondrous sight;
Broad gates with burnished gold displayed,
And courts with turkises inlaid;
With gleaming silver, gems, and rows
Of crystal stairs and porticoes.
In semblance of a Rákshas dame
The city's guardian Goddess came,—
For she with glances sure and keen
The entrance of a foe had seen,—
And thus with fury in her eye
Addressed him with an angry cry:
'Who art thou? what has led thee, say,
Within these walls to find thy way?
Thou mayst not enter here in spite
Of Rávaṇ and his warriors' might.'
'And who art thou?' the Vánar cried,
By form and frown unterrified;
'Why hast thou met me by the gate,
And chid me thus infuriate?'
He ceased: and Lanká made reply:
'The guardian of the town am I,
Who watch for ever to fulfil
My lord the Rákshas monarch's will.
But thou shalt fall this hour, and deep
Shall be thy never-ending sleep.'
Again he spake: 'In spite of thee
This golden city will I see,
Her gates and towers, and all the pride
Of street and square from side to side,
And freely wander where I please
Amid her groves of flowering trees;
On all her beauties sate mine eye,
Then, as I came, will homeward hie.'
Swift with an angry roar she smote
With her huge hand the Vánar's throat.
The smitten Vánar, rage-impelled,
With fist upraised the monster felled:
But quick repented, stirred with shame
And pity for a vanquished dame.
When with her senses troubled, weak
With terror, thus she strove to speak:
'O spare me thou whose arm is strong:
O spare me, and forgive the wrong.

[1] So in Paradise Lost Satan when he has stealthily entered the garden of Eden assumes the form of a cormorant.

The brave that law will ne'er transgress
That spares a woman's helplessness.
Hear, best of Vánars, brave and bold,
What Brahmá's self of yore foretold:
'Beware,' he said, 'the fatal hour
When thou shalt own a Vánar's power.
Then is the giants' day of fear,
For terror and defeat are near.'
Now, Vánar chief, o'ercome by thee,
I own the truth of heaven's decree.
For Sítá's sake will ruin fall
On Rávaṇ, and his town, and all.'

CANTO IV.

WITHIN THE CITY.

The guardian goddess thus subdued,
The Vánar chief his way pursued,
And reached the broad imperial street
Where fresh-blown flowers were bright and sweet.
The city seemed a fairer sky
Where cloud-like houses rose on high,
Whence the soft sound of tabors came
Through many a latticed window frame,
And ever and anon rang out
The merry laugh and joyous shout.
From house to house the Vánar went
And marked each varied ornament,
Where leaves and blossoms deftly strung
About the crystal columns hung.
Then soft and full and sweet and clear
The song of women charmed his ear,
And, blending with their dulcet tones,
Their anklets' chime and tinkling zones.
He heard the Rákshas minstrels sing
The praises of their matchless king;
And softly through the evening air
Came murmurings of text and prayer.
Here moved a priest with tonsured head,
And there an eager envoy sped,
Mid crowds with hair in matted twine
Clothed in the skins of deer and kine,—
Whose only arms, which none might blame,
Were blades of grass and holy flame.[1]
There savage warriors roamed in bands
With clubs and maces in their hands,
Some dwarfish forms, some huge of size,
With single ears and single eyes.
Some shone in glittering mail arrayed
With bow and mace and flashing blade;
Fiends of all shapes and every hue,
Some fierce and foul, some fair to view.

[1] Priests who fought only with the weapons of religion, the sacred grass used like the verbena of the Romans at sacred rites and the consecrated fire to consume the offering of ghee.

He saw the grisly legions wait
In strictest watch at Rávaṇ's gate,
Whose palace on the mountain crest
Rose proudly towering o'er the rest,
Fenced with high ramparts from the foe,
And lotus-covered moats below.
But Hanumán, unhindered, found
Quick passage through the guarded bound,
Mid elephants of noblest breed,
And gilded car and neighing steed.

CANTO VI.[1]

THE COURT.

The palace gates were guarded well
By many a Rákshas sentinel,
And far within, concealed from view,
Were dames and female retinue
For charm of form and face renowned;
Whose tinkling armlets made a sound,
Clashed by the wearers in their glee,
Like music of a distant sea.
The hall beyond the palace gate,
Rich with each badge of royal state,
Where lines of noble courtiers stood,
Showed like a lion-guarded wood.
There the wild music rose and fell
Of drum and tabor and of shell,
Through chambers at each holy tide
By solemn worship sanctified.
Through grove and garden, undismayed,
From house to house the Vánar strayed,
And still his wondering glances bent
On terrace, dome, and battlement:
Then with a light and rapid tread
Prahasta's[1] home he visited,
And Kumbhakarṇa's[2] courtyard where
A cloudy pile rose high in air;
And, wandering o'er the hill, explored
The garden of each Rákshas lord.
Each court and grove he wandered through,
Then nigh to Rávaṇ's palace drew.
She-demons watched it foul of face,
Eace armed with sword and spear and mace,
And warrior fiends of every hue,
A strange and fearful retinue.
There elephants in many a row,
The terror of the stricken foe,
Huge Airávat,[3] deftly trained
In battle-fields, stood ready chained.
Fair litters on the ground were set
Adorned with gems and golden net.
Gay bloomy creepers clothed the walls;
Green bowers were there and picture halls,
And chambers made for soft delight.
Broad banners waved on every height,
And from the roof like Mandar's hill
The peacock's cry came loud and shrill.[4]

CANTO VII.

RÁVAṆ'S PALACE.

He passed within the walls and gazed
On gems and gold that round him blazed,
And many a latticed window bright
With turkis and with lazulite.

---

[1] I omit Canto V. which corresponds to chapter XI. in Gorresio's edition. That scholar justly observes: "The eleventh chapter, Description of Evening, is certainly the work of the Rhapsodists and an interpolation of later date. The chapter might be omitted without any injury to the action of the poem, and besides the metre, style, conceits and images differ from the general tenour of the poem; and that continual repetition of the same sounds at the end of each hemistich which is not exactly rime, but assonance, reveals the artificial labour of a more recent age.' The following sample will probably be enough. I am unable to show the difference of style in a translation:

Fair shone the moon, as if to lend
His cheering light to guide a friend,
And, circled by the starry host,
Looked down upon the wild sea-coast.
The Vánar chieftain raised his eyes,
And saw him sailing through the skies
Like a bright swan who joys to take
His pastime on a silver lake;
Fair moon that calms the mourner's pain,
Heaves up the waters of the main,
And o'er the life beneath him throws
A tender light of soft repose,
The charm that clings to Mandar's hill,
Gleams in the sea when winds are still,
And decks the lilly's opening flower,
Showed in that moon her sweetest power.

[1] One of the Rákshas lords.

[2] The brother Rávaṇ.

[3] Indra's elephant.

[4] Rávaṇ's palace appears to have occupied the whole extent of ground, and to have contained within its outer walls the mansions of all the great Rákshas chiefs. Rávaṇ's own dwelling seems to have been situated within the enchanted chariot Pushpak; but the description is involved and confused, and it is difficult to say whether the chariot was inside the palace or the palace inside the chariot.

Through porch and ante-rooms he passed
Each richer, fairer than the last;
And spacious halls were lances lay,
And bows and shells, in fair array:
A glorious house that matched in show
All Paradise displayed below.
Upon the polished floor were spread
Fresh buds and blossoms white and red,
And women shone, a lovely crowd,
As lightning flashes through a cloud:
A palace splendid as the sky
Which moon and planets glorify:
Like earth whose towering hills unfold
Their zones and streaks of glittering gold;
Where waving on the mountain brows
The tall trees bend their laden boughs,
And every bough and tender spray
With a bright load of bloom is gay,
And every flower the breeze has bent
Fills all the region with its scent.
Near the tall palace pale of hue
Shone lovely lakes where lilies blew,
And lotuses with flower and bud
Gleamed on the bosom of the flood.
There shone with gems that flashed afar
The marvel of the Flower-named[1] car,
Mid wondrous dwellings still confessed
Supreme and nobler than the rest.
Thereon with wondrous art designed
Were turkis birds of varied kind,
And many a sculptured serpent rolled
His twisted coil in burnished gold.
And steeds were there of noblest form
With flying feet as fleet as storm:
And elephants with deftest skill
Stood sculptured by a silver rill,
Each bearing on his trunk a wreath
Of lilies from the flood beneath.
There Lakshmí,[2] beauty's heavenly queen,
Wrought by the artist's skill, was seen
Beside a flower-clad pool to stand
Holding a lotus in her hand.

CANTO VIII.

THE ENCHANTED CAR.

There gleamed the car with wealth untold
Of precious gems and burnished gold;
Nor could the Wind-God's son withdraw
His rapt gaze from the sight he saw,
By Viśvakarmá's[1] self proclaimed
The noblest work his hand had framed.
Uplifted in the air it glowed
Bright as the sun's diurnal road.
The eye might scan the wondrous frame
And vainly seek one spot to blame,
So fine was every part and fair
With gems inlaid with lavish care.
No precious stones so rich adorn
The cars wherein the Gods are borne.
Prize of the all-resistless might
That sprang from pain and penance rite,[2]
Obedient to the master's will
It moved o'er wood and towering hill,
A glorious marvel well designed
By Viśvakarmá's artist mind,
Adorned with every fair device
That decks the cars of Paradise.
Swift moving as the master chose
It flew through air or sank or rose,[3]
And in its fleetness left behind
The fury of the rushing wind:
Meet mansion for the good and great,
The holy, wise, and fortunate.
Throughout the chariot's vast extent
Were chambers wide and excellent,
All pure and lovely to the eyes
As moonlight shed from cloudless skies.
Fierce goblins, rovers of the night
Who cleft the clouds with swiftest flight
In countless hosts that chariot drew,
With earrings clashing as they flew.

CANTO IX.

THE LADIES' BOWER.

Where stately mansions rose around,
A palace fairer still he found,
Whose royal height and splendour showed
Where Rávan's self, the king, abode.
A chosen band with bow and sword
Guarded the palace of their lord,
Where Rákshas dames of noble race
And many a princess fair of face
Whom Rávan's arm had torn away
From vanquished kings in slumber lay.

---

[1] Pushpak from *pushpa* a flower. The car has been mentioned before in Rávan's expedition to carry off Sítá, Book III. Canto XXXV.

[2] Lakshmí is the wife of Vishnu and the Goddess of Beauty and Felicity. She rose, like Aphrodite, from the foam of the sea. For an account of her birth and beauty, see Book I. Canto XLV.

[1] Viśvakarmá is the architect of the Gods, the Hephæstos or Mulciber of the Indian heaven.

[2] Rávan in the resistless power which his long austerities had endowed him with, had conquered his brother Kuvera the God of Gold and taken from him his greatest treasure this enchanted car.

[3] Like Milton's heavenly car:
'Itself instinct with spirit.'

There jewelled arches high o'erhead
An ever-changing lustre shed
From ruby, pearl, and every gem
On golden pillars under them.
Delicious came the tempered air
That breathed a heavenly summer there,
Stealing through bloomy trees that bore
Each pleasant fruit in endless store.
No check was there from jealous guard,
No door was fast, no portal barred;
Only a sweet air breathed to meet
The stranger, as a host should greet
A wanderer of his kith and kin
And woo his weary steps within.
He stood within a spacious hall
With fretted roof and painted wall,
The giant Rávaṇ's boast and pride,
Loved even as a lovely bride.
'Twere long to tell each marvel there,
The crystal floor, the jewelled stair,
The gold, the silver, and the shine
Of chrysolite and almandine.
There breathed the fairest blooms of spring;
There flashed the proud swan's silver wing,
The splendour of whose feathers broke
Through fragrant wreaths of aloe smoke.
'Tis Indra's heaven,' the Vánar cried,
Gazing in joy from side to side;
'The home of all the Gods is this,
The mansion of eternal bliss.'
There were the softest carpets spread,
Delightful to the sight and tread,
Where many a lovely woman lay
O'ercome by sleep, fatigued with play.
The wine no longer cheered the feast,
The sound of revelry had ceased.
The tinkling feet no longer stirred,
No chiming of a zone was heard.
So when each bird has sought her nest,
And swans are mute and wild bees rest,
Sleep the fair lilies on the lake
Till the sun's kiss shall bid them wake.
Like the calm field of winter's sky
Which stars unnumbered glorify,
So shone and glowed the sumptuous room
With living stars that chased the gloom.
'These are the stars,' the chieftain cried,
'In autumn nights that earth-ward glide,
In brighter forms to reappear
And shine in matchless lustre here.'
With wondering eyes a while he viewed
Each graceful form and attitude.
One lady's head was backward thrown,
Bare was her arm and loose her zone.
The garland that her brow had graced
Hung closely round another's waist.
Here gleamed two little feet all bare
Of anklets that had sparkled there,
Here lay a queenly dame at rest
In all her glorious garments dressed,
There slept another whose small hand
Had loosened every tie and band,
In careless grace another lay
With gems and jewels cast away,
Like a young creeper when the tread
Of the wild elephant has spread
Confusion and destruction round,
And cast it flowerless to the ground.
Here lay a slumberer still as death,
Save only that her balmy breath
Raised ever and anon the lace
That floated o'er her sleeping face.
There, sunk in sleep, an amorous maid
Her sweet head on a mirror laid,
Like a fair lily bending till
Her petals rest upon the rill.
Another black-eyed damsel pressed
Her lute upon her heaving breast,
As though her loving arms were twined
Round him for whom her bosom pined.
Another pretty sleeper round
A silver vase her arms had wound,
That seemed, so fresh and fair and young
A wreath of flowers that o'er it hung.
In sweet disorder lay a throng
Weary of dance and play and song,
Where heedless girls had sunk to rest
One pillowed on another's breast,
Her tender cheek half seen beneath
Red roses of the falling wreath,
The while her long soft hair concealed
The beauties that her friend revealed.
With limbs at random interlaced
Round arm and leg and throat and waist,
That wreath of women lay asleep
Like blossoms in a careless heap.

CANTO X.

RÁVAṆ ASLEEP.

Apart a dais of crystal rose
With couches spread for soft repose,
Adorned with gold and gems of price
Meet for the halls of Paradise.
A canopy was o'er them spread
Pale as the light the moon beams shed,
And female figures,[1] deftly planned,
The faces of the sleepers fanned.
There on a splendid couch, asleep
On softest skins of deer and sheep,
Dark as a cloud that dims the day
The monarch of the giants lay,
Perfumed with sandal's precious scent
And gay with golden ornament.

[1] Women, says Válmíki. But the Commentator says that automatic figures only are meant. Women would have seen Hanumán and given the alarm.

His fiery eyes in slumber closed,
In glittering robes the king reposed
Like Mandar's mighty hill asleep
With flowery trees that clothe his steep.
Near and more near the Vánar drew
The monarch of the fiends to view,
And saw the giant stretched supine
Fatigued with play and drunk with wine.
While, shaking all the monstrous frame,
His breath like hissing serpents' came.
With gold and glittering bracelets gay
His mighty arms extended lay
Huge as the towering shafts that bear
The flag of Indra high in air.
Scars by Airávat's tusk impressed
Showed red upon his shaggy breast.
And on his shoulders were displayed
The dints the thunder-bolt had made.[1]
The spouses of the giant king
Around their lord were slumbering,
And, gay with sparkling earrings, shone
Fair as the moon to look upon.
There by her husband's side was seen
Mandodarí the favourite queen,
The beauty of whose youthful face
Beamed a soft glory through the place.
The Vánar marked the dame more fair
Than all the royal ladies there,
And thought, 'These rarest beauties speak
The matchless dame I come to seek.
Peerless in grace and splendour, she
The Maithil queen must surely be.'

CANTO XI.

THE BANQUET HALL.

But soon the baseless thought was spurned
And longing hope again returned :
'No: Ráma's wife is none of these,
No careless dame that lives at ease.
Her widowed heart has ceased to care
For dress and sleep and dainty fare.
She near a lover ne'er would lie
Though Indra wooed her from the sky.
Her own, her only lord, whom none
Can match in heaven, is Raghu's son.'
Then to the banquet hall intent
On strictest search his steps he bent.
He passed within the door, and found
Fair women sleeping on the ground,
Where wearied with the song, perchance,
The merry game, the wanton dance,
Each girl with wine and sleep oppressed
Had sunk her drooping head to rest.
That spacious hall from side to side
With noblest fare was well supplied,
There quarters of the boar, and here
Roast of the buffalo and deer.
There on gold plate, untouched as yet,
The peacock and the hen were set.
There deftly mixed with salt and curd
Was meat of many a beast and bird,
Of kid and porcupine and hare,
And dainties of the sea and air.
There wrought of gold, ablaze with shine
Of precious stones, were cups of wine.
Through court and bower and banquet hall
The Vánar passed and viewed them all ;
From end to end, in every spot,
For Sítá searched, but found her not.

CANTO XII.

THE SEARCH RENEWED.

Again the Vánar chief began
Each chamber, bower, and hall to scan.
In vain : he found not her he sought,
And pondered thus in bitter thought :
'Ah me the Maithil queen is slain:
She, ever true and free from stain,
The fiend's entreaty has denied,
And by his cruel hand has died.
Or has she sunk, by terror killed,
When first she saw the palace filled
With female monsters evil-miened
Who wait upon the robber fiend ?
No battle fought, no might displayed,
In vain this anxious search is made ;
Nor shall my steps, made slow by shame,
Because I failed to find the dame,
Back to our lord the king be bent,
For he is swift to punishment.
In every bower my feet have been,
The dames of Rávan have I seen ;
But Ráma's spouse I seek in vain,
And all my toil is fruitless pain.
How shall I meet the Vánar band
I left upon the ocean strand ?
How, when they bid me speak, proclaim
These tidings of defeat and shame?
How shall I look on Angad's eye?
What words will Jámbaván reply?
Yet dauntless hearts will never fail
To win success though foes assail,
And I this sorrow will subdue
And search the palace through and through,
Exploring with my cautious tread
Each spot as yet unvisited.'
Again he turned him to explore
Each chamber, hall, and corridor,
And arbour bright with scented bloom,
And lodge and cell and picture-room.

[1] Rávan had fought against Indra and the Gods, and his body was still scarred by the wounds inflicted by the tusks of Indra's elephant and by the fiery bolts of the Thunderer.

With eager eye and noiseless feet
He passed through many a cool retreat
Where women lay in slumber drowned;
But Sítá still was nowhere found.

CANTO XIII.

DESPAIR AND HOPE.

Then rapid as the lightning's flame
From Rávan's halls the Vánar came.
Each lingering hope was cold and dead,
And thus within his heart he said:
'Alas, my fruitless search is done:
Long have I toiled for Raghu's son;
And yet with all my care have seen
No traces of the ravished queen.
It may be, while the giant through
The lone air with his captive flew,
The Maithil lady, tender-souled,
Slipped struggling from the robber's hold,
And the wild sea is rolling now
O'er Sítá of the beauteous brow.
Or did she perish of alarm
When circled by the monster's arm?
Or crushed, unable to withstand
The pressure of that monstrous hand?
Or when she spurned his suit with scorn,
Her tender limbs were rent and torn,
And she, her virtue unsubdued,
Was slaughtered for the giant's food.
Shall I to Raghu's son relate
His well-beloved consort's fate,
My crime the same if I reveal
The mournful story or conceal?
If with no happier tale to tell
I seek our mountain citadel,
How shall I face our lord the king,
And meet his angry questioning?
How shall I greet my friends, and brook
The muttered taunt, the scornful look?
How to the son of Raghu go
And kill him with my tale of woe?
For sure the mournful tale I bear
Will strike him dead with wild despair,
And Lakshman, ever fond and true,
Will, undivided, perish too.
Bharat will learn his brother's fate,
And die of grief disconsolate,
And sad Śatrughna with a cry
Of anguish on his corpse will die.
Our king Sugríva, ever found,
True to each bond in honour bound,
Will mourn the pledge he vainly gave,
And die with him he could not save.
Then Rumá his divoted wife
For her dead lord will leave her life,
And Tárá, widowed and forlorn,
Will die in anguish, sorrow-worn.
On Angad too the blow will fall
Killing the hope and joy of all.
The ruin of their prince and king
The Vánars' souls with woe will wring,
And each, o'erwhelmed with dark despair,
Will beat his head and rend his hair.
Each, graced and honoured long, will miss
His careless life of easy bliss,
In happy troops will play no more
On breezy rock and shady shore,
But with his darling wife and child
Will seek the mountain top, and wild
With hopeless desolation, throw
Himself, his wife, and babe, below.
Ah no: unless the dame I find
I ne'er will meet my Vánar kind.
Here rather in some distant dell
A lonely hermit will I dwell,
Where roots and berries will supply
My humble wants until I die;
Or on the shore will raise a pyre
And perish in the kindled fire.
Or I will strictly fast until
With slow decay my life I kill,
And ravening dogs and birds of air
The limbs of Hanumán shall tear.
Here will I die, but never bring
Destruction on my race and king.
But still unsearched one grove I see
With many a bright Aśoka tree,
There will I enter in, and through
The tangled shade my search renew.
Be glory to the host on high,
The Sun and Moon who light the sky,
The Vasus[1] and the Maruts'[2] train,
Ádityas[3] and the Aśvins[4] twain.
So may I win success, and bring
The lady back with triumphing.'

CANTO XIV.

THE AŚOKA GROVE.

He cleared the barrier at a bound;
He stood within the pleasant ground,

[1] The Vasus are a class of eight deities, originally personifications of natural phenomena.

[2] The Maruts are the winds or Storm-Gods.

[3] The Ádityas were originally seven deities of the heavenly sphere of whom Varuṇa is the chief. The name Áditva was afterwards given to any God, specially to Súrya the Sun.

[4] The Aśvins are the Heavenly Twins, the Castor and Pollux of the Hindus.

And with delighted eyes surveyed
The climbing plants and varied shade.
He saw unnumbered trees unfold
The treasures of their pendent gold,
As, searching for the Maithil queen,
He strayed through alleys soft and green;
And when a spray he bent or broke
Some little bird that slept awoke.
Whene'er the breeze of morning blew,
Where'er a startled peacock flew,
The gaily coloured branches shed
Their flowery rain upon his head
That clung around the Vánar till
He seemed a blossom-covered hill.[1]
The earth, on whose fair bosom lay
The flowers that fell from every spray,
Was glorious as a lovely maid
In all her brightest robes arrayed.
He saw the breath of morning shake
The lilies on the rippling lake
Whose waves a pleasant lapping made
On crystal steps with gems inlaid.
Then roaming through the enchanted ground,
A pleasant hill the Vánar found,
And grottoes in the living stone
With grass and flowery trees o'ergrown.
Through rocks and boughs a brawling rill
Leapt from the bosom of the hill,
Like a proud beauty when she flies
From her love's arms with angry eyes.
He clomb a tree that near him grew
And leafy shade around him threw.
'Hence,' thought the Vánar, 'shall I see
The Maithil dame, if here she be,
These lovely trees, this cool retreat
Will surely tempt her wandering feet.
Here the sad queen will roam apart,
And dream of Ráma in her heart.'

CANTO XV.

SÍTÁ.

Fair as Kailása white with snow
He saw a palace flash and glow,
A crystal pavement gem-inlaid,
And coral steps and colonnade,
And glittering towers that kissed the skies,
Whose dazzling splendour charmed his eyes.
There pallid, with neglected dress,
Watched close by fiend and giantess,
Her sweet face thin with constant flow
Of tears, with fasting and with woe;
Pale as the young moon's crescent when
The first faint light returns to men:
Dim as the flame when clouds of smoke
The latent glory hide and choke;
Like Rohiní the queen of stars
Oppressed by the red planet Mars;
From her dear friends and husband torn,
Amid the cruel fiends, forlorn,
Who fierce-eyed watch around her kept,
A tender woman sat and wept.
Her sobs, her sighs, her mournful mien,
Her glorious eyes, proclaimed the queen.
'This, this is she,' the Vánar cried,
'Fair as the moon and lotus-eyed,
I saw the giant Rávan bear
A captive through the fields of air.
Such was the beauty of the dame;
Her form, her lips, her eyes the same.
This peerless queen whom I behold
Is Ráma's wife with limbs of gold.
Best of the sons of men is he,
And worthy of her lord is she.'

CANTO XVI.

HANUMÁN'S LAMENT.

Then, all his thoughts on Sítá bent,
The Vánar chieftain made lament:
'The queen to Ráma's soul endeared,
By Lakshman's pious heart revered,
Lies here,—for none may strive with Fate,
A captive, sad and desolate.
The brothers' might full well she knows,
And bravely bears the storm of woes,
As swelling Gangá in the rains
The rush of every flood sustains.
Her lord, for her, fierce Báli slew,
Virádha's monstrous might o'erthrew.
For her the fourteen thousand slain
In Janasthán bedewed the plain.
And if for her Ikshváku's son
Destroyed the world 'twere nobly done.
This, this is she, so far renowned,
Who sprang from out the furrowed ground,[1]
Child of the high-souled king whose sway
The men of Mithilá obey:
The glorious lady wooed and won
By Daśaratha's noblest son;
And now these sad eyes look on her
Mid hostile fiends a prisoner.
From home and every bliss she fled
By wifely love and duty led,
And, heedless of a wanderer's woes,
A life in lonely forests chose.
This, this is she so fair of mould,
Whose limbs are bright as burnished gold,

---

[1] The poet forgets that Hanumán has reduced himself to the size of a cat.

[1] Sítá 'not of woman born,' was found by King Janak as he was turning up the ground in preparation for a sacrifice. See Book II. Canto CXVIII.

Whose voice was ever soft and mild,
Who sweetly spoke and sweetly smiled.
O, what is Ráma's misery! how
He longs to see his darling now!
Pining for one of her fond looks
As one athirst for water-brooks.
Absorbed in woe the lady sees
No Rákshas guard, no blooming trees.
Her eyes are with her thoughts, and they
Are fixed on Ráma far away.'

CANTO XVII.

SÍTA'S GUARD.

His pitying eyes with tears bedewed,
The weeping queen again he viewed,
And saw around the prisoner stand
Her demon guard, a fearful band:
Some earless, some with ears that hung
Low as their feet and loosely swung:
Some fierce with single ears and eyes,
Some dwarfish, some of monstrous size:
Some with their dark necks long and thin
With hair upon the knotty skin:
Some with wild locks, some bald and bare,
Some covered o'er with bristly hair:
Some tall and straight, some bowed and bent
With every foul disfigurement:
All black and fierce with eyes of fire,
Ruthless and stern and swift to ire:
Some with the jackal's jaw and nose,
Some faced like boars and buffaloes:
Some with the heads of goats and kine,
Of elephants, and dogs, and swine:
With lions' lips and horses' brows,
They walked with feet of mules and cows:[1]
Swords, maces, clubs, and spears they bore
In hideous hands that reeked with gore,
And, never sated, turned afresh
To bowls of wine and piles of flesh.
Such were the awful guards who stood
Round Sítá in that lovely wood,
While in her lonely sorrow she
Wept sadly neath a spreading tree.
He watched the spouse of Ráma there
Regardless of her tangled hair,
Her jewels stripped from neck and limb,
Decked only with her love of him.

[1] Somewhat similarly has Ariosto described the band of monsters at the gate of the city of Alcina:

"Non fu veduta mai piú strana torma,
Piú monstruosi volti e peggio fatti;
Alcum dal collo in giú d'uomini han forma,
Con viso altri di simie, altri di gatti;
Stampano alcun con pié caprigni l'orma;
Alcuni sin centauri agili ed atti."

Orlando Furioso. Canto VI.

CANTO XVIII.

RÁVAN.

While from his shelter in the boughs
The Vánar looked on Ráma's spouse
He heard the gathered giants raise
The solemn hymn of prayer and praise.—
Priests skilled in rite and ritual, who
The Vedas and their branches[1] knew.
Then, as loud strains of music broke
His sleep, the giant monarch woke.
Swift to his heart the thought returned
Of the fair queen for whom he burned;
Nor could the amorous fiend control
The passion that absorbed his soul.
In all his brightest garb arrayed
He hastened to that lovely shade,
Where glowed each choicest flower and fruit,
And the sweet birds were never mute,
And tall deer bent their heads to drink
On the fair streamlet's grassy brink.
Near that Aśoka grove he drew,—
A hundred dames his retinue,
Like Indra with the thousand eyes
Girt with the beauties of the skies.
Some walked beside their lord to hold
The chouries, fans, and lamps of gold,
And others purest water bore
In golden urns, and paced before.
Some carried, piled on golden plates,
Delicious food of dainty cates;
Some wine in massive bowls whereon
The fairest gems resplendent shone.
Some by the monarch's side displayed,
Wrought like a swan, a silken shade:
Another beauty walked behind,
The sceptre to her care assigned.
Around the monarch gleamed the crowd
As lightnings flash about a cloud,
And each made music as she went
With zone and tinkling ornament.
Attended thus in royal state
The monarch reached the garden gate,
While gold and silver torches, fed
With scented oil a soft light shed.[2]

[1] The six *Angas* or subordinate branches of the Vedas are 1. *Sikshá*, the science of proper articulation and pronunciation: 2. *Chhandas*, metre: 3. *Vyákaraṇa*, linguistic analysis or grammar: 4. *Nirukta*, explanation of difficult Vedic words: 5. *Jyotisha*, Astronomy, or rather the Vedic Calendar: 6. *Kalpa*, ceremonial.

[2] There appears to be some confusion of time here. It was already morning when Hanumán entered the grove, and the torches would be needless.

He, while the flame of fierce desire
Burnt in his eyes like kindled fire,
Seemed Love incarnate in his pride,
His bow and arrows laid aside.[1]
His robe, from spot and blemish free
Like Amrit foamy from the sea,[2]
Hung down in many a loosened fold
Inwrought with flowers and bright with gold.
The Vánar from his station viewed,
Amazed, the wondrous multitude,
Where, in the centre of that ring
Of noblest women, stood the king,
As stands the full moon fair to view,
Girt by his starry retinue.

CANTO XIX.

SITÁ'S FEAR.

Then o'er the lady's soul and frame
A sudden fear and trembling came,
When, glowing in his youthful pride,
She saw the monarch by her side.
Silent she sat, her eyes depressed,
Her soft arms folded o'er her breast,
And,—all she could,—her beauties screened
From the bold gazes of the fiend.
There where the wild she-demons kept
Their watch around, she sighed and wept.
Then, like a severed bough, she lay
Prone on the bare earth in dismay,
The while her thoughts on love's fleet wings
Flew to her lord the best of kings.
She fell upon the ground, and there
Lay struggling with her wild despair,
Sad as a lady born again
To misery and woe and pain,
Now doomed to grief and low estate,
Once noble fair and delicate:
Like faded light of holy lore,
Like Hope when all her dreams are o'er:
Like ruined power and rank debased,
Like majesty of kings disgraced:
Like worship foiled by erring slips,
The moon that labours in eclipse:
A pool with all her lilies dead,
An army when its king has fled:
So sad and hopeless, wan and worn,
She lay among the fiends forlorn.

[1] Rávan is one of those beings who can "limb them as they will" and can of course assume the loveliest form to please human eyes as well as the terrific shape that suits the king of the Rákshases.

[2] White and lovely as the Amrit or nectar recovered from the depths of the Milky Sea when churned by the assembled Gods. See Book I. Canto XLV.

CANTO XX.

RÁVAN'S WOOING.

With amorous look and soft address
The fiend began his suit to press:
'Why wouldst thou, lady lotus-eyed,
From my fond glance those beauties hide!
Mine eager suit no more repel;
But love me, for I love thee well.
Dismiss, sweet dame, dismiss thy fear;
No giant and no man is near.
Ours is the right by force to seize
What dames soe'er our fancy please.[1]
But I with rude hands will not touch
A lady whom I love so much.
Fear not, dear queen: no fear is nigh:
Come, on thy lover's love rely.
Some little sign of favour show,
Nor lie enamoured of thy woe.
Those limbs upon the cold earth laid,
Those tresses twined in single braid,[2]
The fast and woe that wear thy frame,
Beseem not thee, O beauteous dame.
For thee the fairest wreaths were meant,
The sandal and the aloe's scent,
Rich ornaments and pearls of price,
And vesture meet for Paradise.
With dainty cates shouldst thou be fed,
And rest upon a sumptuous bed.
All festive joys to thee belong,
The music, and the dance and song.
Rise, pearl of women, rise and deck
With gems and chains thine arms and neck.
Shall not the dame I love be seen
In vesture worthy of a queen?
Methinks when thy sweet form was made
His hand the wise Creator stayed;
For never more could he design
A beauty meet to rival thine.
Come, let us love while yet we may,
For youth will fly and charms decay.
Come, cast thy grief and fear aside,
And be my love, my chosen bride.
The gems and jewels that my hand
Has reft from every plundered land,—
To thee I give them all this day,
And at thy feet my kingdom lay.

[1] Rávan in his magic car carrying off the most beautiful women reminds us of the magician in *Orlando Furioso*, possessor of the flying horse:

"Volando talor s'alza ne le stelle,
E poi quasi talor la terra rade;
E ne porta con lui tutte le belle
Donne che trova per quelle contrade."

[2] Indian women twisted their long hair in a single braid as a sign of mourning for their absent husbands.

The broad rich earth will I o'errun,
And leave no town unconquered, none;
Then of the whole an offering make
To Janak,[1] dear, for thy sweet sake.
In all the world no power I see
Of God or man can strive with me.
Of old the Gods and Asurs set
In terrible array I met:
Their scattered hosts to earth I beat,
And trod their flags beneath my feet.
Come, taste of bliss and drink thy fill,
And rule the slave who serves thy will.
Think not of wretched Ráma: he
Is less than nothing now to thee.
Stript of his glory, poor, dethroned,
A wanderer by his friends disowned,
On the cold earth he lays his head,
Or is with toil and misery dead.
And if perchance he lingers yet,
His eyes on thee shall ne'er be set.
Could he, that mighty monarch, who
Was named Hiraṇyakaśipu,
Could he who wore the garb of gold
Win Glory back from Indra's hold?[2]
O lady of the lovely smile,
Whose eyes the sternest heart beguile,
In all thy radiant beauty dressed
My heart and soul thou ravishest.
What though thy robe is soiled and worn,
And no bright gems thy limbs adorn,
Thou unadorned art dearer far
Than all my loveliest consorts are.
My royal home is bright and fair;
A thousand beauties meet me there.
But come, my glorious love, and be
The queen of all those dames and me.'

CANTO XXI.

SÍTÁ'S SCORN.

She thought upon her lord and sighed,
And thus in gentle tones replied:
'Beseems thee not, O King, to woo
A matron, to her husband true.
Thus vainly one might hope by sin
And evil deeds success to win.
Shall I, so highly born, disgrace
My husband's house, my royal race?

[1] Janak, king of Mithilá, was Sítá's father.

[2] Hiraṇyakaśipu was a king of the Daityas celebrated for his blasphemous impieties. When his pious son Prahláda praised Vishnu the Daitya tried to kill him, when the God appeared in the incarnation of the man-lion and tore the tyrant to pieces.

Shall I, a true and loyal dame,
Defile my soul with deed of shame?'
Then on the king her back she turned,
And answered thus the prayer she spurned:
'Turn, Rávaṇ, turn thee from thy sin;
Seek virtue's paths and walk therein.
To others dames be honour shown;
Protect them as thou wouldst thine own.
Taught by thyself, from wrong abstain
Which, wrought on thee, thy heart would pain.[1]
Beware: this lawless love of thine
Will ruin thee and all thy line;
And for thy sin, thy sin alone,
Will Lanká perish overthrown.
Dream not that wealth and power can sway
My heart from duty's path to stray.
Linked like the Day-God and his shine,
I am my lord's and he is mine.
Repent thee of thine impious deed;
To Ráma's side his consort lead.
Be wise: the hero's friendship gain,
Nor perish in his fury slain.
Go, ask the God of Death to spare,
Or red bolt flashing through the air,
But look in vain for spell or charm
To stay my Ráma's vengeful arm.
Thou, when the hero bends his bow,
Shalt hear the clang that heralds woe,
Loud as the clash when clouds are rent
And Indra's bolt to earth is sent.
Then shall his furious shafts be sped,
Each like a snake with fiery head,
And in their flight shall hiss and flame
Marked with the mighty archer's name.[2]
Then in the fiery deluge all
Thy giants round their king shall fall.'

[1] Do unto others as thou wouldst they should do unto thee, is a precept frequently occurring in the old Indian poems.

This charity is to embrace not human beings only, but bird and beast as well: "He prayeth best who loveth best all things both great and small."

[2] It was the custom of Indian warriors to mark their arrows with their ciphers or names, and it seems to have been regarded as a point of honour to give an enemy the satisfaction of knowing who had shot at him. This passage however contains, if my memory serves me well, the first mention in the poem of this practice, and as arrows have been so frequently mentioned and described with almost every conceivable epithet, its occurrence here seems suspicious. No mention of, or allusion to writing has hitherto occurred in the poem.

CANTO XXII.

RÁVAṆ'S THREAT.

Then anger swelled in Rávaṇ's breast,
Who fiercely thus the dame addressed:
'Tis ever thus: in vain we sue
To woman, and her favour woo.
A lover's humble words impel
Her wayward spirit to rebel.
The love of thee that fills my soul
Still keeps my anger in control,
As charioteers with bit and rein
The swerving of the steed restrain.
The love that rules me bids me spare
Thy forefeit life, O thou most fair.
For this, O Sítá, have I borne
The keen reproach, the bitter scorn,
And the fond love thou boastest yet
For that poor wandering anchoret;
Else had the words which thou hast said
Brought death upon thy guilty head.
Two months, fair dame, I grant thee still
To bend thee to thy lover's will.
If when that respite time is fled
Thou still refuse to share my bed,
My cooks shall mince thy limbs with steel
And serve thee for my morning meal.'[1]
The minstrel daughters of the skies
Looked on her woe with pitying eyes,
And sun-bright children of the Gods[2]
Consoled the queen with smiles and nods.
She saw, and with her heart at ease,
Addressed the fiend in words like these;
'Hast thou no friend to love thee, none
In all this isle to bid thee shun
The ruin which thy crime will bring
On thee and thine, O impious King?
Who in all worlds save thee could woo
Me, Ráma's consort pure and true,
As though he tempted with his love
Queen Sachí[3] on her throne above?
How canst thou hope, vile wretch, to fly
The vengeance that e'en now is nigh,
When thou hast dared, untouched by shame,
To press thy suit on Ráma's dame?
Where woods are thick and grass is high
A lion and a hare may lie;
My Ráma is the lion, thou
Art the poor hare beneath the bough.
Thou raillest at the lord of men,
But wilt not stand within his ken,
What! is that eye unstricken yet
Whose impious glance on me was set?
Still moves that tongue that would not spare
The wife of Daśaratha's heir?'
Then, hissing like a furious snake,
The fiend again to Sítá spake:
'Deaf to all prayers and threats art thou,
Devoted to thy senseless vow,
No longer respite will I give,
And thou this day shalt cease to live;
For I, as sunlight kills the morn,
Will slay thee for thy scathe and scorn.'
The Rákshas guard was summoned: all
The monstrous crew obeyed the call,
And hastened to the king to take
The orders which he fiercely spake:
'See that ye guard her well, and tame,
Like some wild thing, the stubborn dame,
Until her haughty soul be bent
By mingled threat and blandishment.'[1]
The monsters heard: away he strode,
And passed within his queens' abode.

[1] This threat in the same words occurs in Book III. Canto LVI.

[2] Rávaṇ carried off and kept in his palace not only earthly princesses but the daughters of Gods and Gandharvas.

[3] The wife of Indra.

[1] These four lines have occurred before. Book III. Canto LVI.

CANTO XXIII.

THE DEMONS' THREATS.

Then round the helpless Sítá drew
With fiery eyes the hideous crew,
And thus assailed her, all and each,
With insult, taunt, and threatening speech:
'What! can it be thou prizest not
This happy chance, this glorious lot,
To be the chosen wife of one
So strong and great, Pulastya's son?
Pulastya—thus have sages told—
Is mid the Lords of Life[2] enrolled.
Lord Brahmá's mind-born son was he,
Fourth of that glorious company.
Viśravas from Pulastya sprang,—
Through all the worlds his glory rang.
And of Viśravas, large-eyed dame!
Our king the mighty Rávaṇ came.
His happy consort thou mayst be:
Scorn not the words we say to thee.'
One awful demon, fiery-eyed,
Stood by the Maithil queen and cried:
'Come and be his, if thou art wise,
Who smote the sovereign of the skies,
And made the thirty Gods and three,[3]
O'ercome in furious battle, flee.

[2] Prajápatis are the ten lords of created beings first created by Brahmá; somewhat like the Demiurgi of the Gnostics.

[3] "This is the number of the Vedic divinities mentioned in the Rig-veda. In

Thy lover turns away with scorn
From wives whom grace and youth adorn.
Thou art his chosen consort, thou
Shalt be his pride and darling now.'
Another, Vikatá by name,
In words like these addressed the dame:
'The king whose blows, in fury dealt,
The Nágas[1] and Gandharvas[2] felt,
In battle's fiercest brunt subdued,
Has stood by thee and humbly wooed.
And wilt thou in thy folly miss
The glory of a love like this?
Scared by his eye the sun grows chill,
The wanderer wind is hushed and still.
The rains at his command descend,
And trees with new-blown blossoms bend.
His word the hosts of demons fear,
And wilt thou, dame, refuse to hear?
Be counselled; with his will comply,
Or, lady, thou shalt surely die.'

CANTO XXIV.

SÍTÁ'S REPLY.

Still with reproaches rough and rude
Those fiends the gentle queen pursued:
'What! can so fair a life displease,
To dwell with him in joyous ease?
Dwell in his bowers a happy queen
In silk and gold and jewels' sheen?
Still must thy woman fancy cling
To Ráma and reject our king?
Die in thy folly, or forget
That wretched wandering anchoret.
Come, Sitá, in luxurious bowers
Spend with our lord thy happy hours;
The mighty lord who makes his own
The treasures of the worlds o'erthrown.'
Then, as a tear bedewed her eye,
The hapless lady made reply:
'I loathe, with heart and soul detest
The shameful life your words suggest.
Eat, if you will, this mortal frame:
My soul rejects the sin and shame.
A homeless wanderer though he be,
In him my lord, my life I see,
And, till my earthly days be done,
Will cling to great Ikshváku's son.
Then with fierce eyes on Sítá set
They cried again with taunt and threat:
Each licking with her fiery tongue
The lip that to her bosom hung,
And menacing the lady's life
With axe, or spear or murderous knife:
'Hear, Sítá, and our words obey.
Or perish by our hands to-day,
Thy love for Raghu's son forsake,
And Rávan for thy husband take,
Or we will rend thy limbs apart
And banquet on thy quivering heart.
Now from her body strike the head,
And tell the king the dame is dead.
Then by our lord's commandment she
A banquet for our band shall be.
Come, let the wine be quickly brought
That frees each heart from saddening
thought.
Then to the western gate repair,
And we will dance and revel there.'

CANTO XXV.

SÍTÁ'S LAMENT.

On the bare earth the lady sank,
And trembling from their presence shrank
Like a strayed fawn, when night is dark,
And hungry wolves around her bark.

Ashṭaka I. Súkta XXXIV. the Rishi Hiranyastúpa invoking the Aśvins says: A' Násatyá tribhirekádaśairiha devebhiryátam: "O Násatyas (Aśvins) come hither with the thrice eleven Gods." And in Súkta XLV. the Rishi Praskanva addressing his hymn to Agni (ignis, fire), thus invokes him: "Lord of the red steeds, propitiated by our prayers lead hither the thirty-three Gods." This number must certainly have been the actual number in the early days of the Vedic religion; although it appears probable enough that the thirty-three Vedic divinities could not then be found co-ordinated in so systematic a way as they were arranged more recently by the authors of the Upanishads. In the later ages of Brahmanism the number went on increasing without measure by successive mythical and religious creations which peopled the Indian Olympus with abstract beings of every kind. But through lasting veneration of the word of the Veda the custom remained of giving the name of "the thirty-three Gods" to the immense phalanx of the multiplied deities." GORRESIO.

[1] Serpent-Gods who dwell in the regions under the earth.

[2] In the mythology of the epics the Gandharvas are the heavenly singers or musicians who form the orchestra at the banquets of the Gods, and they belong to the heaven of Indra in whose battles they share.

Then to a shady tree she crept,
And thought upon her lord and wept.
By fear and bitter woe oppressed
She bathed the beauties of her breast
With her hot tears' incessant flow,
And found no respite from her woe.
As shakes a plantain in the breeze
She shook, and fell on trembling knees;
While at each demon's furious look
Her cheek its native hue forsook.
She lay and wept and made her moan
In sorrow's saddest undertone,
And, wild with grief, with fear appalled,
On Ráma and his brother called:
'O dear Kauśalyá,[1] 'hear me cry!
Sweet Queen Sumitrá,[2] list my sigh!
True is the saw the wise declare:
Death comes not to relieve despair.
'Tis vain for dame or man to pray;
Death will not hear before his day;
Since I, from Ráma's sight debarred,
And tortured by my cruel guard,
Still live in hopeless woe to grieve
And loathe the life I may not leave.
Here, like a poor deserted thing,
My limbs upon the ground I fling,
And, like a bark beneath the blast,
Shall sink oppressed with woes at last.
Ah, blest are they, supremely blest,
Whose eyes upon my lord may rest;
Who mark his lion port, and hear
His gentle speech that charms the ear.
Alas, what antenatal crime,
What trespass of forgotten time
Weighs on my soul, and bids me bow
Beneath this load of misery now?'

CANTO XXVI.

SÍTÁ'S LAMENT.

'I Ráma's wife, on that sad day,
By Rávan's arm was borne away,
Seized, while I sat and feared no ill,
By him who wears each form at will.
A helpless captive, left forlorn
To demons' threats and taunts and scorn,
Here for my lord I weep and sigh.
And worn with woe would gladly die.
For what is life to me afar
From Ráma of the mighty car?
The robber in his fruitless sin
Would hope his captive's love to win.
My meaner foot shall never touch
The demon whom I loathe so much.
The senseless fool! he knows me not,
Nor the proud soul his love would blot.

[1] The mother of Ráma.
[2] The mother of Lakshman.

Yea, limb from limb will I be rent,
But never to his prayer consent:
Be burnt and perish in the fire,
But never meet his base desire.
My lord was grateful, true and wise,
And looked on woe with pitying eyes;
But now, recoiling from the strife,
He pities not his captive wife.
Alone in Janasthán he slew
The thousands of the Rákshas crew.
His arm was strong, his heart was brave,
Why comes he not to free and save?
Why blame my lord in vain surmise
He knows not where his lady lies.
O, if he knew, o'er land and sea
His feet were swift to set me free;
This Lanká, girdled by the deep,
Would fall consumed, a shapeless heap,
And from each ruined home would rise
A Rákshas widow's groans and cries.'

CANTO XXVII.

TRIJAṬÁ'S DREAM.

Their threats unfeared, their counsel spurned,
The demons' breasts with fury burned.
Some sought the giant king to bear
The tale of Sítá's fixt despair.
With threats and taunts renewed the rest
Around the weeping lady pressed.
But Trijaṭá, of softer mould,
A Rákshas matron wise and old,
With pity for the captive moved,
In words like these the fiends reproved:
'Me, me,' she cried, 'eat me, but spare
The spouse of Daśaratha's heir.
Last night I dreamt a dream; and still
The fear and awe my bosom chill;
For in that dream I saw foreshown
Our race by Ráma's hand o'erthrown.
I saw a chariot high in air,
Of ivory exceeding fair.
A hundred steeds that chariot drew
As swiftly through the clouds it flew,
And, clothed in white, with wreaths that shone,
The sons of Raghu rode thereon.
I looked and saw this lady here,
Clad in the purest white, appear
High on the snow-white hill whose feet
The angry waves of ocean beat.
And she and Ráma met at last
Like light and sun when night is past.
Again I saw them side by side:
On Rávan's car they seemed to ride,
And with the princely Lakshman flee
To northern realms beyond the sea.

Then Rávaṇ, shaved and shorn, besmeared
With oil from head to foot. appeared.
He quaffed, he raved: his robes were red:
Fierce was his eye, and bare his head.
I saw him from his chariot thrust;
I saw him rolling in the dust.
A woman came and dragged away
The stricken giant where he lay,
And on a car which asses drew
The monarch of our race she threw.
He rose erect, he danced and laughed,
With thirsty lips the oil he quaffed,
Then with wild eyes and streaming mouth
Sped on the chariot to the south.[1]
Then, dropping oil from every limb,
His sons the princes followed him,
And Kumbhakarṇa,[2] shaved and shorn,
Was southward on a camel borne.
Then royal Lanká reeled and fell
With gate and tower and citadel.
This ancient city, far-renowned:
All life within her walls was drowned;
And the wild waves of ocean rolled
O'er Lanká and her streets of gold.
Warned by these signs I bid you fly;
Or by the hand of Ráma die,
Whose vengeance will not spare the life
Of one who vexed his faithful wife.
Your bitter taunts and threats forgo:
Comfort the lady in her woe,
And humbly pray her to forgive;
For so you may be spared and live.'

CANTO XXX.[3]

HANUMÁN'S DELIBERATION.

The Vánar watched concealed: each word
Of Sítá and the fiends he heard,
And in a maze of anxious thought
His quick-conceiving bosom wrought:
'At length my watchful eyes have seen,
Pursued so long, the Maithil queen,
Sought by our Vánar hosts in vain
From east to west, from main to main.
A cautious spy have I explored
The palace of the Rákhshas lord,
And thoroughly learned, concealed from sight,
The giant monarch's power and might.
And now my task must be to cheer
The royal dame who sorrows here.
For if I go, and soothe her not,
A captive in this distant spot,
She, when she finds no comfort nigh,
Will sink beneath her woes and die.
How shall my tale, if unconsoled
I leave her, be to Ráma told?
How shall I answer Raghu's son,
'No message from my darling, none?'
The husband's wrath, to fury fanned,
Will scorch me lifeless where I stand.
Or if I urge my lord the king
To Lanká's isle his hosts to bring,
In vain will be his zeal, in vain
The toil, the danger, and the pain.
Yea, this occasion must I seize
That from her guard the lady frees,[1]
To win her ear with soft address
And whisper hope in dire distress.
Shall I, a puny Vánar, choose
The Sanskrit men delight to use?
If, as a man of Bráhman kind,
I speak the tongue by rules refined,
The lady, yielding to her fears,
Will think 'tis Rávan's voice she hears.
I must assume my only plan—
The language of a common[2] man.
Yet, if the lady sees me nigh,

---

[1] In the south is the region of Yama the God of Death, the place of departed spirits.

[2] Kumbhakarṇa was one of Rávaṇ's brothers.

[3] I omit the 28th and 29th Cantos as an unmistakeable interpolation. Instead of advancing the story it goes back to Canto XVII. containing a lamentation of Sítá after Rávaṇ has left her, and describes the the auspicious signs sent to cheer her, the throbbing of her left eye, arm, and side. The Canto is found in the Bengal recension. Gorresio translates it, and observes: "I think that Chapter XXVIII.—The Auspicious Signs—is an addition, a later interpolation by the Rhapsodists. It has no bond of connexion either with what precedes or follows it, and may be struck out not only without injury to, but positively to the advantage of the poem. The metre in which this chapter is written differs from that which is generally adopted in the course of the poem.'

[1] The guards are still in the grove, but they are asleep; and Sítá has crept to a tree at some distance from them.

[2] "As the reason assigned in these passages for not addressing Sítá in Sanskrit such as a Bráhman would use is not that she would not understand it, but that it would alarm her and be unsuitable to the speaker, we must take them as indicating that Sanskrit, if not spoken by women of the upper classes at the time when the Rámáyaṇa was written (whenever that may have been), was at least understood by them, and was commonly spoken by men of the priestly class, and other educated persons. By the Sanskrit proper to

In terror she will start and cry;
And all the demon band, alarmed,
Will come with various weapons armed,
With their wild shouts the grove will fill,
And strive to take me, or to kill.
And, at my death or capture, dies
The hope of Ráma's enterprise.
For none can leap, save only me,
A hundred leagues across the sea.
It is a sin in me, I own,
To talk with Janak's child alone,
Yet greater is the sin if I
Be silent, and the lady die.
First I will utter Ráma's name,
And laud the hero's gifts and fame.
Perchance the name she holds so dear
Will soothe the faithful lady's fear.'

CANTO XXXI.

HANUMAN'S SPEECH.

Then in sweet accents low and mild
The Vánar spoke to Janak's child:
'A noble king, by sin unstained,
The mighty Daśaratha reigned.
Lord of the warrior's car and steed,
The pride of old Ikshváku's seed.
A faithful friend, a blameless king,
Protector of each living thing.
A glorious monarch, strong to save,
Blest with the bliss he freely gave.
His son, the best of all who know
The science of the bended bow,
Was moon-bright Ráma, brave and strong,
Who loved the right and loathed the wrong.
Who ne'er from kingly duty swerved,
Loved by the lands his might preserved.
His feet the path of law pursued;
His arm rebellious foes subdued.
His sire's command the prince obeyed
And, banished, sought the forest shade,
Where with his wife and brother he
Wandered a saintly devotee.
There as he roamed the wilds he slew
The bravest of the Rákshas crew.
The giant king the prince beguiled,
And stole his consort, Janak's child.
Then Ráma roamed the country round,
And a firm friend, Sugríva, found,
Lord of the Vánar race, expelled
From his own realm which Báli held.
He conquered Báli and restored
The kingdom to the rightful lord.
Then by Sugríva's high decree
The Vánar legions searched for thee,
Sampáti's counsel bade me leap
A hundred leagues across the deep.
And now my happy eyes have seen
At last the long-sought Maithil queen.
Such was the form, the eye, the grace
Of her whom Ráma bade me trace.'
He ceased: her flowing locks she drew
To shield her from a stranger's view;
Then, trembling in her wild surprise,
Raised to the tree her anxious eyes.

an [ordinary] man, alluded to in the second passage, may perhaps be understood not a language in which words different from Sanskrit were used, but the employment of formal and elaborate diction." MUIR'S *Sanskrit Texts*, Part II. p. 166.

CANTO XXXII.

SÍTÁ'S DOUBT.

Her eyes the Maithil lady raised
And on the monkey speaker gazed.
She looked, and trembling at the sight
Wept bitter tears in wild affright.
She shank a while with fear distraught,
Then, nerved again, the lady thought:
'Is this a dream mine eyes have seen,
This creature, by our laws unclean?
O, may the Gods keep Ráma, still,
And Lakshman, and my sire, from ill!
It is no dream: I have not slept,
But, trouble-worn, have watched and wept
Afar from that dear lord of mine
For whom in ceaseless woe I pine,
No art may soothe my wild distress
Or lull me to forgetfulness.
I see but him: my lips can frame
No syllable but Ráma's name.
Each sight I see, each sound I hear,
Brings Ráma to mine eye or ear.
The wish was in my heart, and hence
The sweet illusion mocked my sense.
'Twas but a phantom of the mind,
And yet the voice was soft and kind.
Be glory to the Eternal Sire,[1]
Be glory to the Lord of Fire,
The mighty Teacher in the skies,[2]
And Indra with his thousand eyes,
And may they grant the truth to be
E'en as the words that startled me.'

[1] Svayambhu, the Self-existent, Brahmá.

[2] Vrihaspati or Váchaspati, the Lord of Speech and preceptor of the Gods.

CANTO XXXIII.

THE COLLOQUY.

Down from the tree Hanúmán came
And humbly stood before the dame.
Then joining reverent palm to palm
Addressed her thus with words of balm:
'Why should the tears of sorrow rise,
Sweet lady, to those lovely eyes,
As when the wind-swept river floods
Two half expanded lotus buds?
Who art thou, O most fair of face?
Of Asur,[1] or celestial race?
Did Nága mother give thee birth?
For sure thou art no child of earth.
Do Rudras[2] claim that heavenly form?
Or the swift Gods[3] who ride the storm?
Or art thou Rohiṇí[4] the blest,
That star more lovely than the rest,—
Reft from the Moon thou lovest well
And doomed a while on earth to dwell?
Or canst thou, fairest wonder, be
The starry queen Arundhatí,[5]
Fled in thy wrath or jealous pride
From her dear lord Vaśishṭha's side?
Who is the husband, father, son
Or brother, O thou loveliest one,
Gone from this world in heaven to dwell,
For whom those eyes with weeping swell?
Yet, by the tears those sweet eyes shed,
Yet, by the earth that bears thy tread,[6]
By calling on a monarch's name,
No Goddess but a royal dame.
Art thou the queen, fair lady, say,
Whom Rávaṇ stole and bore away?
Yea, by that agony of woe,
That form unrivalled here below,
That votive garb, thou art, I ween,
King Janak's child and Ráma's queen.'

Hope at the name of Ráma woke,
And thus the gentle lady spoke:
'I am that Sítá wooed and won
By Daśaratha's royal son,
The noblest of Ikshváku's line;
And every earthly joy was mine.
But Ráma left his royal home
In Daṇḍak's tangled wilds to roam.
Where with Sumitrá's son and me,
He lived a saintly devotee.
The giant Rávaṇ came with guile
And bore me thence to Lanká's isle.
Some respite yet the fiend allows,
Two months of life, to Ráma's spouse.
Two moons of hopeless woe remain.
And then the captive will be slain.'

CANTO XXXIV.

HANUMÁN'S SPEECH.

Thus spoke the dame in mournful mood,
And Hanumán his speech renewed:
'O lady, by thy lord's decree
I come a messenger to thee.
Thy lord is safe with steadfast friends,
And greeting to his queen he sends,
And Lakshmaṇ, ever faithful bows
His reverent head to Ráma's spouse.'
Through all her frame the rapture ran,
As thus again the dame began:
'Now verily the truth I know
Of the wise saw of long ago:
'Once only in a hundred years
True joy to living man appears.'
He marked her rapture-beaming hue,
And nearer to the lady drew.
But at each onward step he took
Suspicious fear her spirit shook.
'Alas, Alas,' she cried in fear,
'False is the tale I joyed to hear.
'Tis Rávaṇ, 'tis the fiend, who tries
To mock me with a new disguise.
If thou, to wring my woman's heart,
Hast changed thy shape by magic art,
And wouldst a helpless dame beguile,
The wicked deed is doubly vile.
But no: that fiend thou canst not be:
Such joy I had from seeing thee.
But if my fancy does not err,
And thou art Ráma's messenger,
The glories of my lord repeat:
For to these ears such words are sweet.'
The Vánar knew the lady's thought,[1]
And gave the answer fondly sought:

---

[1] The Asurs were the fierce enemies of the Gods.

[2] The Rudras are manifestations of Śiva.

[3] The Maruts or Storm Gods.

[4] Rohiṇí is an asterism personified as the daughter of Daksha and the favourite wife of the Moon. The chief star in the constellation is Aldebaran.

[5] Arundhatí was the wife of the great sage Vaśishṭha, and regarded as the pattern of conjugal excellence. She was raised to the heavens as one of the Pleiades.

[6] The Gods do not shed tears; nor do they touch the ground when they walk or stand. Similarly Milton's angels marched above the ground and "the passive air upbore their nimble tread."

Virgil's 'vera incessu patuit dea' may refer to the same belief.

[1] That a friend of Ráma would praise him as he should be praised, and that if the stranger were Rávaṇ in disguise he would avoid the subject.

'Bright as the sun that lights the sky,
Dear as the Moon to every eye.
He scatters blessings o'er the land
Like bounties from Vaiśravaṇ's[1] hand.
Like Vishṇu strong and unsubdued,
Unmatched in might and fortitude.
Wise, truthful as the Lord of Speech,
With gentle words he welcomes each.
Of noblest mould and form is he,
Like love's incarnate deity.
He quells the fury of the foe,
And strikes when justice prompts the blow.
Safe in the shadow of his arm
The world is kept from scathe and harm.
Now soon shall Rávaṇ rue his theft,
And fall, of realm and life bereft.
For Ráma's wrathful hand shall wing
His shafts against the giant king.
The day, O Maithil Queen, is near
When he and Lakshmaṇ will be here,
And by their side Sugríva lead
His countless hosts of Vánar breed.
Sugríva's servant, I, by name
Hanúmán, by his order came.
With desperate leap I crossed the sea
To Lanká's isle in search of thee.
No traitor, gentle dame, am I:
Upon my word and faith rely.'

CANTO XXXV.

HANUMAN'S SPEECH.

With joyous heart she heard him tell
Of the great lord she loved so well,
And in sweet accents, soft and low,
Spoke, half forgetfool of her woe:
'How didst thou stand by Ráma's side?
How came my lord and thou allied?
How met the people of the wood
With men on terms of brotherhood?
Declare each grace and regal sign
That decks the lords of Raghu's line.
Each circumstance and look relate:
Tell Ráma's form and speech, and gait.'
'Thy fear and doubt,' he cried, 'dispelled,
Hear, lady, what mine eyes beheld.
Hear the imperial signs that grace
The glory of Ikshváku's race.
With moon-bright face and lotus eyes,
Most beautiful and good and wise,
With sun-like glory round his head,
Long-suffering as the earth we tread,
He from all foes his realm defends,
Yea, o'er the world his care extends.
He follows right in all his ways,
And ne'er from royal duty strays.
He knows the lore that strengthens kings;
His heart to truth and honour clings.
Each grace and gift of form and mind
Adorns that prince of human kind;
And virtues like his own endue
His brother ever firm and true.
O'er all the land they roamed distaught,
And thee with vain endeavour sought,
Until at length their wandering feet
Trod wearily our wild retreat.
Our banished king Sugríva spied
The princes from the mountain side.
By his command I sought the pair
And led them to our monarch there.
Thus Ráma and Sugríva met,
And joined the bonds that knit them yet,
When each besought the other's aid,
And friendship and alliance made.
An arrow launched from Ráma's bow
Laid Báli dead, Sugríva's foe.
Then by commandment of our lord
The Vánar hosts each land explored.
We reached the coast: I crossed the sea,
And found my way at length to thee.'[1]

CANTO XXXVI.

RÁMA'S RING.

'Receive,' he cried, 'this precious ring,[2]
Sure token from thy lord the king:
The golden ring he wont to wear:
See, Ráma's name engraven there.'
Then, as she took the ring he showed,
The tears that spring of rapture flowed.
She seemed to touch the hand that sent
The dearly valued ornament,
And with her heart again at ease,
Replied in gentle words like these:
'O thou, whose soul no fears deter,
Wise, brave, and faithful messenger!
And hast thou dared, o'er wave and foam,
To seek me in the giants' home?
In thee, true messenger, I find
The noblest of thy woodland kind,
Who couldst, unmoved by terror, brook
On Rávaṇ, king of fiends, to look.

---

[1] Kuvera the God of Gold.

[1] Sítá of course knows nothing of what has happened to Ráma since the time when she was carried away by Rávaṇ. The poet therefore thinks it necessary to repeat the whole story of the meeting between Ráma and Sugríva, the defeat of Báli, and subsequent events. I give the briefest possible outline of the story.

[2] DE GUBERNATIS thinks that this ring which the Sun Ráma sends to the Dawn Sítá is a symbol of the sun's disc.

Now may we commune here as friends,
For he whom royal Ráma sends
Must needs be one in danger tried,
A valiant, wise, and faithful guide.
Say, is it well with Ráma still?
Lives Lakshman yet untouched by ill?
Then why should Ráma's hand be slow
To free his consort from her woe?
Why spare to burn, in search of me,
The land encircled by the sea?
Can Bharat send no army out
With banners, cars and battle shout?
Cannot thy king Sugríva lend
His legions to assist his friend?'

His hands upon his head he laid
And thus again his answer made:
'Not yet has Ráma learnt where lies
His lady of the lotus eyes,
Or he like Indra from the sky
To Śachí's[1] aid, to thee would fly.
Soon will he hear the tale, and then,
Roused to revenge, the lord of men
Will to the giants' island lead
Fierce myriads of the woodland breed,
Bridging his conquering way, and make
The town a ruin for thy sake.
Believe my words, sweet dame; I swear
By roots and fruit, my woodland fare,
By Meru's peak and Vindhya's chain,
And Mandar of the Milky Main,
Soon shalt thou see thy lord, though now
He waits upon Prasravaṇ's[2] brow,
Come glorious as the breaking morn,
Like Indra on Airávat[3] borne.
For thee he looks with longing eyes;
The wood his scanty food supplies.
For thee his brow is pale and worn,
For thee are meat and wine forsworn.
Thine image in his heart he keeps,
For thee by night he wakes and weeps.
Or if perchance his eyes he close
And win brief respite from his woes,
E'en then the name of Sítá slips
In anguish from his murmuring lips.
If lovely flowers or fruit he sees,
Which women love, upon the trees,
To thee, to thee his fancy flies,
And 'Sítá! O my love!' he cries.'

[1] Śachí is the loved and lovely wife of Indra, and she is taken as the type of a woman protected by a jealous and all-powerful husband.

[2] The mountain near Kishkindhá.

[3] Airávat is the mighty elephant on which Indra delights to ride.

CANTO XXXVII.

SÍTÁ'S SPEECH.

'Thou bringest me,' she cried again,
'A mingled draught of bliss and pain;
Bliss, that he wears me in his heart,
Pain, that he wakes and weeps apart.
O, see how Fate is king of all,
Now lifts us high, now bids us fall,
And leads a captive bound with cord
The meanest slave, the proudest lord.
Thus even now Fate's stern decree
Has struck with grief my lord and me.
Say, how shall Ráma reach the shore
Of sorrow's waves that rise and roar,
A shipwrecked sailor, wellnigh drowned
In the wild sea that foams around?
When will he smite the demon down,
Lay low in dust the giants' town,
And, glorious from his foes' defeat,
His wife, his long-lost Sítá, meet?
Go, bid him speed to smite his foes
Before the year shall reach its close.
Ten months are fled: but two remain,
Then Ravaṇ's captive must be slain.
Oft has Vibhíshaṇ,[1] just and wise,
Besought him to restore his prize.
But deaf is Rávaṇ's senseless ear:
His brother's rede he will not hear.
Vibhíshaṇ's daughter[2] loves me well:
From her I learnt the tale I tell.
Avindhya[3] prudent, just, and old,
The giant's fall has oft foretold;
But Fate impels him to despise
His word on whom he most relies.
In Ráma's love I rest secure,
For my fond heart is true and pure,
And him, my noblest lord, I deem
In valour, power, and might supreme.'

As from her eyes the waters ran,
The Vánar chief again began:
'Yea, Ráma, when he hears my tale,
Will with our hosts these walls assail.
Or I myself, O Queen, this day
Will bear thee from the fiend away,
Will lift thee up, and take thee hence
To him thy refuge and defence;
Will take thee in my arms, and flee
To Ráma far beyond the sea;
Will place thee on Prasravaṇ hill
Where Raghu's son is waiting still.'

[1] Vibhíshaṇ is the wicked Rávaṇ's good brother.

[2] Her name is Kalá, or in the Bengal recension Nandá.

[3] One of Rávaṇ's chief councillors.

'How canst thou bear me hence?' she cried,
'The way is long, the sea is wide.
To bear my very weight would be
A task too hard for one like thee.'[1]
Swift rose before her startled eyes
The Vánar in his native size,
Like Mandar's hill or Meru's height,
Encircled with a blaze of light.
'O come,' he cried, 'thy fears dispel,
Nor doubt that I will bear thee well.
Come, in my strength and care confide,
And sit in joy by Ráma's side.'
Again she spake: 'I know thee now,
Brave, resolute, and strong art thou;
In glory like the Lord of Fire
With storm-swift feet which naught may tire
But yet with thee I may not fly:
For, borne so swiftly through the sky,
Mine eyes would soon grow faint and dim,
My dizzy brain would reel and swim,
My yielding arms relax their hold,
And I in terror uncontrolled
Should fall into the raging sea
Where hungry sharks would feed on me.
Nor can I touch, of free accord,
The limbs of any save my lord.
If, by the giant forced away,
In his enfolding arms I lay,
Not mine, O Vánar, was the blame;
What could I do, a helpless dame?
Go, to my lord my message bear,
And bid him end my long despair.'

CANTO XXXVIII.

SÍTÁ'S GEM.

Again the Vánar chief replied,
With her wise answer satisfied:
'Well hast thou said: thou canst not brave
The rushing wind, the roaring wave.
Thy woman's heart would sink with fear
Before the ocean shore were near.
And for thy dread lest limb of thine
Should for a while be touched by mine,
The modest fear is worthy one
Whose cherished lord is Raghu's son.
Yet when I sought to bear thee hence
I spoke the words of innocence,
Impelled to set the captive free
By friendship for thy lord and thee.
But if with me thou wilt not try
The passage of the windy sky,
Give me a gem that I may show,
Some token which thy lord may know.'
Again the Maithil lady spoke,
While tears and sobs her utterance broke:
'The surest of all signs is this,
To tell the tale of vanished bliss.
Thus in my name to Ráma speak:
'Remember Chitrakúṭa's peak,
And the green margin of the rill[1]
That flows beside that pleasant hill,
Where thou and I together strayed
Delighting in the tangled shade.
There on the grass I sat with thee
And laid my head upon thy knee.
There came a greedy crow and pecked
The meat I waitd to protect.
And, heedless of the clods I threw,
About my head in circles flew,
Until by darling hunger pressed
He boldly pecked me on the breast.
I ran to thee in rage and grief
And prayed for vengeance on the thief.
Then Ráma[2] from his slumber rose
And smiled with pity at my woes.
Upon my bleeding breast he saw
The scratches made by beak and claw.
He laid an arrow on his bow,
And launched it at the shameless crow.
That shaft, with magic power endued,
The bird, where'er he flew, pursued,
Till back to Raghu's son he fled
And bent at Ráma's feet his head.[3]
Couldst thou for me with anger stirred
Launch that dire shaft upon a bird,
And yet canst pardon him who stole
The darling of thy heart and soul?
Rise up, O bravest of the brave,
And come in all thy might to save.
Come with the thunders of thy bow,
And smite to earth the Rákshas foe.'
She ceased; and from her glorious hair
She took a gem that sparkled there:
A token which her husband's eyes
With eager love would recognize.
His head the Vánar envoy bent
In low obeisance reverent,
And on his finger bound the gem
She loosened from her diadem.

[1] Hanumán when he entered the city had in order to escape observation condensed himself to the size of a cat.

[1] The brook Mandákiní, not far from Chitrakúṭa where Ráma sojourned for a time.

[2] The poet here changes from the second person to the third.

[3] The whole long story is repeated with some slight variations and additions from Book II. Canto XCVI. I give here only the outline.

CANTO XLI.[1]

THE RUIN OF THE GROVE.

Dismissed with every honour due
The Vánar from the spot withdrew.
Then joyous thought the Wind-God's son:
'The mighty task is wellnigh done.
The three expedients I must leave;
The fourth alone can I achieve.[2]
These dwellers in the giants' isle
No arts of mine can reconcile.
I cannot bribe: I cannot sow
Dissension mid the Rákshas foe.
Arts, gifts, address, these fiends despise;
But force shall yet their king chastise.
Perchance he may relent when all
The bravest of his chieftains fall.
This lovely grove will I destroy,
The cruel Rávaṇ's pride and joy.
The garden where he takes his ease
Mid climbing plants and flowery trees
That lift their proud tops to the skies,
Dear to the tyrant as his eyes.
Then will he rouse in wrath, and lead
His legions with the car and steed
And elephants in long array,
And seek me thirsty for the fray.
The Rákshas legions will I meet,
And all his bravest host defeat;
Then, glorious from the bloody plain,
Turn to my lord the king again.'

Then every lovely tree that bore
Fair blossoms, from the soil he tore,
Till each green bough that lent its shade
To singing birds on earth was laid.
The wilderness he left a waste,
The fountains shattered and defaced:
O'erthrew and levelled with the ground
Each shady seat and pleasure-mound.
Each arbour clad with climbing bloom,
Each grotto, cell, and picture room,
Each lawn by beast and bird enjoyed,
Each walk and terrace was destroyed.
And all the place that was so fair
Was left a ruin wild and bare,
As if the fury of the blast
Or raging fire had o'er it passed.

CANTO XLII.

THE GIANTS ROUSED.

The cries of startled birds, the sound
Of tall trees crashing to the ground,
Struck with amaze each giant's ear,
And filled the isle with sudden fear.
Then, wakened by the crash and cries,
The fierce shefiends unclosed their eyes,
And saw the Vánar where he stood
Amid the devastated wood.
The more to scare them with the view
To size immense the Vánar grew;
And straight the Rákshas warders cried
Janak's daughter terrified:
Whose envoy, whence, and who is he,
Why has he come to talk with thee?
Speak, lady of the lovely eyes,
And let not fear thy joy disguise.'

Then thus replied the Maithil dame
Of noble soul and perfect frame:
'Can I discern, with scanty skill,
These fiends who change their forms at will?
'Tis yours to say: your kin you meet;
A serpent knows a serpent's feet.

I weet not who he is: the sight
Has filled my spirit with affright.'
Some pressed round Sítá in a ring;
Some bore the story to their king:
'A mighty creature of our race,
In monkey form, has reached the place.
He came within the grove,' they cried,
'He stood and talked by Sítá's side,
He comes from Indra's court to her,
Or is Kuvera's messenger;
Or Ráma sent the spy to seek
His consort, and her wrongs to wreak.
His crushing arm, his trampling feet
Have marred and spoiled that dear retreat,
And all the pleasant place which thou
So lovest is a ruin now.
The tree where Sítá sat alone
Is spared where all are overthrown.
Perchance he saved the dame from harm:
Perchance the toil had numbed his arm.'

Then flashed the giant's eye with fire
Like that which lights the funeral pyre.
He bade his bravest Kinkars[1] speed

---

[1] I omit two Cantos of dialogue. Sítá tells Hanumán again to convey her message to Ráma and bid him hasten to rescue her. Hanumán replies as before that there is no one on earth equal to Ráma, who will soon come and destroy Rávaṇ. There is not a new idea in the two Cantos: all is reiteration.

[2] The expedients to vanquish an enemy or to make him come to terms are said to be four: conciliation, gifts, disunion, and force or punishment. Hanumán considers it useless to employ the first three and resolves to punish Rávaṇ by destroying his pleasure-grounds.

[1] Kinkar means the special servant of a sovereign, who receives his orders im-

And to his feet the spoiler lead.
Forth from the palace, at his hest,
Twice forty thousand warriors pressed,
Burning for battle, strong and fierce,
With clubs to crush and swords to pierce.
They saw Hanumán near a porch,
And, thick as moths around a torch,
Rushed on the foe with wild attacks
Of mace and club and battle-axe.
As round him pressed the Rákshas crowd,
The wondrous monkey roared aloud,
That birds fell headlong from the sky:
Then spake he with a mighty cry:
'Long life to Daśaratha's heir,
And Lakshmaṇ, ever-glorious pair!
Long life to him who rules our race,
Preserved by noblest Ráma's grace!
I am the slave of Kosal's king,[1]
Whose wondrous deeds the minstrels sing.
Hanúmán I, the Wind-God's seed:
Beneath this arm the foemen bleed.
I fear not, unapproached in might,
A thousand Rávaṇs ranged for fight,
Although in furious hands they rear
The hill and tree for sword and spear.
I will, before the giants' eyes,
Their city and their king chastise;
And, having communed with the dame,
Depart in triumph as I came.'

At that terrific roar and yell
The heart of every giant fell.
But still their king's command they feared,
And pressed around with arms upreared.
Beside the porch a club was laid:
The Vánar caught it up, and swayed
The weapon round his head, and slew
The foremost of the Rákshas crew.
Thus Indra vanquished, thousand-eyed,
The Daityas who the Gods defied.
Then on the porch Hanúmán sprang,
And loud his shout of triumph rang.
The giants looked upon the dead,
And turning to their monarch fled.
And Rávan with his spirit wrought
To frenzy by the tale they brought,
Urged to the fight Prahasta's son,
Of all his chiefs the mightiest one.

mediately from his master. The Bengal recension gives these Rákskases an epithet which the Commentator explains 'as generated in the mind of Brahmá.'

[1] Ráma *de jure* King of Kosal of which Ayodhyá was the capital.

CANTO XLIII.

THE RUIN OF THE TEMPLE.

The Wind-God's son a temple[1] scaled
Which, by his fury unassailed,
High as the hill of Meru, stood
Amid the ruins of the wood;
And in his fury thundered out
Again his haughty battle-shout:
'I am the slave of Kosal's king
Whose wondrous deeds the minstrels sing.'
Forth hurried, by that shout alarmed,
The warders of the temple armed
With every weapon haste supplied,
And closed him in on every side,
With bands that strove to pierce and strike
With shaft and axe and club and pike.
Then from its base the Vánar tore
A pillar with the weight it bore.
Against the wall the mass he dashed,
And forth the flames in answer flashed,
That wildly ran o'er roofs and wall
In hungry rage consuming all.
He whirled the pillar round his head
And struck a hundred giants dead.
Then high upheld on air he rose
And called in thunder to his foes:
'A thousand Vánar chiefs like me
Roam at their will o'er land and sea.
Terrific might we all possess:
Our stormy speed is limitless.
And all, unconquered in the fray,
Our king Sugríva's word obey.
Backed by his bravest myriads, he
Our warrior lord will cross the sea.
Then Lanká's lofty towers, and all
Your hosts and Rávaṇ's self shall fall.
None shall be left unslaughtered; none
Who braves the wrath of Raghu's son.'

CANTO XLIV.

JAMBUMÁLÍ'S DEATH.

Then Jambumálí, pride and boast
For valour of the Rákshas host,
Prahasta's son supremely brave,
Obeyed the hest that Rávaṇ gave:
Fierce warrior with terrific teeth,
With saguine robes and brilliant wreath.
A bow like Indra's own,[2] and store

[1] *Chaityaprásáda* is explained by the Commentator as the place where the Gods of the Rákshases were kept. Gorresio translates it by 'un grande edificio.'

[2] The bow of Indra is the rainbow.

Of glittering shafts the chieftain bore.
And ever as the string he tried
The weapon with a roar replied,
Loud as the crashing thunder sent
By him who rules the firmament.
Soon as the foeman came in view
Borne on a car which asses drew.
The Vánar chieftain mighty-voiced
Shouted in triumph and rejoiced.
Prahasta's son his bow-string drew,
And swift the winged arrows flew.
One in the face the Vánar smote,
Another quivered in his throat.
Ten from the deadly weapon sent
His brawny arms and shoulders rent.
Then as he felt each galling shot
The Vánar's rage waxed fiercely hot.
He looked, and saw a mass of stone
That lay before his feet o'erthrown.
The mighty block he raised and threw,
And crashing through the air it flew.
But Jambumálí shunned the blow,
And rained fresh arrows from his bow.
The Vánar's limbs were red with gore:
A Sál tree from the earth he tore,
And, ere he hurled it undismayed,
Above his head the missile swayed.
But shafts from Jambumálí's bow
Cut through it ere his hand could throw,
And thigh and arm and chest and side
With streams of rushing blood were dyed.
Still unsubdued though wounded oft
The shattered trunk he raised aloft,
And down with well-directed aim
On Jambumálí's chest it came.
There crushed upon the trampled grass
He lay an undistinguished mass;
The foeman's eye no more could see
His head or chest or arm or knee;
And bow and car and steeds[1] and store
Of glittering shafts were seen no more.
When Jambumáli's death he heard,
King Rávan's heart with rage was stirred.
And forth his general's sons he sent,
For power and might preëminent.

CANTO XLV.

THE SEVEN DEFEATED.

Forth went the seven in brave attire,
In glory brilliant as the fire,
Impetuous chiefs with massive bows,
The quellers of a host of foes:
Trained from their youth in martial lore,
And masters of the arms they bore:
Each emulous and fiercely bold.
And banners wrought with glittering gold
Waved o'er their chariots, drawn at speed
By coursers of the noblest breed.
On through the ruins of the grove
At Hanumán they fiercely drove,
And from the ponderous bows they strained
A shower of deadly arrows rained.
Then scarce was seen the Vánar's form
Enveloped in the arrowy storm.
So stands half veiled the Mountains' King
When rainy clouds about him cling.
By nimble turn, by rapid bound
He shunned the shafts that rained around,
Eluding, as in air he rose,
The rushing chariots of his foes.
The mighty Vánar undismayed
Amid his archer foemen played,
As plays the frolic wind on high
Mid bow-armed[1] clouds that fill the sky.
He raised a mighty roar and yell
That fear on all the army fell,
And then, his warrior soul aglow
With fury, rushed upon the foe,
Some with his open hand he beat
To death, and trampled with his feet;
Some with fierce nails he rent and slew,
And others with his fists o'erthrew;
Some with his legs, as on he rushed,
Some with his bulky chest he crushed:
While some struck senseless by his roar
Dropped on the ground and breathed no more.
The remnant, seized with sudden dread,
Turned from the grove and wildly fled.
The trampled earth was thickly strown
With steed and car and flag o'erthrown,
And the red blood in rivers flowed
From slaughtered fiends o'er path and road.

CANTO XLVI.

THE CAPTAINS.

Mad with the rage of injured pride
King Rávan summoned to his side
The valiant five who led his host,
Supreme in war and honoured most.
'Go forth,' he cried, 'with car and steed,
And to my feet this monkey lead.
But watch each chance of time and place
To seize this thing of silvan race.
For from his wondrous exploits he
No monkey of the woods can be,

[1] We were told a few lines before that the chariot of Jambumálí was drawn by asses. Here horses are spoken of. The Commentator notices the discrepancy and says that by horses asses are meant.

[1] Armed with the bow of Indra, the rainbow.

But some new kind of creature meant
To work us woe, by Indra sent.
Gandharvas, Nágas, and the best
Of Yakshas have our might confessed.
Have we not challenged and subdued
The whole celestial multitude?
Yet will you not, if you are wise,
A chief of monkey race despise.
For I myself have Báli known,
And King Sugríva's power I own.
But none of all their woodland throng
Was half so terrible and strong.'
  Obedient to the words he spake
They hastened forth the foe to take.
Swift were the cars whereon they rode,
And bright their weapons flashed and glowed.
They saw: they charged in wild career
With sword and mace and axe and spear.
From Durdhar's bow five arrows sped
And quivered in the Vánar's head.
He rose and roared: the fearful sound
Made all the region echo round.
Then from above his weight he threw
On Durdhar's car that near him drew.
The weight that came with lightning speed
Crushed pole and axle, car and steed.
It shattered Durdhar's head and neck,
And left him lifeless mid the wreck.
Yúpáksha saw the warrior die,
And Virúpáksha heard his cry,
And, mad for vengeance for the slain,
They charged their Vánar foe again.
He rose in air: they onward pressed
And fiercely smote him on the breast.
In vain they struck his iron frame:
With eagle swoop to earth he came,
Tore from the ground a tree that grew
Beside him, and the demons slew.
Then Bhásakarṇa raised his spear,
And Praghas with a laugh drew near,
And, maddened at the sight, the two
Against the undaunted Vánar flew.
As from his wounds the torrents flowed,
Like a red sun the Vánar showed.
He turned, a mountain peak to seize
With all its beasts and snakes and trees.
He hurled it on the pair: and they
Crushed, overwhelmed, beneath it lay.

CANTO XLVII.

THE DEATH OF AKSHA.

But Rávaṇ, as his fury burned,
His eyes on youthful Aksha[1] turned,
Who rose impetuous at his glance
And shouted for his bow and lance.
He rode upon a glorious car
That shot the light of gems afar.
His pennon waved mid glittering gold
And bright the wheels with jewels rolled,
By long and fierce devotion won
That car was splendid as the sun.
With rows of various weapons stored;
And thought-swift horses whirled their lord
Racing along the earth, or rose
High through the clouds whene'er he chose.
Then fierce and fearful war between
The Vánar and the fiend was seen.
The Gods and Asurs stood amazed,
And on the wondrous combat gazed.
A cry from earth rose long and shrill,
The wind was hushed, the sun grew chill.
The thunder bellowed from the sky,
And troubled ocean roared reply.
Thrice Aksha strained his dreadful bow,
Thrice smote his arrow on the foe,
And with full streams of crimson bled
Three gashes in the Vánar's head.
Then rose Hanúmán in the air
To shun the shafts no life could bear.
But Aksha in his car pursued.
And from on high the fight renewed
With storm of arrows, thick as hail
When angry clouds some hill assail.
Impatient of that arrowy shower
The Vánar chief put forth his power,
Again above his chariot rose
And smote him with repeated blows.
Terrific came each deadly stroke:
Breast neck and arm and back he broke;
And Aksha fell to earth, and lay
With all his life-blood drained away.

CANTO XLVIII.

HANUMA'N CAPTURED.

To Indrajít[1] the bold and brave
The giant king his mandate gave:
'O trained in warlike science, best
In arms of all our mightiest,
Whose valour in the conflict shown
To Asurs and to Gods is known,
The Kinkars whom I sent are slain,
And Jambumálí and his train;
The lords who led our giant bands
Have fallen by the monkey's hands;
With shattered cars the ground is spread,
And Aksha lies amid the dead.
Thou art my best and bravest: go,
Unmatched in power, and slay the foe.'

[1] Rávaṇ's son.

[1] 'Conqueror of Indra,' another of Rávaṇ's sons.

He heard the hest: he bent his head;
Athirst for battle forth he sped.
Four tigers fierce, of tawny hue,
With fearful teeth, his chariot drew.
Hanúmán heard his strong bow clang,
And swiftly from the earth he sprang,
While weak and ineffective fell
The archer's shafts though pointed well.
The Rákshas saw that naught might kill
The wondrous foe who mocked his skill,
And launched a magic shaft to throw
A binding spell about his foe.
Forth flew the shaft: the mystic charm
Stayed his swift feet and numbed his arm.
Through all his frame he felt the spell,
And motionless to earth he fell.
Nor would the reverent Vánar loose
The bonds that bound him as a noose.
He knew that Brahmá's self had charmed
The weapon that his might disarmed.
They saw him helpless on the ground,
And all the giants pressed around,
And bonds of hemp and bark were cast
About his limbs to hold him fast.
They drew the ropes round feet and wrists;
They beat him with their hands and fists,
And dragged him as they strained the cord
With shouts of trumph to their lord.[1]

CANTO XLIX.

RÁVAṆ.

On the fierce king Hanúmán turned
His angry eyes that glowed and burned.
He saw him decked with wealth untold
Of diamond and pearl and gold,
And priceless was each wondrous gem
That sparkled in his diadem.
About his neck rich chains were twined,
The best that fancy e'er designed,
And a fair robe with pearls bestrung
Down from his mighty shoulders hung.
Ten heads he reared,[2] as Mandar's hill
Lifts woody peaks which tigers fill.
Bright were his eyes, and bright, beneath,
The flashes of his awful teeth.
His brawny arms of wondrous size
Were decked with rings and scented dyes,
His hands like snakes with five long heads
Descending from their mountain beds.
He sat upon a crystal throne
Inlaid with wealth of precious stone,
Whereon, of noblest work, was set
A gold-embroidered coverlet.
Behind the monarch stood the best
Of beauteous women gaily dressed,
And each her giant master fanned,
Or waved a chourie in her hand.
Four noble courtiers[1] wise and good
In counsel, near the monarch stood,
As the four oceans ever stand
About the sea-encompassed land.
Still, though his heart with rage was fired,
The Vánar marvelled and admired:
'O, what a rare and wondrous sight!
What beauty, majesty, and might!
All regal pomp combines to grace
This ruler of the Rákshas race.
He, if he scorned not right and law,
Might guide the world with tempered awe;
Yea, Indra and the Gods on high
Might on his saving power rely.'

CANTO L.

PRAHASTA'S QUESTIONS.

Then fierce the giant's fury blazed
As on Hanúmán's form he gazed;
And shaken by each wild surmise
He spake aloud with flashing eyes:
'Can this be Nandi[2] standing here,
The mighty one whom all revere?
Who once on high Kailása's hill
Pronounced the curse that haunts me still?
Or is the woodland creature one
Of Asur race, or Bali's[3] son?
The wretch with searching question try:
Learn who he is, and whence; and why
He marred the glory of the grove,
And with my captains fiercely strove.'

---

[1] The *sloka* which follows is probably an interpolation, as it is inconsistent with the questioning in Canto L.:

He looked on Rávaṇ in his pride,
And boldly to the monarch cried:
'I came an envoy to this place
From him who rules the Vánar race.

[2] The ten heads of Rávaṇ have provoked much ridicule from European critics. It should be remembered that Spenser tells us of "two brethren giants" "The one of which had two heads, the other three;" and Milton speaks of the "four-fold visaged Four," the four Cherubic shapes each of whom had four faces.

[1] Durdhar, or as the Bengal recension reads Mahodara, Prahasta, Mahápárśva, and Nikumbha.

[2] The chief attendant of Śiva.

[3] Bali, not to be confounded with Báli the Vánar, was a celebrated Daitya or demon who had usurped the empire of the three worlds, and who was deprived of two thirds of his dominions by Vishṇu in the Dwarf-incarnation.

Prahasta heard his lord's behest.
And thus the Vánar chief addressed:
'O monkey stranger be consoled:
Fear not, and let thy heart be bold.
If thou by Indra's mandate sent
Thy steps to Lanká's isle hast bent,
With fearless words the cause explain,
And freedom thou shalt soon regain.
Or if thou comest as a spy
Despatched by Vishṇu in the sky,
Or sent by Yama, or the Lord
Of Riches, hast our town explored;
Proved by the prowess thou hast shown
No monkey save in form alone;
Speak boldly all the truth, and be
Released from bonds, unharmed and free.
But falsehood spoken to our king
Swift punishment of death will bring.'

He ceased: the Vánar made reply;
'Not Indra's messenger am I,
Nor came I hither to fulfil
Kuvera's hest or Vishṇu's will.
I stand before the giants here
A Vánar e'en as I appear.
I longed to see the king: 'twas hard
To win my way through gate and guard.
And so to gain my wish I laid
In ruin that delightful shade.
No fiend, no God of heavenly kind
With bond or chain these limbs may bind.
The Eternal Sire himself of old
Vouchsafed the boon that makes me bold.
From Brahmá's magic shaft released[1]
I knew the captor's power had ceased.
The fancied bonds I freely brooked,
And thus upon the king have looked.
My way to Lanká have I won,
A messenger from Raghu's son.'

CANTO LI.

HANUMÁN'S REPLY.

'My king Sugríva greets thee fair,
And bids me thus his rede declare.
Son of the God of Wind, by name
Hanúmán, to this isle I came.
To set the Maithil lady free
I crossed the barrier of the sea.
I roamed in search of her and found
Her weeping in that lovely ground.
Thou in the lore of duty trained,
Who hast by stern devotion gained
This wondrous wealth and power and fame
Shouldst fear to wrong another's dame.
Hear thou my counsel, and be wise:
No fiend, no dweller in the skies
Can bear the shafts by Lakshmaṇ shot,
Or Ráma when his wrath is hot.
O Giant King, repent the crime
And soothe him while there yet is time.
Now be the Maithil queen restored
Uninjured to her sorrowing lord.
Soon wilt thou rue thy dire mistake:
She is no woman but a snake.
Whose very deadly bite will be
The ruin of thy house and thee.
Thy pride has led thy thoughts astray,
That fancy not a hand may slay
The monarch of the giants, screened
From mortal blow of God and fiend.
Sugríva still thy death may be:
No Yaksha, fiend, or God is he.
And Ráma from a woman springs,
The mortal seed of mortal kings.
O think how Báli fell subdued;
Think on thy slaughtered multitude.
Respect those brave and strong allies;
Consult thy safety, and be wise.
I, even I, no helper need
To overthrow, with car and steed,
Thy city Lanká half divine:
The power but not the will is mine.
For Raghu's son, before his friend
The Vánar monarch, swore to end
With his own conquering arm the life
Of him who stole his darling wife.
Turn, and be wise, O Rávaṇ turn;
Or thou wilt see thy Lanká burn,
And with thy wives, friends, kith and kin
Be ruined for thy senseless sin.'

CANTO LII.

VIBHÍSHAṆ'S SPEECH.

Then Rávaṇ spake with flashing eye:
'Hence with the Vánar: let him die.'
Vibhíshaṇ heard the stern behest,
And pondered in his troubled breast;
Then, trained in arts that soothe and please
Addressed the king in words like these:

'Revoke, my lord, thy fierce decree,
And hear the words I speak to thee.
Kings wise and noble ne'er condemn
To death the envoys sent to them.
Such deed the world's contempt would draw
On him who breaks the ancient law.[1]
Observe the mean where justice lies,
And spare his life but still chastise.'

---

[1] When Hanumán was bound with cords, Indrajit released his captive from the spell laid upon him by the magic weapon.

[1] "One who murders an ambassador (*rája bhata*) goes to Taptakumbha (the hell of heated caldrons)." WILSON'S *Vishṇu Puráṇa*, Vol. II. p. 217.

Then forth the tyrant's fury broke,
And thus in angry words he spoke:
'O hero, when the wicked bleed
No sin or shame attends the deed.
The Vánar's blood must needs be spilt,
The penalty of heinous guilt.'

Again Vibhíshan made reply:
'Nay, hear me, for he must not die.
Hear the great law the wise declare:
'Thy foeman's envoy thou shalt spare.'
'Tis true he comes an open foe;
'Tis true his hands have wrought us woe,
But law allows thee, if thou wilt,
A punishment to suit the guilt.
The mark of shame, the scourge, the brand,
The shaven head, the wounded hand.
Yea, were the Vánar envoy slain,
Where, King of giants, were the gain?
On them alone, on them who sent
The message, be the punishment.
For spake he well or spake he ill,
He spake obedient to their will.
And, if he perish, who can bear
Thy challenge to the royal pair?
Who, cross the ocean and incite
Thy death-doomed enemies to fight?'

CANTO LIII.

THE PUNISHMENT.

King Rávan, by his pleading moved,
The counsel of the chief approved:
'Thy words are wise and true: to kill
An envoy would beseem us ill.
Yet must we for his crime invent
Some fitting mode of punishment.
The tail, I fancy, is the part
Most cherished by a monkey's heart.[1]
Make ready: set his tail aflame,
And let him leave us, as he came,
And thus disfigured and disgraced
Back to his king and people haste.'

The giants heard their monarch's speech;
And, filled with burning fury, each
Brought strips of cotton cloth, and round
The monkey's tail the bandage wound.
As round his tail the bands they drew
His mighty form dilating grew
Vast as the flame that bursts on high
Where trees are old and grass is dry.
Each band and strip they soaked in oil,
And set on fire the twisted coil.
Delighted as they viewed the blaze,
The cruel demons stood at gaze:
And mid loud drums and shells rang out
The triumph of their joyful shout.
They pressed about him thick and fast
As through the crowded streets he passed,
Observing with attentive care
Each rich and wondrous structure there,
Still heedless of the eager cry
That rent the air, The spy! the spy!

Some to the captive lady ran,
And thus in joyous words began:
'That copper-visaged monkey, he
Who in the garden talked with thee,
Through Lanká's town is led a show,
And round his tail the red flames glow.'
The mournful news the lady heard
That with fresh grief her bosom stirred.
Swift to the kindled fire she went
And prayed before it reverent:
'If I my husband have obeyed,
And kept the ascetic vows I made,
Free, ever free, from stain and blot,
O spare the Vánar; harm him not.'

Then leapt on high the flickering flame
And shone in answer to the dame.
The pitying fire its rage forbore:
The Vánar felt the heat no more.
Then, to minutest size reduced,[1]
The bonds that bound his limbs he loosed,
And, freed from every band and chain,
Rose to his native size again.
He seized a club of ponderous weight
That lay before him by the gate,
Rushed at the fiends that hemmed him round,
And laid them lifeless on the ground.
Through Lanká's town again he strode,
And viewed each street and square and road,—
Still wreathed about with harmless blaze,
A sun engarlanded with rays.

"It will be remembered that the envoys of King David had the half of their beards shaved off by Hanun, King of Ammon. (2 Sam. X.)" WHEELER, *Hist. of India*, Vol. II. 342.

[1] I have not attempted to tone down anything in this Canto. I give a faithful translation.

[1] "Behold a wonder! they but now who seemed
In bigness to surpass earth's giant sons,
Now less than smallest dwarfs in narrow room
Throng numberless."

Paradise Lost, I, 776.

CANTO LIV.

THE BURNING OF LANKÁ.

'What further deed remains to do
To vex the Rákshas king anew?
The beauty of his grove is marred,
Killed are the bravest of his guard.
The captains of his host are slain;
But forts and palaces remain.
Swift is the work and light the toil
Each fortress of the foe to spoil.'

Reflecting thus, his tale ablaze
As through the cloud red lightning plays,
He scaled the palaces and spread
The conflagration where he sped.
From house to house he hurried on,
And the wild flames behind him shone.
Each mansion of the foe he scaled,
And furious fire its roof assailed
Till all the common ruin shared:
Vibhíshan's house alone was spared.
From blazing pile to pile he sprang,
And loud his shout of triumph rang,
As roars the doomsday cloud when all
The worlds in dissolution fall.
The friendly wind conspired to fan
The hungry flames that leapt and ran,
And spreading in their fury caught
The gilded walls with pearls inwrought,
Till each proud palace reeled and fell
As falls a heavenly citadel.

Loud was the roar the demons raised
Mid walls that split and beams that blazed,
As each with vain endeavour strove
To stay the flames in house or grove.
The women, with dishevelled hair,
Flocked to the roofs in wild despair,
Shrieked out for succour, wept aloud,
And fell, like lightning from a cloud.
He saw the flames ascend and curl
Round turkis, diamond, and pearl,
While silver floods and molten gold
From ruined wall and latice rolled.
As fire grows fiercer as he feeds
On wood and grass and crackling reeds,
So Hanumán the ruin eyed
With fury still unsatisfied.

CANTO LV.

FEAR FOR SÍTÁ.

But other thoughts resumed their sway
When Lanká's town in ruin lay;
And, as his bosom felt their weight,
He stood a while to meditate:
'What have I done?', he thought with shame;
'Destroyed the town with hostile flame.
O happy they whose firm control
Checks the wild passion of the soul;
Who on the fires of anger throw
The cooling drops that check their glow.
But woe is me, whom wrath could lead
To do this senseless shameless deed.
The town to fire and death I gave,
Nor thought of her I came to save,—
Doomed by my own rash folly, doomed
To perish in the flames consumed.
If I, when anger drove me wild,
Have caused the death of Janak's child,
The kindled flame shall end my woe,
Or the deep fires that burn below,[1]
Or my forsaken corse shall be
Food for the monsters of the sea.
How can I meet Sugríva? how
Before the royal brothers bow,—
I whose rash deed has madly foiled
The noble work in which we toiled?
Or has her own bright virtue shed
Its guardian influence round her head?
She lives untouched,—the peerless dame
Flame has no fury for the flame.[2]
The very fire would ne'er consent
To harm a queen so excellent,—
The high-souled Ráma's faithful wife,
Protected by her holy life.
She lives, she lives. Why should I fear
For one whom Raghu's sons hold dear?
Has not the pitying fire that spared
The Vánar for the lady cared?'

Such were his thoughts: he pondered long,
And fear grew faint and hope grew strong
Then round him heavenly voices rang,
And, sweetly tuned, his praises sang:
'O glorious is the exploit done
By Hanumán the Wind-God's son.
The flames o'er Lanká's city rise:
The giants' home in ruin lies.
O'er roof and wall the fires have spread,
Nor harmed a hair of Sítá's head.'

CANTO LVI.

MOUNT ARISHṬA.

He looked upon the burning waste,
Then sought the queen in joyous haste,
With words of hope consoled her heart,
And made him ready to depart.

---

[1] The fire which is supposed to burn beneath the sea.

[2] Sítá is likened to the fire which is an emblem of purity.

He scaled Arishṭa's glorious steep
Whose summits beetled o'er the deep.
The woods in varied beauty dressed
Hung like a garland round his crest,
And clouds of ever changing hue
A robe about his shoulders threw.
On him the rays of morning fell
To wake the hill they loved so well,
And bid unclose those splendid eyes
That glittered in his mineral dyes.
He woke to hear the music made
By thunders of the white cascade,
While every laughing rill that sprang
From crag to crag its carol sang.
For arms, he lifted to the stars
His towering stems of Deodárs,
And morning heard his pealing call
In tumbling brook and waterfall.
He trembled when his woods were pale
And bowed beneath the autumn gale,
And when his vocal reeds were stirred
His malancholy moan was heard.

Far down against the mountain's feet
The Vánar heard the wild waves beat;
Then turned his glances to the north,
Sprang from the peak and bounded forth.
The mountain felt the fearful shock
And trembled through his mass of rock.
The tallest trees were crushed and rent
And headlong to the valley sent,
And as the rocking shook each cave
Loud was the roar the lions gave.
Forth from the shaken cavern came
Fierce serpents with their tongues aflame;
And every Yaksha, wild with dread,
And Kinnar and Gandharva, fled.

CANTO LVII.

HANUMAN'S RETURN.

Still, like a winged mountain, he
Sprang forward through the airy sea,[1]
And rushing through the ether drew
The clouds to follow as he flew,
Through the great host around him spread,
Grey, golden, dark, and white, and red.
Now in a sable cloud immersed,
Now from its gloomy pall he burst,
Like the bright Lord of Stars concealed
A moment, and again revealed.
Sunábha[1] passed, he neared the coast
Where waited still the Vánar host.
They heard a rushing in the skies,
And lifted up their wondering eyes.
His wild triumphant shout they knew
That louder still and louder grew,
And Jámbaván with eager voice
Called on the Vánars to rejoice:
'Look he returns, the Wind-God's son,
And full success his toils have won;
Triumphant is the shout that comes
Like music of a thousand drums.'

Up sprang the Vánars from the ground
And listened to the wondrous sound
Of hurtling arm and thigh as through
The region of the air he flew,
Loud as the wind, when tempests rave,
Roars in the prison of the cave.
From crag to crag, from height to height,
They bounded in their mad delight,
And when he touched the mountain's crest,
With reverent welcome round him pressed.
They brought him of their woodland fruits,
They brought him of the choicest roots,
And laughed and shouted in their glee
The noblest of their chiefs to see.
Nor Hanumán delayed to greet
Sage Jámbaván with reverence meet;
To Angad and the chiefs he bent
For age and rank preëminent,
And briefly spoke: 'These eyes have seen,
These lips addressed, the Maithil queen.'
They sat beneath the waving trees,
And Angad spoke in words like these:
'O noblest of the Vánar kind
For valour power and might combined,
To thee triumphant o'er the foe
Our hopes, our lives and all we owe.
O faithful heart in perils tried,

[1] 'I omit two stanzas which continue the metaphor of the sea or lake of air. The moon is its lotus, the sun its wild-duck, the clouds are its water-weeds, Mars is its shark and so on. Gorresio remarks: 'This comparison of a great lake to the sky and of celestial to aquatic objects is one of those ideas which the view and qualities of natural scenery awake in lively fancies. Imagine one of those grand and splendid lakes of India covered with lotus blossoms, furrowed by wild-ducks of the most vivid colours, mantled over here and there with flowers and water weeds &c., and it will be understood how the fancy of the poet could readily compare to the sky radiant with celestial azure the blue expanse of the water, to the soft light of the moon the tender hue of the lotus, to the splendour of the sun the brilliant colours of the wild-fowl, to the stars the flowers, to the clouds the weeds that float upon the water &c.'

[1] Sunábha is the mountain that rose from the sea when Hanumán passed over to Lanká.

Which toil nor fear could turn aside,
Thy deed the lady will restore,
And Ráma's heart will ache no more.'[1]

CANTO LXI.

THE FEAST OF HONEY.

They rose in air: the region grew
Dark with their shadow as they flew,
Swift to a lovely grove[2] they came
That rivalled heavenly Nandan's[3] fame;
Where countless bees their honey stored,—
The pleasance of the Vánars' lord,
To every creature fenced and barred,
Which Dadhimukh was set to guard,
A noble Vánar, brave and bold,
Sugríva's uncle lofty-souled.
To Angad came with one accord
The Vánars, and besought their lord
That they those honeyed stores might eat
That made the grove so passing sweet.
He gave consent: they sought the trees
Thronged with innumerable bees.
They rifled all the treasured store,
And ate the fruit the branches bore,
And still as they prolonged the feast
Their merriment and joy increased.
Drunk with the sweets, they danced and bowed,
They wildly sang, they laughed aloud.
Some climbed and sprang from tree to tree,
Some sat and chattered in their glee.
Some scaled the trees which creepers crowned,
And rained the branches to the ground.
There with loud laugh a Vánar sprang
Close to his friend who madly sang.
In doleful mood another crept
To mix his tears with one who wept.
Then Dadhimukh with fury viewed
The intoxicated multitude.
He looked upon the rifled shade,
And all the ruin they had made;
Then called with angry voice, and strove
To save the remnant of the grove.
But warning cries and words were spurned,
And angry taunt and threat returned.
Then fierce and wild contention rose:
With furious words he mingled blows.
They by no shame or fear withheld,
By drunken mood and ire impelled,
Used claws, and teeth, and hands, and beat
The keeper under trampling feet.

[1] Three Cantos of repetition are omitted.

[2] *Madhuvan* the 'honey-wood.'

[3] Indra's pleasure-ground or elysium.

CANTO LXV.

THE TIDINGS.

On to Prasravan's hill they sped
Where blooming trees their branches spread.
To Raghu's sons their heads they bent
And did obeisance reverent.
Then to their king, by Angad led,
Each Vánar chieftain bowed his head;
And Hanumán the brave and bold
His tidings to the monarch told;
But first in Ráma's hand he placed
The gem that Sítá's brow had graced:
'I crossed the sea: I searched a while
For Sítá in the giants' isle.
I found her vext with taunt and threat
By demon guards about her set.
Her tresses twined in single braid,
On the bare earth her limbs were laid.
Sad were her eyes: her cheeks were pale
As shuddering flowers in winter's gale.
I stood beside the weeping dame,
And gently whispered Ráma's name:
With cheering words her grief consoled,
And then the whole adventure told.
She weeps afar beyond the sea,
And her true heart is still with thee.
She gave a sign that thou wouldst know,
She bids thee think upon the crow,
And bright mark pressed upon her brow
When none was nigh but she and thou.
She bids thee take this precious stone,
The sea-born gem thou long hast known.
'And I', she said, 'will dull the sting
Of woe by gazing on the ring.
One little month shall I sustain
This life oppressed with woe and pain;
And when the month is ended, I
The giants' prey must surely die.'

[1] Three Cantos consisting of little but repetitions are omitted. Dadhimukh escapes from the infuriated monkeys and hastens to Sugríva to report their misconduct. Sugríva infers that Hanumán and his band have been successful in their search, and that the exuberance of spirits and the mischief complained of, are but the natural expression of their joy. Dadhimukh obtains little sympathy from Sugríva, and is told to return and send the monkeys on with all possible speed.

CANTO LXVI.

RÁMA'S SPEECH.

There ceased the Vánar : Ráma pressed
The treasured jewel to his breast,
And from his eyes the waters broke
As to the Vánar king he spoke:
'As o'er her babe the mother weeps,
This flood of tears the jewel steeps.
This gem that shone on Sítá's head
Was Janak's gift when we were wed,
And the pure brow that wore it lent
New splendour to the ornament.
This gem, bright offspring of the wave,
The King of Heaven to Janak gave,
Whose noble sacrificial rite
Had filled the God with new delight.
Now, as I gaze upon the prize,
Methinks I see my father's eyes.
Methinks I see before me stand
The ruler of Videha's land.[1]
Methinks mine arms are folded now
Round her who wore it on her brow.
Speak, Hanumán, O say, dear friend,
What message did my darling send?
O speak, and let thy words impart
Their gentle dew to cool my heart.
Ah, 'tis the crown of woe to see
This gem and ask 'Where, where is she?'
If for one month her heart be strong,
Her days of life will yet be long.
But I, with naught to lend relief,
This very day must die of grief.
Come, Hanumán, and quickly guide
The mourner to his darling's side.
O lead me—thou hast learnt the way—
I cannot and I will not stay.
How can my gentle love endure,
So timid, delicate, and pure,
The dreadful demons fierce and vile
Who watch her in the guarded isle?
No more the light of beauty shines
From Sítá as she weeps and pines.
But pain and sorrow, cloud on cloud,
Her moonlight glory dim and shroud.
O speak, dear Hanumán, and tell
Each word that from her sweet lips fell.
Her words, her words alone can give
The healing balm to make me live.'[2]

---

[1] Janak was king of Videha or Mithilá in Behar.

[2] The original contains two more Cantos which end the Book, Canto LXVII begins thus: 'Hanumán thus addressed by the great-souled son of Raghu related to the son of Raghu all that Sítá had said.' And the two Cantos contain nothing but Hanumán's account of his interview with Sítá, and the report of his own speeches as well as of hers.

BOOK VI.[1]

CANTO I.

RÁMA'S SPEECH.

The son of Raghu heard, consoled,
The wondrous tale Hanúmán told;
And, as his joyous hope grew high,
In friendly words he made reply:
'Behold a mighty task achieved,
Which never heart but his conceived.
Who else across the sea can spring,
Save Váyu[2] and the Feathered King?[3]
Who, pass the portals strong and high
Which Nágas,[4] Gods, and fiends defy,
Where Rávan's hosts their station keep,—
And come uninjured o'er the deep?
By such a deed the Wind-God's son
Good service to the king has done,
And saved from ruin and disgrace
Lakshman and me and Raghu's race.
Well has he planned and bravely fought,
And with due care my lady sought.
But of the sea I sadly think,
And the sweet hopes that cheered me sink.
How can we cross the leagues of foam
That keep us from the giant's home?
What can the Vánar legions more
Than muster on the ocean shore?'

CANTO II.

SUGRÍVA'S SPEECH.

He ceased: and King Sugríva tried
To calm his grief, and thus replied:
'Be to thy nobler nature true,
Nor let despair thy soul subdue.
This cloud of causeless woe dispel,
For all as yet has prospered well,
And we have traced thy queen, and know
The dwelling of our Rákshas foe.
Arise, consult: thy task must be
To cast a bridge athwart the sea,
The city of our foe to reach
That crowns the mountain by the beach;

---

[1] The Sixth Book is called in Sanskrit *Yuddha-Kánda* or *The War*, and *Lanká-Kánda*. It is generally known at the present day by the latter title.

[2] Váyu is the God of Wind.

[3] Garuda the King of Birds.

[4] Serpent-Gods.

And when our feet that isle shall tread,
Rejoice and deem thy foeman dead.
The sea unbridged, his walls defy
Both fiends and children of the sky,
Though at the fierce battalions' head
Lord Indra's self the onset led.
Yea, victory is thine before
The long bridge touch the farther shore,
So fleet and fierce and strong are these
Who limb them as their fancies please.
Away with grief and sad surmise
That mar the noblest enterprise,
And with their weak suspicion blight
The sage's plan, the hero's might.
Come, this degenerate weakness spurn,
And bid thy dauntless heart return,
For each fair hope by grief is crossed
When those we love are dead or lost.
Arise, O best of those who know,
Arm for the giant's overthrow.
None in the triple world I see
Who in the fight may equal thee;
None who before thy face may stand
And brave the bow that arms thy hand.
Trust to these mighty Vánars: they
With full success thy trust will pay,
When thou shalt reach the robber's hold,
And loving arms round Sítá fold.'

CANTO III.

LANKÁ.

He ceased: and Raghu's son gave heed,
Attentive to his prudent rede:
Then turned again, with hope inspired,
To Hanumán, and thus inquired:
'Light were the task for thee, I ween,
To bridge the sea that gleams between
The mainland and the island shore.
Or dry the deep and guide us o'er.
Fain would I learn from thee whose feet
Have trod the stones of every street,
Of fenced Lanká's towers and forts,
And walls and moats and guarded ports,
And castles where the giants dwell,
And battlemented citadel.
O Váyu's son, describe it all,
With palace, fort, and gate, and wall.'
He ceased: and, skilled in arts that guide
The eloquent, the chief replied:
'Vast is the city, gay and strong,
Where elephants unnumbered throng,
And countless hosts of Rákshas breed
Stand ready by the car and steed,
Four massive gates, securely barred,
All entrance to the city guard,
With murderous engines fixt to throw
Bolt, arrow, rock to check the foe,
And many a mace with iron head
That strikes at once a hundred dead.
Her golden ramparts wide and high
With massy strength the foe defy,
Where inner walls their rich inlay
Of coral, turkis, pearl display.
Her circling moats are broad and deep,
Where ravening monsters dart and leap.
By four great piers each moat is spanned
Where lines of deadly engines stand.
In sleepless watch at every gate
Unnumbered hosts of giants wait,
And, masters of each weapon, rear
The threatening pike and sword and spear.
My fury hurled those ramparts down,
Filled up the moats that gird the town,
The piers and portals overturned,
And stately Lanká spoiled and burned.
Howe'er we Vánars force our way
O'er the wide seat of Varuṇ's[1] sway,
Be sure that city of the foe
Is doomed to sudden overthrow,
Nay, why so vast an army lead?
Brave Angad, Dwivid good at need,
Fierce Mainda, Panas famed in fight,
And Níla's skill and Nala's might,
And Jámbaván the strong and wise,
Will dare the easy enterprise.
Assailed by these shall Lanká fall
With gate and rampart, tower and wall.
Command the gathering, chief: and they
In happy hour will haste away.'

CANTO IV.

THE MARCH.

He ceased; and spurred by warlike pride
The impetuous son of Raghu cried:
'Soon shall mine arm with wrathful joy
That city of the foe destroy.
Now, chieftain, now collect the host,
And onward to the southern coast!
The sun in his meridian tower
Gives glory to the Vánar power.
The demon lord who stole my queen
By timely flight his life may screen.
She, when she knows her lord is near,
Will cling to hope and banish fear,
Saved like a dying wretch who sips
The drink of Gods with fevered lips.
Arise, thy troops to battle lead:
All happy omens counsel speed.
The Lord of Stars in favouring skies
Bodes glory to our enterprise.
This arm shall slay the fiend; and she,
My consort, shall again be free.

[1] The God of the sea.

Mine upward-throbbing eye foreshows
The longed-for triumph o'er my foes.
Far in the van be Níla's post,
To scan the pathway for the host,
And let thy bravest and thy best,
A hundred thousand, wait his hest.
Go forth, O warrior Níla, lead
The legions on through wood and mead
Where pleasant waters cool the ground,
And honey, flowers, and fruit abound.
Go, and with timely care prevent
The Rákshas foeman's dark intent.
With watchful troops each valley guard
Ere brooks and fruits and roots be marred,
And search each glen and leafy shade
For hostile troops in ambuscade.
But let the weaklings stay behind:
For heroes is our task designed.
Let thousands of the Vánar breed
The vanguard of the armies lead:
Fierce and terrific must it be
As billows of the stormy sea.
There be the hill-huge Gaja's place,
And Gavaya's, strongest of his race,
And, like the bull that leads the herd,
Gaváksha's, by no fears deterred.
Let Rishabh, matchless in the might
Of warlike arms, protect our right,
And Gandhamádan next in rank
Defend and guide the other flank.
I, like the God who rules the sky
Borne on Airávat,[1] mounted high
On stout Hanumán's back will ride,
The central host to cheer and guide.
Fierce as the God who rules below,
On Angad's back let Lakshman show
Like him who wealth to mortals shares,[2]
The lord whom Sárvabhauma[3] bears.
The bold Sushen's impetuous might,
And Vegadarśí's piercing sight,
And Jámbaván whom bears revere,
Illustrious three, shall guard the rear.'

He ceased: the royal Vánar heard,
And swift, obedient to his word,
Sprang forth in numbers none might tell
From mountain, cave, and bosky dell,
From rocky ledge and breezy height,
Fierce Vánars burning for the fight.
And Ráma's course was southward bent
Amid the mighty armament.
On, joyous, pressed in close array
The hosts who owned Sugríva's sway,
With nimble feet, with rapid bound
Exploring, ere they passed, the ground,
While from ten myriad throats rang out
The challenge and the battle shout.

[1] Indra's elephant.

[2] Kuvera, God of wealth.

[3] Kuvera's elephant.

On roots and honeycomb they fed,
And clusters from the boughs o'erhead,
Or from the ground the tall trees tore
Rich with the flowery load they bore.
Some carried comrades, wild with mirth,
Then cast their riders to the earth,
Who swiftly to their feet arose
And overthrew their laughing foes,
While still rang out the general cry,
'King Rávan and his fiends shall die.'
Still on, exulting in the pride
Of conscious strength, the Vánars hied,
And gazed where noble Sahya, best
Of mountains, raised each towering crest.
They looked on lake and streamlet, where
The lotus bloom was bright and fair,
Nor marched—for Ráma's hest they feared
Where town or haunt of men appeared.
Still onward, fearful as the waves
Of Ocean when he roars and raves,
Led by their eager chieftains, went
The Vánars' countless armament.
Each captain, like a noble steed
Urged by the lash to double speed,
Pressed onward, filled with zeal and pride,
By Ráma's and his brother's side,
Who high above the Vánar throng
On mighty backs were borne along,
Like the great Lords of Day and Night
Seized by eclipsing planets' might.
Then Lakshman radiant as the morn,
On Angad's shoulders high upborne,
With sweet consoling words that woke
New ardour, to his brother spoke:
'Soon shalt thou turn, thy queen regained
And impious Rávan's life-blood drained,
In happiness and high renown
To dear Ayodhyá's happy town.
I see around exceeding fair
All omens of the earth and air.
Auspicious breezes sweet and low
To greet the Vánar army blow,
And softly to my listening ear
Come the glad cries of bird and deer.
Bright is the sky around us, bright
Without a cloud the Lord of Light,
And Śukra[1] with propitious love
Looks on thee from his throne above.
The pole-star and the Sainted Seven[2]
Shine brightly in the northern heaven,
And great Triśanku,[3] glorious king,

[1] The planet Venus, or its regent who is regarded as the son of Bhrigu and preceptor of the Daityas.

[2] The seven *rishis* or saints who form the constellation of the Great Bear.

[3] Triśanku was raised to the skies to form a constellation in the southern hemisphere. The story is told in Book I. Canto LX.

Ikshváku's son from whom we spring,
Beams in unclouded glory near
His holy priest[1] whom all revere.
Undimmed the two Viśákhás[2] shine,
The strength and glory of our line,
And Nairrit's[3] influence that aids
Our Rákshas fœmen faints and fades.
The running brooks are fresh and fair,
The boughs their ripening clusters bear,
And scented breezes gently sway
The leaflet of the tender spray.
See, with a glory half divine
The Vánars' ordered legions shine,
Bright as the Gods' exultant train
Who saw the demon Tárak slain.
O let thine eyes these signs behold,
And bid thy heart be glad and bold.'
The Vánar squadrons densely spread
O'er all the country onward sped,
While rising from the rapid beat
Of bears' and monkeys' hastening feet
Dust hid the earth with thickest veil,
And made the struggling sunbeams pale.
Now where Mahendra's peaks arise
Came Ráma of the lotus eyes
And the long arm's resistless might,
And clomb the mountain's wood-crowned height.
Thence Daśaratha's son beheld
Where billowy Ocean rose and swelled.
Past Malaya's peaks and Sahya's chain
The Vánar legions reached the main,
And stood in many a marshalled band
On loud-resounding Ocean's strand.
To the fair wood that fringed the tide
Came Daśaratha's son, and cried;
'At length, my lord Sugríva, we
Have reached King Várun's realm the sea,
And one great thought, still-vexing, how
To cross the flood, awaits us now.
The broad deep ocean, that denies
A passage, stretched before us lies.
Then let us halt and plan the while
How best to storm the giant's isle.'
He ceased: Sugríva on the coast
By trees o'ershadowed stayed the host,
That seemed in glittering lines to be
The bright waves of a second sea.
Then from the shore the captains gazed
On billows which the breezes raised
To fury, as they dashed in foam
O'er Varun's realm, the Asurs' home:[1]
The sea that laughed with foam, and danced
With waves whereon the sunbeams glanced:
Where, when the light began to fade,
Huge crocodiles and monsters played;
And, when the moon went up the sky,
The troubled billows rose on high
From the wild watery world whereon
A thousand moons reflected shone:
Where awful serpents swam and showed
Their fiery crests which flashed and glowed,
Illumining the depths of hell,
The prison where the demons dwell.
The eye, bewildered, sought in vain
The bounding line of sky and main:
Alike in shade, alike in glow
Were sky above and sea below.
There wave-like clouds by clouds were chased,
Here cloud-like billows roared and raced;
Then shone the stars, and many a gem
That lit the waters answered them.
They saw the great-souled Ocean stirred
To frenzy by the winds, and heard,
Loud as ten thousand drums, the roar
Of wild waves dashing on the shore.
They saw him mounting to defy
With deafening voice the troubled sky,
And the deep bed beneath him swell
In fury as the billows fell.

CANTO V.

RÁMA'S LAMENT.

There on the coast in long array
The Vánars' marshalled legions lay,
Where Níla's care had ordered well
The watch of guard and sentinel,
And Mainda moved from post to post
With Dwivid to protect the host.

Then Ráma stood by Lakshman's side,
And mastered by his sorrow cried:
'My brother dear, the heart's distress,
As days wear on, grows less and less.
But my deep-seated grief, alas,
Grows fiercer as the seasons pass.
Though for my queen my spirit longs,
And broods indignant o'er my wrongs,
Still wilder is my grief to know
That her young life is passed in woe.
Breathe, gentle gale, O breathe where she
Lies prisoned, and then breathe on me,

[1] The sage Viśvámitra, who performed for Triśanku the great sacrifice which raised him to the heavens.

[2] One of the lunar asterisms containing four or originally two stars under the regency of a dual divinity Indrágni, Indra and Agni.

[3] The lunar asterism Múla, belonging to the Rákshases.

[1] The Asurs or demons dwell imprisoned in the depths beneath the sea.

And, though my love I may not meet,
Thy kiss shall be divinely sweet.
Ah, by the giant's shape appalled,
On her dear lord for help she called.
Still in mine ears the sad cry rings
And tears my heart with poison stings.
Through the long daylight and the gloom
Of night wild thoughts of her consume
My spirit, and my love supplies
The torturing flame which never dies.
Leave me, my brother; I will sleep
Couched on the bosom of the deep,
For the cold wave may bring me peace
And bid the fire of passion cease.
One only thought my stay must be,
That earth, one earth, holds her and me,
To hear, to know my darling lives
Some life-supporting comfort gives,
As streams from distant fountains run
O'er meadows parching in the sun.
Ah when, my foeman at my feet,
Shall I my queen, my glory, meet,
The blossom of her dear face raise
And on her eyes enraptured gaze,
Press her soft lips to mine again,
And drink a balm to banish pain!
Alas, alas! where lies she now,
My darling of the lovely brow?
On the cold earth, no help at hand,
Forlorn amid the Rákshas band,
King Janak's child still calls on me,
Her lord and love, to set her free.
But soon in glory will she rise
A crescent moon in autumn skies,
And those dark rovers of the night,
Like scattered clouds shall turn in flight.'

CANTO VI.

RÁVAṆ'S SPEECH.

But when the giant king surveyed
His glorious town in ruin laid,
And each dire sign of victory won
By Hanumán the Wind-God's son,
He vailed his angry eyes oppressed
By shame, and thus his lords addressed:
'The Vánar spy has passed the gate
Of Lanká long inviolate,
Eluded watch and ward, and seen
With his bold eyes the captive queen.
My royal roof with flames is red,
The bravest of my lords are dead,
And the fierce Vánar in his hate
Has left our city desolate.
Now ponder well the work that lies
Before us, ponder and advise.
With deep-observing judgment scan
The peril, and mature a plan.
From counsel, sages say, the root,
Springs victory, most glorious fruit.
First ranks the king, when woe impends
Who seeks the counsel of his friends,
Of kinsmen ever faithful found,
Or those whose hopes with his are bound,
Then with their aid his strength applies,
And triumphs in his enterprise.
Next ranks the prince who plans alone,
No counsel seeks to aid his own,
Weighs loss and gain and wrong and right,
And seeks success with earnest might.
Unwisest he who spurns delays,
Who counts no cost, no peril weighs,
Speeds to his aim, defying fate,
And risks his all, precipitate.
Thus too in counsel sages find
A best, a worst, a middle kind.
When gathered counsellors explore
The way by light of holy lore,
And all from first to last agree,
Is the best counsel of the three.
Next, if debate first waxes high,
And each his chosen plan would try
Till all agree at last, we deem
This counsel second in esteem.
Worst of the three is this, when each
Assails with taunt his fellow's speech;
When all debate, and no consent
Concludes the angry argument.
Consult then, lords; my task shall be
To crown with act your wise decree.
With thousands of his wild allies
The vengeful Ráma hither hies;
With unresisted might and speed
Across the flood his troops will lead,
Or for the Vánar host will drain
The channels of the conquered main.'

CANTO VII.

RÁVAṆ ENCOURAGED.

He ceased: they scorned, with blinded eyes,
The foeman and his bold allies,
Raised reverent hands with one accord,
And thus made answer to their lord:
'Why yield thee, King, to causeless fear?
A mighty host with sword and spear
And mace and axe and pike and lance
Waits but thy signal to advance.
Art thou not he who slew of old
The Serpent-Gods, and stormed their hold;
Scaled Mount Kailása and o'erthrew
Kuvera[1] and his Yaksha crew,

[1] The God of Riches, brother and enemy of Rávaṇ and first possessor of Pushpak the flying car.

Compelling Śiva's haughty friend
Beneath a mightier arm to bend?
Didst thou not bring from realms afar
The marvel of the magic car,
When they who served Kuvera fell
Crushed in their mountain citadel?
Attracted by thy matchless fame
To thee, a suppliant, Maya came,
The lord of every Dánav band,
And won thee with his daughter's hand.
Thy arm in hell itself was felt,
Where Vásuki[1] and Śankha dwelt,
And they and Takshak, overthrown,
Were forced thy conquering might to own.
The Gods in vain their blessing gave
To heroes bravest of the brave,
Who strove a year and, sorely pressed,
Their victor's peerless might confessed.
In vain their magic arts they tried,
In vain thy matchless arm defied.
King Varuṇ's sons with fourfold force,
Cars, elephants, and foot, and horse,
But for a while thy power withstood,
And, conquered, mourned their hardihood.
Thou hast encountered, face to face,
King Yama[2] with his murdering mace.
Fierce as the wild tempestuous sea,
What terror had his wrath for thee,
Though death in every threatening form,
And woe and torment, urged the storm?
Thine arm a glorious victory won
O'er the dread king who pities none;
And the three worlds, from terror freed,
In joyful wonder praised thy deed.
The tribe of Warriors, strong and dread
As Indra's self, o'er earth had spread;
As giant trees that towering stand
In mountain glens, they filled the land.
Can Raghu's son encounter foes
Fierce, numerous, and strong as those?
Yet, trained in war and practised well,
O'ermatched by thee, they fought and fell.
Stay in thy royal home, nor care
The battle and the toil to share;
But let the easy fight be won
By Indrajit[3] thy matchless son.
All, all shall die, if thou permit,
Slain by the hand of Indrajit.'

---

[1] King of the Serpents. Śankha and Takshak are two of the eight Serpent Chiefs.

[2] The God of Death, the Pluto of the Hindus.

[3] Literally Indra's conqueror, so called from his victory over that God.

CANTO VIII.

PRAHASTA'S SPEECH.

Dark as a cloud of autumn, dread
Prahasta joined his palms and said:
'Gandharvas, Gods, the hosts who dwell
In heaven, in air, in earth, in hell,
Have yielded to thy might, and how
Shall two weak men oppose thee now?
Hanumán came, a foe disguised,
And mocked us heedless and surprised,
Or never had he lived to flee
And boast that he has fought with me.
Command, O King, and this right hand
Shall sweep the Vánars from the land,
And hill and dale, to Ocean's shore,
Shall know the death-doomed race no more.
But let my care the means devise
To guard thy city from surprise.'

Then Durmukh cried, of Rákshas race:
'Too long we brook the dire disgrace.
He gave our city to the flames,
He trod the chambers of thy dames.
Ne'er shall so weak and vile a thing
Unpunished brave the giants' king.
Now shall this single arm attack
And drive the daring Vánars back,
Till to the winds of heaven they flee,
Or seek the depths of earth and sea.'
Then, brandishing the mace he bore,
Whose horrid spikes were stained with gore,
While fury made his eyeballs red,
Impetuous Vajradanshṭra said:

'Why waste a thought on one so vile
As Hanumán the Vánar, while
Sugríva, Lakshmaṇ, yet remain,
And Ráma mightier still, unslain?
This mace to-day shall crush the three,
And all the host will turn and flee.
Listen, and I will speak: incline,
O King, to hear these words of mine,
For the deep plan that I propose
Will swiftly rid thee of thy foes.
Let thousands of thy host assume
The forms of men in youthful bloom,
In war's magnificent array
Draw near to Raghu's son, and say:
'Thy younger brother Bharat sends
This army, and thy cause befriends.'
Then let our legions hasten near
With bow and mace and sword and spear,
And on the Vánar army rain
Our steel and stone till all be slain.
If Raghu's sons will fain believe,
Entangled in the net we weave,
The penalty they both must pay,
And lose their forfeit lives to-day.'

Then with his warrior soul on fire,
Nikumbha spoke in burning ire :
'I, only I, will take the field,
And Raghu's son his life shall yield.
Within these walls, O Chiefs, abide,
Nor part ye from our monarch's side.'

CANTO IX.

VIBHÍSHAṆ'S COUNSEL.

A score of warriors[1] forward sprang,
And loud the clashing iron rang
Of mace and axe and spear and sword,
As thus they spake unto their lord :
'Their king Sugríva will we slay,
And Raghu's sons, ere close of day,
And strike the wretch Hanúmán down,
The spoiler of our golden town.'
But sage Vibhíshaṇ strove to calm
The chieftains' fury ; palm to palm
He joined in lowly reverence, pressed[2]
Before them, and the throng addressed :
'Dismiss the hope of conquering one
So stern and strong as Raghu's son.
In due control each sense he keeps
With constant care that never sleeps.
Whose daring heart has e'er conceived
The exploit Hanumán achieved,
Across the fearful sea to spring,
The tributary rivers' king?
O Rákshas lords, in time be wise,
Nor Ráma's matchless power despise.
And say, what evil had the son
Of Raghu to our monarch done,
Who stole the dame he loved so well
And keeps her in his citadel ;
If Khara in his foolish pride
Encountered Ráma, fought, and died,
May not the meanest love his life
And guard it in the deadly strife?
The Maithil dame, O Rákshas King,
Sore peril to thy realm will bring.
Restore her while there yet is time,
Nor let us perish for thy crime.
O, let the Maithil lady go
Ere the avenger bend his bow
To ruin with his arrowy showers
Our Lanká with her gates and towers.
Let Janak's child again be free
Ere the wild Vánars cross the sea,
In their resistless might assail
Our city and her ramparts scale.
Ah, I conjure thee by the ties
Of brotherhood, be just and wise.
In all my thoughts thy good I seek,
And thus my prudent counsel speak.
Let captive Sítá be restored
Ere, fierce as autumn's sun, her lord
Send his keen arrows from the string
To drink the life-blood of our king.
This fury from thy soul dismiss,
The bane of duty, peace, and bliss.
Seek duty's path and walk therein,
And joy and endless glory win.
Restore the captive, ere we feel
The piercing point of Ráma's steel.
O spare thy city, spare the lives
Of us, our friends, our sons and wives.'
Thus spake Vibhíshaṇ wise and brave:
The Rákshas king no answer gave,
But bade his lords the council close,
And sought his chamber for repose.

CANTO. X

VIBHÍSHAṆ'S COUNSEL.

Soon as the light of morning broke,
Vibhíshaṇ from his slumber woke,
And, duty guiding every thought,
The palace of his brother sought.
Vast as a towering hill that shows
His peaks afar, that palace rose.
Here stood within the monarch's gate
Sage nobles skilful in debate.
There strayed in glittering raiment through
The courts his royal retinue,
Where in wild measure rose and fell
The music of the drum and shell,
And talk grew loud, and many a dame
Of fairest feature went and came
Through doors a marvel to behold,
With pearl inlaid on burning gold :
Therein Gandharvas or the fleet
Lords of the storm might joy to meet.
He passed within the wondrous pile,
Chief glory of the giants' isle ;
Thus, ere his fiery course be done,
An autumn cloud admits the sun.

---

[1] Their names are Nikumbha, Rabhasa, Súryaśatru, Suptaghna, Yajnakopa, Mahápárśva, Mahodara, Agniketu, Raśmiketu, Durdharsha, Indraśatru, Prahasta, Virupáksha, Vajradanshṭra, Dhúmráksha, Durmukha, Mahábala.

[2] Similarly Antenor urges the restoration of Helen :

> 'Let Sparta's treasures be this hour restored,
> And Argive Helen own her ancient lord.
> As this advice ye practise or reject,
> So hope success, or dread the dire effect.'

POPE'S *Homer's Iliad*, Book VII.

He heard auspicious voices raise
With loud accord the note of praise,
And sages, deep in Scripture, sing
Each glorious triumph of the king.
He saw the priests in order stand,
Curd, oil, in every sacred hand;
And by them flowers were laid and grain,
Due offerings to the holy train.
Vibhíshan to the monarch bowed,
Raised on a throne above the crowd:
Then, skilled in arts of soft address,
He raised his voice the king to bless,
And sate him on a seat where he
Full in his brother's sight should be.
The chieftain there, while none could hear,
Spoke his true speech for Rávan's ear,
And to his words of wisdom lent
The force of weightiest argument:

'O brother, hear! since Ráma's queen
A captive in thy house has been,
Disastrous omens day by day
Have struck our souls with wild dismay.
No longer still and strong and clear
The flames of sacrifice appear,
But, restless with the frequent spark,
Neath clouds of smoke grow faint and dark.
Our ministering priests turn pale
To see their wonted offerings fail,
And ants and serpents creep and crawl
Within the consecrated hall.[1]
Dried are the udders of our cows,
Our elephants have juiceless brows,[2]
Nor can the sweetest pasture stay
The charger's long unquiet neigh.
Big tears from mules and camels flow
Whose staring coats their trouble show,
Nor can the leech's art restore
Their health and vigour as before.
Rapacious birds are fierce and bold:
Not single hunters as of old,
In banded troops they chase the prey,
Or gathering on our temples stay.
Through twilight hours with shriek and howl
Around the city jackals prowl,
And wolves and foul hyænas wait
Athirst for blood at every gate.
One sole atonement still may cure
These evils, and our weal assure.
Restore the Maithil dame, and win
An easy pardon for thy sin.'

The Rákshas monarch heard, and moved
To sudden wrath his speech reproved:
'No danger, brother, can I see:
The Maithil dame I will not free.
Though all the Gods for Ráma fight,
He yields to my superior might.'
Thus the tremendous king who broke
The ranks of heavenly warriors spoke,
And, sternly purposed to resist,
His brother from the hall dismissed.

CANTO XI.

THE SUMMONS.

Still Rávan's haughty heart rebelled,
The counsel of the wise repelled,
And, as his breast with passion burned,
His thoughts again to Sítá turned.
Thus, to each sign of danger blind,
To love and war he still inclined.
Then mounted he his car that glowed
With gems and golden net, and rode
Where, gathered at the monarch's call,
The nobles filled the council hall.
A host of warriors bright and gay
With coloured robes and rich array,
With shield and mace and spear and sword,
Followed the chariot of their lord.
Mid the loud voice of shells and beat
Of drums he raced along the street,
And, ere he came, was heard afar
The rolling thunder of his car.
He reached the doors: the nobles bent
Their heads before him reverent:
And, welcomed with their loud acclaim,
Within the glorious hall he came.
He sat upon a royal seat
With golden steps beneath his feet,
And bade the heralds summon all
His captains to the council hall.
The heralds heard the words he spake,
And sped from house to house to wake
The giants where they slept or spent
The careless hours in merriment.
These heard the summons and obeyed:
From chamber, grove, and colonnade,
On elephants or cars they rode,
Or through the streets impatient strode.
As birds on rustling pinions fly
Through regions of the darkened sky,
Thus cars and mettled coursers through
The crowded streets of Lanká flew.
The council hall was reached, and then,
As lions seek their mountain den,
Through massy doors that opened wide,
With martial stalk the captains hied.
Welcomed with honour as was meet
They stooped to press their monarch's feet,

[1] The *Agnisálá* or room where the sacrificial fire was kept.

[2] The exudation of a fragrant fluid from the male elephant's temples, especially at certain seasons, is frequently spoken of in Sanskrit poetry. It is said to deceive and attract the bees, and is regarded as a sign of health and masculine vigour.

And each a place in order found
On stool, on cushion, or the ground.
Nor did the sage Vibhíshaṇ long
Delay to join the noble throng.
High on a car that shone like flame
With gold and flashing gems he came,
Drew near and spoke his name aloud,
And reverent to his brother bowed.

CANTO XII.

RÁVAṆ'S SPEECH.

The king in counsel unsurpassed
His eye around the synod cast,
And fierce Prahasta, first and best
Of all his captains, thus addressed:
'Brave master of each warlike art,
Arouse thee and perform thy part.
Array thy fourfold forces[1] well
To guard our isle and citadel.'
The captain of the hosts obeyed,
The troops with prudent skill arrayed;
Then to the hall again he hied,
And stood before the king and cried:
'Each inlet to the town is closed
Without, within, are troops disposed.
With fearless heart thine aim pursue
And do the deed thou hast in view.'
Thus spoke Prahasta in the zeal
That moved him for the kingdom's weal.
And thus the monarch, who pursued
His own delight, his speech renewed:
'In ease and bliss, in toil and pain,
In doubts of duty, pleasure, gain,
Your proper path I need not tell.
For of yourselves ye know it well.
The Storm-Gods, Moon, and planets bring
New glory to their heavenly king,[2]
And, ranged about your monarch, ye
Give joy and endless fame to me.
My secret counsel have I kept,
While senseless Kumbhakarṇa slept.
Six months the warrior's slumbers last
And bind his torpid senses fast;
But now his deep repose he breaks,
The best of all our champions wakes.
I captured, Ráma's heart to wring,
This daughter of Videha's king.
And brought her from that distant land[3]
Where wandered many a Rákshas band.
Disdainful still my love she spurns.
Still from each prayer and offering turns.
Yet in all lands beneath the sun
No dame may rival Sítá, none,
Her dainty waist is round and slight,
Her cheek like autumn's moon is bright.
And she like fruit in graven gold
Mocks her[1] whom Maya framed of old.
Faultless in form, how firmly tread
Her feet whose soles are rosy red!
Ah, as I gaze her beauty takes
My spirit, and my passion wakes.
Looking for Ráma far away
She sought with tears a year's delay,
Nor gazing on her love-lit eye
Could I that earnest prayer deny.
But baffled hopes and vain desire
At length my patient spirit tire.
How shall the sons of Raghu sweep
To vengeance o'er the pathless deep?
How shall they lead the Vánar train
Across the monster-teeming main?
One Vánar yet could find a way
To Lanká's town, and burn and slay.
Take counsel then, remembering still
That we from men need fear no ill;
And give your sentence in debate,
For matchless is the power of fate.
Assailed by you the Gods who dwell
In heaven beneath our fury fell.
And shall we fear these creatures bred
In forests, by Sugríva led?
E'en now on ocean's farther strand,
The sons of Daśaratha stand.
And follow, burning to attack
Their giant foes, on Sítá's track.
Consult then, lords for ye are wise:
A seasonable plan devise,
The captive lady to retain,
And triumph when the foes are slain.
No power can bring across the foam
Those Vánars to our island home;
Or if they madly will defy
Our conquering might, they needs must die.'
Then Kumbhakarṇa's anger woke,
And wroth at Rávaṇ's words he spoke:
'O Monarch, when thy ravished eyes
First looked upon thy lovely prize,
Then was the time to bid us scan
Each peril and mature a plan.
Blest is the king who acts with heed,
And ne'er repents one hasty deed;
And hapless he whose troubled soul
Mourns over days beyond control.

---

[1] Consisting of warriors on elephants, warriors in chariots, charioteers, and infantry.

[2] Indra, generally represented as surrounded by the Maruts or Storm-Gods.

[3] Janasthán, where Ráma lived as an ascetic.

[1] Máyá, regarded as the paragon of female beauty, was the creation of Maya the chief artificer of the Daityas or Dánavs.

Thou hast. in beauty's toils ensnared,
A desperate deed of boldness dared;
By fortune saved ere Ráma's steel
One wound, thy mortal bane, could deal.
But, Rávan, as the deed is done,
The toil of war I will not shun.
This arm, O rover of the night,
Thy foemen to the earth shall smite,
Though Indra with the Lord of Flame,
The Sun and Storms, against me came.
E'en Indra, monarch of the skies,
Would dread my club and mountain size,
Shrink from these teeth and quake to hear
The thunders of my voice of fear.
No second dart shall Ráma cast:
The first he aims shall be the last.
He falls, and these dry lips shall drain
The blood of him my hand has slain;
And Sítá, when her champion dies,
Shall be thine undisputed prize.'

CANTO XIII.

RÁVAN'S SPEECH.

But Mahápárśva saw the sting
Of keen reproach had galled the king;
And humbly, eager to appease
His anger, spoke in words like these:
'And breathes there one so cold and weak
The forest and the gloom to seek
Where savage beasts abound, and spare
To taste the luscious honey there?
Art thou not lord? and who is he
Shall venture to give laws to thee?
Love thy Videhan still, and tread
Upon thy prostrate foeman's head.
O'er Sítá's will let thine prevail,
And strength achieve if flattery fail.
What though the lady yet be coy
And turn her from the proffered joy?
Soon shall her conquered heart relent
And yield to love and blandishment.
With us let Kumbhakarna fight,
And Indrajit of matchless might.
We need not other champions: they
Shall lead us forth to rout and slay.
Not ours to bribe or soothe or part
The foeman's force with gentle art,
Doomed, conquered by our might, to feel
The vengeance of the warrior's steel.'
The Rákshas monarch heard, and moved
By flattering hopes the speech approved:
'Hear me,' he cried, 'great chieftain, tell
What in the olden time befell,—
A secret tale which, long suppressed,
Lies prisoned only in my breast.
One day—a day I never forget—
Fair Punjikasthalá[1] I met,
When, radiant as a flame of fire,
She sought the palace of the Sire.
In passion's eager grasp I tore
From her sweet limbs the robes she wore,
And heedless of her prayers and cries
Strained to my breast the vanquished prize
Like Naliní[2] with soil distained,
The mansion of the Sire she gained,
And weeping made the outrage known
To Brahmá on his heavenly throne.
He in his wrath pronounced a curse,—
That lord who made the universe:
'If, Rávan, thou a second time
Be guilty of so foul a crime,
Thy head in shivers shall be rent:
Be warned, and dread the punishment.
Awed by the threat of vengeance still
I force not Sítá's stubborn will,
Terrific as the sea in might;
My steps are like the Storm-Gods' flight;
But Ráma knows not this, or he
Had never sought to war with me.
Where is the man would idly brave
The lion in his mountain cave,
And wake him when with slumbering eyes
Grim, terrible as Death, he lies?
No, blinded Ráma knows me not:
Ne'er has he seen mine arrows shot;
Ne'er marked them speeding to their aim
Like snakes with cloven tongues of flame
On him those arrows will I turn,
Whose fiery points shall rend and burn.
Quenched by my power when I assail
The glory of his might shall fail,
As stars before the sun grow dim
And yield their feeble light to him.'

CANTO XIV.

VIBHÍSHAN'S SPEECH.

He ceased: Vibhíshan ill at ease
Addressed the king in words like these:
'O Rávan, O my lord, beware
Of Sítá dangerous as fair,
Nor on thy heedless bosom hang
This serpent with a deadly fang.
O King, the Maithil dame restore
To Raghu's matchless son before
Those warriors of the woodlands, vast
As mountain peaks, approaching fast,
Armed with fierce teeth and claws, enclose
Thy city with unsparing foes.
O, be the Maithil dame restored
Ere loosened from the clanging cord

[1] One of the Nymphs of Indra's heaven
[2] The Lotus River, a branch of the heavenly Gangá.

The vengeful shafts of Ráma fly,
And low in death thy princes lie.
In all thy legions hast thou one
A match in war for Raghu's son?
Can Kumbhakarṇa's self withstand,
Or Indrajit, that mighty hand?
In vain with Ráma wilt thou strive:
Thou wilt not save thy soul alive
Though guarded by the Lord of Day
And Storm-Gods' terrible array,
In vain to Indra wilt thou fly,
Or seek protection in the sky,
In Yama's gloomy mansion dwell,
Or hide thee in the depths of hell.'
He ceased: and when his lips were closed
Prahasta thus his rede opposed:
'O timid heart, to counsel thus!
What terrors have the Gods for us?
Can snake, Gandharva, fiend appal
The giants' sons who scorn them all?
And shall we now our birth disgrace,
And dread a king of human race?'
Thus fierce Prahasta counselled ill:
But sage Vibhíshaṇ's constant will
The safety of the realm ensued;
Who thus in turn his speech renewed:
'Yes, when a soul defiled with sin
Shall mount to heaven and enter in,
Then, chieftain, will experience teach
The truth of thy disdainful speech.
Can I, or thou, or these or all
Our bravest compass Ráma's fall,
The chief in whom all virtues shine,
The pride of old Ikshváku's line,
With whom the Gods may scarce compare
In skill to act, in heart to dare?
Yea, idly mayst thou vaunt thee, till
Sharp arrows winged with matchless skill
From Ráma's bowstring, fleet and fierce
As lightning's flame, thy body pierce.
Nikumbha shall not save thee then,
Nor Rávaṇ, from the lord of men.
O Monarch, hear my last appeal,
My counsel for thy kingdom's weal.
This sentence I again declare:
O giant King, beware, beware!
Save from the ruin that impends
Thy town, thy people, and thy friends;
O hear the warning urged once more:
To Raghu's son the dame restore.'

CANTO XV.

INDRAJIT'S SPEECH.

He ceased: and Indrajit the pride
Of Rákshas warriors thus replied:
'Is this a speech our king should hear,
This counsel of ignoble fear?
A scion of our gloriuos race
Should ne'er conceive a thought so base,
But one mid all our kin we find,
Vibhíshaṇ, whose degenerate mind
No spark of gallant pride retains,
Whose coward soul his lineage stains.
Against one giant what can two
Unhappy sons of Raghu do?
Away with idle fears, away!
Matched with our meanest, what are they?
Beneath my conquering prowess fell
The Lord of earth and heaven and hell.[1]
Through every startled region dread
Of my resistless fury spread;
And Gods in each remotest sphere
Confessed the universal fear.
Rending the air with roar and groan,
Airávt[2] to the earth was thrown.
From his huge head the tusks I drew,
And smote the Gods with fear anew.
Shall I who tame celestials' pride,
By whom the fiends are terrified,
Now prove a weakling little worth,
And fail to slay those sons of earth?'
He ceased: Vibhíshaṇ trained and tried
In war and counsel thus replied:
'Thy speech is marked with scorn of truth,
With rashness and the pride of youth.
Yea, to thy ruin like a child
Thou pratest, and thy words are wild.
Most dear, O Indrajit, to thee
Should Rávaṇ's weal and safety be,
For thou art called his son, but thou
Art proved his direst foeman now,
When warned by me thou hast not tried
To turn the coming woe aside.
Both thee and him 'twere meet to slay,
Who brought thee to this hall to-day,
And dared so rash a youth admit
To council where the wisest sit.
Presumptuous, wild, devoid of sense,
Filled full of pride and insolence,
Thy reckless tongue thou wilt not rule
That speaks the counsel of a fool.
Who in the fight may brook or shun
The arrows shot by Raghu's son
With flame and fiery vengeance sped,
Dire as his staff who rules the dead?
O Rávaṇ, let thy people live,
And to the son of Raghu give
Fair robes and gems and precious ore,
And Sítá to his arms restore.'

[1] *Trilokanátha*, Lord of the Three Worlds, is a title of Indra.

[2] The celestial elephant that carries Indra.

CANTO XVI.

RÁVAṆ'S SPEECH.

Then, while his breast with fury swelled,
Thus Rávaṇ spoke, as fate impelled:

'Better with foes thy dwelling make,
Or house thee with the venomed snake,
Than live with false familiar friends
Who further still thy foeman's ends.
I know their treacherous mood, I know
Their secret triumph at thy woe.
They in their inward hearts despise
The brave, the noble, and the wise,
Grieve at their bliss with rancorous hate,
And for their sorrows watch and wait:
Scan every fault with curious eye,
And each slight error magnify.
Ask elephants who roam the wild
How were their captive friends beguiled.
'For fire,' they cry, 'we little care,
For javelin and shaft and snare:
Our foes are traitors, taught to bind
The trusting creatures of their kind.'
Still, still, shall blessings flow from cows,[1]
And Bráhmans love their rigorous vows;
Still woman change her restless will,
And friends perfidious work us ill.
What though with conquering feet I tread
On every prostrate foeman's head;
What though the worlds in abject fear
Their mighty lord in me revere?
This thought my peace of mind destroys
And robs me of expected joys.
The lotus of the lake receives
The glittering rain that gems its leaves,
But each bright drop remains apart:
So is it still with heart and heart.
Deceitful as an autumn cloud
Which, though its thunderous voice be loud,
On the dry earth no torrent sends,
Such is the race of faithless friends.
No riches of the bloomy spray
Will tempt the wandering bee to stay
That loves from flower to flower to range;
And friends like thee are swift to change.
Thou blot upon thy glorious line,
If any giant's tongue but thine
Had dared to give this base advice,
He should not live to shame me twice.'

Then just Vibhíshaṇ in the heat
Of anger started from his seat,
And with four captains of the band
Sprang forward with his mace in hand;
Then, fury flashing from his eye,
Looked on the king and made reply:

'Thy rights, O Rávaṇ, I allow:
My brother and mine elder thou.
Such, though from duty's path they stray,
We love like fathers and obey,
But still too bitter to be borne
Is thy harsh speech of cruel scorn.
The rash like thee, who spurn control,
Nor check one longing of the soul,
Urged by malignant fate repel
The faithful friend who counsels well.
A thousand courtiers wilt thou meet,
With flattering lips of smooth deceit:
But rare are they whose tongue or ear
Will speak the bitter truth, or hear.
Unclose thy blinded eyes and see
That snares of death encompass thee.
I dread, my brother, to behold
The shafts of Ráma, bright with gold,
Flash fury through the air, and red
With fires of vengeance strike thee dead.
Lord, brother, King, again reflect,
Nor this mine earnest prayer reject,
O, save thyself, thy royal town,
Thy people and thine old renown.'

[1] As producers of the *ghí*, clarified butter or sacrificial oil, used in fire-offerngs.

CANTO XVII.

VIBHÍSHAṆ'S FLIGHT.

Soon as his bitter words were said,
To Raghu's sons Vibhíshaṇ fled.[1]
Their eyes the Vánar leaders raised
And on the air-borne Rákhshas gazed,
Bright as a thunderbolt, in size
Like Meru's peak that cleaves the skies,
In gorgeous panoply arrayed
Like Indra's self he stood displayed,
And four attendants brave and bold
Shone by their chief in mail and gold.
Sugríva then with dark surmise
Bent on their forms his wondering eyes,
And thus in hasty words confessed
The anxious doubt that moved his breast:
'Look, look ye Vánars, and beware:
That giant chief sublime in air
With other four in bright array
Comes armed to conquer and to slay.'

[1] This dessertion to the enemy is somewhat abrupt, and is narrated with brevity not usual with Válmíki. In the Bengal recension the preceding speakers and speeches differ considerably from those given in the text which I follow. Vibhíshaṇ is kicked from his seat by Rávaṇ, and then, after telling his mother what has happened, he flies to Mount Kailása where he has an interview with Śiva, and by his advice seeks Ráma and the Vánar army.

Soon as his warning speech they heard,
The Vánar chieftains undeterred
Seized fragments of the rock and trees,
And made reply in words like these:
'We wait thy word: the order give,
And these thy foes shall cease to live.
Command us, mighty King, and all
Lifeless upon the earth shall fall.'

Meanwhile Vibhíshan with the four
Stood high above the ocean shore.
Sugríva and the chiefs he spied,
And raised his mighty voice and cried:
'From Rávan, lord of giants, I
His brother, named Vibhíshan, fly.
From Janasthán he stole the child
Of Janak by his art beguiled,
And in his palace locked and barred
Surrounds her with a Rákshas guard.
I bade him, plied with varied lore,
His hapless prisoner restore.
But he, by Fate to ruin sent,
No credence to my counsel lent,
Mad as the fevered wretch who sees
And scorns the balm to bring him ease.
He scorned the sage advice I gave,
He spurned me like a base-born slave.
I left my children and my wife,
And fly to Raghu's son for life.
I pray thee, Vánar chieftain, speed
To him who saves in hour of need,
And tell him famed in distant lands
That suppliant here Vibhíshan stands.'
The Rákshas ceased: Sugríva hied
To Raghu's noble son and cried:
'A stranger from the giant host,
Borne o'er the sea, has reached the coast;
A secret foe, he comes to slay,
As owls attack their heedless prey.
'Tis thine, O King, in time of need
To watch, to counsel, and to lead,
Our Vánar legions to dispose,
And guard us from our crafty foes.
Vibhíshan from the giants' isle,
King Rávan's brother, comes with guile,
And, feigning from his king to flee,
Seeks refuge, Raghu's son, with thee.
Arise, O Ráma, and prevent
By bold attack his dark intent,
Who comes in friendly guise prepared
To slay thee by his arts ensnared.'

Thus urged Sugríva famed for lore
Of moving words, and spoke no more.
Then Ráma thus in turn addressed
The bold Hanúmán and the rest:
'Chiefs of the Vánar legions, each
Of you has heard Sugríva's speech.
What think ye now? In time of fear,
When peril and distress are near,
In every doubt the wise depend
For counsel on a faithful friend.'

They heard his gracious words, and then
Spake reverent to the lord of men:
'O Raghu's son, thou knowest well
All things of heaven and earth and hell.
'Tis but thy friendship bids us speak
The counsel Ráma need not seek.
So duteous, brave, and true art thou,
Heroic, faithful to thy vow,
Deep in the scriptures, trained and tried,
Still in thy friends wilt thou confide.
Let each of us in turn impart
The secret counsel of his heart,
And strive to win his chief's assent,
By force of wisest argument.'

They ceased and Angad thus began:
'With jealous eye the stranger scan:
Not yet with trusting heart receive
Vibhíshan, nor his tale believe.
These giants wandering far and wide
Their evil nature falsely hide,
And watching with malignant skill
Assail us when we fear no ill.
Well ponder every hope and fear
Until thy doubtful course be clear;
Then own his merit or detect
His guile, and welcome or reject.'
Then Śarabha the bold and brave
In turn his prudent sentence gave:
'Yea, Ráma, send a skilful spy
With keenest tact to test and try.
Then let the stranger, as is just,
Obtain or be refused thy trust.'
Then he whose heart was rich in store
Of scripture's life-directing lore,
King Jámbaván, stood forth and cried:
'Suspect, suspect a foe allied
With Rávan lord of Lanká's isle,
And Rákshas sin and Rákshas guile.'
Then Mainda, wisest chief, who knew
The wrong, the right, the false, the true,
Pondered a while, then silence broke,
And thus his sober counsel spoke:
'Let one with gracious speech draw near
And gently charm Vibhíshan's ear,
Till he the soothing witchery feel
And all his secret heart reveal.
So thou his aims and hopes shalt know,
And hail the friend or shun the foe.'

'Not he,' Hanúmán cried, 'not he
Who taught the Gods[1] may rival thee,
Supreme in power of quickest sense,
First in the art of eloquence.
But hear me soothly speak, O King,
And learn the hope to which I cling.
Vibhíshan comes no crafty spy:
Urged by his brother's fault to fly,
With righteous soul that loathes the sin,
He fled from Lanká and his kin.

[1] Vrihaspati the preceptor of the Gods.

If strangers question, doubt will rise
And chill the heart of one so wise.
Marred by distrust the parle will end,
And thou wilt lose a faithful friend.
Nor let it seem so light a thing
To sound a stranger's heart, O King.
And he, I ween, whate'er he say,
Will ne'er an evil thought betray.
He comes a friend in happy time,
Loathing his brother for his crime.
His ear has heard thine old renown,
The might that struck King Báli down,
And set Sugríva on the throne,
And looking now to thee alone
He comes thy matchless aid to win
And punish Rávan for his sin.
Thus have I tried thy heart to move,
And thus Vibhíshan's truth to prove.
Still in his friendship I confide;
But ponder, wisest, and decide.'

CANTO XVIII.

RÁMA'S SPEECH.

Then Ráma's rising doubt was stilled,
And friendly thoughts his bosom filled.
Thus, deep in Scripture's lore, he spake:
'The suppliant will I ne'er forsake,
Nor my protecting aid refuse
When one in name of friendship sues.
Though faults and folly blot his fame,
Pity and help he still may claim.'
  He ceased: Sugríva bowed his head
And pondered for a while, and said:
  'Past number be his faults or few,
What think ye of the Rákshas who,
When threatening clouds of danger rise,
Deserts his brother's side and flies?
Say, Vánars, who may hope to find
True friendship in his faithless kind?'
  The son of Raghu heard his speech:
He cast a hasty look on each
Of those brave Vánar chiefs, and while
Upon his lips there played a smile,
To Lakshman turned and thus expressed
The thoughts that moved his gallant breast:
'Well versed in Scripture's lore, and sage,
And duly reverent to age,
Is he, with long experience stored,
Who counsels like this Vánar lord.
Yet here, methinks, for searching eyes
Some deeper, subtler matter lies.
To you and all the world are known
The perils of a monarch's throne,
While foe and stranger, kith and kin
By his misfortune trust to win.
By hope of such advantage led,
Vibhíshan o'er the sea has fled.
He in his brother's stead would reign,
And our alliance seeks to gain;
And we his offer may embrace,
A stranger and of alien race.
But if he comes a spy and foe,
What power has he to strike a blow
In furtherance of his close design?
What is his strength compared with mine
And can I, Vánar King, forget
The great, the universal debt;
Ever to aid and welcome those
Who pray for shelter, friends or foes?
Hast thou not heard the deathless praise
Won by the dove in olden days,
Who conquering his fear and hate
Welcomed the slayer of his mate,
And gave a banquet, to refresh
The weary fowler, of his flesh?
Now hear me, Vánar King, rehearse
What Kandu[1] spoke in ancient verse,
Saint Kanva's son who loved the truth
And clave to virtue from his youth:
'Strike not the suppliant when he stand
And asks thee with beseeching hands
For shelter: strike him not although
He were thy father's mortal foe.
No, yield him, be he proud or meek,
The shelter which he comes to seek,
And save thy foeman, if the deed
Should cost thy life, in desperate need.'
And shall I hear the wretched cry,
And my protecting aid deny?
Shall I a suppliant's prayer refuse,
And heaven and glory basely lose?
No, I will do for honour sake
E'en as the holy Kandu spake,
Preserve a hero's name from stain,
And bliss in heaven and glory gain.
Bound by a solemn vow I sware
That all my saving help should share
Who sought me in distress and cried,
'Thou art my hope, and none beside.'
Then go, I pray thee, Vánar King,
Vibhíshan to my presence bring.
Yea, were he Rávan's self, my vow
Forbids me to reject him now.'
  He ceased: the Vánar king approved
And Ráma toward Vibhíshan moved.
So moves, a brother God to greet,
Lord Indra from his heavenly seat.

---

[1] In Book II. Canto XXI, Kandu is me tioned by Ráma as an example of fill obedience. At the command of his fath he is said to have killed a cow.

CANTO XIX.

VIBHÍSHAṆ'S COUNSEL.

When Raghu's son had owned his claim
Down from the air Vibhíshaṇ came,
And with his four attendants bent
At Ráma's feet most reverent.
'O Ráma,' thus he cried, 'in me
Vibhíshaṇ Rávaṇ's brother see.
By him disgraced thine aid I seek,
Sure refuge of the poor and weak.
From Lanká, friends, and wealth I fly,
And reft of all on thee rely.
On thee, the wretch's firmest friend,
My kingdom, joys, and life depend.'

With glance of favour Ráma eyed
The Rákshas chief and thus replied:
'First from thy lips I fain would hear
Each brighter hope, each darker fear.
Speak, stranger, that I well may know
The strength and weakness of the foe.'

He ceased: the Rákshas chief obeyed,
And thus in turn his answer made:
'O Prince, the Self-existent gave
This boon to Rávaṇ; he may brave
All foes in fight; no fiend or snake,
Gandharva, God, his life may take.
His brother Kumbhakarṇa vies
In might with him who rules the skies.
The captain of his armies—fame
Perhaps has taught the warrior's name—
Is terrible Prahasta, who
King Maṇibhadra's[1] self o'erthrew.
Where is the warrior found to face
Young Indrajit, when armed with brace
And guard[2] and bow he stands in mail
And laughs at spear and arrowy hail?
Within his city Lanká dwell
Ten million giants fierce and fell,
Who wear each varied shape at will
And eat the flesh of those they kill.
These hosts against the Gods he led,
And heavenly might discomfited.'

Then Ráma cried: 'I little heed
Gigantic strength or doughty deed.
In spite of all their might has done
The king, the captain, and the son
Shall fall beneath my fury dead,
And thou shalt reign in Rávaṇ's stead.
He, though in depths of earth he dwell,
Or seek protection down in hell,
Or kneel before the Sire supreme,
His forfeit life shall ne'er redeem.
Yea, by my brothers' lives I swear,
I will not to my home repair
Till Rávaṇ and his kith and kin
Have paid in death the price of sin.'

Vibhíshaṇ bowed his head and cried:
'Thy conquering army will I guide
To storm the city of the foe,
And aid the tyrant's overthrow.'
Thus spake Vibhíshaṇ: Ráma pressed
The Rákshas chieftain to his breast,
And cried to Lakshmaṇ: 'Haste and bring
Sea-water for the new-made king.'
He spoke, and o'er Vibhíshaṇ's head
The consecrating drops were shed
Mid shouts that hailed with one accord
The giants' king and Lanká's lord.

'Is there no way,' Hanúmán cried,
'No passage o'er the boisterous tide?
How may we lead the Vánar host
In triumph to the farther coast?'
'Thus,' said Vibhíshaṇ, 'I advise:
Let Raghu's son in suppliant guise
Entreat the mighty Sea to lend
His succour and this cause befriend,
His channels, as the wise have told,
By Sagar's sons were dug of old,[1]
Nor will high-thoughted Ocean scorn
A prince of Sagar's lineage born.'

He ceased; the prudent counsel won
The glad assent of Raghu's son.
Then on the ocean shore a bed
Of tender sacred grass was spread,
Where Ráma at the close of day
Like fire upon an altar lay.

CANTO XX.

THE SPIES.

Śárdúla, Rávaṇ's spy, surveyed
The legions on the strand arrayed,
And bore, his bosom racked with fear,
These tidings to the monarch's ear:

'They come, they come. A rushing tide,
Ten leagues they spread from side to side,
And on to storm thy city press,
Fierce rovers of the wilderness.
Rich in each princely power and grace,
The pride of Daśaratha's race,
Ráma and Lakshmaṇ lead their bands,
And halt them on the ocean sands.
O Monarch, rise, this peril meet;
Risk not the danger of defeat.

---

[1] A King of the Yakshas, or Kuvera himself, the God of Gold.

[2] The brace protects the left arm from injury from the bow-string, and the guard protects the fingers of the right hand.

[1] The story is told in Book I. Cantos XL., XLI., XLII.

First let each wiser art be tried:
Bribe them, or win them, or divide.
Such was the counsel of the spy:
And Rávan called to Śuka: 'Fly,
Sugríva lord of Vánars seek,
And thus my kingly message speak:
'Great power and might and fame are
thine,
Brave scion of a royal line,
King Rikśharajas' son, in thee
A brother and a friend I see.
How wronged by me canst thou complain?
What profit here pretend to gain?
If from the wood the wife I stole
Of Ráma of the prudent soul,
What cause hast thou to mourn the theft?
Thou art not injured or bereft.
Return, O King, thy steps retrace
And seek thy mountain dwelling-place.
No, never may thy hosts within
My Lanká's walls a footing win,
A mighty town whose strength defies
The gathered armies of the skies.'

He ceased: obedient Śuka heard;
With wings and plumage of a bird
He rose in eager speed and through
The air upon his errand flew.
Borne o'er the sea with rapid wing
He stood above the Vánar king,
And spoke aloud, sublime in air,
The message he was charged to bear.
The Vánars heard the words he spoke,
And quick redoubling stroke on stroke
On head and pinions hemmed him round
And bore him struggling to the ground.
The Rákshas wounded and distressed
These words to Raghu's son addressed:
'Quick, quick! his Vánar host restrain,
For heralds never must be slain.
To him alone, a wretch untrue,
The punishment of death is due.
Who leaves his master's speech unsaid
And speaks another in its stead.'
Moved by the suppliant's speech and prayer
Up sprang the prince and cried, forbear.
Saved from his wild assailants' blows
Again the Rákshas herald rose,
And borne on light wings to the sky
Addressed Sugríva from on high:
'O Vánar Monarch, chief endued
With power and wondrous fortitude,
What answer is my king, the fear
And scourge of weeping worlds, to hear?'
'Go tell thy lord,' Sugríva cried.
'Thou, Ráma's foe, art thus defied.
His arm the guilty Báli slew;
Thus, tyrant, shalt thou perish too.
Thy sons, thy friends, proud King, and all
Thy kith and kin with thee shall fall;
And, emptied of the giants' brood,
Burnt Lanká be a solitude.
Fly to the Sun-God's pathway, go
And hide thee deep in hell below:
In vain from Ráma shalt thou flee
Though heavenly warriors fight for thee.
Thine arm subdued, securely bold,
The Vulture-king infirm and old:
But will thy puny strength avail
When Raghu's wrathful sons assail?
A captive in thy palace lies
The lady of the lotus eyes:
Thou knowest not how fierce and strong
Is he whom thou hast dared to wrong.
The best of Raghu's lineage, he
Whose conquering hand shall punish thee.'

He ceased: and Angad raised a cry;
'This is no herald but a spy.
Above thee from his airy post
His rapid eye surveyed our host,
Where with advantage he might scan
Our gathered strength from rear to van.
Bind him, Vánars, bind the spy,
Nor let him back to Lanká fly.'

They hurled the Rákshas to the ground,
They grasped his neck, his pinions bound,
And firmly held him while in vain
His voice was lifted to complain.
But Ráma's heart inclined to spare,
He listened to his plaint and prayer,
And cried aloud: 'O Vánars cease;
The captive from his bonds release.'

CANTO XXI.

OCEAN THREATENED.

His hands in reverence Ráma raised
And southward o'er the ocean gazed;
Then on the sacred grass that made
His lowly couch his limbs he laid.
His head on that strong arm reclined
Which Sítá, best of womankind,
Had loved in happier days to hold
With soft arms decked with pearl and gold.
Then rising from his bed of grass,
'This day,' he cried, 'the host shall pass,
Triumphant to the southern shore,
Or Ocean's self shall be no more.'
Thus vowing in his constant breast
Again he turned him to his rest,
And there, his eyes in slumber closed,
Silent beside the sea reposed.
Thrice rose the Day-God, thrice he set,
The lord of Ocean came not yet,
Thrice came the night, but Raghu's son
No answer by his service won.
To Lakshman thus the hero cried,
His eyes aflame with wrath and pride:
'In vain the softer gifts that grace
The good are offered to the base.
Long-suffering, patience, gentle speech

Their thankless hearts can never reach.
The world to him its honour pays
Whose ready tongue himself can praise,
Who scorns the true, and hates the right,
Whose hand is ever raised to smite.
Each milder art is tried in vain:
It wins no glory, but disdain,
And victory owns no softer charm
Than might which nerves a warrior's arm.
My humble suit is still denied
By Ocean's overweening pride.
This day the monsters of the deep
In throes of death shall wildly leap.
My shafts shall rend the serpents curled
In caverns of the watery world,
Disclose each sunless depth and bare
The tangled pearl and coral there.
Away with mercy! at a time
Like this compassion is a crime.
Welcome, the battle and the foe!
My bow! my arrows and my bow!
This day the Vánars' feet shall tread
The conquered Sea's exhausted bed,
And he who never feared before
Shall tremble to his farthest shore.'
  Red flashed his eyes with angry glow:
He stood and grasped his mighty bow,
Terrific as the fire of doom
Whose quenchless flames the world consume.
His clanging cord the archer drew,
And swift the fiery arrows flew
Fierce as the flashing levin sent
By him who rules the firmament.
Down through the startled waters sped
Each missile with its flaming head.
The foamy billows rose and sank,
And dashed upon the trembling bank
Sea monsters of tremendous form,
With crash and roar of thunder storm.
Still the wild waters rose and fell
Crowned with white foam and pearl and shell.
Each serpent, startled from his rest,
Raised his fierce eyes and glowing crest,
And prisoned Dánavs[1] where they dwelt
In depths below the terror felt.
Again upon his string he laid
A flaming shaft, but Lakshman stayed
His arm, with gentle reasoning tried
To soothe his angry mood, and cried:
'Brother, reflect: the wise control
The rising passions of the soul.
Let Ocean grant, without thy threat,
The boon on which thy heart is set.
That gracious lord will ne'er refuse
When Ráma son of Raghu sues.'
He ceased: and voices from the air
Fell clear and loud, Spare, Ráma, spare.

[1] Fiends and enemies of the Gods.

CANTO XXII.

With angry menace Ráma, best
Of Raghu's sons, the Sea addressed:
'With fiery flood of arrowy rain
Thy channels will I dry and drain.
And I and all the Vánar host
Will reach on foot the farther coast.
Thou shalt not from destruction save
The creatures of the teeming wave,
And lapse of time shall ne'er efface
The memory of the dire disgrace.'
  Thus spoke the warrior, and prepared
The mortal shaft which never spared,
Known, mystic weapon, by the name
Of Brahmá, red with quenchless flame.
Great terror, as he strained the bow,
Struck heaven above and earth below,
Through echoing skies the thunder pealed,
And startled mountains rocked and reeled;
The earth was black with sudden night,
And heaven was blotted from the sight.
Then ever and anon the glare
Of meteors shot through murky air,
And with a wild terrific sound
Red lightnings struck the trembling ground.
In furious gusts the fierce wind blew:
Tall trees it shattered and o'erthrew,
And, smiting with a giant's stroke,
Huge masses from the mountain broke.
A cry of terror long and shrill
Came from each valley, plain, and hill;
Each ruined dale, each riven peak
Re-echoed with a wail or shriek.
  While Raghu's son undaunted gazed,
The waters of the deep were raised,
And, still uplifted more and more,
Leapt in wild flood upon the shore.
Still Ráma looked upon the tide
And kept his post unterrified.
Then from the seething flood upreared
Majestic Ocean's form appeared,
As rising from his eastern height
Springs through the sky the Lord of Light.
Attendant on their monarch came
Sea serpents with their eyes aflame.
Like lazulite and burning gold
His form was wondrous to behold.
Bright with each fairest precious stone
A chain about his neck was thrown.
Calm shone his lotus eyes beneath
The blossoms of his heavenly wreath,
And many a pearl and sea-born gem
Flashed in the monarch's diadem.
There Gangá, tributary queen,
And Sindhu[1] by his lord, were seen,

[1] The Indus.

And every stream and brook renowned
In ancient story girt him round.
Then, as the waters rose and swelled.
The king with suppliant hands upheld,
His glorious head to Ráma bent
And thus addressed him reverent:
'Air, ether, fire, earth, water, true
To nature's will, their course pursue;
And I, as ancient laws ordain,
Unfordable must still remain.
Yet, Raghu's son, my counsel hear:
I ne'er for love or hope or fear
Will pile my waters in a heap
And leave a pathway through the deep.
Still shall my care for thee provide
An easy passage o'er the tide,
And like a city's paven street
Shall be the road beneath thy feet.'
He ceased: and Ráma spoke again:
'This spell is ne'er invoked in vain.
Where shall the magic shaft, to spend
The fury of its might, descend?'
'Shoot,' Ocean cried, 'thine arrow forth
With all its fury to the north,
Where sacred Drumakulya lies,
Whose glory with thy glory vies.
There dwells a wild Ábhíra[1] race,
As vile in act as foul of face,
Fierce Dasyus[2] who delight in ill,
And drink my tributary rill.
My soul no longer may endure
Their neighbourhood and touch impure.
At these, O son of Raghu, aim
Thine arrow with the quenchless flame.'
Swift from the bow, as Ráma drew
His cord, the fiery arrow flew.
Earth groaned to feel the wound, and sent
A rush of water through the rent;
And famed for ever is the well
Of Vraṇa[3] where the arrow fell.
Then every brook and lake beside
Throughout the region Ráma dried.
But yet he gave a boon to bless
And fertilize the wilderness:
No fell disease should taint the air,
And sheep and kine should prosper there:
Earth should produce each pleasant root,
The stately trees should bend with fruit;
Oil, milk, and honey should abound,
And fragrant herbs should clothe the ground.
Then spake the king of brooks and seas
To Raghu's son in words like these:
'Now let a wondrous task be done
By Nala, Viśvakarmá's son,
Who, born of one of Vánar race,
Inherits by his father's grace
A share of his celestial art.
Call Nala to perform his part,
And he, divinely taught and skilled,
A bridge athwart the sea shall build.'
He spoke and vanished Nala, best
Of Vánar chiefs, the king addressed:
'O'er the deep sea where monsters play
A bridge, O Ráma, will I lay;
For, sharer of my father's skill,
Mine is the power and mine the will.
'Tis vain to try each gentler art
To bribe and soothe the thankless heart;
In vain on such is mercy spent;
It yields to naught but punishment.
Through fear alone will Ocean now
A passage o'er his waves allow.
My mother, ere she bore her son,
This boon from Viśvakarmá won:
'O Mandarí, thy child shall be
In skill and glory next to me.'
But why unbidden should I fill
Thine ear with praises of my skill?
Command the Vánar hosts to lay
Foundations for the bridge to-day.'
He spoke: and swift at Ráma's hest
Up sprang the Vánars from their rest,
The mandate of the king obeyed
And sought the forest's mighty shade.
Unrooted trees to earth they threw,
And to the sea the timber drew.
The stately palm was bowed and bent,
Aśokas from the ground were rent,
And towering Sáls and light bamboos,
And trees with flowers of varied hues,
With loveliest creepers wreathed and crowned,
Shook, reeled, and fell upon the ground.
With mighty engines piles of stone
And seated hills were overthrown:
Unprisoned waters sprang on high,
In rain descending from the sky:
And ocean with a roar and swell
Heaved wildly when the mountains fell.
Then the great bridge of wondrous strength
Was built, a hundred leagues in length.
Rocks huge as autumn clouds bound fast
With cordage from the shore were cast,
And fragments of each riven hill,
And trees whose flowers adorned them still.
Wild was the tumult, loud the din
As ponderous rocks went thundering in.
Ere set of sun, so toiled each crew,
Ten leagues and four the structure grew;
The labours of the second day
Gave twenty more of ready way,
And on the fifth, when sank the sun,
The whole stupendous work was done.
O'er the broad way the Vánars sped,
Nor swayed it with their countless tread.

[1] Cowherds, sprung from a Bráhman and a woman of the medical tribe, the modern Ahírs.

[2] Barbarians or outcasts.

[3] *Vraṇa* means wound or rent.

Exultant on the ocean strand
Vibhíshan stood, and, mace in hand,
Longed eager for the onward way,
And chafed impatient at delay.
Then thus to Ráma trained and tried
In battle King Sugríva cried:
'Come, Hanumán's broad back ascend;
Let Angad help to Lakshman lend.
These high above the sea shall bear
Their burthen through the ways of air.'
So, with Sugríva, borne o'erhead
Ikshváku's sons the legions led.
Behind, the Vánar hosts pursued
Their march in endless multitude.
Some skimmed the surface of the wave,
To some the air a passage gave.
Amid their ceaseless roar the sound
Of Ocean's fearful voice was drowned,
As o'er the bridge by Nala planned
They hastened on to Lanká's strand,
Where, by the pleasant brooks, mid trees
Loaded with fruit, they took their ease.

CANTO XXIII.

THE OMENS.

Then Ráma, peerless in the skill
That marks each sign of good and ill,
Strained his dear brother to his breast,
And thus with prudent words addressed:
'Now, Lakshman, by the water's side
In fruitful groves the host divide,
That warriors of each woodland race
May keep their own appointed place.
Dire is the danger: loss of friends,
Of Vánars and of bears, impends.
Distained with dust the breezes blow,
And earth is shaken from below.
The tall hills rock from foot to crown,
And stately trees come toppling down.
In threatening shape, with voice of fear,
The clouds like cannibals appear,
And rain in fitful torrents, red
With sanguinary drops, is shed.
Long streaks of lurid light invest
The evening skies from east to west,
And from the sun at times a ball
Of angry fire is seen to fall.
From every glen and brake is heard
The boding voice of beast and bird:
From den and lair night-prowlers run
And shriek against the falling sun.
Up springs the moon, but hot and red
Kills the sad night with woe and dread;
No gentle lustre, but the gloom
That heralds universal doom.
A cloud of dust and vapour mars
The beauty of the evening stars,
And wild and fearful is the sky
As though the wreck of worlds were nigh.
Around our heads in boding flight
Wheel hawk and vulture, crow and kite;
And every bird of happy note
Shrieks terror from his altered throat.
Sword, spear and shaft shall strew the plain
Dyed red with torrents of the slain.
To-day the Vánar troops shall close
Around the city of our foes.'

CANTO XXIV.

THE SPY'S RETURN.

As shine the heavens with autumn's moon
Refulgent in the height of noon,
So shone with light which Ráma gave
That army of the bold and brave,
As from the sea it marched away
In war's magnificent array,
And earth was shaken by the beat
And trampling of unnumbered feet.
Then to the giants' ears were borne,
The mingled notes of drum and horn,
And clash of tambours smote the sky,
And shouting and the battle cry.
The sound of martial strains inspired
Each chieftain, and his bosom fired:
While giants from their walls replied,
And answering shouts the foe defied,
Then Ráma looked on Lanká where
Bright banners floated in the air,
And, pierced with anguish at the view,
His loving thoughts to Sítá flew.
'There, prisoned by the giant, lies
My lady of the tender eyes,
Like Rohiṇí the queen of stars
O'erpowered by the fiery Mars.'
Then turned he to his brother chief
And cried in agony of grief:
'See on the hill, divinely planned
And built by Viśvakarmá's hand.
The towers and domes of Lanká rise
In peerless beauty to the skies.
Bright from afar the city shines
With gleam of palaces and shrines,
Like pale clouds through the region spread
By Vishṇu's self inhabited.
Fair gardens grow, and woods between
The stately domes are fresh and green,
Where trees their bloom and fruit display,
And sweet birds sing on every spray.
Each bird is mad with joy, and bees
Sing labouring in the bloomy trees
On branches by the breezes bowed,
Where the gay Koïl's voice is loud.'
This said, he ranged with warlike art
Each body of the host apart.

'There in the centre,' Ráma cried,
'Be Angad's place by Níla's side.
Let Rishabh of impetuous might
Be lord and leader on the right,
And Gandhamádan, next in rank,
Be captain of the farther flank.
Lakshmaṇ and I the hosts will lead,
And Jámbaván of ursine breed,
With bold Susheṇ unused to fear,
And Vegadarśí, guide the rear.'
Thus Ráma spoke: the chiefs obeyed;
And all the Vanar hosts arrayed
Showed awful as the autumn sky
When clouds embattled form on high.
Their arms were mighty trees o'erthrown,
And massy blocks of mountain stone.
One hope in every warlike breast,
One firm resolve, they onward pressed,
To die in fight or batter down
The walls and towers of Lanká's town.
Those marshalled legions Ráma eyed,
And thus to King Sugríva cried:
'Now, Monarch, ere the hosts proceed,
Let Śuka, Rávaṇ's spy, be freed.'
He spoke: the Vánar gave consent
And loosed him from imprisonment:
And Śuka, trembling and afraid,
His homeward way to Rávaṇ made.
Loud laughed the lord of Lanká's isle:
'Where hast thou stayed this weary while?
Why is thy plumage marred, and why
Do twisted cords thy pinions tie?
Say, comest thou in evil plight
The victim of the Vánars' spite?'
He ceased: the spy his fear controlled,
And to the king his story told:
'I reached the ocean's distant shore,
Thy message to the king I bore.
In sudden wrath the Vánars rose,
They struck me down with furious blows;
They seized me helpless on the ground,
My plumage rent, my pinions bound.
They would not, headlong in their ire,
Consider, listen, or inquire;
So fickle, wrathful, rough and rude
Is the wild forest multitude.
There, marshalling the Vánar bands,
King Ráma with Sugríva stands,
Ráma the matchless warrior, who
Virádha and Kabandha slew,
Khara, and countless giants more,
And tracks his queen to Lanká's shore.
A bridge athwart the sea was cast,
And o'er it have his legions passed.
Hark! heralded by horns and drums
The terrible avenger comes.
E'en now the giants' isle he fills
With warriors huge as clouds and hills,
And burning with vindictive hate
Will thunder soon at Lanká's gate.
Yield or oppose him: choose between
Thy safety and the Maithil queen.'
He ceased: the tyrant's eyeballs blazed
With fury as his voice he raised:
'No, if the dwellers of the sky,
Gandharvas, fiends assail me, I
Will keep the Maithil lady still,
Nor yield her back for fear of ill.
When shall my shafts with iron hail
My foeman, Raghu's son, assail,
Thick as the bees with eager wing
Beat on the flowery trees of spring?
O, let me meet my foe at length,
And strip him of his vaunted strength,
Fierce as the sun who shines afar
Stealing the light of every star.
Strong as the sea's impetuous might
My ways are like the tempest's flight;
But Ráma knows not this, or he
In terror from my face would flee.'

CANTO XXV.[1]

RÁVAṆ'S SPIES.

When Ráma and the host he led
Across the sea had safely sped,
Thus Rávaṇ, moved by wrath and pride,
To Śuka and to Sáraṇ cried:
'O counsellors, the Vánar host
Has passed the sea from coast to coast,
And Daśaratha's son has wrought
A wondrous deed surpassing thought.
And now in truth I needs must know
The strength and number of the foe.
Go ye, to Ráma's host repair
And count me all the legions there.
Learn well what power each captain leads
His name and fame for warlike deeds.
Learn by what artist's wondrous aid
That bridge athwart the sea was made;
Learn how the Vánar host came o'er
And halted on the island shore.
Mark Ráma son of Raghu well;
His valour, strength, and weapons tell.
Watch his advisers one by one,
And Lakshmaṇ, Raghu's younger son.
Learn with observant eyes, and bring
Unerring tidings to your king.'
He ceased: then swift in Vánar guise
Forth on their errand sped the spies.
They reached the Vánars, and, dismayed,
Their never-ending lines surveyd;
Nor would they try, in mere despair,
To count the countless legions there,

[1] Here in the Bengal recension (Gorresio's edition), begins Book VI.

That crowded valley, plain and hill,
That pressed about each cave and rill.
Though sea-like o'er the land were spread
The endless hosts which Ráma led,
The bridge by thousands yet was lined,
And eager myriads pressed behind.
But sage Vibhíshaṇ's watchful eyes
Had marked the giants in disguise.
He gave command the pair to seize,
And told the tale in words like these:
'O Ráma these, well known erewhile,
Are giant sons of Lanká's isle,
Two counsellors of Rávaṇ sent
To watch the invading armament.'
Vibhíshaṇ ceased: at Ráma's look
The Rákshas envoys quailed and shook;
Then suppliant hand to hand they pressed
And thus Ikshváku's son addressed:
'O Ráma, hear the truth we speak:
Our monarch Rávaṇ bade us seek
The Vánar legions and survey
Their numbers, strength, and vast array'.
Then Ráma, friend and hope and guide
Of suffering creatures, thus replied:
'Now giants, if your eyes have scanned
Our armies, numbering every band,
Marked lord and chief, and gazed their fill,
Return to Rávaṇ when ye will.
If aught remain, if aught anew
Ye fain would scan with closer view,
Vibhíshaṇ, ready at your call,
Will lead you forth and show you all.
Think not of bonds and capture; fear
No loss of life, no peril here:
For, captive, helpless and unarmed,
An envoy never should be harmed.
Again to Lanká's town repair,
Speed to the giant monarch there,
And be these words to Rávaṇ told,
Fierce brother of the Lord of Gold:
'Now, tyrant, tremble for thy sin:
Call up thy friends, thy kith and kin,
And let the power and might be seen
Which made thee bold to steal my queen.
To-morrow shall thy mournful eye
Behold thy bravest warriors die,
And Lanká's city, tower and wall,
Struck by my fiery shafts, will fall.
Then shall my vengeful blow descend
Its rage on thee and thine to spend,
Fierce as the fiery bolt that flew
From heaven against the Dánav crew,
Mid those rebellious demons sent
By him who rules the firmament.'
Thus spake Ikshváku's son, and ceased:
The giants from their bonds released
Lauded the king with glad accord,
And hasted homeward to their lord.
Before the tyrant side by side
Śuka and Sáraṇ stood and cried:
Vibhíshaṇ seized us, King, and fain
His helpless captives would have slain.
But glorious Ráma saw us; he,
Great-hearted hero, made us free.
There in one spot our eyes beheld
Four chiefs on earth unparalleled,
Who with the guardian Gods may vie
Who rule the regions of the sky.
There Ráma stood, the boast and pride
Of Raghu's race, by Lakshmaṇ's side.
There stood the sage Vibhíshaṇ, there
Sugríva strong beyond compare.
These four alone can batter down
Gate, rampart, wall, and Lanká's town.
Nay, Ráma matchless in his form,
A single foe, thy town would storm:
So wondrous are his weapons, he
Needs not the succour of the three.
Why speak we of the countless train
That fills the valley, hill and plain,
The millions of the Vánar breed
Whom Ráma and Sugríva lead?
O King, be wise, contend no more,
And Sítá to her lord restore.'

CANTO XXVI.

THE VÁNAR CHIEFS.

'Not if the Gods in heaven who dwell,
Gandharvas, and the fiends of hell
In banded opposition rise
Against me, will I yield my prize.
Still trembling from the ungentle touch
Of Vánar hands ye fear too much,
And bid me, heedless of the shame,
Give to her lord the Maithil dame.'
Thus spoke the king in stern reproof;
Then mounted to his palace roof
Aloft o'er many a story raised,
And on the lands beneath him gazed.
There by his faithful spies he stood
And looked on sea and hill and wood.
There stretched before him far away
The Vánars' numberless array:
Scarce could the meadows' tender green
Beneath their trampling feet be seen.
He looked a while with furious eye,
Then questioned thus the nearer spy:
'Bend, Sáraṇ, bend thy gaze, and show
The leaders of the Vánar foe.
Tell me their heroes' names, and teach
The valour, power and might of each.'
Obedient Sáraṇ eyed the van,
The leaders marked, and thus began:
'That chief conspicuous at the head
Of warriors in the forest bred,
Who hither bends his ruthless eye
And shouts his fearful battle cry:

Whose voice with pealing thunder shakes
All Lanká, with the groves and lakes
And hills that tremble at the sound,
Is Níla, for his might renowned:
First of the Vánar lords controlled
By King Sugríva lofty-souled.
He who his mighty arm extends,
And his fierce eye on Lanká bends,
In stature like a stately tower,
In colour like a lotus flower,
Who with his wild earth-shaking cries
Thee, Rávaṇ, to the field defies,
Is Angad, by Sugríva's care
Anointed his imperial heir:
In wondrous strength, in martial fire
Peer of King Báli's self, his sire;
For Ráma's sake in arms arrayed
Like Varuṇ called to Śakra's aid.
Behind him, girt by warlike bands,
Nala the mighty Vánar stands,
The son of Viśvakarmá, he
Who built the bridge athwart the sea.
Look farther yet, O King, and mark
That chieftain clothed in Sandal bark.
'Tis Śweta, famed among his peers,
A sage whom all his race reveres.
See, in Sugríva's ear he speaks,
Then, hasting back, his post reseeks,
And turns his practised eye to view
The squadrons he has formed anew.
Next Kumud stands who roamed of yore
On Gomatí's[1] delightful shore,
Feared where the waving woods invest
His seat on Mount Sanrochan's crest.
Next him, a chieftain strong and dread,
Comes Chaṇḍa at his legions' head;
Exulting in his warrior might
He hastens, burning for the fight,
And boasts that his unaided powers
Shall cast to earth thy walls and towers.
Mark, mark that chief of lion gait,
Who views thee with a glance of hate
As though his very eyes would burn
The city walls to which they turn:
'Tis Rambha, Vánar king: he dwells
In Krishṇagirí's tangled dells,
Where Vindhya's pleasant slopes are spread
And fair Sudarśan lifts his head.
There, listening with erected ears,
Śarabha, mighty chief, appears.
His soul is burning for the strife,
Nor dreads the jeopardy of life.
He trembles as he moves, for ire,
And bends around his glance of fire.
Next, like a cloud that veils the skies,
A chieftain of terrific size,
Conspicuous mid the Vánars, comes
With battle shout like rolling drums.
'Tis Panas, trained in war and tried,
Who dwells on Páriyátra's side.
He, far away, the chief who throws
A glory o'er the marshalled rows
That ranged behind their captain stand
Exulting on the ocean strand,
Is Vinata the fierce in fight,
Preëminent like Dardur's height.
That chieftain bending down to drink
On lovely Veṇá's verdant brink,
Is Krathan; now he lifts his eyes
And thee to mortal fray defies.
Next Gavaya comes, whose haughty mind
Scorns all the warriors of his kind.
He comes to trample—such his boast—
On Lanká with his single host.'

[1] The Goomtee.

CANTO XXVII.

THE VÁNAR CHIEFS.

'Yet more remain, brave chiefs who stake
Their noble lives for Ráma's sake.
See, glorious, golden-coated, one
Who glisters like the morning sun,
Whom thousands of his race surround,
'Tis Hara for his strength renowned,
Next comes a mighty chieftain, he
Whose legions, armed with rock and tree,
Press on, in numbers passing tale,
The ramparts of our town to scale.
O Rávaṇ, see the king advance
Terrific with his fiery glance,
Girt by the bravest of his train,
Majestic as the God of Rain,
Parjanya, when his host of clouds
About the king, embattled, crowds:
On Rikshaván's high mountain nursed,
In Narmadá[1] he slakes his thirst,
Dhúmra, proud ursine chief, who leads
Wild warriors whom the forest breeds.
His brother, next in strength and age,
In Jámbaván the famous sage.
Of yore his might and skill he lent
To him who rules the firmament,
And Indra's liberal boons repaid
The chieftain for the timely aid.
There like a gloomy cloud that flies
Borne by the tempest through the skies,
Pramáthí stands: he roamed of yore
The forest wilds on Gangá's shore,
Where elephants were struck with dread
And trembling at his coming fled.
There on his foes he loved to sate
The old hereditary hate.[2]

[1] The Anglicized Nerbudda.

[2] According to a Pauranik legend Kesarí Hanumán's putative father had killed an Asur or demon who appeared in the

Look, Gaja and Gaváksha show
Their lust of battle with the foe.
See Nala burning for the fray,
And Nila chafing at delay.
Behind the eager captains press
Wild hosts in numbers numberless,
And each for Ráma's sake would fall
Or force his way through Lanká's wall.'

CANTO XXVIII.

THE CHIEFTAINS.

There Sáraṇ ceased: then Śuka broke
The silence and to Rávaṇ spoke:
'O Monarch, yonder chiefs survey:
Like elephants in size are they,
And tower like stately trees that grow
Where Gangá's nursing waters flow;
Yea, tall as mountain pines that fling
Long shadows o'er the snow-crowned king.
They all in wild Kishkindhá dwell
And serve their lord Sugríva well.
The Gods' and bright Gandharvas' seed,
They take each form that suits their need.
Now farther look, O Monarch, where
Those chieftains stand, a glorious pair,
Conspicuous for their godlike frames;
Dwivid and Mainda are their names.
Their lips the drink of heaven have known,
And Brahmá claims them for his own.
That chieftain whom thine eyes behold
Refulgent like a hill of gold,
Before whose wrathful might the sea
Roused from his rest would turn and flee,
The peerless Vánar, he who came
To Lanká for the Maithil dame,
The Wind-God's son Hanúmán; thou
Hast seen him once, behold him now.
Still nearer let thy glance be bent,
And mark that prince preëminent
Mid chieftains for his strength and size
And splendour of his lotus eyes.
Far through the worlds his virtues shine,
The glory of Ikshváku's line.
The path of truth he never leaves,
And still through all to duty cleaves.
Deep in the Vedas, skilled to wield
The mystic shafts to him revealed:
Whose flaming darts to heaven ascend,
And through the earth a passage rend:
In might like him who rules the sky;
Like Yama, when his wrath grows high:
Whose queen, the darling of his soul,
Thy magic art deceived and stole:
There royal Ráma stands and longs
For battle to avenge his wrongs.
Near on his right a prince, in hue
Like pure gold freshly burnished, view:
Broad is his chest, his eye is red,
His black hair curls about his head:
'Tis Lakshmaṇ, faithful friend, who shares
His brother's joys, his brother's cares.
By Ráma's side he loves to stand
And serve him as his better hand,
For whose dear sake without a sigh
The warrior youth would gladly die
On Ráma's left Vibhíshaṇ view,
With giants for his retinue:
King-making drops have dewed his head,
Appointed monarch in thy stead,
Behold that chieftain sternly still,
High towering like a rooted hill,
Supreme in power and pride of place,
The monarch of the Vánar race.
Raised high above his woodland kind,
In might and glory, frame and mind,
His head above his host he shows
Conspicuous as the Lord of Snows.
His home is far from hostile eyes
Where deep in woods Kishkindhá lies.
A glistering chain which flowers bedeck
With burnished gold adorns his neck.
Queen Fortune, loved by Gods and kings,
To him her chosen favourite clings.
That chain he owes to Ráma's grace,
And Tárá and his kingly place.
In him the great Sugríva know,
Whom Ráma rescued from his foe.'[1]

CANTO XXIX.

ŚÁRDU'LA CAPTURED.

The giant viewed with earnest ken
The Vánars and the lords of men;
Then thus, with grief and anger moved,
In bitter tone the spies reproved:
'Can faithful servants hope to please
Their master with such tales as these?
Or hope ye with wild words to wring
The bosom of your lord and king?
Such words were better said by those
Who come arrayed our mortal foes.
In vain your ears have heard the sage,
And listened to the lore of age,
Untaught, though lectured many a day,
The first great lesson, to obey,
'Tis marvel Rávaṇ reigns and rules
Whose counsellors are blind and fools.
Has death no terrors that ye dare
To tempt your monarch to despair,

---

form of an elephant, and hence arose the hostility between Vánars and elephants.

[1] Here follows the enumeration of Sugriva's forces which I do not attempt to follow. It soon reaches a hundred thousand billions.

From whose imperial mandate flow
Disgrace and honour, weal and woe?
Yea, forest trees, when flames are fanned
About their scorching trunks, may stand;
But naught can set the sinner free
When kings the punishment decree.
I would not in mine anger spare
The traitorous foe-praising pair,
But years of faithful service plead
For pardon, and they shall not bleed.
Henceforth to me be dead: depart,
Far from my presence and my heart.'
Thus spoke the angry king: the two
Cried, Long live Rávan, and withdrew.
The giant monarch turned and cried
To strong Mahodar at his side:
'Go thou, and spies more faithful bring.
More duteous to their lord the king.'
Swift at his word Mahodar shed,
And came returning at the head
Of long-tried messengers, who bent
Before their monarch reverent.
'Go quickly hence,' said Rávan 'scan
With keenest eyes the foeman's plan.
Learn who, as nearest friends, advise
And mould each secret enterprise.
Learn when he wakes and goes to rest,
Sound every purpose of his breast.
Learn what the prince intends to-day:
Watch keenly all, and come away.'
With joy they heard the words he said:
Then with Śárdúla at their head
About the giant king they went
With circling paces reverent.
By fair Suvela's grassy side
The chiefs of Raghu's race they spied,
Where, shaded by the waving wood,
Vibhíshan and Sugríva stood.
A while they rested there and viewed
The Vánars' countless multitude.
Vibhíshan with observant eyes
Knew at a glance the giant spies,
And bade the warriors of his train
Bind the rash foes with cord and chain:
'Śárdúla's is the sin,' he cried.
He neath the Vánars' hands had died,
But Ráma from their fury freed
The captive in his utmost need,
And, merciful at sight of woe,
Loosed all the spies and bade them go.
Then home to Lanká's monarch fled
The giant chiefs discomfited.

CANTO XXX.

SÁRDÚLA'S SPEECH.

They told their lord that Ráma still
Lay waiting by Suvela's hill.
The tyrant, flushed with angry glow,
Heard of the coming of the foe,
And thus with close inquiry pressed
Śárdúla spokesman for the rest:
'Why art thou sad, night-rover? speak:
Has grief or terror changed thy cheek?
Have the wild Vánars' hostile bands
Assailed thee with their mighty hands?
Sárdúla heard, but scarce might speak;
His trembling tones were faint and weak:
'O Giant King, in vain we try
The purpose of the foe to spy.
Their strength and number none may tell,
And Ráma guards his legions well.
He leaves no hope to prying eyes,
And parley with the chiefs denies:
Each road and path a Vánar guard,
Of mountain size, has closed and barred.
Soon as my feet an entrance found
By giants was I seized and bound,
And wounded sore I fell beneath
Their fists and knees and hands and teeth.
Then trembling, bleeding, wellnigh dead
To Ráma's presence was I led.
He in his mercy stooped to save,
And freedom to the captive gave.
With rocks and shattered mountains he
Has bridged his way athwart the sea,
And he and all his legions wait
Embattled close to Lanká's gate.
Soon will the host thy wall assail,
And, swarming on, the rampart scale.
Now, O my King, his consort yield,
Or arm thee with the sword and shield.
This choice is left thee: choose between
Thy safety and the Maithil queen.[1]

CANTO XXXI.

THE MAGIC HEAD.

The tyrant's troubled eye confessed
The secret fear that filled his breast.
With dread of coming woe dismayed
He called his counsellors to aid:
Then sternly silent, deep in thought,
His chamber in the palace sought.
Then, as the surest hope of all,
The monarch bade his servants call

[1] I omit the rest of this canto, which is mere repetition. Rávan gives in the same words his former answer that the Gods, Gandharvas and fiends combined shall not force him to give up Sítá. He then orders Śárdúla to tell him the names of the Vánar chieftains whom he has seen in Ráma's army. These have already been mentioned by Śuka and Sáraṇ.

Vidyujjihva, whom magic skill
Made master of the means of ill.
Then spake the lord of Lanká's isle:
'Come, Sítá with thine arts beguile.
With magic skill and deftest care
A head like Ráma's own prepare.
This head, long shafts and mighty bow,
To Janak's daughter will we show.'
He ceased: Vidyujjihva obeyed,
And wondrous magic skill displayed;
And Rávaṇ for the art he showed
An ornament of price bestowed.
Then to the grove where Sítá lay
The lord of Lanká took his way.
Pale, wasted, weeping, on the ground
The melancholy queen he found,
Whose thoughts in utmost stress of ill
Were fixed upon her husband still.
The giant king approached the dame,
Declared in tones of joy his name;
Then heeding naught her wild distress
Bespake her, stern and pitiless:
'The prince to whom thy fancies cling
Though loved and wooed by Lanká's king,
Who slew the noble Khara,—he
Is slain by warriors sent by me.
Thy living root is hewn away,
Thy scornful pride is tamed to-day.
Thy lord in battle's front has died,
And Sitá shall be Rávaṇ's bride.
Hence, idle thoughts: thy hope is fled;
What wilt thou, Sítá, with the dead?
Rise, child of Janak, rise and be
The queen of all my queens and me.
Incline thine ear, and I will tell,
Dear lady, how thy husband fell.
He bridged his way across the sea
With countless troops to fight with me.
The setting sun had flushed the west
When on the shore they took their rest.
Weary with toil no watch they kept:
Securely on the sands they slept.
Prahasta's troops assailed our foes,
And smote them in their deep repose.
Scarce could their bravest prove their might:
They perished in the dark of night.
Axe, spear, and sword, directed well,
Upon the sleeping myriads fell.
First in the fight Prahasta's sword
Reft of his head thy slumbering lord.
Roused at the din Vibhíshaṇ rose,
The captive of surrounding foes,
And Lakshmaṇ through the woods that spread
Around him with his Vánars fled.
Hanúmán fell: one deadly stroke
The neck of King Sugríva broke,
And Mainda sank, and Dwivid lay
Gasping in blood his life away.
The Vánars died, or fled dispersed
Like cloudlets when the storm has burst.
Some rose aloft in air, and more
Ran to the sea and filled the shore.
On shore, in woods, on hill and plain
Our conquering giants left the slain.
Thus my victorious host o'erthrew
The Vánars, and thy husband slew:
See, rudely stained with dust, and red
With dropping blood, the severed head.'
Then, turning to a Rákshas slave,
The ruthless king his mandate gave;
And straight Vidyujjihva who bore
The head still wet with dripping gore,
The arrows and the mighty bow,
Bent down before his master low.
'Vidyujjihva,' cried Rávaṇ, 'place
The head before the lady's face,
And let her see with weeping eyes
That low in death her husband lies.'
Before the queen the giant laid
The beauteous head his art had made.
And Rávaṇ cried: 'Thine eyes will know
These arrows and the mighty bow.
With fame of this by Ráma strung
The earth and heaven and hell have rung.
Prahasta brought it hither when
His hand had slain thy prince of men.
Now, widowed Queen, thy hopes resign;
Forget thy husband and be mine.'

CANTO XXXII.

SÍTÁ'S LAMENT.

Again her eyes with tears o'erflowed:
She gazed upon the head he showed,
Gazed on the bow so famed of yore,
The glorious bow which Ráma bore.
She gazed upon his cheek and brows,
The eyes of her beloved spouse;
His lips, the lustre of his hair,
The priceless gem that glittered there.
The features of her lord she knew,
And, pierced with anguish at the view,
She lifted up her voice and cried:
'Kaikeyí, art thou satisfied?
Now all thy longings are fulfilled;
The joy of Raghu's race is killed,
And ruined is the ancient line,
Destroyer, by that fraud of thine.
Ah, what offence, O cruel dame,
What fault in Ráma couldst thou blame,
To drive him clad in hermit dress
With Sítá to the wilderness?
Great trembling seized her frame, and she
Fell like a stricken plantain tree.
As lie the dead she lay: at length
Slowly regaining sense and strength,
On the dear head she fixed her eye

And cried with very bitter cry:
'Ah, when thy cold dead cheek I view,
My hero, I am murdered too.
Then first a faithful woman's eyes
See sorrow, when her husband dies.
When thou, my lord, wast nigh to save,
Some stealthy hand thy death wound gave.
Thou art not dead: rise, hero, rise;
Long life was thine, as spake the wise
Whose words, I ween, are ever true,
For faith lies open to their view.
Ah lord, and shall thy head recline
On earth's cold breast, forsaking mine,
Counting her chill lap dearer far
Than I and my caresses are?
Ah, is it thus these eyes behold
Thy famous bow adorned with gold,
Whereon of yore I loved to bind
Sweet garlands that my hands had twined?
And hast thou sought in heaven a place
Amid the founders of thy race,
Where in the home deserved so well
Thy sires and Daśaratha dwell?
Or dost thou shine a brighter star
In skies where blest immortals are,
Forsaking in thy lofty scorn
The race wherein thy sires were born?
Turn to my gaze, O turn thine eye:
Why are thy cold lips silent, why?
When first we met as youth and maid,
When in thy hand my hand was laid,
Thy promise was thy steps should be
Through life in duty's path with me.
Remember, faithful still, thy vow,
And take me with thee even now.
Is that broad bosom where I hung,
That neck to which I fondly clung,
Where flowery garlands breathed their scent,
By hungry dogs and vultures rent?
Shall no funereal honours grace
The parted lord of Raghu's race,
Whose bounty liberal fees bestowed,
For whom the fires of worship glowed?
Kauśalyá wild with grief will see
One sole survivor of the three
Who in their hermit garments went
To the dark woods in banishment.
Then at her cry shall Lakshman tell
How, slain by night, the Vánars fell;
How to thy side the giants crept,
And slew the hero as he slept.
Thy fate and mine the queen will know,
And broken-hearted die of woe.
For my unworthy sake, for mine,
Ráma, the glory of his line,
Who bridged his way across the main,
Is basely in a puddle slain;
And I, the graceless wife he wed,
Have brought this ruin on his head.
Me, too, on him, O Rávan, slay:
The wife beside her husband lay.
By his dear body let me rest,
Cheek close to cheek and breast to breast,
My happy eyes I then will close,
And follow whither Ráma goes.'
Thus cried the miserable dame;
When to the king a warder came,
Before the giant monarch bowed
And said that, followed by a crowd
Of counsellors and lords of state,
Prahasta stood before the gate,
And, sent by some engrossing care,
Craved audience of his master there.
The anxious tyrant left his seat
And hastened forth the chief to meet:
Then summoning his nobles all,
Took counsel in his regal hall.
When Lanká's lord had left the queen,
The head and bow no more were seen.
The giant king his nobles eyed,
And, terrible as Yama, cried:
'O faithful lords, the time is come:
Gather our hosts with beat of drum.
Nigh to the town our foeman draws:
Be prudent, nor reveal the cause.'
The nobles listened and obeyed:
Swift were the gathered troops arrayed,
And countless rovers of the night
Stood burning for the hour of fight.

CANTO XXXIII.

SARAMÁ.

But Saramá, of gentler mood,
With pitying eyes the mourner viewed,
Stole to her side and softly told
Glad tidings that her heart consoled,
Revealing with sweet voice and smile
The secret of the giant's guile.
She, one of those who night and day
Watching in turns by Sítá lay,
Though Rákshas born felt pity's touch,
And loved the hapless lady much.
'I heard,' she said, 'thy bitter cry,
Heard Rávan's speech and thy reply,
For, hiding in the thicket near,
No word or tone escaped mine ear.
When Rávan hastened forth I bent
My steps to follow as he went,
And learnt the secret cause that drove
The monarch from the Aśoka grove.
Believe me, Queen, thou needst not weep
For Ráma slaughtered in his sleep.
Thy lion lord of men defies
By day attack, by night surprise.
Can even giants slay with ease
Vast hosts who fight with brandished trees,
For whom, with eye that never sleeps,
His constant watch thy Ráma keeps?

Lord of the mighty arm and chest,
Of earthly warriors first and best,
Whose fame through all the regions rings,
Proud scion of a hundred kings;
Who guards his life and loves to lend
His saving succour to a friend:
Whose bow no hand but his can strain,—
Thy lord, thy Ráma is not slain.
Obedient to his master's will,
A great magician, trained in ill,
With deftest art surpassing thought
That marvellous illusion wrought.
Let rising hope thy grief dispel:
Look up and smile, for all is well,
And gentle Lakshmí, Fortune's Queen,
Regards thee with a favouring mien.
Thy Ráma with his Vánar train
Has thrown a bridge athwart the main,
Has led his countless legions o'er,
And ranged them on this southern shore.
These eyes have seen the hero stand
Girt by his hosts on Lanká's strand,
And breathless spies each moment bring
Fresh tidings to the giant king;
And every peer and lord of state
Is called to counsel and debate.'
She ceased: the sound, long loud and clear,
Of gathering armies smote her ear,
Where call of drum and shell rang out,
The tambour and the battle shout;
And, while the din the echoes woke,
Again to Janak's child she spoke:
'Hear, lady, hear the loud alarms
That call the Rákshas troops to arms,
From stable and from stall they lead
The elephant and neighing steed,
Brace harness on with deftest care,
And chariots for the fight prepare.
Swift o'er the trembling ground career
Mailed horsemen armed with axe and spear,
And here and there in road and street
The terrible battalions meet.
I hear the gathering near and far,
The snorting steed, the rattling car.
Bold chieftains, leaders of the brave,
Press densely on, like wave on wave,
And bright the evening sunbeams glance
On helm and shield, on sword and lance.
Hark, lady, to the ringing steel,
Hark to the rolling chariot wheel:
Hark to the mettled courser's neigh
And drums' loud thunder far away.
The Queen of Fortune holds thee dear,
For Lanká's troops are struck with fear,
And Ráma with the lotus eyes,
Like Indra monarch of the skies,
With conquering arm will slay his foe
And free his lady from her woe.
Soon will his breast support thy head,
And tears of joy thine eyes will shed.
Soon by his mighty arm embraced
The long-lost rapture wilt thou taste,
And Ráma, meet for highest bliss,
Will gain his guerdon in thy kiss.'

CANTO XXXIV.

SARAMA'S TIDINGS.

Thus Saramá her story told:
And Sítá's spirit was consoled,
As when the first fresh rain is shed
The parching earth is comforted.
Then, filled with zeal for Sítá's sake,
Again in gentle tones she spake,
And, skilled in arts that soothe and please,
Addressed the queen in words like these:
'Thy husband, lady, will I seek,
Say the fond words thy lips would speak,
And then, unseen of any eye,
Back to thy side will swiftly fly.
My airy flights are speedier far
Than Garuda's and the tempest are.'
Then Sítá spake: her former woe
Still left her accents faint and low:
'I know thy steps, which naught can stay,
Can urge through heaven and hell their way.
Then if thy love and changeless will
Would serve the helpless captive still,
Go forth and learn each plot and guile
Planned by the lord of Lanká's isle.
With magic art like maddening wine
He cheats these weeping eyes of mine,
Torments me with his suit, nor spares
Reproof or flattery, threats or prayers.
These guards surround me night and day;
My heart is sad, my senses stray;
And helpless in my woe I fear
The tyrant Rávan even here.'
Then Saramá replied: 'I go
To learn the purpose of thy foe,
Soon by thy side again to stand
And tell thee what the king has planned.'
She sped, she heard with eager ears
The tyrant speak his hopes and fears,
Where, gathered at their master's call,
The nobles filled the council hall;
Then swiftly, to her promise true,
Back to the Aśoka grove she flew.
The lady on the grassy ground,
Longing for her return, she found;
Who with a gentle smile, to greet
The envoy, led her to a seat.
Through her worn frame a shiver ran
As Saramá her tale began:
'There stood the royal mother: she
Besought her son to set thee free,

And to her counsel, tears and prayers,
The elder nobles added theirs:
'O be the Maithil queen restored
With honour to her angry lord.
Let Janasthán's unhappy fight
Be witness of the hero's might.
Hanúmán o'er the waters came
And looked upon the guarded dame.
Let Lanká's chiefs who fought and fell
The prowess of the leader tell.'
In vain they sued, in vain she wept,
His purpose still unchanged he kept.
As clings the miser to his gold,
He would not loose thee from his hold.
No, never till in death he lies,
Will Lanká's lord release his prize.
Soon slain by Ráma's arrows all
The giants with their king will fall,
And Ráma to his home will lead
His black-eyed queen from bondage freed.'
An awful sound that moment rose
From Lanká's fast-approaching foes,
Where drum and shell in mingled peal
Made earth in terror rock and reel.
The hosts within the walls arrayed
Stood trembling, in their hearts dismayed;
Thought of the tempest soon to burst,
And Lanká's lord, their ruin, cursed.

CANTO XXXV.

MÁLYAVÁN'S SPEECH.

The fearful notes of drum and shell
Upon the ear of Rávan fell.
One moment quailed his haughty look,
One moment in his fear he shook.
But, soon recalling wonted pride,
His counsellors he sternly eyed,
And with a voice that thundered through
The council hall began anew:
'Lords, I have heard—your tongues have told—
How Raghu's son is fierce and bold,
To Lanká's shore has bridged his way,
And hither leads his wild array.
I know your might, in battle tried,
Fighting and conquering by my side.
Why now, when such a foe is near,
Looks eye to eye in silent fear?'
He ceased: his mother's sire, well known
For wisdom in the council shown,
Mályaván, sage and faithful guide,
Thus to the monarch's speech replied:
'Long reigns the king in safe repose,
Unmoved by fear of vanquished foes,
Whose feet by saving knowledge led
In justice path delight to tread:
Who knows to sheath the sword or wield,
To offer peace, to strike or yield:
Prefers, when foes are stronger, peace,
And bids a doubtful conflict cease.
Now, King, the choice before thee lies,
Make peace with Ráma, and be wise.
This day the captive queen restore
Who brings the foe to Lanká's shore.
The Sire by whom the worlds are swayed
Of yore the Gods and demons made.
With these Injustice sided; those
Fair Justice for her champions chose.
Still Justice dwells with Gods above;
Injustice, fiends and giants love.
Thou, through the worlds that fear thee, long
Hast scorned the right and loved the wrong,
And Justice, with thy foes allied,
Gives might resistless to their side.
Thou, guided by thy wicked will,
Hast found delight in deeds of ill,
And sages in their holy rest
Have trembled, by thy power oppressed.
But they, who check each vain desire,
Are clothed with might which burns like fire.
In them the power and glory live
Which zeal and saintly fervour give.
Their constant task, their sole delight
Is worship and each holy rite,
To chant aloud the Veda hymn,
Nor let the sacred fires grow dim.
Now through the air like thunder ring
The echoes of the chants they sing.
The vapours of their incense rise
And veil with cloudy pall the skies,
And Rákshas might grows weak and faint
Killed by the power of sage and saint.
By Brahmá's boon thy life was screened
From God, Gandharva, Yaksha, fiend;
But Vánars, men, and bears, arrayed
Against thee now, thy shores invade.
Red meteors, heralds of despair,
Flash frequent through the lurid air,
Foretelling to my troubled mind
The ruin of the Rákshas kind.
With awful thunderings overhead
Clouds black as night are densely spread,
And oozing from the gloomy pall
Great drops of blood on Lanká fall.
Dogs roam through house and shrine to steal
The sacred oil and curd and meal.
Cats pair with tigers, hounds with swine,
And asses' foals are born of kine.
In these and countless signs I trace
The ruin of the giant race.
'Tis Vishnu's self who comes to storm
Thy city, clothed in Ráma's form;
For, well I ween, no mortal hand
The ocean with a bridge has spanned.
O giant King, the dame release,
And sue to Raghu's son for peace.'

CANTO XXXVI.

RÁVAṆ'S REPLY.

But Rávaṇ's breast with fury swelled,
And thus he spake by Death impelled,
While, under brows in anger bent,
Fierce glances from his eyes were sent:
'The bitter words which thou, misled
By friendly thought, hast fondly said,
Which praise the foe and counsel fear,
Unheeded fall upon mine ear.
How canst thou deem a mighty foe
This Ráma who, in stress of woe,
Seeks, banished as his sire decreed,
Assistance from the Vánar breed?
Am I so feeble in thine eyes,
Though feared by dwellers of the skies,—
Whose might in many a battle shown
The glorious race of giants own?
Shall I for fear of him restore
The lady whom I hither bore,
Exceeding fair like Beauty's Queen[1]
Without her well-loved lotus seen?
Around the chief let Lakshmaṇ stand,
Sugríva, and each Vánar band,
Soon, Málgaván, thine eyes will see
This boasted Ráma slain by me.
I in the brunt of war defy
The mightiest warriors of the sky;
And if I stoop to combat men,
Shall I be weak and tremble then?
This mangled trunk the foe may rend,
But Rávaṇ ne'er can yield or bend,
And be it vice or virtue, I
This nature never will belie.
What marvel if he bridged the sea?
Why should this deed disquiet thee?
This, only this, I surely know,
Back with his life he shall not go.'

Thus in loud tones the king exclaimed,
And mute stood Málgaván ashamed.
His reverend head he humbly bent,
And slowly to his mansion went.
But Rávaṇ stayed, and deep in care
Held counsel with his nobles there,
All entrance to secure and close,
And guard the city from their foes.
He bade the chief Prahasta wait,
Commander at the eastern gate.
To fierce Mahodar, strong and brave,
To keep the southern gate, he gave,
Where Mahápárśva's might should aid
The chieftain with his hosts arrayed.
To guard the west—no chief more fit—
He placed the warrior Indrajit,
His son, the giant's joy and boast,
Surrounded by a Rákshas host:
And mighty Sáran hastened forth
With Śuka to protect the north.[1]
'I will myself,' the monarch cried,
'Be present on the northern side.'
These orders for the walls' defence
The tyrant gave, then parted thence,
And, by the hope of victory fired,
To chambers far within, retired.

[1] Lakshmí is the Goddess both of beauty and fortune, and is represented with a lotus in her hand.

CANTO XXXVII.

PREPARATIONS.

Lords of the legions of the wood,
The chieftains with Vibhíshaṇ stood,
And, strangers in the foeman's land,
Their hopes and fears in council scanned:
'See, see where Lanká's towers ascend,
Which Rávaṇ's power and might defend,
Which Gods, Gandharvas, fiends would fail
To conquer, if they durst assail.
How shall our legions pass within,
The city of the foe to win,
With massive walls and portals barred
Which Rávaṇ keeps with surest guard?'
With anxious looks the walls they eyed:
And sage Vibhíshaṇ thus replied:
'These lords of mine[2] can answer: they
Within the walls have found their way,
The foeman's plan and order learned,
And hither to my side returned.
Now, Ráma, let my tongue declare
How Rávaṇ's hosts are stationed there.
Prahasta heads, in warlike state,
His legions at the eastern gate.
To guard the southern portal stands
Mahodar, girt by Rákshas bands,
Where mighty Mahápárśva, sent
By Rávaṇ's hest, his aid has lent.
Guard of the gate that fronts the west
Is valiant Indrajit, the best
Of warriors, Ravaṇ's joy and pride;
And by the youthful chieftain's side
Are giants, armed for fierce attacks
With sword and mace and battle-axe.
North, where approach is dreaded most,
The king, encompassed with a host
Of giants trained in war, whose hands
Wield maces, swords and lances, stands.

[1] The poet appears to have forgotten that Śuka and Sáraṇ were dismissed with ignominy in Canto XXIX., and have not been reinstated.

[2] The four who fled with him. Their names are Anala, Panasa, Sampáti, and Pramati.

All these are chiefs whom Rávaṇ chose
As mightiest to resist his foes;
And each a countless army[1] leads
With elephants and cars and steeds.'
Then Ráma, while his spirit burned
For battle, words like these returned:
'The eastern gate be Níla's care,
Opponent of Prahasta there.
The southern gate, with troops arrayed
Let Angad, Báli's son, invade.
The gate that fronts the falling sun
Shall be by brave Hanúmán won;
Soon through its portals shall he lead
His myriads of Vánar breed.
The gate that fronts the north shall be
Assailed by Lakshmaṇ and by me.
For I myself have sworn to kill
The tyrant who delights in ill.
Armed with the boon which Brahmá gave,
The Gods of heaven he loves to brave.
And through the trembling worlds he flies,
Oppressor of the just and wise.
Thou, Jámbaván, and thou, O King
Of Vánars, all your bravest bring,
And with your hosts in dense array
Straight to the centre force your way.
But let no Vánar in the storm
Disguise him in a human form.
Ye chiefs who change your shapes at will,
Retain your Vánar semblance still.
Thus, when we battle with the foe,
Both men and Vánars will ye know,
In human form will seven appear;
Myself, my brother Lakshmaṇ here;
Vibhishaṇ, and the four he led
From Lanká's city when he fled.'
Thus Raghu's son the chiefs addressed:
Then, gazing on Suvela's crest,
Transported by the lovely sight,
He longed to climb the mountain height.

CANTO XXXVIII.

THE ASCENT OF SUVELA.

'Come let us scale,' the hero cried,
'This hill with various metals dyed.
This night upon the breezy crest
Sugríva, Lakshmaṇ, I, will rest,
With sage Vibhíshaṇ, faithful friend,
His counsel and his lore to lend.
From those tall peaks each eager eye
The foeman's city shall espy,
Who from the wood my darling stole
And brought long anguish on my soul.'

Thus spake the lord of men, and bent
His footsteps to the steep ascent,
And Lakshmaṇ, true in weal and woe,
Next followed with his shafts and bow.
Vibhíshaṇ followed, next in place,
The sovereign of the Vánar race,
And hundreds of the forest kind
Thronged with impetuous feet, behind.
The chiefs in woods and mountains bred
Fast followed to Suvela's head,
And gazed on Lanká bright and fair
As some gay city in the air.
On glittering gates, on ramparts raised
By giant hands, the chieftains gazed.
They saw the mighty hosts that, skilled
In arts of war, the city filled,
And ramparts with new ramparts lined,
The swarthy hosts that stood behind.
With spirits burning for the fight
They saw the giants from the height,
And from a hundred throats rang out
Defiance and the battle shout.
Then sank the sun with dying flame,
And soft the shades of twilight came,
And the full moon's delicious light
Was shed upon the tranquil night.

CANTO XXXIX.

LANKÁ.

They slept secure: the sun arose
And called the chieftains from repose.
Before the wondering Vánars, gay
With grove and garden, Lanká lay,
Where golden buds the Champak showed
And bright with bloom Asoka glowed,
And palm and Sál and many a tree
With leaf and flower were fair to see.
They looked on wood and lawn and glade
On emerald grass and dusky shade,
Where creepers filled the air with scent,
And luscious fruit the branches bent,
Where bees inebriate loved to throng,
And each sweet bird was loud in song.
The wondering Vánars passed the bound
That circled that enchanting ground,
And as they came a sweet breeze through
The odorous alleys softly blew.
Some Vánars, at their king's behest,
Onward to bannered Lanká pressed,
While, startled by the strangers' tread,
The birds and deer before them fled.
Earth trembled at each step they took,
And Lanká at their shouting shook.
Bright rose before their wondering eyes
Trikúṭa's peak that kissed the skies,
And, clothed with flowers of every hue,
Afar its golden radiance threw.
Most fair to see, the mountain's head

[1] The numbers here are comparatively moderate: ten thousand elephants, ten thousand chariots, twenty thousand horses and ten million giants.

A hundred leagues in length was spread.
There Rávaṇ's town, securely placed,
The summit of Trikúṭa graced.
O'er leagues of land she stretched in pride,
A hundred long and twenty wide.
They saw a lofty wall enfold
The city, built of blocks of gold.
They saw the beams of morning fall
On dome and fane within the wall,
Bright with the shine that mansion gives
Where Vishṇu in his glory lives.
White-crested like the Lord of Snows
Before them Rávaṇ's palace rose.
High on a thousand pillars raised
With gold and precious stone it blazed,
Guarded by giant warders, crown
And ornament of Lanká's town.

CANTO XL.

RÁVAṆ ATTACKED.

Still stood the son of Raghu where
Suvela's peak rose high in air,
And with Sugríva turned his eye
To scan each quarter of the sky.
There on Trikúṭa, nobly planned
And built by Viśvakarmá's hand,
He saw the lovely Lanká, dressed
In all her varied beauty, rest.
High on a tower above the gate
The tyrant stood in kingly state.
The royal canopy displayed
Above him lent its grateful shade,
And servants, from the giant band,
His cheek with jewelled chowries fanned.
Red sandal o'er his breast was spread,
His ornaments and robe were red :
Thus shows a cloud of darksome hue
With golden sunbeams flashing through.
While Ráma and the chiefs intent
Upon the king their glances bent,
Up sprang Sugríva from the ground
And reached the turret at a bound.
Unterrified the Vánar stood,
And wroth, with wondrous hardihood,
The king in bitter words addressed,
And thus his scorn and hate expressed :
'King of the giant race, in me
The friend and slave of Ráma see.
Lord of the world, he gives me power
To smite thee in thy fenced tower.'
While through the air his challenge rang,
At Rávaṇ's face the Vánar sprang,
Snatched from his head the kingly crown
And dashed it in his fury down.
Straight at his foe the giant flew,
His mighty arms about him threw,
With strength resistless swung him round
And dashed him panting to the ground.
Unharmed amid the storm of blows
Swift to his feet Sugríva rose.
Again in furious fight they met :
With streams of blood their limbs were wet,
Each grasping his opponent's waist.
Thus with their branches interlaced,
Which, crimson with the flowers of spring,
From side to side the breezes swing,
In furious wrestle you may see
The Kinśuk and the Seemul tree.[1]
They fought with fists and hands, alike
Prepared to parry and to strike.
Long time the doubtful combat, waged
With matchless strength and fury, raged.
Each fiercely struck, each guarded well,
Till, closing, from the tower they fell,
And, grasping each the other's throat,
Lay for an instant in the moat.
They rose, and each in fiercer mood
The sanguinary strife renewed.
Well matched in size and strength and skill
They fought the dubious battle still.
While sweat and blood their limbs bedewed
They met, retreated, and pursued :
Each stratagem and art they tried,
Stood front to front and swerved aside.
His hand a while the giant stayed
And called his magic to his aid.
But brave Sugríva, swift to know
The guileful purpose of the foe,
Gained with light leap the upper air,
And breath and strength and spirit there;
Then, joyous as for victory won,
Returned to Raghu's royal son.

CANTO XLI.

RÁMA'S ENVOY.

When Ráma saw each bloody trace
On King Sugríva's limbs and face,
He cried, while, sorrowing at the view,
His arms about his friend he threw :
'Too venturous chieftain, kings like us
Bring not their lives in peril thus ;
Nor, save when counsel shows the need,
Attempt so bold, so rash a deed.
Remember, I, Vibhíshaṇ, all
Have sorrowed fearing for thy fall.
O do not—for us all I speak—
These desperate adventures seek.
'I could not,' cried Sugríva, 'brook
Upon the giant king to look,

[1] The Kinśuk, also called Paláśa, is the Butea Frondosa, a tree that bears beautiful red crescent-shaped blossoms and is deservedly a favourite with poets. The Seemul or Śálmalí in the silk-cotton tree which also bears red blossoms.

Nor challenge to the deadly strife
The fiend who robbed thee of thy wife.'
'Now Lakshman, marshal,' Ráma cried,
'Our legions where the woods are wide,
And stand we ready to oppose
The fury of our giant foes.
This day our armies shall ascend
The walls which Rávaṇ's powers defend,
And floods of Rákshas blood shall stain
The streets encumbered with the slain.'
Down from the peak he came, and viewed
The Vánars' ordered multitude.
Each captain there for battle burned,
Each fiery eye to Lanká turned.
On, where the royal brothers led
To Lanká's walls the legions sped.
The northern gate, where giant foes
Swarmed round their monarch, Ráma chose
Where he in person might direct
The battle, and his troops protect.
What arm but his the post might keep
Where, strong as he who sways the deep,[1]
Mid thousands armed with bow and mace,
Stood Rávaṇ mightiest of his race?
The eastern gate was Níla's post,
Where marshalled stood his Vánar host,
And Mainda with his troops arrayed,
And Dwivid stood to lend him aid.
The southern gate was Angad's care,
Who ranged his bold battalions there.
Hanúmán by the port that faced
The setting sun his legions placed,
And King Sugríva held the wood
East of the gate where Rávaṇ stood.
On every side the myriads met,
And Lanká's walls of close beset
That scarce the roving gale could win
A passage to the hosts within.
Loud as the angry ocean's roar
When wild waves lash the rocky shore,
Ten thousand thousand throats upsent
A shout that tore the firmament,
And Lanká with each grove and brook
And tower and wall and rampart shook.
The giants heard, and were appalled:
Then Raghu's son to Angad called,
And, led by kingly duty,[2] gave
This order merciful as brave:
'Go, Angad, Rávaṇ's presence seek,
And thus my words of warning speak:
'How art thou changed and fallen now,
O Monarch of the giants, thou
Whose impious fury would not spare
Saint, nymph, or spirit of the air;
Whose foot in haughty triumph trod
On Yaksha, king, and Serpent God:

[1] Varuṇa.

[2] The duty of a king to save the lives of his people and avoid bloodshed until milder methods have been tried in vain.

How art thou fallen from thy pride
Which Brahmá's favour fortified!
With myriads at thy Lanká's gate
I stand my righteous ire to sate,
And punish thee with sword and flame,
The tyrant fiend who stole my dame.
Now show the might, employ the guile,
O Monarch of the giants' isle,
Which stole a helpless dame away:
Call up thy power and strength to-day.
Once more I warn thee, Rákshas King,
This hour the Maithil lady bring,
And, yielding while there yet is time,
Seek, suppliant, pardon for the crime,
Or I will leave beneath the sun
No living Rákshas, no, not one.
In vain from battle wilt thou fly,
Or borne on pinions seek the sky;
The hand of Ráma shall not spare;
His fiery shaft shall smite thee there.'
He ceased: and Angad bowed his head;
Thence like embodied flame he sped,
And lighted from his airy road
Within the Rákshas king's abode.
There sate, the centre of a ring
Of counsellors, the giant king.
Swift through the circle Angad pressed,
And spoke with fury in his breast:
'Sent by the lord of Kosal's land,
His envoy here, O King, I stand,
Angad the son of Báli: fame
Has haply taught thine ears my name.
Thus in the words of Ráma I
Am come to warn thee or defy:
Come forth, and fighting in the van
Display the spirit of a man.
This arm shall slay thee, tyrant: all
Thy nobles, kith and kin shall fall:
And earth and heaven, from terror freed,
Shall joy to see the oppressor bleed.
Vibhíshaṇ, when his foe is slain,
Anointed king in peace shall reign.
Once more I counsel thee: repent,
Avoid the mortal punishment.
With honour due the dame restore,
And pardon for thy sin implore.'
Loud rose the king's infuriate cry:
'Seize, seize the Vánar: let him die.'
Four of his band their lord obeyed,
And eager hands on Angad laid.
He purposing his strength to show
Gave no resistance to the foe,
But swiftly round his captors cast
His mighty arms and held them fast.
Fierce shout and cry around him rang:
Light to the palace roof he sprang,
There his detaining arms unwound,
And hurled the giants to the ground.
Then, smiting with a fearful stroke,
A turret from the roof he broke,—
As when the fiery levin sent

By Indra from the clouds has rent
The proud peak of the Lord of Snow,—
And flung the stony mass below.
Again with loud terrific cry
He sprang exulting to the sky,
And, joyous for his errand done,
Stood by the side of Raghu's son.

CANTO XLII.

THE SALLY.

Still was the cry, 'The Vánar foes
Around the leaguered city close.'
King Rávan from the terrace gazed
And saw, with eyes where fury blazed,
The Vánar host in serried ranks
Press to the moat and line the banks,
And, first in splendour and in place,
The lion lord of Raghu's race.
And Ráma looked on Lanká where
Gay flags were streaming to the air,
And, while keen sorrow pierced him through,
His loving thoughts to Sítá flew :
'There, there in deep affliction lies
My darling with the fawn-like eyes.
There on the cold bare ground she keeps
Sad vigil and for Ráma weeps.'
Mad with the thought, 'Charge, charge,' he cried.
'Let earth with Rákshas blood be dyed.'
Responsive to his call rang out
A loud, a universal shout,
As myriads filled the moat with stone,
Trees, rocks, and mountains overthrown,
And charging at their leader's call
Pressed forward furious to the wall.
Some in their headlong ardour scaled
The rampart's height, the guard assailed,
And many a ponderous fragment rent
From portal, tower, and battlement.
Huge gates adorned with burnished gold
Were loosed and lifted from their hold ;
And post and pillar, with a sound
Like thunder, fell upon the ground.
At every portal, east and west
And north and south, the chieftains pressed
Each in his post appointed led
His myriads in the forest bred.
'Charge, let the gates be opened wide :
'Charge, charge, my giants,' Rávan cried.
They heard his voice, and loud and long
Rang the wild clamour of the throng,
And shell and drum their notes upsent,
And every martial instrument.
Forth, at the bidding of their lord
From every gate the giants poured,
As, when the waters rise and swell,
Huge waves preceding waves impel.
Again from every Vánar throat
A scream of fierce defiance smote
The welkin : earth and sea and sky
Reëchoed with the awful cry.
The roar of elephants, the neigh
Of horses eager for the fray,
The frequent clash of warriors' steel,
The rattling of the chariot wheel.
Fierce was the deadly fight : opposed
In terrible array they closed,
As when the Gods of heaven enraged
With rebel fiends wild battle waged.
Axe, spear, and mace were wielded well ;
At every blow a Vánar fell.
But shivered rock and brandished tree
Brought many a giant on his knee,
To perish in his turn beneath
The deadly wounds of nails and teeth.

CANTO XLIII.

THE SINGLE COMBATS.

Brave chiefs of each opposing side
Their strength in single combat tried.
Fierce Indrajit the fight began
With Angad in the battle's van.
Sampátí, strongest of his race,
Stood with Prajangha face to face.
Hanúmán, Jambumálí met
In mortal opposition set.
Vibhíshan, brother of the lord
Of Lanká, raised his threatening sword,
And singled out, with eyes aglow
With wrath, Śatrughna for his foe.
The mighty Gaja Tapan sought,
And Níla with Nikumbha fought.
Sugríva, Vánar king, defied
Fierce Praghas long in battle tried,
And Lakshman fearless in the fight
Encountered Virúpáksha's might.
To meet the royal Ráma came
Wild Agniketu fierce as flame ;
Mitraghana, he who loved to strike
His foeman and his friend alike ;
With Raśmiketu, known and feared
Where'er his ponderous flag was reared ;
And Yajnakopa whose delight
Was ruin of the sacred rite.
These met and fought, with thousands more,
And trampled earth was red with gore.
Swift as the bolt which Indra sends
When fire from heaven the mountain rends
Smote Indrajit with furious blows
On Angad queller of his foes.
But Angad from his foeman tore
The murderous mace the warrior bore,

And low in dust his coursers rolled,
His driver, and his car of gold.
Struck by the shafts Prajangha sped,
The Vánar chief Sampáti bled,
But, heedless of his gashes, he
Crushed down the giant with a tree.
Then car-borne Jambumáli smote
Hanumán on the chest and throat;
But at the car the Vánar rushed,
And chariot, steeds, and rider crushed.
Sugríva whirled a huge tree round,
And struck fierce Praghas to the ground.
One arrow shot from Lakshmaṇ's bow
Laid mighty Virúpáksha low.
His giant foes round Ráma pressed
And shot their shafts at head and breast;
But, when the iron shower was spent,
Four arrows from his bow he sent,
And every missile, deftly sped;
Cleft from the trunk a giant head.[1]

CANTO XLIV.

THE NIGHT.

The lord of Light had sunk and set:
Night came; the foeman struggled yet;
And fiercer for the gloom of night
Grew the wild fury of the fight.
Scarce could each warrior's eager eye
The foeman from the friend descry.
'Rákshas or Vánar? say;' cried each,
And foe knew foeman by his speech.
'Why wilt thou fly? O warrior, stay:
'Turn on the foe, and rend and slay:'
Such were the cries, such words of fear
Smote through the gloom each listening ear.
Each swarthy rover of the night
Whose golden armour flashed with light,
Showed like a towering hill embraced
By burning woods about his waist.
The giants at the Vánars flew,
And ravening ate the foes they slew:
With mortal bite like serpent's fang,
The Vánars at the giants sprang,
And car and steeds and they who bore
The pennons fell bedewed with gore.
No serried band, no firm array
The fury of their charge could stay.
Down went the horse and rider, down
Went giant lords of high renown.
Though midnight's shade was dense and
dark,
With skill that swerved not from the mark
Their bows the sons of Raghu drew,
And each keen shaft a chieftain slew.
Uprose the blinding dust from meads
Ploughed by the cars and trampling steeds,
And where the warriors fell the flood
Was dark and terrible with blood.
Six giants[1] singled Ráma out,
And charged him with a furious shout
Loud as the roaring of the sea
When every wind is raging free.
Six times he shot: six heads were cleft;
Six giants dead on earth were left.
Nor ceased he yet: his bow he strained,
And from the sounding weapon rained
A storm of shafts whose fiery glare
Filled all the region of the air;
And chieftains dropped before his aim
Like moths that perish in the flame.
Earth glistened where the arrows fell,
As shines in autumn nights a dell
Which fireflies, flashing through the gloom,
With momentary light illume.
But Indrajit, when Báli's son[2]
The victory o'er the foe had won,
Saw with a fury-kindled eye
His mangled steeds and driver die;
Then, lost in air, he fled the fight,
And vanished from the victor's sight.
The Gods and saints glad voices raised,
And Angad for his virtue praised;
And Raghu's sons bestowed the meed
Of honour due to valorous deed.
Compelled his shattered car to quit,
Rage filled the soul of Indrajit,
Who brooked not, strong by Brahmá's grace
Defeat from one of Vánar race.
In magic mist concealed from view
His bow the treacherous warrior drew,
And Raghu's sons were first to feel
The tempest of his winged steel.
Then when his arrows failed to kill
The princes who defied him still,
He bound them with the serpent noose,[3]
The magic bond which none might loose.

CANTO XLV.

INDRAJIT'S VICTORY.

Brave Ráma, burning still to know
The station of his artful foe,

[1] I have omitted several of these single combats, as there is little variety in the details and each duel results in the victory of the Vánar or his ally.

[1] Yajnaśatru, Mahápárśva, Mahodar, Vajradanshṭra, Śuka, and Sáraṇ.

[2] Angad.

[3] A mysterious weapon consisting of serpents transformed to arrows which deprived the wounded object of all sense and power of motion.

Gave to ten chieftains, mid the best
Of all the host, his high behest.
Swift rose in air the Vánar band:
Each region of the sky they scanned:
But Rávan's son by magic skill
Checked them with arrows swifter still,
When streams of blood from chest and side
The dauntless Vánars' limbs had dyed,
The giant in his misty shroud
Showed like the sun obscured by cloud.
Like serpents hissing through the air,
His arrows smote the princely pair;
And from their limbs at every rent
A stream of rushing blood was sent.
Like Kinśuk trees they stood, that show
In spring their blossoms' crimson glow.
Then Indrajit with fury eyed
Ikshváku's royal sons, and cried:
'Not mighty Indra can assail
Or see me when I choose to veil
My form in battle: and can ye,
Children of earth, contend with me?
The arrowy noose this hand has shot
Has bound you with a hopeless knot;
And, slaughtered by my shafts and bow,
To Yama's hall this hour ye go.'
He spoke, and shouted. Then anew
The arrows from his bowstring flew,
And pierced, well aimed with perfect art,
Each limb and joint and vital part.
Transfixed with shafts in every limb.
Their strength relaxed, their eyes grew dim.
As two tall standards side by side,
With each sustaining rope untied,
Fall levelled by the howling blast,
So earth's majestic lords at last
Beneath the arrowy tempest reeled,
And prostrate pressed the battle field.

CANTO XLVI.

INDRAJIT'S TRIUMPH.

The Vánar chiefs whose piercing eyes
Scanned eagerly the earth and skies,
Saw the brave brothers wounded sore
Transfixed with darts and stained with gore.
The monarch of the Vánar race,
With wise Vibhíshan, reached the place;
Angad and Níla came behind,
And others of the forest kind,
And standing with Hanúmán there
Lamented for the fallen pair.
Their melancholy eyes they raised;
In fruitless search a while they gazed.
But magic arts Vibhíshan knew;
Not hidden from his keener view,
Though veiled by magic from the rest,
The son of Rávan stood confessed.
Fierce Indrajit with savage pride
The fallen sons of Raghu eyed,
And every giant heart was proud
As thus the warrior cried aloud:
'Slain by mine arrows Ráma lies,
And closed in death are Lakshman's eyes.
Dead are the mighty princes who
Dúshan and Khara smote and slew.
The Gods and fiends may toil in vain
To free them from the binding chain.
The haughty chief, my father's dread,
Who drove him sleepless from his bed,
While Lanká, troubled like a brook
In rain time, heard his name and shook:
He whose fierce hate our lives pursued
Lies helpless by my shafts subdued.
Now fruitless is each wondrous deed
Wrought by the race the forests breed,
And fruitless every toil at last
Like cloudlets when the rains are past.'
Then rose the shout of giants loud
As thunder from a bursting cloud,
When, deeming Ráma, dead, they raised
Their voices and the conqueror praised.
Still motionless, as lie the slain,
The brothers pressed the bloody plain.
No sigh they drew, no breath they heaved,
And lay as though of life bereaved.
Proud of the deed his art had done,
To Lanká's town went Rávan's son,
Where, as he passed, all fear was stilled,
And every heart with triumph filled.
Sugríva trembled as he viewed
Each fallen prince with blood bedewed,
And in his eyes which overflowed
With tears the flame of anger glowed.
'Calm,' cried Vibhíshan, 'calm thy fears,
And stay the torrent of thy tears.
Still must the chance of battle change,
And victory still delight to range.
Our cause again will she befriend
And bring us triumph in the end.
This is not death: each prince will break
The spell that holds him, and awake;
Nor long shall numbing magic bind
The mighty arm, the lofty mind.'
He ceased: his finger bathed in dew
Across Sugríva's eyes he drew.
From dulling mist his vision freed,
And spoke these words to suit the need:
'No time is this for fear: away
With fainting heart and weak delay.
Now, e'en the tear which sorrow wrings
From loving eyes destruction brings.
Up, on to battle at the head
Of those brave troops which Ráma led.
Or guardian by his side remain
Till sense and strength the prince regain.
Soon shall the trance-bound pair revive,
And from our hearts all sorrow drive.
Though prostrate on the earth he lie,

Deem not that Ráma's death is nigh ;
Deem not that Lakshmí will forget
Or leave her darling champion yet.
Rest here and be thy heart consoled ;
Ponder my words, be firm and bold.
I. foremost in the battle field,
Will rally all who faint or yield.
Their staring eyes betray their fear ;
They whisper each in other's ear.
They, when they hear my cheering cry
And see the friend of Ráma nigh,
Will cast their gloom and fears away
Like faded wreaths of yesterday.'
 Thus calmed he King Sugríva's dread;
Then gave new heart to those who fled.
Fierce Indrajit, his soul on fire
With pride of conquest, sought his sire,
Raised reverent hands, and told him all,
The battle and the princes' fall.
Rejoicing at his foes' defeat
Upsprang the monarch from his seat,
Girt by his giant courtiers: round
His warrior son his arms he wound,
Close kisses on his head applied,
And heard again how Ráma died.

CANTO XLVII.

SÍTÁ.

Still on the ground where Ráma slept
Their faithful watch the Vánars kept.
There Angad stood o'erwhelmed with grief
And many a lord and warrior chief ;
And, ranged in densest mass around,
Their tree-armed legions held the ground.
Far ranged each Vánar's eager eye,
Now swept the land, now sought the sky,
All fearing, if a leaf was stirred,
A Rákshas in the sound they heard.
The lord of Lanká in his hall,
Rejoicing at his foeman's fall,
Commanded and the warders came
Who ever watched the Maithil dame.
'Go,' cried the Rákshas king, ' relate
To Janak's child her husband's fate.
Low on the earth her Ráma lies,
And dark in death are Lakshman's eyes.
Bring forth my car and let her ride
To view the chieftains side by side.
The lord to whom her fancy turned
For whose dear sake my love she spurned,
Lies smitten, as he fiercely led
The battle, with his brother dead.
Lead forth the royal lady : go,
Her husband's lifeless body show.
Then from all doubt and terror free
Her softening heart will turn to me.'
 They heard his speech: the car was brought ;
That shady grove the warders sought
Where, mourning Ráma night and day,
The melancholy lady lay.
They placed her in the car and through
The yielding air they swiftly flew.
The lady looked upon the plain,
Looked on the heaps of Vánar slain,
Saw where, triumphant in the fight,
Thronged the fierce rovers of the night,
And Vánar chieftains, mournful-eyed,
Watched by the fallen brothers' side.
There stretched upon his gory bed
Each brother lay as lie the dead,
With shattered mail and splintered bow,
Pierced by the arrows of the foe.
When on the pair her eyes she bent,
Burst from her lips a wild lament.
Her eyes o'erflowed, she groaned and sighed
And thus in trembling accents cried :

CANTO XLVIII.

SÍTÁ'S LAMENT.

' False are they all, proved false to-day,
The prophets of my fortune, they
Who in the tranquil time of old
A blessed life for me foretold,
Predicting I should never know
A childless dame's, a widow's woe,
False are they all, their words are vain.
For thou, my lord and life, art slain.
False was the priest and vain his lore
Who blessed me in those days of yore
By Ráma's side in bliss to reign ;
For thou, my lord and life, art slain.
They hailed me happy from my birth,
Proud empress of the lord of earth.
They blessed me—but the thought is pain—
For thou, my lord and life, art slain.
Ah, fruitless hope ! each glorious sign
That stamps the future queen is mine,
With no ill-omened mark to show
A widow's crushing hour of woe.
They say my hair is black and fine,
They praise my brows' continuous line ;
My even teeth divided well,
My bosom for its graceful swell.
They praise my feet and fingers oft ;
They say my skin is smooth and soft,
And call me happy to possess
The twelve fair marks that bring success.
But ah, what profit shall I gain ?
Thou, O my lord and life, art slain.
The flattering seer in former days
My gentle girlish smile would praise,

---

1 On each foot, and at the root of each finger.

And swear that holy water shed
By Bráhman hands upon my head
Should make me queen, a monarch's bride:
How is the promise verified?
Matchless in might the brothers slew
In Janasthán the giant crew.
And forced the indomitable sea
To let them pass to rescue me.
Theirs was the fiery weapon hurled
By him who rules the watery world;[1]
Theirs the dire shaft by Indra sped;
Theirs was the mystic Brahmá's Head.[2]
In vain they fought, the bold and brave:
A coward's hand their death-wounds gave.
By secret shafts and magic spell
The brothers, peers of Indra, fell.
That foe, if seen by Ráma's eye
One moment, had not lived to fly.
Though swift as thought, his utmost speed
Had failed him in the hour of need.
No might, no tear, no prayer may stay
Fate's dark inevitable day.
Nor could their matchless valour shield
These heroes on the battle field.
I sorrow for the noble dead,
I mourn my hopes for ever fled;
But chief my weeping eyes o'erflow
For Queen Kauśalyá's hopeless woe.
The widowed queen is counting now
Each hour prescribed by Ráma's vow,
And lives because she longs to see
Once more her princely sons and me.'
  Then Trijaṭá,[3] of gentler mould
Though Rákshas born, her grief consoled:
'Dear Queen, thy causeless woe dispel:
Thy husband lives, and all is well.
Look round: in every Vánar face
The light of joyful hope I trace.
Not thus, believe me, shine the eyes
Of warriors when their leader dies
An Army, when the chief is dead,
Flies from the field dispirited.
Here, undisturbed in firm array,
The Vánars by the brothers stay.
Love prompts my speech: no longer grieve;
Ponder my counsel, and believe.
These lips of mine from earliest youth
Have spoken, and shall speak, the truth.
Deep in my heart thy gentle grace
And patient virtues hold their place.
Turn, lady, turn once more thine eye:
Though pierced with shafts the heroes lie,
On brows and cheeks with blood-drops wet
The light of beauty lingers yet.
Such beauty ne'er is found in death,
But vanishes with parting breath.
O, trust the hope these tokens give;
The heroes are not dead, but live.'
  Then Sítá joined her hands, and sighed,
'O, may thy words be verified!'
The car was turned, which fleet as thought
The mourning queen to Lanká brought.
They led her to the garden, where
Again she yielded to despair,
Lamenting for the chiefs who bled
On earth's cold bosom with the dead.

CANTO XLIX.

RÁMA'S LAMENT.

Ranged round the spot where Ráma fell
Each Vánar chief stood sentinel.
At length the mighty hero broke
The trance that held him, and awoke.
He saw his senseless brother, dyed
With blood from head to foot, and cried:
'What have I now to do with life
Or rescue of my prisoned wife,
When thus before my weeping eyes,
Slain in the fight, my brother lies?
A queen like Sítá I may find
Among the best of womankind,
But never such a brother, tried
In war, my guardian, friend, and guide.
If he be dead, the brave and true,
I will not live but perish too.
How, reft of Lakshmaṇ, shall I meet
My mother, and Kaikeyí greet?
My brother's eager question brook,
And fond Sumitrá's longing look?
What shall I say, o'erwhelmed with shame
To cheer the miserable dame?
How, when she hears her son is dead,
Will her sad heart be comforted?
Ah me, for longer life unfit
This mortal body will I quit;
For Lakshmaṇ slaughtered for my sake,
From sleep of death will never wake.
Ah when I sank oppressed with care,
Thy gentle voice could soothe despair.
And art thou, O my brother, killed?
Is that dear voice for ever stilled?
Cold are those lips, my brother, whence
Came never word to breed offence?
Ah, stretched upon the gory plain
My brother lies untimely slain;
Numbed is the mighty arm that slew
The leaders of the giant crew.
Transfixed with shafts, with blood-streams red,
Thou liest on thy lowly bed:

---

[1] Varuṇ.

[2] The name of one of the mystical weapons the command over which was given by Viśvámitra to Ráma, as related in Book I.

[3] One of Sítá's guard, and her comforter on a former occasion also.

So sinks to rest, his journey done,
Mid arrowy rays the crimson sun.
Thou, when from home and sire I fled,
The wood's wild ways with me wouldst tread:
Now close to thine my steps shall be,
For I in death will follow thee.
Vibhíshaṇ now will curse my name,
And Ráma as a braggart blame,
Who promised—but his word is vain—
That he in Lanká's isle should reign.
Return, Sugríva: reft of me
Lead back thy Vánars o'er the sea,
Nor hope to battle face to face
With him who rules the giant race.
Well have ye done and nobly fought,
And death in desperate combat sought.
All that heroic might can do,
Brave Vánars, has been done by you.
My faithful friends I now dismiss:
Return: my last farewell is this.'
Bedewed with tears was every cheek
As thus the Vánars heard him speak.
Vibhíshaṇ on the field had stayed
The Vánar hosts who fled dismayed.
Now lifting up his mace on high
With martial step the chief drew nigh.
The hosts who watched by Ráma's side
Beheld his shape and giant stride.
'Tis he, 'tis Rávaṇ's son, they thought:
And all in flight their safety sought.

CANTO L.

THE BROKEN SPELL.

Sugríva viewed the flying crowd,
And thus to Angad cried aloud:
'Why run the trembling hosts, as flee
Storm-scattered barks across the sea?'
'Dost thou not mark,' the chief replied,
'Transfixed with shafts, with blood-streams dyed,
With arrowy toils about them wound,
The sons of Raghu on the ground?'
That moment brought Vibhíshaṇ near:
Sugríva knew the cause of fear,
And ordered Jámbaván, who led
The bears, to check the hosts that fled.
The king of bears his hest obeyed:
The Vánars' headlong flight was stayed.
A little while Vibhíshaṇ eyed
The brothers fallen side by side.
His giant fingers wet with dew
Across the heroes' eyes he drew,
Still on the pair his sad look bent,
And spoke these words in wild lament:
'Ah for the mighty chiefs brought low
By coward hand and stealthy blow!
Brave pair who loved the open fight,
Slain by that rover of the night.
Dishonest is the victory won
By Indrajit my brother's son.
I on their might for aid relied,
And in my cause they fought and died.
Lost is the hope that soothed each pain:
I live, but live no more to reign,
While Lanká's lord, untouched by ill,
Exults in safe defiance still.'
'Not thus,' Sugríva said, 'repine,
For Lanká's isle shall still be thine.
Nor let the tyrant and his son
Exult before the fight be done.
These royal chiefs, though now dismayed,
Freed from the spell by Garuḍ's aid,
Triumphant yet the foe shall meet
And lay the robber at their feet.'
His hope the Vánar monarch told,
And thus Vibhíshaṇ's grief consoled.
Then to Susheṇ who at his side
Expectant stood, Sugríva cried:
'When these regain their strength and sense,
Fly, bear them to Kishkindhá hence.
Here with my legions will I stay,
The tyrant and his kinsmen slay,
And, rescued from the giant king,
The Maithil lady will I bring,
Like Glory lost of old, restored
By Śakra, heaven's almighty lord.'
Susheṇ made answer: 'Hear me yet:
When Gods and fiends in battle met,
So fiercely fought the demon crew,
So wild a storm of arrows flew,
That heavenly warriors faint with pain,
Sank smitten by the ceaseless rain.
Vrihaspati,[1] with herb and spell,
Cured the sore wounds of those who fell.
And, skilled in arts that heal and save,
New life and sense and vigour gave.
Far, on the Milky Ocean's shore,
Still grow those herbs in boundless store;
Let swiftest Vánars thither speed
And bring them for our utmost need.
Those herbs that on the mountain spring
Let Panas and Sampáti bring,
For well the wondrous leaves they know.
That heal each wound and life bestow.
Beside that sea which, churned of yore,
The amrit on its surface bore,
Where the white billows lash the land,
Chandra's fair height and Droṇa stand.
Planted by Gods each glittering steep
Looks down upon the milky deep.
Let fleet Hanúmán bring us thence
Those herbs of wondrous influence.'
Meanwhile the rushing wind grew loud,
Red lightnings flashed from banks of cloud.
The mountains shook, the wild waves rose,
And smitten with resistless blows

---

[1] The preceptor of the Gods.

Unrooted fell each stately tree
That fringed the margin of the sea.
All life within the waters feared:
Then, as the Vánars gazed, appeared
King Garuḍ's self, a wondrous sight,
Disclosed in flames of fiery light.
From his fierce eye in sudden dread
All serpents in a moment fled.
And those transformed to shafts that bound
The princes vanished in the ground.
On Raghu's sons his eyes he bent,
And hailed the lords armipotent.
Then o'er them stooped the feathered king,
And touched their faces with his wing.
His healing touch their pangs allayed,
And closed each rent the shafts had made.
Again their eyes were bright and bold,
Again the smooth skin shone like gold.
Again within their shell enshrined
Came memory and each power of mind;
And, from those numbing bonds released,
Their spirit, zeal, and strength increased.
Firm on their feet they stood, and then
Thus Ráma spake, the lord of men:

'By thy dear grace in sorest need
From deadly bonds we both are freed.
To these glad eyes as welcome now
As Aja[1] or my sire art thou.
Who art thou, mighty being? say,
Thus glorious in thy bright array.'
He ceased: the king of birds replied,
While flashed his eye with joy and pride:
'In me, O Raghu's son, behold
One who has loved thee from of old:
Garuḍ, the lord of all that fly,
Thy guardian and thy friend am I.
Not all the Gods in heaven could loose
These numbing bonds, this serpent noose,
Wherewith fierce Rávaṇ's son, renowned
For magic arts, your limbs had bound.
Those arrows fixed in every limb
Were mighty snakes, transformed by him.
Blood-thirsty race, they live beneath
The earth, and slay with venomed teeth.
On, smite the lord of Lanká's isle,
But guard you from the giants' guile
Who each dishonest art employ
And by deceit brave foes destroy.
So shall the tyrant Rávaṇ bleed,
And Sítá from his power be freed.'
Thus Garuḍ spake: then, swift as thought,
The region of the sky he sought,
Where in the distance like a blaze
Of fire he vanished from the gaze.

Then the glad Vánars' joy rang out
In many a wild tumultuous shout,
And the loud roar of drum and shell
Startled each distant sentinel.

[1] Ráma's grandfather.

CANTO LI.

DHU'MRA'KSHA'S SALLY.

King Rávaṇ, where he sat within,
Heard from his hall the deafening din,
And with a spirit ill at ease
Addressed his lords in words like these:
'That warlike shout, those joyous cries,
Loud as the thunder of the skies,
Upsent from every Vánar throat,
Some new-born confidence denote.
Hark, how the sea and trembling shore
Re-echo with the Vánars' roar.
Though arrowy chains, securely twined
Both Ráma and his brother bind,
Still must the fierce triumphant shout
Disturb my soul with rising doubt.
Swift envoys to the army send,
And learn what change these cries portend.'
Obedient, at their master's call,
Fleet giants clomb the circling wall.
They saw the Vánars formed and led:
They saw Sugríva at their head,
The brothers from their bonds released:
And hope grew faint and fear increased.
Their faces pale with doubt and dread,
Back to the giant king they sped,
And to his startled ear revealed
The tidings of the battle field.
The flush of rage a while gave place
To chilling fear that changed his face:
'What?' cried the tyrant,' are my foes
Freed from the binding snakes that close
With venomed clasp round head and limb,
Bright as the sun and fierce like him:
The spell a God bestowed of yore,
The spell that never failed before?
If arts like these be useless, how
Shall giant strength avail us now
Go forth, Dhúmráksha, good at need,
The bravest of my warriors lead:
Force through the foe thy conquering way,
And Ráma and the Vánars slay.'
Before his king with reverence due
Dhúmráksha bowed him, and withdrew.
Around him at his summons came
Fierce legions led by chiefs of fame.
Well armed with sword and spear and mace,
They hurried to the gathering place,
And rushed to battle, borne at speed
By elephant and car and steed.

CANTO LII.

DHU'MRA'KSHA'S DEATH.

The Vánars saw the giant foe
Pour from the gate in gallant show,

Rejoiced with warriors' fierce delight
And shouted, longing for the fight.
Near came the hosts and nearer yet:
Dire was the tumult as they met,
As, serried line to line opposed,
The Vánars and the giants closed.
Fierce on the foe the Vánars rushed,
And, wielding trees, the foremost crushed;
But, feathered from the heron's wing,
With eager flight from sounding string,
Against them shot with surest aim
A ceaseless storm of arrows came:
And, pierced in head and chest and side,
Full many a Vánar fell and died.
They perished slain in fierce attacks
With sword and pike and battle-axe;
But myriads following undismayed
Their valour in the fight displayed.
Unnumbered Vánars rent and torn
With shaft and spear to earth were borne.
But crushed by branchy trees and blocks
Of jagged stone and shivered rocks
Which the wild Vánars wielded well
The bravest of the giants fell.
Their trampled banners strewed the fields,
And broken swords and spears and shields;
And, crushed by blows which none might stay,
Cars, elephants, and riders lay.
Dhúmráksha turned his furious eye
And saw his routed legions fly.
Still dauntless, with terrific blows,
He struck and slew his foremost foes.
At every blow, at every thrust,
He laid a Vánar in the dust.
So fell they neath the sword and lance
In battle's wild Gandharva[1] dance,
Where clang of bow and clash of sword
Did duty for the silvery chord,
And hoofs that rang and steeds that neighed
Loud concert for the dancers made.
So fiercely from Dhúmráksha's bow
His arrows rained in ceaseless flow,
The Vánar legions turned and fled
To all the winds discomfited.
Hanúmán saw the Vánars fly:
He heaved a mighty rock on high.
His keen eyes flashed with wrathful fire,
And, rapid as the Wind his sire,
Strong as the rushing tempests are,
He hurled it at the advancing car.
Swift through the air the missile sang:
The giant from the chariot sprang,
Ere crushed by that terrific blow
Lay pole and wheel and flag and bow.
Hanúmán's eyes with fury blazed:
A mountain's rocky peak he raised,
Poised it on high in act to throw,
And rushed upon his giant foe.
Dhúmráksha saw: he raised his mace
And smote Hanúmán on the face,
Who maddened by the wound's keen pang
Again upon his foeman sprang;
And on the giant's head the rock
Descended with resistless shock.
Crushed was each limb: a shapeless mass
He lay upon the blood-stained grass.

CANTO LIII.

VAJRADANSHTRA'S SALLY.

When Rávan in his palace heard
The mournful news, his wrath was stirred;
And, gasping like a furious snake,
To Vajradanshṭra thus he spake:
'Go forth, my fiercest captain, lead
The bravest of the giants' breed.
Go forth, the sons of Raghu slay
And by their side Sugríva lay.'
He ceased: the chieftain bowed his head
And forth with gathered troops he sped.
Cars, camels, steeds were well arrayed,
And coloured banners o'er them played.
Rings decked his arms: about his waist
The life-protecting mail was braced,
And on the chieftain's forehead set
Glittered his cap and coronet.
Borne on a bannered car that glowed
With golden sheen the warrior rode,
And footmen marched with spear and sword
And bow and mace behind their lord.
In pomp and pride of warlike state
They sallied from the southern gate,
But saw, as on their way they sped,
Dread signs around and overhead.
For there were meteors falling fast,
Though not a cloud its shadow cast;
And each ill-omened bird and beast,
Forboding death, the fear increased.
While many a giant slipped and reeled,
Falling before he reached the field.
They met in mortal strife engaged,
And long and fierce the battle raged.
Spears, swords uplifted, gleamed and flashed,
And many a chief to earth was dashed.
A ceaseless storm of arrows rained,
And limbs were pierced and blood-distained.
Terrific was the sound that filled
The air, and every heart was chilled,
As hurtling o'er the giants flew
The rocks and trees which Vánars threw.
Fierce as a hungry lion when
Unwary deer approach his den,

[1] The Gandharvas are warriors and Minstrels of Indra's heaven.

Angad, his eyes with fury red,
Waving a tree above his head,
Rushed with wild charge which none could stay
Where stood the giants' dense array.
Like tall trees levelled by the blast
Before him fell the giants fast,
And earth that streamed with blood was strown
With warriors, steeds, and cars o'erthrown.

CANTO LIV.

VAJRADANSHṬRA'S DEATH.

The giant leader fiercely rained
His arrows and the fight maintained.
Each time the clanging cord he drew
His certain shaft a Vánar slew.
Then, as the creatures he has made
Fly to the Lord of Life for aid,
To Angad for protection fled
The Vánar hosts dispirited.
Then raged the battle fiercer yet
When Angad and the giant met.
A hundred thousand arrows, hot
With flames of fire, the giant shot;
And every shaft he deftly sent
His foeman's body pierced and rent.
From Angad's limbs ran floods of gore:
A stately tree from earth he tore,
Which, maddened as his gashes bled,
He hurled at his opponent's head.
His bow the dauntless giant drew;
To meet the tree swift arrows flew,
Checked the huge missile's onward way,
And harmless on the earth it lay.
A while the Vánar chieftain gazed,
Then from the earth a rock he raised
Rent from a thunder-splitten height,
And cast it with resistless might.
The giant marked, and, mace in hand,
Leapt from his chariot to the sand,
Ere the rough mass descending broke
The seat, the wheel, the pole and yoke.

Then Angad seized a shattered hill,
Whereon the trees were flowering still,
And with full force the jagged peak
Fell crashing on the giant's cheek.
He staggered, reeled, and fell: the blood
Gushed from the giant in a flood.
Reft of his might, each sense astray,
A while upon the sand he lay.
But strength and wandering sense returned
Again his eyes with fury burned,
And with his mace upraised on high
He wounded Angad on the thigh.
Then from his hand his mace he threw,
And closer to his foeman drew.
Then with their fists they fought, and smote
On brow and cheek and chest and throat.
Worn out with toil, their limbs bedewed,
With blood, the strife they still renewed,
Like Mercury and fiery Mars
Met in fierce battle mid the stars.

A while the deadly fight was stayed:
Each armed him with his trusty blade
Whose sheath with tinkling bells supplied,
And golden net, adorned his side;
And grasped his ponderous leather shield
To fight till one should fall or yield.
Unumbered wounds they gave and took:
Their wearied bodies reeled and shook.
At length upon the sand that drank
Streams of their blood the warriors sank,
But as a serpent rears his head
Sore wounded by a peasant's tread,
So Angad, fallen on his knees,
Yet gathered strength his sword to seize;
And, severed by the glittering blade,
The giant's head on earth was laid.

I omit Cantos LV., LVI., LVII., and LVIII. which relate how Akampan and Prahasta sally out and fall. There is little novelty of incident in these Cantos and the result are exactly the same as before. In Canto LV. Akampan, at the command of Rávaṇ, leads forth his troops. Evil omens are seen and heard. The enemies meet, and many fall on each side, the Vánars transfixed with arrows, the Rákshases crushed with rocks and trees.

In Canto LVI. Akampan sees that the Rákshases are worsted, and fights with redoubled rage and vigour. The Vánars fall fast under his "nets of arrows." Hanumán comes to the rescue. He throws mountain peaks at the giant which are dexterously stopped with flights of arrows; and at last beats him down and kills him with a tree.

In Canto LVII. Rávaṇ is seriously alarmed. He declares that he himself, Kumbhakarṇa or Prahasta, must go forth. Prahasta sallies out vaunting that the fowls of the air shall eat their fill of Vánar flesh.

In Canto LVIII. the two armies meet. Dire is the conflict; ceaseless is the rain of stones and arrows. At last Níla meets Prahasta and breaks his bow. Prahasta leaps from his car, and the giant and the Vánar fight on foot. Níla with a huge tree crushes his opponent who falls like a tree when its roots are cut.

CANTO LIX.

RÁVAṈ'S SALLY.

They told him that the chief was killed,
And Rávaṇ's breast with rage was filled.
Then, fiercely moved by wrath and pride,
Thus to his lords the tyrant cried:
'No longer, nobles, may we show
This lofty scorn for such a foe
By whom our bravest, with his train
Of steeds and elephants, is slain.'
Myself this day will take the field,
And Raghu's sons their lives shall yield.'
High on the royal car, that glowed
With glory from his face, he rode;
And tambour shell and drum pealed out,
And joyful was each giant's shout.
A mighty host, with eyeballs red
Like flames of kindled fire, he led.
He passed the city gate, and viewed,
Arrayed, the Vánar multitude,
Those wielding massy rocks, and these
Armed with the stems of uptorn trees,
And Ráma with his eyes aglow
With warlike ardour viewed the foe,
And thus the brave Vibhíshaṇ, best
Of weapon-wielding chiefs, addressed:
'What captain leads this bright array
Where lances gleam and banners play,
And thousands armed with spear and sword
Await the bidding of their lord?'
'Seest, thou,' Vibhíshaṇ answered, 'one
Whose face is as the morning sun,
Preëminent for hugest frame?
Akampan[1] is the giant's name,
Behold that chieftain, chariot-borne,
Whom Brahmá's chosen gifts adorn.
He wields a bow like Indra's own;
A lion on his flag is shown,
His eyes with baleful fire are lit:
'Tis Rávaṇ's son, 'tis Indrajit.
There, brandishing in mighty hands
His huge bow, Atikáya stands.
And that proud warrior o'er whose head
A moon-bright canopy is spread;
Whose might, in many a battle tried,
Has tamed imperial Indra's pride;
Who wears a crown of burnished gold,
Is Lanká's lord the lofty-souled.'
He ceased: and Ráma knew his foe,
And laid an arrow on his bow:
'Woe to the wretch,' he cried, 'whom fate
Abandons to my deadly hate.'
He spoke, and, firm by Lakshmaṇ's side,
The giant to the fray defied.
The lord of Lanká bade his train
Of warriors by the gates remain,
To guard the city from surprise
By Ráma's forest-born allies.
Then as some monster of the sea
Cleaves swift-advancing billows, he
Charged with impetuous onset through
The foe, and cleft the host in two.
Sugríva ran, the king to meet:
A hill uprooted from its seat
He hurled, with trees that graced the height
Against the rover of the night;
But cleft with shafts that checked its way
Harmless upon the earth it lay.
Then fiercer Rávaṇ's fury grew,
An arrow from his side he drew,
Swift as a thunderbolt, aglow
With fire, and launched it at the foe.
Through flesh and bone a way it found,
And stretched Sugríva on the ground.
Sushen and Nala saw him fall,
Gaváksha, Gavaya heard their call,
And, poising hills, in act to fling
They charged amain the giant king.
They charged, they hurled the hills in vain:
He checked them with his arrowy rain,
And every brave assailant felt
The piercing wounds his missiles dealt.
Then smitten by the shafts that came
Keen, fleet, and thick, with certain aim,
They fled to Ráma, sure defence
Against the oppressor's violence,
Then, reverent palm to palm applied,
Thus Lakshmaṇ to his brother cried:
'To me, my lord, the task entrust
To lay this giant in the dust.'
'Go, then,' said Ráma, 'bravely fight;
Beat down this rover of the night.
But he, unmatched in bold emprise,
Fears not the Lord of earth and skies.
Keep on thy guard: with keenest eye
Thy moments of attack espy.
Let hand and eye in due accord
Protect thee with the bow and sword.'
Then Lakshmaṇ round his brother threw
His mighty arms in honour due,
Bent lowly down his reverent head,
And onward to the battle sped.
Hanúmán from afar beheld
How Rávaṇ's shafts the Vánars quelled:
To meet the giant's car he ran,
Raised his right arm and thus began:
'If Brahmá's boon thy life has screened
From Yaksha, God, Gandharva, fiend,
With these contending fear no ill,
But tremble at a Vánar still.'
With fury flashing from his eye
The lord of Lanká made reply:
'Strike, Vánar, strike: the fray begin,
And hope eternal fame to win.
This arm shall prove thee in the strife

---

[1] 'It is to be understood,' says the commentator, 'that this is not the Akampan who has recently been slain.'

And end thy glory and thy life.'
'Remember,' cried the Wind-God's son,
'Remember all that I have done,
My prowess, King, thou knowest well,
Shown in the fight when Aksha[1] fell.'
With heavy hand the giant smote
Hanúmán on the chest and throat,
Who reeled and staggered to and fro,
Stunned for a moment by the blow,
Till, mustering strength, his hand he reared
And struck the foe whom Indra feared.
His huge limbs bent beneath the shock,
As mountains, in an earthquake, rock,
And from the Gods and sages pealed
Shouts of loud triumph as he reeled.
But strength returning nerved his frame:
His eyeballs flashed with fiercer flame.
No living creature might resist
That blow of his tremendous fist
Which fell upon Hanúmán's flank:
And to the ground the Vánar sank,
No sign of life his body showed:
And Rávan in his chariot rode
At Níla; and his arrowy rain
Eell on the captain and his train.
Fierce Níla stayed his Vánar band,
And, heaving with his single hand
A mountain peak, with vigorous swing
Hurled the huge missile at the king.
Hanúmán life and strength regained,
Burned for the fight and thus complained:
'Why, coward giant, didst thou flee
And leave the doubtful fight with me?'
Seven mighty arrows keen and fleet
The giant launched, the hill to meet;
And, all its force and fury stayed,
The harmless mass on earth was laid.
Enraged the Vánar chief beheld
The mountain peak by force repelled,
And rained upon the foe a shower
Of trees uptorn with branch and flower.
Still his keen shafts which pierced and rent
Each flying tree the giant sent:
Still was the Vánar doomed to feel
The tempest of the winged steel.
Then, smarting from that arrowy storm,
The Vánar chief condensed his form,[2]
And lightly leaping from the ground
On Rávan's standard footing found;
Then springing unimpeded down
Stood on his bow and golden crown.
The Vánar's nimble leaps amazed
Ikshváku's son who stood and gazed.
The giant, raging in his heart,
Laid on his bow a fiery dart;
The Vánar on his flagstaff eyed,
And thus in tones of fury cried:
'Well skilled in magic lore art thou:
But will thine art avail thee now?
See if thy magic will defend
Thy life against the dart I send.'
Thus Rávan spake, the giant king,
And loosed the arrow from the string.
It pierced, with direst fury sped,
The Vánar with its flaming head.
His father's might, his power innate
Preserved him from the threatened fate.
Upon his knees he fell, distained
With streams of blood, but life remained.
Still Ravan for the battle burned:
At Lakshman next his car he turned,
And charged amain with furious show,
Straining in mighty hands his bow.
'Come,' Lakshman cried, 'assay the fight:
Leave foes unworthy of thy might.'
Thus Lakshman spoke: and Lanká's lord
Heard the dread thunder of the cord,
And mad with burning rage and pride
In hasty words like these replied:
'Joy, joy is mine, O Raghu's son:
Thy fate to-day thou canst not shun.
Slain by mine arrows thou shalt tread
The gloomy pathway of the dead.'
Thus as he spoke his bow he drew,
And seven keen shafts at Lakshman flew.
But Raghu's son with surest aim
Cleft every arrow as it came.
Thus with fleet shafts each warrior shot
Against his foe, and rested not.
Then one choice weapon from his store,
By Brahmá's self bestowed of yore,
Fierce as the flames that end the world,
The giant king at Lakshman hurled.
The hero fell, and racked with pain,
Scarce could his hand his bow retain.
But sense and strength resumed their seat
And, lightly springing to his feet,
He struck with one Tremendous stroke
And Rávan's bow in splinters broke.
From Lakshmans's cord three arrows flew
And pierced the giant monarch through.
Sore wounded Rávan closed, and round
Ikshváku's son his strong arms wound.
With strength unrivalled, Brahma's gift,
He strove from earth his foe to lift.
'Shall I,' he cried, 'who overthrow
Mount Meru and the Lord of Snow,
And heaven and all who dwell therein,
Be foiled by one of Ráma's kin?'
But though he heaved, and toiled, and strained,
Unmoved Ikshváku's son remained.
His frame by those huge arms compressed
The giant's God-given force confessed,
But conscious that himself was part

[1] Rávan's son, whom Hanumán killed when he first visited Lanká.

[2] Níla was the son of Agni the God of Fire, and possessed, like Milton's demons, the power of dilating and condensing his form at pleasure.

Of Vishṇu, he was firm in heart.
The Wind-God's son the fight beheld,
And rushed at Rávaṇ, rage-impelled.
Down crashed his mighty hand: the foe
Full in the chest received the blow.
His eyes grew dim, his knees gave way,
And senseless on the earth he lay.
The Wind-God's son to Ráma bore
Deep-wounded Lakshmaṇ stained with gore.
He whom no foe might lift or bend
Was light as air to such a friend.
The dart that Lakshmaṇ's side had cleft,
Untouched, the hero's body left,
And flashing through the air afar
Resumed its place in Rávaṇ's car;
And, waxing well though wounded sore,
He felt the deadly pain no more.
And Rávaṇ, though with deep wounds pained,
Slowly his sense and strength regained,
And furious still and undismayed
On bow and shaft his hand he laid.
Then Hanumán to Ráma cried:
'Ascend my back, great chief, and ride
Like Vishṇu borne on Garuḍ's wing,
To battle with the giant king.'
So, burning for the dire attack,
Rode Ráma on the Vánar's back,
And with fierce accents loud and slow
Thus gave defiance to the foe,
While his strained bowstring made a sound
Like thunder when it shakes the ground:
'Stay, Monarch of the giants, stay,
The penalty of sin to pay.
Stay: whither wilt thou fly, and how
Escape the death that waits thee now?'
No word the giant king returned:
His eyes with flames of fury burned.
His arm was stretched, his bow was bent,
And swift his fiery shafts were sent.
Red torrents from the Vánar flowed:
Then Ráma near to Rávaṇ strode,
And, with keen darts that never failed,
The chariot of the king assailed.
With surest aim his arrows flew:
The driver and the steeds he slew,
And shattered with the pointed steel
Car, flag and pole and yoke and wheel.
As Indra hurls his bolt to smite
Mount Meru's heaven-ascending height,
So Ráma with a flaming dart
Struck Lanká's monarch near the heart,
Who reeled and fell beneath the blow
And from loose fingers dropped his bow.
Bright as the sun, with crescent head,
From Ráma's bow an arrow sped,
And from his forehead, proud no more,
Cleft the bright coronet he wore.
Then Ráma stood by Rávaṇ's side
And to the conquered giant cried:
'Well hast thou fought: thine arm has slain
Strong heroes of the Vánar train.
I will not strike or slay thee now,
For weary, faint with fight art thou.
To Lanká's town thy footsteps bend,
And there the night securely spend.
To-morrow come with car and bow,
And then my prowess shalt thou know.'
He ceased: the king in humbled pride
Rose from the earth and naught replied.
With wounded limbs and shattered crown
He sought again his royal town.

CANTO LX.

KUMBHAKARṆA ROUSED.

With humbled heart and broken pride
Through Lanká's gate the giant hied,
Crushed, like an elephant beneath
A lion's spring and murderous teeth,
Or like a serpent neath the wing
And talons of the Feathered King.
Such was the giant's wild alarm
At arrows shot by Ráma's arm;
Shafts with red lightning round them curled,
Like Brahmá's bolts that end the world.
Supported on his golden throne,
With failing eye and humbled tone,
'Giants,' he cried, 'the toil is vain,
Fruitless the penance and the pain,
If I whom Indra owned his peer,
Secure from Gods, a mortal fear.
My soul remembers, now too late,
Lord Brahmá's words which spoke my fate:
'Tremble, proud Giant,' thus they ran,
'And dread thy death from slighted man.
Secure from Gods and demons live,
And serpents, by the boon I give.
Against their power thy life is charmed,
But against man is still unarmed.'
This Ráma is the man foretold
By Anaraṇya's[1] lips of old:
'Fear, Rávaṇ, basest of the base:
For of mine own imperial race
A prince in after time shall spring
And thee and thine to ruin bring.
And Vedavatí,[2] ere she died
Slain by my ruthless insult, cried:

---

[1] An ancient king of Ayodhyá said by some to have been Prithu's father.

[2] The daughter of King Kuśadhwaja. She became an ascetic, and being insulted by Rávaṇ in the woods where she was

'A scion of my royal line
Shall slay, vile wretch, both thee and thine.'
She in a later birth became
King Janak's child, now Ráma's dame.
Nandíśvara[1] foretold this fate,
And Umá[2] when I moved her hate,
And Rambhá,[3] and the lovely child
Of Varuṇ[4] by my touch defiled.
I know the fated hour is nigh:
Hence, captains, to your stations fly.
Let warders on the rampart stand:
Place at each gate a watchful band;
And, terror of immortal eyes,
Let mightiest Kumbhakarṇa rise.
He, slumbering, free from care and pain,
By Brahmá's curse, for months has lain.
But when Prahasta's death he hears,
Mine own defeat and doubts and fears,
The chief will rise to smite the foe
And his unrivalled valour show.
Then Raghu's royal sons and all
The Vánars neath his might will fall.'
The giant lords his hest obeyed,
They left him, trembling and afraid,
And from the royal palace strode
To Kumbhakarṇa's vast abode.
They carried garlands sweet and fresh,
And reeking loads of blood and flesh.
They reached the dwelling where he lay,
A cave that stretched a league each way,
Sweet with fair blooms of lovely scent
And bright with golden ornament.
His breathings came so fierce and fast,
Scarce could the giants brook the blast.
They found him on a golden bed
With his huge limbs at length outspread.
They piled their heaps of venison near,
Fat buffaloes and boars and deer.
With wreaths of flowers they fanned his face,
And incense sweetened all the place.
Each raised his mighty voice as loud
As thunders of an angry cloud,
And conchs their stirring summons gave
That echoed through the giant's cave.
Then on his breast they rained their blows,
And high the wild commotion rose
When cymbal vied with drum and horn,
And war cries on the gale upborne
Through all the air loud discord spread,
And, struck with fear, the birds fell dead.
But still he slept and took his rest.
Then dashed they on his shaggy chest
Clubs, maces, fragments of the rock:
He moved not once, nor felt the shock.
The giants made one effort more
With shell and drum and shout and roar.
Club, mallet, mace, in fury plied,
Rained blows upon his breast and side.
And elephants were urged to aid,
And camels groaned and horses neighed.
They drenched him with a hundred pails,
They tore his ears with teeth and nails.
They bound together many a mace
And beat him on the head and face;
And elephants with ponderous tread
Stamped on his limbs and chest and head.
The unusual weight his slumber broke:
He started, shook his sides, and woke;
And, heedless of the wounds and blows,
Yawning with thirst and hunger rose,
His jaws like hell gaped fierce and wide,
Dire as the flame neath ocean's tide.
Red as the sun on Meru's crest
The giant's face his wrath expressed,
And every burning breath he drew
Was like the blast that rushes through
The mountain cedars. Up he raised
His awful head with eyes that blazed
Like comets, dire as Death in form
Who threats the worlds with fire and storm.
The giants pointed to their stores
Of buffaloes and deer and boars,
And straight he gorged him with a flood
Of wine, with marrow, flesh, and blood.
He ceased: the giants ventured near
And bent their lowly heads in fear.
Then Kumbhakarṇa glared with eyes
Still heavy in their first surprise,
Still drowsy from his troubled rest,
And thus the giant band addressed.
'How have ye dared my sleep to break?
No trifling cause should bid me wake.
Say, is all well? or tell the need
That drives you with unruly speed
To wake me. Mark the words I say,
The king shall tremble in dismay,

---

performing penance, destroyed herself by entering fire, but was born again as Sítá to be in turn the destruction of him who had insulted her.

[1] Nandíśvara was Śiva's chief attendant. Rávaṇ had despised and laughed at him for appearing in the form of a monkey, and the irritated Nandíśvara cursed him and foretold his destruction by monkeys.

[2] Rávaṇ once upheaved and shook Mount Kailása the favourite dwelling place of Śiva the consort of Umá, and was cursed in consequence by the offended Goddess.

[3] Rambhá, who has several times been mentioned in the course of the poem, was one of the nymphs of heaven, and had been insulted by Rávaṇ.

[4] Punjikasthalá was the daughter of Varuṇ. Rávaṇ himself has mentioned in this book his insult to her, and the curse pronounced in consequence by Brahmá,

The fire be quenched and Indra slain
Ere ye shall break my rest in vain.'
Yúpáksha answered : 'Chieftain, hear ;
No God or fiend excites our fear.
But men in arms our walls assail :
We tremble lest their might prevail.
For vengeful Ráma vows to slay
The foe who stole his queen away,
And, matchless for his warlike deeds,
A host of mighty Vánars leads.
Ere now a monstrous Vánar came.
Laid Lanká waste with ruthless flame,
And Aksha, Rávaṇ's offspring, slew
With all his warrior retinue.
Our king who never trembled yet
For heavenly hosts in battle met,
At length the general dread has shared,
O'erthrown by Ráma's arm and spared.'
He ceased: and Kumbhakarṇa spake :
'I will go forth and vengeance take ;
Will tread their hosts beneath my feet,
Then triumph-flushed our king will meet.
Our giant bands shall eat their fill
Of Vánars whom this arm shall kill.
The princes' blood shall be my draught,
The chieftains' shall by you be quaffed.'
He spake, and, with an eager stride
That shook the earth, to Rávaṇ hied.

CANTO LXI.

THE VÁNARS' ALARM.

The son of Raghu near the wall
Saw, proudly towering over all,
The mighty giant stride along
Attended by the warrior throng ;
Heard Kumbhakarṇa's heavy feet
Awake the echoes of the street ;
And, with the lust of battle fired,
Turned to Vibhíshaṇ and inquired :
'Vibhíshaṇ, tell that chieftain's name
Who rears so high his mountain frame;
With glittering helm and lion eyes,
Preëminent in might and size
Above the rest of giant birth,
He towers the standard of the earth ;
And all the Vánars when they see
The mighty warrior turn and flee.'
'In him,' Vibhíshaṇ answered, 'know
Viśravas' son, the Immortals' foe,
Fierce Kumbhakarṇa, mightier far
Than Gods and fiends and giants are.
He conquered Yama in the fight,
And Indra trembling owned his might.
His arm the Gods and fiends subdued,
Gandharvas and the serpent brood.
The rest of his gigantic race
Are wondrous strong by God-giving grace;
But nature at his birth to him
Gave matchless power and strength of limb.
Scarce was he born, fierce monster, when
He killed and ate a thousand men.
The trembling race of men, appalled,
On Indra for protection called ;
And he, to save the suffering world,
His bolt at Kumbhakarṇa hurled.
So awful was the monster's yell
That fear on all the nations fell,
He, rushing on with furious roar,
A tusk from huge Airávat tore,
And dealt the God so dire a blow
That Indra reeling left his foe,
And with the Gods and mortals fled
To Brahmá's throne dispirited.
'O Brahmá,' thus the suppliants cried,
'Some refuge for this woe provide.
If thus his maw the giant sate
Soon will the world be desolate.'
The Self-existent calmed their woe,
And spake in anger to their foe :
'As thou wast born, Paulastya's son,
That worlds might weep by thee undone,
Thou like the dead henceforth shalt be ;
Such is the curse I lay on thee.'
Senseless he lay, nor spoke nor stirred;
Such was the power of Brahmá's word.
But Rávaṇ. troubled for his sake,
Thus to the Self-existent spake :
'Who lops the tree his care has reared
When golden fruit has first appeared ?
Not thus, O Brahmá, deal with one
Descended from thine own dear son.[1]
Still thou, O Lord, thy word must keep ;
He may not die, but let him sleep.
Yet fix a time for him to break
The chains of slumber and awake.'
He ceased : and Brahmá made reply :
'Six months in slumber shall he lie,
And then arising for a day
Shall cast the numbing bonds away.'
Now Rávaṇ in his doubt and dread
Has roused the monster from his bed,
Who comes in this the hour of need
On slaughtered Vánars flesh to feed.
Each Vánar, when his awe-struck eyes
Behold the monstrous chieftain, flies.
With hopeful words their minds deceive,
And let our trembling hosts believe
They see no giant, but, displayed,
A lifeless engine deftly made.'
Then Ráma called to Níla: 'Haste,
Let troops near every gate be placed,
And, armed with fragments of the rock
And trees, each lane and alley block.'

[1] Pulastya was the son of Brahmá and father of Viśravas or Paulastya the father of Rávaṇ and Kumbhakarṇa.

Thus Ráma spoke: the chief obeyed,
And swift the Vánars stood arrayed,
As when black clouds their battle form,
The summit of a hill to storm.

CANTO LXII.

RÁVAN'S REQUEST.

Along bright Lanká's royal road
The giant, roused from slumber, strode,
While from the houses on his head
A rain of fragrant flowers was shed.
He reached the monarch's gate whereon
Rich gems and golden fretwork shone.
Through court and corridor that shook
Beneath his tread his way he took,
And stood within the chamber where
His brother sat in dark despair.
But sudden, at the grateful sight
The monarch's eye again grew bright.
He started up, forgot his fear,
And drew his giant brother near.
The younger pressed the elder's feet
And paid the King observance meet,
Then cried: 'O Monarch, speak thy will,
And let my care thy word fulfil.
What sudden terror and dismay
Have burst the bonds in which I lay?'
Fierce flashed the flame from Rávaṇ's eye.
As thus in wrath he made reply:
'Fair time, I ween, for sleep is this,
To lull thy soul in tranquil bliss,
Unheeding, in oblivion drowned,
The dangers that our lives surround.
Brave Ráma, Daśaratha's son,
A passage o'er the sea has won,
And, with the Vánar monarch's aid,
Round Lanká's walls his hosts arrayed.
Though never in the deadly field
My Rákshas troops were known to yield,
The bravest of the giant train
Have fallèn by the Vánars slain.
Hence comes my fear. O fierce and brave,
Go forth, our threatened Lanká save.
Go forth, a dreadful vengeance take:
For this, O chief, I bade thee wake.
The Gods and trembling fiends have felt
The furious blows thine arm has dealt.
Earth has no warrior, heaven has none
To match thy might, Paulastya's son.'

CANTO LXIII.

KUMBHAKARṆA'S BOAST.

Then Kumbhakarṇa laughed aloud
And cried: 'O Monarch, once so proud,
We warned thee, but thou wouldst not hear;
And now the fruits of sin appear.
We warned thee, I, thy nobles, all
Who loved thee, in thy council hall.
Those sovereigns who with blinded eyes
Neglect the foe their hearts despise,
Soon, falling from the their high estate,
Bring on themselves the stroke of fate.
Accept at length, thy life to save,
The counsel sage Vibhíshaṇ gave,
The prudent counsel spurned before,
And Sítá to her lord restore.'[1]
The monarch frowned, by passion moved
And thus in angry words reproved:
'Wilt thou thine elder brother school,
Forgetful of the ancient rule
That bids thee treat him as the sage
Who guides thee with the lore of age?
Think on the dangers of the day,
Nor idly throw thy words away:
If, led astray, by passion stirred,
I in the pride of power have erred;
If deeds of old were done amiss,
No time for vain reproach is this.
Up, brother; let thy loving care
The errors of thy king repair.'
To calm his wrath, his soul to ease,
The younger spake in words like these:
'Yea, from our bosoms let us cast
All idle sorrow for the past.
Let grief and anger be repressed:
Again be firm and self-possessed.
This day, O Monarch, shalt thou see
The Vánar legions turn and flee,
And Ráma and his brother slain
With their hearts' blood shall dye the plain.
Yea, if the God who rules the dead,
And Varuṇ, their battalions led;
If Indra with the Storm-Gods came
Against me, and the Lord of Flame,
Still would I fight with all and slay
Thy banded foes, my King, to-day.
If Raghu's son this day withstand
The blow of mine uplifted hand,
Deep in his breast my darts shall sink,
And torrents of his life-blood drink.
O fear not, in my promise trust:
This arm shall lay him in the dust,
Shall leave the fierce Sugríva dyed
With gore, and Lakshmaṇ by his side,
And strike the great Hanúmán down,
The spoiler of our glorious town.'[2]

---

[1] I omit a tedious sermon on the danger of rashness and the advantages of prudence, sufficient to irritate a less passionate hearer than Rávaṇ.

[2] The Bengal recension assigns a very different speech to Kumbhakarṇa and makes him say that Nárad the messenger of the Gods had formerly told him that

CANTO LXIV.

MAHODAR'S SPEECH.

He ceased: and when his lips were closed
Mahodar thus his rede opposed:
'Why wilt thou shame thy noble birth
And speak like one of little worth?
Why boast thee thus in youthful pride
Rejecting wisdom for thy guide?
How will thy single arm oppose
The victor of a thousand foes,
Who proved in Janasthán his might
And slew the rovers of the night?
The remnant of those legions, they
Who saw his power that fatal day,
Now in this leaguered city dread
The mighty chief from whom they fled.
And wouldst thou meet the lord of men,
Beard the great lion in his den,
And, when thine eyes are open, break
The slumber of a deadly snake?
Who may an equal battle wage
With him, so awful in his rage,
Fierce as the God of Death whom none
May vanquish, Daśaratha's son?
But, Rávaṇ, shall the lady still
Refuse compliance with thy will?
No, listen, King, to this design
Which soon shall make the captive thine.
This day through Lanká's streets proclaim
That four of us[1] of highest fame
With Kumbhakarṇa at our head
Will strike the son of Raghu dead.
Forth to the battle will we go
And prove our prowess on the foe.
Then, if our bold attempt succeed,
No further plans thy hopes will need.
But if in vain our warriors strive,
And Raghu's son be left alive,
We will return, and, wounded sore,
Our armour stained with gouts of gore,
Will show the shafts that rent each frame,
Keen arrows marked with Ráma's name,
And say we giants have devoured
The princes whom our might o'erpowered.
Then let the joyful tidings spread
That Raghu's royal sons are dead.
To all around thy pleasure show,
Gold, pearls, and precious robes, bestow.
Gay garlands round the portals twine,
Enjoy the banquet and the wine.
Then go, the scornful lady seek,
And woo her when her heart is weak.
Rich robes and gold and gems display,
And gently wile her grief away.
Then will she feel her hopeless state,
Widowed, forlorn, and desolate;
Know that on thee her bliss depends,
Far from her country and her friends;
Then, her proud spirit overthrown,
The lady will be all thine own.'

CANTO LXV.

KUMBHAKARṆA'S SPEECH.

But haughty Kumbhakarṇa spurned
His counsel, and to Rávaṇ turned:
'Thy life from peril will I free
And slay the foe who threatens thee.
A hero never vaunts in vain,
Like bellowing clouds devoid of rain.
Nor, Monarch, be thine ear inclined
To counsellors of slavish kind,
Who with mean arts their king mislead
And mar each gallant plan and deed.
O, let not words like his beguile
The glorious king of Lanká's isle.'
  Thus scornful Kumbhakarṇa cried,
And Rávaṇ with a laugh replied:
'Mahodar fears and fain would shun
The battle with Ikshváku's son.
Of all my giant warriors, who
Is strong as thou, and brave and true?
Ride, conqueror, to the battle ride,
And tame the foeman's senseless pride.
Go forth like Yama to the field,
And let thine arm thy trident wield.
Scared by the lightning of thine eye
The Vánar hosts will turn and fly;
And Ráma, when he sees thee near,
With trembling heart will own his fear.'
  The champion heard, and, well content,
Forth from the hall his footsteps bent.
He grasped his spear, the foeman's dread,
Black iron all, both shaft and head,
Which, dyed in many a battle, bore
Great spots of slaughtered victims' gore.
The king upon his neck had thrown
The jewelled chain which graced his own,
And garlands of delicious scent
About his limbs for ornament.
Around his arms gay bracelets clung,
And pendants in his ears were hung.
Adorned with gold, about his waist
His coat of mail was firmly braced,
And like Náráyaṇ[1] or the God
Who rules the sky he proudly trod.
Behind him went a mighty throng
Of giant warriors tall and strong,

Vishṇu himself incarnate as Daśaratha's son should come to destroy Rávaṇ.

[1] Mahodar, Dwijihva, Sanhráda, and Vitardan.

[1] A name of Vishnu.

On elephants of noblest breeds,
With cars, with camels, and with steeds;
And, armed with spear and axe and sword
Were fain to battle for their lord.[1]

CANTO LXVI.

KUMBHAKARṆA'S SALLY.

In pomp and pride of warlike state
The giant passed the city gate.
He raised his voice: the hills, the shore
Of Lanká's sea returned the roar.
The Vánars saw the chief draw nigh
Whom not the ruler of the sky,
Nor Yama, monarch of the dead,
Might vanquish, and affrighted fled.
When royal Angad, Báli's son,
Saw the scared Vánars turn and run,
Undaunted still he kept his ground,
And shouted as he gazed around:
'O Nala, Níla, stay, nor let
Your souls your generous worth forget.
O Kumud and Gaváksha, why
Like base-born Vánars will ye fly?
Turn, turn, nor shame your order thus:
This giant is no match for us.'
They heard his voice: the flight was stayed;
Again for war they stood arrayed,
And hurled upon the foe a shower
Of mountain peaks and trees in flower.
Still on his limbs their missiles rained:
Unmoved, their blows he still sustained,
And seemed unconscious of the stroke
When rocks against his body broke.
Fierce as the flame when woods are dry
He charged with fury in his eye.
Like trees consumed with fervent heat
They fell beneath the giant's feet.
Some o'er the ground, dyed red with gore,
Fled wild with terror to the shore,
And, deeming that all hope was lost,
Ran to the bridge they erst had crossed.
Some clomb the trees their lives to save,
Some sought the mountain and the cave;
Some hid them in the bosky dell,
And there in deathlike slumber fell.
When Angad saw the chieftains fly
He called them with a mighty cry:
'Once more, O Vánars, charge once more,
On to the battle as before.
In all her compass earth has not,
To hide you safe, one secret spot.
What! leave your arms? each nobler dame
Will scorn her consort for the shame.
This blot upon your names efface,
And keep your valour from disgrace.
Stay, chieftains; wherefore will ye run,
A band of warriors scared by one?'
Scarce would they hear: they would not stay,
And basely spoke in wild dismay:
'Have we not fought, and fought in vain
Have we not seen our mightiest slain?
The giant's matchless force we fear,
And fly because our lives are dear.'
But Báli's son with gentle art
Dispelled their dread and cheered each heart.
They turned and formed and waited still
Obedient to the prince's will.

CANTO LXVII.

KUMBHAKARṆA'S DEATH.

Thus from their flight the Vánars turned,
And every heart for battle burned,
Determined on the spot to die
Or gain a warrior's meed on high.
Again the Vánars stooped to seize
Their weapons, rocks and fallen trees;
Again the deadly fight began,
And fiercely at the giant ran.
Unmoved the monster kept his place:
He raised on high his awful mace,
Whirled the huge weapon round his head
And laid the foremost Vánars dead.
Eight thousand fell bedewed with gore,
Then sank and died seven hundred more.
Then thirty, twenty, ten, or eight
At each fierce onset met their fate,
And fast the fallen were devoured
Like snakes by Garud's beak o'erpowered.
Then Dwivid from the Vánar van,
Armed with an uptorn mountain, ran,
Like a huge cloud when fierce winds blow,
And charged amain the mountain foe.
With wondrous force the hill he threw:
O'er Kumbhakarna's head it flew,
And falling on his host afar
Crushed many a giant, steed, and car.
Rocks, trees, by fierce Hanúmán sped,
Rained fast on Kumbhakrna's head.
Whose spear each deadlier missile stopped,
And harmless on the plain it dropped.

[1] There is so much commonplace repetition in these Sallies of the Rákshas chieftains that omissions are frequently necessary. The usual ill omens attend the sally of Kumbhakarna, and the Canto ends with a description of the terrified Vánars' flight which is briefly repeated in different words at the beginning of the next Canto.

Then with his furious eyes aglow
The giant rushed upon the foe,
Where, with a woody hill upheaved,
Hanúmán's might his charge received.
Through his vast frame the giant felt
The angry blow Hanúmán dealt.
He reeled a moment, sore distressed,
Then smote the Vánar on the breast,
As when the War-God's furious stroke
Through Krauncha's hill a passage broke.[1]
Fierce was the blow, and deep and wide
The rent: with crimson torrents dyed,
Hanúmán, maddened by the pain,
Roared like a cloud that brings the rain,
And from each Rákshas throat rang out
Loud clamour and exultant shout.
Then Níla hurled with mustered might
The fragment of a mountain height;
Nor would the rock the foe have missed,
But Kumbhakarna raised his fist
And smote so fiercely that the mass
Fell crushed to powder on the grass.
Five chieftains of the Vánar race[2]
Charged Kumbhakarna face to face,
And his huge frame they wildly beat
With rocks and trees and hands and feet.
Round Rishabh first the giant wound
His arms and hurled him to the ground,
Where speechless, senseless, wounded sore,
He lay his face besmeared with gore.
Then Níla with his fist he slew,
And Śarabh with his knee o'erthrew,
Nor could Gaváksha's strength withstand
The force of his terrific hand.
At Gandhamádan's eager call
Rushed thousands to avenge their fall,
Nor ceased those Vánars to assail
With knee and fist and tooth and nail.
Around his foes the giant threw
His mighty arms, and nearer drew
The captives subject to his will:
Then snatched them up and ate his fill.
There was no respite then, no pause:
Fast gaped and closed his hell-like jaws:
Yet, prisoned in that gloomy cave,
Some Vánars still their lives could save:
Some through his nostrils found a way,
Some through his ears resought the day.
Like Indra with his thunder, like
The God of Death in act to strike,
The giant seized his ponderous spear,
And charged the foe in swift career.
Before his might the Vánars fell,
Nor could their hosts his charge repel.
Then trembling, nor ashamed to run,
They turned and fled to Raghu's son.

When Báli's warrior son[1] beheld
Their flight, his heart with fury swelled.
He rushed, with his terrific shout,
To meet the foe and stay the rout.
He came, he hurled a mountain peak,
And smote the giant on the cheek.
His ponderous spear the giant threw:
Fierce was the cast, the aim was true;
But Angad, trained in war and tried,
Saw ere it came, and leapt aside.
Then with his open hand he smote
The giant on the chest and throat.
That blow the giant scarce sustained;
But sense and strength were soon regained.
With force which nothing might resist
He caught the Vánar by the wrist,
Whirled him, as if in pastime, round,
And dashed him senseless on the ground.
There low on earth his foe lay crushed:
At King Sugríva next he rushed,
Who, waiting for the charge, stood still,
And heaved on high a shattered hill.
He looked on Kumbhakarna dyed
With streams of blood, and fiercely cried:
'Great glory has thine arm achieved,
And thousands of their lives bereaved.
Now leave a while thy meaner foes,
And brook the hill Sugríva throws.'

He spoke, and hurled the mass he held:
The giant's chest the stroke repelled.
Then on the Vánars fell despair,
And Rákshas clamour filled the air.
The giant raised his arm, and fast
Came the tremendous[2] spear he cast.
Hanúmán caught it as it flew,
And knapped it on his knee in two.
The giant saw the broken spear:
His clouded eye confessed his fear;
Yet at Sugríva's head he sent
A peak from Lanká's mountain rent.

---

[1] Karttikeya the God of War, and the hero and incarnation Paraśurama are said to have cut a passage through the mountain Krauncha, a part of the Himálayan range, in the same way as the immense gorge that splits the Pyrenees under the towers of Marboré was cloven at one blow of Roland's sword Durandal.

[2] Rishabh, Śarabh, Níla, Gaváksha, and Gandhamádan.

[1] Angad. The text calls him the son of the son of him who holds the thunderbolt, *i. e.* the grandson of Indra.

[2] Literally, weighing a thousand *bháras*. The *bhára* is a weight equal to 2000 *palas*, the *pala* is equal to four *karśas*, and the *karśa* to 11375 French grammes or about 176 grains troy. The spear seems very light for a warrior of Kumbhakarna's strength and stature and the work performed with it.

The rushing mass no might could stay :
Sugriva fell and senseless lay.
The giant stooped his foe to seize,
And bore him thence, as bears the breeze
A cloud in autumn through the sky.
He heard the sad Immortals sigh,
And shouts of triumph long and loud
Went up from all the Rákshas crowd.
Through Lanká's gate the giant passed
Holding his struggling captive fast,
While from each terrace, house, and tower
Fell on his haughty head a shower
Of fragrant scent and flowery rain,
Blossoms and leaves and scattered grain.[1]
By slow degrees the Vánars' lord
Felt life and sense and strength restored.
He heard the giants' joyful boast :
He thought upon his Vánar host.
His teeth and feet he fiercely plied,
And bit and rent the giant's side,
Who, mad with pain and smeared with gore,
Hurled to the ground the load he bore.
Regardless of a storm of blows
Swift to the sky the Vánar rose,
Then lightly like a flying ball
High overleapt the city wall,
And joyous for deliverance won
Regained the side of Raghu's son.
And Kumbhakarṇa, mad with hate
And fury, sallied from the gate,
The carnage of the foe renewed
And filled his maw with gory food.
Slaying, with headlong frenzy blind,
Both Vánar foes and giant kind.
Nor would Sumitrá's valiant son[2]
The might of Kumbhakarṇa shun,
Who through his harness felt the sting
Of keen shafts loosened from the string.
His heart confessed the warrior's power,
And, bleeding from the ceaseless shower
That smote him on the chest and side,
With words like these the giant cried :
'Well fought, well fought, Sumitrá's son;
Eternal glory hast thou won,
For thou in desperate fight hast met
The victor never conquered yet,
Whom, borne on huge Airávat's back,
E'en Indra trembles to attack.
Go, son of Queen Sumitrá, go :
Thy valour and thy strength I know.
Now all my hope and earnest will
Is Ráma in the fight to kill.
Let him beneath my weapons fall,
And I will meet and conquer all.'
The chieftain, of Sumitrá born,
Made answer as he laughed in scorn :
Yea, thou hast won a victor's fame
From trembling Gods and Indra's shame.
There waits thee now a mightier foe
Whose prowess thou hast yet to know.
There, famous in a hundred lands,
Ráma the son of Raghu stands.'
Straight at the king the giant sped,
And earth was shaken at his tread.
His bow the hero grasped and strained,
And deadly shafts in torrents rained.
As Kumbhakarṇa felt each stroke
From his huge mouth burst fire and smoke;
His hands were loosed in mortal pain
And dropped his weapons on the plain.
Though reft of spear and sword and mace
No terror changed his haughty face.
With heavy hands he rained his blows
And smote to death a thousand foes.
Where'er the furious monster strode
While down his limbs the red blood flowed
Like torrents down a mountain's side,
Vánars and bears and giants died.
High o'er his head a rock he swung,
And the huge mass at Ráma flung.
But Ráma's arrows bright as flame
Shattered the mountain as it came.
Then Raghu's son, his eyes aglow
With burning anger, charged the foe,
And as his bow he strained and tried
With fearful clang the cord replied.
Wroth at the bowstring's threatening clang
To meet his foe the giant sprang.
High towering with enormous frame
Huge as a wood-crowned hill he came.
But Ráma firm and self-possessed
In words like these the foe addressed :
'Draw near, O Rákshas lord, draw near,
Nor turn thee from the fight in fear.
Thou meetest Ráma face to face,
Destroyer of the giant race.
Come, fight, and thou shalt feel this hour,
Laid low in death, thy conqueror's power.'
He ceased: and mad with wrath and pride
The giant champion thus replied :
'Come thou to me and thou shalt find
A foeman of a different kind.
No Khara, no Virádha.—thou
Hast met a mightier warrior now.
The strength of Kumbhakarṇa fear,
And dread the iron mace I rear.
This mace in days of yore subdued
The Gods and Dánav multitude.
Prove, lion of Ikshváku's line.
Thy power upon these limbs of mine.
Then, after trial, shalt thou bleed,
And with thy flesh my hunger feed.'
He ceased: and Ráma, undismayed,
Upon his cord those arrows laid

---

[1] The custom of throwing parched or roasted grain, with wreaths and flowers, on the heads of kings and conquerors when they go forth to battle and return is frequently mentioned by Indian poets.

[2] Lakshman.

Which pierced the stately Sál trees through,
And Báli king of Vánars slew.
They flew, they smote, but smote in vain
Those mighty limbs that felt no pain.
Then Ráma sent with surest aim
The dart that bore the Wind-God's name.
The missile from the giant tore
His huge arm and the mace it bore,
Which crushed the Vánars where it fell:
And dire was Kumbhakarṇa's yell.
The giant seized a tree, and then
Rushed madly at the lord of men.
Another dart, Lord Indra's own,
To meet his furious onset thrown,
His left arm from the shoulder lopped,
And like a mountain peak it dropped.
Then from the bow of Ráma sped
Two arrows, each with crescent head;
And, winged with might which naught could stay,
They cut the giant's legs away.
They fell, and awful was the sound
As those vast columns shook the ground;
And sky and sea and hill and cave
In echoing roars their answer gave.
Then from his side the hero drew
A dart that like the tempest flew—
No deadlier shaft has ever flown
Than that which Indra called his own—
Nor could the giant's mail-armed neck
The fury of the missile check.
Through skin and flesh and bone it smote
And rent asunder head and throat.
Down with the sound of thunder rolled
The head adorned with rings of gold,
And crushed to pieces in its fall
A gate, a tower, a massive wall.
Hurled to the sea the body fell;
Terrific was the ocean's swell,
Nor could swift fin and nimble leap
Save the crushed creatures of the deep.
Thus he who plagued in impious pride
The Gods and Bráhmans fought and died.
Glad were the hosts of heaven, and long
The air re-echoed with their song.[1]

[1] I have abridged this long Canto by omitting some vain repetitions, commonplace epithets and similes and other unimportant matter. There are many verses in this Canto which European scholars would rigidly exclude as unmistakeably the work of later rhapsodists. Even the reverent Commentator whom I follow ventures to remark once or twice: *Ayam śloka prakshipta iti bahavah*, 'This *śloka* or verse is in the opinion of many interpolated.'

CANTO LXVIII.

RÁVAṆ'S LAMENT.

They ran to Rávaṇ in his hall
And told him of his brother's fall:
'Fierce as the God who rules the dead,
Upon the routed foe he fed:
And, victor for a while, at length
Fell slain by Ráma's matchless strength.
Now like a mighty hill in size
His mangled trunk extended lies,
And where he fell, a bleeding mass,
Blocks Lanká's gate that none may pass.'
The monarch heard: his strength gave way;
And fainting on the ground he lay.
Grieved at the giants' mournful tale,
Long, shrill was Atikáya's wail;
And Triśiras in sorrow bowed
His triple head, and wept aloud.
Mahodar, Mahápárśva shed
Hot tears and mourned their brother dead.
At length, his wandering sense restored,
In loud lament cried Lanká's lord:
'Ah chief, for might and valour famed,
Whose arm the haughty foeman tamed,
Forsaking me, thy friends and all,
Why hast thou fled to Yama's hall?
Why hast thou fled to taste no more
The slaughtered foeman's flesh and gore?
Ah me, my life is done to-day:
My better arm is lopped away.
Whereon in danger I relied,
And, fearless, Gods and fiends defied.
How could a shaft from Ráma's bow
The matchless giant overthrow,
Whose iron frame so strong of yore
The crushing bolt of Indra bore?
This day the Gods and sages meet
And triumph at their foe's defeat.
This day the Vánar chiefs will boast
And, with new ardour fired, their host
In fiercer onset will assail
Our city, and the ramparts scale.
What care I for a monarch's name,
For empire, or the Maithil dame?
What joy can power and riches give,
Or life that I should care to live,
Unless this arm in mortal fray
The slayer of my brother slay?
For me, of Kumbhakarṇa reft,
Death is the only solace left;
And I will seek, o'erwhelmed with woes,
The realm to which my brother goes.
Ah me ill-minded, not to take
His counsel when Vibhíshaṇ spake
When he this evil day foretold
My foolish heart was overbold:
I drove my sage adviser hence,
And reap the fruits of mine offence.'

CANTO LXIX.

NARÁNTAK'S DEATH.

Pierced to the soul by sorrow's sting
Thus wailed the evil-hearted king.
Then Triśiras stood forth and cried :
'Yea, father, he has fought and died,
Our bravest : and the loss is sore :
But rouse thee, and lament no more.
Hast thou not still thy coat of mail,
Thy bow and shafts which never fail?
A thousand asses draw thy car
Which roars like thunder heard afar.
Thy valour and thy warrior skill,
Thy God-given strength, are left thee still.
Unarmed, thy matchless might subdued
The Gods and Dánav multitude.
Armed with thy glorious weapons, how
Shall Raghu's son oppose thee now?
Or, sire, within thy palace stay ;
And I myself will sweep away
Thy foes, like Garud when he makes
A banquet of the writhing snakes.
Soon Raghu's son shall press the plain,
As Narak[1] fell by Vishṇu slain,
Or Śambar[2] in rebellious pride
Who met the King of Gods[3] and died.'
The monarch heard : his courage grew,
And life and spirit came anew.
Devántak and Narántak heard,
And their fierce souls with joy were stirred;
And Atikáya[4] burned to fight,
And heard the summons with delight ;
While from the rest loud rang the cry,
'I too will fight,' and I,' 'and I.'
The joyous king his sons embraced,
With gold and chains and jewels graced,
And sent them forth with stirring speech
Of benison and praise to each.
Forth from the gate the princes sped
And ranged for war the troops they led.
The Vánar legions charged anew,
And trees and rocks for missiles flew.
They saw Narántak's mighty form
Borne on a steed that mocked the storm.
To check his charge in vain they strove :
Straight through their host his way he clove,
As springs a dolphin through the tide :
And countless Vánars fell and died,
And mangled limbs and corpses lay
To mark the chief's ensanguined way.
Sugrívá saw them fall or fly
When fierce Narántak's steed was nigh,
And marked the giant where he sped
O'er heaps of dying or of dead.
He bade the royal Angad face
That bravest chief of giant race.
As springs the sun from clouds dispersed,
So Angad from the Vánars burst.
No weapon for the fight he bore
Save nails and teeth, and sought no more.
'Leave, giant chieftain,' thus he spoke,
'Leave foes unworthy of thy stroke,
And bend against a nobler heart
The terrors of thy deadly dart.'
Narántak heard the words he spake :
Fast breathing, like an angry snake,
With bloody teeth his lips he pressed
And hurled his dart at Angad's breast.
True was the aim and fierce the stroke,
Yet on his breast the missile broke.
Then Angad at the giant flew,
And with a blow his courser slew :
The fierce hand crushed through flesh and bone,
And steed and rider fell o'erthrown.
Narántak's eyes with fury blazed:
His heavy hand on high he raised
And struck in savage wrath the head
Of Báli's son, who reeled and bled,
Fainted a moment and no more:
Then stronger, fiercer than before
Smote with that fist which naught could stay,
And crushed to death the giant lay.

[1] Narak was a demon, son of Bhúmi or Earth, who haunted the city Prágjyotisha.

[2] Śambar was a demon of drought.

[3] Indra.

[4] Devántak (Slayer of Gods) Narántak (Slayer of Men) Atikáya (Huge of Frame) and Triśiras (Three Headed) were all sons of Rávaṇ.

CANTO LXX.

THE DEATH OF TRIŚIRAS.

Then raged the Rákshas chiefs, and all
Burned to avenge Narántak's fall.
Devántak raised his club on high
And rushed at Angad with a cry.
Behind came Triśiras, and near
Mahodar charged with levelled spear.
There Angad stood to fight with three :
High o'er his head he waved a tree,
And at Devántak, swift and true
As Indra's flaming bolt, it flew.
But, cut by giant shafts in twain,
With minished force it flew in vain.
A shower of trees and blocks of stone
From Angad's hand was fiercely thrown ;
But well his club Devántak plied
And turned each rock and tree aside.
Nor yet, by three such foes assailed,

The heart of Angad sank or quailed.
He slew the mighty beast that bore
Mahodar: from his head he tore
A bleeding tusk, and blow on blow
Fell fiercely on his Rákshas foe.
The giant reeled, but strength regained,
And furious strokes on Angad rained,
Who, wounded by the storm of blows,
Sank on his knees, but swiftly rose.
Then Triśiras, as up he sprang,
Drew his great bow with awful clang,
And fixed three arrows from his sheaf
Full in the forehead of the chief.
Hanúmán saw, nor long delayed
To speed with Níla to his aid,
Who at the three-faced giant sent
A peak from Lanká's mountain rent.
But Triśiras with certain aim
Shot rapid arrows as it came:
And shivered by their force it broke
And fell to earth with flash and smoke.
Then as the Wind-God's son came nigh,
Devántak reared his mace on high.
Hanúmán smote him on the head
And stretched the monstrous giant dead.
Fierce Triśiras with fury strained
His bow, and showers of arrows rained
That smote on Níla's side and chest:
He sank a moment, sore distressed;
But quickly gathered strength to seize
A mountain with its crown of trees.
Crushed by the hill, distained with gore,
Mahodar fell to rise no more.
Then Triśiras raised high his spear
Which chilled the trembling foe with fear,
And, like a flashing meteor through
The air at Hanumán it flew.
The Vánar shunned the threatened stroke,
And with strong hands the weapon broke.
The giant drew his glittering blade:
Dire was the wound the weapon made
Deep in th Vánar's ample chest,
Who, for a moment sore oppressed,
Raised his broad hand, regaining might,
And struck the rover of the night.
Fierce was the blow: with one wild yell
Low on the earth the monster fell.
Hanúmán seized his fallen sword
Which served no more its senseless lord,
And from the monster triple-necked
Smote his huge heads with crowns bedecked.
Then Maháparśva burned with ire:
Fierce flashed his eyes with vengeful fire.
A moment on the dead he gazed,
Then his black mace aloft was raised,
And down the mass ef iron eame
That struck and shook the Vánar's frame.
Hanúmán's chest was wellnigh crushed,
And from his mouth red torrents gushed;
Yet served one instant to restore
His spirit: from the foe he tore
His awful mace, and smote, and laid
The giant in the dust dismayed.
Crushed were his jaws and teeth and eyes:
Breathless and still he lay as lies
A summit from a mountain rent
By him who rules the firmament.

CANTO LXXI.

ATIKÁYA'S DEATH.

But Atikáya's wrath grew high
To see his noblest kinsmen die.
He, fiercest of the giant race,
Presuming still on Brahmá's grace:
Proud tamer of the Immortals' pride,
Whose power and might with Indra's vied,
For blood and vengeful carnage burned,
And on the foe his fury turned.
High on a car that flashed and glowed
Bright as a thousand suns he rode.
Around his princely brows was set
A rich bejewelled coronet.
Gold pendants in his ears he wore;
He strained and tried the bow he bore,
And ever, as a shaft he aimed,
His name and royal race proclaimed.
Scarce might the Vánars brook to hear
His clanging bow and voice of fear:
To Raghu's elder son they fled,
Their sure defence in woe and dread.
Then Ráma bent his eyes afar
And saw the giant in his car
Fast following the flying crowd
And roaring like a rainy cloud.
He, with the lust of battle fired,
Turned to Vibhíshan and inquired:
'Say, who is this, of mountain size,
This archer with the lion eyes?
His car, which strikes our host with awe,
A thousand eager coursers draw.
Surrounded by the flashing spears
Which line his car, the chief appears
Like some huge cloud when lightnings play
About it on a stormy day;
And the great bow he joys to hold
Whose bended back is bright with gold,
As Indra's bow makes glad the skies,
That best of chariots glorifies.
O see the sunlike splendour flung
From the great flag above him hung,
Where, blazoned with refulgent lines,
Ráhu[1] the dreadful Dragon shines.
Full thirty quivers near his side,
His car with shafts is well supplied;

[1] The demon of eclipse who seizes the Sun and Moon.

And flashing like the light of stars
Gleam his two mighty scimitars.
Say, best of giants, who is he
Before whose face the Vánars flee?'
Thus Ráma spake. Vibhíshan eyed
The giants chief, and thus replied:
'This Ráma, this is Rávan's son:
High fame his youthful might has won.
He, best of warriors, bows his ear
The wisdom of the wise to hear.
Supreme is he mid those who know
The mastery of sword and bow.
Unrivalled in the bold attack
On elephant's or courser's back,
He knows, beside, each subtler art,
To win the foe, to bribe, or part.
On him the giant hosts rely,
And fear no ill when he is nigh.
This peerless chieftain bears the name
Of Atikáya huge of frame,
Whom Dhanyamáliní of yore
To Rávan lord of Lanká bore.'
Roused by his bow-string's awful clang,
To meet their foes the Vánars sprang.
Armed with tall trees from Lanká's wood,
And rocks and mountain peaks, they stood.
The giant's arrows, gold-bedecked,
The storm of hurtling missiles checked;
And ever on his foemen poured
Fierce tempest from his clanging cord;
Nor could the Vánar chiefs sustain
His shafts' intolerable rain.
They fled: the victor gained the place
Where stood the lord of Raghu's race,
And cried with voice of thunder: 'Lo,
Borne on my car, with shaft and bow,
I, champion of the giants, scorn
To fight with weaklings humbly born.
Come forth your bravest, if he dare,
And fight with one who will not spare.'
Forth sprang Sumitrá's noble child,[1]
And strained his ready bow, and smiled;
And giants trembled as the clang
Through heaven and earth reëchoing rang.
The giant to his string applied
A pointed shaft, and proudly cried;
'Turn, turn, Sumitrá's son and fly,
For terrible as Death am I.
Fly, nor that youthful form oppose,
Untrained in war, to warriors' blows.
What! wilt thou waste thy childish breath
And wake the dormant fire of death?
Cast down, rash boy, that useless bow:
Preserve thy life; uninjured go.'
He ceased: and stirred by wrath & pride
Sumitrá's noble son replied:
'By warlike deed, not words alone,
The valour of the brave is shown.
Cease with vain boasts my scorn to move,
And with thine arm thy prowess prove.
Borne on thy car, with sword and bow,
With all thine arms, thy valour show.
Fight, and my deadly shafts this day
Low in the dust thy head shall lay,
And, rushing fast in ceaseless flood,
Shall rend thy flesh and drink thy blood.'
His giant foe no answer made,
But on his string an arrow laid.
He raised his arm, the cord he drew,
At Lakshman's breast the arrow flew.
Sumitrá's son, his foemen's dread,
Shot a fleet shaft with crescent head,
Which cleft that arrow pointed well,
And harmless to the earth it fell.
A shower of shafts from Lakshman's bow
Fell fast and furious on the foe
Who quailed not as the missiles smote
With idle force his iron coat.
Then came the friendly Wind-God near,
And whispered thus in Lakshman's ear:
'Such shafts as these in vain assail
Thy foe's impenetrable mail.
A more tremendous missile try,
Or never may the giant die.
Employ the mighty spell, and aim
The weapon known by Brahmá's name.'
He ceased: Sumitrá's son obeyed:
On his great bow the shaft was laid,
And with a roar like thunder, true
As Indra's flashing bolt, it flew.
The giant poured his shafts like rain
To check its course, but all in vain.
With spear and mace and sword he tried
To turn the fiery dart aside.
Winged with a force which naught could check.
It smote the monster in the neck,
And, sundered from his shoulders, rolled
To earth his head and helm of gold.

CANTO LXXII.

RÁVAN'S SPEECH.

The giants bent, in rage and grief,
Their eyes upon the fallen chief:
Then flying wild with fear and pale
To Rávan bore the mournful tale.
He heard how Atikáya died,
Then turned him to his lords, and cried:
'Where are they now—my bravest—where,
Wise to consult and prompt to dare?
Where is Dhúmráksha, skilled to wield
All weapons in the battle field?
Akampan, and Prahasta's might,
And Kumbhakarna bold in fight?
These, these and many a Rákshas more,
Each master of the arms he bore,

[1] Lakshman.

Who every foe in fight o'erthrew,
The victors none could e'er subdue,
Have perished by the might of one,
The vengeful arm of Raghu's son.
In vain I cast mine eyes around,
No match for Ráma here is found,
No chief to stand before that bow
Whose deadly shafts have caused our woe.
Now, warriors, to your stations hence;
Provide ye for the wall's defence,
And be the Aśoka garden, where
The lady lies, your special care.
Be every lane and passage barred,
Set at each gate a chosen guard.
And with your troops, where danger calls,
Be ready to defend the walls.
Each movement of the Vánars mark;
Observe them when the skies grow dark;
Be ready in the dead of night,
And ere the morning bring the light.
Taught by our loss we may not scorn
These legions of the forest-born.'
He ceased: the Rákshas lords obeyed;
Each at his post his troops arrayed:
And, torn with pangs that pierced him through
The monarch from the hall withdrew.

CANTO LXXIII.

INDRAJIT'S VICTORY.

But Indrajit the fierce and bold
With words like these his sire consoled:
'Dismiss, O King, thy grief and dread,
And be not thus disquieted.
Against this numbing sorrow strive,
For Indrajit is yet alive;
And none in battle may withstand
The fury of his strong right hand.
This day, O sire, thine eyes shall see
The sons of Raghu slain by me.'
He ceased: he bade the king farewell:
Clear, mid the roar of drum and shell,
The clash of sword and harness rang
As to his car the warrior sprang.
Close followed by his Rákshas train
Through Lanká's gate he reached the plain.
Then down he leapt, and bade a band
Of giants by the chariot stand:
Then with due rites, as rules require,
Did worship to the Lord of Fire.
The sacred oil, as texts ordain,
With wreaths of scented flowers and grain,
Within the flame in order due,
That mightiest of the giants threw.
There on the ground were spear and blade,
And arrowy leaves and fuel laid,
An iron ladle deep and wide,
And robes with sanguine colours dyed.
Beside him stood a sable goat:
The giant seized it by the throat,
And straight from the consuming flame
Auspicious signs of victory came.
For swiftly, curling to the right,
The fire leapt up with willing light
Undimmed by smoky cloud, and, red
Like gold, upon the offering fed.
They brought him, while the flame yet glowed,
The dart by Brahmá's grace bestowed,
And all the arms he wielded well
Were charmed with text and holy spell.
Then fiercer for the fight he burned,
And at the foe his chariot turned,
While all his followers lifting high
Their maces charged with furious cry.
Dire, yet more dire the battle grew,
As rocks and trees and arrows flew.
The giant shot his shafts like rain,
And Vánars fell in myriads slain.
Sugríva, Angad, Níla felt
The wounds his hurtling arrows dealt.
His shafts the blood of Gaya drank;
Hanúmán reeled and Mainda sank.
Bright as the glances of the sun
Came the swift darts they could not shun.
Caught in the arrowy nets he wove.
In vain the sons of Raghu strove;
And Ráma, by the darts oppressed,
His brother chieftain thus addressed:
'See, first this giant warrior sends
Destruction mid our Vánar friends,
And now his arrows thick and fast
Their binding net around us cast.
To Brahmá's grace the chieftain owes
The matchless power and might he shows;
And mortal strength in vain contends
With him whom Brahmá's self befriends.
Then let us still with dauntless hearts
Endure this storm of pelting darts.
Soon must we sink bereaved of sense;
And then the victor, hurrying hence,
Will seek his father in his hall
And tell him of his foemen's fall.'
He ceased: o'erpowered by shaft and spell
The sons of Raghu reeled and fell.
The Rákshas on their bodies gazed;
And, mid the shouts his followers raised,
Sped back to Lanká to relate
In Rávan's hall the princes' fate.

CANTO LXXIV.

THE MEDICINAL HERBS.

The shades of falling night concealed
The carnage of the battle field,

Which, bearing each a blazing brand,
Hanúmán and Vibhíshan scanned,
Moving with slow and anxious tread
Among the dying and the dead.
Sad was the scene of slaughter shown
Where'er the torches' light was thrown.
Here mountain forms of Vánars lay
Whose heads and limbs were lopped away
Arms legs and fingers strewed the ground,
And severed heads lay thick around.
The earth was moist with sanguine streams.
And sighs were heard and groans and screams.
There lay Sugríva still and cold,
There Angad, once so brave and bold.
There Jámbaván his might reposed,
There Vegadarśí's eyes were closed;
There in the dust was Nala's pride,
And Dwivid lay by Mainda's side.
Where'er they looked the ensanguined plain
Was strewn with myriads of the slain;[1]
They sought with keenly searching eyes
King Jámbaván supremely wise.
His strength had failed by slow decay,
And pierced with countless shafts he lay.
They saw, and hastened to his side,
And thus the sage Vibhíshan cried:
'Thee, monarch of the bears, we seek:
Speak if thou yet art living, speak.'
Slow came the aged chief's reply;
Scarce could he say with many a sigh:
'Torn with keen shafts which pierce each limb,
My strength is gone, my sight is dim;
Yet though I scarce can raise mine eyes,
Thy voice, O chief, I recognize.
O, while these ears can hear thee, say,
Has Hanumán survived this day?'
'Why ask,' Vibhíshan cried, 'for one
Of lower rank, the Wind-God's son?
Hast thou forgotten, first in place,
The princely chief of Raghu's race?
Can King Sugríva claim no care,
And Angad, his imperial heir?'
'Yea, dearer than my noblest friends
Is he on whom our hope depends.
For if the Wind-God's son survive,
All we though dead are yet alive.
But if his precious life be fled
Though living still we are but dead:
He is our hope and sure relief.'
Thus slowly spoke the aged chief:
Then to his side Hanúmán came,
And with low reverence named his name.
Cheered by the face he longed to view
The wounded chieftain lived anew.
'Go forth,' he cried, 'O strong and brave,
And in their woe the Vánars save.
'No might but thine, supremely great,
May help us in our lost estate.
The trembling bears and Vánars cheer,
Calm their sad hearts, dispel their fear.
Save Raghu's noble sons, and heal
The deep wounds of the winged steel.
High o'er the waters of the sea
To far Himálaya's summits flee.
Kailása there wilt thou behold,
And Rishabh with his peaks of gold.
Between them see a mountain rise
Whose splendour will enchant thine eyes;
His sides are clothed above, below,
With all the rarest herbs that grow.
Upon that mountain's lofty crest
Four plants, of sovereign powers possessed,
Spring from the soil, and flashing there
Shed radiance through the neighbouring air.
One draws the shaft: one brings again
The breath of life to warm the slain:
One heals each wound; one gives anew
To faded cheeks their wonted hue.
Fly, chieftain, to that mountain's brow
And bring those herbs to save us now.'
Hanúmán heard, and springing through
The air like Vishnu's discus[1] flew.
The sea was passed: beneath him, gay
With bright-winged birds, the mountains lay,
And brook and lake and lonely glen,
And fertile lands with toiling men.
On, on he sped: before him rose
The mansion of perennial snows.
There soared the glorious peaks as fair
As white clouds in the summer air.
Here, bursting from the leafy shade,
In thunder leapt the wild cascade.
He looked on many a pure retreat
Dear to the Gods' and sages' feet:
The spot where Brahmá dwells apart,
The place whence Rudra launched his dart;[2]
Vishnu's high seat and Indra's home,
And slopes where Yama's servants roam.
There was Kuvera's bright abode;
There Brahmá's mystic weapon glowed.
There was the noble hill whereon

---

[1] In such cases as this I am not careful to reproduce the numbers of the poet, which in the text which I follow are 670000000; the Bengal recension being content with thirty million less.

[1] The discus or quoit, a sharp-edged circular missile is the favourite weapon of Vishnu.

[2] To destroy Tripura the triple city in the sky, air and earth, built by Maya for a celebrated Asur or demon, or as another commentator explains, to destroy Kandarpa or Love.

Those herbs with wondrous lustre shone,
And, ravished by the glorious sight,
Hanúmán rested on the height.
He, moving down the glittering peak,
The healing herbs began to seek ;
But, when he thought to seize the prize,
They hid them from his eager eyes.
Then to the hill in wrath he spake :
'Mine arm this day shall vengeance take,
If thou wilt feel no pity, none,
In this great need of Raghu's son.'
He ceased : his mighty arms he bent
And from the trembling mountain rent
His huge head with the life it bore,
Snakes, elephants, and golden ore.
O'er hill and plain and watery waste
His rapid way again he traced,
And mid the wondering Vánars laid
His burthen through the air conveyed.
The wondrous herbs' delightful scent
To all the host new vigour lent.
Free from all darts and wounds and pain
The sons of Raghu lived again,
And dead and dying Vánars healed
Rose vigorous from the battle field.

CANTO LXXV.

THE NIGHT ATTACK.

Sugríva spake in words like these :
'Now, Vánar lords, the occasion seize.
For now, of sons and brothers reft,
To Rávan little hope is left ;
And if our host his gates assail
His weak defence will surely fail.'
At dead of night the Vánar bands
Rushed on with torches in their hands.
Scared by the coming of the host
Each giant warder left his post.
Where'er the Vánar legions came
Their way was marked with hostile flame
That spread in fury to devour
Palace and temple, gate and tower.
Down came the walls and porches, down
Came stately piles that graced the town.
In many a house the fire was red,
On sandal wood and aloe fed,
And scorching flames in billows rolled
O'er diamonds and pearls and gold.
On cloth of wool, on silk brocade,
On linen robes their fury preyed.
Wheels, poles and yokes were burned, and all
The coursers' harness in the stall ;
And elephants' and chariots' gear,
The sword, the buckler, and the spear.
Scared by the crash of falling beams,
Mid lamentations, groans and screams,
Forth rushed the giants through the flames
And with them dragged bewildered dames
Each, with o'erwhelming terror wild,
Still clasping to her breast a child.
The swift fire from a cloud of smoke
Through many a gilded lattice broke,
And. melting pearl and coral, rose
O'er balconies and porticoes.
The startled crane and peacock screamed
As with strange light the courtyard gleamed,
And fierce unusual glare was thrown
On shrinking wood and heated stone.
From burning stall and stable freed
Rushed frantic elephant and steed,
And goaded by the driving blaze
Fled wildly through the crowded ways.
As earth with fervent heat will glow
When comes her final overthrow ;
From gate to gate, from court to spire
Proud Lanká was one blaze of fire,
And every headland, rock and bay
Shone bright a hundred leagues away.
Forth, blinded by the heat and flame
Ran countless giants huge of frame ;
And, mustering for fierce attack,
The Vánars charged to drive them back,
While shout and scream and roar and cry
Reëchoed through the earth and sky.
There Ráma stood with strength renewed,
And ever, as the foe he viewed,
Shaking the distant regions rang
His mighty bow's tremendous clang.
Then through the gates Nikumbha hied,
And Kumbha by his brother's side,
Sent forth—the bravest and the best—
To battle by the king's behest.
There fought the chiefs in open field,
And Angad fell and Dwivid reeled.
Sugríva saw : by rage impelled
He crushed the bow which Kumbha held.
About his foe Sugríva wound
His arms, and, heaving from the ground
The giant, hurled him o'er the bank ;
And deep beneath the sea he sank.
Like mandar hill with furious swell
Up leapt the waters where he fell.
Again he rose : he sprang to land
And raised on high his threatening hand:
Full on Sugríva's chest it came
And shook the Vánar's massy frame,
But on the wounded bone he broke
His wrist—so furious was the stroke.
With force that naught could stay or check,
Sugríva smote him neath the neck.
The fierce blow crashed through flesh and bone
And Kumbha lay in death o'erthrown.
Nikumbha saw his brother die,
And red with fury flashed his eye.
He dashed with mighty sway and swing

His axe against the Vánar king ;
But shattered on that living rock
It split in fragments at the shock.
Sugríva, rising to the blow,
Raised his huge hand and smote his foe.
And in the dust the giant lay
Gasping in blood his soul away.[1]

CANTO XCIII.

RÁVAN'S LAMENT.

They sought the king, a mournful train,
And cried, 'My lord, thy son is slain.
By Lakshman's hand, before these eyes,
The warrior fell no more to rise.
No time is this for vain regret :
Thy hero son a hero met ;
And he whose might in battle pressed
Lord Indra and the Gods confessed,
Whose power was stranger to defeat,
Has gained in heaven a blissful seat.
The monarch heard the mournful tale :
His heart was faint, his cheek was pale ;
His fleeting sense at length regained,
In trembling tones he thus complained :
'Ah me, my son, my pride : the boast
And glory of the giant host.
Could Lakshman's puny might defeat
The foe whom Indra feared to meet?
Could not thy deadly arrows split
Proud Mandar's peaks, O Indrajit,
And the Destroyer's self destroy?
And wast thou conquered by a boy?
I will not weep : thy noble deed
Has blessed thee with immortal meed
Gained by each hero in the skies
Who fighting for his sovereign dies.
Now, fearless of all meaner foes.
The guardian Gods[1] will taste repose :
But earth to me, with hill and plain,
Is desolate, for thou art slain.
Ah, whither hast thou fled, and left
Thy mother, Lanká, me bereft ;
Left pride and state and wives behind,
And lordship over all thy kind?
I fondly hoped thy hand should pay
Due honours on my dying day :
And couldst thou, O beloved, flee
And leave thy funeral rites to me?
Life has no comfort left me, none,
O Indrajit my son, my son.'
Thus wailed he broken by his woes :
But swift the thought of vengeance rose.
In awful wrath his teeth he gnashed,
And from his eyes red lightning flashed.
Hot from his mouth came fire and smoke,
As thus the king in fury spoke :
'Through many a thousand years of yore
The penance and the pain I bore,
And by fierce torment well sustained
The highest grace of Brahmá gained,
His plighted word my life assured,
From Gods of heaven and fiends secured.
He armed my limbs with burnished mail
Whose lustre turns the sunbeams pale,
In battle proof gainst heavenly bands
With thunder in their threatening hands.
Armed in this mail myself will go
With Brahmá's gift my deadly bow,
And, cleaving through the foes my way,
The slayers of my son will slay.'
Then, by his grief to frenzy wrought,
The captive in the grove he sought.
Swift through the shady path he sped :
Earth trembled at his furious tread.
Fierce were his eyes : his monstrous hand
Held drawn for death his glittering brand.

---

[1] I have briefly despatched Kumbha and Nikumbha, each of whom has in the text a long Canto to himself. When they fall Rávan sends forth Makaráksha or Crocodile-Eye, the son of Khara who was slain by Ráma in the forest before the abduction of Sítá. The account of his sallying forth, of his battle with Ráma and of his death by the fiery dart of that hero occupies two Cantos which I entirely pass over. Indrajit again comes forth and, rendered invisible by his magic art slays countless Vánars with his unerring arrows. He retires to the city and returns bearing in his chariot an effigy of Sítá, the work of magic, weeping and wailing by his side. He grasps the lovely image by the hair and cuts it down with his scimitar in the sight of the enraged Hanumán and all the Vánar host. At last after much fighting of the usual kind Indrajit's chariot is broken in pieces, his charioteer is slain, and he himself falls by Lakshman's hand, to the inexpressible delight of the high-souled saints, the nymphs of heaven and other celestial beings.

[1] The Lokapálas are sometimes regarded as deities appointed by Brahmá at the creation of the word to act as guardians of different orders of beings, but more commonly they are identified with the deities presiding over the four cardinal and four intermediate points of the compass, which, according to Manu V. 96, are 1, Indra, guardian of the East : 2, Agni, of the South-east ; 3, Yama, of the South ; 4, Súrya, of the South-west ; 5, Varuṇa, of the West ; 6, Pavana or Váyu, of the North-west ; 7, Kuvera, of the North ; 8, Soma or Chandra, of the North-east.

There weeping stood the Maithil dame:
She shuddered as the giant came.
Near drew the rover of the night
And raised his sword in act to smite;
But, by his nobler heart impelled,
One Rákshas lord his arm withheld:
'Wilt thou, great Monarch,' thus he cried,
'Wilt thou, to heavenly Gods allied,
Blot for all time thy glorious fame,
The slayer of a gentle dame?
What! shall a woman's blood be spilt
To stain thee with eternal guilt,
Thee deep in all the Veda's lore?
Far be the thought for evermore.
Ah look, and let her lovely face
This fury from thy bosom chase.'
He ceased: the prudent counsel pleased
The monarch, and his wrath appeased;
Then to his council hall in haste
The giant lord his steps retraced.[1]

CANTO XCVI.

RÁVAṆ'S SALLY.

The groans and cries of dames who wailed
The ears of Lanká's lord assailed,
For from each house and home was sent
The voice of weeping and lament.
In troubled thought his head he bowed,
Then fiercely looking on the crowd
Of nobles near his throne he broke
The silence, and in fury spoke:
'This day my deadly shafts shall fly,
And Raghu's sons shall surely die.
This day shall countless Vánars bleed
And dogs and kites and vultures feed.
Go, bid them swift my car prepare,
Bring the great bow I long to bear:
And let my host with sword and shield
And spear be ready for the field.'
From street to street the captains passed
And Rákshas warriors gathered fast,
With spear and sword to pierce and strike,
And axe and club and mace and pike.[2]

Then Rávaṇ's warrior chariot[1] wrought
With gold and rich inlay was brought.
Mid tinkling bells and weapons' clang
The monarch on the chariot sprang,
Which, decked with gems of every hue,
Eight steeds of noble lineage drew.
Mid roars of drum and shell rang out
From countless throats a joyful shout,
As, girt with hosts in warlike pride,
Through Lanká's streets the tyrant hied.
Still, louder than the roar of drums,
Went up the cry 'He comes, he comes,
Our ever conquering lord who trod
Beneath his feet both fiend and God.'
On to the gate the warriors swept
Where Raghu's sons their station kept.
When Rávaṇ's car the portal passed
The sun in heaven was overcast.
Earth rocked and reeled from side to side
And birds with boding voices cried.
Against the standard of the king
A vulture flapped his horrid wing.
Big gouts of blood before him dropped,
His trembling steeds in terror stopped.
The hue of death was on his cheek,
And scarce his flattering tongue could speak,
When, terrible with flash and flame,
Through murky air a meteor came.
Still by the hand of Death impelled
His onward way the giant held.
The Vánars in the field afar
Heard the loud thunder of his car,
And turned with warriors' fierce delight
To meet the giant in the fight.
He came: his clanging bow he drew
And myriads of the Vánars slew.
Some through the side and heart he cleft,
Some headless on the plain were left.
Some struggling groaned with mangled thighs,
Or broken arms or blinded eyes.[2]

[1] I omit two Cantos in the first of which Ráma with an enchanted Gandharva weapon deals destruction among the Rákshases sent out by Ravaṇ, and in the second the Rákshas dames lament the slain and mourn over the madness of Rávaṇ.

[2] I omit several weapons for which I cannot find distinctive names, and among them the *Sataghní* or *Centicide*, supposed by some to be a kind of fire-arms or rocket, but described by a commentator on the Mahábhárata as a stone or cylindrical piece of wood studded with iron spikes.

[1] The chariots of Ravaṇ's present army are said to have been one hundred and fifty million in number with three hundred million elephants, and twelve hundred million horses and asses. The footmen are merely said to have been 'unnumbered.'

[2] I omit Cantos XCVII., XCVIII., and XCIX, which describe in the usual way three single combats between Sugríva and Angad on the Vánar side and Virúpáksha, Mahodar, and Mahápárśva on the side of the giants. The weapons of the Vánars are trees and rocks: the giants fight with swords, axes, and bows and arrows. The details are generally the same as those of preceding duels. The giants fall, one in each Canto.

CANTO C.

RÁVAṆ IN THE FIELD.

The plain with bleeding limbs was spread,
And heaps of dying and of dead.
His mighty bow still Ráma strained,
And shafts upon the giants rained.
Still Angad and Sugríva, wrought
To fury, for the Vánars fought.
Crushed with huge rocks through chest and side
Mahodar, Mahápárśva died.
And Virúpáksha stained with gore
Dropped on the plain to rise no more.
When Rávaṇ saw the three o'erthrown
He cried aloud in furious tone:
'Urge, urge the car, my charioteer,
The haughty Vánars' death is near.
This very day shall end our griefs
For leaguered town and slaughtered chiefs.
Ráma the tree whose lovely fruit
Is Sítá, shall this arm uproot,—
Whose branches with protecting shade
Are Vánar lords who lend him aid.'
Thus cried the king: the welkin rang
As forth the eager coursers sprang,
And earth beneath the chariot shook
With flowery grove and hill and brook.
Fast rained his shafts: where'er he sped
The conquered Vánars fell or fled.
On rolled the car in swift career
Till Raghu's noble sons were near.
Then Ráma looked upon the foe
And strained and tried his sounding bow.
Till earth and all the region rang
Re-echoing to the awful clang.
His bow the younger chieftain bent,
And shaft on shaft at Rávaṇ sent.
He shot: but Rávaṇ little recked;
Each arrow with his own he checked.
And headless, baffled of its aim,
To earth the harmless missile came;
And Lakshmaṇ stayed his arm o'erpowered
By the thick darts the giant showered.
Fierce waxed the fight and fiercer yet,
For Rávaṇ now and Ráma met,
And each on other poured amain
The tempest of his arrowy rain.
While all the sky above was dark
With missiles speeding to their mark
Like clouds, with flashing lightning twined
About them, hurried by the wind.
Not fiercer was the wondrous fight
When Vritra fell by Indra's might.
All arts of war each foeman knew,
And trained alike, his bowstring drew.
Red-eyed with fury Lanká's king
Pressed his huge fingers on the string,
And fixed in Ráma's brows a flight
Of arrows winged with matchless might.
Still Raghu's son endured, and bore
That crown of shafts though wounded sore.
O'er a dire dart a spell he spoke
With mystic power to aid the stroke.
In vain upon the foe it smote
Rebounding from the steelproof coat.
The giant armed his bow anew,
And wondrous weapons hissed and flew,
Terrific, deadly, swift of flight,
Beaked like the vulture and the kite,
Or bearing heads of fearful make,
Of lion, tiger, wolf and snake.[1]
Then Ráma, troubled by the storm
Of flying darts in every form
Shot by an arm that naught could tire,
Launched at the foe his dart of fire,
Which, sacred to the Lord of Flame,
Burnt and consumed where'er it came.
And many a blazing shaft beside
The hero to his string applied.
With fiery course of dazzling hue
Swift to the mark each missile flew,
Some flashing like a shooting star,
Some as the tongues of lightning are;
One like a brilliant plant, one
In splendour like the morning sun.
Where'er the shafts of Ráma burned
The giant's darts were foiled and turned.
Far into space his weapons fled,
But as they flew struck thousands dead.

CANTO CI.

LAKSHMAṆ'S FALL.

When Rávaṇ saw his darts repelled,
With double rage his bosom swelled.
He summoned, wroth but undismayed,
A mightier charm to lend its aid.
And, fierce as fire before the blast,
A storm of missiles thick and fast,
Spear, pike and javelin, mace and brand,
Came hurtling from the giant's hand.
But, mightier still, the arms employed
By Raghu's son their force destroyed,
And every dart fell dulled and spent
By powers the bards of heaven had lent.
With his huge mace Vibhíshaṇ slew
The steeds that Rávaṇ's chariot drew.

---

[1] It is not very easy to see the advantage of having arrows headed in the way mentioned. Fanciful names for war-engines and weapons derived from their resemblance to various animals are not confined to India. The "War-wolf" was used by Edward I. at the siege of Brechin, the "Cat-house" and the "Sow" were used by Edward III. at the seige of Dunbar.

Then Rávaṇ hurled in deadly ire
A ponderous spear that flashed like fire:
But Ráma's arrows checked its way,
And harmless on the earth it lay.
The giant seized a mightier spear,
Which Death himself would shun with fear.
Vibhíshaṇ with the stroke had died,
But Lakshmaṇ's hand his bowstring plied,
And flying arrows thick as hail
Smote fiercely on the giant's mail.
Then Rávaṇ turned his aim aside,
On Lakshmaṇ looked and fiercely cried:
'Thou, thou again my wrath hast braved,
And from his death Vibhíshaṇ saved.
Now in his stead this spear receive
Whose deadly point thy heart shall cleave.'
He ceased: he hurled the mortal dart
By Maya forged with magic art.
The spear, with all his fury flung,
Swift, flickering like a serpent's tongue,
Adorned with many a tinkling bell,
Smote Lakshmaṇ, and the hero fell.
When Ráma saw, he heaved a sigh,
A tear one moment dimmed his eye.
But tender grief was soon repressed
And thoughts of vengeance filled his breast.
The air around him flashed and gleamed
As from his bow the arrows streamed;
And Lanká's lord, the foeman's dread,
O'erwhelmed with terror turned and fled.

CANTO CII.

LAKSHMAṆ HEALED.

But Ráma, pride of Raghu's race,
Gazed tenderly on Lakshmaṇ's face,
And, as the sight his spirit broke,
Turned to Susheṇ and sadly spoke:
'Where is my power and valour? how
Shall I have heart for battle now,
When dead before my weeping eyes
My brother, noblest Lakshmaṇ, lies?
My tears in blinding torrents flow,
My hand unnerved has dropped my bow.
The pangs of woe have blanched my cheek,
My heart is sick, my strength is weak.
Ah me, my brother! Ah, that I
By Lakshmaṇ's side might sink and die:
Life, war and conquest, all are vain
If Lakshmaṇ lies in battle slain.
Why will those eyes my glances shun?
Hast thou no word of answer, none?
Ah, is thy noble spirit flown
And gone to other worlds alone?
Couldst thou not let thy brother seek
Those worlds with thee? O speak, O speak
Rise up once more, my brother, rise,
Look on me with thy loving eyes.
Were not thy steps beside me still
In gloomy wood, on breezy hill?
Did not thy gentle care assuage
Thy brother's grief and fitful rage?
Didst thou not all his troubles share,
His guide and comfort in despair?'
As Ráma, vanquished, wept and sighed
The Vánar chieftain thus replied:
'Great Prince, unmanly thoughts dismiss,
Nor yield thy soul to grief like this.
In vain those burning tears are shed:
Our glory Lakshmaṇ is not dead.
Death on his brow no mark has set,
Where beauty's lustre lingers yet.
Clear is the skin, and tender hues
Of lotus flowers his palms suffuse.
O Ráma, cheer thy trembling heart;
Not thus do life and body part.
Now, Hanumán, to thee I speak:
Hie hence to tall Mahodaya's[1] peak
Where herbs of sovereign virtue grow
Which life and health and strength bestow.
Bring thou the leaves to balm his pain,
And Lakshmaṇ shall be well again.'
He ceased: the Wind-God's son obeyed
Swift through the clouds his way he made.
He reached the hill, nor stayed to find
The wondrous herbs of healing kind,
From its broad base the mount he tore
With all the shrubs and trees it bore,
Sped through the clouds again and showed
To wise Susheṇ his woody load.[2]
Susheṇ in wonder viewed the hill,
And culled the sovereign salve of ill.
Soon as the healing herb he found,
The fragrant leaves he crushed and ground.
Then over Lakshmaṇ's face he bent,
Who, healed and strengthened by the scent
Of that blest herb divinely sweet,
Rose fresh and lusty on his feet.

CANTO CIII.

INDRA'S CAR.

Then Raghu's son forgot his woe:
Again he grasped his fallen bow
And hurled at Lanká's lord amain
The tempest of his arrowy rain.

---

[1] Apparently a peak of the Himalaya chain.

[2] This exploit of Hanumán is related with inordinate prolixity in the Bengal recension (Gorresio's text). Among other adventures he narrowly escapes being shot by Bharat as he passes over Nandigráma near Ayodhyá. Hanumán stays Bharat in time, and gives him an account of what has befallen Ráma and Sítá in the forest and in Lanká.

Drawn by the steeds his lords had brought,
Again the giant turned and fought,
And drove his glittering chariot nigh
As springs the Day-God through the sky.
Then, as his sounding bow he bent,
Like thunderbolts his shafts were sent,
As when dark clouds in rain time shed
Fierce torrents on a mountain's head.
High on his car the giant rode,
On foot the son of Raghu strode.
The Gods from their celestial height
Indignant saw the unequal fight.
Then he whom heavenly hosts revere,
Lord Indra, called his charioteer:
'Haste, Mátali,' he cried, 'descend;
To Raghu's son my chariot lend.
With cheering words the chief address;
And all the Gods thy deed will bless.'
He bowed; he brought the glorious car
Whose tinkling bells were heard afar;
Fair as the sun of morning, bright
With gold and pearl and lazulite.
He yoked the steeds of tawny hue
That swifter than the tempest flew.
Then down the slope of heaven he hied
And stayed the car by Ráma's side.
'Ascend, O Chief,' he humbly cried,
'The chariot which the Gods provide.
The mighty bow of Indra see,
Sent by the Gods who favour thee;
Behold this coat of glittering mail,
And spear and shafts which never fail.'
Cheered by the grace the Immortals showed
The chieftain on the chariot rode.
Then as the car-borne warriors met
The awful fight raged fiercer yet.
Each shaft that Rávaṇ shot became
A serpent red with kindled flame,
And round the limbs of Ráma hung
With fiery jaws and quivering tongue.
But every serpent fled dismayed
When Raghu's valiant son displayed
The weapon of the Feathered King,[1]
And loosed his arrows from the string.
But Rávaṇ armed his bow anew,
And showers of shafts at Ráma flew,
While the fierce king in swift career
Smote with a dart the charioteer.
An arrow shot by Rávaṇ's hand
Laid the proud banner on the sand,
And Indra's steeds of heavenly strain
Fell by the iron tempest slain.
On Gods and spirits of the air
Fell terror, trembling, and despair.
The sea's white billows mounted high
With froth and foam to drench the sky.
The sun by lurid clouds was veiled,
The friendly lights of heaven were paled;
And, fiercely gleaming, fiery Mars
Opposed the beams of gentler stars.
Then Ráma's eyes with fury blazed
As Indra's heavenly spear he raised.
Loud rang the bells: the glistering head
Bright flashes through the region shed.
Down came the spear in swift descent:
The giant's lance was crushed and bent.
Then Rávaṇ's horses brave and fleet
Fell dead beneath his arrowy sleet.
Fierce on his foeman Ráma pressed,
And gored with shafts his mighty breast,
And spouting streams of crimson dyed
The weary giant's limbs and side.[1]

[1] As Garuḍ the king of birds is the mortal enemy of serpents the weapon sacred to him is of course best calculated to destroy the serpent arrows of Rávaṇ.

[1] I omit Cantos CIV. and CV. in which the fight is renewed and Rávaṇ severely reprimands his charioteer for timidity and want of confidence in his master's prowess, and orders him to charge straight at Ráma on the next occasion.

CANTO CVI.

GLORY TO THE SUN.

There faint and bleeding fast, apart
Stood Rávaṇ raging in his heart.
Then, moved with ruth for Ráma's sake,
Agastya[2] came and gently spake:
'Bend, Ráma, bend thy heart and ear
The everlasting truth to hear
Which all thy hopes through life will bless
And crown thine arms with full success.
The rising sun with golden rays,
Light of the worlds, adore and praise:
The universal king, the lord
By hosts of heaven and fiends adored.
He tempers all with soft control:
He is the Gods' diviner soul;
And Gods above and fiends below
And men to him their safety owe.
He Brahmá, Vishṇu, Śiva, he
Each person of the glorious Three,
Is every God whose praise we tell,
The King of Heaven,[3] the Lord of Hell:[4]
Each God revered from times of old,
The Lord of War,[5] the King of Gold:[6]

[2] The celebrated saint who has on former occasions assisted Ráma with his gifts and counsel.

[3] Indra.

[4] Yama.

[5] Kárttikeya.

[6] Kuvera.

Mahendra, Time and Death is he,
The Moon, the Ruler of the Sea.[1]
He hears our praise in every form,—
The manes,[2] Gods who ride the storm,[3]
The Aśvins,[4] Manu,[5] they who stand
Round Indra,[6] and the Sádhyas'[7] band
He is the air, and life and fire,
The universal source and sire :
He brings the seasons at his call,
Creator, light, and nurse of all.
His heavenly course he joys to run,
Maker of Day, the golden sun.
The steeds that whirl his car are seven,[8]
The flaming steeds that flash through heaven.
Lord of the sky, the conqueror parts
The clouds of night with glistering darts.
He, master of the Vedas' lore,
Commands the clouds' collected store :
He is the rivers' surest friend ;
He bids the rains, and they descend.
Stars, planets, constellations own
Their monarch of the golden throne.
Lord of twelve forms,[9] to thee I bow,
Most glorious King of heaven art thou.
O Ráma, he who pays aright
Due worship to the Lord of Light
Shall never fall oppressed by ill,
But find a stay and comfort still.
Adore with all thy heart and mind
This God of Gods, to him resigned ;
And thou his saving power shalt know
Victorious o'er thy giant foe.'[10]

CANTO CVIII.

THE BATTLE.

He spoke, and vanished : Ráma raised
His eyes with reverence meet, and praised
The glorious Day-God full in view :
Then armed him for the fight anew.
Urged onward by his charioteer
The giant's foaming steeds came near,
And furious was the battle's din
Where each resolved to die or win.
The Rákshas host and Vánar bands
Stood with their weapons in their hands,
And watched in terror and dismay
The fortune of the awful fray.
The giant chief with rage inflamed
His darts at Ráma's pennon aimed ;
But when they touched the chariot made
By heavenly hands their force was stayed.
Then Ráma's breast with fury swelled ;
He strained the mighty bow he held,
And straight at Rávaṇ's banner flew
An arrow as the string he drew—
A deadly arrow swift of flight,
Like some huge snake ablaze with light,
Whose fury none might e'er repel,—
And, split in twain, the standard fell.
At Ráma's steeds sharp arrows, hot
With flames of fire, the giant shot.
Unmoved the heavenly steeds sustained
The furious shower the warrior rained,
As though soft lotus tendrils smote
Each haughty crest and glossy coat.
Then volleyed swift by magic art,
Tree, mountain peak and spear and dart,
Trident and pike and club and mace
Flew hurtling straight at Ráma's face.
But Ráma with his steeds and car
Escaped the storm which fell afar
Where the strange missiles, as they rushed
To earth, a thousand Vánars crushed.

[1] Varuṇ.

[2] The Pitris, forefathers or spirits of the dead, are of two kinds, either the spirits of the father, grandfathers and great-grandfathers of an individual or the progenitors of mankind generally, to both of whom obsequial worship is paid and oblations of food are presented.

[3] The Maruts or Storm-Gods.

[4] The Heavenly Twins, the Castor and Pollux of the Hindus.

[5] The Man *par excellence*, the representative man and father of the human race regarded also as God.

[6] The Vasus, a class of deities originally personifications of natural phenomena.

[7] A class of celestial beings who dwell between the earth and the sun.

[8] The seven horses are supposed to symbolize the seven days of the week.

[9] One for each month in the year.

[10] This Canto does not appear in the Bengal recension. It comes in awkwardly and may I think be considered as an interpolation, but I paraphrase a portion of it as a relief after so much fighting and carnage, and as an interesting glimpse of the monotheistic ideas which underlie the Hindu religion. The hymn does not readily lend itself to metrical translation, and I have not attempted here to give a faithful rendering of the whole. A literal version of the text and the commentary given in the Calcutta edition will be found in the Additional Notes.

A canto is here omitted. It contains fighting of the ordinary kind between Ráma and Rávaṇ, and a description of sights and sounds of evil omen foreboding the destruction of the giant.

CANTO CIX.

THE BATTLE.

With wondrous power and might and skill
The giant fought with Ráma still.
Each at his foe his chariot drove,
And still for death or victory strove.
The warriors' steeds together dashed,
And pole with pole reëchoing clashed.
Then Ráma launching dart on dart
Made Rávaṇ's coursers swerve and start.
Nor was the lord of Lanká slow
To rain his arrows on the foe,
Who showed, by fiery points assailed,
No trace of pain, nor shook nor quailed.
Dense clouds of arrows Ráma shot
With that strong arm which rested not,
And spear and mace and club and brand
Fell in dire rain from Rávaṇ's hand.
The storm of missiles fiercely cast
Stirred up the oceans with its blast,
And Serpent-Gods and fiends who dwell
Below were troubled by the swell.
The earth with hill and plain and brook
And grove and garden reeled and shook:
The very sun grew cold and pale,
And horror stiled the rising gale.
God and Gandharva, sage and saint
Cried out, with grief and terror faint:
O may the prince of Raghu' line
Give peace to Bráhmaṇs and to kine,
And, rescuing the worlds, o'erthrow
The giant king our awful foe.'
  Then to his deadly string the pride
Of Raghu's race a shaft applied.
Sharp as a serpent's venomed fang
Straight to its mark the arrow sprang,
And from the giant's body shred
With trenchant steel the monstrous head.
There might the triple world behold
That severed head adorned with gold.
But when all eyes were bent to view,
Swift in its stead another grew.
Again the shaft was pointed well:
Again the head divided fell;
But still as each to earth was cast
Another head succeeded fast.
A hundred, bright with fiery flame,
Fell low before the victor's aim,
Yet Rávaṇ by no sign betrayed
That death was near or strength decayed.
The doubtful fight he still maintained,
And on the foe his missiles rained.
In air, on earth, on plain, on hill,
With awful might he battled still;
And through the hours of night and day
The conflict knew no pause or stay.

CANTO CX.

RÁVAṆ'S DEATH.

Then Mátali to Ráma cried:
'Let other arms the day decide.
Why wilt thou strive with useless toil
And see his might thy efforts foil?
Launch at the foe thy dart whose fire
Was kindled by the Almighty Sire.'
He ceased: and Raghu's son obeyed:
Upon his string the hero laid
An arrow, like a snake that hissed,
Whose fiery flight had never missed:
The arrow Saint Agastya gave
And blessed the chieftain's life to save:
That dart the Eternal Father made
The Monarch of the Gods to aid;
By Brahmá's self on him bestowed
When forth to fight Lord Indra rode.
'Twas feathered with the rushing wind;
The glowing sun and fire combined
To the keen point their splendour lent;
The shaft, ethereal element,
By Meru's hill and Mandar, pride
Of mountains, had its weight supplied.
He laid it on the twisted cord,
He turned the point at Lanká's lord,
And swift the limb-dividing dart
Pierced the huge chest and cleft the heart,
And dead he fell upon the plain
Like Vritra by the Thunderer slain.
The Rákshas host when Rávaṇ fell
Sent forth a wild terrific yell,
Then turned and fled, all hope resigned,
Through Lanká's gates, nor looked behind.
His voice each joyous Vánar raised,
And Ráma, conquering Ráma, praised.
Soft from celestial minstrels came
The sound of music and acclaim.
Soft, fresh, and cool, a rising breeze
Brought odours from the heavenly trees,
And ravishing the sight and smell
A wondrous rain of blossoms fell:
And voices breathed round Raghu's son:
'Champion of Gods, well done, well done.'

CANTO CXI.

VIBHÍSHAṆ'S LAMENT.

Vibhíshan saw his brother slain,
Nor could his heart its woe contain.
O'er the dead king he sadly bent
And mourned him with a loud lament:
'O hero, bold and brave,' he cried,
'Skilled in all arms, in battle tried,
Spoiled of thy crown, with limbs outspread,

Why wilt thou press thy gory bed?
Why slumber on the earth's cold breast,
When sumptuous couches woo to rest?
Ah me, my brother over bold,
Thine is the fate my heart foretold:
But love and pride forbade to hear
The friend who blamed thy wild career.
Fallen is the sun who gave us light,
Our lordly moon is veiled in night.
Our beacon fire is dead and cold:
A hundred waves have o'er it rolled.
What could his light and fire avail
Against Lord Ráma's arrowy hail?
Woe for the giants' royal tree,
Whose stately height was fair to see.
His buds were deeds of kingly grace,
His bloom the sons who decked his race.
With rifled bloom and mangled bough
The royal tree lies prostrate now.'
'Nay, idly mourn not,' Ráma cried,
'The warrior king has nobly died,
Interpid hero, firm through all.
So fell he as the brave should fall;
And ill beseems it chiefs like us
To weep for those who perish thus.
Be firm: thy causeless grief restrain,
And pay the dues that yet remain.'
Again Vibhíshan sadly spoke:
'His was the hero arm that broke
Embattled Gods' and Indra's might,
Unconquered ere to-day in fight.
He rushed against thee, fought and fell,
As Ocean, when his waters swell,
Hurling his might against a rock,
Falls spent and shattered by the shock
Woe for our king's untimely end,
The generous lord the trusty friend:
Our sure defence when fear arose,
A dreaded scourge to stubborn foes.
O, let the king thy hand has slain
The honours of the dead obtain.'
Then Ráma answered. 'Hatred dies
When low in dust the foeman lies.
Now triumph bids the conflict cease,
And knits us in the bonds of peace.
Let funeral rites be duly paid.
And be it mine thy toil to aid.'

CANTO CXII.

THE RÁKSHAS DAMES.

High rose the universal wail
That mourned the monarch's death, and, pale
With crushing woe, her hair unbound,
Her eyes in floods of sorrow drowned,
Forth from the inner chambers came
With trembling feet each royal dame.
Heedless of those who bade them stay
There falling by their husband's side,
'Ah, King! ah dearest lord!' they cried.
Like creepers shattered by the storm
They threw them on his mangled form.
One to his bleeding bosom crept
And lifted up her voice and wept.
About his feet one mourner clung.
Around his neck another hung.
One on the giant's severed head.
Her pearly tears in torrents shed
Fast as the drops the summer shower
Pours down upon the lotus flower.
'Ah, he whose arm in anger reared
The King of Gods and Yama feared.
While panic struck their heavenly train,
Lies prostrate in the battle slain.
Thy haughty heart thou wouldst not bend,
Nor listen to each wiser friend.
Ah, had the dame, as they implored,
Been yielded to her injured lord,
We had not mourned this day thy fall,
And happy had it been for all.
Then Ráma and thy friends content
In blissful peace their days had spent.
Thine injured brother had not fled.
Nor giant chiefs and Vánars bled.
Yet for these woes we will not blame.
Thy fancy for the Maithil dame,
Fate, ruthless Fate, whom none may bend
Has urged thee to thy hapless end.'

CANTO CXIII.

MANDODARI'S LAMENT.

While thus they wept, supreme in place,
The loveliest for form and face,
Mandodari drew near alone,
Looked on her lord and made her moan:
'Ah Monarch, Indra feared to stand
In fight before thy conquering hand.
From thy dread spear the Immortals ran;
And art thou murdered by a man?
Ah, 'twas no child of earth, I know,
That smote thee with that mortal blow.
'Twas Death himself in Ráma's shape,
That slew thee: Death whom none escape.
Or was it he who rules the skies
Who met thee, clothed in man's disguise?
Ah no, my lord, not Indra: he
In battle ne'er could look on thee.
One only God thy match I deem:
'Twas Vishṇu's self, the Lord Supreme,
Whose days through ceaseless time extend
And ne'er began and ne'er shall end:
He with the discus, shell, and mace,
Brought ruin on the giant race.
Girt by the Gods of heaven arrayed
Like Vánar hosts his strength to aid,

And slew the king whom Fate had doomed.
In Janasthán when Khara died
With giant legions by his side,
No mortal was the unconquered foe
In Ráma's form who struck the blow.
When Hanumán the Vánar came
And burnt thy town with hostile flame,
I counselled peace in anxious fear:
I counselled, but thou wouldst not hear.
Thy fancy for the foreign dame
Has brought thee death and endless shame.
Why should thy foolish fancy roam?
Hadst thou not wives as fair at home?
In beauty, form and grace could she,
Dear lord, surpass or rival me?
Now will the days of Sítá glide
In tranquil joy by Ráma's side:
And I—ah me, around me raves
A sea of woe with whelming waves.
With thee in days of old I trod
Each spot beloved by nymph and God;
I stood with thee in proud delight
On Mandar's side and Meru's height;
With thee, my lord, enchanted strayed
In Chaitraratha's[1] lovely shade,
And viewed each fairest scene afar
Transported in thy radiant car.
But source of every joy wast thou,
And all my bliss is ended now.
 Then Ráma to Vibhíshaṇ cried:
'Whate'er the ritual bids, provide.
Obsequial honours duly pay,
And these sad mourners' grief allay.
Vibhíshaṇ answered, wise and true.
For duty's changeless law he knew:
'Nay one who scorned all sacred vows
And dared to touch another's spouse,
Fell tyrant of the human race,
With funeral rites I may not grace.'
 Him Raghu's royal son, the best
Of those who love the law, addressed:
'False was the rover of the night,
He loved the wrong and scorned the right.
Yet for the fallen warrior plead
The dauntless heart, the valorous deed.
Let him who ne'er had brooked defeat,
The chief whom Indra feared to meet,
The ever-conquering lord, obtain
The honours that should grace the slain.'
Vibhíshaṇ bade his friends prepare
The funeral rites with thoughtful care.
Himself the royal palace sought
Whence sacred fire was quickly brought,
With sandal wood and precious scents
And pearl and coral ornaments.
Wise Bráhmans, while the tears that flowed
Down their wan cheeks their sorrow sowed,
Upon a golden litter laid
The corpse in finest ropes arrayed.
Thereon were flowers and pennons hung,
And loud the monarch's praise was sung.
Then was the golden litter raised,
While holy fire in order blazed,
And first in place Vibhíshaṇ led
The slow procession of the dead.
Behind, their cheeks with tears bedewed,
Came sad the widowed multitude.
Where, raised as Bráhmans ordered, stood
Piled sandal logs, and scented wood,
The body of the king was set
High on a deerskin coverlet.
Then duly to the monarch's shade
The offerings for the dead they paid,
And southward on the eastern side
An altar formed and fire supplied.
Then on the shoulder of the dead
The oil and clotted milk were shed.
All rites were done as rules ordain:
The sacrificial goat was slain.
Next on the corpse were perfumes thrown
And many a flowery wreath was strown;
And with Vibhíshaṇ's ready aid
Rich vesture o'er the king was laid.
Then while the tears their cheeks bedewed
Parched grain upon the dead they strewed;
Last, to the wood, as rules require,
Vibhíshaṇ set the kindling fire.
 Then having bathed, as texts ordain,
To Lanká went the mourning train.
Vibhíshaṇ, when his task was done,
Stood by the side of Raghu's son.
And Ráma, freed from every foe,
Unstrung at last his deadly bow,
And laid the glittering shafts aside,
And mail by Indra's love supplied.

CANTO CXIV.

VIBHÍSHAṆ CONSECRATED.

Joy reigned in heaven where every eye
Had seen the Lord of Lanká die.
In cars whose sheen surpassed the sun's
Triumphant rode the radiant ones;
And Rávaṇ's death, by every tongue,
And Ráma's glorious deeds were sung.
They praised the Vánars true and brave,
The counsel wise Sugríva gave.
The deeds of Hanumán they told,
The valiant chief supremely bold,
The strong ally, the faithful friend.
And Sítá's truth which naught could bend.
 To Mátali, whom Indra sent,
His head the son of Raghu bent:
And he with fiery steeds who clove
The clouds again to Swarga drove.

[1] The garden of Kuvera, the God of Riches.

Round King Sugríva brave and true
His arms in rapture Ráma threw,
Looked on the host with joy and pride,
And thus to noble Lakshman cried .
'Now let king-making drops be shed,
Dear brother, on Vibhíshan's head
For truth and friendship nobly shown,
And make him lord of Rávan's throne.'
This longing of his heart he told :
And Lakshman took an urn of gold
And bade the wind-fleet Vánars bring
Sea water for the giants' king.
The brimming urn was swiftly brought :
Then on a throne superbly wrought
Vibhíshan sat, the giants' lord,
And o'er his brows the drops were poured.
As Raghu's son the rite beheld
His loving heart with rapture swelled :
But tenderer thoughts within him woke,
And thus to Hanumán he spoke :
'Go to my queen : this message give :
Say Lakshman and Sugríva live.
The death of Lanká's monarch tell,
And bid her joy, for all is well.'

CANTO CXV.

SITA'S JOY.

The Vánar chieftain bowed his head,
Within the walls of Lanká sped,
Leave from the new-made king obtained,
And Sítá's lovely garden gained.
Beneath a tree the queen he found,
Where Rákshas warders watched around.
Her pallid cheek, her tangled hair,
Her raiment showed her deep despair.
Near and more near the envoy came
And gently hailed the weeping dame.
She started up in sweet surprise,
And sudden joy illumed her eyes,
For well the Vánar's voice she knew,
And hope reviving sprang and grew.
'Fair Queen' he said, 'our task is done :
The foe is slain and Lanká won.
Triumphant mid triumphant friends
Kind words of greeting Ráma sends.
'Blest for thy sake, O spouse most true,
My deadly foe I met and slew.
Mine eyes are strangers yet to sleep :
I built a bridge athwart the deep
And crossed the sea to Lanká's shore
To keep the mighty oath I swore.
Now, gentle love, thy cares dispel,
And weep no more, for all is well.
Fear not in Rávan's house to stay,
For good Vibhíshan now bears away,
For constant truth and friendship known :
Regard his palace as thine own.'
He greets thee thus thy heart to cheer,
And urged by love will soon be here.'
Then flushed with joy the lady's cheek,
Her eyes o'erflowed, her voice was weak ;
But struggling with her sobs she broke
Her silence thus, and faintly spoke :
'So fast the flood of rapture came,
My trembling tongue no words could frame.
Ne'er have I heard in days of bliss
A tale that gave such joy as this.
More precious far than gems and gold
The message which thy lips have told.'
His reverent hands the Vánar raised
And thus the lady's answer praised :
'Sweet are the words, O Queen, which thou
True to thy lord, hast spoken now,
Better than gems and pearls of price,
Yea, or the throne of Paradise.
But, lady, ere I leave this place,
Grant me, I pray, a single grace.
Permit me, and this vengeful hand
Shall slay thy guards, this Rákshas band,
Whose cruel insult threat and scorn
Thy gentle soul too long has borne.'
Thus, stern of mood, Hanumán cried :
The Maithil lady thus replied :
'Nay, be not wroth with servants : they,
When monarchs bid must needs obey,
And, vassals of their lords, fulfil
Each fancy of their sovereign will.
To mine own sins the blame impute,
For as we sow we reap the fruit.
The tyrant's will these dames obeyed
When their fierce threats my soul dismayed.'
She ceased : with admiration moved
The Vánar chief her words approved :
'Thy speech,' he cried, 'is worthy one
Whom love has linked to Raghu's son.
Now speak, O Queen, that I may know
Thy pleasure, for to him I go.'
The Vánar ceased : then Janak's child
Made answer as she sweetly smiled :
'My first, my only wish can be,
O chief, my loving lord to see.'
Again the Vánar envoy spoke,
And with his words new rapture woke :
'Queen, ere this sun shall cease to shine
Thy Ráma's eyes shall look in thine.
Again the lord of Raghu's race
Shall turn to thee his moon-bright face.
His faithful brother shalt thou see
And every friend who fought for thee,
And greet once more thy king restored
Like Śachí[1] to her heavenly lord.'
To Raghu's son his steps he bent
And told the message that she sent.

[1] The consort of Indra.

CANTO CXVI.

THE MEETING.

He looked upon that archer chief
Whose full eye mocked the lotus leaf,
And thus the noble Vánar spake:
'Now meet the queen for whose dear sake
Thy mighty task was first begun,
And now the glorious fruit is won.
O'erwhelmed with woe thy lady lies,
The hot tears streaming from her eyes.
And still the queen must long and pine
Until those eyes be turned to thine.'
But Ráma stood in pensive mood,
And gathering tears his eyes bedewed.
His sad looks sought the ground: he sighed
And thus to King Vibhíshan cried:
'Let Sítá bathe and tire her head
And hither to my sight be led
In raiment sweet with precious scent,
And gay with golden ornament.'
The Rákshas king his palace sought,
And Sítá from her bower was brought.
Then Rákshas bearers tall and strong,
Selected from the menial throng,
Through Lanká's gate the queen, arrayed
In glorious robes and gems, conveyed.
Concealed behind the silken screen,
Swift to the plain they bore the queen,
While Vánars, close on every side,
With eager looks the litter eyed.
The warders at Vibhíshan's hest
The onward rushing throng repressed,
While like the roar of ocean loud
Rose the wild murmur of the crowd.
The son of Raghu saw and moved
With anger thus the king reproved:
'Why vex with hasty blow and threat
The Vánars, and my rights forget?
Repress this zeal, untimely shown:
I count this people as mine own.
A woman's guard is not her bower,
The lofty wall, the fenced tower:
Her conduct is her best defence,
And not a king's magnificence.
At holy rites, in war and woe,
Her face unveiled a dame may show;
When at the Maiden's Choice [1] they meet,
When marriage troops parade the street.
And she, my queen, who long has lain
In prison racked with care and pain,
May cease a while her face to hide,
For is not Ráma by her side?
Lay down the litter: on her feet
Let Sítá come her lord to meet,
And let the hosts of woodland race
Look near upon the lady's face.'
Then Lakshman and each Vánar chief
Who heard his words were filled with grief.
The lady's gentle spirit sank,
And from each eye in fear she shrank,
As, her sweet eyelids vailed for shame,
Slowly before her lord she came.
While rapture battled with surprise
She raised to his her wistful eyes.
Then with her doubt and fear she strove,
And from her breast all sorrow drove.
Regardless of the gathering crowd,
Bright as the moon without a cloud,
She bent her eyes, no longer dim,
In joy and trusting love on him.

[1] The Swayamvara, Self-choice or election of a husband by a princess or daughter of a Kshatriya at a public assembly of suitors held for the purpose. For a description of the ceremony see *Nala and Damayanti* an episode of the Mahábhárat translated by the late Dean Milman, and *Idylls from the Sanskrit*.

CANTO CXVII.

SÍTÁ'S DISGRACE.

He saw her trembling by his side,
And looked upon her face and cried:
'Lady, at length my task is done,
And thou, the prize of war, art won.
This arm my glory has retrieved,
And all that man might do achieved;
The insulting foe in battle slain
And cleared mine honour from its stain.
This day has made my name renowned
And with success my labour crowned.
Lord of myself, the oath I swore
Is binding on my soul no more.
If from my home my queen was reft,
This arm has well avenged the theft,
And in the field has wiped away
The blot that on mine honour lay.
The bridge that spans the foaming flood,
The city red with giants' blood;
The hosts by King Sugríva led
Who wisely counselled, fought and bled;
Vibhíshan's love, our guide and stay—
All these are crowned with fruit to-day.
But, lady, 'twas not love for thee
That led mine army o'er the sea.
'Twas not for thee our blood was shed,
Or Lanká filled with giant dead.
No fond affection for my wife
Inspired me in the hour of strife.
I battled to avenge the cause
Of honour and insulted laws.
My love is fled, for on thy fame
Lies the dark blot of sin and shame;
And thou art hateful as the light

That flashes on the injured sight.
The world is all before thee: flee:
Go where thou wilt, but not with me.
How should my home receive again
A mistress soiled with deathless stain?
How should I brook the foul disgrace,
Scorned by my friends and all my race?
For Rávan bore thee through the sky,
And fixed on thine his evil eye.
About thy waist his arms he threw,
Close to his breast his captive drew,
And kept thee, vassal of his power,
An inmate of his ladies' bower.'

CANTO CXVIII.

SÍTÁ'S REPLY.

Struck down with overwhelming shame
She shrank within her trembling frame.
Each word of Ráma's like a dart
Had pierced the lady to the heart;
And from her sweet eyes unrestrained
The torrent of her sorrows rained.
Her weeping eyes at length she dried,
And thus mid choking sobs replied:
'Canst thou, a high-born prince, dismiss
A high-born dame with speech like this?
Such words befit the meanest hind,
Not princely birth and generous mind.
By all my virtuous life I swear
I am not what thy words declare.
If some are faithless, wilt thou find
No love and truth in womankind?
Doubt others if thou wilt, but own
The truth which all my life has shown.
If, when the giant seized his prey,
Within his hated arms I lay,
And felt the grasp I dreaded, blame
Fate and the robber, not thy dame.
What could a helpless woman do?
My heart was mine and still was true.
Why when Hanumán sent by thee
Sought Lanká's town across the sea,
Couldst thou not give, O lord of men,
Thy sentence of rejection then?
Then in the presence of the chief
Death, ready death, had brought relief,
Nor had I nursed in woe and pain
This lingering life, alas in vain.
Then hadst thou shunned the fruitless strife
Nor jeopardied thy noble life,
But spared thy friends and bold allies
Their vain and weary enterprise.
Is all forgotten, all? my birth,
Named Janak's child, from fostering earth?
That day of triumph when a maid
My trembling hand in thine I laid?
My meek obedience to thy will,
My faithful love through joy and ill,
That never failed at duty's call—
O King, is all forgotten, all?'
  To Lakshman then she turned and spoke
While sobs and sighs her utterance broke:
'Sumitrá's son, a pile prepare,
My refuge in my dark despair.
I will not live to bear this weight
Of shame, forlorn and desolate.
The kindled fire my woes shall end
And be my best and surest friend.'
  His mournful eyes the hero raised
And wistfully on Ráma gazed,
In whose stern look no ruth was seen,
No mercy for the weeping queen.
No chieftain dared to meet those eyes,
To pray, to question or advise.
  The word was passed, the wood was piled
And fain to die stood Janak's child.
She slowly paced around her lord,
The Gods with reverent act adored,
Then raising suppliant hands the dame
Prayed humbly to the Lord of Flame:
'As this fond heart by virtue swayed
From Raghu's son has never strayed,
So, universal witness, Fire
Protect my body on the pyre,
As Raghu's son has idly laid
This charge on Sítá, hear and aid.'
  She ceased: and fearless to the last
Withim the flame's wild fury passed.
Then rose a piercing cry from all
Dames, children, men, who saw her fall
Adorned with gems and gay attire
Beneath the fury of the fire.

CANTO CXIX.

GLORY TO VISHṆU.

The shrill cry pierced through Ráma's ears
And his sad eyes o'erflowed with tears,
When lo, transported through the sky
A glorious band of Gods was nigh.
Ancestral shades,[1] by men revered,
In venerable state appeared,
And he from whom all riches flow,[2]
And Yama Lord who reigns below:
King Indra, thousand-eyed, and he
Who wields the sceptre of the sea,[3]
The God who shows the blazoned bull,[4]
And Brahmá Lord most bountiful
By whose command the worlds were made:
All these on radiant cars conveyed,

[1] The Pitris or Manes, the spirits of the dead.
[2] Kuvera, the God of Wealth.
[3] Varun, God of the sea.
[4] Mahádeva or Śiva whose ensign is a bull.

Brighter than sun-beams, sought the place
Where stood the prince of Raghu's race,
And from their glittering seats the best
Of blessed Gods the chief addressed:
'Couldst thou, the Lord of all, couldst thou,
Creator of the worlds, allow
Thy queen, thy spouse to brave the fire
And give her body to the pyre?
Dost thou not yet, supremely wise,
Thy heavenly nature recognize?
They ceased: and Ráma thus began:
'I deem myself a mortal man,
Of old Ikshváku's line, I spring
From Daśaratha Kosal's king.'
He ceased: and Brahmá's self replied:
'O cast the idle thought aside.
Thou art the Lord Náráyan, thou
The God to whom all creatures bow.
Thou art the saviour God who wore
Of old the semblance of a boar;
Thou he whose discus overthrows
All present, past and future foes;
Thou Brahmá, That whose days extend
Without beginning, growth or end;
The God, who, bears the bow of horn,
Whom four majestic arms adorn;
Thou art the God who rules the sense
And sways with gentle influence;
Thou all-pervading Vishnu Lord
Who wears the ever-conquering sword;
Thou art the Guide who leads aright,
Thou Krishna of unequalled might.
Thy hand, O Lord, the hills and plains,
And earth with all her life sustains;
Thou wilt appear in serpent form
When sinks the earth in fire and storm.
Queen Sítá of the lovely brows
Is Lakshmí thy celestial spouse.
To free the worlds from Rávan thou
Wouldst take the form thou wearest now.
Rejoice: the mighty task is done:
Rejoice, thou great and glorious one.
The tyrant, slain, thy labours end:
Triumphant now to heaven ascend.
High bliss awaits the devotee
Who clings in loving faith to thee,
Who celebrates with solemn praise
The Lord of ne'er beginning days.
On earth below, in heaven above
Great joy shall crown his faith and love.
And he who loves the tale divine
Which tells each glorious deed of thine
Through life's fair course shall never know
The fierce assault of pain and woe.'[1]

[1] The Address to Ráma, both text and commentary, will be found literally translated in the Additional Notes. A paraphrase of a portion is all that I have attempted here.

CANTO CXX.

SITA' RESTORED.

Thus spoke the Self-existent Sire:
Then swiftly from the blazing pyre
The circling flames were backward rolled,
And, raising in his gentle hold
Alive unharmed the Maithil dame,
The Lord of Fire embodied came.
Fair as the morning was her sheen,
And gold and gems adorned the queen.
Her form in crimson robes arrayed,
Her hair was bound in glossy braid.
Her wreath was fresh and sweet of scent,
Undimmed was every ornament.
Then, standing close to Ráma's side,
The universal witness cried:
'From every blot and blemish free
Thy faithful queen returns to thee.
In word or deed, in look or mind
Her heart from thee has ne'er declined.
By force the giant bore away
From thy lone cot his helpless prey,
And in his bowers securely kept
She still has longed for thee and wept.
With soft temptation, bribe and threat,
He bade the dame her love forget:
But, nobly faithful to her lord,
Her soul the giant's suit abhorred.
Receive, O King, thy queen again,
Pure, ever pure from spot and stain.'
Still stood the king in thoughtful mood
And tears of joy his eyes bedewed.
Then to the best of Gods the best
Of warrior chiefs his mind expressed:
''Twas meet that mid the thousands here
The searching fire my queen should clear;
For long within the giant's bower
She dwelt the vassal of his power.
For else had many a slanderous tongue
Reproaches on mine honour flung,
And scorned the king who, love-impelled,
His consort from the proof withheld.
No doubt had I, but surely knew
That Janak's child was pure and true,
That, come what might, in good and ill
Her faithful heart was with me still.
I knew that Rávan could not wrong
My queen whom virtue made so strong.
I knew his heart would sink and fail,
Nor dare her honour to assail,
As Ocean, when he raves and roars,
Fears to o'erleap his bounding shores.
Now to the worlds her truth is shown,
And Sítá is again mine own.
Thus proved before unnumbered eyes,
On her pure fame no shadow lies.
As heroes to their glory cleave,
Mine own dear spouse I ne'er will leave.'

He ceased: and clasped in fond embrace
On his dear breast she hid her face.

CANTO CXXI.

DAŚARATHA.

To him Maheśvar thus replied:
'O strong-armed hero, lotus-eyed,
Thou, best of those who love the right,
Hast nobly fought the wondrous fight.
Dispelled by thee the gloom that spread
Through trembling earth and heaven is fled.
The worlds exult in light and bliss,
And praise thy name, O chief, for this.
Now peace to Bharat's heart restore,
And bid Kausalyá weep no more.
Thy face let Queen Kaikeyí see,
Let fond Sumitrá gaze on thee.
The longing of thy friends relieve,
The kingdom of thy sires receive.
Let sons of gentle Sítá born
Ikshváku's ancient line adorn.
Then from all care and foemen freed
Perform the offering of the steed.
In pious gifts thy wealth expend,
Then to the home of Gods ascend.
Thy sire, this glorious king, behold.
Among the blest in heaven enrolled.
He comes from where the Immortals dwell:
Salute him, for he loves thee well.'
His mandate Raghu's sons obeyed,
And to their sire obeisance made,
Where high he stood above the car
In wondrous light that shone afar.
His limbs in radiant garments dressed
Whereon no spot of dust might rest.
When on the son he loved so well
The eyes of Daśaratha fell,
He strained the hero to his breast
And thus with gentle words addressed:
'No joy to me is heavenly bliss,
For there these eyes my Ráma miss.
Enrolled on high with saint and sage,
Thy woes, dear son, my thoughts engage.
Kaikeyí's guile I ne'er forget:
Her cruel words will haunt me yet,
Which sent thee forth, my son, to roam
The forest far from me and home.
Now when I look on each dear face,
And hold you both in fond embrace,
My heart is full of joy to see
The sons I love from danger free.
Now know I what the Gods designed,
And how in Ráma's form enshrined
The might of Purushottam lay,
The tyrant of the worlds to slay.
Ah, how Kausalyá will rejoice
To hear again her darling's voice,
And, all thy weary wanderings o'er,
To gaze upon thy face once more.
Ah blest, for ever blest are they
Whose eyes shall see the glorious day
Of thy return in joy at last.
Thy term of toil and exile past.
Ayodhyá's lord, begin thy reign,
And day by day new glory gain.'
He ceased: and Ráma thus replied:
'Be not this grace, O sire, denied.
Those hasty words, that curse revoke
Which from thy lips in anger broke:
'Kaikeyí, be no longer mine:
I cast thee off, both thee and thine.'
O father, let no sorrow fall
On her or hers: thy curse recall.'
'Yea, she shall live, if so thou wilt,'
The sire replied, 'absolved from guilt.'
Round Lakshman then his arms he threw
And moved by love began anew:
'Great store of merit shall be thine,
And brightly shall thy glory shine;
Secure on earth thy brother's grace,
And high in heaven shall be thy place.
Thy glorious king obey and fear:
To him the triple world is dear.
God, saint, and sage, by Indra led,
To Ráma bow the reverent head,
Nor from the Lord, the lofty-souled,
Their worship or their praise withhold.
Heart of the Gods, supreme is he,
The One who ne'er shall cease to be.'
On Sítá then he looked and smiled;
'List to my words' he said, 'dear child,
Let not thy gentle breast retain
One lingering trace of wrath or pain.
When by the fire thy truth he proved,
By love for thee his will was moved.
The furious flame thy faith confessed
Which shrank not from the awful test:
And thou, in every heart enshrined,
Shalt live the best of womankind.'
He ceased: he bade the three adieu,
And home to heaven exulting flew.

CANTO CXXII.

INDRA'S BOON.

Then Indra, he whose fiery stroke
Slew furious Páka, turned and spoke:
'A glorious day, O chief, is this,
Rich with the fruit of lasting bliss.
Well pleased are we: we love thee well
Now speak, thy secret wishes tell.'
Thus spake the sovereign of the sky,
And this was Ráma's glad reply:
'If I have won your grace, incline
To grant this one request of mine.
Restore, O King: the Vánar dead
Whose blood for me was nobly shed.

To life and strength my friends recall,
And bring them back from Yama's hall.
When, fresh in might the warriors rise,
Prepare a feast to glad their eyes.
Let fruits of every season glow,
And streams of purest water flow.'
Thus Raghu's son, great-hearted, prayed,
And Indra thus his answer made:
'High is the boon thou seekest: none
Should win this grace but Raghu's son.
Yet, faithful to the word I spake,
I grant the prayer for thy dear sake.
The Vánars whom the giants slew
Their life and vigour shall renew.
Their strength repaired, their gashes healed
Whose torrents dyed the battle field,
The warrior hosts from death shall
Like sleepers when their slumber flies.'
Restored from Yama's dark domain
The Vánar legions filled the plain,
And, round the royal chief arrayed,
With wondering hearts obeisance paid.
Each God the son of Raghu praised,
And cried as loud his voice he raised:
'Turn, King, to fair Ayodhyá speed,
And leave thy friends of Vánar breed.
Thy true devoted consort cheer
After long days of woe and fear.
Bharat, thy loyal brother, see,
A hermit now for love of thee.
The tears of Queen Kauśalyá dry,
And light with joy each stepdame's eye;
Then consecrated king of men
Make glad each faithful citizen.'
They ceased: and borne on radiant cars
Sought their bright home amid the stars.

CANTO CXXIII.

THE MAGIC CAR.

Then slept the tamer of his foes
And spent the night in calm repose.
Vibhíshan came when morning broke,
And hailed the royal chief, and spoke:
'Here wait thee precious oil and scents,
And rich attire and ornaments.
The brimming urns are newly filled,
And women in their duty skilled,
With lotus-eyes, thy call attend,
Assistance at thy bath to lend.'
'Let others,' Ráma cried, 'desire
These precious scents, this rich attire.
I heed not such delights as these,
For faithful Bharat, ill at ease,
Watching for me is keeping now
Far far away his rigorous vow.
By Bharat's side I long to stand,
I long to see my fatherland.
Far is Ayodhyá: long, alas,
The dreary road and hard to pass.'
'One day,' Vibhíshan cried, 'one day
Shall bear thee o'er that length of way.
Is not the wondrous chariot mine,
Named Pushpak, wrought by hands divine,
The prize which Rávan seized of old
Victorious o'er the God of Gold?
This chariot, kept with utmost care,
Will waft thee through the fields of air,
And thou shalt light unwearied down
In fair Ayodhyá's royal town.
But yet if aught that I have done
Has pleased thee well, O Raghu's son;
If still thou carest for thy friend,
Some little time in Lanká spend;
There after toil of battle rest
Within my halls an honoured guest.'
Again the son of Raghu spake:
'Thy life was perilled for my sake.
Thy counsel gave me priceless aid:
All honours have been richly paid.
Scarce can my love refuse, O best
Of giant kind, thy last request.
But still I yearn once more to see
My home and all most dear to me;
Nor can I brook one hour's delay:
Forgive me, speed me on my way.'
He ceased: the magic car was brought,
Of yore by Viśvakarmá wrought.
In sunlike sheen it flashed and blazed;
And Raghu's sons in wonder gazed.

CANTO CXXIV.

THE DEPARTURE.

The giant lord the chariot viewed,
And humbly thus his speech renewed:
'Behold, O King, the car prepared:
Now be thy further will declared.'
He ceased: and Ráma spake once more:
'These hosts who thronged to Lanká's shore
Their faith and might have nobly shown,
And set thee on the giants' throne.
Let pearls and gems and gold repay
The feats of many a desperate day,
That all may go triumphant hence
Proud of their noble recompense.'
Vibhíshan, ready at his call,
With gold and gems enriched them all.
Then Ráma clomb the glorious car
That shone like day's resplendent star.
There in his lap he held his dame
Vailing her eyes in modest shame.
Beside him Lakshman took his stand,
Whose mighty bow still armed his hand.
'O King Vibhíshan,' Ráma cried,
'O Vánar chiefs, so long allied,

My comrades till the foemen fell,
List, for I speak a long farewell.
The task, in doubt and fear begun,
With your good aid is nobly done.
Leave Lanká's shore, your steps retrace,
Brave warriors of the Vánar race.
Thou, King Sugríva, true, through all,
To friendship's bond and duty's call,
Seek far Kishkindha with thy train
And o'er thy realm in glory reign.
Farewell, Vibhíshan, Lanká's throne
Won by our arms is now thine own,
Thou, mighty lord, hast nought to dread
From heavenly Gods by Indra led.
My last farewell, O King, receive,
For Lanká's isle this hour I leave.'
Loud rose their cry in answer: 'We,
O Raghu's son, would go with thee.
With thee delighted would we stray
Where sweet Ayodhyá's groves are gay,
Then in the joyous synod view
King-making balm thy brows bedew;
Our homage to Kauśalyá pay,
And hasten on our homeward way.'
Their prayer the son of Raghu heard,
And spoke, his heart with rapture stirred:
'Sugríva, O my faithful friend,
Vibhíshan and ye chiefs, ascend.
A joy beyond all joys the best
Will fill my overflowing breast,
If girt by you, O noble band,
I seek again my native land.'
With Vánar lords in danger tried
Sugríva sprang to Ráma's side,
And girt by chiefs of giant kind
Vibhíshan's step was close behind.
Swift through the air, as Ráma chose,
The wondrous car from earth arose.
And decked with swans and silver wings
Bore through the clouds its freight of kings.

CANTO CXXV.

THE RETURN.

Then Ráma, speeding through the skies,
Bent on the earth his eager eyes:
'Look, Sítá, see, divinely planned
And built by Viśvakarmá's hand;
Lanká the lovely city rest
Enthroned on Mount Trikúta's crest.
Behold those fields, ensanguined yet,
Where Vánar hosts and giants met.
There, vainly screened by charm and spell,
The robber Rávan fought and fell.
There knelt Mandodarí[1] and shed
Her tears in floods for Rávan dead.
And every dame who loved him sent
From her sad heart her wild lament.
There gleams the margin of the deep,
Where, worn with toil, we sank to sleep.
Look, love, the unconquerd sea behold,
King Varun's home ordained of old,
Whose boundless waters roar and swell
Rich with their store of pearl and shell.
O see, the morning sun is bright
On fair Hiranyanábha's[1] height,
Who rose from Ocean's sheltering breast
That Hanumán might stay and rest.
There stretches, famed for evermore,
The wondrous bridge from shore to shore.
The worlds, to life's remotest day,
Due reverence to the work shall pay,
Which holier for the laps of time
Shall give release from sin and crime.
Now thither bend, dear love, thine eyes
Where green with groves Kishkindhá lies,
The seat of King Sugríva's reign,
Where Báli by this hand was slain.[2]
There Rishyamúka's hill behold
Bright gleaming with embedded gold.
There too my wandering foot I set,
There King Sugríva first I met,
And, where yon trees their branches wave,
My promise of assistance gave.
There, flushed with lilies, Pampá shines
With banks which greenest foliage lines,
Where melancholy steps I bent
And mourned thee with a mad lament.
There fierce Kabandha, spreading wide
His giant arms, in battle died.
Turn, Sítá, turn thine eyes and see
In Janasthán that glorious tree:
There Rávan, lord of giants, slew
Our friend Jatáyus brave and true,
Thy champion in the hopless strife,
Who gave for thee his noble life.
Now mark that glade amid the trees
Where once we lived as devotees.
See, see our leafy cot between
Those waving boughs of densest green,
Where Rávan seized his prize and stole
My love the darling of my soul.
O, look again: beneath thee gleams
Godávarí the best of streams,
Whose lucid waters sweetly glide
By lilies that adorn her side.
There dwelt Agastya, holy sage,
In plantain-sheltered hermitage.
See Śarabhanga's humble shed

[1] Rávan's queen.

[1] Or Maináka.

[2] Here, in the North-west recension, Sítá expresses a wish that Tárá and the wives of the Vánar chiefs should be invited to accompany her to Ayodhyá. The car decends, and the Vánar matrons are added to the party. The Bengal recension ignores this palpable interruption.

Which sovereign Indra visited.
See where the gentle hermits dwell
'Neath Atri's rule who loved us well ;
Where once thine eyes were blest to see
His sainted dame who talked with thee.
Now rest thine eyes with new delight
On Chitrakúṭa's woody height,
See Jumna flashing in the sun
Through groves of brilliant foliage run.
Screened by the shade of spreading boughs
There Bharadvája keeps his vows,
There Gangá, river of the skies,
Rolls the sweet wave that purifies,
There Śringavera's towers ascend
Where Guha reigns, mine ancient friend.
I see, I see thy glittering spires,
Ayodhyá, city of my sires.
Bow down, bow down thy head, my sweet,
Our home, our long-lost home to greet.'

CANTO CXXVI.

BHARAT CONSOLED.

But Ráma bade the chariot stay,
And halting in his airy way,
In Bharadvá's holy shade
His homage to the hermit paid.
'O saint,' he cried, 'I yearn to know
My dear Ayodhyá's weal and woe.
O tell me that the people thrive,
And that the queens are yet alive.'

Joy gleamed in Bhardvája's eye,
Who gently smiled and made reply :
'Thy brother, studious of thy will.
Is faithful and obedient still.
In tangled twine he coils his hair :
Thy safe return is all his care.
Before thy shoes he humbly bends,
And to thy house and realm attends.
When first these dreary years began,
When first I saw the banished man,
With Sítá, in his hermit coat,
At this sad heart compassion smote.
My breast with tender pity swelled :
I saw thee from thy home expelled,
Reft of all princely state, forlorn,
A hapless wanderer travel-worn,
Firm in thy purpose to fulfil
Thy duty and thy father's will.
But boundless is my rapture now :
Triumphant, girt with friends, art thou.
Where'er thy wandering steps have been,
Thy joy and woe mine eyes have seen.
Thy glorious deeds to me art known,
The Bráhmans saved, the foes o'erthrown.
Such power have countless seasons spent
In penance and devotion lent.
Thy virtues, best of chiefs, I know,
And now a boon would fain bestow.
This hospitable gift[1] receive :
Then with the dawn my dwelling leave.
The bended head of Ráma showed
His reverence for the grace bestowed ;
Then for each brave companion's sake
He sought a further boon and spake :

'O let that mighty power of thine
The road to fair Ayodhyá line
With trees where fruit of every hue
The Vánars' eye and taste may woo,
And flowers of every season, sweet
With stores of honeyed juice, may meet.'
The hero ceased : the hermit bent
His reverend head in glad assent ;
And swift, as Bharadvája willed,
The prayer of Ráma was fulfilled.
For many a league the lengthening road
Trees thick with fruit and blossom showed
With luscious beauty to entice
The taste like trees of Paradise.
The Vánars passed beneath the shade
Of that delightful colonnade,
Still tasting with unbounded glee
The treasures of each wondrous tree.

CANTO CXXVII.

RÁMA'S MESSAGE.

But Ráma, when he first looked down
And saw afar Ayodhya's town,
Had called Hanumán to his side,
The chief on whom his heart relied,
And said : 'Brave Vánar, good at need,
Haste onward, to Ayodhyá speed,
And learn, I pray, if all be well
With those who in the palace dwell.
But as thou speedest on thy way
Awhile at Śringavera stay.
Tell Guha the Nishádas' lord,
That victor, with my queen restored,
In health and strength with many a friend
Homeward again my steps I bend.
Thence by the road that he will show
On to Ayodhyá swiftly go.
There with my love my brother greet,
And all our wondrous tale repeat.
Say that victorious in the strife
I come with Lakshman and my wife.
Then mark with keenest eye each trace
Of joy or grief on Bharat's face.
Be all his gestures closely viewed,

[1] The *arghya*, a respectful offering to Gods and venerable men consisting of rice, dúrvá grass, flowers etc., with water.

Each change of look and attitude.
Where breathes the man who will not cling
To all that glorifies a king?
Where beats the heart that can resign
An ancient kingdom, nor repine
To lose a land renowned for breeds
Of elephants and warrior steeds?
If, won by custom day by day,
My brother Bharat thirsts for sway,
Still let him rule the nations, still
The throne of old Ikshváku fill.
Go, mark him well: his feelings learn,
And, ere we yet be near return.'
He ceased: and, garbed in human form,
Forth sped Hanúmán swift as storm.
Sublime in air he rose, and through
The region of his father flew.
He saw far far beneath his feet
Where Gangá's flood and Jumna meet,
Descending from the upper air
He entered Śringavera, where
King Guha's heart was well content
To hear the message Ráma sent.
Then, with his mighty strength renewed,
The Vánar chief his way pursued.
Válúkiní was far behind,
And Gomatí with forests lined,
And golden fields and pastures gay
With flocks and herds beneath him lay.
Then Nandigráma charmed his eye
Where flowers were bright with every dye,
And trees of lovely foliage made
With meeting boughs delightful shade,
Where women watched in trim array
Their little sons' and grandsons' play.
His eager eye on Bharat fell
Who sat before his lonely cell.
In hermit weed, with tangled hair,
Pale, weak, and worn with ceaseless care.
His royal pomp and state resigned
For Ráma still he watched and pined,
Still to his dreary vows adhered,
And royal Ráma's shoes revered.
Yet still the terror of his arm
Preserved the land from fear and harm.
The Wind-God's son, in form a man,
Raised reverent hands and thus began:
'Fond greeting, Prince, I bring to thee,
And Ráma's self has sent it: he
For whom thy spirit sorrows yet
As for a hapless anchoret
In Daṇḍak wood, in dire distress,
With matted hair and hermit dress.
This sorrow from thy bosom fling,
And hear the tale of joy I bring.
This day thy brother shalt thou meet
Exulting in his foe's defeat,
Freed from his toil and lengthened vow,
The light of victory on his brow,
With Sítá, Lakshmaṇ and his friends
Homeward at last his steps he bends.'
Then joy, too mighty for control,
Rushed in full flood o'er Bharat's soul;
His reeling sense and strength gave way,
And fainting on the earth he lay.
At length upspringing from the ground,
His arms about Hanúmán wound,
With tender tears of rapture sprung,
He dewed the neck to which he clung:
'Art thou a God or man,' he cried,
'Whom love and pity hither guide?
For this a hundred thousand kine,
A hundred villages be thine.
A score of maids of spotless lives
To thee I give to be thy wives,
Of golden hue and bright of face,
Each lovely for her tender grace.'
He ceased a while by joy subdued,
And then his eager speech renewed:

CANTO CXXVIII.

HANUMÁN'S STORY.

'In doubt and fear long years have passed,
And glorious tidings come at last.
True, true is now the ancient verse
Which men in time of bliss rehearse:
'Once only in a hundred years
Great joy to mortal men appears.'
But now his woes and triumph tell,
And loss and gain as each befell.'
He ceased: Hanúmán mighty-souled
The tale of Ráma's wanderings told
From that first day on which he stood
In the drear shade of Daṇḍak wood.
He told how fierce Virádha fell;
He told of Śarabhanga's cell
Where Ráma saw with wondering eyes
Indra descended from the skies.
He told how Súrpanakhá came,
Her soul aglow with amorous flame,
And fled repulsed, with rage and tears,
Reft of her nose and severed ears.
He told how Ráma's might subdued
The giants' furious multitude;
How Khara with the troops he led
And Triśiras and Dúshaṇ bled:
How Ráma, tempted from his cot,
The golden deer pursued and shot,
And Rávaṇ came and stole away
The Maithil queen his hapless prey,
When, as he fought, the dame to save,
His noble life Jaṭáyus gave:
How Ráma still the search renewed,
The robber to his hold pursued,
Bridging the sea from shore to shore,
And found his queen to part no more.[1]

[1] I have abridged Hanumán's outline of Ráma's adventures, with the details of which we are already sufficiently acquainted.

CANTO CXXIX.

THE MEETING WITH BHARAT.

O'erwhelmed with rapture Bharat heard
The tale that all his being stirred,
And, heralding the glad event,
This order to Śatrughna sent :
'Let every shrine with flowers be gay
Let incense burn and music play.
Go forth, go forth to meet your king,
Let tabours sound and minstrels sing.
Let bards swell high the note of praise
Skilled in the lore of ancient days.
Call forth the royal matrons : call
Each noble from the council hall.
Send all we love and honour most,
Send Bráhmans and the warrior host,
A glorious company to bring
In triumph home our lord the king.'
Great rapture filled Śatrughna's breast,
Obedient to his brother's hest.
'Send forth ten thousand men' he cried,
'Let brawny arms be stoutly plied,
And, smoothing all with skilful care,
The road for Kosal's king prepare.
Then o'er the earth let thousands throw
Fresh showers of water cool as snow,
And others strew with garlands gay
With loveliest blooms our monarch's way.
On tower and temple porch and gate
Let banners wave in royal state,
And be each roof and terrace lined
With blossoms loose and chaplets twined.'
The nobles hasting forth fulfilled
His order as Śatrughna willed.
Sublime on elephants they rode
Whose gilded girths with jewels glowed.
Attended close by thousands more
Gay with the gear and flags they bore.
A thousand chiefs their steeds bestrode,
Their glittering cars a thousand showed,
And countless hosts in rich array
Pursued on foot their eager way.
Veiled from the air with silken screens
In litters rode the widowed queens.
Kausalyá first, acknowledged head
And sovereign of the household, led :
Sumitrá next, and after, dames
Of lower rank and humbler names.
Then compassed by a white-robed throng
Of Bráhmans, heralded with song,
With shouts of joy from countless throats,
And shells' and tambours' mingled notes,
And drums resounding long and loud,
Exulting Bharat joined the crowd.
Still on his head, well-trained in lore
Of duty, Ráma's shoes he bore.
The moon-white canopy was spread
With flowery twine engarlanded,
And jewelled chouries, meet to hold
O'er Ráma's brow, shone bright with gold,
Though Nandigráma's town they neared,
Of Ráma yet no sign appeared.
Then Bharat called the Vánar chief
And questioned thus in doubt and grief :
'Hast thou uncertain, like thy kind,
A sweet delusive guile designed ?
Where, where is royal Ráma? show
The hero, victor of the foe.
I gaze, but see no Vánars still
Who wear each varied shape at will.'
In eager love thus Bharat cried,
And thus the Wind-God's son replied :
'Look, Bharat, on those laden trees
That murmur with the song of bees ;
For Ráma's sake the saint has made
Untimely fruits, unwonted shade.
Such power in ages long ago
Could Indra's gracious boon bestow.
O, hear the Vánars' voices, hear
The shouting which proclaims them near
E'en now about to cross they seem
Sweet Gomatí's delightful stream.
I see, I see the car designed
By Brahmá's own creative mind,
The car which, radiant as the moon,
Moves at the will by Brahmá's boon ;
The car which once was Rávaṇ's pride,
The victor's spoil when Rávaṇ died.
Look, there are Raghu's sons : between
The brothers stands the rescued queen.
There is Vibhíshaṇ full in view,
Sugríva and his retinue.'
He ceased : then rapture loosed each tongue :
From men and dames, from old and young,
One long, one universal cry,
'Tis he, 'tis Ráma, smote the sky.
All lighted down with eager speed
From elephant and car and steed,
And every joyful eye intent
On Ráma's moonbright face was bent.
Entranced a moment Bharat gazed :
Then reverential hands he raised,
And on his brother humbly pressed
The honours due to welcome guest.
Then Bharat clomb the car to greet
His king and bowed him at his feet,
Till Ráma raised him face to face
And held him in a close embrace.
Then Lakshmaṇ and the Maithil dame
He greeted as he spoke his name.[1]
He greeted next, supreme in place,
The sovereign of the Vánar race,
And Jámbaván and Báli's son,

[1] In these respectful salutations the person who salutes his superior mentions his own name even when it is well known to the person whom he salutes.

And lords and chiefs, omitting none.[1]
Sugríva to his heart he pressed
And thus with grateful words addressed:
'Four brothers, Vánar king, were we,
And now we boast a fifth in thee.
By kindly acts a friend we know:
Offence and wrong proclaim the foe.'
To King Vibhíshan then he spake:
'Well hast thou fought for Ráma's sake.'
Nor was the brave Śatrughna slow
His reverential love to show
To both his brothers, as was meet,
And venerate the lady's feet.
Then Ráma to his mother came,
Saw her pale cheek and wasted frame,
With gentle words her heart consoled,
And clasped her feet with loving hold.
Then at Sumitrá's feet he bent,
And fair Kaikeyí's, reverent,
Greeted each dame from chief to least,
And bowed him to the household priest.
Up rose a shout from all the throng:
'O welcome, Ráma, mourned so long,
Welcome, Kausalyá's joy and pride,'
Ten hundred thousand voices cried.
Then Bharat placed, in duty taught,
On Ráma's feet the shoes he brought:
'My king,' he cried, 'receive again
The pledge preserved through years of pain,
The rule and lordship of the land
Entrusted to my weaker hand.
No more I sigh o'er sorrows past,
My birth and life are blest at last
In the glad sight this day has shown,
When Ráma comes to rule his own.'
He ceased: the faithful love that moved
The prince's soul each heart approved;
Nor could the Vánar chiefs refrain
From tender tears that fell like rain.
Then Ráma, stirred with joy anew,
His arms about his brother threw,
And to the grove his course he bent
Where Bharat's hermit days were spent.
Alighting in that pure retreat
He pressed the earth with eager feet.
Then, at his hest, the car rose high
And sailing through the northern sky
Sped homeward to the Lord of Gold
Who owned the wondrous prize of old.[2]

[1] I have omitted the chieftains' names as they could not be introduced without padding. They are Mainda, Dwivid, Níla Rishabh, Sushen, Nala, Gaváksha, Gandhamádan, Śarabh, and Panas.

[2] The following addition is found in the Bengal recension: But Vaiśravan (Kuvera) when he beheld his chariot said unto it: 'Go, and carry Ráma, and come unto me when my thought shall call thee. And the chariot returned unto Ráma;' and he honoured it when he had heard what had passed.

CANTO CXXX.

THE CONSECRATION.

Then, reverent hand to hand applied,
Thus Bharat to his brother cried:
'Thy realm, O King, is now restored,
Uninjured to the rightful lord.
This feeble arm with toil and pain,
The weighty charge could scarce sustain,
And the great burthen wellnigh broke
The neck untrained to bear the yoke.
The royal swan outspeeds the crow:
The steed is swift, the mule is slow,
Nor can my feeble feet be led
O'er the rough ways where thine should tread.
Now grant what all thy subjects ask:
Begin, O King, thy royal task.
Now let our longing eyes behold
The glorious rite ordained of old,
And on the new-found monarch's head
Let consecrating drops be shed.'
He ceased: victorious Ráma bent
His head in token of assent.
He sat, and tonsors trimmed with care
His tangles of neglected hair.
Then, duly bathed, the hero shone
With all his splendid raiment on.
And Sitá with the matrons' aid
Her limbs in shining robes arrayed.
Sumantra then, the charioteer,
Drew, ordered by Śatrughna, near,
And stayed within the hermit grove
The chariot and the steeds he drove.
Therein Sugríva's consorts, graced
With gems, and Ráma's queen were placed
All fain Ayodhyá to behold:
And swift away the chariot rolled.
Like Indra Lord of Thousand Eyes,
Drawn by fleet lions through the skies,
Thus radiant in his glory showed
King Ráma as he homeward rode,
In power and might unparalleled.
The reins the hand of Bharat held:
Above the peerless victor's head
The snow-white shade Śatrughna spread,
And Lakshman's ever-ready hand
His forehead with a chourie fanned.
Vibhíshan close to Lakshman's side
Sharing his task a chourie plied.
Sugríva on Śatrunjay came,
An elephant of hugest frame:
Nine thousand others bore, behind,
The chieftains of the Vánar kind
All gay, in forms of human mould,
With rich attire and gems and gold.

Thus borne along in royal state
King Ráma reached Ayodhyá's gate
With merry noise of shells and drums
And joyful shouts, He comes, he comes.
A Bráhman host with solemn tread,
And kine the long procession led,
And happy maids in ordered bands
Threw grain and gold with liberal hands.
Neath gorgeous flags that waved in rows
On towers and roofs and porticoes,
Mid merry crowds who sang and cheered
The palace of the king they neared.
Then Raghu's son to Bharat, best
Of duty's slaves, these words addressed :
'Pass onward to the monarch's hall,
The high-souled Vánars with thee call,
And let the chieftains, as is meet,
The widows of our father greet.
And to the Vánar king assign
Those chambers, best of all, which shine
With lazulite and pearl inlaid,
And pleasant grounds with flowers and shade.'

He ceased : and Bharat bent his head ;
Sugríva by the hand he led
And passed within the palace where
Stood couches which Śatrughna's care,
With robes and hangings richly dyed,
And burning lamps, had seen supplied.
Then Bharat spake : 'I pray thee, friend,
Thy speedy messengers to send,
Each sacred requisite to bring
That we may consecrate our king.'
Sugríva raised four urns of gold,
The water for the rite to hold,
And bade four swiftest Vánars flee
And fill them from each distant sea.
Then east and west and south and north
The Vánar envoys hastened forth.
Each in swift flight an ocean sought
And back through air his treasure brought,
And full five hundred floods beside
Pure water for the king supplied.
Then girt by many a Bráhman sage,
Vasishṭha, chief for reverend age,
High on a throne with jewels graced
King Ráma and his Sítá placed.
There by Jábáli, far revered,
Vijay and Kaśyap's son appeared ;
By Gautam's side Kátyávan stood,
And Vámadeva wise and good,
Whose holy hands in order shed
The pure sweet drops on Ráma's head.
Then priests and maids and warriors, all
Approaching at Vasishṭha's call,
With sacred drops bedewed their king,
The centre of a joyous ring,
The guardians of the worlds, on high,
And all the children of the sky
From herbs wherewith their hands were filled
Rare juices on his brow distilled.
His brows were bound with glistering gold
Which Manu's self had worn of old,
Bright with the flash of many a gem,
His sire's ancestral diadem.
Śatrughna lent his willing aid
And o'er him held the regal shade :
The monarchs whom his arm had saved
The chouries round his forehead waved.
A golden chain, that flashed and glowed
With gems the God of Wind bestowed :
Mahendra gave a glorious string
Of fairest pearls to deck the king,
The skies with acclamation rang,
The gay nymphs danced, the minstrels sang.
On that blest day the joyful plain
Was clothed anew with golden grain.
The trees the witching influence knew,
And bent with fruits of loveliest hue,
And Ráma's consecration lent
New sweetness to each flowret's scent.
The monarch, joy of Raghu's line,
Gave largess to the Bráhmans, kine
And steeds unnumbered, wealth untold
Of robes and pearls and gems and gold.
A jewelled chain, whose lustre passed
The glory of the sun, he cast
About his friend Sugríva's neck :
And, Angad Bálí's son to deck,
He gave a pair of armlets bright
With diamond and lazulite.
A string of pearls of matchless hue
Which gleams like tender moonlight threw
Adorned with gems of brightest sheen,
He gave to grace his darling queen.
The offering from his hand received
A moment on her bosom heaved ;
Then from her neck the chain she drew,
A glance on all the Vánars threw,
And wistful eyes on Ráma bent
As still she held the ornament.
Her wish he knew, and made reply
To that mute question of her eye :
'Yea, love ; the chain on him bestow
Whose wisdom truth and might we know,
The firm ally, the faithful friend
Through toil and peril to the end.

Then on Hanúmán's bosom hung
The chain which Sítá's hand had flung :
So may a cloud, when winds are still
With moon-lit silver gird a hill.
To every Vánar Ráma gave
Rich treasures from the mine and wave :
And with their honours well content
Homeward their steps the chieftains bent.
Ten thousand years Ayodhyá, blest
With Ráma's rule, had peace and rest.
No widow mourned her murdered mate,
No house was ever desolate.
The happy land no murrain knew,
The flocks and herds increased and grew.

The earth her kindly fruits supplied,
No harvest failed, no children died.
Unknown were want, disease, and crime:
So calm, so happy was the time.[1]

---

[1] Here follows in the original an enumeration of the chief blessings which will attend the man or woman who reads or hears read this tale of Ráma. These blessings are briefly mentioned at the end of the first Canto of the first book, and it appears unnecessary to repeat them here in their amplified form. The Bengal recension (Gorresio's edition) gives them more concisely as follows: 'This is the great first poem blessed and glorious, which gives long life to men and victory to kings, the poem which Válmíki made. He who listens to this wondrous tale of Ráma unwearied in action shall be absolved from all his sins. By listening to the deeds of Ráma he who wishes for sons shall obtain his heart's desire, and to him who longs for riches shall riches be given. The virgin who asks for a husband shall obtain a husband suited to her mind, and shall meet again her dear kinsfolk who are far away. They who hear this poem which Válmíki made shall obtain all their desires and all their prayers shall be fulfilled.'

APPENDIX.

RAVAṆ DOOMED.

SECTION XIII.

Afterwards R*i*shy*a*-shr*i*ng*a* said again to the King "I will perform another sacrificial act to secure thee a son." Then the son of V*i*bhand*u*k*a*, of subdued passions, seeking the happiness of the king, proceeded to perform the sacrifice for the accomplishment of his wishes. Hither were previously collected the gods, with the G*u*ndh*u*rv*a*s, the Siddh*a*s and the sages, for the sake of receiving their respective shares, Br*u*hm*a* too, the sovereign of the gods, with Sthan*oo*, and Narayan*a*, chief of beings and the four supporters of the universe, and the divine mothers of all the celestials, met together there. To the *U*shw*a*-medh*a*, the great sacrifice of the magnanimous monarch, came also *I*ndr*a* the glorious one, surrounded by the M*u*r*oo*ts. R*i*shy*a*-shr*i*ng*a* then supplicated the gods assembled for their share of the sacrifice (saying), "This devout king D*u*sh*a*-r*u*tha, who, through the desire of offspring, confiding in you, has performed sacred austerities, and who has offered to you the sacrifice called *U*shw*a*-medh*a*, is about to perform another sacrifice for the sake of obtaining sons. To him thus desirous of offspring be pleased to grant the blessing: I supplicate you all with joined hands. May he have four sons, renowned through the universe." The gods replied to the sage's son supplicating with joined hands, "Be it so: thou, O brahman, art ever to be regarded by us, as the king is in a peculiar manner. The lord of men by this sacrifice shall obtain the great object of his desires. Having thus said, the gods preceded by *I*ndr*a*, disappeared.

They all then having seen that (sacrifice) performed by the great sage according to the ordinance went to Pr*u*jap*u*t*i* the lord of mankind, and with joined hands addressed Br*u*hma the giver of blessings, "O Br*u*hm*a*, the Raksh*u*s Rav*u*n*a* by name, to whom a blessing was awarded by thee, through pride troubleth all of us the gods, and even the great sages, who perpetually practise sacred austerities. We, O glorious one, regarding the promise formerly granted by thy kindness that he should be invulnerable to the gods, the Dan*u*v*a*s and the Y*u*ksh*a*s have born (*sic*) all, (his oppression); this lord of Raksh*u*ses therefore distresses the universe; and, inflated by this promise unjustly vexes the divine sages, the Y*u*ksh*a*s, and G*u*ndh*u*rv*a*s, the *U*soor*a*s, and men: where Rav*u*n*a* remains there the sun loses his force, the winds through fear of him do not blow; the fire ceases to burn; the rolling ocean, seeing him, ceases to move its waves. 'Vishr*u*van*a*, distressed by his power, has abandoned L*u*nka and fled. O divine one save us from Rav*u*n*a*, who fills the world with noise and tumult. O giver of desired things, be pleased to contrive a way for his destruction."

Br*u*hm*a* thus informed by the dev*a*s, reflecting. replied, Oh! I have devised the method for slaying this outrageous tyrant. Upon his requesting, "May I be invulnerable to the divine sages, the G*u*ndh*u*rv*a*s, the Y*u*ksh*a*s, the Raksh*u*ses and the serpents," I replied "Be it so." This Rakshus, through contempt, said nothing respecting man; therefore this wicked one shall be destroyed by man. The gods, preceded by Shukra, hearing these words spoken by Bruhma, were filled with joy.

At this time Vishnoo the glorious, the lord of the world, arrayed in yellow, with hand ornaments of glowing gold, riding on Vinuteya, as the sun on a cloud, arrived with his conch, his discus, and his club in his hand. Being adored by the excellent celestials, and welcomed by Bruhma, he drew near and stood before him. All the gods then addressed Vishnoo, "O Mudhoo-sooduna, thou art able to abolish the distress of the distressed. We intreat thee, be our sanctuary, O Uchyoota." Vishnoo replied, "Say, what shall I do?" The celestials hearing these his words added further, "The virtuous, the encourager of excellence, eminent for truth, the firm observer of his vows, being childless, is performing an Ushwa-medha for the purpose of obtaining offspring. For the sake of the good of the universe, we intreat thee, O Vishnoo, to become his son. Dividing thyself into four parts, in the wombs of his three consorts equal to Huri, Shree, and Keertee, assume the sonship of king Dusha-rutha, the lord of Uyodhya, eminent in the knowledge of duty, generous and illustrious, as the great sages. Thus becoming man, O Vishnoo, conquer in battle Ravuna, the terror of the universe, who is invulnerable to the gods. This ignorant Rakshus Ravuna, by the exertion of his power, afflicts the gods, the Gundhurvas, the Siddhas, and the most excellent sages; these sages, the Gundhurvas, and the Upsaras, sporting in the forest Nunduna have been destroyed by that furious one. We, with the sages, are come to thee seeking his destruction. The Siddhas, the Gundhurvas, and the Yukshas betake themselves to thee, thou art our only refuge; O Deva, afflicter of enemies, regard the world of men, and destroy the enemy of the gods."

Vishnoo, the sovereign of the gods, the chief of the celestials, adored by all beings, being thus supplicated, replied to all the assembled gods (standing) before Bruhma, "Abandon fear; peace be with you; for your benefit having killed Ravuna the cruel, destructively active, the cause of fear to the divine sages, together with all his posterity, his courtiers and counsellors, and his relations, and friends, protecting the earth, I will remain incarnate among men for the space of eleven thousand years."

Having given this promise to the gods, the divine Vishnoo, ardent in the work, sought a birth-place among men. Dividing himself into four parts, he whose eyes resemble the lotos and the pulasa, the lotos petal-eyed, chose for his father Dusha-ratha the sovereign of men. The divine sages then with the Gundhurvas, the Roodras, and the (different sorts of) Upsaras, in the most excellent strains, praised the destroyer of Mudhoo, (saying) "Root up Ravuna, of fervid energy, the devastator, the enemy of Indra swollen with pride. Destroy him, who causes universal lamentation, the annoyer of the holy ascetics, terrible, the terror of the devout Tupuswees. Having destroyed Ravuna, tremendously powerful, who causes universal weeping, together with his army and friends, dismissing all sorrow, return to heaven, the place free from stain and sin, and protected by the sovereign of the celestial powers."

Thus far the Section, containing the plan for the death of Ravuna.

CAREY AND MARSHMAN.

CAPUT XIV.

RATIO NECANDI RAVANAE EXCOGITATA.

Prudens ille, voluminum sacrorum gnarus, responsum quod dederat aliquamdiu meditatus, mente ad se revocata regem denuo est effatus: Parabo tibi aliud sacrum, genitale, prolis masculae adipiscendae gratia, cum carminibus in ATHARVANIS exordio expressis rite peragendum. Tum coepit modestus Vibhândaci filius, regis commodis intentus, parare sacrum, quo eius desiderium expleret. Iam antea eo convenerant, ut suam quisque portionem acciperent, Dî cum fidicinum coelestium choris, Beatique cum Sapientibus; Brachman Superûm regnator, Sthânus nec non augustus Nârâyanus, Indrasque almus, coram visendus Ventorum cohorte circumdatus, in magno isto sacrificio equino regis magnanimi. Ibidem vates ille deos, qui portiones suas accipiendi gratia advenerant, apprecatus, En! inquit, hicce rex Dasarathus filiorum desiderio castimoniis adstrictus, fidei plenus, vestrum numen adoravit sacrificio equino. Nunc iterum accingit se ad aliud sacrum peragendum: quamobrem aequum est, ut filios cupienti vos faveatis. Ille ego, qui manus supplices tendo, vos universos pro eo apprecor: nascantur ei filii quatuor, fama per triplicem mundum clari. Divi supplicem vatis filium invicem affari: Fiat quod petis! Tu nobis, virsancte, imprimis es venerandus, nec minus rex ille; compos fiet voti sui egregii hominum princeps. Ita locuti Dî Indra duce, ex oculis evanuerunt.

Superi vero, legitime in concilio congregati, BRACHMANEM mundi creatorem his verbis compellarunt: Tuo munere auctus, O Brachman! gigas nomine Râvanas, prae superbia nos omnes vexat, pariterque Sapientes castimoniis gaudentes. A te propitio olim ex voto ei hoc munus concessum fuit, ut ne a diis, Danuidis, Geniisve necari posset. Nos, oraculum tuum reveriti, facinora eius qualiacunque toleramus. At ille gigantum tyrannus ternos mundos gravibus iniuriis vexat Deos, Sapientes, Genios, Fidicines coelestes, Titanes, mortales denique, exsuperat ille aegre cohibendus, tuoque munere demens. Non ibi calet sol, neque Ventus prae timore spirat, nec flagrat ignis, ubi Râvanas versatur. Ipse oceanus, vagis fluctibus redimitus, isto viso stat immotus; eiectus fuit e sede sua Cuvêrus, huius robore vexatus. Ergo ingens nobis periculum imminet ab hoc gigante visu horribili; tuum est, alme Parens! auxilium parare, quo hic deleatur. Ita admonitus ille a diis universis, paulisper meditatus, Ehem! inquit, hancce inveni rationem nefarium istum necandi. Petierat is a me, ut a Gandharvis, a Geniis, a Divis, Danuibus Gigantibusque necari non posset, et me annuente voto suo potitus est. Prae contemptu vero monstrum illud homines non commemoravit: ideo ab homine est necandus; nullum aliud exstat leti genus, quod ei sit fatale. Postquam audiverant gratum hunc sermonem BRACHMANIS ore prolatum, Dî cum duce suo Indra summopere gaudio erecti sunt. Eodem temporis momento Vishnus, istuc accessit, splendore insignis, concham, discum et clavum manibus gestans, croceo vestitu, mundi dominus, vulturis Vinateii dorso, sicuti sol nimbo, vectus, armillas ex auro candente gerens, salutatus a Superûm primoribus. Quem laudibus celebratum reverenter Dî universi compellarunt. Tu animantium afflictorum es vindex, Madhûs interfector! quamobrem nos afflicti te apprecamur. Sis praesidio nobis numine tuo inconcusso. Dicite, inquit Vishnus, quid pro vobis facere me oporteat. Audito eius sermone, Dî hunc in modum respondent: Rex quidam, nomine Dasarathus, austeris castimoniis sese castigavit, litavit sacrificio equino, prolis cupidus et prole carens. Nostro hortatu tu, Vishnus, conditionem natorum eius subeas; ex tribus eius uxoribus, Pudicitiae, Venustatis et Famae similibus, nasci velis, temetipsum quadrifariam dividens. Ibi tu in humanam naturam conversus Râvanam, gravissimam mundi pestem, diis insuperabilem, O Vishnus! proelio caede. Gigas ille vecors Râvanas Deos cum Fidicinum choris, Beatos et Sapientes praestantissimos vexat, audacia superbiens. Etenim ab hoc furioso Sapientes Fidicines et nymphae, ludentes in Nandano viridario, sunt proculcati. Tu es nostrum omnium summa salus, divine bellator! Ut deorum hostes extinguas, ad sortem humanam animum converte. Augustus ille Nârâyanus, diis hunc in modum coram hortantibus, eosdem apto hoc sermone compellavit: Quare, quaeso, hac in re negotium vestrum a me potissimum, corporea specie palam facto, est peragendum? aut unde tantus vobis terror fuit iniectus? His verbis a Vishnû interrogati Dî talia proferre: Terror nobis instat, O Vishnus! a Râvana mundi direptore; a quo nos vindicare, corpore humano assumpto, tuum est. Nemo alius coelicolarum praeter te hunc scelestum enecare potis est. Nimirum ille, O hostium domitor! per diuturnum tempus sese excruciaverat severissima abstinentia, qua magnus hicce rerum Parens propitius ipsi redditus est. Itaque almus votorum sponsor olim ei concessit securitatem ab ommibus animantibus, hominibus tamen exceptis. Hinc illum, voti compotem, non aliunde quam ab homine necis periculum urget: tu ergo, humanitate assumpta eum interfice. Sic monitus Vishnus, Superûm princeps, quem mundus universus adorat, magnum Parentem ceterosque deos, in concilio congregatos, recti auctores, affatur: Mittite timorem; bene bobis eveniat! Vestrae salutis gratia, postquam praelio necavero Râvanam cum filiis nepotibusque, cum amicis, ministris, cognatis sociisque, crudelem istum aegre cohibendum, qui divinis Sapientibus terrorem incutit, per decem millia annorum decies centenis additis, commorabor in mortalium sedibus, orbem terrarum imperio regens. Tum divini sapientes et Fidicines coniuncti cum Rudris nympharumque choris celebravere Madhûs interfectorem hymnis, quales sedem aetheriam decent.

"Râvanam illum insolentem, acri impetu actum, superbia elatum, Superûm hostem, tumultus cientem, bonorum piorumque pestem, humanitate assumpta pessumdare tuum est."

Schlegel.

CAPITOLO XIV.

IL MEZZO STABILITO PER UCCIDERE RAVANO.

Ma Riscyasringo soggiunse poscia al re: T'appresterò io un altro rito santissimo, genitale, onde tu conseguisca la prole che tu brami. E in quel punto stèsso il saggio figliulo di Vibhândaco, intento alla prosperità del re, pose mano al sacro rito per condurre ad effetto il suo desiderio. Già erano prima, per ricevere ciascuno la sua parte, quì convenuti al gran sacrifizio del re magnanimo l'Asvamedha, i Devi coi Gandharvî, i Siddhi e i Muni, Brahma Signor dei Suri, Sthânu e l' Augusto Nârâyana, i quattro custodi dell' universo e le Madri degli Iddii, i Yaesi insieme cogli Dei, e il sovrano, venerando Indra, visibile, circondato dalla schiera dei Maruti. Quivi così parlò Riscyasringo agli Dei venuti a partecipare del sacrifizio: Questo è il re Dasaratha, che per desiderio di progenie già s' astrinse ad osservanze austere, e testè pieno di fede ha a voi. O eccelsi, sacrificato con un Asvamedha. Ora egli, sollecito d' aver figli, si dispone ad adempiere un nuovo rito; vogliate essere favorevole a lui che sospira progenie. Io alzo a voi supplici le mani, e voi tutti per lui imploro: nascano a lui quattro figli degni d'essere celebrati pei tre mondi. Risposero gli Dei al supplichevole figliuolo del Risci: Sia fatto ciò che chiedi; a te ed al re parimente si debbe da noi, O Brahmano, sommo pregio; conseguirà il re per questo sacro rito il suo suppremo desiderio. Ciò detto disparvero i Numi preceduti da Indra.

Poichè videro gli Dei compiersi debitamente dal gran Risci l'oblazione, venuti al cospetto di Brahma facitor del mondo, signor delle creature, così parlarono reverenti a lui dator di grazie: O Brahma, un Racsaso per nome Râvano, cui tu fosti largo del tuo favore, è per superbia infesto a noi tutti e ai grandi Saggi penitenti. Un dì, O Nume, augusto, tu propizio a lui gli accordasti il favore, ch' egli bramava, di non poter essere ucciso dagli Dei, dai Dânavi nè dai Yacsi: noi venerando i tuoi oracoli, ogni cosa sopportiamo da costui. Quindi il signor dei Racsasi infesta con perpetue offese i tre mondi, i Devi, i Risci, i Yacsi ed i Gandharvi, gli Asuri e gli uomini: tutti egli opprime indegnamente inorgoglito pel tuo dono. Colà dove si trova Râvano, più non isfavilla per timore il sole, più non spira il vento, più non fiammeggia il fuoco: l' oceano stesso, cui fan corona i vasti flutti, veggendo costui, tutto si turba e si commuove. Stretto dalla forza di costui e ridotto allo stremo dovette Vaisravano abbandonare Lancâ. Da questo Râvano, terror del mondo, tu ne proteggi, O almo Nume: degna, O dator d'ogni bene, trovar modo ad estirpar costui. Fatto di queste cose conscio dai Devi, stette alquanto meditando, poi rispose Brahma: Orsù! è stabilito il modo onde distruggere questo iniquo. Egli a me chiese, ed io gliel concessi, di non poter essere ucciso dai Devi, dai Risci, dai Gandharvi, dai Yacsi, dai Racsasi nè dai Serpenti; ma per disprezzo non fece menzione degli uomini quel Racso: or bene, sarà quell' empio ucciso da un uomo. Udite le fauste parole profferte da Brahma, furono per ogni parte liete gli Iddii col loro duce Indra. In questo mezzo quì sopravvenne raggiante d'immensa luce il venerando Visnu, pensato da Brahma nell' immortal sua mente, siccome atto ad estirpar colui; Allora Brahma colla schiera de' Celesti così parlò a Visnu: Tu sei il conforto delle gente oppresse, O distruttor di Madhu: noi quindi a te supplichiamo afflitti: sia tu nostro sostegno, O Aciuto. Dite, loro rispose Visnu, quale cosa io debba far per voi; e gli Dei, udite queste parole, così soggiunsero: Un re per nome Dasaratha, giusto, virtuoso, veridico e pio, non ha progenie e la desidera: ei già s' impose durissime penitenze, ed ora ha sacrificato con un Asvamedha: tu, per nostro consiglio, O Visnu, consenti a divenir suo figlio: fatte di te quattro parti, ti manifesta, O invocato dalle genti, nel seno delle quattro sue consorti, simili alla venusta Dea. Così esortato dagli Dei quivi presenti, l'augusto Nârâyana loro rispose queste opportune parole: Quale opra s'ha da me, fatto visible nel mondo, a compiere per voi, O Devi? e d'onde in voi cotal terrore? Intese le parole di Visnu, così risposero gli Dei: Il nostro terrore, O Visnu, nasce da un Racsaso per nome Râvano, spavento dell' universo. Vestendo umano corpo, tu debbi esterminar costui. Nessuno fra i Celesti, fuorchè tu solo, è valevole ad uccidere quell' iniquo. Egli, O domator de' tuoi nemici, sostenne per lungo tempo acerbissime macerazioni : per esse fu di lui contento l'augusto sommo Genitore ; e un dì gli accordò propizio la sicurezza da tutti gli esseri, eccettutine gli uomini. Per questo favore a lui concesso non ha egli a temere offesa da alcuna parte, fuorchè dall' uomo, perciò, assumendo la natura umana, costui tu uccidi. Egli, il peggior di tutti i Racsasi, insano per la forza che gli infonde il dono avuto, da travaglio ai Devi ed ai Gandharvi, ai Risci, ai Muni ed ai mortali. Egli, sicuro da morte pel favore ottenuto, è turbatore dei sacrifizj, nemico ed uccisor dei Brahmi, divoratore degli uomini, peste del mondo. Da lui furono assaliti re coi loro carri ed elefanti ; altri percossi e fugati si dispersero per ogni dove. Da lui furono divorati Risci ed Apsarase : egli insomma oltracotato continuamente e quasi per ischerzo tutti travaglia i sette mondi. Perciò, O terribile ai nemici è stabilita la morte di costui per opra d'un uomo ; poich' un dì per superbia del dono tutti sprezzò gli uomini. Tu, O supremo fra i Numi, dei, umanandoti, estirpare questo tremendo, superbo Râvano, oltracotato, a noi nemico, terrore e flagello dei penitenti.

GORRESIO.

XIV.

De nouveau Rishyaçringa tint ce langage au Monarque : " Je vais célébrer un autre sacrifice, afin que le ciel accorde à tes vœux les enfants que tu souhaites." Cela dit, cherchant le bonheur du roi et pour l'accomplissement de son désir, le fils puissant de Vibhándaka se mit à célébrer ce nouveau sacrifice.

Là auparavant, étaient venus déjà recevoir une part de l' offrande les Dieux, accompagnés des Gandharvas, et les Siddhas avec les Mounis divins, Brahma, le monarque des Souras, l' immuable Śiva, et l' auguste Náráyana, et les quatre gardiens vigilants du monde, et les mères des Immortels, et tous les Dieux, escortés des Yakshas, et le maître éminent du ciel, Indra, qui se manifestait aux yeux, environné par l' essaim des Maroutes. Alors ce jeune anachorète avait supplié tous les Dieux, que le désir d'une part dans l' offrande avait conduits á l' açwamédha, cette grande cérémonie de ce roi magnanime ; *et, dans ce moment, l' époux de Śántá les conjurait ainsi pour la seconde fois* : " Cet homme *en prières*, c'est le roi Daçaratha, qui est privé de fils. Il est rempli d' une foi vive ; il s'est infligé de pénibles austérités ; il vous a déjà servi, divinités augustes, le sacrifice d'un açwa-médha, et maintenant il s'étudie encore à vous plaire avec ce nouveau sacrifice dans l'espérance que vous lui donnerez les fils, où tendent ses désirs. Versez donc sur lui votre bienveillance et daignez sourire à son vœu pour des fils. C'est pour lui que moi ici, les mains jointes, je vous adresse à tous mes supplications : envoyez-lui quatre fils, qui soient vantés dans les trois mondes ! "

" Oui ! répondirent les Dieux au fils suppliant du rishi ; tu mérites que nous t'écoutions avec faveur, toi, brahme saint, et même, en premier lieu, ce roi. Comme récompense de ces différents sacrifices, le monarque obtendra cet objet le plus cher de ses désirs."

Ayant aussi parlé et vu que le grand saint avait mis fin suivant les rites à son *pieux* sacrifice, les Dieux, Indra à leur tête, s'évanouissent dans le vide des airs et se rendent vers l' architecte des mondes, le souverain des créatures, le donateur des biens, vers Brahma enfin, auquel tous, les mains jointes, ils adressent les paroles suivantes : " O Brahma, un rakshasa, nommé Râvana, tourne au mal les grâces, qu'il a reçues de toi. Dans son orgueil, il nous opprime tous ; il opprime avec nous les grands anchorètes, qui se font un bonheur des macérations: car jadis, ayant su te plaire, O Bhagavat, il a reçu de toi ce don incomparable. "Oui, as-tu dit, exauçant le vœu du mauvais Génie ; Dieu, Yaksha ou Démon ne pourra jamais causer ta mort !" Et nous, par qui ta parole est respectée, nous avons tout supporté de ce roi des rakshasas, qui écrase de sa tyrannie les trois mondes, ou il promène l' injure impunément. Enorgueilli de ce don victorieux, il opprime indignement les Dieux, les rishis, les Yakshas, les Gandharvas, les Asouras et les enfants de Manou. Là ou se tient Râvana, la peur empêche le soleil d' échauffer, le vent craint de souffler, et le feu n'ose flamboyer. A son aspect, la guirlande même des grands flots tremble au sein de la mer. Accablé par sa vigueur indomptable, Kouvéra défait lui a cédé Lanká. Sauve-nous donc, ô toi, qui reposes daus le bonheur absolu ; sauve-nous de Râvana, le fléau des mondes. Daigne, ô toi, qui souris aux vœux du suppliant, daigne imaginer un expédient pour ôter la vie à ce cruel Démon." Les Dieux ayant ainsi dénoncé leurs maux à Brahma, il réfléchit un instant et leur tint ce langage : "Bien, voici que j'ai découvert un moyen pour tuer ce Génie scélérat. Que ni les Dieux, a-t-il dit, ni les rishis, ni les Gandharvas ni les Yakshas, ni les rakshasas, ni les Nágas même ne puissent me donner la mort ! Soit lui ai-je répondu. Mais, par dédain pour la force humaine, les hommes n'ont pas été compris daus sa demande. C'est donc par la main d' un homme, qu'il faut immoler ce méchant." Ainsi tombée de la bouche du créateur, cette parole salutaire satisfit pleinement le roi des habitants du ciel et tous les Dieux avec lui. Lá, dans ce même instant, survint le fortuné Visnou, revêtu d' une splendeur infinie ; car c'était a lui, que Brahma avait pensé dans son âme pour la mort du tyran. Celui-ci donc avec l'essaim des Immortels adresse à Vishnou ces paroles : "Meurtrier de Madhou, comme tu aimes á tirer de l' affliction les êtres malheureux, nous te supplions, nous qui sommes plongés dans la tristesse, Divinité auguste, sois notre asyle !" "Dites! reprit Vishnou; que dois-je faire ?" Ayant oui les paroles de l' ineffable, tous les Dieux repondirent : "Il est un roi nommé Daçaratha ; il a embrassé une très-duré pénitence ; il a célébré même le sacrifice d' un açwa-medha, parce qu'il n'a point de fils et qu' il veut en obtenir du ciel. Il est inébranlable dans sa piété, il est vanté pour ses vertus ; la justice est son caractère, la verité est sa parole. Acquiesce donc à notre demande, ô toi, Vishnou, et consens à naître comme son fils. Divisé en quatre portions de toi-même, daigne, ô toi, qui foules aux pieds tes ennemis, daigne t' incarner dans le sein de ses trois épouses, belles comme la déesse de la beauté." Náráyana, le maître, *non perceptible aux sens, mais qui alors s' était rendu* visible, Náráyana répondit cette parole salutaire aux Dieux, qui i invitaient à cet *heroïque avatára.* Quelle chose, une fois revêtu de cette incarnation, faudra-t-il encore que je fasse pour vous, et de quelle part vient la terreur, qui vous trouble ainsi ?' A ces mots du grand Vishnou : "C'est le démon Rávana, reprirent les Dieux ; c'est lui, Vishnou, cette désolation des mondes, qui nous inspire un tel effroi. Enveloppe-toi d' un corps, humain, et qu'il te plaise arrâcher du monde cette blessante épine; car nul autre que toi parmi les habitants du ciel n'est capable d'immoler ce pécheur. *Sache que* longtemps il s'est imposé la plus austére pénitence, et *que* par elle il s'est rendu agréable au suprême ayeul de toutes les créatures. Aussi le distributeur ineffable des grâces lui a-t-il accordé ce don insigne d'être invulnérable à tous les êtres, l' homme seul excepté. Puisque, doué ainsi de cette faveur, la mort terrible et sûre ne peut venir à lui de nulle autre part que de l'homme, va, dompteur *puissant* de tes ennemis, va dans la condition humaine, et tue-le. Car ce don, auquel on ne peut résister, élevant au plus haut point l' ivresse de sa force, le vil rakshasa tourmente les Dieux, les rishis, les Gandharvas, les hommes sanctifiés par la pénitence ; et, quoique, destructeur des sacrifices, lacérateur des Saintes Ecritures, ennemi des brahmes, dévorateur des hommes, cette faveur incomparable sauve de la mort Rávana le triste fléau des mondes. Il ose attaquer les rois, que défendent les chars de guerre, que remparent les éléphants : d' autres blessés et mis en fuite, sont dissipés ça et là devant lui. Il a dévoré des saints, il a dévoré même une foule d'apsaras. Sans cesse, dans son délire, il s'amuse à tourmenter les sept mondes. Comme *on vient de nous apprendre qu'* il n' a point daigné parler d'eux ce jour, que lui fut donnée cette faveur, *dont il abuse,* entre dans un corps humain, ô toi, qui peux briser tes ennemis, et jette sans vie à tes pieds, roi puissant des treize Dieux, ce Rávana superbe, d'une force épouvantable, d'un orgueil immense, l' ennemi de tous les ascètes, ce ver, *qui les ronge*, cette cause de leurs gémissements."

Ici, dans le premier tome du saint Râmâyana, Finit le quatorzième chapitre, nommé : UN EXPÉDIENT POUR TUER RÁVANA.

HIPPOLYTE FAUCHE.

UTTARAKÁṆḌA.

The Rámáyan ends, epically complete, with the triumphant return of Ráma and his rescued queen to Ayodhyá and his consecration and coronation in the capital of his forefathers. Even if the story were not complete, the conclusion of the last Canto of the sixth Book, evidently the work of a later hand than Válmíki's, which speaks of Ráma's glorious and happy reign and promises blessings to those who read and hear the Rámáyan, would be sufficient to show that, when these verses were added, the poem was considered to be finished. The Uttarakáṇḍa or Last Book is merely an appendix or a supplement and relates only events antecedent and subsequent to those described in the original poem. Indian scholars however, led by reverential love of tradition, unanimously ascribe this Last Book to Válmíki, and regard it as part of the Rámáyan.

Signor Gorresio has published an excellent translation of the Uttarakáṇḍa, in Italian prose, from the recension current in Bengal ;[1] and Mr. Muir has epitomized a portion of the book in the Appendix to the Fourth Part of his Sanskrit Texts (1862). From these scholars I borrow freely in the following pages, and give them my hearty thanks for saving me much wearisome labour.

---

[1] *The Academy*, Vol. III., No. 43, contains an able and interesting notice of this work from the pen of the Professor of Sanskrit in the University of Cambridge : 'The *Uttarakáṇḍa*,' Mr. Cowell remarks, 'bears the same relation to the *Rámáyaṇa* as the Cyclic poems to the *Iliad*. Just as the *Cypria* of Stasinus, the *Æthiopis* of Arctinus, and the little *Iliad* of Lesches completed the story of the

"After Ráma had returned to Ayodhyá and taken possession of the throne, the rishis [saints] assembled to greet him, and Agastya, in answer to his questions recounted many particulars regarding his old enemies. In the Krita Yuga (or Golden Age) the austere and pious Brahman-rishi Pulastya, a son of Brahmá, being teased with the visits of different damsels, proclaimed that any one of them whom he again saw near his hermitage should become pregnant. This had not been heard by the daughter of the royal rishi Trinavindu, who one day came into Pulastya's neighbourhood, and her pregnancy was the result (Sect. 2, vv. 14 ff.). After her return home, her father, seeing her condition, took her to Pulastya, who accepted her as his wife, and she bore a son who received the name of Viśravas. This son was, like his father, an austere and religious sage. He married the daughter of the muni Bharadvája, who bore him a son to whom Brahmá gave the name of Vaiśravaṇ=Kuvera (Sect. 3, vv. 1 ff). He performed austerities for thousands of years, when he obtained from Brahmá as a boon that he should be one of the guardians of the world (along with Indra, Varuṇa, and Yama) and the god of riches. He afterwards consulted his father Viśravas about an abode, and at his suggestion took possession of the city of Lanká, which had formerly been built by Viśvakarman for the Ráxasas, but had been abandoned by them through fear of Vishṇu, and was at that time unoccupied. Ráma then (Sect. 4) says he is surprised to hear that Lanká had formerly belonged to the Ráxasas, as he had always understood that they were the descendants of Pulastya, and now he learns that they had also another origin. He therefore asks who was their ancestor, and what fault they had committed that they were chased away by Vishṇu. Agastya replies that when Brahmá created the waters, he formed certain beings,—some of whom received the name of Ráxasas,—to guard them. The first Ráxasa kings were Heti and Praheti. Heti married a sister of Kála (Time). She bore him a son Vidyutkeśa, who in his turn took for his wife Lankaṭankaṭá, the daughter of Sandhyá (V. 21). She bore him a son Sukeśa, whom she abandoned, but he was seen by Śiva as he was passing by with his wife Párvatí, who made the child as old as his mother, and immortal, and gave him a celestial city. Sukeśa married a Gandharví called Devavatí who bore three sons, Mályavat, Sumáli and Máli. These sons practised intense austerities, when Brahmá appeared and conferred on them invincibility and long life. They then harassed the gods. Viśvakarman gave them a city, Lanká, on the mountain Trikúṭa, on the shore of

---

Iliad, and not only added the series of events which preceded and followed it, but also founded episodes of their own on isolated allusions in Homer, so the *Uttarakáṇḍa* is intended to complete the *Rámáyaṇa*, and at the same time to supplement it by intervening episodes to explain casual allusions or isolated incidents which occur in it. Thus the early history of the giant Rávaṇa and his family fills nearly forty Chapters, and we have a full account of his wars with the gods and his conquest of Lanká, which all happened long before the action of the poem commences, just as the *Cypria* narrated the birth and early history of Helen, and the two expeditions of the Greeks against Troy; and the latter chapters continue the history of the hero Ráma after his triumphant return to his paternal kingdom, and the poem closes with his death and that of his brothers, and the founding by their descendants of various kingdoms in different parts of India.'

the southern ocean, which he had built at the command of Indra....The three Ráxasas, Mályavat and his two brothers, then began to oppress the gods, rishis, etc.; who (Sect. 6, v. 1 ff.) in consequence resort for aid to Mahádeva, who having regard to his protégé Sukeśa the father of Mályavat, says that he cannot kill the Ráxasas, but advises the suppliants to go to Vishṇu, which they do, and receive from him a promise that he will destroy their enemies. The three Ráxasa kings, hearing of this, consult together, and proceed to heaven to attack the gods. Vishṇu prepares to meet them. The battle is described in the seventh section. The Ráxasas are defeated by Vishṇu with great slaughter, and driven back to Lanká, one of their leaders, Máli, being slain. Mályavat remonstrates with Vishṇu, who was assaulting the rear of the fugitives, for his unwarrior-like conduct, and wishes to renew the combat (Sect. 8, v. 3 ff.). Vishṇu replies that he must fulfil his promise to the gods by slaying the Ráxasas and that he would destroy them even if they fled to Pátála. These Ráxasas, Agastya says, were more powerful than Rávaṇa, and, could only be destroyed by Náráyaṇa, *i. e.* by Ráma himself, the eternal, indestructible god. Sumáli with his family lived for a long time in Pátála, while Kuvera dwelt in Lanká. In section 9 it is related that Sumáli once happened to visit the earth, when he observed Kuvera going in his chariot to see his father Viśravas. This leads him to consider how he might restore his own fortunes. He consequently desires his daughter Kaikasí to go and woo Viśravas, who receives her graciously. She becomes the mother of the dreadful Rávaṇa, of the huge Kumbhakarṇa, of Súrpaṇakhá, and of the righteous Vibhíshaṇa, who was the last son. These children grow up in the forest. Kumbhakarṇa goes about eating rishis. Kuvera comes to visit his father, when Kaikasí takes occasion to urge her son Rávaṇa to strive to become like his brother (Kuvera) in splendour. This Rávaṇa promises to do. He then goes to the hermitage of Gokarṇa with his brothers to perform austerity. In section 10 their austere observances are described: after a thousand years' penance Rávaṇa throws his head into the fire. He repeats this oblation nine times after equal intervals, and is about to do it the tenth time, when Brahmá appears, and offers a boon. Rávaṇa asks immortality, but is refused. He then asks that he may be indestructible by all creatures more powerful than men; which boon is accorded by Brahmá together with the recovery of all the heads he had sacrificed and the power of assuming any shape he pleased. Vibhíshaṇa asks as his boon that "even amid the greatest calamities he may think only of righteousness, and that the weapon of Brahmá may appear to him unlearnt, etc. The god grants his request, and adds the gift of immortality. When Brahmá is about to offer a boon to Kumbhakarṇa, the gods interpose, as, they say, he had eaten seven Apsarases and ten followers of Indra, besides rishis and men; and beg that under the guise of a boon stupefaction may be inflicted on him. Brahmá thinks on Sarasvatí, who arrives and, by Brahmá's command, enters into Kumbhakarṇa's mouth that she may speak for him. Under this influence he asks that he may receive the boon of sleeping for many years, which is granted. When however Sarasvatí has left him. and he recovers his own consciousness, he perceives that he has been deluded. Kuvera by his father's advice, gives up the city of Lanká to Rávaṇa."[1] Rávaṇa marries (Sect. 12,) Mandodarí the beautiful daughter of the Asur Maya whose

[1] MUIR, *Sanskrit Texts*, Part IV., pp. 414 ff.

name has several times occurred in the Rámáyan as that of an artist of wonderful skill. She bears a son Meghanáda or the Roaring Cloud who was afterwards named Indrajit from his victory over the sovereign of the skies. The conquest of Kuvera, and the acquisition of the magic self-moving chariot which has done much service in the Rámáyan, form the subject of sections XIII., XIV. and XV. "The rather pretty story of Vedavatí is related in the seventeenth section, as follows: Rávaṇa in the course of his progress through the world, comes to the forest on the Himálaya, where he sees a damsel of brilliant beauty, but in ascetic garb, of whom he straightway becomes enamoured. He tells her that such an austere life is unsuited to her youth and attractions, and asks who she is and why she is leading an ascetic existence. She answers that she is called Vedavatí, and is the vocal daughter of Vrihaspati's son, the rishi Kuśadhvaja, sprung from him during his constant study of the Veda. The gods, gandharvas, etc., she says, wished that she should choose a husband, but her father would give her to no one else than to Vishṇu, the lord of the world, whom he desired for his son-in-law. Vedavatí then proceeds: "In order that I may fulfil this desire of my father in respect of Náráyaṇa, I wed him with my heart. Having entered into this engagement I practise great austerity. Náráyaṇa and no other than he, Purushottama, is my husband. From the desire of obtaining him, I resort to this severe observance." Rávaṇa's passion is not in the least diminished by this explanation and he urges that it is the old alone who should seek to become distinguished by accumulating merit through austerity, prays that she who is so young and beautiful shall become his bride; and boasts that he is superior to Vishṇu. She rejoins that no one but he would thus contemn that deity. On receiving this reply he touches the hair of her head with the tip of his finger. She is greatly incensed, and forthwith cuts off her hair and tells him that as he has so insulted her, she cannot continue to live, but will enter into the fire before his eyes. She goes on "Since I have been insulted in the forest by thee who art wicked-hearted, I shall be born again for thy destruction. For a man of evil desire cannot be slain by a woman; and the merit of my austerity would be lost if I were to launch a curse against thee. But if I have performed or bestowed or sacrificed aught may I be born the virtuous daughter, not produced from the womb, of a righteous man." Having thus spoken she entered, the blazing fire. Then a shower of celestial flowers fell (from every part of the sky). It is she, lord, who, having been Vedavatí in the Kṛita age, has been born (in the Treta age) as the daughter of the king of the Janakas, and (has become) thy [Ráma's] bride; for thou art the eternal Vishṇu. The mountain-like enemy who was [virtually] destroyed before by her wrath, has now been slain by her having recourse to thy superhuman energy." On this the commentator remarks: "By this it is signified that Sítá was the principal cause of Rávaṇa's death; but the function of destroying him is ascribed to Ráma." On the words, "thou art Vishṇu," in the preceding verse the same commentator remarks: "By this it is clearly affirmed that Sítá was Laxmí. This is what Paráśara says: "In the god's life as Ráma, she became Sítá, and in his birth as Krishṇa [she became] Rukmiṇí."[1]

In the following section (XVIII.) "Rávaṇa is described as violently interrupting a sacrifice which is being performed by king Marutta, and the assembled

[1] MUIR, *Sanskrit Texts*, Part IV., 391, 392.

gods in terror assume different shapes to escape; Indra becomes a peacock, Yama a crow, Kuvera a lizard, and Varuṇa a swan; and each deity bestows a boon on the animal he had chosen. The peacock's tail recalls Indra's thousand eyes; the swan's colour becomes white, like the foam of the ocean (Varuṇa being its lord); the lizard obtains a golden colour; and the crow is never to die except when killed by a violent death, and the dead are to enjoy the funeral oblations when they have been devoured by the crows."[1]

Rávaṇ then attacks Arjuna or Kárttavírya the mighty king of Máhishmatí on the banks of the Narmadá, and is defeated, captured and imprisoned by Arjuna. At the intercession of Pulastya (Sect. XXII.) he is released from his bonds. He then visits Kishkindhá where he enters into alliance with Báli the King of the Vánars: "We will have all things in common," says Rávaṇ, "dames, sons, cities and kingdoms, food, vesture, and all delights." His next exploit is the invasion of the kingdom of departed spirits and his terrific battle with the sovereign Yama. The poet in his description of these regions with the detested river with waves of blood, the dire lamentations, the cries for a drop of water, the devouring worm, all the tortures of the guilty and the somewhat insipid pleasures of the just, reminds one of the scenes in the under world so vividly described by Homer, Virgil, and Dante. Yama is defeated (Sect. XXVI.) by the giant, not so much by his superior power as because at the request of Brahmá Yama refrains from smiting with his deadly weapon the Rákshas enemy to whom that God had once given the promise that preserved him. In the twenty-seventh section Rávaṇ goes "under the earth into Pátála the treasure-house of the waters inhabited by swarms of serpents and Daityas, and well defended by Varuṇ." He subdues Bhogavatí the city ruled by Vásuki and reduces the Nágas or serpents to subjection. He penetrates even to the imperial seat of Varuṇ. The God himself is absent, but his sons come forth and do battle with the invader. The giant is victorious and departs triumphant. The twenty-eighth section gives the details of a terrific battle between Rávaṇ and Mándhátá King of Ayodhyá, a distinguished ancestor of Ráma. Supernatural weapons are employed on both sides and the issue of the conflict is long doubtful. But at last Mándhátá prepares to use the mighty weapon "acquired by severe austerities through the grace and favour of Rudra." The giant would inevitably have been slain. But two pre-eminent Munis Pulastya and Gálava beheld the fight through the power given by contemplation, and with words of exhortation they parted King Mándhátá and the sovereign of the Rákshases. Rávaṇ at last (Sect. XXXII.) returns homeward carrying with him in his car Pushpak the virgin daughters of kings, of Rishis, of Daityas, and Gandharvas whom he has seized upon his way. The thirty-sixth section describes a battle with Indra, in which the victorious Meghanáda son of the giant, makes the King of the Gods his prisoner, binds him with his magic art, and carries him away (Sect. XXVII.) in triumph to Lanká. Brahmá intercedes (Sect. XXXVIII.) and Indrajit releases his prisoner on obtaining in return the boon that sacrifice to the Lord of Fire shall always make him invincible in the coming battle. In sections XXXIX., XL, "we have a legend related to Ráma by the sage Agastya to account for the stupendous strength of the monkey Hanumat, as it had been described in the *Rámáyaṇa*. Ráma naturally wonders (as

[1] See *Academy*, III., 43.

perhaps many readers of the *Rámáyaṇa* have done since) why a monkey of such marvellous power and prowess had not easily evercome Báli and secured the throne for his friend Sugríva. Agastya replies that Hanumat was at that time under a curse from a Rishi, and consequently was not conscious of his own might."[1] The whole story of the marvellous Vánar is here given at length, but nothing else of importance is added to the tale already given in the Rámáyaṇa. The Rishis or saints then (Sect. XL.) return to their celestial seats, and the Vánars, Rákshases and bears also (Sect. XLIII.) take their departure. The chariot Pushpak is restored to its original owner Kuvera, as has already been related in the Rámáyaṇ.

The story of Ráma and Sítá is then continued, and we meet with matter of more human interest. The winter is past and the pleasant spring-time is come, and Ráma and Sítá sit together in the shade of the Aśoka trees happy as Indra and Śachí when they drink in Paradise the nectar of the Gods. "Tell me, my beloved," says Ráma, "for thou wilt soon be a mother, hast thou a wish in thy heart for me to gratify?" And Sítá smiles and answers: "I long, O son of Raghu, to visit the pure and holy hermitages on the banks of the Ganges and to venerate the feet of the saints who there perform their rigid austerities and live on roots and berries. This is my chief desire, to stand within the hermits' grove were it but for a single day." And Ráma said: "Let not the thought trouble thee: thou shalt go to the grove of the ascetics." But slanderous tongues have been busy in Ayodhyá, and Sítá has not been spared. Ráma hears that the people are lamenting his blind folly in taking back to his bosom the wife who was so long a captive in the palace of Rávaṇ. Ráma well knows her spotless purity in thought, word, and deed, and her perfect love of him; but he cannot endure the mockery and the shame and resolves to abandon his unsuspecting wife. He orders the sad but still obedient Lakshmaṇ to convey her to the hermitage which she wishes to visit and to leave her there, for he will see her face again no more. They arrive at the hermitage, and Lakshmaṇ tells her all. She falls fainting on the ground, and when she recovers her consciousness sheds some natural tears and bewails her cruel and undeserved lot. But she resolves to live for the sake of Ráma and her unborn son, and she sends by Lakshmaṇ a dignified message to the husband who has forsaken her: "I grieve not for myself," she says "because I have been abandoned on account of what the people say, and not for any evil that I have done. The husband is the God of the wife, the husband is her lord and guide; and what seems good unto him she should do even at the cost of her life."

Sítá is honourably received by the saint Válmíki himself, and the holy women of the hermitage are charged to entertain and serve her. In this calm retreat she gives birth to two boys who receive the names of Kuśa and Lava. They are carefully brought up and are taught by Válmíki himself to recite the Rámáyaṇ. The years pass by: and Ráma at length determines to celebrate the Aśvamedha or Sacrifice of the Steed. Válmíki, with his two young pupils, attends the ceremony, and the unknown princes recite before the delighted father the poem which recounts his deeds. Ráma inquires into their history and recognizes them as his sons. Sítá is invited to return and solemnly affirm her innocence before the great assembly.

"But Sítá's heart was too full; this second ordeal was beyond even her power to submit to, and the poet rose above the ordinary Hindu level of women

---

[1] *Academy*, Vol. III., No. 43.

when he ventured to paint her conscious purity as rebelling: "Beholding all the spectators, and clothed in red garments, Sítá clasping her hands and bending low her face, spoke thus in a voice choked with tears: 'as I, even in mind, have never thought of any other than Ráma, so may Mádhaví the goddess of Earth, grant me a hiding-place.' As Sítá made this oath, lo! a marvel appeared. Suddenly cleaving the earth, a divine throne of marvellous beauty rose up, borne by resplendent dragons on their heads; and seated on it, the goddess of Earth, raising Sítá with her arm, said to her, 'Welcome to thee!' and placed her by her side. And as the queen, seated on the throne, slowly descended to Hades, a continuous shower of flowers fell down from heaven on her head."[1]

"Both the great Hindu epics thus end in disappointment and sorrow. In the *Mahábhárata* the five victorious brothers abandon the hardly won throne to die one by one in a forlorn pilgrimage to the Himálaya; and in the same way Ráma only regains his wife, after all his toils, to lose her. It is the same in the later Homeric cycle—the heroes of the *Iliad* perish by ill-fated deaths. And even Ulysses, after his return to Ithaca, sets sail again to Thesprotia, and finally falls by the hand of his own son. But in India and Greece alike this is an afterthought of a self-conscious time, which has been subsequently added to cast a gloom on the strong cheerfulness of the heroic age."[2]

"The termination of Ráma's terrestrial career is thus told in Sections 116 ff. of the Uttarakáṇḍa. Time, in the form of an ascetic, comes to his palace-gate, and asks, as the messenger of the great rishi (Brahmá) to see Ráma. He is admitted and received with honour, but says, when he is asked what he has to communicate, that his message must be delivered in private, and that any one who witnesses the interview is to lose his life. Ráma informs Laxmaṇa of all this, and desires him to stand outside. Time then tells Ráma that he has been sent by Brahmá to say that when he (Ráma, *i. e.* Vishṇu) after destroying the worlds was sleeping on the ocean, he had formed him (Brahmá) from the lotus springing from his navel, and committed to him the work of creation; that he (Brahmá) had then entreated Ráma to assume the function of Preserver, and that the latter had in consequence become Vishṇu, being born as the son of Aditi, and had determined to deliver mankind by destroying Rávaṇa, and to live on earth ten thousand and ten hundred years; that period, adds Time, was now on the eve of expiration, and Ráma could either at his pleasure prolong his stay on earth, or ascend to heaven and rule over the gods. Ráma replies, that he had been born for the good of the three worlds, and would now return to the place whence he had come, as it was his function to fulfil the purposes of the gods. While they are speaking the irritable rishi Durvásas comes, and insists on seeing Ráma immediately, under a threat, if refused, of cursing Ráma and all his family.

Laxmaṇa, preferring to save his kinsman, though knowing that his own death must be the consequence of interrupting the interview of Ráma with Time, enters the palace and reports the rishi's message to Ráma. Ráma comes out, and

---

[1] E. B. Cowell. *Academy*, No. 43.

The story of Sítá's banishment will be found roughly translated from the *Raghuvaṅśa*, in the Additional Notes.

[2] E. B. Cowell. *Academy*, Vol. III, No. 43.

when Durvásas has got the food he wished, and departed, Ráma reflects with great distress on the words of Time, which require that Laxmaṇa should die. Laxmaṇa however exhorts Ráma not to grieve, but to abandon him and not break his own promise. The counsellors concurring in this advice, Ráma abandons Laxmaṇa, who goes to the river Sarayú, suppresses all his senses, and is conveyed bodily by Indra to heaven. The gods are delighted by the arrival of the fourth part of Vishṇu. Ráma then resolves to install Bharata as his successor and retire to the forest and follow Laxmaṇa. Bharata however refuses the succession, and determines to accompany his brother. Ráma's subjects are filled with grief, and say they also will follow him wherever he goes. Messengers are sent to Śatrughna, the other brother, and he also resolves to accompany Ráma; who at length sets out in procession from his capital with all the ceremonial appropriate to the "great departure," silent, indifferent to external objects, joyless, with Śrí on his right, the goddess Earth on his left, Energy in front, attended by all his weapons in human shapes, by the Vedas in the forms of Brahmans, by the Gáyatrí, the Omkára, the Vashaṭkára, by rishis, by his women, female slaves, eunuchs, and servants. Bharata with his family, and Śatrughna, follow together with Brahmans bearing the sacred fire, and the whole of the people of the country, and even with animals, etc., etc. Ráma, with all these attendants, comes to the banks of the Sarayú. Brahmá, with all the gods and innumerable celestial cars, now appears, and all the sky is refulgent with the divine splendour. Pure and fragrant breezes blow, a shower of flowers falls. Ráma enters the waters of the Sarayú; and Brahmá utters a voice from the sky, saying: "Approach, Vishṇu; Rághava, thou hast happily arrived, with thy godlike brothers. Enter thine own body as Vishṇu or the eternal ether. For thou art the abode of the worlds: no one comprehends thee, the inconceivable and imperishable, except the large-eyed Máyá thy primeval spouse." Hearing these words, Ráma enters the glory of Vishṇu with his body and his followers. He then asks Brahmá to find an abode for the people who had accompanied him from devotion to his person, and Brahmá appoints them a celestial residence accordingly."[1]

[1] Muir, *Sanskrit Texts,* Part IV., Appendix.

ADDITIONAL NOTES.

QUEEN FORTUNE.

'A curious festival is celebrated in honour of this divinity (Lakshmî) on the fifth lunar day of the light half of the month Mâgha (February), when she is identified with Saraswatí the consort of Brahmá, and the goddess of learning. In his treatise on festivals, a great modern authority, Raghunandana, mentions, on the faith of a work called *Samvatsara-sandipa*, that Lakshmî is to be worshipped in the forenoon of that day with flowers, perfumes, rice, and water; that due honour is to be paid to inkstand and writing-reed, and no writing to be done. Wilson, in his essay on the *Religious Festivals of the Hindus* (works, vol. ii, p. 188. ff.), adds that on the morning of the 2nd February, the whole of the pens and inkstands, and the books, if not too numerous and bulky, are collected, the pens or reeds cleaned, the inkstands scoured, and the books wrapped up in new cloth, are arranged upon a platform, or a sheet, and strewn over with flowers and blades of young barley, and that no flowers except white are to be offered. After performing the necessary rites,.........all the members of the family assemble and make their prostrations; the books, the pens, and ink having an entire holiday; and should any emergency require a written communication on the day dedicated to the divinity of scholarship, it is done with chalk or charcoal upon a black or white board.'

CHAMBERS'S ENCYCLOPÆDIA. *Lakshmî.*

INDRA.

'The Hindu Jove or Jupiter Tonans, chief of the secondary deities. He presides over swarga or paradise, and is more particularly the god of the atmosphere and winds. He is also regent of the east quarter of the sky. As chief of the deities he is called Devapati, Devadeva, Surapati, etc.; as lord of the atmosphere, Divaspati; as lord of the eight Vasus or demigods, Fire, etc., Vásava; as breaking cities into fragments, Purandara, Puranda; as lord of a hundred sacrifices (the performance of a hundred Aśvamedhas elevating the sacrficer to the rank of Indra) Śatakratu, Śatamakha; as having a thousand eyes, Sahasráksha; as husband of Śachí, Śachípati. His wife is called Śachí, Indráṇí, Śakráṇí, Maghoni, Indraśakti, Pulomajá, and Paulomí. His son is Jayanta. His pleasure garden or elysium is Nandana; his city, Amarávatí; his palace, Vaijayantá; his horse, Uchchaihśravas; his elephant, Airávata; his charioteer, Mátali.'

PROFESSOR M. WILLIAMS'S English-Sanskrit Dictionary. *Indra.*

VISHṆU.

'The second person of the Hindu triad, and the most celebrated and popular of all the Indian deities. He is the personification of the preserving power, and became incarnate in nine different forms, for the preservation of mankind in various emergencies. Before the creation of the universe, and after its temporary annihilation, he is supposed to sleep on the waters, floating on the serpent Seṣha, and is then identified with Náráyaṇa. Brahmá, the creator, is fabled to spring at that time from a lotus which grows from his navel, whilst thus asleep ....His ten avatárs or incarnations are:

1. The Matsya, or fish. In this avatár Vishṇu descended in the form of a fish to save the pious king Satyavrata, who with the seven Rishis and their wives had taken refuge in the ark to escape the deluge which then destroyed the earth. 2, The Kúrma, or Tortoise. In this he descended in the form of a tortoise, for the purpose of restoring to man some of the comforts lost during the flood. To this end he stationed himself at the bottom of the ocean, and allowed the point of the great mountain Mandara to be placed upon his back, which served as a hard axis, whereon the gods and demons, with the serpent Vásuki twisted round the mountain for a rope, churned the waters for the recovery of the amrita or nectar, and fourteen other sacred things. 3. The Varáha, or Boar. In this he descended in the form of a boar to rescue the earth from the power of a demon called 'golden-eyed,' Hiraṇyáksha. This demon had seized on the earth and carried it with him into the depths of the ocean. Vishṇu dived into the abyss, and after a contest of a thousand years slew the monster. 4. The Narasinha, or Man-lion. In this monstrous shape of a creature half-man, half-lion, Vishṇu delivered the earth from the tyranny of an insolent demon called Hiraṇyakaśipu. 5. Vámana, or Dwarf. This avatár happened in the second age of the Hindús or Tretáyug, the four preceding are said to have occurred in the first or Satyayug; the object of this avatár was to trick Bali out of the dominion of the three worlds. Assuming the form of a wretched dwarf he appeared before the king and asked, as a boon, as much land as he could pace in three steps. This was granted; and Vishṇu immediately expanding himself till he filled the world, deprived Bali at two steps of heaven and earth, but in consideration of some merit, left Pátála still in his dominion. 6. Parasuráma. 7. Rámchandra, 8. Kṛishṇa, or according to some Balaráma. 9. Buddha. In this avatár Vishṇu descended in the form of a sage for the purpose of making some reform in the religion of the Brahmins, and especially to reclaim them from their proneness to animal sacrifice. Many of the Hindús will not allow this to have been an incarnation of their favourite god. 10. Kalki, or White Horse. This is yet to come. Vishṇu mounted on a white horse, with a drawn scimitar, blazing like a comet, will, according to prophecy, end this present age, viz. the fourth or Kaliyug, by destroying the world, and then renovating creation by an age of purity.'

WILLIAMS'S DICTIONARY, *Vishṇu*.

ŚIVA.

A celebrated Hindú God, the Destroyer of creation, and therefore the most formidable of the Hindú Triad. He also personifies reproduction, since the Hindú philosophy excludes the idea of total annihilation without subsequent regeneration. Hence he is sometimes confounded with Brahmá, the creator or first person of the Triad. He is the particular God of the Tántrikas, or followers of the books called Tantras. His worshippers are termed Śaivas, and although not so numerous as the Vaishṇavas, exalt their god to the highest place in the heavens, and combine in him many of the attributes which properly belong to the other deities. According to them Śiva is Time, Justice, Fire, Water, the Sun, the Destroyer and Creator. As presiding over generation, his type is the Linga, or Phallus, the origin probably of the Phallic emblem of Egypt and Greece. As the God of generation and justice, which latter character he shares with the god Yama, he is represented riding a white bull. His own colour, as well as that of the bull, is generally white, referring probably to the unsullied purity of Justice.

35

His throat is dark-blue; his hair of a light reddish colour. and thickly matted together, and gathered above his head like the hair of an ascetic. He is sometimes seen with two hands, sometimes with four, eight, or ten. and with five faces. He has three eyes, one being in the centre of his forehead, pointing up and down. These are said to denote his view of the three divisions of time, past, present, and future. He holds a trident in his hand to denote, as some say, his relationship to water, or according to others, to show that the three great attributes of Creator, Destroyer, and Regenerator are combined in him. His loins are enveloped in a tiger's skin. In his character of Time, he not only presides over its extinction, but also its astronomical regulation. A crescent or half-moon on his forehead indicates the measure of time by the phases of the moon; a serpent forms one of his necklaces to denote the measure of time by years, and a second necklace of human skulls marks the lapse and revolution of ages, and the extinction and succession of the generations of mankind. He is often represented as entirely covered with serpents, which are the emblems of immortality. They are bound in his hair, round his neck, wrists, waist, arms and legs; they serve as rings for his fingers, and earrings for his ears, and are his constant companions. Śiva has more than a thousand names which are detailed at length in the sixty-ninth chapter of the Śiva Purāṇa.—WILLIAMS'S DICTIONARY, *Śiva.*

APSARASES.

'Originally these deities seem to have been personifications of the vapours which are attracted by the sun, and form into mist or clouds: their character may be thus interpreted in the few hymns of the Rigveda where mention is made of them. At a subsequent period when the Gandharva of the Rigveda who personifies there especially the Fire of the Sun, expanded into the Fire of Lightning, the rays of the moon and other attributes of the elementary life of heaven as well as into pious acts referring to it, the Apsarasas become divinities which represent phenomena or objects both of a physical and ethical kind closely associated with that life; thus in the *Yajurveda* Sunbeams are called the Apsarasas associated with the Gandharva who is the Sun; Plants are termed the Apsarasas connected with the Gandharva Fire: Constellations are the Apsarasas of the Gandharva Moon: Waters the Apsarasas of the Gandharva Wind, *etc. etc.*....................In the last Mythological epoch when the Gandharvas have saved from their elementary nature merely so much as to be musicians in the paradise of Indra, the Apsarasas appear among other subordinate deities which share in the merry life of Indra's heaven, as the wives of the Gandharvas, but more especially as wives of a licentious sort, and they are promised therefore, too, as a reward to heroes fallen in battle when they are received in the paradise of Indra; and while, in the Rigveda, they assist Soma to pour down his floods, they descend in the epic literature on earth merely to shake the virtue of penitent Sages and to deprive them of the power they would otherwise have acquired through unbroken austerities.'—GOLDSTÜCKER'S *Sanskrit Dictionary.*

VISHṆU'S INCARNATION AS RÁMA.

'Here is described one of the *avatárs*, descents or manifestations of Vishṇu in a visible form. The word *avatár* signifies literally *descent.* The *avatár* which is here spoken of, that in which, according to Indian traditions, Vishṇu descended and appeared upon earth in the corporeal form of Ráma, the hero of the Rámáyana, is the seventh in the series of Indian *avatárs*. Much has been said before now of these *avatárs*, and through deficient knowledge of the ideas and doctrines of India, they have been compared to the sublime dogma of the Christian Incarnation. This is one of the grossest errors that ignorance of the ideas and beliefs of a people has produced. Between the *avatárs* of India and the Christian Incarnation there is such an immensity of differnce that it is impossible to find any reasonable analogy that can approximate them. The idea of the *avatárs* is intimately united with that of the Trimúrti ; the bond of connection between these two ideas is an essential notion common to both, the notion of Vishṇu. What is the Trimúrti ? I have already said that it is composed of three Gods, Brahmá (masculine), Vishṇu the God of *avatárs*, and Śiva. These three Gods, who when reduced to their primitive and most simple expression are but three cosmogonical personifications, three powers or forces of nature, these Gods, I say, are here found, according to Indian doctrines, entirely external to the true God of India, or Brahma in the neuter gender. Brahma is alone, unchangeable in the midst of creation: all emanates from him, he comprehends all, but he remains extraneous to all: he is Being and the negation of beings. Brahma is never worshipped ; the indeterminate Being is never invoked ; he is inaccessible to the prayers as the actions of man ; humanity, as well as nature, is extraneous to him. External to Brahma rises the Trimúrti, that is to say, Brahmá (masculine) the power which creates. Vishṇu the power which preserves, and Śiva the power which destroys: theogony here commences at the same time with cosmogony. The three divinities of the Trimúrti govern the phenomena of the universe and influence all nature. The real God of India is by himself without power ; real efficacious power is attributed only to three divinities who exist externally to him. Brahmá, Vishṇu, and Śiva, possessed of qualities in part contradictory and attributes that are mutually exclusive, have no other accord or harmony than that which results from the power of things itself, and which is found external to their own thoughts. Such is the Indian Trímúrti. What an immense difference between this Triad and the wonderful Trinity of Christianity ! Here there is only one God, who created all, provides for all, governs all. He exists in three Persons equal to one another, and intimately united in one only infinite and eternal substance. The Father represents the eternal thought and the power which created, the Son infinite love, the Holy Spirit universal sanctification. This one and triune God completes by omnipotent power the great work of creation which, when it has come forth from His hands, proceeds in obedience to the laws which He has given it, governed with certain order by His infinite providence.

The immense difference between the Trimúrti of India and the Christian Trinity is found again between the *avatárs* of Vishṇu and the Incarnation of Christ. The *avatár* was effected altogether externally to the Being who is in India regarded as the true God. The manifestation of one essentially cosmogonical divinity wrought for the most part only material and cosmogonical prodigies. At one time it takes the form of the gigantic tortoise which sustains Mount Mandar from sinking in the ocean; at another of the fish which raises the lost Veda from the bottom of the sea, and saves mankind from the waters. When these *avatárs* are not cosmogonical they consist in some protection accorded to men or Gods, a protection which is neither universal nor permanent. The very manner in which the *avatár* is effected corresponds to its material nature, for instance the mysterious vase and the magic liquor by means of which the *avatár* here spoken of takes place. What are the forms which Vishṇu takes in his descents? They are the simple forms of life; he becomes a tortoise, a boar, a fish, but he is not obliged to take the form of intelligence and liberty, that is to say, the form of man. In the *avatár* of Vishṇu is discovered the inpress of pantheistic ideas which have always more or less prevailed in India. Does the *avatár* produce a permanent and definitive result in the world? By no means. It is renewed at every catastrophe either of nature or man, and its effects are only transitory.......... To sum up then, the Indian *avatár* is effected externally to the true God of India, to Brahma; it has only a cosmogonical or historical mission which is neither lasting nor decisive; it is accomplished by means of strange prodigies and magic transformations; it may assume promiscuously all the forms of life; it may be repeated indefinitely. Now let the whole of this Indian idea taken from primitive tradition be compared with the Incarnation of Christ and it will be seen that there is between the two an irreconcilable difference. According to the doctrines of Christianity the Everlasting Word, Infinite Love, the Son of God, and equal to Him, assumed a human body, and being born as a man accomplished by his divine act the great miracle of the spiritual redemption of man. His coming had for its sole object to bring erring and lost humanity back to Him; this work being accomplished, and the divine union of men with God being re-established, redemption is complete and remains eternal.

The superficial study of India produced in the last century many erroneous ideas, many imaginary and false parallels between Christianity and the Brahmanical religion. A profounder knowledge of Indian civilization and religion, and philological studies enlarged and guided by more certain principles have dissipated one by one all those errors. The attributes of the Christian God, which by one of those intellectual errors, which Vico attributes to the vanity of the learned, had been transferred to Vishṇu, have by a better inspired philosophy been reclaimed for Christianity, and the result of the two religions, one immovable and powerless, the other diffusing itself with all its inherent force and energy, has shown further that there is a difference, a real opposition, between the two principles.'—Gorresio.

KUŚA AND LAVA, *Page* 10.

As the story of the banishment of Sítá and the subsequent birth in Válmíki's hermitage of Kuśa and Lava the rhapsodists of the Rámáyan, is intimately connected with the account in the introductory cantos of Válmíki's composition of the poem, I shall, I trust, be pardoned for extracting it from my rough translation of Kálidása's Raghuvańśa, parts only of which have been offered to the public.

'Then, day by day, the husband's hope grew high,
Gazing with love on Sítá's melting eye:
With anxious care he saw her pallid cheek,
And fondly bade her all her wishes speak.
'Once more I fain would see,' the lady cried,
'The sacred groves that rise on Gangá's side,

Where holy grass is ever fresh and green,
And cattle feeding on the rice are seen :
There would I rest awhile, where once I strayed
Linked in sweet friendship to each hermit maid.'
And Ráma smiled upon his wife, and sware,
With many a tender oath, to grant her prayer.
It chanced, one evening, from a lofty seat
He viewed Ayodhyá stretched before his feet :
He looked with pride upon the royal road
Lined with gay shops their glittering stores that showed,
He looked on Sarjú's silver waves, that bore
The light barks flying with the sail and oar ;
He saw the gardens near the town that lay,
Filled with glad citizens and boys at play.
Then swelled the monarch'bosom with delight,
And his heart triumphed at the happy sight.
He turned to Bhadra, standing by his side,—
Upon whose secret news the king relied,—
And bade him say what people said and thought
Of all the exploits that his arm had wrought.
The spy was silent, but, when questioned still.
Thus spake, obedient to his master's will :
'For all thy deeds in peace and battle done
The people praise thee, King, except for one :
This only act of all thy life they blame,—
Thy welcome home of her, thy ravished dame.'
Like iron yielding to the iron's blow,
Sank Ráma, smitten by those words of woe.
His breast, where love and fear for empire vied,
Swayed, like a rapid swing, from side to side.
Shall he this rumour scorn, which blots his life,
Or banish her, his dear and spotless wife ?
But rigid Duty left no choice between
His perilled honour and his darling queen.
Called to his side, his brothers wept to trace
The marks of anguish in his altered face.
No longer bright and glorious as of old,
He thus addressed them when the tale was told :
'Alas! my brothers, that my life should blot
The fame of those the Sun himself begot ;
As from the labouring cloud the driven rain
Leaves on the mirror's polished face a stain.
E'en as an elephant who loathes the stake
And the strong chain he has no power to break,
I cannot brook this cry on every side,
That spreads like oil upon the moving tide.
I leave the daughter of Videha's King,
And the fair blossom soon from her to spring,

As erst, obedient to my sire's command,
I left the empire of the sea-girt land.
Good is my queen, and spotless ; but the blame
Is hard to bear, the mockery and the shame.
Men blame the pure Moon for the darkened ray,
When the black shadow takes the light away.
And, O my brothers, if ye wish to see
Ráma live long from this reproach set free,
Let not your pity labour to control
The firm sad purpose of his changeless soul.'

Thus Ráma spake. The sorrowing brothers heard
His stern resolve, without an answering word;
For none among them dared his voice to raise,
That will to question:—and they could not praise.
'Beloved brother,' thus the monarch cried
To his dear Lakshmaṇ, whom he called aside.—
Lakshman, who knew no will save his alone
Whose hero deeds through all the world were known :—
'My queen has told me that she longs to rove
Beneath the shade of Saint Válmíki's grove :
Now mount thy car, away my lady bear ;
Tell all, and leave her in the forest there.'

The car was brought, the gentle lady smiled,
As the glad news her trusting heart beguiled.
She mounted up : Sumantra held the reins ;
And forth the coursers bounded o'er the plains.
She saw green fields in all their beauty dressed,
And thanked her husband in her loving breast.
Alas! deluded queen! she little knew
How changed was he whom she believed so true ;
How one she worshipped like the Heavenly Tree
Could, in a moment's time, so deadly be.
Her right eye throbbed,—ill-omened sign, to tell
The endless loss of him she loved so well,
And to the lady's saddening heart revealed
The woe that Lakshmaṇ, in his love, concealed.
Pale grew the bloom of her sweet face,—as fade
The lotus blossoms,—by that sign dismayed.
'Oh, may this omen,'—was her silent prayer,—
'No grief to Ráma or his brothers bear!'

When Lakshmaṇ, faithful to his brother, stood
Prepared to leave her in the distant wood,
The holy Gangá, flowing by the way,
Raised all her hands of waves to bid him stay.
At length with sobs and burning tears that rolled
Down his sad face, the king's command he told ;
As when a monstrous cloud, in evil hour,

Rains from its labouring womb a stony shower.
She heard, she swooned, she fell upon the earth,
Fell on that bosom whence she sprang to birth.
As, when the tempest in its fury flies,
Low in the dust the prostrate creeper lies,
So, struck with terror sank she on the ground,
And all her gems, like flowers, lay scattered round.
But Earth, her mother, closed her stony breast,
And, filled with doubt, denied her daughter rest.
She would not think the Chief of Raghu's race
Would thus his own dear guiltless wife disgrace.
Stunned and unconscious, long the lady lay,
And felt no grief, her senses all astray.
But gentle Lakshmaṇ, with a brother's care,
Brought back her sense, and with her sense, despair.
But not her wrongs, her shame, her grief, could wring
One angry word against her lord the King:
Upon herself alone the blame she laid,
For tears and sighs that would not yet be stayed.
To soothe her anguish Lakshmaṇ gently strove;
He showed the path to Saint Válmiki's grove;
And craved her pardon for the share of ill
He wrought, obedient to his brother's will.
'O, long and happy, dearest brother, live!
I have to praise', she cried, 'and not forgive:
To do his will should be thy noblest praise;
As Vishṇu ever Indra's will obeys.
Return, dear brother: on each royal dame
Bestow a blessing in poor Sítá's name,
And bid them, in their love, kind pity take
Upon her offspring, for the father's sake.
And speak my message in the monarch's ear,
The last last words of mine that he shall hear:
'Say, was it worthy of thy noble race
Thy guiltless queen thus lightly to disgrace?
For idle tales to spurn thy faithful bride,
Whose constant truth the searching fire had tried?
Or may I hope thy soul refused consent,
And but thy voice decreed my banishment?
Hope that no care could turn, no love could stay
The lightning stroke that falls on me to-day?
That sins committed in the life that's fled
Have brought this evil on my guilty head?
Think not I value now my widowed life,
Worthless to her who once was Rama's wife.
I only live because I hope to see
The dear dear babe that will resemble thee.
And then my task of penance shall be done,

With eyes uplifted to the scorching sun;
So shall the life that is to come restore
Mine own dear husband, to be lost no more.'
And Lakshmaṇ swore her every word to tell,
Then turned to go, and bade the queen farewell.
Alone with all her woes, her piteous cries
Rose like a butchered lamb's that struggling dies.
The reverend sage who from his dwelling came
For sacred grass and wood to feed the flame,
Heard her loud shrieks that rent the echoing wood,
And, quickly following, by the mourner stood.
Before the sage the lady bent her low,
Dried her poor eyes, and strove to calm her woe.
With blessings on her hopes the blameless man
In silver tones his soothing speech began:
'First of all faithful wives, O Queen, art thou;
And can I fail to mourn thy sorrows now?
Rest in this holy grove, nor harbour fear
Where dwell in safety e'en the timid deer.
Here shall thine offspring safely see the light,
And be partaker of each holy rite.
Here, near the hermits' dwellings, shalt thou lave
Thy limbs in Tonse's sin-destroying wave,
And on her isles, by prayer and worship, gain
Sweet peace of mind, and rest from care and pain.
Each hermit-maiden with her sweet soft voice,
Shall soothe thy woe, and bid thy heart rejoice:
With fruit and early flowers thy lap shall fill,
And offer grain that springs for us at will.
And here, with labour light, thy task shall be
To water carefully each tender tree,
And learn how sweet a nursing mother's joy
Ere on thy bosom rest thy darling boy.'

....

That very night the banished Sítá bare
Two royal children, most divinely fair.

....

The saint Válmíki, with a friend's delight,
Graced Sítá's offspring with each holy rite.
Kuśa and Lava—such the names they bore—
Learnt, e'en in childhood, all the Vedas' lore;
And then the bard, their minstrel souls to train,
Taught them to sing his own immortal strain.
And Ráma's deeds her boys so sweetly sang,
That Sítá's breast forgot her bitterest pang.

....

Then Sítá's children, by the saint's command,
Sang the Rámáyan, wandering through the land.
How could the glorious poem fail to gain
Each heart, each ear that listened to the strain!
So sweet each minstrel's voice who sang the praise
Of Ráma deathless in Válmíki's lays.
Ráma himself amid the wondering throng
Marked their fair forms, and loved the noble song,
While, still and weeping, round the nobles stood,
As, on a windless morn, a dewy wood.
On the two minstrels all the people gazed,
Praised their fair looks and marvelled as they praised;
For every eye amid the throng could trace
Ráma's own image in each youthful face.
Then spoke the king himself and bade them say
Who was their teacher, whose the wondrous lay.
Soon as Válmíki, mighty saint, he saw,
He bowed his head in reverential awe.
'These are thy children' cried the saint, 'recall
Thine own dear Sítá, pure and true through all.
'O holy father,' thus the king replied,
'The faithful lady by the fire was tried;
But the foul demon's too successful arts
Raised light suspicions in my people's hearts.
Grant that their breasts may doubt her faith no more,
And thus my Sítá and her sons restore.'

Raghuvanśa Cantos XIV, XV.

PARAŚURA'MA, PAGE 87.

'He cleared the earth thrice seven times of the Kshatriya caste, and filled with their blood the five large lakes of Samanta, from which he offered libations to the race of Bhrigu. Offering a solemn sacrifice to the King of the Gods Paraśuráma presented the earth to the ministering priests. Having given the earth to Kaśyapa, the hero of immeasurable prowess retired to the Mahendra mountain, where he still resides; and in this manner was there enmity between him and the race of the Kshatriyas, and thus was the whole earth conquered by Paraśuráma.' The destruction of the Kshatriyas by Paraśuráma had been provoked by the cruelty of the Kshatriyas. *Chips from a German Workshop, Vol.* II. p. 334.

The scene in which he appears is probably interpolated for the sake of making him declare Ráma to be Vishṇu. 'Herr von Schlegel has often remarked to me,' says Lassen, 'that without injuring the connexion of the story all the chapters [of the Rámáyan] might be omitted in which Ráma is regarded as an incarnation of Vishṇu. In fact, where the incarnation of Vishṇu as the four sons of Daśaratha is described, the great sacrifice is already ended, and all the priests remunerated at the termination, when the new sacrifice begins at which the Gods appear, then withdraw, and then first propose the incarnation to Vishṇu.

If it had been an original circumstance of the story, the Gods would certainly have deliberated on the matter earlier, and the celebration of the sacrifice would have continued without interruption.' LASSEN, *Indische Alterthumskunde, Vol. I.* p. 489.

YAMA, PAGE 68.

Son of Vivasvat=Jima son of Vivanghvat, the Jamshíd of the later Persians.

FATE, PAGE 68.

'The idea of fate was different in India from that which prevailed in Greece. In Greece fate was a mysterious, inexorable power which governed men and human events, and from which it was impossible to escape. In India Fate was rather an inevitable consequence of actions done in births antecedent to one's present state of existence, and was therefore connected with the doctrine of metempsychosis. A misfortune was for the most part a punishment, an expiation of ancient faults not yet entirely cancelled.' GORRESIO.

VIŚVÁMITRA, PAGE 76.

'Though of royal extraction, Viśvámitra conquered for himself and his family the privileges of a Brahman. He became a Brahman, and thus broke through all the rules of caste. The Brahmans cannot deny the fact, because it forms one of the principal subjects of their legendary poems. But they have spared no pains to represent the exertions of Viśvámitra, in his struggle for Brahmanhood, as so superhuman that no one would easily be tempted to follow his example. No mention is made of these monstrous penances in the Veda, where the struggle between Visvámitra, the leader of the Kuśikas or Bharatas, and the Brahman Vaśishṭha, the leader of the white-robed Tritsus, is represented as the struggle of two rivals for the place of Purohita or chief priest and minister at the court of King Sudás, the son of Pijavana.' *Chips from a German Workshop, Vol. II.* p. 336.

HOUSEHOLD GODS, PAGE 102.

'No house is supposed to be without its tutelary divinity, but the notion attached to this character is now very far from precise. The deity who is the object of hereditary and family worship, the *Kuladevatá*, is always one of the leading personages of the Hindu mythology, as Śiva, Vishṇu or Durgá, but the *Grihadevatá* rarely bears any distinct appellation. In Bengal, the domestic god is sometimes the *Sálagrám* stone, sometimes the *tulasi* plant, sometimes a basket with a little rice in it, and sometimes a water-jar—to either of which a brief adoration is daily addressed, most usually by the females of the family. Occasionally small images of Lakshmi or Chaṇḍí fulfil the office, or should a snake appear, he is venerated as the guardian of the dwelling. In general, however, in former times, the household deities were regarded as the unseen spirits of ill, the ghosts and goblins who hovered about every spot, and claimed some particular sites as their own. Offerings were made to them in the open air, by scattering a little rice with a short formula at the close of all ceremonies to keep them in good humour.

The household gods correspond better with the genii locorum than with the lares or penates of antiquity.'

H. H. WILSON.

PAGE 107.

Śaivya, a king whom earth obeyed,
Once to a hawk a promise made.

The following is a free version of this very ancient story which occurs more than once in the *Mahábhárat:*

THE SUPPLIANT DOVE.

Chased by a hawk there came a dove
With worn and weary wing,
And took her stand upon the hand
Of Káśí's mighty king.
The monarch smoothed her ruffled plumes
And laid her on his breast,
And cried, 'No fear shall vex thee here,
Rest, pretty egg-born, rest!
Fair Káśí's realm is rich and wide,
With golden harvests gay,
But all that's mine will I resign
Ere I my guest betray.'
But panting for his half won spoil
The hawk was close behind,
And with wild cry and eager eye
Came swooping down the wind:
'This bird', he cried, 'my destined prize,
'Tis not for thee to shield:
'Tis mine by right and toilsome flight
O'er hill and dale and field.
Hunger and thirst oppress me sore,
And I am faint with toil:
Thou shouldst not stay a bird of prey
Who claims his rightful spoil.
They say thou art a glorious king,
And justice is thy care:
Then justly reign in thy domain,
Nor rob the birds of air.'
Then cried the king: 'A cow or deer
For thee shall straightway bleed,
Or let a ram or tender lamb
Be slain, for thee to feed.
Mine oath forbids me to betray
My little twice-born guest:
See how she clings with trembling wings
To her protector's breast.'
'No flesh of lambs,' the hawk replied,
'No blood of deer for me;
The falcon loves to feed on doves,
And such is Heaven's decree.
But if affection for the dove

Thy pitying heart has stirred,
Let thine own flesh my maw refresh,
Weighed down against the bird.'
He carved the flesh from off his side,
And threw it in the scale,
While women's cries smote on the skies
With loud lament and wail.
He hacked the flesh from side and arm,
From chest and back and thigh,
But still above the little dove
The monarch's scale stood high.
He heaped the scale with piles of flesh,
With sinews, blood, and skin,
And when alone was left him bone
He threw himself therein.
Then thundered voices through the air;
The sky grew black as night;
And fever took the earth that shook
To see that wondrous sight.
The blessed Gods, from every sphere,
By Indra led, came nigh;
While drum and flute and shell and lute
Made music in the sky.
They rained immortal chaplets down,
Which hands celestial twine,
And softly shed upon his head
Pure Amrit, drink divine.
Then God and Seraph, Bard and Nymph
Their heavenly voices raised,
And a glad throng with dance and song
The glorious monarch praised.
They set him on a golden car
That blazed with many a gem;
Then swiftly through the air they flew,
And bore him home with them.
Thus Káśí's lord, by noble deed,
Won heaven and deathless fame:
And when the weak protection seek
From thee, do thou the same.

Scenes from the Rámáyan, &c.

PAGE 108.

The ceremonies that attended the consecration of a king *(Abhikshepa lit. Sprinkling over)* are fully described in Goldstücker's Dictionary, from which the following extract is made: 'The type of the inauguration ceremony as practised at the Epic period may probably be recognized in the history of the inauguration of *Ráma*, as told in the *Rámáyaṇa*, and in that of the inauguration of *Yudhishthira*, as told in the *Mahábhárata*. Neither ceremony is described in these poems with the full detail which is given of the vaidik rite in the *Aitareya-Bráhmaṇam;* but the allusion that Ráma was inaugurated by *Vasishṭha* and the other Bráhmaṇas in the same manner as Indra by the Vasus.........and the observation which is made in some passages that a certain rite of the inauguration was performed 'according to the sacred rule'...........admit of the conclusion that the ceremony was supposed to have taken place in conformity with the vaidik injunction......... As the inauguration of *Ráma* was intended and the necessary preparations for it were made when his father Daśaratha was still alive, but as the ceremony itself, through the intrigues of his step-mother *Kaikeyí,* did not take place then, but fourteen years later, after the death of *Daśaratha*, an account of the preparatory ceremonies is given in the *Ayodhyákáṇḍa* (Book II.) as well as in the *Yuddha-Káṇḍa* (Book VI.) of the Rámáyaṇa, but an account of the complete ceremony in the latter book alone. According to the *Ayodhyákáṇḍa,* on the day preceding the intended inauguration *Ráma* and his wife *Sítá* held a fast, and in the night they performed this preliminary rite: *Ráma* having made his ablutions, approached the idol of *Náráyaṇa,* took a cup of clarified butter, as the religious law prescribes, made a libation of it into the kindled fire, and drank the remainder while wishing what was agreeable to his heart. Then, with his mind fixed on the divinity he lay, silent and composed, together with *Sítá,* on a bed of Kuśa-grass, which was spread before the altar of Vishṇu, until the last watch of the night, when he awoke and ordered the palace to be prepared for the solemnity. At day-break reminded of the time by the voices of the bards, he performed the usual morning devotion and praised the divinity. In the meantime the town Ayodhyá had assumed a festive appearance and the inauguration implements had been arranged..............golden water-jars, an ornamented throne-seat, a chariot covered with a splendid tiger-skin, water taken from the confluence of the Ganges and Jumna, as well as from other sacred rivers, tanks, wells, lakes, and from all oceans, honey, curd, clarified butter, fried grain, Kuśa-grass, flowers, milk; besides, eight beautiful damsels, and a splendid furious elephant: golden and silver jars, filled with water, covered with *Udumbara* branches and various lotus flowers, besides a white jewelled *chourie*, a white splendid parasol, a white bull, a white horse, all manner of musical instruments and bards............In the preceding chapter.......there are mentioned *two* white *chouries* instead of one, and all kinds of seeds, perfumes and jewels, a scimitar, a bow, a litter, a golden vase, and a blazing fire, and amongst the living implements of the pageant, instead of the bards, gaudy courtesans, and besides the eight damsels, professors of divinity, Bráhmaṇas, cows and pure kinds of wild beasts and birds, the chiefs of town and country-people and the citizens with their train.'

PAGE 109.

Then with the royal chaplains they
Took each his place in long array.

The twice-born chiefs, with zealous heed,
Made ready what the rite would need.

'Now about the office of a Purohita (house-priest). The gods do not eat the food offered by a king, who has no house-priest (Purohita). Thence the king even when (not) intending to bring a sacrifice, should appoint a Bráhman to the office of house-priest.' HAUG'S *Aitareya Bráhmanam. Vol. II. p.* 528.

PAGE 110.

There by the gate the Sáras screamed.

The Sáras or Indian Crane is a magnificent bird easily domesticated and speedily constituting himself the watchman of his master's house and garden. Unfortunately he soon becomes a troublesome and even dangerous dependent, attacking strangers with his long bill and powerful wings, and warring especially upon 'small infantry' with unrelenting ferocity.

PAGE 120.

My mothers or my sire the king.

All the wives of the king his father are regarded and spoken of by Ráma as his mothers.

PAGE 125.

Such blessings as the Gods o'erjoyed
Poured forth when Vritra was destroyed.

'Mythology regards Vritra as a demon or Asur, the implacable enemy of Indra, but this is not the primitive idea contained in the name of Vritra. In the hymns of the Veda Vritra appears to be the thick dark cloud which Indra the God of the firmament attacks and disperses with his thunderbolt.' GORRESIO.

'In that class of Rig-veda hymns which there is reason to look upon as the oldest portion of Vedic poetry, the character of Indra is that of a mighty ruler of the firmament, and his principal feat is that of conquering the demon *Vritra*, a symbolical personification of the cloud which obstructs the clearness of the sky, and withholds the fructifying rain from the earth. In his battles with Vritra he is therefore described as 'opening the receptacles of the waters,' as 'cleaving the cloud' with his 'far-whirling thunderbolt,' as 'casting the waters down to earth,' and 'restoring the sun to the sky.' He is in consequence 'the upholder of heaven, earth, and firmament,' and the god 'who has engendered the sun and the dawn.' CHAMBERS'S CYCLOPÆDIA. *Indra*.

'Throughout these hymns two images stand out before us with overpowering distinctness. On one side is the bright god of the heaven, as beneficent as he is irresistible; on the other the demon of night and of darkness, as false and treachorous as he is malignant.........The latter (as his name Vritra, from var, to veil, indicates) is pre-eminently the thief who hides away the rain-clouds.........But the myth is yet in too early a state to allow of the definite designations which are brought before us in the conflicts of Zeus with Typhôn and his monstrous progeny, of Apollôn with the Pythôn, of Bellerophôn with Chimaira of Oidipous with the Sphinx, of Hercules with Cacus, of Sigurd with the dragon Fafnir; and thus not only is Vritra known by many names, but he is opposed sometimes by Indra, sometimes by Agni the fire-god, sometimes by Trita, Brihaspati, or other deities; or rather these are all names of one and the same god:

πολλῶν ὀνομάτων μορφὴ μία.

Cox's *Mythology of the Aryan Nations. Vol. II. p. 326.*

PAGE 125.

And that prized herb whose sovereign power
Preserves from dark misfortune's hour.

'And yet more med'cinal is it than that Moly,
That Hermes once to wise Ulysses gave;
He called it Hæmony, and gave it me,
And bade me keep it as of sovereign use
'Gainst all enchantment, mildew, blast, or damp,
Or ghastly furies' apparition.' *Comus.*

The *Moly* of Homer, which Dierbach considers to have been the *Mandrake*, is probably a corruption of the Sanskrit *Múla* a root.

PAGE 136.

True is the ancient saw: the Neem
Can ne'er distil a honeyed stream.

The Neem tree, especially in the Rains, emits a strong unpleasant smell like that of onions. Its leaves however make an excellent cooling poultice, and the Extract of Neem is an admirable remedy for cutaneous disorders.

PAGE 152.

Who of Nisháda lineage came.

The following account of the origin of the Nishádas is taken from Wilson's *Vishṇu Puráṇa*, Book I. Chap. 15. 'Afterwards the Munis beheld a great dust arise, and they said to the people who were nigh: "What is this?" And the people answered and said: "Now that the kingdom is without a king, the dishonest men have begun to seize the property of their neighbours. The great dust that you behold, excellent Munis, is raised by troops of clustering robbers, hastening to fall upon their prey." The sages, hearing this, consulted, and together rubbed the thigh of the king (Vena), who had left no offspring, to produce a son. From the thigh, thus rubbed, came forth a being of the complexion of a charred stake, with flattened features (like a negro), and of dwarfish stature. "What am I to do," cried he eagerly to the Munis. "Sit down (nishída)," said they. And thence his name was Nisháda. His descendants, the inhabitants of the Vindhyá mountain, great Muni, are still called Nishádas and are characterized by the exterior tokens of depravity.' Professor Wilson adds, in his note on the passage: 'The Matsya says that there were born outcast or barbarous races, Mlechchhas, as black as collyrium. The Bhágavata describes an individual of dwarfish stature, with short arms and legs, of a complexion as black as a crow, with projecting chin, broad flat nose, red eyes, and tawny hair, whose descendants were mountaineers and foresters. The Padma (Bhúmi Khaṇḍa) has a similar description; adding to the dwarfish stature and black complexion, a wide mouth, large ears, and a protuberant belly. It also particularizes his posterity as Nishádas, Kirátas, Bhillas, and other barbarians and Mlechchhas, living in woods and on mountains. These passages intend, and do not much exaggerate, the uncouth appearance of the Gonds, Koles, Bhils, and other uncivilized tribes, scattered along the forests and mountains of Central India from Behar to Khandesh, and who are, not improbably, the predecessors of the present occupants of the cultivated portions of the country. They are always very black, ill-shapen, and dwarfish, and have countenances of a very African character.'

Manu gives a different origin of the Nisháđas as the offspring of a Bráhman father and a Śúdra mother. See Muir's *Sanskrit Texts*, Vol. I. p. 481.

PAGE 157.

Beneath a fig-tree's mighty shade,
With countless pendent shoots displayed.

'So counselled he, and both together went
Into the thickest wood; there soon they chose
The fig-tree: not that kind for fruit renowned,
But such as at this day, to Indians known,
In Malabar or Deccan spreads her arms
Branching so broad and long, that in the ground
The bended twigs take root, and daughters grow
About the mother tree, a pillared shade
High overarched, and echoing walks between.'

Paradise Lost, Book IX.

PAGE 161.

Now, Lakshmaṇ, as our cot is made,
Must sacrifice be duly paid.

The rites performed in India on the completion of a house are represented in modern Europe by the familiar 'house-warming.'

PAGE 169.

I longed with all my lawless will
Some elephant by night to kill.

One of the regal or military caste was forbidden to kill an elephant except in battle.

Thy hand has made no Bráhman bleed.

'The punishment which the Code of Manu awards to the slayer of a Brahman was to be branded in the forehead with the mark of a headless corpse, and entirely banished from society; this being apparently commutable for a fine. The poem is therefore in accordance with the Code regarding the peculiar guilt of killing Brahmans; but in allowing a hermit who was not a *Dwija* (twice-born) to go to heaven, the poem is far in advance of the Code. The youth in the poem is allowed to read the Veda, and to accumulate merit by his own as well as his father's pious acts; whereas the exclusive Code reserves all such privileges to *Dwijas* invested with the sacred cord.' Mrs. SPEIR'S *Life in Ancient India*, p. 107.

PAGE 174.

THE PRAISE OF KINGS.

'Compare this magnificent eulogium of kings and kingly government with what Samuel says of the king and his authority: And Samuel told all the words of the LORD unto the people that asked of him a king.

And he said, This will be the manner of the king that shall reign over you: He will take your sons, and appoint them for himself, for his chariots, and to be his horsemen; and some shall run before his chariots.

And he will appoint him captains over thousands, and captains over fifties, and will set them to ear his ground, and to reap his harvest, and to make his instrument of war, and instruments of his chariots.

And he will take your daughters to be confectionaries, and to be cooks, and to be bakers.

And he will take your fields, and your vineyards and your oliveyards, even the best of them; and give them to his servants.

And he will take the tenth of your seed, and of your vineyards, and give to his officers, and to his servants.

And he will take your men-servants, and your maid-servants, and your goodliest young men, and your asses, and put them to his work.

He will take the tenth of your sheep: and ye shall be his servants.

And ye shall cry out in that day because of your king which ye shall have chosen you. I. *Samuel*, VIII.

In India kingly government was ancient and consecrated by tradition: whence to change it seemed disorderly and revolutionary: in Judæa theocracy was ancient and consecrated by tradition, and therefore the innovation which would substitute a king was represented as full of dangers.' GORRESIO.

ŚÁLMALÍ, PAGE 176.

According to the Bengal recension Śálmalí appears to have been another name of the Vipáśá. Śálmali may be an epithet signifying rich in Bombax heptaphyllon. The commentator makes another river out of the word.

BHARAT'S RETURN, PAGE 178.

'Two routes from Ayodhyá to Rájagriha or Girivraja are described. That taken by the envoys appears to have been the shorter one, and we are not told why Bharat returned by a different road. The capital of the Kekayas lay to the west of the Vipáśá. Between it and the Śatadru stretched the country of the Báhíkas. Upon the remaining portion of the road the two recensions differ. According to that of Bengal there follow towards the east the river Indamatí, then the town Ajakála belonging to the Bodhi, then Bhulingá, then the river Śaradaṇḍá. According to the other instead of the first river comes the Ikshumatí.........instead of the first town Abhikála, instead of the second Kulingá, then the second river. According to the direction of the route both the above-mentioned rivers must be tributaries of the Śatadrú.........The road then crossed the Yamuná (Jumna), led beyond that river through the country of the Panchálas, and reached the Ganges at Hástinapura, where the ferry was. Thence it led over the Rámagangá and its eastern tributaries, then over the Gomatí, and then in a southern direction along the Máliní, beyond which it reached Ayodhyá. In Bharat's journey the following rivers are passed from west to east: *Kuṭikoshṭiká*, *Uttániká*, *Kuṭiká*, *Kapívatí*, *Gomatí* according to Schlegel, and *Hiraṇyavatí*, *Uttáriká*, *Kuṭilá*, *Kapívatí*, *Gomatí* according to Gorresio. As these rivers are to be looked for on the east of the Ganges, the first must be the modern *Koh*, a small affluent of the Rámagangá, over which the highway cannot have gone as it bends too far to the north. The Uttániká or Uttáriká must be the Rámagangá, the Kuṭiká or Kuṭilá its eastern tributary Kośilá, the Kapívatí the next tributary which on the maps has different names, *Gurra* or above Kailás, lower down *Bhaigu*. The Gomatí (Goomtee) retains its old name. The Máliní, mentioned only in the envoys' journey, must have been the western tributary of the Sarayú now called Chuká.' LASSEN'S *Indische Alterthumskunde*, Vol. II. p. 524.

PAGE 183.

What worlds await thee, Queen, for this?

'Indian belief divided the universe into several worlds *(lokáh)*. The three principal worlds were heaven, earth, and hell. But according to another division there were seven: Bhúrloka or the earth, Bhuvarloka or the space between the earth and the sun, the seat of the Munis, Siddhas, &c., Svarloka or the heaven of Indra between the sun and the polar star, and the seventh Brahmaloka or the world of Brahma. Spirits which reached the last were exempt from being born again.' GORRESIO.

PAGE 203.

When from a million herbs a blaze
Of their own luminous glory plays.

This mention of lambent flames emitted by herbs at night may be compared with Lucan's description of a similar phenomenon in the Druidical forest near Marseilles, *(Pharsalia*, III. 420.*)*.

Non ardentis fulgere incendia silvae.

Seneca, speaking of Argolis, (Thyestes, Act IV), says :—

Tota solet
Micare flamma silva, et excelsae trabes
Ardent sine igni.

Thus also the bush at Horeb (Exod. II.) flamed, but was not consumed.

The Indian explanation of the phenomenon is, that the sun before he sets deposits his rays for the night with the deciduous plants. See *Journal of R. As. S. Bengal*, Vol. II. p. 339.

PAGE 219.

We rank the Buddhist with the thief.

Schlegel says in his Preface: 'Lubrico vestigio insistit V. Cl. *Heerenius, prof. Gottingensis*, in libro suo de commerciis veterum populorum (OPP. Vol. HIST. XII, pag. 129,) dum putat, ex mentione sectatorum Buddhae secundo libro Rameidos iniecta de tempore, quo totum carmen sit conditum, quicquam legitime concludi posse............Sunt versus spurii, reiecti a Bengalis in sola commentatorum recensione leguntur. Buddhas quidem mille fere annis ante Christum natun vixit: sed post multa demumsecula, odiointernecivo inter Brachmanos et Buddhae sectatores orto, his denique ex India pulsis, fingi potuit iniquissima criminatio, eos animi immortalitatem poenasque et praemia in vita futura negare. Praeterea metrum, quo concinnati sunt hi versus, de quo metro mox disseram, recentiorem aetatem arguit.................................... Poenitet me nunc mei consilii, quod non statim ab initio,...........eiecerim cuncta disticha diversis a sloco vulgari metris composita. Metra sunt duo: pariter ambo constant quatuor hemistichiis inter se aequalibus, alterum undenarum syllabarum, alterum duodenarum, hunc in modum:

⏓ — ⏑ — | — ⏑ ⏑ — | ⏑ — ⏓

⏑ — ⏑ — | — ⏑ ⏑ — | ⏑ — ⏑ ⏓

Cuius generis versus in primo et secundo Rameidos libro nusquam nisi ad finem capitum apposita inveniuntur, et huic loco unice sunt accommodata, quasi peroratio, lyricis numeris assurgens, quo magis canorae cadant clausulae : sicut musici in concentibus extremis omnium vocum instrumentorumque ictu fortiore aures percellere amant. Igitur disticha illa non ante divisionem per capita illatam addi potuerunt: hanc autem grammaticis deberi argumento est ipse recensionum dissensus, manifesto inde ortus, quod singuli editores in ea constituenda suo quisque iudicio usi sunt; praeterquam quod non credibile est, poetam artis suae peritum narrationem continuam in membra tam minuta dissecuisse. Porro discolor est dictio: magniloquentia affectatur, sed nimis turgida illa atque effusa, nec sententiarum pondere satis suffulta. Denique nihil fere novi affertur : amplificantur prius dicta, rarius aliquid ex capite sequente anticipatur. Si quis appendices hosce legendo trausiliat, sentiet slocum ultimum cum primo capitis proximi apte coagmentatum, nec sine vi quadam inde avulsum. Eiusmodi versus exhibet utraque recensio, sed modo haec modo illa plures paucioresve numero, et lectio interdum magnopere variat.'

"The narrative of Ráma's exile in the jungle is one of the most obscure portions of the Rámáyana, inasmuch as it is difficult to discover any trace of the original tradition, or any illustration of actual life and manners, beyond the artificial life of self-mortification and selfdenial said to have been led by the Brahman sages of olden time. At the same time, however, the story throws some light upon the significance of the poem, and upon the character in which the Brahmanical author desired to represent Ráma ; and consequently it deserves more serious consideration than the nature of the subject-matter would otherwise seem to imply.

According to the Rámáyana, the hero Ráma spent more than thirteen years of his exile in wandering amongst the different Brahmanical settlements, which appear to have been scattered over the country between the Ganges and the Godáveri ; his wanderings extending from the hill of Chitra-kúṭa in Bundelkund, to the modern town of Nasik on the western side of India, near the source of the Godáveri river, and about seventy-five miles to the north-west of Bombay. The appearance of these Brahmanical hermitages in the country far away to the south of the Raj of Kasala, seems to call for critical inquiry. Each hermitage is said to have belonged to some particular sage, who is famous in Brahmanical tradition. But whether the sages named were really contemporaries of Ráma, or whether they could possibly have flourished at one and the same period, is open to serious question. It is of course impossible to fix with any degree of certainty the relative chronology of the several sages, who are said to have been visited by Ráma ; but still it seems tolerably clear that some belonged to an age far anterior to that in which the Rámáyana was composed, and probably to an age anterior to that in which Ráma existed as a real and living personage ; whilst, at least, one sage is to be found who could only have existed in the age during which the Rámáyana was produced in its present form. The main proofs of these inferences are as follows. An interval of many centuries seems to have elapsed between the composition of the Rig-Veda and that of the Rámáyana ; a conclusion which has long been proved by the evidence of language, and is generally accepted by Sanskrit scholars. But three of the sages, said to have been contemporary with Ráma, namely, Viśvámitra, Atri and Agastya, are frequently mentioned in the hymns of the Rig-Veda; whilst Válmíki, the sage dwelling at Chitra-kúṭa, is said to have been himself the composer of the Rámáyana. Again, the sage Atri, whom Ráma visited immediately after his departure from Chitra-kúṭa, appears in the genealogical list preserved in the Mahá Bhárata, as the progenitor of the Moon, and consequently as the first ancestor of the Lunar race: whilst his grandson Buddha [Budha] is said to have married Ilá, the daughter of Ikhsváku who was himself the remote ancestor of the Solar race of Ayodhyá, from whom Ráma was removed by many generations, These conclusions are not perhaps based upon absolute proof, because they are drawn from untrustworthy authorities; but still the chronological difficulties have been fully apprehended by the Pundits, and an attempt has been made to reconcile all contradictions by representing the sages to have lived thousands of years, and to have often re-appeared upon earth in different ages widely removed from each other. Modern science refuses to accept such explanations; and consequently it is impossible to escape the conclusion that if Válmíki composed the Rámáyaṇa in the form of Sanskrit in which it has been preserved, he could not have flourished in the same age as the sages who are named in the Rig-Veda." WHEELER'S *History of India, Vol.* II, 229.

PAGE 249.

And King Himálaya's Child.

Umá or Párvatí, was the daughter of Himálaya and Mená. She is the heroine of Kálidása's *Kumára-Sambhava* or *Birth of the War-God.*

PAGE 250.

Strong Kumbhakarṇa slumbering deep
In chains of never-ending sleep.

"Kumbhakarṇa, the gigantic brother of the titanic Rávaṇ,—named from the size of his ears which could contain a *Kumbha* or large water-jar—had such an appetite that he used to consume six months' provisions in a single day. Brahmá, to relieve the alarm of the world, which had begun to entertain serious apprehensions of being eaten up, decreed that the giant should sleep six months at a time and wake for only one day during which he might consume his six months' allowance without trespassing unduly on the reproductive capabilities of the earth." *Scenes from the Rámáyan*, p. 153, 2nd Edit.

PAGE 257.

Like Śiva when his angry might
Stayed Daksha's sacrificial rite.

The following spirited version of this old story is from the pen of Mr. W. Waterfield;

"[This is a favorite subject of Hindú sculpture, especially on the temples of Shiva, such as the caves of Elephanta and Ellora. It, no doubt, is an allegory of the contest between the followers of Shiva and the worshippers of the Elements, who observed the old ritual of the Vedas; in which the name of Shiva is never mentioned.]

Daksha for devotion
  Made a mighty feast ;
Milk and curds and butter,
  Flesh of bird and beast,

Rice and spice and honey,
  Sweetmeats ghí and gur,[1]
Gifts for all the Bráhmans,
  Food for all the poor.

At the gates of Gangá[2]
  Daksha held his feast ;
Called the gods unto it,
  Greatest as the least.

All the gods were gathered
  Round with one accord ;
All the gods but Umá,
  All but Umá's lord.

Umá sat with Shiva
  On Kailása hill ;
Round them stood the Rudras
  Watching for their will.

Who is this that cometh
  Lilting to his lute ?
All the birds of heaven
  Heard his music, mute.

Round his head a garland
  Rich of hue was wreathed :
Every sweetest odour
  From its blossoms breathed.

'Tis the Muni Nárad ;
  'Mong the gods he fares,
Ever making mischief
  By the tales he bears.

"Hail to lovely Umá !
  Hail to Umá's lord !
Wherefore are they absent
  For her father's board ?

"Multiplied his merits
  Would be truly thrice,
Could he gain your favour
  For his sacrifice."

Worth of heart was Umá :
  To her lord she spake :—
"Why dost thou, the mighty,
  Of no rite partake ?

"Straight I speed to Daksha
  Such a sight to see :
If he be my father,
  He must welcome thee."

Wondrous was in glory
  Daksha's holy rite ;
Never had creation
  Viewed so brave a sight.

Gods, and nymphs, and fathers,
  Sages, Bráhmans, sprites,—
Every diverse creature
  Wrought that rite of rites.

Quickly then a quaking
  Fell on all from far ;
Umá stood among them
  On her lion car.

"Greeting, gods and sages,
  Greeting, father mine !
Work hath wondrous virtue,
  Where such aids combine.

"Guest-hall never gathered
  Goodlier company ;
Seemeth all are welcome,
  All the gods but me."

Spake the Muni Daksha,
  Stern and cold his tone ;—
"Welcome thou, too, daughter,
  Since thou com'st alone.

"But thy frenzied husband
  Suits another shrine ;
He is no partaker
  Of this feast of mine.

"He who walks in darkness
  Loves no deeds of light ;
He who herds with demons
  Shuns each kindly sprite.

"Let him wander naked,—
  Wizard weapons wield,—
Dance his frantic measure
  Round the funeral field.

"Art thou yet delighted
  With the reeking hide,
Body smeared with ashes,
  Skulls in necklace tied ?

"Thou to love this monster ?
  Thou to plead his part !
Know the moon and Gangá
  Share that faithless heart.

"Vainly art thou vying
  With thy rivals' charms :
Are not coils of serpents
  Softer than thine arms ?"

Words like these from Daksha
  Daksha's daughter heard :
Then a sudden passion
  All her bosom stirred.

Eyes with fury flashing,
  Speechless in her ire,
Headlong did she hurl her
  'Mid the holy fire.

Then a trembling terror
  Overcame each one,
And their minds were troubled
  Like a darkened sun ;

[1] Ghí : clarified butter. Gur : molasses.

[2] Haridwar (Anglicè Hurdwar) where the Ganges enters the plain country.

And a cruel Vision,
Face of lurid flame,
Umá's Wrath Incarnate,
From the altar came.

Fiendlike forms by thousands
Started from his side,
'Gainst the sacrificers
All their might they plied;

Till the saints availed not
Strength like theirs to stay,
And the gods distracted
Turned and fled away.

Hushed were hymns and chanting,
Priests were mocked and spurned;
Food defiled and scattered;
Altars overturned.—

Then, to save the object
Sought at such a price,
Like a deer in semblance
Sped the sacrifice.

Soaring toward the heavens,
Through the sky it fled?
But the Rudras chasing
Smote away its head.

Prostrate on the pavement
Daksha fell dismayed:—
"Mightiest, thou hast conquered;
Thee we ask for aid.

"Let not our oblations
All be rendered vain;
Let our toilsome labour
Full fruition gain."

Bright the broken altars
Shone with Shiva's form;
"Be it so!" His blessing
Soothed that frantic storm.

Soon his anger ceases,
Though it soon arise;—
But the Deer's Head ever
Blazes in the skies."

Indian Ballads and other Poems.

URVAŚI, PAGE 286.

"The personification of Urvasî herself is as thin as that of Eôs or Selênê. Her name is often found in the Veda as a mere name for the morning, and in the plural number it is used to denote the dawns which passing over men bring them to old age and death. Urvasî is the bright flush of light overspreading the heaven before the sun rises, and is but another form of the many mythical beings of Greek mythology whose names take us back to the same idea or the same root. As the dawn in the Vedic hymns is called Urûkî, the far-going (Têlephassa, Têlephos), so is she also Uruasî, the wide-existing or wide-spreading; as are Eurôpê, Euryanassa, Euryphassa, and many more of the sisters of Athênê and Aphroditê. As such she is the mother of Vasishtha, the bright being, as Oidipous is the son of Iokastê; and although Vasishtha, like Oidipous, has become a mortal bard or sage, he is still the son of Mitra and Varuna, of night and day. Her lover Purûravas is the counterpart of the Hellenic Polydeukês; but the continuance of her union with him depends on the condition that she never sees him unclothed. But the Gandharvas, impatient of her long sojourn among mortal men resolved to bring her back to their bright home; and Purûravas is thus led unwitingly to disregard her warning. A ewe with two lambs was tied to her couch, and the Gandharvas stole one of them; Urvasî said, "They take away my darling, as if I lived in a land where there is no hero and no man." They stole the second, and she upbraided her husband again. Then Purûravas looked and said, "How can that be a land without heroes or men where I am?" And naked he sprang up; he thought it was too long to put on his dress. Then the Gandharvas sent a flash of lighting, and Urvasî saw her husband naked as by daylight. Then she vanished. "I come back," she said, and went. 'Then he bewailed his vanished love in bitter grief.' Her promise to return was fulfilled, but for a moment only, at the Lotos-lake, and Purûravas in vain beseeches her to tarry longer. 'What shall I do with thy speech?' is the answer of Urvasî. 'I am gone like the first of the dawns. Purûravas, go home again. I am hard to be caught like the winds. Her lover is in utter despair; but when he lies down to die, the heart of Urvasî was melted, and she bids him come to her on the last night of the year. On that night only he might be with her; but a son should be born to him. On that day he went up to the golden seats, and there Urvasî told him that the Gandharvas would grant him one wish, and that he must make his choice. 'Choose thou for me,' he said; and she answered, 'Say to them, Let me be one of you.'

Cox's *Mythology of the Aryan Nations.* Vol. I. p. 397.

PAGE 324.

The sovereign of the Vánar race.

"Vánar is one of the most frequently occurring names by which the poem calls the monkeys of Ráma's army. Among the two or three derivations of which the word Vánar is susceptible, one is that which deduces it from वन which signifies a wood, and thus Vánar would mean a forester, an inhabitant of the wood. I have said elsewhere that the monkeys, the Vánars, whom Ráma led to the conquest of Ceylon were fierce woodland tribes who occupied the mountainous regions of the south of India, where their descendants may still be seen. I shall hence forth promiscuously employ the word *Vánar* to denote those monkeys, those fierce combatants of Ráma's army." GORRESIO.

PAGE 326.

No change of hue, no pose of limb
Gave sign that aught was false in him.
Concise, unfaltering, sweet and clear,
Without a word to pain the ear,
From chest to throat, nor high nor low,
His accents came in measured flow.

Somewhat similarly in *The Squire's Tale:*

'He with a manly voice said his message,
After the form used in his language,
Withouten vice of syllable or of letter.
And for his talë shouldë seem the better
Accordant to his wordës was his chere,
As teacheth art of speech them that it lere.

PAGE 329.

RÁMA'S ALLIANCE WITH SUGRÍVA.

"The literal interpretation of this portion of the Rámáyana is indeed deeply rooted in the mind of the Hindu. He implicitly believes that Ráma is Vishnu, who became incarnate for the purpose of destroying the demon Rávana; that he permitted his wife to be captured by Rávana for the sake of delivering the gods and Bráhmans from the oppressions of the Rákshasa; and that he ultimately assembled an army of monkeys, who were the progeny of the gods, and led them against the strong-hold of Rávana at Lanká, and delivered the world from the tyrant Rákshasa, whilst obtaining ample revenge for his own personal wrongs.

One other point seems to demand consideration, namely, the possibility of such an alliance as that which Ráma is said to have concluded with the monkeys. This possibility will of course be denied by modern critics, but still it is interesting to trace out the circumstances which seem to have led to the acceptance, of such a wild belief by the dreamy and marvel loving Hindú. The south of India swarms with monkeys of curious intelligence and rare physical powers. Their wonderful instinct for organization, their attachment to particular localities, their occasional journeys in large numbers over mountains and across rivers, their obstinate assertion of supposed rights, and the ridiculous caricature which they exhibit of all that is animal and emotional in man, would naturally create a deep impression......... Indeed the habits of monkeys well deserve to be patiently studied; not as they appear in confinement, when much that is revolting in their nature is developed, but as they appear living in freedom amongst the trees of the forest, or in the streets of crowded cities, or precincts of temples. Such a study would not fail to awaken strange ideas; and although the European would not be prepared to regard monkeys as sacred animals, he might be led to speculate as to their origin by the light of data, which are at present unknown to the naturalist whose observations have been derived from the menagerie alone.

Whatever, however, may have been the train of ideas which led the Hindú to regard the monkey as a being half human and half divine, there can be little doubt that in the Rámáyana the monkeys of southern India have been confounded with what may be called the aboriginal people of the country. The origin of this confusion may be easily conjectured. Perchance the aborigines of the country may have been regarded as a superior kind of monkeys; and to this day the features of the Marawars, who are supposed to be the aborigines of the southern part of the Carnatic, are not only different from those of their neighbours, but are of a character calculated to confirm the conjecture. Again, it is probable that the army of aborigines may have been accompanied by outlying bands of monkeys impelled by that magpie-like curiosity and love of plunder which are the peculiar characteristics of the monkey race; and this incident may have given rise to the story that the army was composed of Monkeys."

Wheeler's *History of India. Vol. II. pp.* 316 *ff.*

THE FALL OF BÁLI, Page 342.

"As regards the narrative, it certainly seems to refer to some real event amongst the aboriginal tribes; namely, the quarrel between an elder and younger brother for the possession of a Ráj; and the subsequent alliance of Ráma with the younger brother. It is somewhat remarkable that Ráma appears to have formed an alliance with the wrong party, for the right of Báli was evidently superior to that of Sugríva; and it is especially worthy of note that Ráma compassed the death of Báli by an act contrary to all the laws of fair fighting. Again, Ráma seems to have tacitly sanctioned the transfer of Tárá from Báli to Sugríva, which was directly opposed to modern rule, although in conformity with the rude customs of a barbarous age; and it is remarkable that to this day the marriage of both widows and divorced women is practised by the Marawars, or aborigines of the southern Carnatic, contrary to the deeply-rooted prejudice which exists against such unions amongst the Hindús at large."

Wheeler's *History of India. Vol. II.* 324

THE VÁNAR HOST, PAGE 370.

"The splendid Marutas form the army of Indras, the red-haired monkeys and bears that of Râmas; and the mythical and solar nature of the monkeys and bears of the Râmâyaṇam manifests itself several times. The king of the monkeys is a sun-god. The ancient king was named Bâlin, and was the son of Indras. His younger brother Sugrívas, he who changes his shape at pleasure (Kâmarúpas), who, helped by Râmas, usurped his throne, is said to be own child of the sun. Here it is evident that the Vedic antagonism between Indras and Vishṇus is reproduced in a zoological and entirely apish form. The old Zeus must give way to the new, the moon to the sun, the evening to the morning sun, the sun of winter to that of spring; the young son betrays and overthrows the old one.........Râmas, who treacherously kills the old king of the monkeys, Bâlin, is the equivalent of Vishṇus, who hurls his predecessor Indras from his throne; and Sugrívas, the new king of the monkeys resembles Indras when he promises to find the ravished Sítá, in the same way as Vishṇus in one of his incarnations finds again the lost vedás. And there are other indications in the Râmâyaṇam of opposition between Indras and the monkeys who assist Râmas. The great monkey Hanumant, of the reddish colour of gold, has his jaw broken, Indras having struck him with his thunderbolt and caused him to fall upon a mountain, because, while yet a child, he threw himself off a mountain into the air in order to arrest the course of the sun, whose rays had no effect upon him. (The cloud rises from the mountain and hides the sun, which is unable of itself to disperse it; the tempest comes, and brings flashes of lightning and thunder-bolts, which tear the cloud in pieces.)

The whole legend of the monkey Hanumant represents the sun entering into the cloud or darkness, and coming out of it. His father is said to be now the wind, now the elephant of the monkeys (Kapikunjaras), now Keśarin, the long-haired sun, the sun with a mane, the lion sun (whence his name of *Keśariṇah putrah*). From this point of view, Hanumant would seem to be the brother of Sugrívas, who is also the offspring of the sun........................

All the epic monkeys of the *Râmâyaṇam* are described in the twentieth canto of the first book by expressions which very closely resemble those applied in the Vedic hymns to the Marutas, as swift as the tempestuous wind, changing their shape at pleasure, making a noise like clouds, sounding like thunder, battling, hurling mountain-peaks, shaking great uprooted trees, stirring up the deep waters, crushing the earth with their arms, making the clouds fall. Thus Bâlin comes out of the cavern as the sun out of the cloud.................

But the legend of the monkey Hanumant presents another curious resemblance to that of Samson. Hanumant is bound with cords by Indrajit, son of Rávaṇas; he could easily free himself, but does not wish to do so. Rávaṇas to put him to shame, orders his tail to be burned, because the tail is the part most prized by monkeys..

The tail of Hanumant, which sets fire to the city of the monsters, is probably a personification of the rays of the morning or spring sun, which sets fire to the eastern heavens, and destroys the abode of the nocturnal or winter monsters."
DE GUBERNATIS, *Zoological Mythology*, Vol. II, pp. 100 ff.

"The Jaitwas of Rajputana, a tribe politically reckoned as Rajputs, nevertheless trace their descent from the monkey-god Hanuman, and confirm it by alleging that their princes still bear its evidence in a tail-like prolongation of the spine; a tradition which has probably a real ethnological meaning, pointing out the Jaitwas as of non-Aryan race." * TYLOR'S *Primitive Culture*, Vol. I. p. 341.

PAGE 372.

The names of peoples occurring in the following *ślokas* are omitted in the metrical translation:

'Go to the Brahmamálas,[1] the Videhas,[2] the Málavas,[3] the Káśikośalas,[4] the Mágadhas,[5] the Puṇḍras,[6] and the Angas,[7] and the land of the weavers of silk, and the land of the mines of silver, and the hills that stretch into the sea, and the towns and the hamlets that are about the top of Mandar, and the Karṇaprávaraṇas,[8] and the Oshṭhakarṇakas,[9] and the Ghoralohamukhas,[10] and the

---

* Campbell in 'Journ. As. Soc. Bengal,' 1866, Part ii. p. 132; Latham, 'Descr. Eth.' Vol. ii. p. 456; Tod, 'Annals of Rajasthan,' Vol. i. p. 114.

[1] Said by the commentator to be an eastern people between the Himálayan and Vindhyan chains.

[2] Videha was a district in the province of Behar, the ancient Mithilá or the modern Tirhoot.

[3] The people of Malwa.

[4] "The Káśikośalas are a central nation in the Váyu Puráṇa. The Rámáyaṇa places them in the east. The combination indicates the country between Benares and Oude.............. Kośala is a name variously applied. Its earliest and most celebrated application is to the country on the banks of the Sarayú, the kingdom of Ráma, of which Ayodhyá was the capital.........In the Mahábhárata we have one Kośala in the east and another in the south, besides the Prák-Kośalas and Uttara Kośalas in the east and north. The Puráṇas place the Kośalas amongst the people on the back of Vindhya; and it would appear from the Váyu that Kuśa the son of Ráma transferred his kingdom to a more central position; he ruled over Kośala at his capital of Kúśasthali of Kuśavatí, built upon the Vindhyan precipices." WILSON'S *Vishṇu Puráṇa*, Vol. II. pp. 157, 172.

[5] The people of south Behar.

[6] The Puṇḍras are said to be the inhabitants of the western provinces of Bengal. "In the *Aitareyabráhmaṇa*, VII. 18, it is said that the elder sons of Viśvamitra were cursed to become progenitors of most abject races, such as Andhras, Puṇḍras, Śabaras, Pulindas, and Mútibas." WILSON'S *Vishṇu Puráṇa* Vol. II. 170.

[7] Anga is the country about Bhagulpore, of which Champá was the capital.

[8] A fabulous people, 'men who use their ears as a covering.' So Sir John Maundevile says: "And in another Yle ben folk that han gret Eres and long, that hangen down to here knees,' and Pliny, lib. iv. c. 13: "In quibus nuda alioquin corpora prægrandes ipsorum aures tota contegunt." Strabo calls them ἐνωτόκοιτοι. Isidore calls them Panotii.

[9] 'Those whose ears hang down to their lips.'

[10] 'The Iron-faces.'

swift Ekapádakas.[1] and the strong imperishable Eaters of Men, and the Kirátas[2] with stiff hair-tufts, men like gold and fair to look upon : And the Eaters of Raw Fish, and the Kirátas who dwell in islands, and the fierce Tiger-men[3] who live amid the waters.'

PAGE 374.

'Go to the Vidarbhas[4] and the Rishṭikas[5] and the Mahishikas,[6] and the Matsyas[7] and Kalingas[8] and the Kauśikas[9]...............and the Andhras[10] and the Puṇḍras[11] and the Cholas[12] and the Paṇḍyas[13] and the Keralas.[14] 'Go to the

---

[1] 'The One-footed.'

"In that Contree," says Sir Jhon Maundevile, "ben folk, that han but o foot and thei gon so fast that it is marvaylle : and the foot is so large that it schadeweth alle the Body azen the Sonne, when thei wole lye and rest hem." So Pliny, Natural History, lib. vii. c. 2 : speaks of Hominum gens............singulis cruribus, miræ pernicitatis ad saltum ; eosdemque Sciopodas vocari, quod in majori æstu, humi jacentes resupini, umbrâ se pedum protegant."

These epithets are, as Professor Wilson remarks, "exaggerations of national ugliness, or allusions to peculiar customs, which were not literally intended, although they may have furnished the Mandevilles of ancient and modern times."

Vishṇu Puráṇa, Vol. II. p. 162.

[2] The Kirrhadæ of Arrian : a general name for savage tribes living in woods and mountains

[3] Said by the commentator to be half tigers half men.

[4] The kingdom seems to have corresponded with the greater part of Berar and Khandesh.

[5] The Bengal recension has Kishikas, and places them both in the south and the north.

[6] The people of Mysore.

[7] "There are two Matsyas, one of which, according to the Yantra Samráj, is identifiable with Jeypoor. In the Digvijaya of Nakula he subdues the Matsyas further to the west, or Gujerat." WILSON'S *Vishṇu Puráṇa*, Vol. II. 158. Dr. Hall observes : "In the *Mahábhárata Sabhá-parwan*, 1105 and 1108, notice is taken of the king of Matsya and of the Aparamatsyas ; and, at 1082, the Matsyas figure as an eastern people. They are placed among the nations of the south in the *Rámáyaṇa Kishkindhá-káṇda*, XLI., II, while the Bengal recension, *Kishkindhá-káṇda*, XLIV., 12, locates them in the north."

[8] The Kalingas were the people of the upper part of the Coromandel Coast, well known, in the traditions of the Eastern Archipelago, as Kling. Ptolemy has a city in that part, called Caliga ; and Pliny Calingæ proximi mari."

WILSON'S *Vishṇu Puráṇa*, Vol. II. 156, Note.

[9] The Kauśikas do not appear to be identifiable.

[10] The Andhras probably occupied the modern Telingana,

[11] The Puṇḍras have already been mentioned in Canto XL.

[12] The inhabitants of the lower part of the Coromandel Coast ; so called, after them, Cholamaṇḍala

[13] A people in the Deccan.

[14] The Keralas were the people of Malabar proper.

Mlechchhas[1] and the Pulindas[2] and the Śúrasenas,[3] and the Prasthalas and the Bharatas and Madrakas[4] and the Kámbojas[5] and the Yavanas[6] and the towns of the Śakas[7] and the Varadas.'[8]

NORTHERN KURUS, PAGE 378.

Professor Lassen remarks (in the Zeitschrift für die Kunde des Morgenlandes, ii. 62): "At the furthest accessible extremity of the earth appears Harivarsha with the northern Kurus. The region of Hari or Vishṇu belongs to the system of mythical geography: but the case is different with the Uttara Kurus. Here there is a real basis of geographical fact; of which fable has only taken advantage, without creating it. The Uttara Kurus were formerly quite independent of the mythical system of *dvípas*, though they were included in it at an early date." Again the same writer says at p. 65: "That the conception of the Uttara Kurus is based upon an actual country and not on mere invention, is proved (1) by the way in which they are mentioned in the Vedas; (2) by the

---

[1] A generic term for persons speaking any language but Sanskrit and not conforming to the usual Hindu institutions.

[2] "Pulinda is applied to any wild or barbarous tribe. Those here named are some of the people of the deserts along the Indus; but Pulindas are met with in many other positions, especially in the mountains and forests across Central India, the haunts of the Bheels and Gonds. So Ptolemy places the Pulindas along the banks of the Narmadá, to the frontiers of Larice, the Láṭá or Lár of the Hindus,—Khandesh and part of Gujerat." WILSON'S *Vishṇu Puráṇa*, Vol. II. 159, Note.

Dr. Hall observes that "in the Bengal recension of the *Rámáyaṇa* the Pulindas appear both in the south and in the north. The real *Rámáyaṇa* K.-k., XLIII., speaks of the northern Pulindas."

[3] The Śúrasenas were the inhabitants of Mathurá, the Suraseni of Arrian.

[4] These the Mardi of the Greeks and the two preceding tribes appear to have dwelt in the north-west of Hindustan.

[5] The Kámbojas are said to be the people of Arachosia. They are always mentioned with the north-western tribes.

[6] "The term Yavanas, although, in later times, applied to the Mohammedans, designated formerly the Greeks.... The Greeks were known throughout Western Asia by the term יון Yavan, or Ion, 'Ιάονες; the यवन of the Hindus.......... That the Macedonian or Bactrian Greeks were most usually intended is not only probable from their position and relations with India, but from their being usually named in concurrence with the north-western tribes, Kámbojas, Daradas, Páradas, Báhlíkas, Śakas &c., in the Rámáyaṇa, Mahábhárata, Puráṇas, Manu, and in various poems and plays." WILSON'S *Vishṇu Puraṇa*, Vol. II. p. 181, Note.

[7] These people, the Sakai and Sacæ of classical writers, the Indo-Scythians of Ptolemy, extended, about the commencement of our era, along the west of India, from the Hindu Kosh to the mouths of the Indus.

[8] The corresponding passage in the Bengal recension has instead of Varadas Daradas the Dards or inhabitants of the modern Dardistan along the course of the Indus, above the Himálayas, just before it descends to India.

existence of Uttara Kuru in historical times as a real country; and (3) by the way in which the legend makes mention of that region as the home of primitive customs. To begin with the last point the Mahábhárata speaks as follows of the freer mode of life which women led in the early world, Book I. verses 4719—22: 'Women were formerly unconfined and roved about at their pleasure, independent. Though in their youthful innocence they abandoned their husbands, they were guilty of no offence; for such was the rule in early times. This ancient custom is even now the law for creatures born as brutes, which are free from lust and anger. This custom is supported by authority and is observed by great ṛishis, and it is *still practised among the northern Kurus.*'

"The idea which is here conveyed is that of the continuance in one part of the world of that original blessedness which prevailed in the golden age. To afford a conception of the happy condition of the southern Kurus it is said in another place (M.-Bh. i. 4346.) "The southern Kurus vied in happiness with the northern Kurus and with the divine ṛishis and bards."

Professor Lassen goes on to say: "Ptolemy (vi. 16.) is also acquainted with *Uttara Kuru.* He speaks of a mountain, a people, and a city called *Ottorakorra.* Most of the other ancient authors who elsewhere mention this name, have it from him. It is a part of the country which he calls Serica; according to him the city lies twelve degrees west from the metropolis of Sera, and the mountain extends from thence far to the eastward. As Ptolemy has misplaced the whole of eastern Asia beyond the Ganges, the *relative* position which he assigns will guide us better that the absolute one, which removes *Ottorakorra* so far to the east that a correction is inevitable. According to my opinion the *Ottorakorra* of Ptolemy must be sought for to the east of Kashgar." Lassen also thinks that Magasthenes had the Uttara Kurus in view when he referred to the Hyperboreans who were fabled by Indian writers to live a thousand years. In his Indian antiquities, (Ind. Alterthumskunde, i. 511, 512, and note,) the same writer concludes that though the passages above cited relative to the Uttara Kurus indicate a belief in the existence of a really existing country of that name in the far north, yet that the descriptions there given are to be taken as pictures of an ideal paradise, and not as founded on any recollections of the northern origin of the Kurus. It is probable, he thinks, that some such reminiscences originally existed, and still survived in the Vedic era, though there is no trace of their existence in latter times." MUIR'S *Sanskrit Texts,* Vol. II. pp. 336, 337.

PAGE 428.

Trust to these mighty Vánars.

The corresponding passage in the Bengal recension has "these silvans in the forms of monkeys, vánaráh kapirúpinah." "Here it manifestly appears," says Gorresio, "that these hosts of combatants whom Ráma led to the conquest of Lanká (Ceylon) the kingdom and seat of the Hamitic race, and whom the poem calls monkeys, were in fact as I have elsewhere observed, inhabitants of the mountainous and southern regions of India, who were wild-looking and not altogether unlike monkeys. They were perhaps the remote ancestors of the Malay races."

Page 431.

"Art thou not he who slew of old
The Serpent-Gods, and stormed their hold."

All these exploits of Rávaṇ are detailed in the *Uttarakáṇḍa*, and epitomized in the Appendix.

Page 434.

Within the consecrated hall.

The Bráhman householder ought to maintain three sacred fires, the *Gárhapatya*, the *Ahavaniya* and the *Dakshiṇa*. These three fires were made use of in many Brahmanical solemnities, for example in funeral rites when the three fires were arranged in prescribed order.

Page 436.

Fair Punjikasthalá I met.

"I have not noticed in the Uttara Káṇḍa any story about the daughter of Varuṇa, but the commentator on the text (VI 60, 11) explains the allusion to her thus:

"The daughter of Varuṇa was Punjikásthalí. On her account, a curse of Brahmá, involving the penalty of death, [was pronounced] on the rape of women." Muir, *Sanskrit Texts,* Part IV. Appendix.

Page 452.

"Shall no funereal honours grace
The parted lord of Raghu's race?"

"Here are indicated those admirable rites and those funeral prayers which Professor Müller has described in his excellent work, *Die Todtenbestattung bei den Brahmanen.* Sítá laments that the body of Ráma will not be honoured with those rites and prayers, nor will the Bráhman priest while laying the ashes from the pile in the bosom of the earth, pronounce over them those solemn and magnificent words: "Go unto the earth, thy mother, the ample, wide, and blessed earth..........And do thou, O Earth, open and receive him as a friend with sweet greeting: enfold him in thy bosom as a mother wraps her child in her robes." Gorresio.

Page 462.

Each glorious sign
That stamps the future queen is mine.

We read in Josephus that Cæsar was so well versed in chiromancy that when one day a *soi-disant* son of Herod had audience of him, he at once detected the impostor because his hand was destitute of all marks of royalty.

Page 466.

In battle's wild Gandharva dance.

"Here the commentator explains: 'the battle resembled the dance of the Gandharvas,' in accordance with the notion of the Gandharvas entertained in his day. They were regarded as celestial musicians enlivening with their melodies

Indra's heaven and the banquets of the Gods. But the Gandharvas before becoming celestial musicians in popular tradition, were in the primitive and true signification of the name heroes. spirited and ardent warriors, followers of Indra, and combined the heroical character with their atmospherical deity. Under this aspect the dance of the Gandharvas may be a very different thing from what the commentator means, and may signify the horrid dance of war." GORRESIO.

The Homeric expression is similar, "to dance a war-dance before Ares."

PAGE 470.

By Anaraṇya's lips of old.

"The story of Anaraṇya is told in the Uttara Kaṇḍa of the Rámáyaṇa.... Anaraṇya a descendant of Ixváku and King of Ayodhyá, when called upon to fight with Rávaṇa or acknowledge himself conquered, prefers the former alternative; but his army is overcome, and he himself is thrown from his chariot.

When Rávana triumphs over his prostrate foe, the latter says that he has been vanquished not by him but by fate, and that Rávaṇa is only the instrument of his overthrow; and he predicts that Rávaṇa shall one day be slain by his descendant Ráma." *Sanskrit Texts*, IV., Appendix.

PAGE 497.

"With regard to the magic image of Sítá made by Indrajit, we may observe that this thoroughly oriental idea is also found in Greece in Homer's Iliad, where Apollo forms an image of Æneas to save that hero beloved by the Gods; it occurs too in the Æneid of Virgil where Juno forms a fictitious Æneas to save Turnus:

Tum dea nube cava tenuem sine viribus umbram
In faciem Æneæ (visu mirabile monstrum)
Dardaniis ornat telis; clipeumque jubasque
Divini assimulat capitis; dat inania verba;
Dat sine mente sonum, gressusque effingit euntis.

(*Æneidos*, lib X.)"

GORRESIO.

PAGE 489.

"*To Raghu's son my chariot lend.*"

"Analogous to this passage of the Rámáyaṇa, where Indra sends to Ráma his own chariot, his own charioteer, and his own arms, is the passage in the Æneid where Venus descending from heaven brings celestial arms to her son Æneas when he is about to enter the battle:

At Venus æthereos inter dea candida nimbos
Dona ferens aderat;..
....
Arma sub adversa posuit radiantia quercu.
Ille, deæ donis et tanto lætus honore,
Expleri nequit, atque oculos per singula volvit,
Miraturque, interque manus et brachia versat
Terribilem cristis galeam flammasque vomentem,
Fatiferumque ensem, loricam ex ære rigentem.

(*Æneidos*, lib. VIII.)'

GORRESIO.

PAGE 489.

Agastya came and gently spake.

"The Muni or saint Agastya, author of several Vedic hymns, was celebrated in Indo-Sanskrit tradition for having directed the first brahmanical settlements in the southern regions of India; and the Mahábhárata gives him the credit of having subjected those countries, expelled the Rákshases, and given security to the solitary ascetics, who were settled there. Hence Agastya was regarded in ancient legend as the conqueror and ruler of the southern country. This tradition refers to the earliest migrations made by the Sanskrit Indians towards the south of India. To Agastya are attributed many marvellous mythic deeds which adumbrate and veil ancient events; some of which are alluded to here and there in the Rámáyana." GORRESIO.

The following is the literal translation of the Canto, text and commentary, from the Calcutta edition:

Having found Ráma weary with fighting and buried in deep thought, and Rávaṇ standing before him ready to engage in battle, the holy Agastya, who had come to see the battle, approached Ráma and spoke to him thus: "O mighty Ráma, listen to the old mystery by which thou wilt conquer all thy foes in the battle. Having daily repeated the Ádityahridaya (the delighter of the mind of the Sun) the holy prayer which destroys all enemies (of him who repeats it) gives victory, removes all sins, sorrows and distress, increases life, and which is the blessing of all blessings, worship the rising and splendid sun who is respected by both the Gods and demons, who gives light to all bodies and who is the rich lord of all the worlds. (To the question why this prayer claims so great reverence; the sage answers) Since yonder* sun is full of glory and all gods reside in him (he being their material cause) and bestows being and the active principle on all creatures by his rays; and since he protects all deities, demons and men with his rays.

He is Brahmá,[1] Vishṇu,[2] Siva,[3] Skanda,[4] Prajápati,[5] Mahendra,[6] Dhanada,[7] Kála,[8] Yama,[9] Soma,[10] Apám Pati *i. e.* The lord of waters, Pitris,[11] Vasus,[12]

---

* From the word yonder it would appear that the prayer is to be repeated at the rising of the Sun.

[1] The creator of the world and the first of the Hindu triad.

[2] He who pervades all beings; or the second of the Hindu triad who preserves the world.

[3] The bestower of blessings; the third of the Hindu triad and the destroyer of the world.

[4] A name of the War-God; also one who urges the senses to action.

[5] The lord of creatures; or the God of sacrifices.

[6] A name of the King of Gods; also all-powerful.

[7] The giver of wealth. A name of the God of riches.

[8] One who directly urges the mental faculties to action.

[9] One who moderates the senses; also the God of the regions of the dead.

[10] One who produces nectar (amrita) or one who is always possessed of light; or one together with Umá (Ardhanárísvara).

[11] The names or spirits of departed ancestors.

[12] Name of a class of eight Gods; also wealthy.

Sádhyas,[1] Aśvins,[2] Maruts,[3] Manu,[4] Váyu,[5] Vahni,[6] Prajá,[7] Práṇa,[8] Ritukartá,[9] Prabhákara,[10] (Thou,[11] art) Aditya,[12] Savitá,[13] Súrya,[14] Khaga,[15] Púshan,[16] Gabhastimán,[17] Suvarṇasadriśa,[18] Bhánu,[19] Hiraṇyaretas,[20] Divákara,[21] Haridaśva,[22] Sahasrárchish,[23] Saptasapti,[24] Marichimán,[25] Timironmathana,[26] Sambhu,[27] Twashṭá,[28] Mártaṇḍa,[29] Anśumán,[30] Hiraṇyagarbha,[31] Siśira,[32] Tapana,[33] Ahaskara,[34] Ravi,[35] Agnigarbha,[36] Aditiputra,[37] Sankha,[38] Siśiranáśana,[39] Vyomanátha,[40] Tamobhedí,[41] Rigyajussámapáraga,[42] Ghana-

---

[1] They who are to be served by Yogís ; or a class of Gods named Sádhyas.
[2] The two physicians of the Gods : or they who pervade all beings.
[3] They who are immortal : or a class of Gods forty-nine in number.
[4] Omniscient ; or the first king of the world.
[5] He that moves ; life ; or the God of wind.
[6] The God of fire.
[7] Lord of creatures.
[8] One who prolongs our lives.
[9] The material cause of knowledge and of the seasons.
[10] One who shines. The giver of light.
[11] The hymn entitled the Ádityahridaya begins from this verse and the words, thou art, are understood in the beginning of this verse.
[12] One who enjoys all (pleasurable) objects ; The son of Aditi, the lord of the solar disk.
[13] One who creates the world i. e. endows beings with life or soul, and by his rays causes rain and thereby produces corn.
[14] One who urges the world to action or puts the world in motion, who is omnipresent.
[15] One who walks through the sky ; or pervades the soul.
[16] One who nourishes the world i. e. is the supporter.
[17] One having rays (Gabhasti) or he who is possessed of the all-pervading goddess Lakshmí.
[18] One resembling gold.
[19] One who is resplendent or who gives light to other objects.
[20] One whose seed (Retas) is gold ; or quicksilver, the material cause of gold.
[21] One who is the cause of day.
[22] One whose horses are of tawny colour ; or one who pervades the whole space or quarters.
[23] One whose knowledge is boundless or who has a thousand rays.
[24] One who urges the seven (Práṇas) that is the two eyes, the two ears, the nostrils, and the organ of speech, or whose chariot, is drawn by seven horses.
[25] Vide Gabhastimán.
[26] One who destroys darkness, or ignorance.
[27] One from whom our blessings or the enjoyments of Paradise come.
[28] The architect of the gods ; or one who lessens the miseries of our birth and death.
[29] One who gives life to the lifeless world.
[30] One who pervades the internal and external worlds; or one who is resplendent.
[31] He who is identified with the Hindu triad, i. e. the creator (Brahmá) the supporter (Vishṇu) and the destroyer (Śiva).
[32] Cold or good natured. He is so called because he allays the three sorts of pain.
[33] One who is the lord of all.
[34] Vide Divákara.
[35] One who teaches Brahmá and others the Vedas.
[36] One from whom Rudra the destroyer or the third of the Hindu triad springs.
[37] One who is knowable through Aditi i. e. the eternal Brahmavidyá.
[38] Great happiness or the sky.
[39] The destroyer of cold or stupidity.
[40] The Lord of the sky.
[41] Vide Timironmathana.
[42] One who is known through the Upanishads.

vrishti.[1] Apám-Mitra,[2] Vindhyavíthíplavangama,[3] Átapí,[4] Mandalí,[5] Mrityu (death), Pingala,[6] Sarvatápana,[7] Kavi,[8] Viśva,[9] Mahátejas,[10] Rakta,[11] Sarvabhavodbhava.[12] The Lord of stars, planets, and other luminous bodies, Viśvabhávana,[13] Tejasvinám-Tejasví,[14] Dwádaśátman:[15] I salute thee. I salute thee who art the eastern mountain. I salute thee who art the western mountain. I salute thee who art the Lord of all the luminous bodies. I salute thee who art the Lord of days.

I respectfully salute thee who art Jaya,[16] Jayabhadra,[17] Haryaśva,[18] O Thou who hast a thousand rays, I repeatedly salute thee. I repeatedly and respectfully salute thee who art Áditya, I repeatedly salute thee who art Ugra,[19] Víra,[20] and Sáranga.[21] I salute thee who openest the lotuses (or the lotus of the heart). I salute thee who art furious. I salute thee who art the Lord of Brahmá, Śiva and Vishņu. I salute thee who art the sun, Ádityavarchas,[22] splendid, Sarvabhaksha,[23] and Raudravapush.[24]

I salute thee who destroyest darkness, cold and enemies; whose form is boundless; who art the destroyer of the ungrateful; who art Deva;[25] who art the Lord of the luminous bodies, and who appearest like the heated gold. I salute thee who art Hari,[26] Viśvakarman,[27] the destroyer of darkness, and who art splendid and Lokasákshin.[28] Yonder sun destroys the whole of the material world and also creates it. Yonder sun dries (all earthly things), destroys them and causes rain with his rays. He wakes when our senses are asleep; and resides within all beings. Yonder sun is Agnihotra[29] and also the fruit obtained by the

---

[1] He who is the cause of heavy rain.
[2] He who is a friend to the good, or who is the cause of water.
[3] One who moves in the solar orbit.
[4] One who determines the creation of the world: or who is possessed of heat.
[5] One who has a mass of rays; or who has Kaustubha and other precious stones as his ornaments.
[6] He who urges all to action; or who is yellow in colour.
[7] One who is the destroyer of all.
[8] One who is omniscient; or a poet.
[9] One who is identified with the whole world.
[10] One who is of huge form.
[11] One who pleases all by giving nourishment; or who is red in colour.
[12] One who is the cause of the whole world.
[13] One who protects the whole world.
[14] The most glorious of all that are glorious.
[15] One who is identical with the twelve months.
[16] One who gives victory over all the worlds to those who are faithfully devoted to him; or the porter of Brahmá, named Jaya.
[17] One who is identical with the blessing which can be obtained by conquering all the worlds; or with the porter of Brahmá named Jayabhadra.
[18] One who has Hanúmán as his conveyance.
[19] One who controls the senses; or is furious with those who are not his devotees.
[20] He who is free in moving the senses; or urges all beings to action.
[21] He who can be known through the Praņava (the mystical Om-kára.)
[22] One who is the knowledge of Brahmá.
[23] One who devours all things.
[24] He who is the destroyer of all pains; and of love, and hate, the causes of pain; and ignorance which is the cause of love and hate.
[25] One who is bliss; or the mover.
[26] One who destroys ignorance and its effects.
[27] The doer of all actions.
[28] One who beholds the universe; who is a witness of good and bad actions.
[29] Sacrifice of the five sensual fires.

performer of Agnihotra. He is identified with the gods, sacrifices, and the fruit of the sacrifices. He is the Lord of all the duties known to the world, If any man, O Rághava, in calamities, miseries, forests and dangers, prays to yonder sun, he is never overwhelmed by distress.

Worship, with close attention Him the God of gods and the Lord of the world; and recite these verses thrice, whereby thou wilt be victorious in the battle. O brave one, thou wilt kill Rávaṇa this very instant."

Thereupon Agastya having said this went away as he came. The glorious Ráma having heard this became free from sorrow. Rághava whose senses were under control, being pleased, committed the hymn to memory, recited it facing the sun, and obtained great delight. The brave Ráma having sipped water thrice and become pure took his bow, and seeing Rávaṇa, was delighted, and meditated on the sun.

PAGE 490.

His horses poured their burning tears.

I have omitted the Canto from which this line is taken because it describes signs and portents similar to those which have occurred in preceding books. But the weeping of the horses is new and is too Homeric to be passed by unnoticed. I borrow the following extract from De Quincey: "The old Homeric superstition which connects horses by the closest sympathy, and even by prescience, with their masters—that superstition which Virgil has borrowed from Homer in his beautiful episode of Mezentins (*Rhæbe diu*, res si qua diu mortalibus ulla est, Viximus)—still lingers unbroken in Crete. Horses foresee the fates of riders who are doomed, and express their prescience by weeping in a human fashion. The horses of Achilles weep in "Iliad" xvii., on seeing Automedon their beloved driver prostrate on the ground. With this view of the horse's capacity, it is singular, that in Crete this animal by preference should be called το αλογου, the brute, or irrational creature. But the word ἵππος has, by some accident, been lost in the modern Greek. As an instance both of the disparaging name, and of the ennobling superstition, take the following stanza from a Cretan ballad of 1825, written in the modern Greek:—

"Ωντεν εκαβαλλικευε,
Εκλαιε τ' αλογο του.
Και τοτεσα το εγνωρισε
Πως ειναι ὁ θανατος του"

"Upon which he mounted, and his horse wept; and then he saw clearly how this should bode his death."

Under the same old Cretan faith, Homer in "Iliad" xvii. 437, says:—

"Δάκρυα δέ σφι
Θερμὰ κατὰ βλεφάρων χαμάδις ῥέε μυρομένοιΐν
Ἡνιόχοιο πόθῃ".

"Tears, scalding tears, trickled to the ground from the eyelids of them (the horses), fretting through grief for the loss of their charioteer."

DE QUINCEY. *Homer and the Homeridæ.*

Page 492.

Rávaṇ's Funeral.

"In the funeral ceremonies of India the fire was placed on three sides of the pyre; the *Dakshiṇa* on the south, the *Gárhapatya* on the west, and the *A'havaníya* on the east. The funeral rites are not described in detail here, and it is therefore difficult to elucidate and explain them. The poem assigns the funeral ceremonies of Aryan Brahmans to the Rákshases, a race different from them in origin and religion, in the same way as Homer sometimes introduces into Troy the rites of the Grecian cult." Gorresio.

Mr. Muir translates the description of the funeral from the Calcutta edition, as follows: "They formed, with Vedic rites, a funeral pile of faggots of sandal-wood, with *padmaka* wood, *uśira* grass, and sandal, and covered with a quilt of deer's hair. They then performed an unrivalled obsequial ceremony for the Ráxasa prince, placing the sacrificial ground to the S. E. and the fire in the proper situation. They cast the ladle filled with curds and ghee on the shoulder[1] of the deceased; he (?) placed the car on the feet, and the mortar between the thighs. Having deposited all the wooden vessels, the [upper] and lower fire-wood, and the other pestle, in their proper places, they departed. The Ráxasas having then slain a victim to their prince in the manner prescribed in the Śástras, and enjoined by great rishis, cast [into the fire] the coverlet of the king saturated with ghee. They then, Vibhíshaṇa included, with afflicted hearts, adorned Rávaṇa with perfumes and garlands, and with various vestments, and besprinkled him with fried grain. Vibhíshaṇa having bathed, and having, with his clothes wet, scattered in proper form *tila* seeds mixed with *darbha* grass, and moistened with water, applied the fire [to the pile]."

Page 496.

The following is a literal translation of Brahmá's address to Ráma according to the Calcutta edition, text and commentary:

"O Ráma, how dost thou, being the creator of all the world, best of all those who have profound knowledge of the Upanishads and all-powerful as thou art, suffer Sítá to fall in the fire? How dost thou not know thyself as the best of the gods? Thou art one of the primeval Vasus,[2] and also their lord and creator. Thou art thyself the lord and first creator of the three worlds. Thou art the eighth (that is Mahádeva) of the Rudras;[3] and also the fifth[4] of the Sádhyas.[5] (The poet describes Ráma as made of the following gods) The Aśvinikumáras (the twin divine physicians of the gods) are thy ears; the sun and the moon are thy eyes; and thou hast been seen in the beginning and at the end of creation. How dost thou neglect the daughter of Videha (Janaka) like a man whose actions are directed by the dictates of nature?" Thus addressed by Indra, Brahmá and

---

[1] "According to A'pastamba (says the commentator) it should have been placed on the nose: this must therefore have been done in conformity with some other Sútras."

[2] A class of eight gods.

[3] A class of eleven gods called Rudras.

[4] Named Víryaván.

[5] A class of divine devotees named Sádhyas.

the other gods, Ráma the descendant of Raghu, lord of the world and the best of the virtuous, spoke to the chief of the gods. "As I take myself to be a man of the name of Ráma and son of Daśaratha, therefore, sir, please tell me who I am and whence have I come." "O thou whose might is never failing," said Brahmá to Kákutstha the foremost of those who thoroughly know Brahmá, "Thou art Náráyaṇa,[1] almighty, possessed of fortune, and armed with the discus. Thou art the boar[2] with one tusk; the conqueror of thy past and future foes. Thou art Brahmá true and eternal or undecaying. Thou art Viśvaksena,[3] having four arms; Thou art Hrishíkeśa,[4] whose bow is made of horn: Thou art Purusha,[5] the best of all beings; Thou art one who is never defeated by any body; Thou art the holder of the sword (named Nandaka). Thou art Vishṇu (the pervader of all); blue in colour: of great might; the commander of armies; and lord of villages. Thou art truth. Thou art embodied intelligence, forgiveness, control over the senses, creation, and destruction. Thou art Upendra[6] and Madhusúdana.[7] Thou art the creator of Indra, the ruler over all the world, Padmanábha,[8] and destroyer of enemies in the battle. The divine Rishis call thee shelter of refugees, as well as the giver of shelter. Thou hast a thousand horns,[9] a hundred heads.[10] Thou art respected of the respected; and the lord and first creator of the three worlds. Thou art the forefather and shelter of Siddhas,[11] and Sádhyas[12] Thou art sacrifices; Vashaṭkára,[13] Omkára.[14] Thou art beyond those who are beyond our senses. There is none who knows who thou art and who knows thy beginning and end. Thou art seen in all material objects, in Bráhmans, in cows, and also in all the quarters, sky and streams. Thou hast a thousand feet, a hundred heads, and a thousand eyes. Thou hast borne the material objects and the earth with the mountains; and at the bottom of the ocean thou art seen the great serpent, O Ráma, Thou hast borne the three worlds, gods, Gandharvas,[15] and demons. I am, O Ráma, thy heart; the goddess of learning is thy tongue; the gods are the hairs of thy body; the closing of thy eyelids is called the night: and their opening is called the day. The Vedas are thy Sanskáras.[16] Nothing can exist without thee. The whole world is thy body; the surface of the earth is thy stability.

---

1 One who resides in the waters.

2 The third incarnation of Vishṇu, that bore the earth on his tusk.

3 One whose armies are everywhere.

4 One who controls the senses.

5 He who resides in the heart, or who is full, or all-pervading.

6 Vámana, or the Dwarf incarnation of Vishṇu.

7 The killer of Madhu, a demon.

8 He from whose navel, the lotus, from which Brahmá was born, springs.

9 He who has a thousand horns. The horns are here the Sákhás of the Sáma-veda.

10 One who has a hundred heads. The heads are here meant to devote a hundred commandments of the Vedas.

11 Siddhas are those who have already gained the summit of their desires.

12 Sádhyas are those that are still trying to gain the summit.

13 A mystic syllable uttered in Mantras.

14 A mystic syllable made of the letters अ, उ, म, which respectively denote Brahmá, Vishṇu, and Śiva.

15 A class of divine gods.

16 Sanskáras are those sacred writings through which the divine commands and prohibitions are known.

O Śrívatsalakshaṇa, fire is thy anger, and the moon is thy favour. In the time of thy incarnation named Vámana, thou didst pervade the three worlds with thy three steps; and Mahendra was made the king of paradise by thee having confined the fearful Bali.[1] Sítá (thy wife) is Lakshmí; and thou art the God Vishṇu,[2] Krishṇa,[3] and Prajápati. To kill Rávaṇ thou hast assumed the form of a man; therefore, O best of the virtuous, thou hast completed this task imposed by us (gods). O Ráma, Rávaṇa has been killed by thee; now being joyful (e. i. having for some time reigned in the kingdom of Ayodhyá,) go to paradise. O glorious Ráma, thy power and thy valour are never failing. The visit to thee and the prayers made to thee are never fruitless. Thy devotees will never be unsuccessful. Thy devotees who obtain thee (thy favour) who art first and best of mankind, shall obtain their desires in this world as well as in the next. They who recite this prayer, founded on the Vedas (or first uttered by the sages), and the old and divine account of (Ráma) shall never suffer defeat."

THE MEETING, PAGE 503.

The *Bharat-Miláp* or meeting with Bharat, is the closing scene of the dramatic representation of Ráma's great victory and triumphant return which takes place annually in October in many of the cities of Northern India. The Rám-Lílá or Play of Ráma, as the great drama is called, is performed in the open air and lasts with one day's break through fifteen successive days. At Benares there are three nearly simultaneous performances, one provided by H. H. the Maharajah of Benares near his palace at Ramnaggur, one by H. H. the Maharajah of Vizianagram near the Missionary settlement at Sigra and at other places in the city, and one by the leading gentry of the city at Chowká Ghát near the College. The scene especially on the great day when the brothers meet is most interesting: the procession of elephants with their gorgeous howdahs of silver and gold and their magnificently dressed riders with priceless jewels sparkling in their turbans, the enthusiasm of the thousands of spectators who fill the streets and squares, the balconies and the housetops, the flowers that are rained down upon the advancing car, the wild music, the shouting and the joy, make an impression that is not easily forgotten.

Still on his head, well trained in lore
Of duty, Ráma's shoes he bore.

Ráma's shoes are here regarded as the emblems of royalty or possession. We may compare the Hebrew "Over Edom will I cast forth my shoe." A curiously similar passage occurs in LYSCHANDER'S *Chronicon Greenlandiæ Rhythmicon:*

"Han sendte til Irland sin skiden skoe,
Og böd den Konge, som der monne boe,
Han skulde dem hæderlig bære
Pan Juuledag i sin kongelig Pragt,
Og kjende han havde sit Rige og Magt
Af Norges og Quernes Herre."

[1] Bali, a demon whom Vámana confined in Pátála.
[2] Vishṇu, the second of the Hindu triad.
[3] Krishṇa, (black coloured) one of the ten incarnations of Vishṇu.

He sent to Ireland his dirty shoes,
And commanded the king who lived there
To wear them with honour
On Christmas Day in his royal state,
And to own that he had his kingdom and power
From the Lord of Norway and the Isles.

Notes & Queries, March 30, 1872.

I end these notes with an extract which I translate from Signor Gorresio's Preface to the tenth volume of his Rámáyan, and I take this opportunity of again thankfully acknowledging my great obligations to this eminent Sanskritist from whom I have so frequently borrowed. As Mr. Muir has observed, the Bengal recension which Signor Gorresio has most ably edited is throughout an admirable commentary on the genuine Rámáyan of northern India, and I have made constant reference to the faithful and elegant translation which accompanies the text for assistance and confirmation in difficulties:

"Towards the southern extremity and in the island of Lanká (Ceylon) there existed undoubtedly a black and ferocious race, averse to the Aryans and hostile to their mode of worship: their ramifications extended through the islands of the Archipelago, and some traces of them remain in Java to this day.

The Sanskrit-Indians, applying to this race a name expressive of hatred which occurs in the Vedas as the name of hostile, savage and detested beings, called it the Rákshas race: it is against these Rákshases that the expedition of Ráma which the Rámáyan celebrates is directed. The Sanskrit-Indians certainly altered in their traditions the real character of this race: they attributed to it physical and moral qualities not found in human nature; they transformed it into a race of giants; they represented it as monstrous, hideous, truculent, changing forms at will, blood-thirsty and ravenous, just as the Semites represented the races that opposed them as impious, horrible and of monstrous size. But notwithstanding these mythical exaggerations. which are partly due to the genius of the Aryans so prone to magnify everything without measure, the Rámáyan in the course of its epic narration has still preserved and noted here and there some traits and peculiarities of the race which reveal its true character. It represents the Rákshases as black of hue, and compares them with black clouds and masses of black collyrium; it attributes to them curly woolly hair and thick lips, it depicts them as loaded with chains, collars and girdles of gold. and the other bright ornaments which their race has always loved, and in which the kindred races of the Soudan still delight. It describes them as worshippers of matter and force. They are hostile to the religion of the Aryans whose rites and sacrifices they disturb and ruin...Such is the Rákshas race as represented in the Rámáyan; and the war of the Aryan Ráma forms the subject of the epic, a subject certainly real and historical as far as regards its substance, but greatly exaggerated by the ancient myth. In Sanskrit-Indian tradition are found traces of another struggle of the Aryans with the Rákshas races, which preceded the war of Ráma. According to some pauranic legends, Kárttavírya a descendant of the royal tribe of the Yádavas, contemporary with Paraśuráma and a little anterior to Ráma, attacked Lanká and took Rávaṇ prisoner. This well shows how ancient and how deeply rooted in the Aryan race is the thought of this war which the Rámáyan celebrates.

"But," says an eminent Indianist[1] whose learning I highly appreciate, "the Rámáyan is an allegorical epic, and no precise and historical value can be assigned to it. Sítá signifies the furrow made by the plough, and under this symbolical aspect has already appeared honoured with worship in the hymns of the Rig-veda; Ráma is the bearer of the plough (this assertion is entirely gratuitous; these two allegorical personages represented agriculture introduced to the southern regions of India by the race of the Kosalas from whom Ráma was descended; the Rákshases on whom he makes war are races of demons and giants who have little or nothing human about them; allegory therefore predominates in the poem, and the exact reality of an historical event must not be looked for in it." Such is Professor Weber's opinion. If he means to say that mythical fictions are mingled with real events,

Forsan in alcun vero suo arco percuote,

as Dante says, and I fully concede the point. The interweaving of the myth with the historical truth belongs to the essence, so to speak, of the primitive epopeia. If Sítá is born, as the Rámáyan feigns, from the furrow which King Janak opened when he ploughed the earth, not a whit more real is the origin of Helen and Æneas as related in Homer and Virgil, and if the characters in the Rámáyan exceed human nature, and in a greater degree perhaps than is the case in analogous epics, this springs in part from the nature of the subject and still more from the symbol-loving genius of the orient. Still the characters of the Rámáyan, although they exceed more or less the limits of human nature, act notwithstanding in the course of the poem, speak, feel, rejoice and grieve according to the natural impulse of human passions. But if by saying that the Rámáyan is an allegorical epic, it is meant that its fundamental subject is nothing but allegory, that the war of the Aryan Ráma against the Rákshas race is an allegory, that the conquest of the southern region and of the island of Lanká is an allegory, I do not hesitate to answer that such a presumption cannot be admitted and that the thing is in my opinion impossible. Father Paolino da S. Bartolommeo,[2] had already, together with other strange opinions of his own on Indian matters, brought forward a similar idea, that is to say that the exploit of Ráma which is the subject of the Rámáyan was a symbol and represented the course of the sun: thus he imagined that Brahmá was the earth, Vishṇu the water, and that his avatárs were the blessings brought by the fertilizing waters, etc. But such ideas, born at a time when Indo-sanskrit antiquities were enveloped in darkness, have been dissipated by the light of new studies. How could an epic so dear in India to the memory of the people, so deeply rooted for many centuries in the minds of all, so propagated and diffused through all the dialects and languages of those regions, which had become the source of many dramas which are still represented in India, which is itself represented every year with such magnificence and to such crowds of people in the neighbourhood of Ayodhyá, a poem welcomed at its very birth with such favour, as the legend relates, that the recitation of it by the first wandering Rhapsodists has consecrated and made famous all the places celebrated

---

[1] A. Weber, *Akademische Vorlesungen*, p. 181.

[2] Systema brahmanicum, liturgicum, mythologicum, civile, exmonumentis Indicis, etc,

by them, and where Ráma made a shorter or longer stay, how, I ask, could such an epic have been purely allegorical? How, upon a pure invention, upon a simple allegory, could a poem have been composed of about fifty thousand verses, relating with such force and power the events, and giving details with such exactness? On a theme purely allegorical there may easily be composed a short mythical poem, as for example a poem on Proserpine or Psyche: but never an epic so full of traditions and historical memories, so intimately connected with the life of the people, as the Rámáyan.[1] Excessive readiness to find allegory whenever some traces of symbolism occur, where the myth partly veils the historical reality, may lead and often has led to error. What poetical work of mythical times could stand this mode of trial? could there not be made, or rather has there not been made a work altogether allegorical, out of the Homeric poems? We have all heard of the ingenious idea of the anonymous writer, who in order to prove how easily we may pass beyond the truth in our wish to seek and find allegory everywhere, undertook with keen subtlety to prove that the great personality of Napoleon I. was altogether allegorical and represented the sun. Napoleon was born in an island, his course was from west to east, his twelve marshals were the twelve signs of the zodiac, etc.

I conclude then, that the fundamental theme of the Rámàyan, that is to say the war of the Aryan Ráma against the Rákshases, an Hamitic race settled in the south, ought to be regarded as real and historical as far as regards its substance, although the mythic element intermingled with the true sometimes alters its natural and genuine aspect.

How then did the Indo-Sanskrit epopeia form and complete itself? What elements did it interweave in its progress? How did it embody, how did it clothe the naked and simple primitive datum? We must first of all remember that the Indo-European races possessed the epic genius in the highest degree, and that they alone in the different regions they occupied produced epic poetry...But other causes and particular influences combined to nourish and develop the epic germ of the Sanskrit-Indians. Already in the Rig-veda are found hymns in which the Aryan genius preluded, so to speak, to the future epopeia, in songs that celebrated the heroic deeds of Indra, the combats and the victories of the tutelary Gods of the Aryan races over enemies secret or open, human or superhuman, the exploits and the memories of ancient heroes. More recently, at certain solemn occasions, as the very learned A. Weber remarks, at the solemnity, for example of the Aśvamedha or sacrifice of the horse, the praises of the king who ordained the great rite were sung by bards and minstrels in songs composed for the purpose, the memories of past times were recalled and honourable mention was made of the just and pious kings of old. In the *Bráhmaṇas*, a sort of prose commentaries annexed to the Vedas, are found recorded stories and legends which allude to historical events of the past ages, to ancient memories, and to mythical events. Such popular legends which the *Bráhmaṇas* undoubtedly gathered from tradition admirably suited the epic tissue with which they were interwoven by successive hands......Many and various mythico-historical traditions, suitable for epic development, were diffused among the Aryan races, those for example which are relat-

[1] Not only have the races of India translated or epitomized it, but foreign nations have appropriated it wholly or in part, Persia, Java, and Japan itself.

ed in the four chapters containing the description of the earth, the Descent of the Ganges, etc. The epic genius however smetimes created beings of its own and gave body and life to ideal conceptions. Some of the persons in the Rámáyan must be, in my opinion, either personifications of the forces of nature like those which are described with such vigour in the *Sháhnámah*, or if not exactly created, exaggerated beyond human proportions ; others, vedic personages much more ancient than Ráma, were introduced into the epic and woven into its narrations, to bring together men who lived in different and distant ages, as has been the case in times nearer to our own, in the epics, I mean, of the middle ages.

In the introduction I have discussed the antiquity of the Rámáyan ; and by means of those critical and inductive proofs which are all that an antiquity without precise historical dates can furnish I have endeavoured to establish with all the certainty that the subject admitted, that the original composition of the Rámáyan is to be assigned to about the twelfth century before the Christian era. Not that I believe that the epic then sprang to life in the form in which we now possess it ; I think, and I have elsewhere expressed the opinion, that the poem during the course of its rhapsodical and oral propagation appropriated by way of episodes, traditions, legends and ancient myths......But as far as regards the epic poem properly so called which celebrates the expedition of Ráma against the Rákshases I think that I have sufficiently shown that its origin and first appearance should be placed about the twelfth century B. C. ; nor have I hitherto met with anything to oppose this chronological result, or to oblige me to rectify or reject it......But an eminent philologist already quoted, deeply versed in these studies, A. Weber, has expressed in some of his writings a totally different opinion ; and the authority of his name, if not the number and cogency of his arguments, compels me to say something on the subject. From the fact or rather the assumption that Megasthenes[1] who lived some time in India has made no mention either of the Mahábhárat or the Rámáyan Professor Weber argues that neither of these poems could have existed at that time ; as regards the Rámáyan, the unity of its composition, the chain that binds together its different parts, and its allegorical character, show it, says Professor Weber, to be much more recent than the age to which I have assigned it, near to our own era, and according to him, later than the Mahábhárat. As for Megasthenes it should be observed, that he did not write a history of India, much less a literary history or anything at all resembling one, but a simple description, in great part physical, of India : whence, from his silence on literary matters to draw inferences regarding the history of Sanskrit literature would be the same thing as from the silence of a geologist with respect to the literature of a country whose valleys, mountains, and internal structure he is exploring, to conjecture that such and such a poem or history not mentioned by him did not exist at his time. We have only to look at the fragments of Megasthenes collected and published by Schwanbeck to see what was the nature and scope of his *Indica*..................But only a few fragments of Megasthenes are extant ; and to pretend that they should be argument and proof enough to judge the antiquity of a poem is to press the laws of criticism too far. To Professor Weber's argument as to the more or

[1] In the third century B. C.

less recent age of the Rámáyan from the unity of its composition, I will make one sole reply, which is that if unity of composition were really a proof of a more recent age, it would be necessary to reduce by a thousand years at least the age of Homer and bring him down to the age of Augustus and Virgil; for certainly there is much more unity of composition, a greater accord and harmony of parts in the Iliad and the Odyssey than in the Rámáyan. But in the fine arts perfection is no proof of a recent age: while the experience and the continuous labour of successive ages are necessary to extend and perfect the physical or natural sciences, art which is spontaneous in its nature can produce and has produced in remote times works of such perfection as later ages have not been able to equal."

INDEX OF PRINCIPAL NAMES.

A.

B.

C.

D.

L.

M.

N.

O.

P

W.

Y.